C000126949

ISBN 978-0-266-95870-3
PIBN 10915684

THE

AMERICAN STATE REPORTS,

CONTAINING THE

CASES OF GENERAL VALUE AND AUTHORITY,

SUBSEQUENT TO THOSE CONTAINED IN THE "AMERICAN
DECISIONS" AND THE "AMERICAN REPORTS,"

DECIDED IN THE

COURTS OF LAST RESORT

OF THE SEVERAL STATES.

SELECTED, REPORTED, AND ANNOTATED

By A. C. FREEMAN,

AND THE ASSOCIATE EDITORS OF THE "AMERICAN DECISIONS."

Vol. XLV.

SAN FRANCISCO:
BANCROFT-WHITNEY COMPANY,
LAW PUBLISHERS AND LAW BOOKSELLERS.
1895.

SAN FRANCISCO:
THE FILMER-ROLLINS ELECTROTYPE COMPANY,
TYPOGRAPHERS AND STEREOTYPERS.

AMERICAN STATE REPORTS.

VOL. XLV.

SCHEDULE

showing the original volumes of reports in which the cases herein selected and re-reported may be found, and the pages of this volume devoted to each state.

SCHEDULE

SHOWING IN WHAT VOLUMES OF THIS SERIES THE CASES REPORTED IN THE SEVERAL VOLUMES OF OFFICIAL REPORTS MAY BE FOUND.

State reports are in parentheses, and the numbers of this series in bold-faced figures.'

ALABAMA. — (83) **3**; (84) **5**; (85) **7**; (86) **11**; (87) **13**; (88) **16**; (89) **18**; (90, 91) **24**; (92) **25**; (93) **30**; (94) **33**; (95) **36**; (96, 97) **38**; (98) **39**; (99) **42**.

ARKANSAS. — (48) **3**; (49) **4**; (50) **7**; (51) **14**; (52) **20**; (53) **22**; (54) **26**; (55) **29**; (56) **35**; (57) **38**; (58) **41**; (59) **43**.

CALIFORNIA. — (72) **1**; (73) **2**; (74) **5**; (75) **7**; (76) **9**; (77) **11**; (78, 79) **12**; (80) **13**; (81) **15**; (82) **16**; (83) **17**; (84) **18**; (85) **20**; (86) **21**; (87, 88) **22**; (89) **23**; (90, 91) **25**; (92, 93) **27**; (94) **28**; (95) **29**; (96) **31**; (97) **33**; (98) **35**; (99) **37**; (100) **38**; (101) **40**; (102) **41**; (103) **42**; (104) **43**; (105) **45**.

COLORADO. — (10) **3**; (11) **7**; (12) **13**; (13) **16**; (14) **20**; (15) **22**; (16) **25**; (17) **31**; (18) **36**; (19) **41**.

CONNECTICUT. — (54) **1**; (55) **3**; (56) **7**; (57) **14**; (58) **18**; (59) **21**; (60) **25**; (61) **29**; (62) **36**; (63) **38**; (64) **42**.

DELAWARE. — (5 Houst.) **1**; (6 Houst.) **22**; (7 Houst.) **40**; (9 Houst.) **43**.

FLORIDA. — (22) **1**; (23) **11**; (24) **12**; (25, 26) **23**; (27) **26**; (28) **29**; (29) **30**; (30) **32**; (31) **34**; (32) **37**; (33) **39**; (34) **43**.

GEORGIA. — (76) **2**; (77) **4**; (78) **6**; (79) **11**; (80, 81) **12**; (82) **14**; (83, 84) **20**; (85) **21**; (86) **22**; (87) **27**; (88) **30**; (89) **32**; (90) **35**; (91, 92, 93) **44**.

IDAHO. — (2) **35**.

ILLINOIS. — (121) **2**; (122) **3**; (123) **5**; (124) **7**; (125) **8**; (126) **9**; (127) **11**; (128) **15**; (129) **16**; (130) **17**; (131) **19**; (132) **22**; (133, 134) **23**; (135) **25**; (136) **29**; (137) **31**; (138, 139) **32**; (140, 141) **33**; (142) **34**; (143, 144, 145) **36**; (146, 147) **37**; (148) **39**; (149, 150) **41**; (151) **42**; (152) **43**; (154) **45**.

INDIANA. — (112) **2**; (113) **3**; (114) **5**; (115) **7**; (116) **9**; (117, 118) **10**; (119) **12**; (120, 121) **16**; (122) **17**; (123) **18**; (124) **19**; (125) **21**; (126, 127) **22**; (128) **25**; (129) **28**; (130) **30**; (131) **31**; (132) **32**; (133) **36**; (134) **39**; (135) **41**; (136) **43**; (137) **45**.

IOWA. — (72) **2**; (73) **5**; (74) **7**; (75) **9**; (76, 77) **14**; (78) **16**; (79) **18**; (80) **20**; (81) **25**; (82) **31**; (83) **32**; (84) **35**; (85) **39**; (86) **41**; (87) **43**; (88) **45**.

KANSAS. — (37) **1**; (38) **5**; (39) **7**; (40) **10**; (41) **13**; (42) **16**; (43) **19**; (44) **21**; (45) **23**; (46) **26**; (47) **27**; (48) **30**; (49) **33**; (50) **34**; (51) **37**; (52) **39**; (53) **42**; (54) **45**.

KENTUCKY. — (83, 84) **4**; (85) **7**; (86) **9**; (87) **12**; (88) **21**; (89) **25**; (90) **29**; (91) **34**; (92) **36**; (93) **40**; (94) **42**; (95) **44**.

LOUISIANA. — (39 La. Ann.) **4**; (40 La. Ann.) **8**; (41 La. Ann.) **17**; (42 La. Ann.) **21**; (43 La. Ann.) **26**; (44 La. Ann.); **32**; (45 La. Ann.) **40**.

MAINE. — (79) **1**; (80) **6**; (81) **10**; (82) **17**; (83) **23**; (84) **30**; (85) **35**; (86) **41**.

MARYLAND. — (67) **1**; (68) **6**; (69) **9**; (70) **14**; (71) **17**; (72) **20**; (73) **25**; (74) **28**; (75) **32**; (76) **35**; (77) **39**; (78) **44**; (80) **45**.

MASSACHUSETTS. — (145) **1**; (146) **4**; (147) **9**; (148) **12**; (149) **14**; (150) **15**; (151) **21**; (152) **23**; (153) **25**; (154) **26**; (155) **31**; (156) **32**; (157) **34**; (158) **35**; (159) **38**; (160) **39**; (161) **42**; (162) **44**.

MICHIGAN. — (60, 61) **1**; (62) **4**; (63) **6**; (64, 65) **8**; (66, 67) **11**; (68, 69, 75) **13**; (70) **14**; (71, 76) **15**; (72, 73, 74) **16**; (77, 78) **18**; (79) **19**; (80) **20**; (81, 82, 83) **21**; (84) **22**; (85, 86, 87) **24**; (88) **26**; (89) **28**; (90, 91) **30**; (92) **31**; (93) **32**; (94) **34**; (95, 96) **35**; (97) **37**; (98) **39**; (99) **41**; (100) **43**; (101) **45**.

MINNESOTA. — (36) **1**; (37) **5**; (38) **8**; (39, 40) **12**; (41) **16**; (42) **18**; (43) **19**; (44) **20**; (45) **22**; (46) **24**; (47) **28**; (48) **31**; (49) **32**; (50) **36**; (51, 52) **38**; (53) **39**; (54) **40**; (55) **43**; (56) **45**.

MISSISSIPPI. — (65) **7**; (66) **14**; (67) **19**; (68) **24**; (69) **30**; (70) **35**; (71) **42**.

MISSOURI. — (92) **1**; (93) **3**; (94) **4**; (95) **6**; (96) **9**; (97) **10**; (98) **14**; (99) **17**; (100) **18**; (101) **20**; (102) **22**; (103) **23**; (104, 105) **24**; (106) **27**; (107) **28**; (108, 109) **32**; (110, 111) **33**; (112) **34**; (113, 114) **35**; (115) **37**; (116, 117) **38**; (118) **40**; (119, 120) **41**; (121) **42**; (122) **43**; (123) **45**.

MONTANA. — (9) **18**; (10) **24**; (11) **28**; (12) **33**; (13) **40**; (14) **43**.

NEBRASKA. — (22) **3**; (23, 24) **8**; (25) **13**; (26) **18**; (27) **20**; (28, 29) **26**; (30) **27**; (31) **28**; (32, 33) **29**; (34) **33**; (35) **37**; (36) **38**; (37) **40**; (38) **41**; (39, 40) **42**; (41) **43**.

NEVADA. — (19) **3**; (20) **19**; (21) **37**.

NEW HAMPSHIRE. — (64) **10**; (62) **13**; (65) **23**.

NEW JERSEY. — (43 N. J. Eq.) **3**; (44 N. J. Eq.) **6**; (50 N. J. L.) **7**; (51 N. J. L.; 45 N. J. Eq.) **14**; (46 N. J. Eq.; 52 N. J. L.) **19**; (47 N. J. Eq.) **24**; (53 N. J. L.) **26**; (48 N. J. Eq.) **27**; (49 N. J. Eq.) **31**; (54 N. J. L.) **33**; (50 N. J. Eq.) **35**; (55 N. J. L.) **39**; (51 N. J. Eq.) **40**; (56 N. J. L.) **44**.

NEW YORK. — (107) **1**; (108) **2**; (109) **4**; (110) **6**; (111) **7**; (112) **8**; (113) **10**; (114) **11**; (115) **12**; (116, 117) **15**; (118, 119) **16**; (120) **17**; (121) **18**; (122) **19**; (123) **20**; (124, 125) **21**; (126) **22**; (127) **24**; (128, 129) **26**; (130, 131) **27**; (132, 133) **28**; (134) **30**; (135) **31**; (136) **32**; (137) **33**; (138) **34**; (139) **36**; (140) **37**; (141) **38**; (142) **40**; (143) **42**; (144) **43**; (145) **45**.

NORTH CAROLINA. — (97, 98) **2**; (99, 100) **6**; (101) **9**; (102) **11**; (103) **14**; (104) **17**; (105) **18**; (106) **19**; (107) **22**; (108) **23**; (109) **26**; (110) **28**; (111) **32**; (112) **34**; (113) **37**; (114) **41**; (115) **44**.

NORTH DAKOTA. — (1) **26**; (2) **33**; (3) **44**.

OHIO. — (45 Ohio St.) **4**; (46 Ohio St.) **15**; (47 Ohio St.) **21**; (48 Ohio St.) **29**; (49 Ohio St.) **34**; (50 Ohio St.) **40**.

OREGON. — (15) **3**; (16) **8**; (17) **11**; (18) **17**; (19) **20**; (20) **23**; (21) **26**; (22) **29**; (23) **37**; (24) **41**; (25) **42**.

PENNSYLVANIA. — (115, 116, 117 Pa. St.) **2**; (118, 119 Pa. St.) **4**; (120, 121 Pa. St.) **6**; (122 Pa. St.) **9**; (123, 124 Pa. St.) **10**; (125 Pa. St.) **11**; (126 Pa. St.) **12**; (127 Pa. St.) **14**; (128, 129 Pa. St.) **15**; (130, 131 Pa. St.) **17**; (132, 133, 134 Pa. St.) **19**; (135, 136 Pa. St.) **20**; (137, 138 Pa. St.) **21**; (139, 140, 141 Pa. St.) **23**; (142, 143 Pa. St.) **24**; (144, 145 Pa. St.) **27**; (146 Pa. St.) **28**; (147, 150 Pa. St) **30**; (151 Pa. St.) **31**; (148 Pa. St.) **33**; (149, 152, 153 Pa. St.) **34**; (154, 155 Pa. St.) **35**; (156 Pa. St.) **36**; (157 Pa. St.) **37**; (158 Pa. St.) **38**; (159 Pa. St.) **39**; (160 Pa. St.) **40**;

(161 Pa. St.) **41**; (162 Pa. St.) **42**; (163 Pa. St.) **43**; (164, 165 Pa. St.) **44**; (166 Pa. St.) **45**.

RHODE ISLAND. — (15) **2**; (16) **27**; (17) **33**.

SOUTH CAROLINA. — (26) **4**; (27, 28, 29) **13**; (30) **14**; (31, 32) **17**; (33) **26**; (34) **27**; (35) **28**; (36) **31**; (37) **34**; (38) **37**; (39) **39**; (40) **42**; (41) **44**.

SOUTH DAKOTA. — (1) **36**; (2) **39**; (3) **44**.

TENNESSEE. — (85) **4**; (86) **6**; (87) **10**; (88) **17**; (89) **24**; (90) **25**; (91) **30**; (92) **36**; (93) **42**; (94) **45**.

TEXAS. — (68) **2**; (69; 24 Tex. App.) **5**; (70; 25, 26 Tex. App.) **8**; (71) **10**; (27 Tex. App.) **11**; (72) **13**; (73, 74) **15**; (75) **16**; (76) **18**; (77; 28 Tex. App.) **19**; (78) **22**; (79) **23**; (29 Tex. App.) **25**; (80, 81) **26**; (82) **27**; (30 Tex. App.) **28**; (83) **29**; (84) **31**; (85) **34**; (31 Tex. Cr. Rep.) **37**; (86; 32 Tex. Cr. Rep.) **40**.

VERMONT. — (60) **6**; (61) **15**; (62) **22**; (63) **25**; (64) **33**; (65) **36**; (66) **44**.

VIRGINIA. — (82) **3**; (83) **5**; (84) **10**; (85) **17**; (86) **19**; (87) **24**; (88) **29**; (89) **37**; (90) **44**.

WASHINGTON. — (1) **22**; (2) **26**; (3) **28**; (4) **31**; (5) **34**; (6) **36**; (7) **38**; (8) **40**; (9) **43**; (10) **45**.

WEST VIRGINIA. — (29) **6**; (30) **8**; (31) **13**; (32, 33) **25**; (34) **26**; (35) **29**; (36) **32**; (37) **38**; (38, 39) **45**.

WISCONSIN. — (69) **2**; (70, 71) **5**; (72) **7**; (73) **9**; (74, 75) **17**; (76, 77) **20**; (78) **23**; (79) **24**; (80) **27**; (81) **29**; (82) **33**; (83) **35**; (84) **36**; (85, 86) **39**; (87) **41**; (88) **43**.

WYOMING. — (3) **31**.

AMERICAN STATE REPORTS.

VOL. XLV.

CASES REPORTED.

AMERICAN STATE REPORTS.
VOL. XLV.

CASES

IN THE

SUPREME COURT

OF

CALIFORNIA.

———

JORY *v.* SUPREME COUNCIL AMERICAN LEGION OF HONOR.

[105 CALIFORNIA, 20.]

BENEFICIAL ASSOCIATIONS.—A CHANGE IN BENEFICIARIES cannot be made except by a substantial compliance with the regulations of the society, and yet courts of equity recognize exceptions to this general principle. Equity does not demand impossible things, and will consider as done that which should have been done, and, when a member has complied with all the requirements of the rules for the purpose of making a substitution of beneficiaries within his power, he has done all that a court of equity demands.

BENEFICIAL ASSOCIATIONS.—A BENEFICIARY CANNOT PREVENT a change of beneficiaries by obtaining a benefit certificate of a member of a beneficial association and refusing to surrender it to him for the purpose of making that change of beneficiary which he was entitled to make. If the member does all that is within his power to do to effect a change in beneficiaries, and fails to surrender the certificate and have a new one issued only because such certificate is in the possession of the original beneficiary, who refuses to surrender it, the beneficiary thus thwarting the wishes of the member will not be allowed to profit thereby, and his rights to the proceeds of the certificate are subordinate to those of the new beneficiaries selected by the member, and to whom the issue of a proper certificate was prevented only by the act of the original beneficiary in refusing to surrender the old certificate.

BENEFICIAL ASSOCIATIONS—VESTED RIGHTS.—A BENEFICIARY, designated as such by a member of a mutual benefit association, does not thereby acquire any vested rights so as to defeat a subsequent change of beneficiaries effected at the instance of such member, unless the original beneficiary was made such on account of some contract, or has some equities recognized by the courts, and which it would be inequitable to disappoint.

BENEFICIAL ASSOCIATIONS.—THE PAYMENT OF ASSESSMENTS of a member of a beneficial association by a person whom he has designated as a beneficiary in the event of his death does not give such person any vested rights in the certificate, nor deprive the member of the power to change the beneficiaries, unless such payments were made pursuant to some contract. Otherwise they are to be regarded as mere gifts.

APPELLATE PROCEDURE—HARMLESS ERRORS.—The admission in evidence of the statements of a person not a party to the action does not entitle the unsuccessful litigant to a new trial or a reversal of the judgment if such statements relate to an issue upon which there is no conflict in the evidence, and were in harmony with the theory of all the parties to the action.

John H. Dickinson and Henry E. Monroe, for the appellant.

H. W. Hutton, for the respondent.

²⁴ GAROUTTE, J. The right of ownership to the proceeds of a two thousand dollar benefit certificate, issued by a mutual benefit society, known as the American Legion of Honor, forms the subject of this litigation. The society is not an active party to the litigation, having paid the money into court, and being entirely satisfied with the court's adjudication as to whom it belongs. The respondent and appellant are brother and sister, and the beneficiary certificate was taken out by the mother, *Emily Kate Jory,* and made payable upon her death to the daughter appellant, or any other member of the mother's family whom she might thereafter in her lifetime designate.

The by-laws of the society provide that members may, at any time when in good standing, surrender their benefit certificates, and have new ones issued, payable to such beneficiary dependent upon them as they may direct, subject, however, to the provisions of section 2: "Such change to be made upon petition to the supreme secretary, signed by the member desiring to make the change, attested by the secretary of the subordinate council, and having the seal of the subordinate council attached, substantially in accordance with the form prescribed in this section. . . . . The fee to be paid for a new certificate issued shall be one dollar, and must **²⁵** accompany the petition. No change of beneficiary shall be made in any other manner than herein prescribed; . . . . provided, that in case of the loss or destruction of the old certificate satisfactory evidence of such loss or destruction shall be produced by affidavit or otherwise before a new certificate be issued. . . . . No act of a subordinate council in the admission of any member to membership in this order, and no act of any member done for the purpose of changing his or her beneficiary, shall be recognized by or deemed binding upon the supreme council, or as entitling the person admitted, or the new beneficiary named, to any benefits from this order, unless such acts shall be in strict accordance with the provisions contained in the laws and constitution prescribed by the supreme council, nor until such acts have been ratified and approved by the supreme council."

Several years after this certificate was issued the mother became desirous of changing the beneficiary named therein, to wit, the appellant daughter, and to substitute therefor the respondent son; and in furtherance of such desire, and for the purpose of complying with the laws of the society, she attempted to secure control of the original certificate which was then in the keeping of her daughter appellant, in order that she might surrender the same to the society; but she was unsuccessful in this endeavor. Upon this question the court found the fact to be that "she (the daughter) refused to redeliver the same to the said *E*mily Kate Jory, although frequently requested so to do by her as alleged in said amended complaint, but kept and concealed the same for the purpose of endeavoring to prevent her said mother from designating the plaintiff herein as the beneficiary thereunder, and securing the said two thousand dollars herself, and so kept and concealed it until after her mother's death, as alleged in the amended complaint on file herein." And this finding is supported by the evidence.

²⁶ Being unable to secure the original certificate, the mother regularly took all the other steps required by the laws of the order for the purpose of changing the beneficiary, and accompanied her application for a change with an affidavit stating the reason why the original certificate was not surrendered, and further stating therein that she made her son, the respondent herein, her sole beneficiary under said certificate. The society still refused to issue the new certificate upon the ground that the original was neither lost nor destroyed, and yet had not been surrendered. Matters remained *in statu quo* until the death of the mother, when this litigation arose between the children, and was decided by the trial court in favor of the son.

Laying aside any question of interest in the original beneficiary certificate resting in the daughter by virtue of matters

arising in parol between the mother and the daughter, we are
clear that as between the original beneficiary, the daughter,
and the proposed new beneficiary, the son, the proceeds of
this policy belong to the son.   As between them there was a
substitution of beneficiaries in the eyes of a court of equity.
If the Legion of Honor was here as an aggressive party, insisting as against the claims of the son upon a strict compliance with its by-laws before it could be compelled to take
money from its treasury, possibly a different question would
be presented; but, as between these parties litigant, the court
will administer justice from the standpoint of equity, and
bring to the solution of this question those broad principles
upon the basis of which equity always deals.   The general
rule unquestionably is that a change of a beneficiary cannot
be made by the insured unless a substantial compliance with
the laws and regulations of the society is had; yet courts
of equity have recognized various exceptions to this general
principle, and the facts of this case bring it squarely within
one of the well-recognized exceptions.   This exception is
builded upon the principle that equity does not demand impossible things, and [27] will consider that done which ought
to have been done; and is embraced within the proposition
that when the insured complies with all the requirements of
the rules for the purpose of making the substitution of beneficiaries, with which he has the power to comply, he has done
all that a court of equity demands: See *Supreme Conclave* v.
Cappella, 41 Fed. Rep. 1, approved in *McLaughlin* v. *Mc-
Laughlin*, 104 Cal. 171; 43 Am. St. Rep. 83; *Grand Lodge* v.
Child, 70 Mich. 163; *Isgrigg* v. *Schooley*, 125 Ind. 95; *Marsh*
v. *American Legion of Honor*, 149 Mass. 512.

The present case comes squarely within this exception,
and in principle is identical with some of the cases we have
cited.   For the purpose of changing the beneficiary, the
insured complied in detail with every rule of the society,
save the single one of surrendering the certificate, and this
she was unable to do after using due diligence to that end.
Impossibilities are not required, and if the certificate had
been lost or destroyed, and thus the surrender made impossible, equity would have treated the surrender as duly made;
and in legal effect the certificate was lost in this case.   But
there is another well-settled principle of equity equally fatal
to appellant's claims.   No person can take advantage of his
own wrong.   No man is allowed to come into a court of

equity and reap beneficial results from his own iniquity. If Mrs. Jory had the right to make the change of benefi-ciaries, and did all that it was possible for her to do toward making such change, but was prevented by the acts of ap-pellant from a consummation of her intentions, then appel-lant will not be allowed to derive any benefit from her fraudulent conduct. If a fraud of her own practicing pre-vented a legal substitution of beneficiaries, then as against her an equitable substitution will be held to have taken place.

If the insured, Mrs. Jory, had a legal right to make a change of beneficiaries at the time she attempted so to do, then the maxims of equity which we have applied to the facts of the case dispose of this litigation fully and entirely. But, as a further ground of defense to [28] the action, it is insisted by appellant that her mother had no such right. Appellant says she had a vested interest in the certificate, and rights under it which could not be taken away from her by a legal substitution of beneficiaries, even if such substitution had been made by the insured. Under this claim of the appellant the question as to an actual substitution would seem to be immaterial; for if the insured had proceeded under the rules and laws of the order, and obtained a substi-tution of beneficiaries perfect in all its parts, still, as between the parties here litigating, it would not be conclusive as establishing title to its proceeds in the holder thereof, for we are in a court of equity and administering justice to these parties according to their equities.

The principle here under consideration is the most recent growth of mutual benefit association law, a branch of the law which in itself is young in years; and we know of nothing in the law which deprives a person contemplating member-ship in a mutual benefit association from so contracting with the proposed beneficiary as that when such certificate is issued, equities in favor of the beneficiary are born of such merit that the insured member has no power to defeat them. The few authorities shedding light upon this question declare the rights of the beneficiary are such as to create a vested in-terest in the proceeds of the certificate: *Smith* v. *National Ben. Soc.*, 123 N. Y. 85; *Maynard* v. *Vanderwerker*, 24 N. Y. Supp. 932. Possibly this is not a correct declaration of the prin-ciple of law applicable to the conditions; for a second benefici-ary might be substituted, wholly innocent of the contractual

relations existing between the insured and the first beneficiary, and his substitution give rise to the creation of equities
in his behalf, all controlling upon a judicial disposition of
the rights of the parties concerned.   If the original beneficiary's interest was vested, no subsequent conditions could possibly arise which would defeat his right, and for this reason
we think it can hardly be termed a vested interest.   The
whole matter seems to be rather [29] a question of equities,
and the stronger and better equity must prevail.   The illustration we have used does not arise in the present case, for we
here have no clash of equities.   The second beneficiary possesses no equities.   He is a volunteer pure and simple.   His
status during the life of the insured is well described in
Smith v. National Ben. Soc., 123 N. Y. 85, where the court
said: "The designation was in the nature of an inchoate or
unexecuted gift, revocable at any moment by the donor,
and wholly within his control."   We think a court of equity
should declare the insured estopped from substituting a
second beneficiary of the character here involved, whenever
sound equities are extant in favor of the first beneficiary;
and, such estoppel being in force against the insured, it is
equally in force and may be successfully urged against the
volunteer beneficiary.

The respondent is a volunteer beneficiary, and it only
remains for us to ascertain from the record what the appellant's equities are, as disclosed by the evidence.   She claims
by her answer that she and her mother entered into a mutual
agreement, whereby each should join a mutual benefit society
and make the other a beneficiary under the certificates issued,
and that said agreement was carried out.   Appellant further
alleges that she paid all initiation fees, dues, and assessments
upon the benefit certificate taken out by her mother.   If these
moneys were paid out by appellant under and by virtue of a
contract between the parties, and in pursuance of this agreement and scheme for mutual insurance, then she has equities which entitle her to recognition in a court of justice, for
it would be a gross imposition and fraud upon her to allow
the insured to change her beneficiary under these circumstances.   Though wrong and injustice form an unpleasant
sight to a court of equity, yet that court will never close its
eyes because the sight is an unpleasant one, but rather with
vision all the keener will reach out its strong arm to protect
the wronged and innocent party.

In this case, after hearing all the evidence, the court [30] made its findings of fact, holding that appellant failed to prove either that there was a contract of mutual insurance entered into by the mother and the daughter, or that she, the daughter, paid the assessments, dues, etc., upon her mother's certificate other than the small sum of fourteen dollars. In the absence of a contract of some character inuring to the benefit of a beneficiary, the mere fact of payment of assessments by such an one is not sufficient to create equities in his favor, for the courts of the land say such payments are to be treated as gifts; and in the present case the basis of whatever rights to which the appellant may be entitled is the contract of mutual insurance. But the evidence of appellant upon both branches of her claim is weak, vague, and unsatisfactory. The mother, sister, and a younger brother were living together. They all earned more or less money by their labors, which for years was placed in a common fund, and all outlays for living expenses, payment of assessments upon these certificates, and incidental expenses were taken therefrom. It is not apparent that the appellant had any money of her own. She had no independent source of revenue, and after the brother's death the source from which the money to meet the assessments was drawn is not clearly located in her. As to the contract for a mutual insurance, the evidence is even more unsatisfactory than it is as to the source of the funds from which the assessments were paid; and, without entering into a detailed review of the evidence, we will say that the finding of the court in this regard is satisfactory to us. These matters are set up in the answer as an affirmative equitable defense to plaintiff's cause of action, and the burden rested upon her to prove them by a preponderance of evidence; and upon a consideration of the insufficiency of the evidence to support the findings of fact we are not prepared to say that the evidence even preponderates in her favor. The evidence bearing upon this branch of the case was confined almost entirely to the testimony of the parties interested, and their prior [31] statements and admissions. The witnesses were before the court, and we think it pre-eminently a case where great deference should be shown to the judgment of the trial court upon the weight of evidence. For these reasons we will not disturb the findings of fact, and appellant's claim of existing equities has failed for want of proof.

It is stated that the court committed an error in admitting in evidence statements made by Mrs. Jory prior to her death, to the effect that she had asked appellant several times for the certificate, and that appellant would not give it up. Conceding the evidence objectionable, as being hearsay, still no harm to appellant arose by its admission. There is an abundance of other evidence in the record, showing a demand upon her for the certificate, and substantially nothing to the contrary. While she may have formally denied in her answer the allegation of demand made in the complaint, and while she may also have stated at the trial that no demand was made upon her, the whole record is opposed to the statement, and the whole theory of her own case, both in pleading and evidence, is opposed to it; for her case rests upon the claim that her mother was not entitled to the certificate, but that it was her own separate property, of which she was entitled to the absolute and exclusive control. She does not state in her evidence that she would have given it up to her mother if it had been demanded, but, upon the contrary, it is conclusively shown, both by her pleading and evidence, that she would not have done so if a demand had been made. Under these circumstances the statements of her mother as to a demand were not prejudicial, even conceding them to be erroneous.

It is ordered that the judgment and order be affirmed.

HARRISON, J., and VAN FLEET, J., concurred.

MUTUAL BENEFIT ASSOCIATION — BENEFICIARIES — HOW CHANGED.—The laws of a mutual benefit society prescribing a mode of changing beneficiaries must be followed. A change cannot be made in any other manner: *Mc-Laughlin* v. *McLaughlin*, 104 Cal. 171; 43 Am. St. Rep. 83, and note; *Thomas* v. *Thomas*, 131 N. Y. 205; 27 Am. St. Rep. 582; *Rollins* v. *McHutton*, 16 Col. 203; 25 Am. St. Rep. 260, and note. See, also, the extended note to *Bankers'* *etc. Assn.* v. *Stapp*, 19 Am. St. Rep. 786.

MUTUAL BENEFIT ASSOCIATION—BENEFICIARIES—VESTED RIGHTS.—An appointee in a certificate of a benefit society has no vested interest in the sum payable thereunder of which he cannot be deprived without his consent: *Sabin* v. *Phinney*, 134 N. Y. 423; 30 Am. St. Rep. 681, and note, with the cases collected.

GREEN v. BERGE.

[105 CALIFORNIA, 52.]

APPELLATE PROCEDURE, ADVERSE PARTY, WHO IS—CODEFENDANTS.—Under a statute requiring every notice of appeal to be served on the adverse party or his attorney, a plaintiff against whom a judgment has been entered in favor of one of two codefendants, and in whose favor judgment is entered against the other codefendant, need not serve a notice of appeal on the defendant against whom judgment has been entered. He is not an adverse party, because the reversal of the judgment in favor of the other defendant cannot increase his liability nor otherwise prejudice him.

APPELLATE PROCEDURE.—AN ADVERSE PARTY WITHIN THE MEANING OF THE STATUTE REGULATING APPEALS is a party whose interest in relation to the subject of the appeal is in conflict with the reversal or modification of the judgment or order from which the appeal is prosecuted.

LATERAL SUPPORT—LIABILITY OF CONTRACTOR FOR REMOVING.—If a contractor employed by a lotowner to excavate on his own land and up to the line of an adjacent proprietor makes such excavation, and thereafter, and after his contract is wholly completed, the lot of the adjacent proprietor falls in to his injury, such contractor is answerable to him in damages though his work was performed in a careful manner, and the injuries might have been averted after the work was done had the person who contracted for doing it added the proper support.

LATERAL SUPPORT—NEGLIGENCE.—To excavate on one's land so as to deprive the land of his neighbor of lateral support is negligence, unless the excavator furnishes the support required.

LATERAL SUPPORT.—A LOTOWNER AND A CONTRACTOR ARE JOINTLY ANSWERABLE for depriving the land of an adjacent proprietor of lateral support.

ACTION against Berge, the owner of a lot, and Buckman, a contractor, to recover for injuries suffered by plaintiff from an excavation made by the contractor on the lot of Berge up to the line of the plaintiff's lot, and without either defendant taking any measures to prevent the falling in of plaintiff's lot by reason of such excavation and want of lateral support. The trial court rendered judgment against the lotowner, but held that Buckman, the contractor, who actually did the work, was not liable for the damages suffered by plaintiff. The plaintiff appealed, but served his notice of appeal upon the defendant Buckman only.

Alexander D. Keyes, for the appellant.

J. C. Bates, for the respondent.

[55] TEMPLE, C. This appeal is from a portion of the judgment upon the judgment-roll.

The action was brought to recover damages for excavating

upon a lot, adjoining plaintiff's lot, so negligently that the ground constituting a portion of plaintiff's lot fell into the excavation of its own weight.

Berge was the owner of the lot upon which the excavating was done, and Buckman performed the work under a contract.

The case was tried without a jury, and, among other facts, the court found that on the 14th of May, 1891, Berge entered into a contract with Buckman in writing, whereby for a stipulated price Buckman agreed to grade his lot. That in the contract nothing was said in regard to the duty of supporting the bank toward plaintiff's lot. That Buckman performed the work to the satisfaction of Berge, and in all respects in a careful, skillful, and workmanlike manner.

That the work was completed on the fourteenth day of August, 1891, and on that day was accepted by Berge, who then gave Buckman a writing, in which he stated that the work was done to his satisfaction.

That Berge did not, after the completion of the work, provide for any lateral support to plaintiff's land, which by the excavation had been deprived of its natural support.

That in the month of December a great part of the earth of plaintiff's lot, solely by its own weight and by reason of its said lack of lateral support, gave way, and fell into the excavation, to the injury of plaintiff in the sum of one thousand dollars.

Thereupon, the court gave judgment in favor of plaintiff against Berge for one thousand dollars, but also ordered judgment in favor of Buckman against plaintiff for his costs.

Plaintiff appeals from that part of the judgment [56] which is in favor of Buckman, and now contends that upon the findings she is entitled to a joint judgment against both defendants for the amount of damage found by the court.

1. Respondent makes a preliminary objection to the jurisdiction of this court to entertain the appeal, on the ground that the notice of appeal was not served on the codefendant of appellant.

"An appeal is taken by filing with the clerk of the court in which the judgment or order appealed from is entered, a notice stating the appeal from the same or some specific part thereof, and serving a similar notice on the adverse party or his attorney." Is appellant's codefendant an adverse party? The appeal cannot result in a modification of the judgment against him. If the appeal be successful, the only possible result would be either that a new trial would be awarded as to the appellant, or a joint judgment would be entered against both defendants in lieu of the present judgment against Berge. This would in no way affect the liability of Berge upon the judgment, though it might give him the advantage of a codefendant. This is not an adverse interest.

This question was decided in *Senter* v. *De Bernal*, 38 Cal. 637, where it was said, quoting from *Thompson* v. *Ellsworth*, 1 Barb. Ch. 627: "The adverse party . . . . means the party whose interest in relation to the subject of appeals is in conflict with the reversal of the order or decree appealed from, or the modification sought for by the appeal."

This case has been often referred to with approbation since, and indeed it would be difficult to reach any other conclusion.

2. It is contended by the respondent—and this appears to be the view taken by the lower court—that the duty of sustaining the land of the adjoining owner rested upon the lotowner, who caused the natural support of the land to be removed. That Buckman had a right to presume that Berge would perform his duty. [57] He undertook to do a part of the work only, and there was nothing unlawful in what he did. If there was any thing unlawful it was on the part of the lotowner who did the excavating, but did not take measures to support the adjoining land. The land did not cave in until the work had been completed and accepted. The lotowner could then have added the support, and Buckman had a right to presume he would do so. It was found that the work was done in a careful manner, and that there was nothing in the mode of doing the work which increased the liability of the land to slide into the excavation.

This view seems plausible, but, stated in another way, it does not have that appearance. Buckman removed the natural support of the soil. This support was an incident to plaintiff's ownership. It was not lawful to do this except by the owner of adjoining land, nor then except by taking reasonable precautions to sustain the land: Civ. Code, sec. 832. No such precautions were taken, and the work was therefore unlawful, and caused the injury.

The authorities sustain this view. In *Dalton* v. *Angus*, 6 L. R. App. C. 740, the Lord Chancellor said: "The action was brought by reason of the falling of the plaintiff's house

through the excavation of the adjoining land of the commissioners in the course of certain work, executed for them by
the appellant, Dalton, under a contract, and for Dalton by
subcontractors. The commissioners disputed their liability
for the acts of Dalton, and Dalton disputed his liability for
the acts of his subcontractors. The same point arose under
very similar circumstances in *Bower* v. *Pete*, 1 Q. B. Div. 321,
and was decided adversely to the contention of appellants.
It follows from that decision (as to the correctness of which
I agree with both the courts below) that, if the plaintiffs are
entitled to recover at all, they are entitled to recover against
both the commissioners and Dalton."

In *Aston* v. *Nolan*, 63 Cal. 269, the work of excavating was
done under a contract similar to the contract in this [58] case.
That is, it was a contract for excavating which contained no
provisions in regard to supporting the land of the adjoining
lot. It was held that the contractor was liable, and that
since the contract implied that the work should be done in a
lawful manner, that is, in taking reasonable care to support
the earth of the adjoining lot, that the owner of the lot was
not liable. Some would be disposed to question that decision
so far as it holds that the lotowner could thus relieve himself
from the duty he owed to his coterminous owner. That point,
however, is not involved here. The case is authority for the
proposition that the contractor is responsible.

Independently of the statute the adjoining lotowner who
caused the excavation to be made would be responsible for
any damage which might result, irrespective of the question
of negligence in making the excavation: *Gilmore* v. *Driscoll*,
122 Mass. 199; 23 Am. Rep. 312; *Foley* v. *Wyeth*, 2 Allen, 131;
79 Am. Dec. 771; *Carlin* v. *Chappel*, 101 Pa. St. 348; 47 Am.
Rep. 722; *Richardson* v. *Vermont Cent. R. R. Co.*, 25 Vt. 465;
60 Am. Dec. 283.

Here the only neglect necessary to give a cause of action
is the neglect to furnish the support required by the statute
(*Aston* v. *Nolan*, 63 Cal. 269; *Conboy* v. *Dickinson*, 92 Cal.
600), and, of course, to make the excavation otherwise must
be negligence.

A landowner has an interest in adjoining land for the
lateral support of his soil. This is a limitation upon the
rights of landowners. Whoever deprives him of this support for his land, otherwise than as the statute has prescribed,
performs an unlawful act. The general rule is that all who

unite in such acts are wrongdoers, and are responsible in damages. Respondent knew, or should have known, that to make the excavation without supplying the support was unlawful. Having participated in it, he cannot avoid responsibility by pleading that he did the work under a contract.

Except the case of *Aston* v. *Nolan*, 63 Cal. 269, all the [59] authorities I have been able to find hold that the landowner who causes such an excavation to be made cannot relieve himself of responsibility by any contract he could make. Cooley, in his work on Torts, speaking of the exceptions to the rule that the master is not liable for the negligence of an independent contractor, or the servants of such contractor, says: "He must not contract for that, the necessary or probable effect of which would be to injure others, and he cannot by any contract relieve himself of duties resting upon him as owner of real estate, not to do or suffer to be done upon it that which will constitute a nuisance, and, therefore, an invasion of the rights of others."

In a note to this he cites the case of such an excavation as an instance.

But admitting that *Aston* v. *Nolan*, 63 Cal. 269, goes too far, I do not see how that will relieve Buckman. It makes it a case where both are wrongdoers and both responsible.

I think the judgment should be modified so as to make it a joint judgment against both defendants.

SEARLS, C., and VANCLIEF, C., concurred.

For the reasons given in the foregoing opinion the judgment is modified so as to make it a joint judgment against both defendants.

McFARLAND, J., DE HAVEN, J., FITZGERALD, J.

Hearing in Bank denied. ____

APPEAL—ADVERSE PARTIES—WHO ARE.—Every party whose interest in relation to the judgment appealed from is in conflict with the reversal or modification sought by the appeal is an adverse party, and must be served with a notice of appeal under a statute requiring the appellant to serve such notice on the adverse party. The notice must be served on all persons whose interests are adverse to the party appealing: *The Victorian*, 24 Or. 121; 41 Am. St. Rep. 838, and note.

LATERAL SUPPORT.—This question is thoroughly discussed in the monographic note to *Larson* v. *Metropolitan etc. Ry. Co.*, 33 Am. St. Rep. 446–476.

CUNNINGHAM *v.* KENNEY.
[105 CALIFORNIA, 118.]

CONTRACT OF BAILMENT, ENTIRETY OF.—A contract to store hay for a specified period is an entirety, and no compensation therefor can be recovered when, because of the destruction of the warehouse, the contract to keep the hay for the time designated has not been, and cannot be, performed.

A. S. Kittredge, for the appellants.

W. L. Gill, for the respondent.

[119] The COURT. This is an action to recover three hundred and sixty-nine dollars and forty-five cents, as bailees, for the price of storage by defendant of certain hay in the warehouse of plaintiffs. Defendant had judgment, from which judgment and from an order denying their motion for a new trial plaintiffs appealed.

The cause was tried by the court without a jury. The findings, which are supported by the evidence without conflict, show:

1. That in 1888 the plaintiffs and their grantor and [120] E. J. Swift, deceased, of whose estate T. V. Mathews is administrator, were the owners of a warehouse in the county of Santa Clara.

2. On or about September 1, 1888, defendant delivered to plaintiffs for storage in said warehouse certain hay, upon the terms and conditions expressed in an agreement in writing, of which the following is a copy:

"YNIGO RANCHO WAREHOUSE,
"MOUNTAIN VIEW, Oct. 17, 1888.

"This is to certify that Mr. Daniel Kenney has this day stored in sections — of the Ynigo Rancho Warehouse 3,016 bales wheat hay, weighing 720,000 lbs. balers' weight, subject to the following conditions: The warehouse owner will not be responsible for loss or damage to hay from effect of water, fire, damp, or other causes. Hay stored only for the season ending June 1st of each year. Rate, $1.00 on balers' weight. Storage payable only in gold coin of the United States, and must be paid before withdrawal of the hay. Weighing, 25 cents extra.

"M. W. WILCOX, Manager,
"37 North First street, San Jose."

3. Said hay remained on storage under said agreement

until the seventeenth day of March, 1889, when, without the fault of defendant, the said warehouse and hay were wholly destroyed by fire.

The answer of defendant charged plaintiffs with negligence, upon which issue the court did not find, deeming it unimportant, and holding as a conclusion of law that the contract of storage was an entire and not a severable contract, and that as the warehouse and hay having burned before the time for the storing of said hay expired, the agreement of plaintiffs to store the hay until June 1, 1889, was never performed or complied with by them and the storage never earned.

The following extract from the opinion of the learned judge who tried the case in the court below contains a correct exposition of the law applicable to the case, and is adopted as the opinion of the court.

[121] "To defeat the plaintiffs' claim defendant insists, among other things, that the plaintiffs did not perform the contract, and hence cannot recover upon it.

"I am of opinion the point is well taken. As I understand the contract it is an entire one. The terms are, that, for a compensation of one dollar per ton, the plaintiffs agreed to store the hay for the season ending June 1, 1889.

"It is the duty of a bailee, at the end of the term for which property is stored, to return it to the bailor. While the law relieves the bailee at the suit of the bailor from liability for the value of the article stored when it is destroyed by fire without his fault, and when he has exercised reasonable care toward its preservation, it does not permit him to recover compensation for its custody and care when he is unable, through the loss, to perform the contract he has undertaken. His right to recover compensation is to be determined from the contract itself, and, in order to recover, he must show performance according to its terms.

"The industry of counsel has furnished no authority which holds that a warehouseman agreeing to store property for a given time can recover the compensation provided by the contract when the property was lost by fire before the term of storage had expired.

"The case of *Schmidt* v. *Blood*, 9 Wend. 268, 24 Am. Dec. 154, cited by counsel, does not so hold. The only point, aside from the question of negligence, involved in that case, was whether the warehouseman, after part of the goods stored had been stolen without his fault, had a lien upon the remainder for the compensation due for the whole, and the court held that he had.

"From that decision it can only be inferentially argued that if he had the right to compensation, but it may be with equal force argued that the compensation may have been earned and the contract performed before the goods were stolen. As the terms and conditions of the contract in that case are not set forth, and the point in dispute here was not 122 directly involved in that case, it cannot be considered as authority.

"The case at bar comes, I am satisfied, under the rule announced in *Archer* v. *McDonald*, 36 Hun, 194. In that case McDonald agreed to store for Archer from October until May from fifteen thousand to thirty thousand barrels of lime, and to deliver it at the end of his wharf in May. For this he was to receive fifteen cents per barrel. In November, after twenty thousand barrels had been received, they caught fire without any fault of McDonald, and were ruined by slacking. In that case the court held that the contract was an entire one, and that not only was McDonald not entitled to recover any compensation, but that Archer was entitled to recover back the money he had paid on account for storage.

"I see no difference in principle between the case cited and the case at bar.

"It is true that in both cases during all the time the articles were in possession of the warehouseman they had incurred liability and responsibility in the care of the property, and it seems inequitable that they are entitled to no compensation, as it seems to be equally inequitable to allow them compensation for services not performed.

"That, however, is not the fault of the law, but of the warehousemen. They could have provided in their contract for contingencies, and for a proportionate compensation for proportionate service. They have not done so. The court cannot make contracts for the parties; it can only determine such contracts as they have made.

"In this case the plaintiffs have seen fit to enter into a contract entire in its terms, and their rights must be measured by it. As the plaintiffs failed to perform their contract and store the property for the time specified in their contract, they are not entitled to recover. The defendant is entitled to a judgment for his costs, and it is so ordered.

"W. G. LORIGAN, Superior Judge."

123 The foregoing reasons render a finding upon the question of negligence of no importance to the result.

The judgment and order appealed from are affirmed.

CONTRACTS—WHEN ENTIRE.—See the extended note to *Gill* v. *Benjamin,* 54 Am. Rep. 624. A later discussion of this question will be found in *Fullmer* v. *Poust,* 155 Pa. St. 275; 35 Am. St. Rep. 881, and note, and *Pierson* v. *Crooks,* 115 N. Y. 539; 12 Am. St. Rep. 831.

BOLTON *v.* GILLERAN.

[105 CALIFORNIA, 244.]

MUNICIPAL CORPORATION — DELEGATION OF AUTHORITY. — The legislative department of a city cannot delegate to any other officer or body the authority to determine the necessity of making a street improvement, or the extent or character of any improvement which it may itself direct to be made.

STREET ASSESSMENTS.—IF A RESOLUTION OF INTENTION TO DO STREET WORK LEAVES IT UNCERTAIN what is to be done, all subsequent proceedings are unauthorized. The legislative body must determine not only the character and extent of the improvement which it will authorize, but also the amount of the burden which is to be imposed therefor by assessment upon adjacent property to bear the expense of the improvement, though the clerical or ministerial act of apportioning the assessment may be determined by another official.

STREET ASSESSMENTS.—IF A RESOLUTION OF INTENTION to do street work refers to the specifications, and these declare that if the soil be of improper nature for a foundation it shall be removed to a sufficient depth, and two tiers of three-inch planks be laid, and the discretion to determine what planking shall be required is left to the superintendent of streets, the proceedings based upon such resolution are void.

CLOUD ON TITLE — VOID STREET ASSESSMENTS. — An action may be sustained to remove, as a cloud upon plaintiff's title, a street assessment valid upon its face, but void because of informalities in the proceedings preceding it. Though the plaintiff has a perfect defense in an action for the enforcement of the assessment, he is not required to wait until such action is brought, but may himself invoke the equitable aid of the court to remove the cloud, and enjoin the holder of the assessment from asserting any claim based thereon.

J. C. Bates, for the appellant.

Ash & Mathews, for the respondents Conklin & Co.

Frs. E. Spencer, C. T. Bird, and D. W. Burchard, for the respondents Gilleran *et al.*

245 HARRISON, J. The board of supervisors of the city and county of San Francisco passed a resolution of intention

June 1, 1891, to construct sewers in Fell street, and certain connecting streets, "according to plans and specifications prepared by Charles S. Tilton, city engineer." After an order for said improvement of the streets had been passed, the board of supervisors caused notice for sealed proposals to do the work to be given, and, **247** upon receiving bids therefor, awarded the contract to the respondents, Conklin & Co. After the completion of their contract the superintendent of streets made an assessment therefor, which, after being recorded, was delivered to the said respondents. A portion of the expense for doing the work was assessed against certain lands of the plaintiff, and this action was brought by her to obtain a judgment declaring that the contract made with said respondents for the work be declared null and void, and that the assessment be declared not to be a lien upon any of her said property. Judgment was rendered in favor of the defendants, from which the plaintiff has appealed upon the judgment-roll without any bill of exceptions.

The legislature of the state has conferred upon the "legislative department of the government of any city," which in San Francisco is the board of supervisors, the exclusive authority for the improvement of its streets. This legislative department of the city has no power to delegate to any other officer or body the authority to determine upon the necessity of making such improvement, or the character or extent of any improvement which it may itself direct to be made. In the language of Mr. Dillon (Dillon on Municipal Corporations, sec. 96): "It is not competent for the council to pass an ordinance delegating or leaving to any officer or committee of the corporation the power to determine the mode, manner, or plan of the improvement." Accordingly, it has been held that no valid assessment upon property can be made under an order directing the improvement "where necessary" (*Richardson* v. *Heydenfeldt*, 46 Cal. 68); or "excepting such portions of the above-described work which have been already done in a suitable manner" (*Foss* v. *Chicago*, 56 Ill. 354); or for constructing curbs "where the same are not now in good and sound condition" (*Bryan* v. *Chicago*, 60 Ill. 507); or where, in constructing a drain, certain pieces of lumber were to be set "at equidistant points of not more than four feet" (*Village of Hyde Park* v. *Carton*, 132 Ill. **248** 103); or improving "such portions of the sidewalks as the city engineer may direct" (*Hydes* v. *Joyes*, 4

Bush, 464; 96 Am. Dec. 311); or "in such manner as the city superintendent shall direct": *Thompson* v. *Schermerhorn*, 6 N. Y. 92; 55 Am. Dec. 385.   See, also, *Phelps* v. *Mayor*, 112 N. Y. 221; *City of Kankakee* v. *Potter*, 119 Ill. 324; *McCrowell* v. *City of Bristol*, 89 Va. 652.   The legislative body must determine, not only the character and extent of the improvement which it will authorize, but also the amount of the burden which is to be imposed therefor by the assessment upon the adjacent property to defray the expense of the improvement.   This power of assessment is referable to the power of taxation, and is itself a legislative power which must not only find express authority for its exercise, but which can be neither exercised by an executive officer, nor delegated to such officer by the legislative body of the municipality.   The clerical or ministerial act of apportioning the assessment upon the lands to be charged therewith may be performed by another official, but whether the assessment shall be imposed upon the lands, and the amount of such assessment, must be determined by the legislative body.   A prominent consideration before this body, in determining whether an improvement shall be made upon a street, is the amount of its expense and the advantage that will accrue therefrom to the property which is to be charged with that expense; and, unless it can know to a reasonable degree of certainty what the expense will .be, it will be unable to exercise any intelligent discretion in determining whether the improvement should be made.   Hence, it becomes necessary for the legislative body to know the probable expense of the improvement before it will order it to be made, and, after the improvement has been ordered, the actual expense must be approved by this body and fixed in the contract for doing the work as the data upon which the assessment is to be calculated.   This includes not only the price at which the work is to be done, but also the items of the material [249] and work which enter into its construction, so that the official who is to apportion the expense shall have no other function than to compute the amounts that have been previously approved by the legislative body.

This power and the exercise of this discretion in the city and county of San Francisco has been conferred upon the board of supervisors, and must be exercised by that body, and cannot be delegated by it to the superintendent of streets. By section 2 of the street improvement act of this state (Stats.

1889, p. 157) the authority to direct improvements is given
to the city council of any municipality, which, in section 34
of the act, is declared to include "any body or board which
under the law is the legislative department of the government
of any city"; and section 3 requires as the initiatory or jurisdictional step, that the board of supervisors shall pass a
resolution of intention "describing the work" which they
propose to order done, and that "before passing any resolution for the construction of said improvements, plans, and
specifications, and careful estimates of the cost and expenses
thereof, shall be furnished to said city council, if required by
it, by the city engineer of said city, and, for the work of constructing sewers, specifications shall always be furnished by
him." Section 5 provides that, before awarding any contract,
a notice with "specifications" shall be given, inviting proposals for doing the work ordered; and the city council is authorized to reject all proposals, if it deem it for the public
good, and can award a contract only to the lowest responsible
bidder. This contract is to be entered into by the superintendent of streets with the bidder to whom it has been
awarded, and, after its completion, the superintendent is to
apportion the expense of the work, as fixed by the contract,
upon the lands liable to be assessed therefor.

The proceedings in the present case show a wide departure
from these provisions. The work which was "described" in
the resolution of intention was the construction of sewers
upon certain designated streets, "of ²⁵⁰ the materials and
dimensions hereinafter described," and "according to plans
and specifications prepared by C. S. Tilton, city engineer."
One of these specifications was in the following terms: "If
the soil be of improper nature for a foundation it shall be
removed to a sufficient depth, and two tiers of three-inch
planks be laid, one tier transversely and the other tier longitu-
dinally, to be securely spiked with six-inch cut spikes where
the foundation is not sufficiently secure, and upon these
planks will rest a bed of concrete which must be laid to conform to the invert, and to be to a depth below the center of
the invert, as shown on plans." In the notice for proposals
calling for bids these specifications were referred to, and bidders were required to estimate for the entire work, and state
for how much they would construct the sewers per lineal foot
"if on stable foundation," and for how much per lineal foot
"if planking and concrete should be required," "correctly

computing and carrying out the aggregate amount for the
entire work." Under this notice Conklin & Co. presented a
bid in which they offered to take the entire work at the following prices: " Per lineal foot, for the five-foot circular brick
sewer, if on stable foundation, $9.83; per lineal foot, for the
five-foot circular brick sewer, if planking and concrete should
be required, $12.78; per lineal foot, for the 4 x 5 foot elliptical-
shaped brick sewer, if on stable foundation, $8.50; per lineal
foot, for the 4 x 5 foot elliptical-shaped brick sewer, if planking and concrete should be required, $11.45; per lineal foot,
for the 3 x 5 foot egg-shaped brick sewer, if on stable foundation, $7.20; per lineal foot, for the 3 x 5 foot egg-shaped brick
sewer, if planking and concrete should be required, $10.24 ";
and a contract therefor was awarded to them at those prices,
and was afterward entered into between them and the superintendent of streets.

A mere glance at these proceedings shows that the amount
of tax which is to be imposed upon the lands for the expense
of the improvement was not determined by the supervisors
in their award of the contract, but [251] that they gave to
the superintendent of streets the discretion to determine
that amount to the extent of fully one-third thereof. For
the 5 foot circular sewer which was to be constructed for
$9.83 per lineal foot the superintendent was allowed to add
$2.95 for each foot, according as he should determine whether
the foundation was stable, or whether there should be a foundation of plank and concrete, and he was given the same discretion to determine whether the cost of the 4 x 5 foot elliptical
brick sewer should be $8.50 or $10.45, while the cost of the
3 x 5 egg-shaped sewer could be increased by him from $7.20
to $10.24, an increase of nearly 50 per cent. This discre-
tion was not controlled by any fixed rules, but its exercise
was intrusted solely to his own judgment or volition. The
specifications gave no indication of the amount of "stable
foundation" on which the sewers were to be laid, or what
character of ground should be regarded as "stable foundation," or the extent of the ground for which "planking and
concrete" would be required. These matters were to be determined by the superintendent of streets alone, nor were the
conditions for his determination fixed. What constituted an
"improper" nature for a foundation, or what would be a
"sufficient depth " to which it was to be removed, or the
place in which the foundation was not "sufficiently secure,"

were elements of uncertainty which prevented any previous
determination of the cost. It is not sufficient to say that the
character of the ground in which the sewers were to be constructed was not known to the board of supervisors. It was
their duty to cause its character to be examined before ordering the improvement, and not to leave the character of the
improvement to depend upon the subsequent examination by
some other officer. The statute requires that before they
shall pass any resolution for the construction of the improvements they shall cause " careful estimates of the costs and
expenses thereof " to be furnished them by the city engineer.
This necessarily includes an examination of the character of
the ground in which the sewer is to be [252] constructed, and
is to be a guide for their deliberation. It might be that upon
such an examination, and in view of the extraordinary expense that would result therefrom, they would deem it best
not to order the improvement, or would cause the construction
of a different kind of sewer, or would enlarge the district
upon which the expense should be laid. In any event they
were not justified in divesting themselves of the responsibility that the statute has imposed upon them. A contract
in terms like the present gives to the superintendent of streets
the opportunity to make the cost of the improvement greater
or less, according to his desire to favor or injure the contractor, vests him with an illegal discretion, tends to prepare
the way for an unfair assessment, and opens wide the door
to fraud and favoritism. If there is any profit in doing the
work at the higher figure the natural effect of such a contract
is to induce the contractor to put planking and concrete
upon the whole line of work, while, if it is without profit, he
would be disposed to consider the entire foundation stable.
Under such a notice for proposals bidders can have no intelligent basis upon which to calculate the cost of the work, and
all competition for doing the work is practically destroyed.
The statute gives to the owners of the land to be assessed the
right to take the contract at the price at which it was
awarded to the successful bidder. This implies that the
owners shall be definitely informed of the work which is to
be done, and of the amount for which the assessment is to be
made, in order that they may intelligently consider whether
it will be to their advantage to take the contract; but if there
are no data from which to determine the amount of material
that will be required in doing the work, or if the cost thereof,

to the extent of at least one-third, is to depend upon the
volition of an officer who may or may not be friendly to
them, they would naturally hesitate to place themselves in
the position of depending upon his friendship or antagonism,
and would thus fail to receive the advantage which the statute intended to confer upon them. [253] We cannot better
express the result of upholding such a proceeding than in the
words of the supreme court of Illinois in *Foss* v. *Chicago*, 56
Ill. 358:

"*E*very such covert, irresponsible, discretionary power as
here assumed is wholly inconsistent with a proper exercise
of the high and sovereign power of taxation or eminent domain. It might be used, and it does not affect the principle
whether it was so used or not, as a cover to an unfair estimate or assessment. It might be used as the instrument of
favoritism in letting the contracts for the work. Some of the
parties might be made to understand that the portions of the
work already done were not done in a suitable manner, and
that it would all have to be removed, while others might be
informed that if they got the contract the portions already
done would he considered as done in a suitable manner, and
be so much clear gain."

The right of the plaintiff to maintain the action is clearly
established. The statute makes the assessment a lien upon
her lands, and there is nothing upon the face of the assessment to show that the lien is not in all respects valid. If,
by reason of matters outside of the assessment as it is recorded, this apparent lien may be shown not to be a valid
encumbrance, the assessment constitutes a cloud upon her
title which she is entitled to have removed; and although
she can assert the same matters as a defense to any action
for the enforcement of the assessment, she is not required to
wait until such action may be brought, and, in the mean
time, suffer the injury of having the title to her lands impaired by this apparent lien, but may herself invoke the
equitable aid of the court to remove the cloud, and to enjoin
the holder of the assessment from asserting any claim upon
her lands by virtue thereof.

The judgment is reversed.

GAROUTTE J., and VAN FLEET, J., concurred.

Hearing in Bank denied.

MUNICIPAL CORPORATIONS—DELEGATION OF AUTHORITY.—If a municipality is given the right to exercise a certain authority in such manner and by such officers and agents as it may from time to time choose, appoint, or direct, it can delegate the exercise of its powers to a board of officers: *Lynch* v. *Forbes*, 161 Mass. 302; 42 Am. St. Rep. 402; but the power to pass ordinances for improving, grading, and paving streeets is a legislative power vested in the city council and cannot be delegated: *Hydes* v. *Joyes*, 4 Bush, 464; 96 Am. Dec. 311, and note. See, to the same effect, *Thompson* v. *Schermerhorn*, 6 N. Y. 92; 55 Am. Dec. 385, and note.

MUNICIPAL CORPORATIONS — STREET ASSESSMENTS — RESOLUTION OF INTENTION.—If work not included in the resolution of intention is done upon a street, and the expense thereof included in an assessment, such assessment cannot be enforced unless all the work is properly included therein in cases where there is no difficulty in determining what was the cost of the work authorized: *Mason* v. *Sioux Falls*, 2 S. Dak. 640; 39 Am. St. Rep. 802.

CLOUD ON TITLE—ILLEGAL STREET ASSESSMENT.—Where the illegality of a municipal assessment is apparent on the record of the proceedings, and requires no extrinsic evidence to show it, such assessment is not a cloud upon title, and the remedy of the owner is by action at law, and not by suit in equity: *Murphy* v. *Mayor*, 6 Houst. 108; 22 Am. St. Rep. 345.

CHILDERS *v.* SAN JOSE MERCURY PRINTING AND PUBLISHING COMPANY.

[105 CALIFORNIA, 284.]

MALICE MAY BE DIVIDED INTO TWO DISTINCT CLASSES, to wit, malice in law and malice in fact.

MALICE IN LAW is implied from a wrongful act done intentionally, without just cause or excuse.

LIBEL.—MALICE IN LAW IS CONCLUSIVELY PRESUMED FROM the publication of a libel imputing to another the commission of a crime, where the publication is not a privileged one.

LIBEL.—MALICE IN FACT IS MATERIAL in an action for libel only to establish the right to exemplary damages, or to defeat defendant's plea that the publication was privileged.

LIBEL—DAMAGES.—TWO CLASSES OF DAMAGES may be recovered in an action for libel, to wit, actual or compensatory damages and exemplary damages.

LIBEL.—FROM THE PUBLICATION OF A FALSE CHARGE OF A FELONY NOT PRIVILEGED, the right to sustain an action for the actual damages suffered thereby necessarily arises.

LIBEL.—EXEMPLARY DAMAGES may be awarded for the publication of a false charge which is libelous *per se*, and not a privileged communication.

LIBEL.—AN INSTRUCTION in a libel suit that damages may be awarded as an example to others, and as a punishment for the act done, should not be given, if there is an issue respecting malice in fact in the publication of the libel. Malice in fact is never presumed.

D. M. Delmas, H. V. Morehouse, and John E. Richards, for the appellant.

W. M. R. Parker and Charles E. Nougues, for the respondent.

286 GAROUTTE, J.   This is an appeal from a judgment of the superior court of the county of Monterey, in favor of the plaintiff and against the defendant herein, for the sum of two thousand dollars damages for an alleged **287** libel, and from an order denying the defendant's motion for a new trial.

The defendant published in a daily issue of the *San Jose Mercury,* a newspaper printed and published in the city of San Jose, an article to the effect that the plaintiff, William Childers, had committed the offense of burglary, upon the previous night, in said city of San Jose, by breaking and entering a business house of said city.   Plaintiff by his complaint charged said publication to be a libel upon him, and brought this action for damages.

It is now insisted that the court misunderstood the law bearing upon the questions here involved, and that the following instructions, which were given to the jury, are unsound as declarations of legal principles: "1. All libels and slanders are conclusively presumed to be in some degree malicious; 2. Said publication was a libel upon the plaintiff, and entitles him to a verdict in his favor; 3. Damages in such a case as this are given: 1. To compensate the plaintiff for his injuries, if he has suffered any, and 2. As an example to others similarly situated, and as a punishment for a wrongful act done; 4. In this action, if you find for the plaintiff, and if you find that the defendant has been guilty of oppression, fraud, or malice, actual or presumed, in addition to the actual damages sustained by the plaintiff, you may give him damages for the sake of example, and by way of·punishing the defendant.   As I have already charged you, the law presumes the existence of malice from the fact of the publication of the false, unprivileged, and defamatory article in a newspaper regarding the person so charged; 5. The plaintiff in this case has not alleged or attempted to prove any special damages, but simply claims a verdict for exemplary or punitive damages.   Such damages are given for the sake of example, and by way of punishing the defendant."

The foregoing instructions are taken from various portions of the body of law given by the court to the jury, and are collected and numbered for our convenience.   There is no

question in this case but that the [288] publication was not a
privileged one, and the court was justified in so stating to the
jury.

Malice, as pertaining to actions of libel and slander, is a
question both intricate and important, and especially so,
when it, in its various classifications, is considered in connection with the legal principles bearing upon the question
of exemplary or punitive damages. Malice may be divided
into two distinct classes, to wit, malice in law and malice in
fact. Malice in law may be defined as a wrongful act, done
intentionally, without just cause or excuse: *Bell* v. *Fernald,*
71 Mich. 267; *King* v. *Patterson,* 49 N. J. L. 417; 60 Am.
Rep. 622. Such malice is necessary to the life of every cause
of action for libel, and is conclusively presumed in publications of the character here involved. In *King* v. *Patterson,*
49 N. J. L. 417, 60 Am. Rep. 622, it is said: "On the other
hand, where the publication imputes a crime so as to be
actionable *per se,* or is actionable only on averment and proof
of special damages, if the publication is not justified by proof
of its truth, or by the privileged occasion of publication, the
law in such cases presumes malice such as is essential to
the action. In such cases good faith and an honest belief in
the truth of the publication will be no defense. The absence
of a malicious motive may protect against exemplary damages, but will not bar the action."

Malice in fact is only material in libel as establishing a
right to recover exemplary damages, or to defeat defendant's
plea that a publication is privileged. Malice in fact may be
defined as a spiteful or rancorous disposition which causes an
act to be done for mischief: *Lick* v. *Owen,* 47 Cal. 252. As
will be observed hereafter, malice in fact may be established
by evidence aliunde, or it may appear from the face of the
publication itself.

Two classes of damages may be recovered in actions of
libel, to wit, actual or compensatory damages and exemplary.
damages. Special damages as a branch of actual damages
may be recovered when actual pecuniary loss has been sustained, and is specially pleaded. The [289] remaining branch
of actual damages embraces recovery for loss of reputation,
shame, mortification, injury to feelings, etc., and, while special damages must be alleged and proven, general damages
for outrage to feelings and loss of reputation need not be
alleged in detail, and may be recovered in the absence of

actual proof; and to the amount that the jury estimates will fairly compensate plaintiff for the injury done: *Wilson* v. *Fitch*, 41 Cal. 386.

Exemplary damages may be recovered when malice on the part of the defendant is established as a fact, and by the express provisions of section 3294 of the Civil Code this malice may be "actual or presumed." We assume that the word "actual," as used in this section of the code, means "express." In criminal law malice is an element of murder, and this malice may be either express or implied. It is implied when no considerable provocation for the killing appears, or when the circumstances of the killing show an abandoned and malignant heart. We are inclined to believe that the "presumed malice" of section 3294 closely assimilates to the implied malice of the criminal law. It is an inference of fact to be drawn from the libelous character of the publication; and, if the article is libelous *per se*, we see no reason why the law should not declare that upon its introduction in evidence a *prima facie* case of malice in fact is established; for, even though it be presumed malice, it is malice in fact, and has all the dignity and gravity of express or actual malice, proven aliunde. We conclude that presumed malice is equally a question of fact with actual malice, and upon being established equally forms the foundation for the recovery of exemplary damages.

This publication charged plaintiff with the commission of a felony. It was false, not privileged, and libelous *per se*. Upon such a state of facts the cause of action for actual damages is conclusively established: *Wilson* v. *Fitch*, 41 Cal. 386; *Dixon* v. *Allen*, 69 Cal. 527; *Mowry* v. *Raabe*, 89 Cal. 609. And the amount and measure of damages are the only questions left for litigation. [290] In this publication malice in law is not only conclusively presumed, but such malice in fact is implied or presumed as to establish *prima facie* the right of plaintiff to exemplary damages. In other words, the existence of malice in fact is sufficiently shown by the publication to make the question an issue before the jury. That exemplary damages may be based alone upon a publication libelous *per se* we have many authorities from many states: *Samuels* v. *Evening Mail Assn.*, 75 N. Y. 604; *Bergmann* v. *Jones*, 94 N. Y. 51; *Warner* v. *Press Pub. Co.*, 132 N. Y. 181; *Evening News Assn.* v. *Tryon*, 42 Mich. 549; 36 Am. Rep. 450; *Buckley* v. *Knapp*, 48 Mo. 152; *Clements* v. *Maloney*, 55 Mo.

352; *Schmisseur* v. *Kreilich*, 92 Ill. 347; *Snyder* v. *Fulton*, 34
Md. 128; 6 Am. Rep. 314; *Nolan* v. *Traber*, 49 Md. 460; 33
Am. Rep. 277. In *Warner* v. *Press Pub. Co.*, 132 N. Y. 181,
the principle is thus declared: "The plaintiff gave evidence
of malice when she proved the falsity of the libelous publication, and, in the absence of evidence on the part of the defendant tending to show that it had neither the desire nor
the intention to wrong her, it would have been the duty of the
court to instruct the jury that the plaintiff might be awarded
exemplary damages in their discretion; but testimony was
adduced on the part of the defendant, tending to prove the
absence of actual malice on his part toward the plaintiff,
which, taken in connection with the evidence of malice which
the law imputed when the falsity of the libel was established,
presented a question of fact whether malice existed in the
publication. If found to exist, then, in their discretion, the
jury could award exemplary damages." While there may
be authority in some states opposed to the principle declared
in the foregoing citation, yet in this state, in view of section
3294 of the Civil Code, to which we have adverted, there
would seem to be no question as to the true rule.

Do the instructions of the court stand the test when gauged
by the legal principles we have declared? As to those instructions, numbers one and two are correct. [291] Number three
is correct, if malice in fact is assumed to have been established by the evidence, but the court was not justified in
making such an assumption. Malice in fact was an issue
before the jury, and, if found by the jury to be an element of
the case, then, and then only, was the instruction correct, and
the case one for exemplary damages. Instruction number
four is correct in all save the last clause. The court first
tells the jury that if malice, actual or presumed, has been
proven, exemplary damages may be recovered, and then commits the error by saying that the publication is such that
malice is presumed; in other words, conclusively presumed.
This is true of malice in law, but the court in this instruction was dealing with malice in fact, as bearing upon exemplary damages, and the presumption of malice in fact from
the libelous character of the publication is not conclusive,
but disputable. The defendant had the right to rebut this
presumption by any proper evidence. He attempted so to do
in this case, and, if he was successful in that regard to the
satisfaction of the jury, malice in fact was no longer an ele-

ment in the case. The fifth instruction is not entirely correct, but probably too favorable to the defendant. For, while the plaintiff did not claim special damages, he did claim compensatory damages to the extent of the injury to his feelings, etc., and, in the absence of malice in fact, under his pleading these compensatory damages were all that he was entitled to recover.

For the foregoing reasons the judgment and order are reversed and the cause remanded for a new trial.

HARRISON, J., and VAN FLEET, J., concurred.

Hearing in Bank denied. ———

MALICE IN LAW AND IN FACT: See the extended note to *McAllister* v. *Detroit Free Press Co.*, 15 Am. St. Rep. 337, 338.

LIBEL—MALICE, WHEN IMPLIED.—From a libelous publication the law implies malice and infers damage if the publication is false, except in cases of privileged communications: *Upton* v. *Hume*, 24 Or. 420; 41 Am. St. Rep. 863, and note.

LIBEL—DAMAGES.—When libelous words charge an actionable crime, actual damages, including mental suffering and loss of character, are recoverable, even in the absence of malice: *Belo* v. *Fuller*, 84 Tex. 450; 31 Am. St. Rep. 75, and note. This question is thoroughly discussed in the extended note to *McAllister* v. *Detroit Free Press Co.*, 15 Am. St. Rep. 339, 342, and *Terwiliger* v. *Wards*, 72 Am. Dec. 426.

LIBEL OR SLANDER—EXEMPLARY DAMAGES—WHEN RECOVERABLE FOR. Exemplary damages may be recovered in an action for slander when defamatory words are spoken with implied, as well as express, malice: *Callahan* v. *Ingram*, 122 Mo. 355; 43 Am. St. Rep. 583, and note. To the same effect with regard to libel, *Cotulla* v. *Kerr*, 74 Tex. 89; 15 Am. St. Rep. 819. See, also, the extended note to *McAllister* v. *Detroit Free Press Co.*, 15 Am. St. Rep. 341.

———

ADAMS v. GRAND LODGE.

[105 CALIFORNIA, 321.]

BENEFIT ASSOCIATIONS.—IF A BENEFICIARY HAS EQUITIES DERIVED from a member of a mutual benefit association, and which it would be inequitable for him to disregard, he cannot disregard or weaken them by a change of his beneficiary; at least, when the second beneficiary is a mere volunteer or acquires his interest with notice of the pre-existing equities.

BENEFICIAL ASSOCIATION, BENEFICIARY MAY HOLD IN TRUST.—If a member of a beneficial association designates a person as beneficiary for the purpose of securing a debt due to a firm of which the person so designated is a member, the firm is in equity to be treated as the real beneficiary, and hence the death of the person so designated does not deprive the firm or the surviving member of the equitable interest,

nor entitle the heirs of such member of the association to the fund
falling due on his death on the ground that the death of the person
named as beneficiary resulted in there being no one named as beneficiary on the death of a member of the association, and therefore presented a case in which his heirs were entitled to the fund on account of
his failure to designate a beneficiary.

BENEFIT ASSOCIATIONS—WAIVER.—A CHANGE OF BENEFICIARY in a mutual benefit association cannot be treated as invalid for the reason that
the application therefor was not filed within the time, if the association has waived this condition, and the contest arising for decision is
between rival claimants to the fund after it has been paid into court to
be awarded to the person found entitled thereto.

W. H. Cobb and Clinton L. White, for the appellant.

William H. Jordan, for the respondent.

Eugene N. Deuprey, for Grand Lodge, etc., defendant.

C. W. Baker, for the administrator of estate of John Mc-
Neill, deceased.

[322] GAROUTTE, J. The plaintiff, as successor in interest
of the firm of Adams, McNeill & Co., brought this action to
recover the sum of two thousand dollars, due and payable
upon a beneficiary certificate issued by a. society known as
the Ancient Order of United Workmen. The party insured
was Joshua H. Smith, and the original beneficiary named
in the certificate of membership was Caroline H. Smith, his
wife, the present intervenor and appellant. Subsequently
Smith requested the grand lodge to substitute one John Mc-
Neill as the beneficiary in the place and stead of his wife,
Caroline. This [323] request was complied with, and said
McNeill received a new certificate, made payable to himself
upon the death of Smith. A few years thereafter McNeill
died, and, in about a like period after McNeill's death, Smith
died. No new beneficiary was named in Smith's certificate
of insurance after the death of McNeill, and upon this ground
the intervenor and appellant, Mrs. Smith, representing the
heirs and devisees of her late husband, appears in the action,
claiming that the insured died without a named beneficiary,
and that therefore the proceeds of the certificate belong to
the heirs of the insured. The defendant, the grand lodge,
appeared in the action by answer, and offered to pay the
money to whomsoever the court might decree upon final
judgment; while the defendant, Bronner, administrator of
the estate of John McNeill, deceased, answered, but failed to
appear at the trial.

Respondent Adams' claims are fairly illustrated and dependent upon the following facts, which we quote from the findings made by the trial court, and which, in our opinion, are fully supported by the evidence introduced at the trial. After finding that Smith was indebted to the firm of Adams, McNeill & Co., in a large sum of money, the findings further declare.

"1. That the said beneficiary certificate, so issued to the said Joshua H. Smith, and so made payable to the said John McNeill, was intended by the said Smith and the said Mc Neill for the benefit of the said firm of Adams, McNeill & Co., and not otherwise, and that the said certificate was held by the said John McNeill in trust for the said firm of Adams, McNeill & Co., of which said firm the said McNeill was at said time a member, as heretofore found, and that the same was so held in trust by the said McNeill with a full knowledge and consent of defendant, the grand lodge of the Ancient Order of United Workmen of California.

" 2. That it is a fact that the said firm of Adams, McNeill & Co. received said beneficiary certificate, and caused the same to be held by the said John McNeill in ³²⁴ trust for them, as aforesaid, in payment of the said indebtedness to the said firm of the said Joshua H. Smith, and not otherwise, and that since the issuing of said certificate the said firm of Adams, McNeill & Co. and plaintiff, as its successor in interest, have furnished the funds with which to pay all assessments and dues required of the said Joshua H. Smith by the defendant, grand lodge of the Ancient Order of Workmen, to keep the said beneficiary-certificate in full force and effect."

The application of principles of law to litigation arising out of mutual benefit associations is a matter of very recent growth, and especially is this so of that branch of mutual benefit law which directly presents itself for our consideration in the present case. By reason of these things, and by reason of the additional fact that litigation involving these questions is to a great extent at the present time engrossing the attention of courts all over the country, and demanding decision largely without the aid of precedent, we find ourselves, to some extent at least, journeying upon untrodden and devious paths. At the same time we see no reason why those broad and benign principles of equity which, as it were, are the guardians of the law, should not deal with this case as with other cases, and likewise weigh and measure its merits, rendering unto all parties that justice to which they are entitled.

The Ancient Order of United Workmen is not an active party to the litigation. It has no interest whatever in the result. In effect it has paid the fund into the hands of the court, and is now a stranger to the action. We then have a certain fund of money to which the plaintiff and the intervenor both claim title, and their respective claims of ownership are to be litigated in the same way, and finally adjudicated and determined upon the same general principles, as though the common source of title of this money came through a ·bequest or gift rather than from a mutual benefit association. We had occasion in the recent case of *Jory* v. *Supreme Council A. L. of H.*, 105 Cal. 20, *ante*, p. 17, to give some [325] of the matters here involved careful attention, and in that case we arrived at the conclusion that the relations existing between the insured and the beneficiary might be such as to create equities in favor of the beneficiary which the insured would be estopped from defeating; at least as in favor of a subsequently named beneficiary who possessed no equities. Under the authority of that case it cannot be questioned but that if McNeill was a beneficiary possessing such equities, no subsequent act of Smith's, even though it had culminated in the issuance of a new certificate by the order to another beneficiary, could have defeated his equities, conceding, of course, this last beneficiary to be a pure volunteer.

According to the findings of fact McNeill was the beneficiary in name only, and the real beneficiary was Adams, McNeill & Co. Even conceding that, as against the order, McNeill was the real and only beneficiary, that is not the condition here presented. The order is not here as an aggressive party, standing strictly upon its legal rights, and demanding the letter of its bond. As we have said, it is practically not a party to the action at all. But the conditions facing us are simply these: Two litigants, standing upon a common level, submit to a court of equity their respective claims of ownership to a special fund of money, and ask that court to do justice, in the light and under the guidance of those equitable principles which form the glory of that forum. Looking at the case from that standpoint of vision, it presents but little difficulty. If McNeill in terms had been named beneficiary in the certificate, as trustee for Adams, McNeill & Co., there would be no question as to the ownership of the fund. Neither can there be any question but that a certificate could be made payable to Mc-Neill, as guardian of a named minor, or as trustee of Adams, McNeill & Co. If McNeill had lived until the death of Smith, and litigation had arisen between him and Adams, McNeill & Co. as to the ownership of this fund, a court of equity, without hesitation, would have given it to the partnership, and the [326] fact that the trust was not expressed upon the face of the certificate would have been wholly immaterial. The court, under such circumstances, would declare that McNeill was a mere naked trustee of the real beneficiary, and that the real beneficiary was entitled to the money. Such is the principle governing here, and in the eyes of a court of equity the fact that the trustee died prior to the death of Smith makes no difference in the conditions. The real beneficiary still lived and was alive at the death of Smith, and it is the duty of the court to protect such a one.

It is insisted that the certificate issued to McNeill by the order was invalid, for the reason that the application for a change of beneficiary was not filed in the grand lodge within thirty days of its date, and thus was not filed in compliance with the provisions of the constitution of the order. A sufficient answer to such contention by the intervenor is that this provision of the law was one that could be waived by the order, and, when the order issued the certificate upon the application, the provision was waived.

The declaration of trust made by McNeill, defining his relations with the firm as to the beneficiary certificate, was properly admitted in evidence. The administrator of McNeill's estate was a party defendant, and filed a verified answer denying the trust relations, and, under these circumstances, the paper was competent evidence. There is nothing further disclosed by the record demanding our attention.

The judgment and order are affirmed.

HARRISON, J., and VAN FLEET, J., concurred.

Hearing in Bank denied. ____

BENEFIT ASSOCIATIONS—CHANGE OF BENEFICIARY.—A beneficiary designated as such by a member of a mutual benefit association does not thereby acquire any vested rights so as to defeat a subsequent change of beneficiaries effected at the instance of such member, unless the original beneficiary was made such on account of some contract, or has some equities recognized by the courts, and which it would be inequitable to disappoint: *Jory* v. *Supreme Council*, 105 Cal. 20; *ante*, 17, and note. See the note to *Union Mut. Assn.* v. *Montgomery*, 14 Am. St. Rep. 527.

BENEFIT ASSOCIATIONS—WAIVER OF CONDITIONS AS TO CHANGE OF BENEFICIARY.—A benefit association may waive formalities required by its charter to be complied with in changing a beneficiary, and pay the benefit to the new beneficiary, although the new direction as to its payment was not made by the assured in the mode pointed out by the organic law of the association: *Manning* v. *Ancient Order of United Workmen*, 86 Ky. 136; 9 Am. St. Rep. 270.

MERRIMAN *v.* WALTON.
[105 CALIFORNIA, 403.]

JUDGMENT, RELIEF AGAINST FOR FRAUD.—If, contrary to the agreement of counsel for both parties, judgment is entered in a justice's court, and the fact of its entry is concealed from the defendant by the joint misrepresentation of the plaintiff and of the justice of the peace until the time for appeal has expired, equity will grant relief by enjoining the assertion of such judgment.

JUDGMENT, RELIEF AGAINST IN EQUITY.—Though a party against whom a judgment was procured by fraud was entitled to be relieved therefrom by motion in the case in which judgment was entered, this does not preclude a court of equity from granting relief after such motion has been made and denied.

JUDGMENT, RELIEF AGAINST IN EQUITY.—Though a party could have had a judgment against him annulled by certiorari he was not compelled to resort to that remedy in preference to proceeding in equity to have the enforcement of such judgment enjoined.

JUDGMENT, PARTIES TO SUIT FOR RELIEF FROM.—Though a judgment is entered against two defendants, one of them may maintain an action to enjoin its assertion against him on account of fraud practiced upon him without joining his codefendant as a party to such action.

Gedford & Thompson, for the appellants.

Coghlan & Hutchinson, for the respondent.

406 HARRISON, J. The defendant, Walton, commenced an action against the plaintiff and another in a justice's court, and, after the defendants therein had answered the complaint, the justice set the case for trial on the 28th of February, but on the morning of that day it was agreed between the attorneys for the respective parties that the trial should be postponed, and that the cause should be transferred to another township. On the next day the attorneys for the plaintiff herein received a letter from the justice, purporting to have been written the previous day, in which he stated

that the case was to be transferred to another township, and
thereupon the attorneys for Walton agreed to take such steps
as would be necessary to effect the transfer. Instead of so
doing, however, they had on the previous day, without any
knowledge on the part of the plaintiff herein, or of his attorneys, appeared before the justice and caused judgment by
default to be entered by the justice against the defendants
therein for the full amount asked for in the complaint. At
the time that the justice wrote the above letter, and at the
time of the [407] agreement on the part of Walton's attorneys
to effect the transfer to another township, it was known to
them that such judgment had been entered. Other inter-
views were subsequently had between the attorneys for the
respective parties regarding the transfer of the cause, in
which Walton's attorneys, for the purpose of misleading and
deceiving the attorneys of the plaintiff herein, represented
that they were seeking to effect the transfer of the cause, and
in which they concealed the fact that the judgment had been
entered, and by reason of their statements and deceptions
the plaintiff herein did not learn that the judgment had
been entered until more than thirty days after its entry, and
when the time for an appeal therefrom had expired. Upon
learning this fact the plaintiff herein moved the justice to
set aside the judgment, and recall an execution that had
been issued thereon, and on the 18th of April this motion
was granted, but on the next day the justice, without any
notice to the plaintiff herein or his attorneys, vacated this
order. Thereupon the plaintiff brought this action to per-
petually enjoin Walton from enforcing the said judgment
against him or his property. A demurrer to the complaint
was overruled, and, the defendants declining to answer, judgment was rendered in favor of the plaintiff, from which this
appeal has been taken.

The complaint shows that the judgment in the justice's
court was obtained by a fraud practiced upon the plaintiff
herein by the attorneys of Walton, with the assistance of the
justice, in a manner which entitles the plaintiff to the equitable relief sought; and the appellant does not attempt to
controvert the power of a court of equity to afford the relief
sought by the plaintiff, but rests his defense upon the proposition that the plaintiff is not entitled to equitable relief if he
could obtain the same relief at law. It is a familiar rule
that a separate action to restrain the enforcement of a judg-

ment will not be sustained when the same relief can be obtained through a motion or other proceeding [408] in the action in which the judgment was obtained; and, in a jurisdiction in which legal and equitable relief is dispensed in different tribunals, a court of equity will not grant relief against a judgment when the same relief can be obtained by the aid of the court that rendered the judgment. But, under the system of procedure which obtains in this state, where the various kinds of relief are administered by the same tribunal, and where there is but one form of civil action for the enforcement or protection of civil rights (Code Civ. Proc., sec. 307), a party who presents a complaint showing his right to the relief asked is not to be denied that relief because he might have sought it under a different form of action: See *Thompson* v. *Laughlin*, 91 Cal. 313.

When the plaintiff learned that the judgment had been entered against him the time for an appeal had expired, and, even if the justice had the power to grant his motion to open the judgment, his subsequent action vacating this order was equivalent to a denial of the motion, and from this order there was no appeal to the superior court. The rule under which a court of equity declines to interfere until after the application for relief has been made to the court in which the judgment was rendered has no application when relief has been sought and denied in that court. The denial of that court to grant relief gives to the court of equity the same authority to interfere as if the other court was powerless to render aid.

Even if the plaintiff could have had the judgment annulled upon certiorari, he was not compelled to resort to that remedy, especially where he would not thereby obtain as effective relief as by the course herein pursued.

The objection that the codefendant of the plaintiff is not a party to this action is without merit. The judgment in the justice's court is restrained only so far as it affects the plaintiff herein and his property, leaving the [409] judgment against his codefendant in full effect, to be enforced at any time.

The judgment is affirmed.

GAROUTTE, J., and VAN FLEET, J., concurred.

JUDGMENTS—RELIEF FROM IN EQUITY FOR FRAUD.—A judgment will not be set aside or annulled in equity on account of any fraud which is not extrinsic or collateral to the questions examined or determined in the original action: *Pico* v. *Cohn*, 91 Cal. 129; 25 Am. St. Rep. 159, and note; *Fealey* v. *Fealey*, 104 Cal. 354; 43 Am. St. Rep. 111, and note. A party to a judgment obtained by fraud can avail himself of that fraud only in a direct proceeding to vacate and set aside the judgment: *Shultz* v. *Shultz*, 136 Ind. 323; 43 Am. St. Rep. 320, and note. An extended discussion of the power of equity to relieve against judgments at law will be found in the monographic note to *Oliver* v. *Pray*, 19 Am. Dec. 603.

JOHNSTON *v.* FISH.

[105 CALIFORNIA, 420.]

GROWING CROPS—RIGHT OF ADVERSE POSSESSOR.—The owner of land who is not in possession thereof is not entitled to the fruits of the land, and if the disseisee rents it to another, and enters into a cropping contract with him, and he raises crops thereon, he is entitled to them, and they cannot be recovered from him, though subsequently in an action of ejectment a judgment is given in favor of the landowner for the possession of the property. The owner's remedy after the disseisin is restricted to the recovery of the value of the use and occupation of his land.

GROWING CROPS OF LANDS IN ADVERSE POSSESSION.—The fact that one who rents lands from a disseisee and raises crops thereon knows that another person claims to be the owner of such land does not entitle the latter, though found to be such owner, to such crops, because the disseisee is entitled to all crops grown while he maintains his adverse possession, and his tenant or other successor in interest has the same right.

Eli R. Chase, S. Tinning, W. H. H. Hart, Aylett R. Cotton, Nowlin & Fassett, and Rodgers & Patterson, for the appellants.

Estee & Miller and John B. Mhoon, for the respondent.

[421] HARRISON, J   Action to recover damages from defendants for the conversion of certain hay.

The plaintiff's right of action grows out of the following facts: Prior to March 1, 1881, Henry Benson had been for many years the owner of a tract of land in Contra Costa county, which on that day he conveyed to one Jones. In May of the same year Jones conveyed it to the defendants herein. The conveyance from Benson to Jones was procured by the fraud of the latter, and on the 1st of September of that year Benson took possession of the land, claiming it as his own, upon the ground that by reason of the fraud he was entitled to disregard his conveyance, and remained in possession until evicted under a judgment in ejectment by the defendants herein in March, 1883. Shortly after Benson went into possession of the land the defendants herein brought an action of forcible entry against him, which was tried before a jury, and a verdict and judgment rendered in his favor November 12, 1881. In April, 1883, this verdict was set aside and a new trial ordered, but no further step was taken in the action until 1887, when the action was dismissed. November 21, 1881, the defendants commenced an action in ejectment against Benson and others for the recovery of the land and damages for the withholding thereof. The plaintiff herein was made a defendant in this action, but upon his disclaimer he was dismissed from the action November 29, 1881. A cross-complaint was filed in the action in behalf of Benson, to avoid his conveyance to Jones on the ground of fraud; and upon the trial of this issue a decision was rendered February 19, 1883, in favor of the plaintiffs therein, upon the ground that they were *bona fide* purchasers from Jones for [422] value, and after this decision the trial of the issues in the ejectment was had, in which the plaintiffs withdrew their claim for damages, and judgment was rendered in their favor March 22, 1883. On the 1st of December, 1881, the plaintiff herein made a cropping contract with Benson for the cultivation of the land, under which he sowed a portion thereof to hay, which he harvested in the following summer. By the terms of this agreement the plaintiff was to have two-thirds of the crop, and Benson the remaining third; and, after the hay had been cut and stacked, the plaintiff bought from Benson his third of the crop. Subsequently thereto, and while the hay was still on the ground, the defendants herein brought an action of claim and delivery against Benson for the hay, in which, under their direction, the sheriff took possession thereof, and subsequently delivered it to them. This action was brought before the trial was had in the ejectment suit, and issue was joined therein by Benson, but no further proceedings were had therein until 1887, when, upon the stipulation of Benson, judgment for the possession of the hay was entered against him. The present action was commenced in January, 1883, and judgment was rendered in favor of the plaintiff for the value of the hay, assessed at the sum of four thousand dollars.

There is no substantial difference between the facts in this case and those presented in *Page* v. *Fowler*, 39 Cal. 412, 2 Am. Rep. 462, and under the principles laid down in that

case the plaintiff's right of recovery must be sustained:
See, also, *Martin* v. *Thompson*, 62 Cal. 618; 45 Am. Rep.
663; *Emerson* v. *Whitaker*, 83 Cal. 147; *Groome* v. *Almstead*,
101 Cal. 425; *Stockwell* v. *Phelps*, 34 N. Y. 366; 90 Am.
Dec. 710. Benson's entry upon the land in September,
1881, was made under his claim that, by reason of the
fraud perpetrated on him by Jones, his conveyance to Jones
was avoided, and that he still remained the owner of the
land. Such an entry was not a mere trespass, but it was
made under a claim of right adverse to the whole world, and
constituted a disseisin of the real owners. The subsequent
423 determination in the ejectment suit that the real owners
of the land at that time, the defendants herein, were not
affected by the fraud of Jones, for the reason that they were
bona fide purchasers for value, does not change the character
of Benson's entry, or the fact that it was an actual disseisin,
The findings of fraud made by the court in the ejectment suit
fully show that as between Benson and Jones he could successfully defend his possession of the land. While he thus
held possession of the land he had the right to dispose of its
fruits, and any one dealing with him, therefore, became the
owner of what he might purchase from him. He could either
cultivate the land himself, or employ others to do it for him,
and he could recompense those whom he employed, either
by giving them a definite quantity of the product of the land,
or by an aliquot part of the whole. A person entering into a
cropping contract with him would have the same right to the
share agreed upon as his proportion, as if he had purchased
and paid for the same. The real owner of the land could not
deprive him of this share, any more than he could take from
him such portion of the crop as he had purchased from the
occupant. The law gives to the plaintiff in ejectment the
right to recover from the defendant, either in the same action
or in another, the value of the use and occupation of the land,
which is termed " damages," for the withholding thereof; but,
while the title to the land is undetermined, the owner out of
possession is not entitled to the fruits of the land, nor can he,
after he has established his right to the possession, recover
the fruits of the land from one who has purchased them from
an occupant while such occupant was in the adverse possession. Such a rule would give to the real owner the gross
product of the land, irrespective of the labor and expense
required in its production. As was said in *Page* v. *Fowler*,

39 Cal. 412, 2 Am. Rep. 462: "The very fact that he may
recover the rents and profits of the land shows that he cannot recover the crops, for, as was well said in the case of
Stockwell v. *Phelps*, 34 N. Y. 363, 90 Am. Dec. 710, the owner
of the [424] land in such cases does not recover the value of
the crops raised and harvested, but the value of the use and
occupation of the land; and the annual crops of grain and
grass, which contain both the value of the use of the land
and the labor of the farmer, do not, under such circumstances, belong to the owner of the land. It would be an
oppressive rule to require every one who, after years of litigation perhaps may be found to have a bad title, to pay the
gross value of all the crops he has raised; and it would be an
inconvenience to the public if the bad title of the farmer to
his land attached to the crops he offered for sale, and rendered it necessary to have an abstract of his title to make it
safe to purchase his produce." In *Brothers* v. *Hurdle*, 10 Ired.
490, 51 Am. Dec. 400, the court said: "But when one who is
in the adverse possession gathers a crop in the course of hus-
bandry, or severs a tree or other thing from the land, the
thing severed becomes a chattel, but it does not become the
property of the owner of the land, for his title is divested—
he is out of possession, and has no right to the immediate
possession of the thing, nor can he bring any action until he
regains possession. The owner of the land cannot sue for the
thing severed in trover or detinue as a chattel, for it is not
his chattel. It did not become so at the time it was severed,
and the title to it as a chattel cannot pass to him afterward,
when he regains the possession, by force of the *just post lim-
inii.*"

The fact that the plaintiff herein knew that the defendants
claimed to be the owners of the land, as against Benson, does
not impair his right of recovery. If, as against Benson,
they had no right to the fruits of the land which he gathered
while it was held adversely to them, they would have no
right against his vendee, since Benson could give to his vendee as good a title as he himself possessed, and it is equally
immaterial whether the hay cut from the land was a volunteer crop or had been sown by the plaintiff. The right to the
fruits of the land does not depend upon the amount of labor
expended by the occupant in their production. The [425]
apples or strawberries picked by him belong to him as fully
as the potatoes or corn which he may have planted; and the

hay which he cuts is his, whether it is an annual crop, or whether the land was sown to hay for the first time while in his occupancy. The judgment against Benson for the possession of the hay in the action of claim and delivery against him does not aid the defendants herein. At the time that action was begun Benson had no interest in the hay, the plaintiff herein being the owner of two-thirds thereof under the original contract, and having acquired the other third by purchase from Benson.

The evidence fully sustains the finding of the court that the value of the hay at the time it was taken by the defendants was four thousand dollars. The defendants themselves alleged in the affidavit for its seizure in the claim and delivery action against Benson that it was of the value of five thousand dollars, and its value is stated at that amount in the judgment recovered in that action in their favor.

The judgment and order are affirmed.

GAROUTTE, J., and VAN FLEET, J., concurred.

Hearing in Bank denied. ____

GROWING CROPS ON LAND HELD ADVERSELY—TITLE TO.—Crops raised on land by the labor of one in adverse possession under a claim of right belong to him, and are not the property of the rightful owner of the soil: *Faulcon v. Johnston*, 102 N. C. 264; 11 Am. St. Rep. 737, and note.

MASTERSON v. MUNRO.
[105 CALIFORNIA, 431.]

CONVEYANCE—DESCRIPTION—CONFLICT IN.—If a parcel of land is described as being subdivision No. 25, as designated on a map of a block of land on file, and is also described by metes and bounds, and there is a conflict between the two descriptions, the former prevails.

W. C. Burnett, L. G. Burnett, and R. H. Taylor, for the appellants.

Naphtaly, Freidenrich & Ackerman, for the respondent.

432 The COURT. This is an action in ejectment, the land in controversy consisting of a strip ten feet by twenty-five feet. Both parties claim through deeds from Ottinger and Brooks. The deed to respondent and the deed to the predecessor of appellant Margaret were dated each and acknowledged September 30, 1862. Respondent and appellant bought their respective

lots at an auction sale, and the particular tract in dispute is
included in both deeds. Ottinger and Brooks were the owners of one hundred vara lot No. 149, situated at the corner of
Second and Townsend streets in San Francisco, and for the
purpose of selling the same to [433] advantage made a plan or
map of the lot, subdividing the same into smaller lots, numbered consecutively from one upwards, and caused this map
to be filed in the office of the county recorder. After the map
had been filed the property was offered for sale at public
auction at the auction rooms of John Middleton & Son, where
there was an enlarged copy of the map, and the lots were
sold by reference to said map. Upon this map a street called
"Stanford street" was laid out parallel with Second street,
and one hundred and sixty feet distant therefrom. At this
auction sale the plaintiff purchased lot No. 25, and the defendant's grantor purchased lot 22; and, as is stated in appellants' brief, "lots 22 and 25 comprised an area of twenty-five
feet by one hundred and sixty feet, running through from the
east line of Stanford street to the west line of Second street,
the south line of each lot being one hundred and twenty-five
feet north of Townsend street." The conveyance to the
defendant's grantor describes the land by metes and bounds,
with a depth of eighty feet, and also describes it as "being
subdivision No. 22 of the one hundred vara lot known upon
the official map of said city as No. 149," and the conveyance
to the plaintiff describes the land purchased by him as subdivisions 24 and 25, as represented upon the same map, with
a depth of ninety feet.

Under the foregoing circumstances the contradiction of the
descriptions in appellants' deed must be resolved in favor of
the description which refers to the official plat or map. Appellant's predecessor purchased subdivision 22 of a certain
tract of land as shown by the official map. He bought at
public auction with the map before him, and it is clearly evident that the description by courses and distances was intended to describe subdivision 22. If a party purchases a
certain numbered block of land according to the official map
of the city, and his purchase is also described in the deed, a
further description of the block by metes and bounds, or
courses and distances, would be subordinate to the description [434] of the block by its number, and would have to give
way in case of conflict. The present case involves the same
principle.

We might further suggest, if other grounds were necessary to sustain the judgment, that the acts of the respondent in and about the premises in the exercise of his possession are strongly indicative of the creation of a title by prescription; but we do not find it necessary to enter into a discussion of that question in detail. .

The order denying the motion for a new trial is affirmed.

DEEDS.—RULES FOR CONSTRUING INCONSISTENT AND UNCERTAIN DISCRIPTIONS IN: See the extended note to *Heaton* v. *Hodges*, 30 Am. Deo. 734.

IN RE PHILBROOK.

[105 CALIFORNIA, 471.]

ATTORNEYS, FREEDOM OF SPEECH, ABUSE OF.—A brief filed in the supreme court which, in effect, denounces one of the judges thereof, and attributes to him vile motives, and charges him with being *particeps criminis* to a scheme of villainy of which his election as such judge was a part, when there is nothing in the evidence to support such charge, is contemptuous and unbearable, and an entirely unwarranted abuse of the freedom of speech.

ATTORNEY AT LAW, DISBARMENT OF FOR LANGUAGE USED IN ARGUMENT. An attorney who, in a brief, charges a member of the court with being, while an attorney, *particeps criminis* in a vile scheme and conspiracy against justice, and declares that unless the other judges pronounce the transaction in question illegal and void, all persons to whom knowledge of the case may come will no longer suspect, but will know, that the courts may be corrupted, and will point to their decision as proof, is guilty of a breach of his duty as an attorney at law to maintain the respect due to courts of justice and judicial officers, to abstain from offensive language, and to advance no fact prejudicial to the honor or reputation of a party or witness unless required by the justice of the case, and may, as a punishment, be suspended from his office as an attorney at law.

PROCEEDING against Horace W. Philbrook as an attorney at law. In a brief filed in the supreme court on the 13th of November, 1894, in the case of *Rankin, Administrator of Levinson* v. *Newman*, the attorney, among other things, said: "It is not enough for courts of justice to be, in fact, pure. In addition to the fact there must exist the fullest confidence in their purity. It is not enough for judges to be, in fact, strong enough to resist temptation. They must not allow themselves to be tempted. Examine carefully and thoroughly the secret transaction of September 6, 1890. It was without an extenuating circumstance. You have before you here the proof of what its contrivers and users think of courts of justice and of judges. You behold their evil and most contemptuous confidence. They rely solely upon the corrupting force of their corrupt contrivance, the secret transaction of September 6, 1890; and solely upon that reliance they have been ever since September 6, 1890, and still are, as confident of a final judgment for the Newmans as if they already had it locked up at home. And is it not probable, then, that many others think with them that the courts may be corrupted, the judgments of judges perverted, and that others, still more numerous, suspect it? But if this secret transaction of September 6, 1890, is not declared illegal and void upon the rules and principles declared in *Egerton* v. *Earl Brownlow*, then all to whom knowledge of the case shall come will no longer merely suspect or even think that the courts may be corrupted; they will know it; they may point to the decision here as full proof of it; for it will be established that such practices are permissible, and, if permissible, they are sure to have effect." The attention of the court being called to this language, it filed an order referring to the brief in question, and directing the attorney to appear before the court to show cause why he should not be removed from his office as an attorney at law, and disbarred from further practicing in the courts of the state. The order being served upon the attorney, he appeared and presented an argument in his own behalf, after which the court pronounced its opinion.

R. Y. Hayne, for the prosecution.

Horace W. Philbrook, in propria persona, contra.

⁴⁷³ The COURT. Horace W. Philbrook, a licensed attorney, having filed in this court a certain brief, in which he appeared to have violated his duty as an attorney, was cited to appear before the court on the seventeenth day of December, A. D. 1894, at 10 o'clock A. M., to show cause why he should not be removed from his office as an attorney at law, and disbarred from further practicing law before the courts of this state. The citation was served on him ten days previous to said December 17th. On said day he appeared, and as he did not ask any continuance, but announced himself ready, the matter was proceeded with. A committee from the Bar Association of San Francisco requested to be allowed to appear "for the purpose of seeing that said matter is properly presented," and their request was granted. The respondent,

Philbrook, filed a written answer to the citation, and he was allowed to make an oral argument in his own defense, without restriction of time, his argument occupying the greater part of two days. The committee of the Bar Association argued that he should be disbarred. In the citation attention was called to certain pages of the brief which contained the objectionable matter, and a part of it was quoted. The respondent did not offer any apology or make any excuse; but in his written answer, and in his oral argument, he boldly contended that his brief was unobjectionable and contained nothing which he had not the right to put there. His argument was, for the most part, a reiteration of the assertions and language of the brief.

The brief in question was filed by said Philbrook as attorney for the appellant in a certain action now pending here on appeal, No. 15857, entitled, *"Rankin, special* [474] *administrator of the estate of John Levinson, deceased, plaintiff and appellant, v. Wm. J. Newman and Benjamin Newman, defendants and respondents."* Levinson, deceased, had, in his lifetime, been a copartner with the said Newmans, under the firm name of Newman & Levinson; and said action grew out of a difference about the settlement of the business and affairs of the partnership, and was decided by the trial court in favor of the Newmans. A motion for a new trial had been made by Philbrook's client in the trial court, and had been there denied; and the appeal was taken from the order denying the motion for a new trial. This appeal has not yet been argued or submitted in this court, and its merits are not before us, although the transcript in the case, and also the transcripts in two other appeals between the same parties, in which the Newmans were also successful in the trial court, are made parts of the said Philbrook's answer in this present proceeding.

The objectionable parts of the said brief for which respondent, Philbrook, was cited as aforesaid consist mainly: 1. Of offensive, scandalous, and contemptuous language concerning Hon. Ralph C. Harrison, one of the justices of this court; and 2. Of language contemptuous of all the other justices of the court, in that it broadly intimates that they may be improperly influenced in deciding said appeal, and boldly threatens them with evil consequences to themselves if they should decide the appeal adversely to the appellant. It also contains language highly reprehensible concerning the learned judge of the superior court who heard and determined said action at *nisi prius*, and his answer contains such language concerning another learned judge of the superior court who decided the other cases mentioned in said Philbrook's answer.

During the year A. D. 1890 the Hon. Ralph C. Harrison, now a justice of this court, was, and for many years prior thereto had been, a practicing lawyer at the San Francisco bar; and during nearly all of that year he was the attorney of one Raveley, executor of said [475] John Levinson, deceased, above mentioned. On the sixth day of September of that year (1890) a settlement was made by and between the said executor, Raveley, and the surviving partners, the said Newmans, at which two certain paper writings were executed, which were in the handwriting of Justice Harrison, and signed by him as a witness. There were articles of copartnership of the said firm of Newman & Levinson, existing and in force at the time of the death of Levinson, which provided, or at least purported to provide, for the disposition of the interest in the firm property and business of either partner upon his death. At that time, and prior thereto, the respondent here, Philbrook, was the attorney for certain legatees of said Levinson, and it appears that Philbrook thought that the estate was entitled to a share of the "goodwill" of the said firm, while Justice Harrison was of the opinion that under the said articles of copartnership the estate of Levinson had no interest in the goodwill, but was entitled only to its share of the partnership property, to be ascertained as provided in said articles. It is clear that this was the only point of difference existing at the time of said settlement. It was a pure question of law, as to which it was the duty of Justice Harrison to advise his client—the executor—according to his best judgment.

But it happened that a few weeks before the said 6th of September Justice Harrison had been nominated by one of the two leading and nearly equally powerful political parties of the state as a candidate for the office of associate justice of the supreme court, and upon this circumstance respondent, Philbrook, has built up in his imagination a gigantic conspiracy, which, he contends, gives him the right, under the claim of free argument, to assail Justice Harrison while a member of this court by every offensive epithet which his somewhat wide vocabulary supplies, and to ascribe to him

the vilest motives and conduct. He assumes and asserts
that Justice Harrison, his client Raveley, the Newmans, and
their attorneys, Reinstein and Eisner, entered into a [476] conspiracy to do a wrong, which conspiracy was founded upon
the considerations that the former had been nominated as a
candidate for justice of this court, that he was practically
sure of election, and that if he should draw up said paper
writings, and witness them, any superior judge, before whom
any litigation concerning the matter might come, would be
deterred from doing right by the knowledge that one of the
conspirators was a justice of the supreme court, and that
upon appeal the other justices of this court would be swerved
from their duty because one of the alleged conspirators would
be associated with them on the bench. And it is contended
that on account of this imaginary state of facts, founded on
no evidence, and without any probable cause, respondent had
free rein to indulge in whatever insulting and contemptuous
language his fancy may conjure up concerning a justice of
this court.

It is impracticable to here reproduce any considerable
amount of the language used in the brief; but a few specimens
will be quoted. Having characterized Justice Harrison as one
of the chief conspirators, he denounces what he calls the "secret transaction of September 6th" as "this most impudent
and unspeakably wicked scheme." Having said, "There they
all were, Ralph C. Harrison, Milton S. Eisner, William J. Newman, Benjamin Newman, and executor Raveley, secretly as-
sembled solely by reason of the fact that Ralph C. Harrison
was about to become a justice of the supreme court, etc., he
asks: "Could a more villainous deed than that be conceived?"
He speaks of Justice Harrison and the others as "corrupt,
depraved, and wicked persons," and of the former as "particeps criminis." And again he says: "It was done criminally; and it was necessary to the scheme that Ralph C.
Harrison should become a justice of the supreme court."
Again, he says that "every man present at that secret transaction of Saturday, September 6, 1890, knew what they were
all about; knew that he was a participant in one of the foulest
and blackest of crimes; that he was helping plant a [477] dag-
ger for the breast of justice." Again, speaking of that transaction, he asks: "Can it be that we shall find in it a clew to
the secret of supreme success, the very crown of success, in
the practice of the law?" And again: "Why expect men

to wear themselves out with the intemperate study of law books, as they have hitherto been written, when there is open the easier, surer, and more profitable field of low cunning by which helpless women and fatherless children may be betrayed, robbed, and made outlaws by one single stroke?" Again, he asks how far matters have gone "when so vile a scheme is contrived to pervert the courts, when it raises its head openly, plants its vile body openly in the very temple of justice, wears no other disguise than unblushing audacity and brazen impudence."

The foregoing quotations give a fair idea of the character of the brief, and of the temper and animus which inspired it; and in all that respondent has presented, in his answer, in his argument, and in the several transcripts which he made parts of his answer, he has been unable to show any ground, any decent pretext, for the outrageous verbal assaults which he has made upon a member of this court. Nothing appears in connection with the transaction so often alluded to in the brief which places Justice Harrison in any other light than that of an upright and honorable lawyer, faithfully attending to the interests of his client, and advising him according to his best judgment. He also gave some testimony at the trial; but section 282 of the Code of Civil Procedure enjoins upon an attorney "to abstain from all offensive personality, and to advance no fact prejudicial to the honor or reputation of a party or witness unless required by the justice of the cause with which he is charged." The parts of the brief to which we have alluded are, therefore, contemptuous and unbearable, and entirely unwarranted under any claim of free speech. We appreciate the right of counsel to fully argue their cases, to comment on witnesses whoever they may be, and to present views and press arguments [478] within any reasonable bounds of propriety There need be no difficulty in this court on that subject. It would be hard, no doubt, to designate a line that would in all cases properly divide free speech from license. But there is no trouble in the case at bar on that score, for the conduct of the respondent is, beyond doubt, entirely on the side of unbridled license. Of course, the fact that an attorney has been elected a justice of this court does not shield him from any fair criticism of his conduct when an attorney; but, when there is such unwarrantable language as that used by respondent, it is manifest that it was used because the person assailed was a justice of this court, and with intent to commit a contempt of this court. As respondent has, in the same connection, assailed not only all the members of this court and the two superior judges above referred to, but also certain reputable lawyers who were at one time associated with him in the litigation, and a special administrator who was appointed at his own instance and out of his own office, charity might possibly suggest that he is the victim of abnormal suspicion and distrust. But no such defense is made; and moreover, his brief and argument show a bright intellect and a clear mind. His conduct, therefore, exhibits only a sheer intent to be maliciously contemptuous.

With respect to the other members of the court the language of the brief is not only generally contemptuous, but contains a direct attempt to influence them by threats of injury unless they shall adopt his views of the case. He says in his brief: "And let this be borne in mind by every justice who takes part in the decision: You were not, any more than I, either directly or indirectly a party to the secret transaction of September 6, 1890, 'and we that have free souls, it touches us not.' It will never be in any, even the slightest, degree your act, your child, nor will you in even the slightest degree be responsible for it, unless you adopt it as your own. Though it is a lure, prepared to be held out to you as a lure, it touches you not unless you accept it." And [479] again, having said that it is not enough for courts to be pure, but that there must be "the fullest confidence in their purity," he says: "But if this recent transaction of September 6, 1890, is not declared illegal and void upon the rules and principles declared in *Egerton* v. *Earl Brownlow*, then all to whom knowledge of the case may come will no longer merely suspect or even think that the courts may be corrupted; they will know it; they may point to the decision here as full proof of it; for it will be established that such practices are permissible, and if permissible they are sure to have their effect." This is a palpable attempt to influence a decision of this court by base appeals to the supposed timidity of its justices, and made, too, by an officer of the court. It is intolerable. It cannot be suffered by any occupant of the bench who has a just sense of his duty to the people to preserve the due dignity of their courts, and the free course of justice. An attempt to influence a judge through fear of physical injury is no graver offense than such an attempt against his reputation.   A high-spirited man might have perfeet physical courage and yet might, possibly, despite all his efforts against it, be to some extent insensibly affected by dread of the loss of his reputation and good name.   Neither attempt can be for a moment countenanced without a manifest injury to the cause of justice.   When people come into courts as litigants they have the right to expect the best judgments of their judges, uninfluenced except by legitimate arguments made openly before them by counsel.   They must expect those errors which will sometimes inevitably be committed by minds which are not infallible; but they should be able to feel sure that the impartiality of the court will not be disturbed by any influence of fear or favor.   And clearly nothing tends more to disturb that impartiality than a menace that the decision of a cause a certain way will destroy or greatly injure the good name of the judge who shall make it.   And when the punishment of such an offense is clearly within the jurisdiction of the court, as in the case of one of its own officers, it must impose the penalty or neglect its imperative duty.

We exceedingly regret the necessity of this proceeding.   It would have been much more agreeable for us to have devoted the time given to its hearing to other business.   But to have overlooked it would have been to violate our duty, invite future disrespect and indignities, and establish a precedent which would have embarrassed the court if offenses of a similar character should be called to its attention in the future. It may be not out of place to say that we have been lenient to the respondent for past offenses of a character similar to the one now before us, though not so flagrant; and that his attention has heretofore been directly called to his disregard of his duties as an attorney in this respect.   In a petition for rehearing he used disrespectful language toward a commissioner of the court who had prepared the opinion in the case, for which, perhaps, he should have been called to account at the time; and more recently we were compelled to strike out his brief in another case for disrespectful language.   And even now we regret that we cannot see some escape from the necessity of imposing the penalty which seems to be imperatively demanded.

Our conclusion is that by filing said brief the respondent, Philbrook, has violated his duty as an attorney " to maintain the respect due to the courts of justice and judicial officers,"

nd to abstain from offensive personality, and to advance no
act prejudicial to the honor or reputation of a party or wit-
ess, unless required by the justice of the cause with which
e is charged," as declared in section 282 of the Code of Civil
rocedure; and that for such reason he should be suspended
om his office of attorney at law.

It is ordered and adjudged that the said respondent,
orace W. Philbrook, be, and be hereby is, suspended from
his office as attorney and counselor at law, and prohibited
from practicing as an attorney and counselor at law in any
and all of the courts of this state for the [481] period of three
(3) years from this date, and thereafter until the further
order of this court removing such suspension.

FITZGERALD, J.,   GAROUTTE, J.,
McFARLAND, J.,   VAN FLEET, J.,
DE HAVEN, J.

On January 10, 1895, Beatty, C. J., filed the following concurring opinion:

BEATTY, C. J. My views of this case differ in some particulars from those of my associates.

It was not because of Mr. Philbrook's assault upon a member of this court—gross and unjustifiable as I deemed it to
be—that I joined in the order citing him to show cause. So
far as that part of his offense was concerned, I should have
waited until the final determination of the appeal in *Rankin*
v. *Newman*, before deciding what, if any, action it was necessary or proper to take.

But, as is clearly shown in the opinion of the court (*In re
Philbrook*), Mr. Philbrook did not confine himself to an
assault upon Justice Harrison in his character of attorney for
Levinson's executor, and as advisor and participant in the
settlement of the executor with the surviving partners. He
went much further; he distinctly threatened the other members of the court with public infamy and disgrace if they did
not decide the cause of *Rankin* v. *Newman* in his favor. This
he did, not only in the express terms of that part of his brief
set forth in the citation, but indirectly and by every sort of
implication through page after page of that portion of his
brief to which his attention was directed by the reference to
said pages.

In his long and carefully prepared answer in writing Mr.
Philbrook makes no retraction or qualification of this objec-

tionable language, but, on the contrary, distinctly reavows every thing he has said.

He claims—and I fully concede the claim—that if a justice of this court has been a party, or attorney, or [482] witness, or in any other manner so connected with a cause which is on appeal here as justly to subject him to criticism, counsel charged with the presentation of such cause must be allowed the same freedom of criticism as in the case of any other person. But the logic of this proposition is that the fact that such party or witness is a member of this court is wholly irrelevant; it has nothing to do with the case. Mr. Philbrook, however, does not hold himself bound by the logic of his proposition. He does not criticise Justice Harrison's conduct as attorney for Levinson's executor the same as if he were not a member of this court, but apparently because he is a member of the court he assails him with the bitterest invective, for the purpose of giving point and force to the proposition to which his whole argument tends, that we cannot affirm the order of the superior court without making ourselves participants of the fraud which he charges, and thereby giving all men reason to know that the courts of the country are corrupt.

In this consists the offense of which, in my opinion, the court was compelled to take cognizance on its own motion—a step to which, I may say, we resorted with great reluctance. The law which in such cases makes us the judges of offenses against the court places us in an extremely delicate and invidious position, but it leaves us no alternative except to allow the court and the people of the state in whose name and by whose authority it acts, to be insulted with impunity, or to exercise the authority conferred by law for the purpose of compelling attorneys to "maintain the respect due to courts of justice and judicial officers."

If an attorney were to approach a court or a judge with the offer of a bribe to decide a cause in his favor, or if he were to menace a judge with personal violence or pecuniary loss if he decided against him, it cannot be doubted that all men would concede the propriety of depriving him of his privileges as an attorney, and if this is so it cannot be denied that some penalty is incurred [483] by an attorney who reinforces his argument by announcing to the court with endless repetition that an adverse decision will make the judges par-

ticipants of a fraud and sharers in the infamy of its perpe-
trators.

It is not necessary, however, to elaborate this proposition
here. It is plainly enough set forth in the opinion of the
court, and does not even need exposition, for it must be obvious to the meanest apprehension that threats or menaces of
any character addressed to a court as a part of, or in aid of,
the argument upon the law and facts of a case is an obstruction to the free and unbiased consideration which every cause
should receive; and that if such means of influencing the
action of the court should become common, as they might if
allowed to pass unrebuked, no rights would remain secure.

Mr. Philbrook himself, by his tardy disclaimer, made in
the course of his oral argument, seems to admit the justice
of these views.

But as above stated he makes no disclaimer or retraction
in his written answer to the citation, which remains a public
record of the court. On the contrary, he therein deliberately
reaffirms and insists upon the propriety of every word contained in his brief. He claims, of course, never to have
understood until his attention was called to it by a brother
attorney during a recess of the court taken just before the
close of his argument, that he was charged with having men-
aced the judges with any disagreeable consequences to themselves in case of an adverse decision. He asks us to believe
that, with one of the most offensive passages of his brief set
before his eyes in the terms of the citation, and with ten days
for the careful reconsideration which he says in his answer
he has given to the matter, he never saw what is patent to
the observation of every one else.

It is difficult to credit Mr. Philbrook with such simplicity
of understanding, but it may be true that he has become so
blinded by his animosity against [484] Justice Harrison, and
so dominated by the belief that the "secret transaction of
September 6, 1890," as he terms it, was a gross and wicked
fraud, that he has lost the capacity of regarding any other
aspect of the case. Indeed his conduct during the hearing
of the citation would seem to indicate that this is so. For,
after devoting the greater part of two days to a vindication
and renewal of his assault upon Justice Harrison, he interrupted the course of his argument for a few moments to inform
the court that during the recess a brother attorney in whom
he had confidence had informed him that to some minds the

language of his brief might convey the idea of a threat. He, however, professed not to see it even after his attention had been so directed to the matter, but offered, if the court differed with him, to cancel the offensive passages in the briefs on file, and in those which he had distributed among his friends.

In my opinion this retraction was wholly insufficient. Mr. Philbrook had not only been informed by a brother attorney of the offensive construction which might be put upon his brief, he had been notified at the opening of the proceedings by the argument of Mr. Hayne that such was the construction placed upon it by the committee of the Bar Association, and he was plainly informed from the bench that it was understood in the same way by the court. If, in spite of these plain intimations, he was still unable to see what was so clearly apparent to others, it ought to have occurred to him that he would do well to take further advice of those in whom he had confidence as to the propriety of modifying his written answer, and of introducing into that permanent record a plain and unequivocal retraction or disavowal of the intention to threaten the court. That he has never done so, nor offered to do so, leaves his offense entirely unmitigated in my eyes, and imposes upon the court the necessity of inflicting the due penalty. As to the character of the penalty I concur in the view of the court that it should be suspension of his privileges as an attorney.

⁴⁸⁵ Upon the other branch of the case I should have had nothing to say if Mr. Philbrook had not, by devoting himself to that exclusively and ignoring every thing else, challenged the judgment and opinion of the court. Under the circumstances I cannot pass it over in silence without seeming to dissent from the views of my associates, and, therefore, I feel bound to add that, while I fully concede the right of Mr. Philbrook to attack the settlement between Levinson's executor and the Newmans, and to argue the propositions of fact and of law upon which he arraigns the conduct of Justice Harrison, I see nothing in the case to justify the conclusion that the advice given to the executor as to the construction of the partnership agreement, and his duty to settle according to such construction, was not entirely proper.

The proposition of law for which Mr. Philbrook contends, viz: That notwithstanding such settlement may have been entirely free from fraud, in fact it must be held fraudulent in law—a constructive fraud—because advised and witnessed by a gentleman who was then a candidate for the supreme bench, is one which it is open to him to argue, and since it is involved in the appeal of *Rankin* v. *Newman,* I express no opinion concerning it.

It appears from Mr. Philbrook's own showing that at the time of the settlement neither he nor his clients, the mother and sisters of Levinson, were claiming or had ever suggested that the articles of partnership were invalid. On the contrary, they were then and afterward asserting their validity, and claiming under them. Nor did they then claim or suggest that the inventory made in pursuance of the said articles was false or incorrect in any particular, except in the omission of the item of the "goodwill," the whole controversy being merely as to the proper construction of an agreement, then conceded to be valid and binding, with reference to the single question whether or not it embraced or excluded the "goodwill." As to this matter the difference between them was open, express, and well understood, [486] and there is not the slightest reason to suppose that Judge Harrison's opinion was less honest or less sound than that of Mr. Philbrook. Mr. Philbrook, indeed, is not entirely consistent with himself in this matter, for, unless I have misapprehended his position, he is now claiming that the Newmans, by the exercise of undue influence, induced their dying and partially demented partner to execute an agreement which sacrificed his interest in the goodwill; and, if this is so, it is scarcely consistent to claim that Judge Harrison misconstrued it, or that he can be blamed for the advice given to the executor at a time when neither Mr. Philbrook nor any one else had ever suggested fraud or undue influence in the procurement of the agreement.

I concur in the judgment.

Rehearing denied.

Grounds of Disbarment of Attorneys and Counselors at Law.

The proceedings and the judgment in the principal case attracted great attention in the state wherein the judgment was pronounced, and its effect was attempted to be annulled by an act which received the sanction of the two houses of the legislature, but was not approved by the governor. That the words for which the attorney was called to account were such as to warrant some action on the part of the court was, we think, never seriously questioned by any member of the bar, but there was doubt whether, upon his substantial plea of guilty, he should not have been regarded merely as having committed a contempt of the court, and punished as for a contempt, instead of being deprived of his right to continue in the practice of his profession. We have in previous notes cited the principal authorities, at least up to the date of such notes, upon the subject of the disbarment of attorneys: Note to *State* v. *Kirke*, 95 Am. Dec. 335; note to *Burns* v. *Allen*, 2 Am. St. Rep. 850. The great importance of the subject, nevertheless, in our judgment, justifies its further consideration for the purpose of ascertaining and stating the principles which may properly influence the action of the courts, and the nature and general purpose of the proceedings, and the authority of the court to take them and to enter and enforce appropriate orders and judgments to the end of rendering their decisions effective. When the ground of disbarment is like that in question in the principal case, an unfortunate condition has arisen from which there can be no termination which will not to a certain extent injuriously affect the administration of justice. If the court should remain silent under insinuations like those contained in the briefs in that case, it would with many persons be accepted as an admission, or at least an unwillingness to meet an unpleasant issue, and, on the other hand, to take action by administering appropriate remedies is sure to give rise to accusations that freedom of speech is being unwarrantably restricted, and that the right of counsel to fully present his case to the extent that it should be heard upon the merits, though such hearing may be to the discredit of judicial officers, is being unconstitutionally impaired.

POWER OF THE COURTS.—In various decisions the general statement is made that the power of disbarring attorneys is inherent in the courts, or, at least, that it is a power necessarily possessed by all courts having authority to admit attorneys to practice: *Ex parte Robinson*, 19 Wall. 505; *Davis* v. *State*, 92 Tenn. 634; *Penobscot Bar* v. *Kimball*, 64 Me. 140; *Scott* v. *State*, 86 Tex. 321; *State* v. *Kirke*, 12 Fla. 278; 95 Am. Dec. 314. If, indeed, the power is an inherent one, like, for instance. that of punishing contempts, then it must be that the grant by the state or national constitutions to the courts of the authority to exercise judicial functions includes with it the power to disbar attorneys, or to strike them from the roll, and that the legislature cannot limit this power, so far, at least, as to compel the courts to continue on the roll persons notoriously unfit to aid them in the administration of justice. The cases which we have cited do not, however, necessarily go this far, and cannot fairly be regarded as authority for any thing beyond the proposition that courts have, in the absence of statutory or constitutional limitations upon their power, authority to prevent from practicing before them persons who have been found unfit, either because of defects in moral character or otherwise, to discharge the duties of their profession. In truth the only decisions which have fallen within our observation necessarily in point, respecting the question now under discussion, affirm the right of the legislature to limit the power of the court to disbar attorneys, and to compel them to permit the acting as attorneys of persons who have confessedly been false to their obligations as such. Thus, in the case of *Kane* v. *Haywood*, 66 N. C. 1, it appeared that an attorney had collected a large sum of money, and that he had lost it in some way which he was unable to describe, for the reason, as he alleged, that he had been "mad drunk during a period of eighteen months," during which time he suggested that he might either have burned up the money, or put it in some secret place to keep himself from destroying it, which place he had not been able to discover. A rule was applied for, at the hearing of which a motion was made that the attorney be disbarred and deprived of his license to practice as such in the courts of the state. In answer to this motion an act of the legislature of the state was produced which declared: "No person who shall have been duly licensed to practice law as an attorney shall be disbarred or deprived of his license so to practice law, either permanently or temporarily, unless he shall have been convicted, or in open court confessed himself guilty, of some criminal offense showing him to be unfit to be trusted in the discharge of the duties of his profession." The court held that the words " convicted or in open court confessed himself guilty of some criminal offense," meant either that he had been convicted or had pleaded guilty when charged upon an indictment, and therefore that the confession of the attorney respecting the misappropriation of the money was not a confession of a criminal offense within the meaning of the statute, and that the operation of the statute was to take from the court the common-law power of disbarring an attorney, except upon such conviction or confession. The constitutionality of the statute was regarded as established by the preceding case of *Ex parte Schenck*, 65 N. C. 353. In this case the law relied upon was not discussed in the opinion of the court to any considerable extent, the only observation respecting it being that "the recent act above referred to does not take away any of the inherent powers of the courts which are absolutely essential to the administration of justice, and is not such an encroachment upon the rights of the judicial department of the government as to warrant us in declaring it to be unconstitutional and void."

It is true that the power to disbar attorneys is not inherent in courts of justice in the sense that they cannot exist in the absence of that power. The English courts did not originally exercise the power for the reason that at first litigants were required to appear in person, and were not permitted to be heard by attorney: *State* v. *Kirke*, 12 Fla. 278; 95 Am. Dec. 314; and at a later day, when attorneys were allowed to appear, their appointment did not proceed from the courts; but, if the legislative authority may authorize persons to appear as attorneys, we do not think this authority can be regarded as so absolute as to impose upon the courts the necessity of continuing upon their rolls persons who are clearly unfit to represent litigants. The case to which we have referred is a striking illustration of this truth. If it were true, as the attorney pleaded, that he had disposed of the moneys of his client while "mad drunk for the period of eighteen months," he had probably not committed any crime for the punishment of which the courts of the state had jurisdiction, and yet, whether a criminal or not, his absolute unfitness to discharge the duties of an attorney was established beyond controversy, and we think that in such a case the legislature cannot deprive the court of the power of disbarring the attorney without divesting it of an authority which is inherently vested in it by virtue of the constitution of the state giving it authority to exercise judicial functions, and to preserve the respect due to judicial officers and proceedings.

The Disbarment of an Attorney is not the Punishment of a Crime or other misdeed, though the act on account of which the disbarment is made may be of a criminal character or otherwise proper to be punished should appropriate proceedings be commenced for the purpose of establishing the guilt of the offender. The inquiry when proceedings for disbarment are prosecuted is, in effect, whether or not the accused is a proper person to be permitted to continue in the practice of his profession. His admission to practice was equivalent to a judgment that he possessed the mental and moral qualities required of an attorney and counselor at law. Had it been established at the hearing of his application for admission that he was deficient in either of these respects the court should have denied him the right to practice before it, not as a punishment for his deficiency, but because the administration of justice would probably be prejudiced rather than promoted by such admission. If the deficiency is discovered after the admission, there is still the same public policy to be subserved, except that it is to undo what ought not to have been done in the beginning, and in the undoing of it there is as little of the object of punishment as there would have been in denying the application for admission in the first instance. "It is not by way of punishment, but the courts in such cases exercise their discretion whether a man they have formerly admitted is a proper person to be continued on the rolls or not": *Ex parte Brounsall*, Cowp. 829; *In re Weare*, 2 Q. B. 439, for 1893; *Scott v. State*, 86 Tex. 321. "The power of disbarment is not exercised by the courts for the purpose of enforcing remedies between parties, but to protect the courts and the public against the official ministration of an attorney guilty of unworthy practices in his profession": *Davis v. State*, 92 Tenn. 640; *Ex parte Wall*, 107 U. S. 265, 273; *Ex parte Robinson*, 19 Wall. 512.

FOR ACTS NOT PERFORMED AS AN ATTORNEY.—If it be true, as stated in the preceding paragraph, that the purpose of the disbarment of an attorney is to remove a person shown to be unfit for the discharge of the duties of that office, then it must follow: 1. That though the person has committed a crime or other misdeed justifying his punishment, he may, nevertheless, continue as an attorney if appropriate action respecting such misdeed may be punishment alone, and the fact that he has been guilty may exist without necessarily evincing his unfitness to discharge the duties of an attorney; and 2. That where his unfitness is established he may and should be stricken from the rolls, though his wrongful act did not occur in the discharge of the duties of his profession, and does not amount to a crime punishable by law. As an illustration of the first proposition, it has been held that while it is true that the same professional conduct by an attorney may be the ground for disbarment, and may likewise constitute a contempt of court, yet an attorney may be guilty of a contempt of court without giving just cause for his disbarment, as by inserting scandalous matters in his written pleadings: *People v. Berry*, 17 Col. 322; *Ex parte Robinson*, 19 Wall. 512. An illustration of the second proposition is to be found in *In re Weare*, 2 Q. B. 439, for 1893, in which an order was made striking the name of a solicitor from the roll upon the ground that he had allowed himself "to be the landlord of brothels, and that he let his houses to tenants when he knew that those tenants were using them as brothels." The order was appealed from, and the judgment of the appellate court was delivered by Lord Esher, master of the rolls. He first considered the question whether the keeping of a brothel was a common-law offense and indictable as such, and answering this question in the affirmative, proceeded to consider and determine whether the offense for which a solicitor may be stricken from the rolls must be one committed in his character as such, and, after stating that this was the contention on the part of the appellant, answered: "That would seem to me to be a very strange doctrine, if it were true, that a person convicted of a crime, however horrible, must, if it be not connected with his professional character, be allowed by the court still to be a member of a profession which ought to be free from all suspicion." After referring to the cases of *Rex v. Southerton*, 6 East, 126; *In re Hill*, L. R. 3 Q. B. 543; *In re A Solicitor*, 61 L. T. 842, the master of the rolls further said: "All these cases seem to me to show that it is not necessary that the offense, or, at all events, if it be a criminal offense, should be committed by the offending party in his character as an attorney; the question is whether it is such an offense as makes it unfit that he should remain a member of this strictly honorable profession. Where a man has been convicted of a criminal offense, that *prima facie*, at all events does make him a person unfit to be a member of the honorable profession." In a concurring opinion Lindley, L. J., added: "The question is, whether a man is a fit and proper person to remain on the roll of solicitors and practice as such. That is the question. Now, asking that question, how can we say that a person who acts as that man is proved to have acted, is a fit and proper person to remain on the rolls of solicitors? What respectable solicitor could, without loss of self-respect, knowing the facts, meet him in business? And what right have we to impose upon respectable solicitors the duty of meeting him in business. I have no hesitation whatever in saying that the decision of the divisional court was correct." Lopes, L. J., also concurring, said: "It has been suggested that the power to strike off the roll only exists where there has been some professional misconduct. It appears to me that to hold that the jurisdiction of the court to strike off the roll extends only to professional misconduct and neglect of duty as a solicitor, would be placing too narrow a limit upon that most salutary disciplinary power that the court exercises over its officers. To my mind the question which the court in cases like this ought always to put to itself is this: Is the court, having regard to the circumstances brought before it, any longer justified in holding out the solicitor in question as a fit and proper person to be intrusted with the important duties and grave responsibilities which belong to a solicitor?" In the case of *In re Hill*, L. R. 3 Q. B. 543, the act for which disbarment was sought was performed by an attorney while acting as clerk of a firm of attorneys, and consisted in the appropriation to his own use of moneys which he had received from the sale of certain property. The rule applicable to such proceedings was thus stated by Chief Justice Cockburn: "When an attorney does that which involves dishonesty, it is for the interest of the suitors that the court should interpose and prevent a man guilty of such misconduct from acting as attorney of the court. In this case, if the delinquent had been proceeded against criminally upon the facts admitted by him, it is plain that he would have been convicted of embezzlement; and upon that conviction being brought before us, we should have been bound to act. If there had been a conflict of evidence upon the affidavits that might be a very sufficient reason why the court should not interfere until the conviction had taken place; but we have the person against whom the application is made admitting the facts." In this case, however, the judges were of opinion that as the offense had been committed several years previous to the application for disbarment, and as the offender had ever since behaved himself "with perfect propriety in his character as an attorney in the various transactions in which he had been engaged," and that the other circumstances in the case indicated that the offense was a departure from his ordinary course of conduct, and it not appearing at the time the application was made that his character was such as to indicate his unfitness to remain upon the rolls, the application for his disbarment should be denied. The American courts are in accord with those of England upon this subject, and in general concur in the declaration made by the court of appeals of Kentucky that, "It would be unjust to the profession, the purity and integrity of which it is the duty of all courts to preserve, and a disregard of the public welfare, to permit an attorney who has forfeited his right to public confidence to continue the practice of his profession": *Baker* v. *Commonwealth*, 10 Bush, 592; *Ex parte Cole*, 1 McCrary, C. C. 405; *State* v. *Finley*, 30 Fla. 325; *People* v. *Harvey*, 41 Ill. 277; *Rice* v. *Commonwealth*, 18 B. Mon. 473; *Mill's case*, 1 Mich. 394; *Sharon* v. *Hill*, 24 Fed. Rep. 726.

BAD CHARACTER.—It follows as a necessary result of the proposition that unfitness to continue at the bar is a sufficient cause of disbarment that no conviction or admission of any specific crime punishable as such need be shown, and that the action of the court in ordering a disbarment is not only justified, but is absolutely required when a member of it is shown to be of bad moral character of so serious a nature as to make it probable that he will be guilty of dishonest conduct in the discharge of the duties of his profession. "The duties imposed upon members of the bar clothe them with important fiduciary responsibilities, and make them amenable to obligations that other members of the community do not share. In no other calling should so strict an adherence to ethical and moral obligations be exacted, or so high a degree of accountability be enforced. A good moral character is one of the essential requisites to admission to the bar in this state, and the tenure of office thereby conferred is during good behavior; and when it appears upon full investigation that an attorney has forfeited his 'good moral character,' and has by his conduct shown himself unworthy of his office, it becomes the duty of the court to revoke the authority it gave him upon his admission. 'It is a duty they owe to themselves, the bar and the public, to see that a power which may be wielded for good or for evil is not intrusted to incompetent or dishonest hands'": *People* v. *Keegan* 18 Col. 237; 36 Am. St. Rep. 274; *Matter of Wool*, 36 Mich. 299. "When an attorney commits an act, whether in the discharge of his duties as such or not, showing such want of professional or personal honesty as renders him unworthy of public confidence, it is not only the province, but the duty, of the court, upon this fact being made to appear, to strike his name from the roll of attorneys. Nor is it necessary that the offense should be of such a nature as would subject him to an indictment. He has by his own misconduct divested himself of qualifications that are indispensable to the practice of his profession; and while he may regard the judgment depriving him of that right as a punishment for the offense, the action of the court is based alone upon the ground of public policy, and for the public good. It would be carrying the doctrine too far to hold that an attorney must be free from every vice, and to strike him from the roll of attorneys because he may indulge in irregularities affecting, to some extent, his character, when such delinquencies do not affect his personal or professional integrity. To warrant a removal his character must be bad in such respect as to show him to be unsafe and unfit to be intrusted with the powers and duties of his profession; and it is not essential that this misconduct or bad character should be in respect to some deceit, malpractice, or misdemeanor practiced or committed in the e ercise of his profession only; but in the exercise of a sound discretion, the court should only entertain such charges as are in their nature gross, and unfit a person for an honest discharge of the high and responsible trust reposed in an attorney": *State* v. *McClaugherty*, 33 W. Va. 250.

The Commission of Any Crime, if Intentional and Willful, shows a disregard of the law, and indicates an unfitness to be intrusted with its administration, and while there are crimes of a serious nature which it is possible for an attorney to commit without his being of a bad moral character with respect to the duties of his profession, yet there is, perhaps, no crime which the law characterizes as infamous for which an attorney may not be stricken from the rolls. His conviction establishes, *prima facie*, his unfitness to be continued on the rolls, but the court before acting will inquire into the nature of the crime, and not strike off the offender as a matter of course: *In re Weare*, 2 Q. B. 439, for 1893. As a general rule, a conviction of a felony or other infamous crime must be accepted as a sufficient cause for disbarment: *In re McCarthy*, 42 Mich. 71. Therefore, accepting a challenge to fight and fighting a duel, resulting in the killing of his antagonist, was held to be a cause of disbarment, though at the time and place where the question was presented and determined these acts were certainly not by any means conclusive evidence of a bad or criminal character: *Smith* v. *State*, 1 Yerg. 228. We cannot undertake to enumerate the crimes which have been held to justify a disbarment, but the following may be mentioned as illustrations of the rule upon the subject: Subornation of perjury: *State* v. *Holding*, 1 McCord, 379; forgery in erasing from a letter the word "not": *Baker* v. *Commonwealth*, 10 Bush, 592; participating in the unlawful hanging of a prisoner: *Ex parte Wall*, 107 U. S. 265; misappropriating moneys though received as bailee, and not in the course of business as an attorney: *In re O——*, 73 Wis. 602; obtaining money under false pretenses: *People* v. *Ford*, 54 Ill. 520; and fraudulently attempting to retain it for his own use: *People* v. *Murphy*, 119 Ill. 159; forging a deposition or affidavit to be used in court: *People* v. *Leary*, 84 Ill. 190; *Penobscot Bar* v. *Kimball*, 64 Me. 140; *Ex parte Walls*, 64 Ind. 461; assisting in a scheme to defraud creditors: *Ex parte Burr*, 2 Cranch C. C. 388; compounding a felony: *Rex* v. *Vaugn*, 1 Wils. 221; embezzling moneys received as a collector of taxes: *Delano's case*, 58 N. H. 5; 42 Am. Rep. 555; *In re Davies*, 93 Pa. St. 121; 39 Am. Rep. 729; treasonable and disloyal acts: *Cohen* v. *Wright*, 22 Cal. 293. It is not, however, as already suggested, every criminal act which will justify a disbarment. Thus the court refused to disbar an attorney because of the mere publication of a libel: *Ex parte* ——, 2 Dowl. Pr. 110; and in another case it was said that acts merely discreditable, but not infamous and not connected with an attorney's duties, did not justify the striking his name from the rolls: *Dickens' case*, 67 Pa. St. 169; 5 Am. Rep. 420. To this, however, we cannot assent without adding the qualification that the discreditable acts must be such that it may fairly be inferred that, though the attorney is guilty of them, his moral character is not such as will probably lead him into an abuse of the privileges of his profession, or a disregard of his duties either to the court or to his clients.

The Pardon of one found guilty of a crime or the serving of a sentence must result in his release from imprisonment, and therefore in the termination of all punishment which the law is authorized to directly inflict, and the operation of the statute of limitations may prevent his prosecution, though he has never suffered punishment, but neither necessarily nor ordinarily changes a criminal character to a moral and law-abiding one. Therefore, though a conviction for an infamous crime upon which the disbarment of an attorney has been based has been followed by his pardon, yet this does not entitle him to an annulment of the order of disbarment, nor to his reinstatement on the rolls of the court, and therefore the disbarment will continue in full force, unless, indeed, the court, upon investigation, may reach the conclusion that the previous conviction was unjust, and that the attorney did not have the criminal character which it indicates: *In the Matter of——*, 86 N. Y. 563. Nor can a plea of the statute of limitations be interposed with success to proceedings for disbarment: *In re Lowenthal*, 78 Cal. 429.

Misappropriation of Moneys.—No form of professional wrongdoing has been so frequently the cause of disbarment as the misappropriation of moneys received by attorneys in their professional character. There can be no question that this is a disregard of duty, and a sufficient cause for the action of the courts under a statute authorizing the disbarment of an attorney for a violation of his duties as such: *In re Treadwell*, 67 Cal. 353. If the misappropriation takes place under such circumstances as to constitute the crime of embezzlement, the disbarment of the offender is called for under the rule that the courts will not retain on their rolls attorneys guilty of infamous crimes. If the statute declares that disbarment may take place because of deceit practiced toward a court, judge, or party, the receipt of moneys belonging to a client and making false statements concerning them to excuse or conceal the fact of their not being remitted after such receipt, a disbarment may be justified because of deceit: *Slemmer* v. *Wright*, 54 Iowa, 164. Whether any crime has thereby been committed or not, the retention and misappropriation of moneys, and the failure to pay them, unless the circumstances are such as to preclude the idea that the attorney in default is free from all wrongful intent, and has been guilty of nothing but mere negligence or inadvertence, shows that he is not fit to be intrusted with the discharge of the duties of a profession which so frequently calls for action as a fiduciary agent, and that it would be extremely dangerous to permit him to remain where those who trust him are so likely to be exposed to pecuniary loss, and while there are statutes making the refusal to pay over on demand moneys collected by an attorney a cause for disbarment (*People* v. *Ryalls*, 8 Col. 332), no statute is necessary to warrant such disbarment where there has been any actual appropriation to his own use of moneys collected by an attorney, and which it was his duty to turn over to a person for whose benefit the collection was made: *Jeffries* v. *Laurie*, 27 Fed. Rep. 195; *Guilford* v. *Sims*, 10 Com. B. 370; *People* v. *Palmer*, 61 Ill. 255; *People* v. *Cole*, 84 Ill. 327; *Re Moore*, 72 Cal. 359; *In re Temple*, 33 Minn. 343; *Anonymous*, 10 Jur. 198; Q. B. 1 D. & R. 529. The offense when committed establishes the character of the attorney and his unfitness to be trusted, and while the payment of the moneys fraudulently obtained and withheld releases the attorney from civil liability, it is not a purgation of his offense, nor does it prove that he has become a fit person to remain on the rolls: *Anonymous*, 31 L. T. 730. The misappropriation becomes specially grievous when it appears that the moneys have been intrusted to an attorney for some special purpose, and by his neglect to use them for that purpose some valuable right or remedy has been lost to his client: *State* v. *Baum*, 14 Mont. 12, or some misrepresentation or other fraud has been resorted to, either to obtain possession of the money misappropriated: *In re Chandler*, 22 Beav. 253; 2 Jur. N. S. 366; 25 L. J. Ch. 296; *In re Tyler*, 71 Cal. 353; or to conceal either the fact that they have been received or that they have been misappropriated: *Baker* v. *State*, 90 Ga. 153. If moneys are collected by a member of a firm of attorneys and misappropriated by one of their number, while all are liable to the client, only one of them may be morally answerable for the misappropriation, and, where this is the case, the guilt of one member cannot justify the disbarment of the innocent members, nor can they be disbarred because they have not satisfied their civil liability by paying over the moneys for which they are so answerable, but in the misappropriation of which they are not implicated: *In re Luce*, 83 Cal. 303; *Klingensmith* v. *Kepler*, 41 Ind. 341; *Porter* v. *Vance*, 14 Lea. 629.

Whether Criminal Prosecution Must Precede Disbarment.—Whether the guilt of an attorney must be established by his previous conviction when the charge upon which his disbarment is sought involves an indictable offense is a question upon which there has been judicial dissension, and in respect to which there is, unfortunately, still some want of harmony. In some of the states statutes have been enacted which have received a construction restrictive of the power of the courts. Thus, in California, among other grounds for the removal or suspension of an attorney, enumerated in the Code of Civil Procedure, is "his conviction of a felony or misdemeanor involving moral turpitude, in which case the record of conviction shall be conclusive evidence": Cal. Code Civ. Proc., sec. 287. This has been treated by the courts of that state as a limitation upon their authority, or at least as a sufficient excuse for declining to act until after the guilt of the accused has been made the subject of inquiry in a criminal prosecution against him: *In re Tilden* (Cal., June 19, 1891), 5 Pac. Rep. 687; *In re Stephens*, 102 Cal. 264. Even then, before the court will act, the judgment of conviction must have become final. Therefore, proceedings for disbarment instituted during the pendency of an appeal from a judgment of conviction are premature: *People v. Treadwell*, 66 Cal. 400. This statute, if susceptible of the construction thus given it, appears to us to be an attempted unconstitutional invasion of the prerogatives of the court, because it compels the continuance as officers of such court of persons guilty of infamous crimes involving moral turpitude. The case first cited was submitted upon objections to the sufficiency of the charge, and the public conscience was shocked by what, in law, amounted to an assertion by the accused that until convicted it was not material whether he was guilty of the crime charged, and by the court that it was powerless to purge its rolls of unconvicted criminals. It is our judgment that the clause of the statute in question, instead of being a shameful restriction upon the power of the court, was intended to compel its action by denying its right to exonerate an attorney when the record of his conviction was produced. Among other causes of disbarment declared by the same statute were "any violation of the oath taken by him, or of his duties as such attorney and counselor." The oath referred to included an affirmation that the attorney would "faithfully discharge the duties of an attorney and counselor at law to the best of his knowledge and ability." In the Tilden case the charge was of stealing a paper in a cause then pending in court with felonious intent. In the charge against Stephens was involved the accusation that he, after collecting moneys for his client, had misrepresented the amount of such collection for the purpose of defrauding that client. The attorney was willing to meet the accusation, but the court, apparently in the fear that it might be resorted to as a mere agency for collection, refused to act, on the ground that it was asked "to lay aside the important and pressing business, with which every moment of its time is fully occupied, in order to investigate, in the first instance, a charge which may be tried and determined in the courts of the country"; and it thus gave ground for the imputation that a civil action before a justice of the peace to recover a small sum of money was a more appropriate and deserving proceeding than one directed to the striking from the roll of attorneys one who, if the charges were true, was unquestionably unworthy to be retained there. We are happy to say that in another state having a precisely identical statute it has not been found any insuperable objection to proceeding to the disbarment of an attorney, though for an indictable offense: *State v. Winton*, 11 Or. 456; 50 Am. Rep. 486.

In England, upon several occasions, the courts refused to proceed against an attorney when the offense with which he was charged was one proper for an indictment against him, and from these refusals the inference was drawn that in no case would a court proceed against an attorney for an indictable offense until it had been the subject of a criminal prosecution: *Anonymous*, 5 Barn. & Adol. 1088; *Ex parte* ——, 2 Dowl. Pr. 110; *Short* v. *Pratt*, 1 Bing. 102; *Matter of Knight*, 1 Bing. 142; and following these decisions, and somewhat influenced by special statutes, some of the American courts refused to act in the absence of such prosecution: *Anonymous*, 7 N. J. L. 162; *Beene* v. *State*, 22 Ark. 149; *Ex parte Steinman*, 95 Pa. St. 220; 40 Am. Rep. 637. The reasons given were that if an attorney were called upon to answer upon oath a charge of this character, he might be required to give evidence against himself which could be used in aid of his conviction should a prosecution subsequently be instituted. More recent decisions in England show that the position of the courts of that country was misapprehended; and that the rule to be deduced from all their decisions was correctly stated in *Ex parte Wall*, 107 U. S. 280, in the following language: "An attorney will be struck off the rolls if convicted of felony, or if convicted of a misdemeanor involving want of integrity, even though the judgment be arrested or reversed for error; and also, without a previous conviction, if he is guilty of gross misconduct in his profession, or of acts which, though not done in his professional capacity, gravely affect his character as an attorney; but in the latter case, if the acts charged are indictable, and are fairly denied, the court will not proceed against him until he has been convicted by a jury; and will in no case compel him to answer under oath to a charge for which he may be indicted," citing *Stephens* v. *Hill*, 10 Mees. & W. 28; 1 D. P. S. 669; 6 Jur. 585; *In re Blake*, 3 El. & E. 34; *In re Hill*, L. R. 3 Q. B. 543. In America, except when restrained by statute, it is believed the courts may and will proceed to disbar an attorney on account of his criminal act, though it might have been the subject of an indictment, and the fact that there has not been a criminal prosecution will in no case constitute a sufficient answer to the proceeding for disbarment: *Ex parte Wall*, 107 U. S. 265; *Fields* v. *State*, Mart. & Y. 168; *In re Percy*, 36 N. Y. 651; *Smith* v. *State*, 1 Yerg. 228; *Penobscot Bar* v. *Kimball*, 64 Me. 140; *Matter of Niles*, 3 Daly, 435; *State* v. *Finley*, 30 Fla. 302; *Ex parte Walls*, 64 Ind. 461; *Perry* v. *State*, 3 G. Greene, 550; *Delano's case*, 58 N. H. 5; 42 Am. Rep. 555. See, also, *In re Davies*, 93 Pa. St. 116; 39 Am. Rep. 729; *In re Serfass*, 116 Pa. St. 455. We cannot understand how any other view should at any time have found judicial favor. The courts have always disclaimed disbarment as a means of punishment, and have proceeded solely on the ground that it is their duty to strike from their rolls the names of all attorneys shown to be unfit to remain thereon. Nor do we understand that they have ever required this unfitness to be established beyond a reasonable doubt. Yet if conviction must precede disbarment, the guilt of the accused must be established according to the rules of criminal procedure, a part of which is that all the members of a jury shall be satisfied of guilt beyond a reasonable doubt. It seems strangely inconsistent to hold that an attorney may be proceeded against upon some more trivial ground of disbarment, such, for instance, as his failure to maintain the respect due to courts and judicial officers, and suspended or disbarred upon the judgment of the court most likely to be biased against him, and yet that when accused of being a thief, forger, or perjurer, he may in effect interpose a demurrer confessing the charge, and be exonerated from answering on the ground that it is not stealing, forging, or committing perjury which makes him unfit to be continued on the rolls, but only his final conviction of some of those offenses.

Unprofessional Conduct is often spoken of as a ground of disbarment. Of course, all conduct which may justify a disbarment is unprofessional, but this term is usually employed to denote wrongful conduct not amounting to a crime, punishable by the rules of any criminal code, but, nevertheless, in contravention of the ethics of the profession. A familiar instance of this is taking advantage of the confidence reposed by the client, or even of some special hallucination by which he is known to be affected, and thereupon giving him dishonest advice upon which his action may operate to his own injury, and to the benefit of the attorney: *In re Snyder*, 24 Fed. Rep. 910; *Strout* v. *Proctor*, 71 Me. 288; *In re Burris*, 101 Cal. 624; *In re Collins*, 7 De Gex, M. & G. 558. To act toward a client otherwise than with the utmost good faith is indisputably unprofessional, and therefore any advice given by an attorney which he does not himself believe to be correct, and any action whatever taken by him with a view of injuriously affecting his client, or of obtaining some advantage for the attorney to the prejudice of his client, justifies a disbarment: *Fairfield County Bar* v. *Taylor*, 60 Conn. 11. Nor can an attorney, without being guilty of unprofessional conduct, use, to the prejudice of his client, information obtained while acting as such, nor seek profit either by working on the fears of the client that such a use may be made, nor by opening negotiations with his adversary for employment, and holding out the inducement that he has become possessed of knowledge while in the service of his client which may make his employment against that client specially effective: *United States* v. *Costen*, 38 Fed. Rep. 24; *In re O* ——, 73 Wis. 602. After appearing as the attorney for one litigant an attorney must not subsequently appear in the same controversy for his adversary: *People* v. *Spencer*, 61 Cal. 128. So it has been held that interfering between a client and his attorney by slandering the latter, and inducing the client to forsake him, is unprofessional, and may justify a disbarment: *Baker* v. *State*, 90 Ga. 153. The relation of attorney and client is of a confidential nature, and therefore any contract between them during the continuance of that relation is closely scrutinized to the end that the attorney may not gain any advantage either from his superior knowledge or from the confidence reposed in him, and there have been instances in which because of his entering into contracts with his client of a highly advantageous character to himself he has been deemed to have acted from unconscionable motives, and to be unfit to be continued in his profession, as where, shortly after his client became of age, the attorney accepted from him the loan of a large sum of money: *In re A Solicitor*, 1 Q. B. 254. An attorney who, receiving seventeen hundred dollars for arrears of pensions collected for his client, had paid him less than one-third of that amount, and who justified his action on the ground that the agreement between him and the client was to the effect that he should retain all over eight dollars per month, it not appearing that the client knew of the amount to which he was entitled, was adjudged to have entered into an unconscionable agreement with his client, and to have thereby indicated the presence "of a depraved professional morality": *In re* ——, 86 N. Y. 563. An attorney may also be guilty of unprofessional conduct by an advertisement indicating that he can obtain special favors to which litigants are not entitled by law, as where he advertises that he can procure divorces without publicity, and for causes not sanctioned by law: *People* v. *Goodrich,* 79 Ill. 148; *People* v. *MacCabe,* 18 Col. 186; 36 Am. St. Rep. 270.

Under the Head of Unprofessional.Conduct may be Included all attempts on the part of an attorney to pollute the administration of justice by a resort to any form of device for the purpose of preventing a decision of a cause upon the merits, as by deceiving the court or the adverse party or his counsel, or by testimony known to be false or forged, or by tampering with witnesses, or fraudulently avoiding their presence in court when it is suspected that their evidence will be against the interests of the attorney or his client. It is not possible to specify all the fraudulent devices which may fall within the spirit of this rule and for a resort to which upon base motives an attorney may be disbarred. The following illustrations will serve to place the existence of the rule, beyond controversy, and to indicate the circumstances in which it may with propriety be applied: Inducing a witness to absent himself from the trial after the service of a subpœna upon him, and receiving indemnity against the consequences of his disobedience to such subpœna: *Stephens* v. *Hill,* 10 Mees. & W. 28; 1 Dowl. N. S. 669; 6 Jur. 585; causing the wife of a client to visit the family of a judge and to seek by conversation to be had in his presence to commit him to the cause of the client in advance of its trial: *Ex parte Cole,* 1 McCrary C. C. 405; obliterating a record and antedating a writ to avoid the effect of the statute of limitations: *Ex parte Brown,* 1 How. (Miss) 303; offering in evidence for the purpose of procuring a divorce testimony known to the attorney to be false and perjured: *People* v. *Beattie,* 137 Ill. 553; 31 Am. St. Rep. 384; writing out in advance of the taking of a deposition answers to be made by witnesses to be examined, and reading, or causing to be read, those answers when the deposition was taken, although it was not shown that the answers were either false or believed to be so, the attorney having, however, from time to time, furnished sums of money to the witnesses: *Matter of Eldridge,* 82 N. Y. 161; 37 Am. Rep. 558; conspiring and attempting to get the attorney of his adversary drunk for the purpose of gaining an advantage in a cause to be tried: *Dickens' case,* 67 Pa. St. 169; 5 Am. Rep. 420; inducing a United States commissioner to believe that he had authority to issue a writ of habeas corpus and to admit a prisoner to bail, and thus bringing about his escape: *State* v. *Burr,* 19 Neb. 593; presenting mutilated copies of papers to a court for the purpose of deceiving and misleading it: *In re Henderson,* 88 Tenn. 531; making, for the purpose of obtaining a continuance, a showing known to be false: *Baker* v. *State,* 90 Ga. 153; substituting the name of his client for his own name in an affidavit to procure alimony: *People* v. *Leary,* 84 Ill. 190; obtaining a change of the place of trial by the use of a forged affidavit: *Ex parte Walls,* 64 Ind. 461; collusion in the manufacture of deceptive evidence for the purpose of enabling a husband to secure a divorce: *In re Gale,* 75 N. Y. 526; presenting an affidavit containing a statement known to be false in making or supporting a claim for pre-emption. *In re Keegan,* 31 Fed. Rep. 129; taking a retainer not to appear on behalf of a municipality in certain pending suits commenced by an attorney in his name while he was the official attorney of such city, though such retainer was taken after he went out of office, and he never had any personal knowledge of the suits: *In re Cowdrey,* 69 Cal. 52; 58 Am. Rep. 545; and offering such retainer and procuring its acceptance: *In re Whittemore,* 69 Cal. 67; procuring a judgment with knowledge that thereby a fraud was being attempted against certain creditors: *People* v. *Keegan,* 18 Col. 237; 36 Am. St. Rep. 274; assisting a husband to impose upon his wife, and to cause her to believe herself to be legally divorced, and for that purpose forging the name of an officer of the court to a paper purporting to be a copy of a decree annulling the marriage: *Matter of Peterson*, 3 Paige, 510; joining in a conspiracy to cheat and defraud tradesmen, including among its overt acts the collusive signing of judgments and issuing writs of execution thereon: *In re King*, 8 Q. B. 129; 10 Jur. 7; 15 L. J. Q. B. 2; pretending to strike an averment out of a complaint when told that it was false, and procuring his client to verify such complaint, in the belief that such averment had been stricken therefrom: *People* v. *Pearson*, 55 Cal. 472. Misconduct of the class of which we are here speaking may be to subserve a purpose personal to the attorney, and not involving any action or proceeding in which he is representing another, as where he produces a license from a court of another state and procures his admission to practice thereon, though such license has been revoked in the state wherein it was granted: *In re Lowenthal*, 61 Cal. 122; *Dean* v. *Stone* (Oklahoma, Feb. 2, 1894), 35 Pac. Rep. 578. It is essential to support a disbarment in this class of cases that the action of the attorney should have been prompted by unworthy motives, and he cannot be disbarred because he made a motion which was not supported by the facts: *Fletcher* v. *Daingerfield*, 20 Cal. 427; or corrected a decree after it had been signed, by inserting immaterial words omitted therefrom, through clerical oversight: *State* v. *Finley*, 30 Fla. 325.

Contempts and Calumnies of Courts and Judges.—We reach now the consideration of a class of causes or alleged causes of disbarment arising out of the conduct of attorneys towards judges and courts not involving the practice of any deception upon them, or any scheme to corrupt or embarrass the administration of justice by misrepresentation, deceit, or the use of false or forged testimony, or the suppression of unfavorable evidence of any character, but rather by the use of offensive language to a judge or court, or the attributing to him or it of unworthy motives, and the seeking thereby to bring judicial tribunals or officers into contempt by disparaging their motives or learning, or both. If courts may disbar for any of these causes, it is evident that they should proceed with very great caution, and decline to act otherwise than by inflicting punishment as for a contempt, except in very aggravated or extraordinary cases. The administration of justice demands fearless advocates and a freedom of speech which shall be absolutely untrammeled, provided that it be addressed to questions which may fairly be deemed to be involved in the cause, and not consist of mere denunciations upon extrinsic matters not presented by the evidence or record before the court. In every other class of proceedings for disbarment courts have insisted that the object of the proceedings and judgment was not for the punishment of the attorney, but rather for the revocation of a license which would not have been granted in the first place had the court known that the attorney was deficient in mental or moral qualities, and that the disbarment is for the protection of the public, or, at least, that portion thereof whose business may require their interest to be represented before judicial tribunals by persons of ability, learning, and integrity. If it be true that disbarment cannot be justified on the ground that it is an infliction of just punishment for misdeeds, then the instances in which a court may proceed to strike the name of an attorney from the rolls because of his acts or words involving a contempt of, or want of confidence in, such court, or any member thereof, must be extremely rare. In so far as an act done or word spoken may merit punishment, a court should proceed to punish, as it may always do, by virtue of its inherent power to deal with persons found guilty of contempt. We may agree with the opinion of the court in the principal case that the course practiced by the attorney was "intolerable," that "it cannot be suffered by any occupant of the bench who has a just sense of his duty to the public to preserve the due dignity of their courts," without assenting to the order of disbarment;—for intolerable acts may be punished and the dignity of the court may be preserved by summary proceedings to punish contempts, but if we agree with the court that the attorney was guilty "of a palpable attempt to influence the decision of the court by base appeals to the timidity of its justices," then from the order of disbarment there can be no dissent, because he who seeks to influence the action of a court by the means suggested proves the existence of a wrongdoer of a depraved and corrupt moral nature, seeking to accomplish his objects, even in the halls of justice, by depraved and dishonest methods; and giving assurance that he will continue in the future what he has attempted in the past. There can be, and there is, no doubt that every action on the part of an attorney for the purpose of coercing a judge in the decision of a cause, whether it consists of a personal attack, or of threats, or of any other means of intimidation, indicates an unquestionable unfitness for the discharge of the duties of an attorney, and requires his disbarment: *Ex parte Cole*, 1 McCrary C. C. 405. That misconduct toward a judge or court may constitute a sufficient cause of disbarment, though it relates to a past act or decision, and therefore cannot have the purpose of influencing or coercing it, we do not deny, but as disbarment is not for punishment, but for purification, an act cannot justify it, "although in contravention of the rights of the court," unless it has been "induced by a vicious or immoral incentive": *Watson* v. *Citizens' Savings Bank*, 5 S. C. 159. The act of an attorney toward a private citizen may be of so vicious a nature, and exhibit such a defiance of law and of right that it could proceed only from a vicious, lawless culprit so manifestly at war with law and right that it is worse than folly to retain him as an officer of the court to aid it in the administration of justice. Similar acts done to a judge do not any the less indicate the unfitness of the doer to be continued in the office of attorney. Therefore, a personal attack upon a judge for his action as such, or a threatening him with personal chastisement for his conduct during the trial of a cause, is a sufficient cause of disbarment: *Beene* v. *State*, 22 Ark. 149; *Bradley* v. *Fisher*, 13 Wall. 335. In determining the case last cited the court said: "But on the other hand the obligations which attorneys impliedly assume, if they do not by express declaration take upon themselves, when they are admitted to the bar, is not merely to be obedient to the constitution and the laws, but to maintain at all times the respect due to courts of justice and judicial officers. This obligation is not discharged by merely observing the rules of courteous demeanor in open court, but it includes abstaining out of court from all insulting language and offensive conduct toward the judges personally for their judicial acts.' 'In matters collateral to official duty,' said Chief Justice Gibson in the *Case of Austin*, 5 Rawle 191, 28 Am. Dec. 657, 'the judge is on a level with the members of the bar as he is with his fellow-citizens, his title to distinction and respect resting on no other foundation than his virtues and qualities as a man. But it is nevertheless evident that professional fidelity may be violated by acts which fall without the line of professional functions, and which may have been performed out of the pale of the court. Such would be the consequences of beating or insulting a judge in the street for a judgment in court. No one would pretend that an attempt to control the deliberation of the bench, by the apprehension of violence, and subject the judges to the power of those who are, or ought to be, subordinate to them, is compatible with professional duty, or the judicial independence so indispensable to the administration of justice.   And an enormity of the sort, practiced but on a single judge, would be an offense as much against the court, which is bound to protect all its members, as if it had been repeated on the person of each of them, because the consequence to suitors and the public would be the same; and whatever may be thought in such a case of the power to punish for contempt, there can be no doubt of the existence of a power to strike the offending attorney from the roll.'"

Under a statute authorizing the justices of the supreme court at their discretion to strike the name of an attorney or counselor at law from the roll for misconduct in office, an attorney was charged with and found guilty of addressing a judge upon the street in abusive, insulting, and threatening language concerning his judicial action in a cause still pending and undetermined and threatening to expose him by publishing accusations in the newspapers.   The court, in determining that the case was a proper one for its action, said: "The right of lawyers, in common with other persons, to criticise, in a legitimate manner the conduct and rulings of judicial officers is recognized, but this right never extends to nor justifies indignities to such officers concerning proceedings in court, which indignities would properly be characterized as outrages if perpetrated upon private citizens concerning other matters" :   *People* v. *Green*, 7 Col. 237; 49 Am. Rep. 351.   A case very closely resembling the principal case is that of *People* v. *Green*, 9 Col. 506, in which an attorney was prosecuted for charging a judge and an attorney with bribery in proceedings pending in a court, and for attempting to remove such judge and attorney when there was in fact no foundation or probable cause for the charges thus made.   As in the principal case the final action of the court was apparently influenced by the fact that the offender had been before it on a previous occasion for conduct of a somewhat similar character.   In determining upon his disbarment, the court said: "Neither the letter nor the spirit of the attorney's privilege permits him to enter our courts and spread upon judicial records charges of a shocking and felonious character against brother attorneys, and against judges engaged in the administration of justice, upon mere rumors, coupled with facts which should, of themselves, create no suspicion of official corruption in a just and fair mind.   And although, in actions of libel and slander, it has been thought wise to exempt them from liability for defamatory words, published or spoken, in the course of judicial proceedings, provided such words are material, in a disbarment proceeding, the recognition of such a privilege could neither secure justice nor advance the independence of the bar.   On the contrary, its inevitable tendency would be to destroy the respect due to the profession as well as to the bench, and cripple the influence and usefulness of both."   In some of the statutes undertaking to specify in a generel way the duties of attorneys, they are required to maintain at all times the respect due to courts of justice and judicial officers.   This is understood to be among their duties by the common law, and disbarments have been based upon a violation of this duty, though it has not been enjoined by any statute of the state otherwise than by the general adoption of the common law as a rule of decision in the absence of statutes conflicting with it.   Hence an attorney who, when advised of a decision of the supreme court against his client, responded,   "Yes; that's a son of a bitch of a court—one bribed and the other I don't know what," was disbarred: *In re Brown*, 3 Wyo. 121.

It is in a general sense true that it is the duty of attorneys to maintain the respect due to courts and judicial tribunals, but the courts ought to assist them in so doing by being respectable. The rule was never intended to protect judges from adverse criticism, and can never be properly applied unless the offensive language is not only insulting in its nature, but is either employed for the purpose of intimidating a court or judge or of subjecting judicial proceedings to contempt, and arousing a suspicion or conviction that such proceedings are corrupt, and thereby inciting the public to acts of lawlessness in defense or vindication of supposed rights, rather than resorting to the legally constituted tribunals for redress. An attorney as well as any other citizen has a perfect right to criticise the actions and decisions of courts and judges, though neither has any right to indulge in calumny without reasonable cause, nor to express his views in a manner indicative of malevolence or other wrongful incentive to action, rather than manifesting his disapproval of what he, upon probable cause, believes to be either the mistaken or deliberately wrongful action of the court or judge. As between an attorney and his client he may discuss the fitness of a judge before whom a cause is to be brought for trial, "and the peculiar influences which may work upon his mind in favor of the one side or the other to a controversy": *Ex parte Cole*, 1 McCrary C. C. 405. An attorney may address a letter to a judge expressed in respectful language, stating that he has lost the confidence of the public, and suggesting the propriety of his resigning from office: *Austin's case*, 5 Rawle, 91; 28 Am. Dec. 657. And a mere libel upon a judge is not a cause of disbarment unless its object is shown to have been "the acquirement of an influence over a judge in the exercise of his judicial functions by the instrumentality of popular prejudices," and a disbarment therefor will not be ordered where it is found that the motives of the libel were "a desire for notoriety, partisan malice, and a willful, headlong zeal to promote partisan interests": *Ex parte Steinman*, 95 Pa. St. 220; 40 Am. Rep. 637. There are decisions which go very far toward affirming that an attorney may employ very extreme language of and concerning a judge and his motives and rules of action as such, provided the language was not used in court, but is a mere expression of the ill-feeling and ill opinion of one man toward another: *Jackson* v. *State*, 21 Tex. 668. This case is an extreme one, and, perhaps, cannot be approved unless on the ground that the language complained of was used during an exciting political contest, and in a part of the country where political adversaries are somewhat prone to employ exaggerated terms of disapproval. There is, however, we think, no doubt that though language used toward a court or judge is unjustifiable, and constitutes a contempt, such as may, and ought to, be punished, yet that the punishment therefor can never properly include the disbarment of the offender, unless his conduct is such as to establish his unfitness to discharge the duties of his profession: *Ex parte Robinson*, 19 Wall. 505.

MATTINGLY *v.* PENNIE.

[105 CALIFORNIA, 514.]

TARE DECISIS.—The decision of an appellate court on appeal as to a question of fact does not become the law of the case.

BROKER, WHEN ENTITLED TO COMMISSIONS.—To entitle a broker, under a contract authorizing him to sell stocks and to receive as his commission all he could obtain above a designated price, to recover such commission when no sale is actually consummated, he must prove that he found a purchaser ready, willing, and able to buy the property on the terms fixed, and either that he procured from that person a valid contract binding him to make the purchase, or that he brought the vendor and the proposed purchaser together so that the vendor might have secured such contract had he so desired. Readiness and willingness to purchase can be shown only by an offer on the part of the purchaser to the vendor to enter into the contract of purchase, or by the execution on the part of the purchaser of a valid contract of purchase.

CONTRACT WITH BROKER PREVENTING PERFORMANCE.—A broker authorized to sell property, and who informs his principal that there is a party willing to purchase on the terms upon which the principal had authorized the sale to be made, but without stating who is the proposed purchaser, cannot recover his commissions, though the principal refused to make the sale, if the purchaser never entered into any valid and enforceable contract of purchase, and never made any offer to the principal to do so. The refusal of the principal does not entitle the broker to the benefit which would have accrued to him upon performance, if he on his part had not so far performed his contract as to obtain a valid contract of purchase.

JURY TRIAL.—A court should not instruct a jury that evidence of the oral admissions of a party should be received with caution, when it is the only kind of evidence which in the nature of the case his adversary could procure.

EVIDENCE—DECLARATIONS ACCOMPANYING ACTS.—If, in an action to recover compensation as broker, the plaintiff claims that the principal repudiated the contract authorizing the broker to sell certain stocks, it is competent for the defendant to prove that he kept such stocks in the hands of a third person for delivery to any purchaser whom the broker might produce, and he may also prove in connection with those acts any declaration made at the time as characterizing those acts as a part of the *res gestæ*.

Naphtaly, Freidenrich & Ackerman, John A. Wright, and William H. H. Hart, for the appellant.

D. William Douthitt and Edward J. Pringle, for the respondent.

⁵¹⁶ VAN FLEET, J. This is an action to recover the sum of one hundred and twenty-five thousand dollars, commissions for the sale of mining stocks. Plaintiff alleges that, by a written contract with Thomas H. Blythe, defendant's intes-

tate, he was authorized to negotiate a sale of said stocks fo
three hundred thousand dollars, and was to receive as hi
commission all that he could obtain for the stock above tha
price; that he procured a purchaser at the net price of fou
hundred and twenty-five thousand dollars, who was ready
willing, and able to pay that sum for the stock; and tha
Blythe refused to make the sale or convey the stock to th
purchaser.

The cause was tried before a jury, and a verdict was ren
dered for the defendant. Plaintiff appealed to this court
and the judgment was reversed and the cause remanded fo:
a new trial: *Mattingly* v. *Roach*, 84 Cal. 207. A second tria'
was had before a jury, which resulted in a verdict for the
plaintiff for the full amount claimed. The defendant appeals
and assigns error in the instructions and other rulings of the
court, and insufficiency of the evidence to justify the verdict

Respondent contends that on the former appeal the ques·
tion of the sufficiency of the evidence to sustain a verdict for
plaintiff was decided in favor of plaintiff; that plaintiff's evi·
dence was substantially the same on the last trial as on the
first; and that the decision on that point has become the law
of the case, and precludes us from now considering the suffi·
ciency of that evidence.

The facts upon which this contention is based are these:
On the former appeal plaintiff (then appellant) contended
that a certain instruction, given at the request [517] of defend·
ant, was erroneous. In reply defendant (then respondent)
urged that the evidence would not have supported a verdict
for plaintiff even if the instruction in question had not been
given, and that, therefore, the alleged error was without
prejudice to plaintiff. In response to that objection we said
that, in our opinion, plaintiff had produced testimony tend·
ing to sustain his side of the case, that no motion for nonsuit
had been made, and that the case was properly submitted to
the jury for its determination as to the facts. The instruc·
tion in question was held erroneous, and the judgment was
reversed for that reason alone.

It is settled beyond controversy that a decision of this
court on appeal, as to a question of fact, does not become the
law of the case. But plaintiff contends that the question thus
presented of the insufficiency of the evidence to support a
verdict for plaintiff was a question of law, and was the very
fact in judgment on that appeal. Assuming, without decid-

ing, that that view is correct, we are, nevertheless, of opinion
that the point now presented is not the same as that so supposed to have been decided on the former appeal, and that
we are therefore now entitled to consider it without being
concluded by the former decision. We adhere to what was
said on that subject in *Wixon* v. *Devine*, 80 Cal. 388, and will
not extend the application of the doctrine of the "law of the
case" beyond the cases in which it has hitherto been held
to apply.

On the former appeal defendant was not entitled to dispute the correctness of the rulings of the court below, or of
the theory on which the case had been submitted to the jury.
The verdict being in his favor, he could not assign error; and,
on plaintiff's appeal, we were bound to assume the correctness of the instructions given at plaintiff's request. Those
instructions, whether correct or otherwise, were binding upon
the jury; and plaintiff was entitled to a verdict in accordance with those instructions, if the evidence warranted it:
Emerson v. *Santa Clara County*, 40 Cal. 543; *Aguierre* v.
Alexander, 58 [518] Cal. 21, 30; *Declez* v. *Save*, 71 Cal. 552.
On that appeal, therefore, the only question which we could
possibly consider as to the sufficiency of the evidence was
whether the evidence was sufficient, under the instructions
actually given and not objected to by plaintiff, to have supported a verdict in his favor had one been rendered. On the
present appeal defendant contends that the theory on which
the case was given to the jury, which was substantially the
same as at the first trial, was incorrect, and that the instructions were contrary to law; and that the evidence is insufficient to justify a verdict for plaintiff, under the rules of law
as they should have been given to the jury. It is evident
that no such question was or could have been considered or
decided on the former appeal; and, if there are any expressions in the former opinion which at first glance might appear to refer to that question, they must be confined in their
application to the question then actually before the court.

In addition to these considerations we are also of opinion
that as to at least one material point—the alleged repudiation of the contract by Blythe—the evidence is, as we shall
show, materially different from that on the former trial.

For these reasons we think that we are at liberty to consider the points made by appellant without further reference
to the former opinion.

1. At the request of the plaintiff the court gave the jury the following instruction: "The authority given to the plaintiff by exhibit B to sell the stock of the Blue Jacket Mining Company for a sum not less than three hundred thousand dollars did not authorize the plaintiff to execute in the name of Thomas H. Blythe any written contract with a purchaser or to bind Blythe to a purchaser, but only to procure a purchaser, and this might be done verbally by bargain with the purchaser."

It is evident that the question of the power of plaintiff to bind Blythe by a contract of sale of the stock does not arise in this case; and this instruction therefore means, and must have been understood by the jury [519] to mean, that plaintiff would fully perform the conditions of his contract with Blythe, and earn his commissions by merely obtaining from a purchaser a verbal bargain to buy the stock.

The court also, at the request of plaintiff, gave the following instruction: "If the jury believe that the plaintiff found a purchaser who was able, ready, and willing to purchase and pay for the stock of the Blue Jacket mine at five hundred thousand dollars, or any sum above three hundred thousand dollars, before the fifteenth day of February, 1883, and informed Thomas H. Blythe of the fact in season, so that a sale could have been consummated before the fifteenth day of February, 1883, and the said Blythe refused to make a sale, then the plaintiff is entitled to recover."

These instructions do not correctly state the law. In order to entitle a broker, under such a contract, to recover commissions where no sale has actually been consummated, it is incumbent on him to prove that he found a purchaser ready, willing, and able to buy the property on the terms fixed, and either that he procured from that person a valid contract binding him to purchase the property upon those terms, or that he brought the vendor and the proposed purchaser together so that the vendor might have secured such contract if he desired. On no other terms can he recover: *Gunn* v. *Bank of California*, 99 Cal. 349. The readiness and willingness of a person to purchase the property can be shown only by an offer on his part to purchase; and unless he has actually entered into a contract binding him to purchase, or has offered to the vendor, and not merely to the broker, to enter into such a contract, he cannot be considered a "purchaser." Such a contract, in this case, would be within the statute of frauds, and must be in writing (Code Civ. Proc., sec. 1973, subd. 4; Civ. Code, sec. 1739), there being no pretense that the purchaser had received any part of the stock or paid any part of the price. The court should have instructed the [520] jury in accordance with these principles, and the above instructions were erroneous.

2. It follows also from these principles that the evidence did not justify the verdict. The evidence produced by plaintiff at the most tended only to show that plaintiff, within the time limited, found a person in London who offered verbally to purchase the stock for four hundred and twenty-five thousand dollars net; that plaintiff communicated that fact to Blythe without in any way naming or pointing out the purchaser; and that Blythe thereupon refused to make the sale. No contract was obtained from the supposed purchaser which could bind him in any way, nor was it shown that Blythe was aware who he was, or did any thing to prevent plaintiff from performing the condition of the contract. Counsel for plaintiff contend that the evidence shows that Blythe unequivocally refused to perform his contract; and they claim that, under section 1512 of the Civil Code, his refusal to perform entitled plaintiff to all the benefits which he would have obtained if the contract had been performed by both parties. Such is not the law. In some cases of bilateral contracts a refusal on the part of one party to perform the contract has been held to amount to a prevention of performance by the other party. But where, as here, the contract is unilateral, the party to whom the promise is made cannot recover without proof of performance of the condition upon which the promise depends; and in such cases a mere refusal by the promisor to perform, or even an entire repudiation by him of the contract, does not of itself amount to prevention. In no event could plaintiff become entitled to commissions without procuring a purchaser in the manner before pointed out. If he had procured such a purchaser Blythe's refusal to sell would not have strengthened plaintiff's case; as he did not procure one, and was not prevented by an act of Blythe from procuring one, the alleged refusal is immaterial.

But we do not think that the evidence tends to show [521] that Blythe repudiated the contract, or even refused to sell the stock as he had agreed. The only testimony on this subject is that of plaintiff's witness Ledden, who testified that he

took to Blythe a letter from plaintiff stating that plaintiff
had sold the stock in London for five hundred thousand dollars, and that the money was ready in London to pay for it;
that Blythe thereupon became angry, and "said he would not
sell it." The witness asked "if he was going to carry out the
conditions of the letter, and he said 'No.' He said that the
amount was too small, or something to that effect—that he
had to divide up the amount that he was to get with several
parties, and that he would not carry out the condition. He
said that perhaps other arrangements could be made that
would be satisfactory to him, or something to that effect."
The witness remembered nothing further as to the contents
of the letter, though he thought it contained something more.
The only other testimony concerning the contents of the letter was that of the plaintiff and the witness Wand, neither
of whom could state any thing further concerning them.

It is evident that that testimony, if believed, proved nothing, unless in connection with the contents of the letter referred to. If that letter contained nothing beyond the bare
statement testified to by the witnesses, Blythe's language
amounted to nothing, for there was nothing for him to act
upon. If, on the other hand, it contained a statement of the
conditions of the sale, as the witness Ledden seems to imply,
then, without knowing what were the conditions so stated, it
is impossible to determine whether Blythe's refusal was justified or not. It appears by the testimony of plaintiff's witness,
Borgen, the supposed purchaser, that the money was to be
payable in London. If the letter so stated then Blythe was
justified in refusing to accept the proposition, for, under his
contract, he was entitled to payment in San Francisco. It
should be observed that on the former trial the witness Ledden
testified that Blythe [522] said that "if the money was in
hand he would not accept it"; and we considered that such
a statement would excuse the plaintiff from sending or tendering the money to him at San Francisco. But the witness
did not so testify on the last trial, and there is now nothing
in the testimony to show that Blythe in any way repudiated
his contract; certainly nothing tending to show any act on his
part which could have prevented plaintiff from procuring a
purchaser.

The evidence is also insufficient to show that the supposed
purchaser had the ability to purchase the stock at the price
named. The only evidence on that point is his own testi-

mony. He did not claim that he himself had any property or means adequate for that purpose; but he said that he made the purchase on behalf of a "syndicate," and expected to obtain the necessary funds from that syndicate. His testimony, taken most favorably for plaintiff, was that he had never had the money in his hands, that no persons had ever actually subscribed the money, but that, through that syndicate, he "would have been prepared" when the time arrived "to complete the purchase"—"to find the money required." That testimony amounted to nothing more than a statement of his belief that persons not bound by contract to do so would have advanced the money; and it is clearly not such evidence as, under section 1835 of the Code of Civil Procedure, would justify the jury in finding that he had the ability to pay. Moreover, he testified that he was unable to remember the name of a single one of the persons forming the syndicate, and that, since the commencement of this action, he had destroyed all memoranda by which he could have refreshed his memory on the subject. Under these circumstances his testimony was clearly not "satisfactory," within the meaning of section 1835, and should not have been submitted to the jury.

There are many other serious objections urged against the evidence given for plaintiff which it is not necessary to consider, as those already mentioned are [523] sufficient for the purposes of this appeal. It is enough to say that the evidence was not sufficient to support plaintiff's case on any material issue.

3. The court, at the request of plaintiff, instructed the jury that "evidence of the oral admissions of a party ought to be received with caution by the jury." This instruction was evidently predicated upon certain testimony introduced by defendant, tending to prove oral admissions by plaintiff that he had never found a purchaser for the stock. It is in the precise language of subdivision 4 of section 2061 of the Code of Civil Procedure, which authorizes the court to give it "on all proper occasions." Counsel for defendant contend that, under the decision in *Kauffman* v. *Maier*, 94 Cal. 269, 282, it was a charge with respect to a matter of fact, and therefore forbidden by the constitution. It is not necessary to consider that question in this case, for we are of opinion that this was not a "proper occasion," within the meaning of that section for the giving of such an instruction.

The plaintiff's case depended entirely upon oral testimony as to transactions with the deceased Blythe. That testimony was of such a nature as to make direct contradiction absolutely impossible. No documents of any kind were produced to substantiate it nor was it corroborated by any independent fact. Plaintiff's claim was never heard of until more than a year after the appointment of an administrator on Blythe's estate, not even by parties who were jointly interested in the alleged commissions. Under such circumstances the only kind of evidence which defendant could possibly obtain was testimony of the kind referred to in this instruction That testimony was of at least as high a character as that produced by plaintiff. Indeed, plaintiff's whole case rested upon the unsupported testimony of a single witness as to a conversation between Blythe and himself when they were alone. No weaker kind of testimony could be produced; and it was clearly not a proper occasion for the court, under such circumstances, to give to the jury an instruction in disparagement of the testimony [524] by which alone defendant could meet the testimony adduced by plaintiff.

4. The court erred in sustaining plaintiff's objections to the questions propounded by the defendant to the witness Hart. It was competent for defendant to show that the stock was kept in the hands of a third person for delivery to any purchaser whom plaintiff might procure under the contract. That would be a circumstance tending to contradict the claim that Blythe had repudiated his contract. While it is true that defendant could not be permitted to prove the mere declarations of the deceased in his own favor, he was certainly entitled to prove his acts under the contract, and any declaration made at the time, and characterizing those acts as a part of the *res gestæ.*

Some other points are urged by appellant, some of which are sufficiently covered by what has been said, and others will not probably arise on another trial.

The appeal from the judgment, having been taken more than one year after the entry of judgment, is dismissed. The order denying a new trial is reversed and the cause remanded for a new trial.

McFARLAND, J., and FITZGERALD, J., concurred.

GAROUTTE, J., concurring. The evidence in the record is wholly insufficient to support plaintiff's complaint. Of the many elements of the case absolutely necessary to be proven in order to establish a cause of action, hardly one is sufficiently made out. Yet plaintiff has recovered a judgment for more than one hundred thousand dollars upon this evidence, and insists that the validity of such judgment be ratified by the court. To obviate the results which would necessarily flow from this dearth of evidence, to wit., a reversal of the judgment, the principle of the law of the case is invoked, and a former decision of this court relied upon, wherein it is said that "the plaintiff produced testimony tending to prove his side of the case": Citing the testimony [525] *Mattingly* v. *Roach*, 84 Cal. 207. Conceding the evidence to be the same upon both appeals, still I do not think this declaration of the court should be held equivalent to a declaration that plaintiff by the evidence established a *prima facie* case for a recovery. At that time the matter under consideration was the validity of an instruction, and the sufficiency of the evidence only incidentally arose upon the discussion of that question. While in a certain sense the language of the court is not *obiter*, still it is closely allied to it. The sufficiency of the evidence was not the direct question with which the court was dealing, and it is entirely apparent from the context, that the court, in making the statement quoted, never intended to so pass upon the sufficiency of plaintiff's evidence, as to forever foreclose a trial court, or this court, from declaring it insufficient to establish a *prima facie* case.

If the court did not intend to make any law of that kind for the case, to hold that such law was made would be treating the doctrine here invoked most kindly and liberally, while, upon the contrary, it has been recognized always and everywhere as a harsh doctrine, and one which has nothing to commend it to the favor of courts.

I concur in the judgment.

Chief Justice BEATTY and Justice HARRISON being disqualified took no part in the decision of the foregoing cause.

Rehearing denied.

———

STARE DECISIS—RULES GOVERNING.—For a discussion of this subject, see the extended notes to *Gee* v. *Williamson*, 27 Am. Dec. 631, and *Gould* v. *Sternburg*, 15 Am. St. Rep. 142.

BROKERS—WHEN ENTITLED TO COMMISSIONS.—A real estate broker is entitled to his commissions when a purchaser is introduced who is ready, willing, and able to buy on the terms authorized by the principal, and no binding written contract of sale is required if the principal is in a situation to execute it himself: *Gelatt* v. *Ridge*, 117 Mo. 553; 38 Am. St. Rep. 683, and note, with the cases collected.

BROKERS—CONTRACT WITH.—EFFECT OF PREVENTING PERFORMANCE: See the extended note to *Kalley* v. *Baker*, 28 Am. St. Rep. 547.

PEOPLE *v.* HECHT.

[105 CALIFORNIA, 621.]

CONSTITUTIONAL LAW—INELIGIBILITY OF PART OF A BOARD OF FREEHOLD-ERS.—Under a constitution providing for the election of a board of freeholders to consist of fifteen members, and prescribing the qualifications necessary to render a person eligible to be a member of such board, the fact that two of the persons so elected are not eligible does not prevent the remainder from constituting a valid, constitutional board of freeholders.

PUBLIC OFFICERS.—WORDS GIVING A JOINT AUTHORITY to three or more public officers may be construed as giving it to a majority, unless other-wise expressed.

BOARD OF FREEHOLDERS—DE FACTO MEMBERS.—If persons elected as mem-bers of a board of freeholders for the purpose of proposing a charter for a municipality are ineligible, but receive their certificates of election, and qualify as freeholders, and enter upon the discharge of their duties, they thereby become *de facto* officers, whose acts are not less binding than those of officers *de jure* so far as they involve the public and third persons.

Robert Ash, for the appellants.

City and County Attorney Harry T. Creswell, Henry N. Clement, and William F. Gibson, for the respondents.

622 SEARLS, C. This is a proceeding by quo warranto brought in the superior court to determine by what authority the defendants, as individuals or as a board, are acting as a board of fifteen freeholders to prepare and propose a charter for the city and county of San Francisco.

Two several demurrers were interposed to the complaint: one by and on behalf of William B. Bourn and I. W. Hell-man, two of the defendants, and the other by all the defend-ants.

The demurrers, and each of them, were sustained by the court, and the relator declining to amend, final judgment went for the defendants, from which judgment the plaintiffs appeal.

The complaint, which, for the purposes of this case, is to be taken as true, avers in substance as follows:

1. The city and county of San Francisco is, and at all the times herein mentioned has been, a municipal corporation duly organized and existing under and by virtue of an act of the legislature of the state of California, approved April 19, 1856, and the several acts of said legislature amendatory thereof and supplementary thereto, and contains a population of three hundred thousand inhabitants.

2. On the eleventh day of September, 1894, the properly constituted authorities of said city and county of San Francisco, by due proceedings, ordered that a board ⁶²³ of fifteen freeholders, who shall have been at least five years qualified electors thereof, should be elected by the qualified voters of said city and county, at the general election on the sixth day of November, 1894, whose duty it should be to prepare and propose, within ninety days after such election, a charter for such city and county under and by virtue of section 8 of article 11 of the constitution of the state of California.

3. Thereafter, and in due time, forty-three persons were regularly nominated as candidates for the said officers of board of freeholders, certificates of such nominations duly filed as required by law, all of whom were believed to possess the qualifications required by law to fill said offices.

4. The names of the persons so nominated were placed upon the ballots as candidates for said office.

5. On the twenty-fifth day of October, 1894, a proclamation was duly made, issued, and published by the proper officers, as required by law, that there would be chosen and elected on the sixth day of November, 1894, a board of fifteen freeholders.

6. At the general election of November 6, 1894, the said persons so nominated were voted for by the qualified voters of said city and county, each receiving the number of votes mentioned in the complaint.

7. The vote was duly canvassed, and the defendants herein declared duly elected to fill said office.

8. Thereafter defendants, and each of them, received certificates of election, duly qualified and organized as a board of fifteen freeholders, and entered upon the discharge of their duties as such board, and are still so acting and preparing a charter.

9. The defendants are not now, and never have been, a legally constituted board of fifteen freeholders, but have usurped the functions of said board without authority or right; that no board was chosen by the voters as required by the election and article of the constitution referred to herein, for the reasons:

a. Defendant I. W. Hellman was ineligible to said **624** office in that he had not been for at least five years a qualified elector of said city and county; that he had been such qualified elector for but three years, and that prior to said three years he had been a resident and elector of the city of Los Angeles, California.

b. The defendant W. B. Bourn was ineligible because he had not been for five years a qualified elector of the city and county of San Francisco, as required by the constitution; that he had been an elector but two years, and that prior thereto he was a resident and elector of the county of Napa, California.

c. The remaining defendants and members of the board are but thirteen in number, and do not constitute a board of fifteen freeholders.

d. The above-named thirteen defendants are all eligible and qualified to hold the office as members of the board aforesaid, and have accepted the certificates and acknowledged the right of said defendants Bourn and Hellman as members of said board, and are sitting with said Bourn and Hellman as members of said board, and claim that said persons are and constitute a board of fifteen freeholders.

The general demurrer of all the defendants is upon the ground "that said complaint does not state facts sufficient to constitute a cause of action."

The separate demurrer of Hellman and Bourn is upon the ground that the "said complaint does not state facts sufficient to constitute a cause of action against these defendants, or either of them."

Section 8 of article 11 of the constitution of the state of California, as amended, and the ratification thereof declared September 30, 1892, is in part as follows: "Any city containing a population of more than three thousand five hundred inhabitants may frame a charter for its own government, consistent with and subject to the constitution and laws of this state, by causing a board of fifteen freeholders, who shall have been for at least five years qualified electors thereof, to be elected by the qualified voters of said city at any general or special [625] election, whose duty it shall be, within ninety days after such election, to prepare and propose a charter for such city, which shall be signed in duplicate by the members of such board, or a majority of them," etc.

The first question for consideration relates to the eligibility of the defendants I. W. Hellman and William B. Bourn as freeholders under the constitutional provision.

They had not been for at least five years qualified voters of the city and county in which the election was held, and for which the charter was to be prepared.

The language used by the framers of the constitution in relation to the qualification essential to eligibility to the office or position of a freeholder is plain and unequivocal, and the authority to prescribe the qualification is not open to doubt.

The reason of the rule is apparent, and need not be stated.

The defendants Hellman and Bourn, not having been for at least five years qualified electors of the city and county of San Francisco, were ineligible to the office of freeholder, and their separate demurrer should have been overruled.

2. Do the remaining thirteen members, who were regularly elected, constitute a legal board, with authority to act?

The contention of appellant is, that, in order to constitute a valid board, it is essential that fifteen qualified members be elected, and, that without such number thus qualified, there can be no constitutional board, and hence that the thirteen members should be inhibited from acting either with or without the two who are disqualified.

We think this position is unwarranted under the language of the constitution, and not in consonance with public policy or the analogies in similar cases.

It is true the constitution provides for the election of a board of fifteen freeholders, but the persons who are, when elected and qualified, to constitute such board, are [626] elected and must qualify as individuals, and the entity known as the board has no legal existence until it is organized by the individuals who come clothed with the insignia of authority afforded by a certificate or other adequate proof of an election.

The electors select the persons who are to constitute the board, but do not create the board. That is done by the organization of the members.

When the electors have elected, by a plurality of all the votes cast, fifteen members to constitute the board, and furnished them with the evidence of said action, their power in the premises is exhausted, and the requirement of the constitution is so far complied with that it only remains for the persons so selected, or a majority of them, to organize and exercise the power which, by virtue of their election, is .vested in them.

An interpretation which holds that the ineligibility, or death, or unwillingness to act of a single member thus selected invalidates the entire election, would work great hardship, and tend to thwart the will of the electors in many instances, and should not be indulged unless rendered imperative by the mandate of the constitution.

The same constitution (article 11, section 5) provides that the legislature, by general and uniform laws, shall provide for the election or appointment in the several counties of " boards of supervisors," etc.

Other portions of the constitution provide for a supreme court, " which shall consist of a chief justice and six associate justices."

Again, " the senate shall consist of forty members, and the assembly of eighty members."

It would, we think, hardly be contended that because the constitution provides for a board of supervisors that an election for supervisors, in which a single member elected was disqualified, would either invalidate the election of other members, or prevent their organizing and acting as a board.

Like considerations apply to the election of members [627] of the senate and assembly, and to the election, organization, and action of the supreme court.

The code provides that " words giving a joint authority to three or more public officers or other persons are construed as giving such authority to a majority of them, unless it is otherwise expressed in the act giving the authority": Pol. Code, sec. 15.

The earlier doctrine was that where a board of commissioners was created by the legislature, and discretionary powers conferred upon them to decide upon matters of public interest, and the law had made no provision that a majority should constitute a quorum, all must be present and consult, though a majority might decide: *People* v. *Coghill*, 47 Cal. 363, and cases cited.

The rule prior to its modification by the code may be stated thus:

The power or authority given to public officers, commissioners, or committeemen was a joint authority to be exercised by all of them, and (except as provided by statute) all must meet and deliberate; but this done, a majority could decide.

To the exercise of this joint authority it was sometimes held, and it would seem logically, that the existence of a full board was necessary.

If the authority was in contemplation of law to be exercised by all the members, then there should be members capable and competent to its exercise; but under our code this authority, although joint where given to three or more, is to be "construed as giving such authority to a majority of them" unless it is otherwise expressed in the act giving the authority. If a majority possesses all the authority of the whole, then such majority must be competent to its exercise.

For all practical purposes the majority becomes the full board. It is the receptacle—the reservoir—of all the authority conferred upon the whole, and its action, it is submitted, cannot be stayed by the nonaction, failure to qualify, absence, death, or want of eligibility of the minority.

[628] These were the very obstacles intended to be surmounted by the statute.

Since the enactment of the code it was held in *People* v. *Harrington*, 63 Cal. 257, that the action of a quorum was the action of the board of supervisors, and that the action of a majority of such quorum, though not constituting a majority of the board, was valid and binding.

In *State* v. *Huggins*, Harp. (S. C.) 139, the facts were that, of eighteen managers of elections appointed by the legislature, two had refused to qualify, one was dead, and one disqualified to serve, and the court held that a majority, viz., eight of the remaining fourteen, properly formed a board to determine on the validity of a contested election; a majority of the managers qualified to serve being all that is required by the legislature.

Colcock, J., in the course of his opinion, said: " Now, if necessity and public convenience may require that, where all the managers of these elections are alive and have qualified, a majority may act, does not the same reason operate to authorize the managers of an election to act where some of

those who have been nominated are dead or have not qualified?"

Words giving a joint authority to three or more public
officers will be construed as giving it to the majority, unless
otherwise expressed: *Talcott* v. *Blanding,* 54 Cal. 289.

If the authority is given to and may be exercised by the
majority, and that the minority, if present and acting, cannot defeat it, it must follow that such minority cannot, by
absence or failure to qualify, defeat the will of the majority.
This doctrine was illustrated in *City of Oakland* v. *Carpen-
tier,* 13 Cal. 540, where it was argued that, as the charter
provided that a board of five trustees should be elected, etc.,
and as only four qualified, their acts were void for want of
a legal organization. The court disposed of the question by
saying: "We can see no reason for holding that a majority
of the members elected to this board should not as well be
629 held empowered to act at the first as at any subsequent
meeting of it."

There is nothing inherent in the duties to be discharged by
the freeholders to invoke a more strict rule of construction
against them than would be called for in the case of other
boards or bodies invested with public functions.

The provision of the constitution is self-acting: *People* v.
Hoge, 55 Cal. 612. The constitution does not in terms require the joint action of all the members of the board of freeholders. It does provide that the charter prepared by them
must be "signed in duplicate by the members of such board,
or a majority of them."

Under the doctrine which was formerly upheld by many
of the courts, that all the members of a board, committee,
or commission, must meet and deliberate, though a majority could decide, the contention of appellant in support of
the theory that the presence and action of all the members
is necessary to an organization may be upheld. The con-
sensus of modern opinion, however, is believed to be that,
where a majority may act, such majority may organize and
act. This is believed to be the very object of the 'fifteenth
section of the Political Code.

Again, the office of freeholder is created by the constitution. It is a *de jure* office. When Hellman and Bourn were
elected by a plurality of the qualified electors, received their
certificates of election, and qualified and participated in the
action of the board, they were there under color of office and

sumptively entitled to the office. They were *de facto* icers in the discharge of the duties of a *de jure* office, d as such their acts while they remained such were as lid and binding as those of *de jure* officers. There must be *de jure* office to be filled before there can be a *de facto* icer.

If the former exists, and the latter holds it under and pur- ant to a regular commission purporting to empower him act, his acts in such office, until his right thereto is judi- ally determined, the law holds upon [630] principles of policy id justice to be valid so far as they involve the public and ird parties, notwithstanding the personal liability of the in- mbent for intruding into such office. A leading case upon e subject of officers *de facto* is that of *State* v. *Carroll*, 38)nn. 449, 9 Am. Rep. 409, in which Butler, C. J., after an haustive discussion of the doctrine, and a review of the nglish and American cases, uses the following language: A definition sufficiently accurate and comprehensive to)ver the whole ground must, I think, be substantially as llows: An officer *de facto* is one whose acts, though not hose of a lawful officer, the law, upon principles of policy nd justice, will hold valid so far as they involve the in- erests of the public and third persons where the duties of he office were exercised: 1 . . . . 2 . . . . 3. Under color)f a known election or appointment, void because the officer vas not eligible, ... such ineligibility . . . . being un- :nown to the public."

We reach the following conclusion: 1. The thirteen free- 1olders, constituting, as they do, a majority of all the mem-)ers of the board, were competent to organize and act as a)oard of freeholders under the constitution and law, and nay lawfully prepare and propose a charter for the city and :ounty of San Francisco; 2. I. W. Hellman and William B. 3ourn were not eligible to the office of freeholder, and, al- .hough regularly elected and commissioned, are not *de jure*)fficers of the board; 3. Said Hellman and Bourn, having)een elected.and commissioned, became *de facto* members of .he board, and as such their acts were and are valid as to .he public and third parties.

We are asked by the counsel in the event of holding that Bourn and Hellman are not entitled to their seats, to indi- :ate: 1. Whether or not Patrick Reddy and J. C. Whiting, vho received the next highest number of votes, are entitled to demand and receive certificates of election; and, if not, then 2. How shall the vacancies be filled?

631 The first query seems to be settled in this state: *Saunders* v. *Haynes*, 13 Cal. 145; *Crawford* v. *Dunbar*, 52 Cal. 36.

We must, however, decline to pass upon either of the foregoing propositions, for the reason that they are not involved in the issues presented in the case, and any thing which might be said would be mere *obiter dictum*, and of no binding force should the same questions again arise.

The judgment appealed from should be affirmed as to all the defendants except I. W. Hellman and William B. Bourn, and reversed as to said two last-named defendants, with directions to the court below to overrule the separate demurrer of said I. W. Hellman and William B. Bourn, with leave to answer.

HAYNES, C., concurred.

For the reasons given in the foregoing opinion the judgment appealed from is affirmed as to all the defendants except I. W. Hellman and William B. Bourn, and reversed as to said two last-named defendants, with directions to the court below to overrule the separate demurrer of said I. W. Hellman and William B. Bourn, with leave to answer.

McFARLAND, J.,   GAROUTTE, J.,
VAN FLEET, J.,   HENSHAW, J.,
BEATTY, C. J.

OFFICERS DE FACTO—BINDING EFFECT OF ACTS OF.—Acts of officers *de facto* are valid and binding when they concern the public, or the rights of strangers and third persons who have an interest in the acts done: *King* v. *Philadelphia Co.*, 154 Pa. St. 160; 35 Am. St. Rep. 817, and note; *Butler* v. *Walker*, 98 Ala. 358; 39 Am. St. Rep. 61, and note. To the same effect, *Gorman* v. *People*, 17 Col. 596; 31 Am. St. Rep. 350, and note.

CASES

SUPREME COURT

OF

ILLINOIS.

NIAGARA FIRE INSURANCE COMPANY *v.* BISHOP.

[154 ILLINOIS, 9.]

APPELLATE PROCEDURE.—To bring before the supreme court of Illinois for review the rulings of the trial court upon a question of law, written propositions must be submitted to it to be held as law in the decision of the cause, and the court must then write on such proposition either "refused" or "held," and the party objecting to the action of the court in this respect must except thereto.

APPELLATE PROCEDURE—PRESUMPTION THAT ERROR WAS MATERIAL.—If, when a case is tried before a court without a jury, one of the parties presents propositions of law to the court, to which, though correct, it refuses its assent, the error will be presumed to have been material and prejudicial, unless it appears that the party excepting thereto was not injured thereby.

INSURANCE—ARBITRATION.—A SPECIAL COVENANT IN A POLICY OF INSURANCE TO SUBMIT EVERY MATTER in dispute to arbitration is no bar to a suit for damages, and is invalid as an attempt to oust the courts of their jurisdiction.

INSURANCE—ARBITRATION AS TO VALUES.—A stipulation in a policy of insurance that amounts or values shall be submitted to arbitration is valid, and such arbitration may be made a condition precedent to the right to recover.

INSURANCE—ARBITRATION, EXCUSE FOR NOT OBTAINING AWARD.—If a policy of insurance provides that the amount of a loss shall be ascertained by arbitration the insured may recover though the arbitrators have not agreed, if he can show that their failure to agree has been brought about by the instrumentality of the insurer for the purpose of preventing an award, or that he has acted in bad faith in interposing obstacles so that no award could be made.

INSURANCE—ARBITRATION, DUTY OF THE INSURED IN CASE OF DISAGREEMENT.—If the appraisers chosen by the insurer and the insured cannot agree upon an umpire it is not the duty of the assured to propose the selection of other appraisers unless the policy so provides.

INSURANCE, ARBITRATION, ACT OF THE APPRAISER CHOSEN BY THE IN-
SURER.—If an appraiser chosen by an insurer acts as though he was the
agent of the insurer, and refuses to agree to a disinterested umpire, or
otherwise prevents the appointment of such an umpire, the insured is
entitled to maintain an action upon his policy without obtaining an
award fixing the amount of his loss.

APPELLATE PROCEDURE—HARMLESS ERROR.—Though the court errs in refusing to affirm as a proposition of law that a party is precluded from
maintaining an action upon a policy of insurance until there has been
an appraisal, unless such appraisal has been waived by agreement of
the parties, or prevented by the fraud of the defendant, the error will
be treated as harmless if it appears that the appraiser chosen by the
insurer regarded himself as acting as his agent, and refused either to
agree upon a reasonable appraisement or to appoint a disinterested
umpire.

ACTION to recover upon a policy of insurance for a loss arising
out of a peril insured against. The policy contained a stipulation that the company should not be liable unless the loss
or damage should have been ascertained, in case of a difference
of opinion between the insurer and the insured, by appraisers
chosen by them, and that, in the event of the disagreement
of such appraisers, they should select a competent and disinterested umpire, and with him should estimate and appraise
the loss. The loss occurred in February, 1892. On the 10th
of June following, the insurer selected an appraiser, and notified the appellee to select one in his behalf, which was done
accordingly. The appraiser so selected visited the ground
and began an estimate of the cost of material and construction. The appraisers differing widely, the one selected by
the insurer returned after a few days to Chicago without
agreeing upon an estimate. The selection of an umpire was
then discussed between the appraisers, but none was selected,
because they could not agree upon the locality from which
he should be chosen. On the 10th of August following this
action was brought. Judgment for the plaintiff, defendant
appealed.

Paden & Gridley and George L. Paddock, for the appellant.

Botsford & Wayne and Charles Wheaton, for the appellee.

[14] MAGRUDER, J. This cause was tried by agreement before the court without a jury; and, therefore, both matters
of law and fact were submitted to be tried by the court. In
order to bring before this court for review a ruling of the
trial court upon a question of law, written propositions must
be submitted to the court to be held as law in the decision of

the case.   If the court shall be of the opinion that a proposition so submitted is not the law he shall write upon it
"refused"; and if he is of the opinion that a proposition so
submitted is the law he must write upon it "held."   To the
action of the court in this regard either party may except.
If either party submits to the court a correct proposition of
law, which the court refuses to hold as such, its refusal may
be assigned as error in this court.   In view of the many
decisions made by this court to the effect that, where there
is a trial before the court without a jury, a party desiring to
present a question of law to the supreme court as having
been passed upon [15] by the court below must submit propositions of law to the trial court, as provided for in section 41
of the Practice Act; it cannot be said that the refusal of the
trial court to hold a correct proposition of law to be such is
an immaterial error, unless it appears that the complaining
party is not injured thereby: 2 Starr and Curtis' Annotated
Statutes, 1808; *Northwestern etc. Mut. Aid Assn.* v. *Hall,* 118
Ill. 169; *Montgomery* v. *Black,* 124 Ill. 57; *Knowles* v. *Knowles,*
128 Ill. 110; *Exchange Nat. Bank* v. *Chicago Nat. Bank,* 131
Ill. 547.   .

In the case at bar the plaintiff did not submit to the court
any written propositions to be held as law in the decision of
the case.   The defendant submitted eleven written propositions to be held as law, but each and every one of them was
marked "refused" by the trial court.   We do not deem it
necessary to discuss all of them.   Most of them were objectionable, and were properly marked "refused."   The second
and eighth were as follows:

"2. The court holds, as a matter of law, that where the
parties in a contract of insurance fix on a certain mode by
which the amount of loss shall be ascertained, as in the
present case, the party that seeks an enforcement of the
agreement must show that he has done every thing on his
part which could be done to carry it into effect.   He cannot
compel the payment of the amount claimed unless he shall
procure the kind of evidence required by the contract, or
show that by time or by accident, or some fault on the part
of the insurer, he is unable to do so."

"8. The court holds, as a matter of law, that where the
evidence shows that the parties to a contract of insurance like
the one sued upon in this case, disagree upon the amount of
the loss, and by agreement between themselves submit the

matter of ascertaining the amount of loss to appraisers, as provided in the policy, the insured is precluded from beginning suit to recover for the amount of the loss until such appraisal has been made [16] according to contract, or abandoned by agreement of parties, or prevented by the defendant."

We are unable to see why these propositions do not announce correct principles of law. A general covenant in a policy of insurance to submit every matter in dispute to arbitration is held to be no bar to a suit for damages, and to be invalid as an attempt to oust the courts of their jurisdiction. But an agreement, which provides for the determination of amounts or values, is lawful, and may be made a condition precedent to the right of recovery, either in terms or by necessary implication: May on Insurance, sec. 493; Wood on Insurance, sec. 493; *Old Saucelito etc. Co.* v. *Commercial Union etc. Co.*, 66 Cal. 253; *Hanover Fire Ins. Co.* v. *Lewis*, 28 Fla. 209. Such agreements do not oust the courts of their jurisdiction, and, where the contract is, that no suit shall be maintained until an award is made fixing the amount of the claim, the contract will be respected by the courts: *Chippewa Lumber Co.* v. *Phœnix Ins. Co.*, 80 Mich. 118; *Adams* v. *South British etc. Ins. Co.*, 70 Cal. 198; *Wolff* v. *Liverpool etc Ins. Co.*, 50 N. J. L. 453.

Of course, the plaintiff will be relieved from the obligation of complying with the contract to submit to arbitration and have an award made, if he shows a valid excuse for not doing so. Such excuse will be found in conduct on the part of the defendant, which has the effect of preventing an appraisal from being had, or an award from being made.

In *Johnson* v. *Humboldt Ins. Co.*, 91 Ill. 92, 33 Am. Rep. 47, where the language of the policy provided that an action should not be brought until after an award was obtained fixing the amount of the claim, we said: "Such an award is an indispensable prerequisite to the bringing of a suit or action, unless the assured should be prevented by the company."

Where the policy provided, as does the one in this case, for the selection of appraisers in case of a failure to agree, and for the reference by the appraisers of their differences to an umpire selected by themselves, and for the payment [17] of the loss within a certain time after the adjustment, it was held that the money could not be sooner demanded, "unless the adjustment provided for was waived, refused, or prevented by the company": *Gasser* v. *Sun Fire Office*, 42 Minn. 315.

In *Hamilton* v. *Liverpool etc. Ins. Co.*, 136 U. S. 242, where the policy contained a stipulation that differences as to the amount of any loss or damage should be submitted to two competent and impartial persons, chosen one by each party, and the two so chosen to select an umpire in case of disagreement, and the award of any two of them in writing to be binding and conclusive as to the amount, just as in the case at bar it is provided that "the award in writing of any two shall determine the amount of such loss," the supreme court of the United States, speaking through Mr. Justice Gray, said: "Such a stipulation, not ousting the jurisdiction of the courts, but leaving the general question of liability to be judicially determined, and simply providing a reasonable method of estimating and ascertaining the amount of the loss, is unquestionably valid, according to the uniform current of authority in England and in this country: *Scott* v. *Ave· ·*, 5 H. L. Cas. 811; *Viney* v. *Bignold*, L. R. 20 Q. B. Div. 172; *Delaware etc. Canal Co.* v. *Pennsylvania Coal Co.* 50 N. Y. 250; *Reed* v. *Washington etc. Ins. Co.*, 138 Mass. 572, 576; *Wolff* v. *Liverpool etc. Ins. Co.*, 50 N. J. L. 453; *Hall* v. *Norwalk Fire Ins. Co.*, 57 Conn. 105, 114. The case comes within the general rule long ago laid down by this court: ' Where the parties in their contract fix on a certain mode by which the amount to be paid shall be ascertained, as in the present case, the party that seeks an enforcement of the agreement must show that he has done every thing on his part which could be done to carry it into effect. He cannot compel the payment of the amount claimed, unless he shall procure the kind of evidence required by the contract, or show that by time or accident he is unable to do so ': *United States* v. *Robson*, 9 Pet. 319.''

[18] It will be noticed that the language of the second refused proposition is exactly the same as that in the foregoing quotation from *United States* v. *Robeson*, 9 Pet. 319, except the following words at the close, " or some fault on the part of the insurer he is unable to do so." Wherever the plaintiff can show that the disagreement has been brought about by the instrumentality of the company for the purpose of preventing an award, or that the company has been acting in bad faith, or interposing obstacles so that no award can be

had, he will have a right to resort to his action: *Davenport* v. *Long Island Ins. Co.*, 10 Daly, 535.

The issue made by the sixth plea and the replication thereto was ꞁ ꞌether the appellant refused, without good and sufficient cause, to go on and complete said appraisement, and by neglect, delay, and unfair action defeated the appraisal, and whether the inability of the appraisers to agree was owing to any fault, connivance, or collusion on the part of appellant. As propositions 2 and 8 were in line with the issue thus made by the pleadings and with the authorities hereinbefore referred to, we are inclined to think that those propositions should have been marked " held " and not " refused."

The evidence tends to show that the failure of the appraisers to select an umpire was due to the fact that Donlin, the appraiser chosen by appellant, desired to appoint an umpire living in Bloomington, or Chicago, or some distant city, while Hoag, the appraiser who had been chosen by appellee, was in favor of some man as umpire whose residence was in Elgin, or near the place where the fire occurred.

It was said in *Davenport* v. *Long Island Ins. Co,.* 10 Daly, 535, that, upon the failure of the appraisers to agree upon an umpire, it is the duty of the insured at least to propose to the company the selection of new appraisers. We are unable to subscribe to this doctrine, so far as the policy upon which the present suit has been brought is concerned. [19] The contract here only requires the parties to choose appraisers once, and not twice.

Counsel for appellant claim that the appraisers are not agents of the parties selecting them, and, therefore, that the insurance company cannot be held responsible for the act of the appraiser selected by it, either in refusing to agree with the other appraiser, or in failing to agree upon an umpire. It has been held, that where the appraiser nominated by the company insists upon the appointment of an umpire living at a great distance from the scene of the loss, and refuses to agree to persons named by the plaintiff's appraiser without excuse, his conduct amounts to a refusal to proceed with the appraisal, and the plaintiff will not be required to wait longer before bringing his action: *McCullough* v. *Phœnix Ins. Co.*, 113 Mo. 606; *Uhrig* v. *Williamsburgh City Fire Ins. Co.*, 101 N. Y. 362.

In *Bishop* v. *Agricultural Ins. Co.*, 130 N. Y. 488, the

appraisers selected by the plaintiff and the insurance company failed to agree upon an umpire. Upon the trial there was evidence tending to show that the company "through its appraiser, Langworthy, refused to agree upon a disinterested umpire"; and the court said: "If this was true, the fact that an appraisal had not been made was not a defense to the action." It was there held that, as the question of fact was submitted to the jury under conservative instructions, and they had found for the plaintiff, the verdict would not be disturbed.

We are inclined to agree with counsel for appellant in the contention that a person nominated as an arbitrator ought not to consider himself as the agent for the person on whose behalf he is nominated: Kyd on Awards, 75. "The arbitrators selected, one by each side, ought not to consider themselves the agents or advocates of the party who appoints them. When once nominated they ought to perform the duty of deciding impartially between the parties, and they will be looked upon as acting [20] corruptly if they act as agents or take instructions from the other side": Russell on Arbitrators, 6th ed., 221. But while it is true that an arbitrator or appraiser is not to be regarded as the agent of the party appointing him simply by reason of the fact of his appointment, yet an arbitrator or appraiser may act in such a partial manner, and so manifestly in the interest of the party appointing him, that it may become a question of fact to be submitted to the jury, or to be determined by the court sitting without a jury, whether he conducts himself as an agent to such an extent that the party appointing him shall be held responsible for his acts. If an insurance company selects a man for appraiser, who, instead of acting as such, conducts himself in the interest of the company and as an agent for the company, the company will be held responsible for such conduct on his part as inures to the benefit of the company. If the evidence proves that he prevents an agreement, or the appointment of an umpire, by methods which show him to be the agent of the company, his acts will be regarded as those of his principal.

We think that the propositions of law upon this subject submitted by appellant were properly refused, because they assume that Donlin was not in fact the agent of the company, without leaving it to be determined from the evidence whether he so acted as to be justly regarded as such agent.

If the propositions in question had simply announced that appraisers appointed as those here were appointed "should not be advocates for the parties appointing them," we cannot see that they would have been objectionable.

There is evidence in the record tending very strongly to show that appellee was delayed for about five months after the fire occurred by the adjuster of the company; that some time in June Donlin was appointed appraiser by the company and Hoag by appellee; that some time afterward Donlin came out to Elgin and went to the [21] ruins and made some measurements, but returned to Chicago without attempting to make an appraisal; that two days afterward he again came to Elgin and had a meeting with Hoag, objecting to the values as too high and to the amount of depreciation as insufficient, and "broke off the figuring," and refused to close the examination as to prices, and left Elgin abruptly, saying: "I will go back and see our people, and I will write you a proposition to-morrow that will do"; that Donlin never afterward returned to Elgin, or renewed the effort to agree upon an appraisal, but in a day or two, and about August 1st wrote to Hoag, proposing to close up "the E. L. Bishop loss" at a low figure, "or we will have to agree upon a third man as umpire"; that after his proposal was rejected as "unreasonable and unjust," and after he was requested to return "and proceed with the appraisement without delay," he wrote, on August 5th, suggesting, in the matter of selecting an umpire, the names of men in Bloomington and Chicago, whose standing, competency, and reliability were unknown to Hoag.

It thus appears that there was evidence tending to show a relation of agency between Donlin and the companies represented by him, and tending to show that, while acting as such agent, rather than as an impartial arbitrator, he prevented an appraisal and the appointment of an umpire. If this was true the companies are responsible for the result produced by his conduct. Whether the award was thus prevented by the companies was the main question of fact in the case. The issue made by the sixth and seventh pleas was the principal issue. It is so admitted by counsel for appellant in their brief in this court. The issues formed by the other pleas are immaterial. The propositions of law submitted to the court bear upon the issue formed by the sixth and seventh pleas. It is not pretended that there was any thing dishonest or fraudulent about the loss, nor is it denied that the loss was total: *McCullough* v. *Phœnix Ins. Co.,* 113 Mo. 606.   [22] Counsel for appellant thus state their position: "The award of appraisers is a condition precedent to begin-ning the suit, unless such award is prevented by the insurer in some way."

It is manifest from what has been said that, under the pleadings in this case, the court below could not have ren-dered the judgment in favor of the plaintiff without finding that the appraisal was prevented by appellant. As there is evidence tending to support this finding, the judgment of the appellate court affirming the judgment of the trial court is conclusive, so far as we are concerned, as to the fact that the appraisal was prevented by the appellant: Practice Act, sec. 89; 2 Starr and Curtis' Annotated Statutes, 1851; 3 Starr and Curtis' Annotated Statutes, 991; *Powell* v. *McCord,* 121 Ill. 330.

Hence the appellant could not have been injured by the refusal of the trial court to hold as law the second and eighth propositions, because, even if the trial court had been of the opinion that the award of the appraisers was not a condition precedent to the bringing of suit, yet, if it found that the making of the award was prevented by the company, the effect as to the plaintiff's right to bring the suit was the same as though the court had been of the opposite opinion. When a proposition announces that it is the duty of the plaintiff to do a certain thing before beginning suit, unless he is pre-vented from doing it by the defendant, and when the proof shows that he was prevented from doing it by the defendant, the abstract rule as to his duty becomes of no practical im-portance in the determination of the question whether the suit was properly brought.

The judgment of the appellate court is affirmed.

INSURANCE—CONDITION AS TO ARBITRATION—VALIDITY OF.—A condition in a policy of insurance providing for arbitration cannot deprive the in-sured of his right of action unless clearly made a condition precedent to the existence of such right: *Birmingham etc. Ins. Co.* v. *Pulver,* 126 Ill. 329; 9 Am. St. Rep. 598, and note. A provision in an insurance policy requiring all differences arising between the parties as to their rights and liabilities to be submitted to arbitration is disregarded as against public policy; but when such provision only requires that the value of a thing which might be in-volved in litigation under the contract may be determined by arbitration, it does not oust the jurisdiction of the courts, and is valid: *Randall* v. *American etc. Ins. Co.*, 10 Mont. 340; 24 Am. St. Rep. 50, and note. This questio will be found fully discussed in the extended notes to *Utter v. Traveler Ins. Co.*, 8 Am. St. Rep. 922; *Commercial etc. Ins. Co. v. Hocking*, 2 Am. S Rep. 569; and the shorter notes to *Continental Ins. Co. v. Wilson*, 23 Am St. Rep. 723, and *Nurney v. Fireman's Fund Ins. Co.*, 6 Am. St. Rep. 341.

City of Pekin *v.* McMahon.

[154 Illinois, 141.]

Landlord, Liability of, to Trespassers.—A private owner or occupan of land is under no obligation to strangers to place guards around ex cavations thereon. He is not required to keep his premises in a saf condition for the benefit of trespassers or those who come upon ther without invitation, either express or implied, and merely to seek the own pleasure or gratify their own curiosity.

Landowner, Children, Duty to of Trespassing.—Though a child c tender years meeting with injury on the premises of a private owne is a technical trespasser, yet the owner is liable if the things causin injury have been left exposed and unguarded, and are of such a char acter as to be an attraction to a child, appealing to his childish curios ity and instincts.

Children—Liability of Landowner to.—If the land of a private owne is in a thickly settled portion of a city, adjacent to a public street o alley, and has upon it dangerous machinery or a dangerous pit or pon at a point near such street or alley, of such character as to be attract ive to children of tender years, incapable of exercising ordinary care and he has notice of its attractions for children of that class, he is un der obligation to use reasonable care to protect them from injury whe coming upon such premises, though they may be trespassers thereon.

Municipal Corporations.—Children, Liability of for Keeping Plac Dangerous to.—A municipal corporation owning part of a block o land in a thickly settled portion of a city in which it has dug an exca vation with steep banks in which water has accumulated and stood whereon logs and other material floated, and this excavation was nea to public streets from which it might be reached without any hin derance or obstruction, and was attractive to children and also dangerou to them, is answerable for injuries suffered by a child of tender year who is attracted to such excavation, when the municipality has notic both of its dangerous character and of the fact that children wer attracted there for the purpose of playing with and upon the water and that its depth was sufficient to drown them in case of their fallin therein, if incapable of swimming.

Negligence Causing Injury to Child of Tender Years.—Question fo the Jury.—When a child of tender years has entered upon premise of a dangerous character, attractive to children, and the owner of suc premises is sought to be made answerable for damages suffered, th question, whether he has been guilty of negligence, and whether th premises were sufficiently attractive to entice children into dange and to suggest to the owner the probability of the occurrence of a accident, are for the jury.

EGLIGENCE, CONTRIBUTORY OF PARENT.—That the parent of a child of tender years was guilty of negligence contributing to an accident may be shown in bar to an action brought by such parent as administrator of such child.

HILDREN, NEGLIGENCE, WHEN CHARGEABLE WITH. — A CHILD MORE THAN SEVEN YEARS of age is bound to exercise such care as children of his age, capacity, and intelligence are capable of exercising, and whether he did so or not is a question to be submitted to the jury.

A MUNICIPAL CORPORATION HOLDING PROPERTY AS A PRIVATE PERSON IS CHARGEABLE with the same duties and obligations devolving upon individuals,.and is therefore answerable for injuries sustained by a private person by reason of its negligence in respect to such property, if, under such circumstances a private owner would have been thus answerable.

MUNICIPAL CORPORATIONS, ORDINANCE AS EVIDENCE AGAINST.—If in an action against a city the condition in which it had put and left its private property is claimed to have been a nuisance, an ordinance declaring a similar condition of the property of a private person within the municipal limits to be a nuisance is admissible in evidence as tending to prove that the condition of its premises constituted them a nuisance.

AN EXECUTION CANNOT ISSUE AGAINST A MUNICIPAL CORPORATION.

ACTION by the administrator of the estate of Frank Mc-Mahon to recover damages for the death of the decedent through the alleged negligence of the defendant, the city of Pekin. That city was the owner of four lots in a certain block therein, bounded on the north by a public alley and on the west and south by public streets. These streets were improved and open for travel. The lots were in a thickly settled portion of the city. The municipality before taking possession of the lots in 1887 had built a sewer, and thereafter made an excavation for the purpose of obtaining gravel to be used upon the streets. This excavation was about two hundred feet long and one hundred feet wide; its banks were steep, and water could accumulate therein to the depth of fourteen feet. There had been a fence around the property, but it was permitted to get out of repair and to have an opening therein at one point of the width of forty feet and in another of at least thirty feet. There was a driveway across the property which the public had been in the habit of using for the purpose of going across the lots, instead of going round about them upon the public streets, and boys had been in the habit of playing upon planks and logs which had fallen into the water and remained floating thereon. The city authorities had been notified by parents residing in the vicinity that the place was dangerous to their children. The decedent, being eight years and two months old, went with another

child to play, and, stepping upon a log in the water, it rolle
and threw him therein, and as a consequence his life wa
lost. Judgment for the plaintiff; the defendant appealed.

G. W. Cunningham, W. L. Prettyman, and William Do
Maus, for the appellant.

T. N. Green and W. R. Curran, for the appellee.

[147] MAGRUDER, J. 1. The main question in the case arise
out of the refusal of the trial court to give the second an
third instructions asked by the defendant: Is an individua
landowner obliged to respond in damages for the death of
child occurring upon his premises under such circumstance
as are developed by the testimony in this case?

The general rule is well settled that the private owner o
occupant of land is under no obligations to strangers to plac
guards around excavations upon his land. The law does no
require him to keep his premises in safe condition for th
benefit of trespassers, or those who come upon them withou
invitation, either express or implied, and merely to seek thei
own pleasure or gratify their own curiosity: 1 Thompson o
Negligence, 303; 2 Shearman and Redfield on Negligence
4th ed., sec. 715. An exception, however, to this general rul
exists in favor of children. Although a child of tender year:
who meets with an injury upon the premises of a privat
owner, may be a technical trespasser, yet the owner may b
liable, if the things causing the injury have been left ex
posed and unguarded, and are of such a character as to b
an attraction to the child, appealing to his childish curiosit
and [148] instincts. Unguarded premises, which are thu
supplied with dangerous attractions, are regarded as boldin
out implied invitations to such children. " The owner c
land, where children are allowed or accustomed to play, par
ticularly if it is unfenced, must use ordinary care to keep i
in safe condition; for they, being without judgment an
likely to be drawn by childish curiosity into places of dange:
are not to be classed with trespassers, idlers, and mere 1
censees": 2 Shearman and Redfield on Negligence, 4th ed
sec. 705; 4 Am. & Eng. Ency. of Law, 53, and cases in note
In such case the owner should reasonably anticipate the in
jury which has happened: 1 Thompson on Negligence, 30:

There is conflict in the decisions upon this subject, som
courts holding in favor of the liability of the private owne:

and others ruling against it. Where the land of a private owner is in a thickly settled city, adjacent to a public street or alley, and he has upon it, or suffers to be upon it, dangerous machinery or a dangerous pit or pond of water, or any other dangerous agency, at a point thereon near such public street or alley, of such a character as to be attractive to children of tender years incapable of exercising ordinary care, and he is aware or has notice of its attractions for children of that class, we think that he is under obligations to use reasonable care to protect them from injury when coming upon said premises, even though they may be technical trespassers. To charge him with such an obligation under such circumstances is merely to apply the well-known maxim, *Sic utere tuo ut alienum non lædas.* It is true, as a general rule, that a party guilty of negligence is not liable if he does not owe the duty which he has neglected to the person claiming damages: *Williams* v. *Chicago etc. R. R. Co.*, 135 Ill. 491; 25 Am. St. Rep. 397. But, though the private owner may owe no duty to an adult under the facts stated, the cases, known as the "turntable" cases hold that such duty is due from him to a child of tender years.

149 The leading one of the turntable cases is *Railroad Co.* v. *Stout*, 17 Wall. 657; there the company was held liable in an action by a child about six years old, who had injured his foot while playing with a turntable belonging to the company, although it was contended that he was a trespasser, and had received the injury because of his own negligence, and that the company owed him no duty; it appearing that the turntable was located upon the private grounds of the company in a settlement of from one hundred to one hundred and fifty persons, about eighty rods from the depot, near two traveled roads, and was a dangerous machine, and was not guarded or fastened, and that a servant of the company had previously seen boys playing there and had forbidden them to do so; and it was further held, that the care and caution required of a child is according to his maturity and capacity, and is to be determined by the circumstances of each case; that the fact of the child being a technical trespasser made no difference in his right of recovery; that the question of the defendant's negligence was one for the jury to determine; and that the jury were justified in believing that children would probably resort to the turntable, and that the defendant should have anticipated their resort to it, from the fact that several boys were at play there when the accident occurred, and had played there on other occasions within the observation, and to the knowledge, of defendant's employees.

To the same effect are the following cases: *Keffe* v. *Milwaukee etc. Ry. Co.*, 21 Minn. 207; 18 Am. Rep. 393; *Kansas Cent. Ry. Co.* v. *Fitzsimmons*, 22 Kan. 686; 31 Am. Rep. 203; *Koons* v. *St. Louis etc. R. R.*, 65 Mo. 592; *Union Pac. Ry. Co.* v. *Dunden*, 37 Kan. 1; *Evanisch* v. *G. C. & S. F. Ry. Co.*, 57 Tex. 123; *Ferguson* v. *Columbus etc. Ry. Co.*, 75 Ga. 637; 77 Ga. 102; *St. Louis etc. R. R. Co.* v. *Bell*, 81 Ill. 76; 25 Am. Rep. 269.

In many if not all of the foregoing "turntable" cases, stress is laid upon the facts that the turntable was in a public or open and frequented place; that it was dangerous [150] and left unfastened, and when in motion was attractive to children by reason of their love of motion " by other means than their own locomotion"; and that the servants of the railroad companies knew, or had reason to believe, that it was attractive to children, and that children were in the habit of playing on or about it.   The doctrine of the cases is that the child cannot be regarded as a voluntary trespasser, because he is induced to come upon the turntable by the defendant's own conduct.   "What an express invitation would be to an adult the temptation of an attractive plaything is to a child of tender years": *Keffe* v. *Milwaukee etc. Ry. Co.*, 21 Minn. 207; 18 Am. Rep. 393; *Union Stock Yards etc. Co.* v. *Rourke*, 10 Ill. App. 474.

We are unable to see any substantial difference between the turntable cases and the case at bar.   Here was a half block of ground in a populous city, bounded on two sides by public streets and on the third side by a public alley; with an opening of some forty feet in the fence upon the street on the south side, and an opening of equal dimensions in the fence upon the alley on the north side; with a causeway running from one opening to the other diagonally across the premises, inviting approach, and actually used for passage by men and teams.   Upon this half block was a dangerous pond or pit, in which the water was always five or six feet deep, and sometimes fourteen feet deep.   Logs and timbers floated about in this pond, and boys had for some time been in the habit of playing upon them in the water.   The city authorities had been notified of its attractiveness to children.

.and of its dangerous character. They not only suffered the
pond to remain undrained, but the fences around it to be
broken down in some places, and to be actually removed in
others. The deceased boy, Frank McMahon, is proven to
have entered the premises at the opening in the fence on the
alley. This opening was only seventeen feet from the barn
of Soady, where he dismounted from the wagon on which he
had been riding. The place where he was seen playing in
[151] the water was only a few feet from this opening on the
public alley. The love of motion, which attracts a child to
play upon a revolving turntable will also attract him to experiment with a floating plank or log which he finds in a
pond within his easy reach.

The doctrine of the "turntable" cases is sustained by
other cases where the injuries complained of were caused by
agencies of a different character. Such are *Mackey* v. *City of
Vicksburg*, 64 Miss. 777; *Birge* v. *Gardner*, 19 Conn. 507; 50
Am. Dec. 261; *Daley* v. *Norwich etc. R. R. Co.*, 26 Conn. 591;
68 Am. Dec. 413; *Bransom* v. *Labrot*, 81 Ky. 638; 50 Am.
Rep. 193; *Powers* v. *Harlow*, 53 Mich. 507; 51 Am. Rep. 154;
Hydraulic Works Co. v. *Orr*, 83 Pa. St. 332; *Whirley* v. *White-
man*, 1 Head, 610.

There are very respectable authorities on the other side of
the question here under consideration. Such are *Gillespie*
v. *McGowan*, 100 Pa. St. 144; 45 Am. Rep. 365; *Hargreaves*
v. *Deacon*, 25 Mich. 1; *Klix* v. *Nieman*, 68 Wis. 271; 60 Am.
Rep. 854; *Schmidt* v. *Kansas City Dis. Co.*, 90 Mo. 284; 59
Am. Rep. 16; *Indianapolis* v. *Emmelman*, 108 Ind. 530; 58
Am. Rep. 65; *Clark* v. *Richmond*, 83 Va. 355; 5 Am. St. Rep.
281; *Clark* v. *Manchester*, 62 N. H. 577; *Frost* v. *Eastern R. R.
Co.*, 64 N. H. 220; 10 Am. St. Rep. 396. Some of these cases
are distinguishable from the case at bar. In the Pennsylvania case, a child, seven years and ten months old, fell into
a well in the field of a private owner, one hundred feet from
the public highway and three hundred feet from the nearest
house, and not concealed in any way so as to escape notice;
the scene of the accident was at a comparatively remote
point, and the court below had held that the plaintiff could
not be guilty of contributory negligence as matter of law
instead of submitting the question to the jury; moreover, the
case is inconsistent with the ruling of the same court in the
previous case of *Hydraulic Works Co.* v. *Orr*, 83 Pa. St. 332.

In the Michigan case a child of tender years fell into a cis-

tern on property "not immediately adjoining a highway";
and it is expressly said: "We express no opinion concerning cases where the nature of the business is such as to present peculiar attraction to children," etc. So, [152] in the
Missouri case, it was expressly stated that the agency causing the accident was not shown by the evidence to be "attractive to children." The supreme court of New Hampshire
expressly repudiates the doctrine of the "turntable" cases.
Such also seems to be the position of the court in the Wisconsin case. In the Indiana case the excavation into which
the child fell was in a shallow stream which was part of a
public street, and it was held that the city was liable for that
reason; and, consequently, what was said as to excavations
upon private property was not necessary to the decision of
the case; it was said, however, that "whoever does any thing
. . . . immediately adjacent to a public street to attract
children of the vicinity into danger, which they cannot appreciate, owes the duty of protecting them by suitably guarding the source of danger." In the Virginia case, where the
action was against the city of Richmond, the city was held
not to be liable because the child climbed up from the sidewalk upon a brick wall and fell into the area beyond it, thereby receiving the injuries complained of. But whether the
cases, which hold to the rule of nonliability under such facts
as appear in this record, can be clearly distinguished from
the case at bar or not, we are not disposed to follow them in
view of the authorities on the other side.

We do not regard the case of St. Louis etc. R. R. Co. v.
Bell, 81 Ill. 76, 25 Am. Rep. 269, as opposing, but rather as
indorsing, the doctrine of the "turntable" cases; that case
was decided when this court so far considered questions of
fact as to determine whether the verdict of a jury was contrary to the weight of the evidence or not; and we held that
"in view of the isolated position in which the turntable was
located, the proofs fail to show that appellant was guilty of
such want of care as could lawfully charge it with damages
for this accident."

The question whether a defendant has or has not been
guilty of negligence in case of such an accident upon [153] his
land to a child of tender years is for the jury. Involved in
this question is the further question whether or not the premises were sufficiently attractive to entice children into danger,
and to suggest to the defendant the probability of the occur-

nce of such accident; and, therefore, such further question
also a matter to be determined by the jury: *Mackey* v.
ity of Vicksburg, 64 Miss. 777; *Railroad Co.* v. *Stout*, 17 Wall.
57. The subject of the attractiveness of the premises was
bmitted to the jury by the instructions given for the
laintiff in the case at bar.

It was also submitted to the jury by such instructions to
etermine whether the deceased or his parents were guilty
f contributory negligence. In answer to special interroga-
ories submitted by the city, the jury found specially that
he deceased, Frank McMahon, at the time of his death, was
iot of sufficient age and ability to exercise ordinary care and
iscretion in taking care of himself, and was without fault
n his part, and did not, at that time, have discretion, in-
elligence, information, and knowledge sufficient to enable
iim to know that it was dangerous for him to play in the
vater on the premises, and to be at the place of drowning;
hat he necessarily and unavoidably fell into the pit and was
drowned; that the premises were not sufficiently fenced to
warn him of his danger in entering thereon; and that his
parents, at the time of his drowning, were without fault in
respect to the same.

In *Chicago City Ry. Co.* v. *Wilcox*, 138 Ill. 370, we held that,
where a suit for damages, caused by the negligence of the defendant, is brought by a child of tender years, the negligence
of his parents cannot be imputed to him in support of the
defense of contributory negligence. Here, however, the suit
is brought by the father as administrator of a deceased child.
In such a case the contributory negligence of the parent, if
it exist, may be shown in bar of the action: *Chicago City Ry.
Co.* v. *Wilcox*, 138 Ill. 370. The question whether the parents
were guilty of such contributory [154] negligence, having been
fairly left to the jury, has been decided adversely to the appellant, and cannot be reviewed here.

Whether, as matter of law, a child seven years old, or under
that age, can be justly held to be incapable of negligence, it
is not necessary to decide. But where a child has passed the
age of seven years, as was the case with appellee's deceased
intestate, we are of the opinion that he is bound to use such
care as children of his age, capacity, and intelligence are
capable of exercising, and that the question whether he has
done so or not should be submitted to the jury: *Kerr* v. *Forgue*,
54 Ill. 482; 5 Am. Rep. 146; *Chicago City Ry. Co.* v. *Wilcox*,

138 Ill. 370; 2 Thompson on Negligence, 1181, 1182; *Railroad Co.* v. *Stout*, 17 Wall. 657; *Birge* v. *Gardner*, 19 Conn. 507; 50 Am. Dec. 261; *Daley* v. *Norwich etc. R. R. Co.*, 26 Conn. 591; 68 Am. Dec. 413; *Union Stock Yards etc. Co.* v. *Rourke*, 10 Ill. App. 474; *Evanisch* v. *G. C. & S. F. Ry. Co.*, 57 Tex. 123; *Kansas Cent. Ry. Co.* v. *Fitzsimmons*, 22 Kan. 686; 31 Am. Rep. 203. It was so submitted here, and the instructions given for the plaintiff are in accordance with these views.

2. A municipal corporation holding property as a private owner is chargeable with the same duties and obligations which devolve on individuals. Where it owns, leases, or controls lands, houses, docks, piers, water and gas works it is liable, in respect to the care of the same, for injuries arising from neglect, in the same manner as an individual owner is liable, and must respond in the same way for creating or suffering nuisances: Cooley on Torts, marg. pp. 619, 620; 15 Am. & Eng. Ency. of Law, 1155, and cases cited; *Mackey* v. *City of Vicksburg*, 64 Miss. 777; *Clark* v. *Manchester*, 62 N. H. 577.

3. The plaintiff introduced in evidence, on the trial below, section 8 of the city ordinances of the city of Pekin, which is as follows:

"8. Any owner or occupant, or person in possession, of any uninclosed lot or parcel of land in said city, who shall, by digging or removing earth, sand, or gravel from any such lot or parcel of land, make, or cause to be made, [155] in such uninclosed lot or parcel of land any pit or hole of such depth and character as to be considered dangerous, unsightly, or a source of annoyance to the persons residing in the vicinity thereof or adjacent thereto, shall be deemed guilty of creating a nuisance; and any owner, occupant, or possessor of any such uninclosed lot or parcel of land who shall refuse or neglect to remedy or abate said nuisance, by filling up or covering or securely fencing the same, after being notified so to do by the superintendent of police, or by any member of the police force, or any person aggrieved thereby, shall be subject to a penalty of not less than five dollars nor more than fifty dollars, and a further penalty of two dollars for every day, after the first conviction, that said nuisance shall by him be continued."

It is claimed that the court erred in admitting this ordinance in evidence. The declaration alleged that defendant

had negligently permitted large quantities of water to accumulate in the pit upon the lots in question, "so that the same became a nuisance and dangerous to the lives . . . . of children
of tender years," etc.   The plea of the general issue had the
effect of putting it at issue whether the excavation was a
nuisance or not; and the ordinance was to some extent evidence of the affirmative of such issue.   Moreover, in its
notice of special matters of defense, the defendant had stated
that the premises "were nearly inclosed upon the north and
south sides thereof."   Under the ordinance it was an owner's
duty, after notice, to "securely," and not partially or inef-
fectually, fence the same.   We are not satisfied that the
admission of the ordinance injured the defendant.   In connection with the other proof as to the character and condition
of the excavation upon the lots it had a tendency to show
what the character and condition of the excavation ought to
have been under the requirements exacted by the city itself
of private owners of [156] land.   The city was thereby estopped
from denying its duty under the circumstances.

4. The judgment of the circuit court was unquestionably
erroneous in ordering execution to issue against the city.
The appellate court has found that this order was a mistake
of the circuit clerk, and has entered an order making the
necessary correction and directing the circuit court to amend
its record accordingly.   The final judgment of the appellate
court affirms the judgment of the circuit court as thus modified.   We do not think that there was any error in such
action of the appellate court.

The judgment of the appellate court is affirmed.

REAL PROPERTY—LIABILITY OF OWNERS TO TRESPASSERS.—The owner
of private grounds is under no obligation to keep them in a safe condition
for the benefit of trespassers, or those who may go upon them uninvited for
motives of curiosity or private convenience, in no way connected with the
owner: *Railway Co.* v. *Ferguson*, 57 Ark. 16; 38 Am. St. Rep. 217, and note;
Faris v. *Hoberg*, 134 Ind. 269; 39 Am. St. Rep. 261, and note.   And to the
same effect, *Benson* v. *Baltimore Traction Co.*, 77 Md. 535; 39 Am. St. Rep. 436.

REAL PROPERTY—DUTY OF OWNER TOWARD CHILDREN.—If an infant
trespasses on the premises of another, and is there injured by something
that he does while so trespassing, he cannot recover of the owner of the
premises unless the injury was wantonly inflicted, or was due to his recklessly careless conduct: *McGuiness* v. *Butler*, 159 Mass. 233; 38 Am. St.
Rep. 412, and note.   See, also, the extended notes to *Westbrook* v. *Mobile etc.
R. R. Co.*, 14 Am. St. Rep. 596, and *Plummer* v. *Dill*, 32 Am. St. Rep.
470.   These cases are not in harmony with the principal case.   The subject
received further consideration in *Walsh* v. *Fitchburgh R. R.*, 145 N. Y. 301,

post, p. 615, a "turntable case," and the decision there pronounced was also a denial of the landowners' liability.

NEGLIGENCE—DUTY OF PARENT TO PROTECT CHILD.—It is the duty of a parent to shield his young child from danger, and if, by his own carelessness and neglect, he contributes to his loss of his child's services he is *in pari delicto* with a negligent defendant, and cannot recover for an injury to the child: *Johnson* v. *Reading etc. Ry.*, 160 Pa. St. 647; 40 Am. St. Rep. 752, and note. If the negligence of a parent contributes to the death of a child too young to be able to take care of himself his testator cannot recover therefor against another to whose negligence such death was due: *Grant* v. *Fitchburg*, 160 Mass. 16; 39 Am. St. Rep. 449, and note.

NEGLIGENCE—CHILDREN.—A child is held to such care and prudence only as are usual among children of his age and capacity: *Haynes* v. *Raleigh Gas Co.*, 114 N. C. 203; 41 Am. St. Rep. 786, and note.

EXECUTION AGAINST PROPERTY OF MUNICIPAL CORPORATION.—The property of a municipal corporation is subject to be taken in execution if payment of judgments against it is not otherwise provided for; although property held by it for public use cannot be so taken: *Darlington* v. *Mayor*, 31 N. Y. 164; 88 Am. Dec. 248.

MANDEL *v.* SWAN LAND AND CATTLE COMPANY.
[154 ILLINOIS, 177.]

CORPORATIONS—CONFLICT OF LAWS.—THE LIABILITY OF STOCKHOLDERS of a corporation must be determined by the laws of the state or country which created it.

CORPORATIONS.—A STOCKHOLDER'S LIABILITY FOR CALLS UPON HIS SUBSCRIPTION to the corporate stock, though created by statute, is contractual in its nature.

CORPORATIONS—STOCKHOLDER'S LIABILITY, ENFORCING IN ANOTHER STATE OR COUNTRY.—If a stockholder is liable in the state or country in which the corporation has been created to an action to compel the payment of calls upon his subscription for stock, such liability may be enforced by action in any other state or country, unless by such enforcement wrong or injury will be done to the citizens of the state or country whose courts are resorted to, or the policy of its laws will be contravened or impaired.

CORPORATIONS, FOREIGN, PERSONAL LIABILITY OF STOCKHOLDERS WHOSE SHARES HAVE BEEN FORFEITED.—If by the statutes of a country in which a corporation was created, upon failure of a stockholder to pay a call upon his unpaid subscription, the corporation has a right to forfeit his stock and also to recover, notwithstanding such forfeiture, all calls owing upon the stock at the time of forfeiture, the corporation may, though his stock has been forfeited, maintain an action in this state to recover the amount of calls unpaid at the time of the forfeiture.

CORPORATIONS—CONFLICT OF LAWS.—If the right to recover interest from calls of stock subscriptions after such stock has been forfeited is not conferred by the statutes of the country in which the corporation was created, but only by a by-law of the corporation, and this right is in conflict with the current legislation of the country in which the action is brought, the courts of such country will not permit the recovery of such interest.

CORPORATION, FOREIGN—CONFLICT OF LAWS—STOCKHOLDER'S LIABILITY.
A statute of this state providing that foreign corporations doing business shall be subject to all the liabilities, restrictions, and duties that
may be imposed upon corporations of like character organized under
the general laws of this state does not prohibit a citizen of this state
from becoming a stockholder in a foreign corporation, nor relieve him
from liabilities imposed by the laws of the country in which the corporation was created, and to which he has submitted by his voluntary
action in becoming a stockholder.

EVIDENCE.—A STATEMENT BY A WITNESS AS TO THE CONTENTS OF A REG-
ISTRY of the members of a corporation, of the minutes of a directors'
meeting, and of entries on books of account is not admissible when the
original or a certified copy can be produced.

Otis & Graves, for the appellant.

Swift, Campbell, Jones & Martin, for the appellee.

[181] PHILLIPS, J.   The appellee was a corporation organized in Scotland under the Companies' Act of 1862 of the
United Kingdom, in which appellants became shareholders.
The capital stock of the company was £600,000, divided into
60,000 shares, of £10 each.   The appellant Mandel became
the owner of 380 shares, the appellant Henry L. Frank became the owner of 140 shares, Louis E. Frank was the owner
of 395 shares, and Joseph E. Friend was the owner of 99
shares.   On these shares calls had been made and paid,
amounting to the sum of £6 per share.   On the 11th of
October, 1887, a call was made of £1 2s per share by the
directors, which not being paid, they, by a resolution of the
board passed September 4, 1888, declared the stock forfeited.
On the 24th of March, 1890, the appellee instituted its actions of assumpsit in the circuit court of Cook county to
recover from each of said several appellants the amount
owing on their stock by [182] reason of the calls so made, and
filed its declarations setting up the foregoing facts, to which
the defendants therein filed pleas of general issue and *nul tiel*
corporation, and on trial before the judge, a jury being waived,
appellee recovered judgments, whereupon appeals were prosecuted to the appellate court for the first district, where the
several judgments were affirmed, and these appeals are now
prosecuted to this court.   The same questions of law are presented in the several cases.

By stipulation certain portions of the acts of parliament of
Great Britain, comprising what is generally known as the
"Companies' Act of 1862," with its amendments, were in evi-
dence, from which it appears that seven or more persons, by

subscribing their names to a memorandum of association, and otherwise complying with the statute in respect of registration, may form an incorporated company, with or without limited liability. The act contains the usual provisions prescribing the powers and duties of corporations, the manner in which they can be created, their business conducted, and how their affairs may be wound up and put into liquidation in case of insolvency. By a schedule to this act, known as "Table A," certain regulations for the management, government, and control of the business affairs of corporations organized under this law are given, which each corporation was at liberty to adopt or make other and different regulations in lieu thereof. These regulations contained in "Table A" are substantially by-laws regulating the manner in which the corporate business may be conducted. The appellee did not adopt the regulations in "Table A," but expressly provided they should not apply, and this they were authorized to do by the act.

The appellee introduced the evidence of sundry witnesses, by deposition, who testified, in substance, that the books of the company showed that the appellant Mandel was the owner of 380 shares of the capital stock of the company, of the par value of £10 per share, on [183] which only £6 per share had been paid in, and that a call was made by the directors on the stock of the appellant on the eleventh day of October, 1887, of £1 2s per share, which was not paid, and that in September, 1888, the same was duly forfeited for nonpayment of the call, but the corporate books and records themselves were not offered in evidence on the trial. The only indebtedness of the appellant to the company was for the call made upon the shares standing in his name, for nonpayment of which they were forfeited more than a year before the commencement of suit, and all previous calls had been paid by appellant. No attempt was made to show the amount realized by the company from forfeiture and resale of the stock of appellant, or in what manner it was disposed of, or its value, and the witness Dun, the secretary, refused to answer cross-interrogatories seeking to ascertain what disposition of the forfeited shares had been made by the company, and how much it had realized from such resale. Objections were duly interposed by the appellant to certain designated portions of the depositions, and the court was asked to suppress the same, on the ground that parol state-

ments of the contents of the corporate books and records
were offered in evidence, instead of producing the original
books themselves.   The minute-book itself was not offered in
evidence on the trial, though shown to be in the possession
of appellee.

Appellant asked the court to hold propositions of law numbered one to eight, inclusive, which was refused, and there
was a finding and judgment for the appellee for the sum of
$2,570.61, being the full amount of the call, with interest
thereon at six per cent per annum, without any credit for the
amount received by the company from the forfeiture and resale of the shares.   Motions for a new trial and in arrest of
judgment having been overruled by the court, this appeal is
prosecuted from the judgment.   This suit was instituted by
the company itself, and the rights of creditors are not involved.

[184] It is urged by appellant that no action can be maintained by a corporation to recover upon a call made upon its
stockholders, where, for the same call, the stock has been, by
resolution of the board of directors of the corporation, declared forfeited for nonpayment of that call.   The appellee being a foreign corporation, the general rule is that the liability
of stockholders in such corporation must be determined by
the law of the state which created it.   The law of such foreign
state cannot operate beyond its own territory, and its right to
do business in this state or create relations between itself
and citizens of this state, as members, exists by comity alone.
The liability of a stockholder to the corporation for calls
made has but slight analogy to a debt, but is a statutory
liability, the form and extent of which is dependent upon the
particular phraseology of the statute creating the liability.
It is not a penalty, but a liability that is contractual, and
will ordinarily be enforced by the courts of all the states,
unless where a wrong or injury will be done to the citizens of
the state in which the calls are sought to be enforced, or the
policy of the laws of such state will be contravened or impaired.   This rule is so uniformly held that the citation of
authorities is unnecessary.

The general rule in the states of this country is, that where
a corporation has a right, under the statute creating it, to
declare a forfeiture of shares for nonpayment of calls, it may
exercise its option to forfeit the stock or bring its action to
collect the amount of the calls, but cannot forfeit the stock

and afterward sue at law, as the exercise of the first option would end the relation between the parties and exclude a resort to the other: *Small* v. *Herkimer Mfg. Co.,* 2 N. Y. 330; *Buffalo R. R. Co.* v. *Dudley,* 14 N.Y. 336;. *Rutland etc. R. R. Co.* v. *Thrall,* 35 Vt. 536. But it never has been held that a right to do both cannot be given. When the act of incorporation gives the right to declare a forfeiture, and at the same time [185] reserves to the company the right to collect all calls made prior to such declaration, it must be held that the positive enactment will control, and any principle adopted as a mere equitable rule must yield to such express provision. This corporation, in its articles of association, expressly provided that "the regulations contained in the table marked 'A,' in the first schedule to the Companies' Act of 1862, shall not apply to the company." The table marked "A," in the first schedule to the Companies' Act, is practically a system for the government of a company organized under that act. Section 14 of the act authorizes incorporators thereunder, by their articles of association, to adopt all or any of the provisions contained in the table marked "A," in the first schedule. Section 15 of the act is as follows: "In the case of a company limited by shares, if the memorandum of association is not accompanied by articles of association, or in so far as the articles do not exclude or modify the regulations contained in the table marked 'A,' in the first schedule hereto, the last-mentioned regulations shall, so far as the same are applicable, be deemed to be the regulations of the company, in the same manner and to the same extent as if they had been inserted in articles of association, and the articles had been duly registered." Section 17 of "Table A" provides, if a member fail to pay any call, as made, the directors may serve a notice on him requiring him to pay such call, together with interest and expenses. Section 18 is as to the notice provided for in section 17. Section 19 provides for forfeiture for noncompliance with above notice, whilst section 20 provides that any share so forfeited shall be the property of the company. Section 21 is as follows: "Any member whose shares have been forfeited, shall, notwithstanding, be liable to pay to the company all calls owing upon such shares at the time of forfeiture." Sections 34, 35, 36, and 37 of the articles as adopted by this corporation are practically and substantially an adoption of sections 17, 18, 19, and [186] 20 of "Table A," of the first schedule to the act

1862, whilst in lieu of section 21 the following act of asso.
tion is adopted as section 39: "Any member whose shares
ve been forfeited, shall, notwithstanding, be liable to pay,
d shall forthwith pay, to the company all calls, install-
ints, interest, and expenses owing upon or in respect of
h shares at the time of the forfeiture, together with inter-
; thereon from the time of forfeiture until payment, at
e rate of five per cent per annum, and the directors may
force the payment thereof, if they think fit."

No provisions of the act are pleaded or offered in evidence
iich authorize a recovery of calls after a declaration of for-
ture other than section 21 of "Table A," and a right of
covery in such case, being in conflict with the current of
gislation here, cannot depend on a by-law merely, but to be
iforced must exist in the act authorizing the incorporation
the company. The provisions of section 21 of the act au-
iorize a recovery, after forfeiture, of all calls owing upon
ich forfeited shares at the time of forfeiture, but it has no
rovision authorizing a recovery for interest and expenses
iereafter accruing. If the by-law adopted as section 39
epends for its existence upon some other provision of the
ompanies' Act of 1862, such other provision should have
een properly incorporated into the record. There is no pro-
ision that authorizes a recovery for calls, installments, inter-
st, and expenses, and a judgment for $2,570.61 on a call of
1 2s on 380 shares cannot be sustained, even under section
1 of "Table A."

Appellant further insists that appellee, being a foreign cor-
oration, can exercise no rights except such as are conferred on
corporation created by a statute of this state. Beach, in his
ork on Private Corporations, states the rule in reference to
tockholders in foreign corporations as follows: "Where a per-
on becomes a stockholder in a corporation organized under
ie laws of [187] a foreign state he must be held to contract
ith reference to all the laws of the state under which the cor-
oration is organized and which enter into its constitution,
nd the extent of his individual liability as a shareholder to
ie creditors of the company must be determined by the laws
f that state, not because such laws are in force in the other
tate, but because he has voluntarily agreed to the terms of
he company's constitution. It is equally clear, both upon
rinciple and authority, that this liability may be enforced
y creditors wherever they can obtain jurisdiction of the

necessary parties. This does not depend upon any principle of comity, but upon the right to enforce in another juris- · diction a contract validly entered into. The validity, interpretation, and effect of the act imposing the liability are determined by the law of the state creating the corporation": Beach on Private Corporations, sec. 148. And the author cites many authorities which sustain his statement of the rule. The statute of this state which provides that "foreign corporations doing business in this state shall be subject to all the liabilities, restrictions, and duties that may be imposed upon corporations of like character organized under the general laws of this state, and shall have no other or greater powers," does not prohibit a citizen of this state from becoming a stockholder in a foreign corporation, nor relieve him in any way from a contract liability resulting from his voluntary action in becoming such stockholder. The statute, by the term "doing business," has reference to the business for which the corporation was organized, and not to the form of its by-laws with reference to its relations to its own members, or a resort to the courts of this state to recover a contract liability. The principle as announced and the rule as stated in *Stevens* v. *Pratt*, 101 Ill. 206, *Granite State Provident Assn.* v. *Lloyd*, 145 Ill. 620, and *Santa Clara Female Academy* v. *Sullivan*, 116 Ill. 375, 56 Am. Rep. 776, are not inconsistent with what is here said, as in each of those cases active business was entered on of the character for which [188] the corporation was organized. Appellee would not be doing business in this state by resorting to the courts here to enforce a contract liability, nor would the purchase of shares of stock by appellant of one holding such shares, and their transfer on the books of the company in a foreign jurisdiction, bring such company within this state doing business, within the meaning of section 26 of the act entitled "Corporations."

The contention of appellant that calls could not be made by this corporation until the entire amount of stock had been subscribed cannot be sustained, as by section 5 of the articles of association authorized by the act of parliament "the registered holders of shares in the company, for the time being, whatever the number issued or subscribed for, shall be associated and shall form the company, and the business of the company may be commenced as soon as the directors think fit." Under this provision of the articles, made in accordance with the act, it is not a condition precedent to the right to make a call that all the stock must be subscribed for or the shares allotted: Buckley's Companies' Act, 4th ed., 19; *Ornamental Pyrographic Co.* v. *Brown,* 2 Hurl. & C. 63; 32 L. J. Ex. 190. There is nothing in the articles of association which states the subscribers shall not be associated, for the purposes of the company, till a particular event happens, such as a subscription to or the allotment of a particular number of shares, as was the case in *Pierce* v. *Jersey Water Works,* L. R. 5 Ex. 209, and in *North Stafford etc. Coal Co.* v. *Ward,* L. R. 3 Exch. 172. It cannot be held a defense to an action for a call here that the capital is not fully subscribed or allotted.

It was not error to refuse to hold as law the propositions submitted by appellant.

Previous to the commencement of the trial a motion was made by appellant to suppress and strike out certain portions of the answers of Finley Dun, Thomas Murray, George Milne, and John Reed, witnesses for appellee. [189] The motion as to Dun's deposition was, that in his answer to the fifth and eighth interrogatories he purported to give the contents of the register of members of the company, and the minutes of a meeting of the board of directors and a resolution adopted, and by his answer to the seventh interrogatory he purported to give copies of the books of account and original entries of the plaintiff, and because of his refusal to answer the third cross-interrogatory. The objections to the depositions of Murray and Milne, in their answers to the seventh interrogatory, were the same as made to the answers of Dun to the fifth and eighth interrogatories, and the deposition of Reed was objected to for the reason that in his answer to the eighth interrogatory he was permitted to give what purports to be the contents of the postage-book by him referred to, etc. The motion to suppress depositions was overruled, and an objection to the answers made on trial, which objection was also overruled.

By section 15 of chapter 57 of the Revised Statutes of Illinois, " the papers, entries, and records of any corporation or incorporated association may be proved by a copy thereof, certified under the hand of the secretary, clerk, cashier, or other keeper of the same. If the corporation or incorporated association has a seal the same shall be affixed to such certificate." By section 18 of the same chapter it is provided that "any such papers, entries, records, and ordinances may be proved by copies, examined and sworn to by credible witnesses." In addition to the evidence authorized by the statute, the original books would be admissible, and in case of loss or destruction the contents might be proven, and under certain circumstances, where there is an omission to make any record on the subject, parol evidence may be heard: *Ratcliff* v. *Teters*, 27 Ohio St. 66; *Bank of United States* v. *Dandridge*, 12 Wheat. 64. The original books, and the evidence provided for by sections 15 and 18 of the statute, are original evidence, and evidence of a secondary nature [190] is not to be resorted to where there is in the possession of a party evidence of a higher and more satisfactory character. Proof of the papers, entries, and records of a private corporation in possession of that corporation cannot be shown by an opinion or conclusion of a witness. The evidence must be primary, original evidence. Certain parts of the depositions of Dun, Murray, and Milne should have been suppressed, where they stated a conclusion as to what is shown by the records. The evidence of Reed was as to mailing notice, and the entries as to his mailing letters, etc., are a mere memorandum to which he could refer to refresh his recollection, and not a record of which copies must be made. It was not error to overrule the motion to suppress his deposition.

For the errors indicated, the judgments of the appellate court and circuit court of Cook county must be reversed, and the cause remanded to the circuit court of Cook county for new trial.

Mr. Justice BAKER. I dissent. I think that the judgment should be affirmed.

CORPORATIONS—ENFORCING INDIVIDUAL LIABILITY OF STOCKHOLDER IN FOREIGN JURISDICTION.—When a special remedy is given creditors of a corporation against its stockholders, the liability of the latter cannot be enforced in any state except that in which the corporation was organized: *Fowler* v. *Lamson*, 146 Ill. 472; 37 Am. St. Rep. 163, and extended note fully discussing the subject. See, also, the extended note to *Prince* v. *Lynch*, 99 Am. Dec. 433.

CORPORATIONS—STOCKHOLDER'S LIABILITY FOR CALLS—NATURE OF.—This question is discussed at length in the extended notes to *Franklin Glass Co.* v. *Alexander*, 9 Am. Dec. 97, and *Thompson* v. *Reno Sav. Bank*, 3 Am. St. Rep. 806.

CORPORATIONS.—Personal liability of a stockholder whose shares have been forfeited: See the extended notes to *Thompson* v. *Reno Sav. Bank*, 3 Am. St. Rep. 821, 823, and *Franklin Glass Co.* v. *Alexander*, 9 Am. Dec. 97. The forfeiture of stock of a corporation extinguishes all rights and liabilities of the shareholder and of the corporation to recover on it: *Germantown etc. Ry. Co.* v. *Fitler*, 60 Pa. St. 124; 100 Am. Dec. 546.

COLEMAN *v.* HOWE.

[154 ILLINOIS, 458.]

CORPORATIONS—STOCKHOLDER'S LIABILITY.—ANY DEVICE by which members of a corporation seek to avoid the liability which the law imposes upon them is void as to creditors.

CORPORATIONS.—STOCKHOLDERS' LIABILITY CONTINUES UNTIL THEIR STOCK HAS BEEN IN GOOD FAITH FULLY PAID UP, and cannot be avoided by agreements between themselves that shares of the capital stock shall be regarded as fully paid up.

CORPORATIONS.—PAYMENT FOR THE STOCK OF A CORPORATION MAY BE MADE in property as well as in money.

CORPORATIONS—STOCK, PAYMENT FOR IN OVERVALUED PROPERTY.—If property contributed or paid for the capital stock of a corporation is not valued in good faith a stockholder may be compelled to respond to the creditors of the corporation for the par value of the stock, less the actual value of the property taken in exchange for it.

CORPORATIONS—STOCK.—FRAUD IN TAKING PROPERTY IN PAYMENT OF STOCK will be presumed where the value of such property is well known, or might have been easily learned, and it has been taken at an exaggerated valuation. Where an overvaluation is so great that a fraudulent intent appears on its face and is not explained the court will hold it to be fraudulent as a matter of law. If stock of the par value of $300,000 is issued for property worth only one-fourth of that sum the overvaluation is so gross that it must be regarded as fraudulent on its face.

CORPORATIONS. — A PURCHASER OF STOCK WHICH HAS NOT BEEN FULLY PAID UP, or which has been paid for in property at a gross overvaluation, who has notice of the facts, is liable to the same extent as the party who transfers it to him.

CORPORATIONS—STOCK AGREED TO BE REGARDED AS PAID IN FULL.—An agreement between stockholders that stock issued for certain property shall be regarded as paid in full cannot be sustained, as against creditors of the corporation, if such property was not valued in good faith. The issuing of paid-up shares at less than their par value is a fraud upon the creditors.

CORPORATIONS.—THE LIABILITY OF STOCKHOLDERS TO CREDITORS IS SEVERAL. Hence a creditor of a corporation may maintain a suit against a stockholder who has not paid for his stock in full, and may compel him to pay the balance due, if it does not exceed the amount of the liability of the corporation to the creditor, and the stockholder has no right to have the other stockholders made parties to the suit, nor to restrict a recovery against him to his proportion of the debt due such creditor.

BILL in equity by certain judgment creditors of the Illinois Agricultural Works, a corporation, against certain stockholders therein to enforce their liability upon the stock held by them upon an allegation that such stock remained unpaid to the extent of fifty per cent of the face value. The three members of the firm of Coleman, Post & Reed formed a partnership for the purpose of manufacturing agricultural machinery, and received a donation of a tract of land worth

$6,000 or $7,000, and put into the business about $60,000.
In November, 1884, their property and business was worth
not more than $75,000 and their indebtedness amounted to
$70,000. In September, 1884, they formed a corporation
which they styled, "Illinois Agricultural Works," and designated its capital stock at the sum of $300,000 and claimed
to have subscribed therefor as following: Coleman, 1,500
shares, Post, 1,000 shares, and Reed, 500 shares, each share
being of the par value of $100. No money was paid by any
of them to the corporation, but in consideration of the stock
received by them they transferred to it the property of the
firm. Afterward an agreement was entered into with Tracy,
Mendenhall, Smith, and Mrs. Coleman to take stock at fifty
cents on the dollar. The corporation assumed the indebtedness of the old firm. On September 22, 1884, stock was
issued to Coleman, Post, Reed, Tracy, Smith, and Mendenhall. The stock so issued, upon some objection being made
by Tracy, was surrendered and destroyed, and a new issue
made on October 23, 1884, to the former partners, to wit:
Coleman, 1,500 shares, Post, 1,000 shares, Reed, 500 shares.
The stock so issued was surrendered November 10, 1884,
with assignments on the back of the certificates to one-half
of the shares amounting to $150,000 with Mendenhall as
trustee, and on the same day new certificates were issued as
follows: To Coleman, 750 shares, to Post, 500 shares, to Reed,
250 shares, and to Mendenhall, trustee, 1,500 shares. The
certificate so issued to him as trustee was surrendered November 27, 1884. On November 24, 1884, a certificate for
200 shares was issued to Mrs. Coleman, and for 100 shares to
Smith, and subsequently 50 shares were issued to Mendenhall, 100 shares to Tracy, and 1,050 shares to Mendenhall,
trustee. For the stock issued to Smith, Tracy, Mendenhall,
and Coleman there was no question that they had not paid any
thing in excess of fifty per cent of its face value. The 1,050
shares remaining in the name of Mendenhall, as trustee, belonged to the corporation, and nothing had been paid for it.
The intention was to sell it for the benefit of the corporation
in the market at fifty cents on the dollar.

Greene & Humphrey, James H. Matheny, and *Brown, Wheeler
& Brown,* for the appellants.

W. L. Gross and *Crea & Ewing,* for the appellees.

[467] MAGRUDER, J.   The capital stock of an insolvent corporation is a trust fund for the payment of its debts. If a stockholder has not paid his subscription in full he is liable for the debts of the corporation to the extent of the unpaid portion of his subscription. It is the duty of the directors of a corporation to manage its capital stock as a trust fund for the benefit of its shareholders while it exists, and of its creditors in case of its dissolution. [468] This trust fund consists not only of the capital paid in, but also of that which the shareholder has promised to pay in. The unpaid stock is as much a part of the corporate assets as the money which has been paid upon the stock. The obligation of a subscriber to pay his subscription cannot be released or surrendered to him by the trustees of the corporation. Nor will stockholders be permitted to agree among themselves that their shares shall be taken at a nominal value, or be nonassessable, when such agreement operates to the injury of creditors: *Upton* v. *Tribilcock*, 91 U. S. 45; *Sanger* v. *Upton*, 91 U. S. 56. "Any device by which the members of a corporation seek to avoid the liability which the law imposes upon them is void as to creditors, whether binding or not as between themselves. Of this character is an agreement among the members that the shares of the capital stock of the corporation shall be regarded as fully paid up,". when in fact they are not fully paid: *Union etc. Ins. Co.* v. *Frear Stone Mfg. Co.*, 97 Ill. 537; 37 Am. Rep. 129. The question presents itself in this case, whether the stock held by the appellants was stock which had been in good faith fully paid up, or whether it must be regarded as stock upon which only fifty per cent had been paid, and upon which fifty per cent remained unpaid, as a fund liable to be subjected by the appellees to the payment of their judgments.

It is held that stock may be paid for in property as well as in money: 2 Morawetz on Private Corporations, sec. 825; 23 Am. & Eng. Ency. of Law, 794. In the present case the capital stock was paid for in property alone. Property worth not more than $75,000 was conveyed in exchange for capital stock amounting to $300,000. There was here an overvaluation of the property which formed the consideration for the issue of the stock. Cases may arise where stock is issued for property taken at an overvaluation, which will justify the courts in compelling the stockholders to respond to the creditors for the [469] par value of the stock less the actual value of the property taken in exchange for it. Such will not be the case where there is entire good faith in making the valuation. But if the property contributed is not valued in good faith the shares of stock will not be fully paid up, either in law or fact, by the contribution of such property. A declaration by the corporation that the shares are paid up will not avail against the creditors in case of insolvency: 2 Morawetz on Private Corporations, sec. 825. "The courts have inflexibly enforced the rule that payment of stock subscriptions is good as against creditors only where payment has been made in money, or what may be fairly considered as money's worth": *Wetherbee* v. *Baker,* 35 N. J. Eq. 501.

Some of the cases hold, that overvaluation will not render the stockholder liable for the difference between the actual and accepted values unless there is affirmative proof of fraud *aliunde.* But other cases hold what we regard as the better view, namely, that, where property, whose value is well known or can be easily learned, is taken at an exaggerated estimate, a strong presumption is raised that the valuation is not in good faith and is made for a fraudulent purpose. This presumption will be conclusive unless rebutted by satisfactory evidence explanatory of the apparent fraud. Where the overvaluation is so great that the fraudulent intent appears on its face, and is not explained, the court will hold it to be fraudulent as matter of law: 1 Cook on Stock and Stock. holders, sec. 47; 23 Am. & Eng. Ency. of Law, 859, 860; *Douglass* v. *Ireland,* 73 N. Y. 104; *Boynton* v. *Andrews,* 63 N. Y. 93; *Boynton* v. *Hatch,* 47 N. Y. 232; *Osgood* v. *King,* 42 Iowa, 478. In *Boynton* v. *Andrews,* 63 N. Y. 93, stock for $100,000 was issued for property worth $50,000, and it was held that there was a gross overvaluation, and that the transaction was fraudulent in law on its face. In the case at bar the proof shows clearly that stock for $300,000 was issued for property worth only $75,000, an overvaluation [470] so gross that we cannot but regard it as fraudulent on its face; and its real value was well understood by the parties transferring it to the corporation. It is said that there was value in certain patents held by Post, under which the machinery was manufactured, and in the prospect of future profits from the business, but these considerations were of small moment when it is remembered that the property was not conveyed clear of encumbrance, but was subject to $70,000 of firm debts before its transfer, and was still subject to them after the transfer by reason of the assumption of their payment by the corporation.

The proof shows that the appellees, Tracy, Smith, Mendenhall, and Mrs. Coleman, were fully aware of the overvaluation. Tracy knew the value of the plant. As a banker he had loaned the firm money upon the property as security. Smith had made a personal inspection of the property and was told about it by Post and by Tracy, the latter being his agent who invested in the stock for him. Mrs. Coleman not only inspected the plant and the books, but was informed by her husband of the exact condition of affairs. The same information was possessed by Mendenhall who conferred with both Post and Coleman. These parties cannot be regarded as innocent purchasers of the stock without notice of the real value of the property upon which it was based. The very fact that, before the corporation was organized and before any stock was subscribed for, they agreed in advance to pay only fifty cents on the dollar for the stock afterward issued to them, shows that they knew of the overvaluation of the property by at least fifty per cent; for they were all aware that the original subscribers paid no money for their stock, but took it in exchange for the plant.

Counsel claim that the stockholders cannot be held liable on account of the overvaluation unless fraud is shown, and that, even if the proof shows a fraudulent [471] overvaluation there is no allegation of fraud in the bill. The bill distinctly charges that the corporation was organized with a capital stock of $300,000, and that the shares were not paid for in full by the original subscribers, and that appellants took their shares at fifty cents on the dollar, knowing that the original subscribers had not paid for them in full, and knowing that the debts of appellees existed against the corporation. The proof sustains the charge. If there is a fraudulent overvaluation of the property taken by the corporation for the stock, the stockholder is liable for the difference between the actual value and the accepted value of such property, and consequently his stock is regarded as unpaid stock to the extent of that difference. Hence, proof of fraudulent overvaluation is proof that the stock is unpaid. Under the allegation that the stock is unpaid any proof that it is unpaid, even though it be proof of the unpaid difference referred to as growing out of a fraudulent overvaluation, may be legitimately introduced.

It is not necessary, however, to hold in this case that appellants are liable for more than fifty cents on the dollar of their stock as being unpaid. They received stock of the face value of $45,000 for which they paid only $22,500. The decree of the circuit court and the judgment of the appellate court have found them liable to pay about $20,000 of the sum of $22,500 toward the discharge of the judgments of appellees, upon the theory that the latter amount represented the extent to which the stock held by appellants was unpaid. Their claim, however, is that they cannot be regarded as original stockholders, or original subscribers to the stock, but that they purchased it at second hand as paid-up stock from Mendenhall, trustee, at fifty cents on the dollar, and are, therefore, *bona fide* holders of it.

A purchaser or assignee of stock which has not been fully paid does not become liable to the corporate creditors for the unpaid balance, where the stock has been [472] issued as fully paid, and he has acquired the same in good faith and without notice that it has not been fully paid. But, where a person purchasing stock issued as paid up has notice that it has not been paid, his liability is the same as that of the party who transferred it to him: 1 Cook on Stock and Stockholders, 3d ed., secs. 49, 50; *Jackson* v. *Traer*, 64 Iowa, 469; 52 Am. Rep. 449. The equitable doctrine that the capital stock is a trust fund that may be followed by the creditors of the corporation, and that any balance remaining unpaid thereon may be reached by such creditors, applies not only to original subscribers to the stock, but also to purchasers or assignees with notice of the fact that all of the stock has not been paid for. We do not think that, under the evidence in this case, the appellants can be regarded as such *bona fide* purchasers without notice. In the first place the stock was issued to them directly by the corporation, as belonging, not to the original subscribers, but to the corporation itself. In the second place, if it be regarded as having been issued by Mendenhall, the trustee, the scheme, by which it was placed in the hands of the trustee, was a mere device for evading the law, and for giving to the stock the appearance of being fully paid up, when one-half of it was unpaid. As matter of fact, the original subscribers for the stock never really owned more than half of it; and that they were to get half of the original issue at fifty cents on the dollar was known to appellants before its issue. Not only was it understood, before the corporation was organized and before it acquired any property, that appellants were to take stock at fifty cents on the dollar, but the issue of all the stock to the promoters, and its surrender, and its reissue to them and to the appellants, and to the trustee, were steps taken with the knowledge of appellants, and by arrangement with them and with the trustee.

In *Alling* v. *Wenzel*, 133 Ill. 264, it appeared that, before stock was issued, it was transferred upon the books to [473] the company itself, and was called "treasury stock"; that the corporation sold portions of it at less than its par value; that the parties procuring it from the corporation knew that the corporation was not receiving par value therefor, and took it from the company at less than its face value; and we held that "the plan . . . . pursued was but a device to evade the law, and to defeat its useful and wholesome provisions." The original subscribers for the $300,000 of stock surrendered it to the corporation. Half of it was reissued to them, and the stock acquired by appellants was a part of the other half retained by the corporation. Not only were the certificates of stock issued directly to appellants by the corporation, but their names were entered on the stock-book as original subscribers and not as transferees. They thereby became subrogated to the rights and assumed the liabilities of original subscribers to the stock: *Upton* v. *Hansbrough*, 3 Biss. 429.

The transaction by which the appellants received stock of the face value of $45,000 for one-half that amount amounted to nothing more than an agreement between them and the corporation, that the remaining fifty per cent of the stock should not be called for. Such an agreement cannot be sustained as against creditors. The issue of paid-up shares at less than their par value is a fraud upon the creditors: *Union etc. Ins. Co.* v. *Frear Stone Mfg. Co.*, 97 Ill. 537; 37 Am. Rep. 129; *Jewell* v. *Rock River Paper Co.*, 101 Ill. 57; *Scovill* v. *Thayer*, 105 U. S. 143; *Jackson* v. *Traer*, 64 Iowa, 469; 52 Am. Rep. 449; *Clapp* v. *Peterson*, 104 Ill. 26.

There is evidence in the record that Coleman told appellee Loeb, the holder of the largest judgment against the corporation, that the new stockholders, the present appellants, had paid but fifty cents on the dollar for their stock, and were perfectly good for the other fifty cents. Loeb was thereby assured that his debt was secure, and did not press for the payment of his claim. Such representations were calculated to induce the creditors to rely [474] upon the respon-

sibility of the corporation, which had assumed the payment
of their debts.

It is claimed that the decree was erroneous in assessing
the entire amount of the claims of appellees against appellants, and assessing nothing against Coleman and Post. We
understand counsel to abandon this objection so far as Reed
is concerned; Reed could not be found and was not served,
and the bill was dismissed as to him.   In *Hatch* v. *Dana*,
101 U. S. 205, it was held that where a creditor's bill is
filed upon return of execution *nulla bona* by the creditor of
a corporation to reach the unpaid balance due upon a subscription for stock it is not necessary to make all the stockholders defendants.   It is sufficient if those stockholders are
defendants whose unpaid subscriptions it is sought to reach.
It may be otherwise where the proceeding is under the statute to wind up the corporation, because there all the shareholders, so far as they can be ascertained, should be made parties
so that "complete justice may be done by equalizing the burdens, and in order to prevent a multiplicity of suits": *Hatch*
v. *Dana*, 101 U. S. 205.   But the liability of a stockholder
for unpaid stock is several, and not joint.   In case of a
suit by creditor's bill to reach such unpaid stock, " there is
not the same reason for requiring all the stockholders to be
made defendants.   In such a case no stockholder can be compelled to pay more than he owes": *Hatch* v. *Dana*, 101 U. S.
205.   " The creditor is subrogated to the place of the debtor
corporation, and the proceeding is in the nature of an equitable attachment by which the debts due the company may
be applied to the payment of its own debts": *Patterson* v.
Lynde, 112 Ill. 196.   The doctrine of the case of *Hatch* v.
Dana, 101 U. S. 205, has been substantially indorsed by this
court: *Clapp* v. *Peterson*, 104 Ill. 26; *Hickling* v. *Wilson*, 104
Ill. 54; *Patterson* v. *Lynde*, 112 Ill. 196; *Young* v. *Farwell*,
139 Ill. 326.   The stockholder who is made a defendant to
the creditor's bill may file a cross-bill and bring in the stockholders who are not parties, and enforce contributions [475]
from them: *Young* v. *Farwell*, 139 Ill. 326.   But if he neglects
to do so the remedy against himself does not fail.

In the case at bar Post and Coleman were made defendants and served, and default was entered against them.   The
appellate court say in their opinion affirming this decree:
"The first hearing resulted in a dismissal of the bill as to
all the defendants.   The present appellees brought that rec-

ord to this court by a writ of error, and the only question then contested was as to the liability of the present appellants. The reversal opened the whole case, and when the cause was remanded it was to be heard anew. Notice of the motion to reinstate was served upon the appellants, but not upon Post, or upon Coleman in his personal capacity, and the cause proceeded to a second hearing in this shape, no further attention being paid to Post and Coleman. Whether this was by design or from mere oversight we cannot ascertain from the record, but it is hardly presumable that a matter so apparent was overlooked. . . . . Reed was dropped out of the case early in its history. By going to a hearing upon reinstatement without notice to Coleman and Post the contesting parties dropped them also from the case. No other fair inference arises from such action, and having tried the case in this condition without suggestion of irregularity in the court below, neither side should be permitted to make objection on that account for the first time in this court." Such being the condition of the record, appellants suffered no injury from the failure to take a decree against Coleman and Post, inasmuch as the evidence shows that they were insolvent. If the liability of appellants upon their unpaid stock could be reached under a bill of this kind in case Coleman and Post had not been made parties at all the result is practically the same here under a decree, which does not embrace them within its terms, in view of their insolvency.

476 Even under the stricter rule which prevails where the proceeding is to wind up the corporation under section 25 of the corporation act, if any stockholder shall not have property enough to satisfy his portion of the debts, then the amount shall be divided equally among all the remaining stockholders: 1 Starr & Curtis' Annotated Statutes, 613.

We find no error in the record which would justify us in reversing the judgment. Accordingly, the decree of the circuit court and the judgment of the appellate court are affirmed.

Judgment affirmed. ____

CORPORATIONS—LIABILITY OF SUBSCRIBERS FOR STOCK PAID FOR IN PROPERTY.—Where corporate stock subscriptions are made payable in property it must be taken at a reasonable money value, and any intentional overvaluation is not permissible, and if grossly excessive and intentionally made, though without actual fraud, it is invalid as to corporation creditors, who may proceed against the stockholders individually as for unpaid stock

subscriptions: *Elyton Land Co.* v. *Birmingham Warehouse etc. Co.*, 92 Ala.
407; 25 Am. St. Rep. 65, and note.

CORPORATIONS—UNPAID SUBSCRIPTIONS—AGREEMENTS BETWEEN STOCK-
HOLDERS—RIGHTS OF CREDITORS.—Any arrangement between the stockholders and the corporation to issue stock as fully paid for though only
partly paid for in fact, by which the corporation does not get the benefit of
the full price of the stock in good faith, may be valid and binding between
the corporation and the stockholders, but it is invalid as to the creditors of
the former, and may be set aside at their instance: *Elyton Land Co.* v. *Birmingham Warehouse etc. Co.*, 92 Ala. 407; 25 Am. St. Rep. 65, and note.

CORPORATIONS—THE LIABILITY OF STOCKHOLDERS UPON THEIR SUBSCRIP-
TIONS FOR STOCK IS SEVERAL, not joint: *Baines* v. *Babcock*, 95 Cal. 531; 29
Am. St. Rep. 158, and note. To the same effect, see *Willis* v. *Mabon*, 48
Minn. 140; 31 Am. St. Rep. 626, and note. See, also, the extended note to
Thompson v. *Reno Sav. Bank*, 3 Am. St. Rep. 837.

The subject of the payment for stock in a corporation was considered in
several recent Tennessee cases. In the first of these, *Kalley* v. *Fletcher*, 94
Tenn. 1, it was decided not only that shares of stock might be issued in payment for property or services, but that it was presumed that the transaction
was made in good faith, and the property or services paid for at a fair valuation, and that creditors of a corporation seeking, after its insolvency, to
compel the holder of such shares to contribute to the payment of the debts
of the corporation must affirmatively establish that the transaction by
which the stockholders received their stock was fraudulent, and that the
burden of proof, therefore, was upon such creditors to show that the overvaluation was intentional, and consequently fraudulent. These views were
substantially reiterated in *Shields* v. *Clifton Hill Land Co.*, 94 Tenn. 160,
post, p. 700, and in *Jones* v. *Whitworth*, 94 Tenn. 602, in which it was said:
"We think the true rule is, and should be, that creditors of an insolvent
corporation, or its assignee for the benefit of corporate creditors, can have
relief against a stock subscriber who has paid his subscription in property
which the corporation was legally authorized to buy only upon allegation
and proof that the property was sold at an overvaluation which was intentionally fraudulent, or which was so gross as to be constructively fraudulent,
as against corporate creditors. The bill should allege facts making a case
of actual or constructive fraud: *Phelan* v. *Hazard*, 5 Dill. 50; *Coit* v. *Amalgamating Co.*, 119 U. S. 343; *Coffin* v. *Ransdell*, 110 Ind. 417; *Gogebec Inv.
Co.* v. *Iron Chief Min. Co.*, 78 Wis. 427; 23 Am. St. Rep. 419–421; *Elyton
Land Co.* v. *Birmingham etc. Co.*, 92 Ala. 407; 25 Am. St. Rep. 82, 83.

LONG *v.* HESS.

[154 ILLINOIS, 482.]

APPELLATE PROCEDURE.—IF DEPOSITIONS ARE ADMITTED IN EVIDENCE against the objections of a party, but upon all the evidence judgment is rendered in his favor, from which his adversary appeals, the appellee, if he assigns no cross-errors, must be deemed to have acquiesced in the decision of the trial court, and the depositions must be treated as having been rightfully admitted in evidence.

CONFLICT OF LAWS—HUSBAND AND WIFE.—If an antenuptial contract is entered into between parties living in a foreign country, which does not purport on its face to provide respecting acquisitions to be made by them after their marriage, such acquisitions, if made in this country, will be controlled by its laws, and be in no respect affected by the antenuptial contract.

CONFLICT OF LAWS—ADOPTED CHILDREN.—Though children adopted in a foreign country may have acquired the status of children and heirs at law of a person there residing, yet, if he subsequently removes to another country, and there acquires property, it is subject to the laws of that country, and the right of the owner to dispose of it by will, though by so doing he may disinherit the children.

SUIT in chancery by William Long and Catherine Gleim against the children of Jacob Hess and Christina Hess, widow, and Louis Hess, executor of the estate of Jacob Hess, deceased, to set aside the will of said decedent, and to declare a trust in favor of the complainants, in two-sixths of the estate of the testator. He died in March, 1891, in Illinois, having for many years previous to that date been a resident of that state, and the owner of real property situate therein, and which by his last will he devised to his widow for life, and subject to the payment of one hundred dollars to each of the complainants; the remainder was to be divided among his four children. The claim of the complainants was that, while they and the decedent were residents and natives of the grand duchy of Hesse, an antenuptial agreement had been entered into between the decedent and Christina Hess, then the widow of one Bernhardt Lang; that the complainants were the children of the widow by her former marriage, and that by the antenuptial contract they had acquired interests in the estate of the decedent which he was not at liberty to dispose of by his will. The contract in question specified the property which the contracting parties then had; that the children of the bride by her first marriage should have an advancement of one hundred florins; that " as to every thing else the said two children of the first marriage and those begotten

in this marriage shall inherit equally, share and share alike.
In all other cases not especially enumerated herein the contracting parties subject themselves to the general laws of
Germany, especially the rules and customs of the country."
The marriage contract and the propriety and adequacy of
the allowance to the children appeared to have been the subject of further controversy before local tribunals in Germany,
the final result of which was a declaration by all the parties and sanctioned by the local authorities, among the provisions of which were: 1. "The groom, Jacob Hess, assumes
the parentage of the two children"; and 2. Their advancement was to be paid to them when they were twenty-five
years of age. The wife, Christina, in 1851, sold the property
which she then owned in Germany, and came with her husband and children, including the complainants, to America,
first settling in New York, and afterward, in the year 1858,
removed to La Salle county, Illinois. There she resided with
her husband up to the time of his death, and he accumulated
the property which is the subject of the controversy, and it
was not claimed that any portion of the proceeds of the property which she sold in Germany formed any part of the estate
which the husband owned at the time of his death. The
complainants contended that by the antenuptial contract
they had acquired vested rights in the estate of Jacob Hess
which he could not destroy by his will, and that they were,
notwithstanding such will, entitled to the same portion of his
estate as if he had died intestate. A decree was entered dismissing the bill of the complainants, from which they prosecuted this appeal.

Richolson & Seeley and *Brewer & Strawn,* for the appellants.

F. P. Snyder and *W. H. Stead, H. N. Ryon & Son,* for the
appellees.

⁴⁹⁰ BAILEY, J. The defendants, in whose favor the decree
was rendered, now urge, with a considerable degree of earnestness, that the court below erred in refusing to suppress the
deposition taken in Germany, on the ground that the manner in which it was taken was a clear departure from that
prescribed by the statute for taking the depositions of foreign
witnesses. All we need say upon that point is, that the
question thus raised is not before us for decision. The court
below refused to suppress the deposition, and considered it as

evidence on the final hearing, but upon all the evidence as thus presented the decision of the court was in the defendants' favor, and the complainants have appealed. The defendants have assigned no cross-errors, and they must, therefore, be deemed to be content with the decision of their motion to suppress, and so, for all the purposes of this appeal, the deposition, however irregularly it may have been taken, must be regarded as having been rightfully retained and considered as evidence at the hearing.

491 The only question presented by the record is as to the legal effect upon the property acquired by Jacob Hess in this state of the antenuptial contract entered into in Germany between him and his then intended wife. It is claimed that the contract, when considered in connection with the judicial proceedings had thereon, constituted, in legal effect, an adoption of the complainants by Hess, so as to place them upon the same footing, so far as succession to his property and estate was concerned, with the children afterward born of the marriage then in contemplation; and it is further contended that by the rules of law in force where the contract was made, and which entered into and formed a part of it, the property then owned by Hess and by his intended wife, as well as that afterward acquired by them, became communal property, in which the children of the family, both natural and adopted, acquired a vested right, and that Hess could not, by will, divest their right to succeed to such estate as he might leave at his death.

After considering all the evidence we are left in very grave doubt whether the laws of the grand duchy of Hesse, upon which reliance is placed, are sufficiently proved. But waiving that point, and assuming that the proof is sufficient, and that the rules of law prevailing in Hesse at the date of the contract were as the complainants contend, the question remains whether the antenuptial contract should be enforced in this state as to property, and especially real property, subsequently acquired by Hess in this state.

It should be remembered that at the date of the contract the parties were living at Beerfelden, in the grand duchy of Hesse, and, so far as appears, were intending to remain there permanently. There is nothing, either in the contract itself or in the evidence, having the least tendency to show that their removal to any other place was then contemplated. The evidence furnished by the contract is all in the direction

of showing that their intention [492] was to make Beerfelden
their permanent home. The agreement on the part of the
bride was "to receive the groom to live at her house," and
the contract, after certain stipulations as to the property
brought into the marriage by the groom, and as to the rights
of the children of the bride by her former marriage, concludes
with the provision that "in all other cases not especially
enumerated herein the contracting parties subject themselves
to the general laws of Germany, especially the rules and customs of the country." In point of fact Jacob Hess, after
his marriage, took up his residence at his wife's house, and
made that his domicile, and thereupon engaged at that
place in the business of a baker, which he carried on for
five years. He then sold out his property there and emigrated to the United States.

It should also be observed that there is a total absence of
any express provision in the contract making it applicable
to the future acquisitions of the contracting parties. It deals
with the property they then possessed, but makes no reference to such as they might afterward gain. The only language in the contract on which any reliance is placed as
having reference to future acquisitions is the following:
"As regards their worldly success and subsistence, the bride
agrees to receive the groom to live at her house." If these
words are correctly translated from the original German, in
which the contract was written—and we have heard no suggestion that they are not—they are, to say the least, extremely ambiguous, and we are able to put upon them no
rational construction which would make out of them an agreement to subject the future acquisitions of the parties to the
provisions of the contract. The most probable and natural
interpretation of the words would seem to be that, with a
view to providing for the worldly success and the subsistence
of the family, the bride agreed to receive the groom to live
at her house. They cannot, without importing into them
a meaning which does not appear upon their face, be held
[493] to have any direct reference to the future acquisitions
of the contracting parties, and especially their acquisitions
after emigrating from their then residence and making their
permanent domicile in a foreign country.

The property rights of husband and wife, as affected by
the marriage contract itself, or by an antenuptial agreement,
where the marriage or the antenuptial agreement has been

entered into in a foreign country, have always presented questions of no little perplexity and difficulty. Story, in his treatise on the Conflict of Laws, section 143, says: "The principal difficulty is not so much to ascertain what rule ought to govern in cases of express nuptial contract, at least where there is no change of domicile, as what rule ought to govern in cases where there is no such contract, or no contract which provides for the emergency. Where there is an express nuptial contract, that, if it speaks fully to the very point, will generally be admitted to govern all the property of the parties, not only in the matrimonial domicile, but in every other place, under the same limitations and restrictions as apply to other cases of contract. But where there is no express nuptial contract at all, or none speaking to the very point, the question, what rule ought to govern, is surrounded .with more difficulty." The learned author then, after an extended examination of the opinions of the leading law writers in this country and in Europe, and also of the decisions of the supreme court of Louisiana (the only court which, at that time, seems to have given these questions elaborate and careful consideration), lays down the following propositions, which, as he says, although not universally established or recognized in America, have much domestic authority for their support, and have none in opposition to them:

" 1. Where there is a marriage between parties in a foreign country, and an express contract respecting their rights and property, present and future, that, as a matter of contract, will be held equally valid everywhere, unless, [494] under the circumstances, it stands prohibited by the laws of the country where it is sought to be enforced. It will act directly on movable property everywhere. But as to immovable property in a foreign territory it will, at most, confer only a right of action, to be enforced according to the jurisprudence *rei sitæ*. 2. Where such an express contract applies, in terms or intent, only to present property, and there is a change of domicile, the law of the actual domicile will govern the rights of the parties as to all future acquisitions. 3. Where there is no express contract, the law of the matrimonial domicile will govern as to all the rights of the parties to their present property in that place, and as to all personal property everywhere, upon the principle that movables have no situs, or rather, that they accompany the person everywhere. As to immovable property the law *rei sitæ* will prevail. 4. Where there is no change of domicile the same rule will apply to future acquisitions as to present property. 5. But where there is a change of domicile the law of the actual domicile, and not the matrimonial domicile, will govern as to all future acquisitions of movable property, and as to all immovable property the law *rei sitæ*": Story on Conflict of Laws, sec. 184, et seq.

The propositions thus laid down by Judge Story seem to have received the general approval of the courts of this country, so far as there has been occasion to consider them since he wrote. Thus, in *Fuss* v. *Fuss*, 24 Wis. 256, 1 Am. Rep. 180, parties domiciled in Prussia were married there, and afterward entered into a postnuptial contract, whereby each granted and transferred to the other all real and personal property which should belong to the donator on the day of his death. The wife, at the time, owned real estate in Prussia, over which, by the laws of that country, she had full control and right of disposal. Several years afterward the property was sold, the husband taking the money and investing it in land in Wisconsin, to which the parties removed, and on which they resided until the [495] husband's death. He also, during his lifetime, acquired other property, both real and personal, situate in Wisconsin, which he owned on the day of his death. By his last will the husband devised and bequeathed all his property, both real and personal, to his widow for life, with remainder to the brothers and sisters of the testator. On bill filed by the widow, claiming that, by force of the postnuptial contract, she was entitled to an estate in fee in the lands, and to the absolute ownership of the personal property left by her husband, it was held that there was nothing in the contract which spoke to the very point; that it contained nothing which manifested any intention in the parties to regulate or control by it, according to the law of their matrimonial domicile, the future acquisitions and gains of property in any foreign state or territory, or any property which should be held by the husband in such state or territory, and, consequently, that the property acquired and owned by the husband in Wisconsin in his own name was subject to be disposed of by him, by will or otherwise, according to the laws of that state, and that the widow's rights therein were not determined by the contract.

In *Castro* v. *Illies*, 22 Tex. 479, 73 Am. Dec. 277, substantially the same doctrine was laid down, although, as that

case arose out of a controversy between a wife claiming under
an antenuptial contract and execution creditors of the husband, the decision is not in all respects so directly in point
as the one last cited. There parties domiciled in Paris,
France, executed an antenuptial contract and married in
Paris. Some years afterward they emigrated to this country
and became domiciled in Texas, where the husband subsequently acquired certain real property. It was claimed that
by the rules of the French law the contract vested in the
wife a certain interest in the property acquired by her husband which was not subject to seizure for her husband's
debts, but it was held that as there were in the contract no
words "speaking to the [496] very point"—that is, no words
making the contract specifically applicable to property subsequently acquired by the husband in state or country
foreign to that in which the contract was made—it had no
operation upon lands subsequently acquired by the husband
in Texas.

In *Besse* v. *Pellochoux*, 73 Ill. 285, 24 Am. Rep. 242, an
antenuptial contract was made between parties domiciled in
Switzerland in regard to property to be occupied during the
marriage, it appearing that the contract contemplated no
change of domicile, but was to be performed in the place
where it was made, and it was held that the contract did not
affect real estate acquired in this state by the husband after
their emigration to this country. In the opinion the doctrine
laid down by Judge Story was cited with approval, and it
was said that in that case there was nothing in the contract
" speaking to the very point"—that manifested any intention
that all future acquisitions of property in foreign countries
should be controlled by it: See, also, *Lyon* v. *Knott*, 26 Miss.
548; *Kneeland* v. *Ensley*, Meigs, 620; 33 Am. Dec. 168; *Saul*
v. *Creditors*, 5 Mart., N. S., 569; 16 Am. Dec. 212; *Le Breton*
v. *Miles*, 8 Paige, 261; *Gale* v. *Davis*, 4 Mart., O. S., 645.

The case of *Decouche* v. *Savetier*, 3 Johns. Ch. 190; 8 Am.
Dec. 478, is one where an antenuptial contract, entered into by
the parties in Paris, was enforced in this country in favor of
the wife, to the exclusion of the husband's relatives. But
there the contract expressly provided " that there shall be a
community of property between them, according to the custom of Paris, which is to govern the disposition of the property, though the parties should hereafter settle in countries
where the laws and usages are different or contrary." There

the intention to make the contract applicable to property afterward acquired in foreign countries was expressly made to appear by " words speaking to the very point."

Considerable reliance is placed by the complainants upon the case of *Scheferling* v. *Huffman*, 4 Ohio St. 241, 62 Am. Dec. 281, [497] where an antenuptial contract entered into by the parties in Germany, in which it was agreed that all the property of the intended wife which she then owned or which should be mutually acquired by the parties during coverture should be the property of the wife, was sustained and enforced, and held to apply to the property acquired by them in the state of Ohio after their emigration to this country. It will be noticed, however, that in that case the contract, by its express terms, was made applicable not only to the property then owned by the intended wife, but also to all property acquired during the continuance of the marriage. It is therefore clearly distinguishable from the present case, where no express provision is made applicable to property acquired in this state after the parties became domiciled here.

We are therefore of the opinion that the antenuptial contract in this case is not applicable to real property acquired by Hess in this state after his emigration to this country, but that such property was subject to disposition by him, by deed or will, according to the laws of this state. His will, therefore, must be held to be valid, so as to vest in his devisees a title which must prevail over any rights derived by the complainants from the antenuptial contract.

We are unable to see that any peculiar force is to be given to the fact that the complainants, at the time Jacob Hess and wife emigrated to this country, were infants, and therefore incapable of consenting to a change of their domicile, or of waiving any rights which were secured to them by the contract. As the contract cannot be held to have any application to the property sought to be reached in this case, no rights of theirs were affected by their being brought to this country, and they had nothing to waive. Even if it be admitted that, by reason of their legal adoption by Jacob Hess, they would have been entitled to succeed to his estate, at [498] his death, as his heirs at law, the antenuptial contract furnished no obstacle to the exercise by Hess of his right to dispose of his estate by will, and he having done so, nothing was left to descend to the complainants as his heirs at law. Although the complainants may have acquired the status of adopted children and heirs at law by the contract and judicial proceedings had in Germany, their inheritance of after-acquired real estate situated in this state must be in accordance with our laws, and by our laws a testator has an absolute right to dispose of his property by will, even to the exclusion alike of his natural or his adopted children.

We are of the opinion that the decree of the circuit court is justified by the evidence, and it will accordingly be affirmed.

———

ADOPTION—EXTRATERRITORIAL EFFECT OF.—A child adopted or legitimized can, outside of the jurisdiction of his adoption or legitimation, maintain no claim as heir of the person or persons to whom such law made him the lawful child or heir: *Van Matre v. Sankey*, 39 Am. St. Rep. 229.

———

HOBART *v.* HOBART.

[154 ILLINOIS, 610.]

WILLS.—THE PROOF OF A CODICIL TO A WILL ESTABLISHES THE WILL without further proof if both are written on the same paper, and the codicil clearly and unmistakably refers to the will so as to prevent all doubt of its identity. In such case the codicil operates as a republication of the will, and gives to it the same force as if it had been executed at the date of the codicil, the two instruments being regarded as one and their speaking from the date of the latter.

WILLS.—PROOF OF THE HANDWRITING OF A DECEASED WITNESS is *prima facie* sufficient, especially when the signatures of the witnesses are attached to a clause stating that the will was written, signed, and sealed in their presence.

WILLS.—IT IS NOT NECESSARY THAT A TESTATOR SHOULD HAVE ACKNOWLEDGED HIS SIGNATURE to the will if he produces a paper which he declares to be his will, and asks the witnesses to sign it, and states that it is not necessary for them to know what is in it.

WILLS—PRESUMPTION OF SIGNING.—If a testator produces a paper which he declares to be his last will, and asks the subscribing witnesses to sign it as such, and they do so in his presence, it will be presumed that it was already signed by him, though the witnesses cannot remember whether they saw his signature or not.

Ewing & Wight, for the appellant.

Kerrick & Spencer, for the appellees.

⁶¹² MAGRUDER, J. Harrison E. Hobart, of McLean county, died testate on December 22, 1892. On January 9, 1893, his widow, Lynda A. Hobart, presented his will and codicil thereto for probate to the county court of that county, where it was admitted to probate. From the order admitting it to

probate, the appellant here, Francke B. Hobart, one of the sons of the testator, took an appeal to the circuit court of said county. The circuit court, after evidence introduced and hearing had, affirmed the order of the county court, and directed that the will and codicil be admitted to probate. Upon appeal to the appellate court the latter court affirmed the order of the circuit court, and from the judgment of the appellate court the present appeal is prosecuted.

The original will was dated October 17, 1885. By its terms the testator gave and bequeathed to his wife, Lynda, all his real estate consisting of two tracts of land, one containing forty acres and the other containing sixty acres, and all his personal property, "including horses, cattle, moneys, credits, bank accounts," and to his sons, Howard E. Hobart and Francke B. Hobart, each the sum of one hundred dollars. The original will was signed "Harrison Earl Hobart [SEAL]." Its attesting clause and the subscriptions thereto are as follows:

"The above and foregoing instrument was, at the date thereof, signed, sealed, published and declared by the said Harrison Earl Hobart as and for his last will and testament, in presence of us, who, at his request and in his [613] presence, and in the presence of each other, have subscribed our names as witnesses.

"Mrs. Maris B. Howard, Farmer City, Ill.
"Marshal F. Howard, Farmer City, Ill."

The codicil to the will and the attesting clause and signatures thereto are as follows:

"CODICIL.

"The within will made this 9th day of June, one thousand eight hundred and eighty-eight (1888). I hereby will or give or direct that the property willed to my wife, Lynda Adams Hobart, in the within instrument, after her decease I give to my son, Howard Earl Hobart.

"HARRISON EARL HOBART. [L. S.]

"Written, signed, and sealed in the presence of
"Mordecia Tamling, Normal, McLean Co., Ill.
"Betsey A. Tamling, Normal, McLean Co., Ill."

1. Objection is made that the proof introduced was of the codicil only, and not of the will. It was shown that the original will and the codicil and attestations were all written upon the same paper. The codicil refers to the will, and

changes it in part only. When the codicil is written on the same paper as the will, or clearly and unmistakably refers to the will so as to preclude all doubt of its identity, proof of the codicil establishes the will without further proof, except such portions thereof as are revoked or altered by the codicil. In such case the codicil operates as a republication of the original will, and gives to it the same force as if it had been executed at the date of the codicil, the two instruments being regarded as one and as speaking from the date of the codicil. "Adding a codicil brings the will to it, and makes it a will from the time of executing the codicil": *Duncan* v. *Duncan*, 23 Ill. 364; 76 Am. Dec. 699; 1 Redfield on Law of Wills, marg. p. 288; 3 Am. & Eng. Ency. of Law, 301. It follows that, if the codicil in the case at bar was duly executed and attested, such portions of the original will as were not changed by it were thereby reaffirmed.

[*614] 2. Objection is made that the record does not show the testimony of the two subscribing witnesses to the codicil. It is proven that Mordecia Tamling, one of the subscribing witnesses to the codicil, died in February, 1890, more than two years before the death of the testator. The sixth section of the act in regard to wills (2 Starr and Curtis' Annotated Statutes, 2469) provides that "in all cases where any one or more of the witnesses to any will . . . . shall die or remove to parts unknown, so that his or her testimony cannot be procured, it shall be lawful . . . . to admit proof of the handwriting of any such deceased or absent witness, as aforesaid, and such other secondary evidence as is admissible in courts of justice to establish written contracts generally, in similar cases," etc. Here, Betsey A. Tamling, the other subscribing witness, swore that the signature of her husband, Mordecia Tamling, to the attestation of the codicil was in his handwriting. His handwriting was also proven by the testimony of two other witnesses. Proof of the handwriting of the deceased witness is *prima facie* sufficient, especially where the signatures of the witnesses are attached to an attesting clause that the will or codicil was written, signed, and sealed in their presence: *Ela* v. *Edwards*, 16 Gray, 91. The death of the witness merely changes the form of the proof. It permits secondary evidence to be introduced of the due attestation and execution of the will. The attestation is then to be shown, as it would be in case of deeds, by proof of the handwriting of the witness. As to him it is to be presumed,

that he duly attested the will in the presence of the testator. As was said by the supreme court of Massachusetts in *Nicker-son* v. *Buck*, 12 Cush. 332: "As regards this witness, if nothing appears in other parts of the evidence to control the presumption resulting from proof of his handwriting, it may be taken that, as to his attestation, it was properly made to the signature by the testator": *Robinson* v. *Brewster*, 140 Ill. 649; 33 Am. St. Rep. 265.

[615] Without deciding that, under section 6 above quoted, other secondary evidence besides proof of the handwriting of the deceased witness is necessary in all cases, it is sufficient to say that in this case there was such other secondary evidence. Betsey A. Tamling, the survivor of the subscribing witnesses, and two other witnesses swore in the circuit court that the signature to the will was in the handwriting of the testator. Counsel for appellant insist that the circuit court erred in receiving the evidence of the other witnesses besides Mrs. Tamling to the testator's signature, upon the ground that, under the decisions of this court, where the appeal is to the circuit court from an order of the probate court admitting the will to probate, the evidence in the circuit court to prove the will must be confined to that of the subscribing witnesses: *Andrews* v. *Black*, 43 Ill. 256; *Weld* v. *Sweeney*, 85 Ill. 50. This undoubtedly is the rule where both the subscribing witnesses are alive, or not in "parts unknown." But under the circumstances of this case, where one of the subscribing witnesses was deceased, we are inclined to think that proof, upon the hearing in the circuit court, of the testator's signature to the will by other testimony than that of the subscribing witness who survived, comes under what the statute denominates "such other secondary evidence as is admissible in courts of justice to establish written contracts generally in similar cases."

3. It is contended that the proof, introduced to establish the execution of the codicil, ought to have shown that the testator signed it in the presence of the attesting witnesses, or that he acknowledged the signature thereto to be his act and deed, and that the proponents were bound to show affirmatively that the will was signed when it was attested.

Section 2 of the act in regard to wills provides that "all wills . . . . shall be reduced to writing and signed by the testator or testatrix, or by some person in his or her presence, and by his or her direction, and attested in [616] the presence

of the testator or testatrix by two or more credible witnesses,
two of whom declaring on oath or affirmation, before the
county court of the proper county, that they were present and
saw the testator or testatrix sign said will, testament, or
codicil in their presence, or acknowledged the same to be his
or her act and deed, and that they believed the testator or
testatrix to be of sound mind and memory at the time of
signing or acknowledging the same, shall be sufficient proof
of the execution of said will, etc., to admit the same to record."

We think that the words "the same," following the word
"acknowledged," in section 2, refer back to the words "said
will," so that the clause would mean: "Or acknowledged the
said will to be his or her act and deed." The question has
sometimes arisen, whether, under a local statute or code, the
requirement is that the testator acknowledge the signature to
the will to be his act and deed, or that he acknowledge the
will to be his act and deed. In England the statute of 1
Victoria upon this subject requires the signature of the testator to be made or acknowledged: 1 Jarman on Wills, marg.
pp. 83, 84. In New York, and perhaps in some of the other
states, the statute requires that there must be an acknowledgment of the signature: Schouler on Wills, 2d ed., sec.
325. Decisions based upon these statutes have held, in substance, that there is not a sufficient acknowledgment of the
signature by the testator when he produces a will and requests the witnesses to sign it, unless his signature is visibly
apparent on the face of the paper, and is seen, or can be seen,
by the witnesses, especially if he does not explain the instrument to them: Schouler on Wills, 2d ed., secs. 321–325; 1
Williams on Executors, marg. p. 88; 1 Jarman on Wills,
Bigelow's 6th ed., marg. p. 84. But we are inclined to think
that these decisions are not applicable where the statute, as
is the case with that in this state, merely requires that the
testator acknowledged the will or codicil to be his act and
deed, and [617] does not specifically and in terms require the
signature to be acknowledged. A man may acknowledge an
entire written instrument to be his act and deed without
necessarily calling the attention of those before whom he
produces it to any particular part of such instrument. But
if he is required to make acknowledgment of a specified part
of it, it may be requisite that attention should be directed to
that part.

Mrs. Tamling swore that her signature to the attesting clause was in her handwriting, and her husband's in his handwriting; that the testator and his wife brought the will to her house and were both present in the room when it was signed by the witnesses; that she and her husband signed it as witnesses in a few moments of each other; that the signature to the will produced in court is the signature of the testator; that she signed it in her own house; that the testator had it when she and her husband first saw it; that the testator and his wife were going away, and wanted us to sign the will before they went; that "we were talking about it altogether"; that "they laid it on the table, and when he got ready to take it, he took it up"; that he was certainly of sound mind and memory when she signed her name; "we were talking that he was going away he was making preparation to go out, and his will was made, and he came there, and wanted we should sign the will; he said that it was not necessary for us to know what was in the will; he said he had talked with a lawyer, and if you was acquainted with a person so as to trust their word you could sign it; we knew it was his will; they said they wanted us to sign the will; I saw nothing but the place to write our names; there was nothing said about whether Mr. Hobart had signed it; as to seeing where he had signed it we did n't pay any attention to that; he did not sign it in our presence; it was all done before he came there; he did no writing after he came there; I suppose I saw his signature, but I paid no attention to it; 618 I can't say positively whether I saw his signature or not; I did n't think any thing about it; I sat down to write my name; there were papers laid on the will; we did n't move it; I don't know whether it was designed to conceal it; there was room enough for us to see to write—that was all that I know any thing about; there was some talk that there was no danger about signing any thing when the individual told us what was in the document we put our names to; I did n't ask him any questions; I can't say positively that I did n't see whether it was signed or not; I did n't think any thing about that; we had advised, and we had talked about various things; Mr. Hobart told us it was his will and wanted us to witness it; whether he had signed it at that time or not I don't think there was any thing said about any thing like it; I supposed of course it was straight and all right; I have no distinct recollection of our attention being called to the question whether or not he had signed it; there was nothing said about it."

While it is true that the witness cannot remember seeing the signature, yet she cannot say positively that she did not see it. It is clear, however, that the testator produced before the subscribing witnesses an instrument in writing which· he stated to be his will, and asked them to sign it as witnesses. A will must be reduced to writing, and signed by the testator, or by some one in his presence and under his direction. The words "said will," in section 2, refer back to a will reduced to writing and signed. An instrument not in writing and not signed is not a will. When the testator called the paper his will, it will be presumed, in the absence of any evidence to the contrary, that he had signed it, inasmuch as a signature was necessary to justify him in calling it a will. Included in the declaration of the testator to the witnesses that the paper was his will was the further declaration that he had signed it. Where the testator declares to the witnesses that the instrument is his will, [619] or requests them to attest his will, such declaration or request implies that the same has been signed by him: *Nickerson* v. *Buck*, 12 Cush. 332. In the latter case it was said: "The request to these witnesses to attest his will was quite enough to authorize the inference that he had executed a paper as a will, and was equivalent to his acknowledgment that he had signed some paper as a will." The fact that a testator seeks the attestation of witnesses and gives directions to them as to signing their names, furnishes strong presumptive proof that he had signed the will: *Dewey* v. *Dewey*, 1 Met. 349; 35 Am. Dec. 367. Where a testator took a paper from his desk and asked a witness to sign it, and pointed out the place where he wished him to put his name, and the witness did so, not knowing what the paper was, and not noticing the signature on the paper, it was held that there was a good attestation of the will: *Ela* v. *Edwards*, 16 Gray, 91.

In addition to the presumption that the testator, Hobart, had signed the will, arising from his declaration that it was his will, and from his request to the witnesses to sign it, there is proof that the signature to the will produced is his, and that the two subscribing witnesses signed the attestation clause in his presence. Thus, a *prima facie* case is made in favor of the due execution of the will; and this *prima facie* case is not overcome by the mere fact that the subscribing witness here testifying failed to notice whether the will was signed or not, and cannot remember whether she saw the signature or not: *Mundy* v. *Mundy*, 15 N. J. Eq. 292; *Raudebaugh* v. *Shelley*, 6 Ohio St. 307; *Hogan* v. *Grosvenor*, 10 Met. 56; 43 Am. Dec. 414; *Osborn* v. *Cook*, 11 Cush. 532; 59 Am. Dec. 155; *Dickie* v. *Carter*, 42 Ill. 376; *Allison* v. *Allison*, 46 Ill. 61; 92 Am. Dec. 237; *Holloway* v. *Galloway*, 51 Ill. 159; *Yoe.* v. *McCord*, 74 Ill. 33; *Canatsey* v. *Canatsey*, 130 Iil. 397.

We are inclined to hold that the evidence was sufficient to authorize the admission of the will to probate.

Accordingly, the judgment of the appellate court is affirmed.

WILLS—PROOF OF BY PROOF OF CODICIL.—Proof of a codicil establishes the will, or such portions of it as are not revoked by the codicil, when the codicil is written on the same paper as the will, or clearly refers to and identifies the will: *Duncan* v. *Duncan*, 23 Ill. 364; 76 Am. Dec. 699, and note. A codicil duly executed, if attached to a paper which was never signed, attested, and published as a will, will have the effect of giving force and operation to the whole as one will: *Beall* v. *Cunningham*, 3 B. Mon. 390; 39 Am. Dec. 469.

WILLS—ATTESTATION—PROVING HANDWRITING OF WITNESSES.—If the witnesses to a will cannot be found, their handwriting may be proved, and the jury left to determine whether the will was published with the requisite formalities: *Pearson* v. *Wightman*, 1 Mill Coust. 336; 12 Am. Dec. 636. If the witnesses to a will are dead or beyond the jurisdiction of the court their handwriting should be proved: *Jackson* v. *Vickory*, 1 Wend. 406; 19 Am. Dec. 522; *Tynan* v. *Paschal*, 27 Tex. 286; 84 Am. Dec. 619.

WILLS—SUBSCRIBING WITNESSES—NECESSITY FOR KNOWLEDGE OF CONTENTS OF WILL.—A will need not be read by or to the subscribing witnesses, nor is it necessary that they should know its contents: *Higdon's Will*, 6 J. J. Marsh. 444; 22 Am. Dec. 84.

WILLS—EXECUTION OF.—It is not necessary that a subscribing witness should see the testator sign the will. It is sufficient that the will be produced, signed by the testator, and in such a way that his signature may be seen by the witnesses, and that he request them to witness it as his will: *Simmons* v. *Leonard*, 91 Tenn. 183; 30 Am. St. Rep. 875, and note. But see on this subject, *Matter of Mackay*, 110 N. Y. 611; 6 Am. St. Rep. 409.

CASES

IN THE

SUPREME COURT

OF

INDIANA.

SPRINGER v. BYRAM.

[137 Indiana, 15.]

APPEAL—WHEN ASSIGNMENT OF ERROR MAY BE CONSIDERED AS A WHOLE. On an appeal from a judgment of the superior court in general term, reversing a judgment of that court in special term overruling a motion for a new trial, the assignment of error in general term being that the court in special term erred in overruling appellant's motion for a new trial, which was sustained as a whole, and not by piecemeal, the supreme court may consider such assignment as a whole.

APPEAL—BILL OF EXCEPTIONS—MOTION FOR NEW TRIAL.—The supreme court is not precluded from considering a statement of offered evidence in a motion for a new trial, because of a slight difference between the phraseology of the motion and that of the bill of exceptions relating to the statement of testimony offered to be proved, if the substance is the same in each.

PHYSICIAN AND PATIENT.—COMMUNICATIONS MADE BY A PATIENT to his physician for the purpose of professional aid and advice are privileged. The immunity extends to all facts, whether learned directly from the patient, or acquired by the physician through his own observation or examinations.

WITNESSES—PHYSICIAN AND PATIENT—PRIVILEGE AS TO CONVERSATION HEARD BY THIRD PERSON.—Third persons who hear conversations between parties sustaining confidential relations to each other, as physician and patient, whether such third persons are necessarily present as officers or as indifferent bystanders, may testify to what they heard.

ELEVATOR ACCIDENT—NEGLIGENCE—NOTICE OF RULES.—In an action for damages incurred by the plaintiff, a newsboy, while attempting to take passage in an elevator, it is competent, where the question of negligence is at issue, to show that plaintiff was notified, prior to the accident, of the fact that newsboys were not allowed to ride in the elevator, and that he could not do so.

W. V. Rooker and H. Dailey, for the appellant.

G. W. Stubbs and C. E. Averill, for the appellees.

[16] DAILEY, J. This is an action for personal injuries alleged to have been sustained by the appellant, while being transported in a passenger elevator in a public office building owned and operated by the appellees.

The facts disclosed by the record in this cause briefly stated are these:

In November, 1889, the appellees, Byram and Cornelius, were the owners of an office building situated on East Market street, in the city of Indianapolis. The north half of this building was four stories in height, including the basement, and the south half but three stories. The building was known as the "Thorpe Block," and was rented for office purposes to attorneys and persons of other occupations. Each half of the block was provided with convenient stairways, giving access to each floor of the block, and, in the north half, was also situated a passenger elevator, in use for the convenience and benefit of appellees' tenants, and also giving access to each of the four floors of the block. The elevator was [17] propelled by hydraulic pressure, and moved in a shaft built for that purpose, next to the west wall of the building. This shaft was separated from the halls, on the several floors, by sliding doors of open wire, the rest of the opening of the several halls being protected by either wirework or paneled woodwork. The elevator was operated by a person employed by the appellees for that purpose, who controlled its movements by means of a rope which opened and closed the valves of the hydraulic apparatus, and which passed through the car near the door of ingress and egress. The appellant, Harry M. Springer, was a boy of the age of twelve years and six months, attending the public schools and selling newspapers in the afternoons.

On the twenty-third day of November, 1889, the appellant was in the Thorpe Block, and on what is known as the second floor, and attempted to enter the elevator. In making this attempt he fell partly upon the floor of the elevator, and was carried up and against the framework over the door, receiving injuries, to recover damages for which this action was brought.

Appellant's complaint is in three paragraphs: 1. Charging negligence of defendants in the use of their property and premises, in the matter complained of; 2. Charging willful and wanton disregard of plaintiff's situation by the defendants, while he was on and using their property and premises;

3. Charging defendants with negligence as carriers of the plaintiff.

Each paragraph shows that plaintiff was rightfully on the premises, and each also charges a resulting injury to the plaintiff without his fault. A demurrer, for want of facts was filed to the second and third paragraphs of the complaint, and overruled, and defendants answered in general denial.

[18] Upon these issues the cause was tried at the March term, 1891, of the superior court of Marion county, before a jury, which returned a verdict for the appellant.

Appellees filed a motion for a new trial, which was overruled, and judgment was rendered and entered on the verdict. From this judgment, at special term, appellees appealed to the general term of the superior court, where the judgment at special term was reversed for error in overruling appellees' motion for a new trial. From this judgment of reversal at the general term the appellant has appealed to this court, and by proper assignment of error has presented for review the correctness of the decision of the court in general term in reversing the judgment of the special term, and directing a new trial of the cause.

From the opinion of the court in general term it appears that the only question presented by the assignment of errors in general term, which was considered and determined by the court, was the action of the court, in special term, in overruling appellee's motion for a new trial. The overruling of that motion by the court, in special term, was held to be erroneous, and the assignment of error made in this court presents for review all matters properly assigned as errors in the motion for a new trial. Appellant's brief proceeds upon the theory that the only matters which this court can consider on this appeal are the particular points or reasons in the motion for a new trial, which the opinion of the court in general term shows were expressly considered by that court, and which that opinion shows were the basis of the action of the general term in reversing the judgment at special term. To this theory we cannot give assent. Clearly it was not incumbent upon the court in general term, after it had found an error for which the judgment in special term should be reversed, to investigate [19] the sufficiency of the remaining reasons for a new trial, and pass upon the questions as to whether or not they were severally well taken. The instruc-

tions of the general term, as shown by its judgment, required
the court, in special term, to sustain the defendant's motion
for a new trial. This, we think, clearly indicates the error
for which the judgment was reversed, and appellant's assignment of error, in this court, brings to us for review all
the questions properly presented by appellees' motion for a
new trial. In other words, the judgment of the court, in general term, sufficiently shows the decision of that court to
have been that there was error of the court in special term,
in refusing to sustain the motion, as stated, of the appellees
for a new trial.

A new trial was ordered upon a consideration of the errors
assigned by the appellees in general term, viz: "3. The court,
in special term, erred in overruling appellant's motion for a
new trial of this cause."

The general term found this assignment of error well taken,
and sustained it as a whole—not in piecemeal; and there was
no ruling of the court in general term upon which these
appellees had any reason to assign cross-errors. The questions
presented to the general term were those presented by the
assignment of errors in that court.

In the case of *Wesley* v. *Milford*, 41 Ind. 413 (416), it is
said: " The appeal to this court being allowed from the judgment of the general term only, we think it must follow that
whatever errors are assigned in this court must be predicated
upon the assignment of errors in the general term, and the
action of that court in general term thereon."

This being so, it is clear that the action of the court in
general term, upon the errors assigned in that court, is what
this court passes upon, and not the several and [20] particular
matters which may have been embraced and covered by the
assignments of error in the special term. To present to this
court questions which were presented in the motion for a new
trial, and to separate and set apart for the consideration of
the court a portion of the reasons assigned in such motion,
is equivalent to presenting to this court, for the first time,
as grounds for reversal, matters which must be assigned as
reason for a new trial.

The appellant's assignment of error in this court and his
complaint here is: "That said general term of said court
erred in reversing the judgment of the special term of said
superior court, and remanding said cause for another trial to
said special term."

The question is not whether the reasons given by the court are sound or unsound, but, rather, upon a consideration of the matters presented by the assignment of errors in the general term, Did the court reach a right conclusion and enter a judgment to which these appellees were entitled, upon the errors assigned in that court?

The first assignment in appellees' motion for a new trial embraces alleged errors of law occurring and excepted to by the defendants at the time, and comprised in subdivisions "A" to "S," inclusive.

The first three subdivisions each relate to the correctness of the ruling of the trial court in excluding the testimony of the two witnesses, Scott and Goth, with reference to a conversation sought to be proved, between the appellant and Dr. Sutcliffe, in the ambulance, almost immediately after the accident, in the presence and hearing of the witnesses interrogated, in reference thereto, and included the statement of the appellant as to the manner in which his injuries were received. The objection to the offered testimony was sustained upon [21] the theory that it was incompetent to prove a conversation between a physician and his patient.

In defining who are incompetent to testify, section 497 of the Revised Statutes of 1881 reads: " 3. Attorneys, as to confidential communications made to them in the course of their professional business, and as to advice given in such cases; 4. Physicians, as to matter communicated to them, as such, by patients, in the course of their professional business, or advice given in such cases."

It has been held that communications made through a third person from a client to a solicitor are privileged, if otherwise entitled to be so. Also, whoever represents a lawyer in confidence or correspondence with the client, is under the same protection as the lawyer himself. The privilege extends to the attorney's clerk, interpreter, assistant attorney, or other agent while in the discharge of his duty: 19 Am. & Eng. Ency. of Law, 131, 132.

At common law confidential communications made by a patient to a physician are not privileged. The common law in this state has been changed by statute: 19 Am. & Eng. Ency. of Law, 131, 132.

It was said, in *Masonic Mut. etc. Assn.* v. *Beck*, 77 Ind. 203, 40 Am. Rep. 295, that the object of these statutes seems to be to place the communications made to physicians in the course

of their professional employment upon the same footing with
communications made by clients to their attorneys in the
course of their employment.

"The privilege may attach, notwithstanding the presence
of third persons in the sickroom, where the consultation is
had ": *Cahen v. Continental etc. Ins. Co.*, 41 N. Y. Super. Ct.
296.

If the attending physician calls in another physician for
consultation the communications made to the latter [22] are
privileged: *Ætna Life Ins. Co. v. Deming*, 123 Ind. 384; *Ray-
mond v. Burlington etc. Ry. Co.*, 65 Iowa, 152; *Renihan v.
Dennin*, 103 N. Y. 573; 57 Am. Rep. 770.

Where there are two physicians the patient does not, by
calling one of his physicians as a witness, waive his privilege
to object to the testimony of the other: *Pennsylvania etc. Ins.
Co. v. Wiler*, 100 Ind. 92; 50 Am. Rep. 769; *Mellor v. Missouri
Pac. Ry. Co.*, 105 Mo. 455; *Record v. Village of Saratoga
Springs*, 46 Hun, 448.

Communications made by a patient to his physician, for
the purpose of professional aid and advice, are privileged,
because intended to be private and confidential, and can never
be divulged without the consent of the patient, it being the
privilege of the patient, and not of the physician. The privilege of exemption from testifying to declarations made and
facts actually known is extended to a physician who derives
his knowledge from the communications of a patient who
applies and makes disclosures to him in his professional
character. The immunity extends to all such facts, whether
learned directly from the patient himself or acquired by the
physician through his own observation or examination: 7
Am. & Eng. Ency. of Law, 508.

Neither can disclosures be made by other persons whose
intervention is strictly necessary to enable the parties to
communicate with each other.

In *Cotton v. State*, 87 Ala. 75, the court said: "The rule
as to the inviolability of professional confidences applies, as
between attorney and client, only to communications made
and received for the purposes of professional action and aid,
and the secrecy imposed extends to no other persons than
those sustaining to each other the confidential relationship,
except the necessary organs of communication between them,
such as interpreters and their own agents and clerks."

[22] Further it does not extend. It is settled law that if

parties sustaining confidential relations to each other hold their conversation in the presence and hearing of third persons, whether they be necessarily present as officers or indifferent bystanders, such third persons are not prohibited from testifying to what they heard: *Cotton* v. *State*, 87 Ala. .75; *House* v. *House*, 61 Mich. 69; 1 Am. St. Rep. 570; *In re McCarthy*, 55 Hun, 7; *Commonwealth* v. *Griffin*, 110 Mass. 181; *Hoy* v. *Morris*, 13 Gray, 519; 74 Am. Dec. 650; *Oliver* v. *Pate*, 43 Ind. 132 (142); Wharton's Criminal Evidence, sec. 398; 1 Lawson's Rights, Remedies, and Practice, sec. 147.

From the record it appears that the witnesses Scott and Goth, whose testimony was rejected or excluded by the court, were employees of one C. E. Kregelo, an undertaker, of the city of Indianapolis, who sent an ambulance to convey the appellant to his home, and these witnesses were in charge of it. It does not appear from the transcript that they were in the employ of either the physician or the injured party, or that even their principal was attending him for hire. Scott and Goth were, for aught that appears, disinterested bystanders, and were competent to testify, and the weight of their statements was to be determined by the jury.

Counsel for appellant seek to shut out the consideration of this question because of slight differences between the phraseology of the motion for a new trial and that of the bill of exceptions, relating to the testimony offered to be proved by the appellees. The offer, on the trial, is in these words: " Now we offer to prove, may the court please, by this witness (Scott), that in the ambulance, in the presence of this witness and Dr. Sutcliffe and of Mr. Goth, this boy, the plaintiff in this case, stated that he attempted to get on the elevator while it was in motion, and that that was the way in which he got hurt, and, further, that nobody was to blame; that [24] his brother said that nobody was to blame except himself; that it was his own fault; that he tried to get on the elevator while it was in motion; and that he was playing in the halls at the time, and had been playing about the elevator."

The words, as made in the motion for a new trial, are: " We offer to prove . . . that in the ambulance, in the presence of this witness and Dr. Sutcliffe and Mr. Goth, this boy (the plaintiff in this case) stated that he attempted to get into the elevator while it was in motion; and that that was the way he got hurt, and, further, that nobody was to blame except himself; that it was his own fault; that he was hurt in trying to get into the elevator while it was in motion; and that he was playing in the halls at the time, and had been playing about the elevator."

In the late case of *Ohio etc. Ry. Co.* v. *Stein,* 133 Ind. 243, it is said: "It is not the practice, and it is not incumbent on a party, in a motion for a new trial, to set out in detail a verbatim copy of the evidence admitted over objection, or offered and refused, or a verbatim statement of the objections made to its introduction. It is sufficient if the evidence be referred to with such certainty as to call the attention of the court to it, and to the ruling in relation thereto, so that the judge could not mistake the matter and the ruling alluded to and complained of by the party filing the motion." We also cite *Clark* v. *Bond,* 29 Ind. 555 (557); *Meyer* v. *Bohlfing,* 44 Ind. 238 (239).

We think the statement of the offered evidence, in the motion for a new trial, was sufficiently explicit to inform the court of the question sought to be raised by the motion. The matter offered to be proved in the trial court was not objectionable because it sought to incorporate a [25] statement of the brother, made in the ambulance, in the presence of the appellant.

If statements are made in the presence and hearing of a person affecting his rights, and under such circumstances as call for a reply, what he said, or if he failed to say any thing, may be proven as in the nature of an admission: *Pierce* v. *Goldsberry,* 35 Ind. 317; *Puett* v. *Beard,* 86 Ind. 104; *Surber* v. *State,* 99 Ind. 71; *Broyles* v. *State,* 47 Ind. 251; *Conway* v. *State,* 118 Ind. 482.

In 1 Rice on Evidence, page 424, the author says: "The act or declaration of another person, and within the observation of a party, and his conduct in relation thereto, is relevant if, under all the circumstances of the case, he would have been likely to have been affected by the act or the declaration."

Subdivision F calls in question the ruling of the court in sustaining the appellant's objection to the following question propounded to Earl Spain, a witness called on behalf of appellees: "If, at any time, say the week before the day he was hurt, he tried to get into the elevator, tell the jury what you said to him."

Appellees then offered to prove by the witness, in answer to the above question, that "about a week before this acci-

dent occurred, the appellant did try to get in, and asked to
get in, the elevator, and was then told that he would not be
allowed to; that newsboys were not allowed to ride in that
elevator, and that he could not; and that he did, in spite of
that injunction, get in, and was put out."

This evidence was excluded on the ground that it was not
material and competent under the issues in this case.

The only issue tendered by the complaint was that of negligence. Under the allegations of the complaint [26] charging
negligence it was incumbent upon the appellant, in order to
charge the appellees with a breach of duty toward him, to
show that he was rightfully attempting to use the elevator
in the Thorpe Block. If his attempted use of that elevator
was wrongful, then the only legal duty on the part of the
appellees was not to willfully injure him. If it was necessary for appellant to show that he was rightfully attempting
to use the same, then clearly appellees had the right to have
any evidence which tended to show that appellant was not
rightfully engaged in its use go to the jury, under the general denial.

It will be observed, from a reading of the several paragraphs of the complaint, that it charges these appellees, as
carriers of passengers, with a breach of duty on their part as
such, in this, that "plaintiff was invited by the defendants
to enter said elevator, and be transported therein."

Under the issue tendered by the complaint it was only
necessary for the appellant to show an implied invitation on
the part of the appellees for him to enter and be transported
therein; and, if this be true, then certainly it was competent
for appellees to show that appellant was notified of the fact
prior to the accident, that newsboys were not allowed to ride
in the elevator, and that he could not do so. If, as a matter
of fact, he had been so warned; if he knew that appellees
did not allow newsboys to ride in the elevator, in what respect was there a rightful attempt, on his part, to use the
elevator contrary to the knowledge which he had? The
mere fact that he was permitted to enter the building and
ply his vocation of newsboy cannot alone be held to bind
the appellees to carry him in their elevator, whether they
wished or not. It would be just as reasonable to conclude
that if a person were admitted upon a train of [27] cars as
a passenger, and provided with a passenger-car, he could
insist upon and be at liberty to ride in the baggage-car or

upon an engine, or occupy a berth in a sleeper without a
permit. If the appellees had a rule with respect to their
elevator, by which they required the person in charge to refuse
its use to newsboys in the building, such rule would have to
be brought to the attention or knowledge of the boy in
some way before he would be bound by such rule; but we
think it is clear that after he has been apprised of appellees'
rule, to the effect that he cannot be carried in their elevator,
it would be binding upon him. This rule has been uniformly sustained in the case of common carriers of passengers, and where a passenger has taken a position upon a
train contrary to known rules of the carrier to the contrary,
and has been injured in consequence of the violation of such
rules, it has been held without exception, we believe, that
there was no right of recovery. It has also been frequently
held that where a person is invited to ride upon a train of
cars by an employee who had no authority to give such invitation, the party accepting the same was either a trespasser
or a mere licensee, to whom the carrier owed no duty to
exercise care: *Waterbury* v. *New York etc. R. R. Co.*, 21
Blatchf. 314; 17 Fed. Rep. 671; *Eaton* v. *Delaware etc. R. R.
Co.*, 57 N. Y. 382; 15 Am. Rep. 513; *Duff* v. *Allegheny etc.
R. R. Co.*, 91 Pa. St. 458; 36 Am. Rep. 675; *Woodruff* v.
Bowen, 136 Ind. 431; *Pennsylvania R. R. Co.* v. *Langdon*, 92
Pa. St. 21; 37 Am. Rep. 651; *Hickey* v. *Boston etc. R. R. Co.*,
14 Allen, 429; *Gulf etc. Ry. Co.* v. *Campbell*, 76 Tex. 174;
Faris v. *Hoberg*, 134 Ind. 269; 39 Am. St. Rep. 261; *Fluker*
v. *Georgia etc. Co.*, 81 Ga. 461; 12 Am. St. Rep. 328; *Robert-
son* v. *New York etc. R. R. Co.*, 22 Barb. 91; *Chicago etc. Ry.
Co.* v. *West*, 125 Ill. 320; 8 Am. St. Rep. 380; *Cooper* v. *Lake
Erie etc. R. R. Co.*, 136 Ind. 366.

Under the issues it was certainly a material fact which
[28] the appellees had a right to show, whether or not this
appellant had knowledge, a week before the injury, of the
fact that newsboys were not allowed in the elevator. It
tended to negative any proof he might have offered, showing
he was rightfully attempting to ride at the time of the accident complained of, and also tended to show that as to any
use of the elevator he was a trespasser.

The refusal of the court, at the special term, to admit this
testimony deprived appellees of a valuable element of their
defense that there was no invitation to appellant to ride, and
that he was not permitted to do so. It was harmful error to

sustain appellant's objection to the question and exclude the evidence offered.

Subdivision "Q" of the first reason for a new trial challenges instruction number 3, and, indeed, the whole series of instructions is criticised by the appellees, but this opinion has already been extended beyond the limits intended, and we will not consider the objections presented to the instructions.

We think the decision of the court in general term, reversing the judgment of the special term, correct, and it is affirmed.

PHYSICIAN AND PATIENT—PRIVILEGED COMMUNICATIONS—WHAT ARE NOT.—Communications made to physicians in the course of their professional employment stand upon the same footing as communications made by clients to their attorneys in the course of their employment. A communication made by a patient to a physician, in order to be privileged, must be made to the latter for the purpose of enabling him to perform his professional duty: See monographic note to *Thompson* v. *Ish*, 17 Am. St. Rep. 565–571, on when a physician may and may not testify; note to *Birmingham Union Ry. Co.* v. *Hale*, 24 Am. St. Rep. 752. A conversation between two persons in the presence of an attorney employed by them to draw a paper in connection with the subject of the conversation is not privileged: See note to *Hanson* v. *Bean*, 38 Am. St. Rep. 519.

ELEVATOR ACCIDENTS.—If any considerable doubt exists as to whether or not the plaintiff is guilty of contributory negligence that question should be submitted to the jury for its determination: *People's Bank* v. *Morgolofski*, 75 Md. 432; 32 Am. St. Rep. 403, and note.

WILMORE *v.* STETLER.

[137 INDIANA, 127.]

ESTOPPEL—GUARDIAN AND WARD—HEIRS—ACCEPTING PROCEEDS OF UNAUTHORIZED SALE OF LANDS.—Heirs who, with knowledge, accept the proceeds of an unauthorized sale of their lands are estopped from disputing the validity of the sale. They cannot retain the purchase money and also recover the land. Hence, where the guardian of a woman of unsound mind sold certain land, under order of court, having alleged, under oath, that it all belonged to his ward, when in fact she owned but a one-third interest therein with her children, the heirs of her deceased husband, and the guardian, after the death of his ward, paid to the heirs their full share of such proceeds, after they became of age, which they accepted, knowing what their interest in the land was, and that such money was the proceeds of the sale of their interests therein, and their full shares thereof; such facts show a ratification of the sale by the heirs, and estop them from attacking its validity. They cannot retain the proceeds of the sale, and recover their two-thirds interest in the land.

J. W. Ryan, W. A. Thompson, A. O. Marsh, J. W. Thompson, J. T. France, and *J. T. Merryman,* for the appellants.

J. Morris, R. C. Bell, J. M. Barrett, and *S. M. Morris,* for the appellee.

[127] OLDS, J. The appellants brought this action in the court below, averring in their complaint that one Addison G. Wilmore died testate, at the county of Adams, seised of certain real estate; that he left surviving him, as his heirs at law, his widow, Eleanor, appellants, and Ellen, who died in 1871, his children.

A copy of the will is set out, and it is charged that the widow took under the law, and not under the will; that in 1868, after the death of her husband, Eleanor was declared [128] of unsound mind, and a guardian was appointed for her; that the guardian applied to the Randolph common pleas court for an order to sell the real estate of which Wilmore died seised; that the court ordered the guardian to sell the interest of his ward in the lands he had described in his petition; that said Eleanor had no interest in the real estate except the one-third interest inherited from her husband; that the appellants had never transferred or conveyed the interest in this real estate, which had descended from their father and sister Ellen; that the guardian of Eleanor pretended to sell the entire fee of the real estate; that one Lewis Edwards purchased the real estate at guardian's sale; that at the time he purchased he had notice and knowledge that appellants, and the sister since dead, had and held an interest in said real estate, as the heirs at law of Addison G. Wilmore; that Lewis Edwards afterward conveyed a part of this real estate to appellee, who holds possession of said part, and claims the entire fee therein, and denies appellants' right and title to said real estate, or any part thereof; that the claim of appellee is a cloud upon the appellants' interest in, and title to, said real estate.

The relief asked was for partition, to quiet title, and possession of their interest in the land.

A demurrer was filed to the complaint, which was overruled, and the appellee answered in six paragraphs.

The appellants demurred to paragraphs of answer, and the court overruled the demurrer to the second, fourth, and fifth paragraphs of answer, to which ruling the appellants excepted.

The fourth paragraph pleads the fifteen years' statute of limitation, and the fifth paragraph pleads the twenty years' statute. They are general pleas of the statutes, alleging that the cause of action did not accrue within the fifteen and twenty years, without alleging adverse [129] possession. It is contended by appellants that the complaint is for partition between tenants in common, and that the answers are not good, while the appellee contends that the action is not for partition, but for possession and to quiet title, and even if held to be in partition the paragraphs of answer are good.

There was a special verdict returned finding the facts, and owing to the view we take of the case it matters not whether there was error in ruling on the demurrers to these paragraphs of answer or not, for if error it was harmless. We have recently considered and passed upon the question as to the sufficiency of answers of this character in actions for partition, in the case of *Peden* v. *Cavens*, 134 Ind. 494; 39 Am. St. Rep. 276: See, also, *Patterson* v. *Nixon*, 79 Ind. 251 (256); *Nutter* v. *Hawkins*, 93 Ind. 260; Wood's Limitations of Actions, sec. 266, p. 559.

The next question discussed by counsel relates to the sufficiency of the second paragraph of answer.

The complaint sets out a copy of the will; alleges the death of the testator; the survivorship of the widow and children; the insanity of the widow; the appointment of Adamson as her guardian; the petition to sell the real estate, including that in controversy. The petition to sell, which is sworn to, alleges that Mrs. Wilmore owned the land in fee simple. The answer admitted the foregoing facts. It averred that the court ordered the whole of said real estate to be sold by the guardian; that the guardian did, pursuant to the order of the court, cause the fee simple of said land to be sold for three thousand five hundred dollars, being four hundred dollars more than its appraised and actual value in fee simple, to Lewis Edwards; that the sale was reported to, and approved and confirmed by, said court; that one-third of the purchase money was paid in hand and the balance properly secured and afterward paid and the [130] land conveyed to said Edwards; that some five hundred dollars of interest accrued on the purchase was applied to the support of the appellants and their insane mother, in accordance with the terms of the will of Addison P. Wilmore; that the said Adamson ceased to be guardian of said insane widow; that one Bodkins, the uncle of Mrs. Wilmore was appointed the successor of said Adamson in said trust, to whom Adamson paid the money by him received as the purchase money of said land, being four thousand one hundred and forty-six dollars and more; that after the appellants became of full age, and after the death of Mrs. Wilmore, the said Bodkins settled with them and paid to each over one thousand dollars, being the purchase money of said land received by him from said Adamson; that said appellants accepted said money so paid them by said Bodkins, knowing it to be the proceeds of the sale of said real estate, and knowing at the same time what their interest in said real estate was, and that the money received and accepted by them was the proceeds of the sale of their interest therein, and their full shares thereof.

This paragraph of answer is based on the theory that the appellants, by accepting the money, ratified the sale and estopped them from attacking its validity, and while retaining the money recover the land, and thus receive and retain both the money and the land, and this paragraph of answer presents the controlling question in the case; for if by the acceptance of the money the appellants, who are the heirs, ratified the sale and estopped themselves from recovering the land while retaining the proceeds derived from the sale, it puts an end to the case, and the many other questions so ably discussed by counsel are immaterial. If the appellants ratified the sale and estopped themselves from recovering the lands, by accepting the money, such ratification and estoppel took place at the time of accepting the money, and it is [131] immaterial how many years had elapsed afterward and between that time and the commencement of this suit. Nor is it material as to what construction should be placed upon the will. That this answer is good we think there can be but little doubt.

The petition of the guardian of Mrs. Wilmore to sell the real estate in controversy was sworn to, and alleged that she owned the whole of the land. The court ordered the whole of the real estate to be sold. It was duly appraised and sold for more than the full appraised value, and the sale was approved and confirmed by the court. The money was retained by the guardian, and loaned, and the accumulated interest added to it, only expending a small amount for the support of Mrs. Wilmore, and after her death the guardian paid to the appellants, who, it is claimed, owned the undivided two-thirds of the land sold, the purchase money received, with

the unexpended interest, and said heirs accepted it, knowing
it to be the proceeds of the sale of said land, and knowing at
the same time what their interest in the land was, and that
the money received and accepted by them was the proceeds
of the sale of their interests therein and their full shares
thereof.

In the face of such a state of facts as are alleged in this
paragraph of answer, to allow the appellants to maintain an
action for and recover the two-thirds interest in the land
from the purchaser for value, whose money they had received,
would be such a wrong and injustice as it would seem no
court ought or would tolerate, even if the sale was invalid and
subject to being set aside, had the heirs not received the proceeds of the sale.

The doctrine ruling in this case is well stated in the case
of *Palmerton* v. *Hoop*, 131 Ind. 23 (28), though the facts in
that case differ some from the facts in the case at bar.

It is held, in that case, that the party could not recover
[132] for two reasons: 1. Because she was a party to the proceedings to sell; and 2. It is said by the court that "She is
also estopped from claiming the land by reason of accepting,
and still retaining, a part of the price for which it was sold.
She cannot have both the land and the purchase price."
That is just what the appellants contend they have the right
to do in this case, viz., retain the purchase money and also
recover the land, and, if they cannot be permitted to do so,
then the answer is clearly good as a defense to the action.

In *Bumb* v. *Gard*, 107 Ind. 575, it is said: "Where an
heir, having full knowledge that all of the estate in the land
has been sold on petition of the administrator, receives and
retains the purchase money remaining after the payment of
debts, he cannot avoid the sale. He cannot have both the
money and the land. Equity will not uphold such a claim.
In accordance with this general doctrine it has often been
held that an heir who has full knowledge of his right, and,
with such knowledge, receives and retains the purchase
money, cannot vacate the sale and obtain the land. This
principle is often applied in analogous cases."

The case at bar is analogous to the class of cases cited.
It could be no different in equity if the widow, under claim
of right or ownership, had, in her lifetime, sold and conveyed
for full value the whole of the land to a purchaser, and then
paid the full amount of the purchase money over to the heirs,

they knowing at the time that she had no legal right to convey their interest, but that she had, in fact, conveyed it and received full value for it, and the heirs, with full knowledge of the facts and their rights, accept and retain the purchase money so paid, and while so retaining it seek to recover the land. In either case it would be inequitable to allow the heirs [133] to recover the land without refunding the purchase money.

It is contended by counsel for appellant that the cases holding that the heirs or legal owners are estopped by the receipt of the purchase money in cases where the land was attempted to be sold as the property of the parties afterward receiving the money. This fact, it seems to us, can make no difference. In either case, if the sale was void, it would pass no title. The principle applies where there has been an illegal sale of the parties' land, and they, with knowledge of the facts, receive and retain the purchase money.

The case of *Pepper* v. *Zahnsinger*, 94 Ind. 88, is a case, as we think, directly in point. There the administrator sold the whole of the land, and afterward paid to the widow the one-third, or nearly the one-third, of the purchase money, and she received and retained it, and it was held that she was estopped from recovering the land. It is true, in that case, she directed the administrator to sell it, but he conveyed only as administrator, and the court held that the sale of the widow's interest was void, and the estoppel rested, on the grounds of the receipt and retention of the purchase money, with knowledge of the facts.

In *Karns* v. *Olney*, 80 Cal. 90, 13 Am. St. Rep. 101, the court says: " It is a well-settled rule of estoppel that one who with knowledge accepts the proceeds of an unauthorized sale of his property is estopped to dispute the validity of the sale."

It would seem unnecessary to multiply authorities on this question: *Smith* v. *Warden*, 19 Pa. St. 424; *State* v. *Stanley*, 14 Ind. 409; *Rowe* v. *Majr*, 92 Ind. 206; *Kent* v. *Taggart*, 68 Ind. 163; *Armstrong* v. *Cavitt*, 78 Ind. 476; *Bryan* v. *Uland*, 101 Ind. 477.

Maple v. *Kussart*, 53 Pa. St. 348, 91 Am. Dec. 214, is a case where the [134] administrator sold the land of the widow, which he had no right to do, and she received the purchase price for which it sold, and it was held that she was estopped from claiming the land. In that case the court says that "It is a maxim of common honesty, as well as of law, that a

party cannot have the price of the land sold and the land
itself. Accordingly, it has been uniformly held that if one
receives the purchase money of land sold he affirms the sale,
and he cannot claim against it, whether void or only voidable."

We think the facts pleaded show an affirmance of the sale
and an estoppel on the part of the appellants from claiming
the land.

Counsel for appellant, in an able brief, cite numerous authorities and draw distinctions, endeavoring to show that the
parties are not estopped. We do not agree with their theory,
and deem it unnecessary to take up the decisions cited, and
draw the distinctions in each. It is possible that the doctrine announced in some cases, carried to its full length, may
conflict with the rule laid down in some of the cases cited;
but that this case falls clearly within the rule laid down in
the decisions we have cited and quoted from there can be
no doubt.

The next question presented arises on the special verdict.
It is unnecessary to set this verdict out in full. It clearly
supports the second paragraph of answer, and entitles the
appellee to judgment on the theory upon which the paragraph is based and which we have discussed.

The jury finds that said Adamson, guardian, paid to his
successor, Bodkins, the proceeds of the sale of said real estate,
being four thousand one hundred and fifty-four dollars and
nineteen cents; that Bodkins made settlement with the appellants in relation thereto, and distributed and paid over to
each of them the sum of one thousand and thirty-six dollars and seventy-one cents, making in all four thousand one
hundred and fifty-four dollars and nineteen cents; that prior
to the settlement and [135] receipt of the money, and at the
time thereof, the appellants and each of them knew their
rights in and to said land so sold by said guardian of their
mother; that at the same time each of them knew that the
money so paid and distributed to them was money derived
from the sale of the land; that the purchaser believed the
land was being sold and purchased by him in fee; that before
the commencement of this suit the appellants knew that the
money paid to them was derived from the sale of said land,
and with full knowledge of their interests in and rights to
said lands, they have retained the money, still have it, and
have never offered to pay it back, or any part thereof, to the

purchaser or his grantee, or either. Some distinction is
sought to be made as to the language of the verdict, so as to
construe it as not showing but that the heirs may not have
known that they were receiving any pay except for their
mother's one-third. The verdict will not bear the construction contended for by appellant's counsel. It is further contended that as one of the heirs died after the sale, and before
the settlement, as to appellant's interest in the share of the
deceased heir a different rule applies. We do not think so.
The appellants received all of the purchase money, both the
amount received for sale of their own interests and that of
the interest of the deceased heir, and they affirmed the sale
as well in so far as it relates to the share derived from the
other heir as that portion derived from their father.

There is no error in the record.

Judgment affirmed.

ON PETITION FOR A REHEARING.

DAILEY, J. Counsel very earnestly petition for a rehearing
in this case, and present two able briefs in which [136] they
criticise the opinion of the court for holding that the appellants ratified the guardian's sale of the real estate in litigation,
and estopped themselves from recovering in this proceeding
by accepting and retaining the proceeds derived from the sale
after they became adults. From the facts shown by the
record it is evident that the appellants had known, for years
prior to the settlement with their guardian, that Edwards,
and those claiming under him, as grantees, had been occupying the premises as their own under color of title created by
the guardian's deed and subsequent conveyances. They
knew the value of the land and the amount paid for it by
Edwards. They also knew that, besides the mother's interest in the two hundred acres in question, she had no real
estate except a small piece in Randolph county inherited
from her father, the income of which was fifteen dollars per
year, that belonged to her at the time of her death.

With a full knowledge of these facts and their rights they
settled with their guardian, in relation thereto, and received
from him, in full of the proceeds of the real estate they seek
to recover and interest thereon, the sum of four thousand
one hundred and forty-six dollars and eighty-four cents.
Did, then, the acceptance of the purchase money, knowing
it was the price paid for their land at its full value, confirm

the sale and estop the appellants, while retaining it, to assert the right to the land ? It is an old proverb that "you cannot eat your cake and have it, too."

Equity will no more allow the appellants to retain the proceeds of the sale with such knowledge, and claim the land also, than it would allow them, with like knowledge, to claim the land and accept the proceeds. They should, if they desired to claim the land, have tendered back to the purchaser the accepted purchase money as soon as they knew the facts. Men are bound by principles of [137] common honesty in business transactions, and such laws of conduct are vindicated and sanctioned by the courts.

In *Deford* v. *Mercer*, 24 Iowa, 118, 92 Am. Dec. 460, the court assumed that a sale made by a guardian was void, but found that before the plaintiffs had instituted their suit to recover the land sold by their guardian they had received from him the purchase money for it, and were estopped to claim the tract.

The court said: "If there is any thing well founded in conscience or in law, it is that they are estopped in equity from claiming the land after having voluntarily accepted the money which arose from or was the product of the sale of the land: *France* v. *Haynes*, 67 Iowa, 139."

It is the law of other courts as well, that one who, with knowledge, accepts the proceeds of an unauthorized sale of his property, is estopped to dispute the validity of the sale: *Schenck* v. *Sautter*, 73 Mo. 46; *Moore* v. *Hill*, 85 N. C. 218; *Field* v. *Doyon*, 64 Wis. 560; *Booth* v. *Wiley*, 102 Ill. 84.

In *Hoffmire* v. *Holcomb*, 17 Kan. 378, the court held that where a mortgagor accepted the surplus of the proceeds arising from the sale of the mortgaged premises in a foreclosure proceeding, he was estopped to question the validity of the sale or to recover the land sold. In this connection we cite *Walling* v. *Burgess*, 122 Ind. 299.

In *Goodman* v. *Winter*, 64 Ala. 410 (436, 437), 38 Am. Rep. 13, the tenant for life was the mother of the remaindermen, and the sale and conveyance was made by her and her husband, the father, the natural guardian of the remaindermen.

The court said: "The wrongful alienation by the tenant for life, while incapable of operating to their injury, clothed them with these several distinct, conflicting rights. If they accepted the investment made by the life tenant, or claimed a lien

on the premises conveyed, for the purchase money [138] the life
tenant had received and invested, the wrongful alienation was
ratified and confirmed.   During infancy the remaindermen
were thus clothed with inconsistent and conflicting rights,
between which they were incapable of electing, and yet having the right of electing when they attained majority. While
an infant cannot make an election, a court of equity has
undoubted jurisdiction to make an election for him: 1 Lead.
Cas. Eq., pt. 2, p. 1169.

"It is also true that an infant may not create an estoppel;
yet, under circumstances, the benefits of a particular transaction may have been so appropriated to his advantage that
he will not be heard to gainsay it. A sale of lands, descended
to him, may have been made, under an order of court, void
for want of jurisdiction; the purchaser cannot repudiate his
contract to pay the purchase money, unless the infant is
brought before a court of equity, and an election made for
him, whether the sale shall be confirmed or repudiated:
Lamkin v. *Reese*, 7 Ala. 170; *Bland* v. *Bowie*, 53 Ala. 153;
McCully v. *Chapman*, 58 Ala. 325; *Merritt* v. *Horne*, 5 Ohio
St. 307; 67 Am. Dec. 298.

"No adult, infant, lunatic, or married woman can be permitted to receive, hold, and enjoy the proceeds of a sale of
property, whether the sale is by an order of a court irregular
and void, or by the wrongful act of an individual, without
being estopped from a repudiation of the sale.

"In *Commonwealth* v. *Shuman*, 18 Pa. St. 346, it is said:
'Equitable estoppels of this character apply to infants, as well
as adults; to insolvent trustees and guardians, as well as
persons acting for themselves; and have place, as well when
the proceeds received arise from a sale by authority of law
as where they spring from the act of the party.'

"Of course it must appear that the sale is for the [139]
benefit of the infant, or the court would not prevent him from
asserting his title, though it would protect the purchaser by
decreeing him a lien or trust for the repayment of such
sums as had been applied to the benefit of the infant."

It is true the doctrine of *caveat emptor* applies to a purchase at a guardian's sale.   But this has nothing to do with
what Edwards believed at the time he was buying the land,
nor with his actual good faith in making the investment.
The guardian who swore that Mrs. Wilmore owned the land
in fee was, in a legal sense, presumed to know the will, and

ıe interest which the ward took under it, as was the attorey who prepared the petition and the court which ordered ıe sale. But these are not controlling facts in this case.

Appellee is now better informed than was his grantor at ıe time he bought, and rests his title upon the facts that his rantor paid to the guardian the full value of the land, and that ıey accepted the sum so paid when of full age, with knowlige of their rights, and the source from which the money aid and accepted was derived. It would be unreasonable) suppose that Edwards, in paying for the land he bought, iving for it four hundred dollars more than its appraised alue in fee, was acting in bad faith, because the law, for ɔme purposes, would hold him cognizant of facts of which, ı truth, he was ignorant. While he was uninformed of the ıw governing the construction of the testator's will, and the xtent of the title he acquired by his purchase, he evidently elieved he was acquiring a good title to the whole of the ract, as the jury have found by their special verdict.

It is doubtless true, in most instances, that equitable esoppels are usually based upon "a fraudulent purpose and a raudulent result," and if the element of fraud is wanting, here is no estoppel if both parties were equally [140] cognizant of the facts and the declarations, or silence produced no hange in the conduct of the other, he acting solely upon his ıwn judgment. But such is not the doctrine of this and kinIred cases, because the rule so applied would be inequitable ınd unjust. This belongs to the class in which it is held hat an estoppel may arise upon matters that transpire after he purchase, and on which the purchaser did not make the nvestment.

Inasmuch as the judgment in this case rests upon the secınd paragraph of the answer pleading ratification it is not ıecessary we should determine the sufficiency of the fourth ınd fifth paragraphs, which rely upon the statute of limitaion as a defense.

Petition overruled.   ___

ESTOPPEL BY RATIFICATION AFTER RECEIVING PROCEEDS OF UNAUTHORZED SALE.— One who with knowledge accepts the proceeds of an unauthorzed sale of his property is estopped to dispute the validity of such sale: *Carns* v. *Olney*, 80 Cal. 90; 13 Am. St. Rep. 101. This principle seems to e borne out by the monographic note to *Craig* v. *Van Bebber*, 18 Am. St. Lep. 700, 715, discussing the ratification of contracts by infants, and the ffect of accepting the consideration after attaining majority.

BROWN *v.* STATE.

[137 INDIANA, 240.]

JUROR—INTOXICATION OF VITIATES VERDICT.—The conduct of a juror, during the trial of a cause, after the court has adjourned for the day, in
drinking liquors until he becomes intoxicated, though he is in his seat
on the next morning, upon the convening of court, renders the verdict
invalid. Upon proof of such misconduct it should be set aside, and a
new trial granted, especially in a prosecution for murder, where such
verdict is "guilty," and fixes the death penalty.

J. F. Cox, for the appellant.

A. G. Smith, attorney general, F. W. Cady, and D. L. Cady,
for the state.

240 COFFEY, J. The appellant was indicted in the Bar-
tholomew circuit court upon a charge of murder in the first
degree. A trial of the cause, by jury, resulted in a verdict of
guilty, fixing the death penalty. Over a motion for a new
trial the court rendered judgment on the verdict, and named
a day on which the sentence should be executed. From the
judgment thus rendered the appellant prosecutes this appeal, and assigns as error: 1. That the circuit court erred in
overruling a motion to quash the indictment; 2. That the
court erred in overruling the appellant's motion for a new
trial.

The indictment is, substantially, such as has often been
held sufficient by this court. It would unnecessarily encumber this opinion to set it out here, as no good purpose would
be subserved thereby. We think it is a good indictment for
murder in the first degree, and the court did not err in overruling a motion to quash it.

The trial of the cause began on the twelfth day of December, 241 1893. The time of the court was consumed in hearing evidence from that date to the fifteenth day of the month.
Without any objection the jury was permitted to separate
at each adjournment of court. After hearing the evidence
from 9 o'clock in the forenoon until 4:30 in the afternoon
on Wednesday, the thirteenth day of the month, one of the
jurors, about 8 o'clock, and after court had adjourned for
the day, became intoxicated and was known to be intoxicated up to 10 o'clock of that evening. At the convening of
court on the next morning the juror was in his seat, and
remained on the jury and assisted in making the verdict
against the appellant.

It is contended by the appellant that this was such irregularity and misconduct on the part of the jury as vitiates the verdict. It is said that the misconduct of one juror, so far as it may affect the verdict in contemplation of law, is the misconduct of all: Moore's Criminal Law, sec. 417.

It seems to be well settled in this state, as well as in other jurisdictions, that drinking intoxicating liquor during the recess of the court is not such misconduct of the jury as vitiates the verdict, unless the drinking is to such an extent as to produce intoxication; but, where a juror drinks to such an extent as to become intoxicated, such conduct renders the verdict invalid, and the court, upon proof of such misconduct, should set it aside and grant a new trial: *Creek* v. *State*, 24 Ind. 151; *Davis* v. *State*, 35 Ind. 496; 9 Am. Rep. 760; *Huston* v. *Vail*, 51 Ind. 299; *Pratt* v. *State*, 56 Ind. 179; *Carter* v. *Ford etc. Co.*, 85 Ind. 180; *Pelham* v. *Page*, 6 Ark. 535: 4 Crim. Law Mag., secs. 10, 11; *State* v. *Cucuel*, 31 N. J. L. 249; *Jones* v. *State*, 13 Tex. 168; 62 Am. Dec. 550.

In the case of *Ryan* v. *Harrow*, 27 Iowa, 494, 1 Am. Rep. 302, the court [242] declined to enter into the question as to whether the juror drank to intoxication, but said: "The drinking of intoxicating liquor by one or more of the jurors, during the discharge of their duties as such, constituted sufficient ground for setting aside the verdict and ordering a new trial. The view we take of the case will relieve us of the duty of determining whether the charge of intoxication is sustained by the record. And we are glad to escape so unpleasant an investigation, which might result in convincing us that the administration of the law in our state has been disgraced by the drunkenness of those appointed to decide, in a court of justice, upon the rights of their fellow-citizens. We had hoped that such things were of the past, and would only be remembered as rare instances existing in the traditions of frontier days."

In the case of *Jones* v. *State*, 13 Tex. 168, 62 Am. Dec. 550, it was said by the supreme court of Texas, after a quotation from Scotland's most popular bard: "Yes, it is but too true, that it (intoxicating liquor) will make a man bold and reckless, not only of consequences personally, but also of the rights of those whose life and most valuable interests, property, and reputation are at stake; and its effect is so very different on different men, that it would be dangerous in the extreme to attempt to lay down any rule by which it could or should be determined whether a juror had drank too much or not; and the only safe rule is to exclude it entirely."

In this case we are not required to go to the extent to which these cases lead us. It is not denied by the state that the juror in question was intoxicated, as charged in the affidavits filed in support of the motion for a new trial.

In the administration of the law it sometimes becomes necessary to take human life upon the assumption [243] that the good of society demands it; but, when life is to be taken, the legal proceedings leading to such a result should be free from any error the nature of which could result in injury to the accused. No more solemn duty could be imposed upon a tribunal than that of passing the death sentence upon a fellow-being, and, when this duty is to be performed, there should be no reasonable doubt that the unfortunate subject of the sentence has had a fair and impartial trial.

In this case one of the jurors charged with the duty of impartially trying the appellant, at a time when he should have kept his mental faculties in a condition to retain the evidence in the cause and carefully ponder and weigh it, became intoxicated by the intemperate use of intoxicating liquor. In this condition it is perfectly plain that he was in no condition to give the case a fair consideration.

While it does not appear that he was still intoxicated when he took his seat in the jury-box on the next morning, we have no means of knowing the extent to which his mental faculties were beclouded by the previous night's debauch. It is enough to say that the appellant was entitled to have this juror consider and pass upon his case with faculties unimpaired by drunkenness during the progress of the trial.

The record in the cause is not of such a character as to warrant us in saying that the intoxication of the juror did not injuriously affect the appellant.

There was much evidence introduced at the trial of the cause, of an apparently reliable character, tending to prove that the appellant, at the time of the commission of the alleged crime for which he was convicted, was a person of unsound mind.

In our opinion the circuit court erred in overruling [244] the appellant's motion for a new trial on account of the misconduct of the jury trying the cause.

Judgment reversed, with directions to the circuit court to sustain the appellant's motion for a new trial.

NEW TRIAL—MISCONDUCT OF JURY—USE OF INTOXICATING LIQUORS.—
The use of intoxicating liquors by the jurors during the progress of the
trial of a cause, before their retirement to deliberate upon their verdict,
does not justify the remanding of the case for a new trial, in the absence of
a showing that such misconduct did influence the verdict, or could have
done so, taking all the circumstances of the case into consideration: *Brad-
shaw* v. *Degenhart*, 15 Mont. 267; monographic note to *Hilton* v. *Southwick,*
35 Am. Dec. 258, discussing the subject; note to *Davis* v. *State*, 9 Am. Rep.
765. That the excessive use, by the jury, of intoxicating liquors, after
they have retired to deliberate upon a verdict, will vitiate it, see *State* v.
Broussard, 41 La. Ann. 81; 17 Am. St. Rep. 396, and note. .

CAYLOR *v.* LUZADDER.

[137 INDIANA, 319.]

SURVEYS.—A DEFICIENCY IN A QUARTER SECTION OF LAND, as shown by the
original survey and plat, should be borne by the several tracts in proportion to the quantities supposed to be contained therein by the
government and its purchasers, who have assumed the lines to be correct. Hence, where, by the original survey and the plat of the surveyor
general, the east line of a certain quarter section was 38 and 5-100 chains
in length, and the west line was 38 and 48-100 chains, the half quarter
line not being established, nor the corners thereof located, and the plat
assigned 20 chains to the east line of said quarter at the south end
thereof, 20 chains to the west line at the south end thereof, 18 and 5-100
chains to said east line at the north end thereof, and 18 and 48-100
chains to said west line at the north end thereof, when, in fact, the
east and west lines of said quarter section were each but 37 chains in
length, and contained 6 and 49-100 acres less than shown by said original survey and plat, the original plat marking the southern portion of
said quarter section as containing 80 acres and the northern portion as
containing 72 and 49-100 acres, and being each so respectively described by the government patent and subsequent conveyances; such
deficiency of 6 and 49-100 acres in said quarter section should be deducted proportionally from said north and south one-half quarters, upon
the basis of 80 and 72 and 49-100 acres respectively.
SURVEYS.—"PROPORTIONATE MEASUREMENT" IS A MEASUREMENT having
the same ratio to that recorded in the original field notes, as the length
of the chain used in the new measurement has to the length of the
chain used in the original survey, assuming that the original measurement was correctly made.

E. L. Watson and J. E. Watson, for the appellant.

J. W. Thompson, for the appellee.

320 HACKNEY, J. This was an appeal from a survey affecting the lands of the parties. Without moving to dismiss
the appeal, or objecting to the record, the appellant appeared

and joined in an agreed statement of facts, and asked the decision and judgment of the circuit court.

The absence from the record of a notice of the time of the survey affected the question of jurisdiction over the person of the appellant, and was waived by his appearance. There was a record certified by the surveyor, on appeal, which, though possibly informal, was sufficient to invoke the jurisdiction of the circuit court over the subject matter. The submission of the cause without objection to the informality of the record, and giving the appellee an opportunity to perfect the record, was a waiver of such informality: *Ricketts* v. *Dorrell*, 59 Ind. 427.

From the agreed facts it appeared that the appellant owned the south half and the appellee owned the north half of the northwest quarter of section 1, township 21, north of range 12 east. The dividing line between these two tracts is the disputed point in the case. By the original survey and the plat of the surveyor general the east line of said quarter section was $38\frac{5}{100}$ chains in length, and the west line was $38\frac{48}{100}$ chains, and while the half quarter line was not established, nor the corners thereof located, the said plat assigned 20 chains to the east line and to the west line [321] of said quarter at the south end thereof, and assigned $18\frac{5}{100}$ chains to said east line at the north end thereof, and $18\frac{48}{100}$ chains to said west line at the north end thereof. It is agreed that the east line of said quarter section was in fact but 37 chains in length, and the west line was but 37 chains in length, or that said quarter section contained $6\frac{49}{100}$ acres less than shown by said original survey and plat. It is also agreed that said plat marked the southern portion of said quarter section as containing 80 acres, and the northern portion as containing $72\frac{49}{100}$ acres.

The patent issued by the government for the south half of said quarter section described it as containing 80 acres, and that issued for the north half described it as containing $72\frac{49}{100}$ acres, and the various conveyances thereafter so described said tracts.

The lower court found and adjudged upon the agreed facts that the deficiency of $6\frac{49}{100}$ acres in said quarter section should be deducted proportionately from said north and south half quarters upon the basis of 80 and $72\frac{49}{100}$ acres respectively.

The appellant insists that no part of said deficiency should be deducted from his tract, but that the whole thereof should be deducted from the north half of said quarter section, upon the rule that interior lots in fractional sections shall be made to contain the legal number of acres, and that the deficiency or overplus is charged against or credited to the outer lots of such sections.

The principal case cited in support of that rule is *Keesling* v. *Truitt*, 30 Ind. 306. The rule is not questioned, and has been reaffirmed in *Grover* v. *Paddock*, 84 Ind. 244.

The application of the rule to the facts here involved [322] is the important question. There seems to be a well-recognized distinction between this rule, as applied to original surveys, whether in the making of such surveys or in allotting the deficiency or overplus when the correctness of such surveys is not questioned, and that where such original surveys are found to have been erroneous or the original corners and lines are wholly lost.

This distinction was recognized in *Bailey* v. *Chamblin*, 20 Ind. 33; *Jones* v. *Kimble*, 19 Wis. *429 (452); *Moreland* v. *Page*, 2 Iowa, 139; *Westphal* v. *Schultz*, 48 Wis. 75; *James* v. *Drew*, 68 Miss. 518; 24 Am. St. Rep. 287. See, also, Hodgman's Land Surveying, sec. 8, p. 282, and Dorr's Surveyor's Guide, 8, 12, 21–23.

The surveyor general was not required to, and did not, locate the half quarter posts or line, and, having surveyed the quarter, established the lines, and located the corners thereof, these defined irrevocably the boundaries or limits of the quarter; the purchasers and the government acted upon the assumption that the lines were correctly measured and returned by the deputy surveyor; in this all were alike deceived; the length of lines is less than that so acted upon, and, by every principle of equity, the deficiency should be borne by the several tracts in proportion to the quantities so presumed to be contained therein at the time of the purchase.

This theory has been expressly adopted by the commissioner of the general land-office since June 2, 1887, if not since an earlier period. In the instructions of Commissioner Sparks, of that date, it is said: "In the subdivision of quarter sections the quarter quarter corners are to be placed at points equidistant between the section and quarter section corners; and between the quarter corners and the common center of the section, except on the last half mile of the lines closing on the north or west boundaries of a township, where they [323] should be placed at 20 chains, proportionate measurement, to the north or west of the quarter section corner."

" Proportionate measurement " is defined as " a measurement having the same ratio to that recorded in the original field notes as the length of the chain used in the new measurement has to the length of the chain used in the original survey, assuming that the original measurement was correctly made": See Copp's Public Land Laws, 1890, p. 1041.

We conclude, therefore, that the circuit court adopted the proper rule, and that its judgment should be affirmed.

Accordingly the judgment is affirmed.

SURVEYS—DEFICIENCY—EXCESS.—If lines of a survey are found to be either shorter or longer than stated in the original plat or field notes, the causes contributing to such mistake will be presumed to have operated equally in all parts of the original plat or survey, and every lot or parcel must bear the burden or receive the benefit of a corrected resurvey, in the proportion which its frontage, as stated in the original plat or field notes, bears to the whole frontage as there set forth: *Pereles* v. *Magoon*, 78 Wis. 27; 23 Am. St. Rep. 389, and note. This rule applies to government surveys: *James* v. *Drew*, 68 Miss. 518; 24 Am. St. Rep. 287.

McIlhinny *v.* McIlhinny.

[137 INDIANA, 411.]

DEEDS.—THE RULE IN SHELLEY'S CASE is this: Where a freehold is limited to one for life, and by the same instrument the inheritance is limited, either mediately or immediately, to heirs, or heirs of his body, the first taker takes the whole estate, either in fee simple or fee tail; and the words "heirs" or "heirs of the body" are words of limitation, and not of purchase. This rule is the law of Indiana, but courts everywhere are inclined to circumscribe its operation within the strict limits of its own boundaries.

DEEDS—"ISSUE" AS A WORD OF PURCHASE OR LIMITATION—IN APPLYING THE RULE IN SHELLEY'S CASE there is a material distinction between wills and deeds. As to wills the rule will not be allowed to override the manifest and clearly expressed intention of the testator, which will always be carried into effect if it can be ascertained. The word "issue," when used in a will, may be a word of purchase, or it may be a word of limitation, depending on the testator's intention; but when used in a deed it is always a word of purchase.

DEEDS—RULE IN SHELLEY'S CASE—REMAINDERS, VESTED AND CONTINGENT. A deed creating a life estate in a daughter, with remainder over to the issue of her body born alive, but in the event of her dying without such issue, then with remainder over to another, is not within the rule in Shelley's case, the word "issue" being a word of purchase and not of limitation. Under such a deed there is limited on such life estate a

contingent remainder to the issue of the daughter's body born alive,
and on such life estate there is also limited to such other person a
remainder contingent on "issue" not being born alive of the body of
the daughter.   Upon "issue" of her body being born alive, the contingent remainder as to such issue becomes a vested remainder by such
birth, and the contingent remainder of such other person ceases to
exist, and the remainderman has, and can have, no further interest.
The remainder limited to the "issue" of her body born alive, though it
becomes vested in such "issue" by the birth, is subject to be opened
up to let in those afterward born alive of her body, before the termination of her life estate

G. C. Florea and L. L. Broaddus, for the appellant.

R. Conner and H. L. Frost, for the appellee.

⁴¹¹ McCabe, J.   Suit by appellee to quiet title against
appellant.

The overruling of appellant's exceptions to the conclusions
of law stated on a special finding by the court is assigned
here for error.

⁴¹² The substance of the special finding is that on the
twenty-first day of December, 1881, one William Merrill, the
father of appellee, was the owner in fee simple and in possession of the real estate described in the complaint, which was
sixty-five acres of land; that on said day, while he was such
owner, he and his wife executed to his daughter, Annie
Merrill, then aged fourteen years, a deed for said real estate,
reading as follows:

"This indenture witnesseth that we, William Merrill and
Annie Merrill, his wife, of Fayette county, in the state of
Indiana, convey and warrant to Annie Merrill, junior, of
Fayette county, Indiana, for and during her life, with remainder over to the issue of her body born alive, but in the
event of the said Annie Merrill, junior, dying without issue
of her body born alive, then with remainder over to John
Merrill for and in consideration of the sum of eight thousand
dollars as an advancement made to the said Annie Merrill,
junior, by the said William Merrill in his estate the following
real estate in Fayette county, in the state of Indiana, to wit:
[then follows a description of the land]

" In witness whereof the said William Merrill and Annie
Merrill, his wife, have hereunto set their hands and seals,
this 21st day of December, A. D. 1881.

                                   " William Merrill.
                                   " Annie Merrill."

That the execution of said deed was duly acknowledged before the proper officer on the same day by the grantors; that the plaintiff, Anna C. McIlhinny, is the same person named in said deed as Annie Merrill, junior; that at the time of said deed the plaintiff was an unmarried daughter of said William Merrill, and did not have born to her any children until the twenty-seventh day of July, 1890; on that day Jennie L. McIlhinny was born to the plaintiff, she being the plaintiff's first and only child, and is now [413] living; that after the execution of the deed the appellee took possession of the premises conveyed; that the defendant, John Merrill, is the John Merrill mentioned in the deed; that John Payne is now, and was before the beginning of the suit, the legal and qualified guardian of said Jennie L. McIlhinny; that the appellee has not parted with the title to said real estate conveyed to her by said deed, but is still the owner of whatever title said deed conveyed to her; that John Merrill and John Payne, appellant's guardian, both claimed, prior to bringing the suit, that the appellee was not the owner in fee simple, and that they had some interest in the land; that said claims cast a cloud upon the title of appellee in fee simple.

The conclusions of law are " that appellee, Annie C. McIlhinny, was, at the beginning of the suit, and is now, the owner in fee simple of the real estate described in the complaint, setting out the description by metes and bounds; and that said John Merrill and Jennie L. McIlhinny have no interest in said real estate."

It is contended by the appellee's counsel that the rule in Shelley's case applies to the deed, and that by that rule a title in fee simple vested in the first taker by virtue of the deed. The appellant's counsel contend that the rule in Shelley's case does not apply, and, if that rule does not apply, the plainly expressed intention of the grantor was to vest a life estate in the appellee with remainder over in fee to the issue of her body born alive.

It is not denied by the appellee's counsel that such was the apparent and plainly expressed intent of the grantor, but invoking the aid of the rule in Shelley's case, and quoting from Chancellor Kent, they say: "And yet it [the rule in Shelley's case] is admitted to interfere, in most cases, with the presumed, and in many others with [414] the declared, intention of the parties to the instrument to which it is applied."

They, therefore, conclude if the deed in question falls within the rule in Shelley's case the question of intention is foreign to the discussion in this case.

The rule in Shelley's case is this: " Where a freehold is limited to one for life, and by the same instrument the inheritance is limited, either mediately or immediately, to heirs or heirs of his body, the first taker takes the whole estate, either in fee simple or fee tail; and the words ' heirs,' or ' heirs of the body,' are words of limitation, and not of purchase": *Andrews* v. *Spurlin*, 35 Ind. 262.

In *Ridgeway* v. *Lanphear*, 99 Ind. 251 (253), this court said: " The rule in *Shelley's case*, 1 Coke, 88, is the law of this state, and, in all cases where the facts make it applicable, we must enforce it, although we may think there was not much reason for it at the time of its adoption, and none at all under the existing system of tenures and conveyances. But, in accepting the rule, we take it as construed and enforced by the courts which formulated and proclaimed it. Pressed by the evils wrought by the rule, and shocked by the great number of instances in which it operated to utterly overthrow the intention of the testator, these courts, centuries ago, affirmed that there existed an important difference between wills and deeds, and that the rule should not be so strictly enforced in the case of a will as in the case of a deed. It has long stood as the law that there is a material distinction between wills and deeds, and that the rule in Shelley's case will not be allowed to override the manifest and clearly expressed intention of the testator, but that the intention will always be carried into effect if it can be ascertained. It is true that where the words used are such as to bring the case within the rule, it will [415] be given full force and effect, but where the context clearly shows that the testator annexed a different meaning, that meaning will be adopted, and the rule will not be allowed to fustrate his intention."

But the appellee insists that *King* v. *Rea*, 56 Ind. 1, is parallel to, and directly supports, the conclusions of law stated by the trial court in the case at bar. It must be confessed that if that case was correctly decided the judgment in this case must be affirmed. One of the deeds involved in that case, executed by Andrew Wallace, read: " Conveys and warrants to Martha W. Rea, during her life, in remainder to the issue of her body, their heirs and assigns forever." The court held that Martha W. Rea, by the deed from Andrew

Wallace, took a fee simple in the lands, and that the words "issue of her body" must be held as words of limitation, and not words of purchase.

It was held in *Gonzales* v. *Barton*, 45 Ind. 295, Downey, C. J., delivering the opinion of the court, that the words "lawful issue" were words of limitation, and not words of purchase.˙ This court, in following that case, lost sight of the fact that that case was one involving the construction of a will, and the distinction between the force of the word "issue" when used in a deed and when used in a will. It has long been established law that when used in a will the word "issue" may be a word of purchase or it may be a word of limitation, depending on the testator's intention as expressed in the context. But when used in a deed it is always a word of purchase: Elphinstone's Interpretation of Deeds, 318, 319; *Bagshaw* v. *Spencer*, 2 Atk. 582; *Doe* v. *Collis*, 4 Term Rep. 294; *Rowle's case*, 11 Coke, 79, *b;* 11 Am. & Eng. Ency. of Law, 876, 877, and authorities there cited; 2 Washburn on Real Property, 5th ed., top pp. 654, 655.

It is also held in *Nelson* v. *Davis*, 35 Ind. 478, and in **416** *Shimer* v. *Mann*, 99 Ind. 190; 50 Am. Rep. 82, that the word "issue" is very frequently a word of purchase. It was properly enough held in *Gonzales* v. *Barton*, 45 Ind. 295, that the word "issue" in the will involved in that case, under the context therein, was a word of limitation, and not a word˙ of purchase. Quite a large number of English cases are therein cited to support that construction of the word, but they are all will cases. It is quite natural that in the light of all those cases construing the word "issue" to be a word of limitation, and not a word of purchase, the distinction between the force and effect of the word when used in a will and when used in a deed should escape the notice of the court in citing *Gonzales* v. *Barton*, 45 Ind. 295, in support of the ruling in *King* v. *Rea*, 56 Ind. 1, and therefore this court felt constrained to say "this case must be followed."

The legitimate offspring and fruit borne by *King* v. *Rea*, 56 Ind. 1, is *Fletcher* v. *Fletcher*, 88 Ind. 418, which is also cited and relied upon by the appellee here.

In that case, Stoughton J. Fletcher and Allen M. Fletcher sued their minor children to quiet title to real estate, showing that at the date of the execution of the deed they were unmarried, and neither of them ever had any children born unto them, but that since the execution of said deed, both of them had become married and had children born unto them, who are still living, naming them as defendants.

The deed was by Stoughton A. Fletcher and wife, who "convey and warrant to Stoughton J. and Allen M. Fletcher, during their lives, one undivided moiety each, and then, after their death, to their children respectively, in fee simple, for the sum of $39,000, the following real estate in Marion county, in the state of Indiana." Then follows a description of the land.

417 "In witness whereof, the said Stoughton A. Fletcher and Julia A. Fletcher, his wife, have hereunto set their hands and seals, this 30th day of December, A. D. 1873.

> "S. A. FLETCHER.
> "JULIA A. FLETCHER."

The foregoing deed is such as, at common law, would be a conditional fee, and was called a fee tail or estate tail, the quality of which is defined to be that it is liable to be defeated by the failure of the contingency or condition on which it is made to depend; and, in that event, at common law, it reverted to the donor: 1 Washburn on Real Property, 5th ed., 106, 107, and authorities there cited; 6 Am. & Eng. Ency. of Law, 879, and authorities there cited.

By our statute (2 Burns' Rev. Stats. 1894, sec. 3378), "estates tail are abolished; and any estate which, according to the common law, would be adjudged a fee tail, shall hereafter be adjudged a fee simple; and if no valid remainder shall be limited thereon, shall be a fee simple absolute."

Now, as the contingency of the grantees in the foregoing deed, leaving children surviving, might never have happened, the estate was a conditional one, and, at common law, would have been a fee tail or estate tail, and but for the latter clause of the above-quoted statute abolishing such estates it would be a fee simple absolute in the first takers, and their children would have taken nothing.

The question then arises, Was there a valid remainder limited thereon? If there was, then the first takers did not take a fee simple absolute, unless the rule in Shelley's case applies.

Section 3380 of the same statute provides that "a remainder may be limited on a contingency, which, in **418** case it should happen, will operate to abridge or determine the precedent estate."

Accordingly, it has been held by this court, and so ruled

at common law, that a valid remainder might be limited on a particular estate for life, to unborn children, and, on their birth during the life tenancy, the remainder would immediately vest. The remainder is contingent before, and vested after, the birth of the remainderman: *Amos* v. *Amos*, 117 Ind. 19, 37; 20 Am. & Eng. Ency. of Law, 854, 855; 2 Washburn on Real Property, 5th ed., 610, 611; *Glass* v. *Glass*, 71 Ind. 392.

It follows that the deed in the Fletcher case limited a valid remainder upon the particular estate granted, and the children to whom it was limited being unborn it was a contingent remainder until their birth, when it became vested unless this manifest intent was defeated by the operation of the rule in Shelley's case. That rule is cited along with *King* v. *Rea*, 56 Ind. 1, as authority for the conclusion reached.

That the rule in Shelley's case has no application to that case is too plain for argument. The word "children," used in the deed, has always been held in this court and the courts of England as a word of purchase, and not a word of limitation: *Sorden* v. *Gatewood*, 1 Ind. 107; *Doe on Demise* v. *Jackman*, 5 Ind. 283; 3 Am. & Eng. Ency. of Law, 229–233, and authorities there cited.

The result is, if we follow the two cases of *King* v. *Rea*, 56 Ind. 1, and *Fletcher* v. *Fletcher*, 88 Ind. 418, we shall extend the rule in Shelley's case farther in this state than it was ever extended in England or in this country, so far as we have been able to discover.

While it is a rule of law too firmly established to be shaken by the courts, and which the courts should enforce, [419] not because it is just or wholesome, but because it is law, yet its operation more frequently defeats the just and undoubted intention of grantors and testators than any other effect it has. For this reason the courts everywhere are inclined to circumscribe its operation within the strict limits of its own boundaries.

It follows from what we have said that there was no word of limitation used in the deed to the appellee, but that the word "issue," used therein, being a word of purchase, the rule in Shelley's case does not apply; therefore, we are left free to give effect to the manifest intent of the grantor therein, William Merrill. That intention is very clearly expressed to create a life estate in his daughter, the appellee here, with remainder over to the issue of her body born alive, but, in the event of her dying without such issue born alive then with remainder over to John Merrill. Such a deed, as we have seen, would have conveyed what is known at common law as a conditional estate or fee, called an estate tail, liable to be defeated by the failure of the condition, namely, issue of her body born alive, and failure of the contingent remainderman, John Merrill, to be living at the termination of her life estate. In such case, at common law, the estate would revert, as we have seen, to the donor. But our statute, as we have seen, changes that feature of the estate, and makes it a fee simple in the first taker, the appellant, unless there was a valid remainder over limited to the issue of her body, or, on failure of such issue, to John Merrill.

As we have already seen, the remainder limited was a valid one, both under the statute and at the common law. It was contingent at the date of the deed, and became vested by the birth of the appellant as issue of appellee's body born alive. Having become vested in appellant, the contingency on which John Merrill's interest [420] depended, his contingent interest has ceased, and he has, and can have, no further interest: 2 Washburn on Real Property, 629; 20 Am. & Eng. Ency. of Law, 850, and authorities there cited.

The remainder vested in appellant on her birth, subject to be opened up to let in those afterward born alive, or issue of appellee's body, before the termination of her life estate: 20 Am. & Eng. Ency. of Law, 855, and authorities there cited.

In so far as *King* v. *Rea*, 56 Ind. 1, is inconsistent with this opinion, it is modified, and *Fletcher* v. *Fletcher*, 88 Ind. 418, in so far as it conflicts with this opinion, is overruled.

It is but just to the learned judge of the trial court to say that he was under legal compulsion to follow the cases just referred to so long as they stood unmodified and not overruled by this court. Hence, he was fully justified in holding, in line with those cases, that the rule in Shelley's case applied, and that the appellee took a fee simple.

We are of opinion that the trial court erred in its conclusions of law.

The judgment is reversed and the cause remanded, with instructions to the trial court to restate its conclusions of law in accordance with this opinion.

THE RULE IN SHELLEY's CASE, as stated by Mr. Preston, is as follows: In any instrument, if a freehold be limited to the ancestor for life and the inheritance to his heirs, either mediately or immediately, the first taker takes the whole estate; if it be limited to the heirs of his body he takes a fee tail; if to his heirs, a fee simple: See monographic note to *Carpenter* v. *Van Olinder*, 11 Am. St. Rep. 100, where the rule is stated in other forms. In a will the word "issue" is either a word of purchase or of limitation, as will best answer the intention of the devisor, though in the case of a deed it is universally a word of purchase: Note to *Carpenter* v. *Van Olinder*, 11 Am. St. Rep. 104, treating at length of the rule in Shelley's case. This rule is repudiated in some of the states: *Wilkerson* v. *Clark*, 80 Ga. 367; 12 Am. St. Rep. 258; but is the law of Indiana: *Earnhart* v. *Earnhart*, 127 Ind. 397; 22 Am. St. Rep. 652, 653. As to the legal war carried on by the bench and bar between the "Shelleyites" and the "anti-Shelleyites," see note to *Leathers* v. *Gray*, 9 Am. St. Rep. 35.

REMAINDERS—VESTED AND CONTINGENT.—Vested remainders exist when the estate is invariably fixed to remain to a determinate person after the particular estate is spent. In cases of vested remainders a present interest passes to a fixed person, or class of persons, to be enjoyed in future. Contingent remainders exist when no present interest passes, and the estate in remainder is limited to take effect either to a dubious and uncertain person, or upon a dubious and uncertain event, so that the particular estate may chance to be determined and the remainder never take effect: *Chapin* v. *Crow*, 147 Ill. 219; 37 Am. St. Rep. 213; note to *Ducker* v. *Burnham*, 37 Am. St. Rep. 146.

ÆTNA POWDER COMPANY *v.* HILDEBRAND.

[137 INDIANA, 462.]

CONTRACTS—CONSIGNMENT FOR SALE VESTS TITLE, WHEN—PROCEEDS NOT A TRUST FUND.—Under a contract by which goods are consigned to one person to sell for another as agent upon commission, the consignee to guarantee all sales, and to make a report at the end of each sixty days of the amount of sales, and to pay for the same, less commissions, with his notes, the proceeds of the sales vest in the consignee. Upon the sale taking place the relation of principal and agent ceases, and the relation of debtor and creditor arises as to the proceeds thereof, whether the notes are executed or not. Hence, if the consignee becomes insolvent, the consignor cannot follow such proceeds as a trust fund, but must proceed as a common creditor.

A PLEADING MUST PROCEED UPON SOME ONE SINGLE DEFINITE THEORY, and it must be good upon that theory, or it will be held insufficient on demurrer, though it may be sufficient on some other theory.

F. H. Blackledge and W. W. Thornton, for the appellant.

S. M. Chambers, S. O. Pickens, C. W. Moores, U. J. Hammond, and E. St. G. Rogers, for the appellees.

⁴⁶² McCABE, J. Jacob S. Hildebrand and James L. Fugate had been partners in the mercantile hardware business

in Indianapolis for many years. Becoming embarrassed and insolvent, one of them, Jacob S., filed a petition in the superior court against the other, James L., alleging their insolvency and asking a dissolution of the partnership and the appointment of a receiver to take charge of and wind up the affairs of said partnership. Whereupon such proceedings were had at special term as that Alonzo P. Hendrickson was duly appointed receiver for, and who took possession of, the assets of said firm.

The appellant, the Ætna Powder Company, appeared and filed an intervening petition asking to make Edwin [463] St. George Rogers and Philip M. Hildebrand parties defendant.

The substance of the intervening petition is that the appellant had, on the eleventh day of February, 1886, entered into a written contract with the firm of Hildebrand & Fugate, a copy of which, as an exhibit, is filed with the petition, and by which, it is claimed, the appellant constituted said firm the agent and trustee of appellant to sell, as such agent, powders manufactured by appellant.

It is further alleged that said contract continued in force until the twenty-fifth day of September, 1893, when it was terminated by appellant; that appellant, during that time, furnished to said firm many thousands of pounds of its high explosive powders to sell in accordance with the terms of said contract; that said firm, pursuant to said contract, on the first day of May, 1893, in writing, reported to appellant that for the sixty days immediately preceding that date there was due from them to appellant, on sales made of said powder so furnished after deducting their commissions and other lawful charges, the sum of six hundred and seventy-seven dollars and twenty-seven cents. And on July 1, 1893, a like report was made by said firm showing that for the sixty days immediately preceding that date, there was due from them to appellant on sales made of said powders so furnished, after deducting their commissions and other lawful charges, the sum of five hundred and fifteen dollars and seven cents. And that on the first day of September, 1893, a like report was made by said firm; that for the sixty days immediately preceding that date there was due from said firm to appellant, on sales of said powders so furnished, after deducting their commissions and other lawful charges, the sum of three hundred and thirteen dollars and fifty-five cents; that from the last report to the termination of the contract the

amount reported as due appellant on account of sales in
that time, after deducting commissions and other charges,
[464] amounted to the sum of twenty-six dollars and forty
cents, amounted in all to sixteen hundred and ninety-four
dollars and fifty-four cents, all of which is due appellant
and remains wholly unpaid; that no note was at any time
executed by said firm to appellant for all or any part of
said sums so reported due appellant on powder sold by said
firm, as aforesaid; that of the moneys due on said sales of
powders during the sixty days immediately preceding said
May 1, 1893, and the sixty days immediately preceding
September 18, 1893, said firm collected, before the appointment of the receiver, large sums, the amounts of which appellant is unable to state, which amounts so collected they
placed and deposited with moneys of said firm, either in or
out of bank, or both, and never remitted or paid the same to
appellant; and that parts of such amounts thus collected,
but how much appellant is unable to state, said firm, without
the consent of appellant, used for the purpose of purchasing
goods, wares, and merchandise for their said business, and
the goods thus purchased became a part thereof, and are now
a part of the assets of said firm, and the moneys derived
from the sale by said firm of the goods, wares, and merchandise thus purchased were either used by said firm in their
said business or were on hand at the time said receiver was
appointed, but whether all of said fund was used or kept, or
whether a part was used and a part kept, or whether said
receiver has received parts of the amounts of said sales since
his appointment, appellant is unable to state; that the receiver had taken possession of all the accounts and contracts
of sale of said powders that had been made during the sixty
days previous to said May 1, 1893, and from that date to said
September 18, 1893, the date of the last report, which had
been uncollected and unsatisfied, and has, as such receiver,
collected and received a part or the whole of the amount due
thereon, and now has the same in his possession, but how
much [465] he has thus collected appellant is unable to state;
that before the appointment of said receiver said firm of Hildebrand & Fugate had executed a mortgage upon all of the
assets of said firm to Philip M. Hildebrand and Edwin St.
George Rogers, including the property that had been purchased by said firm, with the moneys collected by said firm
on said contracts of sale of said powders; that said mortgage

was executed to said Philip M. Hildebrand and Rogers to secure debts and obligations of said firm to said mortgagees due before the execution of said mortgage; and that the same was not given for an extension of time of payment of said indebtedness nor for any new obligation or indebtedness.

Prayer that appellant's claim be declared a preferred one to all other creditors and to the mortgagees' claim.

The contract on which the petition is founded reads as follows:

"It is this day agreed between the Ætna Powder Company of Chicago, Ill., and Jacob S. Hildebrand and James S. Fugate, copartners, composing the firm of Hildebrand & Fugate, at Indianapolis, Indiana, jointly and severally as follows:

"The said Ætna Powder Company, for their part, agree to consign to the said Hildebrand & Fugate, to sell as agents, such powders of the kinds manufactured by the Ætna Powder Company, as shall be needed, and pay the freight on the same to Indianapolis; that said Ætna Powder Company will establish a scale of prices below which the goods so consigned shall not be sold, and that they hereby reserve the right to change the same at any time, and will, and hereby do, authorize the said Hildebrand & Fugate to sell the goods so consigned at the prices so established.

"The said Ætna Powder Company further agree that they will allow the said Hildebrand & Fugate, as a commission for selling the goods so consigned, and for guaranteeing all sales made by them, the sum of ten per cent of the gross sales of all powder known and branded as Ætna High Explosive, with an additional allowance of thirty cents per case for cartage. The said Hildebrand & Fugate, for their part, agree to act as agents for the said Ætna Powder Company for the sale of the powder so consigned to them; to use due diligence in selling; to guarantee all sales made, and to become the agents for the sale of no other high explosive powder while they retain the agency as above. The said Hildebrand & Fugate also agree to adhere strictly to such scale of prices as are furnished by the Ætna Powder Company.

"The said Hildebrand & Fugate furthermore agree to make no charges for storing, selling, or delivery other than the commission above specified, and to be responsible for the good and safe keeping of the powder after the delivery to them, unavoidable accidents (occurring from no neglect or carelessness on their part) excepted.

"The said Hildebrand & Fugate furthermore agree to make a true and correct report to said Ætna Powder Company of all sales, at the end of each sixty days, of the amount of sales for that time, reporting the full selling price of all sold, and to pay for the same, less their commissions as above, with their sixty day note.

"It is further agreed that either party being desirous of terminating this contract must give a reasonable notice to the other, and make satisfactory arrangements for the disposition of property and full settlements of mutual accounts.

"In witness of the above we have hereunto set our hands at ——, this the 11th day of February, 1886.

"[Sign in duplicate]ᵢ   HILDEBRAND & FUGATE."

A demurrer to the petition, for want of facts sufficient, ⁴⁶⁷ was sustained by the special term, and the appellant standing by the demurrer, and refusing to plead further, the appellees had judgment upon the demurrer. On appeal to the general term the judgment was affirmed, holding that the demurrer was rightly sustained to the petition. That ruling of the general term is assigned here for error.

The appellant contends that the contract on which the petition is founded creates the relation of principal and agent between the appellant and the firm of Hildebrand & Fugate for the sale of the powders mentioned therein; and that by the terms of that contract the title to the goods remained in appellant as consignor until sold by such firm as such agent; and that the proceeds of such sales vested in appellant as soon as the sales were made; and that the firm of Hildebrand & Fugate became trustee to collect and pay over to appellant such proceeds, less their commissions and other lawful charges. And appellant further contends that the fund arising from such sales is a trust fund, which the appellant, as *cestui que trust,* may follow into whatever shapes or forms it may pass, so long as it can be identified; and that the facts stated in the petition, while they show that the fund has become commingled and consolidated with the funds and assets of the insolvent firm, yet that equity will fasten the trust upon the estate of the failing partnership by making appellant a preferred creditor so as to get the alleged trust fund out of the estate in the hands of the receiver.

Both of these propositions are disputed by the appellees. They concede that the contract does create an agency; that the firm of Hildebrand & Fugate was thereby made the agent of appellant to sell their powders; that the property in the goods consigned remained in appellant as the consignor until the sale took [468] place; and that thereupon said firm ceased to be an agent as to so much and such part of the goods consigned as had been sold by such consignees, and they thereupon became the debtor of the consignor, the appellant, for the price stipulated in the contract, less their commissions and lawful charges.

The appellant's learned counsel concede that this would be the legal status and result under and by virtue of the terms of the contract, if its terms had been complied with by Hildebrand & Fugate in executing to appellant the sixty day notes at the stipulated times for the amount of the sales of powder by them made, less their commissions and lawful charges.

The concession, then, is that while the relation of principal and agent is created by the contract to sell goods by Hildebrand & Fugate, as such agents for appellant, and that the property in the goods remained in the appellant until a sale took place, in pursuance of the contract of agency, yet that, when that contract was carried out, the relation of principal and agent ceased at that point, and, by virtue of the contract, a new relation arose, namely, that of debtor and creditor, for the amount for which the goods sold, less commissions and charges.

The only difference, therefore, between counsel on both sides as to this point is that appellant's counsel contend that a different relation between the parties than that provided in the contract may arise or be created by the act of one of the parties thereto without any new contract, or the modification of the old by mutual agreement of both.

Such a doctrine is at variance with the plainest and most familiar elementary principles of the law of contracts.

It is manifest that the contract fixes the relations between [469] the parties thereto at every stage of the transactions provided for therein. It is also manifest that the failure to execute the notes at the times specified in the contract to pay the proceeds of the sales made during the several periods specified therein, to the appellant, less the commissions and charges, does not change the terms of the contract, nor does it release the obligation of the firm of Hildebrand & Fugate to pay appellant such amounts. If it did, then Hildebrand & Fugate, having made improvident sales on credit to purchasers who afterward proved insolvent and unable to pay, could take advantage of their own wrong, refuse to execute the notes in violation of their contract, and then insist on throwing the loss on the appellant in further violation of their contract. The terms of the contract vest the property of the proceeds of the sales, whether made for cash in hand or on credit, in the firm of Hildebrand & Fugate, and obligate them to pay in sixty days after the close of each period specified during which sales were made.

The obligation thus created is not that of an agent to his principal, but that of a debtor to his creditor. Their failure to execute the notes therefor, pursuant to the contract, does not change their respective relations to each other, nor the obligation of Hildebrand & Fugate to pay.

The appellant's learned counsel attempt to liken the transaction to a sale of personal property, where the title to the property will not pass until the terms of the sale are complied with. For instance, if a sale of such property is made for cash in hand, or for notes to be executed for the purchase price. In such a case it is said the title will not pass until the purchase price is paid or the notes executed. And they apply this principle to the proceeds of the sales of powder. But the contract in [470] this case provides for the vesting of the title to the proceeds of sales in Hildebrand & Fugate before the time for the execution of the notes or the payment of the money. It makes no provision for a report of even the names of the purchasers of the powder, much less the amounts purchased by each, nor the obligations entered into by each to pay therefor. Had the contract contemplated that the appellant in any event had, or was to have, any title to or interest in such proceeds, it would most likely have contained such a provision. It clearly contemplated that Hildebrand & Fugate assumed all risks of the solvency and honesty of the purchasers of powder as their debtors, and that appellant assumed all risks of the solvency and honesty of Hildebrand & Fugate, as appellant's debtors, for the proceeds of sales of powder, less commissions and charges.

The case of *Nutter* v. *Wheeler*, 2 Low. 346, is very much like the present case in every respect.

The court, in that case, on pages 348 and 349, said: "And it is plain that the goods sent to Boston by the defendants, from time to time, remained their property until they were sold, and that when a sale occurred Gear became immediately the debtor at a fixed price, and was bound to pay at a definite time, and that he never consulted with them about terms or purchasers, or any thing else, except the variations of the trade price; never accounted to them or was expected to account as agent, or was subject to their directions, excepting as to the tools remaining in his hands undisposed of. As to those goods sent to Boston, he may be described as a bailee, having power to sell as principal.   Until a sale was made, the property in the goods remained in the defendants, and they were well justified in reclaiming those which remained on hand at the time of the failure of Gear.   But, after the goods were sold, the agreement appears to have [471] been that Gear's credit only was looked to.   Perhaps there were conveniences in this mode of conducting the business.   Whatever profit or loss Gear might make, or whatever credit he might give, the defendants had a fixed price and a fixed time of payment.   He never consulted them about his sales, or rendered any account of sales.   The prohibition against selling below the trade price is a very common one between a manufacturer and those who buy of him to sell again, and is intended to prevent a ruinous competition between sellers of the same article.   I have often known this arrangement to be made by a patentee and his various licensees.   It has but little tendency to prove agency. . . . . But the real inquiry in all cases is, whether the credit was given to the person sought to be charged by the person seeking to charge him. . . . . If the relation of the parties was such as I have considered it, then, even as to the goods which had once been consigned to Gear, he should be considered as the purchaser, subject only to the understanding that he was neither the owner of them, nor liable to pay for them until he had succeeded in finding a purchaser; but when he did sell he immediately became the principal, and the defendants ceased to have the rights of a consignor, and could not follow the goods or their proceeds as undisclosed principals."

Among the authorities cited in the above opinion is the late English case of *Ex parte White*, L. R. 6 Ch. App. 397. That case was almost an exact parallel to the case at bar, and it was there held that the proceeds of such sales vested

202 PowDEB Co. v. HILDEBRAND. [Indiana,

in the person who had been agent until the sale was made, and that thereupon he became a debtor.

It was said by that high court, on pages 400 and 401, that: "Mr. Nevill was not to pay immediately; and if he sold for cash, it seems to me impossible that Towle & Co. [472] could have any right to say, 'You have sold the goods for cash; therefore, hand over the money to us at once.' Nevill would have said, 'No; the bargain between us is that I am to give you an account at the end.of the month, and to pay you at the end of another month. My selling for hard cash does not alter the nature of the bargain between you and me, or entitle you to call upon me to hand the moneys over to you, or to put the moneys *in medio* and keep them for you.' The proceeds of sale were his own moneys, ... and he was at liberty to deposit them with a banker, or deal with them as he pleased." On appeal to the House of Lords this case was affirmed: 21 Week. Rep. 465. To the same effect is *In re Linforth*, 4 Saw. 370.

We are, therefore, of opinion that the proceeds of the sales of powder under the contract were the property of the firm of Hildebrand & Fugate, and that the appellant has only a claim as a common creditor against the assets of said firm in the hands of the receiver of the firm.

The appellant's counsel suggest that the court below ought to be reversed, even though we should reach the conclusions above stated, because it is claimed the intervening petition states facts sufficient to enable appellant to obtain an allowance of the claim as a common creditor of the firm. But the theory upon which the intervening petition proceeds is wholly at variance with such an allowance. It proceeds upon the theory that no such relation as debtor and creditor ever existed between the appellant and the firm of Hildebrand & Fugate; that the relation was that of principal and agent, trustee and *cestui que trust*. It proceeds upon the theory that the proceeds of the sales of powder always belonged, and still belong, to the appellant in equity, and that the firm of Hildebrand & Fugate held them as trustee for appellant's [473] benefit; and it seeks to follow them into the assets of that firm in the hands of its receiver, and invokes the aid of equity to fasten the trust upon them and hold them for appellant's benefit.

It is a familiar and well-established rule that a pleading must proceed upon some one single definite theory, and it must be good upon that theory or it will be held insufficient on demurrer, however sufficient it might be on some other theory: *Feder* v. *Field*, 117 Ind. 386; *First Nat. Bank etc.* v. *Root*, 107 Ind. 224; *Louisville etc. Ry. Co.* v. *Godman*, 104 Ind. 490; *Chicago etc. R. R. Co.* v. *Bills*, 104 Ind. 13; *Leeds* v. *City of Richmond*, 102 Ind. 372; *Holderman* v. *Miller*, 102 Ind. 356; *Bremmerman* v. *Jennings*, 101 Ind. 253.

The idea of making the intervening petition the basis for an allowance of the claim to appellant as a common creditor seems to be an afterthought put forth in the reply brief for the first time.

The intervening petition, for the reasons already stated, does not state facts sufficient to constitute a cause of action, or to entitle appellant to any relief on the theory upon which it proceeds.

The conclusion reached makes it wholly unnecessary to pass on the very interesting question so ably discussed in the briefs as to whether equity would follow a fund and fasten a trust upon it under the circumstances described in the intervening petition, and we intimate no opinion thereon. It is sufficient to end our inquiry in that direction when we reach the conclusion we have, that the proceeds of the sales of powder never were a trust fund. We are, therefore, of opinion that the general term did not err in affirming the ruling of the special term in sustaining the demurrer to the intervening petition.

The judgment of the general term is affirmed.

———

CONSIGNMENT FOR SALE VESTS TITLE, WHEN.—A consignment is not a sale. It consists of one person's sending goods to another to be sold or disposed of by the latter for and on account of the former. The agent employed to sell goods or merchandise consigned or delivered to him, by or for his principal, for a compensation, is commonly called a factor; but the simple fact of consignment of goods to the consignee is by no means notice to him that the consignor holds him, as a purchaser of the goods, for their price: *Peck* v. *Ritchey*, 66 Mo. 114. In commercial transactions the house that receives and sells any commodity for another party guarantees the price, less the agreed commissions, but gives no security to make this guaranty good. The responsibility of the house, and of every member of it, is pledged to the consignor, and their credit is accepted as satisfactory when the consignment is made: *Gould* v. *Lee*, 55 Pa. St. 99. The mere shipment of goods does not always vest the property in the consignee, though he is a purchaser, as there may be some condition unperformed, or circumstances inducing the shipper to retain in his own hands the ultimate appointment of the consignment: *Steamboat John Owen* v. *Johnson*, 2 Ohio St. 142. Hence, a consignee of goods for sale incurs no liability until he has accepted the consignment: *Du Peirat* v. *Wolfe*, 29 N. Y. 436. Nor can he receive any benefit from it until acceptance: *Bank of Rochester* v. *Jones*, 4 N. Y. 497; 55 Am. Dec. 290. But after acceptance he is bound by the terms prescribed by the shipper, and cannot refuse to comply with the orders which accompany the consignment: *Loraine* v. *Cartwright*, 3 Wash. C. C. 151; *Walker* v. *Smith*, 4 Dall. 389; *Cotton* v. *Hiller*, 52 Miss. 7; *Weed* v. *Adams*, 37 Conn. 378; *Beadles* v. *Hartmus*, 7 Baxt. 476. It must be observed, however, that the action of the consignee in accepting or refusing a consignment does not affect the consignor's title to the goods consigned, though an acceptance of the consignment does fix a liability upon the consignee: *Chaffe* v. *Heyner*, 31 La. Ann. 594. The factor, therefore, has, ordinarily, no property or interest in the goods beyond his commissions, and cannot control the right of the principal over them (*Walter* v. *Ross*, 2 Wash. C. C. 283; *Cobb* v. *Illinois Cent. R. R. Co.*, 88 Ill. 394; *Beadles* v. *Hartmus*, 7 Baxt. 476; *Ogden* v. *Coddington*, 2 E. D. Smith, 317; *Bonner* v. *Marsh*, 10 Smedes & M. 376; 48 Am. Dec. 754; *Bank of Rochester* v. *Jones*, 4 N. Y. 497; 55 Am. Dec. 290; *Stafford* v. *Webb*, Hill & D. Supp. 213), as the title is in him: *Sturm* v. *Boker*, 150 U. S. 312; *Walter* v. *Ross*, 2 Wash. C. C. 283; *Cobb* v. *Illinois Cent. R. R. Co.*, 88 Ill. 394; *Benny* v. *Rhodes*, 18 Mo. 147; 59 Am. Dec. 293; *Lindley* v. *Downing*, 2 Ind. 418; *Bonner* v. *Marsh*, 10 Smedes & M. 376; 48 Am. Dec. 754; *Bank of Rochester* v. *Jones*, 4 N. Y. 497; 55 Am. Dec. 290; *Stafford* v. *Webb*, Hill & D. Supp. 213; *Cayuga County Nat. Bank* v. *Daniels'* 47 N. Y. 631; *Bevan* v. *Cullen*, 7 Pa. St. 281.

The consignor is liable for the freight: *Hayward* v. *Middleton*, 1 Mill Const. 186. And the consignee, having no title, would have no cause of action against a carrier for negligence or delay in transportation: *Cobb* v. *Illinois Cent. R. R. Co.*, 88 Ill. 394; *Ogden* v. *Coddington*, 2 E. D. Smith, 317. Neither can the title of the principal be divested by the factor's transfer of the goods to pay a private debt: *Benny* v. *Rhodes*, 18 Mo. 147; 59 Am. Dec. 293. As a factor, when he receives goods for sale on commission, he undertakes to account for those he may sell, and to pay over the proceeds, and to redeliver the residue on demand: *Lindley* v. *Downing*, 2 Ind. 418. As the consignment does not involve a change of title it cannot be subjected by the consignee's creditors to the payment of his debts: *Sturm* v. *Boker*, 150 U. S. 312, 330; *Moore* v. *Hillabrand*, 16 Abb. N. C. 477. Neither has the factor any right to pledge the goods of the consignor: *Chicago Taylor Printing Press Co.* v. *Lowell*, 60 Cal. 454; *McCreary* v. *Gaines*, 55 Tex. 485; 40 Am. Rep. 818; *Macky* v. *Dillinger*, 73 Pa. St. 85; *Commercial Bank* v. *Hurt*, 99 Ala. 130; 42 Am. St. Rep. 38. One essential incident to trust property is that the trustee or bailee can never make use of it for his own benefit: *Sturm* v. *Boker*, 150 U. S. 312, 330. Hence, a factor cannot retain the proceeds of a sale of goods consigned to him for the purpose of canceling a debt held by him against the person from whom the trust is derived: *Bell* v. *Powell*, 23 La. Ann. 797; *Succession of Norton*, 24 La. Ann. 218. A factor who receives goods, and, in his own name, ships them to another market to be sold by a subagent, cannot collect the proceeds against the will of the owner. After the sale the subagent is the debtor, and not the trustee, of the principal: *Jackson Ins. Co.* v. *Partee*, 9 Helsk. 296.

Of course, if the factor has made advances upon the merchandise consigned to him for sale, he has a special property or interest in the consignment to the extent of such advances. He has a vested interest in the good, for his protection, and as security for his advances and charges and interests which would enable him to hold the goods against third parties or even the consignor himself; but only so far as would be necessary for his protection and security. His title is, therefore, a qualified one: *Moore* v. *Hillabrand*, 16 Abb. N. C. 477; *Cotton* v. *Hiller*, 52 Miss. 7. The legal title to the property passes to him to carry out certain designated purposes, and he has the right to the undisturbed possession of it until those purposes are effected. The consignee, where he has made advances, has title to the extent of his interest: *Nelson* v. *Chicago etc. R. R. Co.*, 2 Ill. App. 180; *Brooks* v. *Hanover Nat. Bank*, 26 Fed. Rep. 301; *Beadles* v. *Hartmus*, 7 Baxt. 476; *Weed* v. *Adams*, 37 Conn. 378; and is regarded as a purchaser for value: *Hall* v. *Hinks*, 21 Md. 406. A person who advances money upon the faith that the proceeds of goods remaining in the hands of the owner will be applied to his reimbursement, has no such title as will support an action for their delivery: *McCurdy* v. *Brown*, 1 Duer, 101; but the moment that the goods are consigned to him, and put in the possession of a carrier or forwarder, title vests in the consignee, and the consignors would have no right to change the destination of the goods, or even to exercise the right of stoppage *in transitu*, common to consignors, where they have already received, by way of advance, the full amount of the proceeds of the articles: *Stafford* v. *Webb*, Hill & D. Supp. 213.

ACCEPTANCE AND PAYMENT OF DRAFTS—BILLS OF LADING.—It is a common mercantile transaction for the consignor of property, upon its shipment, to draw a bill of exchange or draft upon the consignee, and procure the same to be discounted upon the faith of the bill of lading, which is transferred and delivered with it. In such cases the bank or person discounting the paper acquires the title to the property described in the bill of lading to secure payment, conditioned upon the consignee's accepting the bill or draft. If property is delivered to a carrier, consigned to a factor for sale, the consignee only acquires title thereto in case the shipment is accompanied by an unconditional consignment in pursuance of an agreement to ship; and an owner who has made a prior agreement to consign goods may, notwithstanding, impose any conditions upon the consignment he chooses, and the consignee can only acquire title by performing the conditions. Even where the consignor is indebted to the consignee for advances, and has agreed to ship the goods to the latter for sale, from the proceeds of which the advances are to be repaid, the consignee has no prior security against the goods as against a bank discounting a bill of exchange, drawn by the consignor against the consignee, on the faith of a bill of lading. Whether the delivery of property by a consignor to a carrier vests the title in the consignee is largely a question of intention. The ordinary mercantile transaction of discounting a draft on consignees, and attaching the bill of lading to the draft, in the absence of any further explanation, affords *prima facie* evidence of an intention to pass the title to the goods mentioned in the bill of lading, to the extent of the amount called for by the draft. In support of the above propositions, see note to *Bank of Rochester* v. *Jones*, 55 Am. Dec. 299, 300. If a party consigns goods to another, and draws upon the consignee for funds, accompanying the draft with the delivery of the bill of lading or shipping receipt as collateral security for its payment, the acceptance and payment by the consignee of the draft, accompanied with the bill of lading or shipping receipt, vests in him a special property in the goods sufficient to maintain replevin against an officer who, after such delivery, attaches them upon a writ against the general owner, and, although the draft is not paid until after the officer has levied on the goods, yet if the draft and shipping receipt were delivered to the payee of the draft before the levy, such delivery will be regarded as made for the use of the consignee, and when he pays the draft his right to the goods will relate back to the time of the delivery of the draft and shipping receipt to the payee of the draft, without reference to the fact as to whether the payee of the draft paid any consideration therefor to the owner or not, if the consignee paid it in good faith, without notice of any attachment or levy on the goods: *Peters* v. *Elliott,* 78 Ill. 321.

SALE OR CONSIGNMENT.—The agency to sell goods and return the proceeds, or the specific goods if not sold, stands precisely upon the same footing as a bailment. The title is not changed in either case, and the recognized distinction between bailment and sale "is that when the identical article is to be returned in the same or in some altered form, the contract is one of bailment, and the title to the property is not changed. On the other hand, when there is no obligation to return the specific article and the receiver is at liberty to return another thing of value, he becomes a debtor to make the return, and the title to the property is changed; the transaction is a sale": *Sturm* v. *Boker,* 150 U. S. 312, 329, per Jackson, J. This distinction or test of a bailment was recognized in *Powder Co.* v. *Burkhardt,* 97 U. S. 110; *Barnes Safe & Lock Co.* v. *Bloch etc. Tobacco Co.,* 38 W. Va. 158, 166, *post,* p. 842; *Rahilly* v. *Wilson,* 3 Dill. 420; *Bretz* v. *Diehl,* 117 Pa. St. 589; 2 Am. St. Rep. 706.

It is evident from a consideration of what constitutes a sale and what constitutes a consignment for sale, that the terms and conditions under which the goods are delivered are not always clear, and that the transaction may be either a sale or a consignment for sale, depending upon certain facts which are in dispute, doubt, or uncertainty. In such cases the evidence should be submitted to the jury, and they should determine the issue as to whether the transaction was a sale or a consignment for sale. Especially is this true where the rights of the parties depend upon an agreement between them which can be gathered only from statements and expressions used by them in letters and conversations which are apparently conflicting and inconsistent with each other. Under such circumstances it is the duty of the jury, and not of the court, to find from all the evidence what the agreement really was: *Rauber* v. *Sundback,* 1 S. Dak. 268; *Head* v. *Miller,* 45 Minn. 446; *Yaeger Milling Co.* v. *Brown,* 128 Mass. 171; *Lobdell* v. *Horton,* 71 Mich. 681; *Crosby* v. *President of Delaware etc. Canal Co.,* 119 N. Y. 334; *Holbrook* v. *Wight,* 24 Wend. 169; 35 Am. Dec. 607; *Cobb* v. *Illinois Cent. R. R. Co.,* 88 Ill. 394; *Ellsner* v. *Radcliff,* 21 Ill. App. 195; *Keiser* v. *Esterly,* 160 Pa. St. 100; *Bretz* v. *Diehl,* 117 Pa. St. 589; 2 Am. St. Rep. 706. And evidence showing the nature of the transaction is admissible, as that an order for goods was given in response to a proposition to deliver the goods upon consignment: *Head* v. *Miller,* 45 Minn. 446, or that the consignee, exercising an election, accepted the goods as a purchaser: *Yaeger Milling Co.* v. *Brown,* 128 Mass. 171. Letterheads may also be considered in connection with the letters upon which they are placed in determining whether a consignment of goods has been "solicited" and made: *Simpson* v. *Pegram,* 108 N. C. 407. But, where the contract is clearly expressed in writing, the printed billhead of the invoice cannot control, modify, or alter it: *Sturm* v. *Boker,* 150 U. S. 312, 327. If a party consigns goods to another, sending him a letter of advice, and immediately after draws upon the consignee for funds, and the consignee accepts the drafts, a jury is warranted in finding a contract, and that the title to the goods has vested in the consignee, although there is no express agreement to that effect: *Holbrook* v. *Wight*, 24 Wend. 169; 35 Am. Dec. 607. The acceptance, however, and payment of drafts drawn on general account, without reference to any particular lot of goods forwarded, will not pass the title: *Cobb* v. *Illinois Cent. R. R. Co.*, 88 Ill. 394.

SPECIAL AGREEMENTS—FRAUDULENT AGREEMENTS.—The authorities appear to show clearly that the consignor of goods to be sold on commission does not part with his title by the consignment; that he continues to be the true owner until the goods are sold by the consignee; and that the rule is the same whether the consignee is a *del credere factor*, or is under advances for the principal, or is simply an agent for sale: *Commercial Nat. Bank* v. *Heilbronner*, 108 N. Y. 439; reversing the same case, 20 Jones & S. 388; *Sturm* v. *Boker*, 150 U. S. 312; *Barnes Safe & Lock Co.* v. *Bloch Bros. Tobacco Co.*, 38 W. Va. 158, *post*, p. 842; *Peek* v. *Heim*, 127 Pa. St. 500; 14 Am. St. Rep. 865.

Therefore, a consignment for sale does not vest title except where the facts of the case, such as the contract, the bill of lading, and the invoice, show an intent to give the consignee a right of property, free from any condition whatever: *Cayuga County Nat. Bank* v. *Daniels*, 47 N. Y. 631. It must be observed, however, that a mere agreement to ship, though founded upon a good consideration, gives no title: *Cayuga County Nat. Bank* v. *Daniels*, 47 N. Y. 631; *First Nat. Bank* v. *McAndrews*, 5 Mont. 325; 51 Am. Rep. 51; and that an invoice is not a bill of sale or evidence of a sale. It is a mere detailed statement of the nature, quantity, and cost or price invoiced, and is as appropriate to a bailment as it is to a sale. Hence, standing alone, it is never regarded as evidence of title: *Sturm* v. *Boker*, 150 U. S. 312, 328. But the delivery of a bill of lading to a bank for the purpose of securing the payment of drafts drawn by the consignor upon the consignee, and discounted by the bank, is sufficient to transfer the title to the property covered by the bill of lading, subject to be divested only by acceptance of the draft: *Cayuga County Nat. Bank* v. *Daniels*, 47 N. Y. 631. It thus appears that outside of ordinary consignments for sale the question as to whether a transaction is a sale, or a consignment for sale, depends upon the particular contract between the parties; and after a sale by an agent, which entitles his principal to a cash payment, the principal may take the agent's notes in lieu of cash without converting the agent into a purchaser of the goods, if he was in fact an agent to sell at the time the sale was effected: *National Bank* v. *Goodyear*, 90 Ga. 711.

Some illustrations of the subject taken from the more recent decisions are as follows: A contract by which one person receives goods on consignment to be sold by him as agent of the consignor, monthly reports to be made, the goods to remain on consignment as the property of the consignor until paid for in full by the consignee, and all proceeds of sale to belong to the consignor until he is paid the invoice price in cash, which is payable as sales are made, is one of bailment for sale and agency, and not of absolute sale, although it provides that the compensation of the consignee shall be any surplus over the price named in the contract; that goods removed from his place of business shall be paid for immediately; that he shall pay all expenses, charges, and taxes, and assume all risks of loss or damage, but that upon his failure to sell or to comply with any condition the consignor may terminate the agency, and goods remaining on hand are to be subject to his order free from charges: *National Bank* v. *Goodyear*, 90 Ga. 711. A consignment of goods to a retail dealer to be sold at not less than a certain price for cash, with an agreement that he may retain the excess above that price as commissions, and that he shall return on demand the goods or money received for them, does not constitute a sale as to the creditors of such dealer: *Rosencranz* v. *Hanchett*, 30 Ill. App. 283. The title does not pass, of course, where the goods consigned are to be held as the property of the consignor: *Blood* v. *Palmer*, 11 Me. 414; 26 Am. Dec. 547; or where they do not reach the consignee: *Alexander* v. *Tomlinson*, 40 Ark. 216. Neither does title pass to the consignee where the consignor is to stock the consignee with coal, wood, and bark to be sold at retail, the consignee to be paid so much a ton for doing the business, and the consignee to purchase from the consignor such as may be required, and to account monthly, and the consignor to fix the price, retail and wholesale, not above the lowest market price: *Audenried* v. *Betteley*, 8 Allen, 302; or where the consignee is to sell at a certain price and to have a commission on each machine sold, and to guarantee the notes taken, the unsold machines to be paid for in notes or stored for the consignor at his option: *Weir Plow Co.* v. *Porter*, 82 Mo. 23. Nor does title pass, before delivery, in a shipment of bullion made without notice to the consignee, the proceeds to be credited when a sale shall be made, to advances previously made by the consignee: *First Nat. Bank* v. *McAndrews*, 5 Mont. 325; 51 Am. Rep. 51. A statute providing that if a person transacting business as a trader with the addition of the words "factor," "agent," etc., shall fail to disclose his principal, the goods shall be liable for his debts, is not intended to include the case of an agent holding and selling machinery on commission, although his name has after it on his business sign the words "Mfrs. Agent": *Brown Mfg. Co.* v. *Deering*, 35 W. Va. 255. And if a principal agrees to furnish his agent on consignment certain manufactured articles, at a stipulated price, to be paid for when sold, such articles, when so furnished, remain the property of the principal until sold to a *bona fide* purchaser, and are not subject to the debts of the agent. If the articles are sold to pay such debts the purchaser would get no title as against the principal: *Barnes Safe & Lock Co.* v. *Bloch Bros. Tobacco Co.*, 38 W. Va. 158, *post*, p. 842. For further illustrations which show a consignment and not a sale, see *Denney* v. *Wheelwright*, 60 Miss. 733; *Sturm* v. *Boker*, 150 U. S. 312; note to *Bretz* v. *Diehl*, 2 Am. St. Rep. 711, on distinction between sale and bailment; *Brown Bros. & Co.* v. *Billington*, 163 Pa. St. 76; 43 Am. St. Rep. 780.

On the other hand, the agent or consignee may, by express written contract, fasten upon himself a primary liability for goods consigned to him for sale: *Wheeler & Wilson Mfg. Co.* v. *Laus*, 62 Wis. 635. If he is under an obligation to pay for the goods delivered, and not merely to keep them on deposit or for sale, the transaction is a sale, and not a bailment: *Woodward* v. *Boone*, 126 Ind. 122. So, where the consignee is to settle for all goods on hand at the end of the year by giving his note, and the goods are furnished at schedule prices, the vendors can make no claim to the goods sold or removed from their warehouse by the consignee who has become bankrupt: *In re Linforth*, 4 Saw. 370. Again, a consignee, by the terms of his agency, may be the agent of the consignor until the consigned goods are sold; and when they are sold, become, as between him and the consignor, the purchaser of, and principal debtor for, the goods sold: *Nutter* v. *Wheeler*, 2 Low. 346.

ACTIONS—ATTACHMENT—BANKRUPTCY—LOSS OF GOODS.—As the title to goods in an ordinary consignment for sale is in the consignor, an attachment of the goods or levy of execution upon them, or their proceeds by the creditors of the consignee, is without jurisdiction, and void: *Barnard* v. *Kobbe,* 54 N. Y. 516; *Powell* v. *Brunner,* 86 Ga. 531; *McCollough* v. *Porter,* 4 Watts & S. 177; 39 Am. Dec. 68; *Blood* v. *Palmer,* 11 Me. 414; 26 Am. Dec. 547; *Ellsner* v. *Radcliff,* 21 Ill. App. 195.

The goods may be seized by an attaching creditor of the consignor before they reach the consignee: *Bonner* v. *Marsh,* 10 Smedes & M. 376; 48 Am. Dec. 754; *First Nat. Bank* v. *McAndrews,* 5 Mont. 325; 51 Am. Rep., 51; and the consignor may replevy them from an officer levying an execution on them against the consignee: *Alexander* v. *Tomlinson,* 40 Ark. 216. So, before the property has reached the consignee, the consignor may transfer the title to the goods to a third person, by an assignment of the bill of lading, or even by a delivery thereof with intent to pass the title: *Bank of Rochester* v. *Jones,* 4 N. Y. 497; 55 Am. Dec. 290. Again, in an action involving the title to goods consigned for sale, the assignee or receiver in insolvency can assert no better claim than the consignee: *Head* v. *Miller,* 45 Minn. 446; and the principal of a bankrupt factor may, therefore, recover from the assignee any goods remaining unsold, or any proceeds of a sale of such goods which the assignee has sold, or which can be specifically distinguished from the property of the bankrupt: *Nutter* v. *Wheeler,* 2 Low. 346. Even where the factor is acting under a *del credere* agreement, if nothing more than the relation of principal and factor exists, the principal is entitled to recover in full the proceeds of goods sold by the factor, and which have been collected by the factor's assignee for the benefit of creditors: *Gindre* v. *Kean,* 31 Abb. N. C. 100. But if the agreement between the parties establishes the relation of buyer and seller, instead of that of principal and agent, the principal cannot recover from the assignees of his consignee the proceeds of goods sold by the latter, and collected by such assignees, or recover on the notes of the purchasers of such goods in the hands of the assignees: *In re Linforth,* 4 Saw. 370. If goods have been shipped on a *del credere* commission the title to the unpaid purchase money for goods sold by the factor, remains in the shipper, and, if attached by the creditors of the factor he may recover of the sheriff the amount received by him under the attachment: *Moore* v. *Hillabrand,* 37 Hun, 491.

On the other hand, a factor who has made advances on goods consigned to him for sale has such an interest in them as will support an action by him to recover the goods from one to whom they have been wrongfully delivered: *Fitzhugh* v. *Wiman,* 9 N. Y. 559. He may sue a carrier for their loss, waste, or wrongful conversion: *Adams* v. *Bissell,* 28 Barb. 382; or maintain replevin against an officer who attaches them upon a writ against the general owner: *Peters* v. *Elliott,* 78 Ill. 321; or replevin against an attaching creditor of the consignor, to whom the officer making the attachment had delivered the goods: *Nesmith* v. *Dyeing etc. Co.,* 1 Curt. 130; or trespass for a wrongful attachment by the creditors of the consignor: *Halliday* v. *Hamilton,* 11 Wall 560. The factor's interest, however, being limited to the amount of his advances and charges, an attachment by a creditor of the consignor will bind any surplus left in the hands of the factor after his claims for advances and charges have been satisfied: *Patterson* v. *Perry,* 10 Abb. Pr. 82. It is error, however, in an action of replevin by a consignor where only an alternative judgment for a return of the property or the value thereof is authorized, to direct a verdict for the plaintiff, for the value of goods in the hands of a factor, less the factor's advances and commissions: *Wood* v. *Orser,* 25 N. Y. 348. The rights of the consignee who has refused to accept a shipment of goods to him, and who attaches the goods as an ordinary

creditor, are subordinate to the rights of an intervenor who has advanced on
the goods, and holds, as the transferee of the consignor, the bill of lading:
Chopin v. *Clark,* 31 La. Ann. 846. While goods consigned to a factor for sale
remain the property of the consignor, and are not subject to the debts of the
factor, a consignment made for the purpose of covering up a sale, and preserving a lien in the sellers for the price of the goods, is void, as respects creditors of the buyer: *Peek* v. *Heim,* 127 Pa. St. 500; 14 Am. St. Rep. 865, and
note; *Chickering* v. *Bastress,* 130 Ill. 206; 17 Am. St. Rep. 307.

Another effect of the fact that the title rests in the consignor in a consignment for sale is that the consignee is not liable for loss before acceptance of
the consignment: *Du Peirat* v. *Wolfe,* 29 N. Y. 436; or afterward, where he
has followed the shipper's instructions, and the destruction has not been
caused by the factor's fault: *Milburn Wagon Co.* v. *Evans,* 30 Minn. 89;
Barrows v. *Cushway,* 37 Mich. 481; though he would be liable for loss in
not complying with such directions: *Gordon* v. *Wright,* 29 La. Ann. 812;
Housel v. *Thrall,* 18 Neb. 484. Nor could the factor, if the goods are destroyed while in his possession, claim their value for the benefit of the
owner: *Stone* v. *Mayor etc.,* 25 Wend. 157; *Mayor etc.* v. *Stone,* 20 Wend. 139.
The consignee is not liable for a loss arising from the act of God: *Dunbar* v.
Gregg, 44 Ill. App. 527; but, if he accepts an invoice expressly stating that
the merchandise is at his risk, he will be liable in case of loss: *Reinstein* v.
Watts, 84 Me. 139.

"SALE OR RETURN" CONTRACTS exist where the privilege of purchase or
return is not dependent upon the character or quality of the property sold,
but rests entirely upon the option of the purchaser to retain or return.
In this class of cases the title passes to the purchaser subject to his option
to return the property within a time specified or a reasonable time; and
if, before the expiration of such time, or the exercise of the option given,
the property is destroyed, even by inevitable accident, the buyer is responsible for the price: *Sturm* v. *Boker,* 150 U. S. 312, 329; *Main* v. *Oien,*
47 Minn. 89; *House* v. *Beak,* 141 Ill. 290; 33 Am. St. Rep. 307. Such authorities, however, must be distinguished in determining when a consignment for sale vests title, as they are not in point: *Sturm* v. *Boker,* 150 U. S.
312, 329.

BURROWS *v.* STATE.

[137 INDIANA, 474.]

LARCENY.—THERE CAN BE NO CONVICTION FOR LARCENY WITHOUT PROOF
OF THE VALUE of the stolen property. It must be shown to be of
some value, for the purpose of fixing the grade of the offense, and the
penalty to be imposed. The market value of the article stolen, and
not its original cost, is the test by which to determine the grade of the
larceny.

LARCENY—PROOF OF VALUE—PRESUMPTION.—If the value of articles stolen
is fixed by law, as in the case of gold or silver coin, or national currency, no other proof of their value is necessary; but, in the absence of
any evidence upon the subject of value, the court cannot indulge in
presumptions to supply the omission.

LARCENY—PROOF OF VALUE—PRESUMPTION.—If the value of notes, bills of
exchange, drafts, and checks is not *prima facie* fixed by statute, the

question of their value, in case of larceny, is to be determined by the jury the same as that of any other article of personal property. The fact that the maker of a check has funds in the bank cannot give rise to any presumption affecting its validity or value.

THE GIVING OF A CHECK IS NOT PAYMENT until the money is received on it, or the check is accepted by the bank at which it is made payable.

LARCENY—BANK CHECK—INSTRUCTION.—To instruct the jury, in a prosecution for the larceny of a bank check, that "a check drawn on a bank, when the drawer has money on deposit, as much or more than sufficient to pay the check, is presumptively of some value, in the hands of the person in whose favor it is drawn," is erroneous, as it usurps the functions of the jury by taking away from them the question of value, which it is their province alone to determine.

G. D. Hurley and M. E. Clodfelter, for the appellant.

A. G. Smith, attorney general, and W. S. Moffett, for the state.

⁴⁷⁴ DAILEY, J.   The appellant was indicted in the court below for the alleged larceny of one check on the First National Bank of Salem, New York, for the sum of fifty dollars, bearing date of June 19, 1893, executed to the order of Arthur Le Roy Piser, by L. C. Piser, and charged to have been of the value of fifty dollars.

Plea of not guilty; trial by jury; verdict of guilty, assessing punishment at imprisonment in the state prison for the period of two years; a fine in the sum of one dollar, and disfranchisement for five years.

⁴⁷⁵ There was a motion for a new trial, which was overruled.   Judgment upon the verdict and appeal to this court.

Six errors are assigned.   The first four are predicated upon the overruling of the motion to quash the indictment and the several counts thereof; the fifth upon the overruling of the appellant's motion for a new trial; and the sixth upon the overruling of his motion in arrest of judgment.

Under the fifth specification of error it is contended by counsel for the appellant that the fifth instruction given by the court to the jury of its own motion was clearly erroneous. It is as follows: "A check drawn on a bank, when the drawer has money on deposit, as much or more than sufficient to pay the check, is presumptively of some value in the hands of the person in whose favor it is drawn."

It has long been an established rule of the courts that without proof of the value of stolen property there can be no conviction for larceny.   It is essential to prove the value of the property alleged to have been stolen, in order to determine

the grade of the offense and the penalty to be imposed. In
the absence of any evidence upon the subject of such value
the court or jury could not indulge in presumptions to supply the omission. The goods need not be proved to be of the
value charged in the indictment, but it must be shown that
they are of some value: Bicknell's Criminal Practice, 327;
Moore & Elliott's Indiana Criminal Law, note, sec. 368, p. 238.

The market value of the article stolen, and not its original
cost, is the true criterion by which to determine the grade of
the larceny: Moore & Elliott's Indiana Criminal Law, note
239, citing *Taylor's case*, 1 City H. Rec. 28; *State* v. *Doepke*,
68 Mo. 208; 30 Am. Rep. 785; *Cannon* v. *State*, 18 Tex. App.
172; *People* v. *Cole*, 54 Mich. 238.

[476] There is an exception to this rule, in that the value
of gold or silver coin and national currency generally being
fixed by law, no other proof of their value is necessary:
McCarty v. *State*, 127 Ind. 223; *Collins* v. *People*, 39 Ill. 233;
Grant v. *State*, 55 Ala. 201; *Duvall* v. *State*, 63 Ala. 12.

In all jurisdictions where the value of notes, bills of exchange, drafts, and checks is not *prima facie* fixed by statute,
the question of their value is solely for the jury, and courts
should not invade its province.

In Iowa and Missouri, where these instruments are, by
statute, made subjects of larceny, their value is *prima facie*
fixed by statute at their face value: *State* v. *Pierson*, 59 Iowa,
271; 1 Mo. Rev. Stats., sec. 2539.

In this state section 1878 of Burns' Revised Statutes of
1894 defines what written instruments may be the subject of
larceny, among which are named bills, orders, drafts, checks,
etc. But we have no section of the statute fixing *prima facie*
the value of such instruments. By this section such instruments are considered as personal goods, of which larceny
may be committed, and their value is left to be determined
by the jury, the same as that of any other article of personal
property.

The enactment of laws in Iowa and Missouri, fixing *prima
facie* the value of these choses in action, is a controlling
argument in favor of the necessity of such a law, and equally
as potent a reason, in the absence of it, that the value of this
class of instruments is a question alone for the consideration
of the jury trying the cause. Courts cannot, during the progress of a trial, supply by instruction what they may deem
to be necessary legislative enactments. The court bases its

presumption of law, contained in instruction number 5, upon the contingency that the drawer of the check has on deposit as [477] much money as will pay it, or more than enough for the purpose.

It is a rule of law well established that the giving of a check is not payment until the money is received on it, or the check is accepted by the bank at which it is made payable: *People* v. *Baker*, 20 Wend. 602 (604); *People* v. *Howell*, 4 Johns. 296 (303); *Pearce* v. *Davis*, 1 Moody & R. 365.

In *Harrison* v. *Wright*, 100 Ind. 515, 50 Am. Rep. 805, it was held that the execution of a check is not even an equitable assignment of any part of the funds of the maker to the payee. This being true, the fact that the maker of the check has funds in the bank could not give rise to any presumption affecting its validity. It seems clear upon principle, and by the great weight of authority, that at any time before acceptance and payment the drawer may countermand the check.

In the present case the bank at which the check was made payable, being located in the state of New York, the maker could have availed himself of the right to order the bank not to pay it, or withdraw the money on deposit before it could have been presented for payment.

In our opinion, in the giving of instruction number five, the court usurped the functions of the jury, and took away from them the question of value, which it was their province alone to determine. In criminal cases the jury are the exclusive judges of the facts proven, and of all inferences to be drawn therefrom: *Moore* v. *State*, 85 Ind. 90; *Jackman* v. *State*, 71 Ind. 149; *Faller* v. *Salmons*, 87 Ind. 328; *Union etc. Ins. Co.* v. *Buchanan*, 100 Ind. 63.

This is a constitutional provision, guaranteed in the bill of rights.

Section 64 of Burns' Revised Statutes of 1894 declares that: "In all [478] criminal cases whatever, the jury shall have the right to determine the law and the fact."

It may be remarked that the giving of an erroneous instruction is not cured by the giving of a correct or conflicting one.

In Elliott's Appellate Procedure, section 705, it is said: "The general rule is that the court may cure errors in its instructions by withdrawing, explaining, or correcting them. Where a material instruction is given that is erroneous it should be effectively withdrawn. An error in giving an erroneous instruction is not cured by merely giving another contradicting it. The court cannot, without fatal error, give contradictory instructions to the jury."

In the case at bar it is a conceded fact that the check in controversy was mailed by the maker at his home in New York, addressed to the payee at Crawfordsville, Indiana, payable to order, without any indorsement thereon. There is no testimony that it ever reached its destination, unless the posting of a letter duly addressed and stamped creates a *prima facie* presumption of its receipt by the party addressed within the usual time. As against such presumption there is the positive testimony of the prosecuting witness that it never came into his possession, and that he did not indorse it.

On the trial of the cause it became a material question whether the check in controversy, payable to order, out of the possession of the payee, and without his indorsement thereon, was of any value. The instruction in review in effect told the jury to ignore the testimony of the witnesses as to value, for the reason already indicated that a value was to be presumed.

There are other questions presented by the record, and argued by counsel in their briefs in this case; but, as they [479] may not arise upon another trial of the cause, we deem it unnecessary to decide them.

For the error of the court in the matter herein indicated the judgment of the circuit court is reversed, with instructions to grant a new trial, and for the necessary order for the return of the prisoner. ____

LARCENY—VALUE.—Indictments for larceny must state the value of the property alleged to have been stolen only when the punishment is graduated with reference to its value: *State* v. *Perley,* 86 Me. 427; 41 Am. St. Rep. 564. It is not necessary, in order to sustain a conviction, to prove the value as alleged, but the property stolen must be shown to be of some value, as things of no value are not the subjects of larceny: *Commonwealth* v. *Riggs,* 14 Gray, 376; 77 Am. Dec. 333. Under the Indiana statutes it is only necessary, in an indictment for larceny of money, to describe the money stolen simply as money, giving, of course, the aggregate value; but, if a particular description is given, it must be proved substantially as charged: See note to *State* v. *Segermond,* 10 Am. St. Rep. 175.

CHECK—PAYMENT.—A check on a bank is not payment, unless by express contract it is so received: *Johnson-Brinkman etc. Co.* v. *Central Bank,* 116 Mo. 558; 38 Am. St. Rep. 615.

JONES *v.* KOHLER.

[137 INDIANA, 528.]

PROCESS—NONRESIDENT—SERVICE OF NOTICE BY PUBLICATION.—If a married woman, interested in land, shifts about from place to place, and her whereabouts have been unknown to her friends and acquaintances for about thirty-five years, and notice in an action to quiet title to the land is given to her by publication in her former name, by which she was known in the state, it is sufficient, although her husband had died and she had since married, and taken the name of her second husband.

PROCESS—NONRESIDENT—SERVICE OF NOTICE BY PUBLICATION—PRESUMPTION—ESTOPPEL.—If notice of a judicial proceeding is properly given to a nonresident by publication, the presumption is that the party notified becomes acquainted with the notice, and he is estopped from denying it.

G. H. Voigt and E. B. Stotsenburg, for the appellant.

W. W. Tuley and G. H. Hester, for the appellees.

528 HACKNEY, J.   By the last will and testament of Peter Ross, probated in April, 1858, in providing for all of his children and disposing of all of his property, were made, among others, the following two bequests: "I bequeath to my daughter, Mary Jackson, ... the house and tenements I now occupy, together with four acres of ground, embracing the orchard, provided that she come **529** and live in it and occupy it," and "I bequeath to my son Eli the home place, containing seventy acres, more or less, providing Mary takes the four acres before mentioned to reside on."

Eli took possession of the "home place," and, with his family, occupied it from the death of his father until his death.

At the time of the execution of the will, and for many years thereafter, Mary Jackson shifted about from city to city, and from state to state, without communication with her family, friends, or acquaintances in this state, and with no knowledge on their part as to her whereabouts until in 1891, and in ignorance of any change in her name or of the death of her husband.

After the death of Eli his widow and children sued the heirs of said Peter Ross, including said Mary Jackson, to quiet the title to said "home place," and, in 1878, obtained a decree in all respects regular and unobjectionable, save that the notice to said Mary was by publication to and in the name of Mary Jackson, when, as she claims, her hus-

band, Jackson, had died in 1860, and she was again married.
in 1871 to one Jones.

After the proceeding to quiet title, and in proceedings for
partition, the appellee, Philopœna Kohler, in 1879, became
the purchaser of said "home place," and now holds the same
free from adverse claim, excepting that here made by Mary
Jones in her suit claiming title and demanding partition.

Her complaint ignores the will of her father, and treats
her surviving brothers and sister as owners, in common with
her, of the undivided four-fifths of said land, and she makes
no reference to said proceeding and decree of 1878.

The several answers of Philopœna Kohler set up the ⁵²⁰
will, the decree, and the partition sale, and allege that at the
time of said publication the appellant was known as Mary
Jackson.

The evidence supported the answers, and the court found
for the appellee, Mrs. Kohler.

The argument includes two questions: Did Eli Ross fail to
acquire these lands by reason of the breach of the condition,
if it was a condition, that Mary should take the four acres?
And, was the decree quieting title void as to Mary Jones,
because of the notice to her as Mary Jackson?

If a person is known by more than one name, it is a common rule that service of process by either name is sufficient.
If one by his conduct leads others to believe, with reason,
that a state of facts exists, it will not be permitted that such
an one may deny the existence of that state of facts, and
especially where the decrees of courts have been entered and
investments have been made in reliance upon such facts.

Here it appears that one having property rights within
this state absented herself for more than thirty-five years,
abandoning those rights and withdrawing herself from the
jurisdiction of the state; when she departed she was a married woman, bearing the name of her husband; the presumption of a continuation of life and that state of matrimony
during the allotted time of life, and that her property rights
would be held and treated with reference to such presumptions, created a duty to avoid deceiving others by concealing
changes in such conditions. At least, she could not complain
that others, in perfect good faith, acted upon and with reference to such conditions.

The object in publishing the notice of nonresidence is that
the interested party may observe that the law is about to

deal with his property, and that, if objection can be made [531] to so dealing with it, an opportunity will be afforded. When a publication is made, the presumption must prevail that the interested party becomes acquainted with the notice; at least, such party will be held to have seen it, and to be estopped to deny it.

If Mary Jackson, instead of changing her name by assuming that of a second husband, had procured the change by enactment of a·legislature, without notice of such change to those who might deal, in good faith, with reference to her property, it would be without merit that she could claim to defeat the rights of those so dealing. When it is conceded that the state has the power to take jurisdiction and make disposition of the property of a nonresident, by publishing a notice of the pendency of the cause in which it is proposed to exercise that jurisdiction, and when it is conceded that the publication is held to have reached the nonresident, such nonresident must be held bound by all that the notice contains.

In this instance the notice was given to the interested party in the only name by which she was known within the jurisdiction of this state—the only name by which, as she well knew, she would be dealt with in this state; that name in which she would necessarily be notified of the pendency of legal proceedings, and that name which, when reading the notice, she would, of course, understand to apply to herself.

Under our statute (Rev. Stats. 1881, p. 317; Rev. Stats. 1894, p. 319), neither the summons nor the service thereof may "be adjudged insufficient where there is sufficient substance about either to inform the party on whom it may be served that there is an action instituted against him in court, the name of the plaintiff and the court, and the time when he is required to appear."

This provision applies with equal force where the summons is by publication as where it is by personal service.

[532] We have found but one case which would seem to conflict with our conclusion that the notice in this case was sufficient, and that is the case of *Freeman* v. *Hawkins*, 77 Tex. 498, 19 Am. St. Rep. 769, where the publication was in the name of Mary E. Robinson, who, by a marriage, had taken the name of Freeman. It was there held that because of a statutory requirement that the notice should contain the names of the parties to the action the publication was insufficient.

Our statute does not expressly so require, and we here have the additional fact that the party served by publication was known by the name in which she was served.

Finding the notice sufficient the decree was valid, and a to bar the appellant's recovery.

The judgment of the circuit court is affirmed.

JUDGMENT—SERVICE OF PROCESS BY PUBLICATION— NAME.—A judgment quieting title, in which the name of the owner is incorrectly stated or spelled though the summons is served by publication only, is, nevertheless, binding upon him, if it is the name by which he is designated in the conveyance by which he acquired title. By accepting the conveyance he consents to be known by that name in all proceedings relating to the land so conveyed to him, and, if that name is used in a legal proceeding or notice, he is presumed to understand that it is addressed to him: *Blinn* v. *Chessman*, 49 Minn. 140; 32 Am. St. Rep. 536.

COBURN *v.* STEPHENS.

[137 INDIANA, 683.]

MECHANIC'S LIEN — SUFFICIENCY OF NOTICE.—A mechanic's lien notice is sufficient if it describes the premises, and states the amount due, to whom and from whom, and for what it is due.

MECHANIC'S LIEN—IMPERFECT DESCRIPTION, HOW AIDED BY EXTRINSIC EVIDENCE.—Under proper allegations in the pleadings of an action to enforce a mechanic's lien, an imperfect description of the property in the lien notice may be aided by extrinsic evidence. That is certain which can be made certain.

MECHANIC'S LIEN—CONTRACT WITH OWNER.—If a materialman is seeking to enforce a mechanic's lien against land of the owner, there can be no recovery unless the lien is perfected, and this cannot be done unless a contract is shown to have been made with the owner or his agent.

MECHANIC'S LIEN—LANDLORD AND TENANT.— Except as to his own interest, a tenant, as such, cannot subject the real estate of his landlord to a mechanic's lien.

MORTGAGES—TWO SECURITIES FOR SAME DEBT.—One holding a real estate mortgage and a chattel mortgage, as security for the same debt, does not lose any right under the former by not enforcing the latter.

MORTGAGE — MECHANIC'S LIEN — MERGER. — If the holder of a purchase money mortgage, having priority over a mechanic's lien, takes from his grantee a quitclaim deed to the property after the mechanic's lien has attached, in consideration of such grantee's release from personal liability on the notes secured by the mortgage, a merger does not take place, and equity will preserve the prior lien of the mortgagor. It is only where the fee simple and the lien center in the same person, and where there are no intervening equities, that a merger of the title and the lien will take place.

EVIDENCE—EXCLUSION OF, IS HARMLESS ERROR, WHEN.—A deed of assignment executed by a debtor, and specifying certain debts named therein
to be paid by the trustee, is competent evidence for the purpose of
proving the creditor's claim by such admission on the part of the
assignor, but if the only question at issue is the right to enforce a mechanic's lien upon the debtor's land, the exclusion of the deed is harmless error.

J. Coburn, for the appellant.

M. G. McLain and J. P. Baker, for the appellees.

[684] HOWARD, C. J.   The appellant brought this action to
enforce a materialman's lien against certain real estate owned
by the appellee, Joseph L. Stephens, making the remaining
appellees defendants to answer as to their interests in said
land.

The appellees, Joseph L. Stephens and wife, suffered default.   The appellee, John Chew, answered in general denial,
and filed his cross-complaint, setting up his mortgage on said
real estate, alleged to be prior to the lien claimed by appellant.   The appellee, William H. English, also answered in
general denial, and filed his cross-complaint, setting up his
first mortgage on said land, besides his paramount lien for
taxes.

Special pleas were filed by appellant to the cross-complaint
of the appellee, John Chew, to which special answers said
appellee filed special replies.   Other pleadings were filed
which need not here be further noticed.   Errors and cross-
errors were assigned.

The appellee, John Chew, contends that the complaint and
notice of lien were insufficient; but we think the court did
not err in holding them good.   Several parcels [685] of ground
are named in the notice, but we think they are so described
that we may know that they form one body of land, upon
which the buildings described are located.   The county in
which the lands are situated is not named in the notice, but
in the complaint it is alleged that the lands are in Marion
county, Indiana.   It was the intention of the legislature that
the mechanic's and materialman's lien law should be liberally interpreted in favor of mechanics, materialmen, and
laborers.   Imperfect descriptions of property may therefore be
aided by extrinsic evidence under proper allegations in the
pleadings.   That is sufficiently certain which can be so made
certain: *White* v. *Stanton,* 111 Ind. 540.   The notice is sufficient if it state the amount due, to whom, from whom, and

for what, and describe the premises: *Simonds* v. *Buford*, 18 Ind. 176.

The appellant, in the fourth and fifth paragraphs of his answer to the cross-complaint of the appellee, John Chew, averred that the said Chew, in addition to his mortgage on said real estate, had also a chattel mortgage on certain personal property, forming an additional security for the debt due him by appellee Stephens, but that instead of taking possession of the chattels under his mortgage he suffered them to be wasted by another person, in whose possession they were; and it is assigned as error that the court sustained demurrers to these paragraphs of answer. It is true that the appellee Chew might have taken possession of these chattels and converted them into money in payment, or part payment, of his debt; but, while this might be a benefit to appellant, we do not see that Chew was obliged to realize on those securities. It was rather for him to judge for himself whether his mortgage on the land was sufficient security for the debt due him from Stephens, and appellant cannot complain: *Knarr* v. *Conaway*, 42 Ind. 260.

[686] The appellee John Chew had sold the land described in the complaint to the appellee Stephens; and the mortgage set up in the cross-complaint of John Chew was given to secure the unpaid part of the purchase price for said land. At the time of the filing of appellant's notice of his lien in the recorder's office, and for a long time before, the said purchase money mortgage was on record and unsatisfied, and the purchase money so secured was unpaid, and is still unpaid.

In the second paragraph of his answer to the cross-complaint of the appellee Chew, the appellant averred that since the filing of said cross-complaint the appellees Stephens and wife had, by quitclaim deed, conveyed the mortgaged land to John Chew, and that the consideration for such deed was the amount due on the notes secured by said purchase money mortgage; that said mortgage is, therefore, satisfied by such conveyance, and is merged in the fee simple by such deed, and asking that the mortgage debt be declared satisfied and the mortgage canceled of record.

To this paragraph of answer the appellee Chew replied that he admitted the execution to him by Stephens and wife of the quitclaim deed, but that the only consideration for such deed was the release given by him to Stephens of any personal liability on the notes secured by the mortgage; that Stephens is a nonresident of the state, and is insolvent; that it was further agreed between him and Stephens, at the time of the execution of the deed, that the conveyance was not to have the effect of merging the mortgage in the fee simple, but that the mortgage should remain as a valid and subsisting lien on the land for the security of said debt and the protection of Chew's title.

A demurrer to this paragraph of reply was overruled, and appellant very earnestly contends that such ruling [687] was erroneous. "It is an elementary rule," as laid down in *Lowrey* v. *Byers*, 80 Ind. 443, "that equity will consider an encumbrance as in force if the ends of justice can be thereby attained: *Troost* v. *Davis*, 31 Ind. 34; *Howe* v. *Woodruff*, 12 Ind. 214."

John Chew's purchase money mortgage was filed and recorded December 18, 1886. The alleged contract for furnishing the material for which the lien is claimed was made in July, 1888, so that, under the statute of 1883 (Elliott's Supplement, sec. 1691), then in force, the lien which was filed October 9, 1888, could not relate further back than July, 1888: *Fleming* v. *Bumgarner*, 29 Ind. 424; *Mark* v. *Murphy*, 76 Ind. 534.

The purchase money mortgage in favor of the appellee Chew was, therefore, a lien upon the land sold to appellee Stephens long prior to the earliest time to which the lien claimed by appellant could have related back. Could the deed taken by Chew from Stephens have merged the lien of the mortgage so as to give appellant's materialman's lien a better standing against the land than it had when the notice was filed? We think not.

The agreement set up in the reply made between Chew and Stephens, to the effect that there should be no merger, was for their mutual benefit, and could not, as we think, injuriously affect the rights of appellant, who was not a party to such agreement. Neither do we think that the transfer of title from Stephens to Chew could in any way inure to appellant's advantage to the prejudice of the parties to the agreement. The lien of the mortgage was prior to any lien that appellant might have. In equity this priority of lien could not be lost by reason of Chew becoming the owner both of the fee simple and of the mortgage lien. It is only where the fee simple and the lien center in the same person, and where there are [689] no intervening equities, that a merger of the title and the lien will take place: *Thomas* v. *Simmons*, 103 Ind. 538; *Hanlon* v. *Doherty*, 109 Ind. 37; *Strohm* v. *Good*, 113 Ind. 93; Pomeroy's Equity Jurisprudence, sec. 793.

The first reason given in the motion for a new trial is that the court erred in excluding as evidence a deed of assignment executed by the appellee Stephens, making one Charles Wagner a trustee to take charge of certain personal property, out of which he should pay debts named in said deed of assignment. Amongst the debts so admitted was that of appellant. We are of opinion that appellant was entitled to this evidence for the purpose of proving his claim by such admission on the part of the appellee Stephens. We think, however, that the error was harmless so far as the purposes of the action are concerned. Appellant is not seeking a judgment against Stephens, but to enforce a lien against the land owned by Stephens at the time of filing notice of the intended lien. If the materialman's lien was never perfected, there can be no recovery.

This brings us to another important question in the case. As we have already said, we are of opinion that the complaint and the notice of intention to hold a lien were good in form. But an examination of the evidence leads to the conclusion that the lien was not in fact perfected, for the reason that no contract is shown with Stephens, who was then the owner of the premises.

Appellant offered a great deal of evidence to show that one Poor, who lived upon the farm, was the agent of Stephens, and that the contract for materials was made with Poor, as such agent. We have carefully looked through all this evidence, and we think that none of it, nor all of it taken together, can amount to proof of such agency. From the deposition of Stephens, read in evidence, it appears that Poor was his brother in law, and [689] occupied and farmed the land. Nothing in the deposition shows any agency on the part of Poor. On the contrary, it appears that when Stephens wished to surrender the land to Chew, and to enter into an agreement with him to be released from his personal liability on the mortgage notes, he sent an agent from Ohio, a Mr. Clark, to transact the business. He also states expressly that he never purchased the materials for which the lien is claimed, and never authorized any one to purchase them.

In the newly discovered evidence, on account of which also a new trial is asked, several letters are given. One of these was written by Stephens to an investment company. In this, the only letter shown in the record as written by Stephens, he makes no mention of Poor. On the contrary, in the letter, he appoints the investment company his agent to attend to some financial business for him. We do not think there was any thing in this newly discovered evidence to prove the agency of Poor.

If Poor was Stephens' agent this should be shown by some writing, some language, or act of Stephens himself. No evi‹ dence given or offered showed that Stephens intrusted any business whatever to Poor; and we must find, with the trial court, that no agency was shown.

If Poor was merely the tenant of Stephens, that, of itself, would give him no authority to enter into contract with appellant so as to authorize the filing of a lien upon Stephens' real estate, except, of course, as to any interest therein which the tenant might himself own: *Ogg* v. *Tate*, 52 Ind. 159; *Adams* v. *Buhler*, 116 Ind. 100.

We find no error in the record, and the judgment is affirmed.

———

MECHANIC'S LIEN—NOTICE—DESCRIPTION.—A mechanic's lien notice is sufficient if it contains all of the essential requisites of a lien as prescribed by law: *Johnston* v. *Harrington*, 5 Wash. 73. The description of a building in the notice of a mechanic's lien is sufficient if it enables a person familiar with the location to identify the building as the only one corresponding with such description: *Hughes* v. *Torgerson*, 96 Ala. 346; 38 Am. St. Rep. 105, and note.

MECHANIC'S LIEN—OWNER—LANDLORD AND TENANT.—It is necessary for a materialman, in order to enforce a mechanic's lien, to show that the material was furnished in pursuance of an agreement, express or implied, with the owner or his agent: *Bloomer* v. *Nolan*, 36 Neb. 51; 38 Am. St. Rep. 690, and note. The party with whom the contract is made, by a person furnishing labor or materials, is regarded as the owner of the premises only to the extent of his interest, and that interest only is subject to a mechanic's lien. Hence a tenant for life or years cannot, by contract, create a lien upon the fee. On the contrary, he can create a lien only to the extent of his right and interest in the premises: *Williams* v. *Vanderbilt*, 145 Ill. 238; 36 Am. St. Rep. 486, and note.

CASES

IN THE

SUPREME COURT

OF

IOWA.

HINKLE *v.* AVERY.

[88 IOWA, 47.]

WATERCOURSE, CHANGE IN LOCATION OF.—If for many years, and as a result of natural causes, a watercourse has flowed across the lands of the plaintiff, though it formerly flowed upon the lands of the defendant, and the change in its course came so gradually that it is not easily traced in its history, it must be regarded as a watercourse upon the lands of the plaintiff, which defendant has no right to divert so that it will again flow only upon his lands.

WATERCOURSE, WHAT IS.—If waters from springs uniting run into a ravine, and on reaching low, level land widen and then pass still farther, forming a pond, and beyond the pond flow not into a channel with banks, but along a depression in the earth and over the grass and sod, and the waters thus running are at some places quite narrow, and at others several rods in width, but a current is visible along their entire course, and they again come into a single channel, through which they flow into a river, they form, in contemplation of law, a watercourse which the owner of lands through which they flow has no right to divert and to keep from flowing beyond his lands.

Sloan & Brown and Work & Blake, for the appellant.

Wherry & Walker, for the appellee.

⁴⁸ GRANGER, J. The plaintiff and defendant are owners of adjacent farms, that of the plaintiff being directly west of the defendant's. On the dividing line, for a part of the distance, is what is known as the "Batavia road." North of the lands owned by the parties is land belonging to one Stoop. On the land of the defendant are two springs, from each of which is a flowing stream. On the land of Stoop, directly north of the defendant's land, is a like spring, the stream from which runs south and unites with those from the

(224)

springs on the defendant's land, and the stream thus formed runs through the barn lot of the defendant to the Batavia road on the line between the parties. It is the course of this stream, from this point, over which the contention in the case is. ·The plaintiff's farm consists of two hundred and sixty-three acres; the sixty-three acres being situated just across the Batavia road at the point where the stream reaches it.

The averments of the petition show: "That from time immemorial a natural watercourse or stream of water, supplied in part by a never-failing spring, has flowed in a natural and well-defined channel from the premises of the defendant, in a westerly direction, over and across the aforesaid sixty-three acres of the plaintiff's land, and from thence finding its way into the [49] Des Moines river, thus furnishing, where it flowed over the plaintiff's premises, a perpetual and bountiful supply of living water for the plaintiff's stock kept in said pasture, and being the only natural and continual supply of water above ground available for stock therein, and without which the value of such premises and pasture would be greatly and irreparably impaired." It is also averred that the plaintiff's land was used as a stock farm, on which is kept from one to two hundred head of cattle and horses, depending for water on the aforesaid stream. It is further averred that within the last few years the defendant has, by different methods, diverted the stream from its natural channel, so as to deprive the plaintiff of its legitimate use. The answer is, in its legal effect, a denial. It contains other averments, but, in view of the positions taken in argument, our statement of it is sufficient.

The appellant presents the questions for our consideration as follows: "1. Does the water from the spring form a stream with a well-defined course, confined by banks, so that the defendant did not have any right to divert it, even if its course was over and across the plaintiff's premises? 2. Was the course of the water over and across the plaintiff's premises, as claimed by him, or wholly on the defendant's premises?" We will adopt the inverse order in considering the propositions, the latter being exclusively one of facts.

1. As bearing on this question, much testimony has been taken, and among the witnesses are those who have resided in the neighborhood of the stream for fifty years or more, and were among the first settlers of the state. Much of the testi-

mony is directed to the flow of the water from the spring
onto the defendant's farm at that early period; the spring on
Stoop's place not then being in existence. By the aid of
surveys and excavations it is [50] made to appear that quite
a material change has been made in the natural curvature
of the earth because of deposits, and on account of the wash
from the adjacent hills, and it is a matter of considerable
doubt, at least, if the natural course of these waters has not
been, to some extent, changed thereby. But, however this
may be, and if it be conceded that originally these waters
naturally flowed along on the west side of the Batavia road,
and across the land of the defendant to the river, it is a well-
established fact that for many years, and as a result of
natural causes, they have flowed across the road onto and
over the land of the plaintiff. This fact has existed for so
long a time, and, if the change in the course of the waters
ever came, it was so gradual and so remote from the present,
that the fact is not easily traceable from its history as disclosed by the evidence. From the history of this case we are
led to believe that the question of the flow of this water being
otherwise than as it naturally would be at the present time
was not thought of, or relied upon, as a significant fact in the
case until near the conclusion of the trial of the case in the
district court. This would not, of course, lessen the importance of the fact, if true, but it has a value in finding the fact
where it is one of doubt. We are of the opinion that the flow
of the water was across the land of the plaintiff, so as to
justify the action, if the other proposition is resolved in the
plaintiff's favor.

2. It may be well to restate the proposition in this connection: "Does the water from the spring form a stream with a
well-defined course, confined to banks, so that the defendant
did not have the right to divert it, even if its course was
over and across his premises?" The proposition presents
two inquiries: 1. The particular facts as to the character of
the stream; and 2. Their legal effect upon the rights of the
parties. The water from these springs runs a little more
than a mile to the [51] Des Moines river. It starts and runs
for a few rods in what may be called a ravine, when it
reaches low, level land, and the stream widens. Farther on,
because of the construction of the public highway, it is
brought into such a compass as to pass through a culvert,
and then onto the plaintiff's land, on which is formed, in

part at least by this water, a pond. Beyond this pond the
water flows, not in a channel with banks, but along a depression in the earth, and over the grass or sod. It seems to be
irregular in width, owing to the character of the ground, at
some places quite narrow, and at others several rods in width.
It has had, however, at all times the characteristics of a flowing stream, it may be said, a current that is visible and distinctly traceable. Before reaching the river the water comes
again into a channel or small branch called " Crooked creek,"
and thence into the river.

The legal contention arises over the definition of a " stream
or watercourse," so as to come within the rule whereby one
riparian owner cannot divert it from its natural course to
the damage of another such owner. The doubts as to the
definition are induced by the language of the adjudicated
cases. The appellant's theory is that, to constitute such a
watercourse, there " must be a distinct channel or bed of a
stream with well-defined banks cut through the turf and
into the soil by the flowing of the water, presenting on a casual
glance to every eye unmistakable evidence of frequent action
of running water, and not a mere depression; and such a
flow must be necessary to prevent the flooding of a considerable tract of land." Definitions somewhat similar have
been many times given. Kerr's Injunctions in Equity, page
251, uses this language: "As distinguished from water of a
casual and temporary character, a watercourse is a flow of
water usually flowing in a certain direction, and by a regular channel, having a bed, banks, and sides, and possessing
that unity of character [52] by which the flow on one man's
land can be identified with that on the land of his neighbor."
If we now look to the adjudicated cases to see the application
of the general rule to the facts of particular cases we may be
aided to a proper application of the law to the case in hand.

The appellant cites us to *Gibbs* v. *Williams*, 25 Kan. 214,
37 Am. Rep. 241, as a very conclusive case, and it would
appear that his definition, as we have quoted it, is taken
therefrom. The case deals with surface water, and aims to
indicate the distinction between a watercourse and surface
water from rains and melting snows collected into streams
in ravines and depressions causing a temporary flow, but not
of a character to be known as a watercourse. To this end
the opinion employs language that, if literally applied, and
given application to cases involving the flowage of water from

springs and other streams, would override many well-considered cases, and operate as a denial of what has long been considered established rights of riparian owners of land. The particular language, "with well-defined banks cut through the turf into the soil by the flowage of the water," is mainly relied upon in this case. Reading that case with care, and in connection with *Palmer* v. *Waddell*, 22 Kan. 352, it will be seen that both cases deal with the exceptional question of when surface water caused by rainfalls constitutes a watercourse so as to take it out of the general rule as to surface water, and bring it within the rule as to watercourses. In such a connection the language is apt, and its correctness would not be doubted. *Bloodgood* v. *Ayers*, 108 N. Y. 400, 2 Am. St. Rep. 443, is another case cited by appellant, but the facts are widely different from this case. That was a case of percolating water. There was no flowing stream from the spring, and the case was determined upon an uncertainty as to facts, and not upon the rule of the appellant's contention. [53] *Barkley* v. *Wilcox*, 86 N. Y. 140, 40 Am. Rep. 519, is another case of surface water, and the court defines a "natural watercourse" as "a natural stream flowing in a defined bed or channel, with banks and sides, having permanent sources of supply." This definition closely approximates the facts of this case. Some parts of the way the stream in question has no banks, and, in a literal sense, there may be no channel in places, but in the ordinary acceptance of the term there was a channel. The case of *Hoyt* v. *City of Hudson*, 27 Wis. 656, 9 Am. Rep. 473, contains a definition not met, in a literal sense, by the facts of this case, but the language there used is as to surface water from rains and melting snow.

We now notice a few cases more closely allied to the facts of this case. In *Pyle* v. *Richards*, 17 Neb. 180, it is said: "When water has a definite source, as a spring, and takes a definite channel, it is a watercourse." The case quotes from *Shields* v. *Arndt*, 4 N. J. Eq. 234, as follows: "There must be water as well as land, and it must be a stream usually flowing in a particular direction. It need not flow continually, as many streams in this country are, at times, dry." In Gould on Waters it is said: "Surface water may be said to form a watercourse at the point where it begins to form a well-defined channel, with bed, banks, or sides, and current": See section 263. It is in such a connection that much of the language relied upon by the appellant is used.   The case of *Macomber* v. *Godfrey*, 108 Mass. 219; 11 Am. Rep. 349, is a case in its material facts parallel to this.   It was a brook running from the land of the defendant to that of the plaintiff.   It was a well-defined stream for a part of the way on the defendant's land.   Before reaching the plaintiff's land the water spread out over the surface of the ground a few rods in width, and so ran upon and across the plaintiff's land, which was a level meadow, covering it several rods in width and irrigating it, and [54] in this shape passed onto the land of others.   From the point where the water spread out on the defendant's land to a point beyond the plaintiff's land there was no "defined channel."   A short distance beyond the plaintiff's land the water again formed a small brook, and ran to the river.   In that case it was said: "If the whole of the stream had sunk into the defendant's soil, and no water remained to pass to the plaintiff's land except under the surface, it would have ceased to be a watercourse, and the plaintiffs would have had no right to it."   It was held to be a watercourse with well-defined bed and banks, with its usual course in a channel. The rule of the case is a salutary one.   This case is not different in principle.   In this case the water was spread out over a longer line, but it was not lost in the earth, nor was the identity of the stream lost.   A case closely in point sustaining the rule is *Gillett* v. *Johnson*, 30 Conn. 180.

Our conclusion is that the stream in question is such a one that the plaintiff has the right to its enjoyment, and that because of its diversion the plaintiff's action was, by the district court, properly sustained.   We are not aware of any adjudicated case against this conclusion when properly considered.   The district court, by its decree, gave to each party one-half of the water in the stream, and of that the defendant should not complain.   The judgment is affirmed.

WATERCOURSES — CHANGE IN LOCATION OF. — A stream of water which has been diverted from its natural channel by reason of an unusual freshet, and allowed by an adjoining proprietor to flow over his land for the period of ten years without objection, cannot be restored by him to its original course: *Woodbury* v. *Short*, 17 Vt. 387; 44 Am. Dec. 344.

WATERCOURSES DEFINED.—A watercourse is a living stream with definite banks and channel, and a mouth distinguishable from its source, not necessarily running all the time, but fed from more permanent sources than mere surface water: *Chamberlain* v. *Hemingway*, 63 Conn. 1; 38 Am. St. Rep. 330, and note.

FAWKNER *v.* SMITH WALL PAPER COMPANY.

[88 Iowa, 169]

CONTRACT, EVIDENCE TO VARY.—If a written contract is made for the delivery of goods at wholesale prices evidence is not admissible tending to prove that the parties in the negotiation preceding the execution of the contract had a card on which was printed a list of goods and of prices, and that the agreement was to take the goods at such prices. Such evidence, if admitted and given effect, would vary the terms of a written contract.

CONTRACTS—VARYING.—WHATEVER THE LAW IMPLIES FROM A CONTRACT IN WRITING is as much a part of the contract as that which is therein expressed, and if the contract, with what the law implies, is clear, definite, and complete, it cannot be added to, varied, or contradicted by extrinsic evidence.

CONTRACT PARTLY WRITTEN AND PARTLY ORAL.—Extrinsic evidence is not admissible to show that a contract was partly written and partly oral, if the matter proposed to be made part of the contract by such evidence is inconsistent with the terms of the writing.

A CONTRACT WHICH IS CERTAIN, COMPLETE, AND UNAMBIGUOUS CANNOT BE VARIED by evidence of the situation of the parties, or the subject matter of the contract, and the acts of the parties under it.

J. R. Barcroft and Crom Bowen, for the appellant.

P. F. Bartle, for the appellees.

170 KINNE, J. The question involved in this case was deemed of such importance that a rehearing was granted, and further argument had. The original opinion will be found in 49 N. W. Rep. 1003.

The plaintiff declared upon the following written contract:

"DES MOINES, IOWA, July 11, 1887.

"On demand I promise to deliver to the order of E. F. Fisher eight hundred dollars (less twenty per cent discount), in wallpaper, at wholesale price, good, clean, assorted stock out of my store on Fifth street, Des Moines, Iowa. No storage.   LEW SMITH WALL PAPER Co."

On the same day there was indorsed on the back of said contract a statement signed by Fisher that he had given Towne & McFarland an order for two hundred dollars' worth of said paper, and that it had been delivered to them; also, an assignment of the contract to the plaintiff. It was averred that demand had been made for the balance of the goods at the wholesale price, and that the defendant refused to deliver the goods at said price. Judgment was asked for six hundred dollars and interest.

The defendant admitted the execution of the contract, and the payment of the two hundred dollars, and denied all the other allegations in the petition. He also pleads that, at the date of making the order, and of its acceptance by Fisher, the "wholesale price" for good, clean, assorted wall-paper, and the price upon which [171] said order was based, and at which said paper was to be delivered by the defendant to, and accepted by, the payee was agreed upon, and set forth on a card then shown Fisher, and a copy of same is attached to the answer; that the schedule of prices printed upon the card was then agreed upon between the parties to said order as the then wholesale prices at which paper was to be delivered, and said card accompanied the order, as a part of it, and a part of the contract fixing the wholesale price for said paper. It is also averred that defendant has tendered the six hundred dollars in paper to the plaintiff, in accordance with the contract and terms of said card.

1. The defendant was permitted to prove that, when the contract was made between the parties, he handed the plaintiff's assignor a card, having printed thereon a price list of wall-paper, and that he was to take the paper mentioned in the contract at the prices stated on the card. This evidence was objected to, as it tended to vary and contradict the written contract of the parties. The defendant claims that the evidence was admissible as constituting a part of the contract; that, though it was on a separate piece of paper, still it was in fact but a part of and altogether constituted but one contract. The rules of law touching the admission of parol, contemporaneous evidence, to add to, vary, or contradict the terms of a written contract, are well settled. The difficulty in these cases generally arises, not as to any doubt as to what the law is, but as to whether or not the case presented comes within the rules prohibiting the introduction of such evidence. We do not think the evidence was admissible. It tended to add to, vary, and contradict the written contract. By the terms of the contract the defendant company bound itself to deliver to the plaintiff, whenever he demanded it, wallpaper of the value of eight [172] hundred dollars (less twenty per cent discount), and the price of the paper was by the very wording of the contract to be the wholesale price at the time of such delivery. The instrument, it occurs to us, was in nowise ambiguous or uncertain, so as to call for extrinsic evidence to render certain the meaning of language

which, without it, would be obscure or unintelligible. It required no explanation as to what the "wholesale price" meant. The words "wholesale price" have a fixed, certain, and well-defined meaning in the mercantile world. They mean the price fixed on merchandise by one who buys in large quantities of the producer or manufacturer, and who sells the same to jobbers or to retail dealers therein. Neither can it be successfully claimed that the written contract leaves it a matter of doubt or uncertainty as to what wholesale price should be used in determining the value of the paper. The plaintiff or his assignor, by the plain terms of the contract, had a right to demand its fulfillment whenever he chose so to do. The contract was by its terms to be satisfied by delivery of wallpaper at wholesale price, the delivery to take place on demand. It was then a contract in all respects complete and perfect as to the parties, the subject matter, and the delivery. There is no claim that the schedule of prices, as set forth on the card introduced in evidence, was to be a part of the written contract, and was omitted by accident, mistake, oversight, or fraud. No such issue is presented. The evidence objected to would work a material change in the terms of the contract. It shows that the paper was to be received at a price which was agreed upon when the contract was executed, and outside of the provision of the written contract. It measured the amount of paper that should be received under the written contract by the then wholesale market price, when the written contract measured the amount of paper to be delivered [173] under it by the wholesale price at the time of demand made for the goods.

2. Another thing must be borne in mind in determining as to whether or not the written contract is such that it can be varied by parol evidence, and that is that the law raises certain implications from the terms used in the contract; that whatever the law thus implies from the language used in the writing is as much a part of the contract as that which is expressed therein: *Works* v. *Hershey*, 35 Iowa, 343; *American Emigrant Co.* v. *Clark*, 47 Iowa, 6/3; *Liljengren etc. Lumber Co.* v. *Mead*, 42 Minn. 420. Hence, if the contract as expressed or viewed in the light of what the law thus implies from the language used therein, is clear, definite, and complete, the rule applies that it cannot be added to, varied, or contradicted by extrinsic evidence. We have endeavored to show that this contract is complete in itself, and, when

construed in the light of its legal import, there can be no doubt as to its meaning, and it does not need the aid of extrinsic evidence: 2 Parsons on Contracts, 7th ed., 683, 694.

3. It is said that a contract may rest partly in writing and partly in parol, and that in such cases extrinsic evidence is admissible to establish that part which is not written. This exception is as well settled as the rule itself. But extrinsic evidence in such cases is only admissible when that part of the contract sought to be thus established relates to some matter about which the writing is silent. If the proposed evidence is in any way inconsistent with the terms of the writing, such evidence is inadmissible: *Blair* v. *Buttolph*, 72 Iowa, 31; 7 Am. & Eng. Ency. of Law, 91; 17 Am. & Eng. Ency. of Law, 443, 444; *Taylor* v. *Galland*, 3 G. Greene, 22; *Annis* v. *Annis*, 61 Iowa, 220. In the case at bar the evidence introduced [174] related to a matter as to which the contract itself speaks with certainty. The legal import of the contract determined that the wholesale price therein mentioned should be ascertained as of the date a demand and delivery of the goods was made. It was then impossible that in advance of that time, and at the time the contract was made, the parties could by parol ingraft upon it a provision inconsistent with the written contract as interpreted by the law. As we have said, the rule prohibiting the introduction of contemporaneous parol evidence to add to, change, or contradict a written contract is as clearly applicable when the effect of such evidence is to change the terms of the contract as interpreted by the law, as when it contradicts or varies the expressed provisions of it.

4. The court instructed the jury that if they found that, at the time the written contract was made, a card containing a list of prices of wallpaper was produced and shown to said Fisher, and it was agreed between him and the defendant that said card specified the wholesale price attached, and it was delivered to Fisher with the written contract as a part of it, and the goods were to be furnished under said contract, then the defendant had a right to charge for paper furnished to the plaintiff or his assignor the prices appearing on said card. For the reasons heretofore given this instruction was erroneous.

5. While it is competent in construing a contract to show the situation of the parties, the subject matter of the contract, and acts of the parties under the contract, as tending

to show how they understood it, still this cannot be done to
the extent of varying or contradicting a written contract,
when such contract is certain, complete, and unambiguous.
The case of *Thompson* v. *Locke*, 65 Iowa, 432, was one where
the contract was [175] not complete in all its parts: *Shuier* v.
Dutton, 75 Iowa, 155, 157; *Bigelow* v. *Wilson*, 77 Iowa, 603.

For the reasons given the judgment of the district court is
reversed.

———

CONTRACTS—PAROL EVIDENCE OF PRIOR AGREEMENTS.—Parol evidence is
not admissible to vary a written contract, by showing that it does not accord
with the previous agreement of the parties: *Cream City Glass Co.* v. *Fried-
lander*, 84 Wis. 53; 36 Am. St. Rep. 893, and note, with the cases collected.
See, also, the extended note to *Sullivan* v. *Lear*, 11 Am. St. Rep. 394.

———

MORGAN *v.* ROUNTREE.

[88 IOWA, 249.]

EXEMPTION LAWS ARE TO BE LIBERALLY CONSTRUED in favor of those
claiming their benefit.

HOMESTEAD—MONEYS DUE FOR RENT OF A HOMESTEAD ARE EXEMPT from
execution.

THIS case was presented upon a certificate of the trial
judge as follows: "Where the judgment debtor, who is a resident of this state and the head of a family, is temporarily
absent from her homestead for the period of one year for the
purpose of educating her daughter, and voluntarily executes
a lease of the homestead to a tenant during and for the period
of said absence, are moneys which are due and owing to the
judgment debtor from the tenant for the rent of said homestead accrued under said lease exempt from execution issued
upon a judgment in favor of the plaintiff and against the
judgment debtor?"

W. O. McElroy, for the appellants.

No appearance for the appellee.

[250] GIVEN, J. 1. It is the question certified, and that
alone, which we are to decide. Though plain and pointed,
the result is important, because of its effects, and demands
careful consideration. We regret not to have the benefit of
full arguments, but, as the appellee has submitted without
argument, we must forego the aid that would have come from a

full discussion of the question. It will be observed that there is no question of homestead, nor of abandonment, nor of the right to follow the proceeds of the lease into other property involved. The leased premises were and continued to be a homestead, and the question is simply whether the money due from the garnishee to the defendant is exempt to her. The only ground upon which such an exemption can be claimed is that it is the proceeds of the use of the homestead.

Exemption of property from the payment of debts is purely statutory, and courts may not enlarge the exemption; but, as said in *Kaiser* v. *Seaton*, 62 Iowa, 463, 466, " exemption laws are to be maintained in their spirit as well as letter, and even liberally construed in favor of those claiming their benefit": See, also, *Bevan* v. *Hayden*, 13 Iowa, 125; *Huskins* v. *Hanlon*, 72 Iowa, 37. Looking to the spirit of the law, this court held in *Kaiser* v. *Seaton*, 62 Iowa, 463, that money due as damages for right of way over a homestead was exempt, notwithstanding the character of the homestead was not destroyed as such by the easement. In *Mudge* v. *Lanning*, 68 Iowa, 641, it is held that a judgment for damages against a railway company for setting out fire, by which fences, vines, [251] and trees on a homestead were destroyed, was exempt. The appellants cite and rely upon *Huskins* v. *Hanlon*, 72 Iowa, 37, wherein it is said: " But homestead rights do not presumptively attach to money or choses in action. They are *prima facie* liable for debts, and are only exempt when sold with the intention to use such proceeds in the purchase of another homestead." The question in that case was whether the execution debtor intended to invest the proceeds derived from the sale of his homestead in another homestead, and hence the language of the opinion is limited to that kind of proceeds. Had proceeds derived as damages for right of way or setting out fire been involved they would have been included. That case does not hold that homestead rights may not attach to other money than that derived from the sale of a homestead for the purpose of purchasing another. In that case Hanlon failed to prove an intention to purchase another homestead with the proceeds derived from the sale; it was therefore held that the proceeds were not exempt. *Harkness* v. *Burton*, 39 Iowa, 101, also cited, is not in point. That case holds that a license to remove minerals from the homestead, when its enjoyment does not impair the use of the homestead, may be given by the husband without the assent of his wife.

The appellants have not cited, nor have we found, any case involving the precise question certified. In *Cox* v. *Cook*, 46 Ga. 301, it is held that the crop raised on the homestead was exempt. In *Wade* v. *Weslow*, 62 Ga. 563, it is not only held that crops grown upon the homestead are exempt, but that sheep purchased with the proceeds of the crop and put on the homestead are also exempt. The correctness of this ruling is questioned in *Coates* v. *Caldwell*, 71 Tex. 19; 10 Am. St. Rep. 725. As that question is not involved in this case, we do not consider it. In the latter case it is held that "cotton grown upon the homestead and unpicked [252] is exempt from execution. After it has been picked the exemption ceases, and it is subject to execution." In *Alexander* v. *Holt*, 59 Tex. 205, it is said: "We are of opinion, also, that the crops of corn and cotton growing on the homestead were also exempt, as necessary to its beneficial enjoyment." Chief Justice Hemphill, in *Cobbs* v. *Coleman*, 14 Tex. 598, said that it was "very clear that by these reservations the legislature intended a real, substantial benefit; that by fair construction the grants in the statute must include not only the subject itself, but every thing absolutely essential to its beneficial enjoyment. The same doctrine is also deducible from *Anderson* v. *McKay*, 30 Tex. 186." *Horgan* v. *Amick*, 62 Cal. 401, holds that grain harvested from lands constituting a homestead are not exempt. The reasoning in this case and in *Coates* v. *Caldwell*, 71 Tex. 19, 10 Am. St. Rep. 725, seems to be that to exempt the gathered crop would be to add to it the exemptions of personal property provided in the statute without its being specified therein. It is clear that such crops are not exempt under statutes exempting personal property, unless specified therein. Such crops, if exempt, must, in the absence of such specifications, be so under the law exempting the homestead. The reasoning in these cases seems to us to lose sight of the spirit and purpose of the law exempting homesteads. The conflict in the cases is explained, in part at least, by the differences in the statutes of these states. It will be observed, however, that in none of them is it held that crops, while growing upon the homestead, are not exempt.

2. To answer the question certified we must ascertain the letter and spirit of our statute exempting homesteads. It is

certainly the spirit and purpose to exempt, not only the homestead, but also the use thereof, for without the use the exemption would be valueless. It is not simply as a place of shelter, a place in which to live, that homesteads are exempt, but [253] also as a means of making a living, as is shown by the exemption of one-half an acre in town, forty acres in the country, and the shop or building, when situated on the exempt premises, in which the head of the family carries on his business. The use of the homestead, as well as the homestead itself, is unquestionably exempt so long as the homestead character is maintained. When the homestead is terminated by abandonment or otherwise the exemption ceases, but in this case it was not terminated.

We think it is in harmony with the evident spirit and purpose of our statute to hold that the head of a family owning a homestead has a right to hold as exempt, not only the homestead and its use, but also crops or money which he may derive from its use while the property continues to be his homestead. If the homestead is terminated by abandonment or otherwise the exemption ceases. To hold that the owner of a homestead can only hold as exempt such proceeds of its use as the industry of himself or family has produced would be in many cases to deny the benefits of such exemption entirely. Take the case of an owner who cannot, from any cause, cultivate the homstead garden of forty acres, there is no good reason why he may not rent them to another, and hold the proceeds exempt for the use of his family. This case furnishes another apt illustration; also the case of one having spare room in the homestead, who takes lodgers, or one who, having no use for a stable on the homestead premises, rents it to another. We are clearly of the opinion that proceeds derived from the use of the homestead while it remains such are exempt to the head of a family. Whether property purchased with such proceeds, not otherwise exempt, would be subject to execution we do not determine.

The question certified must be answered in the affirmative, and the judgment of the district court is affirmed.

The Exemption of the Proceeds and Produce of a homestead is a question of very considerable importance, and respecting which the decisions of the courts are inharmonious. If the husband and wife make a voluntary sale of their homestead, and thereby convert its proceeds into personalty, such proceeds do not, in the absence of special statutory provisions to that effect, retain the homestead character, and therefore are not exempt from attachment nor execution: Freeman on Executions, secs. 247 a, 235. In some of the states are statutes modifying this rule, to the extent, at least, of permitting a debtor to retain the proceeds of the voluntary sale of his homestead, while he in good faith retains them with the view of procuring another: *Watkins* v. *Blutschinski*, 40 Wis. 347; *Huskins* v. *Hanlon*, 72 Iowa, 37; *Binzel* v. *Grogan*, 67 Wis. 147

When the homestead or any part of it is converted into money or other personal property without the voluntary act of its owner or owners there is certainly no intentional or implied waiver of the exemption, and equitably, at least, the proceeds of such conversion ought to be regarded as still impressed with and protected by the homestead exemption. Thus, if the property held as a homestead exceed in value the amount which the debtor may hold as exempt, his creditors may, in most states, institute proceedings to segregate the exempt from the nonexempt part, in order that the latter may be reached, and applied to the satisfaction of their demands; and if the property is not susceptible of segregation without substantial prejudice, the whole may be sold, provided the debtor is paid the full amount of the exemption. In such an event the amount thus paid him retains its homestead character, either for some period designated by statute, or until he has, for an unreasonable time, failed to invest it in another homestead: *Walsh* v. *Horine*, 36 Ill. 238; *Mitchell* v. *Milhoan*, 11 Kan. 628; *Freiberg* v. *Walzem*, 85 Tex. 264; 34 Am. St. Rep. 808; *Dearing* v. *Thomas*, 25 Ga. 223; *Keyes* v. *Rines*, 37 Vt. 260; 86 Am. Dec. 707; *Maxey* v. *Loyal*, 38 Ga. 531; *Wright* v. *Westheimer*, 2 Idaho, 962; 35 Am. St. Rep. 269; *Morgan* v. *Stearns*, 41 Vt. 398; *Fogg* v. *Fogg*, 40 N. H. 282; 77 Am. Dec. 715; *Pittsfield Bank* v. *Howk*, 4 Allen, 347; *Mann* v. *Kelsey*, 71 Tex. 609; 10 Am. St. Rep. 800.

A like rule should apply to other involuntary conversions of the homestead or some part of it into money. The most familiar of these is the destruction of buildings or fixtures by fire, while the subject of insurance, and the payment by the insurer for the loss thus occasioned. The proceeds of such an insurance are not within the letter of the statutes· governing homestead exemptions, and hence the decisions refusing to protect them from execution: *Smith* v. *Ratcliff*, 66 Miss. 683; 14 Am. St. Rep. 606; *Wooster* v. *Page*, 54 N. H. 125; 20 Am. Rep. 128. These decisions follow the letter, while they ignore the spirit, of the law. The object of the law was to assure to unfortunate debtors and their dependent and often helpless families the comfort and protection of a home. This object is partly thwarted, if the improvements, without which the family has no shelter, may not be protected by insurance; and if, though so protected when the home is devastated by fire, the family must be left with the ashes, while the creditor is awarded the fruits of the claimant's forethought and provision. The better view, therefore, is that the proceeds of such insurance cannot be reached by a creditor: *Houghton* v. *Lee*, 50 Cal. 101; *Cooney* v. *Cooney*, 65 Barb. 524; *Cameron* v. *Fay*, 55 Tex. 58; *Reynolds* v. *Haines*, 83 Iowa, 342; 32 Am. St. Rep. 311. Part of a homestead may be taken by proceedings in the exercise of the right of eminent domain, or by a wrongdoer removing, injuring, or destroying a building or other fixture. In each case it is believed that the moneys becoming due the homestead claimant are, as was the property on account of which the right to them has accrued, exempt from execution: *Wylie* v. *Grundysen*, 51 Minn. 360; 38 Am. St. Rep. 509; *Brooks* v. *Collins*, 11 Bush, 622; *Mudge* v. *Lanning*, 68 Iowa, 641; *Kaiser* v. *Seaton*, 62 Iowa, 463.

As to certain classes of homestead, the object of the statute is not restricted to affording a mere shelter of the family; and perhaps there is no class of which it may fairly be said that the statute did not intend the debtor to have the advantage accruing from the profitable use of the homestead for such purposes as it might be devoted to without impairing its homestead character or abandoning all exemption rights therein. The principal case goes further than any other falling within our observation in securing to a debtor the profits of his homestead, accruing when he was absent therefrom. We are not inclined to doubt or criticise it on that account. The claimant has a right to the full use of his homestead, and if he denies himself part of this right and thereby becomes entitled to compensation, as when he lets the whole, or some part of it, the courts, in denying creditors the right to garnish or otherwise subject to execution, the proceeds of such letting, inflict no wrong on the creditor. A case, equitably still less subject to doubt, arises when the owner of an agricultural homestead plants and harvests a crop which his creditor undertakes to seize in satisfaction of a debt. By not restricting such a homestead to the dwelling-house and its appurtenances, and in permitting it to extend over lands useful only for the production of crops, the legislature impliedly expressed an intention to include the beneficial use of those lands in the homestead exemption. It is true that in many instances there is an enumeration of the personal property which a debtor is entitled to retain as exempt from execution, and that the produce of the homestead may exceed this enumeration or be of a different character. Hence, some courts have denied that the produce of a homestead is exempt from execution, unless of a character or quantity which would exempt it though it had been acquired from any other source: *Horgan* v. *Amick,* 62 Cal. 401; *Citizens' Nat. Bank* v. *Green,* 78 N. C. 247. Others affirm that the exemption of a homestead extends to the crops grown thereon: *Cox* v. *Cook,* 46 Ga. 301; *Alexander* v. *Nolt,* 59 Tex. 205; and even to other property purchased with the proceeds thereof: *Wade* v. *Weslow,* 62 Ga. 563. The decisions upon the subject,

> "That palter with us in a double sense;
> That keep the word of promise to our ear,
> And break it to our hope,"

are those of the courts of Texas, holding that a crop planted on a homestead is exempt from execution while growing and attached to the soil, and becomes subject to execution as soon as harvested or detached: *Coates* v. *Caldwell,* 71 Tex. 19; 10 Am. St. Rep. 725. Homestead claimants are thereby assured the exemption of their crops so long as they remain attached to the soil, and therefore useless, but lose the exemption on attempting to detach such crops so that they can subserve some useful end.

MARSH v. McNIDER.

[88 IOWA, 390.]

LANDLORD AND TENANT.—ICE FORMED ON A NON-NAVIGABLE STREAM of water belongs to the tenant and not to the landlord, if there is nothing in the lease restricting the tenant's use of the property.

SUIT to restrain the defendants from cutting or removing ice, and to recover damages for ice already cut. Judgment in favor of the defendant.

Cliggitt & Rule, for the appellant.

Richard Wilber, for the appellee.

[394] ROBINSON, C. J.   Clara E. Doud is the owner of that part of a certain tract of land which is west of the center of a stream of water which flows across it.   That stream is about eight rods in width, is not navigable, and is known as "Lime creek."   Mrs. Doud made to the plaintiff a bill of sale of the ice which should be formed in her part of the stream during the winter which commenced in the year 1890. When Mrs. Doud purchased the land, in June of that year, it was occupied by S. M. Fulghum, as subtenant, under a lease which gave him the right to the free and uninterrupted occupation thereof until April, 1891, and the title acquired by the purchase was subject to his rights under the lease. He sold to the defendants the ice which was included in the bill of sale to the plaintiff, and, after the ice was formed, they cut and removed portions of it for their own uses.   The plaintiff contends that the ice was real estate, a part of the land owned by Mrs. Doud; therefore, that the lease gave to the tenant no right to remove it; and that the bill of sale transferred the ownership of it to the plaintiff.

[395] It is well settled that, under some conditions, water and ice are to be regarded as real estate, belonging to the owner of the land which is beneath it: See *State* v. *Pottmeyer,* 33 Ind. 402; 5 Am. Rep. 224, and cases therein cited; 9 Am. & Eng. Ency. of Law, 853.   And, when that is the case, the landowner, or his assign, has the exclusive right to gather and dispose of the ice for his own benefit, subject to the rights of other riparian owners: See *Bigelow* v. *Shaw,* 65 Mich. 341; 8 Am. St. Rep. 902, and cases therein cited.   In this state the owner of land has the right to use so much of the water of a stream flowing over it as is necessary to supply what are termed his "natural wants": *Spence* v. *McDonough,* 77 Iowa,

461; *Ferguson* v. *Firmenich Mfg. Co.*, 77 Iowa, 576; 14 Am.
St. Rep. 319. Where he does not own the soil under the
stream, as where it is meandered, and his ownership does
not include its bed, he has no exclusive right to the ice which
forms in it: *Serrin* v. *Grefe*, 67 Iowa, 197. In such cases,
whoever has lawful access to the stream may use the water
and the ice which forms therein in such manner as does
not interfere with the rights of the riparian owners: *Brown* v.
Cunningham, 82 Iowa, 515.

Whether the ice which forms in a running stream is to be
regarded technically as a part of the land over which it is
formed, or to which it is attached, is a question we do not find
it necessary to determine. It is water congealed, and, although more readily secured and controlled for many purposes than water, it is in most respects subject to the rules
which govern the rights of the riparian proprietor to the
water. Ice may be attached to his land, but it was not produced by the land, drew nothing from it, and will give nothing to it. It is transient by nature, and will soon disappear,
unless prevented by the labor of man. It is a product of the
changing seasons, which the occupier of the soil may use as
he might have used the water from which [396] it was formed.
If he own the land under it, he may use the ice as he might
have used the water, to supply his natural wants, and for
other purposes, so far as he can do so without affecting the
rights of others, as of lower owners on the same stream.
Such use appertains to the land, and belongs to him who has
the right to possess and use it.

In this case that right was conferred upon Fulghum, by
virtue of the lease. It is said that his lease was for ordinary
farming purposes only, but, if that were true, he would have
had the right to use so much of the water and ice as he required for such purposes. The lease, however, does not restrict the tenant to the use of the premises for agricultural
purposes only, but gives him the right to the "free and uninterrupted occupation thereof," and necessarily the right to
use them and their appurtenances. Nothing was reserved,
excepting timber not required for repairing fences. The
leased premises included one-half of the bed of the stream,
and such rights as the owner had in the stream itself. He
retained no right to enter upon the premises to gather ice,
and his grantee acquired none as against the tenant. We
are of the opinion that the lease gave to the tenant the right

to cut and remove the ice in question, and find that such
right was assigned to the defendants. The judgment of the
district court is affirmed.

ICE BELONGS TO THE OWNER OF THE SOIL under the water on which it
forms: *Bigelow* v. *Shaw*, 65 Mich. 341; 8 Am. St. Rep. 902, and note. See,
further, the notes to *Woodman* v. *Pitman*, 1 Am. St. Rep. 352, and *Higgins*
v. *Kusterer*, 32 Am. Rep. 165.

HARKER *v.* BURLINGTON, CEDAR RAPIDS & NORTH-ERN RAILWAY CO.

[88 IOWA, 409.]

MASTER AND SERVANT—RISKS—ASSUMPTION OF.—One who accepts employment with knowledge of its risks does so at his peril, and has no claim
for indemnity on the ground of such risks, and, if he remains in the
service without objection and without promise to him of a change, he
will be deemed to have waived his right to compensation for injuries
which he may sustain by reason of such risks.

NEGLIGENCE IS A FAILURE to do what a reasonable and prudent person
would ordinarily have done under the circumstances, or doing what
such a person would not have done under such circumstances. The
duties are dictated and measured by the exigencies of the occasion.

MASTER AND SERVANT—A SERVANT'S KNOWLEDGE OF A RISK OR DEFECT
DOES NOT EXONERATE the master, if for any reason the servant forgets
it, and is not in fault in so doing at the precise time he suffers thereby,
as where the servant's forgetfulness was due to sudden alarm, or the
urgent demand for speed, or by his duties being such as to necessarily
absorb his attention, leaving him no reasonable opportunity to look for
defects.

MASTER AND SERVANT—NEGLIGENCE, CONTRIBUTORY.—If a railway corporation is guilty of negligence in keeping an awning at a position
dangerous to its employees, and one of them, knowing of such awning
and of its dangerous character, is, by his superior, suddenly called upon
to perform a service exposing him to danger from the awning, and the
mode of giving him his orders is such as to probably confuse him and
at the same time to demand haste in action, whether under such circumstances, in case of his injury from the awning, he is chargeable
with contributory negligence, in not remembering and avoiding it, is a
question for the determination of the jury.

JURY TRIAL.—A VERDICT IS NOT EXCESSIVE which awards plaintiff seven
thousand seven hundred and sixty dollars in an action for personal
injuries, where his expectancy of life is thirty-four years, he was earning sixty-five dollars per month when hurt, and his injuries confined
him to his bed one week, rendered him unable to perform any labor for
three months, and to perform any labor except chores for nine months,
and there is evidence tending to show that his injuries are permanent
and will prevent him from ever doing any but light work.

J. W. Cory and S. K. Tracy, for the appellant.

Parker, Funk & Carlton, for the appellee.

[410] ROBINSON, C. J.   In February, 1890, the plaintiff was in the employment of the defendant, as conductor of a freight train.   His ordinary run was from Estherville to a siding near Hotel Orleans, at Spirit lake, where ice was being loaded, and back to Estherville.   At that time there was a railway platform south of the hotel, over a part of which was an awning about fifty feet in length, constructed to protect passengers who [411] should be there for trains.   On a day of the month named the plaintiff left Estherville with his train, which was made up of empty cars, under orders to set out a part of them on a sidetrack at the Hotel Orleans, and to take the remainder about eighty rods farther west, to a point where ice was being loaded.   When he arrived near the hotel he found loaded cars standing on the main track, between the switches.   He slackened the speed of his train, intending to set out some of the cars, as he had been ordered to do, and to couple onto the cars on the main line.   The engine had been backed from Estherville, was at the west end of the train it was drawing, and had reached the loaded cars.   The plaintiff was on a car near the engine, but, before it reached the platform, he descended, and met one Forrest, who was the trainmaster of the defendant, and his superior in authority.   Forrest said to him: "Damn it; they are waiting for cars down here.   Where have you been?   Couple that engine onto these cars.   Back them right up to the main line.   Take every thing up to the side."   In obedience to that direction the plaintiff coupled the engine, which was moving slowly, to the loaded cars, and stepped out to one side.   Forrest took charge of the train and gave the signal for backing.   The plaintiff then started eastward to go onto the foremost car of his train, when Forrest said to him, "The brakes are set on those cars," referring to those to which the engine had just been coupled.   That was, in effect, an order to loosen the brakes, and the plaintiff at once started westward, running to overtake the loaded cars; climbed up the side of the one next to the engine, to loosen the brakes; and, just as he had reached the top was struck in the back by a corner of the awning, and received the injuries of which he complains.

The plaintiff charges the defendant with negligence, in maintaining the awning in the position in which it [412] was at the time of the accident; in running the train toward it at too rapid a rate of speed while he was upon it; and in ordering him to go upon it, to loosen the brakes, while it was being so run. The defendant denies negligence on its part, and avers that the plaintiff was injured by reason of his own negligence.

1. The car which the plaintiff was climbing when injured was one of the defendant's ordinary boxcars. There is nothing to show that he was ascending it in any way other than the usual manner, and the evidence is ample to sustain the charge of negligence on the part of the defendant in maintaining the awning in the condition in which it was when the accident occurred. That it was so negligent is not denied with any apparent confidence. But the defendant contends that the plaintiff had assumed the usual risks of its service, and the perils which he incurred from structures which were visible and well known to him, and that, by remaining in its service after obtaining the knowledge he possessed of the awning, he waived all right to recover for injuries which he might sustain by reason of its existence. The plaintiff had known of the awning three or four years when he was hurt. He had been employed on the railway of the defendant, from Estherville to Spirit lake, ten or twelve months before the accident, and had unloaded freight under the awning many times. It was familiar to him, and he and his coemployees had frequently spoken of it as dangerous. The accident occurred in the daytime, when the danger he incurred in doing what he attempted while the train was passing the awning could have been seen readily.

The general rule is, as claimed by the appellant, that a person who accepts employment, with knowledge of its risks, does so at his peril, and has no claim on his employer for indemnity on account of such risks, and that if the employee remains in the service of his employer [413] without objection, and without promise of a change, after obtaining knowledge of special hazards not known to him when the service was entered, he will be deemed to have waived a right to compensation for injuries which he may sustain by reason of such hazards: *Wells* v. *Burlington etc. Ry. Co.*, 56 Iowa, 524, and cases therein cited; *Overby* v. *Chesapeake etc. Ry. Co.*, 37 W. Va. 524. But there are exceptions to the general rule, and acts which would be negligent under some circumstances may be the result of reasonable diligence and due care under

others.   An employee may sometimes do without negligence
when ordered by a superior what would be negligence if
done voluntarily: *Raburn* v. *Central Iowa Ry. Co.*, 74 Iowa,
637, 640; *Frandsen* v. *C., R. I. & P. Ry. Co.*, 36 Iowa, 372,
375; *Greenleaf* v. *Illinois Cent. R. R. Co.*, 29 Iowa, 14, 47; 4
Am. Rep. 181.   There are cases where a subordinate may
disobey the order of a superior when to obey would be negligent; as, where the order cannot be obeyed with reasonable
regard for the safety of human life: *Hawley* v. *Chicago etc.
Ry. Co.*, 71 Iowa, 717, 726; *Wescott* v. *New York etc. R. R. Co.*,
153 Mass. 460; Patterson's Railway Accident Law, secs. 334,
335.   But an employee is not required to use the highest degree of care and diligence which is possible.   Absolute per-
fection in that respect is not required: *Greenleaf* v. *Dubuque
etc. R. R. Co.*, 33 Iowa, 52, 57.   "Negligence is the failure to
do what a reasonable and prudent person would ordinarily
have done under the circumstances of the situation, or doing what such a person, under the existing circumstances,
would not have done.   The duties are dictated and measured by the exigencies of the occasion": *Railroad Co.* v.
Jones, 95 U. S. 439.   In 1 Shearman and Redfield on Negligence, section 213, it is said: "The mere technical fact of
the servant's knowledge of a defect is not sufficient to exonerate the master, if, for any reason, the servant forgets it,
and is not in fault in forgetting it, at the precise time [414] he
suffers thereby.   In analogy to the principles already stated
under the head of 'Contributory Negligence' the servant's
rights are not prejudiced by his forgetfulness or failure to
observe a defeat, under the influence of sudden alarm, or of
an urgent demand for speed, or if his duties are such as
necessarily to absorb his whole attention, leaving him no
reasonable opportunity to look for defects": See, also, 1
Shearman and Redfield on Negligence, sec. 89; *Plank* v. *New
York Cent. etc. R. R. Co.*, 60 N. Y. 607; *Snow* v. *Housatonic
R. R. Co.*, 8 Allen, 447; 85 Am. Dec. 720.

In *Hosic* v. *Chicago etc. Ry. Co.*, 75 Iowa, 683; 9 Am. St.
Rep. 518, it appeared that a brakeman had occasion to pass
over a car which was so loaded that the passage could not
be made without danger to himself, and that he must have
known that fact before he went upon the car.   He attempted
to pass over it, but fell from it to the ground, and received
injuries for which he sought to recover.   This court said that
whether he was negligent in what he did depended upon all

the circumstances of the case; that the efficiency of the railway service, and the due protection of life and property, require prompt obedience to orders, and prompt discharge of duties, on the part of employees, especially in regard to the management of moving trains; and that it would not do to make the subordinate judge of the propriety of obeying an order: See, also, *Frandsen* v. *Chicago etc. Ry. Co.*, 36 Iowa, 372, 375.

In this case the remark of Forrest to the plaintiff, when the latter reached Hotel Orleans, showed irritation, by reason of supposed delay on his part, and a necessity for haste. The directions he then received were contrary to those given him at Estherville, and which he had communicated to his brakemen. When he was told that the brakes on the loaded cars were set, and, in effect, to loosen them, he was about one hundred feet east of the awning, and on the same side of the track. The cars were moving westward at an increasing [415] rate of speed, which was then from four to six miles an hour. He ran to overtake the car, which he ascended, and, as he was going up, turned his face toward the east, to see that the brakemen did not cut the trains as they had been ordered to do at Estherville. The only way in which the brakes could be loosened was for some one to climb the car as he was doing, and at the time he was not looking at the awning, and did not think of it. It was natural that he should have been somewhat confused by the language and conduct of Forrest and the haste demanded, and that his mind should have been fully occupied with the effort required to execute the directions given him. Whether, under these circumstances, he was negligent in not remembering and avoiding the awning was clearly a question of fact for the determination of the jury.

The cases upon which appellant relies are not in conflict with the conclusions we reach. In *McKee* v. *Chicago etc. Ry. Co.*, 83 Iowa, 616, it appears that the employee injured exposed himself voluntarily, and, without any occasion to incur unusual risk, placed himself in a position in which he came in contract with a wing fence, of which he had knowledge, and which he would have avoided had he used ordinary care. The facts involved in *Platt* v. *Chicago etc. R. Co.*, 84 Iowa, 694, were that the person injured knew before the accident occurred that the roof of the depot building projected over the track; that he was engaged in pushing a car along the track; that the car was higher and wider than ordinary freight-cars, and that he knew that such was the case; that there was no emergency which required him to expose himself to danger, but that, without looking for, or taking any precautions to avoid, danger, he ascended the car, and was caught between it and the roof of the building, and injured. In *Bengston* v. *Chicago etc. Ry. Co.*, 47 Minn. 486, it was held that the employee had [416] assumed the risks from the acts of negligence which caused his death. In *Overby* v. *Chesapeake etc. Ry. Co.*, 37 W. Va. 524, it was held that the injuries for which a recovery was sought were received in consequence of an effort made by the person injured in direct violation of a rule of the company, with which he had agreed to comply. There was no sudden alarm, no urgent demand for speed, and his duties were not of such a character as necessarily to absorb his attention. The facts involved in *Helfrich* v. *Ogden City Ry. Co.*, 7 Utah, 186, showed that the employee was killed in consequence of gross carelessness on his part. The case of *Fisk* v. *Fitchburg R. R. Co.*, 158 Mass. 238, is also cited. The plaintiff in that case appears to have been injured while engaged in performing the ordinary duties of his employment. He was chargeable with knowledge of the risk which he incurred, and does not appear to have been acting under circumstances which excused his failure to remember it.

2. The amount of the verdict and judgment is seven thousand six hundred and sixty dollars. The appellant contends that it is excessive. When injured, the plaintiff was thirty years of age, his expectancy of life was thirty-four years, and he was earning sixty-five dollars per month, as conductor. He testifies that, in consequence of his injuries, he was confined to his bed one week, was unable to perform labor of any kind for three months, and was unable to perform manual labor, excepting a few chores, for nine months; that he suffered severe pain for about three days, and after that time did not suffer much, unless he was moving; that, since the expiration of nine months from the date of the injury, he has done some light work on a farm, and has hunted ducks for the market, but has been unable to do lifting or heavy [417] work; that the conductor of a freight train is required to do various kinds of lifting, and to set brakes; that he has been unable to do that kind of work; and that the twisting movements required to set brakes causes him great

pain, and for a time disables him to do work of any sort. A physician examined the plaintiff at the time of the trial, which was about one year and ten months after the injury was received, and testified that he did not find any mark or indications of injury, and ascertained nothing in regard to it, excepting what the plaintiff told him; also that a physician should be able to ascertain by such an examination whether the injuries exist as claimed. But he also stated, in effect, that, if the condition of the plaintiff was correctly shown by his testimony, his injuries were probably permanent. The plaintiff and the physicians were the only witnesses who testified in the case, and the jury were authorized to find from the testimony given that the plaintiff was permanently disabled to discharge the duties of conductor of a freight train, or any but light manual labor. If the jury so found we cannot say, in view of all the facts stated, that the amount allowed is excessive: *Collins* v. *City of Council Bluffs*, 35 Iowa, 432; *Rice* v. *City of Des Moines*, 40 Iowa, 638, 646; *Allender* v. *Chicago etc. Ry. Co.*, 43 Iowa, 276, 281; *Funston* v. *Chicago etc. Ry. Co.*, 61 Iowa, 452, 463; *Knapp* v. *Sioux City etc. Ry. Co.*, 71 Iowa, 41, 43; *Reed* v. *Chicago Ry. Co.*, 74 Iowa, 188, 195; *Henry* v. *Sioux City etc. Ry. Co.*, 75 Iowa, 84, 89; 9 Am. St. Rep. 457; *Knott* v. *Dubuque etc. Ry. Co.*, 84 Iowa, 462.

No reason for disturbing the judgment of the district court has been shown. It is, therefore, affirmed.

MASTER AND SERVANT — ASSUMPTION OF RISKS — KNOWN DEFECT.—A servant continuing in an employment with knowledge of a risk, which afterward is the source of an accident to him, cannot recover against the master for the injury: *Titus* v. *Bradford etc. R. R. Co.*, 136 Pa. St. 618; 20 Am. St. Rep. 944, and note. An employee who knew of a defect which caused him injury must be held to have assumed the risk caused thereby: *Taylor etc. Ry Co.* v. *Taylor*, 79 Tex. 104; 23 Am. St. Rep. 316, and note: *Williamson* v. *Newport News etc. Co.*, 34 W. Va. 657; 26 Am. St. Rep. 927; *St. Louis etc. Ry. Co.* v. *Davis*, 54 Ark. 389; 26 Am. St. Rep. 48, and note; *Georgia Pac. Ry. Co.* v. *Davis*, 92 Ala. 300; 25 Am. St. Rep. 47, and note; *Baltimore etc. R. R. Co.* v. *State*, 75 Md. 152; 32 Am. St. Rep. 372, and note, but see *Boss* v. *Northern Pac. R. R. Co.*, 2 N. Dak. 128; 33 Am. St. Rep. 756, and note, and see, also, the extended note to *Shortel* v. *St. Joseph*, 24 Am. St. Rep. 322.

NEGLIGENCE—WHAT IS.—Negligence is the failure to do what a reasonable and prudent person would ordinarily have done under the circumstances, or the doing of what such a person would not have done under those circumstances. This definition does not exclude the idea that one may act upon appearances: *McDonald* v. *International etc. Ry. Co.*, 86 Tex. 1; 40 Am. St. Rep. 803, and note.

Conger v. Crabtree.

[88 Iowa, 536.]

Negotiable Instruments.—An Alteration in a Promissory Note, by filling up a blank for interest after it was executed and contrary to the agreement of the parties, renders it void as between the maker and the party who made the alteration. Such alteration may be shown as against an innocent purchaser for value before maturity.

Negotiable Instruments.—Negligence of Maker Furnishing Opportunity for Alteration.—One who executes a promissory note, leaving interest blanks therein which are afterwards fraudulently filled up, contrary to the agreement of the parties, cannot, as a matter of law, be held to have been so negligent as to preclude him from resisting payment of such note on the ground of such fraudulent alteration. If there was any negligence precluding him from the assertion of this defense the holder of the note must assume the burden of proving such negligence.

Phillips & Phillips, for the appellant.

No appearance for the appellee.

537 Robinson, C. J. The note in suit as it appeared on the trial is in words and figures as follows:

" $100.00.   Des Moines, Iowa, Sept. 3, 1889.

"Six months after date, for value received, I promise to pay to S. E. McCreary, M. D., or order, one hundred (100) dollars, at Des Moines, Iowa, with interest at ten per cent per annum, payable annually, and interest in arrears shall draw ten per cent interest till paid; and in case of nonpayment of interest when due the whole sum of principal and interest to become due and collectible at the holder's option. And, in any action that may be brought for any sum under the provisions of this note by the holder hereof, he shall be entitled to recover of the maker hereof a reasonable sum as attorney's fee, to be taxed by the court.

                                        "Geo. W. Crabtree."

It bore indorsements as follows:

"Pay to J. W. Whitmore or order, without recourse.

                                        S. E. McCreary, M. D."

"Pay to C. M. Conger, or order, without recourse.

                                        "J. W. Whitmore."

538 The plaintiff introduced the note in evidence, and rested. The defendant then introduced evidence which must be regarded, for the purposes of this appeal, as showing that when the note was made and delivered it did not provide for the payment of interest, but contained two blanks, one of which was in the clause in regard to the payment of interest on the principal and the other in the clause which refers to the payment of interest on interest in arrears; that it was agreed between the defendant and the payee of the note that it should not bear interest, and that the blanks for the rate of interest were filled without the knowledge or consent of the maker, after the note was delivered.

It has been held in some cases that the holder of a note has an implied power to fill blanks which were not filled when it was delivered. But whether a power to fill such blanks as those in controversy may exist by implication, in any event, we need not determine. In this case it is shown, clearly, that it was withheld. The filling of the blanks was unauthorized, and was designed to affect the liability of the maker of the note, by increasing the amount for which he was liable. The alteration was therefore material, and a forgery, and rendered the note void, as between the maker and the party who made the alteration: Code, section 3917; *First Nat. Bank* v. *Hall*, 83 Iowa, 645; *Smith* v. *Eals*, 81 Iowa, 235; 25 Am. St. Rep. 486; *Adair* v. *Egland*, 58 Iowa, 314; Tiedeman on Commercial Paper, secs. 391, 394; *McGrath* v. *Clark*, 56 N. Y. 34; 15 Am. Rep. 372; *Cape Ann Nat. Bank* v. *Burns*, 129 Mass. 596. Such an alteration may be shown as against an innocent purchaser for value, before maturity: *Charlton* v. *Reed*, 61 Iowa, 166; 47 Am. Rep. 808; *Knoxville Nat. Bank* v. *Clark*, 51 Iowa, 265; 33 Am. Rep. 129.

It is possible that the maker of an altered note may be estopped to deny liability on account of it because of negligence on his part in delivering it with unfilled blanks, but we do not think it can be said, as a matter [539] of law, that proof that the alteration was made by filling blanks left by the maker, even though they were provided for inserting therein the rate of interest, is alone proof of negligence which will estop him to deny liability. When he shows such an alteration in the note as will make it void as between him and the party who altered it the burden is upon the party asking a recovery thereon to establish the liability of the maker notwithstanding the alteration: *Smith* v. *Eals*, 81 Iowa, 235; 25 Am. St. Rep. 486; *Robinson* v. *Reed*, 46 Iowa, 220; *Scofield* v. *Ford*, 56 Iowa, 370. In *Rainbolt* v. *Eddy*, 34 Iowa, 441, 11 Am. Rep. 152, it was held that the innocent holder for value, before maturity, of a note which had been altered by inserting without authority the words, "ten per ct. inst.," in a blank left in the note by the maker, could recover. The statement of facts in that case is brief, but we are justified in presuming that the defendant assumed the burden of proving that the plaintiff acquired the note with knowledge of its alteration, and what this court said in regard to the burden of proof must be considered as applicable to that case, as it was presented by the pleadings. The petition in this case set out the note, alleged that it was owned by plaintiff, and that it was unpaid, and demanded judgment for its amount. The answer did not deny the making of the note as originally drawn, but pleaded as a defense the alteration, and that it was unauthorized. To the answer the plaintiff filed a general denial. The pleadings did not aver that the defendant was negligent in making and delivering the note with the blanks unfilled, nor that the plaintiff had no notice of the alleged alteration when he purchased it. The evidence showed that the note had been altered without authority, as alleged, and that defense was fully sustained. If negligence on the part of the defendant in making and delivering the note would have estopped him to deny liability thereon the burden of proving the negligence was on plaintiff, under [540] the rule we have stated, and no attempt was made to assume that burden. But, by going to trial on the issues presented by the answer, the plaintiff waived objections to its sufficiency: Code, secs. 2650, 2664, *Linden* v. *Green*, 81 Iowa, 366.

It follows from what we have said that the district court erred in directing a verdict for the plaintiff. Its judgment is, therefore, reversed.

NEGOTIABLE INSTRUMENT—ALTERATION—FILLING UP BLANK FOR INTEREST—EFFECT.—Where the indorsee of a note fills the blanks contained herein so as to change the rate of interest from the legal rate to an excessive rate without the knowledge or consent of the maker the note is vitiated and becomes void: *Hoopes* v. *Collingwood*, 10 Col. 107; 3 Am. St. Rep. 565, and note. This question is further discussed in the extended note to *Jones* v. *Bangs*, 48 Am. Rep. 667, and the notes to *McGrath* v. *Clark*, 15 Am. Rep. 375, and *Readlich* v. *Doll*, 13 Am. Rep. 578.

NEGOTIABLE INSTRUMENTS—LEAVING BLANK SPACES—NEGLIGENCE.—The fact that blank spaces sufficient to admit of alterations in the amount are left in a promissory note at the time when the indorser thereof writes his name upon it does not constitute such negligence on his part as will render him liable to a *bona fide* purchaser for the amount to which the note is fraudulently raised without the indorser's consent or knowledge: *Burrows* v. *Klunk*, 70 Md. 451; 14 Am. St. Rep. 371, and note, with the cases collected.

ORVIS v. PARK COMMISSIONERS.

[88 IOWA, 674.]

MUNICIPAL INDEBTEDNESS, WHAT IS.—If, by a statute, a park commission
is created in cities of a certain class, the members of which are authorized to organize as a board, to elect a treasurer, to certify to the amount
of taxes necessary for park purposes, to acquire property therefor, to
make contracts, to sue and to be sued, to issue bonds for the sale of real
estate, to hold in trust all property within the city dedicated to park
purposes, bonds issued by such commission constitute municipal indebtedness of the city for which the commission acts, and are void if, before
their issue, such city was already indebted to the full amount of the
indebtedness which it was authorized to incur by the constitution of the
state.

William Connor, for the appellant.

Bishop & Wilcoxen, for the appellees.

[675] GRANGER, J. The defendant board of park commissioners was elected by the legal voters of the city of Des
Moines in pursuance of the provisions of chapter 1 of acts of
the twenty-fourth general assembly. The act is entitled, "An
act to establish a board of park commissioners in certain
cities of the first class, defining their powers and prescribing
their duties." It will conduce to clearness if we here state,
somewhat, at least, the claims of counsel as to the character
of this board. By the appellant it is urged that it is an agent
or the instrumentality in aid of, or acting for, the city government, so that the indebtedness created by it becomes the
debt of the city. On the other hand, it is maintained that
by the act creating the board a new [676] municipal corporation
was created, territorially the same as the city of Des Moines,
but entirely independent, and for definite and specified purposes, of which the board is the governing power. It is provided by section 3, article 11, of the constitution of the state,
that "no county or other political or municipal corporation
shall be allowed to become indebted in any manner, or for
any purpose, to an amount in the aggregate exceeding five
per centum on the value of the taxable property within such
county or corporation." If the tax certified to the county
auditor by the board of park commissioners, and the bonds
it proposes to place upon the market, would increase the
indebtedness of the city of Des Moines, as a city, they are
invalid, under the admitted facts of the case, for it is conceded that, aside from such tax and bonds, the city is indebted to the full amount of its constitutional authority. It

is not to be, nor is it, we think, doubted that the bonds, if issued, would constitute a debt payable by the people, and from the taxable resources within the city of Des Moines. If, then, they are to be held valid, it must be on the theory of another legal entity, embodying precisely the same constituent elements as the city of Des Moines, for and on behalf of which the board of park commissioners is a delegated authority. No legal name is attempted to be applied to this independent existence, other than that it is a municipal corporation, and such it is urged to be in argument, and the conclusion of the district court was that the act created another such corporation.

The specific question, then, is: Is the effect of the act of the twenty-fourth general assembly such that, to the territory embraced within the city of Des Moines, there is added a second municipal corporation, independent of the other, in its authority to create indebtedness. We must look to the act for a solution of the problem. By the first section it is provided that in 677 each of the cities of the class specified there shall be elected, by the legal voters of the city, three park commissioners. The second section provides for their organization as a board, and for the election by them of a treasurer who "shall receive, keep, and pay out all moneys belonging to, or under the control of, said commissioners, as ordered by them." It is then provided that the commissioners may certify to the county auditor the per cent of taxes necessary for park purposes, under certain limitations as to amount, which taxes are to be collected and paid over to the treasurer of the board. The board is authorized to acquire real estate or other property within the city, for park purposes, by donation, purchase, or condemnation, and to sell and exchange the same. _The board may make contracts, sue and be sued, and issue bonds for the payment of real estate. By the terms of the act the title to all real estate within the city for park purposes "shall be held by the commissioners in trust for the public, shall be exempt from taxation of every kind and nature, and from all debts and liabilities of the city." The board is, in express terms, invested with full control of the parks in the city. In a word, it may be said that, aside from the selection of the commissioners, the city government, as distinct from the board, is divested of all authority in relation to the parks of the city. We think it very manifest that the board is, by the act, invested with corporate author-

ity, independent of the city government, that is, the general
government of the city, while it seems to be in aid of it.

But from what are we to infer that the legislature intended
that these acts of the board, or the existence of the board
itself, should be with reference to a new municipal corporation, instead of the one already existing? The act contains
no words indicative of a purpose to create a new corporation,
but it does treat of corporations already in existence. It is
said by the appellees [678] that it is to be inferred from the
nature of the authority granted to the board, its powers being of a corporate nature. Why infer a legislative intent to
create a new corporation merely from the nature of the
powers delegated, when the exercise of those powers has
precisely the same relation to, and effect on, the city of Des
Moines, or other cities of that class, as it would have on the
new corporation? There is not a power granted nor duty
assigned under the law that cannot as well be exercised or
discharged in behalf of the present corporations as in behalf
of those contended for under the limitations of the law as to
indebtedness. It is well to plainly say that, barring a supposed or real necessity for avoiding the constitutional inhi-
bition as to the indebtedness of cities, there is neither motive
nor reason to claim that the act ingrafts upon each of the
cities of the class described another and independent corporate organization. It is true that such boards are sometimes incorporated, but in every instance coming to our
notice it has been by an express provision to that effect. It
is also true that corporate existence is sometimes implied
from the nature of the authority to be exercised: Dillon on
Municipal Corporations, 4th ed., sec. 43. But it is never
so implied unless the powers granted "cannot be exercised
and enjoyed" without it: Dillon on Municipal Corporations,
sec. 43. The act makes unmistakable reference to corporate bodies, the people, territory, and property of which are
to be most affected by the legislation; and, viewing the act as
applicable to them, there is not a power granted by it that is
not to be exercised by the board and enjoyed by such corporations, comprising the same persons, properties, and interests as the corporation proposed. This being true, the basis
for an implied corporate existence under any known rule of
law is entirely wanting. By this construction the law is not
overruled, but it stands in all its parts to the benefit of the
people, intended to be benefited by it, [679] with the board of

park commissioners to administer it in accord with the legislative will. ·

If it be said that with such a construction the provisions of the act are not to be fully enjoyed by the city of Des Moines, because of its present debt, it may be said that the law, in none of its parts, purports to be a remedy or aid in such an emergency. We must assume that, if the legislature had such a purpose in view, it would have, in some form, expressed it. Whether or not the legislature could furnish such a relief, we are not to consider, for the act is absolutely without expression or inference relative to the subject. The powers granted by the act are, of course, to be exercised subject to constitutional prohibitions.

As further indicating the intent of the legislature, the appellant refers to the title of the act, and then to the constitutional provision as to what it must contain. It is as follows: "Every act shall embrace but one subject, and matters properly connected therewith, which subject shall be expressed in the title. But if any subject shall be embraced in an act which shall not be expressed in the title, such act shall be void only as to so much thereof as shall not be expressed in the title." The title of the act expresses its subject as the "Board of Park Commissioners" in certain cities. It makes no reference to a corporation to be created by the act, and no one, to read the title, would understand that such a purpose was intended by the act. Hence, if so intended, it would be vulnerable to the constitutional provision. It cannot properly be said that the board of commissioners is the subject of the legislation, if a new corporation was designed by the act, of which the board was held to be the governing body. In such a case the corporation would have been the proper subject of the act, and the means of its government a matter " properly connected therewith." The title, "An act to establish a board of park commissioners in 680 certain cities of the first class," etc., indicates on its face that the subject of legislation is with reference to cities then in existence; and, with a purpose to create new corporations, the title would be misleading, if not deceptive. Speaking of our constitutional provision the court said in *State* v. *Judge of Davis County*, 2 Iowa, 280: "It was designed to prevent surprise in legislation by having matter of one nature embraced in a bill whose title expressed another." Mr. Cooley, in his work on Constitutional Limitations, sixth edition, page 169, says: "Titles to legislative acts, however, have recently, in some states, come to possess very great importance, by reason of constitutional provisions which not only require that they shall correctly indicate the purpose of the law, but which absolutely control, and exclude every thing from effect and operation as law which is incorporated in the body of the act, but is not within the purpose indicated by the title." Our purpose, in this particular branch of the opinion, is not to indicate that the act, because of its title, or the subject itself, is in any way invalid, because unconstitutional, but to more clearly show that the act, in none of its parts, gives evidence of a legislative purpose to create a municipal corporation. The utter silence of the act upon the subject, if it was intended, in the face of the constitutional requirement that it should be prominent, really forbids an inference of such a purpose. The case at times presents the thought of the board of park commissioners being a municipal corporation of itself. The existence of a municipal corporation, in the character of an organized board of persons, independent of a territory and people, could in no way subserve the purposes of the act in question. The board created by this act represents some thing, and that some thing is the city of Des Moines, or some other legal entity for which it exists and acts. If some thing else, what is it? It is said that it is a "park district." The act does not say so, but, on 281 the contrary, it provides for park districts only in case the commissioners do not agree upon "one park for the whole city," where more than one organized township is included in the city. It should be said that the appellees make no claim in this court that the commissioners constitute such a corporation, but are "simply the visible, directing force of the corporation.' They also say, in argument: "The corporation consists of that territory, and all the persons and property included therein, which is coextensive with the boundary line of the particular city coming within the provisions of the act."

There is no phase of the case upon which we can sustain the conclusion that there is a new municipal corporation, by virtue of which the bonds and the indebtedness in excess of the constitutional limit upon the city of Des Moines are valid. A decree should be entered, restraining the sale of the bonds or the levy of a tax for the payment of the interest thereon.

The judgment of the district court is reversed.

IN the note to *Bruce v. City of Hopkinsville,* 44 Am. St. Rep. 222, we considered the question what is municipal indebtedness within the meaning of the constitutional prohibitions and what is the effect of indebtedness created in violation thereof. The question was also determined in *Anderson v. Orient Fire Ins. Co.,* 88 Iowa, 579. This was a suit brought by citizens and taxpayers against officers of a city to restrain the levy of taxes to raise funds for the payment of certain bonds. After disposing of various preliminary questions the court said:

"The constitutional provision on which plaintiffs seek exemption from liability on the bonds in question is article 11, section 3: 'No county or other political or municipal corporation shall be allowed to become indebted in any manner, or for any purpose, to an amount, in the aggregate, exceeding five per centum on the value of the taxable property within such county or corporation, to be ascertained by the last state and county tax lists previous to the incurring of such indebtedness.' Lyon county was organized in 1872. Five per centum of the assessed valuation of taxable property in the county from that time to 1884 was somewhat fluctuating; the lesser amount being for 1872, twenty-four thousand nine hundred and fifty-four dollars and ninety-nine cents, and the greater for 1884, seventy-one thousand eight hundred and seventy-six dollars and thirty-five cents. At various times from 1873 to May, 1885, the county issued bonds, under different legislative acts, for the purpose of funding and refunding its indebtedness upon judgments and outstanding warrants. There was no time between these dates that the bonds of the county, outstanding, did not exceed the constitutional limit of indebtedness.

"On the first day of May, 1885, the county issued a series of one hundred and twenty bonds, of one thousand dollars each, and they were placed in the hands of one Richards, as refunding agent for the county, who negotiated the same, and applied the proceeds to the payment of other outstanding bonds, except a small amount used for commissions and expenses. It is this series of one hundred and twenty bonds that is the subject of this suit. Just the amount of the indebtedness of the county on the first day of May, 1885, when the one hundred and twenty thousand dollars of bonds were issued, does not definitely appear, nor is it material as to the precise amount. It is a fact that it was quite largely in excess of the one hundred and twenty thousand dollars of bonds that were issued, and it is also a fact that the constitutional limitation at that time was seventy-one thousand eight hundred and seventy six dollars and thirty-five cents.

"Another important fact to be stated, in view of the argument, is this: That of the previous issue of bonds, paid off with the proceeds of the one hundred and twenty thousand dollars of bonds in question, were some issued in discharge of judgments existing against the county, and probably bonds issued upon warrants or other evidences of debt within the constitutional limitation; so that it may be said for the purposes of our present consideration, that the bonds in question represent indebtedness both within and without the constitutional limit. A ground of earnest contention by appellants against the judgment of the district court is that, notwithstanding the validity of a part of the indebtedness for which the bonds issued, yet the decree embraces, and declares void, the entire series.

"The case of *Ætna Ins. Company v. Lyon County,* 44 Fed. Rep. 329, tried in the United States circuit court for the northern district of this state, was a law action upon interest coupons of this same series of bonds, and the opinion of the court is a subject of comment and difference between counsel. In that opinion it is said: 'As the case now stands I hold that the facts show that the series of bonds issued by the county and negotiated by B. L. Richards, as agent for the county, represent in part bonds previously issued, and which were enforceable against the county, and in part bonds which were invalid and nonenforceable, but that in the present case, at law, and in the absence of interested parties, it is impossible to determine what part or proportion of the coupons sued on belong to bonds that represent the valid indebtedness refunded therein. While the plaintiff has shown a right of recovery against the county for some amount, it has failed to show a legal right to recover on all the coupons sued on, or any particular number thereof, and hence there is no basis for rendering a judgment at law in the present cause.'

"Counsel do not seem to differ as to the correctness of the rule stated, as applicable to that kind of a proceeding, but their difference is as to the applicability of the same rule to this proceeding, being in equity. Accepting the correctness of the rule as applied, some additional authorities may aid in its application to this case. However, to a full understanding of the opinion in that case, it may be well, in addition to the above quotation, which is that of appellants, to add the following, as a part of the same paragraph: 'It seems to me that the only means of solving the difficulties of the situation is for the plaintiff and the other nonresident bondholders to unite in a proper proceeding against the county and such other bondholders as may refuse to act as complainants; and in such a suit it can be finally determined for what amount the county can be held liable, and the rights of the respective bondholders in and to this sum can be decreed.'

"Since that case was determined, the case of *Doon Township* v. *Cummins,* 142 U. S. 366, has been decided in the supreme court of the United States, and it will be hereafter referred to. The relationship of that case to this, as to the subject matter, is such that, if the two courts are in harmony as to the legal rules for application, the final solution of a problem of great importance to parties in interest will be materially aided.

"Some facts and well-settled rules of law lie at the threshold of this inquiry. It is to be remembered that it is the taxpayer, and not the county, that brings the suit, and also that defendants to the suit are the officers of the county, who are its legal representatives and business agents, and upon whose care and conduct the taxpayer has a right to rely for protection against illegal taxation. These bonds were wrongfully placed upon the market by these officers against whom they now seek relief. It is a rule of law that purchasers of such bonds are bound to take notice of the constitutional limitation of municipal indebtedness, and of such facts as constitute a basis for their issuance, with certain defined exceptions, as to the facts recited in the bonds. In *Buchanan* v. *Litchfield,* 102 U. S. 278, it is said: 'The purchaser of the bonds was certainly bound to take notice, not only of the constitutional limitation upon municipal indebtedness, but of such facts as the authorized official assessments disclosed concerning the valuation of taxable property within the city.' The rule is quoted and approved in *Dixon County* v. *Field,* 111 U. S. 83. In *Lake County* v. *Graham,* 130 U. S. 674, the rule is stated as follows: 'Nothing is better settled than this rule, that the purchaser of bonds, such as these (being county bonds in excess of a constitutional limitation in Colorado) is held to know the constitutional provisions and the statutory restrictions bearing on the question of the authority to issue them.' The same rule, in substance, is announced by this court in the *First Nat. Bank* v. *District Township of Doon,* 86 Iowa, 330;

41 Am. St. Rep. 489, and see authorities there cited.   With such a rule of law to govern, we have the fact that the purchasers of the bonds, through Richards, took them with knowledge that they were illegally issued.

"*Litchfield* v. *Ballou,* 114 U. S. 190, was a suit in equity to establish a lien for the purchase price of such bonds, because of the adjudged illegality of the bonds, on certain water-works of the city, to the construction of which the money had been applied.   Mr. Justice Miller, in the opinion, used these words: 'The holders of the bonds, and agents of the city, are *particeps criminis* in the act of violating that prohibition, and equity will no more raise a resulting trust in favor of the bondholders than the law will raise an implied assumpsit against a public policy so strongly declared.'   The 'declared' public policy refers to the constitutional provision limiting the indebtedness of the city, and while that is a case from Illinois, the constitutional language is the same as ours—that a county 'shall not be allowed to become *indebted, in any manner or for any purpose,* to an amount, including existing indebtedness, in the aggregate exceeding five per centum on the value of its taxable property.'   The following, from the opinion, indicates the scope of this prohibitive language:

" 'It shall not *become indebted.*   Shall not incur any pecuniary liability. It shall not do this in *any manner;* neither by bonds nor notes, nor by expressed or implied promises.   Nor shall it be done for any *purpose.*   There stands the existing indebtedness to a given amount, in relation to the sources of payment, as an impassable obstacle to the creation of any further debt, in any manner or for any purpose whatever.   If this prohibition is worth any thing, it is as effectual against the implied as the express promise, and is as binding in a court of chancery as a court of law.'

"The italicised language is the same in the opinion.   The case being in equity, and dealing with the equitable rights of such holders of bonds, because of the advantages of the corporation from the use of the money paid for the bonds, we may profitably give the case further notice.   It denied to the plaintiff a recovery in any form, and directed the lower court to dismiss the bill.   In the most unmistakable terms it holds that no debt was created because of the purchase of the bonds, either expressed or implied; that if the plaintiff had a right against the city it was for some specific property, as the particular money expended, or the property representing it, 'as property which they have purchased.'   The court below granted the lien on the water-works, and the opinion speaks of it as 'having decreed an indebtedness where none can exist.'   It is further said: 'The money received on the bonds having been expended, with other funds raised by taxation, in erecting the water-works of the city, to impose the amount thereof as a lien upon these public works would be equally a violation of the constitutional prohibition, as to raise against the city an implied assumpsit for money had and received.'   That case is a very significant and conclusive one upon the equitable claim that the county should be held to respond to the extent of its having received, appropriated, and profited by the money paid for the bonds, and we doubt if such a holding would have obtained except for the controlling principle that the bond purchasers, in parting with their money, were parties to a legal fraud upon the taxpayers.   *Doon Township* v. *Cummins,* 142 U. S. 366, is a law action to recover upon interest coupons, and the case involves the application of this same constitutional provision, and the facts are closely allied to the point we are considering.   The district township had issued refunding bonds in excess of the legal limit.   The bonds were sold to Cummins, and the proceeds thereof were placed in the treasury of the district township, and six thousand dollars thereof were applied to the payment of outstanding bonds and coupons, the remaining part of the proceeds of the bonds being applied to other purposes. The circuit court gave judgment for six thousand four hundred and sixty-two dollars and forty cents, being the amount of the coupons sued on, with interest. The case was free from any confusion as to conflicting interests of different bondholders, and the circuit court evidently applied the rule of allowing a recovery where the money for the bonds had been applied to the payment of debts within the constitutional limit. The case, on appeal, was reversed, with instructions to enter judgment for the township.

"The opinion in that case contains some reasoning as to the application of the proceeds of the sale of the bonds, and the consequence to result from a failure of the officers to do their duty in that respect, which we do not find it necessary to approve or disapprove, because in this case the situation is such that there is no pretense of knowing, or being able from the record to know, that any part of the proceeds of the bonds in question, that is, those affected by the judgment in this case, were applied, or intended to be applied, to any legal indebtedness of the county; and the burden of such a showing, even if available, which we do not decide, would be with the holder of such bonds. Under the facts as they appear in this case the bonds are to be treated as void. We are not to be understood as in any manner changing the rule as to the right of a municipal corporation, where its indebtedness is up to, or exceeds, the constitutional limit, to make improvements or otherwise expend its moneys in a way that the legal effect of its action is not to create an indebtedness in excess of the constitutional limit, as is indicated in *Dively* v. *City of Cedar Falls*, 27 Iowa, 227, nor to change the rule as to contracts within the rule as to current revenues, as held in *Grant* v. *City of Davenport*, 36 Iowa, 396.

"The appellants cite many authorities upon familiar rules as to 'laches' and 'clean hands' for those asking equity, but they are entirely inapplicable, and have never, to our knowledge, been applied to a similar state of facts."

CASES

IN THE

SUPREME COURT

OF

KANSAS.

IN RE SIMS.

[54 KANSAS, 1.]

CONTEMPT—CONSTITUTIONAL LAW.—A statute authorizing a county attorney to punish for contempt any witnesses disobeying process or refusing to answer questions when commanded by subpœna issued by such attorney to appear before him as provided by the statute is unconstitutional and void.

CONTEMPT—CONSTITUTIONAL LAW.—The legislature has no power to confer on an executive officer, charged with the searching out violations of law, and inquiring into facts prior to instituting prosecutions, the power, at the same time and as ancillary to the performance of his duties as such prosecuting officer, to commit persons to jail as for a contempt of his authority.

CONTEMPT—POWER OF EXECUTIVE OFFICER TO PUNISH FOR.—The power to punish for contempt is never exercised except by legislative bodies or judicial officers, and cannot be conferred upon an executive officer while acting in his executive capacity.

PETITION in habeas corpus.

O. Foust & Son, for the petitioner.

A. H. Campbell and Ewing & Bennett, for the respondent.

ALLEN, J. The petitioner was restrained of his liberty by the sheriff of Allen county, under a commitment issued by the county attorney for refusal to answer questions propounded to him touching violations of the prohibitory liquor law. Paragraph 2553 of the General Statutes of 1889 makes it the duty of the county attorney, when notified of any violation of the prohibitory law, to issue his subpœna commanding witnesses to appear before him, to swear such witnesses, examine them, reduce their testimony to writing, and cause

(261)

it to be subscribed by such witnesses, and expressly authorizes the county attorney to punish for contempt any witnesses
disobeying his process or refusing to answer questions. If
the testimony so taken discloses the fact that an offense has
been committed he is required forthwith to file the statements
of the witnesses with his complaint or information against the
person having committed the offense, and thereupon to proceed with the prosecution of the offender.

The single question presented for our consideration is,
whether that portion of the statute which authorizes the
county attorney to punish as for contempt is in violation of
the constitution of this state. Nothing is more firmly fixed
in the governmental systems of all English-speaking countries
than the division of powers between the three great departments of government, the executive, legislative, and judicial.
The question before us is whether the legislature has power
to confer on an executive officer charged with the duty of
searching out violations of the law, inquiring into facts, instituting and carrying on prosecutions for violations of the
criminal laws of the state, the power, at the same time and as
ancillary to the performance of his duties as a prosecuting
officer, to commit persons to jail as for a contempt of his
authority. That a proceeding to punish for contempt is in
[5] its nature a criminal proceeding has been directly decided
by this court, *State* v. *Dent*, 29 Kan. 416, as well as by the
courts of other states: *Cartwright's case*, 114 Mass. 230; *Puterbaugh* v. *Smith*, 131 Ill. 199; 19 Am. St. Rep. 30.

The right to appeal from an order punishing for a contempt
has been frequently recognized by this court: *Peyton's Appeal*,
12 Kan. 398; *In re Dalton*, 46 Kan. 253; *State* v. *Henthorn*,
46 Kan. 613; *State* v. *Vincent*, 46 Kan. 618; *In re Nickell*, 47
Kan. 734; 27 Am. St. Rep. 315; *In re Noonan*, 47 Kan. 771;
In re Harmer, 47 Kan. 262; *State* v. *Durein*, 46 Kan. 695.
An appeal to a superior court can only be taken from a judicial decision, never from one involving merely executive or
legislative discretion: *Fulkerson* v. *Commrs. of Harper County*,
31 Kan. 125; *Kent* v. *Commrs. of Labette County*, 42 Kan. 534.
In committing the prisoner for contempt the county attorney
therefore decided a case in its nature criminal, and, in making such decision, assumed to act in a judicial capacity.
That the statute referred to gives him this power in terms is
clear. Is the statute valid? The cases of *In re Abeles*, 12
Kan. 451, and *In re Merkle*, 40 Kan. 27, are cited in support

of the proposition that power to commit for contempt may be given to other than a judicial officer, and it is said that it is not necessary in order to confer judicial power that the legislature should first in terms create a court. The constitution of this state provides that "the judicial power of this state shall be vested in a supreme court, district courts, probate courts, justices of the peace, and such other courts inferior to the supreme court as may be provided by law": art. 3, sec. 1. The legislature, therefore, is at liberty to confer judicial power, and to create courts inferior to the supreme court. It may be conceded that the legislature may confer judicial power on an individual who also fills an executive office. The prior decisions of this court go no further than this. The point here involved, whether executive and judicial power may be mingled and combined, may be exercised by the same person at the same time and in the same proceeding, has never yet been decided by this court.

    * The county attorney is peculiarly an executive officer. He is not only authorized to appear on behalf of the state and prosecute all criminal cases arising in his county, but it is his duty to do so; and the act concerning the sale of intoxicating liquors imposes on him the specific duty of making inquiries and investigations for the purpose of detecting violations of the prohibitory law, to compel witnesses to testify, to reduce their statements to writing, to cause them to be signed by the witnesses, to file them in the district or other court having jurisdiction, and with them his complaint or information, charging offenders with such offenses as the testimony shows they are guilty of. In all these proceedings the county attorney acts as an administrative officer, prosecuting on behalf of the people. It is for the purpose of aiding him in the effectual execution of this duty that the power to commit for contempt is given him. It is given to him, not as a judicial officer, but as county attorney, and for the very purpose of aiding him in performing the duties of that office. Such a combination of powers is not in accordance with the theory of our government nor with the orderly administration of justice as administered in this country and in England. The power to punish for contempt is never exercised except by legislative bodies or judicial officers: *Whitcomb's case*, 120 Mass. 118; 21 Am. Rep. 502; *Langenberg* v. *Decker*, 131 Ind. 471; *Kilbourn* v. *Thompson*, 103 U. S. 168; *Attorney General* v. *McDonald*, 3 Wis. 805.

It is sought to distinguish the case before us from those cited because of provisions in the constitutions of Wisconsin and Indiana with reference to the separation of executive and judicial powers. We think, however, that in our constitution these powers are as clearly separated as though the framers of the constitution had said so in terms. It needs but a suggestion to show that the combination of executive and judicial powers may become tyrany at once. The advancement in the science of government made in modern times is due to the separation of the three great co-ordinate departments. If the legislature may confer on the county [7] attorney one of the highest and most distinctive attributes of judicial power, that of punishing for contempt, to aid him in ascertaining from witnesses the facts with reference to violations of law, might the legislature not also confer on any attorney the power to examine witnesses in civil cases in the same manner, and to commit them for contempt if they refuse to answer his questions? Might it not also give to any executive officer from the governor down the power to subpœna witnesses to inform his judgment and to aid him in any executive decision or determination? And, if the rule is established, can it be doubted that the division between executive and judicial officers will be completely broken down, and all constitutional barriers removed from those forms of oppression which have always attended this combination.

In this very case the county attorney, as a prosecuting officer, issued his subpœna. When the witness came before him, as a prosecuting officer he asked him a question. When the witness refused to answer he at once passed on his own right to ask the question, on its pertinency and propriety, judicially determined that he, as prosecuting attorney, had asked a proper question, and, as a judicial officer, declared and determined that the witness was guilty of a judicial contempt in refusing to answer the question which he himself had asked as a prosecuting attorney. This is a commingling and confusing of executive and judicial functions in a manner incompatible with the constitution, obnoxious to its whole spirit and to the spirit of free institutions, and the act to that extent is void.

The petitioner will be discharged.

HORTON, C. J., and JOHNSTON, J., concurring specially.

Horton, C. J. Paragraph 2543 of the General Statutes of 1889 confers upon county attorneys of the state, when notified of any violation of the provisions of the prohibitory liquor law, the power to inquire into such violation, and for that purpose they are authorized to issue subpœnas for any person they believe [8] has information or knowledge thereof to appear before them and testify. The testimony in every case must be reduced to writing and signed by the witness, the same as a deposition in a civil cause. Power is also attempted to be conferred upon county attorneys to imprison any witness for refusal to testify concerning any violation of the statute, when required to do so: Laws of 1885, c. 149, sec. 8. Paragraph 2543 further provides that, if the testimony taken discloses that any offense has been committed against the provisions of the statute, the county attorney taking the testimony must file the statement of the witness and a complaint or information against the offender in some court of competent jurisdiction. The complaint or information may then be verified by the county attorney upon information and belief.

All of the provisions of the statute are for the purpose of assisting county attorneys in procuring testimony for violations of the act and in preparing their cases for successful prosecution in the court. So far as the power conferred by the statute is ministerial or administrative it is constitutional, and must be obeyed; but, if a witness refuses to testify, I do not think county attorneys have, or ought to have, the power to imprison such a witness for contempt. County attorneys are executive or administrative officers; but the power attempted to be conferred upon them, or any other officer taking depositions or testimony, to commit a witness for refusing to answer, is judicial in character: *Kilbourn* v. *Thompson*, 103 U. S. 168. If the statute is constitutional and open to no legal objection county attorneys have the power to ask questions of the witnesses brought before them, and then to pass upon the competency or pertinency of the same, and, if the witness refuses to answer, to imprison him in the county jail, there to remain until he submits to testify. It is an old maxim of the law that "no man can be a judge in his own cause." This wise maxim is infringed upon by conferring on a prosecuting attorney judicial power to commit a witness called before him to testify in a case which he is preparing for trial, or in which he proposes, if his investigation war-

rants, to file ⁹ a complaint or information. In such a proceeding, on the examination of a witness, the prosecuting
attorney has a pecuniary, professional, and official interest.
He is not acting disinterestedly. The statute would be very
similar, and liable to like objection, if it authorized notaries
public and attorneys at law to personally take depositions or
perpetuate testimony in actions they were intending to commence for the other parties. In a civil action no deposition
or affidavit can be taken before a relative, or an attorney of
either party, or before any one interested in the event of the
proceeding: Civ. Code, sec. 350; *Foreman* v. *Carter*, 9 Kan.
681; *Warner* v. *Warner*, 11 Kan. 121. The rule in criminal
cases ought to be as strict.

The legislature has full authority to confer the power to
imprison a witness for contempt, prescribed in paragraph
2543, upon justices of the peace, probate judges, notaries
public, clerks of courts, or any individual, not the prosecuting attorney or interested in the proceeding. I fully concur
in the judgment pronounced in *In re Clayton*, 59 Conn. 510,
21 Am. St. Rep. 128, but some of the reasons given are not
satisfactory to me. In that case the examination was taken
before a police judge, not before a prosecuting attorney or
any one interested in commencing criminal proceedings upon
the testimony which it was sought to compel the witness to
disclose. I am of the opinion, as observed in that case, that
"it is the duty of all good citizens, when legally required
so to do, to testify to any facts within their knowledge affecting public interest, and no one has a natural right to be protected in his refusal to discharge this duty. Public policy
does not forbid, but on the contrary often requires, legislation to facilitate the administration of justice." But the
power to compel a citizen to testify should be exercised
legally, not unconstitutionally. If this ruling shall in any
way interfere with full and successful investigations on the
part of county attorneys of violations of the provisions of
the prohibitory liquor law, it can be remedied speedily.
The legislature will convene in a few months, and the power
to imprison recusant witnesses, attempted to be conferred
upon county attorneys by paragraph 2543, may, as before ¹⁰
stated, be constitutionally and legally imposed upon any
officer or individual not the county attorney or otherwise
interested in the proceeding.

My attention has been called recently to the case of *De*

Camp v. *Archibald,* 50 Ohio St. 618, 40 Am. St. Rep. 692, ruling that the power to commit a person for contempt for refusing to answer is not judicial in character. That decision, although made by an able court, is not supported by logical reasoning, is not in line with our own decisions, and is opposed to the great weight of authority.

JOHNSON, J. In the enactment of the provisions authorizing the county attorney to make preliminary inquiry as to the commission of offenses the legislature appears to have proceeded upon the theory that the duties imposed and power conferred in that respect were not judicial in character. If they were executive or merely quasi judicial in their nature, the objections urged against the statute would be without force; and the fact that they were imposed and conferred upon an executive officer indicates the legislative view, and may be some argument that they are not judicial. Some of the steps in the preliminary inquiry are clearly the exercise of executive functions, and whether or not any of them are judicial·must be determined from their nature, rather than from the position or station of the one by whom the act is to be performed. Assuming that the authority to punish for contempt was an incident to the exercise of executive power, the legislature vested it in the county attorney; and this is not to be wondered at, in view of the fact that the supreme court of Ohio, in a recent case, has determined that the exercise of such authority is not the exercise of judicial power: *De Camp* v. *Archibald,* 50 Ohio St. 618; 40 Am. St. Rep. 692. Although I entertain the highest respect for that tribunal I am unable to reach the same conclusion.

The authority to hear and determine a controversy upon both the facts and the law is judicial power. When the witness [11] refuses to answer the question proposed, the county attorney must then determine upon the propriety of the question, and whether, under the circumstances, an answer should be compelled. At that stage of the proceedings an issue is formed, and a controversy arises between the state and the witness. A contempt of court is a substantive criminal offense, and to adjudicate a case of contempt and to impose punishment for such offense is generally said to be the highest exercise of judicial power. The county attorney not only inquires and decides, but he is given full power to enforce his decision, and that by one of the most severe methods known to the law. The authority to try one accused of a criminal offense, pronounce judgment against him, and enforce that judgment by imprisonment, is surely an exercise of judicial power. If, then, the power is to be regarded as judicial, it can only be exercised by one of the tribunals mentioned in section 1 of article 3 of the constitution. Under this constitutional provision the legislature may vest judicial power in such courts as it may see fit to create, provided only that they are inferior to the supreme court. Can the county attorney be regarded as a court within the meaning of this constitutional provision?

The contention of the state that the legislature may create a court or confer judicial power without designating the tribunal created as a court must be conceded: *Malone* v. *Murphy*, 2 Kan. 250; *State* v. *Young*, 3 Kan. 445. I am unable, however, to sustain the position of the petitioner, and hold that the vesting of judicial power in an executive officer, and requiring him to perform both executive and judicial functions, is a sufficient objection to the statute. It is highly important to separate the legislative, judicial, and executive functions, and that the officer of one department should not exercise the functions conferred upon another. Under our system, however, the absolute independence of the departments, and the complete separation of the powers is impracticable, and was not intended.

"It is true, with some exceptions, that the legislature cannot [12] exercise judicial or executive power, that the courts cannot exercise legislative or executive power, and that the executive department cannot exercise legislative or judicial power; but it is not true that they are entirely separate from each other, or independent of each other, or that one of them may not in some instances control one of the others": *Martin* v. *Ingham*, 38 Kan. 654.

The governor has been vested with some judicial functions, and the legislature acts judicially when it tries a charge of contempt, and adjudges punishment therefor. Ministerial duties have been placed upon courts, and while scrupulous care should be used to prevent an officer of one department from intruding to any extent upon the duties conferred upon an officer of another department, nothing in our state constitution, as there is in that of some other states, prevents the vesting of more than one function in a single individual. Illustrations of conferring more than one of these powers upon the same person are numerous. It has been held that the mayor of a city of the second class might, while acting as mayor, exercise the powers of a court, although the statute did not in terms create him a court: *Prell* v. *McDonald*, 7 Kan. 426; 12 Am. Rep. 423. Judicial powers have been conferred on county commissioners and coroners, whose duties are mainly ministerial. Probate judges, whose duties are mostly judicial, have had conferred upon them many ministerial duties, and legislation giving such powers has been upheld: *In re Johnson*, 12 Kan. 102; *Intoxicating Liquor cases*, 25 Kan. 759; 37 Am. Rep. 284.

Other instances might be cited, but these are sufficient to show that the legislature may confer judicial powers upon an executive officer, provided such duties are not inconsistent with those required of such officer. No case has been sustained, however, where the new duties conferred upon an officer were incompatible with those already imposed by such office. When the petitioner refused to answer the question, and a controversy arose, he was, in effect, accused of an offense. The state was the plaintiff, and the petitioner the defendant. [13] The county attorney is the representative of the state, and required to appear in all prosecutions in its behalf. When the issue was thus formed, the positions of county attorney and judge became antagonistic, and the duties of the respective places incompatible. It is not within the power of the legislature to make a judge an arbiter in his own cause, and to give an attorney for one of two adverse parties the power to determine the controversy is wholly inconsistent with our system of jurisprudence. The legislature has not clothed the county attorney with the paraphernalia of a court, and it does not seem to have been its purpose to invest him with the attributes of a judicial tribunal. Manifestly, it proceeded upon the theory that the powers conferred were such as might be carried out by an executive officer, and are not "judicial" within the meaning of the constitution.

As that view cannot be sustained, and as the authority to punish for contempt must be regarded as the exercise of judicial power, it follows that the statute cannot be upheld.

———

CONTEMPT—WHO MAY PUNISH FOR.—The common council of a city has no power to commit and punish for a contempt, and a statute which attempts to confer such authority is unconstitutional and void: *Whitcomb's case,* 120 Mass. 118; 21 Am. Rep. 502. See, also, the extended note to *Burns* v. *Allen,* 2 Am. St. Rep. 847, where the power of the legislature to punish for contempt is discussed.

STATE *v.* CONKLING.
[54 KANSAS, 108.]

APPEAL DOES NOT LIE from a discharged and satisfied judgment.

JUDGMENTS — DISCHARGE OF — RIGHT TO APPEAL.—One found guilty of contempt, who pays, under protest, the fine adjudged against him, cannot reserve the right to appeal. No appeal lies from a discharged judgment.

L. M. Conkling, for the appellant.

C. W. Fairchild, county attorney, for the state.

[108] JOHNSTON, J.   An attachment was issued by the district court of Kingman county for I. G. Conkling, requiring him to appear before the court to answer a charge of contempt; and on December 26, 1891, he was adjudged guilty of contempt in obstructing a receiver of the court, and was sentenced to pay a fine of fifty dollars, and stand committed until it was paid.   Motions for a new trial and to arrest the judgment of the court were made and overruled.   Afterward, on December 29, 1891, I. G. Conkling appeared in open court, and paid the fine assessed against him.   The statement was then made that he paid the fine under protest, and that he reserved the right to appeal, and all rights that he might be entitled to in the premises.   He has attempted to bring the case here on appeal.

It appears that the sentence of the law has been executed, and nothing is left for further controversy.   By his own act Conkling has satisfied and discharged the judgment entered against him.   His protest and attempt to reserve the right of appeal are unavailing.   The statute does not provide for nor [109] contemplate an appeal from a discharged judgment. Neither payment nor protest was necessary to protect his rights.   Under the statute the judgment of conviction which was entered against him would have been stayed by the mere taking of an appeal, without any order of the court or the giving of a bond: Gen. Stats. 1889, par. 5349.   The appeal will be dismissed.

All the justices concurring.

JUDGMENTS—APPEAL AFTER SATISFACTION—*Judgment Plaintiff.*—The rule is almost universal that one in whose favor a judgment is rendered, by accepting or receiving satisfaction thereof, or seeking satisfaction by having an execution issued to compel such payment, is estopped from prosecuting an appeal from such judgment. The ground upon which this estoppel or waiver of the right of appeal is based is that one cannot be permitted to accept and retain the fruits of a judgment in his favor and at the same time insist that it is erroneous: *Murphy* v. *Murphy*, 45 Ala. 123; *Knox* v. *Steele*, 18 Ala. 815; 54 Am. Dec. 181; *Cassell* v. *Fagin*, 11 Mo. 207; 47 Am. Dec. 151; *Corwin* v. *Shoup*, 76 Ill. 246; *Ind. School Dist. of Altoona* v. *District Township of Delaware*, 44 Iowa, 201; *Lamprey* v. *Henk*, 16 Minn. 405; *Estate of Baby*, 87 Cal. 200; 22 Am. St. Rep. 239; *Carll* v. *Oakley*, 97 N. Y. 633; *Fly* v. *Bailey*, 36 Tex. 119; *Garner* v. *Garner*, 38 Ind. 139; *Moore* v. *Floyd*, 4 Or. 260; *Shingler* v. *Martin*, 54 Ala. 354. In *Buckman* v. *Alwood*, 44 Ill. 183, it was said to be settled doctrine "that where a party recovering judgment or a decree accepts the benefits thereof voluntarily, and knowing the facts, he is estopped to afterward reverse the judgment or decree on error; that the acceptance operates as, and may be pleaded as, a release of errors." A person who sues out an execution and enforces a judgment in his favor, thereby elects to take it as it was rendered, and cannot afterward appeal from such judgment: *Hall* v. *Lacy*, 37 Pa. St. 366. The issuing of an execution upon a judgment rendered in his favor, after bringing an appeal therefrom, is a waiver of the right of the plaintiff in the judgment to prosecute such appeal: *Knapp* v. *Brown*, 45 N. Y. 207. Or, if the judgment plaintiff accepts or receives the fruits of the judgment after taking an appeal therefrom, he thereby waives the appeal: *Alexander* v. *Alexander*, 104 N. Y. 643; *People* v. *Burns*, 78 Cal. 645. A party cannot avail himself of the fruits of that part of a judgment favorable to him, and then by appeal seek to reverse such portions of the judgment as militate against him: *Holt* v. *Rees*, 46 Ill. 181; *Webster-Glover etc. Co.* v. *St. Croix County*, 71 Wis. 317. In this last case the court said, at page 319, that "a party cannot proceed to enforce and have the benefit of such portions of a judgment as are in his favor, and appeal from those against him. In other words, the right to proceed on a judgment and enjoy its fruits, and the right to appeal therefrom, are totally inconsistent. The election to pursue one course must be deemed an abandonment of the other." A party may be concluded and estopped to appeal by his acquiescence in a decree affecting his rights made during the progress of the case, under which he takes part of the fund decreed to him, making no objection until the final decree is rendered in the case, a number of years thereafter: *Burton* v. *Brown*, 22 Gratt. 1. Some of the cases maintain that although a plaintiff accepts the sum to which he has been declared entitled by the judgment, yet he may be permitted to appeal for the purpose of showing that he is entitled to a larger amount than has been awarded him: *Clowes* v. *Dickenson*, 8 Cow. 328; *Higbie* v. *Westlake*, 14 N. Y. 281; *Catlin* v. *Wheeler*, 49 Wis. 507; *Tarleton* v. *Goldthwaite*, 23 Ala. 346; 58 Am. Dec. 296; *Meaders* v. *Gray*, 60 Miss. 400; 45 Am. Rep. 414; *Erwin* v. *Lowry*, 7 How. 172; *Clifft* v. *Wade*, 51 Tex. 15. The reason for this rule is thus stated in *Knapp* v. *Brown*, 45 N. Y. 207-210, where it is said that "*Clowes* v. *Dickenson*, 8 Cow. 328, was an appeal by a party from a decree in chancery awarding him a specified sum of money, who had demanded and received payment from the opposite parties and afterward appealed from the decree. A motion to dismiss the appeal was denied by the court. The appellant did not seek to obtain a reversal of the decree, but its modification, so as to award him a larger sum. It thus appears that in any event he was entitled to retain the sum received, and that the only question that could arise upon the appeal was whether he was not entitled to recover more. Hence, his act in demanding and receiving payment of the judgment was not inconsistent with his appeal." The case of *Higbie* v. *Westlake*, 14 N. Y. 281, cited above, is based upon the same reasoning. It must be observed, however, that the cases which maintain this rule involve appeals from decrees or orders in chancery or probate courts, and generally include the right of heirs, distributees, or creditors, to recover a greater sum than has been awarded them by the lower court. The cases draw the distinction between the right to appeal from a decree in chancery, after accepting the fruits of the decree, and the right to appeal from a judgment at law, after receiving its benefits. The rule, as said in the beginning, is universal that a judgment plaintiff, upon receiving the amount awarded to him by a judgment at law, thus satisfying such judgment, waives the right to prosecute an appeal therefrom. The distinction noted is pointed out in *Tarleton* v. *Goldthwaite*, 23 Ala. 346; 58 Am. Dec. 296; *Knapp* v. *Brown*, 45 N. Y. 207; *Shingler* v. *Martin*, 54 Ala. 354, where it was said: "It is well settled as the practice of this court that if a judgment be rendered in favor of a party in a lower court, especially in an action at law, and he coerces or receives payment of the amount thereof, he will not be permitted to maintain an appeal from the same judgment; and even if judgment of reversal has been rendered here, in the appeal, before the court is informed that such payment has been made, this court, on being advised thereof, will withhold the certificate of reversal, and set aside its judgment, if the money collected be not, within a time prescribed by it, paid back to the appellee. True, this is a power which will not be exercised in some peculiar cases from the probate and chancery courts, in which it is apparent or admitted that the appellants are entitled to recover all they have received, and perhaps more." It has been decided that a party who recovers a judgment before a justice of the peace may appeal therefrom, although he has accepted the fruits of the judgment, and the reason given is that on appeal to the circuit court the case is heard *de novo:* that the court does not sit as a court of error. Hence the doctrine that accepting the benefit of a judgment is a release of error therein has no application to such appeals: *Kasting* v. *Kasting*, 47 Ill. 438.

Judgment Defendant.—Although there is undoubtedly a conflict in the cases, the doctrine supported by the great weight of authority is that a judgment defendant does not waive the right to appeal and to reverse the judgment for error, by paying the amount thereof, either before or after taking his appeal, no matter whether the payment is made voluntarily or after execution has issued and been served upon him: *Hayes* v. *Nourse*, 107 N. Y. 577; 1 Am. St. Rep. 891; *Burrows* v. *Mickler*, 22 Fla. 572; 1 Am. St. Rep. 217; *Schermerhorn* v. *Wheeler*, 5 Daly, 472; *Clark* v. *Ostrander*, 1 Cow. 437; 13 Am. Dec. 546; *Richeson* v. *Ryan*, 14 Ill. 73; 56 Am. Dec. 493; *Hutch* v. *Jacobson*, 94 Ill. 584; *Page* v. *People*, 99 Ill. 418; *Armes* v. *Chappel*, 28 Ind. 469; *Dickensheets* v. *Kaufman*, 29 Ind. 154; *Hill* v. *Starkweather*, 30 Ind. 434; *Belton* v. *Smith*, 45 Ind. 291; *Kelly* v. *Bloom*, 17 Abb. Pr. 229; *Burch* v. *Newbury*, 4 How. Pr. 145; *Grim* v. *Semple*, 39 Iowa, 570; *Mayor etc.* v. *Riker*, 38 N. J. L. 225; 20 Am. Rep. 386. The reason for the rule is clearly stated in *Richeson* v. *Ryan*, 14 Ill. 74, 56 Am. Dec. 493, where the court said: "Ryan recovered a judgment against Richeson. The latter paid the judgment before an execution issued, and then sued out a writ of error to reverse it. Did the payment operate as a release of errors? If the judgment had been collected by execution there would not be a doubt of the right of Richeson to prosecute the writ of error. A payment under such circumstances would be compulsory, and would not preclude him from afterwards reversing the judgment, if erroneous, and then maintaining an action to recover back the amount paid. The payment in question must equally be considered as made under legal compulsion. The judgment fixed the liability of Richeson, and he could only avoid payment by procuring its reversal. He was not bound to wait until payment should be demanded by the sheriff. He was at liberty to pay off the judgment at once, and thereby prevent the accumulation of costs. By so doing he did not waive his right to remove the record to this court, for the purpose of having the validity of the proceedings tested and determined." In *Grim v. Semple*, 39 Iowa, 570-572, the court said: "Suppose a judgment is rendered against a party, and he cannot give security to supersede its enforcement while he prosecutes an appeal, and an execution is therefore issued, and his property is about to be sold under it—his homestead, it may be. Now, can it be claimed that if he shall pay off the judgment, he is thereby deprived of an appeal. Surely this cannot be the law." In this case it was decided that the payment of a judgment after levy of execution, and shortly before the time fixed for sale, is not a voluntary payment so as to defeat the right of the judgment defendant to appeal: *Grim v. Semple*, 39 Iowa, 570. "One against whom a judgment is entered, if he fails to satisfy it, must expect to see his property seized and sold at a sacrifice, and it is difficult to conceive how his payment of the judgment can give rise to any estoppel against his seeking to avoid it for error. . . . . The better view we think is, that though execution has not issued, the payment of a judgment must be regarded as compulsory, and therefore as not releasing errors nor depriving the payor of his right to appeal": 2 Freeman on Judgments, sec. 480 a.

The performance of the requirements of a peremptory writ of mandate is not a bar to an appeal from the judgment awarding the writ: *County Commrs. v. Johnson*, 21 Fla. 577. In *Hatch v. Jacobson*, 94 Ill. 584, the parties agreed, after judgment rendered against the defendant, that if the time for the payment of the money for which the decree found defendant liable should be extended he would pay the amount, and it was decided that this agreement to pay such amount was not so far voluntary on his part as to operate as a release of errors and a waiver of the right to appeal.

Compliance with a decree in equity does not deprive the party against whom it is rendered of his right to appeal: *Peer v. Cookerow*, 14 N. J. Eq. 361; *White v. Jones*, 4 Call. 253; 2 Am. Dec. 564; nor does a party lose his right to appeal from a decree by executing a conveyance as commanded thereby: *O'Hara v. MacConnell*, 93 U. S. 150. A judgment defendant who gives a mortgage to secure the payment of a fine adjudged against him, and has the judgment marked "paid," does not thereby waive or lose his right to appeal: *Floyd v. State*, 32 Ark. 200.

A few cases agree with and maintain the doctrine pronounced in the principal case, namely, that the voluntary payment of a judgment in either a civil or criminal case, by the judgment defendant is a release of errors, and a waiver or bar of the right to appeal from such judgment. This ruling is put upon the ground that such voluntary payment satisfies and extinguishes the judgment, leaving nothing to appeal from, and that an appeal thereafter taken or pending at the time of the payment is void, and must be dismissed on motion: *Sager v. Moy*, 15 R. I. 528; *Morton v. Supe.*

rior Court, 65 Cal. 496; *Borgalthous* v. *Farmers' etc. Ins. Co.,* 36 Iowa, 260; *State* v. *Westfull,* 37 Iowa, 575. Although we entirely disagree with the reasoning and the rule laid down in these cases, yet it may be good law that a judgment debtor who makes part payment on a judgment to gain a special advantage, as to postpone a levy of execution, thereby estops himself from prosecuting an appeal and waives all error committed by the trial court in rendering the judgment: *Smith* v. *O'Brien,* 146 Mass. 294; *Bennett* v. *Van Syckel,* 18 N. Y. 481. An appeal may be dismissed, if, after it is taken, the judgment has been paid and satisfied by agreement of the parties, and the only object of the hearing in the appellate court is to save the attorney for the appellant his costs: *Cock* v. *Palmer,* 19 Abb. Pr 372. It may be provided by statute that voluntary acquiescence in a judgment or decree by paying the money or doing the thing adjudged or decreed bars the right of the party thus acquiescing in judgment to appeal therefrom. Such a provision exists in at least one state: Louisiana Code of Practice, art. 567: *Succession of De Egana,* 18 La. Ann. 59; *Buntin* v. *Johnson,* 27 La. Ann. 625.

KENNETT *v.* PETERS.

[54 KANSAS, 119.]

TROVER—SUFFICIENCY OF COMPLAINT.—A complaint in trover must allege that plaintiff was the owner, or in possession, or entitled to the immediate possession of, the property when converted.

TROVER—ALLEGATIONS OF POSSESSION.—A complaint in an action of trover brought by one not in possession at the time the chattels were converted must allege that he was entitled to the immediate possession of the property at that time.

TROVER—ALLEGATIONS OF OWNERSHIP.—A complaint in an action of trover by one not the absolute owner of the property must allege that he had a special ownership or interest therein at the time of the conversion and must state the facts in relation thereto.

MORTGAGE OF CHATTELS—TROVER FOR CONVERSION—PLEADING.—A chattel mortgagee does not become the absolute owner of the mortgaged property upon condition broken, nor does he then become entitled to the immediate possession of the property unconditionally. Therefore, he cannot maintain trover for its conversion without alleging his special ownership and interest therein at the time of the conversion, and stating the facts in relation thereto. A general allegation of ownership is insufficient to maintain the action.

PLEADING.—IF A COMPLAINT IS DEFECTIVE for want of material averments, and such averments are not supplied by the answer, the complaint is not cured thereby.

JUDGMENTS—REVIEW.—A judgment, if shown to be correct by the pleadings and evidence, cannot be disturbed on appeal, notwithstanding errors may have occurred upon the trial.

JUDGMENT—REVIEW.—If a complaint is fatally defective, and does not support the judgment, alleged errors occurring upon the trial cannot be examined upon appeal at the instance of the plaintiff.

ACTION by H. Kennett against Peters & Co., C. W. Lord, and other defendants. The complaint alleged that "plaintiff says that he is and was the owner, and entitled to the possession of 36 head of steers, one and two years old, of the value of $850; 29 head of hogs, of the value of $260; 10 cows, of the value of $200; 6 calves, of the value of $70, and 2 bulls, of the value of $50; all of the total value of $1,430. On and about the 11th day of September the defendants unlawfully obtained possession of said property, refused to deliver it to plaintiff, and converted it to their own use, to the damage of plaintiff $1,500, for which he asks judgment with interest, from September 11, 1888, and costs of suit." The defendants filed general denials, and, upon the trial, recovered a verdict and judgment in their favor. Plaintiff appealed.

Kennett, Peck & Matson, for the appellant.

Ellis & Cook and D. C. Chipman, for the appellee.

[121] HORTON, C. J.   It is claimed that the petition does not state facts sufficient to constitute a cause of action, and that, under an allegation of general ownership, a chattel mortgage permitting the property to remain in possession of the mortgagor until default in payment of the debt secured thereby is not evidence to sustain the same. The points are well taken. The petition fails to state that the plaintiff was the owner of or in the possession of the property on the date of the conversion; fails to state that the plaintiff was entitled to the immediate possession of the property at the time of the conversion; fails to state the year in which the conversion occurred, and fails to state the special ownership or interest in the property.   In trover plaintiff must either have the possession, or the immediate right of possession, of the property to entitle him to recover: *Wilson* v. *Fuller,* 9 Kan. 176, 190, 191; *Hoisington* v. *Armstrong,* 22 Kan. 110, 113; Chitty on Pleading, 167; *Owens* v. *Weedman,* 82 Ill. 409–417; *Middlesworth* v. *Sedgwick,* 10 Cal. 392.

The precedents from all the books upon pleadings require that the petition must show that the plaintiff was in the actual possession of the property at the time of the conversion, or, if not in possession, that he was entitled to the immediate possession of the property: 2 Estee's Pleading and Practice, sec. 2098; Maxwell on Code Pleading, 637.   Swan on Pleadings expressly states that the petition for the conversion of chattels must allege, "if the plaintiff was not in possession," that he "was entitled to the immediate possession of the property."

The petition does not state that the plaintiff was the owner of the property at the time of the conversion, but merely charges that the conversion was on "the eleventh day of September." The year is omitted: *Sawyer* v. *Robertson*, 11 Mont. 416; *Smith* v. *Force*, 31 Minn. 119; Bouvier's Institutes, sec. 3538; *Cruger* v. *Hudson Riv. R. R. Co.*, 12 N. Y. 191–201. Cobbey on the Law of Replevin, section 601, says: "Where the plaintiff claims as sole owner he must stand [122] or fall on that claim, and cannot, if his alleged title turns out to be invalid as against the true owner, fall back upon an alleged lien. The claim of title is a waiver of any lien, and, in any event, before he can claim the chattel by virtue of the lien, the false claim of title must be abandoned, the title of the true owner conceded, and the claim reduced to one of lien."

Our statute provides that, in an affidavit for an order for the delivery of property, the plaintiff must show that he is the owner of the property, or has a special ownership or interest therein, stating the facts in relation thereto: Civ. Code, sec 177. The code prescribes that there can be no feigned issues in pleadings, and that all pleadings must be written statements by the parties of the facts constituting their respective claims: Civ. Code, secs. 11, 84. A petition in replevin, or for conversion, ought to advise the defendant of the nature of the plaintiff's claim to the property, to the end that he can intelligently defend. Of course the proof must sustain the material allegations of the judgment: *Kern* v. *Wilson*, 73 Iowa, 490.

The plaintiff's interest in the property, upon the evidence offered, was only that of a mortgagee. There are authorities in some of the states holding that, after condition broken, the title to mortgaged personal property becomes absolute in the mortgagee, without redemption. Our statute contemplates a different rule: *Wolfley* v. *Rising*, 12 Kan. 535; *Kern* v. *Wilson*, 73 Iowa, 490. In the mortgages offered, the possession of the property was retained by the mortgagor until condition broken; therefore, although the plaintiff, under the statute, had the legal title to the property referred to in his mortgages, if they were sufficient in description and embraced the property sold, he was not entitled to the possession of the property until he had shown to the satisfaction

of the court that the indebtedness, or a part thereof, secured
by the mortgage was due and unpaid, but even then his title
was not absolute. We are referred to *Miller* v. *Adamson*, 45
Minn. 99, in support of the claim that a plaintiff may, in
replevin or trover, allege generally he is the owner [123] of the
property, and prove either general or special ownership. The
decision is not satisfactory to us.

According to the common and usual practice as it exists in
this state a plaintiff in replevin sets forth in his petition the
facts which constitute his special interest or ownership in the
property: *Lewis* v. *Burnham*, 41 Kan. 546, 548; *Ream* v. *Mc-
Elhone*, 50 Kan. 409; *Coder* v. *Stotts*, 51 Kan. 382.

"A party to an action should not be allowed to obtain benefits from contradictory and inconsistent allegations deliberately made by himself in his pleadings. Our civil code does
not contemplate any such thing. The spirit of our civil
code is that a party shall state in his pleadings the real facts
of his case, and not falsehoods or fictions; and when each
party states what he believes to be true, and the real facts of
his case, the court may know precisely where the parties differ": *Losch* v. *Pickett*, 36 Kan. 216; *Wilson* v. *Fuller*, 9 Kan.
176; *Wolfley* v. *Rising*, 12 Kan. 535; *Hoisington* v. *Armstrong*,
22 Kan. 110.

Where the petition is defective for want of material averments, and such averments are not supplied by the answer,
the petition is not cured thereby: *Wilhite* v. *Williams*, 41
Kan. 288; 13 Am. St. Rep. 281. The general denials filed
by the defendants did not supply the omissions in the petition. Upon the petition and the evidence introduced, the
defendants were entitled to verdict and judgment. When
the pleadings and the evidence show that the judgment is
correct it will be sustained, notwithstanding errors may
have occurred upon the trial: *Kilpatrick etc. Dry Goods Co.*
v. *Kahn*, 53 Kan. 274; *Commiskey* v. *McPike*, 20 Mo. App.
82–84; *Johnson* v. *Simpson*, 77 Ind. 412, 417. If a verdict
had been rendered for the plaintiff we might have permitted
the petition to be amended to conform to the facts proved,
but, when a petition is fatally defective and will not support
a judgment, this court will not examine, at the instance of
the plaintiff, alleged errors occurring upon the trial. The
attention of the district court and counsel was directly called
to the defects in the petition and to the incompetency of the
evidence, according to the record now before us. No [124]

amendments were made to the petition, and no request was made therefor. Under all the circumstances the judgment of the district court will be affirmed.

All the justices concurring.

———

TROVER—NECESSARY TITLE AND POSSESSION.—Trover and conversion cannot be maintained when the plaintiff has neither the right of property in, nor the right of possession to, the chattels alleged to have been converted: *Johnson-Brinkman Commission Co.* v. *Central Bank*, 116 Mo. 558; 38 Am. St. Rep. 615, and note. This question will be found fully discussed in the extended notes to *Bolling* v. *Kirby*, 24 Am. St. Rep. 798, and *Hostler* v. *Skull*, 1 Am. Dec. 585.

APPEAL — WHEN JUDGMENT WILL BE SUSTAINED. — A judgment rendered on insufficient grounds will, if correct, be affirmed: *Railway Co.* v. *Wilson*, 90 Tenn. 271; 25 Am. St. Rep. 693.

———

ATCHISON, TOPEKA & SANTA FE RAILROAD COMPANY *v.* HAGUE.

[54 KANSAS, 284.]

NEGLIGENCE—ACCIDENT AT RAILROAD CROSSING—EVIDENCE.—In an action against a railroad company to recover for personal injuries received in a collision with a train at a highway crossing, alleged to have been caused by the failure of the train hands to give the necessary signals of approach, evidence is admissible to show that, as the same train approached another crossing one and one-half miles from the place of the accident and only two minutes later, no signal was given of its approach.

RAILROAD COMPANIES—DUTY TO GIVE SIGNALS AT CROSSINGS.—The performance of statutory requirements as to the giving of signals is not always the full measure of the duty of a railroad company toward the public at highway crossings. Circumstances may arise when the giving of other warnings or signals may be necessary and obligatory upon the company.

RAILROAD COMPANIES—NEGLIGENCE—SPEED OF TRAIN.—Cases may arise when the speed of a train may be considered by a jury, in connection with the location and other surrounding circumstances upon a question of negligence; but, in the absence of proof that the train in question was run at an excessive or dangerous rate of speed at the time of an accident, the submission of the question to the jury as to the liability of the railroad company for running its trains at a dangerous rate of speed is improper and may be prejudicial.

RAILROAD COMPANIES—DUTY AT CROSSINGS.—A person approaching a railroad crossing has a right to assume that, in handling the cars, the railroad company acts with proper care and that all reasonable and necessary signals of approach will be given by those in charge of the train; but such person must make vigilant use of his senses, so far as he has opportunity to ascertain if there is a present danger in crossing, and, if he neither sees nor hears any indications of a moving train, he cannot be charged with negligence in assuming that there is none near enough to make the crossing dangerous.

RAILROAD COMPANIES—ACCIDENT AT CROSSING—EVIDENCE OF SIGNALS.— In an action against a railroad company to recover for personal injury received in a collision with a train at a crossing, alleged to have been caused by a failure to give the necessary signals of the approach of the train, positive evidence that such signals were given outweighs negative evidence that they were not heard by other witnesses.

RAILROAD COMPANIES — ACCIDENT AT CROSSING — CONTRIBUTORY NEGLI- GENCE.—In an action against a railroad company to recover for personal injury received in a collision at a crossing alleged to have been caused by the failure of the train hands to give the necessary signals of ap- proach, if the evidence fails to show that the negligence of the company was so gross as to amount to wantonness, or a reckless disregard of the plaintiff's safety, he is not entitled to recover if he was guilty of con- tributory negligence at the time of the accident.

RAILROAD COMPANIES — ACCIDENT AT CROSSING — CONTRIBUTORY NEGLI- GENCE.—Ordinarily it is not the duty of a traveler on a highway on approaching a railroad crossing to stop and listen before attempting to cross, and his failure to stop is not negligence *per se;* but there are cases where, by reason of obstructions or noises in the vicinity, a trav- eler is required to stop and listen before attempting to cross, and whether such reason exists in a particular case is a matter for the jury to determine.

A. A. Hurd and R. Dunlap, for the appellant.

J. W. Parker and S. T. Seaton, for the appellee.

290 JOHNSTON, J.   W. J. Hague brought this action against the Atchison, Topeka & Santa Fé Railroad Company to re- cover damages for injury to his person and property by rea- son of an accident occurring at a railroad crossing. The crossing is over a country road, about half a mile west of De Soto. The railroad lies between the river and a bluff, and the road or highway runs along the top of the bluff, parallel with the railroad, for a considerable distance, and when about half a mile away from the village it turns north, and crosses the railroad track, toward the river. From the top of the **291** bluff there is quite a steep descent, through a cut, until a point about seventy-five feet from the track is reached, when it becomes level with the track. On the day of the accident the plaintiff and another man were driving a team of mules, attached to an ordinary wagon, along this high- way, and as they entered the cut, going down the decline, the mules were pushed into a trot, or were going faster than an ordinary walk, until they reached the track. Although the wagon made considerable noise Hague did not stop to listen, but he claims to have looked and listened, and that he did not hear or see any thing that indicated the approach of a train. As he was about to cross the track an extra train passed by, which struck and killed one of the mules, broke the harness and wagon, and also injured him. In his petition Hague alleged that the accident resulted from the negligence of the railroad company in failing to sound the whistle eighty rods from the public road, or give any other signal of approach, and that the company ran this extra passenger train over the crossing at a speed of fifty miles an hour, in wanton disregard of those who might be upon the crossing. The case was tried with a jury, and a verdict was rendered in favor of Hague for three hundred dollars. The principal controversy upon the facts was as to whether the company had given the necessary signals on approaching this crossing, and also as to whether Hague had used his senses and exercised that degree of care to avoid injury which the condition of the crossing and the circumstances required.

The first assignment of error is based upon rulings of the court permitting two witnesses to testify that, as the same train approached a crossing, which was a mile and a half west of the one at which the accident occurred, no signal was given of its approach. While the writer doubts the admissibility of testimony showing negligence at other crossings than where the accident occurred, the majority of the court are of opinion than its admission was not erroneous. It is held that, as the crossings were so close together, and as the crossing west of [292] the one at which the accident occurred was passed over by the same train in charge of the same engineer and fireman within a period of two minutes, the failure to give signals at the second crossing is some testimony of negligence at the first. The same view was taken by the supreme court of Wisconsin, where testimony was admitted of a failure to give signals on approaching a crossing three miles away from the one at which the accident occurred. It was said that such evidence " had a direct bearing upon that question, and had some weight, and might properly have had, against the testimony of the defendant's witnesses that the bell was rung and whistle blown at the crossing in question, and supporting the plaintiff's witnesses that they were not. It related to the manner in which this locomotive was managed and run on this very trip, and near the place of the accident, in using such signals at street or road crossings, and would establish more than a possibility—from which a probability could be inferred—that no such signals were used at the Lyons crossing, and would create a strong and direct probability that they were not, because it was not customary to use such signals at other like crossings": *Bower* v. *Chicago etc. Ry. Co.*, 61 Wis. 457. See, also, *Savannah etc. Ry. Co.* v. *Flannagan*, 82 Ga. 579; 14 Am. St. Rep. 183.

Several errors are assigned on the giving and refusal of instructions. The court refused to charge the jury that the railroad company owed any other duty or obligation to the public on approaching a highway or country road than those prescribed by the legislature, and that, if it had performed its statutory duty of sounding the whistle at a distance of at least eighty rods from the crossing as it approached thereto, no other signal or precaution was required. We are unable to adopt the theory that the performance of the statutory requirements is the full measure of the company's duty toward the public at crossings. Circumstances may arise where the giving of other warnings or signals may be necessary and obligatory upon the company. If those in charge of a train should discover a person upon a crossing who had not heard the signal, and was unconscious of the approach of the train, or should see a loaded vehicle stuck fast upon the track, the giving of the statutory [293] signal eighty rods away would not be the entire measure of the company's duty. It would be reasonable and right to require them in such instance to give additional warnings, and in some instances to slacken the speed of the train, so as to avoid injury to persons or property that might be upon the crossing: 1 Rorer on Railways, 529, and cases cited.

The trial court instructed the jury that, even if the whistle was sounded, as required by law, yet, if they "believe that other precautions, such as ringing the bell, blowing the whistle oftener and nearer the crossing, moderating the speed of the train, etc., one or more of them was reasonably required at the time and crossing in question to secure the safety of persons who might be at the crossing, and, if you find that such precautions are not taken, the defendant would still be guilty of negligence." A just criticism is made upon this instruction, on account of the uncertainty of its language with respect to what other precautions may be required of the company. It not only means the ringing of the bell and blowing of the whistle oftener and nearer the crossing, moderating the speed of the train, but it uses the term "etc.," thus leaving the jury to infer that other precautions than those named might be required by the jury. Under this indefinite charge the jury, or some of them, may have based their finding of negligence upon a failure to place a flagman or a gate at the crossing of this country road, or upon some vague, shifting, or supposed duty or obligation.

Complaint is made of the charge of the court with refer- ence to the speed of the train. The jury were instructed that if the train which caused the injury was running at a rate of speed in excess of that which a due regard for the public safety demanded, or at a rate which was excessive or danger- ous in that locality, it would constitute negligence on the part of the company. Cases may arise where the speed of a train may be considered by a jury, in connection with the location and other surrounding circumstances, upon a ques- tion of negligence. In densely populated districts, such as towns and cities, public safety requires the speed to be mod- erated. This [294] crossing, as we have seen, however, was in the country, where there was no statutory or municipal regu- lation with respect to the speed of trains. In such cases there is no limit upon the speed at which trains may be run, except that of a careful regard for the safety of trains and passengers.

"The movement of trains must be regulated by the rail- road companies in the exercise of a business discretion, and upon consideration of the competition they have to encounter, and the necessities of modern business. We do not think a jury may fix the maximum rate of speed at which a train may be moved in the open country, or that a high rate of speed is negligence *per se*. But, while railroad companies may move their trains at such rate of speed as the character of their machinery and roadbed may make practicable, they must not forget that increased speed for the train means increased danger to those who must cross the tracks, and that increased care on their part to guard against accidents becomes a duty": *Childs* v. *Pennsylvania R. R. Co.*, 150 Pa. St. 73.

In this case we find nothing in the testimony to require the submission of the question of speed to the jury. While witnesses differed somewhat as to the speed of the train, none of them placed it at a higher rate than fifty miles an hour; and while it is stated by one witness that the rate was faster than some other trains were run, there is no proof that it was excessive or dangerous. In the absence of such testimony the submission of the question of speed to the jury was improper, and may have been prejudicial.

Complaint is made of an instruction which stated that Hague had a right to assume that in handling the cars the railroad company would act with proper care, and that all reasonable and necessary signals of approach would be given by those in charge of the train. This instruction, without qualification, might have been erroneous, but the court coupled with it the statement that, though he might make that assumption, he was required to make vigilant use of his senses, so far as there was an opportunity, to ascertain if there was a present danger in crossing; and, if he neither saw nor heard [295] any indications of a moving train, he is not to be charged with negligence in assuming that there was none near enough to make the crossing dangerous. With this qualification it cannot be held that the instruction was improper: 4 Am. & Eng. Ency. of Law, 924.

Complaint is also made that the court failed to give an instruction with reference to the relative value of positive and negative testimony. It is true, as contended, that positive evidence that the statutory signals were given in general outweighs negative evidence that they were not heard by other witnesses.

"The testimony of one who was in a position to hear, and who was giving special attention to the sounding of the whistle, that it was not sounded, while negative in form, is a positive statement of fact; and where the witnesses had equal opportunity to hear the whistle, and are equally credible, it is generally of as much value as the testimony of one who states that it was sounded": *Kansas City etc. R. R. Co. v. Lane*, 33 Kan. 702.

From the testimony in the present case an instruction with reference to the difference between positive and negative evidence might have been properly given, but the one which was submitted was somewhat objectionable in form, and we cannot say that its refusal was error.

There is good cause for complaint of a charge of the court as to gross negligence. The jury were told that, if the negligence was so gross as to amount to wantonness or a reckless disregard of the plaintiff's safety, the plaintiff would be entitled to recover, although he was guilty of ordinary negligence. There is nothing in the testimony which warranted the giving of this instruction. It is clear, and conceded, that the engineer or fireman in charge of the train did not know that any one was at the crossing, and was not aware of the peril of the plaintiff. The speed cannot be held to be excessive or dangerous, and a mere oversight or omission to give the statutory signals, if such was the case, does not furnish any evidence of such recklessness and wantonness as would relieve Hague from the exercise of ordinary diligence. Both the engineer and the fireman testify positively that the whistle **296** sounded for that crossing, and that the bell was rung, but upon this question there is a dispute. However, there is nothing in the testimony to show that they were not at their proper places in the cab, keeping a lookout upon the track for obstructions, and certainly nothing to show malice or such wanton negligence as would justify the instruction that was given.

The final contention—that the verdict is not sustained by sufficient evidence—requires but little attention. It is true that the case is close, upon the facts, both as to whether the company performed its duty by giving proper warning at the crossing and as to whether plaintiff below was guilty of contributory negligence. It is earnestly contended that it was the duty of Hague, in approaching the railroad track, not only to look and listen for the train, but to stop before he reached the railroad track. In the wagon which he was driving down the hill were barrels, and as the mules were in a sort of a trot and the wagon with the barrels made a rumbling noise, it is contended that it was his duty to stop the wagon so that he could hear an approaching train. Ordinarily it is not the duty of a traveler on approaching a railroad track to stop, but there may be cases where, by reason of obstructions or noises in the vicinity, that he would be required to stop and listen before crossing the track. Whether the surroundings of this crossing and the circumstances and conditions which existed at the time of the accident required Hague to stop was a proper matter for the consideration of the jury.

Under the testimony in the case it cannot be said, as a matter of law, that the failure to stop was negligence *per se;* and, hence, it cannot arbitrarily be said that plaintiff is not entitled to recover.

In view of the errors that have been pointed out the judgment must be reversed and the cause remanded for another
trial.

All the justices concurring.

RAILROADS—DUTY TO GIVE SIGNALS AT CROSSINGS.—A train should give
timely notice of its approach to a public highway by the usual signals, and
the company will be liable in damages to one injured by a failure to give
such signals unless it can be affirmatively shown that ordinary care was not
taken by the person injured to avoid accident: *Philadelphia etc. R. R. Co.
v. Hagan*, 47 Pa. St. 244; 86 Am. Dec. 541, and note; *Brown* v. *Texas etc.
Ry. Co.*, 42 La. Ann. 350; 21 Am. St. Rep. 374, and note; *Hinkle* v. *Richmond etc. R. R. Co.*, 109 N. C. 472; 26 Am. St. Rep. 581, and note. See
further on this subject the extended notes to *Welsch* v. *Hannibal etc. R. R.
Co.*, 37 Am. Rep. 443, and *Tetherow* v. *St. Joseph etc. Ry. Co.*, 14 Am. St. Rep.
625.

RAILROADS—DUTY OF PERSONS ABOUT TO CROSS TO LOOK AND LISTEN.—
A person about to cross a railroad is bound to look and listen, and a failure
to do so is such negligence as will bar his recovery for an injury which might
have been avoided had he done so: *Mynning* v. *Detroit etc. R. R. Co.*, 64 Mich.
93; 8 Am. St. Rep. 804, and note; *Hinkle* v. *Richmond etc. R. R. Co.*, 109
N. C. 472; 26 Am. St. Rep. 581, and note; *Brown* v. *Texas etc. Ry. Co.*, 42
La. Ann. 350; 21 Am. St. Rep. 374, and note. See also the extended notes
to *Tolman* v. *Syracuse etc. R. R. Co.*, 50 Am. Rep. 653, and *Ernst* v. *Hudson River R. R. Co.*, 90 Am. Dec. 780.

RAILROADS—NEGLIGENCE—SPEED OF TRAINS.—The general rule is that
negligence cannot be inferred from the rate of speed alone at which railway
trains are run: *Dyson* v. *New York etc. R. R. Co.*, 57 Conn. 9; 14 Am. St.
Rep. 82; *McDonald* v. *International etc. Ry. Co.*, 86 Tex. 1; 40 Am. St. Rep.
803, and note. See also the notes to *Peyton* v. *Texas etc. Ry. Co* , 17 Am.
St. Rep. 435, and *McMarshall* v. *Chicago etc. Ry. Co.*, 20 Am. St. Rep. 453.

WINSLOW *v.* BROMICH.

[54 KANSAS, 300.]

FIXTURES.—SUGAR-WAGONS used in a sugar-mill for the purpose of holding
syrup and conveying it from place to place by being pushed by hand on
the floor of the mill, if similar to wagons used in other sugar-mills, and
necessary to their operation, and not run upon rails, nor actually nor
constructively annexed to the realty, or to any thing appurtenant
thereto, but merely furnished for necessary use in the mill, and not to
enhance the value of the realty, are personal property and not fixtures.

FIXTURES—TESTS.—One of the tests of whether personal property retains
its character or becomes a fixture is the use to which it is put. If it is
placed on the realty, to improve it and make it more valuable, it is generally deemed a fixture. If it is placed there for a use that does not
enhance the value of the realty it generally retains its character of
personal property.

H. G. Ney and L. S. Webb, for the appellant.

S. B. Isenhart, for the appellees.

305 HORTON, C. J. This was a controversy in the court below over sugar-wagons. They were furnished by Joseph Bromich to the American Sugar Company, manufacturing sugar at Minneola, in this state. They were constructed of sheet and cast iron, being four feet long, three feet wide, and twenty-six inches deep, with three adjustable wheels on each wagon. They were used in the mill for the purpose of holding the syrup and conveying it from place to place on the floor of the mill until it was converted into sugar. The wheels of the sugar-wagons were low, about eight inches in diameter, and the wagons, when in use, were pushed by hand from place to place within the mill. These wagons were of the same character as other similar wagons used in other sugar-mills, and such mills cannot be successfully operated without such wagons or other vessels of like character.

The question for our determination is whether the sugar-wagons were personal property or fixtures. If personal property, then C. W. Winslow is entitled to judgment for costs, but if fixtures, the judgment in favor of Joseph Bromich and the Densmore Brothers must be affirmed. The supreme court of Ohio, in *Teaff* v. *Hewitt*, 1 Ohio St. 529, 59 Am. Dec. 634, says: "The following requisites will be found the safest criterion of a fixture: 1. Actual annexation to the realty, or something appurtenant thereto; 2. Appropriation to the use or purpose of that part of the realty which it is connected; 3. The intention of the party making the annexation to make the article a permanent accession to the freehold; this intention being inferred from the nature of the articles affixed, the relation and situation of the party making the annexation, the structure and mode of annexation, and the purpose or use for which the annexation has been made." See, also, *Eaves* v. *Estes*, 10 Kan. 314; 15 Am. Rep. 345.

In *Atchison etc. R. R. Co.* v. *Morgan*, 42 Kan. 23; 16 Am. St. Rep. 471, it was observed: "One of the tests of whether personal property retains its character or becomes a fixture is the uses to which it is put. If it is placed on the realty to improve it and make it more **306** valuable it is some evidence that it is a fixture; but, if it is placed there for a use that does not enhance the value of the realty, this is some evidence that it is personal property. . . . . The simple fact of annexation to the realty is not the sole and controlling test of whether a certain article is a fixture or not, is very well illustrated by the fact that trees growing in a nursery and kept there for sale are personal property, while trees no larger, if transplanted to an orchard, become real estate. On the other hand, there are very many things, although not attached to the realty, which become real property by their use—keys to a house, blinds and shutters to the windows, fences and fence rails, etc."

The sugar-wagons, as we understand the agreed facts, were placed in the mill for use, not to enhance the value. They are movable, and if taken out will not disturb the mill or in any way injure the building. They do not run upon wooden or iron rails attached to the building, nor are they connected in their operation by bands or in any other way with the permanent machinery. They are not like the wheels or stones to a mill, or the keys to a house, or the blinds and shutters to windows. Being adapted to convey syrup from place to place in the mill, they must be considered in the same class as buckets, kettles, barrels, and similar vessels used for like purposes. As the sugar-wagons were not actually or constructively annexed to the realty, or something appurtenant thereto, but merely furnished for necessary use in the mill, and not intended to enhance the value of the realty, we must hold them to be personal property, and not fixtures: *Walker* v. *Sherman*, 20 Wend. 636; *Haeussler* v. *Missouri Glass Co.*, 52 Mo. 452; *Graves* v. *Pierce*, 53 Mo. 423; *Ex parte Astbury*, L. R. 4 Ch. App. 630; Ewell's Fixtures (1876), 22, 23; 1 Jones on Mortgages, secs. 444–449.

The judgment of the district court will be reversed, and the cause remanded with direction to the court below to render judgment for C. W. Winslow.

All the justices concurring.

FIXTURES—TEST OF.—The chief test by which to determine whether an article is a fixture is to inquire whether the party annexing it intended it to be a permanent accession to the freehold. This intention is to be inferred from the nature of the article affixed, the relation and situation of the parties making the annexation, and the policy of the law in relation thereto, the structure and mode of annexation, and the purpose for which it was made: *Fifield* v. *Farmers' Nat. Bank*, 148 Ill. 163; 39 Am. St. Rep. 166, and note, with the cases collected.

WALLACE *v.* TRAVELERS' INSURANCE COMPANY.

[54 KANSAS, 442.]

HOMESTEADS—ALIENATION OF ENCUMBRANCE OF BY HUSBAND UNDER POWER OF ATTORNEY.—A power of attorney given by a wife to her husband to "sign deeds and mortgages, with full power and authority to do and perform all and any acts whatsoever requisite and necessary to be done in and about the premises, as fully and to all intents and purposes as I might or could do if present, with full power of substitution and ratification, hereby ratifying and confirming all that my said attorney or his substitutes shall lawfully do, or cause to be done, by virtue hereof," but not describing any real estate, nor referring in any way to their homestead, is too general and indefinite to authorize the husband to execute a mortgage on the homestead signed by him for himself and as attorney in fact for his wife. A mortgage so executed is void.

Wells & Wells, for the appellant.

Webb & Caldwell, for the appellees.

444 JOHNSTON, J. This was an action to recover upon promissory notes, and to foreclose two mortgages executed by James D. Wallace and Georgia P. Wallace, by her attorney in fact, James D. Wallace, one of which mortgages was owned **445** by the Travelers' Insurance Company, and the other by Angell Matthewson & Co. The insurance company recovered a judgment against the Wallaces for eighteen hundred and fifty-two dollars, and Angell Matthewson & Co. recovered a judgment for one hundred and seventy dollars. The mortgages were foreclosed, and it was decreed that the property should be sold, and the proceeds applied, 1. To the payment of the costs and to the taxes due against the property; 2. To the payment of the judgment of the insurance company; and 3. To the payment of the judgment of Angell Matthewson & Co. A review of the rulings made upon the trial is asked, and the principal question is as to the validity of the mortgages that were foreclosed. They were executed in February, 1887, and were signed by James D. Wallace, and by him as attorney in fact for his wife. The power of attorney under which Wallace signed the name of his wife was executed on July 18, 1884, at Bushnell, Illinois, in which Georgia P. Wallace appointed her husband as her lawful attorney, " to sign deeds and mortgages, notes, checks, releases, etc., to loan moneys, to sue and be sued, to collect rents, make contracts, giving and granting unto my said attorney full power and authority to do and perform all and any acts and things whatsoever requisite and necessary to

be done in and about the premises, as fully and to all intents
and purposes as I might or could do if present, with full
power of substitution and ratification, hereby ratifying and
confirming all that my said attorney or his substitutes shall
lawfully do or cause to be done by virtue hereof."

The power of attorney was duly acknowledged, and, having
been transmitted to Kansas, was duly recorded in Crawford
county, on the ninth day of August, 1884. The testimony
tends to show that the Wallaces owned the property in dispute, and had occupied it as a homestead for several months
before the power of attorney was executed and recorded;
and it is further shown that Mrs. Wallace and her child
continued to live there until after this action was begun.
The contention now is, that a conveyance of a homestead by
virtue of a power of attorney is a nullity, and further, that if
the homestead may be alienated under a power of attorney,
the [446] authority conferred in this instance is too general
and indefinite to authorize the execution of a mortgage upon
real estate.

If a mortgage upon a homestead may be executed by
either husband or wife through a power of attorney from the
other, and if the power given by the wife to the husband in
this case is sufficient in form and substance, the mortgages
in question must be held to be good. It is conceded that the
wife executed the power of attorney, and it is not questioned
that it remained unrevoked and in full force when the mortgages were executed. It is strongly urged, however, that the
preservation of the homestead rights requires that there shall
be the concurrent personal consent of each spouse when the
conveyance or mortgage is executed. Under our constitution
joint consent is indispensable, and it is said that, as it is the
policy of the law to preserve to every family a homestead, the
restrictions which have been made upon the alienation of the
same should be strictly complied with. It is therefore said
that good policy requires that, before the title of the homestead shall be divested, or any interest transferred or affected,
there shall be consultation between husband and wife, and
the personal consent of each obtained at the time the transfer
or contract is made. The claim is that neither can act by
proxy, and that, when a power of attorney is executed by one,
only the consent of such a one is then expressed, and that,
when the conveyance is subsequently made by the other
spouse, he or she only consents, and therefore there is a lack

of that contemporaneous joint consent which the constitution requires: *Gagliardo* v. *Dumont*, 54 Cal. 496. Then again, it is urged that the power of attorney in this instance fails to describe any real estate, or to show that the homestead was within the contemplation of the wife when the power of attorney was executed. It is said that, while she gave her husband authority to sign mortgages, it does not appear that she intended to encumber her own property, or to do more than authorize the sale or mortgage of the property the title of which was in her husband. The majority of the court, therefore, hold that the power of attorney in the present case is insufficient to express [447] that joint consent which the constitution and statutes of this state require in the alienation or encumbrance of a homestead.

The writer is unable to agree with this conclusion. Neither the husband nor the wife, acting alone, can execute a conveyance or mortgage of the homestead which is of any validity, and no construction should be placed upon the constitutional restraints on alienation which will to any extent dwarf the homestead rights. It is clear that to encumber the homestead there must be a joint consent of both when the encumbrance is executed. How must that consent be given? Can the wife authorize another to express her consent, and, if so, may she confer that authority upon her husband? In some states not only is consent required, but it is necessary that both, acting contemporaneously, shall sign the same joint instrument. In others, in addition to her signature, she must, in a private examination, express to an officer taking the acknowledgment that she knowingly and voluntarily signs the instrument. In still others, in order to convey or encumber the homestead, there must be in the instrument itself a renunciation of the homestead right, or an express stipulation that the homestead is intended to be conveyed or affected by the instrument. The constitution of our state does not expressly provide how the consent shall be given, nor have we any statutory provision which requires that the husband and wife shall contemporaneously sign the same joint instrument. In *Ott* v. *Sprague*, 27 Kan. 624, it was recognized that a husband and wife might alienate the homestead by two separate instruments, when it was intended by both that such instruments should operate together as a single instrument; and, being so connected, they might together be considered as the joint consent of both.

It has been decided that "neither the statutes nor the constitution requires that the alienation of a homestead with the joint consent of the husband and wife must be in writing": *Perrine* v. *Mayberry*, 37 Kan. 262. In *Pilcher* v. *Atchison etc. R. R. Co.*, 38 Kan. 516, 5 Am. St. Rep. 770, it was held that it was not essential [448] that the joint consent should be expressed in writing, and it was said that "consent is best evidenced by a writing to that effect; but the constitution does not in express terms require that it shall be so done, and hence it can be established by such facts and circumstances as the necessity of particular cases requires": See, also, *Dudley* v. *Shaw*, 44 Kan. 683. Of course real property must be conveyed in the manner prescribed by statute, and in respect to conveying real property or any interest which she may have therein, the wife stands upon an equal footing with the husband, and is governed by the same rule. The statute provides how the consent of parties may be expressed in order to make an effective conveyance of real estate, and there is an express provision that any person having an interest may do so by an attorney in fact: Gen. Stats. of 1889, par. 1112. In *Munger* v. *Baldridge*, 41 Kan. 236, 13 Am. St. Rep. 273, it was held that a married woman might not only convey her inchoate interest in her husband's real estate through a power of attorney, but that she was free to select whomsoever she pleased as her agent or attorney for that purpose, and that no reason existed why her husband might not act in that capacity. In that case the statutory relations between husband and wife were considered, and it was held that nothing in the law or its policy forbids that the husband should act as the agent or attorney of the wife in conveying real estate. It was said: "The statutes of Kansas recognize no conflict of interest between them, nor any necessity to protect the wife against the act of the husband. They do not contemplate that she may be led to convey her interest through fear, compulsion, or the undue influence of her husband; and hence we have no enactment, as some states do, that in making a conveyance she must undergo a private examination by an officer to learn whether she is intimidated by her husband or is executing the conveyance against her will. On the contrary, the law proceeds upon the theory of confidence, good faith, and honest dealing between husband and wife; and while there may be cases where the husband may take advantage of this confidence, yet it is almost as liable to occur through his obtaining [449] her signature to the deed of conveyance as it would be in procuring from her a power of attorney authorizing him to convey the same property. We conclude that the wife can appoint her husband as her agent and attorney in fact to convey the inchoate interest which she holds in his real estate, and that an instrument duly executed by himself and by him for her, under such authority, is effectual to transfer such interest."

As our law authorizes the husband to act for the wife in the conveyance of real estate, and no exception is made with reference to the conveyance of the homestead, no reason is seen why he may not consent for her, and sign her name to a mortgage or conveyance of the homestead. The authorities generally are to the effect that, where the constitution fails to provide the method of giving consent, compliance with the general provisions of the legislature as to the means of conveying real estate is sufficient. The power of attorney, when properly executed and acknowledged, is a continuing consent which remains in the attorney until the power is withdrawn or revoked. In signing the instrument the husband acted for himself, and also, under the authority conferred, acted for his wife. At the time the conveyance was executed she was present in him, consenting to the conveyance, and, as he signed the instrument at the same time, it would appear that there was that joint consent which the constitution requires.

It is said that considerable time elapsed from the execution of the power of attorney before the mortgage was made, but it was duly acknowledged and recorded, and, standing on the public record as it did, the wife cannot shut her eyes to its existence, and the public had a right to rely on its validity: *Patton* v. *King*, 26 Tex. 685; 84 Am. Dec. 596; *Warren* v. *Jones*, 69 Tex. 462; *Jones* v. *Robbins*, 74 Tex. 615.

In regard to the last objection it may be said, that while the power conferred is general, it cannot be held invalid. The power granted is to sign any deeds, mortgages, and releases which she might or could do if present, and, to that end, the husband was given full power and authority to do any [450] and all acts and things whatsoever necessary to accomplish that purpose. This power of attorney was recorded in the office of the register of deeds of the county in which the lands mortgaged were situate, and, within the rule of *Munger* v. *Baldridge*, 41 Kan. 236, 13 Am. St. Rep. 273, is sufficient authority for the conveyance or encumbrance of any land

within that county.   It is therefore the opinion of the writer
that the judgment of the district court was right.   But, as a
majority of the court hold the power of attorney to be invalid
for the purposes intended, there must be a reversal of the
judgment of the district court, and a new trial of the cause.

HORTON, C. J.   The testimony in this case, and that offered
upon the trial by the defendant below, which was rejected,
emphasizes the gross injustice of holding that the power of
attorney executed by the wife, and preserved in the record
before us, is sufficient to express the joint consent of husband
and wife which the constitution and the statutes of the state
require in the alienation or encumbrance of a homestead
occupied as a residence by the family.

In 1884 the father of Mrs. Georgia P. Wallace, the wife of
James D. Wallace, gave and transferred to her the real estate
described in the mortgages.   Soon after, Mrs. Wallace, with
her minor child and husband, occupied the property as her
actual residence, and has ever since continued to occupy the
same.   During the latter part of the year 1884 she made a
visit to the state of Illinois.   While she was there visiting,
and before her return, her husband, J. D. Wallace, wrote her
several letters, in which he informed her, among other family
matters, that he had bought some town lots out at a little
town called Caldwell, in this state, and desired to sell them;
that he could not sell them unless he had authority from her
so to do, or her signature to a deed therefor; that he did not
know what person he would be able to make a sale of them
to, and could not safely have deeds of conveyance executed.
He sent her the power of attorney in the record, without her
signature, and assured her that he did not want to interfere
with any of [451] her property or money whatever, and stated
that he did not intend to in any manner alienate her homestead.   Mrs. Wallace signed and acknowledged the power of
attorney on the 18th of July, 1884, and returned it to her
husband.   He placed it on record in Crawford county, in this
state, where the land is situated, on August 9, 1884.   On the
3d of February, 1887—three years afterward—her husband,
without the knowledge or consent of his wife, made an application to the Travelers' Insurance Company, through its
agents, Angell Matthewson & Co., for a loan on the homestead
in the sum of thirteen hundred and fifty dollars, at a time
when it was actually occupied by the family.   The applica-

tion was granted, and the mortgages executed by James D. Wallace in person, and also by him for his wife, as her attorney in fact. Wallace then deserted his wife, and has not lived with her since, and she does not know of his whereabouts. The mortgages described the property as "the homestead of the grantors."

The power of attorney, executed by the wife to the husband, does not describe any real estate nor refer in any way to the homestead of the family. This court has decided that two separate and independent conveyances by the husband and wife would not be sufficient to alienate the homestead: *Ott* v. *Sprague*, 27 Kan. 620. This court has also said: " The wife cannot, even after the execution of a mortgage of the homestead hy·the husband, ratify the mortgage of the homestead by the husband so as to breathe life into its existence. Such a mortgage will be void." It must be conceded that, if the husband had encumbered the homestead under the power of attorney by a deed from his wife alone, the mortgage would be void. Not so, if the real estate was not actually occupied by the family as a residence. The alienation or encumbrance of a homestead must be with the "joint consent of husband and wife"; therefore, the conveyance or alienation of a homestead must be the consenting acts of the husband and wife. If the wife may delegate to her husband the power to act for her in the conveyance or alienation of the homestead, the power of attorney must expressly **452** or by necessary implication confer the power to consent with him, or to act with his consent, in such conveyance or alienation.

The cases of *Munger* v. *Baldridge*, 41 Kan. 236, 13 Am. St. Rep. 273, and *Wilkinson* v. *Elliott*, 43 Kan. 590, 19 Am. St. Rep. 158, are not decisive of this case upon the facts disclosed. In the Munger case there was no transfer or conveyance of any homestead. The power of attorney in that case was definite in giving power to transfer the wife's interest in any lands and tenements the title to which was in the husband, and in which Mrs. Munger had any interest as his wife. In the Wilkinson case the deed did not convey a homestead, because the general finding of the trial court was interpreted by this court as meaning that the homestead had been voluntarily abandoned. Under all the circumstances, I do not think that the power of attorney executed by the wife alone, in and of itself, was sufficient to ·

give authority to the husband, or any one else, to convey the homestead of the family.

ALLEN, J.   The constitutional provision requiring the joint consent of husband and wife to any alienation of the homestead must be given effect in accordance with its letter and spirit.   The legislature could not, under the guise of a mere regulation of the mode in which that consent might be expressed, do away with the substance of the requirement. Joint consent clearly implies the concurrent action and mental accord of husband and wife.   The provision was not incorporated in the fundamental law for the benefit of either husband or wife alone, or both of them together, but for the children as well—for the whole family as a social unit.   The vast importance of preserving to each family a dwelling place to which every member might look for shelter, secured against improvident alienation and encumbrance, was recognized by the framers of the constitution.   Nothing tends more surely to preserve social order, to encourage virtue, industry, and independence, than a home owned by the occupants.

In order to sustain the judgment in this case it must be 453 held, in effect, that the wife may transfer to her husband the power to assent for her, as well as himself, to the alienation of the homestead, to determine all questions as to time, terms, and purpose of the sale, and to make this assent without the benefit of consultation with her.   The facts that the power of attorney was executed, that it was subject to revocation at any time, and that it remained in full force, without any attempt at revocation, up to the date of the mortgage, may seem to some minds to present a logical chain carrying the action of the wife when executing the power of attorney on through a period of years, and finally giving it effect through the action of her husband as an assent to the encumbrance.   Yet it is clear in this case that the wife had no knowledge of the proposed mortgage, and never, in fact, gave to it any intelligent assent.   The assent required by the constitution is not a blind action, performed without knowledge, or a fair opportunity to know the consequences, but must be an intelligent concurrence on the part of the wife in the conveyance.   That a homestead cannot be conveyed or encumbered by the husband and wife acting separately, at different times and places, through separate instru-

ments, has been settled by this court: *Ott* v. *Sprague*, 27
Kan. 620; *Howell* v. *McCrie*, 36 Kan. 636; 59 Am. Rep. 584.
The power of attorney executed by the wife in this case is
just as separate and distinct from the mortgage afterward
executed by her husband as were the separate instruments
executed by husband and wife in the cases above cited.
The only way that joint or concurrent action can be deduced
from them is by making the wife constructively present at
the execution of the mortgage, and constructively concurring and assenting to that which she doubtless would have
refused to assent to had she known of the purposes of her
husband in executing it. The power of attorney contains
no reference whatever to the homestead. It is as general as
such an instrument could be made. We are not required,
in this case, to go to the length of holding that the joint
consent of husband and wife must always, of necessity, be
expressed at the same time and place, and through the
same [434] instrument. As was said by Mr. Justice Valentine in the opinion in *Ott* v. *Sprague*, 27 Kan. 620: " It might
be that a husband and wife, by two separate instruments,
could alienate the homestead, when it was intended by both
that such instruments should operate together as a single
instrument; for in such a case it might, perhaps, be said
that the separate consent of each had such a connection with
each other that they might together be considered as the joint
consent of both."

It is not necessary, either, that we should decide in this
case that the husband could not be authorized by the wife,
in any manner, to attach her signature to a deed. But it is
necessary in all cases that the husband and wife assent
jointly; that both shall know of the proposed alienation;
that both shall assent to it; that each shall assent with the
knowledge and concurrence of the . other. The minds of
husband and wife must meet and concur in the alienation
or encumbrance, just as minds of contracting parties must
meet and concur in entering into any valid contract; and
one mind cannot be made, through agency, or by any legal
abdication of its rights, to vest in the other the power to act
singly in fact with the same effect as the concurrent action
of both. One mind clearly cannot act in a dual capacity.
The very purpose of the constitutional provision is to require
that the proposed alienation shall be made known to the wife
as well as to the husband; that it shall be considered from

her standpoint; that her views, feelings, and wishes shall be brought to bear on the case; and that, unless she yields her assent, no alienation shall take place.

POWERS OF ATTORNEY—CONSTRUCTION OF.—Powers of attorney are to be strictly construed, and are limited to the particular acts authorized: *Frost* v. *Erath Cattle Co.*, 81 Tex. 505; 26 Am. St. Rep. 831, and note; *Gilbert* v. *How*, 45 Minn. 121; 22 Am. St. Rep. 724, and extended note.

HOMESTEAD.—CONVEYANCE OF BY HUSBAND ALONE, WHEN INVALID: See *Pipkin* v. *Williams*, 57 Ark. 242; 38 Am. St. Rep. 241, and note.

WEA GAS COAL AND OIL COMPANY *v.* FRANKLIN LAND COMPANY.

[51 KANSAS, 533.]

HOMESTEADS—LEASE OF BY HUSBAND.—A lease for years of a homestead is an alienation of an interest therein, to which the joint consent of husband and wife is essential. Such a lease, if signed by the husband alone, though with the knowledge and consent of the wife, and though she was ready and willing to have signed it, if she had been requested so to do, is null and void.

HOMESTEADS—CONVEYANCE OF.—A deed jointly executed by husband and wife conveying their homestead, though made subsequently to a lease of the homestead, signed by the husband alone, conveys a perfect title to the purchaser.

H. Stevens, for the appellant.

H. C. Mecham, for the appellee.

⁵³⁵ JOHNSTON, J. There is little in the additional findings of fact to change the view that was taken when the case was here before: *Franklin Land Co.* v. *Wea Gas etc. Co.*, 43 Kan. 518. It appears that there was but one lease executed by Dunn, and that that one and the lease referred to in the Wadsworth contract are identical. And it further appears that the officers of the land company had knowledge of the execution and delivery of a paper purporting to be the lease executed by Dunn to the oil company. It is shown beyond question, however, that no lease was in fact executed, and nothing subsequently done gave any life or validity to the lease signed by Robert Dunn. The paper was not signed by Mrs. Dunn, and there was not that joint consent necessary to give validity to an alienation of the homestead. It was held when the case was here before that a lease of a homestead, such as Dunn attempted to give, is of no validity unless given with

the joint consent of husband and wife. It is true that the wife was ready to sign the lease, and would have signed it if her husband had requested her to do so, but she was not requested to sign it, and did not join in its execution. It is manifest that at that time none of the parties thought that her signature or consent was essential to the validity of the lease, and it is clear that no legal consent was sought or obtained from her. As the lease was absolutely void, Dunn and wife were at liberty to convey a complete title to a purchaser. In the conveyance which they executed no reservation or exception was made. While the land company had learned of this lease when it bought, it knew that it was one without validity as to both Mr. and Mrs. Dunn, and that no rights could be built upon it. It had a right to assume that the oil company could not maintain possession under the lease against the Dunns or any person who might hold under them. The lease being absolutely void, the Dunns held a complete title, and the effect of their conveyance was the transfer of the whole interest [536] which was vested in them. It is true that they are not here asking to avoid the lease, but, where "the owner of a homestead has sold the same, the purchaser has a right, for the purpose of establishing his own title, to show that at the date of his purchase the land was a homestead, and therefore not subject to a judgment lien or forced sale. He does this, not for the benefit of his grantor, but for the protection of his own right and title": *Elwell* v. *Hitchcock*, 41 Kan. 130.

There is a finding that there was a mutual mistake in not excepting the lease from the terms of general warranty in the deed executed by Dunn and wife. But this is unimportant in this action. The deed has never been reformed, nor have any of the parties to the same set up the mistake or asked for its correction. None of the parties to that instrument were parties in this action, and hence the finding is without force. Whether the exception of the lease from the terms of general warranty would have validated the lease is a doubtful question, which we need not decide. The reference to the lease in the Wadsworth contract does not help the oil company, and the doctrine of estoppel has no application. It was not a party to that contract, did not, and had no right to rely upon it, and, as was shown in the former opinion, was not in any way affected adversely by the recital contained in that contract. As the lease was an absolute nullity it neither passed any estate or interest to the oil company, nor did it have any operation against the Dunns or their grantees by estoppel or otherwise. We think the district court reached a correct conclusion upon the facts in the case, and therefore its judgment will be affirmed.

All the justices concurring.

HOMESTEADS—CONVEYANCE OF WITHOUT JOINDER OF WIFE.—A conveyance of an interest in a homestead, executed by the husband alone, is invalid for any purpose: *McKenzie* v. *Hows*, 70 Miss. 388; 35 Am. St. Rep. 654, and note. To the same effect, see *Pipkin* v. *Williams*, 57 Ark. 242; 38 Am. St. Rep. 241, and note. See, further, the extended notes to *Alt* v. *Banholzer*, 12 Am. St. Rep. 684, and *Poole* v. *Gerrard*, 65 Am. Dec. 484.

NATIONAL BANK OF ST. JOSEPH *v.* DAKIN.
[54 KANSAS, 656.]

NEGOTIABLE INSTRUMENTS—UNAUTHORIZED USE—RIGHT OF HOLDER OF AS COLLATERAL.—A payee of a negotiable note who indorses it in blank before maturity, and intrusts it to others upon condition that the proceeds be applied to a particular use, is liable to an innocent holder who takes it in the due course of business as collateral security or in payment of a debt, and such holder takes it free from all equities and defenses between the antecedent parties, although it may have been wrongfully used or diverted from the purpose for which it was intended by the parties to whom it was intrusted.

NEGOTIABLE INSTRUMENTS—COLLATERAL SECURITY.—A pre-existing debt is a sufficient consideration for the transfer of collaterals as security for its payment.

W. C. Don Carlos, for the appellant.

J. V. Coon, for the appellees.

656 JOHNSTON, J. D. D. Bemis, who was the owner of a quarter section of land in Phillips county, executed a mortgage thereon to Judith Dakin to secure the payment of a debt. Afterward he sold one-half of the tract to W. J. Gould, and as a part of the purchase price took Gould's note for seven hundred dollars, payable in five years, with annual interest at the rate of eight per cent per annum, and took a mortgage on the same land to secure the payment of the note. It was stipulated and agreed in writing by the parties that the seven hundred dollars debt to be paid by Gould should be paid to Judith Dakin, to extinguish the mortgage debt due to her, and to satisfy and discharge a part of the original mortgage which Bemis executed to her. There was a further stipulation that the note and mortgage given by Gould should be deposited with the banking firm of Bodwell & Hamilton, and that payments made to them thereon should be immediately applied to the satisfaction of the Dakin mortgage debt. Afterward the firm of Bodwell & Hamilton had other dealings with Bemis, and took several notes from him, among which was one for the sum of two thousand and sixty-two dollars, which was secured by another mortgage upon the land previously mortgaged to Judith Dakin. The last-mentioned note was sold and transferred to the First National Bank of Frankfort, and several other of the notes mentioned were used by Bodwell & Hamilton as collateral security to obtain a loan from the National Bank of St. Joseph, Missouri. Default having been made in the payment of the Dakin mortgage, a proceeding in foreclosure was begun, in which all of those interested in the land were made parties. All of the various claims and liens were adjusted without difficulty, except the note for seven hundred dollars due from Gould to Bemis, which, with the mortgage to secure the same was deposited with Bodwell & Hamilton under the contract heretofore mentioned.

From the record, it appears that this seven hundred dollar note, which was payable to the order of Bemis, was indorsed in blank and left [660] with Bodwell & Hamilton, and that, instead of retaining it and collecting and using the proceeds to discharge the Dakin mortgage debt, in accordance with the agreement, they wrongfully indorsed and transferred the same to the National Bank of St. Joseph, Missouri, as collateral security for a loan obtained from that bank, and, subsequently, they made an absolute sale and transfer of the same in payment of a portion of the debt due from them to the National Bank of St. Joseph. Afterward, Bodwell & Hamilton became insolvent, and when the foreclosure proceeding was begun the National Bank of St. Joseph was allowed to interplead and set up the Gould note for seven hundred dollars, and under the mortgage to secure the same they claimed a second lien upon the premises. Some of the other claimants contested the validity of the transfer of the seven hundred dollar note to the National Bank of St. Joseph, alleging that Bemis did not indorse or transfer the note, but merely left the same with Bodwell & Hamilton in trust, the proceeds of which were to be collected by them and used to extinguish the Dakin debt; that they wrongfully diverted the seven hundred dollar note so left with them to the National Bank of St. Joseph, which bank obtained no title or ownership therein. Bemis, the payee of the note, also answered, setting up the fraud of Bodwell & Hamilton, and averring that the note was never indorsed or transferred to the bank as its absolute property, but was only delivered as collateral for the debt of Bodwell & Hamilton, and that the debt has since been paid from other collaterals held by the bank. He further averred that the bank is not a *bona fide* owner or holder for value, but obtained the same unlawfully and in fraud of the rights of Bemis and the other claim-ants.

The main issue on this branch of the case was the validity of the transfer of the Gould note, or whether the bank was a *bona fide* owner and holder of the same. On this issue the court found against the bank that Bemis was the owner, and that there was due to him thereon nine hundred and seventy-six dollars and eighty-eight cents, and decreed that the money when collected should be paid in discharge of the Dakin debt and lien. It is undisputed that the note was [661] negotiable in form; that it was transferred to the bank before due in the regular course of business; that it was received by the bank in good faith, as collateral security for a loan of money by the bank to Bodwell & Hamilton; and that it was finally transferred absolutely in partial payment of the debt for which it was originally transferred as security. It was accepted as security for an actual debt, and there is nothing to show that the bank had any notice of the true ownership of the note, or that Bodwell & Hamilton had put it in circulation in viola-tion of any trust or of any condition under which they held it. Under such circumstances the bank must be regarded as a *bona fide* holder, unaffected by the wrongful transfer of Bodwell & Hamilton, or of any equities existing as between the antecedent parties. Although there was a denial of the allegation of indorsement and transfer by Bemis, the proof is clear that he did indorse it in blank, and in his own testimony he declines to say that he did not so indorse it. Having indorsed a negotiable promissory note in blank and intrusted it to others, he cannot complain if he is held liable to an in-nocent holder for value, although it may have been wrong-fully used or diverted from the purpose for which it was intended. Under the unrestricted indorsement any one without notice of the title had a right to assume that Bodwell & Hamilton were the owners of the same.

"The mere possession of a negotiable instrument payable to order and properly indorsed is *prima facie* evidence that the holder is the owner thereof; that he acquired the same in good faith, for full value, in the usual course of business, before maturity, without notice of any circumstance that would impeach its validity, and that he is entitled to recover upon it its full face value as against any of the antecedent parties": *Mann* v. *Second Nat. Bank*, 34 Kan. 747.

It is true that Bodwell & Hamilton committed a flagrant fraud upon Bemis and the other parties in the transfer of the note, but as Bemis intrusted the paper to others in such form as to enable them to hold themselves out as the absolute owners [662] of the note, he should suffer rather than the bank, which had no notice or knowledge of the wrong. In such cases the rule is, that of two innocent persons, the one who placed it in the power of others to commit the wrong must suffer for his misplaced confidence rather than the one who is not in fault. As far as the testimony goes, nothing on the face of the paper or in the circumstances of the transfer would give rise to any suspicions in regard to the title of Bodwell & Hamilton. They had frequently borrowed money from the bank, and had transferred to it as collateral security numerous promissory notes of their customers, and among them were several others upon which Bemis was liable. The bank having made a loan upon the pledge and transfer of the collateral security, is entitled to the position of a *bona fide* holder for value and to protection against equities, offsets, and other defenses which might have been available between antecedent parties. It is even held that a pre-existing debt affords sufficient consideration for the transfer of collaterals as security for its payment: *Best* v. *Crall*, 23 Kan. 482; 33 Am. Rep. 185; *Swift* v. *Tyson*, 16 Pet. 1; *Goodman* v. *Simonds*, 20 How. 343; *Oates* v. *National Bank*, 100 U. S. 239; *Railroad Co.* v. *National Bank*, 102 U. S. 14; *Spencer* v. *Sloan*, 108 Ind. 183; 58 Am. Rep. 35; *Maitland* v. *Citizens' Nat. Bank*, 40 Md. 540; 17 Am. Rep. 620; Jones on Pledges, sec. 107; Story on Promissory Notes, sec. 195; Daniell on Negotiable Instruments, sec. 824, et seq. If there was no indorsement of the note by Bemis, or if the bank knew of the conditions under which Bodwell & Hamilton held the note, the bank would not be entitled to protection as a holder for value. The testimony

in the record fails to show that the debt which was secured
by the transfer of the note has been paid. Indeed, it would
appear that, if the note should be collected by the bank and
the proceeds applied on what was due to it from Bodwell &
Hamilton, a considerable part of the debt would still remain
unsatisfied. We conclude that the testimony is insufficient
to sustain the judgment that was rendered, and for that reason there must be a reversal and a new trial.

All the justices concurring.

NEGOTIABLE INSTRUMENTS—RIGHTS OF BONA FIDE HOLDERS OF AS SE-
CURITY.—A *bona fide* holder of commercial paper, taken as collateral security
for a debt created either before or at the time of the transfer, is entitled to
enforce payment thereof without regard to equities existing between prior
parties, of which he had no notice: *Crump* v. *Berdan,* 97 Mich. 293; 37 Am.
St. Rep. 345, and note. An indorsee of negotiable paper taken before maturity as collateral security for an antecedent indebtedness, in good faith,
and without notice of defenses, such as fraud, which might have been available as between the original parties, holds the paper free from such defenses:
Rosemond v. *Graham,* 54 Minn. 323; 40 Am. St. Rep. 336.

DAVENPORT *v.* CITY OF OTTAWA.

[54 KANSAS, 711.]

LOTTERY—WHAT IS.—A scheme by which a merchant sells his goods at
usual and ordinary market prices, giving to each customer purchasing
goods to the amount of fifty cents, a key, and, to the customer thus
obtaining the particular key which will unlock a certain box, twenty-
five dollars in coin contained therein, is a lottery, and punishable as
such.

Smart & Muesse, for the appellant.

H. A. Richards, for the appellee.

[716] ALLEN, J. The only question presented for our consideration by the record in this case is, whether the defendant
[717] sold lottery tickets. Counsel for appellant contend that
there are two indispensable elements in the offense: "1. A
pecuniary consideration paid; 2. A determination by chance
what and how much he who pays money is to have for it."
It is urged that the agreed facts show that the defendant was a
merchant conducting a legitimate business, with a large stock
of general merchandise, which he sold for the usual and ordinary prices, and that the scheme of giving the money in the
box to whomsoever should chance to get the key that would

unlock the box was merely in the nature of an advertisement, to draw attention and custom to the defendant's store; that, inasmuch as the defendant received no more in any instance for his goods than their fair and usual market value, no compensation was paid for the chance, but that the keys to the box and the chance to obtain a prize was a free gift to his customers, which he had a perfect right to offer. This argument, while plausible is not sound. The defendant advertised his goods for sale. At the same time he advertised that, to every purchaser of goods to the value of fifty cents or more, paying in cash therefor, a key would be given, and that the person receiving the key which would unlock the box should receive the twenty-five dollars as a free gift. Each sale, then, was a sale, not of the goods, but of a chance to obtain twenty-five dollars.

In this instance it may be conceded that the main purpose of the defendant was to increase his legitimate business by this scheme, and that the sale of merchandise was not used merely as a cover for conducting a lottery. The purpose of the defendant undoubtedly was to attract attention and stimulate trade at his store; but this case must be determined by the legal principles applicable to it. Suppose that, instead of a large stock of general merchandise, on which only moderate profits are made, the defendant kept only such articles as usually bear a very high percentage of profit, and, instead of offering twenty-five dollars, had offered one thousand dollars, on precisely the same terms as this twenty-five dollars was offered: could any one doubt for a moment that those who are inclined to invest small sums for the purpose of gaining large ones would be likely to purchase articles for [718] which they had no special need, merely with the hope of gaining the prize offered? Though the goods, in such a case, should be sold only at the regular retail price, the main business of the defendant would become that of selling chances to draw the one thousand dollars, rather than merchandise for a legitimate profit. The key, with the card attached, was in substance and effect a lottery ticket. Purchasers were given to understand, whether truthfully or not does not affect the case, that one key, and only one of those given out, would unlock the box, and that whoever chanced to get the proper key would get the money. It is said that no element of chance existed, because the right of the purchaser to obtain a prize was, in fact, absolutely determined the instant he received the key. If the key fitted the lock the money was his from that instant. If it did not it was not his.

This contention is not sound, though specious. Neither buyer nor seller was supposed to know which was the true key to the box, and the fact would only be actually determined when the trial was made at the time appointed to unlock the box. But, even if we assume that the chance was determined when the sale was made, it would be equally a lottery, for the fortunate person would at once obtain a right to the prize, though he could not in fact get it until the time appointed. The unfortunate purchaser would at once receive his merchandise and his blank in the lottery. No sound distinction exists between the principle involved in this case and that in the case of *State* v. *Kansas Mercantile Assn.*, 45 Kan. 351; 23 Am. St. Rep. 727. The case of *State* v. *Mumford*, 73 Mo. 647, 39 Am. Rep. 532, is also directly in point. Prizes were offered to subscribers to the Kansas City *Times*, each subscriber receiving a ticket entitling him to participate in a drawing of prizes, and no extra charge above the ordinary subscription price being made. The supreme court of Missouri held this a lottery, and that subscribers to the newspaper bought at the same time, and for one and the same consideration. the newspaper and the ticket in the lottery. So in this case the purchaser, for one undivided price, bought merchandise and a ticket in [719] the scheme which was to determine who should have the prize. These views are also upheld in the cases of *Hudelson* v. *State*, 94 Ind. 426; 48 Am. Rep. 171; *United States* v. *Zeisler*, 30 Fed. Rep. 499; *Bell* v. *State*, 5 Sneed, 507; *Thomas* v. *People*, 59 Ill. 160. Judgment affirmed.

All the justices concurring.

LOTTERIES—WHAT ARE—GIFT ENTERPRISES.—A lottery is a scheme by which, on one's paying money or some other thing of value, he obtains the contingent right to have something of greater value, if an appeal to chance, by lot, or otherwise, under direction of the manager of the scheme, should decide in his favor: *Cross* v. *People*, 18 Col. 321; 36 Am. St. Rep. 292, and note, with the cases collected.

GERMAN FIRE INSURANCE COMPANY *v.* BOARD OF COMMISSIONERS OF SHAWNEE COUNTY.

[54 KANSAS, 732.]

INSURANCE—VIOLATION OF CONDITION IN POLICY.—A fire insurance policy containing a provision forbidding the keeping or use of gasoline on the insured premises is rendered void by the violation of such condition by one in the occupancy of the insured premises with the implied consent of the insured.

ACTION to recover for a total loss by fire upon two policies of insurance upon a building situated upon fair grounds in Shawnee county, and known as the "grand stand." The county commissioners of said county procured the insurance on such premises, and at the time of the loss the premises were occupied by members of the Grand Army of the Republic for the purposes of a reunion without authority from such commissioners, who were entitled to the possession and control of the premises. Judgment for the plaintiffs, and the insurers appealed.

E. F. Ware, for the appellants.

R. B. Welch, D. R. Hite, and H. Keeler, for the appellees.

736 JOHNSTON, J. Each policy contained a condition providing that the insured should not keep or use gasoline upon the premises, and that a violation of the condition would avoid the policy. The facts agreed upon clearly show that the fire which destroyed the property was occasioned by the use of gasoline, and it fairly appears that the gasoline which caused the fire was kept and used upon the premises. The statement respecting it is not as explicit as it might have been, but we think that the fair import is that the lunch counter was a part of the premises. The burning of the grand stand was the subject of controversy, and about which the parties were stipulating, and the manifest meaning of their agreement is, that the fire which burned the grand stand was communicated directly from the gasoline used upon the premises. It is true that the gasoline was not kept and used by the assured, nor by any express authority granted by them, and they, therefore, insist that they should not be held responsible for the use of the forbidden article. Although it is agreed that the board of county commissioners gave no authority for the use of the premises by the Grand Army of the Republic, **737** it is agreed that the fact that the reunion was to be held upon the premises was a matter of general and common knowledge. It had been extensively advertised, and the board of county commissioners knew in advance that it would be held upon the fair grounds. It was held there for a period of several days, and gasoline stoves and lamps were used without hindrance or restriction. The board of county commissioners not only knew that the reunion was to be held upon the fair grounds, as other reunions had been held before, but they would have willingly granted the use of the premises for that purpose, if application had been made. Under such circumstances the members of the Grand Army of the Republic cannot be regarded as strangers or trespassers, nor can the assured escape responsibility for the use of the prohibited articles. The company stipulated in each case that it would not assume the risk of the use of a very dangerous and combustible material. The violation of these conditions by any one who occupied the premises, with the implied consent of the assured, is equivalent to a violation by the assured themselves. Under the facts it must be held that the Grand Army of the Republic occupied and held control of the grounds with at least the implied assent of the board of county commissioners, and when they intrusted the occupation and control of the premises to another the latter became their representative, for whom they must answer as for themselves: *Liverpool etc. Ins. Co.* v. *Gunther*, 116 U. S. 113; *Gunther* v. *Liverpool etc. Ins. Co.*, 134 U. S. 110; *Kelly* v. *Worcester etc. Ins. Co.*, 97 Mass. 284; *Diehl* v. *Adams etc. Ins. Co.*, 58 Pa. St. 443; 98 Am. Dec. 302; *Farmers' etc. Ins. Co.* v. *Simmons*, 30 Pa. St. 299. The condition in the policy that gasoline should not be used on the premises is plain and unambiguous, and the defendants in error expressly agreed that a violation of this condition should operate as a forfeiture of all insurance under the policy. It was a reasonable condition, and they cannot reasonably complain of the enforcement of a forfeiture.

The judgment in each case will be reversed, and the causes remanded, with the direction that judgment shall be entered in each case in favor of the insurance company.

All the justices concurring.

INSURANCE—INCREASE OF RISK BY TENANT.—Where premises are insured to the owner, and his tenant increases the risk, without the consent of the insurer, and a loss occurs while the risk is so increased, the ignorance of the owner that the risk has been increased is no defense to a condition for

forfeiture: *Long* v. *Beeber*, 106 Pa. St. 466; 51 Am. Rep. 532. Increase of
risk due to an act of a tenant, without the knowledge of the owner, will not
avoid the policy unless it contains a stipulation that an increase of risk by
the tenant shall render it void in addition to the condition that it shall be
void if the risk is increased by any means within the knowledge or control
of the insured: *Nebraska etc. Ins. Co.* v. *Christiensen*, 29 Neb. 572; 26 Am.
St. Rep. 407, and note. See, also, *First Congregational Church* v. *Holyoke
etc. Ins. Co.*, 158 Mass. 475; 35 Am. St. Rep. 508, and note.

INSLEY *v.* SHIRE.
[54 KANSAS, 793.]

EXECUTORS AND ADMINISTRATORS—INDIVIDUAL LIABILITY.—In an action
against an executor in his representative capacity it is not competent
to establish and adjudge an individual liability against him.

EXECUTORS AND ADMINISTRATORS—LIABILITY—MISJOINDER OF ACTIONS.
An action by one executor against a coexecutor alleging negligence
and dereliction of duty, and asking that he be removed from his trust,
cannot be joined with an action for an accounting by a partnership in
which the estate has an interest with other persons not connected
therewith.

EXECUTORS AND ADMINISTRATORS—JOINT LIABILITY.—Coexecutors who
give a joint bond are treated in law as one and the same person, and
whatever each one does is to be taken as the act of all.

EXECUTORS AND ADMINISTRATORS—LIABILITY OF COEXECUTOR.—If one
executor by his negligence suffers his coexecutor to waste the estate,
when, by the exercise of reasonable diligence, he could have prevented
it, he is responsible for the loss.

EXECUTORS AND ADMINISTRATORS—ACTIONS BETWEEN.—One executor cannot sue his coexecutor for money or property in his hands belonging
to the estate.

EXECUTORS AND ADMINISTRATORS—ACTIONS BY—PARTIES.—All of the executors should join as plaintiffs in an action for an accounting by a partnership in which the estate is interested, but if the action is brought
by one executor, and his coexecutors are made parties defendant, and
appear without objection to the misjoinder of parties before judgment, the failure to name them as parties plaintiff is not fatal.

EXECUTORS AND ADMINISTRATORS—PARTNERSHIP, EFFECT OF CONTINUANCE
BY EXECUTORS.—If executors, in compliance with a provision of a will,
continue to carry on a partnership business, in which the testator
was a partner, upon the same terms that the business was conducted
in his lifetime, a new partnership is thus created, composed of the
executors and the surviving partner.

EXECUTORS AND ADMINISTRATORS—PARTNERSHIP, DUTIES OF.—If, after the
death of a testator, his partnership business is continued by his executors, they become partners with the surviving partner, and it is the duty
of all of the partners to devote their time and best endeavors to carry
on the business, and promote the prosperity of the partnership. In
the absence of any special agreement between them as to a division of
labor, each must give his time and attention to the conduct of the

business without compensation, and without regard to the relative value of the services of the several partners.

PARTNERSHIP—NEGLIGENCE OF PARTNER.—If partners share alike in the control and labor of the partnership business, one of them cannot sit passively by, indifferent to the interests of the firm, and, after neglecting to use reasonable diligence himself, hold the others responsible to the firm for a like indifference or negligence.

WITNESSES—EXPERT EVIDENCE.—An issue as to business negligence between parties must be determined from facts, and not from the opinions of witnesses.

W. C. Hook and D. M. Valentine, for the appellant.

E. Hagan, Hayden & Hayden, T. A. Hurd, and L. B. & S. E. Wheat, for the appellees.

794 JOHNSTON, J.   In the year 1873 M. H. Insley, Daniel Shire, and E. R. Kellogg formed a partnership under the firm name of Insley, Shire & Co., with a view of carrying on banking and other lines of business at Leavenworth, Kansas. About a year afterward Kellogg withdrew from the firm, and Insley and Shire continued the business as equal partners, without a change in the name of the firm.   The partnership had no established capital, nor was there any fund set aside for that purpose.   Each partner deposited a certain amount of money to his personal credit, subject to be checked out by himself at will.   The two principal lines of business in which the firm was engaged were private banking and the manufacture, construction, and sale of bridges, but it also appears that they were interested in real estate, mining, and other business ventures, some of which were profitable and some unprofitable.   In June, 1882, Shire died, leaving a will, under which Ann M. Shire, James W. Gaw, and Levi Wilson were appointed as executors, who were empowered to manage and **795** control the property of the deceased until it should be distributed in accordance with the provisions of the will, in one of which the testator authorized the executors "to continue my present business as long as they may deem best." The persons appointed duly qualified and gave a joint bond for the faithful performance of their duties, conditioned as required by law.   No inventory of the partnership was made, nor were any steps taken to ascertain what the interest of the deceased was in the partnership.   They did not take the partnership property into their possession, nor was it given over to the possession and control of the surviving partner.   Insley gave no bond, and did not undertake the management of the

partnership estate as he might have done under the statute,
but the executors and Insley together determined to continue
the partnership business as it had been previously carried on
during the lifetime of Shire. Gaw, who was a brother in
law of the testator, was the active executor in carrying out
the provisions of the will, and from February 1, 1884, under
an agreement with his coexecutors, he devoted most of his
time to the partnership business, as the representative of the
Shire interest, for which he was to receive $1,000 annually.
He continued to act in this capacity and to receive the stipulated salary for his services until February, 1887. Heavy
losses were suffered by the partnership prior to December,
1887, when a run was made upon the bank, which compelled
an assignment and transfer of the property for the benefit of
creditors. Soon afterward this action was brought by Ann
M. Shire, as she alleges in her petition, "as well in her individual right as she does as one of the executors of the last
will of Daniel Shire, deceased." It was brought against
James W. Gaw and Levi Wilson, two of the executors of the
last will and testament of Daniel Shire, deceased, and also
M. H. Insley, A. J. Tullock, Samuel C. Milligan, W. H. Chap-
lin, and the First National Bank of Leavenworth, Kansas.
In her petition she stated substantially that the defendants
other than Tullock and the bank had conspired together to
defraud her; that the estate has been [796] mismanaged; that
the business of Insley, Shire & Co. had been negligently conducted, by which great loss had occurred; that the property
and assets of the estate and partnership had been wasted and
diverted, resulting in insolvency and business disaster. She
asked for the appointment of a receiver to take possession of
the property and assets of Insley, Shire & Co; that certain
transfers might be adjudged to be void, and that an accounting should be had of the partnership business, and that the
partnership should be dissolved. A further prayer is that
James W. Gaw and Levi Wilson should be removed from the
position of executors of the estate of Daniel Shire, deceased.
Insley answered, denying the wrong and mismanagement
charged, as did also Gaw and Wilson. The answer of Milligan was a general denial.

After the issues were joined, the cause was referred to a
referee, who, after trial, made an elaborate report of the
facts and law. An accounting of the business was made,
and among other facts it was found that the plaintiff, on

account of her sex and infirmities, had taken no part in the administration of the estate; that James W. Gaw was the controlling and active executor thereof; that the bridge business of Insley, Shire & Co., under the control of Tullock, had been well managed and profitable; that the banking business had been badly managed, the clerks and employees connected with the same having been negligently selected; that they had abstracted and misappropriated large sums of money, and that, from May 1, 1885, to December 6, 1887, the bank had been despoiled of $29,832.98 by and through the fraud of the employees. It was found that Insley had failed to exercise due skill, diligence, and care in supervising the affairs of the bank, by reason of which great losses occurred; that at the close of the partnership business the plaintiff had overdrawn her account in the bank to the extent of $30,104.27, and that she was allowed to so improvidently overdraw her account because of the omission of Insley to keep accurate and intelligible accounts of the business. It was also found that James W. Gaw had failed to exercise ordinary care, diligence, and [797] watchfulness in attending to the partnership business, and had not administered the Shire estate as the law requires; that he did not inform himself of the condition of the partnership business, kept no accounts, and rendered no statements thereof, and that he kept no check upon the bad habits of the employees, although he was paid a salary of $1,000 per annum for the performance of such duties. In regard to the wrongdoing of the employees, there was an express finding that neither Insley nor Gaw "participated in any of the fraudulent transactions herein mentioned or in any of the fruits thereof, nor did they have actual knowledge of the same; but they were negligent as herein stated, and by reason of such negligence are chargeable with such losses as herein found." In the statement of account the referee found, after charging Insley with the illegal abstractions and defalcations of employees and other losses, that there was due from him to the partnership estate $13,465.43; that there was due from Milligan to the partnership the sum of $34,671.89, and it was recommended that judgment should be entered in accordance with these findings; and further, that James W. Gaw ought to be removed from his trust as executor of the Shire estate. The report of the referee was taken up by the district court, and upon the same evidence radical changes were made in the findings of the referee; some were modified, others were

eliminated, and additional findings were also made. The
court materially reduced the liability of Insley, but found
that there was a joint negligence on the part of Insley and
Gaw, by reason of which they were jointly and severally
liable to the partnership in the sum of $8,555, and the court
undertook to determine as between them the individual liability of each. Judgment was accordingly rendered against
them, and it was further adjudged that the firm of Insley,
Shire & Co. should recover of Milligan $39,121.42. Judg-
ment was rendered in favor of the other defendants, and it
was provided that the costs incurred should be paid one-half
out of the assets of the partnership and the other by Insley
and Gaw.

⁷⁹⁸ Several objections are made to the findings, rulings,
and judgment of the trial court. It is urged that in the proceeding there is a mingling of parties and issues not in keeping with good practice nor warranted by the rules of law.
There is good cause for this objection. Ann M. Shire, who is
an executrix, brings an action as executrix against Gaw and
Wilson as coexecutors, alleging waste and unfaithful administration, and asking that they be removed from their trusts
as executors. Although she sues them only as executors, she
attempts to hold them personally liable, and judgment was
actually rendered against Gaw individually. In her petition
she describes them as executors, and from the averments of
the petition and the kind of relief which is asked against
them there can be no question but that they were sued
in their representative capacity. The action having been
brought against them in that capacity, it is not competent to
establish and adjudge an individual liability against them.
She also brings the action in her individual capacity against
the executors of the estate, but whatever this aspect of the
case may count for, it does not warrant a judgment against
them as individuals. The petition which she files, however,
in its whole scope, relates largely to partnership matters, and
its main purpose appears to be to obtain an accounting of
the partnership business. This could not be accomplished
by her as an individual. It is true that she is an heir and
legatee, and is therefore interested in the estate, but there are
several children and other legatees who are also interested,
and who are not parties to the proceeding.

No settlement of the estate has ever been made, nor does
there appear to have been any order of the probate court for

the payment of legacies, or the distribution of the estate. She has no right, as an individual, at this time, to bring an action in behalf of the partnership against its employees for the recovery of money due to the partnership, or for losses occasioned by their neglect or wrongdoing. Although she is jointly concerned in the execution of the trust, she brings an [799] action in her representative capacity against her coexecutors on account of negligence and dereliction of duty for which all were in a measure responsible. Under the law coexecutors are to be treated as one and the same individual, and whatever each one does is to be taken as the act of all—their authority being joint and entire: Schouler on Executors, sec. 400. In this case a joint bond was given, and the effect of this act was to make each executor liable for the default of the others during the continuance of the joint executorship. A separate bond might have been given by each under the statute; yet, as the plaintiff chose to join with the others in the giving of the bond, she made herself liable, although she may have been without fault, for the waste and improper administration of her associates: Schouler on Executors, sec. 406; 7 Am. & Eng. Ency. of Law, 216, and cases cited.

There are cases where one executor is not answerable for the neglect or bad faith of the others, but where one, by his own negligence, suffers another to waste the estate, when by the exercise of reasonable diligence he could have prevented it, he will be held responsible for the loss. One of the reasons why more than one executor is appointed is, that one may watch over and correct the conduct of the other. It would hardly do to say that one who has taken upon himself the execution of a trust may, without incurring responsibility, leave the whole care of the estate upon others. Mrs. Shire, after accepting the trust, could not ignore the duties incumbent upon her and escape liability. She still retains the trust, and yet she seeks to recover against her coexecutors. As a rule one person holding such trust relation cannot sue and recover from another in his representative capacity. " Being coexecutors, the possession of the funds of the estate by either is possession of the other, the possession being in law a joint one." And so it has been held that one executor cannot sue his coexecutor for money or property in his hands belonging to the estate of the deceased: *Taylor* v. *Minton*, 45 Kan. 17. If Gaw was guilty of bad faith, neglect, or wrongdoing the plaintiff could [800] have taken steps to have had him removed in the manner prescribed by statute, and then legatees and distributees could have required him to account for property misappropriated or for losses occurring through his maladministration. Apart from these considerations, Insley was not concerned in the controversy between the coexecutors. He was not an executor, nor did he hold any other direct trust relation to the estate. The questions of whether they acted in bad faith toward each other, and whether they were negligent toward the estate, and for that reason should have been removed from their trusts, has no proper place in the partnership accounting between Insley and those who held the other partnership interests.

There is the further contention that the plaintiff could not maintain an action against Insley for the purpose of obtaining an accounting of the partnership business. This contention is based upon the idea that all of the executors represent the Shire interest in the partnership, and, as the estate is joint and entire, the executors are to be considered in law as one person, and all of them must join as plaintiffs. This is the correct rule, and all three of the representatives of the estate should have joined in bringing the action for an accounting with Insley: 7 Am. & Eng. Ency. of Law, 360, and cases cited; 11 Am. & Eng. Ency. of Law, 1033. No proper objection, however, was made on account of the nonjoinder of Gaw and Wilson, and, as they were made defendants in the action in their representative capacity, and remained in the court throughout the proceeding, while the accounting was being made, the failure to name them as plaintiffs cannot be regarded as a fatal objection. Treating the proceeding, then, as one in which all of the representatives of the estate had joined in asking an accounting of the partnership business, the question remains as to the liability of Insley. Insley and Shire, as we have seen, were equal partners. When Shire died Insley did not give a bond and take possession of the partnership property as surviving partner, as he might have done under the statute. [801] The death of Shire operated to dissolve the partnership, but it appears that by a mutual arrangement, and in accordance with the provisions of the will, the business was continued by the executors upon the same terms as it was during the lifetime of Daniel Shire. This arrangement had the effect of creating a new partnership, composed of the executors on one side and Insley on the other.

Some attempt is made to hold Insley to the liability of a
surviving partner under the law, but, from the testimony, it is
clear that he was not so regarded or treated by any of the parties. He did not assume title and control as surviving partner.
No bond was given by him; no inventory of the partnership
estate was made; and he did not undertake the management
of the partnership estate as surviving partner. On the contrary, all the parties united in the control and possession of
the property; the executors, representing the Shire interest,
and Insley, representing his own, they joined together in carrying on the business until it was discontinued. They were
partners to all intents and purposes, and all alike equally
owed the duties of partners to each other. There was no
agreement for a division of labor between the executors on
one side and Insley upon the other. Insley was not employed
to represent the executors or to attend to the business of the
partnership for the estate. It is true that he devoted most
of his time and attention to the partnership business, but,
from 1885, Gaw was employed on behalf of the estate to
attend to the Shire interest in the partnership, and he
received an annual salary of $1,000 as compensation for his
services. There is a finding by the referee that he undertook to represent the Shire interest in the partnership, and
was continuously so engaged down to the close of the bank.

The claim that Insley was general manager for the firm,
and liable as such, is not sustained by the record. While
he was active in the management of the affairs of the firm,
he was not appointed nor employed as manager, nor did he
hold any official position which made him the representative
of the 802 estate in the firm business. There was no agreement that he should receive compensation as manager or
agent for the firm, and none was allowed or paid. It is true
that, when the controversy arose between the parties, a credit
was entered and a claim for extra services made, but, as
there was no such agreement, it was not allowed, and it
appears to have been abandoned. So far as the partnership
accounting is concerned Insley is to be treated as a one-half
owner and the Shire estate as the owner of the other half
interest. The three executors are to be regarded as one person, and together they sustain the same relation to Insley as
Shire did in his lifetime. Insley owed them, as partners, no
higher duty or any greater diligence than he would have
owed to Shire under similar circumstances if he had been

alive. It was the duty of the partners to devote their time
and best endeavors to carry on the business, and promote the
prosperity of the partnership. In the absence of any special
agreement between them as to the division of labor, each
should give time and attention to the conduct of the business
without compensation, and without regard to the relative
value of the services of the several parties: Parsons on Partnership, 3d ed., 244; 17 Am. & Eng. Ency. of Law, 1056.
Scrupulous good faith and reasonable diligence is required
from each to the other, and all losses caused by culpable
neglect of duty or bad faith on the part of a partner are
chargeable against him in favor of the firm. "A fair degree
of care only, however, is required. An honest mistake of
judgment, or a trivial departure from the partnership agreement in cases of emergency, will not impose the burden of
the losses of the firm upon the deviating partner": 17 Am.
& Eng. Ency. of Law, 1219.

A partner of equal responsibility, and who himself is
indifferent to his own interest or guilty of negligence, is
hardly in a position to claim and recover for the entire losses
resulting from the negligence of both. In this case the duty
of carefully selecting employees and supervising the business
of the partnership rested equally upon Insley and the representatives [803] of the estate; and yet we find that the entire
loss resulting from the fraud and defalcation of employees was
placed upon a single partner. The principal losses resulted
from the action of Milligan in abstracting and purloining
money from the bank. Gaw, who was giving special attention to the interests of the Shire estate, procured the employment of Milligan, who was a relative, and there is testimony
that Milligan was employed and placed on the working force
of the bank as the representative of the Shire estate. It was
as much the duty of those representing the estate to exercise
a watchful care over the conduct of Milligan and other
employees as it was of Insley. The accounts which he fraudulently manipulated and the books which he falsified were
under the eyes and supervision of the partners. Why, then,
should Insley account for all these losses? If Shire had been
alive, and had selected Milligan as an employee, and he had
been guilty of frauds similar to those charged against him,
and if there had been no other division of labor or responsibility between Insley and Shire than did exist while they
were partners, how could Shire have claimed that Insley

should bear all the losses resulting from the frauds and peculations of Milligan?

It appears that the methods by which Milligan abstracted and purloined the money of the firm were so ingenious as to almost baffle the skill of expert accountants, and several weeks were consumed by them before they were able to un-cover the fraud and determine by whom the money was taken. Insley was not a book-keeper nor an expert account-ant, and no reason is seen why he should be held to a higher degree of care with respect to the books than those represent-ing the other interests. Where partners share alike in the control and labor of business one of them cannot sit pas-sively by, indifferent to the interests of the firm, and after neglecting to use reasonable diligence himself, hold the other responsible to the firm for a like indifference or negligence. It does not appear that Insley had any special skill as a banker, and as a partner [804] he cannot be held for the lack of skill in that respect. His partners had a right to expect reasonable care and diligence from him in assisting to carry on the business, but they knew what his capabilities were when they entered into business with him, and therefore have no right to complain of a lack of ability or skill. The charge of bad faith and of conspiracy with Gaw was not sus-tained because there was an express finding that Insley did not participate in any of the fraudulent transactions of the employees or in any of the fruits thereof, and, more than that, that he had no knowledge of the same. It is clear that the accounting was made upon an incorrect theory. The liabil-ity of Insley was extended beyond what was warranted by the evidence or the law, and hence the judgment cannot be sustained.

There were some rulings upon the admission of testimony which were so erroneous as to require a reversal. Testimony was received, over objection, that was unquestionably incom-petent. Witnesses were asked if books were kept in a cer-tain manner, and if money was abstracted, and no exami-nation was made to discover the fraud or robbery, could the witness say that due diligence and care were exercised by the manager? Several other questions were allowed in which the witnesses were asked, in effect, whether those in charge of the bank had exercised due diligence in its man-agement. Aside from the unwarranted assumptions of fact, the testimony related to a matter which was not the subject

of expert testimony.   The question whether the parties were
negligent was the principal point in controversy, and should
have been determined from facts, and not from opinions:
Monroe v. *Lattin,* 25 Kan. 352; *Kansas Pac. Ry. Co.* v. *Peavey,*
29 Kan. 177; 44 Am. Rep. 630; *Dow* v. *Julien,* 32 Kan. 578;
Solomon R. R. Co. v. *Jones,* 34 Kan. 463.

The judgment of the district court against Insley and Gaw
will be reversed, and the cause remanded for further proceedings, in accordance with the views herein expressed.

All the justices concurring.

EXECUTORS AND ADMINISTRATORS—LIABILITY OF COEXECUTORS.—Joint
administrators are responsible jointly and severally, each for his own act
and also for the acts of each other.   To avoid this responsibility for each
other they should execute several bonds: *Clarks* v. *State,* 6 Gill & J. 288;
26 Am. Dec. 576, and note.   Executors and administrators are not liable
for each other's acts unless there be connivance or gross negligence: *Lenoir*
v. *Winn,* 4 Desaus. Eq. 65; 6 Am. Dec. 597.   An executor is liable only for his
own acts or defaults: *Atcheson* v. *Robertson,* 3 Rich. Eq. 132; 55 Am. Dec.
634, and note.   See, especially, the extended notes to *Doolittle* v. *Lewis,* 11
Am. Dec. 389, and *Jones' Appeal,* 42 Am. Dec. 291.

EXECUTORS AND ADMINISTRATORS.   Liability for neglect: See the extended note to *Thomas* v. *White,* 14 Am. Dec. 65.

EXECUTORS AND ADMINISTRATORS—EFFECT OF CARRYING ON PARTNER-
SHIP BY.—Where the executor of a deceased partner carries on the business
with the surviving partners the executor becomes a copartner, and is liable
personally for the debts of the company: *Alsop* v. *Mather,* 8 Conn. 584; 21
Am. Dec. 703, and note.   See the extended note to *Wild* v. *Davenport,* 57
Am. Rep. 560.

CASES

COURT OF APPEALS

OF

MARYLAND.

BALTIMORE & OHIO R. R. Co. *v.* BARGER.

[80 MARYLAND, 23.]

RAILROAD COMPANIES—DAMAGES FOR ASSAULT—EVIDENCE.—In an action against a railroad company by a passenger to recover for an assault made on him by the conductor on a train, evidence to show that on some other occasion, and on a day different from that of the alleged assault, such passenger had used abusive and profane language to, and made threats against, the same conductor, is inadmissible.

RAILROAD COMPANIES—ASSAULT ON PASSENGER BY CONDUCTOR.—A railroad company is liable for an assault made by its conductor upon a passenger, although the assault is provoked by profane and abusive language used by the passenger to the conductor without provocation.

RAILROAD COMPANIES—LIABILITY FOR ASSAULT BY CONDUCTOR—PROVOCATION AS MITIGATION OF DAMAGES.—The provocation offered by a railroad passenger in using profane and abusive language to the conductor on the train, if of such character as to naturally arouse the passions of men of ordinary temperament, and not too remote in time, is admissible in mitigation of damages in an action against the railroad company to recover for such assault.

RAILROAD COMPANIES—ASSAULT BY CONDUCTOR—EXEMPLARY DAMAGES. If, in an action by a passenger to recover of a railroad company for an assault committed by its conductor, the evidence is conflicting as to the provocation offered by the passenger in using profane and abusive language to the conductor the court cannot instruct the jury, as matter of law, not to award punitive damages for the assault. The jury may properly be instructed to consider the character of the assault and the conduct of both parties, and award such punitive or exemplary damages as the circumstances may require.

RAILROAD COMPANIES—ASSAULT BY CONDUCTOR—EXEMPLARY DAMAGES. An assault by a railroad conductor upon a passenger, though provoked by profane and abusive language, is not justified thereby, and renders the railroad company liable in exemplary damages.

J. C. Lane, J. K. Cowen, and H. H. Keedy, Jr., for the appellant.

F. J. Nelson, for the appellee.

[28] BOYD, J.   This was an action brought by Theophilus Barger, the appellee, against the Baltimore & Ohio Railroad Company, for an alleged assault upon him by the conductor in charge of the train on which the appellee was a passenger.   The evidence was conflicting as to the conduct of Barger.   He testified that he was riding on the step of the rear car, as the train was crowded; that when the conductor came out on the platform he handed him his ticket, and remarked to the conductor: "You did not get all your tickets to-night"; that the conductor accused him of applying an opprobious epithet to him, which he denied, and the conductor struck him with his fist and then with his lantern.   The conductor testified that he collected Barger's ticket, who then said to him: "You thieving s—— of a b——, you had better get them all or I'll report you."   He acknowledged that he then struck Barger with his fist, and claimed that the latter grabbed him by the collar, and he (the conductor) then struck him with his lantern, just as the train was leaving Knoxville.   It is admitted that the difficulty occurred between the points embraced in appellee's ticket, which was good from Brunswick to Weverton.   The conductor further testified that when they reached Weverton, he said: "If you want any more [29] out of me I will get down with you"; and Barger replied: "I have got you just where I want you, and will sue the company."

The witness was then asked by the defendant's attorney "if before this, on some other occasion, and on a different day, Barger had used abusive and profane language to him on the train, and made threats against the witness."   That was objected to, and the court refused to let the question be asked or answered.   This ruling of the court is brought here for review by the first bill of exceptions.   Without deciding how far, if at all, that character of testimony would be admissible in a case of this kind, if properly presented, it is manifest that the evidence disclosed in the record is too remote and indefinite.   It was not stated how long before, on what occasion or what day it occurred, although it is affirmatively shown that it was on a day different from that of the assault.   The ruling of the court was therefore clearly right.

If any authority be necessary, the case of *Gaither* v. *Blower,* 11 Md. 536, is in point.

At the conclusion of the testimony the plaintiff offered two and the defendant eight prayers. Both of the former were granted, and all of the defendant's were rejected, with the exception of the seventh. The rulings of the court in these prayers are presented by the second bill of exceptions. The first, third, fourth, and eighth prayers of the defendant deny the right of the plaintiff to recover at all, if the jury believed the facts stated in them.

The first is, in substance, that if the jury believed the plaintiff used foul and abusive language to the conductor which caused or provoked the assault complained of, and that in making said assault the conductor was not acting for the defendant, and within the scope of his duties as conductor, but was carrying out a personal purpose and feeling, the defendant was not liable for such act of the conductor. The theory of that prayer is that the plaintiff had, by his conduct, forfeited his right as a passenger, and the act of the conductor was merely a personal matter between him so and the plaintiff, provoked by the latter, independent of and freed from the relation that had existed between the plaintiff and defendant as passenger and carrier.

To such a doctrine we cannot subscribe, under the circumstances of this case. There may be, and doubtless are, cases in which the conduct of a passenger toward the employee of a railroad company was such that the company would not be liable for the act of the employee. A conductor, for example, would be justified in the defense of his own person, or the property of the company in his charge, in using such force as would be necessary for their protection against a passenger or any one else, without rendering the company liable. Because he occupies the position of a conductor, and his assailant that of a passenger, does not deprive the former of the right of defending himself or the property in his charge, so far as it becomes necessary. But that is not this case. The plaintiff was, at the time of the assault, a passenger on the train which was in charge of this conductor, who was the agent of the company, to see, as far as he reasonably could, that the plaintiff and other passengers were properly treated, and carried to their respective points of destination. If the plaintiff persisted in misbehaving on the train, either by the use of foul and abusive language toward

the conductor, or in any other way calculated to frighten
or materially interfere with the comfort and safety of the
other passengers, after being admonished by the conductor,
the latter would have been justified in ejecting him from the
train. The remedy in such case would be to eject the unruly
passenger—not to assault him, and then let his employer
escape all liability, because he, the conductor, was carrying
out a "personal purpose and feeling," as stated in the prayer.
A conductor of a train doubtless has his patience and for-
bearance severely tested at times; but he must not settle his
own personal difficulties with the passengers, whilst they are
such, any more than he should permit others to do so, when
he could avoid it. If he has the opportunity to prevent
[31] an assault on a passenger in his charge it is his duty to
do so, and his failure to make a reasonable effort to protect
the passenger from such assault would make the company
responsible. If that be a correct statement of the law, as it
undoubtedly is, as settled by the case of the *New Jersey
Steamboat Co.* v. *Brockett*, 121 U. S. 645, and numerous other
authorities, then *a fortiori* the company must be liable if the
conductor makes an assault on one who is still a passenger,
as Barger was.

In the case of *Central Ry. Co.* v. *Peacock*, 69 Md. 257, 9
Am. St. Rep. 425, cited by the appellant, the plaintiff had left
the car and had ceased to be a passenger, and hence, when the
assault was made, the conductor "stepped aside from the line
and scope of his employment," and therefore the company
was not liable. The court indicated very clearly, however,
that if the assault had been made whilst the plaintiff was a
passenger, and the driver (who was also acting as conductor)
was still executing "the contract of transportation," the company would have been responsible. To hold otherwise would
put a passenger at the mercy of the temper of a conductor.

Much of what we have already said applies to the third,
fourth, and eighth prayers. The third is to the effect that if
the plaintiff used grossly profane and abusive language to the
conductor in the presence of other passengers, without any
provocation on the part of the conductor, he forfeited his
right to be carried as a passenger, and the defendant was not
liable for the assault. That was properly rejected for reasons
already stated. The fourth is still more objectionable, as it
is altogether indefinite and too general to guide the jury as to
what would be deemed a sufficient cause of provocation

to relieve the defendant, even if the theory contended for by
it be correct. The eighth is likewise defective, and there is
no legally sufficient evidence to show that the plaintiff used
the language complained of to provoke an assault by the
conductor for the purpose of suing the company. No such
inference could properly be drawn from the [32] expression
used by Barger, as testified to by the conductor, that "I have
got you just where I want you, and will sue the company."

Whilst the language used by the plaintiff, according to the
defendant's evidence, did not justify an assault by the conductor, it was certainly calculated to irritate him and arouse
his passions, and hence it becomes material as to whether the
remaining prayers of the defendant and the second of the
plaintiff properly presented the law applicable to the measure
of damages to be allowed. The second and fifth prayers of
the defendant undertook to confine the recovery to nominal
damages. The second is like the third, and the fifth is the
same as the fourth, excepting the third and fifth deny the
right of the plaintiff to recover at all, whilst the other two
limited his recovery to nominal damages. No authority has
been cited, and we know of none, that would have justified
the court in granting those prayers under the facts in this
case. The sixth prayer asked the court to instruct the jury,
"that from all the evidence in the cause the plaintiff is not
entitled to recover exemplary damages, but such damages
only as will compensate him for the injury done him, in estimating which the jury are at liberty to consider the offensive
language of the plaintiff (if they should find that he used
such language), in mitigation of the damages." We agree
fully with the learned counsel for the appellant in his contention that, if the jury believed the assault was provoked by the
language used by the plaintiff, as testified to by the conductor
and others, they were authorized to take the provocation into
consideration in mitigation of damages. Whilst the law will
not justify an assault on account of words used toward the
assailant, it does recognize, as was said by Le Grand, C. J.,
in 11 Md. 552, "the weakness and infirmities of human nature which subject it to uncontrollable influences when under
great and maddening excitement superinduced by insults
and threats." But this prayer does not properly present the
question. It disregarded the evidence of the plaintiff himself, [33] who denied that he had used the language complained of. The court could not therefore instruct the

jury that "from all the evidence in the cause the plaintiff is not entitled to recover exemplary damages," etc., for, if the jury believed the plaintiff, the assault was wholly unjustifiable, and such an one as would very properly call for exemplary or punitive damages. It may be true that the great preponderance of the testimony in the record contradicts the plaintiff, but it was for the jury, and not for the court, to determine which was true. That prayer was therefore properly rejected.

It only remains to pass upon the plaintiff's prayers. We have already said that the conduct of the plaintiff, as disclosed by the record, did not justify the assault made by the conductor. We think the plaintiff's first prayer is in accord with that conclusion. In some cases the word "assaulted," as used in this prayer, might be objectionable on the ground that the court left it to the jury to find whether or not, while the plaintiff was a passenger on the cars, he was assaulted and struck by the conductor. It is for the court and not for the jury to determine whether certain facts amount in law to an assault: *Handy* v. *Johnson*, 5 Md. 450. But in this case the defendant was not injured thereby, as at most the court, at the instance of the plaintiff, left to the jury to decide, as a matter of fact, what the court on application would doubtless have decided, as a question of law. The word "assault" was moreover evidently not intended in its technical sense, as its context shows; and in the connection in which it was used was not calculated to mislead the jury or injure the defendant.

The only question remaining to be passed upon is the ruling on the second prayer of the plaintiff. That it announces a correct principle of law in the abstract may be admitted, but whether or not it was misleading under the circumstances of this case is not altogether free from doubt. It certainly might have been drawn in a way that would have been more clearly unobjectionable.

It is not every case of assault that authorizes a jury to award exemplary damages. Whilst the provocation of the plaintiff may not justify an assault, yet, if it be of such character as would naturally arouse the anger and passions of men of ordinary temperament, and it is not too remote, it is admissible in mitigation of damages. The authorities differ somewhat as to whether evidence of recent provocation can be admitted in mitigation of compensatory damages. In

Wisconsin it has been held that it ·cannot be: *Corcoran* v. *Harran*, 55 Wis. 122. Whilst in New York (*Kiff* v. *Youmans*, 86 N. Y. 330; 40 Am. Rep. 543), and in Pennsylvania (*Robison* v. *Rupert*, 23 Pa. St. 523), it has been decided that it may mitigate compensatory as well as punitive damages. It is said in *Robison* v. *Rupert*, 23 Pa. St. 523, that "where there is a reasonable excuse for the defendant arising from the provocation or fault of the plaintiff, but not sufficient entirely to justify the act done, there can be no exemplary damages, and the circumstances of mitigation must be applied to the actual damages. If it were not so the plaintiff would get full compensation for damages occasioned by himself." But the authorities agree that sufficient provocation (of which the jury is ordinarily left to judge) will at least mitigate exemplary damages in actions for assaults, and the conduct of a passenger may be such as to preclude his right to exemplary damages for an assault by a conductor or other employee of a railroad company. We are not prepared, however, to say that under the circumstances of this case the conduct of Barger, as disclosed by the evidence of the defendant in the record, was such as would have justified the court below in instructing the jury, as a question of law, that they could not award punitive damages for the assault made on him. The conductor's own testimony shows that he not only struck Barger with his fist when the epithet was applied to him, but he followed it up with a blow over his head with the lantern. It would require very great provocation to justify a conductor in charge of a train using such violence on one in his care. It might have resulted in a riot or other serious trouble on that heavily loaded train, to [35] the great discomfort and danger of the other passengers. If the plaintiff's statement was believed by the jury the defendant was unquestionably liable for punitive damages, and this prayer submitted his theory of the case. By it the jury was at liberty to consider the violent character of the conductor's conduct and the outrage to the feelings of the plaintiff, and thereupon, to award such exemplary or punitive damages as the circumstances in their judgment required.

The defendant had the right to present its theory of the case in mitigation of damages—which is a matter of defense—but its prayers on the subject, as we have already determined, did not properly present the question. It would have been right for the court to have granted an instruction of its own, but it was not required to do so, unless requested by prayers free from the defects pointed out in those that were offered. As the jury were simply told that they were at liberty to consider the character of the assault, and award such punitive or exemplary damages as the circumstances, in their judgment, would require, they could have taken into consideration the conduct of the plaintiff, as well as of the conductor, in making up their verdict, and the amount of the verdict rendered shows they were not inclined to punish the defendant very severely, if they allowed any punitive damages at all. The second prayer of the plaintiff in *Byers* v. *Horner*, 47 Md. 23, used language very similar to that in this prayer, and this court said it ought to have been granted. Taking all the circumstances into consideration, we are of the opinion that there was no error in granting this prayer, and the judgment must be affirmed.

Judgment affirmed with costs.

RAILROADS—LIABILITY TO PASSENGERS FOR ASSAULT BY EMPLOYEES.— A railroad company is liable for a malicious assault on a passenger made by one of its employees: *Williams* v. *Pullman Palace Car Co.*, 40 La. Ann. 417; 8 Am. St. Rep. 538. This rule is illustrated in the following line of cases: *Fick* v. *Chicago etc. Ry. Co.*, 68 Wis. 469; 60 Am. Rep. 878, and extended note; *Western etc. R. R. Co.* v. *Turner*, 72 Ga. 292; 53 Am. Rep. 842; *McKinley* v. *Chicago etc. R. R. Co.*, 44 Iowa, 314; 24 Am. Rep. 748; *Goddard* v. *Grand Trunk Ry. Co*, 57 Me. 202; 2 Am. Rep. 39, and note; *Hanson* v. *European etc. Ry. Co.*, 62 Me. 84; 16 Am. Rep. 404, and note. See, also, the extended notes to the following cases: *Weeks* v. *New York etc. R. R. Co.*, 28 Am. Rep. 112; *Hoffman* v. *New York etc. R. R. Co.*, 41 Am. Rep. 341; *Chicago etc. R. R. Co.* v. *Flexman*, 42 Am. Rep. 36, and *Evansville etc. R. R. Co.* v. *McKee*, 50 Am. Rep. 108. But in a case where the plaintiff, a passenger on defendants' road, applied to the baggage-master to have his trunk checked, which not being done promptly, he became angry and used abusive language, whereupon the baggage-master struck him with a hatchet, it was held that the company was not liable: *Little Miami R. R. Co.* v. *Wetmore*, 19 Ohio St. 110; 2 Am. Rep. 373.

LEWIS *v.* FISHER.

[80 MARYLAND, 139.]

EMPLOYEE, WHO NOT ENTITLED TO PRIVILEGE OF.—Under a statute providing that when a person or corporation shall make an assignment for the benefit of creditors, be adjudged insolvent, or have his or its property taken possession of by a receiver, all moneys due and owing therefrom for wages or salaries to clerks, servants, or employees, contracted not more than three months prior thereto, shall be paid in full, an attorney at law engaged by such person or corporation is not an "employee," nor entitled to any priority for the payment of fees for services rendered.

A. H. Robertson, H. Stockbridge, Jr., and *J. T. Mason*, for the appellant.

C. J. Bonaparte and *W. A. Fisher*, for the appellees.

140 MCSHERRY, J.   Section 15 of article 47 of the code provides, in substance, that, when any person or body corporate shall make an assignment for the benefit of his or its creditors, or shall be adjudged insolvent, or shall have his or its property taken possession of by a receiver "all moneys due and owing from such person or body corporate, for wages or salaries to clerks, servants, or employees, contracted not more than three months anterior to the execution of such assignment, adjudication of insolvency, or appointment of a receiver, shall first be paid in full out of such property or estate," etc.   The appellant, who is an attorney at law, claims to be paid in full the fees due him by the American Casualty Insurance & Security Company, an insolvent corporation, whose assets were placed in the hands of a receiver by a decree of the circuit court of Baltimore city, on November 23, 1893.   Whether he comes within the statute just alluded to, and is, therefore, entitled to a priority in the payment of his claim, is the sole question raised by the pending appeal, and the question is an exceedingly narrow one.

We have before us only the petition of the appellant, together with his itemized account verified by affidavit, and the answer of the receivers.   From these it appears that the claim is made up of two charges for salary for the month of December, 1892, and the month of January, 1893, and nine other charges for services rendered and for retainers in particular cases.   All of these items, except the last six, which aggregate the sum of nine hundred dollars, bear date more than three months prior to November 23, 1893, and are, in

consequence, under the statute, entitled to no priority. The
six items with which we have to deal are not items for salary. Four of the six are for retainers in cases undisposed of,
and the remaining two are for fees in cases previously tried.
The statute has relation to wages or salaries due to clerks,
servants, or employees. The appellant was, confessedly, not
a clerk of the insolvent company; and, unless the sums he
claims were wages or salary, and, unless [141] he was, when
they were earned, a servant or employee within the meaning
and intent of the statute, he is not entitled to claim the benefit of the above provision of the code.

We are not content to dispose of this question by adopting
any of the varying definitions of the terms " wages," ." servants," and " employees," given in different lexicons, because
there are well-recognized rules of construction which ought
to control in the judicial interpretation of the statute. If we
look to the object which the legislature had in view in adopting this particular act, and if we bear in mind the familiar
doctrine that the signification of the words used is to be
gathered therefrom, and also from their association and collocation, there would seem to be but little, if any, difficulty in
disposing of this contention. Now, the title of the original
act which forms the section of the code referred to in the
beginning of this opinion is, "An act to provide for the payment of wages and salaries due employees of insolvent employers," and the obvious scope of the enactment is, in the
language of Bacon, J., in *Coffin* v. *Reynolds*, 37 N. Y. 640,
when discussing a somewhat similar provision of a New York
statute, "to protect the classes most appropriately described
by the words used as those engaged in manual labor as distinguished from officers of the corporation or professional
men engaged in its service; in short to afford additional
relief to a class who usually labor for small compensation,
to whom the moderate pittance of their wages is an object of
interest and necessity, and who are poorly qualified to take
care of their own concerns or look sharply after their employer." "To the language of the act must be applied the
rule common in the construction of statutes, that when two
or more words of analogous meaning are coupled together
they are understood to be used in their cognate sense, express
the same relations, and give color and expression to each
other": *Wakefield* v. *Fargo*, 90 N. Y. 213. Or, as stated by
Lord Bacon, "the coupling of the words together shows that

they are to be understood in the same sense": 4 Bacon's
Abridgment, 26; [142] see, also, *Commonwealth* v. *De Jardin,*
126 Mass. 46; 30 Am. Rep. 652. The word "employee,"
though generally and ordinarily quite comprehensive, cannot,
if regard be had to the principle just stated, be given a wider
meaning than the cognate words "clerks" and "servants"
with which it is associated, but must be restricted in its signification so as to include only persons who perform the same
kind of service that is due from clerks or servants. "A statute which treats of persons of an inferior rank cannot by any
general word be so extended as to embrace a superior; the
class first mentioned is to be taken as the most comprehensive; *specialia generalibus derogant;* Black Intro., sec. 3;
Sandiman v. *Breach,* 7 Barn. & C. 96; *Regina* v. *Cleworth,* 4
Best & S. 927; *Kitchen* v. *Shaw,* 6 Adol. & E. 729; *Bramwell*
v. *Penneck,* 7 Barn. & C. 536: *Williams* v. *Golding,* L. R. 1
Com. P. 69; Broom's Maxims, 625; *Smith* v. *People,* 47 N. Y.
337; Allen, J., *Wakefield* v. *Fargo,* 90 N. Y. 213." Now, by
no possible construction could an attorney at law be included
under the term "clerk," and it is not unreasonable to suppose, looking to the subject matter with which the legislature
was dealing, and to the mischiefs it intended to remedy, that
the word "servant" was used in the sense in which it was
employed in the common law. "The first sort of servants
acknowledged by the laws of England are menial servants,
so called from being *intra mœnia,* or domestics. . . . .
Another species of servants are called apprentices (from *ap-
prendre,* to learn.) . . . . A third species of servants are laborers, who are only hired by the day or week, and do not live *intra
mœnia* as a part of the family. . . . . There is yet a fourth
species of servants, if they may be so called, being rather in
a superior, a ministerial capacity, such as stewards, factors,
bailiffs; whom, however, the law considers as servants *pro
tempore* with regard to such of their acts as affect their master's or employer's property": 1 Blackstone's Commentaries,
c. 14. "Besides these four sorts of servants may be mentioned: 5: Clerks and shopmen, who, however confidentially
[143] they may be employed, are servants in the eye of the law:
6. Merchant seamen; . . . . 7. Persons working in mills and
factories, or mines and collieries": 1 Broom & Hadley's Commentaries, c. 14. Taking these, for the reason suggested, to
be the senses in which the legislature used the term "servant," it is perfectly apparent that an attorney at law is not

included; and as the more general word "employee" must,
by reason of its association and collocation with the two preceding words, be restricted to a meaning synonymous with
their meaning, it follows of necessity that it cannot include a
person of a higher grade of service than the more limited
terms embrace. If this be so, as we think it is, then an attorney at law is not within the statute.

This conclusion is supported by many adjudications construing statutes of a kindred character. Thus, in *Gordon* v.
Jennings, L. R. 9 Q. B. Div. 45, it was held under 33 and 34
Vict., c. 30, which prohibited the attachment of the wages of
any servant, laborer, or workman, that a secretary who was
paid an annual salary in quarterly installments was not included. And in *Aikin* v. *Wasson*, 24 N. Y. 482, it was decided
that under section 10 of the General Railroad Act of 1850,
which made stockholders liable for all debts due or owing to
any of the company's laborers and servants for services performed for it, a contractor to build a part of the road was not
embraced. In *Coffin* v. *Reynolds*, 37 N. Y. 640, a secretary was
held not to be included under the terms "laborers," "servants," and "apprentices." In *Wakefield* v. *Fargo*, 90 N. Y. 213,
a book-keeper and general manager was held not within the
same words. In *People* v. *Remington*, 109 N. Y. 631, by
affirming the lower court, it was held that a superintendent
at an annual salary, an attorney at law, and salesmen on
salaries and commission, are not entitled to preference under
the statute. In *Tod* v. *Kentucky Union Ry. Co.*, 52 Fed.
Rep. 241, contractors were held not to be employees.

[144] But there is another ground upon which the decree
appealed from must be affirmed. We have said that the
items claimed as due and earned within three months prior
to the appointment of the receivers are charges for special
services, and in no sense for wages or salary at all. Obviously
for such fees, even under the widest construction that might
be given to the word "employee," a priority could not be
claimed. Thus, in the recent case of *Louisville etc. R. R. Co.*
v. *Wilson*, 138 U. S. 501, it appeared that a receiver of the
railway was appointed: That the order of appointment provided, "it is further ordered, adjudged, and decreed that the
said receiver, out of the income that shall come into his
hands from the operation of the said railway or otherwise, do
proceed to pay all just claims and accounts for labor, material, supplies, salaries of officers, and wages of employees that

may have been earned or furnished within six months prior
to January 1st, 1885." Mr. Wilson claimed to be paid for
services rendered by him as attorney. In disposing of his
claim the supreme court said: "With respect to the provision in the order of appointment, he claims to come under
the descriptive words therein used, 'wages of employees.'
. . . . On the meaning of the words 'wages of employees,'
he cites the case of *Gurney* v. *Atlantic etc. Ry. Co.*, 58 N. Y.
358, in which an order directing the receiver of a railway
company, thereby appointed, to pay debts owing to the laborers and employees for labor and services, was held broad
enough to include a debt due to Hon. Jeremiah S. Black for
professional services as counsel. Without criticising that
decision, or noticing the special circumstances which seemed
in the judgment of that court to justify the inclusion of professional services within the descriptive words of the appointment, we are of the opinion that the term 'wages of employees,' as used in the order now under consideration, does
not include the services of counsel employed for special purposes: *Vane* v. *Newcombe*, 132 U. S. 220. The terms 'officers'
and 'employees,' both alike refer to those in regular and
continual service. Within [145] the ordinary acceptation of
the terms, one who is engaged to render service in a particular
transaction is neither an officer nor an employee. They imply
continuity of service, and exclude those employed for a special and single transaction. An attorney of an individual,
retained for a single suit, is not his employee. It is true he
has engaged to render services; but his engagement is rather
that of a contractor than that of employee. The services of
the appellee, therefore, did not come within the order appointing the receiver." It will be seen from the above extract that
the supreme court declined to follow the case of *Gurney* v.
Atlantic etc. Ry. Co., 58 N. Y. 358. We may observe with
regard to Gurney's case that it was decided by but four of
the seven judges who sat, the other three having dissented;
and that it apparently ignores, in construing the word "employee," the principle to which we have already alluded, and
which Lord Hale concisely expressed in the phrase *noscitur
a sociis*, or, as applied in that case, that the coupling together
of the words "laborers" and "employees" in the order then
under consideration, indicated that the term "employee," as
there used, was designed to have no broader meaning than
its conjoined and associated term "laborer."

By a *pro forma* decree the circuit court of Baltimore city
adjudged that the appellant was "neither a clerk, servant, or
employee of the American Casualty Insurance & Security
Company of Baltimore, within the meaning of section 15 of
article 47 of the code," and that he was not entitled to any
priority of payment for any portion of his claim. For the
reasons we have assigned we are of opinion that this decree
is right, and we shall accordingly affirm it.

Decree affirmed, with costs above and below.

MASTER AND SERVANT.—RELATION OF, WHEN EXISTS: See the extended
note to *Brown* v. *Smith*, 22 Am. St. Rep. 459.

HOWSER *v.* CUMBERLAND & PENNSYLVANIA RAILROAD COMPANY.

[80 MARYLAND, 146.]

NEGLIGENCE—PRESUMPTION OF FROM ACCIDENT.—A presumption of negligence may arise from an accident, and if the circumstances are of such
a nature that it may be fairly inferred from them that the reasonable
probability is that the accident was caused by the failure of a party to
exercise proper caution, a presumption of negligence arises.

NEGLIGENCE.—PRESUMPTION OF FROM ACCIDENT.—The fact that one while
walking in a footpath beside the roadbed of a railroad, but not upon
its right of way, is injured by cross-ties, which fall from a car attached
to a train passing on such railroad and strike him, raises a presumption of negligence on the part of the railroad company.

ACTION to recover damages for personal injury. At the
close of plaintiff's case the court instructed the jury that
"upon the pleadings in the cause and the evidence given to
the jury by the plaintiff he is not entitled to recover." Verdict and judgment for defendant, and plaintiff appealed.

J. W. S. Cochrane, for the appellant.

R. H. Gordon and *H. K. Douglas*, for the appellee.

148 ROBERTS, J. This appeal brings before us for consideration a single question, yet one of interest and some importance, the determination of which is not entirely free from
difficulty. In the fall of 1892, whilst the defendant was
passing from the place of his employment to his home, he
walked over a footpath on the land of William E. Walsh, in
the city of Cumberland, which had been for twenty years

used by various persons. This path extended along the roadbed of the appellee, but not upon its right of way.

As the plaintiff proceeded on his way to his home the defendant's train was approaching on the outside track, the one nearest to him. Attached to the train was a gondola car loaded with railroad cross-ties; when the car containing the cross-ties got opposite to where he was walking, a part of the ties slipped off of the car and about half a dozen fell upon him and broke one of his legs in two places and otherwise injured him. In the testimony he says "he supposed there was a jar on the track."

The case was tried before a jury, the court, at the instance of the appellee, instructing them "that upon the pleadings in the cause and the evidence given to the jury the plaintiff was not entitled to recover." If the defendant was entitled to recover it was only because of the insufficiency of the proof offered by the plaintiff in that connection. We will now proceed to consider the instruction.

Whilst the general rule undoubtedly is that the burden of proof that the injury resulted from negligence on the part of the defendant is upon the plaintiff, yet in some cases "the very nature of the action may, of itself, and through the presumption it carries, supply the requisite proof": Wharton on Negligence, par. 421.

Thus, when the circumstances are, as in this case, of such a nature that it may be fairly inferred from them that the reasonable probability is that the accident was occasioned by the failure of the appellee to exercise proper caution which it readily could and should have done; and, in the [149] absence of satisfactory explanation on the part of the appellee, a presumption of negligence arises against it. In the case of *Byrne* v. *Boadle*, 2 Hurl. & C. 722, the plaintiff was walking in a public street past the defendant's shop, when a barrel of flour fell upon him from a window above the shop, and seriously injured him. The court held that these facts constituted sufficient *prima facie* evidence of negligence for the jury to cast on the defendant the onus of proving that the accident was not caused by his negligence. Pollock, C. B., said: "There are many accidents from which no presumption of negligence can arise, but this is not true in all cases. It is the duty of persons who keep barrels in a warehouse to take care that they do not roll out, and I think that such a case would, beyond all doubt, afford *prima facie* evidence of neg-

ligence. A barrel could not roll out of a warehouse without
some negligence. So, in building or repairing a house, if a
person passing along the road is injured by something falling
upon him, I think the accident would be *prima facie* evidence
of negligence."

Shortly after this decision a similar case, that of *Scott v.
London Dock Co.*, 3 Hurl. & C. 596, was decided in the exchequer chamber. The plaintiff proved in this case that
while in the discharge of his duties as a customs officer he
was passing in front of a warehouse in the dock, and was
felled to the ground by six bags of sugar falling upon him.
The court said: "There must be reasonable evidence of negligence. But where the thing is shown to be under the management of the defendant or his servants, and the accident is
such as, in the ordinary course of things, does not happen if
those who have the management use proper care, it affords
reasonable evidence, in the absence of explanation by the
defendant, that the accident arose from want of care."

Then followed the leading case of *Kearney v. London,
Brighton etc. Ry. Co.*, L. R. 5 Q. B. 411. This case under-
went great discussion, with a view to the settlement of the
true principle governing it. The facts were, [150] that the
plaintiff was passing on a highway under a railway bridge,
when a brick fell and injured him on the shoulder. A train
had passed over the bridge shortly before the accident. The
bridge had been built three years, and was an iron girder
bridge, resting on iron piers on one side and on a perpendic-
ular brick wall with pilasters on the other, and the brick fell
from the top of one of the pilasters, where one of the girders
rested on it. A motion was made for a nonsuit, on the ground
that there was no evidence of negligence to leave to a jury.
The court of queen's bench, by a divided vote, held that this
was a case to which the maxim *res ipsa loquitur* was applicable; or, in other words, that there was *prima facie* evidence
of negligence. Kelly, C. B., delivering the opinion on the
appeal, said: "We are all agreed that the judgment of the
queen's bench must be affirmed. . . . . The question, therefore, is, whether there was any evidence of negligence on the
part of the defendants, and by that we all understand such
an amount of evidence as to fairly and reasonably support
the finding of the jury. The lord chief justice, in his judgment in the court below, said *res ipsa loquitur*, and I cannot
do better than to refer to that judgment. It appears, without

contradiction, that a brick fell out of the pier of the bridge without any assignable cause, except the slight vibration caused by a passing train. This, we think, is not only evidence, but conclusive evidence, that it was loose; for otherwise so slight a vibration could not have struck it out of its place. No doubt it is humanly possible that the percussion of the iron girder, arising from expansion and contraction, might have gradually shaken out the mortar, and so loosened the brick; but this is merely conjecture. The bridge had been built two or three years, and it was the duty of the defendants, from time to time, to inspect the bridge, and ascertain that the brickwork was in good order, and all the bricks well secured. If there were necessity for other evidence the case is made still stronger by the evidence of the plaintiff, which was uncontradicted on the part of the defendants, that, after the accident, on fitting [151] the brick to its place, several other bricks were found to have fallen out."

And, again, in the case of *Briggs* v. *Oliver*, 4 Hurl. & C. 403, the plaintiff, going to a doorway of a house in which the defendant had offices, was pushed out of the way by his servant, who was watching a packing-case belonging to his master and was leaning against the wall of the house. The plaintiff fell, and the packing-case fell on his foot and injured him. There was no evidence as to who placed the packing-case against the wall or who caused it to fall. The court held that there was a *prima facie* case against the defendant to go to the jury.

We have made full reference to the foregoing cases as showing the views of the English courts upon this question. These and many other English and American cases clearly establish the fact that it is not requisite that the plaintiff's proof, in actions of this kind, should negative all possible circumstances which would excuse the defendant, but it is sufficient if it negatives all probable circumstances which would have this effect: Thompson on Negligence, 1229. It is also well settled that the cause of accident must be connected with the defendant, either by direct evidence that it is his act, or that it is under his control, before it can be presumed that he has been negligent: *Higgs* v. *Maynard*, 12 Jur., N. S., 705; *Welfare* v. *L. B. & S. C. Ry. Co.*, L. R. 4 Q. B. 693; *Smith* v. *Great Eastern Ry. Co.*, L. R. 2 Com. P. 10. When, however, there is no duty upon the plaintiff, as under the facts of this case, or when the duty which he has to per-

form has been performed by him, it is clear that the negligence of the plaintiff is out of the question, and if the
accident is connected with the defendant the question whether
the phrase "*res ipsa loquitur*" applies or not becomes a question of common sense: Whittaker's Smith on Negligence, 422.

The American cases sustaining the maxim *res ipsa loquitur*
are numerous and to the point. In the case of *Cummings* v.
National Furnace Co., 60 Wis. 603, the defendant company
¹⁵² was engaged in unloading iron ore from a vessel by
means of a crane to which was attached a bucket. Whilst
so engaged the bucket tipped and threw its contents upon a
seaman lawfully working upon the deck of the vessel. The
court said: "The accident itself was of such a character as
raised a presumption of negligence either in the character of
the machinery used or in the care with which it was handled,
and as the jury found the fault was not with the machinery,
it follows that it must have been in the handling, otherwise
there is no rational cause shown for its happening.

The leading American case, however, appears to be *Mullen*
v. *St. John*, 57 N. Y. 567; 15 Am. Rep. 530. The opinion of
the court was delivered by Dwight, C., and is a most able
and exhaustive examination of the subject. He cites with
approval many of the English and American cases, to which
reference is made in this opinion. The case was one in
which the walls of a building, without any special circumstances of storm or violence, fell into one of the streets of
the city of Brooklyn, knocking down the plaintiff, who was
on the sidewalk, and seriously injuring her. The court said:
"There was some evidence tending to show that it was out
of repair. Without laying any stress upon the affirmative
testimony, it is as impossible to conceive of this building so
falling, unless it was badly constructed or in bad repair, as
it is to suppose that a seaworthy ship would go to the bottom
in a tranquil sea and without collision. The mind necessarily
seeks for a cause for the fall. That is apparently the bad
condition of the structure. This again leads to the inference
of negligence, which the defendant should rebut."

To like effect are *Lyons* v. *Rosenthal*, 11 Hun, 46; *Edgerton*
v. *New York etc. R. R. Co.*, 39 N. Y. 227; *Kirst* v. *Milwaukee*
etc. Ry. Co., 46 Wis. 489; *Smith* v. *Boston Gas Light Co.*, 129
Mass. 318; *Clare* v. *National City Bank*, 1 Sweeny, 539;
Brehm v. *Great Western R. R. Co.*, 34 Barb. 256; *Sullivan* v.
Vicksburg etc. R. R. Co., 39 La. Ann. 800; 4 Am. St. Rep.

239; *Hays v. Gallagher*, 72 Pa. St. 136; [153] *Thomas* v. *Western Union Tel. Co.*, 100 Mass. 156; *Dixon* v. *Pluns*, 98 Cal. 384; 35 Am. St. Rep. 180.

We have referred to numerous cases as illustrating the views which we entertain, because the question on this appeal has not heretofore been determined by this court. Cases resting in contract have frequently received our consideration, and they are generally free from difficulty, because the mere happening of the accident will be *prima facie* evidence of a breach of contract without further proof, while in those not resting in contract " it must not only appear that the accident happened, but the surrounding circumstances must be such as to raise the presumption of a failure of duty on the part of the defendant toward the plaintiff ": Article, Res Ipsa Loquitur, by Judge Seymour D. Thompson in 10 Central Law Journal, 261. None of the cases herein relate to those resting in contract.

. In all cases of the character we have been considering, the most careful scrutiny should be given to the circumstances attending the accident, and whilst an excellent authority has said that after all the question resolves itself into one of common sense, we would add that it should be of a high order. For it is unquestionably true that the authorities are by no means in accord on the question which arises out of the doctrine of *res ipsa loquitur.*

The facts of this appeal are very meager, but they by no means lie on the border line, nor even close to it. Here you find the plaintiff traversing a path over which the defendant had no dominion, for the plaintiff was rightfully there. The defendant moves its cars over its roadway along said path, and from a gondola car there slips a half dozen railroad cross-ties, falling upon the plaintiff and seriously injuring him.

The plaintiff was guilty of no negligence in being where we was at the time he was injured, and in so far as the defendant's rights are involved, the principle is the same whether he was on the land of Mr. Walsh or on his own land. The accident happened at the hour of noon, as the [154] plaintiff was on his way to his dinner. There is no contention that it did not happen just as the plaintiff has himself represented. The plaintiff had no control over, nor was he in any way connected with, the loading or management of the cars or trains upon defendant's road.

If the cross-ties had been properly loaded there existed no reasonable probability of their falling off. A cross-tie is defined to be a sleeper, connecting and supporting the parallel rails of a railroad: Standard Dictionary, 444. Its figures and dimensions are familiar, and its flat surfaces and weight illustrate how readily they can be loaded so as to form an almost compact body of wood, if reasonable care be exercised in placing them on the flat bottom of the car, and proper lateral support be given them. If by accident the ties had become displaced, it was a duty incumbent upon the defendant and its servants to have readjusted them in such manner as to have prevented the happening of an accident. It was the duty of the defendant and its servants to have carefully loaded said cross-ties upon its cars, and it was equally its duty to have exercised reasonable care in seeing that its train was transported in such condition as to avoid all reasonable probability of injury.

If the presumption arising out of the doctrine of *res ipsa loquitur* finds proper application any where, we think this is a case in which it should be applied. In conclusion, taking the proof as we find it in the record, we think the case should have been permitted to go to the jury with proper instructions from the court. The judgment must be reversed.

Judgment reversed and new trial awarded.

MR. JUSTICE MCSHERRY dissented, stating that he considered it the settled law of Maryland, when the relation of carrier and passenger does not exist, no presumption of negligence can ever arise from the mere fact that an accident has happened and an injury been sustained. When no contractual relation exists between the parties the mere occurrence of an accident resulting in injury furnishes no evidence of causative negligence.

It is incumbent on the plaintiff in such cases not only to show injury, but also to show that the defendant has been guilty of some negligence which is the proximate cause producing such injury. Without such proof no recovery can be had. In the present case no relation of carrier and passenger existed between the plaintiff and defendant. There was no proof of any antecedent negligence on the part of the defendant, and no proof as to what caused the cross-ties to fall from the train and produce the accident and injury complained of.

Under these circumstances, and in the absence of proof of some negligence on the part of the defendant, the court below properly instructed the jury that the plaintiff was not entitled to recover.

Mr. Justice FOWLER concurred in the dissenting opinion expressed by Mr. Justice McSherry.

NEGLIGENCE—PRESUMPTION OF FROM HAPPENING OF ACCIDENT. — This
question is thoroughly discussed in the extended note to *Philadelphia etc.
R. R. Co.* v. *Anderson,* 20 Am. St. Rep. 490; *Huey* v. *Gahlenbeck,* 6 Am. St.
Rep. 794, and the note to *Fleming* v. *Pittsburgh etc. Ry.,* 38 Am. St. Rep.
837.

DEEMS *v.* MAYOR OF BALTIMORE.

[80 MARYLAND, 164.]

INJUNCTION LIES TO RESTRAIN ENFORCEMENT OF MUNICIPAL ORDINANCE
admitted to be invalid, the execution of which injuriously affects private rights.

POLICE POWER — INSPECTION AND DESTRUCTION OF MILK — DUE PROCESS
OF LAW.—Under a statute authorizing a city to provide for the inspection and to regulate the sale of milk, a municipal ordinance providing
for the inspection of milk offered for sale in such city, forbidding the
sale of milk not coming up to a standard or test of purity prescribed,
and authorizing an inspector to destroy all milk found by him to be
impure according to such standard, is a valid exercise of the police
power of the city and state.

CONSTITUTIONAL LAW—DUE PROCESS OF LAW—POLICE POWER.—A constitutional guarantee against the taking of private property without due
process of law cannot be construed as abridging or interfering with the
power of a state or city to pass such laws or ordinances as may be
necessary to protect the health and provide for the safety and good
order of society.

MUNICIPAL ORDINANCES.—VALIDITY.—Under a statute authorizing a city.
to provide by ordinance for the inspection and regulation of the sale of
milk within the city limits, and to provide a fine of not more than one
hundred dollars for each violation of such ordinance, an ordinance
passed in pursuance of the power thus conferred, imposing a fine of not
more than fifty dollars for each violation of its provisions, is valid.

BILL for an injunction to restrain the taking and destruction of milk under and by virtue of the provisions of a
municipal ordinance alleged to be void. This appeal is from
an order of the court below sustaining a demurrer to the
bill.

T. C. Weeks, for the appellant.

*T. G. Hayes, city counselor, and W. S. Bryan, Jr., city
solicitor,* for the appellee.

170 ROBINSON, C. J. In addition to the general powers
conferred on the mayor and city council by section 378,
article 4, of the Code of Public Local Laws, to pass ordinances to preserve the health of the city, the act of 1894,
chapter 53, expressly authorizes them to provide by ordi-

nance for the proper inspection of milk and all other food products offered for sale in the city, and to make such regulations in regard to the sale of the same as they may deem necessary to protect the public health.

It was in pursuance of these powers that ordinance No. 87, now in question, was passed. This ordinance makes it unlawful for any person to sell or offer for sale "any impure, adulterated, sophisticated, or unwholesome milk or other food products." It further provides that only pure, unadulterated, unsophisticated, and wholesome milk shall be sold, and that such article shall be understood to be the natural product of healthy cows, and which has not been deprived of any part of its cream, and to which no additional liquid or solid preservative has been added, [171] and which, at a temperature of 60° Fahrenheit, shall have a specific gravity of not less than 1.029, and not less than twelve per cent of total solids, and not less than three per cent of butter fats. And all milk kept or offered for sale in the city which shall not come up to the standard thus prescribed shall be considered impure, adulterated, sophisticated, or unwholesome.

And the ordinance also provides that the term "adulterated" shall be construed to mean any artificial addition to normal constituents, and the term "sophisticated" to mean the substitution of one product for another, or any abstraction of or artificial change in the normal constituents, and the term "unwholesome" to mean deleterious to health, etc. And it further provides for the appointment of a competent analytical chemist, who shall make such chemical and microscopical examinations as may be required under the ordinance, and for the appointment also of three inspectors of food.

And section 6, as amended, provides: " And milk or food products in the possession of the person or persons so violating, disobeying, refusing, or neglecting to comply with the provisions of this ordinance may be confiscated and destroyed by the inspector examining the same."

The bill of complaint alleges that the appellant is a dairyman, and conducts a retail business for the sale of milk, and that in the pursuit of his business he daily serves milk from his wagons to his customers at their homes in the city.

That on or about the 16th of July, 1894, Patrick R. Welsh, inspector, and William P. Tonry, analyst, on the public highway, took certain milk, the property of the appellant,

"and without making any chemical or microscopical examination thereof, and without due process of law, poured the
said milk out upon the streets and down the gutters of the
city; thereby wasting and destroying the said milk."

The bill also alleges that the said Patrick R. Welsh and
William P. Tonry, under the direction of the board of health,
and under color of ordinance No. 87 as amended, publicly
declared their intention to destroy the milk of the appellant
172 and others, which, after an inspection by them, made by
means of a certain mechanical instrument known as a "lactometer," and by a test taken with "litmus" paper, they
shall conclude not to be of the standard prescribed by the
ordinance. The bill further alleges that the ordinance is an
undue and excessive exercise of the corporation's legislative
powers as conferred by law, and that section 6, as amended,
as absolutely void and no effect.

Besides the general relief the bill prays that an injunction
be issued restraining the mayor and city council, and all
the other defendants, from taking and destroying, without
chemical or microscopical examination first made, and without due process of law first had, any milk or other dairy
product, the property of the complainant, etc.

We cannot agree with the counsel for the appellee that a
court of equity has no jurisdiction to restrain the appellee in
the enforcement of the ordinance in question, even though it
may be conceded to be invalid, and that its execution would
affect injuriously the rights of the appellant and others.   In
Page v. *Mayor etc.*, 34 Md. 558, and in *Holland* v. *Mayor etc.*,
11 Md. 186, 69 Am. Dec. 195, and in other cases, we have
said that "where an ordinance is void, and its provisions are
about to be enforced, any party whose interests are to be injuriously affected thereby may and properly ought to go into
a court of equity. and have the execution of the ordinance
stayed by injunction."

An action at law, it is true, would not lie against the city
authorities to recover damages for the wrongful acts of its
officers in the execution of the ordinance, and for the reason
that the police power to pass such ordinance is delegated by
the state to be exercised not for the benefit or in the interest
of the city in its corporate capacity, but for the public good:
Boehm v. *Mayor etc.*, 61 Md. 259.   There is a broad distinction, however, between an action at law against the city
authorities to recover damages for the wrongful acts of its

officers, and the power of a court of equity to restrain the enforcement of an ordinance admitted to be [173] invalid, and the execution of which affects injuriously private rights.

Nor can there be any question as to the power of the appellee to provide by ordinance for the inspection of milk offered for sale within its corporate limits, and to forbid the sale of any milk which does not come up to the standard or test prescribed by the ordinance. And the real question, it seems to us, under the demurrer is, whether it has the power to direct that milk which is found upon inspection not to come up to the standard, as thus prescribed, shall be destroyed.

What is termed the police power has been the subject of a good deal of consideration by both the federal and state courts, and all agree that it is a difficult matter to define the limits within which it is to be exercised. Every well-organized government has the inherent right to protect the health and provide for the safety and welfare of its people. It has not only the right, but it is a duty and obligation which the sovereign power owes to the public, and as no one can foresee the emergency or necessity which may call for its exercise, it is not an easy matter to prescribe the precise limits within which it may be exercised. It may be said to rest upon the maxim, "*Salus populi suprema lex,*" and the constitutional guarantees for the security of private rights relied on by the appellant have never been understood as interfering with the power of the state to pass such laws as may be necessary to protect the health and provide for the safety and good order of society. "Property of every kind," says Mr. Justice Story, "is held subject to those general regulations which are necessary for the common good and general welfare. And the legislature has the power to define the mode and manner in which every one may use his property": 2 Story on the Constitution.

And in the late case of *Mugler* v. *Kansas*, 123 U. S. 623, after considering the constitutional limitations which declare that no person shall be deprived of his property or liberty without due process of law, the supreme court says these [174] limitations "have never been construed as being incompatible with the principle equally vital, because so essential to the peace and safety, that all property in this country is held under the implied obligation that the owner's use of it shall not be injurious to the community."

To justify such interference with private rights its exercise must have for its immediate object the promotion of the public good, and, so far as may be practicable, every effort should be made to adjust the conflicting rights of the public and the private rights of individuals.   At the same time the emergency may be so great, and the danger to be averted so imminent, that private rights must yield to the paramount safety of the public, and to await, in such cases, the delay necessarily incident to ordinary judicial inquiry, in the determination of private rights, would defeat altogether the object and purposes for which the exercise of this salutary power was invoked.   Whatever injury or inconvenience one may suffer in such cases, he is, in the eye of the law, compensated by sharing the common benefit resulting from the summary exercise of this power, and which, under the circumstances, was absolutely necessary for the protection of the public.

The use of milk as an article of food enters largely, as we all know, in the daily consumption of every household, and there is no more fruitful source of disease than the use of adulterated and unwholesome milk.   And if the appellant's contention be right, that the question whether or not milk, which is daily offered for sale in every part of a large and populous city, comes up to the standard prescribed by the ordinance, must be determined by the ordinary process of judicial investigation, or by chemical analysis, it would be impossible to prevent the danger to the public health necessarily resulting from impure and unwholesome milk.   And it is absolutely necessary, therefore, that the appellee should have power to provide for its inspection by proper means and instruments, and if, upon such inspection, it shall be found not to come up to the standard prescribed by the [175] ordinance, to direct that the offending thing shall be destroyed.

The exercise of such a power is, we think, fully sustained both on principle and authority.   In *Blazier* v. *Miller*, 10 Hun, 435, an ordinance, like the one now before us, authorized the inspector to destroy milk offered for sale, which, upon inspection, was found to be below the proper standard, was sustained on the ground that the destruction of the offending thing was necessary to prevent the imminent danger to life and health, which would result from the use of impure milk.   And in *Mugler* v. *Kansas*, 123 U. S. 623, to which we have heretofore referred, Mr. Justice Harlan says: " The exercise of the police power by the destruction of property, which is itself a public nuisance, or the prohibition of its use in a particular way, whereby its value becomes depreciated, is very different from taking property for public use, or from depriving a person of his property without due process of law."

It is in the exercise of this power that quarantine laws which not only interfere with private rights, but with the liberty of persons, are passed; and also laws which provide for the destruction of infected clothing, to prevent the spread of contagious diseases. And as to the extent and the summary manner in which this power may be exercised to protect the public health, we may refer to *Boehm* v. *Mayor etc.* 61 Md. 264; *Train* v. *Boston Disinfecting Co.*, 144 Mass. 523; 59 Am. Rep. 113; and *Newark etc. Ry. Co.* v. *Hunt*, 50 N. J. L. 308.

The act of 1894, authorizing the appellee to provide for the inspection of milk, and to make such regulations in regard to the same as it may deem necessary, also authorizes the appellee to provide, by a fine of not more than one hundred dollars, for the punishment of all persons violating such regulations. The amount of the fine was left to the discretion of the appellee; provided, however, it was not to exceed one hundred dollars. The ordinance in question provided a fine of not more than fifty dollars, as a punishment for persons violating its provisions, and as the amount [176] of the fine, not to exceed, however, one hundred dollars, was left to its discretion, there can be no objection to the ordinance on this ground.

Order affirmed.   ——

INJUNCTION TO RESTRAIN ENFORCEMENT OF VOID MUNICIPAL ORDINANCE. — A court of equity has jurisdiction to enjoin the enforcement of a city ordinance having for its purpose the destruction of the franchise of a railroad company in which the public has an interest, where the injury to the company will be irreparable: *Port of Mobile* v. *Louisville etc. R. R. Co.*, 84 Ala. 115; 5 Am. St. Rep. 342, and note. The enactment of a void ordinance will not ordinarily be enjoined. The restrictive powers of the courts should be directed against the enforcement rather than the passage of such ordinances: *Stevens* v. *St. Mary's Training School*, 144 Ill. 336; 36 Am. St. Rep. 438.

POLICE POWER — INSPECTION OF MILK. — A law prohibiting the sale of adulterated milk, or milk to which water or any foreign substance has been added, or the sale as pure milk of any milk from which the cream has been removed, is valid: *State* v. *Campbell*, 64 N. H. 402; 10 Am. St. Rep. 419, and note with the cases collected.

MUNICIPAL CORPORATIONS—POWER TO PRESERVE HEALTH AND SAFETY OF ITS INHABITANTS.—The legislature, by the act authorizing the organization of a municipal corporation, expressly delegates to the municipality the power to preserve the health and safety of its inhabitants: *Crawfordsville v. Braden,* 130 Ind. 149; 30 Am. St. Rep. 214; *Charleston v. Werner,* 38 S. C. 488; 37 Am. St. Rep. 776, and note.

CITY & SUBURBAN RAILWAY CO. v. MOORES.

[80 MARYLAND, 348.]

INDEPENDENT CONTRACTOR — LIABILITY FOR NEGLIGENCE OF. — Although work is being performed by an independent contractor, and an injury to a third person is caused by the negligence of his servants, yet the party for whom the work is being done is liable if the injury is such as might have been anticipated by him as a probable consequence of the work let to the contractor, or if it is of such character as must result in creating a nuisance, or if he owes a duty to third persons or the public in the performance of the work.

INDEPENDENT CONTRACTORS—NEGLIGENCE OF—LIABILITY FOR.—The use of a steam-engine by an independent contractor on a turnpike road for hauling materials to be used in repairs or improvements is not a nuisance *per se,* and does not render a turnpike company, for whom the work is being done, liable to a third person for the negligence of the servants of such independent contractor.

G. D. Penniman and M. W. Offutt, for the appellant.

J. Grason and J. S. Ensor, for the appellees.

[352] BOYD, J. This suit was instituted by Minnie Moores and her husband against the City & Suburban Railway Company for injuries sustained by her through the alleged negligence of the defendant's agents. Whilst she was driving along the Baltimore and Yorktown Turnpike Road her horse was frightened at a steam-engine, which was being used for hauling cars containing ballast to be put on the tracks of the railway company. The defendant introduced in evidence two contracts between the president, managers, and company of the Baltimore and Yorktown Turnpike Road and one James B. White, by which the latter contracted to do certain work for the turnpike company, including the delivery of broken stone to be used in ballasting and back-filling the railway tracks constructed on the pike, and also in macadamizing the pike, and claims that the work was being done under these contracts by White as an independent contractor.

The defendant offered two prayers, which were refused by

the cour\ below, which raise the only questions presented for our c>nsideration. The first prayer asked that the jury be instructed that if they found there was a contract between the turnpike company and White for doing certain work upon and adjacent to the bed of said turnpike offered in evidence; that said White conducted the work under the terms of said contract, without any interference on the part of the turnpike company or the defendant in [353] mode or manner of doing the work; and that the injury complained of resulted from the running of an engine engaged in the prosecution of the work, which belonged to and was under the control of said White, then the plaintiff could not recover. The second asked the court to instruct the jury that if they found that the turnpike company and White entered into the agreements offered in evidence to do certain work therein set out; that in the prosecution of the work White used approved and ordinary machinery, and employed competent and skillful workmen in the management and conduct of said machinery; that the work was superintended with the usual and ordinary care incident to the same; that the injury complained of was done during the prosecution of the work in the manner testified to by the plaintiff's witnesses; that the employees in, on, and about said engine were selected and employed by White, and were under his exclusive control, then the plaintiff could not recover, although the jury may believe the whistle was blown on the engine as testified to by plaintiff's witnesses.

It will be observed that both of these prayers go upon the theory that White was a contractor to perform the work being done, which resulted in the alleged injury to Mrs. Moores, independent of and free from any control of the company as to how the work should be done, and hence the defendant was not responsible for the negligence of the servants of White. The general principles applicable to a case where work is to be done by a contractor, upon his own responsibility, who is not subject to the control of the employer as to the manner in which it is to be performed, are so familiar and well established that it would be useless to go into any extended discussion of them. The difficulty generally is to determine who is to be regarded as the master of the wrongdoer under the facts arising in the particular case before the court, and whether there is any such relation existing between the person for whom the work is to be done and the negligent party as to hold the former [354] responsible for damages sustained by third persons through such negligence. Even if the relation of principal and agent, or master and servant, do not, strictly speaking, exist, yet the person for whom the work is done may still be liable if the injury is such as might have been anticipated by him, as a probable consequence of the work let out to the contractor, or, if it be of such character as must result in creating a nuisance, or, if he owes a duty to third persons or the public in the execution of the work.

This case presents some further questions peculiar to itself from the fact that the defendant is not a party to the contracts offered in evidence, so far as disclosed by them, and in this respect differs from the cases cited in argument. The testimony, however, is that the road was being constructed by White, at the time of the accident, for the defendant, and that the work was done under these contracts. It is true that there was nothing in the record to show just what the relations between the turnpike company and the defendant were, or how the latter became interested in the contract.

The railway company may have been an undisclosed principal, as contended by the appellant's counsel; the turnpike company may have owned the railway tracks when the contracts were made, or it may, as the owner of the turnpike road, have contracted for the work to be done on the railway tracks whilst doing the other work for it mentioned in the agreement, under some arrangement with the railroad company. But, however this may be, if the jury believed the work was being done by White under these contracts, we must assume, in order to enable the plaintiff to recover at all, that it was being done for the defendant, and must connect it with the contract. If that be not done, then clearly the defendant is not liable to the plaintiffs, and their only remedy would be against White or the turnpike company, if it is not relieved on the ground that White was an independent contractor.

The mere fact that the railway company owned the [355] tracks on which the engine was being run in performance of those contracts would not make it liable, and it would not be connected with the act which caused the injury to Mrs. Moores, for its mere permission to the turnpike company or its contractor to use the railroad tracks would not make it responsible. If, for example, White had simply contracted to deliver this stone for the purposes of the turnpike company in macadamizing its road, and the engine was being used for that at the time of the accident, it could not be successfully contended that the use of its tracks would have made the defendant liable. We must, therefore, treat the defendant as a party to the contracts, at least as a party having work done for it under them, in disposing of the prayers. Of course, it was for the jury to determine whether, as a matter of fact, the work was being done for White under the contracts, which facts the prayers submitted to the jury.

One way of testing the liability of the defendant is to ascertain whether the turnpike company would have been liable, if it had been sued by the plaintiffs. Under the law, as settled in this state by the case of *Deford* v. *State*, 30 Md. 179, and the numerous decisions elsewhere, many of which are collected together in Wood on Railroads, edition of 1894, page 1152, it would seem clear that White was an independent contractor, and hence the turnpike company would not be responsible by reason of any such relation as master and servant. But, if that be conceded, the question arises whether it owed such a duty to the public, as a turnpike company, as to require it to see that no injury be sustained by persons traveling over its road, through the negligence of the servants of the contractor employed to do the work. It was said by the court in *Baltimore etc. Road* v. *Parks*, 74 Md. 282, that this turnpike company was bound to keep its road in proper repair and safe condition, just as municipal corporations are required to see that their public roads and streets are kept safe for travelers. In *Mayor etc.* v. *O'Donnell*, 53 Md. 110, 36 Am. Rep. 395, the city of Baltimore was held liable for an accident which [356] resulted from a rope being stretched across the street which was being repaired. A lantern had been hung on the rope, but was shortly afterward broken by some boys and not replaced. The city claimed freedom from liability, because the work was being done by an independent contractor, but it was held responsible, because of the duty imposed on it to have the work done properly, and have precautions against accident observed. In the case of *Water Company* v. *Ware*, 16 Wall. 566, the liability of the employer who owes a duty to the public, either under the law or by contract, is fully discussed, and there are many cases in this country and England on this subject. They are to the effect that "when the employer owes certain duties to third persons or to the public in the execution of a work, he cannot relieve himself from liability to the extent of that duty, by committing the work to a contractor."

The evidence of Kinsley, the superintendent in charge for White, shows that "the machinery used in and about the work was of the ordinary kind used for such purposes"; and contract No. 2 requires the contractor "to make all necessary connections with present track to run cars to crusher." We think, therefore, that the turnpike company had reason to believe a steam-engine would be used in the execution of the work. But the use of the steam-engine on that road was not a nuisance *per se*, and there was no such obligation on the turnpike company to the plaintiff or to the public as to prohibit it from using or permitting it to be used for hauling material for repairs or improvements. There was, therefore, no reason why that company could not make these contracts with White, although it knew he was going to use a steam-engine such as this. In *Water Co.* v. *Ware*, 16 Wall. 566, although the plaintiff's horse was frightened by the alleged negligent use of a steam-drill, yet the injury sustained was really caused by the material, dirt, etc., which had been left in the street, and which came within the duty of the defendant to persons traveling on the streets to see that they were kept safe. So in *Mayor etc.* v. *O'Donnell*, [357] 53 Md. 110; 36 Am. Rep. 395. If Mrs. Moores had been injured by piles of stone or other material negligently left in the road by the contractor, then a different question might arise. But the evidence shows that the injury was sustained by the negligent use of the engine in not stopping it, and in blowing the whistle as she approached.

It would be carrying the obligation of the turnpike company beyond that required or authorized by the authorities to hold that its duty to the public required it to see that the servants of White were not thus negligent, although the use of the steam-engine was not a nuisance *per se*, and could be operated so as not likely to do any injury to any one using the road. It would be requiring too much of it to make it take such precautions against accidents when letting out lawful work to an independent contractor. It must be admitted that the work to be done was lawful, and the company had the right to assume that there would not be such negligence as that complained of, which was entirely collateral to and not a probable consequence of the work con-tracted for. To hold the company to such a strict liability would practically forbid it from having such work done by contractors as it would have to keep its own agents on engines to see that there was no negligence on the part of the con-tractors or their servants.

As there was no such duty resting on the turnpike com-pany it follows *a fortiori* that there was none such on the appellant. As we have determined that White should be treated as an independent contractor with the turnpike com-pany, and that the railway company must be regarded as a party to the contracts, if the jury found that the work was being done under them we think the second prayer should have been granted. The first is, perhaps, too general, although intended to raise the same question, but, as there was error in refusing the second, we must therefore reverse the judg-ment.

Judgment reversed and new trial awarded.

MASTER AND SERVANT—LIABILITY OF MASTER FOR NEGLIGENCE OF IN-DEPENDENT CONTRACTOR.—If a person employs an independent contractor to do work for his benefit, which in the ordinary mode of doing it he, as a prudent man, has reason to believe is a nuisance, he is liable for injuries resulting from it to third persons: *James* v. *McMinimy,* 93 Ky. 471; 40 Am. St. Rep. 200, and note. When work to be performed is necessarily dan-gerous and an obligation rests on the employer to keep the place in a safe condition, he is answerable for injury resulting from the dangerous condi-tion in which the work is left, though it is being done by an independent contractor: *Omaha* v. *Jensen,* 35 Neb. 68; 37 Am. St. Rep. 432, and note. See, also, the extended note to *Stone* v. *Cheshire R. R. Corp.,* 51 Am. Dec. 200.

NATIONAL UNION BANK *v.* NATIONAL MECHANICS' BANK.

[80 MARYLAND, 371.]

ASSIGNMENT FOR BENEFIT OF CREDITORS—RIGHTS OF CREDITOR HOLDING COLLATERAL.—In case of an assignment for the benefit of creditors, a creditor who holds collateral security for his debt is entitled to partici-pate in the distribution of the insolvent estate only to the amount of his debt remaining due after deducting the value of his collaterals.

ASSIGNMENT FOR BENEFIT OF CREDITORS—RIGHTS OF CREDITOR HOLDING COLLATERAL.—A creditor who, after the execution of an assignment for the benefit of creditors, sells collaterals held by him as security for his debt, is entitled to participate in the distribution of the insolvent estate only to the extent of the balance remaining due him.

PARTNERSHIP—REAL PROPERTY—RIGHTS OF CREDITORS.—Persons dealing with the members of a partnership have a right, in the absence of some notice or knowledge to the contrary, to assume that public records, showing certain real estate to be the individual property of the members of the firm, inform them correctly as to the ownership of the property, notwithstanding the private understanding between the partners themselves.

PARTNERSHIP REAL ESTATE.—PARTNERS cannot so change the character of real estate originally owned by them as individuals, and not in any way derived from the partnership, as to give priority to firm creditors over separate creditors, simply by making entries in their books and treating it between themselves as partnership property.

PARTNERSHIP REAL ESTATE, WHETHER FIRM OR INDIVIDUAL PROPERTY.— If real property is not purchased with partnership funds for partnership purposes, but is, as far as the public records show, the separate property of the individual partner, and not incident to the business of the firm, the fact that the partners have entered it on the firm books, and treated it as firm property, is not sufficient to change it into partnership property, and, if sold, the proceeds should be applied to the payment of the claims of individual creditors before those of partnership creditors.

PARTNERSHIP REAL ESTATE, WHETHER FIRM OR INDIVIDUAL PROPERTY. If real estate connected with a partnership business necessary for the convenient and proper conduct of the business is treated by the partners as partnership property, is put into the firm business as part of the common stock, and so entered on the firm books as to comply with the statute of frauds, the partnership creditors should have priority over the general creditors of the individual partners in the distribution of the proceeds of the sale of such property, provided it was so used as to give notice to individual creditors that it was treated as partnership property and substantially involved in the partnership business.

PARTNERSHIP—ASSIGNMENT FOR BENEFIT OF CREDITORS—RIGHTS OF CREDITOR—ESTOPPEL.—After a partnership has made an assignment for the benefit of creditors, one who is both a firm and an individual creditor, and who has recommended the ratification of the assignee's sale of certain real estate, is not thereby estopped to claim that such land is not partnership property, as against one who has procured such recommendation by assurances that the creditor's claim would not be affected thereby.

ESTOPPEL IN PAIS CAN BE SET UP and relied upon only by a party who has actually been misled to his injury.

J. N. Steele, W. H. Buckler, J. E. Semmes, and F. K. Carey, for the appellant.

R. Barton, W. Reynolds, and S. Wilmer, for the appellees.

351 BOYD, J. In October, 1893, George W. S. Hoffman, W. E. Hoffman, and John W. Hoffman, partners, trading under the firm name of W. H. Hoffman & Sons, executed a deed of trust, in which their wives joined, to John B. Ramsay and Simon P. Schott, by which they conveyed all their

property, "including all of the joint stock of the copartnership and all of the separate estate of each of the partners in
trust, for the payment of partnership and individual creditors, according to their respective rights and interest therein."

The circuit court of Baltimore city assumed jurisdiction of
the trust, and, after the sale of the property, which will be
more particularly hereafter referred to, an audit was made
distributing the proceeds of sales, etc.   The appellant held,
at the time of the assignment, two notes of the firm, each
being for the sum of five thousand dollars, and indorsed by
George W. S. Hoffman and J. W. Hoffman, individually.
With each note there were deposited bonds of the Gunpowder
Valley Railroad Company, of the par value of seven thousand
five hundred dollars, as collateral security, with the usual
authority to the bank to sell at public or private sale, in case
of default.   The appellant filed its claim for the amount of
the notes, together with costs of protests, against the estates
of the firm and of the individual indorsers.   The National
Mechanics' Bank of Baltimore excepted to the allowance by
the auditor of the claim of appellant, because it had not credited the value of the collateral security held by it, and the
appellant excepted to the audit for the reason, as it alleges,
that the real estate held and owned by the three members of
the firm was their individual property, and not partnership
assets.

³⁸² An agreement was filed in which certain facts are ad-
mitted, and the court below was authorized to pass a *pro
forma* order sustaining the exceptions to the claim of the
appellant and overruling those filed by it.   A *pro forma* order
was accordingly passed, and an appeal taken to this court.

The principal questions presented for our consideration are:
1. Is the appellant entitled to a distribution on its whole
claim, without crediting the value of the securities held by
it as collateral?   2. Is the real estate held by the members
of this firm to be treated as partnership or individual property, so far as the appellant is concerned?

If the appellant had sold the securities held by it between
the dates of the assignment and the distribution there could
be no question about the right of the trustees or the creditors
to require it to credit its claim with the net proceeds of such
sale.   The case of *Third Nat. Bank* v. *Lanahan,* 66 Md. 461,
has established that as the law of this state, whatever may be
the effect of the decisions elsewhere, cited by the appellant,

and it is a just and equitable rule. Such being the case, would there be any equity in permitting the appellant to receive a dividend on its whole claim, simply because it saw proper to delay realizing on its securities until after distribution was made? We think not. The creditor who holds collateral securities for his claim has the advantage over other creditors to the extent of their value, or what he may realize upon them, but he should not be permitted to have, in addition thereto, what in many cases might be equivalent to double dividends or even more. If, for example, the collaterals realized fifty per centum of the creditor's claim, and the debtor's estate would only pay fifty cents on the dollar, the creditor with the security would be paid in full, whilst the others would receive only one-half of their claims. Great inconvenience and cost would oftentimes follow the practice **383** contended for in the distribution of insolvent estates, in addition to the undue advantage given the creditor holding the collateral. For, if the whole claim be distributed, and the dividend exceeded the difference between the value of the collaterals and the amount of the claim, the creditor would have to refund or deduct from his dividend the balance, which would require another audit, thus involving the estate in unnecessary cost and delay. The value of the collaterals would have to be ascertained before the dividend was paid to the creditor, so as to properly protect the insolvent estate, for, if this be not done, and the dividend was more than the difference between the value of the collaterals and the amount of the claim, the trustee would have to look to the creditor holding the collaterals for the excess paid him, and possibly the estate would sustain loss by not being able to recover the amount. The long-established practice in proceedings of this kind in this state requires the creditor, in presenting to the auditor *prima facie* proof of his claim, to swear "that no part of the money intended to be secured by such note hath been received, or any security or satisfaction given for the same, except what (if any) is credited"; following the language required for authenticating claims in the orphans' court. The claim in controversy in this case was supported by the affidavit of the cashier of the bank to the above effect. Such language is not meaningless, but was evidently inserted for the purpose of requiring the creditor either to surrender the securities or credit his claim with their value before it is distributed.

The value of the securities thus held should be ascertained and credited on the claim before distribution is made. That can be easily done by relevant testimony, taken under authority of the court, when no sale has taken place. This was the practice in bankruptcy proceedings, and is not without precedent in other courts: See *In re Bridgman,* 1 Nat. Bank Reg. 312; *Amory* v. *Francis,* 16 Mass. 308; *Farnum* v. *Boutelle,* 13 Met. 159; *First Nat. Bank* v. *Eastern* [384] *R. R. Co.,* 124 Mass. 524, and *Bell* v. *Fleming,* 12 N. J. Eq. 13. There was, therefore, no error in the *pro forma* decree in regard to that ruling.

In considering the question as to the right of the appellant to have the real estate treated as the individual property of the members of the firm, and not as partnership assets, we must bear in mind the fact that W. H. Hoffman was the original owner of all this property, and that, whilst it was thus owned by him, he was in partnership with his three sons, trading under the name of William H. Hoffman & Sons, being the style of the firm subsequently adopted by them. If a deed of trust, similar to the one made by the sons, had been made in the lifetime of the father, by the members of the original firm, it would hardly be contended that the real estate should be treated as partnership property—certainly not as against the individual creditors of William H. Hoffman. By his last will and testament the senior Hoffman charged an annuity upon the "Gunpowder Mill" property, for the purpose of keeping a burying-ground, etc., in proper condition, and made certain provisions for his wife. He directed his executors to ascertain the value of the rest of his property, and gave it, with the exception of one-twentieth thereof left to Peter Vondersmith, his son in law, to his three sons and his daughter, Lydia A. Smyser, to be divided between them equally, share and share alike. He directed that in the division his son, John W. Hoffman, should have the property known as the "Gunpowder Mill" chargeable with the annuity aforesaid, together with certain water rights and four hundred acres of land connected therewith, known as "Paper Mill Hills"; also a part of the tract of the land known as "Laurel Hills," one hundred yards wide, on each side of a stream. He also directed that in the distribution his son, George W. S. Hoffman, was to have the "Marble Vale Mill" property, containing two hundred and eighteen acres, and his son, William E. Hoffman, was to have his "Clipper

Mill," together with a tract of land called "Grist Mill Hills," containing two hundred and fifty-seven acres; also a tract **385** called "Addition to Grant Mill Hills," containing seven and one-quarter acres, and some houses named by him. He provided that the property thus given to his three sons should be taken by them in the distribution at the prices or values fixed by the appraisers, as provided for in his will, and then directed "that all the rest of my property and estate not hereinbefore devised or specially distributed . . . . shall be sold or disposed of by my said executors . . . . and the proceeds of such sale or sales be so distributed among my said four children as to make the share of each, under these provisions of my will, equal the one to the other." Subsequently, his son in law and his daughter conveyed their respective interests to the three sons "as individuals."

It is admitted in the agreed statement of facts that after the father died the three sons continued to trade under the firm name of William H. Hoffman & Sons, and opened on their firm books an account headed "Real Estate," in which they entered all the property so derived by them, and continued the same on their books in that way; "that between the said three sons all the said real estate was always considered in their business as copartnership property, and was treated between themselves as such, but that the title to the same appeared in the land records of Baltimore county, and in the office of the register of wills of Baltimore county, as having been derived by them under the will of their said father, and the conveyances of said Vondersmith and Smyser, as has been hereinbefore stated, and no conveyance was made by them to the said partnership."

It must be conceded that there is nothing on the face of that will that would indicate any intention of the testator to vest the property in his three sons as partners; but, on the contrary, it is apparent that he intended them to own individually certain properties which he directed to be given them, as above stated. The property was, at the time the partnership was formed, the individual property of the three members. So far as the record discloses, nothing has since **386** been done to transfer the property to the firm or vest any interest in it, excepting the entries in the books and the fact that the real estate was considered in the business as copartnership property, and so treated between the members, as above stated. We are therefore met with the inquiry, whether that is sufficient to authorize a court of equity to treat the proceeds of sale as partnership assets when called upon to decide between the creditors of the firm and those of the individual members.

If this property had been purchased with partnership funds for the use and on account of the firm it would be immaterial that the title stood in the name of the individual members, as a court of equity would treat it for all the purposes of the partnership as firm property, and hence it would be liable to the partnership creditors to the exclusion of the individual creditors until the former are satisfied. In that case there would be an implied or constructive trust in favor of the partners as such, which would inure to the benefit of the creditors of the firm. But when it has been acquired in the manner above stated the question arises whether those dealing with the members of the firm have not the right, in the absence of some notice or knowledge to the contrary, to assume that the public records inform them correctly as to the ownership of the property, notwithstanding the private understanding between the partners themselves. Creditors have sometimes suffered great hardships by courts of equity declaring property standing in the name of one person to be in trust for the benefit of others, but such decisions are rendered to prevent injustice being done those whose money purchased the property, and relief is only granted to them when their claims are established by clear, direct, and explicit proof. This court has said: "This strictness of proof is required because of the danger of rendering titles depending upon deeds and other written documents insecure": *Witts* v. *Horney*, 59 Md. 586.

The same reasoning applies to real estate held of record by members of a firm as tenants in common. When it is [387] sought to change such property from individual to partnership property, the record evidence all pointing to it being the former, a court of equity should not act upon doubtful proof, particularly when the rights of strangers or third parties are to be affected. The public records will be of but little avail if the private books and intentions of partners are to entirely control and determine the character of ownership of real estate.

If property is purchased with partnership funds, and conveyed to one or more of the partners as individuals, the entries of the firm books would have great, possibly controlling, weight

as to whether it should be treated as partnership or individual
property, but courts should require more than private entries
and understandings between partners to overcome the public
records in cases such as this.   No one would suppose from
reading the will of William H. Hoffman that the property
belonged to the partnership.   Persons dealing with the individual members would be led to believe from that will that
they owned the property individually, and inasmuch as it
was once the separate property of the members, we are not
prepared to break down all the safeguards and protection intended by our registry acts by announcing as the law of this
state that partners can so change the character of real estate,
originally owned by them as individuals, and not in any way
derived from the partnership, as to give priority to firm creditors over their separate creditors simply by making entries
in their books and treating it between themselves as partnership property, without giving some notice or doing some acts
equivalent to notice, to their individual creditors.   The agreed
statement of facts does not show that the appellant had notice
of any facts that should have put its officers on inquiry.   The
statement is not as full as it might have been.   It does not
even show what business the firm was engaged in, but from
the arguments, and what we gather from the record, we assume that they were manufacturing paper.   Nor is it definitely stated whether the business was conducted in one or
more paper-mills, although it is shown **388** that William H.
Hoffman died owning real estate, consisting of three paper-
mills, farm lands, etc.   It would certainly have been much
more satisfactory if the facts had been fully set out so as to
enable the court to understand the exact character and extent
of the use of the real estate by the firm.   But it is admitted
that the property was acquired under the will of William H.
Hoffman and by the deeds of Mr. Vondersmith and Mrs.
Smyser, and that no conveyance was made by the members
of the firm to the partnership.   As to what uses, if any, this
firm engaged in manufacturing paper, made of the farm,
dwelling-houses, and other property not necessarily incident
to the paper-mills, the record is silent, but it is certain that
without some notice that they were treated as partnership
property, no one dealing with the individual members of the
firm would be expected to so regard it, and the ordinary use
of that kind of property, such as cultivating or renting the
farms, occupying or renting the houses, etc., would not put

creditors on inquiry or be sufficient notice that they were treated as partnership property.

If the paper-mills themselves, and such other real estate as would properly be used in connection with them, were treated by the partners as firm property, and were so used as to give notice to creditors of the individual members of the firm that they had been put into the partnership as part of the common stock, and were entered on the books of the firm in such way as to comply with the statute of frauds, then the partnership creditors might properly be given priority over the separate creditors to the extent of the proceeds of sales of such property. The record does not disclose such facts as would justify us in determining that question, but as the decree must be reversed the court below can authorize testimony to be taken on that subject. We have carefully examined the authorities cited by the counsel for the respective parties, as well as many others, and have found considerable apparent conflict between some of them. But when the facts of them are carefully examined it will be found that the most **389** of them are in accord with our conclusion, which might be summarized as follows:

1. That as the farms, houses, and similar property were not purchased with partnership funds, for partnership purposes, but were, as far as the public records show, the separate property of the individual members, and were not incident to the business of the firm, the fact that the partners entered them on the firm books and treated them as firm property is not sufficient to change them into partnership property, and the proceeds of sales of them should be applied to the payment of the claims of individual creditors prior to those of the partnership creditors.

2. That if the paper-mills, and such other real estate connected therewith as would be necessary for the convenient and proper conduct of the business, were treated by the partners as partnership property, were put into the firm business as part of the common stock, and were so entered in the books of the firm as to comply with the statute of frauds, then the partnership creditors should have priority over the general creditors of the individual partners in the distribution of the proceeds of sales of such property; provided this class of property was so used as to give notice to the latter that it was treated as partnership property, and was substantially involved in the business of the firm.

There is still another question to be disposed of. It is
contended that the appellant is estopped from claiming that
the real estate is individual and not partnership property, by
reason of its signing a recommendation to the court to ratify
its sale reported May 1, 1894, by John B. Ramsay, one of the
trustees.

Mr. Ramsay and Mr. Schott, the trustees, differed as to the
propriety of a sale of the property remaining unsold at the
price which had been offered, the latter thinking that in time
a better price could be obtained, whilst the former thought
it best to sell at once. Mr. Ramsay reported the sale, and
Mr. Schott was required to show cause why it [390] should not
be made. The American National Bank, of which Mr. Schott
was cashier, was the only creditor opposing the sale, and
Mr. Ramsay undertook to secure the concurrence of enough
creditors to overcome the opposition of that bank. Accordingly, the National Mechanics' Bank, of which Mr. Ramsay
was president, and which was the largest creditor, signified,
through its attorneys, who were also attorneys for the trustees, its concurrence in the sale to the officers of the appellant,
which was the next largest creditor, and sought their consent. It was explained to them that by the proposed sale
the creditors of William H. Hoffman & Sons would get about
thirty-three and one-third per cent of their claims, and it
was thought that the concurrence of two such large creditors
would influence the others. The appellant fully understood
that the thirty-three and one-third per cent was to come from
the sale of the property mentioned in these proceedings.
The appellant, the Mechanics' Bank, and another creditor,
signed a paper requesting the court to ratify the sale, whereupon Mr. Ramsay sent out a circular letter to the creditors
of the firm asking their concurrence in the sale, stating that
the proposed sale would pay the creditors about thirty-three
and one-third per cent of their claims, and that these two
banks approved of it. It is admitted that the officers of
the Union Bank asked the counsel for the trustees and Mechanics' Bank whether the signing of the concurrence to the
sale would affect the claim of the Union Bank, and " were
told that it would not, and that it only meant an assent to
said sale at the price proposed. But nothing was said by
either side as to the claim against the property as individual
or firm property."

We do not think the facts stated in the record are sufficient to estop the appellants. It is perfectly apparent that the difference between the trustees was as to the price to be obtained for the property, whether the offer received by Mr. Ramsay should be accepted or they should wait for a better price. There is not a particle of evidence tending to show that the property did not bring its true value, or that **391** any of the creditors have been injured. The only creditor that filed objections to the appellant's claim on this ground is the Mechanics' Bank, which had concurred in the sale before the appellant did. It could not, therefore, claim that it was misled by the act of the appellants. But, before the officers of the appellant signed the recommendation, they inquired of the attorneys representing the Mechanics' Bank and the trustees who were seeking their concurrence whether it would affect the claim of the Union Bank, and were told it would not. There can be no question as to what claim was referred to, as the agreed statement shows that "the claim of the Union Bank was filed long prior to any sale against both the partnership and the indorsers of the notes held by the bank." It would, perhaps, be more equitable to say that the Mechanics' Bank should be estopped from questioning the right of the Union Bank to assert its claim after having induced it to sign the concurrence by the assurance that such act would not affect its claim. But there is no proof that any creditor was either misled or injured by the action of the appellant, and nothing in the record to justify an inference that such was the case.

This court, in *Hardy* v. *Chesapeake Bank*, 51 Md. 590, 34 Am. Rep. 325, in speaking of the doctrine of an estoppel *in pais*, said: " It can therefore only be set up and relied on by a party who has actually been misled to his injury, for if not so misled he can have no ground for the protection that the principle affords." From what we have already said it can be seen that we think that an application of the above principle of law to the facts of this case disposes of the question of estoppel. The decree *pro forma* must be reversed and the cause remanded for further proceeding in accordance with this opinion.

Decree reversed and cause remanded with costs to the appellant.

————

PARTNERSHIP—REAL PROPERTY HELD BY—RIGHTS OF CREDITORS.—To make land partnership property it must have been purchased with partnership funds for partnership purposes, or at least there must have been one of such elements present; a mere designation of it as partnership property by the partners will not make it partnership assets: *Alkire* v. *Kahle*, 123 Ill. 496; 5 Am. St. Rep. 540. Whether land belonging to a firm or conveyed to a firm is to be considered as part of the partnership stock depends on the intention of the parties to be ascertained from their acts or their agreements, express or implied. Land may become part of the partnership stock under a parol agreement of the partners: *Murrell* v. *Mandelbaum*, 85 Tex. 22; 34 Am. St. Rep. 777, and note. See the extended notes to *Greene* v. *Greene*, 13 Am. Dec. 646, and *McCormick's Appeal*, 98 Am. Dec. 197.

ESTOPPEL IN PAIS MAY BE SET UP, WHEN.—To constitute an estoppel *in pais* there must be a false representation or concealment of material facts made to a party ignorant of their truth or falsity, and made with the intent that the latter party would act upon them, and he must have so acted: *Blodgett* v. *Perry*, 97 Mo. 263; 10 Am. St. Rep. 307; *Bynum* v. *Preston*, 69 Tex. 287; 5 Am. St. Rep. 49. Estoppel *in pais* is one that arises from acts, conduct, or declarations of a person by which he designedly induces another to alter his position injuriously to himself: *Rorer Iron Co.* v. *Trout*, 83 Va. 397; 5 Am. St. Rep. 285, and note; *Davis* v. *Davis*, 26 Cal. 23; 85 Am. Dec. 157, and note; *Brown* v. *Wheeler*, 17 Conn. 345; 44 Am. Dec. 550.

SCHAEFFER *v.* FARMERS' MUTUAL FIRE INS. CO.

[80 MARYLAND, 563.]

INSURANCE — PROOF TO SHOW DEFENSE OF FORFEITURE. — An insurance company which resists, on the ground of forfeiture, the payment of a loss against which it has insured, must show both that its policy or written contract contains, either in express terms or by clear implication, some provision forfeiting the policy in specified contingencies, and also that the contingency has arisen.

INSURANCE—USE OF ENGINE—FORFEITURE.—The use on insured premises of an engine regularly employed in grinding bark in a tannery in the process of tanning leather is not ground for forfeiting an insurance policy releasing the company from liability for loss by fire resulting from the use of "any steam-engine temporarily employed for the purpose of threshing out crops of any kind."

INSURANCE — INCREASE OF RISK — FORFEITURE. — Under a policy of fire insurance providing that, if an engine is stationed on the insured premises in proximity to buildings, the president of the company shall appoint a committee to examine and ascertain the amount of the increased risk, and, if increased, the insured shall pay an additional premium, the use of an engine on the insured premises does not of itself necessarily forfeit the policy nor increase the risk; but, if the risk is increased, and loss by fire caused thereby, the insurer, in the event that no additional premium note has been given, is released from liability, unless it has neglected for an unreasonable time after notice to appoint the committee and to make the examination provided for.

INSURANCE — INCREASE OF RISK — DUTY OF INSURER.—Under a policy of fire insurance providing that, if an engine is stationed on premises in proximity to insured buildings, the president of the insurance company shall appoint a committee to examine forthwith, and ascertain the amount of the increased risk, and, if increased, to require the insured to pay an additional premium, it is the imperative duty of such president, upon receiving notice that an engine has been placed near insured buildings, to appoint the committee and have the examination as to increase of risk made forthwith, or at least with proper and due diligence. A failure to do so for an unreasonable time is a waiver of the right to resist, because of such increased risk, an action based on such policy.

INSURANCE — INCREASE OF RISK. — NOTICE GIVEN BY THE INSURED TO A GENERAL AGENT of the insurer, ten days before a loss by fire, of the use of an engine near the insured building, and of his readiness to comply with conditions of the policy concerning an increase of the risk arising from the use of such engine, is notice to the insurer, and the question as to whether such ten days' notice was a reasonable time within which the insurer ought to have required the payment of an additional premium for the increased risk.

INSURANCE—INCREASE IN RISK.—If a risk is materially increased, notice thereof given the insurer by the insured, and no additional premium is required to be given, as provided in the policy, the right to recover for a loss is not defeated, unless it occurs wholly or in part from such increased risk.

INSURANCE—INCREASE IN RISK.—If, under a policy of insurance providing that if an engine is used on the premises in proximity to the insured buildings the insurance company shall appoint a committee to examine and ascertain the amount of the increased risk, and, if increased, to require the insured to pay an additional premium, the risk is increased by the use of an engine, notice is given to the company, and no additional premium is required to be given, solely because of unreasonable delay on the part of the company in making an examination to ascertain the amount of increased risk, the company is liable for a loss caused by such engine, as it cannot set up its own negligent delay as a defense.

INSURANCE — ALTERATION IN PREMISES. — The placing and operating an engine fifty feet away from an insured building is not an alteration of the insured premises, nor the use of them for carrying on a trade or business increasing the risk, unless expressly so declared by the terms of the contract of insurance.

INSURANCE—FORFEITURE—WAIVER.—Without any forfeiture of a policy of insurance there can exist no waiver of a forfeiture.

INSURANCE. — NOTICE TO GENERAL AGENT of an insurer is notice to the insurer himself.

H. M. Clabaugh, G. K. Gaither, Jr., J. M. Roberts, and J. D. Brooks, for the appellant.

J. A. C. Bond, C. T. Reifsnider, and C. T. Reifsnider, Jr., for the appellee.

[569] McSHERRY, J.   The appellant's tannery, barkmill, and stock in trade, which, with other property owned by him, were insured under one and the same policy issued by the appellee, were destroyed by fire on February 27, 1892.

[570] Due preliminary proof of loss was made, and subsequently suit was brought upon the policy to recover the amount of insurance written on that portion of the property which had been burned. During the progress of the trial in the circuit court for Carroll county five exceptions were taken. The second one of these, though it appears in the record, was not signed by the judge. It cannot, therefore, be considered by us beyond its recitals of facts. These, by reason of the unsigned bill of exceptions being connected with the succeeding one, form part of the latter: *Cooper* v. *Holmes*, 71 Md. 20. The first, third, and fourth bills of exception relate to questions of evidence, and the fifth to the several prayers presented by both parties. The verdict and judgment were against the plaintiff, and he has appealed.

It will obviate much unnecessary discussion if we proceed at once to an examination of the fundamental and controlling questions involved in the controversy, instead of considering separately the several exceptions in the order in which they appear in the record.

The defendant resists the claim of the plaintiff on the ground that the unauthorized use by the plaintiff of a steam-engine located about fifty feet away from the barkmill, but connected with the machinery in the latter by a leather band, worked a forfeiture of the policy under the terms and conditions set forth therein and indorsed thereon. And it relies in support of this position on the recent case of *Farmers' Mut. Fire Ins. Co.* v. *Hull*, 77 Md. 498. On the other hand, the plaintiff insists: 1. That the use of the steam-engine for the purpose of grinding bark did not cause a forfeiture; and 2. That, even if a forfeiture did occur, the defendant unequivocally waived it.

It can scarcely be necessary to reaffirm what has been so often and so uniformly decided, that forfeitures by mere implication are never favored in the law. A company which resists, on the ground of forfeiture, the payment of a loss against which it has insured, must show both that its policy or written contract contains, either in express terms or by [571] clear implication, some provision forfeiting the policy in specified contingencies; and also that the insured has brought himself within the scope and conditions of that provision. The policy is a contract between the insurer and the insured, and, as they have written it, and not otherwise, so courts must construe and enforce it. To the policy, then, and to all that forms a part of it, must resort be had to ascertain not only whether a forfeiture is in fact provided for, but the conditions and circumstances under which it becomes applicable and effective.

In the body of the policy now before us there are two causes of forfeiture; and in the conditions of insurance thereto annexed and in the by-laws, made a part thereof by reference, there are three more. Those first alluded to relate, the one to the taking out by the insured, without notice to the insurer, additional insurance on the same property in a different company; and the other: 1. To alterations of the premises, and 2. To their use for the purpose of carrying on therein any trade or business " which, according to the by-laws and conditions, class of hazards or rates thereto annexed, would increase the hazard," unless by the consent of the insurer indorsed upon the policy. Those set forth in the conditions are: 1. Alterations made in any building which increases the risk; 2. The omission for thirty days after demand to pay any assessment levied on the assured's premium note; and 3. The sixteenth condition, which, without qualification, prohibits the use of " any steam-engine temporarily employed for the purpose of threshing out crops of any kind."

Under the policy sued on, which was issued in February, 1887, and covered a period of seven years, the appellant's dwelling-house, household furniture, tenant-house, wagon-shed, barn, hayshed, and other farm buildings and farming implements, together with his tanshop, barkshed, barkmill house, stock in trade, consisting of bark, hides, leather, finished and unfinished, were all insured. The engine used on the premises the day of the fire was not located at the [572] barn or employed for the purpose of threshing out crops of any kind, but was stationed between fifty and sixty feet away from the barkmill house, and was, and for more than a year and a half previously had been, used once a month to furnish the motive power for grinding bark for the plaintiff's tannery. On the day of the fire the engine was in use for grinding bark, and whilst the employees were at dinner, and the engine was not running and its fires were banked, a fire broke out in the barkmill house and consumed the tannery buildings and stock in trade. When first discovered the fire was within the building, whose sides toward the engine were tightly weatherboarded and stripped. Earlier on the same day a slight fire broke out about the same spot, but was promptly extinguished. There was evidence tending to show that the first fire was produced by the friction of the machinery, but there is no evidence whatever in the record to show what caused the second and destructive fire.

It is not pretended that the first of the two causes of forfeiture set forth in the body of the policy, and the second of those contained in the conditions and by-laws, have any relation to the case at bar. There was other insurance in a different company, but it was taken out only after notice had been given to, and a written permit had been procured from, the general agent of the defendant. The third of the causes of forfeiture contained in the conditions, being the one numbered sixteen, was the one under consideration in *Farmers' Mut. Fire Ins. Co.* v. *Hull*, 77 Md. 498. Hull stationed a portable engine within thirty feet of his barn, and connected it by a strap and pulley with machinery in the barn, and used it there in chopping and threshing his grain. The barn was destroyed by fire whilst the engine was so used, and we held that the policy, which was identical in terms with the policy in this case, and was issued by the same company, though, of course, covering different property, was forfeited. The conduct of Hull was directly within the terms of the sixteenth condition indorsed on the policy, and there was no possible escape from the conclusion that his policy was forfeited thereby, and, hence, [573] the only contention in that case was whether the company had waived this forfeiture.

Apart from other provisions of the policy now under examination, it is clear that an engine regularly employed in grinding bark for use in a tannery in the process of tanning leather is not a "steam-engine temporarily employed for the purpose of threshing out crops of any kind," and is not within the sixteenth condition, and is not, therefore, the cause of forfeiture specified therein. It is manifest that this provision was intended to prohibit the use of engines for the purpose of threshing out crops in the vicinity of barns and other equally inflammable farm buildings; and, imposing as it does, a forfeiture for such a use, it must be strictly confined in its application to cases within its terms as written, and is not to be enlarged to include by implication another class of circumstances neither within its letter nor its evident design. In the vital particular that the use made of the engine by the appellant was not a use prohibited or at a place prohibited by the sixteenth condition on the policy, the case at bar is widely distinguishable from Hull's case. That condition cannot control this case unless restrictions and inhibitions which are not there now are first imported into it by mere construction.

That this view of the limited scope and effect of the sixteenth condition is the correct one is made even more apparent by other and different provisions embodied in the seventeenth condition, which was obviously framed to meet a class of cases not covered by the sixteenth condition. Whilst this latter condition provides without qualification of any sort that "this company will not become responsible for any loss or damage by fire . . . . resulting from the use of any steam-engine temporarily employed for the purpose of threshing out crops of any kind," the seventeenth condition distinctly and in terms recognizes the liability of the company for losses or damage by fire resulting from the use of other steam-engines than those referred to in the sixteenth condition, and specifically prescribes what shall be done by [574] the company and by the insured when such other steam-engines are employed; but it nowhere imposes a forfeiture. The seventeenth section or condition is in these words: " That in the event of an engine being stationed on the premises, and in close proximity to the buildings insured by this company, then, in that event, the president of the company shall appoint a committee of three discreet men, who shall be members of this company, who shall proceed forthwith to said property to make a fair and impartial examination, in order to ascertain the amount of increased risk on account of said engine; and, if they shall find that the risk is increased thereby, then they shall take an additional premium note for such increase, upon which the assured shall pay ten per centum at the time of the execution, and the said note to be subject to the same assessments as other notes of said company, to meet losses by fire happening to property insured by this company." The plain meaning of this is, that if an engine other than those referred to in the sixteenth condition is stationed on the insured premises, ascertainment shall be made in the method pointed out, whether the risk has been increased thereby or not; and, if it be found that the risk has been increased, then it is provided, not that the policy shall be forfeited, but that an additional premium note shall be given upon which ten per cent must be paid; but, if

it be found that the risk has not been increased, then neither
is the policy forfeited, nor is an additional premium note
demandable.   The employment, therefore, of such an engine
as the seventeenth clause contemplates does not result under
its terms in a forfeiture of the policy or even necessarily in
increasing the risk; but, if the risk be increased by the use
of such an engine, and loss by fire is occasioned thereby,
then the insurer, in the event that no additional premium
note has been given, will be released from liability under the
policy, unless it has neglected to appoint the committee and
to make the examination provided for; but, if thus released,
it would be upon altogether different principles.   It would
575 be released, if released at all, because it is the settled
law, even in the absence of an express provision on the subject in the policy, that when the erection by the insured of
an adjacent building, and, of course, the use by him of an
adjacent steam-engine, has caused a material increase of
risk by fire to the property insured, and when the loss was
produced by such increase of risk, a recovery on the policy
would be denied: *Washington Fire Ins. Co.* v. *Davison,* 30 Md.
102.   Under this seventeenth clause it becomes the imperative duty of the president of the company, when a steam-
engine has been stationed on the premises in close proximity
to the buildings insured, to appoint a committee of three
members of the company to examine forthwith whether there
has been an increase of risk on account thereof.   Good faith
toward, and frank dealing with, the assured, no less than the
explicit words of the provision itself, require that this duty
should be discharged, if not " forthwith," upon the company
being apprised of the existence of the conditions on which
its performance depends, at least with due and proper diligence thereafter.   Obviously, a failure for an unreasonable
time after notice to do that which it is the company's plain
duty to do forthwith offers no defense to a plaintiff's right to
recover.

   The record shows that ten days before the fire the plaintiff notified the defendant's general agent, whose duty it was
to attend to all its business in his territory, that he, the plaintiff, was then using the engine for grinding bark, and that he
was willing to do and to pay any thing that might be necessary for the protection of the property in the event of fire,
and that he wanted to be made safe in his insurance on the
tanyard.   This was notice to the company: May on Insur-

ance, sec. 152; *Union Mut. Ins. Co.* v. *Wilkinson*, 13 Wall.
222. We are not dealing with the question of the agent's
power or authority to waive or vary a condition of the policy,
but only with the proposition that notice of the character we
are considering given to the general agent of the company is
notice to the company itself. And it was [576] notice to the
company because it was the duty of the agent to communicate it to his principal. It can make no possible difference
that the agent, when so notified, declined to give a permit for
the use of the engine, because under the seventeenth condition no permit was needed, but another method was provided.
Whether the period that elapsed between the date of this
notice and the subsequent fire was a reasonable time within
which the company ought to have appointed the committee
of three members under the seventeenth condition, was a
question of fact for the jury to determine under all the attend-
ant circumstances: *Rokes* v. *Amazon Ins. Co.*, 51 Md. 519;
34 Am. Rep. 323. Under this seventeenth clause, whilst there
was no forfeiture declared or even implied, there are two contingencies presented. There is the contingency that the use
of the engine would increase the risk under which two different
aspects are presented; and there is the opposite contingency
that it would not. In the latter event the policy would in no
way be affected, and the right to recover on it would not be
impaired. In the event that the risk was materially increased
and no additional premium note was given, then the right to
recover was not defeated unless the loss occurred in whole
or in part from that increased risk; and this is a question of
fact for the jury to find. If, again, the risk was materially
increased and notice was given to the company, and no additional premium note was given, solely because of unreasonable delay on the part of the company in making an
examination to ascertain the amount of the increased risk,
and loss resulted by fire occasioned by such increased risk,
still the company would be liable, because it would not be
permitted to invoke in its defense the failure of the plaintiff
to give an additional premium note when that failure was
due exclusively to the company's own omission or neglect to
perform its precedent duty within a reasonable time. In no
view, then, that can be taken of the sixteenth and seventeenth clauses was there a forfeiture of the policy.

The remaining causes of forfeiture stated in the policy and
in the conditions thereto annexed are those which [577] re-

late to alterations in the premises or buildings which increase
the risk, and to the use thereof for the purpose of carrying on
therein any trade or business, which, according to the by-
laws and conditions, class of hazards and rates annexed to
the policy would increase the hazard.   There is no evidence
that there were alterations made in the premises or buildings after they were insured.   When the policy was issued the
buildings used in the tannery business were described in the
policy, and distinctly insured as buildings pertaining to that
occupation, and it is not intimated that they were used thereafter for the purpose of carrying on any different trade or
business.   Nothing, then, in the structures themselves, or in
the business conducted therein, was changed or altered after
the insurance had been granted, and unless placing and
operating the engine fifty or sixty feet away from the barkmill house amount to an alteration in the insured premises, or to a use of them for carrying on a trade, which,
according to the class of hazards and rates annexed to the
policy, would increase the hazard, there is nothing in either
of those provisions which has the slightest reference to the
case at bar.   That the engine so placed and so operated did
not amount to an alteration in the insured premises in the
sense in which the terms used in the policy are invariably
interpreted can admit of no doubt.   Those terms mean an
alteration in the thing insured: *Washington Fire Ins. Co.* v.
Davison, 30 Md. 102.   That an engine employed as this one
was, was not a use of the premises for carrying on a trade
or business, which, according to the by-laws and conditions,
class of hazards and rates annexed to the policy, would
increase the hazard, is equally free from doubt, because the
by-laws and conditions do not expressly or impliedly so
declare, and because there is no class of hazards or rates annexed to the policy at all.   There is consequently no standard
as to what would increase the risk, furnished by any by-law,
condition, class of hazards or rates.   To avoid any misunder-
standing, we repeat that if without notice to the insurer the
use of [578] the engine as described did in fact materially
increase the risk, and if the loss was occasioned by that
increased risk, the insurer would be relieved from liability.
But these are facts to be found by the jury.

As there was no forfeiture of the policy there could be no
waiver of a policy that never existed, and hence the evidence
offered and objected to in the first, third, and fourth excep-

tions tending to prove a waiver was irrelevant, and was for that reason properly excluded. The plaintiff's first, second, and third prayers, which were confined to the question of waiver, were also properly rejected, because there was no question of waiver involved, and there could be none where there had been no forfeiture. The fifth and sixth prayers were wrong, and were properly rejected. As there was no forfeiture, there was no right in the company to cancel the policy, and a delay in an abortive cancellation was of no consequence one way or the other, as respects the plaintiff's right to recover. The fourth and seventh prayers were right, and ought to have been granted. The fourth has relation to the knowledge of the agent being the knowledge of the company; and the seventh refers to the insurance in a different company. All of the defendant's prayers except the second were rejected, and that one ought to have been refused. Its vice is that it construes the policy to mean that the use of the engine, under the circumstances stated, of itself forfeited the policy. We have already discussed that question, and have reached a different conclusion.

For the error in rejecting the plaintiff's fourth and seventh prayers, and in granting the defendant's second, the judgment must be reversed, and a new trial will be awarded.

Judgment reversed, with costs above and below, and new trial awarded.

___

INSURANCE.—FORFEITURES ARE NOT FAVORED, and courts are reluctant to declare and enforce them if by reasonable interpretation it can be avoided: *Coleman* v. *Insurance Co.*, 49 Ohio St. 310; 34 Am. St. Rep. 565, and note; *Duran* v. *Standard etc. Ins. Co.*, 63 Vt. 437; 25 Am. St. Rep. 773, and note. A forfeiture is not favored, and will not be enforced unless specifically and definitely provided for in the contract. *Murray* v. *Home Ben. etc. Assn.*, 90 Cal. 402; 25 Am. St. Rep. 133, and note.

INSURANCE—INCREASE OF RISK—ENGINE ON PREMISES.—Where a dummy-engine had been used on the premises before the issuing of the policy it was held that its subsequent use when required, although such use increased the risk did not avoid the policy under a provision therein that "if the situation or circumstances affecting the risk shall be so altered as to increase the risk," the policy should be void: *Commonwealth* v. *Hide etc. Ins. Co.*, 112 Mass. 136; 17 Am. Rep. 72. To the same effect, see *Whitney* v. *Black River Ins. Co.*, 72 N. Y. 117; 28 Am. Rep. 116, and note.

INSURANCE—ALTERATION OF PREMISES INCREASING THE RISK.—Liability of insured, unless additional premium is paid: See *Merriam* v. *Middlesex etc. Ins. Co.*, 21 Pick. 162; 32 Am. Dec. 252.

INSURANCE.—NOTICE TO or knowledge of the general agent of an insurance company is imputed to the company: *Morrison* v. *Insurance Co.*, 69 Tex. 353; 5 Am. St. Rep. 63, and note.

HELDEN *v.* HELLEN.

[80 MARYLAND, 616.]

CLOUD ON TITLE—WHO MAY MAINTAIN BILL TO REMOVE.—A bill to remove a cloud on title cannot be maintained unless the plaintiff has both the legal title and the possession.

CLOUD ON TITLE—RIGHT OF EXECUTION PURCHASER TO MAINTAIN BILL TO REMOVE.—One claiming title to land under an execution sale cannot maintain a bill against a party in possession claiming under a deed of trust to have such deed declared void and vacated as a cloud on his title. His remedy is by ejectment.

M. Duckett and E. Dent, for the appellant.

C. H. Stanley and R. F. Combs, for the appellee.

619 BRISCOE, J.   The appeal in this case is from an order sustaining a demurrer to a bill in equity. The bill charges that the appellant obtained by deed from Dr. Charles A. Wells and Mrs. Wells, on the 4th of January, 1894, a tract of land situate in Prince George's county, containing one hundred and twenty-nine acres; that Dr. Wells previously purchased the land at sheriff's sale, at the suit of himself against one Thomas A. Mitchell, and on the 27th of June, 1892, obtained the sheriff's deed; that Mitchell, on the 21st of March, 1890, being on that date indebted unto the appellant's grantor, executed an instrument of writing purporting to be a deed of trust, and professing to convey unto William F. Hellen, one of the appellees, this tract of land, together with other lands, to secure to one William W. Hall an indebtedness of seven thousand dollars, covered by six promissory notes from Mitchell to Hall.

It further charges that Mitchell was never indebted to Hall in the sum set forth in the pretended deed of trust, or in any other sum; that the deed of trust is without consideration, was made in prejudice of subsisting creditors, is fraudulent, void, and operates as a cloud upon the appellant's title. The bill then prays that the deed of trust be annulled and set aside; that the notes secured by the deed decreed to be brought in and canceled; that the cloud upon his title to the land be removed, and concludes with a prayer for general relief.   And to this bill a demurrer was interposed, which was sustained by the court, and the bill dismissed.

620 The question, then, presented for our consideration, is whether the plaintiff has presented such a case by the bill as entitles him to the relief he seeks.   It is manifest that the appellant is not entitled to invoke the jurisdiction of a court of equity for "the quieting of title and the removal of a cloud therefrom," because his bill fails to allege that the plaintiff was in the possession of the property at the time the bill was filed, it being well settled in this state, as a general rule, that the jurisdiction of a court of equity cannot be maintained to remove a cloud from title unless the party has the legal title and the possession. If the possession is in another his remedy is by an action of ejectment: *Crook* v. *Brown*, 11 Md. 158; *McCoy* v. *Johnson*, 70 Md. 490; *Livingston* v. *Hall*, 73 Md. 386. And the case of *Steuart* v. *Meyer*, 54 Md. 454, relied upon by the appellant, is not in conflict with this rule as applicable to a case like the one here presented: *Textor* v. *Shipley*, 77 Md. 479.

Nor can there be any question that a creditor who has pursued his remedy at law by an ineffectual execution on his judgment can invoke the aid of a court of equity to have fraudulent conveyances standing in his way and covering up the property set aside and vacated. This relief is fully established by authority: *Trego* v. *Skinner*, 42 Md. 430. But the plaintiff here is in no sense a creditor of Mitchell, the alleged fraudulent grantor. The relation of debtor and creditor between Dr. Wells, the plaintiff's grantor, and Mitchell, the grantor under the deed of trust, ceased to exist, by the execution sale, so far as the property sold and sought to be recovered in this proceeding can be affected. The plaintiff acquired the title of the purchaser at the sheriff's sale, and can assert no better equity than those under whom he claims: *Baxter* v. *Sewell*, 3 Md. 338. And whether the conveyance to the appellee, Helden, was fraudulent or not can be tried in an action of ejectment: *Welde* v. *Scotten*, 59 Md. 73; *Hecht* v. *Colquhoun*, 57 Md. 563; *National Park Bank* v. *Lanahan*, 60 Md. 510.

⁶²¹ In the case of *Polk* v. *Pendleton*, 31 Md. 118, it was distinctly held that a party not in possession of the land, but claiming title to it under an execution sale, could not maintain a bill to have the adverse title of the party in possession claiming under a tax sale declared void, or to have the question of title adjudicated. And in the case of *Thigpen* v. *Pitt*, 1 Jones Eq. 49, the supreme court of North Carolina, in treating of a case somewhat similar to the one here presented, held that where a debtor makes a conveyance of land with intent to defeat his creditors, and they proceed to have the

land sold, treating the conveyance as void, one who becomes a purchaser and takes a sheriff's deed has no right to call on a court of equity to have the fraudulent deed brought in and canceled upon the ground of removing a cloud from his title. "This," says that court, "would be a novel attempt to extend the jurisdiction of equity, and have it try and dispose of a pure legal question." And in the case of *Welde* v. *Scotten*, 59 Md. 76, this court held that an injunction would not be granted to prevent a judgment creditor from selling and purchasing the property under an execution, so as to put himself into a position to test at law, through ejectment, the validity of another's title alleged to be fraudulent. The question was left to be litigated at law. "The real question," said the court in that case, "for us to decide is, should he (the judgment creditor) be prevented by injunction from putting himself into such position that he may have the question of the *bona fides* of the appellee's purchase tested in a court of law, through an action of ejectment. We are all of opinion that he ought not, and that it was error in the circuit court to hold otherwise."

Whatever, then, may be the decisions elsewhere, no case in this state has gone so far as to maintain a bill in equity under the facts and circumstances of this case.

We shall, therefore, affirm the order appealed from, sustaining the demurrer and dismissing the bill with costs.

Order affirmed with costs.

———

CLOUD ON TITLE—WHO MAY MAINTAIN SUIT TO REMOVE.—A cloud upon title is a title or encumbrance, apparently valid, but in fact invalid. "A cloud upon a title is but an apparent defect in it. If the title, sole and absolute in fee, is really in the person moving against the cloud, the density of the cloud can make no difference in the right to have it removed. Any thing of this kind that has a tendency, even in a slight degree, to cast doubt upon the owner's title, and to stand in the way of a full and free exercise of his ownership, is a cloud upon his title" which he has a right to have removed: *Whitney* v. *City of Port Huron*, 88 Mich. 269-272; 26 Am. St. Rep. 291.

To constitute a cloud on title the claim of title made must be apparently valid and based upon an instrument which appears to be valid from the face of the record, the defect in which can only be made to appear by extrinsic proof, for, if the invalidity of the instrument complained of is apparent upon its face, it does not constitute a cloud. The general rule to be deduced from the authorities is, that if the title against which relief is prayed is of such character that, if asserted by action and put in evidence, it would drive the true owner of the property to the production of his own title in order to establish a defense, it constitutes a cloud which he has a right to have removed. If, on the other hand, such title is void on its face, so that an action based upon it would fall of its own weight without extrinsic evidence to show its invalidity, or, when, if such evidence is produced, it must inevitably show the invalidity of such title and destroy its effect, it does not constitute a cloud, and the complainant must, if he would have such title removed, show some special circumstances which entitle him, in the view of a court of equity, to a decree for that purpose: *Lick* v. *Ray*, 43 Cal. 83–88; *Sloan* v. *Sloan*, 25 Fla. 53; *Crooke* v. *Andrews*, 40 N. Y. 547; *Fonda* v. *Sage*, 48 N. Y. 173; *Maloney* v. *Finnegan*, 38 Minn. 70; *Lawrence* v. *Zimpleman*, 37 Ark. 643; *Gamble* v. *Loop*, 14 Wis. 465; *Barnes* v. *Mayo*, 19 Fla. 542; *Guest* v. *Brooklyn*, 69 N. Y. 506; *Moores* v. *Townshend*, 102 N. Y. 387. "The true test is whether, in an action of ejectment founded upon a claim of title, the owner in possession would be required to offer evidence to defeat a recovery. If such proof would be necessary the cloud would exist, but if such proof would not be necessary no cloud would be cast upon the title. If the action would fall of its own weight, without proof in reply, there is no occasion for equitable interference, as in the case where the instrument relied upon is void upon its face, or is the result of proceedings void upon their face and requiring no extrinsic evidence to show their illegality": *Sloan* v. *Sloan*, 25 Fla. 53–67.

The right to remove a cloud from title is, in the absence of statute, purely equitable in its nature, and peculiarly within the jurisdiction of courts of chancery. Hence, relief must be sought in equity: *Loring* v. *Downer*, 1 McAll. 360; *Downing* v. *Wherrin*, 19 N. H. 9; 49 Am. Dec. 139; *Huntington* v. *Allen*, 44 Miss. 654; *Standish* v. *Dow*, 21 Iowa, 363; *Eldridge* v. *Smith*, 34 Vt. 484; *Walker* v. *Peay*, 22 Ark 103. The jurisdiction of equity to remove clouds from title is an independent source or head of jurisdiction, not requiring any accompaniment of fraud, accident, mistake, trust, or account, or any other basis of equitable intervention: *Dull's Appeal*, 113 Pa. St. 510.

In some states statutes have been enacted permitting parties, whether in possession or not, to determine adverse claims and remove clouds from title in an action at law brought under the provisions of such statute. Cases arising under such statutes are not to be considered here. This note is confined to the right to maintain a bill in equity to remove clouds from title. A bill in equity to remove a cloud from title can only be maintained when the pretended title or instrument, alleged to constitute the cloud, is apparently valid on its face, and the party in possession is compelled to resort to extrinsic evidence to show the invalidity of the pretended title and to defend his own. If the pretended claim is invalid on its face, or when it requires that extrinsic facts be proved for the purpose of establishing its validity, a court of equity refuses to interfere on the ground that the facts which are essential to sustain the pretended claim do not exist, and the party in possession is left to his defense in an action at law. This is the general and well-settled rule, subject, perhaps, to some exceptions in special cases: *Murray* v. *Hazell*, 99 N. C. 168; *Busbee* v. *Macy*, 85 N. C. 329; *Briggs* v. *Johnson*, 71 Me. 235; *City of Hartford* v. *Chipman*, 21 Conn. 488; *Lehman* v. *Roberts*, 86 N. Y. 232. "The jurisdiction of a court of equity to afford relief against deeds and other instruments in writing which in their nature and apparent validity operate in such improper and unjust way as to cast doubt upon the right or title of the party complaining arises only when the deed or instrument in question has such present apparent validity and effectiveness, or where it is capable, by reason of such causes, of misuse in the future to his prejudice, and he has no other remedy. If the deed or other instrument is upon its face void, or if the complaining party may have a present legal remedy, a court of equity will not interfere, nor will its authority be interposed where the purpose of the deed or other instrument is clear, and it cannot operate presently or in the future to the injury of such party": *Murray* v. *Hazell,* 99 N. C. 168-171.

Possession Necessary.—A party cannot maintain a bill in equity to remove a cloud from his title unless he has a legal or a perfect equitable title: *Toul-min* v. *Heidelberg,* 32 Miss. 268. If his title is legal it is also settled by an overwhelming array of authority that he must be in possession of the property. In such case there is no necessity for the exercise of equitable jurisdiction, the remedy at law being full and adequate. The validity of the disputed title can be fully tried and determined in an action of ejectment. The jurisdiction of equity to remove clouds from title is intended to reach only persons out of possession, who cannot be compelled to defend their claims at law: *Davis* v. *Sloan,* 95 Mo. 552; *Graves* v. *Ewart,* 99 Mo. 13; *Sloan* v. *Sloan,* 25 Fla. 53; *Weaver* v. *Arnold,* 15 R. I. 53; *Barron* v. *Robbins,* 22 Mich. 35; *Carter* v. *Woolfork,* 71 Md. 283; *Textor* v. *Shipley,* 77 Md. 473; *Clayton* v. *Barr,* 34 W. Va. 290; *Wood* v. *Nicolson,* 43 Kan. 461; *Newman* v. *Westcott,* 29 Fed. Rep. 49; *Smith* v. *McConnell,* 17 Ill. 135; 63 Am. Dec. 340; *United States* v. *Wilson,* 118 U. S. 86; *Moores* v. *Townshend,* 102 N. Y. 387; *Gamble* v. *Hamilton,* 31 Fla. 401; *Daniel* v. *Stewart,* 55 Ala. 278; *McLean* v. *Presley,* 56 Ala. 211; *Plant* v. *Barclay,* 56 Ala. 561; *Allen* v. *Hanks,* 136 U. S. 300; *Haworth* v. *Norris,* 28 Fla. 763; *Peacock* v. *Stott,* 104 N. C. 154; *Sheppard* v. *Nixon,* 43 N. J. Eq. 627; *Beale* v. *Blake,* 45 N. J. Eq. 668; *Thor-ington* v. *City Council of Montgomery,* 82 Ala. 591; *Curry* v. *Peebles,* 83 Ala. 225; *Burton* v. *Gleason,* 56 Ill. 25; *Gage* v. *Schmidt,* 104 Ill. 106; *Oakley* v. *Hurl-but,* 100 Ill. 204; *Kilgannon* v. *Jenkinson,* 51 Mich. 240; *Dyer* v. *Krackauer,* 14 Mo. App. 39; *Clark* v. *Covenant Mut. L. Ins. Co.,* 52 Mo. 272; *Gage* v. *Abbott,* 99 Ill. 366; *McDonald* v. *White,* 130 Ill. 493; *Page* v. *Montgomery,* 46 Mich. 51. In a few of the states one claiming a legal title, though not in possession, may maintain a bill in equity against one in possession to remove a cloud from the title of the former: *De Camp* v. *Carnahan,* 26 W. Va. 839; *Hamilton* v. *Batlin,* 8 Minn. 403; 83 Am. Dec. 787; *Bausman* v. *Kelley,* 38 Minn. 197; 8 Am. St. Rep. 661. "When a party has the only or the better legal title to land, as against that which he wishes to put at rest, he may obtain or regain possession by an action of ejectment, if he is out of possession, and it is reasonable that equity should decline to interfere where he may obtain all the relief he needs at law. If he is in possession, then, as he can bring no action at law, he may ask a court of equity to remove a cloud upon his title, which makes it less valuable, and may prevent his disposing of it to others": *Allen* v. *Hanks,* 136 U. S. 300-311. Before a party is entitled to the aid of equity to remove a cloud upon his title he must have the possession of the land, and the cloud must be with respect to something connected with his own title. If neither himself nor the party holding the title alleged to be a cloud are in possession of the land, equity cannot entertain jurisdiction of his bill: *Marks* v. *Main,* 4 Mackey, 559; *Stearns* v. *Harman,* 80 Va. 48. Actual possession with a claim of ownership in fee establishes a presumptive title, and is sufficient to maintain a bill in equity to remove a cloud upon title: *Loomis* v. *Roberts,* 57 Mich. 284.

The possession necessary to entitle one to remove a cloud on his title must be *bona fide,* and fairly gained: *Watson* v. *Lion Brewing Co.,* 61 Mich. 695. It must have been acquired in a lawful way. If obtained by violence or by the use of unfair or corrupt means a court of equity does not lend its aid. A possession obtained by fraud is treated in equity as no possession: *Hardin* v. *Jones,* 86 Ill. 313; *Gould* v. *Sternburg,* 105 Ill. 488; *Gage* v. *Hamp-*

ton, 127 Ill. 87. The possession of a party is insufficient to maintain such suit if it is merely temporary or nominal, obtained by an act of trespass, and for the sole purpose of instituting the proceeding: *Dyer* v. *Baumeister,* 87 Mo. 134; *Swayze* v. *Bride,* 34 Mo. App. 414; *Watson* v. *Lion Brewing Co.,* 61 Mich. 595.

A stranger to the title to land is not entitled to remove a cloud therefrom: Hence, one in possession, but having no legal or equitable title to the land, cannot maintain a bill in equity to remove a cloud upon such title. In order to prevail he must show either a good legal or equitable title in himself: *Wilkinson* v. *Hiller,* 71 Miss. 678; *Jackson* v. *La Moure Co.,* 1 N. D. 238.

Possession of land by a duly authorized agent of a nonresident owner is sufficient to sustain equitable jurisdiction to remove a cloud upon the title of such owner: *Sloan* v. *Sloan,* 25 Fla. 53.

The possession of one cotenant is sufficient to enable his cotenant out of the actual possession to maintain a suit to remove a cloud upon the title of the land held in cotenancy: *Vallandigham* v. *Johnson,* 85 Ky. 288; *Scott* v. *Scott,* 85 Ky. 385; *Herron* v. *Knapp,* 72 Wis. 553.

Possession and title gained by adverse possession for the necessary period is sufficient to maintain a bill to remove a cloud upon title: *Echols* v. *Hubbard,* 90 Ala. 309; *Normant* v. *Eureka Co.,* 98 Ala. 181; 39 Am. St. Rep. 45; *Walker* v. *Converse,* 148 Ill. 622; *Chicago* v. *Middlebrooke,* 143 Ill. 265. In one instance, however, it was decided that "if a party has acquired another's land under the statute of possessions, he ought to be content with the title which the statute gives him, and he cannot, without some further equity, reinforce it by coming into chancery to compel a release of the title which he has superseded: *Taylor* v. *Staples,* 8 R. I. 170; 5 Am. Rep. 556.

The mere possession of one who has not paid all of the purchase money for the land cannot support a bill against the holder of the legal title to whom such purchase money is unpaid: *Northrop* v. *Andrews,* 39 Kan. 567.

The Holder of a Perfect Equitable Title, Though Out of Possession, may maintain a suit to remove a cloud from his title. Ordinarily, bills to remove clouds from the title to land do not lie in behalf of one out of possession, for the reason that generally, under such circumstances, an action for possession may be maintained at law, judgment in which dissipates the alleged cloud, but if the title which is supposed is purely an equitable one, the remedy at law does not exist, and no recovery can there be had, however meritorious the complainant's title may be in contemplation of a court of equity, and upon this consideration the principle has become well established that chancery may be resorted to for relief against the cloud by the holder of the equitable title, though out of possession, and the legal title is in the defendant in possession: *Mason* v. *Black,* 87 Mo. 329; *Graves* v. *Ewart,* 99 Mo. 13; *Sneathen* v. *Sneathen,* 104 Mo. 201; 24 Am. St. Rep. 326; *Connecticut etc. Ins. Co.* v. *Smith,* 117 Mo. 261; 38 Am. St. Rep. 656; *Lawrence* v. *Zimpleman,* 37 Ark. 643; *Bryan* v. *Winburn,* 43 Ark. 29; *Mathews* v. *Marks,* 44 Ark. 436; *Sale* v. *McLean,* 29 Ark. 612; *Branch* v. *Mitchell,* 24 Ark. 431; *Smith* v. *Orton,* 21 How. 241; *Freeman* v. *Brown,* 96 Ala. 301; *Sloan* v. *Sloan,* 25 Fla. 53. In such cases the relief sought and obtained is not, strictly speaking, the removal of a cloud from the complainant's title. It is rather in the nature of securing a judicial declaration that the legal title is held in trust for, and should be conveyed to, him, or, at least, that it shall not be asserted to his prejudice. The complainant must prove his equitable title. He cannot depend on the weakness of the title of his opponent: *Lawrence* v. *Zimpleman,* 37 Ark. 643; *Gamage* v. *Harris,* 79 Me. 531.

One out of possession whose land is sold under execution, the record under which the purchaser at sheriff's sale claims, not disclosing any infirmity on its face, and recourse being necessary to extrinsic evidence to establish such infirmity, has a right to ask the aid of a court of equity to have the sheriff's deed annulled as a cloud on his title: *Beedle* v. *Mead*, 81 Mo. 297. This doctrine is denied in *Herrington* v. *Williams*, 31 Tex. 448, it being there maintained that a party holding both the legal title and the possession is the only person who can maintain a bill in equity to remove a cloud from his title, and that an equitable claimant, not in possession, has no right to invoke the aid of chancery to remove a cloud cast over his title by other claimants.

If a complainant has the legal title to lands that are wild, unimproved, and unoccupied, he may invoke the aid of a court of equity to remove a cloud from his title, although he has no other than the constructive possession resulting from legal ownership, but it is essential to the maintenance of the bill in such cases that it be alleged and proved that the lands are wild, uncultivated, and unoccupied. The jurisdiction of equity exists in such cases, independent of statutory authority: *Graham* v. *Florida etc. Co.*, 33 Fla. 356; *Mathews* v. *Marks*, 44 Ark. 436; *Shirk* v. *Williamson*, 50 Ark. 562; *Thompson* v. *Woolf*, 8 Or. 455; *Gage* v. *Curtis*, 122 Ill. 520; *Glos* v. *Randolph*, 133 Ill. 197; *Wetherell* v. *Eberle*, 123 Ill. 666; 5 Am. St. Rep. 574; *Johnson* v. *Huling*, 127 Ill. 14; *Lejeune* v. *Harmon*, 29 Neb. 268.

On the other hand, if the deed is void on its face, and does not require the production of any extrinsic proof to show its invalidity, it cannot be said to constitute a cloud on the title of the party in possession, and he cannot maintain a suit in equity to have it set aside and canceled: *Morgan* v. *Lehman*, 92 Ala. 440; *Daniel* v. *Stewart*, 55 Ala. 278; *Murray* v. *Hazell*, 99 N. C. 168; *Scott* v. *Onde. donk*, 14 N. Y. 9; 67 Am. Dec. 106; *Alden* v. *Trubee*, 44 Conn. 455.

Judgments—If the invalidity of a judgment is apparent from the face of the record, a bill in equity cannot be maintained to have it declared void and removed as a cloud upon the title of the party in possession: *Morgan* v. *Lehman*, 92 Ala. 440. If, however, the nullity of the judgment is not shown by the face of the proceedings, and proof of its invalidity rests in parol, equity has jurisdiction to declare it void, and cancel it as a cloud upon the title of the judgment debtor: *Brown* v. *Goodwin*, 75 N. Y. 409; *Fitzgerald* v. *Cummings*, 1 Lea, 232.

If an Assessment and Tax Certificate are void upon their face for uncertainty in description of the land they do not create a cloud, and equity will not interfere for the purpose of canceling them: *Shepardson* v. *Milwaukee Co.*, 28 Wis. 593. Or, if an assessment for local improvement is void upon its face, it does not call for the interference of a court of equity to remove it as a cloud upon the title: *Stuart* v. *Palmer*, 74 N. Y. 183; 30 Am. Rep. 289; *Wells* v. *Buffalo*, 80 N. Y. 253. If the facts which render void an assessment for the purpose of general taxation or for special improvement do not, however, appear from the face of the record, a suit will lie to set the assessment aside as a cloud upon the title: *Chaffee* v. *Detroit*, 53 Mich. 573; *Pier* v. *Fond Du Lac County*, 53 Wis. 421.

A Mortgagor in Possession may invoke the aid of equity to cancel a mortgage on his homestead, as a cloud on his title, provided he refunds the mortgage money, and proves that the mortgage is invalid because of defects in its execution and acknowledgment: *Grider* v. *American Freehold etc. Co.*, 99 Ala. 281; 42 Am. St. Rep. 58. Equity will also entertain a suit to remove, as a cloud upon title, a forged mortgage, purporting to be signed by the holder of the legal title in possession of the land on which the mortgage is given: *Byerly* v. *Humphrey*, 95 N. C. 151. And a mortgagee in possession under a deed absolute in form, though a mortgage, if fairly obtained, may maintain a suit to remove a cloud from the title to the mortgaged land: *Burton* v. *Perry*, 146 Ill. 71. But if the instrument under which he holds was obtained by fraud, as, if it was given to defraud creditors of the mortgagor, he cannot maintain a bill to remove a cloud: *Greenbank* v. *Ferguson*, 58 Fed. Rep. 18.

A Mortgagee Out of Possession after foreclosure cannot, however, maintain a suit to remove a cloud from the title, as against the party in possession, for he has a complete remedy at law by writ of entry: *Russell* v. *Barstow*, 144 Mass. 130.

A party in possession of land, and holding the legal title, cannot maintain a bill to remove a mere verbal claim or oral assertion of ownership to such land as a cloud upon the title. Clouds which may be removed by equity are instruments or other proceedings in writing appearing upon the records or which may be recorded, and which might injuriously affect the title of the true owner, and prevent or retard his alienation of the land: *Parker* v. *Shannon*, 121 Ill. 452; *Cashman* v. *Cashman*, 50 Mo. 663.

The owner of land cannot maintain suit to remove a cloud on the title created by himself: *Bresler* v. *Pitts*, 58 Mich. 347.

A bill to remove a cloud from title cannot be maintained if at the time it is filed a suit at law for the recovery of the land is pending, in which the complainant's legal title may be tested and established, as against the party holding the title claimed to be a cloud: *Normant* v. *Eureka Co.*, 98 Ala. 182; 39 Am. St. Rep. 45.

CASES

SUPREME COURT

OF

MICHIGAN.

MERTZ *v.* BERRY.

[101 MICHIGAN, 82.]

HOMESTEADS—EXEMPTIONS FROM TORTS.—A constitutional provision exempting a homestead from " forced sale on execution or any other final process from a court, for any debt contracted after the adoption of this constitution," exempts the homestead from execution and sale upon all judgments, whether founded in tort or in contract.

BILL to set aside an execution sale of a homestead. Judgment for complainant, and defendant appealed.

E. F. Conely and O. B. Taylor, for the appellant.

Avery Bros. & Walsh, for the appellee.

[82] McGRATH, C. J. The sole question in this case is whether, under our constitution, the homestead is exempted from levy and sale under an execution issued upon a judgment recovered in an action of tort.

The constitution provides (art. 16, sec. 2) that "every homestead . . . . shall be exempt from forced sale on execution, or any other final process from a court, for any debt contracted after the adoption of this constitution."

The statute provides (Howell's Statutes, sec. 7721) that "a homestead . . . . shall not be subject to forced sale on execution, or any other final process from [83] a court, for any debt or debts growing out of or founded upon contract, either express or implied, made after the third day of July, A. D. 1848." This statute was, however, passed in 1848, before the adoption of the present constitution.

Upon examination of the proceedings of the constitutional

convention of 1850 it will be observed that sections 1, 2, and 3 of this article, as first reported, read as follows:

" 1. The personal property of every resident of this state shall be exempted, to the amount of not less than five hundred dollars, from sale on execution or other final process of any court of law or equity.

" 2. The homestead of every family of not less than forty acres, which shall not be included in any city, village, or recorded town plat, or, in lieu thereof, any lot in any city, village, or recorded town plat, shall not be subject to forced sale for any debt hereafter incurred; nor shall the owner of such homestead, if a married man, alienate the same by any deed of conveyance, without the consent of his wife, obtained in due form of law

" 3. The homestead of any family, after the death of the owner thereof, shall likewise be exempt from the payment of his debts contracted after the adoption of this constitution in all cases where any minor children shall survive the death of such owner, for their benefit and support during minority": Constitutional Debates of 1850, p. 240.

When these sections were under consideration it was urged that the first section was retrospective in its action; and to obviate that objection, Mr. Pierce offered the following as an addition thereto: "Issued for the collection of any debt contracted after the adoption of this constitution": Constitutional Debates of 1850, p. 667.

The article was again taken from the table, when a substitute was offered for sections 1, 2, and 3. Thereupon, certain amendments were offered as a substitute for the 34 former substitute, which amendments prevailed. The article was then recommitted, with instructions. The committee immediately reported back the article, "amended agreeably to instructions." The article was then passed, and, under the rule, referred to the committee on arrangement and phraseology. Up to this time it nowhere appears that section 2 had been amended, or that any instructions had been given respecting amendments thereto, except such as appears on pages 740 and 741, which do not relate to this subject. The committee on arrangement and phraseology reported back the article, and, in their report, the language, "for any debt contracted after the adoption of this constitution," first appeared as substituted for the language, "for any debt hereafter incurred." This would appear to have been done to make the language of the three sections uniform.

The subject of exemptions was very fully discussed. The retrospective effect of the first section, as it appeared when first reported, was objected to, but nowhere was any distinction hinted at between debts founded on contract and those founded in tort; and it affirmatively appears that the language added to the first section was appended for the express purpose of obviating the objection raised. The statutes existing at that time relating to the exemption of personal property exempted the property specified from levy and sale " under any execution, or upon any other final process of a court." The statute of 1848, relating to real property, above quoted, was clear and explicit, and clearly applies only to " debts growing out of or founded upon contract, either express or implied, made after," etc. The debates furnish no indication of an intention to make the constitutional provision relating to the exemption of personal property more restrictive than the statutory provisions upon the same subject. Pending [53] the discussion of these sections, which was a protracted one, the second section read, " any debt hereafter incurred "; and, although the section was amended in other particulars, no reference appears to have been made to this language.

The word " debt " is one of large import, including debts of record or judgments: *Gray* v. *Bennett*, 3 Met. 526; *New Jersey Ins. Co.* v. *Meeker*, 37 N. J. L. 301; *In re Estate of Lambie*, 94 Mich. 489. A judgment founded in tort is a debt. What, then, is the office of the language which follows the word " debt "? Is it to qualify the word " debt," or, in other words, to indicate what class of debts the exemption was intended to include, or was it used for the purpose of making the provision prospective, instead of retrospective—in other words, to limit the operation of the provision to debts afterward incurred? In view of the history recited, we are inclined to the latter view. The word " contracted " is sometimes used in a broader sense than that contended for by defendant. A disease may be contracted, while not contracted for. The words " liability contracted," etc., have been said to have a broader signification than the words " debt contracted," etc; but a contract liability is as much a liability growing out of a contract as is a contract debt a debt founded upon contract. In either case, if the word

"contracted" can be said to qualify the word which precedes
it, the result is the same, so far as the limitation of the qualified word is concerned. There are a number of authorities
which hold that under such a provision the homestead is not
exempt from execution issued upon a judgment founded in
tort: *Robinson* v. *Wiley*, 15 N. Y. 489; *Lathrop* v. *Singer*, 39
Barb. 396; *Kenyon* v. *Gould*, 61 Pa. St. 292; *Kirkpatrick* v.
White, 29 Pa. St. 176; *McLaren* v. *Anderson*, 81 Ala. 106;
Williams v. *Bowden*, 69 Ala. 433; *Burton* v. *Mill*, 78 Va. 468.
In Indiana and Georgia the language [36] is, "debts founded
on contract." In Wisconsin the language is, "for any debt
or liability contracted after," etc; and it is there held that
the homestead is exempt from levy and sale upon a judgment
founded in tort: *Smith* v. *Omans*, 17 Wis. 395. In Illinois
the language is the same as ours, but there is another statute
which prohibits an alienation of the homestead in any case
by the husband, except with the consent of the wife, and the
courts of that state have held that, in the light of both of
these laws, it was the evident intent of the legislature to protect the homestead as a shelter for the wife and children,
independently of any acts of the husband. In *Conroy* v.
Sullivan, 44 Ill. 451, the court say: "He [the husband] cannot deprive them of their right to it [the homestead] without
the consent of the wife, either by his contracts or his torts.
There is no more reason, so far as the wife is concerned, for
permitting it to be sold for the husband's tort, than for his
violation of a contract, and it is the evident policy of the law
to forbid its being sold under a judgment and execution in
either case." See, also, *Loomis* v. *Gerson*, 62 Ill. 11. The
Illinois cases have been criticised by some of the text-writers,
but we think the rule laid down by that court is sound.

As a general rule, only such property as the owner or debtor
himself might sell can be taken on execution against him:
Coombs v. *Jordan*, 3 Bland, 284; 22 Am. Dec. 236; *French* v.
Mehan, 56 Pa. St. 286; *Gentry* v. *Wagstaff*, 3 Dev. 270; *Knox*
v. *Hunt*, 18 Mo. 243. It has frequently been held by our own
court that any deed, release, or mortgage, except for purchase
money, of the homestead exemption, by the husband, without
the signature of the wife, is void as to both. As early as the
case of *Beecher* v. *Baldy*, 7 Mich. 488, 506, it was held that
where the householder is a married man he cannot, by any
waiver, consent to a sale on execution, so as to render such
sale valid, without the [37] consent of the wife. Justice Chris-

tiancy, in that case, speaking 'for the court, says: "For, in such case, the validity of the sale would rest upon his consent, in the same manner as if he had conveyed by deed; and, if deeded by him under the like circumstances, the deed would be void, even as to him, without the signature of the wife. Such, we think, is the effect of the express provision of the constitution. . . . . The object of the exemption was quite as much to protect the wife and family as the husband."

Mr. Justice Campbell, in *Penniman* v. *Perce*, 9 Mich. 528, says: "The wife has an absolute and vested interest in the homestead, which her husband has no power to discharge or affect."

We do not think that it was the intention of the framers of the constitution to prohibit a voluntary alienation by the husband, and at the same time permit an involuntary alienation. It was not intended that a mortgage executed by the husband upon the homestead without the consent of the wife should be void, but that in case the husband represented that he was not married, and that the premises mortgaged were not a homestead, a judgment founded upon the fraud, and not upon the contract, could be enforced against the homestead property. In view of the language employed, the light thrown upon the use of the phrase by the record of the proceedings of the convention, the fact that the language of the existing statute upon the same subject was not adopted, and the effect which has already been given to this provision as respects alienation by the husband, the provision must be construed as exempting the homestead from execution and sale upon all judgments, whether founded in tort or in contract. It may be said, also, that this constitution has for nearly fifty years received this construction, and to give it that contended [38] for by defendant would be a surprise to the bar and people of this state.

The decree is affirmed with costs.

The other justices concurred.

HOMESTEADS—FOR WHAT CLAIMS LIABLE—LIENS FOR IMPROVEMENTS.— Under many of the statutory and constitutional provisions of the several states relating to homestead exemptions, real property impressed with a homestead claim is not exempt from a lien in favor of a mechanic, laborer, or materialman who furnishes labor or materials to be used in the improvement of the homestead, and it can therefore be directed to be sold in satisfaction of such lien: *Bonner* v. *Minnier*, 13 Mont. 269; 40 Am. St. Rep. 441;

Dicken v. *Thrasher*, 58 Ga. 360; *Anderson* v. *Seamans*, 49 Ark. 475; *Murray* v. *Rapley*, 30 Ark. 568; *Phelps* v. *Shay*, 32 Neb. 19; *Allen* v. *Harley*, 3 S. C. 412. Some of the cases hold that the claimant, by failing to take the steps necessary to secure a lien upon the premises, under the provisions of the Mechanics' Lien Law, loses the right to subject the premises to such debts: *Sternberger* v. *Gowdy*, 93 Ky. 146; *McPhee* v. *O'Rourke*, 10 Col. 301; 3 Am. St. Rep. 579; *Merchant* v. *Perez*, 11 Tex. 20. There is authority, however, for the proposition that the homestead is not exempt from sale for the satisfaction of a debt contracted for improvements made thereon, although the creditor may have lost his lien as a mechanic for the debt: *Miller* v. *Brown*, 11 Lea, 155. It has been decided in quite a number of cases that, under statutes subjecting homesteads to "mechanics' and laborers'" liens, one who furnishes materials for the construction of a building on realty, either before or after it has been impressed with the homestead character, cannot obtain a lien thereon for the material furnished: *Richards* v. *Shear*, 70 Cal. 187; *Walsh* v. *McMenomy*, 74 Cal. 356; *Coleman* v. *Ballandi*, 22 Minn. 144; *Smith* v. *Lackor*, 23 Minn. 454. It has also been determined that although a constitutional provision subjects the homestead to the liens of mechanics and laborers, yet a statute attempting to give a lien for materials furnished and used in improvements upon a homestead is void, as an unwarranted attempt to enlarge such constitutional provision: *Cumming* v. *Bloodworth*, 87 N. C. 83; *Coleman* v. *Ballandi*, 22 Minn. 144. The doctrine that a materialman cannot obtain a lien against a homestead for material furnished in making improvements thereon, under a statute giving the right to obtain such lien to "mechanics and laborers," is expressly repudiated in *Bonner* v. *Minnier*, 13 Mont. 269; 40 Am. St. Rep. 441; *Phelps* v. *Shay*, 32 Neb. 19.

Antecedent Debts.—It may be considered as well settled that a homestead, as a general rule, is not exempt from a debt reduced to judgment against the homestead claimant before his acquisition or occupation of the homestead as such: *Peterson* v. *Little*, 74 Iowa, 223; *Lamb* v. *McConkey*, 76 Iowa, 47; *O'Shea* v. *Payne*, 81 Mo. 516; *Peake* v. *Cameron*, 102 Mo. 568; *Woodlie* v. *Towles*, 9 Baxt. 592; *Meador* v. *Meador*, 88 Ky. 217; *Croup* v. *Morton*, 53 Iowa, 599. The liability of the homestead for such indebtedness attaches at the date of the creation of the indebtedness, and not at the time of the rendition of the judgment thereon: *Bills* v. *Mason*, 42 Iowa, 329. Statutes in some instances provide that the homestead is exempt from liability for the debts of the owner contracted before the homestead is dedicated or occupied, and decisions are found upholding such statutes (*Estate of Walley*, 11 Nev. 260), or the doctrine provided for in them: *Stokes* v. *Hatcher*, 60 Ga. 617; *Wilson* v. *Sparks*, 72 N. C. 208; *Cusic* v. *Douglass*, 3 Kan. 123; 87 Am. Dec. 464, and extended note treating the topic. While it may be conceded, as established by the great weight of authority, that statutes are valid exempting homesteads from the payment of debts contracted by the owner while the homestead is occupied as such (note to *Vanstory* v. *Thornton*, 112 N. C. 196; 34 Am. St. Rep. 499), yet it has been decided by the highest court in the land that a statute exempting a homestead from the payment of debts contracted before the enactment of the statute creating the homestead is unconstitutional and void, as impairing the obligations of contracts: *Gunn* v. *Barry*, 15 Wall. 610, on appeal from the supreme court of Georgia; *Edwards* v. *Kearzey*, 96 U. S. 595, on appeal from the supreme court of North Carolina. Such is the doctrine of all of the late cases, which also maintain that the homestead is liable to the lien of judgments entered before the homestead had an existence as such. Note to

Vanstory v. *Thornton,* 34 Am. St. Rep. 496; note to *Cusic* v. *Douglass,* 87 Am. Dec. 464, originally reported in 3 Kan. 123.

Purchase Money.—In most of the states constitutional and statutory provisions relating to homestead exemptions expressly provide that the homestead shall not be exempt from liability for purchase money. In the absence of such provisions, the homestead is liable for its purchase price, because equity creates a lien upon it in favor of the vendor even when there is no conventional creation of it. It follows that it is a rule of universal application that, as a general proposition, no homestead right can be acquired in land upon which the purchase money is unpaid, either in whole or in part, as against the party to whom such purchase money is due. Although it is impressed with the homestead character, it remains subordinate to the lien for its unpaid purchase price, whether created by mortgage or otherwise, until removed in a lawful manner, and may be subjected to forced sale to satisfy such lien so long as it exists: *Toms* v. *Fite,* 93 N. C. 274; *Williams* v. *Jones,* 100 Ill. 362; *Campbell* v. *Maginnis,* 70 Iowa, 589; *Bills* v. *Mason,* 42 Iowa, 329; *Bradley* v. *Curtis,* 79 Ky. 327; *McCarty* v. *Brackenridge,* 1 Tex. Civ. App. 170; *McCreery* v. *Fortson,* 35 Tex. 642; *Tunstall* v. *Jones,* 25 Ark. 272; *Hopper* v. *Parkinson,* 5 Nev. 233; *Williams* v. *Young,* 17 Cal. 403; *Alexander* v. *Jackson,* 92 Cal. 514; 27 Am. St. Rep. 158; *Andrews* v. *Akorn,* 13 Kan. 351; *Bush* v. *Scott,* 76 Ill. 524; *Cook* v. *Cook,* 67 Ga. 381; *Nichols* v. *Overacker,* 16 Kan. 59; *Buckingham* v. *Nelson,* 42 Miss. 417; *Austin* v. *Underwood,* 37 Ill. 438; 87 Am. Dec. 254; note to *Magee* v. *Magee,* 99 Am. Dec. 574–576, 665. Money advanced to purchase supplies for the purpose of raising a crop on the homestead has been regarded in the nature of purchase money, and therefore a claim which might be enforced against the homestead: *Stephens* v. *Smith,* 62 Ga. 177. The character of the purchase money debt and of the vendor's right of payment out of the homestead is not affected by changing the form of the evidence of the debt nor by securing it with additional security, real or personal: *Bentley* v. *Jordan,* 3 Lea, 353; *Chase* v. *Abbott,* 20 Iowa, 154; *Burns* v. *Thayer,* 101 Mass. 426; *Wood* v. *Lord,* 51 N. H. 448; *Pratt* v. *Topeka Bank,* 12 Kan. 570; *Weaver's Estate,* 25 Pa. St. 434.

Assignment of Lien.—The weight of authority establishes the proposition that the assignee of a note or note and mortgage given for the purchase price of a homestead is subrogated to all of the rights of the vendor as against the right of homestead exemption in the vendee, and that the assignee may therefore enforce the payment of such note out of the homestead land. It is only just that the assignment of a note given for the purchase price of a homestead carries with it the lien of the vendor, and all the equities and remedies the latter would have had if he had never parted with the claim. This rule is supported by *Bradley* v. *Curtis,* 79 Ky. 327; *Williams* v. *Jones,* 100 Ill. 362; *Bills* v. *Mason,* 42 Iowa, 329; *Wofford* v. *Gains,* 53 Ga. 485; *Sparger* v. *Cumpton,* 54 Ga. 355; *Wynn* v. *Flannegan,* 25 Tex. 778; *Purcell* v. *Dittman,* 81 Ky. 148; *Brooks* v. *Young,* 60 Tex. 32; *Hicks* v. *Morris,* 57 Tex. 658, expressly overruling *Malone* v. *Kaufman,* 38 Tex. 454, asserting the contrary doctrine, which is also maintained in *Skaggs* v. *Nelson,* 25 Miss. 89. If the assignee of a note given for the homestead purchase price surrenders it to the maker, and takes the latter's note in exchange, the homestead is bound by a trust deed given to secure the latter note: *Williams* v. *Jones,* 100 Ill. 363. The new note in such case stands in place of the old one, and is evidence of a debt incurred in the purchase of the homestead: *Wood* v. *Lord,* 51 N. H. 448.

Borrowed Purchase Money.—There is a conflict of authority upon the question as to whether money loaned by a third person to the vendee to enable him to purchase a homestead, or to complete the payment for one already purchased, entitles him to the vendor's lien. The minority of the cases maintain that the person who thus furnishes money to the vendee does not stand in the position of the vendor, so as to be entitled to his lien for the money advanced: *Stansell* v. *Roberts*, 13 Ohio, 148; 42 Am. Dec. 193; *Burnap* v. *Cook*, 16 Iowa, 149; 85 Am. Dec. 507; *Notte's Appeal*, 45 Pa. St. 361; *Lear* v. *Heffner*, 28 La. Ann. 829; *Chapman* v. *Abrahams*, 61 Ala. 108. In *Eyster* v. *Hatheway*, 50 Ill. 525, 99 Am. Dec. 537, it was held, in effect, that homestead purchase money means the price agreed to be paid for the land to the vendor, and not a debt due another generally; therefore, if money is borrowed of a third person, without specifying the purpose for which it is obtained, and is afterward applied by the borrower to the payment of the purchase money due for the homestead, such third party does not stand in the place of the vendor, and is not entitled to his lien, and this ruling has been followed in *Parrott* v. *Kimpf*, 102 Ill. 423; *Winslow* v. *Noble*, 101 Ill. 194. On the other hand, it has been repeatedly decided in Illinois that, if the borrowed money is paid by such third person directly to the vendor for the vendee as the price of the land, it is purchase money, for which the lender has a lien against the homestead: *Austin* v. *Underwood*, 37 Ill. 438; 87 Am. Dec. 254. Or, if the purchase money is advanced by a third person to pay for a homestead in the possession of the vendee, under his promise to secure its repayment out of the land, it is purchase money for which such person has a lien as against the homestead right: *Magee* v. *Magee*, 51 Ill. 500; 99 Am. Dec. 571, and note, 574–576, on vendor's liens against homesteads for purchase money. The majority of the cases maintain the more equitable rule, namely, that money borrowed of a third person by the vendee of a homestead and paid to the vendor, either by the lender or by the vendee in payment of the whole or a part of the purchase price of the land, is purchase money for which such land is liable to such third person, who is subrogated to all of the rights of the vendor: *Lassen* v. *Vance*, 8 Cal. 271; 68 Am. Dec. 322; *Carr* v. *Caldwell*, 10 Cal. 380; 70 Am. Dec. 740; *Bugg* v. *Russell*, 75 Ga. 837; *White* v. *Wheelan*, 71 Ga. 533; *Warhmund* v. *Merritt*, 60 Tex. 24; *Eylar* v. *Eylar*, 60 Tex. 315; *Pridgen* v. *Warn*, 79 Tex. 588; *Hicks* v. *Morris*, 57 Tex. 658, expressly overruling *Malone* v. *Kaufman*, 38 Tex. 454, maintaining the contrary rule; *Whitaker* v. *Elliott*, 73 N. C. 186; *Bradley* v. *Curtis*, 79 Ky. 327; *Nichols* v. *Overacker*, 16 Kan. 54. Perhaps the best rule to follow is that adopted in *Dreese* v. *Myers*, 52 Kan. 126; 39 Am. St. Rep. 336; and in *Carey* v. *Boyle*, 53 Wis. 574. In the last-named case the court, in laying down such rule, said: "It must be understood that the extension of this equity (the lien of the vendor) to a third person is strictly confined to those who furnish or advance the purchase money to the purchaser in such manner that they can be said either to have paid it to the vendor personally, or caused it to be paid on behalf or for the benefit of the purchaser, and to this extent they become parties to the transaction. It must not be a general loan, to be used by the purchaser to pay the consideration of the purchase, or to be used for any other purpose at his pleasure. In such case the simple fact that the money can be traced into the land as having been paid by the purchaser to the vendor, as the whole or part of the purchase money, gives the person who loaned it no such right." To this rule might be added the fact that if money is borrowed of a third person under an express agreement that it is to be used in the purchase of the homestead, or to pay the price thereof, and it is so used, it becomes purchase money, and the party so advancing it is entitled to be subrogated to the rights of the vendor, and may enforce the lien against the homestead against the objection of the owner of the land: *Dreese* v. *Meyers,* 52 Kan. 126; 39 Am. St. Rep. 336; *Nichols* v. *Overacker,* 16 Kan. 54; *Magee* v. *Magee,* 51 Ill. 500; 99 Am. Dec. 571; *Warhmund* v. *Merritt,* 60 Tex. 24.

Taxes.—A homestead is not exempt from sale for taxes or assessments levied against it. A provision to this effect exists in the statutes of most of the states, but independent of statutory enactment there can be no doubt that the homestead must bear its just proportion of taxation: *Lamar* v. *Sheppard,* 80 Ga. 25; *Colquitt* v. *Brown,* 63 Ga. 440; *Douthett* v. *Winter.* 108 Ill. 330; *Tucker* v. *Tucker,* 108 N. C. 235. In *Lufkin* v. *Galveston,* 58 Tex. 545, the court said: "The constitution of the state, article 16, section 50, makes no difference between the homestead and any other real property as to its liability to be sold for taxes that may be due on it. Nor does it draw any distinction between general and special taxes to which it may be subject. The plain import of its terms is, that it is not protected from forced sale for lawful taxes that may be due on it. This instrument throws the most ample protection around the homestead. In return, it clearly intends that it shall bear its just proportionate share in the burdens imposed by the government. It was intended to be alike liable as other real property to all taxes—state, county, or municipal—that could under its restrictions be justly and lawfully laid upon the real estate of a citizen." In this case it was decided that an assessment or tax levied against a homestead to cover the cost of a local improvement in constructing a sidewalk in front of it was a valid lien for which the homestead was liable. And again, in *Perine* v. *Forbush,* 97 Cal. 305, it was decided that it was no defense to an action upon a street assessment that the property against which it is sought to enforce the lien constitutes the homestead of the defendant. The homestead is, however, exempt from sale for taxes, except such as are assessed against the homestead itself, and the sale of it for other taxes, as well as those assessed against it, cannot be upheld: *Wright* v. *Straub,* 64 Tex. 64. In Illinois it has been decided that real estate occupied as a homestead is exempt from sale under execution issued upon a judgment *in personam* against the homestead claimant for state and county taxes due thereon, and that the only way in which such property can be held liable for taxes assessed against it is by proceedings *in rem: Douthett* v. *Winter,* 108 Ill. 330.

Fiduciary Debts.—A homestead is liable for the payment of fiduciary debts created by the owner, if there is in the state a constitutional or statutory provision making the homestead liable for all liabilities incurred by any public officers, officer of a court, other fiduciary, or any attorney at law for money collected: *Commonwealth* v. *Ford,* 29 Gratt 683; *Gilbert* v. *Neely,* 35 Ark. 25; *Schuessler* v. *Dudley,* 80 Ala. 547; 60 Am. Rep. 124; *Vincent* v. *State,* 74 Ala. 274; *Bridewell* v. *Halliday,* 37 La. Ann. 410; *Commonwealth* v. *Cook,* 8 Bush, 220; 8 Am. Rep. 456. Such provisions of law include the sureties of a public officer, and their homesteads may be subjected to sale to pay a fiduciary debt created by their principal by a misappropriation of funds belonging to the public (*Commonwealth* v. *Cook,* 8 Bush, 220; 8 Am. Rep. 456; *Commonwealth* v. *Ford,* 29 Gratt. 683), tax collectors (*Commonwealth* v. *Ford,* 29 Gratt. 683; *Schuessler* v. *Dudley,* 80 Ala. 547; 60 Am. Rep. 124), sheriffs (*Commonwealth* v. *Cook,* 8 Bush. 220; 8 Am. Rep. 456), and guardians (*Gilbert* v. *Neely,* 35 Ark. 24), and the sureties of such officers are within the meaning of this rule. The homestead of an agent is

liable for money or property misappropriated by him in the discharge of a
trust bestowed upon him by his principal: *Bridwell* v. *Halliday*, 37 La. Ann.
410.   But the homestead of an attorney is not subject to liability for money
received by such attorney to indemnify himself against liability as surety
for his client, and by him converted to his own use.   In such case the
money is not received by him in his capacity of attorney, and is not held
by him as a trustee, but as security to protect himself against loss: *Sanders*
v. *Sanders*, 56 Ark. 585.   A surety on the bond of a defaulting officer or fiduciary, who pays the amount of his principal's default, is entitled to be subrogated to the rights of the state, county, or person who might have subjected
the homestead of such principal to the payment of his defalcation, and the
surety may subject the homestead of his principal to the payment of his demand: *Schuessler* v. *Dudley*, 80 Ala. 547; 60 Am. Rep. 124; *Gilbert* v.
Neely, 35 Ark. 24.   Under statutory enactments making the real estate of
a public officer liable for his defalcation or misappropriation of public money,
but not especially mentioning his homestead, it has been decided that his
homestead is not liable for a fiduciary debt, arising from his defalcations in
office: *Reu* v. *Driskell*, 11 Lea 642; *Hume* v. *Gossett*, 43 Ill. 297; and a
homestead assigned to a debtor, in bankruptcy proceedings, is exempt from
liability for a fiduciary debt which has not been discharged by such proceedings: *Simpson* v. *Houston*, 97 N. C. 344; 2 Am. St. Rep. 297.

Torts.—Statutes exempting homesteads from liability for "debts contracted" by the homestead owner do not seem to contemplate the protection of a wrongdoer from liability for his own torts, or for any trespass
committed by him.   Hence a majority of the cases maintain the doctrine,
contrary to that announced in the principal case, that under such statutes
there is no exemption provided from liability for obligations arising from
torts, and that the homestead of the wrongdoer may be subjected to the
payment of such obligations: *Vincent* v. *State*, 74 Ala. 275; *Williams* v.
Bowden, 69 Ala 433; *Meredith* v. *Holmes*, 68 Ala. 190; *Davis* v. *Henson*, 29
Ga. 345; *Ries* v. *McClatchey*, 128 Ind. 125; *McClure* v. *Braniff*, 75 Iowa, 38;
Burton v. *Mill*, 78 Va. 468; *Lathrop* v. *Singer*, 39 Barb. 396; *Robinson* v.
Wiley, 15 N. Y. 489.   Under such statutes the homestead is liable for a
penalty provided by statute against a mortgagee for failure to enter satisfaction of a mortgage upon the margin of the record after payment: *Williams* v. *Bowden*, 69 Ala. 433.   The homestead exemption does not protect
against a demand for damages for a breach of promise to marry, as this is not
a debt contracted, but a quasi tort: *Burton* v. *Mill*, 78 Va. 468.   Nor can a
homestead exemption be claimed against a fine imposed for a violation of criminal law: *Whiteacre* v. *Rector*, 29 Gratt. 714; 26 Am. Rep. 420.   If the homestead is used for the unlawful sale of intoxicating liquors it is liable for fines,
costs, and judgments rendered against the homesteader on account of such
unlawful conduct, and it can make no difference that the homestead is put
to such use by him without the consent of his wife: *McClure* v. *Braniff*, 75
Iowa, 38.

No exemption can be claimed in favor of a homestead against a liability
growing out of a tort, and, if the execution or judgment discloses on its face
that the liability arose out of a tort, the officer may disregard a claim of
homestead exemption interposed by the debtor, and proceed to sell the
property, but he cannot go beyond the face of the judgment or execution to
ascertain the facts: *McLaren* v. *Anderson*, 81 Ala. 106.   On the other hand,
authority is not wanting to support the proposition that under constitutional
or statutory provisions exempting a homestead from liability for debts

"contracted" while it remains such homestead, it is not liable to forced sale to satisfy a judgment rendered against the homestead owner in an action of tort: *Smith* v. *Omans,* 17 Wis. 395; *In re Radway,* 3 Hughes, 609; *Conroy* v. *Sullivan,* 44 Ill. 451; *Loomis* v. *Gerson,* 62 Ill. 11; *Dellinger* v. *Tweed,* 66 N. C. 207; *Gill* v. *Edwards,* 87 N. C. 76. The exemption may be claimed in such case either against a judgment in favor of a private person or in favor of the state: *State* v. *Pitts,* 51 Mo. 133; *Loomis* v. *Gerson,* 62 Ill. 11. The exemption is also good against judgments founded in tort, both as to principal and costs: *In re Radway,* 3 Hughes, 609; *Kruger* v. *Le Blanc,* 75 Mich. 424. The reason for the rule is thus stated in *Loomis* v. *Gerson,* 62 Ill. 11: "We held in *Conroy* v. *Sullivan,* 44 Ill. 451, that the homestead was protected from sale under a judgment obtained against the husband for his tort, as well as under one obtained for violation of his contracts. The object of these homestead laws was to furnish a shelter for the wife and children, which could not be taken away or lost by the act of the husband alone. The principle must equally exempt the homestead from sale under a judgment for a fine and costs rendered in a criminal prosecution for a misdemeanor. The wife is not to suffer for the wrongful act of the husband. The state must submit to the same exemptions of a defendant's property that it imposes upon its citizens."

Miscellaneous.—The professional services of a physician do not constitute a claim for labor so as to subject a homestead to the payment thereof: *Weymouth* v. *Sanborn,* 43 N. H. 171; 80 Am. Dec. 144. The homestead is exempt from liability for alimony decreed in favor of the wife in a divorce suit: *Biffle* v. *Pullam,* 114 Mo. 50; *Byers* v. *Byers,* 21 Iowa, 268; *Stanley* v. *Sullivan,* 71 Wis. 585; 5 Am. St. Rep. 245.

Judgment, Execution, and Attachment Liens, in so far as they attach to homesteads, are treated at considerable length in notes to *Vanstory* v. *Thornton;* 34 Am. St. Rep. 496–506; *Pipkin* v. *Williams,* 38 Am. St. Rep. 247, 248; *Blue* v. *Blue,* 87 Am. Dec. 273–280.

Miller *v.* Scottish Union and National Insurance Company.

[101 Michigan, 49.]

Insurance—Authority of Agent—Notice to Insured.—An insurance company whose agent indorses upon a policy issued by him that a mortgage upon the property is in process of foreclosure, for the purpose of perfecting the title, and delivers such policy to other insurance agents with a statement that it is contrary to his orders to write policies on mortgaged property, but that he will submit it to his company, is liable on the policy for a loss occurring two days later if the policy is delivered to the insured by such agent, and the premium obtained from him without notice of the nature of the transaction or of any limitation on the power of the agent issuing the policy, although it contains a provision that in matters relating to the procuring of insurance no person, unless duly authorized in writing, shall be deemed the agent of the company, and although the company has directed the insurance to be canceled upon receiving notice of the loss.

M. Norris, for the appellant.

McDonell & Hall, for the appellees.

[50] MONTGOMERY, J.   This is an action on a policy of insurance.   The policy was issued from the agency of the company at Bay City, and was duly countersigned by George Washington, the agent at that place.   The plaintiffs made application to Knaggs & Plum, insurance agents at Bay City, to place ten thousand dollars of insurance on their mill. Knaggs & Plum, being unable to place the whole amount in companies represented by them, applied in turn to Mr. Washington to write the policy in question, which he did. On examining the policy Knaggs & Plum called the attention of Mr. Washington to the fact that the mill was mortgaged, and the mortgage in process of foreclosure, and asked that the following indorsement be placed upon the policy: "It is understood that the mortgage on this property is in process of foreclosure, such proceedings being amicable for the purpose of perfecting the title."

Mr. Washington replied that it was contrary to his orders to write on mortgaged mill property, but Knaggs & Plum asked if he could not make an explanation, and get the company to carry it, stating that the policy would be of no value without it.   The agent, Washington, replied that he would submit it to the company, and thereupon made the indorsement, and delivered the policy to Knaggs & Plum, who delivered it to plaintiffs.   Plaintiffs had no notice of this conversation, and paid the premium to Knaggs & Plum.   A fire occurred the second day after the policy was delivered. Notice of this was telegraphed [51] to the company by the agent, Washington, and on the same day it wrote a letter to him, directing that the policy be canceled, and it has since denied liability upon the policy.   The policy contained the following clause: "In any matter relating to the procuring of this insurance no person, unless duly authorized in writing, shall be deemed the agent of this company."

The sole question in this case is whether, under the facts stated, the notice of want of authority to Knaggs & Plum was notice to the plaintiffs.   The circuit judge was of the opinion that the question was ruled by *McGraw* v. *Germania F. Ins. Co.*, 54 Mich. 145.   Counsel for defendant contends that the case referred to has been since overruled in effect, and that, if not, this case is distinguishable from that, in that the present policy contains the provision, above quoted, that in any matter relating to the procuring of the insurance no person, unless duly authorized in writing, shall be deemed the agent of the company.

We do not deem it necessary to decide whether the present case is distinguishable from *McGraw* v. *Germania F. Ins. Co.*, 54 Mich. 145, or whether Knaggs & Plum are to be treated as agents of the insured or the insurer. If it be assumed that they were agents of the plaintiffs, on every principle of equity the defendant is bound by the policy in suit. This is not a case where the broker has misrepresented the risk, or in which the agent of the company has been deceived in any other manner. Nor is it a case where notice of the purpose to cancel has been brought home to the broker. But the sole question is whether the plaintiffs are chargeable with notice of the want of authority on the part of the agent, Washington, to do what he attempted to do. We quite agree with the defendant's counsel [52] that the same rule should obtain in dealing with the acts of agents to obtain insurance as is applied in interpreting the acts of agents in other business transactions, but we do not agree with counsel that any rules governing the conduct of agents will permit the defendant in this case to escape liability on this policy. There can be no doubt that, had the defendant's agent, Washington, delivered the policy directly to plaintiffs, the company would be bound by his act. It was directly within the scope of his apparent authority. We think it is quite clear that the company is bound, notwithstanding the notice to Knaggs & Plum, in this case, upon precisely the same principle, viz., that where one of two innocent parties must suffer by the wrong of the third, it should be that one which has put it in the power of the third party to work the injury. The notice to Knaggs & Plum of want of authority was accompanied by notice to Washington, equally clear, that Knaggs & Plum had limitations placed upon their authority to bind the plaintiffs. The course of business was enough to furnish this notice. It cannot be contended that the defendant's agent did not know that Knaggs & Plum were only empowered to furnish insurance to plaintiffs, and were not empowered to buy waste paper. Knowing this, and being also directly informed by Knaggs & Plum that, without the indorsement in question, the policy would be valueless—a fact which he must be assumed to have known—he intrusted the policy to them, to be delivered to the plaintiffs as a binding contract. If notice to Knaggs & Plum was notice to plaintiffs, certainly notice to Washington of the limitations of their authority was likewise notice to defendant. Yet with this notice he put it in the power of Knaggs & Plum to collect the premium from the plaintiffs upon a policy which he knew, from the nature of Knaggs & Plum's employment, they had no power to accept.

[53] It is undoubtedly a general rule that notice to an agent is equivalent to notice to the principal. Mr. Story states that the rule is based upon the presumption that such notice is communicated to the principal (Story on Agency, sec. 140); and in most cases this is a conclusive presumption, resulting in the general rule that the law imputes to the principal notice of facts which the agent acquires while acting as such agent within the scope of his authority. But, as pointed out in Mechem on Agency, section 721, this rule is subject to exceptions: "And such notice or knowledge will not be imputed, 1. Where it is such as it is the agent's duty not to disclose; and 2. Where the agent's relations to the subject matter, or his previous conduct, render it certain that he will not disclose it; and 3. Where the person claiming the benefit of the notice, or those whom he represents, colluded with the agent to cheat or defraud the principal."

In section 723 the learned author further states: "The rule is based, as has been seen, upon the principle that it is the duty of the agent to communicate to his principal the knowledge possessed by him relating to the subject matter of the agency, and material to the principal's protection and interests. This presumption, however, will not prevail where it is certainly to be expected that the agent will not perform this duty, as where the agent, though nominally acting as such, is in reality acting in his own or another's interest, and adversely to that of his principal." The doctrine of the text is supported by abundant authority: See cases cited in the note.

In *Innerarity* v. *Merchants' Nat. Bank*, 139 Mass. 332, 52 Am. Rep. 710, it is said: "While the knowledge of an agent is ordinarily to be imputed to the principal, it would appear now to be well established that there is an exception to the construction or imputation of notice from the agent to the principal in case of such conduct by the agent as raises a clear presumption that he would not communicate the fact in controversy; as where the communication of such a fact would [54] necessarily prevent the consummation of a fraudulent scheme which the agent was engaged in perpetrating."

An instructive case upon this subject is *Thompson* v. *Cartwright*, 33 Beav. 178. In that case it appeared that one Montriou was the attorney of one Downes, and received a conveyance in Downes' interest. He had knowledge of the existence of a prior encumbrance, and the question was whether his knowledge was the knowledge of Downes. The rule is very clearly stated by the master of the rolls: "I take the rule to be, generally, that the client'must be treated as having had notice of all the facts which, in the same transaction, have come to the knowledge of the solicitor, and that the burden of proof lies on him (the client) to show that there is a probability, amounting to a moral certainty, that the solicitor would not have communicated that fact to his client. The question here is whether the applicant, Mr. Downes, discharges the burden so imposed on him. Upon the whole, I think that he does. Mr. Montriou, as his solicitor, knowing of the mortgage affecting the property, prepares a deed by which the owner of the property covenants that there is no mortgage, charge, or encumbrance on it or affecting it. He prepares this deed, and causes his client, the grantor, to execute to his client, the grantee, a solemn instrument, by which he deliberately puts his hand and seal to an assertion which is false. I think that this amounts to a solemn declaration by Mr. Montriou to his client that he, Mr. Montriou, was ignorant of any charge affecting the property, and that he did not believe that any such charge existed."

This case is not distinguishable in principle from the present. It cannot be doubted that the defendant's agent had every reason to believe that the policy, which was itself an assertion of his authority, would be conveyed to the plaintiffs by Knaggs & Plum as and for a binding contract. Indeed, it could have been placed in their hands by him for no other purpose. To permit the company which he represents to assert now that the plaintiffs had notice, through Knaggs & Plum, of the want of [55] authority, would be to imply notice to the principals which defendant's agent had every reason to anticipate would not in fact be given them. No such injustice can be sanctioned. The conclusion of the circuit judge was right.

The judgment will be affirmed, with costs.

The other justices concurred.

INSURANCE—AUTHORITY OF AGENT—NOTICE TO INSURED.—The acts of
an insurance agent performed within the scope of his apparent power bind
his principal. Persons dealing with the agent without knowledge of any
limitations on his powers are not bound to go beyond his apparent authority, and inquire whether or not he is in fact authorized to do a particular
act for his principal: *Hahn* v. *Guardian Ins. Co.*, 23 Or. 576; 37 Am. St.
Rep. 709, and note; but, where limitations on the powers of an agent are
known to the insured, the company is bound only by acts of the agent within
the scope of the authority conferred: *German Ins. Co.* v. *Heiduk*, 30 Neb.
288; 27 Am. St. Rep. 402, and note.

KEARNEY *v.* CLUTTON.

[101 MICHIGAN, 106.]

WAREHOUSEMEN—LIABILITY OF.—A storage company is not liable in trover
for goods stored with it by a mortgagor, and taken from its custody by
the mortgagee, and by him converted to his use, without the knowledge
or consent of the storage company.

AUCTIONEER'S LIABILITY.—An auctioneer who takes property into his possession from one not the true owner, and sells it in good faith, paying
over the proceeds, less his commissions, is liable in trover to the true
owner, although such auctioneer has no knowledge of want of title in
the party for whom he sells.

TROVER—DIVISION OF VERDICT—INSTRUCTIONS.—In an action of trover
against several defendants for the conversion of goods, if the jury render a verdict for a certain sum against each defendant, without any evidence by which to determine that each defendant converted a specific
part of the goods, the court commits no error in sending the jury back
with an instruction that there is no ground for a division of the verdict
against the defendant.

TROVER—INSTRUCTIONS.—If, in an action of trover against a chattel mortgagee and an auctioneer who sold the goods at foreclosure sale, it is
shown that a portion of the goods sued for were not covered by the
mortgage, it is not error to refuse to submit the question to the jury, at
the request of defendants, as to whether the auctioneer sold goods
amounting to more than the mortgage debt.

CHATTEL MORTGAGE.—DESCRIPTION of property in a chattel mortgage as
"all household and personal effects" is controlled by a subsequent
specific and minute description of the property.

Corliss, Andrus & Leete, W. F. Atkinson, and R. Kelly, for
the appellants.

E. S. Grece and G. H. Penniman, for the appellee.

[107] GRANT, J. This is an action of trover for the conversion of certain household and personal goods. Plaintiff
and her husband, on April 24, 1890, executed a chattel mortgage to one Cromwell Clutton, to secure the payment of an

expressed consideration of one hundred and thirty-five dollars. Shortly afterward Mr. Kearney died. After his death Mrs. Kearney executed to another person a second mortgage upon the goods for the sum of two hundred dollars. She broke up housekeeping, and stored the goods with the defendants Grace, who carried on a storage and cartage business, under the name of the Fidelity Storage Company. Cromwell Clutton, it appears, lived in Dakota, and defendant Jonathan L. Clutton made the loan, and took the mortgage in his name. Jonathan L. Clutton carried on the business in his brother's name, and had an interest in it. Jonathan L., learning that the goods had been removed from the plaintiff's house, requested an interview with the plaintiff. She informed him where the goods were stored, and claims that she then made an agreement with him that proceedings to foreclose the mortgage should be postponed until she had obtained [108] some life insurance which she claimed to be due on a policy upon her husband's life. Defendant Clutton denied this conversation, and testified that plaintiff then informed him that she could not redeem the property. The mortgage was then past due. The defendant Clutton then, in the name of his brother, brought an action of replevin in justice's court against the defendants Grace to recover the property. The writ of replevin was placed in the hands of one William H. Guyott, a constable, for service. He made due return to the writ that he had replevied the goods, and delivered them to the plaintiff, and had made personal service of the writ upon the defendants Grace. The goods were not removed by the constable from the storehouse of the Graces, but, on the day following, defendant Clutton caused them to be removed to the auction-room of the defendant Jerome, where, after notice of sale, they were sold by Jerome, who realized upon the sale eighty-two dollars, which he paid over to Clutton, after deducting his commission. A few days after plaintiff learned of the above proceedings, and related the transaction to some of her friends, who went to Clutton, and exacted from him sixty-five dollars, which he claims was a settlement of the entire transaction, and which was paid over to the plaintiff. She insisted that she did not authorize this settlement, and shortly afterward instituted this action. She recovered verdict and judgment for eight hundred dollars. The jury returned a verdict of five hundred dollars against defendant Clutton, one hundred and fifty dollars against the defendants Grace,

and one hundred and fifty dollars against Jerome. This verdict was objected to by the plaintiff, and, under the instruction of the court, the jury retired, and brought in a verdict
for the whole amount against all the defendants jointly.

1. The verdict and judgment against the defendants Grace
cannot be sustained. There is no evidence connecting them
with any conversion. The second count in [109] the declaration alleges a conspiracy between the defendants to defraud
the plaintiff. There is no evidence tending to show that the
defendants Grace had any knowledge of the replevin suit or
of the sale of the goods. The constable, a witness for plaintiff, flatly contradicts his return to the writ, by testifying that
he did not take the goods under his writ; that he never saw
them; that he made no service upon either of the defendants
Grace; that Clutton told him not to take the goods, but to
leave them there; and that the only service he made was
upon their book-keeper. If the book-keeper had handed this
writ to his employers, or if it had been properly served upon
them, being a valid writ, it would have operated as a complete defense to any action against them. Nor can they be
held for conversion from the fact that they did not notify the
plaintiff that the goods had been so seized. But, as already
shown, plaintiff failed to bring any knowledge of the transaction home to them. If there was any evidence of collusion
and conspiracy, it was between Clutton, the constable, and
the book-keeper, the only parties shown to have had any connection with the replevin suit.

2. In regard to the liability of defendant Jerome a more
difficult question is presented. There is no evidence that he
acted in bad faith or in collusion with Clutton. Clutton took
the goods to his auction-rooms, to be sold by him as agent
and auctioneer, under the foreclosure sale, a copy of which
was posted in Jerome's window. It is argued on behalf of
plaintiff that Jerome is liable, though acting in good faith,
if the taking by Clutton was tortious. It is sought to place
Jerome in the position of an officer who seizes and sells property under a writ. An officer acting under his writ is liable
beyond question when he seizes property under a void execution, or the property of a stranger under a valid execution.
The law considers such officer as the moving party. He is
the [110] only one authorized to make a levy and sale. He
acts at his peril. Counsel cite Cooley on Torts, 451: "One
who buys property must, at his peril, ascertain the owner-

ship; and, if he buys of one who has no authority to sell, his taking possession, in denial of the owner's right, is a conversion. The vendor is equally liable, whether he sells the property as his own or as officer or agent; and so is the party for whom he acts, if he assists in or advises the sale." The learned author cites the following authorities in support of the text: *Billiter* v. *Young*, 6 El. & B. 1; *Cooper* v. *Chitty*, 1 Burr. 23; *Garland* v. *Carlisle*, 4 Clark & F. 693; *Moore* v. *Eldred*, 42 Vt. 13; *Calkins* v. *Lockwood*, 17 Conn. 154; 42 Am. Dec. 729; *Smith* v. *Colby*, 67 Me. 169.

An examination of these authorities discloses that none of them involve the liability of an agent or auctioneer who merely sells the property for another when brought to him for that purpose.

In *Billiter* v. *Young*, 6 El. & B. 1, the defendant was not the sheriff, but plaintiff in the execution under which the sheriff, by his direction, seized and sold the property, the title to which had passed from the defendant in the execution.

In *Cooper* v. *Chitty*, 1 Burr. 23, the sheriff, who had seized goods under similar circumstances, was held liable, the title having passed, by an assignment in bankruptcy, out of the debtor to the assignee before levy and sale.

In *Garland* v. *Carlisle*, 4 Clark & F. 693, decided by the house of lords in 1837, there is an able discussion of the liability of a sheriff who levied upon the goods of a bankrupt. The sheriff was held liable, the court appearing to base their judgment upon the fact that the property seized was in the custody and power of the sheriff, and could not be disposed of by an agreement of the parties to the suit without the permission of the sheriff.

In *Moore* v. *Eldred*, 42 Vt. 13, the defendant was held liable because he had co-operated with the purchaser of the property with the intent to deprive the plaintiffs, the rightful owners, of it.

In *Calkins* v. *Lockwood*, 17 Conn. 154, 42 Am. Dec. 729, the defendant was held liable because he acted for the other defendants as their officer in their service, and because, by their direction, he removed and retained the property.

In *Smith* v. *Colby*, 67 Me. 169, the defendant, the superintendent of a poorhouse, under the direction of the selectmen of the town, removed and carried away a fence upon the plaintiff's land, and refused, upon demand, to return it. He was held in trover, and correctly so, because he alone removed the property.

The above are all the authorities cited in behalf of the plaintiff. No authorities have been cited by either party bearing upon the question. The authorities are not uniform, but the clear weight of authority holds that where an auctioneer receives and takes the property into his possession, and sells it, paying over the proceeds, less his commission, he is liable, although he has no knowledge of want of title in the party for whom he sells and acts in good faith: *Hoffman* v. *Carow*, 22 Wend. 285; *Coles* v. *Clark*, 3 Cush. 399; *Cochrane* v. *Rymill*, 40 L. T., N. S., 744; *Ganly* v. *Ledwidge*, 10 Ir. Com. L. 33. See, also, *Koch* v. *Branch*, 44 Mo. 542; 100 Am. Dec. 324; *Hollins* v. *Fowler*, L. R. 7 H. L. 757. To the contrary are *Rogers* v. *Huie*, 2 Cal. 571; 56 Am. Dec. 363; *Frizzelle* v. *Rundle*, 88 Tenn. 396; 17 Am. St. Rep. 908. See, also, *Ashe* v. *Livingston*, 2 Bay, 80; *Greenway* v. *Fisher*, 1 Car. & P. 190. Where an agent in good faith sold stolen coupons of United States bonds, and paid the proceeds over to the thief, he was held not liable in an action for their conversion: *Spooner* v. *Holmes*, 102 Mass. 503; 3 Am. Rep. 491. The court distinguish between that case and *Coles* v. *Clark*, 3 Cush. 399, upon the ground that the coupons were negotiable promises for the payment of money and that the rule of *caveat emptor* did not apply. The auctioneer may protect himself [112] by requiring indemnity, and we think the rule holding him liable is supported by the better reason.

3. We think the court committed no error in sending the jury back and instructing them that there was no ground for a division of the verdict against defendants. They were either jointly liable or there was no liability as against the defendants Grace and Jerome. There was no testimony by which the jury could determine that each defendant converted a portion of the goods.

4. Defendants' attorneys asked that the following question be submitted to the jury, viz: "Did Jerome sell more than one hundred and thirty-five dollars' worth of goods?" which the court refused. We think this refusal was correct, because it appeared beyond contradiction that goods were seized and sold which were not covered by the chattel mortgage. The property was described in the mortgage as "all household and personal effects," which expression was followed by a specific and minute description of the property. This minute

description limited the expression "all household and personal effects" to the property described, and excluded other property. Dresses and other articles of plaintiff's wardrobe, the family Bible, the family pictures, and other things which were not covered by the mortgage, were seized and sold. As to these she was entitled to recover, regardless of the mortgage.

5. In the event of a new trial it is proper to say that the statement of counsel for the plaintiff, in the presence of the jury, that he proposed to show that the chattel mortgage was obtained by fraud; that it was folded so as to look like a single paper, and that plaintiff thought it was a note and not a mortgage, and other similar statements, were unjustifiable, from the fact that no testimony was offered in support of such statements.

6. Testimony was offered by the plaintiff showing that only sixty-five dollars was in fact obtained upon the chattel mortgage, [113] and that one payment had been made. The defendant Clutton's mortgage was good for the amount actually advanced and still due. The jury should have been instructed that if they found the transaction to be as claimed by the plaintiff, she was entitled to judgment for the value of the goods mortgaged, less the amount of the mortgage and the sixty-five dollars which she had received in the supposed settlement and for the full value of the goods not mortgaged.

Judgment reversed and new trial ordered.

The other justices concurred.

WAREHOUSEMEN.—WHEN LIABLE FOR CONVERSION: See the extended note to *Schmidt* v. *Blood*, 24 Am. Dec. 156.

AUCTIONEERS—LIABILITY FOR SELLING PROPERTY OF ANOTHER.—An auctioneer is liable for selling the property of another unless he can show some other excuse or justification than his good faith and his ignorance of the true owner's title: *Robinson* v. *Bird*, 158 Mass. 357; 35 Am. St. Rep. 495, and note. See, also, the extended note to *Thomas* v. *Kerr*, 96 Am. Dec. 264.

CHATTEL MORTGAGES—DESCRIPTION.—The enumeration of certain specific articles in a mortgage also containing a general description of like articles will not prevent others from passing under the general description: *Harding* v. *Coburn*, 12 Met. 333; 46 Am. Dec. 680, and note. See the extended note to *Barrett* v. *Fisch*, 14 Am. St. Rep. 244.

HEMBEAU *v.* GREAT CAMP OF KNIGHTS OF MAC-
CABEES.

[101 MICHIGAN, 161.]

BENEVOLENT SOCIETIES—BY-LAWS—CONCLUSIVENESS OF DECISIONS OF.—A
by-law of a mutual benefit association providing that the decision of a
tribunal created by the association to pass upon death claims shall be
final, and shall bar a suit in law or equity to recover such claims, is
constitutional and valid.

BENEVOLENT SOCIETIES.—BY-LAWS of a mutual benefit association, assented
to by all parties, making a finding of liability by the association for
death claims by the duly constituted committee of the association a
condition precedent to a right to receive benefits, is constitutional and
valid.

FRAUD CANNOT BE PREDICATED upon the decision of a tribunal constituted
by the parties themselves, either as to the equity or the law of the case
considered, unless such tribunal has acted in bad faith and oppressively.

R. Connor, for the appellant.

Durand & Carton, for the appellee.

[162] MONTGOMERY, J. The defendant is a fraternal and
mutual benefit association, doing business on the assessment
plan. It pays beneficiaries of the class to which deceased
belonged one thousand dollars in case of death. By the laws
of the order beneficiaries are confined to widows, relatives
within the first degree of kinship, and to dependents. Alexander Coderre became a member of the order in 1891, and
named the present plaintiff as beneficiary, claiming [163] that
he was a dependent. Coderre died July 16, 1892. Proofs of
death were made by plaintiff. The executive committee of
the order, which passes on death claims, refused to allow the
claim of plaintiff, on the ground that plaintiff was not, and
never had been, a dependent of Coderre. On appeal to the
great camp this action of the executive committee was sustained. Plaintiff then brought the present suit in the circuit
court for the county of Saginaw, and on the trial the circuit
judge directed a verdict for the defendant, on the ground
that, by his contract, the plaintiff was precluded from maintaining the action.

Among the laws of the order at the time that Coderre became a member of the defendant, and also in force at the
time of his death, was section 83, which provides: " The executive committee shall have power to pass on all death
claims, and if, in their judgment, any such claim is not, on
its face, a valid one, they shall notify the beneficiary or ben-

eficiaries of the deceased member thereof, and give them or their attorneys an opportunity to appear before such committee within sixty days thereafter, and present such evidence as they may have to establish the justness of the said claim; and the said committee shall try, hear, and decide upon the justness or validity of such claim, and such decision shall be binding on such claimant, unless an appeal is taken to the great camp. The notice of the appeal from the decision of the committee must be filed with the great record keeper within sixty days thereafter. The decision of the great camp in all such cases shall be final, and no suit in law or equity shall be commenced or maintained by any member or beneficiary against the great camp."

We think the ruling of the circuit judge was in accordance with the holdings of this court in *Canfield* v. *Knights of Maccabees*, 87 Mich. 626; 24 Am. St. Rep. 186, and *Van Poucke* v. *Netherland etc. Society*, 63 Mich. 378. An attempt has been made to distinguish this case, but we do not discover any difference in principle between the Canfield case and the present. [164] That was a death claim, and the plaintiff was wholly defeated. It was sought to try by the suit at law the question of whether the policy was binding at the time of the death of the deceased. The only possible difference between that and the present case is that in the present case the determination of the great camp was that the policy never was of binding force. But this is not sufficient to distinguish the cases in principle.

The plaintiff contends that this law of the order is invalid as against public policy, for the reason that it attempts to oust the courts of jurisdiction. The same point was made in the Canfield case, and, while it was not much discussed, this court held that the case was controlled by the Van Poucke case. The holding of the courts places contracts of this nature, by which one becomes a member of a mutual association, and entitled to benefits in case of disability, or whose heirs are entitled to benefits in case of death, as upon a different footing than ordinary contracts between individuals. As was said in the case of *Rood* v. *Railway Pass. etc. Benefit Assn.*, 31 Fed. Rep. 63: "This is a purely voluntary association. The members of the association have, by their own organic law, provided a tribunal to hear and determine all claims against it, and I do not think any court can be invoked to review the action of the board in a matter so completely delegated to them. To attempt to enforce by suit any claim which the board of directors has acted upon, or refused to allow or approve, is equivalent to prosecuting an appeal from this board. It was certainly competent for the members of this association to agree among themselves that the action of their board of directors in reference to any claim presented against the association should be final; and there can be no doubt from the language of the clause from the constitution just quoted that they have so agreed." [165] See, also, *Woolsey* v. *Independent Order of Odd Fellows*, 61 Iowa, 492; *Anacosta Tribe* v. *Murbach*, 13 Md. 91; 71 Am. Dec. 625; *Black etc. Society* v. *Vandyke*, 2 Whart. 309; 30 Am. Dec. 263; *Toram* v. *Howard Assn.*, 4 Pa. St. 519; *Lantalum* v. *Insurance Co.*, 22 New Br. 14.

The effect of this agreement would not be to oust the court of jurisdiction in case the great camp should determine that the plaintiff was entitled to benefits, but should refuse to proceed to make payment. But such is not the case here. The plaintiff has submitted his claim to the jurisdiction provided by the laws of the order, and has been defeated therein, and now applies to the courts for redress. We think it was competent, under the decisions cited, for the association to provide a law of its order to which all parties should assent, and which should make a finding of liability by the duly constituted committees of the order a condition precedent to a right to receive benefits.

The plaintiff claims that the decision of this court in *Risser* v. *Hoyt*, 53 Mich. 185, and other cases in which it has been held that the legislature may not impair the right of trial by jury, are inconsistent with the validity of such an engagement as the one under consideration. We fail to see how the cases have any application to the question before us. This is not a case of an attempted exclusion of remedy by the legislature, but a case where the parties have agreed that only on certain terms and under certain conditions shall a member be entitled to receive any benefits, or the beneficiary named be entitled to receive any sum in case of the death of the member.

But it is claimed, further, that the company is guilty of fraud, which takes this case out of the rule laid down in *Canfield* v. *Knights of Maccabees*, 87 Mich. 626; 24 Am. St. Rep. 186. The declaration alleges that, before coming into court, the plaintiff diligently prosecuted his claim for payment, and has exhausted [166] his remedies, before the tribunals provided by the order; and the plaintiff further alleges that "the defendant, in so refusing, as aforesaid, to pay said sum of money to said plaintiff, is acting in violation of the laws, rules, and regulations of said association, and is willfully seeking to defraud said plaintiff." The only respect in which any fraud is alleged is that, at the time Coderre became a member, the agent of the company assured Coderre that the plaintiff was a "dependent" within the meaning of the policy. There is no averment of any facts tending to show fraud on the part of the executive committee or of the great camp. This being so, one of the very questions which they had to determine was the effect of any alleged statements which the plaintiff was able to prove had been made by the agent of the company. Fraud cannot be predicated upon the decision of the tribunal constituted by the parties themselves, either as to the equity or the law of the case considered, unless, in fact, such committee acted in bad faith and oppressively. No such allegations are contained in the declaration, and the case cannot therefore, on this ground, be distinguished from the Canfield case.

The judgment of the court below will be affirmed, with costs.

McGRATH, C. J., GRANT and HOOKER, JJ., concurred. LONG, J., did not sit. ____

INSURANCE—MUTUAL BENEFIT SOCIETIES—VALIDITY AND EFFECT OF BY-LAWS.—It is competent for a mutual benefit society to provide for the presentation of claims to officers designated in its by-laws, and it may also prescribe a mode of procedure, provided such mode is not such as to deprive parties of property rights: *Supreme Council* v. *Forsinger*, 125 Ind. 52; 21 Am. St. Rep. 196.

LYNCH *v.* JUDGE OF PROBATE.

[101 MICHIGAN, 171.]

PUBLICATION OF LEGAL NOTICES—NEWSPAPER, WHAT IS.—A journal published weekly, of general circulation, devoted primarily to the interests of the legal profession and the dissemination of legal news, but also containing matters of interest to the general public, such as personal items, notices of passing events, general trade advertisements, and the like, is a newspaper within the meaning of the Michigan statute providing for the publication of legal notices.

PUBLICATION OF LEGAL NOTICE.—PROBATE COURTS ALONE HAVE JURISDICTION to determine in what particular newspaper probate notices shall be published.

E. F. Conely and *O. B. Taylor*, for the relator.

C. B. Warren, for the respondent.

[172] LONG, J. Petitioner is one of the heirs at law of Timothy Lynch, deceased. On April 23, 1894, a petition was filed in the probate court for Wayne county by Patrick Lynch, a brother of petitioner, praying for the appointment of an administrator, as the deceased died intestate. An order was entered that the matter be set for hearing on May 22, 1894, and that notice of hearing be published in the *Wayne County Legal News*. Petitioner filed a protest against the appointment, on the ground, among others, that the *Wayne County Legal News*, in which the notice was published, was not a newspaper printed and circulating in said county and state, within the meaning of the statute. This protest was overruled, and petitioner made application to the Wayne circuit court for a writ of prohibition against the probate judge, restraining the appointment on that ground. An order to show cause was granted, and the probate judge answered. Upon the hearing, the writ of prohibition was denied. The case now comes here on certiorari to review that finding

[173] Howell's Statutes, section 5801, provides that the probate court shall appoint a time and place for proving any will, and " shall cause public notice thereof to be given by personal service on all persons interested, or by publication under an order of such court in such newspaper printed in this state as the judge shall direct, three weeks successively," etc.

Section 5866 provides that, " When application shall be made to the judge of probate for the appointment of an ad-

ministrator on an intestate estate, or for letters of administration with the will annexed, he shall cause notice of the
same, and of the time and place of hearing thereof, to be
published for three successive weeks in such newspaper as
he may direct."

Section 6808 provides: "All probate and other legal
notices required by law to be published by the judge of probate of any county . . . . shall be published in some newspaper printed in the county where said probate judge shall
hold his court."

Section 9031 provides that, "All legal advertisements
shall be published in a newspaper printed in the county in
which the proceedings are carried on," etc.

These are the only provisions of our statutes relating to
such publication.

The answer of the judge of probate made to the order of
the court below to show cause sets up that the *Wayne County
Legal News* is a newspaper, published weekly in the city of
Detroit, and, while devoted primarily to the interests of the
legal profession and the dissemination of legal knowledge,
yet it is also intended to contain, and does contain, matters
of interest to the general public; that it contains the proceedings of the supreme court of the state of Michigan, the
Wayne circuit court, and the other courts of the city of
Detroit, and also contains notices of future proceedings in
said courts; that it also contains, [174] from time to time,
opinions of the courts of the United States and of the other
states, and also of other counties in Michigan, where the
same are of interest to the legal profession or to the general
public; that it also contains personal items of general interest, and notices of passing events; and respondent asserts,
on information and belief, that it is intended, when the
legislature is in session, to contain the proceedings thereof,
and general items of interest in connection therewith. The
answer further states that it contains a record of real estate
transfers and mortgages, chattel mortgages, and bills of sale,
and also advertisements, not only relating to the legal profession, but general trade advertisements of interest to every
one; that it is intended to circulate, and in fact has a present circulation, among judges, lawyers, bankers, brokers,
real estate agents, merchants, and business men, and is intended to contain items of importance to all, and is on sale
at the news-stands in the city of Detroit. The answer

further asserts that the *Wayne County Legal News* is intended to fill the same position in the county of Wayne, state of Michigan, as is filled at present by the *Chicago Legal News*, the *Toledo Legal News*, the *St. Louis Legal Record*, and other papers of similar nature in other cities; that it is not an innovation in the newspaper field, there being, as respondent asserts, upwards of forty similar journals now published. A copy of the paper is filed with this return, as well as copies of the *Chicago Legal News* and other legal journals, which indicate the actual character of the *Wayne County Legal News*, and the field which it is intended to cover.

Similar provisions to sections 5801 and 5866, above referred to, are to be found in the Revised Statutes of 1846; the other provisions quoted were enacted in 1853 and 1857; so that these statutes were on the statute books long before the newspaper field was occupied by the many [175] thousands of publications we now find in circulation. But a newspaper, even in the days when these statutes were enacted, meant what it means to-day—a sheet of paper printed and distributed at short intervals for conveying intelligence of passing events; a public print that circulates news, advertisements, proceedings of legislative bodies, public documents, and the like. Under the return here, we are unable to say that this paper does not come within this definition. Our statutes are quite similar to those of other states in reference to the publication of such notices. The *Chicago Legal News* was held to be a newspaper within the meaning of the Illinois statute: *Kerr* v. *Hitt*, 75 Ill. 51. The *St. Louis Legal Record* was held to be such a newspaper within the meaning of the Missouri statute in *Kellogg* v. *Carrico*, 47 Mo. 157. See, also, *Hernandez* v. *Drake*, 81 Ill. 34; *Railton* v. *Lauder*, 126 Ill. 219; 26 Ill. App. 655; *Maass* v. *Hess*, 140 Ill. 576; *Benkendorf* v. *Vincenz*, 52 Mo. 441; *Hull* v. *King*, 38 Minn. 349; *Beecher* v. *Stephens*, 25 Minn. 146.

It was said in *Beecher* v. *Stephens*, 25 Minn. 146: "Newspapers are of so many varieties that it would be next to impossible to give any brief definition which would include and describe all kinds of newspapers."

In *Hull* v. *King*, 38 Minn. 349, the court quote this language, and further say: "It would therefore be unsafe to attempt to give any definition of the term, except the very general one that, according to the usage of the business

world and in ordinary understanding, a newspaper is a publication, usually in sheet form, intended for general circulation, and published regularly at short intervals, containing
intelligence of current events and news of general interest.
. . . . But, if a publication contains the general and current
news of the day, it is none the less a newspaper because it is
chiefly devoted to the dissemination of intelligence of a particular kind or to the advocacy of particular principles or
views. Most newspapers are devoted largely to special **176**
interests—political, religious, financial, moral, social, and the
like; and each is naturally patronized mainly by those who
are in accord with the views which it advocates, or who are
most interested in the kind of intelligence to which it gives
special prominence. But, if it gives the general current
news of the day, it still comes within the definition of a newspaper."

In the case of *Kellogg* v. *Carrico*, 47 Mo. 157, the question
was raised as to the validity of a publication in the *St. Louis
County Legal Record and Advertiser*. It was objected that
such paper was not a newspaper. The court said: "The
Legal Record and Advertiser was printed in St. Louis in
the form of a newspaper, and was issued to its subscribers
daily, except Sundays, when the publication was omitted.
It was devoted to the dissemination of general legal intelligence, and engaged extensively in legal advertising, including the publication of notices of sales under deeds of trust,
and sales on execution, and all judicial sales. It was a law
and advertising journal, and so, in a limited sense at least,
a newspaper; for whether a newspaper or not is a question
that cannot be determined by a consideration alone of the
kind of intelligence it disseminated. It is not the particular kind of intelligence published that constitutes one publication a newspaper rather than another. Newspapers are
devoted to the dissemination of intelligence on a great variety
of subjects, such as politics, commerce, temperance, religion,
and so on; and the law and legal topics and occurrences are
not excluded from the range of newspaper enterprise. A
paper devoted to the gathering up and dissemination of legal
news among its readers is, or at least may be, a newspaper. I
regard the *Legal Record* as a newspaper of that character."

The statute of Illinois provides that the publication of
legal notices shall be in a secular newspaper of general circulation, or some paper specially authorized by law to pub-

lish legal notices, and the question was raised as to whether the *Chicago Legal News* came within the definition of a secular newspaper. In the case of *Kerr* v. *Hitt*, 75 Ill. 51, the court said: [177] "The *Chicago Legal News* is published in the city of Chicago, in the county where this proceeding was commenced; is published once a week; is devoted principally to the dissemination of legal intelligence, but makes reference to passing events, contains advertisements, brief notices of legislative bodies, personal and political items of interest to the general reader, as well as the legal profession. Thus it will be seen it comes, substantially at least, within the definition given by lexicographers of a 'newspaper.' It is none the less a newspaper because its chief object is the publication of legal news. Many newspapers published in this and other countries are devoted chiefly to special interests—such as religious and political newspapers; others devoted exclusively to literature—that contain advertisements, news items, personal and political, brief notices of matters of special public concern, and reference to proceedings of legislative and other public bodies. So it is with this journal. Besides legal it contains other items of news, not only connected with the bench and bar, but others of a general interest. It is that class of journal that will circulate among lawyers, real estate, and other business men, for it contains information in regard to sales of real estate, whether under judicial process or under powers. Accordingly, its advertising columns contain notices of sales under trust deeds, on execution, judicial sales under decrees of court, and all manner of notices of legal transactions, as well as a limited number of other advertisements usually found in a newspaper of general circulation."

In the later case of *Railton* v. *Lauder*, 126 Ill. 219, it was held that the *Chicago Daily Law Bulletin* was a newspaper within the meaning of the statute, the purpose of the paper being similar to that of the *Chicago Legal News*.

The court below was bound by the return of the probate judge as to the character of the *Wayne County Legal News*, and by that return it appears that such paper is as much a newspaper within the meaning of our statute as were the *Chicago Legal News* and the *St. Louis Legal Record* newspapers within the meaning of the statutes of [178] Illinois and Missouri. We think the return shows this journal to be a newspaper within the meaning of our statute. It has a general circulation, and contains the general news of the day; and we have no power to determine what particular paper shall publish probate notices. That question is left by statute to the probate court.

We find no error in the record, and the finding of the court below will not be disturbed.

The other justices concurred.

PUBLICATION OF LEGAL NOTICES IN NEWSPAPERS—SUFFICIENCY OF.— This question will be found treated in the extended note to *Lincoln* v. *Wright.* 62 Am. Dec. 321.

HEINLEIN *v.* IMPERIAL LIFE INSURANCE COMPANY.

[101 MICHIGAN, 250.]

INSURANCE—SURRENDER OF POLICY—RIGHT TO REVIVE.—If, after a mother has secured a policy of insurance upon her life payable to her son, if he survives her, and, if not, to her estate, the son pays the premiums on the insurance for and as the agent of his mother, and the insurance company then induces him, through false representations that the policy is a wagering contract and void, to surrender it upon receipt by him of the premiums paid, he is entitled to maintain a bill in equity to revive the policy.

INSURANCE—INSURABLE INTEREST.—PAYMENT OF PREMIUMS on life insurance by the insured renders the policy valid, even though the beneficiary named in the policy has no insurable interest in the life of the insured.

INSURANCE.—PAYMENT OR TENDER OF PAYMENT OF PREMIUM on a life insurance policy is not necessary if the insurer has already declared the policy forfeited, or done any act which is tantamount to a declaration of refusal to receive the premium if tendered, or if he has failed to keep his agreement to notify the insured of the amount of such premium and the day when due.

Tarsney and Wicker, for the appellant.

H. Post, for the appellee.

²⁵¹ McGRATH, C. J.   This is a bill to revive a life insurance policy, issued December 22, 1890, on the life of Margaretha Heinlein, and payable "to Henry Heinlein, Jr., her son, if living; if not living, to the executors, administrator, or assigns of the said insured."

` One Smith, an insurance agent, applied to Henry Heinlein to take out insurance. Heinlein replied that he did not desire to take out a policy, but that his mother had spoken to him about insurance, and he thought that she wanted insurance. Smith requested him to see his mother, and let him know. Afterward Smith, who was accompanied by a physician, met Heinlein, and asked if the latter had been his mother. Heinlein replied that he had, and Smith suggested that they go right up to the house, and they did so. The application was filled out, and the medical examination made. The defendant company declined to take the full amount, viz., ten thousand dollars, but issued a policy for five thousand dollars, and the Berkshire Life took a policy for three thousand dollars, a new application being made out, and another medical examination having been made. The first premium was paid by check on a bank at Saginaw, signed "M. Heinlein, by Henry Heinlein." The insured resided at East Saginaw, and it would appear from the testimony that Henry Heinlein also resided there at the time the policy was taken out. The subsequent premiums were payable quarterly, and were paid by Henry Heinlein, although he testified that he had general charge of his [252] mother's affairs, and paid the premiums in her behalf. The policy seems to have lapsed in 1891, owing to the failure to pay the premium promptly, but a health certificate was furnished, and the policy was restored.

Margaretha Heinlein was taken sick in the spring of 1892, and died July 2d of that year. On June 14, 1892, the president of the defendant company and the secretary thereof and the general agent of the Berkshire Life Company went to Bay City, where complainant then resided, and secured both policies from Henry Heinlein, refunding to him the amount of the premiums paid. It appears that, before going to Bay City, the officers of these companies had been to East Saginaw, and had there learned of the illness of the insured. Upon arriving at Bay City they sought out Smith, who had solicited the insurance, and secured his services to aid in recovering the policies. The interview with Smith is described by him as follows:

"We went up to a room, Mr. Angus and Mr. Oliver and Mr. Early and myself, and Mr. Angus, I think, was the one who broached the subject to me, and told me that they were there to see what could be done with the Heinlein matter. As near as I can remember, Mr. Early showed me the papers, and asked me as to the certificates of health, etc., and wanted to know if I knew that that was graveyard insurance. I told him, 'No sir'; I didn't consider it in that light; that the insurance was solicited in the regular way. He says: 'I understand that this, where the party is paying the premium on his mother, makes it graveyard insurance or speculative insurance.' I told him I did n't think that that was the case —that this was a case of that kind—because, in Mr. Heinlein's statement to me previous to this, he told me what his mother wanted the insurance for—to protect the property of some minor children; that is what she was taking this insurance for. And Mr. Angus said to me, or Mr. Oliver—I could not say which one, the conversation was between the two of them—they said it was graveyard insurance, and that, if he pressed it, they should put it into the courts, and it [253] would be a question whether they would get any thing or not, and stated to me that they wanted to take them up, and would pay for the taking up of the policies, and wanted to know what I thought about it. I says: 'Gentlemen, if I have done any thing wrong in any way, shape, or manner, I am willing to right it.' They wanted to know how I was willing to right it. I told them I was willing to go to Mr. Heinlein, and state to him their statements, and the only condition that I would go would be that they would pay the premiums in full that Mr. Heinlein had paid. And Mr. Early and Mr. Angus talked together, and wanted to know if I would go and do that, and I told them I would, and Mr. Angus signed a check for Mr. Oliver, and Mr. Early signed a check payable to my order."

He says, further: "I told Mr. Heinlein that, as I understood it, we had got ourselves in trouble with that insurance; and he wanted to know how, and I told him Mr. Oliver says we had made a mistake in writing the insurance in that way, making him the beneficiary, as it came under the head of graveyard insurance, and that they wanted to settle the matter, and they would do so by paying him back the entire amount of his premiums that he had paid if he would release the policies, both for the Imperial and for the Berkshire; and Mr. Oliver says to him, 'That is the facts in the case,' as near as I can remember what he said. 'It comes under the head of old folks' insurance, and ain't legitimate business.'"

Complainant testifies that he met Oliver and Smith in the street, and "Smith said: 'You are the man we are looking for.' We went into a store, and Smith says: 'We have got ourselves in a nice box. We have got ourselves in trouble.' I asked him in what way." Oliver is then introduced, and he proceeds to assert that the policies are void; that it was grave-yard insurance; that Heinlein did n't have any insurable in-terest in his mother, and she had no insurable interest in him; that, if the insured should die, Heinlein could recover only the premiums paid in; that they would refund the pre-miums if he would surrender [254] the policies; that, unless he accepted, they would throw it into the courts, and then he would get nothing; that he had insured his mother for a speculation; that they were in haste to leave the city. Hein-lein suggested that the insurance commissioner lived in the city, and that he would go to him for advice; but Oliver said: "There is no use going to him. He cannot help you any in this matter, and, if you don't take what we offer you, why, we will take it and throw it into the court, and you will not get any thing." The matter seems to have been closed out within a few hours. Heinlein went to the office of Shepard & Lyon, attorneys. The parties went with him. Neither Shepard nor Lyon was in. Heinlein then went to the office of a jus-tice of the peace. They went with him, and the matter was then concluded. From the time that Oliver and Smith met Heinlein until the policies were received by them, Heinlein was not out of their sight. Heinlein had a short talk with the justice about the matter. Oliver and Smith were in the room, and Oliver reiterated the assertions as to speculative and graveyard insurance, and exhibited to the justice a pamphlet containing some reference to the subject of specu-lative insurance, and read therefrom.

We think that the facts bring the case within the rules laid down in *Tabor* v. *Michigan M. L. Ins. Co.*, 44 Mich. 324, and that complainant is entitled to the relief prayed: See, also, *Renard* v. *Clink*, 91 Mich. 3; 30 Am. St. Rep. 458. There is no ground for the claim that this was a wager policy. It affirmatively appears that the first premium was paid by the insured, and the fact that the check for the premium was signed as it was, and was, as thus signed, presented and honored, supports Heinlein's claim that he was acting for his mother, had general charge of her affairs, and for her for-warded the other premiums. Mr. May, in his work on Insur-ance, says, at section 112, if the person whose life is insured pays the premiums, there can [255] be no doubt as to the valid-ity of the policy, even if the beneficiary has no interest, since his own interest supports the policy: *Campbell* v. *New England M. L. Ins. Co.*, 98 Mass. 381; *Hogle* v. *Guardian etc. Ins. Co.*, 6

Rob. (N. Y.) 567; *Scott* v. *Dickson*, 108 Pa. St. 6; 56 Am. Rep. 192; *Amick* v. *Butler*, 111 Ind. 578; 60 Am. Rep. 722. It is apparent from the policy itself that the mother's regard for the son's interest was not the only motive for its procurement. The record discloses that the policy was made payable in the event of the death of Henry Heinlein to the estate of the insured, at the special instance of the insured. This fact tends to corroborate what Smith says as to the purpose of the policy.

It is urged, however, that a premium fell due July 1st, following the surrender, which was not paid or tendered. There are two reasons why this contention should not prevail: 1. Payment or tender of payment of premiums is not necessary where the insurers have already declared the policy forfeited, or done any act which is tantamount to a declaration on their part that they will not receive it if tendered: May on Insurance, sec. 358; 2. On February 12, 1892, the company, by its president, had sent a written notice to the insured, which contained the following: " Your premiums on insurance with this company will be collected hereafter at this office, instead of Saginaw bank, and must be here before 12 o'clock noon on day of maturity. You will receive due notice of day when due, amounts," etc.: See May on Insurance, secs. 356, 356 *a*.

The decree of the court below will be reversed, and a decree entered here for the complainant, restoring the policy, and for the amount thereof, with costs of both courts.

The other justices concurred.

INSURANCE—LIFE—INSURABLE INTEREST.—EFFECT OF PAYMENT OF PRE-MIUMS where beneficiary has no interest in life of assured: See the extended note to *Currier* v. *Continental etc. Ins. Co.*, 52 Am. Rep. 141.

INSURANCE — LIFE — WAIVER OF PAYMENT OF PREMIUM. — An action may be maintained upon a policy of insurance after the death of the insured without the payment or tender of the premium due when the action of the company shows that it would have refused a tender if made, as it had already treated the rights of the claimant under the policy as forfeited by the non-payment of the premium: *Greisemer* v. *Mutual Life Ins. Co.*, 10 Wash. 202.

TALMAGE *v.* SMITH.

[101 MICHIGAN, 370.]

ASSAULT—LIABILITY FOR UNINTENTIONAL INJURY.—One who throws a stick
of wood at a trespasser on his premises with intent to inflict an unwarranted injury upon him, though he misses the party intended to be
struck, is liable for an injury inflicted upon another trespasser who is
struck by such stick.

APPEAL—IMMATERIAL ERROR.—In an action to recover for personal injury
a declaration by plaintiff's counsel that the subject matter in dispute
had been submitted to arbitration, by the parties and a certain compensation agreed upon, though inadmissible in evidence, is not reversible error if the jury is cautioned by the court not to take the matter
into account, and the issues are clearly defined and set forth in the
charge.

G. E. Nichols, for the appellant.

F. D. M. Davis and F. C. Miller, for the appellee.

371 MONTGOMERY, J. The plaintiff recovered in an action
of trespass. The case made by plaintiff's proofs was substantially as follows: On the evening of September 17, 1891,
some limekilns were burning a short distance from defendant's premises, in Portland, Ionia county. Defendant had
on his premises certain sheds. He came up to **372** the vicinity of the sheds, and saw six or eight boys on the roof of one
of them. He claims that he ordered the boys to get down,
and they at once did so. He then passed around to where he
had a view of the roof of another shed, and saw two boys
on the roof. The defendant claims that he did not see the
plaintiff, and the proof is not very clear that he did, although
there was some testimony from which it might have been
found that plaintiff was within his view. Defendant ordered
the boys in sight to get down, and there was testimony tending to show that the two boys in defendant's view started to
get down at once. Before they succeeded in doing so, however, defendant took a stick, which is described as being two
inches in width and of about the same thickness, and about
sixteen inches long, and threw it in the direction of the
boys; and there was testimony tending to show that it was
thrown at one of the boys in view of the defendant. The stick
missed him, and hit the plaintiff just above the eye, with such
force as to inflict an injury which resulted in the total loss of
the sight of the eye.

Counsel for the defendant contends that the undisputed

testimony shows that defendant threw the stick without intending to hit anybody, and that, under the circumstances, if it in fact hit the plaintiff, defendant not knowing that he was on the shed, he was not liable.   We cannot understand why these statements should find a place in the brief of defendant's counsel.   George Talmage, the plaintiff's father, testifies that defendant said to him that he threw the stick, intending it for Byron Smith, one of the boys on the roof, and this is fully supported by the circumstances of the case. It is hardly conceivable that this testimony escaped the attention of defendant's counsel.

The circuit judge charged the jury as follows: "If you conclude that Smith did not know the Talmage [373] boy was on the shed, and that he did not intend to hit Smith, or the young man that was with him, but simply, by throwing the stick, intended to frighten Smith and the other young man that was there, and the club hit Talmage, and injured him, as claimed, then the plaintiff could not recover.   If you conclude that Smith threw the stick or club at Smith, or the young man that was with Smith, intended to hit one or the other of them, and you also conclude that the throwing of the stick or club was, under the circumstances, reasonable, and not excessive, force to use toward Smith and the other young man, then there would be no recovery by this plaintiff. But if you conclude from the evidence in the case that he threw the stick, intending to hit Smith, or the young man with him, to hit one of them, and that that force was unreasonable force, under all the circumstances, then Smith, you see (the defendant), would be doing an unlawful act, if the force was unreasonable, because he had no right to use it; then he would be doing an unlawful act.   He would be liable, then, for the injury done to this boy with the stick, if he threw it intending to hit the young man Smith, or the young man that was with Smith on the roof, and the force that he was using, by the throwing of the club, was excessive and unreasonable, under all the circumstances of the case; if it was, and then the stick went on and hit the boy, as it seems to have hit him, if it was unreasonable and excessive, then he would be liable for the consequences of it, because he was doing an unlawful act in the outset; that is, he was using unreasonable and unnecessary force—excessive force— against Smith and the young man to get them off the shed."

We think the charge a very fair statement of the law of the case. The doctrine of contributory negligence could have no place in the case. The plaintiff, in climbing upon the shed, could not have anticipated the throwing of the missile, and the fact that he was a trespasser did not place him beyond the pale of the law. The right of the plaintiff to recover was made to depend upon an intention on the part of the defendant to hit somebody, and to inflict an unwarranted injury upon some one. Under these circumstances, the fact that the injury resulted to another than was intended does not relieve the defendant from [374] responsibility. The cases cited in defendant's brief, we think, support this rule: *Scott* v. *Shepherd*, 3 Wils. 403; 2 W. Black. 892; *Jeffersonville etc. R. R. Co.* v. *Riley*, 39 Ind. 568. The case is to be distinguished from a case of negligence on the part of defendant. The act is found by the jury to have been a willful act.

Plaintiff's counsel, in opening the case, referred to a conversation between the plaintiff's father and the defendant, and stated that they submitted the matter to arbitration, and that a certain compensation was agreed upon between the parties, and this proposition was repeated in the offer of testimony. This the circuit judge ruled out, and held that it was not competent to go to the jury, and cautioned the jury that the proposition should have no weight with them. The ruling of the circuit judge was proper, but we are not prepared to say that the statement of counsel was intended by him to influence the jury improperly, nor do we think, under the circumstances of this case, that it had that result. The circuit judge not only specially cautioned the jury not to take the matter into account, but further defined the issues with exceptional clearness in his charge. Under these circumstances, we think the case falls within the rulings of this court in *Kirchner* v. *Detroit City Ry. Co.*, 91 Mich. 400; *Prentis* v. *Bates*, 93 Mich. 234; *Daniels* v. *Weeks*, 90 Mich. 190.

The judgment will be affirmed, with costs.

McGRATH, C. J., LONG and HOOKER, JJ., concurred. GRANT, J., concurred in the result. ___

ASSAULT—LIABILITY FOR UNINTENTIONAL HARM.—There may be an actionable assault, although there was no specific intent to do harm: *Mercer* v. *Corbin*, 117 Ind. 450; 10 Am. St. Rep. 76, and note; *Vosburg* v. *Putney*, 80 Wis. 523; 27 Am. St. Rep. 47, and note. One who shoots a loaded gun

into a crowd of persons with the intent to harm any of them may be convicted of an assault with intent to do great bodily harm to the person
wounded, although he had no specific intent to wound that particular person: *People* v. *Raher,* 92 Mich. 165; 31 Am. St. Rep. 575, and note, with the
cases collected.

GIBBONS *v.* PEMBERTON.

[101 MICHIGAN, 397.]

CREDITOR'S BILL—ALLEGATION OF OWNERSHIP.—An allegation in a creditor's bill that the judgment debtor executed a deed to the land levied
upon to his sons for a pretended consideration is a sufficient allegation, in the absence of demurrer, that the judgment debtor owned
the land at the time that the conveyance was made.

CREDITOR'S BILL—SUFFICIENCY OF.—A creditor who attaches land previously conveyed by the debtor to his sons, and, after obtaining judgment, files a creditor's bill in aid of an execution issued on such
judgment, need not allege the insolvency of the judgment debtor, nor
have the execution returned *nulla bona* in order to maintain the bill.
The only question to be determined is whether the transfer by the
debtor was in fraud of creditors. If the attachment is not dissolved,
the lien is good as against the debtor, regardless of how much property he may own. His vendees alone can contest the title.

Fletcher & Wanty, for the appellant.

F. Dumon, for the appellee.

398 GRANT, J. In November, 1891, the defendant, Cheney
O. Pemberton, was indebted to the City National Bank of
Greenville in the sum of twelve hundred dollars. The officers
of the bank were pressing him for payment. He asked
further time, which they refused to grant. On the twenty-
third day of that month he conveyed to the codefendants,
his sons, the land in controversy. March 12, 1892, the bank
commenced suit by attachment, and levied upon the land.
Judgment was rendered July 7th, execution duly issued and
levied, and the complainant then filed this bill in aid of the
execution, charging that the conveyance was made without
consideration, and to defraud creditors. Proofs were taken
before a circuit court commissioner, reported to the court,
and the bill dismissed. No reason is given by the court for
its decree of dismissal. The points insisted on by the **399**
defendants are: 1. That the bill does not allege that Cheney
O. Pemberton had any interest in the land at the time of the
conveyance; 2. That it does not allege that Mr. Pemberton was
insolvent; and 3. That the conveyance was not fraudulent.

1. The first point, if valid, should have been raised by demurrer. It is true that the bill does not expressly allege that the judgment debtor was the owner of the premises, but, it does allege that he executed a deed for a pretended con-, sideration of fifteen hundred dollars, by which he pretended to convey the land to his sons. In the absence of a demurrer the allegation was sufficient.

2. It was not necessary to allege the insolvency of the judgment debtor, or to have an execution returned *nulla bona.* The attached property, whether real or personal, is subject to the attachment lien; and the sole question in such cases is whether the transfer by the debtor of the identical property, whether real or personal, was in fraud of creditors. If the attachment is not dissolved the lien is good, as against the debtor, and it makes no difference how much other property he may own. His vendees alone can contest the title.

3. The loan to Mr. Pemberton was made upon the faith of his representation that he was the owner of this land. Mr. Cheney O. Pemberton was examined as a witness for the complainant. We think the fact is clearly established by his testimony that the deed was without consideration, and made for the express purpose of avoiding the payment of the complainant's claim. He does not show that he owned, or had an interest in, any other property, except one hundred and sixty acres of land, in which he had no interest other than as security for signing notes and a bond for another party. November 12, 1891, he wrote to Mr. Moore, the president of the bank, saying that two attachments had been placed upon this land, and asking a renewal of the notes for ninety [400] days. The deed in question was made shortly after the refusal of the bank to make the renewal. Mr. Pemberton testified that when he sold he got promises, but no money; that he took his sons' check for fifteen hundred dollars, and lent it back to them within a week or ten days, and was not positive that he did not give it back to them the same day; that he did not think his sons kept a joint bank account. When asked to produce the check he promptly refused. He said that six hundred dollars of the amount was paid by one of his sons the day he gave his testimony, which was May 15, 1893, and that each of his sons had paid him seven hundred and fifty dollars. Only two hundred dollars, if any, was paid before the attachment. Neither of his sons was a witness. If they were *bona fide* purchasers it was in

their power to place the *bona fides* of the transaction beyond question. Had they paid fifteen hundred dollars it is impossible to believe that they would not have furnished the proof. We cannot avoid the conclusion that the transfer was fraudulent.

Decree reversed, and entered here for the complainant, with costs of both courts.

The other justices concurred.

CREDITOR'S BILL—SUFFICIENCY OF.—The insolvency of cojudgment debtors need not be averred in a bill to set aside a fraudulent conveyance of one insolvent judgment debtor if execution has been levied upon the property fraudulently conveyed: *Vasser* v. *Henderson*, 40 Miss. 519; 90 Am. Dec. 351. See the extended note to *Massey* v. *Gorton*, 90 Am. Dec. 297, where the sufficiency of the allegations in a creditor's bill is thoroughly discussed.

BURROUGHS v. EASTMAN.

[101 MICHIGAN, 419.]

CONSTITUTIONAL LAW—ARREST WITHOUT WARRANT—DUE PROCESS OF LAW.—A provision in a city charter authorizing police officers to arrest without warrant or process all persons who shall, in the presence of such officer, be engaged in the violation of any ordinance of the city, is valid, and not unconstitutional, as authorizing arrest without due process of law.

CONSTITUTIONAL LAW—ARREST WITHOUT WARRANT.—A statute authorizing an arrest without warrant for an offense not amounting to a breach of the peace, if committed in view of an officer, is constitutional and valid.

VERDICT—INCONSISTENCY OF WHEN NOT GROUND FOR EXCEPTION.—An officer who directs another officer to make an arrest, and is found guilty of false imprisonment therefor, cannot complain of the verdict on the ground of its inconsistency in finding that the officer who actually made the arrest is not guilty of the false imprisonment charged against both jointly.

E. F. Uhl, for the appellant.

James E. McBride, for the appellee.

419 MONTGOMERY, J. This is an action for false imprisonment.

The plaintiff was, by defendant's directions, arrested while engaged in giving a performance at a theater in the city of Grand Rapids on Sunday evening. There existed **420** an ordinance of the city of Grand Rapids relative to shows, which prohibited a person or company giving theatrical exhibitions on the first day of the week.

1. The charter of the city provides that police officers, in addition to the power and authority possessed by them at common law, and under the laws of the state in matters of a criminal nature, shall have the power to arrest, without process, all persons who shall, in the presence of the arresting officer, be engaged in the violation of any ordinance of the common council of the city, and that the police officer may detain such persons in custody until complaint can be made, and process issue for their arrest and trial. It will be seen, therefore, that, so far as the legislative power can go, it has been exercised to authorize an arrest without warrant for an offense against the ordinances of the city which is committed in the presence of the officer. It is insisted, however, that the act which attempts to clothe the officer with this power is unconstitutional.

This court has repeatedly held that, in the absence of any statutory power or authority, an officer cannot arrest without warrant, except on suspicion of felony, or in case of an actual breach of the peace committed in the presence of the arresting officer: See *Way's case*, 41 Mich. 304; *Davis* v. *Burgess*, 54 Mich. 514; 52 Am. Rep. 828; *Quinn* v. *Heisel*, 40 Mich. 576; *People* v. *Johnson*, 86 Mich. 175; 24 Am. St. Rep. 116. But whether the legislature may extend the right to the officer to arrest for other misdemeanors, not amounting to a breach of the peace, has not been directly passed upon, unless it be in the case of *Robison* v. *Miner*, 68 Mich. 549. In *People* v. *Johnson*, 86 Mich. 179, 24 Am. St. Rep. 116, the subject is referred to, but, as the record was not in shape to present the question, it was left undecided.

[421] In *Quinn* v. *Heisel*, 40 Mich. 577, Mr. Justice Marston said: " We are not at present prepared to say that an ordinance of the city of Grand Rapids could authorize arrests without process in cases not justified by common-law principles."

But this statement in this case was mere dictum, and, if the query suggested had been answered in the negative, it would not necessarily follow that the legislature of the state might not confer a power which the common council of the city, under the charter then in force, could not have conferred.

In *Robison* v. *Miner*, 68 Mich. 549, it must be conceded, language is employed which might be construed as prohibiting the power of arrest. The statute there under consideration was Act No. 313, Laws of 1887, which contained the peculiar provision that "any person found in the act of violating any of the provisions of this section shall be deemed guilty of a breach of the peace, and punished accordingly, and the arrest therefor may be without process; and this punishment shall be taken to be in excess of all other manner of punishment in this act provided for a violation of the provisions of this section. All officers authorized to make arrests for a breach of the peace shall have like power to make arrests under the provisions of this section as in other cases of a breach of the peace."

These provisions are peculiar and incongruous. It seemed to have been an attempt on the part of the legislature to confer the power of arrest by a process of first declaring that to be a breach of the peace which is not such in fact, and by further providing that a party might be punished for such breach of the peace in addition to and beyond the punishment provided by the same statute. The conclusion that these provisions could not be maintained, in view of the constitutional provision that no person shall be twice put in jeopardy for the same offense, [422] was undoubtedly correct. As was well said by Mr. Justice Campbell, in rendering the opinion of the court: "This statute is practically, if carried out, a general warrant itself, directing all officers to visit houses and business places without other authority, and make searches and arrests, and close up places of business on their own well or ill founded notion that the law has been violated."

But, in the course of this opinion, Justice Campbell used language which seems to favor the contention of plaintiff here, as follows: "The constitution prohibits interference with persons or property without due process of law. The proceedings under this statute are all highly penal, and treated expressly as criminal proceedings. The constitution expressly prohibits the issue of warrants of search or seizure of persons or property except on a sworn showing, which, it has always been held, must be of facts on personal knowledge such as would establish the legal probability of the cause of complaint. If the legislature could evade this by providing for seizures and searches without legal warrant the provision would be useless."

As to the first provision of the constitution referred to in the discussion, it means no more than that a person shall not

be deprived of liberty except by the law of the land. As to
the latter provision, namely, section 26 of article 6, which provides that "no warrant to search any place or to seize any
person or things shall issue without describing them, nor
without probable cause, supported by oath or affirmation,"
we are constrained to say that this section is not susceptible
of the construction which, by implication, is placed upon it
in the opinion of Mr. Justice Campbell. The same provision
was considered by the supreme court of Alabama in the case
of *Williams* v. *State*, 44 Ala. 43, and a contention that such
provision prohibited an arrest without warrant was concisely
disposed of as follows: "The federal and state constitutions
both provide that [423] no warrant shall issue to search any
place, or to seize any person or thing, without probable cause,
supported by oath or affirmation. As a warrant is the process upon which arrests are usually made, and it cannot be
issued without oath, the corollary has been drawn that there
can be no arrest without a warrant. The popular error on
the subject is our excuse for the assertion of the truism that
it is the issue of the warrant, without oath or affirmation,
which is forbidden, and not the arrest without a warrant."

The statute under consideration in that case authorized an
arrest by a policeman without a warrant, on any day and at
any time, for any public offense committed, or a breach of
the peace threatened, in his presence.

It may further be said that, if the constitutional provision
last quoted is to be construed as might be implied from the
language employed by Mr. Justice Campbell, it would exclude all arrests without warrant. The right which existed
at common law to arrest for offenses committed in the presence of the officer has been too often recognized since the
adoption of our constitution to be open to question. Mr. Justice Campbell uses the further language: "So far as arrests
are concerned, a similar principle applies. Under our system we have repeatedly decided, in accordance with constitutional principles as construed everywhere, that no arrest
can be made without warrant, except in cases of felony, or in
cases of breaches of the peace committed in the presence of
the arresting officer. This exception in cases of breaches of
the peace has only been allowed by reason of the immediate
danger to the safety of the community against crimes of violence, and it was confined, even in such cases, to instances

where the violence was committed in the presence of the officer."

This language embodies a correct statement of the rule of common law, but, if it is sought to extend its application to a case where the legislature has authorized the arrest without warrant for offenses, other than breaches of the peace, committed in the view of the arresting officer, [424] we do not find the contention supported by authority. In 1 Bishop's Criminal Procedure, section 184, it is said: "The right of arrest by the officers of the peace is more or less enlarged by statutory regulations in the several states, as well as, of late, in England; or, if not enlarged, defined. A statute enlarging the right—that is, in restraint of personal liberty—is to be strictly construed. But statutes of this sort are generally held to be constitutional."

In *Roberts* v. *State*, 14 Mo. 138, 55 Am. Dec. 97, the power of the municipality to provide by ordinance for the arrest of vagrants without warrant was sustained. The same ruling was made in the case of *Bryan* v. *Bates*, 15 Ill. 87, and *Main* v. *McCarty*, 15 Ill. 441.

In Massachusetts the legislature has from time to time provided by statute for the arrest of persons guilty of a particular offense, including the offense of selling liquor contrary to law, and the offense of drunkenness, and the power of arrest without warrant for the commission of the offense has been repeatedly sustained: See *Jones* v. *Root*, 6 Gray, 435; *Mason* v. *Lothrop*, 7 Gray, 354; *Commonwealth* v. *Cheney*, 141 Mass. 102; 55 Am. Rep. 448. See, also, *Davis* v. *American Soc.*, 75 N. Y. 362.

In *White* v. *Kent*, 11 Ohio St. 550, a statutory provision which conferred the right upon police officers to arrest without process for violations of the city ordinances not amounting to breaches of the peace was upheld. It was said: "It is evident that many ordinances necessary for good order and general convenience, as well as for the preservation of morals and decency, would be almost nugatory if offenders could only be arrested upon warrant."

In *Davis* v. *American Soc.*, 75 N. Y. 362, it was held that a statute authorizing an arrest, without process, of one guilty of cruelty to animals, was valid.

In *O'Connor* v. *Bucklin*, 59 N. H. 589, a statute [425] authorizing an officer, upon view of any crime or breach of the peace or offense against the police of towns, to arrest without warrant, was sustained.

In *State* v. *Cantieny*, 34 Minn. 1, a statute of the state authorizing any peace officer to arrest without warrant for a "public offense committed or attempted in his presence" was construed and upheld, and it was held that an arrest without warrant for such public offense was authorized, even if the offense did not amount to a breach of the peace: See *Wahl* v. *Walton*, 30 Minn. 506. See, also, *Beville* v. *State*, 16 Tex. App. 70; *Wiltse* v. *Holt*, 95 Ind. 469; *Taaffe* v. *Slevin*, 11 Mo. App. 507; *Smith* v. *Donelly*, 66 Ill. 464; *Scircle* v. *Neeves*, 47 Ind. 289; *Jacobs* v. *State*, 28 Tex. App. 79; *Butolph* v. *Blust*, 41 How. Pr. 481; *Ballard* v. *State*, 43 Ohio St. 340; 1 Dillon on Municipal Corporations, secs. 210, 211, 414, and cited in notes.

It will be seen that the question has arisen in many of our sister states, and the power to authorize arrest on view for offenses not amounting to breaches of the peace has been affirmed. Our attention has been called to no case, nor have we in our research found one in which the contrary doctrine has been asserted. We think that, while the language in *Robison* v. *Miner*, 68 Mich. 549, may furnish justification for the contention which is made by the plaintiff here, the language which we have referred to, bearing that construction, was not necessary to a determination of the question there involved, and should not be followed.

The right to arrest without warrant applies as well to felonies made so by statute after the adoption of the constitution as to offenses which are felonies at the common law, and this without express legislation providing for such arrest: *Firestone* v. *Rice*, 71 Mich. 377; 15 Am. St. Rep. 266. This holding is wholly inconsistent with the claim that what is due process of law must be determined by what arrest without warrant was permissible at the time of the adoption of the constitution. **426** It is illogical to say that the legislature may, by defining a particular offense as a felony, or providing for its punishment as such, authorize an arrest without warrant for such offense not committed in the presence of the officer, and yet it may not by statute authorize arrest for a misdemeanor committed in the presence of the officer. The necessity may be as great in the one case as in the other, and the case of *Firestone* v. *Rice*, 77 Mich. 377, 15 Am. St. Rep. 266, illustrates that the rule is not irrevocably or inflexibly fixed by the state of the law as it existed prior to the adoption of the constitution. The same provision of the constitution which protects the person protects the property from invasion without due process of law, and yet statutes which have prescribed what use of property shall constitute a nuisance, and authorized its summary destruction when so used, have been upheld by the courts: *Hart* v. *Mayor etc.*, 9 Wend. 571; 24 Am. Dec. 165; *Meeker* v. *Van Rensselaer*, 15 Wend. 397; *American Print Works* v. *Lawrence*, 21 N. J. L. 248; and fully approved by the federal supreme court in the recent case of *Lawton* v. *Steele*, 152 U. S. 133. See, also, *People* v. *Brooks*, 101 Mich. 98.

2. Appellant also contends that the verdict of the jury finding the defendant guilty should not be allowed to stand because of the inconsistency in the verdict rendered. The actual arrest, which was made by the direction of the defendant Eastman, was made by one Hurley, lieutenant of police. Hurley was joined with defendant Eastman, and upon the trial Eastman was found guilty, and Hurley not guilty. It does not appear whether the plaintiff has rested content with the verdict in favor of Hurley; but, while it may be that the jury rendered an inconsistent verdict, it does not follow that defendant Eastman can take advantage of it. The plaintiff could have *nolle prosequied* the case as against Hurley at any stage, and have proceeded to try the issue as against Eastman. The plaintiff [427] might, after verdict, have moved for a new trial as against defendant Hurley, and a different result might be reached on another trial. We think the point should be overruled.

The circuit judge, however, erred in instructing the jury that the legislature has not the power to authorize an arrest for an offense not amounting to a breach of the peace, without warrant, if committed in view of the officer.

For this reason the judgment will be reversed, with costs, and a new trial ordered.

GRANT and HOOKER, JJ., concurred with MONTGOMERY, J.

MR. CHIEF JUSTICE McGRATH dissented, and contended, that the statute in question authorizing an arrest without warrant for an offense not amounting to a breach of the peace, if committed in the presence of an officer, was unconstitutional and void within the rulings in *Allor* v. *Wayne County Auditors*, 43 Mich. 76; *Robison* v. *Miner*, 68 Mich. 549; *Weimer* v. *Bunbury*, 30 Mich. 201, and *Way's case*, 41 Mich. 299. He also reviewed most of the cases cited by Mr. Justice Montgomery in support of the views expressed in the principal opinion, showing that in every instance some breach of the peace had been committed, and that this was the only reason why the arrests detailed in such cases were upheld as valid, though made without warrant or other process. In discussing the question involved, Mr. Justice McGrath said: "It may well be asked what principle was perpetuated or secured against abrogation or violation, if what constitutes due process of law is made to depend upon the will of the legislature as expressed in any one of our many and varied municipal charters. If this constitutional provision be not regarded as a limitation of the power of the legislature, then the statute is in each instance the test of authority, and the constitutional provision is without office or force. That provision is not necessary to support or protect the statute. The latter is to be construed in subordination to the constitution, and is to be tested by that instrument. The term "due process of law" had a well-settled meaning when the constitution was adopted, of which the framers of that instrument must be presumed to have had knowledge, and with reference to which it must be presumed that they acted. Subsequent legislation cannot change the meaning or effect of a constitutional provision. A statute may provide for a removal from office, or for the taxation or taking of property, without notice or hearing; but, although such would be a process provided by law, it will not be contended that a removal or a taking thereunder would not be a plain violation of the constitution. Such statutory process, when tested by principles which were before the constitution, would be found to lack essential requisites of due process. The constitution nowhere in express terms speaks of notice or a day in court, but, notwithstanding, these are universally recognized as essential incidents of due process. In *Weimer v. Bunbury*, 30 Mich. 201, 213, Mr. Justice Cooley subjected the process under consideration in that case to the test of settled rules which antedated the constitution. Any other test would violate a cardinal rule of constitutional interpretation, subject provisions designed for the protection of persons and property to legislative modification, and make the meaning of a term employed in the fundamental law, which term had, at the time of the adoption of the constitution, a well-known signification, depend upon the language used in a municipal charter or ordinance."

ARREST WITHOUT WARRANT.—An officer is a trespasser if he attempts to make an arrest without a warrant where he is not authorized to do so: *Commonwealth v. Wright*, 158 Mass. 149; 35 Am. St. Rep. 475, and note, with the cases collected. An arrest sought to be made by an officer without a warrant for a crime not committed in his presence, and where it is doubtful if any crime has been committed, is an unlawful arrest: *Cryer v. State*, 71 Miss. 467; 42 Am. St. Rep. 473, and note. See the discussion of this subject to be found in the extended note to *Roberts v. State*, 55 Am. Dec. 104, and the notes to *Wade v. Chaffee*, 5 Am. Rep. 574, and *Doering v. State*, 19 Am. Rep. 672.

DOWNES *v.* HARPER HOSPITAL.

[101 MICHIGAN, 555.]

HOSPITALS—LIABILITY FOR NEGLIGENCE OF MANAGERS OF EMPLOYEES OF.—
An incorporated eleemosynary hospital, organized and maintained for
no private gain, but for the proper care and medical treatment of the
sick, and for that purpose made the manager of a donated trust fund,
is not liable for injury received by a patient therein, through the negligence of its managers or their employees, and the fact that patients who
are able to pay are required to do so does not deprive the corporation
of its eleemosynary character, nor permit a recovery for damages on
account of the existence of contract relations.

J. H. Pound, for the appellant.

E. F. Conely and O. B. Taylor, for the appellee.

⁵⁵⁵ GRANT, J.   Plaintiff's decedent and husband became
insane from disease, and, by advice of his physician, was
⁵⁵⁶ conveyed to Harper Hospital.   He was violent, and was
confined in a room in the third story of the building, which
was especially arranged for such patients, having a framework of iron over the windows.   The deceased wrenched this
iron framework off, jumped from the window, and was killed.
Plaintiff brings this suit to recover damages for the benefit
of herself and children, alleging negligence on the part of the
defendant.

Defendant is a body corporate organized under Act No.
242, Laws of 1863, entitled "An act for the incorporation of
hospitals or asylums in cases where valuable grants or emol-
uments have been made to trustees for such purposes," and,
at the time the alleged right of action is said to have accrued,
was engaged in maintaining at Detroit the hospital commonly
known as "Harper Hospital."

In the declaration it is alleged that on or about January
26, 1890, Downes was ill, and was so disordered in mind from
the effects of disease and pain that he became and was temporarily insane, violent, and dangerous, so that it became
necessary to place him under restraint and skillful medical
treatment to prevent him from harming himself and others,
and to effect his cure; that the defendant, at the request of
plaintiff, and well knowing Downes' mental and physical
condition, received him into Harper Hospital as a patient,
and, in consideration of the payment of two dollars per day,
agreed to give Downes proper medical treatment, and to keep
and restrain him so that he should suffer no bodily injury,

and his life should be preserved from injury which he might inflict upon himself, and to have the room in which he was confined secure, with a proper and sufficient guard, framework, or other suitable protection over the window of such room, and so securely fastened that Downes, when confined in the room, would not be able to tear away the framework or grating over the window and throw himself therefrom, and to keep him [557] properly handcuffed, so that he could not injure himself by tearing away the framework or bars over the window, or by throwing himself out of the window, and also to keep some suitable person constantly in attendance upon him.

It is further alleged that the defendant, in disregard of its alleged duties and obligations, wrongfully, carelessly, and negligently failed to safely keep and care for and give medical attendance to Downes, and so keep and restrain him that his body should suffer no injury, and his life should be preserved from injury which he might produce by his own conduct and actions; that the defendant did not have the room where Downes was confined secure, and with a proper and sufficient guard, framework, or other suitable protection over the window, and so securely fastened that Downes, when confined in the room, could not tear away the framework or grating over the window, and throw himself therefrom; that the defendant did not keep Downes properly handcuffed, so that he could not do himself injury by tearing away the framework or bars and throwing himself out of the window, and did not keep some suitable person constantly in attendance upon him.

It is further alleged that the defendant, well knowing Downes' mental and physical condition, and that he was temporarily insane, violent, and liable to injure himself and others, and to throw himself from the window of the room where he was confined, removed the handcuffs from Downes' wrists, placed him, alone and unattended, in the padded room of the hospital, where insane persons are usually placed, and did not have the grating or framework over the window of such room properly constructed or properly secured and fastened, and that such framework or grating was made and fastened in such an insecure, unsafe, careless, and negligent manner that Downes, while insane, pulled down the ironwork and grating from the [558] window, and threw himself therefrom, falling a distance of about thirty-five feet to the pavement, thereby receiving such injuries as to cause his death on January 29, 1890.

At the conclusion of the evidence the court directed a verdict for the defendant, for the reason that the defendant was a charity, which could not be made liable for a tort.

The organization of the defendant had its origin in two deeds—one executed February 3, 1859, by Walter Harper, and the other by Ann Martin, March 10th, the same year. The lands therein described were conveyed to seven prominent citizens of Detroit in trust for the founding of a hospital. The purpose was stated in the deed by Mr. Harper to be: "The institution, erection, and maintenance of a hospital in the city of Detroit, or in the immediate vicinity thereof, for the succor, care, and relief of such aged, sick, poor persons who shall apply for the benefit of the same, and who shall seem to my trustees hereof to be proper subjects for such aid as their means will enable them to afford."

The particular scheme for founding the hospital and all the details were left to be devised and controlled by the trustees. It also provided for organizing and permanently maintaining a school for the instruction of youth in the different arts and trades, after the manner of what is known in Prussia as the "Flintenberg School." The deeds also provided that, if the legislature should enact a law enabling a corporation to be formed for the purposes named in them, the trustees might convey all the lands and funds to a corporation formed therefor.

The trust was accepted by the trustees, and, under the law above referred to, the trustees conveyed the property to the defendant, a corporation, May 17, 1863. Other bequests have been made to the defendant for the same purpose, which in one year amounted to over one hundred thousand dollars. [559] The corporators receive no compensation or dividends. It is purely an eleemosynary institution, organized and maintained for no private gain, but for the proper care and medical treatment of the sick. Hospital physicians and attendants are, and of course must be, paid. The receipts have not always been sufficient to meet ordinary expenses, and one year a private citizen gave one thousand dollars toward the deficiency. The law under which the defendant is organized recognizes it as a charity, exempts its property from taxation, provides that its funds shall be used faithfully and exclusively for the purposes of its organization, and that it may receive, by gift, grant, or devise, any property, but only for the purpose for which it is incorporated. It has no shares, and is not a stock corporation.

If the contention of the learned counsel for the plaintiff be true, it follows that the charity or trust fund must be used to compensate injured parties for the negligence of the trustees, or architects and builders, upon whose judgment reliance is placed as to lands and strength of materials; of physicians employed to treat patients; and of nurses and attendants. In this way the trust fund might be entirely destroyed, and diverted from the purpose for which the donor gave it. Charitable bequests cannot be thus thwarted by negligence for which the donor is in no manner responsible. If, in the proper execution of the trust, a trustee or an employee commits an act of negligence, he may be held responsible for his negligent act; but the law jealously guards the charitable trust fund, and does not permit it to be frittered away by the negligent acts of those employed in its execution. The trustees of this fund could not by their own direct act divert it from the purpose for which it was given, or for which the act of the legislature authorized the title to be vested in the defendant. It certainly follows that the fund cannot be indirectly diverted by the tortious or negligent acts of the 560 managers of the fund or their employees, though such acts result in damage to an innocent beneficiary. Those voluntarily accepting the benefit of the charity accept it upon this condition.

The fact that patients who are able to pay are required to do so does not deprive the defendant of its eleemosynary character, nor permit a recovery for damages on account of the existence of contract relations. The amounts thus received are not for private gain, but contribute to the more effectual accomplishment of the purpose for which the charity was founded. The wrongdoer, in a case of injury, but not the trust fund, must respond in damages. This proposition seems too clear to require argument or authority. It is not, however, inappropriate to remark that better facilities for the care, cure, and treatment of the sick, both of the poor and of those who are able to pay, are secured by the establishment of hospitals like that of the defendant. These facilities are increased by the receipt of money from those who are able to pay in whole or in part for the benefits received. Several hospitals of this character exist in this state, founded by private munificence. Obviously, they would not have been founded if their donors had known or, or ever supposed, that their charitable purposes might be thwarted by the verdicts of juries for the negligent acts of those who must necessarily be employed in the execution of the charity. The following authorities appear to sustain the above position: *Hospital* v. *Ross*, 12 Clark & F. 507; *McDonald* v. *Massachusetts etc. Hospital*, 120 Mass. 432; 21 Am. Rep. 529; *Gooch* v. *Association etc.*, 109 Mass. 558; *Perry* v. *House of Refuge*, 63 Md. 20; 52 Am. Rep. 495; *Railway Co.* v. *Artist*, 9 Co. Ct. App. 14.

In what we have said we are not to be understood as intimating any opinion as to whether there is any liability of the trustees for the alleged defect in the construction of the room where the deceased was confined, or of those [561] who were intrusted with his care and treatment. This question was not passed on by the court below, and we express no opinion upon it.

The judgment is affirmed.

MCGRATH, C. J., LONG and HOOKER, JJ., concurred. MONTGOMERY, J., did not sit.

———

HOSPITAL—LIABILITY TO INMATES FOR NEGLIGENCE OF ITS EMPLOYEES. The cases discussing this subject are collected in the extended note to *Goddard* v. *Inhabitants*, 30 Am. St. Rep. 402. If a hospital is maintained and a physician employed by a corporation for the purpose of caring for sick or injured employees, the expenses being provided for out of certain moneys retained out of the wages of the employees, and the corporation makes no profit out of the undertaking, but conducts it as a charitable institution, it is not liable for negligence on the part of the physician, but only for a want of care in selecting him: *Richardson* v. *Carbon Hill Coal Co.*, 10 Wash. 648.

———

MIDGLEY *v.* WALKER.

[101 MICHIGAN, 583.]

JOINT TENANCY—EXECUTION AGAINST ONE TENANT.—The individual interest of one of two or more joint tenants is subject to levy and sale upon execution running against such tenant.

C. S. Chase, for the appellants.

J. P. Whittemore, for the appellee.

[583] MCGRATH, C. J. This is a bill filed to remove a cloud from the title of a parcel of land which was deeded to the

complainants, "and the survivor of either of them." Defendant is a purchaser at an execution sale upon a judgment
against William D. Midgley, and the sole question is whether
the individual interest of one of two or more joint tenants is
subject to levy and sale upon execution running against such
tenant.

[584] Our statute (Howell's Statutes, sec. 5560) provides
that, "All grants and devises of lands made to two or more
persons, except as provided in the following section, shall be
construed to create estates in common, and not in joint tenancy, unless expressly declared to be in joint tenancy." The
right of survivorship is, however, expressly granted in the
deed to complainants.

There can be no doubt but that the joint estate may be
severed by the act of the parties, by a conveyance by either
party, by partition under Howell's Statutes, section 7850, or
by a levy and sale upon an execution against one of the parties. Either tenant may convey his share to a cotenant or
to a stranger: 1 Washburn on Real Property, 5th ed., 680; 4
Kent's Commentaries, 363. Each has the power of alienation over his aliquot share, and of charging it with his individual debts, and the joint tenants may sever the tenancy
voluntarily by deed or compel a partition: 4 Kent's Commentaries, 364; *Lake* v. *Craddock,* 1 Lead. Cas. Eq. (Hare &
Wallace's notes) 224. Whether more than the joint estate
could be disposed of upon partition it is not necessary to determine: See *Southerland* v. *Cox,* 3 Dev. 394. The interest
of either is subject to levy and sale on execution: *Thompson*
v. *Mawhinney,* 17 Ala. 363; 52 Am. Dec. 176; *Galusha* v. *Sin-
clear,* 3 Vt. 394; *Bigelow* v. *Topliff,* 25 Vt. 273; 60 Am. Dec.
264; *Baker* v. *Shepherd,* 37 Ga. 12; *Blevins* v. *Baker,* 11 Ired.
291. A sale, however, of the interest of one of several does
not affect the interest of the others: *Carlyle* v. *Patterson,* 3
Bibb, 93; *People* v. *Marshall,* 8 Cal. 51; *White* v. *Brooks,* 43
N. H. 402; *Sneed* v. *Waring,* 2 B. Mon. 522. There can be
neither dower nor curtesy of an estate held in joint tenancy,
and a devise by one joint tenant of his share will be inoperative, inasmuch as the right of survivorship takes precedence:
1 Washburn on Real Property, 5th ed., 681, 682. The same
author lays down the rule that no charge, like a rent or a
right of way or a judgment, created by one [585] cotenant can
bind the estate in the hands of the survivor, unless the
charge be created by the one who becomes such survivor, or

the creator of the charge releases his estate to a cotenant, who, as releasee, accepts, with that part of the estate, the charge inhering therein by his own act. But the charges made by a joint tenant and judgments against him will bind his assignee and himself as survivor: 4 Kent's Commentaries, 360.

The rules which govern holdings by husband and wife jointly have no application. They do not take by moieties, but they are both seised of the entirety: *In re Appeal of Lewis,* 85 Mich. 340; 24 Am. St. Rep. 94.

The decree dismissing the bill is affirmed, with costs to defendant.

The other justices concurred.

JOINT TENANCY—EXECUTION. —A grant of land to husband and wife "in joint tenancy" makes them joint tenants, and the interest of each is subject to execution: *Thornburg* v. *Wiggins,* 135 Ind. 178; 41 Am. St. Rep. 422.

CASES

SUPREME COURT

MINNESOTA.

IN RE HOLT'S WILL.

[56 MINNESOTA, 38.]

AN ATTESTING WITNESS TO A WILL must be competent at the time of attestation. If then competent his subsequent incompetency, from any cause, will not prevent the probate of the will, if it can be otherwise satisfactorily proved. The rule of competency in such cases, in Minnesota, is defined by statute.

WITNESSES—HUSBAND AND WIFE—CONSTRUCTION OF STATUTE.—A statute providing that neither husband nor wife shall be examined as a witness without the consent of the other does not make them incompetent witnesses, nor are they to be classed as such, though their right to be examined is contingent upon the consent of the spouse for or against whom the witness may be offered.

WITNESS TO WILL—COMPETENCY OF MARRIED PERSON.—A married person is not incompetent to attest a will simply because the husband or wife of such person is a beneficiary under the will; and he can become incompetent only upon a single contingency, and that is where such interested party shall become a contestant on the subsequent probate of the will.

LEGACY TO WIFE OF ATTESTING WITNESS IS NOT VOID.—A statute making void a legacy to an attesting witness to a will does not apply to the husband or wife of such witness, as neither has, under existing laws, any present, direct, or certain interest in a legacy to the other.

Jay W. Crane, for the appellant.

Stringer & Seymour, for the respondent.

[34] VANDERBURGH, J. The will in question here contains a legacy to Georgiana Needham, estimated by the testator at about four hundred dollars. The will was attested by two witnesses, one of whom was E. Z. Needham, who is, and was at the time of such attestation, the husband of Georgiana. [35] Mrs. Needham is the proponent of the will, and in the pro-

bate court objection was made by the contestants, appellants here, to the allowance and probate of the will, on the ground that E. Z. Needham, the husband of the proponent, was not a competent witness to the will.

The action of the probate court, allowing the will, having been affirmed by the district court, the case is brought here on appeal from the judgment of the last-named court.

1. The first question presented involves the competency of the attesting witness E. Z. Needham. Undoubtedly, he must have been a competent witness at the time of the execution of the will. This is the established doctrine of the common-law authorities, from the case of *Holdfast* v. *Dowsing*, 2 Strange, 1253, down to the present time: 1 Redfield on Wills, 253; 2 Greenleaf on Evidence, sec. 691; *Morrill* v. *Morrill*, 53 Vt. 78; 38 Am. Rep. 659; and it is clearly recognized in our statute (Probate Code, c. 2, sec. 19), which requires that a will shall be attested and subscribed in the testator's presence by two or more competent witnesses. But, if competent at the time of the execution of the will, their subsequent incompetency, from whatever cause it arises, shall not prevent the probate and allowance of the will, if it is otherwise satisfactorily proven.

The appellants, however, contend that the attesting witnesses must be such as would be competent under the common-law rule, and that they are impliedly not included in the definition of "witness," in General Statutes of 1878, chapter 73, section 6, because their competency is to be determined as of the time of the attestation, and not as of the time when they may be called to testify on the probate of the will. But this construction cannot be upheld. The cases from Massachusetts are not in point, because there the statutes removing the objection to the competency of witnesses on the ground of interest, and of the relation of husband and wife, are expressly declared not to apply to attesting witnesses to a will: *Sullivan* v. *Sullivan*, 106 Mass. 478; 8 Am Rep. 356.

The question of the competency of such witnesses in this state is determined by the statute: Gen. Stats. of 1878, c. 73, secs. 6, 7, 9, 10. An attesting witness is competent, if he be one who would at the same time be competent to testify in court to the facts which he attests; and so the courts hold. Thus, in *Jenkins* v. *Dawes*, 115 Mass. 601, an attesting witness is declared to be one who at the time of the attestation would be competent to testify; and in *Morrill* v. *Morrill*, [36] 53 Vt. 78, 38 Am. Rep. 659, "competency to testify" must exist at the time of the attestation.

The attestation contemplated the subsequent testimony to the facts attested when the will should be proved. The incompetency of the husband or wife to testify, where either was an interested party at the common law, rose out of the unity of interest and of personal relations. This unity of interest may be removed, and yet, owing to the unity and confidential nature of their personal relations, the common-law rule in respect to competency remain, on grounds of public policy: *Lucas* v. *Brooks*, 18 Wall. 453; *Giddings* v. *Turgeon*, 58 Vt. 110.

It is conceded that the unity of interest, so far as relates to property, has been done away with by statute: *Wilson* v. *Wilson*, 43 Minn. 400; and the general disqualification to testify on the ground of interest is removed by the General Statutes of 1878, chapter 73, section 7, but it is denied that the statute has removed the general incompetency growing out of the marriage relation. But the only limitation upon the competency of either is found in the General Statutes of 1878, chapter 73, section 10, which provides that neither party shall be examined without the consent of the other. They are not thereby made incompetent witnesses, nor are they to be classed as such, though their right to be examined is contingent upon the consent of that one for or against whom the witness may be offered. It does not follow that a married person is incompetent to attest a will because the husband or wife of such person is a beneficiary under the will. He can only become incompetent in a single contingency, and that is, in case such interested party shall become a contestant on the subsequent probate of the will. If the latter be not a contesting party he is in no position to raise the objection, and he may not choose to do it if he is; and, if he be one of the proponents, he thereby consents to the testimony of the attesting witnesses. The contingency which would make him incompetent may never arise, and, if it does, it must be deemed to arise subsequent to the act of attestation. In the case at bar, then, what evidence is there that the witness is incompetent? The wife is proponent, and offers to examine her husband as a witness. No question, therefore, in respect to his competency is raised. Incompetency in a witness is not presumed, and the question is to be determined when the offer to examine the witness is made, and then the facts are to be ascertained by the court. The witness is not shown to be incompetent [37] in this case, and his evidence on the probate of the will was properly received. In *Tillotson* v. *Prichard*, 60 Vt. 107, 6 Am. St. Rep. 95, it is held that the wife.of the grantor in a Minnesota deed was a competent attesting witness thereto, under the provisions of the statute we have been considering, and the court say "that she was a competent witness, and might be examined with the consent of her husband." The court also held, as we do, that the plaintiff, by offering the deed in evidence, consented to her being a witness.

2. The appellant also contends that if the husband be a competent witness, then the legacy to his wife should be held void under the statute which annuls beneficial devises, etc., to a subscribing witness on account of the marital relation. But there is nothing in this point. The husband has no direct or certain interest in the legacy to his wife. It is absolutely hers in her own right, and free from his control: Gen. Stats. 1878, c. 69; *Wilson* v. *Wilson*, 43 Minn. 400. The only devises or legacies which the statute annuls are those made to subscribing witnesses, which clearly does not apply to the husband or wife of the legatee.

In England, where husband and wife are competent witnesses (Taylor on Evidence, 1145, 1147), the statute has gone further (1 Vict., c. 26, sec. 15), and also avoids gifts, legacies, and devises to the husband or wife of an attesting witness. It could not be done without the statute.

This legislation assumes both the competency of the witnesses and that they had no interest in the legacies which would have made the same void without the aid of legislation to that effect.

The construction we have adopted is in conformity with the spirit of modern legislation on the general subject of the rights of husband and wife, and the practical results will no doubt be no more serious than in the case of parents or children, who may unquestionably attest deeds and wills for each other: 1 Alb. L. J. 246.

It is a matter largely for the judgment of the legislature. Judgment affirmed. ___

WILLS—COMPETENCY OF ATTESTING WITNESSES—HUSBAND OR WIFE. The competency of attesting witnesses to a will is to be tested upon the state of facts existing at the time of such attestation, and not upon that

existing at the time the will is presented for pròbate.   The husband or wife
of one named as devisee or legatee in a will is not a competent witness to
prove the execution of the will, even as to devisees and bequests made to
persons other than to the wife or husband of such witness, and is not
rendered competent by a release by the devisee or legatee of all his or her
right, title, interest, and claim under the will.   Section 8 of the Illinois
statute of wills provides in substance that any beneficial devise, legacy, or
interest, made or given to a subscribing witness to the execution of-any
will, testament, or codicil, shall, "as to such subscribing witness, and all
persous claiming under him, be null and void."   This provision is construed
as having no application to the interests of any persons other than those
who are attesting witnesses, and does not declare such interests null and
void.   Nor does the further provision of the statute assume to render competent any subscribing witnesses other than those to whom a beneficial
devise, etc., was made or given: *Fisher* v. *Spence*, 150 Ill. 253; 41 Am. St.
Rep. 360, and note.

BARNES *v.* HEKLA FIRE INSURANCE COMPANY.

[56 MINNESOTA, 38.]

REINSURANCE IS A MERE CONTRACT OF INDEMNITY, in which the insurer
reinsures risks in another company, and is solely for the benefit of
the insurer, and not of the policy holders, who have no interest therein,
and cannot sue thereon.

INSURANCE.—IF A CONTRACT OF REINSURANCE includes a promise or agreement to assume and pay the losses of policy holders, actions may be
brought by them, in case of loss, directly against the reinsurer, upon
such promise or undertaking.

INSURANCE—REINSURANCE—REMEDY IN CASE OF LOSS—ELECTION—INSOL-
VENCY.—In case of loss under a contract of reinsurance, which includes
an agreement to pay the losses of policy holders, an action may be
maintained against either company without the plaintiffs being compelled to elect, as the remedies are not inconsistent, though he can have
but one satisfaction, so it is no bar to his action against one of the
companies for him to file his claim in insolvency proceedings against
the other.

NOVATION—REINSURANCE.—A mere agreement whereby one party agrees,
upon a consideration moving from the other, to pay a debt due from
the latter to a third person is not a novation upon the mere consent
to or adoption of such agreement by such third party creditor. This
applies to contracts of reinsurance, and the doctrine of novation is not
applicable.

ACTION upon a policy of insurance. Defendant's second
answer alleged that the plaintiff was a nonresident, and
that the court had no jurisdiction. Its third answer alleged
the reinsurance and insolvency proceedings as stated in the
opinion. Defendant's second and third answers were demurred to upon the ground that they did not state facts sufficient to constitute a defense.

C. D. & Thomas D. O'Brien, for the appellant.

B. H. Schriber, for the respondent.

40 VANDERBURGH, J. The plaintiff demurred to the second and third defenses set up in the defendant's answer, and this appeal is from the order sustaining the demurrer.

The action is brought upon a policy of insurance issued by the defendant to the plaintiff for a loss covered thereby. It is alleged, by way of defense, that subsequent to the date of plaintiff's policy the St. Paul German Insurance Company, a corporation lawfully doing business in this state, had "reinsured the said policy, and promised and agreed with the said plaintiff and this defendant to pay to the plaintiff any loss which she might suffer under said policy, and said agreement was in full force and effect at the time of the pretended occurrence of the fire described in the complaint, if any such fire did occur, and that said plaintiff had always full notice and knowledge thereof." It further appears that thereafter, and before the commencement of this action, the St. Paul German Insurance Company duly made an assignment under the insolvency laws of the state, and that the plaintiff has duly filed and proved her claim in the insolvency proceedings for the loss indemnified against by defendant, and so assumed by the German Insurance Company. It is claimed by the defendant in this action that, by electing to proceed against the estate of the German Insurance Company, the plaintiff has effectually waived her remedy against the defendant upon the policy sued on.

It will be conceded that the agreement between the two companies set out in the answer is not merely a contract of reinsurance, but also to pay, and assume the payment of losses of parties indemnified by policies issued by the defendant company reinsured. Reinsurance is a mere contract of indemnity, in which an insurer reinsures risks in another company. In such a contract the policy holders have no concern, are not the parties for whose benefit the contract of reinsurance is made, and they cannot, therefore, sue thereon. But the agreement alleged in this case is not a mere reinsurance of the risks by the reinsurer, but it embraces also an express agreement to assume and pay losses of the policy holder, and is therefore an agreement upon which he is entitled to maintain an action directly against the reinsurer: *Johannes* v. *Phenix Ins. Co.*, 66 Wis. 50; 57 Am. Rep. 249.

[41] This is not, however, a case where the insurer is put to an election between his remedies against the two companies.

Unless there was a substitution of debtors, in the nature of a novation, between the three parties, upon the plaintiff's consent to the new agreement, the plaintiff has not waived or lost her right of action against the defendant. A creditor is put to an election only where his remedies are inconsistent, and not where they are consistent and concurrent. In the latter case a party may prosecute as many as he has, as in the case of several debtors. And so, if, in this instance, the remedy against the insolvent company, as respects the plaintiff, was merely cumulative, there is no reason why she may not pursue either or both. As between the two companies, the defendant occupies no better position than a surety. It is not like the case of a former suit pending between the same parties. She may have an action against each at the same time, but only one satisfaction; and to this end the court may interpose by a stay, when found necessary. But an action against the party primarily or originally liable in such cases may be necessary, in order to save rights under the statute of limitations, or for like reasons.

The new agreement between the companies referred to, which inured to plaintiff's benefit, lacks the essential elements of novation.

It is not alleged that it was mutually understood or agreed between the two companies that the liability of the defendant should be discharged, and the new promisor should be substituted and accepted as plaintiff's debtor in the place of the defendant. or that plaintiff ever assented to or adopted any such thing.

In some few cases, notably in Rhode Island, it is held that such an agreement necessarily implies an intention to substitute the new for the original debtor, and that the creditor, in assenting to it, adopts it as a substitutional agreement: *Urquhart* v. *Brayton*, 12 R. I. 172; *Wood* v. *Moriarty*, 15 R. L. 522. But this, we think, is importing a stipulation into the agreement by construction which the parties have not made. It is frequently the case that the creditor consents to the arrangement as a favor or for the convenience of his debtor; and we apprehend it would be a surprise to the parties, as well as an injustice, in many cases, if [42] it were held to operate as a release of the original liability; and therefore it should distinctly appear, from the express terms of the agreement, or as a necessary inference from the situation of the parties, and the special circumstances of the case, that such was the intention and understanding of the parties, of which the creditor was chargeable with notice, and this is the generally accepted doctrine of the courts: 11 Am. & Eng. Ency. of Law, 889, 890.

In the early case of *Farley* v. *Cleveland*, 4 Cow. 432, 15 Am. Dec. 387, in which this remedy of a creditor, upon a promise for his benefit made to his debtor, upon a consideration moving from the latter, is elaborately considered, the fact of the subsisting liability of the original debtor is recognized, and held no obstacle to the right of recovery by the third party creditor, and such continued liability is generally assumed by the courts.

The exact ground upon which the direct liability to the creditor in this class of cases should be placed appears to be left in doubt by the cases.

It is called the "American doctrine," because peculiar to the courts of this country, though all do not assent to it, notably those of Massachusetts.

It is an equitable rule, adopted for convenience and to avoid circuity of action and the formality of an assignment by the original debtor of the new agreement with him, and is strictly in accordance with the intention of the parties to the contract in creating a liability in favor of a third party creditor: *Gifford* v. *Corrigan*, 117 N. Y. 264, 265; 15 Am. St. Rep. 508. The same rule of procedure is held applicable, though not uniformly, where the grantee of a mortgagor assumes in his deed to pay off the encumbrance.

The mortgagee may proceed by action directly against the grantee, but the mortgagor still remains liable, and is held to occupy the relation of surety for the grantee, who, as between them, becomes the principal debtor: *Thorp* v. *Keokuk Coal Co.*, 48 N. Y. 257, 258; *Klapworth* v. *Dressler*, 78 Am. Dec. 76, 77, note.

There is no double liability. There is no dividend, as yet, shown in the insolvency proceedings; and there is, of course, nothing to be credited upon the plaintiff's claim. The receipt of a dividend would only operate as a *pro tanto* satisfaction; and, if defendant is required [43] to pay before the dividend, it will be entitled to it, and may be subrogated to the rights of plaintiff therein, so that there need be no embarrassment in adjusting the rights of the parties.

Other questions in the case do not, we think, demand any discussion.

Order affirmed.   ——

CONTRACT OF REINSURANCE AND THE REMEDIES OF THE PARTIES.—It is not the purpose of this note to give any special attention to that part of the law of reinsurance, called double insurance, or to that condition of things whereby an old company sells out to a new one, or becomes consolidated with it, so that the new company becomes liable directly to the insured. "Throughout the modern treatises in all languages, reassurance is distinguished from double insurance, which is a contract entirely different": *Hone* v. *Mutual Safety Ins. Co.*, 1 Sand. 137, 146. Other insurance is treated in the monographic notes to *Funk* v. *Minnesota Farmers' Mut. Fire Assn. Ins. Co.*, 43 Am. Rep. 221-223; *Thomas* v. *Builders' Mut. Fire Ins. Co.*, 20 Am. Rep. 319-323; and the liabilities of successive insurers is discussed in the monographic note to *Alliance etc. Assur. Co.* v. *Louisiana State Ins.*, 28 Am. Dec. 121-125. This note is, therefore, confined to a treatment of the law of those cases in which a risk taken by one insurance company is reinsured in another company.

Nature of Contract—Custom.—One who has assumed a liability under an insurance policy may, for prudential or other reasons, contract with another to relieve him from that liability, and take it upon himself. This is reinsurance. The practice of reinsuring is now a common one, and the policy of reinsurance is a valid contract: *Manufacturers' Ins. Co.* v. *Western Assur. Co.*, 145 Mass. 419-423; *Herckenrath* v. *American Mutual Ins. Co.*, 3 Barb. Ch. 63; *Merry* v. *Prince*, 2 Mass. 176; *Delaware Ins. Co.* v. *Quaker City Ins. Co.*, 3 Grant Cas. 71. A contract of reinsurance to the whole extent of the original insurer's liability is valid, in the absence of usage or stipulation to the contrary: *Insurance Co.* v. *Hibernia Ins. Co.*, 140 U. S. 565. The custom among underwriters in the city of New Orleans, with respect to reinsurance, is to divide the risk and not take the whole of it; and when the application is silent this is always understood: *Louisiana Mut. Ins. Co.* v. *New Orleans Ins. Co.*, 13 La. Ann. 246; *Egan* v. *Firemen's Ins. Co.*, 27 La. Ann. 368. But an open policy of insurance, executed in one state and sent to another, and taking effect by acceptance of risks under it by the insurer's agent there, is not affected by local usage of the place where it was executed: *Insurance Co.* v. *Hibernia Ins. Co.*, 140 U. S. 565. Reinsurance in New York is also held to be a valid contract both as to fire and marine policies. The risk assumed by the first insurers gives them such an insurable interest as renders the reinsurance a valid contract: *Delaware Ins. Co.* v. *Quaker City Ins. Co.*, 3 Grant Cas. 71; *Herckenrath* v. *American Mut. Ins. Co.*, 3 Barb. Ch. 63. An insurance company in that state is authorized to make reinsurance, under the general powers conferred to make contracts of insurance, and all kinds of insurance: *New York etc. Fire Ins. Co.* v. *New York Fire Ins. Co.*, 17 Wend. 359. Reinsurance is a contract of indemnity to the reinsured, and binds the reinsurer to pay to the reinsured the whole loss sustained in respect to the subject insured, to the extent for which he is reinsurer: *Eagle Ins. Co.* v. *Lafayette Ins. Co.*, 9 Ind. 443; but the contract extends no further than the risk taken by the original insurer. He cannot stipulate for indemnity against a risk which he has not assumed: *Commonwealth Ins. Co.* v. *Globe Mut. Ins. Co.*, 35 Pa. St. 475. A policy of reinsurance, "subject to such risks, valuations and conditions, including the risk of premium note, as are or may be taken," by the original underwriters, is not an indemnity against a loss incurred on a different voyage from that originally insured. It covers only the insurable interest of the prior insurers: *Commonwealth Ins. Co.* v. *Globe Mut. Ins. Co.*, 35 Pa. St. 475. There is no privity between the one originally insured and the reinsurer. The liability of the reinsurer is solely to the reinsured: *Strong* v. *Phœnix Ins. Co.*, 62 Mo. 289; 21 Am. Rep. 417; *Herckenrath* v. *American Mut. Ins. Co.*, 3 Barb. Ch. 63; *Delaware Ins. Co.* v. *Quaker City Ins. Co.*, 3 Grant Cas. 71; *Yonkers etc. Fire Ins. Co.* v. *Hoffman Fire Ins. Co.*, 6 Rob. (N. Y.) 316; *Manufacturers' Ins. Co.* v. *Western Assur. Co.*, 145 Mass. 419, 423. The law authorizing reinsurance is not intended for the benefit of individual policy holders, but for the benefit of the whole company insured: *Casserly* v. *Manners*, 48 How. Pr. 219; and, it being competent for an insurance company to reinsure upon its risks, it may transfer its property, including premium notes, as a consideration therefor: *Davenport Fire Ins. Co.* v. *Moore*, 50 Iowa, 619. The failure of an insurance company to comply with a law requiring it to have a certain amount of capital stock, and a certain number of agreements of insurance in order to continue in business, will not prevent it from indemnifying itself by reinsurance for risks already assured: *Davenport Fire Ins. Co.* v. *Moore*, 50 Iowa, 619. An insurable interest can spring from a prior insurance, and may arise from a time policy as well as from any other: *Philadelphia Ins. Co.* v. *Washington Ins. Co.*, 23 Pa. St. 250; *Herckenrath* v. *American Mut. Ins. Co.*, 3 Barb. Ch. 63, 70; *Manufacturers' Ins. Co.* v. *Western Assur. Co.*, 145 Mass. 419. Hence reinsurance is but a modification of the contract of insurance, in which the thing insured is the same as in the original policy; but the subject of indemnity is the risk assumed by the first insurer: *Fame Ins. Co's Appeal*, 83 Pa. St. 396, 407. The insurer's risk is, therefore, the sole object of reinsurance, and forms the consideration of a new and independent contract, distinct from and unconnected with the original insurance: *Jackson* v. *St. Paul etc. Ins. Co.*, 99 N. Y. 124, 130; *New York etc. Fire Ins. Co.* v. *New-York Fire Ins. Co.*, 17 Wend. 359.

It is sometimes required by statute that life insurance companies shall, upon discontinuing business, reinsure their policy holders in a solvent company: *Alliance Mut. Life etc. Society* v. *Welch*, 26 Kan. 632. A contract of reinsurance under a charter not expressly giving power to reinsure is not *ultra vires* where the charter is made subject to a general insurance act which does authorize reinsurance: *Fame Ins. Co's Appeal*, 83 Pa. St. 396, 407. A contract, however, by a mutual benefit association to pay the death losses of another association in consideration of the transfer of the assets and membership of such other association, is, in the absence of express authority in its articles of incorporation, *ultra vires* and void: *Twiss* v. *Guaranty Life Assn.*, 87 Iowa, 733; 43 Am. St. Rep. 418. The better opinion seems to be that a contract for reinsurance is not within the statute of frauds as a contract to answer for the debt or default of another: *Bartlett* v. *Fireman's Fund Ins. Co.*, 77 Iowa, 155; *Commercial Mut. Marine Ins. Co.* v. *Union Mut. Ins. Co.*, 19 How. 318, 321; though the contrary has been held: *Egan* v. *Fireman's Ins. Co.*, 27 La. Ann. 368. These cases refer, of course, to the promise to issue the policy of reinsurance, and the better ruling is based upon the principle that, at common law, a promise for a valuable consideration to make a policy of insurance is no more required to be in writing than a

promise to execute and deliver a bond, or a bill of exchange, or a negotiable
note: *Commercial Mut. Marine Ins. Co. v. Union Mut. Ins. Co.*, 19 How. 318,
321. No distinction exists between policies of reinsurance and other or
first policies in respect to the nature or extent of the proof required; and
an inaccurate description of property,in a policy of reinsurance, will not
necessarily defeat it. If a mistake has been made as to the location of the
property insured, extrinsic evidence may be let in to identify the place:
Yonkers etc. Fire Ins. Co. v. Hoffman Fire Ins. Co., 6 Rob. (N. Y.) 316. The
insured, in a policy of reinsurance, means the reinsured: *Carrington v. Commercial etc. Ins. Co*, 1 Bosw. 152. It is not competent to limit the contract of
reinsurance by proof of a usage whereby the reinsurer pays the same proportion of the entire loss sustained by the original insured that the sum reinsured
bears to the first insurance written by the reinsured. The indiscriminate
resort to testimony of usages and customs of trade to control the construction and the results of contracts "is liable to dangerous abuses," and such
testimony is to be admitted with great caution: *Hone v. Mutual Safety Ins.
Co.*, 1 Sand. 137. One who obtains a policy of reinsurance is bound to communicate all facts within his knowledge, and to conceal no fact material to
the risk. A violation of these requirements will, as in cases of original
insurance, render the policy of reinsurance void: *New York etc. Fire Ins. Co.
v. New York Fire Ins. Co.*, 17 Wend. 359. If the original insurer has
specific information it must be communicated specifically. He must see to
it that the reinsurer's knowledge is substantially as full and particular as
his own: *Sun Mut. Ins. Co. v. Ocean Ins. Co.*, 107 U. S. 485, 505, 510. The
court, however, were divided in opinion on this point, and Justices Miller,
Waite, and Bradley dissented from the majority opinion on the ground
that it proceeded an upon erroneous view of the principles of reinsurance, and
placed the reinsurer in the exact condition of a joint insurer, or of an original insurer of the risk of the party first insured. "In point of fact," said
Mr. Justice Bradley, " the Sun company insured the Ocean company against
the risk which the latter had incurred by its policies, and unless there was
misrepresentation, fraud, or intentional concealment by the Ocean company, the Sun company should pay the loss which the other sustained,
and against the hazard of which it agreed to insure the Ocean company.
The long course of dealing between the two companies showed that the Sun
company was in the habit of reinsuring for the Ocean company without
inquiry into the particulars of the risk, and, in this case, there was no reason
for any special communication of the circumstances of the risk by the Ocean
to the Sun company."

Risk—What Included in.—Reinsurance may be for a less risk than the
original insurance, but not for more: *Philadelphia Ins. Co. v. Washington
Ins. Co.*, 23 Pa. St. 250. And when two insurance companies contract with
each other that one shall share the loss with the other, as to all risks exceeding a certain sum, the contract applies to every risk that has been written
for a sum exceeding the sum so specified: *Continental Ins. Co. v. Ætna Ins.
Co.*, 138 N. Y. 16; reversing the same case, 62 Hun, 554. In this case, one
of marine insurance, the contract was for one of the companies to reinsure
the other to the extent of one-half the amount of each and every risk which
equaled or exceeded in value the sum of fifteen thousand dollars, and in an
action upon the policy it was held that the word "risk" therein referred to
the entered or written value of the cargo, and not simply to such risks as
after a loss and upon adjustment, were found to equal or exceed the sum
named; that it was the intent of defendant's contract that its obligation

should be complete and perfect when the goods were entered for insurance; and not that the existence of any contract whatever should be left to depend upon the extent of the loss. So a contract of reinsurance which clearly includes only risks issued by the first company upon properties situated in one state cannot be extended to risks taken by the first company in such state on properties located elsewhere: *London etc. Fire Ins. Co.* v. *Lycoming Fire Ins. Co.*, 105 Pa. St. 424. A policy of reinsurance, limited to the excess of the original insurer's risk above a certain sum, will not prevent him from reinsuring himself elsewhere within that sum: *Insurance Co.* v. *Hibernia Ins. Co.*, 140 U. S. 565.

General Rights and Liabilities of Reinsurer and Reinsured.—In a contract of reinsurance the risk of the reinsuring company begins when the risk on the original policy begins, unless otherwise specified, and, if the reinsuring policy does not show on its face that it is a policy of reinsurance, parol evidence of the facts of the case is admissible to show that the contract is really one of reinsurance, and so fix the date of the beginning of the risk: *Philadelphia Life Ins. Co.* v. *American etc. Ins. Co.*, 23 Pa. St. 65, 67. When it is provided in a contract of insurance that the loss, if any, shall be payable "*pro rata* at and in the same time and manner as the reinsured," the liability of the company reinsuring accrues at the same time with the liability of the reinsured: *Blackstone* v. *Alemannia Fire Ins. Co.*, 56 N. Y. 104; 4 Daly, 299. Such a provision has no reference to the insolvency of the reinsured. It means that the reinsurer shall have all the advantages of the time and manner of payment specified in the policy of the reinsured: *Cashau* v. *Northwestern Nat. Ins. Co.*, 5 Biss. 476, 479. Under an agreement that the reinsurer shall be liable *pro rata*, and only in the same manner and at the same time as the reinsured, the liability of the reinsurer is limited to indemnity; and the provision as to time means that payment shall be made by the reinsurer in point of time, as the reinsured had contracted to make it; as the liability of the reinsurer is not affected by the insolvency of the reinsured, nor the inability of the latter to fulfill the original contract of insurance: *Blackstone* v. *Alemannia Fire Ins. Co.*, 56 N. Y. 104; 4 Daly, 299; *Illinois Mut. Fire Ins. Co.* v. *Andes Ins. Co.*, 67 Ill. 362; 16 Am. Rep. 620; *Norwood* v. *Resolute Fire Ins. Co.*, 4 Jones & S. 552; *Consolidated etc. Fire Ins. Co.* v. *Cashow*, 41 Md. 59; *Cashau* v. *Northwestern Nat. Ins. Co.*, 5 Biss. 476; *Ex parte Norwood*, 3 Biss. 504. The liability of the reinsurer, except as limited by contract, is the same as the original insurer, and the reinsuring company need pay no more than what the first insuring company is legally bound to pay, as the contract of insurance is not one of profit, but of indemnity: *Ex parte Norwood*, 3 Biss. 504. That a contract of reinsurance is a contract of indemnity is not seriously questioned, but what constitutes indemnity is, under some circumstances, a very serious problem. For example, if the original insurer settles with the insured for less than the loss for which it was liable, or, if it is insolvent and cannot pay in full, how much shall the reinsurer be required to pay? The weight of authority sustains the proposition that the liability, and not the ability, of the insurer is the measure of the reinsurer's liability, at least, where no final settlement has been made: *Ex parte Norwood*, 3 Biss. 504; *Cashau* v. *Northwestern Nat. Ins. Co.*, 5 Biss. 476; *Hone* v. *Mutual Safety Ins. Co.*, 1 Sand. 137; *Eagle Ins. Co.* v. *Lafayette Ins. Co.*, 9 Ind. 443; *Gantt* v. *American Cent. Ins. Co.*, 68 Mo. 503; *Blackstone* v. *Alemannia Fire Ins. Co.*, 56 N. Y. 104; 4 Daly, 299; *Consolidated etc. Fire Ins. Co.* v. *Cashow*, 41 Md. 59; *Strong* v. *American Cent. Ins. Co.*, 4 Mo. App. 7. But in *Illinois Mut. Fire Ins. Co.* v. *Andes*

Ins. Co., 67 Ill. 362, 16 Am. Rep. 620, the court makes a clear distinction between cases in which the insurer has actually settled and those in which full settlement has not been made. In that case the original insurer became liable to pay to the insured the sum of six thousand dollars, but actually discharged its whole liability by the payment of six hundred dollars, and the court held that only six hundred dollars could be recovered from the reinsurer. So, in *Insurance Co.* v. *Insurance Co.* 38 Ohio St. 11, 43 Am. Rep. 413, where the insurer obtained full discharge and satisfaction of all claim against it by the payment of sixty cents on the dollar, and in which the court laid down the rule that where the insuring company discharges its liability by the payment of a less sum than that for which the original insurance was effected, the sum so paid by it will be taken as the amount of damage sustained, and the measure of indemnity to be recovered from the reinsuring company, if such sum does not exceed the amount of actual loss, and the policy contains no provision for prorating loss or limiting liability. Where the insuring company becomes bankrupt at the time of sustaining losses, the reinsuring company may purchase claims against it which it has reinsured for the purpose of using such claims as offsets to its own liability, and such claims so purchased will be a valid counterclaim against its indemnity of reinsurance upon such claims: *In re Cleveland Ins. Co.*, 22 Fed. Rep. 200.

ACTION BY FIRST INSURED—COMPROMISE, SETTLEMENT, OR CONTEST.— Judge Story, in commenting upon the relation sustained by the reinsurers to the reinsured, said: "If notice of a suit, threatened or pending, upon the original policy, be given to the reassurers, they have a fair opportunity to exercise an election whether to contest or admit the claim. It is their duty to act upon such notice, when given, within a reasonable time. If they do not disapprove of the contestation of the suit, or authorize the party reassured to compromise or settle it, they must be deemed to require that it should be carried on; and then, by just implication, they are held to indemnify the party reassured against the costs and expenses necessarily and reasonably incurred in defending the suit": *New York State Marine Ins. Co.* v. *Protection Ins. Co.*, 1 Story, 458, 462. Any judgment rendered against the reinsured in an action against it by the insured would, of course, conclusively establish its liability, and also the liability of the reinsurer upon its policy, "for it is a well-settled rule," says McKee, J., in *Commercial Union Assur. Co.* v. *American Cent. Ins. Co.*, 68 Cal. 430, "that where one is bound to protect another from liability he is bound by the result of a litigation to which such other was a party, provided he had notice of the litigation, and opportunity to control and manage it; the rule being subject to the qualification that the litigation must have been carried on without fraud or collusion, and conducted in a reasonable manner." But it is otherwise where there is no adjudication of the question of liability. The reinsured may not defend the action, although it has agreed with the reinsurer to do so, and in its control and management thereof it may acknowledge its liability by abandoning all defenses to it, and compromising and settling with the party originally insured. This it has a right to do, so far as the question of its own liability is concerned, because there is no privity of contract between the original insured and the reinsurer, and the latter cannot legally object to or prevent such a compromise. But the original insurer has no power, under the authority conferred upon it, to defend the action for the reinsurer and itself, to compromise and settle the claim so as to bind the reinsurer, unless the latter had knowledge of the compromise, and consented to it or approved of it: *Commercial Union Assur. Co.* v. *American Cent. Ins. Co.*, 68 Cal. 430; *Gantt* v. *American Cent. Ins. Co.*, 68 Mo. 503. A judgment, however, against the original insurer is, in the absence of fraud or collusion, binding upon the reinsurer where he has notice of the suit, and an opportunity to defend. The reinsuring company can litigate the question of the liability of the insuring company but once, and the litigation is put to an end where the question has once been fairly tried, with the reinsurer made a party by notice: *Strong* v. *Central Ins. Co.*, 4 Mo. App. 7; *Gantt* v. *American Cent. Ins. Co.*, 68 Mo. 503; *Strong* v. *Phœnix Ins. Co.*, 62 Mo. 289; 21 Am. Rep. 417. These causes show that the reinsurer is liable for the cost and expenses of the defense, under such circumstances, although he is not made a party to the record.

Action Against Reinsurer by Policy Holder.—There is no doubt, as held in the principal case, that a policy holder may sue the reinsurer, in case of loss, upon a contract of reinsurance, which includes a promise or agreement on the part of the reinsurer to assume and pay the losses of the policy holders. This principle has been applied where life has been reinsured: *Glen* v. *Hope Mut. Life Ins. Co.*, 56 N. Y. 379. In that case three policies of life insurance, upon the life of one Joseph F. Hall, were issued on November 11, 1870, by the Craftsmen's Life Assurance Company, each for the sum of five thousand dollars, payable in case of death, within four years, to plaintiffs. In the same month the insuring company reinsured its risk in the Continental Life Insurance Company and the Equitable Life Assurance Society of the United States, to the extent of five thousand dollars in each company. In May, 1872, the Craftsmen's Life Assurance Company entered into an agreement with the defendant whereby the latter reinsured it on all risks for which its policies were outstanding at that date, and in which the reinsurer agreed to assure all such policies, and to pay to the holders thereof all such sums as the reinsured might become liable to pay by force of such policies. The liability for death losses was limited to such deaths as might occur on and after May 25, 1872. Hall died on June 23, 1872. Notice was furnished to the original insurer. On or about August, 1872, the Craftsmen's Life Insurance Company collected and received from the Equitable Life Assurance Society the sum of five thousand dollars, for reinsurance, and on or about October 3, 1872, it collected and received from the Continental Life Insurance Company the sum of five thousand dollars. Plaintiffs then demanded payment of their three policies from the defendant company, which was refused. In an action against the reinsurer to recover the amount of the three policies the court directed a verdict for the plaintiffs, and, on appeal, the judgment was affirmed, the court holding that defendant's liability was unaffected by the fact that the Craftsmen's Life Insurance Company had collected its reinsurance of the other two companies. Whether the defendant had any right, said the court, as against the Craftsmen's company to demand and receive the money paid it on its two reinsurances is not a question now before us for decision, for with that question the plaintiffs have no concern. "The payment of those moneys," said the court, "did not inure to the plaintiff's benefit, and they had no lien upon or specific right to them, and the fact of such payment did not affect their right to resort to the defendant, under its contract with the Craftsmen's company for their benefit": See, also, *Cahen* v. *Continental Life Ins. Co.*, 69 N. Y. 300. In the absence of some special agreement, the reinsurer is liable solely to the reinsured: *Strong* v. *Phoenix Ins. Co.*, 62 Mo. 289; 21 Am. Rep. 417. Thus, in *Carrington* v. *Commercial etc. Ins. Co.*, 1 Bosw. 152, the

American Mutual Insurance Company of Amsterdam having insured the plaintiff against loss or damage by fire, and having issued some nineteen other policies insuring the like number of other persons or firms, its agent, while such policies were in force, entered into an agreement with the defendant company by which the latter reinsured the first-named company upon twenty specified policies, including that of the plaintiff, and it was held that plaintiff could not sue the reinsuring company upon the contract of reinsurance. Such a result necessarily follows from the nature of the contract of reinsurance. It is separate and distinct from the one of original insurance: there is no privity between the policy holder and the reinsurer; and the policy holder has nothing to do with the contract of reinsurance unless he is connected therewith by the terms of the contract itself.

ACTIONS BY REINSURED AGAINST REINSURER.—As the reinsurer is bound to pay to the reinsured the whole loss sustained with respect to the subject insured, to the extent of the reinsurance, it is not necessary for the reinsured to pay the loss, where one occurs, to the first assured before proceeding against the reinsurer: *Eagle Ins. Co.* v. *Lafayette Ins. Co.*, 9 Ind. 443; *Gantt* v. *American Cent. Ins. Co.*, 68 Mo. 503, 534; *Blackstone* v. *Alemannia Fire Ins. Co.*, 56 N. Y. 104; 4 Daly, 299; *In re Eddystone Marine Ins. Co.*, [1892], 2 Ch. 423; *Norwood* v. *Resolute Fire Ins. Co.*, 47 How. Pr. 43; *Hone* v. *Mutual Safety Ins. Co.*, 1 Sand. 137. And the liability of the latter is not affected by the insolvency of the reinsured, his inability to fulfill his own contract with the first insured, or by any release of liability which it may have obtained in a compromise: *Eagle Ins. Co.* v. *Lafayette Ins. Co.*, 9 Ind. 443; *Strong* v. *American Cent. Ins. Co.*, 4 Mo. App. 7. If the reinsured is not liable on the original policy a recovery cannot be had against the reinsurer: *Eagle Ins. Co.* v. *Lafayette Ins. Co.*, 9 Ind. 443. The contract of reinsurance is separate and distinct from that of the original insurance, and the reinsured, in order to recover against the reinsurer, must prove the fact and extent of the loss, in the same manner as the original insurer must have proved it against him: *Yonkers etc. Fire Ins. Co.* v. *Hoffman Fire Ins. Co.*, 6 Rob. (N. Y.) 316. The reinsurer is entitled to make the same defense to an action brought against him on the second policy as the original insurer might have done on the first policy: *Eagle Ins. Co.* v. *Lafayette Ins. Co.*, 9 Ind. 443; *Merchants' Mut. Ins. Co.* v. *New Orleans Mut. Ins. Co.*, 24 La. Ann. 305, 307; *New York State Marine Ins. Co.* v. *Protection Ins. Co.*, 1 Story, 458; *Hone* v. *Mutual Safety Ins. Co.*, 1 Sand. 137; *Hastie* v. *De Peyster*, 3 Caines, 190 b. It is not necessary for the reinsured to pay the loss to the first insured before proceeding against the reinsurer. He may at once resort to his action against the reinsurer, and to such action the reinsurer may make the same defense which the reinsured could make against the original insured; or the reinsured may await a suit by the first insured, give notice of it to his reinsurer, and, on being subjected to damages, recover them, together with the costs and expenses of the litigation against the reinsurer: *Gantt* v. *American Cent. Ins. Co.*, 68 Mo. 503, 534; *Eagle Ins. Co.* v. *Lafayette Ins. Co.*, 9 Ind. 443; *New York State Marine Ins. Co.* v. *Protection Ins. Co.*, 1 Story, 458; *Hastie* v. *De Peyster*, 3 Caines, 190 b; *New York Cent. Ins. Co.* v. *National Protection Ins. Co.*, 20 Barb. 468. But costs and other expenses wantonly and unnecessarily incurred, when there is no reasonable ground of defense, and when there is no express or implied sanction of the defense by the reinsurer, cannot be recovered by the reinsured: *New York State Marine Ins. Co.* v. *Protection Ins. Co.*, 1 Story, 458. Reinsurers are liable only for the amount that the insurer is legally liable: *Merchants' Mut.*

Ins. Co. v. *New Orleans Mut. Ins. Co.*, 24 La. Ann. 305, 307; *Delaware Ins. Co.* v. *Quaker City Ins. Co.*, 3 Grant Cas. 71; *Strong* v. *American Cent. Ins. Co.*, 4 Mo. App. 7, 27. In an action on a policy of reinsurance the true measure of damages is not what the reinsured has paid the original assured, but what he is bound, under his policy, to pay by reason of the loss: *Gantt* v. *American Cent. Ins. Co.*, 68 Mo. 503; *Blackstone* v. *Alemannia Fire Ins. Co.*, 56 N. Y. 104; 4 Daly, 299; *Strong* v. *American Cent. Ins. Co.*, 4 Mo. App. 7; *Eagle Ins. Co.* v. *Lafayette Ins. Co.*, 9 Ind. 443; *Hone* v. *Mutual Safety Ins. Co.*, 1 Sand. 137; *Ex parte Norwood*, 3 Biss. 504; *Cashau* v. *Northwestern Nat. Ins. Co.*, 5 Biss. 476. The reinsurer, however, is entitled to all proper credits. Thus, in a case of marine insurance, where there is a technical total loss, and by abandonment the salvage passes to the insurer, and according to its value practically reduces the amount to be paid by the underwriter, the reinsurer in settling with the insurer is clearly entitled to this credit: *Delaware Ins. Co.* v. *Quaker City Ins. Co.*, 3 Grant Cas. 71. If a policy of reinsurance contains a provision for prorating loss or limiting liability the contract must be construed and enforced as other contracts because the same rules of construction which apply to all other instruments apply equally to an instrument called a policy of insurance: *Yonkers etc. Fire Ins. Co.* v. *Hoffman Fire Ins. Co.*, 6 Rob. (N. Y.) 316, 319. For example, if, in a policy of reinsurance, the underwriter agrees to "reinsure" and to "make good unto the reinsured all such loss or damage (not exceeding the sum specified) as shall happen by fire, the loss or damage to be estimated according to the true and actual cash value of the property at the time the same shall happen," the contract imports on its face that the reinsurer is to make a full indemnity within the amount of risk taken by him. And there being no ambiguity in the terms used, evidence of a local custom among insurers to pay only such a proportion of the actual loss as the amount of reinsurance bears to the original policy cannot be received to control the contract or reduce the amount of a recovery thereon: *Mutual Safety Ins. Co.* v. *Hone*, 2 N. Y. 235. On the other hand, if the insurer reinsures for half the amount of his risk, and a loss occurs, and the original insured sues the insuring company and recovers judgment, the reinsurer is responsible for one-half of the amount of the judgment, that being the proportion or *pro rata* between the amount originally insured and the amount reinsured, agreeably to the terms of the policy of reinsurance: *Consolidated etc. Fire Ins. Co.* v. *Cashow*, 41 Md. 59; *Blackstone* v. *Alemannia Fire Ins. Co.*, 56 N. Y. 104; 4 Daly, 299.

A reinsuring company may be sued by the receiver of an insolvent insuring company for the full amount of the latter's liability without reference to its assets: *Ex parte Norwood*, 3 Biss. 504; *Cashau* v. *Northwestern Nat. Ins. Co.*, 5 Biss. 476. And a court of equity will take jurisdiction of a bill by the assignee of a reinsured company against the reinsuring company to enforce a contract of reinsurance. Thus the Enterprise Insurance Company and the Fame Insurance Company entered into a contract whereby the latter agreed to reinsure the former on all its risks in Ohio, Indiana, Illinois, Missouri, Kentucky, and Pennsylvania, except Philadelphia, and exonerate it from all losses in one class of cases exceeding five thousand dollars, and in others, denominated "extrahazardous" exceeding two thousand five hundred dollars, and, in the cases of dwelling-houses or their contents, to contribute for the payment of losses, if any, in various proportions and amounts. The contract contained this express provision: "The losses, if any, are to be payable *pro rata* to the Enterprise Insurance

Company, at such time and in such manner as the latter company may pay." Losses covered by this agreement occurred by the fire in Chicago, on October 8 and 9, 1871. It was held that the reinsured might go into equity as soon as the claim arises upon him, without waiting to pay the original insured; that the words "may pay" in the contract meant "liable to pay"; and that the sending to the Fame Insurance Company of insurances which they ought not to have had, and the withholding of others which they should have had under the contract, did not work a forfeiture thereof: *Fame Ins. Co's Appeal*, 83 Pa. St. 396. There is no statute of limitations applicable to courts of admiralty, in cases of marine insurance. Hence, a reinsuring company, when sued by the insured company, cannot set up the defense of delay on the part of the plaintiff, where it has brought suit within a reasonable time after the loss: *Ocean Ins. Co.* v. *Sun Mut. Ins. Co.*, 13 Blatchf. 249. As a reinsurer merely substitutes himself for the original insurer, he can make no defense that the latter could not. Therefore, a representation which was true when the original policy was made, but was false when the reinsurance was made, is of no avail to the reinsurer: *Cahen* v. *Continental Life Ins. Co.*, 69 N. Y. 300. Neither can a misrepresentation in the description of the property in the original application be taken advantage of by the reinsurer. The risk of the insurer is the object of reinsurance, and if this was correctly stated, and the insurer has been found legally liable for a loss, the reinsurer must pay: *Jackson* v. *St. Paul & M. Ins. Co.*, 99 N. Y. 124.

CONSTRUCTION AND EFFECT OF PARTICULAR CLAUSES.—Contracts of insurance are construed as other contracts: *Yonkers etc. Fire Ins. Co.* v. *Hoffman Fire Ins. Co.*, 6 Rob. (N. Y.) 316, 319. And ambiguous language in an insurance policy should be construed against the insurer: *Teutonia Ins. Co.* v. *Boylston Mut. Ins. Co.*, 20 Fed. Rep. 148. The subject of the insurance, in a policy of fire insurance, being the interest of the original underwriters in the preservation of the property, a clause inserted in the policy providing that, in case there is any other insurance, prior or subsequent, on the property insured, the reinsured shall be entitled to receive, in the event of a loss, only a proportionate part thereof, refers to a double insurance on the same interest—in other words, to a double reinsurance. Therefore, where there is no other reinsurance, the reinsurer is liable, in the event of a loss, to pay the full amount thereof, if it does not exceed the sum mentioned in his contract: *Mutual Safety Ins. Co.* v. *Hone*, 2 N. Y. 235. A stipulation by a reinsuring company that their insurance is "subject to the same risks, valuations, conditions, and mode of settlement as are or may be adopted or assumed" by the insuring company, overrides a condition relating to preliminary proof of loss, and renders the furnishing of such proof to the reinsurers wholly unnecessary. It not only dispenses with such proof, but fastens the responsibility of the reinsurer to the settlement and adjustment made by the original insurers with the original assured as to the amount of loss: *Consolidated etc. Fire Ins. Co.* v. *Cashow*, 41 Md. 59, 77. If a policy in the common form is used in a contract of reinsurance, except that the word "reinsured" is used in the place of "insured," the requirements of the contract that the parties shall give notice, render an account signed with their own hands and verified by their oath, etc., are sufficiently complied with if the party originally insured gives notice, etc., to his immediate insurer, who forthwith transmits such notice, etc., to the underwriters on the policy of reinsurance: *New York etc. Fire Ins. Co.* v. *New York Fire Ins. Co.*, 17 Wend. 359. A clause in a policy of reinsurance providing that no action "for the recovery of any claim, by virtue of this policy, shall be sustainable until after an award shall have been obtained fixing the amount of such claim," nor unless commenced within twelve months after the loss, does not apply to the contract of reinsurance, and does not affect the liability of the reinsurer, or the right of the insured company to recover: *Jackson* v. *St. Paul etc. Ins. Co.*, 99 N. Y. 124.

SIMS *v.* AMERICAN STEEL BARGE COMPANY.

[56 MINNESOTA, 68.]

FELLOW-SERVANTS—SCAFFOLD-BUILDERS AND SHIP-PLATERS—PRESUMPTION AS TO FACT.—Men composing a crew whose exclusive work and duty it is to put up such staging and scaffolding as is needed, from time to time, for the use of workmen engaged in defendant's general work and business, are not fellow-servants with the men engaged in such work and business such as ship-platers; and the presumption is that a staging found in position at the place where a workman is required to perform his work, and upon which he is obliged to stand to perform it, was built by such crew.

APPEAL—CHANGE OF VENUE.—Unless some abuse of discretion is shown on the part of the trial court in denying the defendant's motion for a change of the place of trial for the convenience of witnesses its ruling thereon will not be considered on appeal, as the matter is purely discretionary.

ACTION to recover damages for an injury, as stated in the opinion. Plaintiff claimed that the negligence of the builders of the staging, in using an unfit plank, was defendant's negligence, and rendered it liable to him. The answer was a general denial. Defendant moved for a change of venue to suit the convenience of witnesses, but its motion was denied. It claimed that the plaintiff and the stage-builders were fellow-servants, and also claimed, after the case was submitted, that there was no evidence that any of its servants built the staging. There was a judgment for the plaintiff, and defendant appealed.

Kitchel, Cohen & Shaw, for the appellant.

C. D. & Thomas D. O'Brien, for the respondent.

[71] COLLINS, J. Plaintiff was a ship-plater in defendant's employ, at its yards in West Superior, Wisconsin. He was injured while "laying off" steel plates upon the deck of a steam barge which defendant corporation was constructing in said yards. The deck beams of steel had been put in, but the spaces between them were open. In order to do his

work, the plaintiff had to go upon a staging made of two or more planks, sixteen or eighteen feet long, laid upon wooden horses about two and a half feet high. These horses rested on planks laid down upon the deck beams. A plank used for staging broke, and plaintiff was precipitated to the hold of the vessel, some eighteen feet, receiving the injuries complained of, and which he attributes to defendant's negligence. Certain it is that the plank in question was defective and unfit for use in such a place. A verdict was rendered against defendant, and it appeals from a judgment entered after the denial of its motion for a new trial.

1. There is nothing in the assignment that the court erred in overruling defendant's motion for a change of place of trial for the convenience of witnesses. There was, so far as appears from the record, no abuse of that discretion which is necessarily vested in a trial court upon the consideration of such a motion.

2. By means of various specifications of error the claim is made that there was no evidence offered or received which tended to show that the defective plank, or the staging in which it was found, were placed in position by the men employed by defendant as builders of necessary staging, or by any other authorized person. The plaintiff did not prove by whom the staging in question was built. He did prove that the materials were furnished by defendant and that the construction of all staging used about the barge was delegated by defendant to one Guinane and a crew of from two to four men, his assistants. Guinane and his crew were not employed in the general work carried on by defendant, their exclusive business being to build such staging and scaffolding as might be needed, from time to time, by other workmen engaged in defendant's general work and [72] business. On the day of the accident plaintiff had gone from near where he was afterward injured, the staging not being then in position, to the other side of the vessel, and had there been at work for something more than an hour. He then went, with his helper, into the yard for a mold, which was to be used at the point where they found the staging built on their return. The helper testified that it was put up while plaintiff and himself were in the yard after the mold. So the facts were that at the time plaintiff was required to perform work at that particular place, and, necessarily, to stand upon and use a staging while performing it, he found the one in question in

position, and used it. It is certainly fair to presume that this staging was built by one or more of the men employed and delegated by the defendant to do that special work when needed, and whose exclusive duty it was to do it, and, unless this is a fair presumption, we must infer that these men wholly failed to do their duty, and also infer that a staging upon the barge may have been erected by an intermeddler. If this was the fact it was incumbent upon the defendant, at least, to offer to show it. The presumption we have referred to was not affected by proof that Guinane himself did not build the staging, nor could he tell who did.

The cases cited by defendant's counsel, *Flynn* v. *Beebe*, 98 Mass. 575, and *Joy* v. *Winnisimmet Co.*, 114 Mass. 63, are not at all analogous to the one at bar.

3. It is urged that within the rules laid down in *Lindvall* v. *Woods*, 41 Minn. 212, and *Fraser* v. *Red River Lumber Co.*, 45 Minn. 235, the plaintiff cannot recover, because the men engaged in building the staging were his fellow-servants. In each of those cases, as well as in *Marsh* v. *Herman*, 47 Minn. 537, the very familiar rule that the master is bound to use due care in furnishing safe structures or instrumentalities with which the servant is to do his work, and is responsible if, through his own negligence, or the negligence of other servants employed to furnish them, they are unsafe, and injury results, was referred to. In *Lindvall* v. *Woods*, 41 Minn. 212, the defendants were declared not liable, because the men were all serving thr same master, under the same control, and all engaged in the same general work—that of grading a railroad. The trestle which fell and caused the injury was not a [73] structure furnished by the defendants for their employees to work upon, but was itself a part of the work the employees were employed to perform. It was built by themselves. In *Fraser* v. *Red River Lumber Co.*, 45 Minn. 235, it was distinctly held that all of the men engaged about defendant's lumber-yard, whether pilers, scalers, sorters, or measurers, were engaged in promoting the same common object, and as to each other, and as to every part of the common enterprise, were fellow-servants. Attention was called in that opinion to an important consideration often overlooked, it was said; and that is, whether the structure, appliance, or instrumentality is one which has been furnished for the work in which the servants are to be engaged, or whether the furnishing and preparation of it is part of the work which they

are employed to perform.   This same distinction was alluded
to in *Marsh* v. *Herman*, 47 Minn. 537, and it was held that
where the general work in which several servants are engaged
includes the construction or preparation of the appliances
with which they are to work, such as constructing a scaffold
on which they are to stand while at work, they must be
deemed fellow-servants in respect to the negligence of one of
them while building such scaffold.   The difference between
the case at bar and those we have referred to, on the facts, is
marked.   The latter are really authorities in plaintiff's favor,
and support his contention that the builders of the scaffold
were not his fellow-servants.   The defendant had undertaken
to furnish a scaffold upon which the plaintiff was to do his
work, and had delegated the construction of such scaffold to
certain men who were employed for no other purpose.   The
defendant master owed to plaintiff, its servant, the duty of
furnishing to him a safe structure, and failed so to do.   The
omission and neglect of Guinane and his crew, to whom this
duty had been specially confided, was that of the master, and
for which it was liable to plaintiff in this action.

Judgment affirmed.   ____

FELLOW-SERVANTS: See monographic note to *Fisk* v. *Central Pac. R. R.
Co.*, 1 Am. St. Rep. 31–33, giving profuse illustrations as to who are and
who are not fellow-servants.   Whether parties are fellow-servants is not to
be determined by the rank or grade of the offending or injured servant,
but is to be determined by the character of the act being performed by the
offending servant: *Jenkins* v. *Richmond etc. R. R. Co.*, 39 S. C. 507; 39 Am.
St. Rep. 750.

APPEAL—DISCRETIONARY ACTION.—In matters where the lower court has
a sound legal discretion the supreme court will not control it, except for a
refusal to exercise it, or abuse thereof if exercised: *English* v. *Smock*, 34 Ind.
115; 7 Am. Rep. 215; *Moody* v. *Fleming*, 4 Ga. 115; 48 Am. Dec. 210; *Winslow* v. *Minnesota etc. R. R. Co.*, 4 Minn. 313; 77 Am. Dec. 519.

_____

In re State Bank.

[56 MINNESOTA, 119.]

BANKS AND BANKING—TITLE TO DRAFTS LEFT AT BANK FOR "COLLEC-
TION AND CREDIT."—A deposit being made by a customer in a bank,
in the ordinary course of business, of money drafts or other negotiable
paper, received and credited as money, the title vests in the bank,
which immediately becomes the owner of the property and a debtor of
the depositor for the amount.   In the absence of any special agreement
this course of dealing would be held to show conclusively that such was
the intention.

BANKS AND BANKING—TITLE TO DRAFTS LEFT AT BANK FOR "COLLECTION
AND CREDIT"—AGREEMENT.—The question as to whether money drafts
or other negotiable paper, deposited by a customer in a bank, is the
property of the bank, is really one of agreement between the parties, as
neither an unrestricted indorsement of the paper by the customer, nor
crediting him with the amount of his account, with the privilege of
drawing against it, is conclusive on the question of ownership. If it is,
in fact, delivered to the bank for collection, or for "collection and
credit," a credit to the customer before collection will be deemed merely
provisional, which the bank may cancel if the paper is not paid.

BANKS AND BANKING—BANK HOLDS DEPOSITOR'S PAPER FOR COLLECTION
AS AGENT, WHEN.—If drafts are left at a bank for collection and credit
under circumstances indicating no understanding that the title shall
pass, a finding is justified that the bank holds the paper for collection,
as agent of the depositor.

APPEAL by George H. Fletcher, assignee of the State Bank
of Minneapolis, from an order directing him to deliver to
Osborne & Clark two drafts in his possession as such assignee. Osborne & Clark were lumber dealers in Minneapolis, and had an account with the bank. In the course
of the business, the bank, on receiving from them their
draft on their customer in another place, due at a future
day, would discount it at the rate of eight per cent a year,
and give them credit for the amount. The bank would then
forward the draft, for acceptance and collection, to some bank
at the place where the customer lived. If the draft was paid
at maturity the money belonged to the state bank. If it was
not paid, the bank charged Osborne & Clark in their account
with the amount, and the draft was returned to them. Two
drafts were drawn, as stated in the opinion, and, according
to the usual practice, one or both of them should have been
charged to the account of Osborne & Clark, and returned
to them. Fletcher was the assignee in trust for creditors.
Osborne & Clark filed a petition alleging that the two drafts
belonged to them, and praying an order that the assignee
deliver them over. The court made findings, and ordered
that the two drafts be delivered to the claimants. Proceedings were stayed, a case made, settled, signed, and filed, and
the assignee appealed. The discussion on appeal was upon
the evidence, whether or not it supported the finding of the
trial court that the parties understood, when the drafts were
drawn, that the title to them was not to pass to the bank.

Hahn & Hawley, for the assignee.

J. L. Dobbin, for the claimants.

[122] MITCHELL, J. The petitioners, having drawn in their own favor two drafts on third parties, payable in sixty days, indorsed them by unrestricted indorsements, and delivered them to the state bank, of which they were customers, and with which they had an open and current bank account. The bank credited the amount of the drafts (less the interest at eight per cent per annum until maturity) to the credit of petitioner's account, against which they were entitled to draw by check; but, as a matter of fact, they never did draw against it, they having a balance to their credit, when the bank failed, much larger than the amount of the drafts.

Before the drafts were paid, and while they were still in its possession, [123] the bank failed, and made an assignment of its property for the benefit of its creditors. The petitioners thereupon stopped payment of the drafts, and now ask that the assignee of the bank be ordered to return them, claiming that they are still their property, and that the bank held them as their agent for collection.

It might, at first sight, strike many that the facts that the indorsements of the petitioners were unrestricted, and that the amount of the drafts was placed to their credit, with a privilege of drawing against it by check would be conclusive that the drafts immediately became the property of the bank; but we are satisfied that upon both principle and authority there is no hard and fast rule on the subject. There is no question but that the general rule is that upon a deposit being made by a customer in a bank, in the ordinary course of business, of money, drafts, or other negotiable paper, received and credited as money, the title vests in the bank, and the money drafts or other paper immediately becomes the property of the bank; and the bank becomes debtor of the depositor for the amount.

And if no other facts appeared except these they would be held to conclusively show an intention of the parties that the paper should immediately become the property of the bank. But, after all, the question is one of the agreement of the parties, either express or implied, from the general course of business between them. There can be no doubt that, if a draft or other paper is delivered to a bank for collection, the mere fact that the indorsement of the owner is unrestricted will not, as between him and the bank, make the latter the owner of the property.

Neither is it conclusive upon the question of ownership of

the paper that before collection the amount of it is credited to the customer's account, against which he has the privilege of drawing by check. It has been frequently held, with the approval of the best text-writers, that if paper is delivered by a customer to a bank for collection or "for collection and credit," a credit of the amount to the customer before and in anticipation of collection will be deemed merely provisional, and the privilege of drawing against it merely gratuitous, and that the bank may cancel the credit or charge back the paper to the customer's account if it is not paid by the maker or drawee: *Giles* v. *Perkins*, 9 East, 12; *Levi* v. *National* [124] *Bank*, 5 Dill. 104; *Balbach* v. *Frelinghuysen*, 15 Fed. Rep. 675.

The right of banks to do this in case of the deposit of checks on other banks, without any special contract, is generally exercised and recognized. This is inconsistent with the idea that the title to the checks passes absolutely to the bank, and is only consistent with the theory that the bank is the agent of the customer for collection, notwithstanding the credit of the latter: 2 Morse on Banks and Banking, sec. 586; *Hoffman* v. *First Nat. Bank*, 46 N. J. L. 604.

Of course, in all such cases, the banker, like a factor, has a lien for advances made on the faith of the paper, and consequently the claim of the customer may be modified by the state of his account. No such question, however, arises in this case; the balance of the petitioner's account, independent of these drafts, being in their favor at the time of the failure of the bank.

The authorities on this subject are quite fully collated in Morse on Banks and Banking, section 573, et seq: See, also, Paley on Principal and Agent, 91, note; and Story on Agency, sec. 228, note 2.

In examinatian of the cases there should be kept in mind the distinction between those where the paper was still in the hands of the bank or its assignee in bankruptcy and those where the bank, clothed by the customer with the indicia of ownership, had transferred the paper or its proceeds to a *bona fide* purchaser. The distinction is clear on principle, and is generally recognized by the authorities.

It remains to apply these principles to the facts of this case. The petitioners commenced doing business with this bank over seven years ago. When they opened an account with the bank they received a pass-book upon which their debits

and credits were entered. On the front leaf of this book is
the following statement: "This bank, in receiving checks or
drafts on deposit or for collection, acts only as your agent,
and, beyond carefulness in selecting agents at other points
and in forwarding to them, assumes no responsibility."

The language of this statement will not admit of the construction claimed for it by the assignee—that it refers only
to the paper left with the bank for collection without credit
to the account of the customer. What was intended by it is
best shown by the testimony of the cashier (afterward president) of the bank. He says: [125] "The intention of it undoubtedly is this: that, if we should have to send the draft for
collection at Chicago or Oshkosh, or wherever the case may
be, and, if the bank up there should send us paper that subsequently turned out to be no good, it would not fall on the
state bank, but on the party who has discounted or sold
it. Question. And you regard yourselves as the agents of
Osborne & Clark? Answer. In case the collecting bank
should fail to collect it. They [the collecting correspondent]
might send a draft on Chicago or New York, and the draft
might be no good when we got it there. That is the reason
that these lines are printed in there."

The purport of all this is, that beyond the exercise of care
in the selection of correspondents and forwarding the paper
to them, the entire risk of collection was on the customer;
and only when the proceeds were actually received by the
bank did it unconditionally assume the relation of debtor
for the amount. It is needless to suggest that the bank could
not be agent for collection and owner of the paper at the
same time. The evidence also is that there was no subsequent conversation between the petitioners and the bank
officers "changing this statement." During the years that
followed, the petitioners were accustomed to deposit paper,
and take credit for it on account, the same as in the case of
these drafts; and, whenever any of the paper came back uncollected, the bank charged it up to their account, or they
gave their check for it, and took back the paper. It does not
appear that such paper was ever protested for nonpayment,
or that the petitioners ever waived protest on it, or that its
return to them in the manner indicated had any reference
to any liability on their part as indorsers. On the contrary,
it appears that this was done in accordance with a general
understanding between the parties that, whenever any of the

paper was not paid, the bank was either to charge it up to the petitioners' account or that they would give their check for it, and take it up.   It does appear that, when the petitioners were doubtful about paper being paid, they would give it to the bank for collection without taking any credit for it.   It likewise appears that, where credit was given for the paper, the bank would enter it among their discounts; while, if no credit was given, they would enter it among their collections.   But as this was a mere matter of book-keeping, of which the petitioners had no knowledge, it is a matter of little or no weight.   There [126] is other evidence having more or less bearing upon the question, but what we have stated is of itself sufficient to justify the findings of the court that the bank held these drafts merely as agents for collection, that it did not assume the absolute relation of debtor for the amount until collected and received, and that the credit before collection was merely conditional or provisional.

Order affirmed.

BANKS AND BANKING—TITLE TO PAPER LEFT FOR COLLECTION.—The title to commercial paper left with a bank for collection passes only by a contract to that effect either proved or inferred from an unequivocal course of dealing: *National Park Bank* v. *Seaboard Bank*, 114 N. Y. 28; 11 Am. St. Rep. 612; monographic note to *First Nat. Bank* v. *Strauss*, 14 Am. St. Rep. 585.   So indorsement for collection of a draft or check is not a transfer of the title to the indorsee, but merely constitutes him the agent of the indorser to present the paper, demand and receive payment, and remit the proceeds.   Nor does a different result follow from the fact that the indorser is credited, and the indorsee charged, with the amount of such draft or check, where it appears that the indorsee does not become unconditionally responsible for such amount until the draft or check is actually paid: *National Butchers' etc. Bank* v. *Hubbell*, 117 N. Y. 384; 15 Am. St. Rep. 515.   As an indorsement to a bank for collection does not, as a general rule, vest title to the property in the bank, the owner may recover it, if the paper passes into the hands of an assignee in insolvency of the bank: *Akin* v. *Jones*, 93 Tenn. 353; 42 Am. St. Rep. 921; *National Butchers' etc. Bank* v. *Hubbell*, 117 N. Y. 384; 15 Am. St. Rep. 515.

EVARTS *v.* ST. PAUL, MINNEAPOLIS & MANITOBA RAILWAY COMPANY.

[56 Minnesota, 141.]

MASTER AND SERVANT—LIABILITY OF MASTER TO A VOLUNTEER FOR THE NEGLIGENCE OF A SERVANT.—A master owes no contract obligation to one voluntarily assisting his servants. Such volunteer assumes all the risks incident to the situation, and cannot recover from the master for an injury caused by a defect in the instrumentalities used, or by the mere negligence of the servants.

MASTER AND SERVANT—LIABILITY OF MASTER FOR INJURY TO VOLUNTEER THROUGH SERVANT'S NEGLIGENCE. — If one volunteers to assist the servants of another, and places himself in a position of danger, though by his own negligence, the master will be liable for a resulting injury where his servants fail to exercise reasonable care to avert the danger, not upon the ground of any contract obligation, but upon the general duty not to inflict a wanton or willful injury on another.

ACTION by Jennie M. Evarts, as administratrix of the estate of her deceased husband, James Evarts, to recover of defendants five thousand dollars for wrongfully causing his death. The jury found a general verdict for the plaintiff, and assessed her damages at five thousand dollars. They also found specially that the conductor, mentioned in the opinion, knew, or in the exercise of ordinary care had reason to believe, when he gave the signal to reverse the engine, that Evarts would be imperiled thereby. The defendant appealed from an order denying its motion for a new trial.

Benton, Roberts & Brown and *W. E. Dodge,* for the appellant.

Larrabee & Gammons, for the respondent.

¹⁴⁴ MITCHELL, J. This was an action to recover damages for the death of plaintiff's intestate, caused by the alleged negligence of the defendant. At the time of his death the deceased was in the employment of the defendant as assistant timekeeper, his duties being to keep an account of the time of men at work upon, and to make measurements of materials used in, construction work. It was no part of his duty to assist in the operation of trains, nor had any conductor of a train authority to direct or employ him to assist in any such work. Neither had he any experience, as brakeman or otherwise, in the operation of trains.

On the day of the accident he was sent by his superior officer from the office to a yard about a mile distant, with an order to the conductor of a construction train to bring certain carloads of stone to a place where construction work was going on.

Having delivered this message he boarded the construction train for the purpose of riding back to the office. The train consisted of thirty-five cars—six flatcars loaded with stone and twenty-nine empty dump-cars. The train was moving easterly, and was made up as follows: At the west end was the engine, with the pilot facing east; then came the dump-cars, and then the six cars loaded with stone, the engine facing the cars and pushing them, the stone being on the front end of the train as it moved east. The deceased was riding on the rear car of stone next to the dump-cars.

When the train approached the destination of the stone the conductor in charge desired to put the six cars of stone upon one track, [145] and the twenty-nine dump-cars upon another parallel track, without bringing any portion of the train to a full stop.

This was to be done after the cars had attained a sufficient rate of speed, by uncoupling the stone-cars, and then reversing the engine, which would check the speed of the dump-cars, while the stone-cars would continue at the previous rate of speed, and pass the switch, onto the desired track, before the dump-cars reached it. To accomplish this the conductor signaled the engineer to "kick" the train, in obedience to which the latter pushed the train rapidly ahead at the rate of from seven to ten miles an hour.

Immediately upon giving this order to the engineer the conductor, as the jury found, ordered Evarts to pull the pin between the stone-cars and the dump-cars, and, in obedience to this order, Evarts stepped down between the stone-car and the dump-car next to it, and stooped down and pulled the pin. While the evidence is not entirely conclusive on the point, yet it would seem that Evarts, while pulling the pin in this stooping position, stood with one foot on each car. Meanwhile the conducter had signaled the engineer to reverse his engine. The engineer promptly obeyed. This, of course, suddenly checked the speed of the dump-cars with a jerk, as the slack between them was taken up. This jerk occurred while Evarts, still partially in a stooping position, was in the act of straightening himself up, holding the pin in one hand. The consequence was that he was thrown upon the ground, and run over by the cars and killed. The evidence is not very clear whether at this time Evarts still had one foot on each car, or, while in the act of straightening himself up, he had placed both feet on the end of the dump-car. The defendant claims that the evidence shows that the latter was the fact. As we view the case the question is not one of importance; but we think the jury would have been at least justified by the evidence in finding that, so suddenly did the whole thing occur, Evarts was still substantially in the same position when thrown from the cars as when the conductor signaled the engineer to reverse his engine.

The evidence was also ample to justify the jury in finding that the conductor knew Evarts' position when he gave the signal to reverse. In any event there is no assignment of error that raises the question of its sufficiency.

[146] The negligence charged against defendant is the act of the conductor in signaling the engineer to reverse the engine when, as is claimed, he either knew, or ought to have known, that the result would be to endanger the life of Evarts.

The theory of the law, and doubtless the correct one, upon which the case was submitted to the jury, was that, as to the acts he was then performing, Evarts was a mere volunteer, and that the defendant owed him no contractual duty as master.

The learned trial judge, over and over again, in the most explicit manner, instructed the jury that plaintiff could not recover unless the conductor, at the time he gave the signal to reverse the engine, knew, or in the exercise of ordinary care ought to have known, that the giving of the signal "would result in jerking Evarts from the train"; "would necessarily produce injury to Evarts"; "would result in injury to Evarts."

This was but another way of saying that plaintiff could not recover unless, with knowledge that Evarts was in a dangerous position, the conductor, who controlled the movements of the cars, failed to exercise reasonable care to avert the danger. This is the law, even as to trespassers: *Hepfel* v. *St. Paul etc. Ry. Co.*, 49 Minn. 263. This duty rests on no contract obligation, but upon the bare obligation, founded upon the dictates of common humanity, to avoid inflicting a willful or wanton injury on another. Had Evarts been a mere trespasser, and the conductor had seen him in such a position of danger, it would have been the duty of the conductor to exercise reasonable care to avert it, and, if he failed to do so, the defendant would have been liable. We fail to see why a volunteer should have any less rights than a mere trespasser. Because a man is a trespasser or a volunteer he is not therefore an outlaw, so as to permit others to willfully or recklessly do him an injury.

It is no doubt the law, as repeatedly held, that, if a person volunteers to assist the servant of another, the master, as such, owes him no duty; that he assumes all the ordinary risks incident to the situation; and that he cannot recover from the master for an injury caused by a defect in the instrumentalities used, or by the mere negligence of the servants: *Church* v. *Chicago etc. Ry. Co.*, 50 Minn. 218.

[147] But it seems to us that this is not inconsistent with the further proposition that if, after discovering such volunteer has placed himself in a position of danger, even through his own negligence, the servants fail to exercise reasonable care to avert the danger, the master will be liable. Such must be the law, unless, as already suggested, a volunteer occupies a less favorable position than a trespasser. There is nothing in *Church* v. *Chicago etc. Ry. Co.*, 50 Minn. 218, inconsistent with this; and, while we have found no case precisely in point, there is nothing inconsistent with it in any of the cases cited by counsel. It is sometimes given as a reason why a master is not liable to a volunteer for the negligence of a servant, that a servant cannot, by his officious conduct, impose a greater duty on the master than that which the latter owes his servant, and that a master is not liable to a servant for the negligence of a fellow-servant. If there is any thing in this "fellow-servant" doctrine that has any bearing on the question, it is at least inapplicable in this state as to railway companies.

It strikes us that the very ingenious argument of counsel for the defendant is all based on one radical fallacy, to wit, that in all respects, and for all purposes, Evarts is to be considered as a skilled and experienced brakeman, and therefore, if he did or failed to do any thing which an experienced brakeman, in the exercise of reasonable care, would have done or omitted to do, he was guilty of negligence which would prevent a recovery; also, that if the conductor of the train did nothing that would have been negligent had Evarts been an experienced brakeman, then he was not guilty of any negligence in this instance.

To the first part of this proposition it is sufficient answer that the question of Evarts' negligence up to the time
the conductor gave the signal to reverse the engine was
wholly immaterial, under the theory upon which the case
was submitted to the jury, to wit, that a recovery could only
be had in case the conductor, when he gave the signal, knew,
or in the exercise of ordinary care had reason to believe, that
Evarts would be imperiled thereby. The court correctly
instructed the jury that "although it may be deemed an act
of negligence on the part of Evarts to have gone there and
performed this duty as a volunteer, because dangerous to
any man unaccustomed to perform it, ... yet if, after he
assumed to do that act, even though he was negligent, and
the conductor, as a matter of fact, saw him in that [148] perilous position, and gave the order, knowing that the effect of
the order would be to throw him from the car, then his negligence would not prevent a recovery." To the matter of
negligence on the part of Evarts after the conductor signaled
the engineer we will refer hereafter.

The second branch of the proposition, viz., that the conductor was not negligent, if he did nothing but what would
have been proper had Evarts been an experienced brakeman,
is clearly incorrect. If he knew, as he did, that Evarts was
inexperienced, and for that reason in greater peril, it was the
conductor's duty to regulate his conduct with reference to
that fact. A position might be perilous to a young boy that
would not be so to a mature man; and, for the same reason,
the conductor should reasonably have anticipated danger to
an inexperienced man like Evarts, when he might not have
done so in the case of an experienced brakeman.

The court, after charging the jury, as already stated, that,
even if Evarts was negligent on account of his inexperience
in attempting to perform so dangerous an act, this would not
prevent a recovery if, as a matter of fact, the conductor saw
him in a perilous position, and gave the order knowing that
the effect of it would be to throw him from the car, added:
"This, then, is the exception to the rule that the plaintiff
cannot recover where he is guilty of contributory negligence;
and I think I may say to you there is no evidence of contributory negligence in this case which you need consider."
This forms the subject of the fourth assignment of error. It
is undoubtedly true that the action of the conductor is to be
judged by the facts existing and known to him when he sig-

naled the engineer, for he was not required to anticipate any subsequent and independent act of negligence on the part of Evarts.

But it seems to us quite clear, from a perusal of the record, that the only negligence on the part of Evarts claimed on the trial was that of an inexperienced man attempting to perform an act essentially dangerous. This was evidently the understanding of the trial court, and, if defendant claimed any other and subsequent act of contributory negligence, the attention of the court ought to have been called to it specifically.

. But in any view of the case we fail to see any evidence of negligence on the part of Evarts other than that of attempting to do a perilous [149] act as to which he was inexperienced—a fact known to the conductor when he gave the signal.

The only other negligence which defendant claims is, that he had placed his feet on the end of the dump-car, when he ought, after drawing the pin, to have gotten back upon the stone-car, where he would have been safer when the jerk came from letting out the slack. If this were so, it is only what might have been reasonably anticipated from an inexperienced man. But, remembering that the burden of proof on this point was on the defendant, and that there is no evidence that Evarts knew, or had reason to suppose, that the signal to reverse the engine would be given so soon, and the further fact that the whole thing was done so quickly that he had not yet had time to regain an erect posture after stooping over to take out the pin, we do not think that the jury would have been justified in finding the specific act of negligence now claimed, even if the question had been submitted to them.

When the jury returned into court for further instructions the judge charged them that unless they could answer the third question intelligently they ought not to, and could not, give a general verdict, because the whole case depended on that question. The question referred to was: "Did the conductor know, or in the exercise of ordinary care have reason to believe, that Evarts would be imperiled by the signal to reverse the engine?" It is contended that this was erroneous, for the reason that it was an instruction that they could not render a verdict for the defendant unless they could answer this question. Of course, the instruction is subject to

this verbal criticism; but what the court evidently meant was
that no verdict for the plaintiff could be rendered unless the
jury could answer the question in the affirmative, and it is
impossible that they could have understood the instruction
otherwise.

Order affirmed.

MASTER AND SERVANT—VOLUNTEERS.—One who assists the servants of
a master, merely as a volunteer, cannot recover from such master for an
injury received by him through the negligence of such servant: See note to
Fox v. *Sandford*, 67 Am. Dec. 597; *Flower* v. *Pennsylvania R. R. Co.*, 69 Pa.
St. 210; 8 Am. Rep. 251; *New Orleans etc. R. R. Co.* v. *Harrison*, 48 Miss.
112; 12 Am. Rep. 356. *Contra: Street Railway Co.* v. *Bolton*, 43 Ohio St. 224;
54 Am. Rep. 803, and note. If, when injured, he was acting in furtherance
of his own or of his master's business he may recover: *Bonner* v. *Bryant*, 79
Tex. 540; 23 Am. St. Rep. 361, and note. One who is a volunteer, or in a
master's employment at the request of the latter's servant or foreman, is not
a trespasser, and he is, for the time being, the servant of the master, and
entitled to the same protection as his other servants: *Johnson* v. *Ashland
Water Co.*, 71 Wis. 553; 5 Am. St. Rep. 243.

MARKS *v.* MARKS.

[56 MINNESOTA, 264.]

DIVORCE—CRUEL AND INHUMAN TREATMENT.—Ill-treatment by the husband, long continued, and consisting of continual scolding and fault-
finding, the use of unkind language, and of many other little acts, if
studied and malicious, and the wife is sensitive, may be cruel and inhuman treatment if it has a serious effect on her health, or causes her
great mental suffering; but, to be a ground for divorce, the effect on her
must be of a serious character. It is error to refuse to admit evidence
of such acts in an action for divorce, although no act of violence is
proved, or any act which would, of itself, prove cruel and inhuman
treatment.

F. B. Hart, for the appellant.

Shaw & Cray, for the respondent.

265 CANTY, J. This is an action for divorce on the ground
of cruel and inhuman treatment. The complaint alleges at
great length, that, during the eleven years of married life
in which the parties lived together, the defendant did constantly worry, annoy, and subject her to personal indignity,
and did daily, by a systematic course of ill-treatment, abuse
her, use unkind language toward her, and find fault with
her; that he was in the habit of berating her for hours at a

time, and often after they retired, until the small hours of
the morning, thereby depriving her of sleep, rest, peace, and
quiet.   It also states many other acts of a similar character,
but states only one act of violence on his part, and alleges
that by reason of such ill-treatment her health was greatly
injured, and her nervous system shattered.

On the trial the plaintiff called the defendant for cross-
examination, under the statute which provides that either
party may so call the other.   On such cross-examination
the witness was asked such questions as: "After you were
married you immediately had trouble?"   "When did you
have your first quarrel with your wife?"   "Did you at any
time have trouble with your wife?"   "How was it as to fre-
quency?"   "Did you ever see your wife in tears during that
winter, from October to March?"—and other questions of
the same character.   To each of these questions the defendant's counsel objected, on the ground that the same was
incompetent and immaterial, and the objections were all
sustained by the court.   The court stated that, before the
plaintiff would be allowed to go into these matters, she must
first prove some act of violence, or some one act that would of
itself prove cruel and inhuman treatment.   Plaintiff's counsel stated that he could not do this, but could prove all the
other allegations of the complaint; and this the court refused to permit him to do, either on such cross-examination
or by other witnesses subsequently called.   Thereupon the
plaintiff rested, and the court dismissed the action.   We are
of the opinion that the court erred in ruling out this evidence.   While the court should act with great caution in
granting a divorce on evidence of this character, where no
266 acts of violence are proven, still such evidence may be
sufficient.   Such a course of ill-treatment, long continued,
where the acts of the husband are studied and malicious,
and the wife is sensitive, may be cruel and inhuman treatment if it has a serious effect on her health, or causes her
great mental suffering; but the effect on her must be of a
serious character.

The evidence was competent, and should have been admitted.   Whether there was sufficient of it when it was all
received to entitle plaintiff to a divorce is another question.

For these errors the order denying the motion for a new
trial should be reversed.   It is so ordered.

MARRIAGE AND DIVORCE—CRUELTY.—What acts of a spouse constitute extreme cruelty within the meaning of a statute making this a ground for a divorce cannot be defined with precision, but each case is to be determined according to its own peculiar circumstances by the court or jury, keeping always in view the intelligence, apparent refinement, and delicacy of sentiment of the complaining party: *Fleming* v. *Fleming,* 95 Cal. 430; 29 Am. St. Rep. 124, and note, showing that, in the absence of bodily violence by a husband, in order to entitle a wife to a divorce, she must show such cruel treatment as produces a degree of mental anguish which threatens to impair her health. The general rule is, that acts, to constitute cruel treatment, must injure or endanger life, limb, or health, or create a reasonable apprehension of such injury: See monographic notes to *Poor* v. *Poor,* 29 Am. Dec. 674–679; *Morris* v. *Morris,* 73 Am. Dec. 627.

GALLOWAY *v.* CHICAGO, MILWAUKEE & ST. PAUL RAILWAY COMPANY.

[56 MINNESOTA, 346.]

RAILROAD COMPANIES—LIABILITY OF, FOR INJURY CAUSED BY MAIL AGENT'S THROWING LOADED MAIL-BAG FROM TRAIN.—While a railway company has no right to interfere with a mail agent in the discharge of his official duties, its duty is to prevent him, while on its trains and premises from continuing any negligent practice, of which it has notice, and which is liable to cause injury to passengers and others lawfully there. Throwing loaded mail-bags out of a moving train upon a platform occupied by the public is of itself a negligent and dangerous practice, and, where injury results from it, the company may be charged with negligence, without showing that a like injury occurred on some former occasion.

EXCESSIVE VERDICT—MAIL-BAG THROWN FROM TRAIN.—A verdict for ten thousand dollars damages for being struck and injured by a mail-bag thrown from the mail-car of a moving railroad train by a United States mail agent while slowing up at the platform of a passenger station is not excessive where the evidence shows that the company had notice of the practice of throwing out loaded mail-bags, and that the result was one which might reasonably have been anticipated.

APPEAL by the defendant railroad company from an order denying its motion for a new trial.

Flandrau, Squires & Cutcheon, W. H. Norris, and F. W. Root, for the appellant.

Davis, Kellogg & Severance, for the respondent.

[346] MITCHELL, J. This was an action for personal injuries occasioned to the plaintiff by being struck by a mail-bag thrown by a United States mail agent from a mail-car belonging to the defendant [347] on one of its passenger trains

at the station on its road at Durand, Wisconsin. At this station the railway track runs north and south, and the depot and platform adjoin it on the west. The platform is of the width of twelve feet on all sides of the depot, and of the width of eight feet extends along the track in two wings— one to the south about seventy-five feet, and one to the north about one hundred feet to the south line of a street which crosses the railway at right angles. The principal part of the village lies north and west of the station. The passenger train run on this road consisted of an engine and tender, mail and express car, baggage-car, and two passenger-coaches, in the order named; the mail end of the combination car being next the tender, the entire length of the train being about equal to the entire length of the platform. Trains from the south usually stopped so that the nose of the engine would be ten or fifteen feet beyond the north end of the platform, out on the street crossing.

On the day in question the plaintiff came from the village to the station, accompanying a young girl, for the purpose of seeing her safely upon the north-bound passenger train. Approaching the station from the north, she stepped up on the north end of the platform just as the train was pulling in from the south, and walked hurriedly along toward the south end of the platform, where the passenger-coaches would be when the train stopped; and, as she claims, when she had reached a point on the platform some twenty or twenty-five feet from the depot, she was struck by a small sack thrown from the mail-car while the train was still in motion.

Inasmuch as the mail agent was not the servant of the defendant, it is not claimed that the railway company would be liable for his negligence, however gross, on this occasion only.

To render it liable, as negligent, for the negligence of the mail agent, this government employee must have practiced a dangerous method of discharging mail-sacks on the platform at this station so habitually or so frequently as to charge the company, as part of its duty to its passengers and others occupying its depot platform by its invitation or license, with notice, actual or implied, of his negligence or recklessness. While the railway company had no power to interfere with the mail agent in the discharge of his official duties, yet it was its right, as well as duty, to prevent him, while on its cars and on its premises, from continuing any negligent practice, [348] of which it had notice, which was liable to cause injury to passengers and others lawfully there. The case comes fully within the rule which enjoins care, not only on the part of the company's servant, but also like care in preventing injury from the wrongful act of others whom it permits to come upon its premises.

The negligence charged against the defendant is that it had notice of a long-continued custom of the mail agents of throwing heavy mail-bags from the cars, while still moving at a high rate of speed, onto the platform occupied by persons lawfully there, in such a reckless and negligent manner as to endanger their safety, and that, notwithstanding such notice, it took no steps to prevent this negligent practice, or to warn people of the danger.

The answer admitted that the platform is a public place for the purposes of railway travel to and from the station, and for the transaction of railway business with the defendant, but denied all the allegations of negligence in the complaint. On the trial the defense was that mail-bags were never thrown from the car upon the platform while the train was in motion, and the plaintiff, instead of being struck by the mail-bag, walked against it, and stumbled over it, while lying on the platform; and, so far as plaintiff's right to recover was concerned, the case was tried squarely and exclusively upon this issue.

We are satisfied that the evidence justified the jury in finding that plaintiff was struck by a mail-bag thrown from the cars while still in motion, and that the practice of throwing mail-bags upon the platform before the train had come to a stop had been so frequent and long continued as to charge the defendant with notice of it. It is not claimed that the company had ever made any attempt to stop this practice, and it is expressly admitted that no notice or warning had been given, either to the plaintiff or the public, that it was the habit of mail clerks to throw out the mail-bags while the train was in motion. Leaving out of account extreme instances testified to, the fair import of the evidence produced in behalf of the plaintiff is that it had for a long time been the practice of the mail clerks to throw out the mail-sacks while the train had still sufficient speed to run from ten to thirty feet after they had thrown the sacks. Hence, in view of the evidence as to where the head of the engine usually stood when brought to a full stop, and as to the length of the engine [349] and tender, the jury was warranted in concluding that the act of the mail clerk on this particular occasion was not an exceptional one, but that the sack or bag was thrown out upon a part of the platform where he had been in the habit of throwing it.

It follows that, if this platform was used by passengers and others rightfully there by defendant's invitation or license, and that this practice of throwing out mail-sacks from a moving train might reasonably be apprehended to result in injury to such persons, then the defendant was guilty of negligence which was the proximate cause of plaintiff's injuries. It was not necessary to charge defendant with negligence to show that on some former occasion a like injury had happened.

The practice of throwing loaded mail-bags out of a moving train upon a platform occupied by the public is itself a dangerous act, and the accident which did happen on this occasion was just such a one as might be reasonably anticipated; at least the jury had a right to so find: *Carpenter* v. *Boston etc. R. R. Co.*, 97 N. Y. 494; 49 Am. Rep. 540; *Snow* v. *Fitchburg R. R. Co.*, 136 Mass. 552; 49 Am. Rep. 40.

Defendant's main contention, however, is that, upon the arrival of a train from the south, this north end of the platform was not used by passengers, and that it had no reason to anticipate that it would be so used. Of course, it stands to reason that on such occasions that part of the platform would be used in part for the purposes of receiving and delivering mail, baggage, and express matter; but it was nowhere suggested, either in the pleadings, or on the trial, or in the requests to charge, that the plaintiff was not rightfully on this part of the platform, or that it was not rightfully used by the public, or that there was any distinction, in that respect, between this and any other part of the platform. On the contrary, it seems to have been assumed and conceded throughout the trial that this part of the platform was rightfully used by passengers and the public generally, precisely the same as any other part of it. Moreover, while there is very little direct evidence as to the use of this part of the platform by passengers on the arrival of trains from the south, yet it appears all through the testimony that it was used by bystanders by the license of the defendant, and by customers by its implied invitation, and it is conceded that plaintiff was lawfully there on this occasion. All persons having duties to perform incidental ³⁵⁰ to the departure and arrival of passengers, and all persons having business with the company on its premises at a station, are entitled to the same protection as passengers, or intended passengers, while there. The plaintiff was a customer of the defendant, within the essence and spirit of the rule, and was entitled to protection as such.

It is claimed that the damages (ten thousand dollars) are excessive. The verdict is certainly a large one. The immediate injury—a wound on the knee—seems, in and of itself, a comparatively small one. But it is claimed, and the evidence tended to prove, that this caused a nervous shock, which resulted in the development of heart disease, and in what the physicians called "traumatic neurosis," which, being translated from Greek into English, simply means a disease of the nerves caused by a wound; that these injuries are permanent, and have rendered the plaintiff a helpless invalid. The cause might seem inadequate to produce such serious consequences. It is one of the class of cases where there is a chance for "malingering," and where about the only available evidence tending to prove the connection of cause and effect, aside from chronological coincidence, is that of medical experts, which, it must be admitted, is often subject to the suspicion of dealing largely in doubtful speculation and surmise. But it is well known that there are many genuine cases of serious and permanent injuries resulting from what at first seem very trivial causes.

In this case the evidence tended to show that the plaintiff was, prior to this accident, a healthy, active woman; that immediately after the accident she was compelled to take to her bed, and has ever since been almost helpless, and has grown worse rather than better; and, while suggestions were made that she was shamming, no substantial evidence was produced to support these assertions.

The expert evidence on behalf of the plaintiff was to the effect that these ailments were real, that they were the result of the injury complained of, and that they were permanent; and the defendant produced practically no evidence to rebut this. If the plaintiff's alleged present diseases are real, and are the proximate result of the injury (and, under the evidence, we cannot say that such are not the facts), the damages awarded are not so large as to warrant this court in saying that they are excessive.

351 A new trial was also asked on the ground of newly discovered evidence, but, as this point is not argued, it must be deemed abandoned. We may say, however, that we have examined the affidavits on the subject, and are clearly of opinion that there was no error in refusing a new trial on that ground.

Order affirmed.

———

Railroads—Liability for Negligence of One not Acting for Company.—A railway corporation is not answerable for the negligence of one of its employees in throwing certain articles from a baggage-car while the train was in motion, and thus inflicting injury on a person standing near the track, if in so doing the employee was not acting in the course of his employment, but was performing a duty voluntarily assumed for a person other than his employer, and from the performance of which the master derived no benefit: *Walker* v. *Hannibal etc. R. R. Co.*, 121 Mo. 575; 42 Am. St. Rep. 547. An express messenger on a railway train is not the servant of the railroad company, and the company is not, therefore, liable for his wrongful acts: *Louisville etc. Ry. Co.* v. *Douglass*, 69 Miss. 723; 30 Am. St. Rep. 582.

———

JOHNSON *v.* NORTHWESTERN MUTUAL LIFE INSURANCE COMPANY.

[56 Minnesota, 365.]

Infants—Recovery upon Contracts of Insurance—Burden of Proof. If the personal contract of an infant, beneficial to himself, is fair and reasonable, and free from any fraud, overreaching, or undue influence by the other party, and has been wholly or partly executed on both sides, and the infant has disposed of what he has received, or · the benefits recovered by him are such that they cannot be restored, as in a contract of insurance, he cannot recover back what he has paid; but the burden is on the other party to show that such was the character of the contract.

Infants—Contracts of—Recovery of Excess.—If the personal contract of an infant, beneficial to himself, is free from any element of fraud or bad faith, and is reasonable and fair except that his payments exceed the value of what he has received, his recovery should be limited to such excess.

Insurance—Infants—Validity of Contract.—A contract of life insurance between an infant and a solvent insurance company, at the ordinary and usual rates, for an amount reasonably commensurate with the infant's estate, or his financial ability to carry it, is a provident, fair, and reasonable contract, which it is proper for the company to make with him, so long as it practices no fraud or other unlawful means to secure it.

INFANTS—CONTRACTS OF—FRAUD.—If the personal contract of an infant involves the element of actual fraud or bad faith, as where it is improvident or calculated to squander his estate, he may recover all that he has parted with or paid.

ACTION to recover the amount of premiums paid by an infant on an insurance policy. The plaintiff, at the age of seventeen years, had his life insured for twenty years, and paid several semi-annual premiums until he became of age, when he elected to avoid the policy. He offered to return it, and demanded the money he had paid. Upon the company's refusal to return it he brought this action. Defendant demurred upon the ground that the complaint did not state facts sufficient to constitute a cause of action. The demurrer was overruled and the defendant appealed.

Lusk, Bunn & Hadley, for the appellant.

Freeman P. Lane and William H. Briggs, for the respondent.

[372] MITCHELL, J. This case was argued and decided at the last term of this court. A reargument was granted for the reasons that although the amount was small the legal principles involved were important; the time permitted for argument under our rules was brief; the case was decided near the end of the term, without perhaps, the degree of consideration that its importance demanded; and, on further reflection, we are not satisfied that our decision was correct.

The former opinion laid down the following propositions, to which we still adhere: 1. That the contract of insurance was of benefit to the infant himself, and was not a contract for the benefit of third parties; 2. The contract, so far as appears on its face, was the usual and ordinary one for life insurance, on the customary terms, and was a fair and reasonable one, and free from any fraud, unfairness, or undue influence on part of the defendant, unless the contrary is to be presumed from the fact that it was made with the infant.

[373] It is not correct, however, to say that the plaintiff has received no benefit from the contract, or that the defendant has parted with nothing of value under it. True, the plaintiff has received no money, and the defendant has paid none to the plaintiff; but the life of the former was insured for four years, and, if he had died during that time, the defendant would have had to pay the amount of the policy to his estate. The defendant carried the risk all that time, and this is the essence of the contract of insurance. Neither does it

follow that the risk has cost the defendant nothing in money, because plaintiff himself was not one of those insured who died.   The case is therefore one of a voidable or rescindable contract of an infant, partly performed on both sides, the benefits of which the infant has enjoyed, but which he cannot return, and where there is no charge of fraud, unfairness, or undue influence on the part of the other party, unless, as already suggested, it is to be presumed from the fact that the contract was made with an infant.

The question is, Can the plaintiff recover back what he has paid, assuming that the contract was in all respects fair and reasonable?   The opinion heretofore filed held that he can. Without taking time to cite or discuss any of our former decisions, it is sufficient to say that none of them commit this court to such a doctrine.   That such a rule goes further than is necessary for the protection of the infant, and would often work gross injustice to those dealing with him, is, to our minds, clear.   Suppose a minor engaged in agriculture should hire a man to work on his farm, and pay him reasonable wages for his services.   According to this rule the minor might recover back what he paid, although retaining and enjoying the fruits of the other man's labor.   Or, again, suppose a man engaged in mercantile business, with a capital of five thousand dollars, should, from time to time, buy and pay for one hundred thousand dollars' worth of goods, in the aggregate, which he had sold, and had got his pay.   According to this doctrine he could recover back the one hundred thousand dollars which he had paid to the various parties from whom he had bought the goods.   Not only would such a rule work great injustice to others, but it would be positively injurious to the infant himself.   The policy of the law is to shield or protect the infant, and not to debar him from the privilege of contracting.

But, if the rule suggested is to obtain, there is no footing on [374] which an adult can deal with him, except for necessaries.   Nobody could or would do any business with him. He could not get his life insured.   He could not insure his property against fire.   He could not hire servants to till his farm.   He could not improve or keep up his land or buildings.   In short, however advantageous other contracts might be to him, or however much capital he might have, he could do absolutely nothing, except to buy necessaries, because nobody would dare to contract with him for any thing else.

It cannot be that this is the law. Certainly it ought not to be.

The following propositions are well settled everywhere as to the rescindable contracts of an infant, and in that category we include all contracts, except for necessaries: 1. That, in so far as the contract is executory on part of an infant, he may always interpose his infancy as a defense to an action for its enforcement. He can always use his infancy as a shield; 2. If the contract has been wholly or partly performed on his part, but is wholly executory on part of the other party, the minor having received no benefits from it, he may recover back what he has paid or parted with; 3. Where the contract has been wholly or partly performed on both sides the infant may always rescind and recover back what he has paid, upon restoring what he has received; 4. A minor on arriving at full age may avoid a conveyance of his real estate, without being required to place the grantee *in statu quo*, although a different rule has sometimes been adopted by courts of equity when the former infant has applied to them for aid in avoiding his deeds. Whether this distinction between conveyances of real property and personal contracts is founded on a technical rule, or upon considerations of policy growing out of the difference between real and personal property, it is not necessary here to consider; 5. Where the contract has been wholly or partly performed on both sides, the infant, if he sues to recover back what he has paid, must always restore what he has received, in so far as he still retains it in specie; 6. The courts will always grant an infant relief where the other party has been guilty of fraud or undue influence. As to what would constitute a sufficient ground for relief under this head [375] and what relief the courts would grant in such cases we will refer to hereafter.

But suppose that the contract is free from all elements of fraud, unfairness, or overreaching, and the infant has enjoyed the benefits of it, but has spent or disposed of what he has received, or the benefits received are, as in this case, of such a nature that they cannot be restored, Can he recover back what he has paid? It is well settled in England that he cannot. This was held in the leading case of *Holmes* v. *Blogg*, 8 Taunt. 508, approved as late as 1890 in *Valentini* v. *Canali*, 24 Q. B. Div. 166. Some obiter remarks of the chief justice in *Holmes* v. *Blogg*, 8 Taunt. 508, to the effect that an infant could never recover back money voluntarily paid, were too broad, and have often been disapproved—a fact which has sometimes led to the erroneous impression that the case itself has been overruled: *Corpe* v. *Overton,* 10 Bing. 252 (decided by the same court), held that the infant might recover back what he had voluntarily paid, but on the ground that the contract in that case remained wholly executory on part of the other party, and hence the infant had never enjoyed its benefits.

In 1 Chitty on Contracts, page 222, the law is stated in accordance with the decision in *Holmes* v. *Blogg,* 8 Taunt. 508. Leake, a most accurate writer, in his work on Contracts, page 553, sums up the law to the same effect. In this country, Chancellor Kent (2 Kent's Commentaries, 240), and Reeves, in his work on Domestic Relations, chapters 2 and 3, title " Parent and Child," state the law in exact accordance with what we may term the " English rule." Parsons in his work on Contracts, volume 1, page 322, undoubtedly states the law too broadly in omitting the qualification, " and enjoys the benefit of it."

At least a respectable minority of the American decisions are in full accord with what we have termed the " English rule": See, among others, *Riley* v. *Mallory,* 33 Conn. 206; *Adams* v. *Beall,* 67 Md. 53; 1 Am. St. Rep. 379; *Breed* v. *Judd,* 1 Gray, 455. But many—perhaps a majority—of the American decisions, apparently thinking that the English rule does not sufficiently protect the infant, have modified it; and some of them seem to have wholly repudiated it, and to hold that although the contract was in all respects fair and reasonable, and the infant had enjoyed the benefits of it, yet, if the [376] infant had spent or parted with what he had received, or if the benefits of it were of such a nature that they could not be restored, still he might recover back what he had paid. The problem with tne courts·seems to have been, on the one hand, to protect the infant from the improvidence incident to his youth and inexperience, and how, on the other hand, to compel him to conform to the principles of common honesty. The result is that the American authorities—at least the later ones—have fallen into such a condition of conflict and confusion that it is difficult to draw from them any definite or uniform rule.

The dissatisfaction with what we have termed the " English rule" seems to be generally based upon the idea that the courts would not grant an infant relief, on the ground of fraud or undue influence, except where they would grant it to an adult on the same grounds, and then only on the same conditions.   Many of the cases, we admit, would seem to support this idea.   If such were the law it is obvious that there would be many cases where it would furnish no adequate protection to the infant.   Cases may be readily imagined where an infant may have paid for an article several times more than it was worth, or where the contract was of an improvident character, calculated to result in the squandering of his estate, and that fact was known to the other party; and yet if he was an adult the court would grant him no relief, but leave him to stand the consequences of his own foolish bargain.   But to measure the right of an infant in such cases by the same rule that would be applied in the case of an adult would be to fail to give due weight to the disparity between the adult and the infant, or to apply the proper standard of fair dealing due from the former to the latter.   Even as between adults, when a transaction is assailed on the ground of fraud, undue influence, etc., their disparity in intelligence and experience, or in any other respect which gives one an ascendency over the other, or tends to prevent the latter from exercising an intelligent and unbiased judgment, is always a most vital consideration with the courts.   Where a contract is improvident and unfair courts of equity have frequently inferred fraud from the mere disparity of the parties.

If this is true as to adults the rule ought certainly to be applied with still greater liberality in favor of infants, whom the law deems [377] so incompetent to care for themselves that it holds them incapable of binding themselves by contract except for necessaries.   In view of this disparity of the parties, thus recognized by law, every one who assumes to contract with an infant should be held to the utmost good faith and fair dealing.   We further think that this disparity is such as to raise a presumption against the fairness of the contract, and to cast upon the other party the burden of proving that it was a fair and reasonable one, and free from any fraud, undue influence, or overreaching.

A similar principle applies to all the relations, where, from disparity of years, intellect, or knowledge, one of the parties to the contract has an ascendency which prevents the other from exercising an unbiased judgment—as, for example, parent and child, husband and wife, guardian and ward. It is true that the mere fact that a person is dealing with an infant creates no "fiduciary relation" between them, in the proper sense of the term, such as exists between guardian and ward; but we think that he who deals with an infant should be held to substantially the same standard of fair dealing, and be charged with the burden of proving that the contract was in all respects fair and reasonable, and not tainted with any fraud, undue influence, or overreaching on his part. Of course, in this as in all other cases, the degree of disparity between the parties in age and mental capacity would be an important consideration. Moreover, if the contract was not in all respects fair and reasonable, the extent to which the infant should recover would depend on the nature and extent of the element of unfairness which characterized the transaction.

If the party dealing with the infant was guilty of actual fraud or bad faith, we think the infant should be allowed to recover back all he had paid, without making restitution, except, of course, to the extent to which he still retained in specie what he had received. Such a case would be a contract essentially improvident, calculated to facilitate the squandering the infant's estate, and which the other party knew or ought to have known to be such, for to make such a contract at all with an infant would be fraud. But if the contract was free from any fraud or bad faith, and otherwise reasonable, except that the price paid by the infant was in excess of the value of what he received, his recovery should be limited to the [378] difference between what he paid and what he received. Such cases as *Medbury* v. *Watrous*, 7 Hill, 110, *Sparman* v. *Keim*, 83 N. Y. 245, and *Heath* v. *Stevens*, 48 N. H. 251, really proceed upon this principle, although they may not distinctly announce it. The objections to this rule are, in our opinion, largely imaginary, for we are confident that in practice it can and will be applied by courts and juries so as to work out substantial justice.

Our conclusion is that where the personal contract of an infant, beneficial to himself, has been wholly or partly executed on both sides, but the infant has disposed of what he has received, or the benefits recovered by him are such that they cannot be restored, he cannot recover back what he has paid, if the contract was a fair and reasonable one, and free from any fraud or bad faith on part of the other party, but that the burden is on the other party to prove that such was the character of the contract; that if the contract involved the element of actual fraud or bad faith, the infant may recover all he paid or parted with, but if the contract involved no such elements, and was otherwise reasonable and fair, except that what the infant paid was in excess of the value of what he received, his recovery should be limited to such excess. It seems to us that this will sufficiently protect the infant, and at the same time do justice to the other party. Of course, in speaking of contracts beneficial to the infant we refer to those that are deemed such in contemplation of law.

Applying these rules to the case in hand we add tha tlife insurance in a solvent company, at the ordinary and usual rates, for an amount reasonably commensurate with the infant's estate, or his financial ability to carry it, is a provident, fair, and reasonable contract, and one which it is entirely proper for an insurance company to make with him, assuming that it practices no fraud or other unlawful means to secure it; and, if such should appear to be the character of this contract, the plaintiff could not recover the premiums which he has paid in, so far as they were intended to cover the current annual risk assumed by the company under its policy.

But it appears from the face of the policy that these premiums covered something more than this. The policy provides that after payment of three or more annual premiums the insured will be entitled to a paid-up nonparticipating policy for as many twentieths [379] of the original sum insured, one thousand dollars, as there have been annual premiums so paid. The complaint alleges the payment of four annual premiums. Hence, the plaintiff was entitled, upon surrender of the original policy, to a paid-up nonparticipating policy for two hundred dollars; and it therefore seems to us that, having elected to rescind, he was entitled to recover back, in any event, the present cash "surrender" value of such a policy. For this reason, as well as that the burden was on the defendant to prove the fair and honest character of the contract, the demurrer to the complaint was properly overruled. The result arrived at in the former opinion was therefore correct, and is adhered to, although on somewhat different grounds.

Order affirmed.

BUCK, J., absent; sick; took no part.

THE trial court gave as its reasons for overruling the demurrer in the principal case that "this contract of insurance was not beneficial to the insured: it was for the benefit of third persons." On the original hearing before the supreme court, Buck, J., said: "We do not see how the court fell into such an error, for the plain provisions of the policy show clearly that it was for the benefit of the plaintiff, for it expressly provides that at the end of twenty years the policy is payable to himself if living, and after ten years he could share in the company's surplus, according to usage, at each distribution, until all contributions to the surplus funds found in the course of making such contributions to have arisen from the policy should have been returned. After three or more annual premiums were paid in cash, if he made default in the payment of any premium on the day it became due, he was entitled to a paid-up nonparticipating policy for as many twentieth parts of the original sum insured as there were complete annual premiums so paid. There were also other benefits which he would receive, which we need not further specify particularly. But, notwithstanding the wrong reason given by the trial court for its decision, if the decision was correct it must stand." His honor then took up the question of the proper construction to be given to contracts between an infant and an adult, and concluded that such contracts are not void, but merely voidable. "As between the two parties," said he, "the defendant so far has profited by the contract. If the plaintiff succeeds in this action the defendant suffers no loss or damage except to return to plaintiff just what it got of him while an infant." The order appealed from was affirmed.

From the majority opinion on rehearing before the supreme court Gilfillan, C. J., dissented in the following language: "I dissent, and especially from the proposition that in any case the contract of a minor is presumed to be fraudulent on the part of the other party to it. If two minors contract together each may avoid the contract. Is that because each is presumed to have fraudulently drawn the other into making it? If a contract be wholly executory when the minor seeks to avoid it, will any amount of proof that it is advantageous to him, and made in good faith and honestly on the part of the adult, prevent the minor avoiding it? If wholly executory when made, will the subsequent performance raise a presumption that it was fraudulent when made? A minor's contract, except for necessaries, is voidable by him only because he is, in law, incapable to bind himself. When he seeks to avoid a contract the question arises, On what conditions shall he do so? In such cases there are two considerations: 1. To afford him full protection from the consequences of his own incapacity; 2. That being done, to prevent him making his legal incapacity a means to defraud others. If the contract be wholly executory both ends will be attained by allowing him to repudiate it, which will leave both parties as they were before it was made. But suppose it partly performed on both sides, he may undoubtedly avoid further performance. But, if he takes the aggressive and seeks to recover what he has parted with in performance, what then? The authorities are agreed that, if he have in specie what he received under it, he must restore it, as a condition of recovering what he parted with. The disagreement in the authorities is in cases where he cannot restore the benefits he has received; where he has expended them, or they are of such a character that they cannot be restored. I am speaking only of contracts relating to the personalty. Since the first argument of this cause, I have come to the conclusion that whether, when he cannot restore what he has received he may recover what he has parted with will depend on the character of the contract. If, from the subject matter or terms of the contract, it is a wasting of his estate, so that to require him to restore what he has received will likewise waste his estate it will not be required of him. But if the contract be, both in subject matter and terms, a provident one, advantageous to the minor, the court, to prevent a fraud on the other party unnecessary to his protection, will not permit him to recover what he has parted with without setting off against it what he has received. Such is this case."

INFANTS—RECOVERY BACK ON CONTRACT OF.—An infant who makes a loan of money may disaffirm his contract and recover back the money: See monographic note to *Craig* v. *Van Bebber,* 18 Am. St. Rep. 605, on contracts of infants.

INFANTS—INSURANCE.—An infant's contract of insurance by which he is insured against fire is not void, but voidable only at the election of the infant. The defense of infancy in such a case is personal, and is not open to the company in an action against it to recover for the loss: See monographic note to *Craig* v. *Van Bebber*, 18 Am. St. Rep. 615.

INFANTS—DISAFFIRMANCE OF CONTRACT—RETURN OF CONSIDERATION.— As to when an infant may and may not disaffirm his contract without a return of the consideration, see *Englebert* v. *Troxell,* 40 Neb. 195; 42 Am. St. Rep. 665.

BARTON *v.* LOVEJOY.

[56 MINNESOTA, 380.]

PARTNERSHIP—RIGHT OF SURVIVING PARTNER TO SELL FIRM REAL ESTATE TO PAY DEBTS—EQUITABLE TITLE.—Upon the death of a partner the surviving partner has the right, if there is not sufficient personalty to pay the firm debts, to sell enough realty for that purpose; and, if he does so, in good faith and for a valuable consideration, though he has obtained no order of court, the equitable title passes to the purchaser, and the devisees or heirs may be compelled to convey the legal title.

Little & Nunn and Hale & Morgan, for the appellants.

Leon E. Lum and Jackson & Atwater, for the respondents.

382 BUCK, J. The plaintiffs brought this action to determine the adverse claims of the defendants to certain vacant premises situated in the counties of Cass, Itasca, and Crow Wing, in this state. It is alleged in the complaint that plaintiffs are the owners in fee of such vacant premises, and they ask that the title be determined to be in them, and forever quieted, and that the defendants, and each of them, be enjoined and barred from asserting any claim whatever in or to said lands. The defendants, Frank L. Lovejoy, Lorin K. Lovejoy, Arthur Lovejoy, and Mary E. Winston answered, and the other defendants were in default.

Mary E. Winston, in her separate answer, alleges that she is the owner of three thirty-seconds of said premises, and the other three defendants in their answer each claims to be the owner in fee of three thirty-seconds of the premises.

On and prior to January 29, 1886, the premises in question were part of the partnership property and assets of the firm of J. J. Howe & Co., but at said time the legal title to said land was held as follows: An undivided three-eighths by Sumner W. Farnham, an undivided three-eighths by James A. Lovejoy, and an undivided two-eighths by Jeremiah J. Howe, one of these plaintiffs. The firm of J. J. Howe & Co. then consisted of the partnership firms of Farnham [383] & Lovejoy owning a six-eighths interest in its property and business, and said J. J. Howe, who owned a two-eighths interest in its said property and business, and the firm of Farnham & Lovejoy consisted of those two persons, who each owned a half interest therein, both firms being engaged in the lumber business. Lovejoy died intestate January 29, 1886, and said J. J. Howe and O. C. Merriman and Winthrop Young were the executors of said will, which, by its terms, authorized said executors to close up and settle the said co-partnership business of Farnham & Lovejoy, and to join with said Farnham in the execution of all contracts, deeds, and mortgages and other papers and instruments that might become necessary for the sale of the lands of said Farnham & Lovejoy, and for the doing of such other acts as might be by said executors deemed necessary and advisable in regard to the business of said partnership.

The will was duly probated, and by its terms made the defendants who have answered the devisees of said James A. Lovejoy. At the time of the death of said Lovejoy his estate and the firm of Farnham & Lovejoy were insolvent, and the firm of J. J. Howe & Co. was largely in debt. On the eleventh day of May, 1887, the plaintiffs entered into a partnership under the firm name of J. J. Howe & Co., and about the fifteenth day of May, 1887, said Farhaum, as surviving partner of said James A. Lovejoy, proceeded to settle up the business of said firm, and to this end he sold to plaintiffs all the interest of said Farnham & Lovejoy in said firm of J. J. Howe & Co. as it existed at the time of said Lovejoy's death, and prior to the date of said sale, for the sum of thirty-eight thousand dollars, and which sum was by said Farnham applied to the payment of the debts of said firm of Farnham &

Lovejoy, and the premises so sold are a part of the copartnership property of J. J. Howe & Co., these plaintiffs. The executors of said Lovejoy, jointly with said Farnham and his
wife, executed a deed to these plaintiffs, in form conveying
to them the legal interest in said lands held by said Farnham
& Lovejoy at the time of said Lovejoy's death. The court
below found as a fact that such sale was made in good faith,
for the best price obtainable, and for the best interest of said
firm of Farnham & Lovejoy. The final account of the executors was duly settled in probate court [384] and they
made return to said court that no money or property had
been received by them from the assets of the firm of Farnham & Lovejoy as the same was insolvent. It does not appear that these defendants, or any of them, or any creditor,
ever in probate court, or elsewhere, objected to the sale made
by Farnham as surviving partner to plaintiffs, nor to the
transfer of the property of Farnham & Lovejoy to plaintiffs.
Upon these facts the court below found for the plaintiffs, and
decreed that the defendants had no right or title as against
the plaintiffs.

We are of the opinion that the decision of the lower court
was correct, and should be affirmed. We shall not attempt to
enter into a full discussion of all the various questions discussed by the respective counsel. It is elementary that where,
in case of the death of a partner, there is not enough personal
property to pay the firm debts, then the surviving partner
has a right to sell the real estate of the firm to do so. If he
sells the real estate of the firm for the purpose of paying the
firm debts without first obtaining an order from the court,
and makes such sale in good faith and for a valuable consideration, then such sale passes the equitable title in the premises to the purchaser. In this case there does not appear to
have been any bad faith on the part of the surviving partner,
nor that he has squandered any of the proceeds of the sale,
nor in any manner diverted the consideration received from
the just payment of the partnership debts. The property
seems to have been sold for its full value. The firm was
hopelessly insolvent, and it was not only the right, but the
duty, of the surviving partner to sell enough property to pay
the debts. If he had not done this the debts could have
been collected by due process of law if there were sufficient
assets, and the same property applied toward paying the

firm debts. If the surviving partner sold the premises in good faith, and, as the court below found, for the best price obtainable, no injury could possibly have resulted to the defendants.

Although the surviving partner, Farnham, sold the premises without an order of the court, yet the heirs have no right to come in and defeat the equitable title which passed upon the sale. The devisees or heirs in such case can be compelled to convey the legal [385] title, or, as in this case, the court properly adjudged and decreed the title to the premises to be in the plaintiffs as against the defendants.

In the case of *Shanks* v. *Klein*, 104 U. S. 18, the law is stated thus: "Real estate purchased with partnership funds for partnership purposes, though the title be taken in the individual name of one or both partners, is, in equity, treated as personal property, so far as necessary to pay the debts of the partnership, and to adjust the equities of the copartners; and, for this purpose, in case of the death of one of the partners, the survivor can sell the real estate so situated; and, though he cannot convey the legal title which passed to the heirs or devisee of the deceased partner, his sale invests the purchaser with the equitable ownership of the real estate, and the right to compel a conveyance of the title from the kin or devisee in a court of equity": See, also, *Hanson* v. *Metcalf*, 46 Minn. 25.

The power and authority which the law confers upon a surviving partner appears to be quite full and extensive for the performance of all the business necessary to a complete settlement of the concern. As against heirs or devisees of the deceased partner he has full control of the partnership property. In this case there does not, as we have said, appear to have been bad faith on the part of the surviving partner, and this statement is strongly confirmed by the fact that the three executors joined with him in the conveyance to the plaintiffs. The answer does not allege any fraud or bad faith on the part of the surviving partner or the executors. It was his duty to proceed without unnecessary delay to settle the partnership affairs in the best possible manner for all parties interested. As his powers were commensurate with his position, and there does not appear to have been any misconduct upon his part, the judgment of the court below is affirmed.

PARTNERSHIP—SALE OF REAL ESTATE BY SURVIVING PARTNER TO PAY DEBTS OF FIRM—TITLE.—The legal title to all partnership property vests, upon the death of any member of the firm, in the survivor or survivors, but it vests in trust for partnership purposes, to wit: The settlement of the affairs of the firm, the payment of its debts, and thereafter the turning over to the representative of the deceased partner his share of the surplus: See monographic note to *Smith* v. *Smith*, 43 Am. St. Rep. 375. Partnership real estate is, in equity, and for partnership purposes, to be treated as personalty: *Rovelsky* v. *Brown*, 92 Ala. 522; 25 Am. St. Rep. 83. The surviving partner may, therefore, sell real estate to pay debts: See monographic note to *Shields* v. *Fuller*, 65 Am. Dec. 300. A surviving partner has a right in equity to dispose of real property belonging to the firm for the payment of the debts where the firm is insolvent, and the deed will convey the equity of the heir of a deceased partner, who may be compelled to make a conveyance: *Andrews* v. *Brown*, 56 Am. Dec. 252.

HEISLER v. AULTMAN.

[56 MINNESOTA, 454.]

PAYMENT OF MORTGAGE OPERATES AS AN ASSIGNMENT, WHEN.—The payment of money due upon a mortgage by one who is not an intermeddler or volunteer operates as a discharge of the mortgage, or in the nature of an assignment of it, as may best serve the purposes of justice and the just intent of the parties.

MORTGAGE SATISFACTION UNDER MISTAKE OF FACT—SUBROGATION.—If one not an intermeddler or volunteer causes a mortgage to be satisfied and discharged in ignorance of the existence of a judgment lien, under circumstances authorizing an inference of a mistake of fact, equity will presume such mistake, and give the party who made it the benefit of the equitable right of subrogation where no superior intervening equities are interfered with.

SUBROGATION OF SURETY WHO PAYS MORTGAGE DEBT—PRIORITY OF MORTGAGE AND JUDGMENT LIENS.—In a case where real property is sold subject to a mortgage the rules of subrogation will be applied when the surety upon a note, given for a part of the purchase price, and secured by a second mortgage upon the property, has paid the note, and taken a deed of the land in indemnification, if the second mortgage has been satisfied and discharged in ignorance of the fact that a judgment against the maker of the note and mortgage, and subordinate to the mortgage liens on the premises, has thereby been promoted and advanced from a third to a second lien, so as to render his interest in the property of no value. The satisfaction and record will be canceled and annulled, and the mortgage lien be placed prior and paramount to the lien of the judgment, or lien acquired by a sale on execution thereunder.

APPEAL from an order denying the defendant's motion for a new trial.

Hale & Morgan and *E. E. Smith*, for the appellant.

J. L. Washburn and *Lorin Cray*, for the respondent.

⁴⁵⁶ COLLINS, J. Stated in chronological order, the controlling facts in this case are as follows: July 28, 1880, defendant corporation duly recovered, and caused to be docketed in the office of the clerk of the district court for Blue Earth county, in this state, a judgment for the sum of $844.09 against one John C. Heisler and another. In March, 1886, said Heisler purchased, and there was duly conveyed to him by warranty deed, a farm in said county, consisting of 110 acres, subject to a mortgage for the sum of $900; and, for the vendor's interest, Heisler agreed to pay the sum of $1,450, to be evidenced by two promissory notes, one for $550, and the other for $900. The plaintiff in this action, at the request of said Heisler, who was her son, signed his said note for $550, as a surety, and it was delivered to the vendor of the ⁴⁵⁷ farm. Heisler also made and delivered to said vendor his note for $900, and, to secure the payment of both notes, executed and delivered a second mortgage on the farm, which was duly recorded. John C. Heisler neglected to pay the note for $550 when it matured, and, upon the commencement of legal proceedings against her to enforce its collection, the plaintiff paid the same. She then paid the note for $900 given to the vendor of the farm, and soon afterward, December 7, 1887, said John C., his wife joining, executed and delivered a warranty deed, whereby they conveyed the farm to the plaintiff, subject to the mortgage first above mentioned. The deed to said John C. Heisler, and the deed from him and his wife to the plaintiff herein, were recorded simultaneously, on January 3, 1888. The court found that the deed last mentioned was accepted by plaintiff to secure and indemnify her for the amounts so paid by her on said notes, that the value of the farm had never exceeded $2,300, and that no part of the sums paid by plaintiff had been repaid to her. On January 21, 1888, the vendor mortgagee executed and delivered a satisfaction of his mortgage, which was duly recorded, the effect on the title, as shown by the record and docket entries, being to promote defendant's judgment, and to make it a second instead of a third lien on the land. The only superior lien was that of the first mortgage, and, as will be seen, the plaintiff's claim or interest in the farm was thus made of no practical value. At no time prior to this was the plaintiff informed of the existence of the judgment, nor had she caused any examination to be made in the clerk's office as to judgments against her son. January 11, 1890,

after this action had been commenced, and defendants had
been informed of plaintiff's equities, the farm was sold to one
Lamb, by the proper sheriff, under and by virtue of an execution duly issued upon the judgment, and to satisfy the
same. The sheriff's certificate of sale was delivered to Lamb,
but defendant was the real purchaser, and shortly afterward
the certificate was duly assigned to it. On these findings the
court below ordered judgment canceling and annulling the
satisfaction of the mortgage and the record of the same, and
restoring and reinstating, of record and otherwise, the mortgage lien as of the date of the record, and as prior and paramount to the lien or claim of defendant by virtue of the
judgment or sale on execution, or otherwise; further, [458] that
plaintiff was the equitable assignee and owner of said mortgage, and that as such she be subrogated to the rights of the
original mortgagee.

This appeal is from an order denying a new trial.

The doctrine of subrogation has recently been considered
by this court in two cases: *Emmert* v. *Thompson*, 49 Minn.
386, 32 Am. St. Rep. 566, and *Wentworth* v. *Tubbs*, 53 Minn.
388. It was said in the first-mentioned case that this doctrine is enforced solely for the purpose of accomplishing
substantial justice, and, being administered upon equitable
principles, it is only when an applicant has an equity to
invoke, and when innocent persons will not be injured, that
a court can interfere. That in this way a court, under a
great variety of circumstances, may relieve one who has acted
under a justifiable or excusable mistake of fact, is well settled, and that it is a common thing for courts of equity to
relieve parties who by mistake have discharged mortgages of
record, and to fully protect them from the consequences of
their acts, where, as before stated, no injury to innocent
parties will result. In *Wentworth* v. *Tubbs*, 53 Minn. 388, it
was said that the doctrine could only be applied in favor of
one who has bought a debt, either expressly or by paying it
under circumstances which render the payment equivalent to
a purchase, and this is solely a question of intention, either
expressed or presumed, from the relation of the party to the
debt, or other circumstances under which payment was made.
These cases come very near sustaining the conclusion reached
by the court below.

The findings are silent as to any express intention of the
plaintiff when paying the $550 note. But she was a surety

only, entitled, upon payment, to the benefit of all securities held by the payee, and, under these circumstances, the payment was simply equivalent to a purchase. Because of the relations of the parties the presumption arises that plaintiff did not intend to extinguish the debt or to release the security. Being, by reason of the payment, entitled to the benefit of the mortgage, to the extent of her interest, but subject to the claim of the holder of the second note, the plaintiff was not an intermeddler or a volunteer, when, in order to fully protect and secure herself, she paid the note last mentioned. And, under the circumstances, this payment must also be regarded as [459] equivalent to a purchase. That it was not intended by the parties to extinguish the claim or to release the security is evidenced by the fact that, immediately after this last-mentioned transaction, plaintiff received a deed of the premises from her son and his wife, which, as found by the court, was taken and received for her indemnification and as security.

A party situated as was plaintiff, who has paid money due upon a mortgage, is entitled, for the purpose of effecting substantial justice, to be substituted in place of the encumbrancer, and to be treated as assignee of the mortgage, and is enabled to hold the same as assignee, notwithstanding the mortgage itself has been canceled. The true principle is that, where money due upon a mortgage is paid, it shall operate as a discharge of the mortgage, or in the nature of an assignment of it, as may best serve the purposes of justice and the just intent of the parties. One who has paid money due upon a mortgage of lands to which he had a title that might have been defeated thereby has the right to hold the lands as if the mortgage subsisted, and had been assigned to him. The mortgage may, for his benefit, be considered as still subsisting, though formally discharged of record, in so far as he ought, in justice, to hold the property: Sheldon on Subrogation, secs. 13, 14, and cases cited; Jones on Mortgages, secs. 858, 869, 881, and cases cited.

Upon the payment of the mortgage plaintiff was entitled to all of the rights of the original mortgagee, and to an assignment of the mortgage. The same was discharged and satisfied in ignorance of the existence of the judgment lien. Having caused it to be satisfied and discharged in ignorance of the existence of the judgment lien, under circumstances authorizing an inference of a mistake of fact, equity will pre-

sume such mistake, and give the party who made it the
benefit of the equitable right of subrogation. To do so in
this case is to prevent manifest injustice and hardship, and
no superior intervening equities are interfered with: See
Barnes v. *Mott*, 64 N. Y. 397; 21 Am. Rep. 625; *Stantons* v.
Thompson, 49 N. H. 272.

Of course it has been observed that defendant obtained
and docketed the judgment several years before its debtor
purchased the real estate in question, and that the mortgage
was a prior and paramount lien up to the time of its satisfaction and discharge. Before the sale this action had been
commenced, and thereby [460] defendant had been informed
of plaintiff's equities. It purchased with full notice. It
could not and did not acquire an intervening superior equity
through the sheriff's certificate. By subrogating the plaintiff
to the rights of the mortgagee it is not placed in a worse
position than it held when the mortgage was alive.

Order affirmed.

BUCK, J., took no part. ____

MORTGAGES—PAYMENT—SUBROGATION.—When a debt secured by mortgage is paid by one under no obligation to pay it he is subrogated to the
rights of the mortgagee in the mortgaged property: See note to *Baker* v.
Baker, 39 Am. St. Rep. 782; though it would be otherwise in the case of a
mere volunteer: See note to *Campbell* v. *Foster Home Assn.*, 43 Am. St.
Rep. 826. Payment by a surety on mortgage notes entitles him to be subrogated to the rights and remedies of the payee of such notes: *Nettleton* v.
Ramsey County etc. Co., 54 Minn. 395; 40 Am. St. Rep. 342.

MORTGAGES—SATISFACTION OF BY MISTAKE.—Where the cancellation of a
mortgage is procured by fraud, or made by mistake or without authority,
and without actual payment and satisfaction, the canceling will be set
aside, and the mortgage enforced. The mistake, however, must be one of
fact, and not of law, and clear evidence of the mistake is required: See
monographic note to *Young* v. *Shaner*, 5 Am. St. Rep. 703-708, on revival
of mortgages when satisfied by mistake, and the enforcement of a new
mortgage as a continuation of the lien of a prior one.

St. Paul & Duluth Railroad Company *v.* City of Duluth.

[56 Minnesota, 494.]

Municipal Corporations—Sewerage, Failure to Provide.—A city is
not liable to the owner of private premises within its boundaries for
failing to provide a system of sewerage to carry away surface water and
the water of perennial streams naturally accumulating thereon.

Swamp-land Owner in City—No Protection Against Tributary Surface Waters and Perennial Streams.—The owner of swamp land
in a city cannot improve it, and then compel the owner of high land
above to keep surface water and the water of perennial streams, naturally tributary to such land, from coming upon it, though the water
is discharged by storm sewers, provided by the city, diverting the
water from natural ravines upon the high land, but returning it to its
common dumping-ground, the plaintiff's premises, at different points
from those at which the ravines terminate, especially where he has to
some extent already adopted the plan of the city, with reference to its
storm sewers.

Action by the railroad company to require the city to
construct and continue its storm sewers underneath its railroad tracks to the bay of Duluth, and to restrain the city
from so constructing new storm sewers as to empty their
waters against its embankment built for its tracks along the
shore of the bay. The matter was referred to a referee,
whose conclusion was against the city. Its motion for a
new trial was denied, and it appealed.

H. F. Greene, city attorney, for the appellant.

Bunn & Hadley and J. D. Armstrong, for the respondent.

⁴⁹⁸ Canty, J. The part of the city of Duluth here in
question is a steep hillside, sloping toward St. Louis bay.
This slope rises six hundred feet above the bay, and extends
back from it more than a mile. In 1870, between the foot of
the hill and the bay, there was a wide margin of marsh or
swamp, covered more or less with the water of the bay.
Between what is now Fourth avenue east and Twelfth avenue west there were on this slope seventeen large ravines,
which were well-defined water channels, in which water ran
down the hill into the swamp below, and there spread out
over the swamp, and flowed off into the bay. In seven of
these ran perennial streams of water, and in the other ten
large volumes of water ran during times of storms, freshets,
and melting snows. There were many other smaller depres-

sions and ravines, which carried more or less surface water at such times into the swamp.

In 1870 the predecessor in interest of the plaintiff constructed its [499] track along on this swamp, parallel to the foot of the hill and the side of the bay, upon piling driven into the swamp. This piling offered no resistance to the free egress of the water. From time to time since, the plaintiff has added other tracks built on piles, and has filled up the right of way under the tracks with embankments of earth, leaving no place or passage for the egress of the water, except one near Tenth avenue west, which is sixteen to eighteen feet wide, and is still crossed by the track, supported on piling. At seven or eight other points plaintiff has put in temporary box culverts of wood across the right of way, not opposite the ravines and natural water channels, but opposite the ends of the storm sewers hereinafter mentioned. The part of the city built on this slope was platted before the railroad was built, with streets running along the side of the slope, parallel with the railroad right of way, and other cross streets running up and down the side of the hill, terminating at the right of way. These streets have since been improved, and now exist as so platted.

The city has also constructed under these cross streets fourteen sewers, which run down the hill, and all of them terminate at plaintiff's right of way, except two, one at Lake avenue and one at Fifth avenue west, which have been extended under the right of way to the bay. Some of the others connect with the box culverts above mentioned, some have no connection, and one or two empty into said bridged open space left across the right of way. These sewers carry off the surface water deposited by rains and snows and the water of the seven perennial streams, all the water having been diverted from the said seventeen ravines into these storm sewers. They are connected only with the catch basins in the streets, not with the houses. There is another system of sanitary sewers running at right angles to these storm sewers, and having no connection with them.

The plaintiff brings this action against the city to enjoin the use by it of these sewers, and the depositing of the water from them on plaintiff's right of way. It is not claimed that these sewers bring any more water onto plaintiff's premises than was brought by the ravines and creeks in a state of nature; but it is claimed that the water has been diverted from the creeks and ravines, and deposited at other points on the premises; that it runs down these sewers ^{500} with great velocity, and strikes the roadbed with great force, tearing it up.

The plaintiff further claims that "it is well settled that the construction of ditches and pipes for the sole purpose of drainage, gathering water in streams or bodies solely to discharge it, and thus dumping it onto another's land, is actionable. Such works are not a reasonable and proper improvement of one's own premises."

The cases cited by counsel are cases where surface water was collected and discharged onto premises where it would not naturally go. The city of Duluth would have no right to discharge surface water on the land of any private owner, unless his land is the natural channel or dumping-ground for it. But the land of plaintiff is such natural dumping-ground. Plaintiff complains that the city is making such of it, but it seems to forget that nature, and not the city, has made this place such dumping-ground, and that the city has never relieved the land of such servitude. It complains that the city diverted the water from its natural channels into these sewers, which deposit the water at different points on its premises from those at which the ravines deposited it; but it forgets that these premises are, so to speak, all channel, and that, while the city diverted the water from its natural channels upon the slope of the hill, it returned the water to that channel—the common dumping-ground—at plaintiff's premises. If plaintiff had improved its right of way with special reference to the ends of the ravines and left openings opposite such ends for the water coming down the ravines, then the plaintiff might be in a position to object to a diversion afterward of the water to the points where the sewers terminate. But it has not done so. It has permitted the city to make these changes, and has to a considerable extent adopted the plan of the city, by closing up all openings for egress of water at the ends of the ravines, and putting in the box culverts opposite the ends of the sewers. Estoppel by conduct, if any exists, is against the plaintiff, not against the city.

The defendant is not liable for failing to relieve plaintiff of the burdens put on plaintiff's premises by nature, or for failing to provide a sewer system for plaintiff's premises. "The duty of providing drainage or sewerage is in its nature judicial or legislative, and consequently a municipal corporation

is not liable for mere nonaction **501** in failing to perform it":
McClure v. *City of Red Wing*, 28 Minn. 194.

It is true that the water comes down against plaintiff's
right of way with considerable velocity, but that is a velocity
given it by the hillside, which was made by nature and
not by the city.

It seems to us that the case is simply this: Can the owner
of a swamp improve it and then compel the owner of the
high land around it to keep the surface water naturally tributary to the swamp from coming from the higher lands upon
the swamp? We think not.

For these reasons the order denying the motion for a new
trial should be reversed.   So ordered.

MUNICIPAL CORPORATIONS—SEWERS—SURFACE WATER.—A city is liable
for collecting surface water by artificial means, such as sewers and drains,
and casting it upon the premises of another in increased and injurious quantities. It is the duty of the city to provide by adequate means for passing
off the water thus concentrated in volume, so as to avoid doing damage to
private property; and if it allows the water to accumulate in large quantities at the mouth of a sewer, and thus overflow private property, the city
is liable in damages: See monographic note to *Chalkley* v. *City of Richmond*,
29 Am. St. Rep. 743, treating of the subject at length. The authorities,
however, show many circumstances under which the owner would be without redress: See *Kansas City* v. *Brady*, 52 Kan. 297; 39 Am. St. Rep. 349,
and note; and monographic note to *Goddard* v. *Inhabitants of Harpswell*,
30 Am St. Rep. 390.

IN RE MINNETONKA LAKE IMPROVEMENT.

[56 MINNESOTA, 513.]

"HIGH-WATER MARK," as a line between a riparian owner and the public,
on fresh-water rivers and lakes, is to be determined by examining the
bed and banks, and ascertaining where the presence and action of the
water are so common and usual as to mark upon the soil of the bed a
character distinct from that of the banks in respect to vegetation as
well as to the nature of the soil itself. It is co-ordinate with the limit
of the bed of the water.

"BED OF THE WATER."—That only is to be considered the "bed of the
water" which the water occupies so long and continuously as to wrest
it from vegetation and destroy its value for agricultural purposes. It
does not include lowlands which, although subject to frequent overflow, are valuable as meadows or pastures.

EMINENT DOMAIN—TAKING LAND IN AID OF NAVIGATION.—The state has
no right, even in aid of navigation, to permanently maintain the waters
of a lake, by artificial means, at a uniform height above high-water
mark, to the material damage of lands of riparian owners. If it does
so, the act constitutes a taking of their property which entitles them to
compensation.

To Support a Special Assessment for a Local Improvement the benefit for which the land is assessed must be secured.   In other words, it must appear that benefits for which persons are asked to pay will be received.   Hence, an assessment for a local benefit, under an act authorizing the waters of a lake to be permanently maintained, by artificial means, at a uniform height above high-water mark, but which makes no provision for compensating riparian owners for injuries to their lands caused by raising the waters, is invalid.

Prescriptive Right to Overflow Lands.—Merely maintaining a dam on one's own land, without thereby raising the water, will not create a prescriptive right upon the lands of another.   It is only the uninterrupted flowing of such lands for the statutory period that will create such a right.

Certiorari to review the confirmation of special assessments for a local improvement.   This remedy was sought as the statute made no provision for an appeal.   The assessors appointed assessed the amount of the condemnation proceedings on the property in Hennepin county, which they deemed specially benefited, taxing different parcels of land with a specific amount.   Objections to a confirmation of the assessment were overruled.   The whole evidence was embodied in a case certified, signed, and filed with the proceedings, and the record was removed to the supreme court by certiorari.

Kellogg & Laybourn, Benton, Roberts & Brown, and W. E. Dodge, for the relators.

Frank M. Nye, county attorney, and Carman N. Smith, for the respondents.

[517] Mitchell, J.   Lake Minnetonka is a large, navigable body of water, situated mainly, but not wholly, in Hennepin county.   The shores of the lake are in some places somewhat steep and abrupt, and in other places low and flat, and bounded by large tracts of lowland, only slightly elevated above the ordinary level of the water in the lake.   These lands form no part of the bed of the lake, but are more or less subject to periodical overflow at certain seasons of the year—during some years in times of high water caused by rains or melting snows; but they are sufficiently dry, when the water subsides, to be susceptible of valuable use as pastures and meadows.   The height of the water in the lake varies [518] in different years and at different seasons of the same year, according as the year or season of the year is wet or dry, the difference between extreme high water and extreme low water, according to observations taken during a series of

years, being something like 6 feet; extreme high water being
223.65, and extreme low water being 217.84, measured from
an arbitrary base line. These changes in the height of the
water are irregular, without fixed quantity or time, except
that they occur periodically, according as the year or the season of the year is wet or dry. The rises of the water, to a
sufficient height to overflow, in whole or in part, those lowlands, are not infrequent, and are liable to occur any year,
usually in the spring; but the water generally subsides later
in the season, so as to render the lands capable of use as
meadows and pastures. The outlet of the lake is Minnehaha
creek, the real point of outlet being about four miles below
the main body of the lake. About a mile below this point
there was a mill and milldam, which had been maintained
for over twenty years. The object of this dam was, apparently, to enable the owners of the mill to use the lake as a
millpond, in which to store the waters of the lake at certain
seasons of the year, and draw them off at others, as required
for the use of the mill.

In 1891 the legislature passed an act (Special Laws 1891,
c. 381) which, after reciting that it was necessary "for the
improvement of navigation, preservation of public health, and
for public advantage, benefit, and use," that the waters of the
lake should be maintained at a uniform height, sufficient to
secure these purposes, authorized the board of county commissioners of Hennepin county to establish and maintain a
uniform height of the water, "not to be above extreme high-
water mark of the waters of said lake." In order to carry
out the purposes of the act the board was authorized to
acquire, by gift, purchase, or condemnation, the dam already
referred to, together with all the rights and easements connected with or appurtenant to the same, and the land on
which the dam was situated, and such other lands adjacent
thereto as might be necessary to enable the board to maintain said waters at the height so established. As will be
seen, the act authorizes the acquisition only of lands on which
the milldam is situated, and lands or rights in land adjacent
thereto, and not of riparian lands, or rights in [519] riparian
lands, on the lake; and, of course, it makes no provision for
the payment of compensation for any such riparian lands or
riparian rights.

The act provides for the assessment, by appraisers appointed by the court, upon such lands in Hennepin county

as they deem specially benefited by the improvement, such sum as they shall deem a just proportion of the total cost of the purchase or condemnation.   Under this act the board of county commissioners established the "uniform height" at which the waters of the lake should be maintained at 220.91, measured from the base line referred to.

This is considerably above average natural low water, and below natural extreme high water in wet seasons.

Of course the effect of maintaining the water at the "uniform height" thus established would be to make such height permanent low water, except, possibly, in very dry times, when the water might altogether cease to run over the dam, and evaporation would reduce it somewhat below that level.

The evidence shows that the effect of uniformly maintaining the water of the lake at the height thus established would be to overflow permanently some of these low riparian lands, or at least to render them so wet as to destroy or seriously impair the value, for pasture or meadow, which they would have if the waters of the lake were left at their natural level.

The board of county commissioners, having acquired the milldam and adjacent lands at a cost of some twelve thousand dollars, caused further proceedings under the act to be had by which assessments for benefits were made against the lands deemed benefited.   Upon application to the court an order was made, against the objections of the appellants, confirming the assessments against their lands, and from this order they appeal.

Various objections to these assessments were interposed, but, as we view the case, it is only necessary to consider one. To support an assessment for benefits against the lands of appellants it must appear that they will receive the benefits for which they are asked to pay.   In other words, if, for any cause, the right to maintain the water at the height fixed by the commissioners cannot be secured under the act the assessments are invalid; for this is the very benefit for which appellants are taxed.

520 As no provision is made for compensation to riparian owners on the lake it follows that, if they are entitled to compensation—in other words, if what is proposed to be done constitutes a taking of their property—the assessments are void.

The respondents claim the right to maintain the water to the height established, without paying compensation to these

riparian owners, on two grounds: 1. That the state has the
right, in aid of navigation, to raise and permanently maintain navigable waters up to ordinary high-water mark without making compensation to riparian owners; 2. That the
owners of the milldam on Minnehaha creek had acquired a
prescriptive right, as against riparian owners, to raise and
maintain the water of the lake at a height as great as that
established by the county commissioners under this act.   The
second proposition may be disposed of very briefly.   In the
first place the court below declined to pass upon it, but based
its decision exclusively on the first ground.   Again, the evidence was, at least, not such as to require a finding that any
such prescriptive right had been acquired.   It, perhaps, did
appear that the milldam had been continuously maintained
for over twenty years at a height sufficient to maintain the
water at the uniform height established by the commissioners.
But merely maintaining a dam on one's own land, without
thereby raising the water, will not create a prescriptive right
upon the lands of another.   It is only the uninterrupted flowing of such lands for the statutory period that will create
such a right.   The evidence tends to show some very considerable intervals during which the water was not maintained
at any such height as is now proposed, and which would,
therefore, interrupt the prescription.   The evidence also tends
to show that, when the mill was in operation, the water was
drawn down by means of gates for power to turn machinery,
and hence, of necessity, the height of the water must have
been, much of the time, below that "uniform height" which
it is now proposed to constantly maintain under this act.

   It remains, then, to consider the first ground, viz., the right
of the state, in aid of navigation, to raise and permanently
maintain the water up to ordinary high-water mark without
making any compensation to riparian owners.   While the
title of a riparian owner on navigable or public waters extends to ordinary low-water mark, [521] yet it is unquestionably true that his title is not absolute, except to ordinary
high-water mark.   As to the intervening space, the title of
the riparian owner is qualified or limited by the public right.
The state may not only use it for purposes connected with
navigation without compensation, but may protect it from
any use of it, even by the owner of the land, that would interfere with navigation.

   It may be conceded, as claimed by respondent, that

"within the banks, and below high-water mark, the public right is supreme, and that damages to riparian proprietors are *damnum absque injuria*." But the question is, What is "high-water mark," as the line between the riparian owner and the public, and below which his title is thus qualified by the public right? It seems to us that it is right here where both the trial court and counsel have fallen into error. It seems to have been assumed that " high-water mark " means the extreme line which the water reaches (even outside its natural channel or bed) in times of high water, caused by rains or melting snows, which are not unusual or extraordinary, but occur annually, or at least frequently, during the wet season. The consequences of any such rule, if applied to our navigable rivers and inland lakes, would be very startling. Take, for example, the Mississippi river. It is subject to periodical, and almost annual, rises, usually in the spring, when the water overflows its banks, and submerges thousands of acres of bottom lands which are, at other seasons of the year, dry and valuable for timber, grass, and even agriculture. The stage of water necessary to overflow these lands is not extraordinary or unusual high water, in the popular sense, for it is liable to occur, and does occur, almost every year. And yet it would hardly be claimed that the title of the owners of these lands is qualified, and that the public might, in aid of navigation, by dams or other artificial means, maintain the water of the river at such a height as to permanently submerge and destroy these lands, without making compensation to the owners. Any such definition of "high-water mark," as a line between riparian owners and the public, is clearly inapplicable to inland fresh-water rivers and lakes, which are subject to frequent rises, causing them to overflow their natural banks.

· "High water," as applied to the sea, or rivers where the tide ebbs and flows, has a definite meaning. It is marked by the periodical flow of the tide, excluding the advance of the water above the line, [522] in the case of the sea, by winds and storms, and, in the case of the river, by floods and freshets. But in the case of fresh-water rivers and lakes—in which there is no ebb and flow of the tide, but which are subject to irregular and occasional changes of height, without fixed quantity or time, except that they are periodical, recurring with the wet or dry seasons of the year—high-water mark, as a line between a riparian owner and the public, is to be determined by examining the bed and banks, and ascertaining where the presence and action of the water are so common and usual, and so long continued in all ordinary years, as to mark upon the soil of the bed a character distinct from that of the banks, in respect to vegetation, as well as respects the nature of the soil itself.

"High-water mark" means what its language imports—a water mark. It is co-ordinate with the limit of the bed of the water; and that only is to be considered the bed which the water occupies sufficiently long and continuously to wrest it from vegetation, and destroy its value for agricultural purposes. Ordinarily the slope of the bank and the character of its soil are such that the water impresses a distinct character on the soil as well as on the vegetation. In some places, however, where the banks are low and flat, the water does not impress on the soil any well-defined line of demarcation between the bed and the banks. In such cases the effect of the water upon vegetation must be the principal test in determining the location of high-water mark as a line between the riparian owner and the public. It is the point up to which the presence and action of the water is so continuous as to destroy the value of the land for agricultural purposes by preventing the growth of vegetation, constituting what may be termed an ordinary agricultural crop—for example, hay: *Howard* v. *Ingersoll*, 13 How. 381; *Stover* v. *Jack*, 60 Pa. St. 339; 100 Am. Dec. 566; *Houghton* v. *Chicago etc. R. R. Co.*, 47 Iowa, 370; *Plumb* v. *McGannon*, 32 U. C. Q. B. 8; Gould on Waters, sec. 45.

The evidence tends to show that what is proposed to be done under this act is to permanently maintain the water at a uniform height above high-water mark, as thus defined, to the material damage of lands of riparian owners. This constitutes a taking of their property which entitles them to compensation: *Weaver* v. *Mississippi & Rum River Boom Co.*, 28 Minn. 534. It follows that [523] the benefits for which appellants' lands have been assessed are not secured to them by the proceedings under this act.

We have assumed as facts what the evidence tends to prove, but it is proper to add that these proceedings are not conclusive on the riparian owners who are not parties to them; and, as the act contains no provision for making them parties, it is impossible, in any proceedings under it, to certainly determine that any benefit is secured to appellants.

Order reversed.   ——

EMINENT DOMAIN—OVERFLOWING LANDS.—Private property cannot be taken under the right of eminent domain, in the absence of the owner's consent, without fully compensating him therefor: See monographic note to *Gainesville etc. Ry. Co.* v. *Hall,* 22 Am. St. Rep. 49. The raising of water, by artificial means, so as to permanently overflow adjacent lands, is a damage for which compensation must be made: See monographic notes to *Sheehy* v. *Kansas City etc. Ry. Co.,* 4 Am. St. Rep. 403; *Vanderlip* v. *City of Grand Rapids,* 16 Am. St. Rep. 611, treating of the subject at some length. And the same damages are to be allowed where lands are permanently overflowed as if they had been taken outright: See monographic note to *Winona etc. R. R. Co.* v. *Waldron,* 88 Am. Dec. 114, on damages in eminent domain cases.

LOCAL ASSESSMENTS may be levied by the legislature for many purposes, but the object must be one productive of special local benefits: Note to *Zigler* v. *Menges,* 16 Am. St. Rep. 371.

—— ——

TATE *v.* CITY OF ST. PAUL.

[56 MINNESOTA, 527.] ·

MUNICIPAL CORPORATIONS — DAMAGES — PUBLIC WORK — SEWERS. — If a public work, for instance, a sewer, as the same was originally planned and constructed, is found to result in direct and physical injury to the property of another, that would not otherwise have happened, and which, from its nature, is liable to be repeated and continuous, but is remediable by a change of plan or the adoption of prudent measures, the corporation is liable for such damages as occur in consequence of the original cause, after notice and an omission to use ordinary care to remedy the evil.

MUNICIPAL CORPORATIONS — DAMAGES — SEWERS. — There is a distinction between injuries incidental to the exercise of municipal legislative functions and direct and positive wrongs. For the former no action will lie; but for the latter the party injured may recover. Hence, a city is liable for damages caused by a sewer of insufficient size in setting back water into the plaintiff's cellar.

ACTION against the city to recover damages to property caused by a sewer of insufficient size. The complaint charged that the injury was caused by the negligence of defendant in not properly designing and building the sewers, and in collecting therein too large an amount and volume of water, and not making sufficient outlets therefor. The city answered by a general denial, and also alleged that the sewers were constructed pursuant to plans and specifications

prepared by the city engineer and approved by the board
of public works and the common council of the city. The
plaintiff obtained a verdict, and his damages were assessed
at three hundred and fifty dollars. The city appealed from
an order denying its motion for a new trial.

Leon T. Chamberlain and Frederic A. Pike, for the appellant.

John L. Townley, for the respondent.

[528] GILFILLAN, C. J.   The action is to recover damages
arising from a sewer laid by defendant, and with which plaintiff had connected, as he had a right to do, setting the water
in it back so that it flooded plaintiff's basements.   The defect
alleged in the sewer was that it was of insufficient capacity
to carry off the water brought into it.   The defect appears to
have existed in the original plan for sewering that part of
the city; that is, the city, in determining upon a system [529]
of sewers, determined upon the sizes required for the main
sewer and for the lateral sewers running into it, and the size
determined on for the former proved too small.

The rule is uniformly conceded that for injuries wholly incidental to, and consequential upon, the exercise by a municipal corporation of the legislative or discretionary powers
intrusted to it (as distinguished from its ministerial acts) no
action will lie against it.   Instances of the application of that
rule are furnished by *Lee* v. *City of Minneapolis,* 22 Minn. 13,
where the power exercised was establishing the grade of a
street under the charter, and *Alden* v. *City of Minneapolis,* 24
Minn. 254, where the city had established a system of grades
for streets and sidewalks, and drains, gutters, catch-basins,
and sewers, and had constructed the streets, sidewalks, drains,
and gutters, and partially completed the sewers.   The complaint was that the sewers, drains, gutters, and catch-basins
were not sufficient to carry off the surface water falling in
rains upon the streets, so that it flowed from the streets upon
plaintiff's lot.

The line between legislative acts and ministerial acts of a
municipal corporation is not very clearly marked by the decisions, nor is it necessary to attempt to trace it in this case.

Some of the earlier cases do not clearly recognize the distinction between injuries incidental to the exercise of municipal and legislative functions and direct and positive wrongs, such, for instance, as trespass, caused by it. The later and better authorities, however, recognize the distinction, and, while adhering to the rule that for the former no action will lie, hold that for the latter the party may recover. The distinction is apparent, though it is not clearly discussed in either of the cases of *O'Brien* v. *City of St. Paul*, 18 Minn. 176, and 25 Minn. 331; 33 Am. Rep. 470; *Kobs* v. *City of Minneapolis*, 22 Minn. 159, and the Lee and Alden cases above cited.

To determine when and upon what plan a public improvement shall be made is, unless the charter otherwise provides, left to the judgment of the proper municipal authorities, and is, in its nature, legislative. And, although the power is vested in the municipality for the benefit and relief of property, error of judgment as to when or upon what plan the improvement shall be made, resulting only [530] in incidental injury to the property, will not be ground of action; as, if, in grading streets to the authorized grades, the plan of the grading is inadequate to drain a lot of the surface water, or even if it make it more difficult and expensive for the owner to drain it, or make access to the lot more difficult, that is a result incidental to the improvement. But for a direct invasion of one's right of property, even though contemplated by, or necessarily resulting from, the plan adopted, an action will lie; otherwise, it would be taking private property for public use without compensation. Thus, if, in cutting a street down a grade, the soil of an abutting lot is precipitated into the cut, or if, in filling up to grade, the slope of the embankment is made to rest on private property, that is a direct invasion of property rights which cannot be justified, even though the plan adopted contemplates, or will necessarily produce, the result.

Judge Dillon, in his work on Municipal Corporations, fourth edition, sections 1047 to 1051, approves the rule laid down in more recent decisions by some of our ablest courts, that if a sewer, whatever its plan, is so constructed as to cause a positive and direct invasion of private property, as by collecting and throwing upon it, to its damage, water or sewage which would not otherwise have flowed or found its way there, the corporation is liable. Conspicuous for their ability, among the cases referred to by him, are *Ashley* v. *Port Huron*, 35 Mich. 296; 24 Am. Rep. 552, and *Seifert* v. *City of Brooklyn*, 101 N. Y. 136; 54 Am. Rep. 664, each, the former especially, a very interesting case: See, also, *Brayton* v. *Fall River*, 113 Mass. 218; 18 Am. Rep. 470; *Lehn* v. *San Francisco*, 66 Cal. 76; *Weis* v. *City of Madison*, 75 Ind. 241; 39 Am. Rep. 135. It is impossible to answer the reasoning of these cases, especially where the injury complained of constitutes a taking. That making one's premises a place of deposit for the surplus waters in the sewers in times of high water, or creating a nuisance upon them so as to deprive the owner of the beneficial use of his property, is an appropriation requiring compensation to be made, see *Weaver* v. *Mississippi etc. Boom Co.*, 28 Minn. 534.

The court below instructed the jury "that where a public work, for instance a sewer, as the same was originally planned and constructed, [531] is found to result in direct and physical injury to the property of another, that would not otherwise have happened, and which, from its nature, is liable to be repeated and continuous, but is remediable by a change of plan or the adoption of prudent measure, the corporation is liable for such damages as occur in consequence of the original cause, after notice and an omission to use ordinary care to remedy the evil."

This is within the rule stated in Dillon and the cases cited, and, as it gives the corporation an opportunity to correct or obviate the error in the original plan before liability, we do not hesitate to approve it. This is as far as we need go in this case.

The evidence was such as to justify a verdict for plaintiff under that charge of the court.

Order affirmed.

————

MUNICIPAL CORPORATIONS—DAMAGES—DEFECTIVE SEWERS.—A city is liable in damages for injury resulting from defective or negligently constructed sewers: *Allen* v. *City of Boston*, 159 Mass. 324; 38 Am. St. Rep. 423; *Chalkley* v. *City of Richmond*, 88 Va. 402; 29 Am. St. Rep. 730, and monographic note thereto discussing the subject at length.

CASES

SUPREME COURT

MISSOURI.

BELL v. CAMPBELL.

[123 MISSOURI, 1.]

FRAUD—UNDUE INFLUENCE.—If an illiterate woman, unacquainted with business affairs and of great age, is induced to execute a mortgage to the sureties on the bond of her son in law, who is threatened by them with criminal prosecution for a defalcation of public funds, after persistent and uninterrupted importunities by such sureties, without an opportunity on her part to advise with disinterested friends, and only to save the son in law from such prosecution, she is entitled to have the mortgage canceled in equity for fraud, and she is not *in pari delicto* with such parties so as to bar her of such relief.

FRAUD—UNDUE INFLUENCE—EQUITABLE RELIEF.—A party is entitled to relief in equity whenever undue advantage is taken of him under circumstances which mislead, confuse, or disturb the just result of his judgment, if proper time is not allowed him, and he acts improvidently, or is importunately pressed, and if those in whom he places confidence make use of strong persuasions, and he is not fully aware of the consequences, but is suddenly drawn in to act without being permitted to consult counsel or disinterested friends.

UNDUE INFLUENCE.—WHATEVER DESTROYS FREE AGENCY and constrains the person whose act is brought in judgment to do what is against his will, and what he would not have done if left to himself, is undue influence whether the control be exercised by physical force, threats, importunity, or any other species of mental or physical coercion.

EQUITY—PARTIES IN PARI DELICTO.—Equity interferes for the relief of the less guilty of parties *in pari delicto*, whose transgression has been brought about by the imposition or undue influence of the party on whom the burden of the original wrong principally rests.

MORTGAGES—CANCELLATION FOR FRAUD—STATUTE OF LIMITATIONS.—If an illiterate and aged woman is induced under undue influence to execute a mortgage indemnifying the sureties on the bond of her son in law who is threatened by them with a criminal prosecution for a misappropriation of public funds, the fact that she does not institute proceedings to cancel the mortgage for fraud until the statute of limita-

(505)

tions has barred the prosecution of the son in law does not bar her of relief.

Mortgages—Cancellation for Fraud—Presumption.—Acquiescence in a mortgage under such circumstances as to render it voidable for fraud and undue influence cannot be presumed from a failure of the mortgagor to move for its cancellation while the same conditions which caused its execution continue.

Negotiable Instruments.—Indorsements of Payment of Interest on Notes is *prima facie* evidence of such payment by the maker thereof, but such presumption is rebutted by the testimony of the maker to the contrary.

Mortgages—Cancellation for Fraud—Defenses.—In an action to cancel a mortgage procured by the fraud and undue influence of the mortgagor's son in law and the sureties on his bond, and executed solely to indemnify such sureties against the result of a threatened criminal prosecution of the son in law for a misappropriation of public funds, such sureties cannot set up as a defense the fact that the mortgagor has failed to reconvey land deeded to him by the son-in-law as a part of the same transaction, and at the same time deny that they are chargeable with any thing done by the son in law in the same matter.

Mortgages—Cancellation for Fraud—Reconveyance.—A mortgagor seeking to cancel a mortgage for fraud and undue influence in its execution must tender a reconveyance of land conveyed to him as part of the same transaction.

Mortgages—Cancellation for Fraud—Reconveyance.—If a mortgagor in an action to cancel a mortgage for fraud and undue influence tenders a quitclaim deed to land conveyed to him as part of the same transaction the court may compel a reconveyance as the price of a decree in his favor.

Action to cancel a deed of trust on a farm and to cancel notes secured thereby, on the ground that they had been obtained by fraud, undue influence, and improper practices. This deed of trust was executed by plaintiff, Mrs. Bell, on June 25, 1888, to the defendant Campbell, as trustee for the Saxton National Bank, and two others, to secure three notes aggregating seven thousand seven hundred dollars due in three years, with interest at eight per cent per annum, payable every ninety days, and given by plaintiff to the several beneficiaries before mentioned. Plaintiff, at the time of executing the deed of trust and notes, was a widow, ignorant, illiterate, unaccustomed to business affairs, and about seventy years of age. She had left the said farm, and had moved to the city, and was at this time living near her son in law, H. C. Carter, who had married her daughter, and who enjoyed her confidence, and attended to her business affairs. Said Carter, prior to June, 1888, was treasurer of the city of St. Joseph, Missouri, and in that capacity had defaulted in the sum of seven thousand

seven hundred dollars. His bondsmen, so far as need be
mentioned here, were A. N. Schuster, president of the Schuster-Hax National Bank; C. F. Burnes, president of the
National Bank; S. C. Woodson, vice-president of the Saxton
National Bank, and S. A. Walker, cashier of the Schuster-
Hax National Bank, all of St. Joseph, Missouri. Shortly
after the defalcation it was agreed between these bondsmen
and Carter that each of the three named banks should lend
Carter one-third of the amount of his defalcation, and that
they would accept a joint deed of trust on the Bell farm as
security. The plaintiff was not informed of this agreement,
or consulted with reference to it. She had no notice of Carter's defalcation until about four days before she signed the
deed of trust and notes secured thereby, nor was she informed
in any way respecting the responsibility she was then called
upon to assume. Carter, when confronted with his defalcation and its consequences, determined to raise money out of
the Bell farm to make it good. For this purpose he sent for
Mrs. Bell, and had her come to his house about four days
before the trust deed and notes were executed, and kept her
there until the transaction was consummated. When she
arrived he began to importune her to execute such instruments. He disclosed to her his situation, the amount of his
defalcation, his •inability to raise the amount without her
help, the likelihood that he would be arrested and imprisoned
unless the money was obtained, and implored her to save him
from disgrace, by giving a mortgage on her farm, but this
she stoutly refused to do. Again and again he renewed his
importunities during the next four days, threatening to commit
suicide unless she consented, and procured his wife and child
to unite their importunities with his incessantly during such
four days. One of his bondsmen, S. C. Woodson, and one Englehart, the mayor of St. Joseph, also importuned Mrs. Bell to
execute the mortgage, assuring her that Carter would not be
suspended from office or prosecuted if his shortage was made
good. Under these trying circumstances, and immediately
after the departure of Woodson and Englehart, a notary
named Hedenberg came to the house with the three notes
and the deed of trust in question, together with a warranty
deed from Carter to plaintiff, which such notary had been
directed by Carter to prepare and bring to the house. Mrs.
Bell showed great hesitation about signing the notes and
mortgage, and the notary was about to leave, but at Carter's

request lingered until the completion of a conversation between Mrs. Bell and Carter. He did not hear this conversation, but at its termination he was recalled for the purpose of
having the notes and mortgage executed. He then signed
and witnessed Mrs. Bell's name to them, and she, though
much agitated, added her mark to her signature as made by
him. These notes and the deed of trust being signed and
duly acknowledged by Mrs. Bell, then, for the first time,
the deed from Carter to her was produced. She then
thought, and afterward continued to think, that such deed
was merely a mortgage on Carter's property. Carter and
wife also executed a note in favor of Mrs. Bell for seven thousand seven hundred dollars, which was handed to her with
Carter's deed, but without her knowledge of its execution
or existence. Hedenberg handed the deed of trust and
notes from Mrs. Bell to Carter. The latter took the note in
favor of the Saxton National Bank, together with the deed of
trust on the Bell farm, to that bank. Woodson then approved
the loan, had the trust deed recorded, and directed a credit
to the Schuster-Hax Bank. Carter on the next day handed
the remaining two notes executed by Mrs. Bell to Mr. Walker,
of the Schuster-Hax Bank. These notes were made payable
to Burnes and Schuster, and by them indorsed to their
respective banks. Walker then got a cashier's check from
the National Bank of St. Joseph, and credited seven thousand
seven hundred dollars to Carter's account therein as city
treasurer. Interest was regularly paid on these notes, but
not by Mrs. Bell, nor out of her money. She heard nothing
more of them until they matured, and upon her failure to
pay them, the farm was advertised and sold under the deed
of trust, Woodson purchasing it at such sale for five thousand
dollars. Pending these foreclosure proceedings, and before
the sale, Mrs. Bell instituted this proceeding to cancel the
notes and deed of trust. Judgment in the court below dismissing plaintiff's petition, and she appealed.

S. S. Brown and J. F. Pitt, for the appellant.

Porter & Woodson and B. R. Vineyard, for the respondents.

[14] SHERWOOD, J. Upon the facts thus presented, a conclusion is to be reached and announced whether plaintiff is
entitled to any relief.

That plaintiff owed the city nothing and the beneficiaries
in the deed of trust nothing stands conceded. That Carter's

bondsmen owed the city seven thousand seven hundred dollars is equally undisputed. And yet this was the sole basis and the groundwork upon which plaintiff was so persistently and constantly importuned for days and days to surrender her little all; to beggar herself in order that the bondsmen might be saved harmless, and she made poor indeed. On the very morning that this most indefensible transaction found its blameworthy consummation this poor, ignorant, illiterate old woman, fast verging on the biblical limit of threescore years and ten, for over three hours was kept on the rack of varying emotions. Within that time every argument that could be advanced was used, every chord of human feeling and affection that could be played upon was struck by the sordid hand of self-interest, or the tremulous hand of anticipated punishment, in the endeavor to swerve her from her purpose; how well it succeeded is matter now of record.

The circumstances of this case clearly bring it within the operation of the principle that condemns and avoids a contract entered into where the obligor is not a free agent; where he stands *in vinculis;* where he is not equal to the task of protecting himself; where the circumstances which surround him at the time are of such extreme necessity or of distress that his will is overcome, his free agency destroyed by some oppression or fraudulent advantage or imposition incident to the transaction; in such case a court of equity will [15] protect him, by setting aside the contract thus made: 1 Story's Equity Jurisprudence, 13th cd., sec. 239.

In instances like the present, where surprise and sudden action are the chief ingredients, where due deliberation is therefore wanting, these incidents are classed by courts of equity under the head of fraud or imposition. Wherever undue advantage is taken of party " under circumstances which mislead, confuse, or disturb the just result of his judgment, and thus expose him to be the victim of the artful, the importunate, and the cunning," where " proper time is not allowed to the party, and he acts improvidently, if he is importunately pressed, if those in whom he places confidence make use of strong persuasions, if he is not fully aware of the consequences, but is suddenly drawn in to act, if he is not permitted to consult disinterested friends or counsel before he is called upon to act in circumstances of sudden emergency or unexpected right or acquisition—in these and many like cases, if there has been great inequality in the bargain, courts of equity will assist the party upon the ground of fraud, imposition, or unconscionable advantage": 1 Story's Equity Jurisprudence, 13th ed., sec. 251, and cases cited.

Other cases announce the same principle and its application to like circumstances as are here presented: *Turley* v. *Edwards*, 18 Mo. App. 676; *Sharon* v. *Gager*, 46 Conn. 189; *Foley* v. *Greene*, 14 R. I. 618; 51 Am. Rep. 419; *Jordan* v. *Elliott*, 15 Cent. L. J. 232; *Meech* v. *Lee*, 82 Mich. 274; *Eadie* v. *Slimmon*, 26 N. Y. 9; 82 Am. Dec. 395; *Coffman* v. *Lookout Bank*, 5 Lea, 232; 40 Am. Rep. 31; *Berlien* v. *Bieler*, 96 Mo. 491.

The true question as announced by Lord Eldon in *Peel* v. ———, 16 Ves. 157, in all such cases is, "whether the mind was not so subdued, that though the execution was the free act of that person, it was an [16] act, speaking the mind, not of that person, but of another."

In *Earle* v. *Norfolk etc. Co.*, 36 N. J. Eq. 192, Van Fleet, V. C., aptly epitomizes this whole doctrine when he says: "Whatever destroys free agency and constrains the person whose act is brought in judgment to do what is against his will, and what he would not have done if left to himself, is undue influence, whether the control be exercised by physical force, threats, importunity, or any other species of mental or physical coercion."

The testimony in this case shows in the most indubitable manner that the act of plaintiff in touching the pen and in acknowledging the deed and the notes was purely automatic and perfunctory. It is urged that if the deed of trust and notes executed by plaintiff had been given through fear of Carter's criminal prosecution, and in order to prevent the same, that then she stands *in pari delicto* with the other parties to the transaction, and, therefore, could have no relief against the enforcement of those writings obligatory.

There are two answers to this contention: 1. Granting that plaintiff did enter into the contract with that purpose in view, she will not be debarred from pursuing her remedy, because she cannot in any event be regarded as equally culpable with the adversary parties. When this is the case a court of equity will interfere and go to the relief of the less guilty party, whose transgression has been brought about by the imposition, undue influence, etc., of the party on whom the burden of the original blameworthiness principally rests:

2 Pomeroy's Equity Jurisprudence, 2d cd., sec. 942; 1 Story's Equity Jurisprudence, 13th ed., sec. 300; *Pinckston* v. *Brown,* 3 Jones Eq., 494; *Kitchen* v. *Greenabaum,* 61 Mo. 115; 2. For reasons already given, plaintiff cannot be regarded [17] as having entered into a binding contract that can prejudice her rights.

It is insisted that plaintiff should have moved more promptly for cancellation of the alleged contract; but we fail to appreciate the force of this position, because the notes had three years to run, evidently made so for a purpose. The statute of limitations would bar any prosecution of Carter at the end of that period. During that time the same prospect of family disgrace was held over plaintiff that was used originally to procure, and was such a potent factor in procuring, the execution of the securities, and, if plaintiff had instituted her proceedings for relief at an earlier date, she would have been confronted by the same situation, the same circumstances of moral duress and imposition which confronted her in the first instance. In such circumstances her failure to move sooner in the matter is not to be accounted acquiescence on her part. On this topic Sir William Grant, M. R., said: "There is, I believe, no case in which, during the continuance of the same situation in which the party entered into the contract, acquiescence has ever gone for any thing; it has always been presumed that the same distress which pressed him to enter into the contract prevented him from coming to set it aside; that it is only when he is relieved from that distress that he can be expected to resist the performance of the contract": *Gowland* v. *De Faria,* 17 Ves. 20.

In *Buck* v. *First Nat. Bank,* 27 Mich. 293, 15 Am. Rep. 189, the note had been given for money of which the defendant claimed her son had robbed the bank, and that such note had been executed upon an understanding that the bank would use its influence to mitigate any punishment the son had incurred a liability in receiving, and, in a suit on that note, the plaintiff bank was allowed to show that [18] when interest on the notes was arranged before the principal became due, defendant did not object to the payment of the notes. But the court said: "We think no such presumption could safely be drawn from this evidence. The notes were negotiable, and if the bank officers should be apprised of an intended defense before they fell due, it would be reasonable to expect they would endeavor to protect themselves by negotiating them. The makers of the notes were consequently interested in keeping silent regarding their defense, and it is as legitimate to refer their action to prudence as to any other motive. The evidence, we think, should not have been received. And for the same reason no inference against the *bona fides* of the defense could safely be drawn from the mere fact of the payment of interest by the makers of the notes before the maturity of the principal. To disclose their defense at that time would have been to defeat it, so far, at least, as concerned the principal."

On this point of acquiescence, or seeming acquiescence, Judge Story says: " But if the party is still acting under the pressure of the original transaction or the original necessity, or if he is still under the influence of the original transaction, and of the delusive opinion that it is valid and binding upon him, then, and under such circumstances, courts of equity will hold him not barred from relief from any such confirmation": 1 Story's Equity Jurisprudence, sec. 345.

As a further proof of plaintiff's acquiescence in the alleged contract the notes are offered in evidence showing indorsements of interest paid thereon. While these indorsements are *prima facie* evidence of payment by the maker, such presumption is rebutted by testimony of plaintiff that she had never had the money to make even one of the payments. Conduct evincing the same sort of cunning is exhibited in the note to the [19] Saxon bank being surreptitiously signed by Carter as co-maker with plaintiff, though no one could tell how or when it was signed by him.

Defendants claim that plaintiff could not exercise the right of rescission without tendering back all she received from Carter, to wit, the warranty deed and note for seven thousand seven hundred dollars. Plaintiff never asked for this deed or note; they were simply part and parcel of an adroit scheme to make an apparent show of a consideration for plaintiff's execution of the deed of trust and the three notes, and were dexterously foisted on plaintiff for that purpose. The evidence shows very clearly that the warranty deed and the note of Carter's for seven thousand seven hundred dollars were executed after plaintiff had executed the three notes and deed of trust, and that she made no use of them and never recorded the deed, and in fact did not even know its nature; thought it was a " mortgage." But it does not lie in defendants' mouths to set up this claim about Carter's property, and still at the same time deny, as they do, that they are chargeable with any thing Carter did in the transaction. Such inconsistent positions will not be tolerated in a court of justice: *Brown* v. *Bowen,* 90 Mo. 190; *McClanahan* v. *West,* 100 Mo. 309, 322, and cases cited.

Nor does it concern defendants in regard to the land of Carter described in the warranty deed; it is not involved in this litigation. A similar ruling was made in *Meech* v. *Lee,* 82 Mich. 274.

Again, the same considerations which would go to over-throw the original contract, would necessarily destroy the one alleged to be auxiliary thereto. Plaintiff could not pro-cure the cancellation of the first and still retain the benefits of the second, nor would the trial court allow her to do so, in the event a decree went for her.

[20] Moreover, plaintiff in her petition recognized this, in which she tendered to Carter a quitclaim deed for the prop-erty that he had conveyed to her, and under this tender the circuit court could have compelled a conveyance and made it the price of the decree it gave her: *Whelan* v. *Reilly,* 61 Mo. 565, and cases cited; *Dwen* v. *Blake,* 44 Ill. 141, and cases cited.

Finally, defendants assert that we ought to defer some-what to the conclusions reached by the lower court; but, while we do this, we do not neglect to review its rulings and the evidence offered in their support; to do otherwise would be to abdicate our jurisdiction in chancery causes: *Benne* v. *Schnecko,* 100 Mo. 250, 258; *McElroy* v. *Maxwell,* 101 Mo. 294, 308, et seq; *Berlien* v. *Bieler,* 96 Mo. 491.

The premises considered, we reverse the decree of the lower court dismissing plaintiff's petition, and remand the cause with directions to take an account of the rents and profits of the farm as is usual in case of a mortgagee in posses-sion, and having adjusted this matter then to enter a decree canceling the deed of trust and notes secured thereby, and to take such other steps as may be necessary and not inconsist-ent with this opinion, in which shall be included the bring-ing in as a party defendant of the purchaser of Mrs. Bell's farm, and the ascertainment and reconveyance by quitclaim deed of whatever land or other securities Mrs. Bell may have received from Carter.

All of this division concur.

UNDUE INFLUENCE—WHAT IS.—If by physical or mental superiority one obtains an advantage in a transaction over another who is enfeebled in mind and body by disease or old age, the person obtaining such advantage is required to show that the transaction was a fair one: *Goodbar* v. *Lidikey,* 136 Ind. 1; 43 Am. St. Rep. 296. Undue influence to vitiate an act must amount to coercion, destroying free agency, or harassing importunity producing compliance for the sake of peace: *Gardner* v. *Gardner,* 22 Wend. 526; 34 Am. Dec. 340, and note.

EQUITY—PARTIES IN PARI DELICTO.—A court of equity will not aid either party to an illegal contract, but will leave them where it finds them: *Brooks* v. *Cooper,* 50 N. J. Eq. 761; 35 Am. St. Rep. 793, and note; *Garrett* v. *Kansas City etc. Min. Co.,* 113 Mo. 330; 35 Am. St. Rep. 713, and note. A court of equity will set aside a conveyance at the instance of the grantor, although it was intended to defeat the law, if the parties did not stand upon an equal footing, and the conveyance was obtained through the false representations of the grantee. In such a case the parties are *in delicto,* but not *in pari delicto: Harper* v. *Harper,* 85 Ky. 160; 7 Am. St. Rep. 583, and extended note.

EQUITY.—CANCELLATION OF INSTRUMENTS: See the note to *Fitzmaurice* v. *Mosier,* 9 Am. St. Rep. 859.

NICHOLS *v.* STEVENS.

[123 MISSOURI, 96.]

JUDGMENTS AGAINST CORPORATIONS — CONCLUSIVENESS AGAINST STOCKHOLDER.—In the absence of fraud or collusion a judgment against a corporation is valid and binding against a stockholder as to his liability for unpaid stock subscriptions, until reversed by him in some direct proceeding for that purpose, and cannot be collaterally attacked.

JUDGMENTS AGAINST CORPORATIONS OBTAINED BY FRAUD — ATTACK BY STOCKHOLDER.—Fraud in obtaining a judgment against a corporation, to enable a stockholder to attack it, either directly or collaterally, must be actual fraud as distinguished from a judgment obtained on false evidence or a forged instrument.

FRAUD—PLEADING.—The facts constituting fraud must be clearly stated, whether it is alleged in a petition as a cause of action or in an answer as a ground of defense.

CORPORATIONS—STOCKHOLDER'S LIABILITY—RELEASE.—The officers or directors of a corporation cannot release a stockholder from liability thereto, to the prejudice of corporation creditors.

PRACTICE—AMENDMENTS—PRESUMPTION.—In the absence of exceptions it is to be presumed on appeal that amendments to pleadings permitted by the court below were properly permitted and made.

APPEAL—MATTERS NOT NOTICED ON.—A recitation in the record on appeal of matters not belonging thereto, but belonging solely to the bill of exceptions, cannot be noticed in an appellate court.

APPEAL—MATTERS NOT REVIEWED ON.—If no objection is raised to a form of pleading and no exception is saved to an amendment thereto permitted by the trial court the point that a change of cause of action is thereby made cannot be urged on appeal.

REMOVAL OF CAUSES.—When a cause has been removed to a federal court, and remanded because the petition for removal does not set up the diverse citizenship of the parties at the commencement of the suit, a second removal on the same ground is not allowable.

REMOVAL OF A CAUSE TO A FEDERAL COURT must be refused if not petitioned for in time.

PLAINTIFF Nichols obtained a judgment against the Texas & Atlantic Refrigerator Car Company based upon two notes for five thousand eight hundred dollars and four thousand two hundred dollars, respectively, executed by said company through its president, J. R. Barrett. This judgment was obtained by default. ·Execution issued thereon, and was returned *nulla bona*, except as to costs and twelve dollars which were credited thereon. Plaintiff then commenced proceedings, under section 2517 of the Revised Statutes of Missouri of 1889, to procure the issuing of executions against Stevens and Mirrick, stockholders in said company, to satisfy said judgment against it. Stevens and Mirrick filed answers, and afterward filed a petition, and gave bond to remove the case to the United States circuit court. In that court the defendants had separate verdicts and judgments rendered against them. Stevens then took his branch of the case to the United States supreme court by writ of error, and Mirrick filed a petition for an injunction to restrain the issuing of execution against him. Before this petition was acted upon the United States supreme court reversed the judgment as to Stevens, and remanded the case to the Missouri state court, on the ground that the case had not been properly removed to the federal courts, and that they had never acquired jurisdiction, because the affidavit for removal did not set forth the diverse citizenship of the parties at the time of the commencement of the suit.

The case being thus remanded, it again came on for hearing before the state court when defendant Stevens filed a verified motion to amend his petition for removal of the case to a federal court, by interlineation showing the facts, before mentioned as omitted.

This motion was denied and an exception preserved. Plaintiff then, on the same day, filed amended motions or petitions against the defendants Stevens and Mirrick, respectively, as follows:

[Title of Court and Cause.]

"Now comes plaintiff, and, leave of court therefor first being had and obtained, for his amended motion or petition states: That the Texas & Atlantic Refrigerator Car Company was, on May 1, 1875, and ever since has been, and now is, a corporation duly created and organized under the laws of the state of Missouri, and having its chief office in Pettis county, Missouri.

"That on the sixth day of May, 1875, said corporation, by its president and duly authorized agents, executed and delivered its certain promissory note, dated on that day, to one J. R. Barrett, whereby it promised, for value received, to pay, three months after the date thereof, to the order of J. R. Barrett, at the Commercial Bank of St. Louis, the sum of fifty-eight hundred dollars, which said note was afterward by J. R. Barrett indorsed and delivered to this plaintiff for a valuable consideration.

"That on the fourteenth day of May, 1875, the said corporation, by its president and duly authorized agent, executed and delivered to said J. R. Barrett its other promissory note, dated on that day, whereby it promised for value received to pay, three months after date thereof, to the order of J. R. Barrett at the Commercial Bank of St. Louis, the sum of forty-two hundred dollars, which said note was afterward by J. R. Barrett indorsed and delivered to this plaintiff for a valuable consideration.

"That, default having been made in the payment of both of said notes, this plaintiff brought suit upon both of said notes in the circuit court of Pettis county, Missouri, on December 11, 1875, against said corporation, and on the twenty-sixth day of January, 1876, at the January term, 1876, of said court obtained judgment on said notes against said corporation for the sum of ten thousand three hundred and seventy-seven and twenty-one one-hundredths dollars ($10,377.21), with ten per cent per annum interest thereon, and for his costs in said suit taxed at the sum of six and seventy-five one-hundredths dollars; that afterward, on the thirty-first day of January, 1876, this plaintiff caused an execution to be issued on said judgment from the office of the clerk of said court, which said execution was, on the first day of February, 1876, placed in the hands of the sheriff of Pettis county, Missouri, and was by said sheriff, on the twenty-fourth day of February, 1876, levied upon all the property of said corporation which could be found in said county; that said sheriff, on the seventh day of March, 1876, sold said property for the sum of twenty-five dollars, of which he applied on the costs the sum

of thirteen dollars, and credited upon said judgment the sum
of twelve dollars, and returned said execution not satisfied as
to the balance of said judgment, 'there being no other goods,
chattels, or property found belonging to the defendant, upon
which to levy this execution.'

" Plaintiff states that except said sum of twelve dollars no
part of said judgment has ever been paid, and that the balance thereof with interest thereon remains unpaid, and is
still due to plaintiff.

" Plaintiff further states that the defendant, Robert S.
Stevens, is a stockholder in said corporation, and has been
ever since said May 1, 1875, holding and owning certificates
of stock therein to the amount of five thousand dollars; that
upon said stock said defendant has paid to said corporation
the sum of one thousand dollars, and that the balance of
said amount of stock subscribed and held by him is still due
and unpaid, and which plaintiff demanded of said defendant
on March 7, 1876.

" Wherefore plaintiff prays the court that it enter its order
and judgment that plaintiff recover of defendant said sum of
four thousand dollars, with interest thereon from March 7,
1876, and for the costs of this proceeding, and that execution
issue therefor in favor of plaintiff against said defendant,
Robert S. Stevens."

The bill of exceptions contains no mention of any exceptions being saved to the action of the court in permitting the
amended motions to be filed. The record, however, recites
that the defendant excepted thereto. Defendants filed separate answers to such amended motions or petitions. Stevens set up three defenses, the first being a denial of the
allegations of the amended motion against him, except of the
incorporation of the company and that he took twenty shares
of stock on which he paid fifty per cent. The second and
third defenses are as follows:

" Defendant, for a second defense to the cause of action
alleged in said petition, states that the pretended judgment
described in said petition was recovered on the two promissory notes described in said petition. That, at the time of
the signing of the name of the Texas & Atlantic Refrigerator
Car Company to said notes and each of them by J. R. Barrett,
said Barrett was the president of said company, and he made
said notes and each of them payable to himself as the payee
thereof, and he, as the payee thereof, indorsed them and each

of them in blank, and he got them, and each of them, discounted at the Commercial Bank of St. Louis, and he received and retained the proceeds of said notes, and has never accounted to said Texas & Atlantic Refrigerator Car Company therefor, as it was and is his duty to do. That said Texas & Atlantic Refrigerator Car Company did not pay said notes, or either of them, at their maturity. That prior to the institution of the suit by plaintiff against the Texas & Atlantic Refrigerator Car Company in this court on said notes, as alleged in plaintiff's petition, said J. R. Barrett had fully paid off and satisfied said notes, and each of them, to said bank, and thereby became the legal owner thereof. That, at the time of said Barrett's paying off and satisfying said notes as aforesaid, he made and entered into the following collusive and corrupt agreement and scheme with the plaintiff who was at said time and at the time that said notes had been discounted at said Commercial Bank of St. Louis the cashier thereof, to wit:

" Said J. R. Barrett was to fully pay off to said bank and take up said notes and deliver them, or cause to be delivered, to the plaintiff for the purpose of having suit brought on them for the use and benefit of said Barrett in the plaintiff's name as the ostensible owner and holder thereof, and the plaintiff was to execute his due bill to said Barrett for the amount of said notes, to wit, for the sum of $10,000, with the distinct understanding between plaintiff and said Barrett that said Barrett would never enforce the collection of said due bill against the plaintiff. That the plaintiff was to institute and prosecute suit on said notes in his own name for the use and benefit of said Barrett against the Texas & Atlantic Refrigerator Car Company, and said company was not to make any defense, although it had a good, legal, and meritorious defense to said notes. That said Texas & Atlantic Refrigerator Car Company had at said time no assets of any kind out of which said judgment could be satisfied, only some unpaid stock held by this defendant and other stockholders therein. That, in pursuance of said agreement and scheme, said J. R. Barrett did, on or about the ninth day of December, 1875, pay off said notes and fully discharge the same to the said Commercial Bank of St. Louis, and the plaintiff took them up, and on the eleventh day of December, 1875, had suit instituted on them in his own name for the use and benefit of said Barrett against said Texas & Atlantic Refrigerator Car

Company in this court, and a summons for said Texas &
Atlantic Refrigerator Car Company was issued in said suit
to the sheriff of Pettis county, Missouri, returnable to the next
term of this court, on the first Monday in January, 1876, and
said summons was by said sheriff personally served on said
J. R. Barrett, as the president of said Texas & Atlantic Refrigerator Car Company, on the eleventh day of December,
1875. That on the twenty-sixth day of January, 1876, a
judgment by default was taken on said notes in the name of
the plaintiff for the sum of $10,377.21, and on the thirty-first
day of January, 1876, an execution was issued thereon, and
the sum of $12 realized on said execution in the manner
alleged in plaintiff's petition, and the execution returned not
satisfied as to the balance of said judgment, 'there being no
other goods or chattels or property found belonging to the
defendant upon which to levy the same.'

"That on the fifteenth day of December, 1875, the plaintiff,
in pursuance of said agreement and scheme, executed his due
bill to said Barrett for the sum of ten thousand dollars, which
said Barrett still holds, but which is to be delivered up to the
plaintiff if he shall succeed in collecting said judgment, or, if
he does not, it is in no event to be collected off the plaintiff.
That, in pursuance of said agreement and scheme, and as
a part thereof, plaintiff has commenced this suit on said judgment against this defendant as a stockholder in said Texas
& Atlantic Refrigerator Car Company for the unpaid balance
on his stock.

"Defendant avers that said J. R. Barrett was the president
of said Texas & Atlantic Refrigerator Car Company at the
time of his getting said notes and each of them discounted
as aforesaid. That he has never accounted to said company
for the proceeds of said notes, or either of them. That, besides said notes, he collected and received large sums of
money belonging to said Texas & Atlantic Refrigerator Car
Company, for which he has never accounted to said company.
That at the time said Barrett paid off and satisfied said notes
as aforesaid said Texas & Atlantic Refrigerator Car Company did not owe nor was it indebted to said Barrett. On
the contrary said Barrett had subscribed for two hundred
and fifty shares of capital stock of the Texas & Atlantic
Refrigerator Car Company on which he has only paid fifty
per cent. That he still owes and is indebted to said company for the balance of said stock. That the plaintiff never

paid any thing for said notes, or either of them, and was not and is not a *bona fide* holder thereof for value, and he took them in pursuance of the agreement and scheme hereinbefore stated. That he had no right, title, interest, or claim in or to said notes, or either of them, at the time when he commenced suit thereon as aforesaid, and he has no title, right, interest, or claim in or to said judgment now. That he instituted and prosecuted said suit in his own name for the exclusive use and benefit of said J. R. Barrett to final judgment in this court in pursuance of said agreement and scheme between him and said Barrett with the intent and for the purpose of fraudulently, improperly, and unjustly preventing this defendant, as a stockholder in said Texas & Atlantic Refrigerator Car Company, from setting up the defenses which the said Texas & Atlantic Refrigerator Car Company had and has to a suit by said Barrett in his own name, either on said notes or on said pretended judgment thereon; and for the purpose of fraudulently, illegally, and unjustly coercing money out of this defendant as a stockholder in said Texas & Atlantic Refrigerator Car Company to pay said pretended judgment to plaintiff when said company did not and does not owe, nor is it indebted to, said Barrett for whose use and benefit the plaintiff is prosecuting this suit.

"That said J. R. Barrett has been all the time and he still is the real party in interest, and he has been ever since the commencement of this suit, and still is prosecuting it in the name of the plaintiff, to prevent this defendant, as a stockholder in said Texas & Atlantic Refrigerator Car Company, from setting up the equities existing between said company, and said J. R. Barrett, as the president thereof and a stockholder therein, and to prevent said Texas & Atlantic Refrigerator Car Company from calling on said Barrett to account to it for the proceeds of said notes and other money belonging to said company, collected by said Barrett as president thereof, and also to prevent said Barrett from being required to pay the unpaid balance on his stock in said company; and the claims and equities which said company had and has against said Barrett would more than offset any claim which said Barrett has against it, either on account of said notes or any other claim; and this defendant avers that, if said Barrett were to settle fairly and account to said Texas & Atlantic Refrigerator Car Company for the money belonging to said company in his hands, that, after allowing all just credits and offsets, he would be found indebted to said company, instead of said company being indebted to him; and that there would be no just claim against said defendant for any unpaid balance on his stock in said Texas & Atlantic Refrigerator Car Company.

"Defendant, for a third defense to plaintiff's right to recover against this defendant on the judgment, described in plaintiff's amended petition, says it was recovered by fraud, and is null and void as to this defendant. Defendant sets up and pleads the foregoing facts as a full and complete bar to the cause of action alleged in plaintiff's petition."

Plaintiff then filed a reply admitting that judgment had been recovered on the notes; that said Barrett was the president of said company, and signed the notes as such to his own order, indorsed in blank, but denying that Barrett received or retained any of the proceeds of such notes, or that he never accounted therefor, and alleged that the whole of such proceeds was received by said company, and used by it in its business. Plaintiff admitted that the company failed to pay the notes at maturity, and denied all other allegations of the answer.

On the trial plaintiff offered in evidence a copy of the record of the proceedings, judgment, execution, and other documents in his favor in the action before mentioned against said company on said notes.

This record was admitted in evidence over the objection of defendant, on the grounds that the court rendering such judgment had no jurisdiction of the subject matter of the suit; that defendant was not a party thereto; that said Barrett was the owner of the notes in question, was president of said company at the time suit was brought; that said suit was brought for his benefit, was rendered by default, and was null and void; that said record was incompetent evidence against defendant, except to show that plaintiff had recovered judgment against said company, and that an execution had issued thereon and had been returned *nulla bona.* Plaintiff also offered in evidence the subscription-book of said company, showing that said defendant had subscribed for fifty shares of stock therein at one hundred dollars per share, on which he had paid one thousand dollars. Plaintiff then rested, and defendant offered a demurrer to the evidence. This demurrer was overruled, and defendant excepted and appealed.

G. A. Madill and J. A. Carr, for the appellant.

G. P. B. Jackson, for the respondent.

[114] Sherwood, J. (Division Two.) This proceeding is grounded upon section 736 of the Revised Statutes of 1879, now section 2517 of the Revised Statutes of 1889, and section 940 of the Revised Statutes of 1879, now section 2782 of the Revised Statutes of 1889, which sections are respectively as follows:

"Sec. 736. If any execution shall have been issued against any corporation, and there cannot be found any property or effects whereon to levy the same, then such execution may be issued against any of the stockholders to the extent of the amount of the unpaid balance of such stock by him or her owned; *provided,* [115] *always,* that no execution shall issue against any stockholder, except upon an order of the court in which the action, suit, or other proceedings shall have been brought or instituted, made upon motion in open court after sufficient notice, in writing, to the person sought to be charged; and, upon such motion, such court may order execution to issue accordingly; *and provided further,* that no stockholder shall be individually liable in any amount over and above the amount of stock owned."

"Sec. 940. No stockholder shall be personally liable for the payment of any debt contracted by any corporation created under this article, which is not to be paid within one year from the time the debt is contracted, nor unless a suit for the collection of such debt shall be brought against such corporation within one year after the debt shall become due; and no suit shall be brought against any stockholder who shall cease to be a stockholder in any such corporation for any debt so contracted, unless the same shall be commenced within two years from the time he shall cease to be a stockholder in such corporation, nor until an execution shall have been returned unsatisfied, in whole or in part."

1. Whatever may have been thought at a former period, and in some jurisdictions, as to the effect upon a stockholder of a judgment rendered against his corporation, at the present time, the execution and organization of a corporation having been established, a judgment against such corporation, being proved, is conclusive evidence of debt against its stockholders, where the plaintiff in the original and the primary and auxiliary actions is the same, in the absence of

collusion, fraud, etc., and not upon original grounds: 1 Freeman on Judgments, 4th ed., sec. 177, and cases cited.   And
a judgment by default against a corporation equals, in [116]
conclusiveness as to a stockholder, one obtained after contest: Authorities *supra.*   Except on the grounds before mentioned it is out of the power of a stockholder to go back into
the original consideration of the judgment against the corporation, that the indebtedness for which the judgment was
rendered was the debt of the president, and not of the corporation: Thompson's Liabilities of Stockholders, secs. 329, 337,
and cases cited; *Donworth* v. *Coolbaugh*, 5 Iowa, 300.

Such judgment against the corporation is valid against a
stockholder, until reversed by him in some direct proceeding
for that purpose, and cannot be attacked collaterally: See
authorities *supra.*

The rule thus announced in the foregoing authorities elim-
inates the defenses relied on by defendant, that Nichols was
not the owner of the notes that were merged in the judgment
against the corporation; that such notes had been paid, or
that the transactions which gave origin to the notes were
fraudulent.   At any rate there was no fraud proved at the
trial, nor does the second defense in the answer show that
the judgment against the corporation was concocted in fraud;
that fraud was practiced in the very act of obtaining the
judgment.   The fraud, in such case, must be actual fraud,
as contradistinguished from a judgment obtained on false
evidence or a forged instrument on the trial: 1 Bigelow on
Fraud, 86, 87; *United States* v. *Throckmorton*, 98 U. S. 61;
Ward v. *Southfield*, 102 N. Y. 287; 2 Story's Equity Jurisprudence, sec. 1579.

The principle, of course, would be the same were a party
defendant to resort to a collateral attack on the judgment
alleged to have been fraudulently obtained, instead of a direct
attack.   And there is abundant authority to sustain the view
that, in modern adjudication, there is no longer any distinction made between the two methods of attack: 1 Bigelow on
Fraud, 94, [117] and cases cited; *Mandeville* v. *Reynolds*, 68
N. Y. 528; *Rogers* v. *Gwinn*, 21 Iowa, 58; *Davis* v. *Headley*,
22 N. J. Eq. 115; *Dobson* v. *Pearce*, 12 N. Y. 165; 62 Am.
Dec. 152; *Ward* v. *Quinlivin*, 57 Mo. 425, 427; 2 Freeman on
Judgments, 4th ed., sec. 576, p. 996; 2 Black on Judgments,
sec. 973; *Spencer* v. *Vigneaux*, 20 Cal. 442.   So that, should
we treat the answer as a collateral attack on the corporation

judgment, the result would not be at all variant from a direct
attack, since in the former, as well as in the latter, the substance of the pleading would have to be the same.

As to the third defense of defendant's answer, it is bad on
grounds already stated, and also on the additional ground
that a simple conclusion of law is pleaded. That it is
necessary to set forth in a petition the facts constituting the
fraud pleaded no one has ever doubted or denied. Logical
and legal consistency, therefore, require that an answer
should as necessarily state the constitutive facts of the fraud
relied on as that a petition should do so. This is the view
taken by Judge Bliss in his work on Pleading, where he says:
"In alleging fraud it will not suffice to say that the party
fraudulently procured, or fraudulently induced, or fraudulently did this or that, or that he committed or was guilty of
fraud; the facts which constitute the fraud must be stated.
Fraud is a conclusion of law. A statement that defendants,
in concert, did by connivance, conspiracy, and combination
beat and defraud the plaintiff out of, etc., does not state the
facts that constituted the cause of action. It does not appear
what they did; the legal conclusion—an epithet only—is
applied to their acts without knowing what they were": Bliss
on Code Pleading, 2d ed., sec. 211; see, also, sec. 339, and
note.

Several authorities in this state support a similar view as
to a petition: *Smith* v. *Sims*, 77 Mo. 269; *Reed* v. *Bott*, 100
Mo. 62; *Hoester* v *Sammelmann*, 101 [118] Mo. 619; *Mateer* v.
Missouri Pac. Ry. Co., 105 Mo. 320; *Williams* v. *Chicago etc.
Ry.*, 112 Mo. 463, 496; 34 Am. St. Rep. 403. No reason is
perceived why the same rule should not as well apply to an
answer as to a petition.

The case of *Montgomery* v. *Tipton*, 1 Mo. 446, holds a general averment of fraud good in an answer, and cites Chitty's
Pleading as authority, and *Pemberton* v. *Staples*, 6 Mo. 59,
follows in its wake; and the same may be said of *Edgell* v.
Sigerson, 20 Mo. 494. The cases in 1 and 6 Missouri were
correctly decided, because we were then practicing under
the common law; not so, however, when Edgell's case was
determined, because that was in 1855, and we had adopted
in substance the New York code in 1849, and, with its adoption, we took with it the construction put upon it by the
courts of that state, which construction is contrary to the
views expressed in Edgell's case: *Pierson* v. *Cooley*, 1 Code

Rep. 91; *Beers* v. *Squire* (1848), 1 Code Rep. 84; *McMurray* v. *Gifford*, 5 How. Pr. 14, and cases cited. See, also, *Lefler* v. *Field*, 52 N. Y. 621. This view is also taken in other code states: See note to Bliss on Code Pleading, sec. 339.

And there is as little reason for making any distinction in this regard between petitions and answers as there is for saying that a petition is not good in equity, unless it sets forth the facts constituting the fraud; but that it may be good at law, because we have in this state but one form of action. If fraud is necessary to be pleaded at all it is just as necessary to plead the constitutive facts when asking for legal relief as there is when asking for equitable relief: See *Clough* v. *Holden*, 115 Mo. 336, 353, 354; 37 Am. St. Rep. 393.

In *Little* v. *Harrington*, 71 Mo. 390, obeying the behests of the code, we disapproved *Fordyce* v. *Hathorn*, 57 Mo. 120, and earlier cases, which asserted that matters in abatement and in bar could not be united in the [119] same answer: *Little* v. *Harrington*, 71 Mo. 390, has frequently been followed since. *Byler* v. *Jones*, 79 Mo. 261; *May* v. *Burk*, 80 Mo. 675; *Young Men's Christian Assn.* v. *Dubach*, 82 Mo. 475; *Cohn* v. *Lehman*, 93 Mo. 574.

For these reasons the answer should be held insufficient both in its second and third defenses, and, if so, the evidence offered in support of those defenses need not be set out at large.

2. The evidence shows that defendant Stevens subscribed for fifty shares of stock in the company. This being the case, his liability was commensurate with that number of shares, and that liability could not be diminished by a release from the president, of which there was no proof. Even the directors of the corporation could not release a stockholder to the prejudice of creditors: *Upton* v. *Tribilcock*, 91 U. S. 45; 1 Beach on Private Corporations, sec. 109; *Hannibal etc. Plank Road Co.* v. *Menefee*, 25 Mo. 547, and other cases.

3. The original motion to obtain execution against Stevens and Mirrick not having been preserved, we can only conjecture as to what it was, and, in the absence of the original, we shall presume that the trial court ruled correctly in permitting the amendment to be made which was made; because there was no exception saved as to the amendment being permitted, or, if there were, it was abandoned by not being

preserved in the bill of exceptions, the only repository known
to the law where matters of mere exception can be preserved.
A recitation in the record of matters not properly belonging
thereto, of matters belonging solely to the bill of exceptions,
cannot be noticed in an appellate court. Matters which are
not in fact a part of the record cannot be made such by the
mere recital of the clerk: *Parkinson* v. *People* (Ill., June 12,
1890), 24 N. E. Rep. 772, and cases cited; *Gould* v. *Howe*, 127
Ill. 251, and cases cited.

[120] 4. It will have been noticed that section 736 of the
Revised Statutes of 1879 requires a motion to be made in
order to have execution issued against a stockholder; that
section is found under the title "Corporations," and under the
special head of "General Powers, Duties, and Liabilities,"
while section 940 of the same chapter is found ranged under
the head of "Manufacturing and Business Companies," and
requires a suit to be brought, etc.

The motion in this case is sufficiently comprehensive to
constitute a petition, and is a petition in all essential particulars, and is to be so treated: *Wilson* v. *St. Louis etc. Ry. Co.*,
108 Mo. 588; 32 Am. St. Rep. 624, and cases cited. So that
no objection can be raised to the form of the pleading, and,
no exceptions having been saved to the amendment of the
motion in the trial court, and the defendant having pleaded
to it and gone to trial, he cannot raise the point of a change
of cause of action, even if such amendment could be regarded
as such change, which is not admitted.

5. It is urged, in regard to the removal of the cause to the
federal court, that error occurred. Several authorities establish the proposition that when a cause has been removed to
a federal court, and has been remanded because the petition
for removal does not set up the diverse citizenship of the parties
at the commencement of the suit, etc., there a second removal
on the same ground is not allowable: *Johnston* v. *Donvan*, 30
Fed. Rep. 395; *St. Paul etc. Ry. Co.* v. *McLean*, 108 U. S. 212,
and cases cited. And, even if this obstacle had not arisen in
this case, one equally fatal is apparent of record, and that is
that Stevens did not file his petition for removal until several
terms of the Pettis circuit court had lapsed: *Woolf* v. *Chisolm*,
30 Fed. Rep. 881; *Austin* v. *Gagan*, 39 Fed. Rep. 626; *Dixon*
v. *Western Union Tel. Co.*, 38 Fed. Rep. 377. And it has also
been held by the [121] federal courts that an extension of
time to the next term could not be granted even by stipula-

tion of parties: *Pullman Palace Car Co.* v. *Speck*, 113 U. S. 84, et seq. This was the ruling under the removal act of 1875, and that of 1887 is much more strict. Refusal of the trial court to permit defendant Stevens to amend his petition for removal was, therefore, proper.

6. The declarations of law asked by defendant need not be discussed in detail, as the principles they involve have been sufficiently touched upon already; there was no error in refusing them.

Therefore judgment affirmed.

BURGESS, J., concurs.

GANTT, P. J., not sitting.

Per CURIAM. (In Bank.) The foregoing opinion delivered in division number two is adopted and approved in Bank.

GANTT, J., not sitting.

BARCLAY, J., concurs in the result.

CORPORATIONS—JUDGMENTS AGAINST—CONCLUSIVENESS AS TO STOCK-HOLDERS.—A judgment establishing the liability of a corporation is conclusive in an action against stockholders for unpaid subscriptions to the capital stock: *Tatum* v. *Rosenthal*, 95 Cal. 129; 29 Am. St. Rep. 97, and note. See the extended note to *Thompson* v. *Reno Sav. Bank*, 3 Am. St. Rep. 815, 858, in which the further question as to the right of the stockholder to attack such judgment for fraud or want of jurisdiction is discussed.

CORPORATIONS—RELEASE OF STOCKHOLDERS.—The obligation of a subscriber to the capital stock of a corporation to pay a subscription cannot be surrendered or released by the directors: *Gogebic Investment Co.* v. *Iron Chief Min. Co.*, 78 Wis. 427; 23 Am. St. Rep. 417. A subscriber to corporate stock can be released from liability only by the consent of all the subscribers: *Cartwright* v. *Dickinson*, 17 Am. St. Rep. 910. See on this subject the extended notes to *Thompson* v. *Reno Sav. Bank*, 3 Am. St. Rep. 821, and *Parker* v. *Thomas*, 81 Am. Dec. 399.

REMOVAL OF CAUSES.—This question is the subject of an extensive note to *Beery* v. *Irick*, 12 Am. Rep. 545-552.

BURDICT *v.* MISSOURI PACIFIC RAILWAY COMPANY.

[123 MISSOURI, 221.]

NEGLIGENCE—TRANSITORY ACTION—PROOF OF LEX LOCI.—A common-law action against a railroad company by an employee to recover for injuries caused by the negligence of the company is transitory in its nature, and may be maintained in a state other than that in which the injury is received without proof of the law of the latter state.

EVIDENCE—PRESUMPTION AS TO COMMON LAW.—It is presumed that the common law prevails in a sister state.

RAILROAD COMPANIES—LIABILITY FOR NEGLIGENCE— CONTRIBUTORY NEGLIGENCE OF SWITCHMAN.—In an action against a railroad company by a switchman to recover for injury received while coupling moving cars, and alleged to have been caused by the negligence of the company in maintaining a ditch across its track, the fact that the plaintiff knew that it was dangerous to walk between moving cars is not such contributory negligence as to bar a recovery, if the coupling could not have been made while the cars were standing still, and was made in the usual way, in a careful and prudent manner.

RAILROAD COMPANIES—NEGLIGENCE—DUTY TO KEEP TRACK IN REPAIR.— A railroad company must exercise reasonable care in maintaining its track in reasonably safe repair, so as to prevent injury to its employees discharging their duties with ordinary care, and for a failure to do so it is liable to them in damages if injury results.

RAILROAD COMPANIES—NEGLIGENCE—DUTY TO KEEP TRACK IN REPAIR.— A railroad company must keep its track in reasonably safe repair, so as to prevent injury to its employees or other persons lawfully upon such track in the discharge of their duties, and for a failure to do so is liable for injury resulting therefrom.

INSTRUCTIONS GIVEN WHICH FAIRLY PRESENT THE LAW of the case need not be repeated, and if other instructions are asked they are properly refused.

DAMAGES—EXCESSIVE VERDICT—REMITTITUR.—If damages awarded are excessive, but the excess is not due to passion or prejudice of the jury, the appellate court may designate such excess, and allow the plaintiff to remit it and take an affirmance for the residue, or submit to a new trial.

E. Robinson, for the appellant.

F. W. Randolph and *Beebe & Watson,* for the respondent.

[226] BURGESS, J. (Division Two.) Action for damages for injuries resulting from alleged negligence on the part of the defendant, in permitting a ditch to be and remain in [227] and across its track, by reason of which it was unsafe for persons engaged in switching cars, that being the kind of work in which plaintiff, as an employee of defendant, was engaged in at the time of the accident.

The answer denied all allegations in the petition, and pleaded contributory negligence on the part of the plaintiff.

On the thirty-first day of August, 1887, the plaintiff, while in the service of defendant, as a switchman, was endeavoring to make a coupling in its switchyards, in Wyandotte, Kansas, he stepped into a ditch which crossed defendant's roadbed, causing his left arm to be caught between the bumpers of the cars, necessitating the amputation of his hand and a part of the forearm. The ditch was about ten inches wide, and twelve inches deep, and extended the entire width of the roadbed. It had been there for at least a year before the accident; looked like a ditch to drain off water.

Plaintiff, at the time of his injury, was working under one Wardell, who was foreman of his crew, and who ordered him to go down the track and couple some cars which were about to be pushed down to some cars that were stationary. They were then at work in defendant's switchyard, known as the "Cypress yards." "He went down to the stationary cars and set the coupling-pin on the drawhead, so that when the link on the moving car should be entered into the drawhead of the stationary car the pin would drop in and make the coupling. Plaintiff entered between the cars when they came together to enter the link. When they came together he entered the link and 'stepped back,' but instead of the pin dropping into the link it jumped up and rested against the bumper on the opposite side. Plaintiff then stepped between the cars, reached over and got the pin, and, while in the act of dropping it into the link, he stepped into the ditch, [228] which was under the stationary car, and his left hand going down with him was caught between the bumpers." Plaintiff also testified that the way he made the coupling was the usual and proper way.

"The cars were moving at the rate of two or three miles per hour or 'a very slow walk,' and had moved only five or six feet before reaching the ditch. After first coming together the slack ran out between the cars, leaving a space between the bumper sufficiently wide to receive his arm, when he stepped into the ditch. Plaintiff was pushed a car length and a half, with his hand between the bumpers, when the slack again ran out of the cars and released him. He got out, was taken to the hospital, where his hand and the lower part of his arm were amputated. He testified that his arm was wholly useless; 'that it bothered him all the time in winter; that it was cold all the time, and always bothered him.' At the time of his injury he was thirty years of age, and had, since he was seventeen years old, worked for railroads, seven years of that period for the defendant."

Under the instructions of the court the jury returned a verdict in favor of plaintiff for twelve thousand five hundred dollars. As a condition to the overruling of the motion for a new trial the court required plaintiff to remit two thousand five hundred dollars, which was done. Defendant appeals to this court.

It is insisted by defendant that the court should have sustained the demurrer to the evidence: 1. Upon the ground that the accident occurred in Kansas, and that there could be no liability, except such as arose from the laws of that state, and that plaintiff was not entitled to recovery without showing what those laws were, and that under them the facts of the case created a liability; 2. That plaintiff's own evidence showed that he was guilty of contributory negligence, and he could not recover for that reason.

[229] A careful examination of the authorities cited by counsel for defendant in his brief in support of the first proposition shows that they do not support that contention. This is not a statutory action; if it were, the authorities cited would be in point. Upon the contrary it is a common-law action, transitory in its nature, and as the common law, in the absence of any thing showing to the contrary, is presumed to exist in Kansas, where the injury occurred, as it does in this state, it was not necessary that plaintiff should introduce any evidence with reference thereto.

The case of *Le Forest* v. *Tolman*, 117 Mass. 109, 19 Am. Rep. 400, was an action brought in Massachusetts against the owner of a dog who had bitten the plaintiff in the state of New Hampshire, and it was held that plaintiff could not recover under the statute of the latter state, nor could he at common law, without proof that the defendant knew that his dog was accustomed to attack and bite mankind.

Hyde v. *Wabash etc. Ry. Co.*, 61 Iowa, 441, 47 Am. Rep. 820, was an action brought in Iowa by the administrator of one Hyde, who was alleged to have been killed by the negligence of defendant in this state, purely a statutory action, and it was held that, as the administrator failed to show that by the laws of this state an action could be maintained for such injury by the administrator, such action could not be maintained in that state.

Davis v. *New York etc. R. R. Co.*, 143 Mass. 301, 58 Am.

Rep. 138, was also a statutory action, and in that case the same rule is announced.

In *Wooden* v. *Western N. Y. etc. R. R. Co.*, 126 N. Y. 10, 22 Am. St. Rep. 803, relied upon by defendant, it is expressly held that an action for the injury to the person in another state is maintainable in New York without proof of the law of the place where the injury occurred, because permitted by the common law which is presumed to exist in the foreign state. It was also held that when the right of action depends [230] upon the statute conferring it, it can only be maintained in another state upon proof that the statute law in the state in which the injury occurred gives the right of action, and is similar to the statute of the state where the action is brought. The question now under consideration was brought before this court in *State* v. *Clay*, 100 Mo. 571, and Sherwood, J., speaking for the court with reference to an instrument of writing executed in the state of Kansas, said: "In the absence of any showing to the contrary it will be presumed that the common law prevails in a sister state": See, also, *Meyer* v. *McCabe*, 73 Mo. 236; *Benne* v. *Schnecko*, 100 Mo. 250; *Wooden* v. *Western N. Y. etc. R. R. Co.*, 126 N. Y. 10; 22 Am. St. Rep. 803. Moreover, the question was not raised by answer on the trial, nor by motion for a new trial, and cannot now be raised for the first time in this court.

With respect to the second proposition, while it is true, as contended by counsel for defendant, that plaintiff admitted in his testimony that he knew that it was dangerous to walk between the cars while in motion, and that he had control of the train, he also stated that he made the coupling in a careful and prudent way; that the coupling could not have been made if the cars had been standing still, and that the way in which it was done was the customary and usual way. Plaintiff knew nothing of the hole in which he stepped, and which was the cause of the accident. Here the facts as disclosed by the evidence admit of different constructions and inferences as to contributory negligence by plaintiff, and that question was properly submitted to the jury: *Mauerman* v. *Siemerts*, 71 Mo. 101; *Nagel* v. *Missouri Pac. Ry. Co.*, 75 Mo. 653; 42 Am. Rep. 418; *Huhn* v. *Missouri Pac. Ry. Co.*, 92 Mo. 440.

The instructions given on behalf of plaintiff are as follows: [231] "1. The court instructs the jury that it was the duty of the defendant railway company to exercise reasonable care in maintaining its roadbed in a reasonably safe condition, in order that its employees, in the exercise of ordinary care, or in the discharge of their duties, could use the same with safety.

"And if the jury believes from the evidence that on the third day of August, 1887, there was a hole in defendant's roadbed, at a point about one hundred and twenty feet (120) south of the switch known as the 'Sixth street switch' in defendant's yards, known as the 'Cypress yards,' and by reason of said hole said roadbed was not reasonably safe for the plaintiff, in the exercise of ordinary care, to use in the discharge of his duties at the time of said injury, and that said hole existed such a length of time that the defendant railway company either knew, or by the exercise of ordinary care might have known, of its existence in time so that by the exercise of ordinary care it could have put the said roadbed in a reasonably safe condition before the injury. And if you further believe from the evidence that the plaintiff, at the time and place aforesaid, was in the employment of the defendant, as switchman, and in the exercise of such care as ordinarily a prudent switchman would exercise under the same or similar circumstances, and that while so engaged in his work he stepped into said hole, and by reason thereof his hand was caught between the bumpers of the cars, and he was injured thereby, he is entitled to recover.

" 2. If the jury believe from the evidence that the injury of plaintiff resulted from the failure of defendant to provide a reasonably safe track for the use of plaintiff in the discharge of his duty, and he was in the exercise of ordinary care, then the injury was not the result of the ordinary risk and danger assumed by plaintiff when he entered into defendant's services.

²³² " 3. If the jury find for the plaintiff, they will assess his damages at such sum as they believe, from the evidence, he has sustained, taking into consideration the pain and anguish, mental and physical, if any, and the loss of his hand, not to exceed the sum of $15,000."

The court gave, at the instance of defendant, the following instructions:

" 1. The court instructs the jury that, before plaintiff can recover in this action, it devolves upon him to prove to the reasonable satisfaction of the jury, by a preponderance of evidence in the case:

" *First.* That there was a hole in defendant's roadbed at the point and of the character set forth in his petition.

" *Second.* That by reason of the existence of said hole the defendant's roadbed was not in a reasonably safe condition.

" *Third.* That the officers, agents, or employees of defendant, whose duty it was to keep defendant's roadbed in a reasonably safe condition, either knew of the existence of said hole or, by the exercise of ordinary and reasonable care, could have known of the existence of said hole.

" *Fourth.* That, in undertaking to make the coupling in question, plaintiff stepped into said hole, and that this fact was the direct and proximate cause of his injury.

"And, if the evidence in the case fails to satisfy the jury of the existence of any of these facts, their verdict should be for the defendant.

" 2. The jury are instructed that the law governing the case is, that the plaintiff, when he entered into the employment of the defendant as one of its switchmen, took upon himself the ordinary risks and perils incident to that business.

233 " 3. The court instructs the jury that if they believe from the evidence in the case that plaintiff's injuries were occasioned by a mere accident, and without fault on anybody's part, then the verdict must be for the defendant.

" 4. Although the jury shall believe from the evidence that defendant's roadbed was out of repair, and that defendant, by the exercise of ordinary care, could have known of such defect in such roadbed, still defendant would not be liable in this action, unless it failed to repair such defect within a reasonable time after, by the exercise of ordinary care and prudence, it might have discovered such defect, and as to what would be a ' reasonable time,' as above used, would be such a length of time as a man of ordinary care and prudence, engaged in managing and operating a railroad, would take under such or like circumstances.

" 5. Even though the jury may believe from the evidence in the case that there was a ditch across defendant's roadbed, as stated in plaintiff's petition, and defendant's employees in charge of said roadbed either knew of the existence of said ditch or, by the exercise of ordinary care, might have known of it, although the jury may believe that plaintiff, in undertaking to make said coupling, stepped into said ditch and that his injuries were caused thereby, still, if the jury further believes from the testimony in the cause that the plaintiff, in going between the cars and trying to make the coupling while the cars were in motion, was not himself in the exercise of ordinary and reasonable care, and that such lack of ordinary and reasonable care on his part directly contributed to his injuries, then he is not entitled to recover, and the verdict will be defendant.

"6. The court instructs the jury that by the term 'ordinary and reasonable care' is meant such as an ordinary, careful, and prudent person would exercise [234] under the same or similar circumstances; and this definition applies as well to the care required of the plaintiff as to that required of defendant.

"7. The court instructs the jury that, while they are the sole judge of the credibility of the witnesses, and of the weight to be given to the testimony, yet it is the exclusive province of the court to define the issues to be determined by the jury, and to instruct the jury on the law applicable to such issues, and it is the duty of the jury, and they have promised in their oaths, to follow the instructions given by the court.

"It is not their province, in determining the questions submitted to them, to indulge in any possible sympathy for the plaintiff, or in any possible prejudice against the defendant; nor should they consider what effect their verdict, in this case, will or may have in any other case against this or any other railroad company, but they are to consider and determine the issues submitted to them in the instructions, and should determine these issues in the same way in all respects as if this were a case between man and man.

"8. The court instructs the jury that by the term 'preponderance of evidence' is meant the greater weight of evidence; and, if the jury believe that the greater weight of evidence is on the side of the defendant, or if the testimony is of such a character or so evenly balanced that the jury are unable to determine on which side the greater weight of it actually is, then, in either such event, the verdict will be for the defendant."

The defendant also asked the court to give the following instructions, which were refused:

"10. The court instructs the jury that there is no evidence in this case that defendant knew that there was a hole or ditch across its track at the point where the alleged injury is said to have occurred, prior to the happening of said accident; and before plaintiff is entitled [235] to recover on that account, they must find and believe from the evidence that said hole or ditch had existed for such a length of time, prior to the happening of said accident, that the defendant, by the exercise of ordinary care and prudence on its part, could have discovered the existence of such hole or ditch.

"11. The court instructs the jury that, if they shall believe from the evidence that plaintiff set the pin with which to make the coupling of the train of cars in question in a slanting position, relying upon the jar of the train of cars to make the coupling, and that that was the usual method and a safe method, of making the coupling, and that the jar of the train of cars upon the first trial did not make such coupling, and that plaintiff controlled the movement and operation of the train of cars, and could have stopped the train of cars until he could have placed it in the position aforesaid the second time, and that he voluntarily undertook to make the coupling without exerting his control over the train of cars, and was injured thereby, then plaintiff voluntarily assumed all risks and dangers incident to the manner of so coupling cars, and, if injured in consequence of such risk, he is not entitled to recover, and your verdict must be for the defendant."

"13. The court instructs the jury that ordinary care and prudence in this case would have required the plaintiff to have looked where he was walking when upon defendant's track for the purpose of coupling its cars, and if you shall believe from the evidence he did not look where he was walking when coupling defendant's cars when he could have done so, and if, by doing so, he could have avoided the injury, then his failure to so look was such contributory negligence on his part as will prevent a recovery in this case, and your verdict must be for the defendant."

[236] It is insisted by counsel that the first instruction given for plaintiff is erroneous; that it was calculated to mislead the jury in that it requires defendant to furnish appliances which will enable its employees to discharge their duties in absolute safety. It was the duty of the defendant to keep its tracks in reasonably safe repair so as to prevent injury to all persons who might lawfully be upon its track, and for failure to do so it is liable for the consequences: *Lewis* v. *St. Louis etc. R. R. Co.*, 59 Mo. 495; 21 Am. Rep.

385; *Gibson* v. *Pacific R. R. Co.*, 46 Mo. 163; 2 Am. Rep. 497. Nothing more was required of defendant by this instruction. Nor is counsel correct in that there was no evidence upon which to predicate it.

There was no error committed in refusing the tenth instruction asked by defendant. It was, in substance, given in its first and fourth; and the issues presented by its eleventh and thirteenth refused instructions were fairly and fully presented in other instructions already given. It is not error to refuse instructions when those given fairly present the law of the case: *State* v. *St. Louis Brokerage Co.*, 85 Mo. 411; *Baum* v. *Fryrear*, 85 Mo. 151. The instructions, taken together, present the law of the case fairly to the jury.

But one other point remains to be disposed of; that is, with respect of the amount of the verdict, which is claimed by defendant to be excessive. The verdict was for twelve thousand five hundred dollars. The court required plaintiff to remit two thousand five hundred dollars, and upon that condition overruled the motion for a new trial. That the verdict was large, there is no question. The hand injured was the left. Plaintiff was thirty years of age at the time, and had been a railroad brakemen for thirteen years. After the injury he was taken to the hospital and his hand amputated. He was then sent to Sedalia to the company's hospital, where he remained for twenty-seven days. He stated that his [237] arm was of no use to him; was cold all the time in winter, and bothered him all the time. The case is free from malice or wanton misconduct on the part of the servants of defendant. There was very little evidence as to the plaintiff's present or former capacity for labor, and none as to the amount of his ordinary wages or earnings, either before or after the accident, or to show that he was not in good health. Nor did it appear how long he was laid up and incapacitated for labor; nor the amount of his medical or other expenses.

In *Murray* v. *Hudson Riv. R. R. Co.*, 47 Barb. 196, the plaintiff, who was a cooper by trade, and by occupation a driver or teamster in the employ of a brewer, received personal injuries resulting in the loss of a hand, for which he received a verdict for eight thousand dollars, and it was held that the verdict should be set aside for excessive damages, and a new trial granted, unless the plaintiff would reduce such damages to the sum of six thousand dollars.

In *Union Pac. Ry. Co.* v. *Milliken*, 8 Kan. 647, an action for injuries to the person where the only permanent disability was the loss of a hand, and where there was neither lengthened sickness nor extraordinary suffering, a verdict of ten thousand dollars was held to be excessive.

Under the authorities cited and the circumstances disclosed by the evidence in this case we think the damages allowed for the injuries still excessive, and that the judgment should be reversed and cause remanded on the ground of excessive damages, unless plaintiff will remit three thousand dollars within thirty days.

All of this division concur, except as to the remittitur upon which there is a difference of opinion, in consequence of which the case is transferred to the court in Bank.

238 BLACK, C. J. (In Bank.) The opinion heretofore filed in this case is now approved by court in Bank. The only question calling for further discussion is the one raised by the objection that the damages are excessive. The claim of defendant is that, when the court has reached the conclusion that the damages are excessive, the judgment should be reversed and a new trial ordered; while the plaintiff insists the court should indicate the excess, and allow him to remit it and take a judgment of affirmance for the residue. There is certainly much conflict in the authorities on this question of practice. It is believed a review of all of them will accomplish no good at this time. Special mention will be made of a few recent decisions only.

Belt v. *Lawes*, 12 Q. B. Div. 356, was heard in the court of appeal in 1884. It was an action for libel. Brett, M. R., said: " The first point in this case is a pure point of law, namely, whether the judgment of the majority of the divisional court can in law stand as it is if the verdict cannot otherwise be impeached, it being founded on the consent of the plaintiff alone that the amount of the damages should be reduced from five thousand pounds to five hundred pounds. In my opinion such judgment can stand. Where the complaint is only that the damages are excessive, and the verdict cannot be otherwise impeached, and it is a case where the plaintiff is entitled to substantial damages, the court has power to refuse a new trial without the consent of the defendant, on the plaintiff's consenting to the amount of the damages being reduced to such an amount as, if it had been given by the jury, the court would not have con-

sidered excessive. It has been argued that this cannot
be the right rule, because it is said that if the damages are
excessive the court [239] must come to the conclusion that
the verdict is wrong, and the inevitable result of that must
be a new trial. But the court is asked to exercise its discretionary power, and to say that the jury have given larger
damages than they ought to have given. The court does not
give damages, but it only says that if the jury had given a
sum which was a part of what they had given the court
would not have been dissatisfied. . . . . I have not the least
doubt that where, as in the present case, the jury have given
damages which are challenged only as being too large, the
court has power to say that if the jury had given less, as
five hundred pounds and not five thousand pounds, the court
would have considered such damages not excessive, and,
therefore, to say, if the plaintiff will consent to the verdict
being for that amount, the defendant will really have no
grievance. I see nothing in principle against reducing the
damages under such circumstances, and it has certainly for
years been the invariable practice of the courts to do so."

For a long time the rule in Wisconsin was that contended
for by the defendant in this case, but it was much modified
by the recent case of *Baker* v. *City of Madison*, 62 Wis. 150,
which was a personal damage suit. There had been three
verdicts, one for three thousand dollars, one for two thousand
five hundred dollars, and the last for six thousand dollars.
The supreme court allowed the plaintiff to remit two thousand
five hundred dollars, and take an affirmance for three thousand five hundred dollars. Lyon, J., in speaking for the
court, alludes to the fact that the appellate courts of many
of the states have adopted the practice of indicating the
excess and giving, or directing the trial court to give, the
plaintiff the option to remit such excess and take an affirmance for the residue. He then uses the following language:
"The main ground upon which the rule of *Potter* v. *Chicago etc. Ry. Co.*, 22 Wis. 615, is rested is, that, if the court
assumes to fix a sum for which the plaintiff may [240] have
judgment, it thereby usurps the functions of the jury. . . . .
Certainly the usurpation is the same if the trial court does
the same thing. Yet the right of the trial court to allow the
plaintiff to remit the excess, and then give him judgment
for the residue, is almost universally recognized, and, so far
as we are advised, such has always been the practice in this

state. . . . . All that we now do is to make the rule of *Potter* v. *Chicago etc. Ry. Co.*, 22 Wis. 615, sufficiently elastic to enable the court, in a proper case, to relieve the plaintiff from the delay and expense of another trial, when the only fault in the verdict is that it gives him too large an amount. If other material errors have been committed, prejudicial to the defendant, or if there is reasonable ground for belief that the jury were moved by improper motives or led astray by ignorance, or if any other grounds exist satisfactory to the court, a new trial will be ordered. In the present case the plaintiff's right of action has been established by a verdict which is free from error affecting such right. The jury honestly awarded him too large damages. Other verdicts indicate the sum he ought to recover. We do not hesitate to give him the option to take his judgment for the proper sum, and thus end the litigation."

The following cases will show that the trend of modern judicial opinion is in the same direction: *Missouri Pac. Ry. Co.* v. *Dwyer,* 36 Kan. 58–74; *Black* v. *Carrolton R. R. Co.*, 10 La. Ann. 33–39; 63 Am. Dec. 586; *Mortimer* v. *Thomas*, 23 La. Ann. 165; *Belknap* v. *Boston etc. R. R. Co.*, 49 N. H. 358–374; *Murray* v. *Hudson River R. R. Co.*, 47 Barb. 196–205; 48 N. Y. 655; 3 Sedgwick on Damages, 8th ed., sec. 1322, and cases cited.

In *Loyd* v. *Hannibal etc. R. R. Co.*, 53 Mo. 514, the plaintiff was allowed to remit in the trial court, and the remittitur there entered was held to be a valid answer to the objection that the damages awarded were excessive. A like objection was overcome by entering a remittitur [241] in this court in the following cases, which were personal damage suits: *Waldhier* v. *Hannibal etc. R. R. Co.*, 87 Mo. 37; *Smith* v. *Wabash etc. Ry. Co.*, 92 Mo. 359, 374; 1 Am. St. Rep. 729. If, as these cases hold, the plaintiff can avoid the objection that the damages are excessive by remitting a part of the judgment of his own volition, no good reason can be seen why this court may not indicate the excess, and then allow the plaintiff, if he desires to do so, to take an affirmance for the balance. Indeed, this course was pursued in *Furnish* v. *Missouri Pac. Ry. Co.*, 102 Mo. 438, 456; 22 Am. St. Rep. 781, where there was a verdict for fifteen thousand dollars, which was deemed excessive, and the court left it to the plaintiff to remit five thousand dollars or submit to a new trial. If these cases are to be respected, and they have never been overruled, they settle this much, at least, that this court will, in a proper case, where the only valid objection is that the damages are excessive, direct the plaintiff to remit the excess. It is true that some observations of a contrary import were made in the late case of *Gurley* v. *Missouri Pac. Ry. Co.*, 104 Mo. 233, but in that case there was error in the instructions, so that the judgment could not have been affirmed had the plaintiff's request to remit been granted.

An argument pressed upon our consideration in this case is this, that, if this court has the right and power to reduce the damages when excessive, it has the right and power to increase them when inadequate. We do not see the force of this line of argument. In one case the court simply says the judgment may stand for a part of the amount found by the jury, while in the other case it would add something never within the terms of the verdict.

If it can be seen and fairly said the jury gave the excessive verdict by reason of prejudice, passion, or any other improper motive, a new trial should be awarded; for the inference would be a fair one that [242] the finding for the plaintiff was also brought about by improper influences, and this is especially so when there is any doubt as to the right of the plaintiff to recover. Indeed, the verdict may be so large and out of all reason as, of itself, to furnish sufficient evidence that it was the result of passion or some other improper influence. But it does not follow that a verdict is necessarily the result of prejudice or passion because it is excessive. It might just as well be said that the mistakes made by appellate judges are the offspring of prejudice. Jurors, like other persons, may, and often do, err, though conscientious in the discharge of their duties. Common experience teaches us that verdicts differ widely, even in the same case, where the evidence as to the extent of the injury is precisely the same, and this, too, when there is nothing whatever from which the conclusion can be fairly drawn that the jurors were under the influence of any improper motive. Nor is there any thing strange in this when it is remembered that no exact guide can be given as to the amount of damages to be allowed. In the very nature of things the amount of damages must, to a large extent, rest with the jury. This court is constantly reviewing verdicts in this class of cases, and is in a position to be able to judge when a verdict is so far beyond those usually allowed in like cases as to be excessive, and litigants

ought to have the benefit of its judgment.   When it is conceded, as it generally is, that an appellate court can say a
given verdict is excessive, it follows that it can designate an
amount which would not be excessive.   If it possesses the
power to say the one thing, it possesses the power to say the
other.   The law is a practical affair, and ought to be administered in a practical way, so as to work out substantial justice by avoiding, as far as possible, the long [243] delays and
accumulated costs incident to reversals and repeated trials.

Indeed, second and third trials, as a general rule, result in
increased verdicts.   Where there is no just complaint save
that the damages are excessive, we are unable to see any
good reason why this court may not indicate the excess and
give the plaintiff the option to remit that excess or submit to
a new trial.   Such a practice is in the interest of justice, and
is the practice heretofore pursued by this court and that now
adopted by many of the state courts of last resort.   In the
case now in hand the plaintiff, if entitled to recover at all, is
entitled to recover substantial damages; the finding in his
favor is well supported by the evidence; there is nothing in
the record from which it can be said the jurors were actuated
by any improper influence; and there is no error, save that
the damages are excessive.   In such a case this court should
designate the excess, and allow the plaintiff to remit it and
take an affirmance for the residue.   The plaintiff having remitted three thousand dollars the judgment is affirmed for
the residue.

BRACE, MACFARLANE, and BURGESS, JJ., concur.

BARCLAY, GANTT, and SHERWOOD, JJ., dissent from what is
said in this supplemental opinion.

———

JUSTICES BARCLAY, GANTT, AND SHERWOOD dissented, on the ground that
in cases where the damages are unliquidated, and there is no legal measure
of damages, the amount to be awarded is solely and exclusively a question
of fact to be determined by the jury, and that the appellate court has no
right to interfere with the amount awarded except in cases where it clearly
appears that the verdict is the result of passion, prejudice, corruption, or
evident mistake, and then only to set the verdict aside and award a new
trial, or make such other disposition of the questions of law presented as
may be lawful and proper.   Under a constitution guaranteeing the right of
trial by jury and not investing the appellate court with power to try and
decide questions of both law and fact, the supreme court has no constitutional authority to review a decision of the jury or trial court upon issues
of fact in cases like the one here presented.   It has no right to constitute
itself a trier of facts, and upon the ground that the verdict, though ren-

dered without passion, prejudice, corruption, or evident mistake, is excessive, indicate and designate the excess, and require the plaintiff to remit that much as a condition of affirmance of the judgment or submit to a new trial. Mr. Justice Barclay, in support of his reasoning and conclusion, quoted at length from the opinions of the supreme court of Missouri and other states as follows:

"In *Dale* v. *St. Louis etc. Ry. Co.* (1876), 63 Mo. 460, the court unanimously said: 'The verdict in this case on the first trial was set aside on account of the damages being, in the opinion of the court, excessive. A second verdict was for the same amount, which the court refused to set aside, and any interference by this court would be a usurpation of the province of the jury': *Goetz* v. *Ambs*, 27 Mo. 34.

"In *Porter* v. *Railroad* (1879), 71 Mo. 83; 36 Am. Rep. 454, we find this ruling: 'There have been three trials of this cause, and three verdicts for plaintiff; the first for ten thousand dollars, the second twelve thousand dollars, and the third for ten thousand dollars; and we could with no propriety say, under these circumstances, that the damages are excessive.'

"In a later case this passage appears: 'The appellant contends that the damages are excessive. There is testimony to support the verdict, and the instructions taken together correctly state the measure of damages. In such cases we cannot interfere': *State* v. *Gaither* (1883), 77 Mo. 306.

"No doubt remarks may be found in some decisions to the effect that the supreme court will not set aside a verdict on the ground of excessive damages, unless the latter are so great as to indicate passion or prejudice on the part of the jury. But those observations occur chiefly in cases where the court declined to interfere, and in which the distinction between the functions of the trial court and of the supreme court under the constitution was not discussed.

"In *Sawyer* v. *Hannibal etc. R. R. Co.* (1866), 37 Mo. 246, 90 Am. Dec. 382, the court advanced an opinion that the damages were excessive, but refrained from placing the reversal of judgment on that ground.

"In *Kennedy* v. *North Missouri R. R. Co.* (1865), 36 Mo. 351, the court used the following language on this subject. 'The ground urged for a reversal, that the damages are too large, is not good here. There was evidence to go to the jury, and where that is the case it is their peculiar province, under proper instructions from the court, to determine the amount. Before we are at liberty to interfere with a verdict it must appear at first blush that the damages are flagrantly excessive, or that the jury have been influenced by passion, prejudice, or partiality. When there is any evidence to support the verdict it will not be disturbed; but this court will interfere when there is no evidence, or when the court below gives an instruction which is not authorized by the evidence.'

"In *Gregory* v. *Chambers* (1883), 78 Mo. 294, and *Pritchard* v. *Hewitt* (1887), 91 Mo. 547, 60 Am. Rep. 265, the court declined to set aside verdicts for wholly inadequate damages. Each verdict was for one dollar. In the former case the verdict was also against the evidence, yet it was rightly held that those were questions of fact, and the ruling thereon by the trial court was conclusive. In the latter decision the court made similar remarks to those in the Kennedy case, as to the want of power in this court to interfere unless the verdict showed passion or prejudice on its face.

"The same theory was approved by a majority of the judges of division one in the very recent judgment in *Boggess* v. *Metropolitan St. Ry. Co.* (1893), 118 Mo. 328.

"In *Gurley* v. *Missouri Pac. Ry. Co.* (1891), 104 Mo. 211, the second division denied the right to require a remittitur on appeal where the damages were excessive, saying: 'We do not think it within our province to assess the damages'; and that 'we have no right to set ourselves up as triers of facts and render another and different verdict.'

"In *Franklin* v. *Fischer* (1892), 51 Mo. App. 345, 348, the St. Louis court of appeals took the same view, declaring that 'to enforce a remittitur on appeal is to destroy the integrity of the verdict, and to substitute our judgment for that of the jury on a question which is eminently a question of fact.'

"If the last two quotations are correct in holding the question under consideration to be one of fact it follows logically and necessarily that it is a question not reviewable in any manner by this court, in actions of this description.

"No basis has ever been stated for a distinction between this question of fact and any other question of fact, with respect to the right of this court to review it.

"Neither the constitution nor any statute makes such a distinction.

"If it be held that this court may reverse the action of the trial judge and jury on one question of fact in actions at law it must be because of the possession of power to review all questions of fact in such cases.

"Where judges of this court consider a finding of fact so far wide of that which they would render in a given case as to appear to them to indicate passion or prejudice of the jury the nature of that finding is not thereby changed, nor does that opinion at once transform an error of fact into an error of law. The gravity of the mistake made by the constitutional triers of the fact does not enlarge the jurisdiction of this court, or authorize it to decide an issue not committed to, but excluded from, its reviewing power by the constitution.

"But the opinion by the majority in the present case does not assert a right to interfere to reduce a verdict where it shows passion or prejudice. The court seems to abandon that position, but it then proceeds to take a far bolder one. It holds that mere excess in the finding is subject to review here and to correction, by substituting the verdict of four judges of this court for the finding and judgment of the trial court, upon a question which is one of fact alone, as many of the strongest and ablest courts in other states have expressly held, as well as our own courts, already quoted.

"The United States supreme court has so declared on several occasions.

"In *Boggess* v. *Metropolitan St. Ry. Co.* (1893), 118 Mo. 340, an excerpt from its opinion on that point in *Railroad* v. *Fraloff* (1879), 100 U. S. 24, will be found. Since the latter ruling the same principle has been several times applied in other cases: *Wabash Ry. Co.* v. *McDaniels* (1882), 107 U. S. 454; *New York etc. R. R. Co.* v. *Winter* (1892), 143 U. S. 60. In *New York etc. R. R. Co.* v. *Winter*, 143 U. S. 65, the issue of excessive damages is expressly held to be one of fact, and hence not reviewable by that court.

"The courts of appeal of the United States have announced the same view in one case where a verdict for eighteen thousand two hundred and fifty dollars for personal injuries was challenged, on the ground that it appeared to have been given by reason of passion and prejudice (*Northern Pac. Ry. Co.* v. *Charless* (1892), 51 Fed. Rep. 562), and in another where a verdict for four thousand dollars for libel was similarly questioned:

Morning Journal Assn. v. *Rutherford* (1892), 51 Fed. Rep. 513. It was held in both instances that the verdicts were not reviewable for excess, because the appellate court had power to review errors of law only.

"In Illinois the supreme court formerly revised verdicts for excessive damages in law actions; but the laws of the state were then amended so as to declare explicitly that the supreme court should have no power to review questions of fact. Since then that court, recognizing that this question is one of fact, have held that it was not reviewable by them: *Chicago etc. Cab Co.* v. *Havelick* (1889), 131 Ill. 179; *Joliet Street Ry. Co.* v. *Call* (1892), 143 Ill. 179; *West Chicago R. R. Co.* v. *Bode* (1894), 150 Ill. 396.

"This is the law in Michigan: 'Whether damages found by a jury are excessive or not does not present a question of law. If no improper testimony affecting the subject of damages has been admitted, and the court has given to the jury proper instruction to guide them in reaching a conclusion, the amount of the damages awarded is beyond the reach of a writ of error': *Hunn* v. *Michigan Cent. R. R. Co.* (1889), 78 Mich. 513.

"In New Hampshire we find the subject thus treated: 'To justify the setting aside of a verdict because of excessive damages it should appear that they were so exorbitant as to warrant the belief that the jury must have been influenced by partiality, passion, or prejudice, or misled by some mistaken view of the merits of the case: Sedgwick on Damages, 601; *Belknap* v. *Boston etc. R. R. Co.*, 49 N. H. 358, 370-375. But neither this objection nor the further objection that the verdict was against the evidence presents any question of law. Such questions of fact are to be determined at the trial term': *Hovey* v. *Brown* (1879), 59 N. H. 114, followed as settled law in *Merrill* v. *Perkins* (1881), 61 N. H. 262, and in *Clark* v. *Manchester* (1887), 64 N. H. 471.

"[Nevertheless, the Belknap case, from the forty-ninth report of that state, appears as a citation in the prevailing opinion here as an authority for a review (on appeal) of that question.]

"In New York, in *Gale* v. *New York Cent. etc. R. R. Co.* (1879), 76 N. Y. 594, 'it was claimed that the damages awarded were excessive. The court stated their opinion to be that the claim was well founded, but that they had no jurisdiction to reverse upon that ground.' To the same purport are *Metcalf* v. *Baker* (1874), 57 N. Y. 662, and *Link* v. *Sheldon* (1892), 136 N. Y. 5.

"This is the view in Oregon: 'Where the verdict of a jury is excessive it is the duty of the *nisi prius* court to set it aside, but its refusal to do so cannot be reviewed by this court. Nothing but questions of law appearing upon the transcript can be reviewed here. The verdict herein may have been much larger than this court would have allowed under the evidence in the case, or in view of the facts found by the jury. Still we have no right to set it aside, or reverse or modify the judgment entered thereon. The jury are judges of the facts, and however widely our view might disagree with theirs, matters nothing. We have no right to invade their province, however sanguine we may be that they have committed error': *Nelson* v. *Oregon Ry. etc. Co.* (1886), 13 Or. 141, followed in *Kumli* v. *Southern Pac. Co.* (1892), 21 Or. 505.

"In Pennsylvania the settled doctrine, governing the action of the supreme court, has been lately stated very tersely, in an action for personal injuries, thus: 'It is enough to say that the only remedy for an excessive verdict is a motion for a new trial, and that the refusal of such trial is not assignable as error': *Vallo* v. *United States Express Co.* (1892), 147 Pa. St. 404; 30 Am. St. Rep. 741.

"In South Carolina, under a constitution conferring jurisdiction on the supreme court, 'for the correction of errors at law' (S. C. Const. 1868, art. 4, sec. 4), it is held that the subject of excessive damages for personal injury 'cannot be reviewed' by the supreme court: *Steele* v. *Charlotte etc. R. R. Co.* (1879), 11 S. C. 589; *Dobson* v. *Cothran* (1891), 34 S. C. 518.

"In all the jurisdiction from which the above cases have been cited excessive damages in actions of this sort are held to belong to the domain of fact.

"3. In Missouri the trial courts have been invested with the power to review such questions upon motion after verdict. They have the power to set aside the verdict if it is against the evidence or the weight of evidence.

"The power of the trial judge to revise a verdict upon the facts, in respect of its amount, is of modern growth. The rule of the old English law was that 'in actions founded upon torts, the jury are the sole judges of the damages, and therefore in such cases the court will not grant a new trial on account of the damages being trifling or excessive': Buller's Nisi Prius, 7th ed., *327.

"The rule is different now in England by virtue of parliamentary legislation, to be noted later in this opinion.

"But, in this state, the trial courts have the undoubted power, and it is often their duty, to vacate findings of damages for personal injuries, when those findings, in the opinion of the court upon the facts, appear so excessive as to indicate that prejudice or other improper motive of the jury entered into the result: Compare *Whipple* v. *Cumberland etc. Co.* (1843), 2 Story, 661; *Porter* v. *Hannibal etc. R. R. Co.* (1879), 71 Mo 66, 83; 36 Am. Rep. 454.

"But if the verdict is merely excessive, that is to say, too great, under the evidence, the trial court in the exercise of its right to review on the weight and sufficiency of evidence may cut it down (if a remittitur by the prevailing party be entered) to a sum which will accord with the evidence on that point.

"The amount of a verdict may sometimes form part of an issue of law; for example, in some actions on contract: *Pratt* v. *Blakey* (1838), 5 Mo. 205; *Hoyt* v. *Reed* (1852), 16 Mo. 294; and in other instances not in view now: Compare *Logan* v. *Small* (1869), 43 Mo. 254; *Todd* v. *Boone Co.* (1844), 8 Mo. 431; *Atwood* v. *Gillespie* (1836), 4 Mo. 423.

"In such cases the supreme court, on appeal (no less than the trial court), may apply the proper corrective, by remittitur or otherwise, which the error of law disclosed may require. Such cases are no authority for reviewing excessive damages here, in a case like that at bar. . . . .

"Since the adoption of the constitution of 1875 the supreme court, in a few instances, has assumed the power to cut down verdicts in actions for personal injuries: *Waldhier* v. *Hannibal etc. R. R. Co.* (1885), 87 Mo. 37; *Furnish* v. *Missouri Pac. Ry. Co.* (1891), 102 Mo. 438; 22 Am. St. Rep. 781. But in neither of those cases was the constitutional objection to such action met, or discussed, or, apparently, considered. In the latter of those decisions the court was not united; and neither of them can, in my opinion, be accepted as having the force of an amendment to the constitution.

"In *Smith* v. *Wabash etc. Ry. Co.* (1887), 92 Mo. 359, 1 Am. St. Rep. 729, the plaintiff remitted a part of his recovery when its amount was challenged as excessive; but the official report does not show that the supreme court forced the remittitur, or considered its power to force a remittitur.

"If law is to be administered with a due regard to the principles which give it life this court should either review all questions of fact or none in actions at law. If it has power under the constitution to act on a question of fact in respect of damages, which the judges here deem excessive, the court should also review the facts in all cases; and thus give all litigants alike the benefit of that reviewing power."'

Mr. Justice Barclay also asserted that the cases cited in the principal opinion were not authority for the doctrine there maintained, and in review-ing them said:

"In testing the strength of the precedents cited to uphold the result reached on the present appeal it should be remarked that the English case last above mentioned was determined under the procedure established by the Judicature Act, which made the trial court that first heard that case, and the court of appeal which reviewed it, merely different branches of the same 'supreme court of-judicature.' As parts of the same court, the court of appeal and divisional courts are invested by the law with power to act upon the verdict in the trial court, in the matter of amount: Supreme Court Judicature Act, 1875; Pub. Gen. Stats. 1875, pp. 830, 831, 1st sched-ule, order 58, secs. 2, 5, 11; *Webster* v. *Friedeberg* (1886), 17 Q. B. Div. 736; *Railroad* v. *Wright* (1886), 11 App. Cas. 152. Thus, for example, in *Phillips* v. *London etc. Ry. Co.* (1879), 5 Q. B. Div. 78, the queen's bench division granted a new trial to a plaintiff who had had a verdict for seven thousand pounds (about thirty-five thousand dollars), for personal injuries sustained in a collision; and that ruling was approved in the court of appeal, on the sole ground that the damages were inadequate.

"The decision in *Belt* v. *Lawes*, 12 Q. B. Div. 356, cannot, therefore, be regarded as any authority whatever upon the right to review excessive damages in appellate courts, organized under our constitution and laws.

"In England, prior to the Judicature Act, in *Britton* v. *South Wales Ry. Co.* (1858), 27 L. J. Ex., N. S., 355, the plaintiff having had a verdict for two thousand pounds sterling before Willes, J., and a jury at *nisi prius*, the court of exchequer (Pollock, C. B., Martin, B., Bramwell, B., and Watson, B.) declared: 'We cannot take the matter of damages out of the hands of the jury when the judge is not dissatisfied with their finding. It is impos-sible to measure the damages in such cases, and we cannot substitute our-selves for both judge and jury.'

"No other point was made, and the foregoing lines embrace the whole opinion in that case.

"Nor is the decision cited from 47 Barbour any authority on the subject in hand, for, by the law of New York then in force, the supreme court (in which the decision was rendered) had power to review the facts, and to reverse judgments on the weight of evidence: *Macy* v. *Wheeler* (1864), 30 N. Y. 237; *Hoyt* v. *Thompson* (1859), 19 N. Y. 211. The citation of the case in 47 Barbour, on appeal to the court of appeals (48 N. Y. 655), merely shows an affirmance of the former decision; but it has no bearing on the power to review the subject of excessive damages in a court having juris-diction of errors of law only. That topic is abundantly treated in other New York cases, already cited in this opinion. In Louisiana, from which another citation appears in the opinion of the learned chief justice, the supreme court has jurisdiction in damage suits to pass on the facts as well as law, and hence may, of course, enforce a remittitur of damages or an additur, as the facts may appear to the court to demand: *Donnell* v. *Sandford* (1856), 11 La. Ann. 645; *Caldwell* v. *Railroad Co.* (1889), 41 La Ann. 624. The remarks quoted from the Wisconsin case should be read along with a later decision in the same state, wherein the court, in declining to set aside a verdict for excess, remarked: 'The rule firmly established in this court by numerous adjudications forbids any interference with the verdict for alleged excessiveness of damages': *Hinton* v. *Railroad* (1886), 65 Wis. 323, 341."

"In my opinion the verdict under review cannot lawfully be disturbed here on account of its amount; and the majority of this court, be it said with the greatest respect, have no constitutional warrant for the order which has compelled the plaintiff to give up a large part of the damages adjudged to him by the jury and the trial court.

"The majority have taken this course without even discussing the question whether, in so doing, the plaintiff's right to a trial by jury has been violated.

"But such a question of constitutional right cannot thus be disposed of without my earnest, but respectful, protest.

"Hence my dissent is entered to the judgment announced by the majority of my brethren."

Mr. Justice Gantt also delivered a dissenting opinion, in which he said: "In *Kennedy* v. *Railroad*, 36 Mo. 351, Judge Wagner said: 'The ground urged for reversal, that the damages are too large, is not good here. There was evidence to go to the jury, and where that is the case it is their peculiar province, under proper instructions from the court, to determine the amount. Before we are at liberty to interfere with a verdict it must appear at first blush that the damages are flagrantly excessive, or that the jury have been influenced by passion, prejudice, or partiality.' In *Graham* v. *Railroad*, 66 Mo. 536, Judge Norton, for the whole court, said: 'It is claimed the damages are excessive.' After quoting the remark from *Kennedy* v. *Railroad*, 36 Mo. 351, he said: 'In the case before us plaintiff's right to recover damages was clearly established, and it does not appear to us that they are so flagrantly excessive, or that the sum assessed is so disproportioned to the injury as to bear marks of passion, prejudice, or corruption on the part of the jury, and, because we cannot say this, the judgment cannot be disturbed on the ground of excessive damages.'

"*Smith* v. *Railroad*, 92 Mo. 359, 1 Am. St. Rep. 729, was placed squarely on the authority of *Miller* v. *Hardin*, 64 Mo. 545. No reference was made to the *Waldhier case*, 87 Mo. 37. *Miller* v. *Hardin*, 64 Mo. 545, was an action of ejectment, and the jury assessed no damages, but the circuit court, in rendering judgment, entered it up for one hundred and five dollars damages. The plaintiff discovered this and asked to remit all of said damages, and it was permitted, but neither of those cases meets the practice to which I am objecting, namely, the enforced remittitur, or the alternative of a reversal. My position is that our jurisdiction in these cases is appellate, and that we are not authorized to assess the damages in a case like this, and that we are utterly without the means to properly fix them. As an original proposition I recognize the force and logic of a position that, as an appellate tribunal, we have no right to pass upon any question of fact in an appeal from a law case, but this court has asserted this jurisdiction in similar cases, since *Lackey* v. *Lane*, 7 Mo. 220, and *McAfee* v. *Ryan*, 11 Mo. 364, under the constitution of 1820, and the people adopted the present constitution with our construction upon it; but I am unwilling to go further than to say that a verdict may be reversed when, upon the record, it appears to be the result of passion, prejudice, corruption, or evident mistake. The rule now announced by our learned chief justice and adopted by the court, in my opinion, goes further than any court in the country, and further, in my opinion, than warranted by the constitution of this state, or the great weight of decisions prior to the *Waldhier case*, 87 Mo. 37, justifies   In *Worster* v. *Canal Bridge*, 16 Pick. 547, the supreme court of Massachusetts said: 'In all cases where there is no rule of law regulating the assessment of damages, and the amount does not depend on computation, the judgment of the jury and not the opinion of the court is to govern, unless the damages are so excessive as to warrant the belief that the jury must have been influenced by partiality or prejudice, or have been misled by some mistaken view of the merits of the case.'"

"In *Nudd* v. *Wells*, 11 Wis. 415, the court said: 'The practice of remitting where the illegal part is clearly distinguishable from the rest, and may be ascertained by the court without assuming the functions of the jury and substituting its judgment for theirs, is well settled. . . . . But it ought not to be carried so far as to allow the court, when a jury has obviously mistaken the law, or the evidence, and rendered a verdict which ought not to stand, to substitute its own judgment for theirs, and after determining upon the evidence what amount ought to be allowed, allow the plaintiff to remit the excess, and then refuse a new trial.   There are authorities that would sustain even this, as *Collins* v. *Railroad Co.*, 12 Barb. 492, and *Clapp* v. *Railroad Co.*, 19 Barb. 461.   But we are unable to see how such a practice can be sustained, in such cases as those were without doing the very thing which they professed not to do; that is, allow the court to substitute its own verdict for a wrong verdict of the jury, and, on the plaintiff's accepting that, refusing a new trial.'

"In *Vinal* v. *Core*, 18 W. Va., 1, that court fully indorsed the above view of the supreme court of Wisconsin and reasserted the same doctrine in *Unfried* v. *Railroad*, 34 W. Va. 260; *Vaulx* v. *Herman*, 8 Lea, 683; *Thomas* v. *Womack*, 13 Tex. 580."

"No amount of argument can disguise the fact that, if we assume to set aside verdicts in this manner, and substitute our findings in lieu of the jury's, we have taken to ourselves the prerogative that was confided by the constitution and the statutes to the jury.   Nor am I able to see the consistency in setting aside the verdict of a jury, dictating a different finding, and yet hesitating, when asked to instruct a jury as to the elements of damages, because we would thereby be invading their province.

"At one time I had thought I would not dissent in this case, but yield my assent because of the former decision of this court in *Furnish* v. *Railroad*, 102 Mo. 438, 22 Am. St. Rep. 781, but when I consider that that decision did not constitute a rule of property, and no vested right would be disturbed by not adhering to it, and because I am convinced that, as judges, we ought not to assume the functions of a jury, and that it has from the organization of the state been considered the peculiar right of a jury to fix the amount of damages in a tort like this, I deem it my duty to say so now.   It has been iterated and reiterated numberless times that 'no measure can be prescribed in such cases except the enlightened consciences of impartial jurors.'   Have we concluded we will substitute the enlightened conscience of the judges of the appellate courts in lieu of that of the jury? It seems so to me, and for that reason I dissent from the practice."

NEGLIGENCE—ACTION FOR WHETHER LOCAL OR TRANSITORY.—Actions for damages for personal injuries or for pecuniary loss resulting from the death of a person caused by the wrongful act or neglect of another are transitory in character: *Cincinnati etc. R. R. Co.* v. *McMullen*, 117 Ind. 439; 10 Am. St. Rep. 67. This question is fully discussed in the extended note to *Morris* v. *Missouri Pac. Ry. Co.*, 22 Am. St. Rep. 22, 24.

EVIDENCE—COMMON LAW—PRESUMPTION AS TO EXISTENCE OF.—The common law is presumed to be the rule of decision in other states unless the contrary is shown: *Thompson* v. *Monrow*, 2 Cal. 99; 56 Am. Dec. 318, and note; *Connor* v. *Trawick*, 37 Ala. 289; 79 Am. Dec. 58, and note; *Ellis* v. *Maxon*, 19 Mich. 186; 2 Am. Rep. 81; *Carpenter* v. *Grand Trunk Ry. Co.*, 72 Me. 388; 39 Am. Rep. 340, and note.

EXCESSIVE DAMAGES—REMISSION OF EXCESS.—Excessive verdict is cured by entering a remittitur in the appellate court for a smaller sum: *Smith* v. *Wabash etc. Ry. Co.*, 92 Mo. 359; 1 Am. St. Rep. 729. Where, on motion for a new trial, the damages appear to be excessive the plaintiff may be permitted to remit the excess, or a portion thereof, and the verdict will stand for the residue: *Doyle* v. *Dixon*, 97 Mass. 208; 93 Am. Dec. 80.

RAILROADS.—LIABILITY FOR INJURY TO BRAKEMAN coupling cars caused by defective track: See *Ragon* v. *Toledo etc. Ry. Co.*, 97 Mich. 265; 37 Am. St. Rep. 336; *Soeder* v. *St. Louis etc. Ry. Co.*, 100 Mo. 673; 18 Am. St. Rep. 724; *Missouri Pac. Ry. Co.* v. *Jones*, 75 Tex. 151; 16 Am. St. Rep. 879; *Kansas City etc. R. R. Co.* v. *Kier*, 41 Kan. 661; 13 Am. St. Rep. 311.

CRUZEN *v.* STEPHENS.

[123 MISSOURI, 337.]

COURTS—PRESUMPTION AS TO ACTS OF.—It is presumed, in the absence of evidence, that a court acts in conformity to, and not in violation of, law.

JUDGMENT cannot be collaterally impeached by oral evidence of facts outside the record of the case in which the judgment was rendered.

JUDGMENTS — NOTICE BY PUBLICATION — COLLATERAL ATTACK.—Under a statute authorizing notice by publication on a return of not found, "the court being first satisfied that process cannot be served," the fact that an order for publication of process is granted upon the unsworn statement of a witness does not make the judgment rendered in the action void in a collateral proceeding, nor is oral evidence admissible in such proceedings to show that the court acted upon an insufficient showing.

JUDGMENTS—COLLATERAL ATTACK.—If a court has power to act on proof of a given fact, its action upon the statement of such fact by an unsworn witness is not for that reason alone entirely void, so as to render its judgment void when questioned collaterally.

PROCESS—NOTICE BY PUBLICATION.—Surplusage in an order for the service of process by publication does not render it void if it is otherwise valid.

PROCESS—NOTICE BY PUBLICATION—COLLATERAL ATTACK.—Service by publication in a tax suit is sufficient, as against collateral attack, if it names the defendants with sufficient definiteness to plainly indicate their identity.

PROCESS—NOTICE BY PUBLICATION—COLLATERAL ATTACK.—Service of process by publication addressed to "Etta R. Fisher and —— Fisher, her husband," is valid on collateral attack.

PROCESS.—Publication of process in a newspaper four consecutive times, with an interval of one week between each publication, is a publication for four weeks.

JUDGMENTS FOR TAXES—COLLATERAL ATTACK.—A tax judgment dealing with the property as one tract instead of subjecting each subdivision to its appropriate part of the taxes is not void on collateral attack.

JUDGMENT FOR TAXES.—SHERIFF'S DEED under a tax judgment conveying all the estate which the sheriff might sell under the judgment is valid to transfer the interests of the defendant in the tax suit.

J. E. Wait, for the appellants.

Alexander & Richardson, for the respondent.

540 BARCLAY, J. This is an action of ejectment for a tract of land in Daviess county. The petition is in ordinary, statutory form: Rev. Stats. 1889, sec. 4631.

The original defendant, Mr. Stephens (who was sued alone), answered, admitting his possession as tenant of the Lyle heirs. The latter also appeared, and became parties defendant on their motion, viz., Messrs. W. H. Lyle and George W. Lyle, and Mrs. Etta R. Fisher and Mr. John Fisher, her husband.

They filed a separate answer, alleging possession of the land by their tenant, Mr. Stephens, and denying the other allegations of the petition.

They then charged that plaintiff's claim of title was under a judgment and sale in a certain tax suit, entitled State ex rel. and to the use of N. B. Brown against " defendants in this answer," which suit terminated in **541** the same court at the February term, 1889; and that plaintiff had no other interest in the property.

The answer then continues thus: " That defendants herein are, and have ever been since 1880, residents of Illinois, and had no information of said suit; that there was no allegation in said petition for taxes; that the defendants were nonresidents, nor was there any order of publication by this court, nor was the tax-book, under which said suit was brought, ever examined and completed as required by law; and the said suit and execution, and the sale thereunder, was, and is, wholly void; and defendants therefore pray that the said deed be set aside, and the cloud which is so made thereby on defendants' title be removed; that the defendants have title to said land, subject to a certain mortgage not yet foreclosed; and defendants ask for such further orders, judgments, and decrees as they may be entitled to." To this answer the plaintiff filed a reply, consisting of a general denial.

Upon the trial it was admitted that the defendants, Lyle and Fisher, were the owners of the land, and that Stephens was their tenant, unless the proceedings in the tax suit and sale thereunder had transferred the title to plaintiff, in which event he should recover. The monthly rents and profits were also agreed upon.

It was further stipulated that the sheriff's deed to plaintiff under the tax sale should be considered in evidence, subject to be finally received or rejected by the court, after hearing all the other evidence and the objections thereto by defendants. The sheriff's deed was then produced in evidence, and plaintiff rested. Defendants then offered the court record and all the papers in the tax suit.

[343] It will not be necessary to set them out at length. The points at which fatal deficiencies therein are said to appear will be noted in the course of the opinion in connection with the discussion of the defendants' objections. At the close of the testimony the court overruled the objections to the sheriff's deed, and gave judgment for plaintiff. Defendants then appealed, after taking the usual steps for a review.

1. The first objection to the sheriff's deed, under the tax judgment, is that the defendants in the judgment were not in court, because the order of publication was granted without proper foundation.

The record shows that a writ of summons was issued January 7, 1889, to all the defendants. The sheriff's return upon the writ was this: "*Non est;* none of the within-named defendants found in my said county."

Thereupon the court ordered publication, February 12, 1889 (at the February term), "it appearing to the court, among other things, that the defendants are nonresidents of this state, so that the ordinary process of law cannot be served," etc., as the order states. No affidavit of nonresidence of defendants was filed. Nor does the petition in that suit allege that fact.

Under the revenue law all notices and process in suits for the collection of back taxes are required to be sued out and served in the same manner as in civil actions in the circuit court; and the proceedings against nonresident or other parties, on whom service cannot be had by ordinary summons, shall be the same as now provided by law in civil actions affecting real estate, etc: Rev. Stats. 1889, sec. 7682, same as Rev. Stats. 1879, sec. 6837.

[543] The sufficiency of the order of publication is hence to be determined by the rule applicable to that subject in the code governing ordinary actions.

The code provides that, in a case to enforce a lien on real property, when "summons shall be issued against any defendant, and the sheriff to whom it is directed shall make return that the defendant or defendants cannot be found, the court, being first satisfied that process cannot be served," shall make an order of publication against such defendants: Rev. Stats. 1889, sec. 2024, same as Rev. Stats. 1879, sec. 3496.

Upon the return of "not found," on the summons to defendants, the court had power to grant the order of publication "being satisfied," as stated in the section last quoted.

The fact that the court made such an order after the return of not found is sufficient of itself to indicate that it was "satisfied" of the required fact; for it should be assumed of a court, in the absence of any showing to the contrary, that it acts in conformity to, not in violation of, the law.

Verbal testimony was put in by defendants, at the trial of this case, with a view to prove that the court made the order of publication without any legal evidence that process could not be served. That verbal testimony was wholly incompetent for that purpose. A judgment cannot be collaterally impeached by such evidence of facts outside the record of the cause in which the judgment was rendered.

But even accepting, for the moment, that verbal testimony, it amounts only to this: that the attorney, representing the collector in the tax suit, informally represented to the court that the defendants were nonresidents, after the sheriff's return had been made; [544] and thereupon the court entered the order of publication. Those facts surely would not nullify the action of the court in that behalf when collaterally attacked.

If the court had power to act on proof of a given fact, its action upon the statement of it by an unsworn witness would not, for that reason alone, be entirely void, so as to render its judicial action a nullity when questioned collaterally. And, if the court was satisfied that defendants were not residents of the state, it might logically and reasonably conclude that they could not be served with ordinary process.

Nor does the recital, in the order of .publication, to the effect that it appeared to the court that defendants were non-residents, vitiate the order. That part of it is simply surplusage. Its material part is that it appeared to the court that the ordinary process of law could not be served.

The record made by the defendants in the case at bar establishes that they were in fact residents of Illinois during the time the tax suit was pending, and for many years before.

There is certainly no injustice done them in applying firmly the presumption of correct action by the circuit judge in making the order of publication in the tax suit, when the record therein does not negative the correctness of that order, and defendants' own admissions now prove conclusively that the order had, at the time, ample support in truth.

2. It is then claimed that the order was void because of its form. In the petition in the tax case, and in the order of publication, the defendants were named thus: "Wm. H. Lile, Gerge W. Lile, Etta R. Fisher, and —— Fisher, her husband."

[345] Defendants insist that this designation of Mr. Fisher is so vague as to render the tax proceedings, judgment, and sale utterly void.

The answer in the case in hand admits that Mr. John Fisher, one of defendants in both cases, is the husband of Etta R. Fisher, and that the present defendants are the same persons who were defendants in the former suit. The object of giving notice by publication is to advise the parties to whom the notice is directed of the proceedings mentioned. If the notice effectively does that it should be held sufficient against any collateral attack.

Judge Vanfleet thus summarizes the rule deducible from principle and well-considered cases: "That the omission of the name of a defendant from the process makes the judgment void in respect to him is plain; but, where he is so described that he would not be misled, it is not void": Vanfleet's Collateral Attack, secs. 356, 361.

It certainly seems to accord with just principles of law and of common sense that, where the notice names the parties defendant with sufficient definiteness to plainly indicate their identity, it should be held good, and not void, when questioned in this collateral way.

Here the notice in effect was directed to Etta R. Fisher

and Mr. Fisher, her husband. It would have been practically no more informative of the identity of John Fisher, her husband, had the blank in the order and in the petition in that case been filled with his first name.

3. It is next urged that the publication of the order in the newspaper was insufficient.

According to the affidavit of the printer and publisher it appeared in the designated paper, the *Gallatin Democrat*, "for four weeks," namely, on March 7, 14, 21, and 28, 1889.

[346] Defendants argue that publication four times, at these intervals, is not publication for "four weeks"; and cite the argument of the court of appeals in *State* v. *Tucker* (1888), 32 Mo. App. 620, claiming that the latter demonstrates that the ruling on this subject in *Haywood* v. *Russell* (1869), 44 Mo. 252 (where such a publication was held good), is unsound, and should not be followed.

Whatever we might think of the ruling in the forty-fourth report as an original proposition, it has been acquiesced in so fully, and been treated as a settled point of practice in making publications in all sorts of proceedings for so many years, that we decline to re-examine it. We consider that the rule it declares has become a rule of property, on the • faith of which great numbers of titles founded on judicial sales depend.

The publication in the tax suit was sufficient under the decision last mentioned, and we refrain from any further discussion of it, without, however, intending to cast any doubt upon its correctness.

4. Defendants also object to the validity of the tax judgment, because the petition and all the subsequent proceedings in that case, including the sale, deal with the property as one tract, a quarter section, instead of subjecting each subdivision to its appropriate part of the taxes. This point is settled against defendants by *Jones* v. *Driskill* (1887), 94 Mo. 190. This criticism, though, perhaps, indicating error or irregularity in the proceedings, does not show a blemish sufficiently serious to avoid the judgment in a collateral action.

5. Defendants also object to the sheriff's deed, on the ground that it conveys nothing by its terms.

It recites the proceedings in the tax suit at great [347] length, describing the land "as the southeast quarter section 13, township 58, range 26," giving the items of tax charges against it, and declaring that the court had decreed that the lien of the state upon said real estate for said taxes be enforced, and the same sold to satisfy said judgment, interest, and costs.

It then continues as follows: "Now, therefore, in consideration of the premises, and of the sum of $97 to me, the said sheriff, in hand paid by the said N. G. Cruzen, the receipt whereof I do hereby acknowledge, and by virtue of the authority in me vested by law, I, Gabe W. Cox, sheriff as aforesaid, do hereby assign, transfer, and convey unto the said N. G. Cruzen all the above-described real estate so stricken off and sold to him that I might sell as sheriff as aforesaid, by virtue of the aforesaid judgment, execution, and notice.

"To have and to hold the right, title, interest, and estate hereby conveyed unto the said N. G. Cruzen, his heirs and assigns, forever, with all the rights and appurtenances thereto belonging. In witness whereof," etc.

It is enough to say that we regard the terms of this deed as sufficient to transfer to plaintiff the interests of the defendants in the tax suit, under the statute law touching the form of such conveyances.

We have discussed all the defendant's assignments of error which appear to call for any remark.

We hold the objections to the tax deed untenable. The learned circuit judge was correct in overruling them.

We affirm the judgment.

BLACK, C. J., and BRACE and MACFARLANE, JJ., concur.

EVIDENCE.—PRESUMPTION AS TO REGULARITY OF JUDICIAL PROCEEDINGS: See the notes to *McGowan* v. *Lufburrow*, 14 Am. St. Rep. 183, and *Hersey* v. *Walsh*, 8 Am. St. Rep. 691. The judgment of a domestic court of general jurisdiction is conclusively presumed to be correct: *Crim* v. *Kessing*, 89 Cal. 478; 23 Am. St. Rep. 491, and note.

JUDGMENT—IMPEACHMENT BY MATTERS OUTSIDE OF THE RECORD.—Judgments of courts of record cannot be contradicted or falsified by proof *aliunde;* they are of too high verity to be impeached by parol proof: *Bank* v. *Patterson*, 8 Humph. 363; 47 Am. Dec. 618, and note. To the same effect see *Kemp* v. *Cook*, 18 Md. 130; 79 Am. Dec. 681.

JUDGMENTS—PROCESS BY PUBLICATION—COLLATERAL ATTACK.—Judgment on process served by publication is not open to collateral attack: *Taylor* v. *Coots*, 32 Neb. 30; 29 Am. St. Rep. 426, and note. See the extended note to *Hahn* v. *Kelly*, 94 Am. Dec. 762.

JURISDICTION—SERVICE BY PUBLICATION.—Jurisdiction over the defendant is acquired in cases of service of summons by publication only when the statutory requirements are successively and accurately taken: *Beckett* v.

Cuenin, 15 Col. 281; 22 Am. St. Rep. 399, and note.   Constructive service
of process by publication addressed to "John McCorkle and —— Mc-
Corkle, his wife," he being then dead, is no notice to her of the pendency of
the action, and a judgment based on such service alone is void as to her:
Thompson v. *McCorkle*, 136 Md. 484; 43 Am. St. Rep. 334, and note.

PROCESS BY PUBLICATION.—Publication once a week for four weeks construed: Note to *Maddox* v. *Sullivan*, 44 Am. Dec. 239.

GIRARD v. ST. LOUIS CAR WHEEL COMPANY.
[123 MISSOURI, 358.]

NEGLIGENCE—PLEA OF RELEASE—FRAUD.—If a plea of release is set up in
an answer alleging an agreement in the nature of a discharge of a cause
of action to recover for personal injury caused by negligence, a reply to
such plea, alleging that such agreement was obtained by fraud, while
plaintiff was unable from the pain and suffering arising from the injury
to comprehend his act in signing it, and that he never assented thereto,
is good and sufficient, in an action at law, without first resorting to
equity for the cancellation of such agreement.

RELEASE OBTAINED BY FRAUD—NECESSITY FOR TENDER BEFORE SUIT.—
A tender of money, or other thing of value, received by virtue of a
release, need not be made before bringing an action at law to recover
for personal injury if the release was obtained by fraud.   It is sufficient to offer its return and to account for it by the judgment.

RELEASE OBTAINED BY FRAUD—NECESSITY FOR TENDER.—If a release is
found to have been obtained by fraud practiced upon one incapable,
because of mental weakness to enter into such a contract, the fruits of
the release need not be refunded before action brought.

RELEASE OBTAINED BY FRAUD—WAIVER OF TENDER.—If a reply of fraud
is made to a plea of release, and no objection is at any time, by pleading or otherwise, made to the sufficiency of plaintiff's case for failure to
tender or return the fruits of such release, and defendant insists upon
its validity as a defense, he thereby waives the necessity for a tender,
especially when the fruits of the release are restored to him by the
judgment.

W. E. Fisse and Lee & Ellis, for the appellant.

A. R. Taylor, for the respondent.

358 BARCLAY, J.   The petition states a case for damages
on account of personal injuries suffered by plaintiff while in
the employ of the defendant company.

It charges as the cause negligence in respect of the operation of certain hoisting machinery, under the direction of
defendant's superintendent, at its shops in St. Louis; and
alleges that, in consequence of that negligence (the particulars of which are not important at this stage of the proceed-

ings), a heavy timber fell upon plaintiff, disabling him from labor, etc.

The answer denies the charge of negligence, and sets up, as a bar to plaintiff's action, a written instrument, signed by plaintiff and by one of defendant's officers, in which (after reciting the fact of plaintiff's injury) the following stipulations appear:

"The said Car Wheel Co., on their part, proposes [364] to furnish and pay for all the medical attendance, necessary for his recovery from said injuries sustained by said accident, and to keep his name on its pay-roll at the uniform wages per day, for all working days, which he has been up to this time credited, and in any other way in their power assist in his recovery, until he is physically sufficiently recovered from said accident, evidenced by physician's certificate, to resume work.

"And that on his part, beyond the above obligation of the St. Louis Car Wheel Co., he relinquishes all other claims whatsoever as to them, and that he agrees to this deliberately, and of his own free will, and without any undue influence from any one.

"The said parties, in evidence of which and in good faith, sign this, the date first herein written."

Defendant alleged compliance with the above agreement, so far as plaintiff had permitted such compliance, and prayed judgment. Plaintiff, by a reply, charged that the said agreement had been obtained from him by gross fraud and misrepresentations of defendant and its agents; that, at the time it was made, he was in the deepest distress and bodily pain, and was unable, through his bodily and mental condition, to understand or comprehend the contents of said agreement, and never did assent to the terms thereof.

These allegations of fraud and incapacity are repeated in several forms with considerable particularity of detail; but the above outline will be sufficient for present purposes. The cause came to trial before Judge Dillon and a jury. It is not necessary to go into the evidence as to the plaintiff's original right of recovery, since no point is made in this court on that branch of the case.

[365] The only questions of any difficulty now submitted concern the rules of law to be applied in view of the so-called release or settlement.

The plaintiff's testimony tended to prove that his injury

occurred September 13, 1889, and the agreement (which we will for convenience call a release) was signed the next day, about noon. The timber which struck plaintiff was about eighteen feet long and six by nine inches thick. It hit him in the back. He was knocked to the ground, senseless. His arm was broken. Blood oozed from his forehead, and his face was scratched. He could not stand. He had to be carried away from the shop. He was put into an ambulance and taken to the city hospital. The next day he was removed to his boarding-house.

He testified that he had no recollection of signing the release; that at that time he was unable to read or comprehend any thing; if he attempted to read he could merely "see a gleam" in front of him; "that for four or five weeks he was not in his proper mind or able to understand things; that during the first week he did not easily recognize people who called on him." He suffered intense pain, which did not begin to abate for two months. His face and jaws were badly swollen, his eyes discolored and almost closed. He had a lump on the back of his head for some time after the mishap. Six or eight days later he found a copy of the release on the floor of his room. He gave it to his attorney soon afterward, and then brought this action, in October, 1891.

Several of his fellow-workmen, who called to see him on the day the release was signed and on the following day, gave various descriptions of his condition; for instance: **366** "He was excited and bewildered." "His mind was not clear." "He was more jovial than was usual with him." "He did not seem rational." "He did n't seem to me to act or talk at the time as I saw him do before."

The defendant's testimony contradicted that above quoted, and tended to prove that plaintiff understood the release, assented to its terms, executed it freely, and that no fraud was practiced upon him. Under the terms of the release defendant employed a physician to treat plaintiff, at a cost of fifty dollars, until the time plaintiff discharged him, shortly before bringing this suit. The defendant further paid ten dollars to another physician who had been called to plaintiff's aid at the shop in the emergency when he was first injured. Defendant also kept plaintiff's name on the pay-roll, and was ready and willing to pay him wages according to the agreement in the release; but he would not, or did not, accept those wages.

The trial court submitted the issue of release upon instructions, under which the jury found that plaintiff signed that paper at the instance of defendant's agents without knowing its contents, and that he never did assent to its terms. They also found that the release was signed when plaintiff was in such a mental condition that he could not comprehend its contents; and that defendant's agents took advantage of that condition to induce him to sign the paper without understanding it, intending thereby to defraud plaintiff of his cause of action set forth in the petition.

On that issue the court gave the following instructions at the instance of defendant, viz:

"4. The jury are instructed, even though you should believe from the evidence the release pleaded by [367] defendant to have been unfair to the plaintiff and not a sufficient recompense for plaintiff's injuries, still, this will not relieve plaintiff from its force and effect as a bar to his recovery in this action. The only way in which plaintiff can affect the conclusiveness of this bar is to satisfy you by a preponderance of evidence that plaintiff, when he signed the release, had not sufficient mental power to know the nature of the instrument he was signing."

"The court instructs the jury that the paper read in evidence, signed by the plaintiff, and termed a release, is on its face a release and discharge of the cause of action sued on in this case. It is a presumption of law that the plaintiff understood and agreed to the terms and contents of said paper when he signed it, and the burden is on the plaintiff to show by a preponderance of evidence that he was not acquainted with the contents of the paper, and that he did not voluntarily agree to release his claim for damages growing out of his injury upon the terms stated in said petition, or that defendant fraudulently procured the execution thereof by him, and, unless the plaintiff has affirmatively so proved these facts to the satisfaction of the jury by a preponderance of proof, they should find for the defendant."

"12. The court instructs the jury, that in determining the question whether the paper offered in evidence and termed a release was freely and voluntarily signed by the plaintiff, they are not at liberty to consider whether the terms of said release were reasonable, nor whether the undertakings of the defendant therein constituted a full and adequate compensation for his injury."

560   GIRARD *v.* ST. LOUIS CAR WHEEL CO.   [Missouri,

The bill of exceptions also shows that, "the cause being submitted to the jury, they found a verdict in favor of plaintiff, such verdict being an award of damages [368] in favor of plaintiff in the sum of $1,562, less the sum of $62, paid by the defendant under the terms of the release given in evidence, leaving the amount of damages $1,500."

The jury also found for the plaintiff on the issues of negligence, under appropriate instructions, which need not be examined, as this appeal does not call in question any rulings on that part of the case.

After the usual motions and exceptions defendant appealed to the St. Louis court of appeals; but, as the judges of that court were divided in opinion (*Girard* v. *St. Louis Car Wheel Co.*, 46 Mo. App. 81), the case was transferred to the supreme court under the provisions of the constitution: Constitutional Amendment, 1884, sec. 6.

1. Defendant's first proposition is that this action for damages is not maintainable, because the release has not been set aside by a decree in equity. In other words, it is claimed that the paper in question is a complete defense at law to the cause of action to which it relates, no matter how the paper may have been obtained. This position has been defended with much ability; but no resources of counsel are sufficient to conceal its inherent weakness.

The testimony for plaintiff tends strongly to prove that he was incapable of understanding the release when he signed it, and that he did not comprehend nor intend to assent to its terms. The jury so found in response to instructions.

Those facts, when established, destroyed the substance of the agreement which the release in form expressed. They took from the apparent contract what was essential to its legal force and validity, namely, the element of assent by the plaintiff. That element is a necessary part of every contract.

[369] Without it a mere writing, expressing some formula of words, imposes no obligation. The signature of plaintiff obtained to such a paper, without the assent of his mind to the act, deprived him of no legal right. He might, indeed, affirm such a signature, or make it his lawful act by his subsequent conduct, the effect of which would be to give to the agreement that assent which was necessary to originate an obligation on his part. But, in the absence of such acts as amounted to an approval of it, he might proceed to enforce his rights,

irrespective of such a paper: *Brewster* v. *Brewster* (1875), 38 N. J. L. 119.

In circumstances such as are here exhibited, a writing, in the form of a release, which never acquired original validity as a contract for want of competent assent to its terms, may be disregarded by a court of law in the administration of justice without the intervention of a court of equity.

The paper in question is, in contemplation of law, nothing more than the form of a contract; and, on finding that the substance, which should give life to an obligation, is wanting the court may cast aside the form and proceed to judgment, notwithstanding the fraud which may have brought the verisimilitude of an obligation into existence: *Hartshorn* v. *Day* (1856), 19 How. 211; *Vandervelden* v. *Chicago etc. Ry. Co.* (1894), 61 Fed. Rep. 54.

A court of law, upon ascertaining such a fraud, may properly pass over it to the conclusion which it considers just; thus, in effect, discarding the fraud as an obstacle to the exercise of its jurisdiction. It is not thought necessary at this day to further argue the correctness of this proposition. It has been repeatedly asserted in earlier decisions in this state, both before and since the adoption of the [370] reformed code of procedure in 1849: *Burrows* v. *Alter* (1842), 7 Mo. 424; *Wright* v. *McPike* (1879), 70 Mo. 175.

They conform to a multitude of precedents elsewhere, many of which are cited in the briefs of counsel, to which may be added, *Thompson* v. *Faussat* (1815), Pet. C. C. 182; *Bliss* v. *New York etc. R. R. Co.* (1894), 160 Mass. 447; 39 Am. St. Rep. 504.

The case of *Blair* v. *Chicago etc. R. R. Co.* (1886), 89 Mo. 383, which is cited as having some tendency to the contrary, goes no further in that direction than to approve the practice of proceeding to first cancel the release for fraud upon allegations stating a cause of action in equity, before trying the other cause of action at law on the merits of the plaintiff's original claim. While that course may be adopted, it is not essential where the alleged fraud goes to the integrity of the release as a legal agreement, which is the case in the present action. The Blair decision does not declare it necessary to go into equity to get rid of a paper executed in such circumstances as here appear.

2. It is next contended that the release must stand, because plaintiff did not, before action brought, offer to refund the

amount paid by defendant for medical services to plaintiff under the terms of that paper.

The verdict gave defendant the benefit of that credit upon the plaintiff's claim, by reducing his damages to that extent (sixty-two dollars); but it is urged that that mode of refunding the fruits of the agreement for a release does not satisfy the requirements of law.

The substance of defendant's contention is that a tender of the benefits received under the release was essential to plaintiff's case; and that without it his action cannot be maintained.

Assuming [as this court is now bound to do in view of the evidence and the findings of the jury] that [371] the release was not the valid act or contract of the plaintiff, then it was, at best, voidable at his option. That is to say, he was at liberty to ignore it in the assertion of his legal rights. His act in bringing the present suit was a plain and unmistakable repudiation of it, and a distinct notice that he discarded and denied the obligation which it apparently imposed: *Ward* v. *Day* (1863), 33 L. J. Q. B. 3; *Clough* v. *London etc. Ry. Co.* (1871), L. R. 7 Exch. 26; *Dawes* v. *Harness* (1875), L. R. 10 C. P. 166. He had done nothing to ratify it or adopt it as his act.

Was he required, in such a case, to seek the defendant's officers and tender back the value of the medical services rendered to him before beginning his action? He has, before judgment, accounted for every thing of value received by him by virtue of the supposed release; and the defendant has had credit therefor, as the verdict of the jury on its face shows.

But the attitude of the defendant throughout, as well as before, the litigation, its plea of release, its setting aside in an envelope the wages of plaintiff each week, all indicate that any tender by plaintiff of repayment for the medical services would have been useless. Since the execution of that paper defendant has continuously asserted and relied upon its validity, and still asserts it.

It has been decisively held in other cases that no preliminary tender can be insisted upon, as a bar to legal action, where the facts show that the tender would have been rejected: *Deichmann* v. *Deichmann* (1871), 49 Mo. 107; *Westlake* v. *St. Louis* (1882), 77 Mo. 47; 46 Am. Rep. 4.

In such a state of the facts a tender would be what Mr.

Bigelow calls an idle ceremony: Bigelow on Fraud, ed. 1888, p. 424.

[372] No distinction should be made, and, in my opinion, none exists in principle, between actions for personal injuries and other actions at law in respect of the right now under consideration, or in respect of the amount of testimony required to sustain a judgment.

A preponderance of evidence is necessary to support an allegation of fraud in a court of law; and it is for the trial judge, in the first instance, to determine whether or not the testimony offered upon that allegation is reasonably sufficient to justify an inference of the fraud charged.

It has been often held in other jurisdiction, that a tender of money [received by virtue of a release of similar tenor to that in question here] need not be made before bringing suit where the release was obtained by fraud; but that it is sufficient to offer its return, and to account for it by the judgment: *Duval* v. *Mowry* (1860), 6 R. I. 479; *Smith* v. *Salomon* (1877), 7 Daly, 216; *Butler* v. *Richmond etc. R. R. Co.* (1891), 88 Ga. 594; *Kley* v. *Healy* (1891), 127 N. Y. 555; *Sheanon* v. *Pacific Mut. L. Ins. Co.* (1892), 83 Wis. 507; *Kirchner* v. *New Home Sewing Machine Co.* (1892), 135 N. Y. 182; *Knoxville etc. R. R. Co.* v. *Acuff* (1892), 92 Tenn. 26.

That certainly is the rule in equity in reference to rescission (*Martin* v. *Martin* (1860), 35 Ala. 560; *Metropolitan El. Ry. Co.* v. *Manhattan Ry. Co.* (1884), 14 Abb. N. C. 224; *Lusted* v. *Chicago etc. Ry. Co.* (1888), 71 Wis. 391), and in equity, as a general rule, a better showing is required of a plaintiff, conditional to granting relief, than is exacted by the practice in courts of law.

It has, moreover, been ruled that where a release is found to have been obtained by fraud practiced upon one incapable, because of mental weakness, to validly enter into such a contract, no necessity exists for refunding the fruits of the release before action brought: *O'Brien* v. *Chicago etc. Ry. Co.* (Iowa, 1894), 57 N. W. [373] Rep. 425; *Johnson* v. *Merry Mt. Granite Co.* (1892), 53 Fed. Rep. 569.

Whether these rulings correctly declare the law applicable to releases of the kind now in question we think it unnecessary to decide, in view of the condition of the record before the court.

3. If it be conceded, for the sake of argument, that a tender was necessary to sustain plaintiff's right to recover upon

his original cause of action, let us see whether the judgment actually reached in the trial court can be supported upon the pleadings, evidence, and findings of the jury, irrespective of the question of a tender.

No objection to the sufficiency of the plaintiff's case, for the want of such tender, was, at any time, interposed in the trial court, unless it may be implied in the request for an instruction that, under the pleadings and evidence, plaintiff was not entitled to recover. But, at that stage of the case, the testimony tending to prove fraud in obtaining from the plaintiff the execution of the release had been admitted under the allegations of the reply.

Upon the facts before the court at that time plaintiff would have been entitled to recover at law, upon the footing of the fraud, a measure of damages at least as great as that which the judgment shows was actually meted out to him.

Plaintiff, at the outset of the proceeding, might have set up his original cause of action, and the fraud by which he was induced to execute the release for it, and, on showing these facts, have lawfully claimed a recovery of the difference between what he received by reason of the release and the damages justly due him upon his former cause of action.

574 That theory would have involved acquiescence in the release which he might have given without waiving his right to recover for the fraud in obtaining it. His right of action for fraud on such a showing could be maintained without any offer to return the fruits of the release.

These positions are sustained by abundant precedents: 1 Wharton on Contracts, sec. 282; *Wabash etc. Union* v. *James* (1893), 8 Ind. App. 449.

The only difference between a recovery on that basis and the judgment reached on the trial under review is one of form. The essential facts to sustain both appear in the plaintiff's pleadings, and were found by the jury. Part of those facts are first stated in the reply; but the only objection made at any time to the reply in the circuit court was on the ground that it admitted the existence of a release uncanceled when the action was brought. That objection we have held to be untenable, for the reasons given in the first paragraph of this opinion.

No objection was made to any of plaintiff's pleadings on the ground that a tender of the fruits of the release was essential to plaintiff's right of recovery, nor was that propo-

sition advanced in the trial court by defendant in any request
for instructions.

By positive law in this state the trial courts are expressly
authorized, where defendant has appeared and answered,
as in this record, to "grant any relief consistent with the
case made by the plaintiff, and embraced within the issues":
Rev. Stats. 1889, sec. 2216.

By the Code of Procedure this court is directed, in every
stage of the action, to "disregard any error or defect in the
pleadings or proceedings which shall not affect the substantial rights of the adverse party": Rev. Stats. 1889, sec.
2100; and, further, not to "reverse the [375] judgment of any
court, unless it shall believe that error was committed by
such court against the appellant or plaintiff in error, and
materially affecting the merits of the action": Rev. Stats.
1889, sec. 2303.

In addition to these very plain and practical rules of decision the statute declares furthermore that it is the duty of
the courts to so construe the provisions of the code of pleading
and practice as "to distinguish between form and substance":
Rev. Stats. 1889, sec. 2117.

In this state of the record and of the law, would it not be
the sheerest technicality, a complete surrender of substance
to barren form, to hold that the judgment should be reversed
for want of a tender, when the facts alleged, proved, and
found show a solid foundation for the result reached, irrespective of the question of a tender?

Viewing the case at bar broadly on its merits the judgment of the trial court seems abundantly supported by the
facts and by the law applicable thereto.

The court would depart from the precepts contained in the
statutes referred to should it reverse the judgment for any of
the objections which have been urged to it here. It should not
be done. In my opinion the judgment ought to be affirmed.

BLACK, C. J., and BRACE and MACFARLANE, JJ., concur in
that result, and express their own views in an opinion filed
along with this.

Judges GANTT, SHERWOOD, and BURGESS dissent, and file
a separate opinion.

MACFARLANE, J., concurring.—I agree to the conclusion
reached by the court that the judgment should be affirmed,
but desire briefly to give my reasons therefor.

The questions insisted upon in this court by defendant are: 1. That an action could not be [376] maintained for damages until the release had been canceled by a decree in equity; and 2, that the release could not be attacked for fraud, either in law or equity, until plaintiff had restored to defendant whatever of considerations he had received thereunder.

An examination of this abstract of record fails to show that any objection was, at any time, by pleading or otherwise, made to the failure of plaintiff to return or tender to defendant the consideration paid under the release. On the other hand, the record does show that the defendant insisted upon the validity of the release throughout the trial, and gave it prominence as a defense. It may, therefore, be reasonably inferred that a tender would have been refused, and was waived. In addition, it affirmatively appears upon the record that the amount paid out by defendant on account of the release was restored to it by a reduction of the judgment which was obtained by plaintiff. Manifestly, defendant was not prejudiced by a failure to make the tender.

We have often said that this court will only consider questions to which exceptions have been saved in the circuit court, or which affirmatively appear upon the record proper. We must, therefore, decline to consider the second proposition.

This leaves simply the question whether the reply properly put in issue the validity of the release; or, in other words, whether a release of the character of this one can be avoided, in an action at law, on the ground of fraud charged in the reply to the answer of defendant setting it up in bar of plaintiff's action. Defendant insists that it is a complete bar until canceled by the decree of a court of equity.

It is undoubtedly true that fraud was one of the original heads of equity jurisdiction. " But," says Blackstone, " every kind of fraud is equally cognizable [377] . . . . in a court of law; and some frauds are cognizable only there, as fraud in obtaining a devise of lands": 3 Blackstone's Commentaries, 431. "Courts of equity and courts of law have a concurrent jurisdiction to suppress and relieve against fraud": Lord Mansfield in *Bright* v. *Eynon*, 1 Burr. *396. This principle has received recognition and approval by this court from the decision of *Montgomery* v. *Tipton*, 1 Mo. 446, to that of *Clough* v. *Holden*, 115 Mo. 336; 37 Am. St. Rep. 393.

This doctrine is not disputed when the fraud is pleaded by way of answer to a cause of action stated in the petition, but it is insisted and argued with much learning and ability that a different rule applies in case the charge of fraud is made to a release when pleaded as a bar to the action. In such case it is argued that the release must be canceled by the decree of a court of equity before the original action can be prosecuted. The principal ground of objection urged to the right to raise the question of fraud by reply is that such a course of proceeding permits questions of fraud to be tried by a jury, instead of a chancellor, and the rescission of a release to be obtained upon evidence which would have been insufficient in a court of equity.

But this objection can be urged with equal plausibility to pleading fraud by answer, which, it is conceded, may be done. When we keep in view the fact that courts of law have jurisdiction to relieve against fraud, it would seem to follow logically that its jurisdiction may be exercised to relieve against a fraudulent contract pleaded as a defense, as well as against a fraudulent contract which is made the subject matter of the suit. It would seem wholly unnecessary and oppressive to drive a plaintiff to another jurisdiction for relief against a defense, of which he may have had no information until the answer was made, when the forum, [378] having all the parties before it, has concurrent jurisdiction of the same subject matter. This is particularly true in jurisdictions wherein legal and equitable rights are administered by one court and in one proceeding, as in this state.

Chitty says: "To a plea of release, he (plaintiff) may reply *non est factum,* or that it was obtained by duress or fraud": 1 Chitty on Pleadings, 16th Am. ed., 608. It is contended by counsel that Mr. Chitty had reference alone to a release obtained pending the suit. It is true the references made are to cases in which pleas *puis darrein continuance* were interposed, but the author's general accuracy in the statement of his proposition forbids my acceptance of any qualification to the broad and general declarations. Bliss, in his work on Code Pleadings, lays down the same rule, section 201.

The rule given by Mr. Chitty has been generally, if not uniformly, followed by the courts of this country. "The pleading of a release first occurs generally in the answer or

plea of the defendant, unless in actions brought to set aside
a release.   And the controverting of the release is usually
made under the plaintiff's reply": 20 Am. & Eng. Ency. of
Law, 766.

The following cases will be found to follow the rule given
by Chitty, *supra*, as applied to a release of claims for damages on account of personal injuries caused by negligence:
Chicago etc. R. R. Co. v. *Lewis*, 109 Ill. 120; *Bussian* v. *Milwaukee etc. Ry. Co.*, 56 Wis. 325; *International etc. R. R. Co.*
v. *Brazzil*, 78 Tex. 314; *Sobieski* v. *St. Paul etc. R. R. Co.*, 41
Minn. 169; *O'Brien* v. *Chicago etc. Ry. Co.* (Iowa, 1894), 57
N. W. Rep. 425; *Mullen* v. *Old Colony R. R. Co.*, 127 Mass.
87; 34 Am. Rep. 349; *Addystone etc. Co.* v. *Copple*, 94 Ky.
292; *Dixon* v. *Brooklyn etc. R. R. Co.*, 100 N. Y. 170; *Bean*
v. *Western etc. R. R. Co.*, 107 N. C. 731; *O'Neil* v. *Lake
Superior Iron Co.*, 63 Mich. 690; *East Tennessee etc. Ry. Co.*
v. *Hayes*, 83 Ga. 558; *St. Louis etc. Ry. Co.* v. *Higgins*, 44
Ark. 296.

The pleading necessary to assert and attack such [379] release has not been directly considered or decided by this
court.   In *Vautrain* v. *St. Louis etc. Ry. Co.*, 8 Mo. App. 538, a
release was pleaded in bar, and the reply charged that it was
obtained by fraud.   No question of the propriety of thus
attacking the release was raised or considered, but the sufficiency of the pleading to put in issue the validity of the
release was, inferentially, at least, conceded.   This decision
was approved by this court without comment: *Vautrain* v.
St. Louis etc. Ry. Co., 78 Mo. 44.

In the case of *Blair* v. *Chicago etc. R. R. Co.*, 89 Mo. 383,
the petition contained two counts, one in equity to set aside the
release and the other for the damages received.   This method
of proceeding was approved by this court.   There can be no
doubt that a plaintiff can elect to have the release set aside
by suit in equity before proceeding at law on the original
cause of action.   The Blair case, then, only settled the question that the two actions may be joined in separate counts
in the same petition.

This court has recognized the right of a plaintiff to plead
fraud in reply to a transaction set up by answer as a bar in
the original cause of action: *Wright* v. *McPike*, 70 Mo. 177;
Williams v. *Chicago etc. Ry. Co.*, 112 Mo. 463; 34 Am. St.
Rep. 403; *Jarrett* v. *Morton*, 44 Mo. 277.

Our conclusion is that the validity of the release was properly put in issue by the reply.

BLACK, C. J., and BRACE, J., concur in this opinion.

JUSTICES BURGESS, GANTT, AND SHERWOOD, dissented on the ground that the release agreement set up as a defense in this case could be set aside only in a court of equity, and that until annulled it is an absolute bar to the action. This conclusion was reached on the ground that in order to maintain an action at law to recover for his injuries plaintiff must show that he has rescinded the fraudulent compromise prior to the commencement of the action, and that, if no rescission is shown, a final determination by the court that he is entitled to more than the sum paid under the agreement of release, is no answer to the objection. In the course of the opinion it was said in effect that when one has received any thing of value, on a settlement of a right of action, and executed a release therefor, the contract of settlement, although obtained by fraud and misrepresentations, constitutes an insuperable barrier against a recovery at law so long as it is not rescinded or avoided by an offer to return the consideration paid for it. This conclusion was based upon the fact that "the authorities are almost unanimous in holding that where money or any other valuable thing is paid on a settlement to obtain a release of any right of action, before the person to whom it is paid and who has the right of action can recover on it, he must return, or offer to return, whatever he has received, if of any value, and this he must do, although the settlement or release was obtained by fraud. And it is also manifest from the decided weight of authority that the offer to return whatever of value has been received as a consideration for the settlement or release must be made before or at the time the suit is brought, and the contract or agreement, in so far as it lies in the power of the party desiring to do so, rescinded." In support of this doctrine the following cases were cited: *Home Ins. Co.* v. *Howard*, 111 Ind. 544; *Gould* v. *Cayuga Nat. Bank*, 86 N. Y. 75; *East Tennessee etc. Ry. Co.* v. *Hayes*, 83 Ga. 558. The case last cited is in all point similar to and in direct opposition to the conclusion reached by the majority of the court in the principal case: *Peterson* v. *Chicago etc. Ry. Co.*, 38 Minn. 511; *Lusted* v. *Chicago etc. Ry. Co.*, 71 Wis. 391; *Coolidge* v. *Brigham*, 1 Met. 547; *Thayer* v. *Turner*, 8 Met. 550; *Thurston* v. *Blanchard*, 22 Pick. 18; 33 Am. Dec. 700; *Estabrook* v. *Swett*, 116 Mass. 303; *Brown* v. *Hartford Ins. Co.*, 117 Mass. 479; *Mullen* v. *Old Colony R. R. Co.*, 127 Mass. 86; 34 Am. Rep. 349; *Cobb* v. *Hatfield*, 46 N. Y. 533; *Evans* v. *Gale*, 17 N. H. 573; 43 Am. Dec. 614; *Morarity* v. *Stofferan*, 89 Ill. 528; *Doane* v. *Lockwood*, 115 Ill. 490; *Hart* v. *Handlin*, 43 Mo. 171; *Jarrett* v. *Morton*, 44 Mo. 275; *Estes* v. *Reynolds*, 75 Mo. 563; *Blair* v. *Chicago etc. R. R. Co.*, 89 Mo. 383; *Cahn* v. *Reid*, 18 Mo. App. 115; *Stevens* v. *Hyde*, 32 Barb. 171; *McMichael* v. *Kilmer*, 76 N. Y. 36; *Graham* v. *Meyer*, 99 N. Y. 611; *Baird* v. *Mayor*, 96 N. Y. 567; *Gifford* v. *Carvill*, 29 Cal. 589; *Bisbee* v. *Ham*, 47 Me. 543; *Tisdale* v. *Buckmore*, 33 Me. 461; *Lee* v. *Lancashire etc. Ry. Co.*, L. R. 6 Ch. 527.

NEGLIGENCE—RELEASE OBTAINED BY FRAUD—NECESSITY FOR TENDER BEFORE SUIT.—If a person injured receives payment for part of the injury, and a receipt is procured from him by fraud purporting to release his whole cause of action, he is not obliged to return the money thus paid to him be-

fore maintaining an action to recover for the residue of his injuries for
which no compensation has been made: *Bliss* v. *New York etc. R. R. Co.*,
160 Mass. 447; 39 Am. St. Rep. 504, and note. What amounts to fraud in
procuring such a release is also discussed in the above-cited case.

HAVENS *v.* GERMANIA FIRE INSURANCE COMPANY.
[123 MISSOURI, 403.]

INSURANCE—WHEN GOVERNED BY STATUTE.—If the facts involved in an
insurance loss bring the case within regulations prescribed by statute,
such statute enters into and forms part of the contract of insurance as
completely as if written into it.

INSURANCE—CONCURRENT POLICIES—EFFECT OF STATUTE UPON.—If several concurrent policies of fire insurance are written with the consent
of the respective insurers, and the property is wholly destroyed by fire,
such policies as well as single policies are governed by a statute making
the amount of insurance written conclusive as to the value of the property insured and the true amount of loss and measure of damages when
so destroyed. In such case the aggregate of the concurrent policies
must be taken as the true value of the property destroyed, and each
insurer is liable for the full amount of his policy.

FIXTURES.—MACHINERY constructed and placed in a mill to be used in and
as a part of it, and which would pass by a grant of the mill, is part of
the real estate upon which the mill is situated, and not personal property.

INSURANCE—VOID CONTRACT AS TO REAL AND PERSONAL PROPERTY.—
Under a statute making the amount of insurance written on real property
conclusive as to its value insurance companies cannot avoid their fixed
liability for losses on such property by agreeing with the owner to denominate it personal property.

INSURANCE—TOTAL LOSS.—Under an insurance upon a mill and the machinery therein against loss by fire the fact that a small part of the machinery has been removed pending improvements prior to the burning of
the mill and machinery then in it does not prevent the mill from being
"wholly destroyed," nor reduce the loss from a total to a partial one;
but the value of the machinery thus removed should be deducted from
the total amount of the policy.

INSURANCE—"WHOLLY DESTROYED"—DEFINITION.—The words "wholly
destroyed," as used in statutes regulating fire insurance and fixing the
liability of the insurer, mean the total destruction of a building as such,
although there is not an absolute extinction of all of its parts.

ACTION on concurrent policies of insurance to recover for
the loss of a mill and the machinery therein totally destroyed by fire while such policies were in full force and
effect. The insurance, aggregating seven thousand dollars,
was procured by one Sage under policies issued by five different insurance companies, each of such policies permitting
concurrent insurance to the extent of ten thousand dollars.

Sage, who was in possession of the mill under a contract for its purchase from its owners, Havens and Richardson, procured such insurance in their names and for their benefit to the extent of their interest in the property, and the remainder for his own benefit. Sage assigned his interest in two of the policies, one to Harrington and the other to McAdam for indebtedness due by him to them. Judgment for plaintiffs, and the insurers appealed. Sage, McAdam, and Harrington, who were adjudged to take nothing by the court below, also appealed.

Warner, Dean & Hagerman, for the appellants.

Gage, Ladd & Small, for the respondents.

416 Gantt, J.   All the policies of insurance sued on in this case were written and issued in November, 1884, after section 6009 of the Revised Statutes of 1879 had become a law of this state. Several of said policies contained a stipulation that in case of loss the damage should be estimated according to the actual cash value of the property at the time of the loss or fire, which should in no case, exceed the cost of replacing or restoring the burnt property, whereas section 6009 of the Revised Statutes of 1879 provided: "Whenever any policy of insurance shall be written to insure any real property, including building or buildings owned separate from the realty, as well as such as are a part of the realty, and the property insured shall be wholly destroyed, and without criminal fault on the part of the insured or his assigns, the amount of the insurance written in such policy shall be taken conclusively to be the true value of the property when insured, and the true amount of loss and measure of damages when destroyed, and the company may either pay the amount written in such policy in cash, or rebuild and restore such building to its original condition as to value, size, plan, and general finish, such work of rebuilding to commence within sixty days after the destruction of such building, and be completed with all possible speed, and to clear and remove all debris from the premises."

It is assumed by the appellants Sage and his assignees that if the conditions as to the subject matter of the insurance and the nature of the loss bring these policies within the terms of this section, then the stipulations of the policy must yield to the statute, and this is not seriously controverted by the insurance companies, their only contention

being that the case is without the statute.   It is now the
established rule that, [417] if the facts bring the case within
the regulations prescribed by law, the statute enters into and
forms a part of the contract of insurance as completely as if
written into it.

Thus, in *White* **v.** *Connecticut Mut. L. Ins. Co.*, 4 Dill. 177,
Judge Dillon, speaking of certain provisions in life insurance
policies issued in this state after the enactment of section
5849 of the Revised Statutes of 1889, said: "The legislature
of Missouri conceived, and we think wisely, that the promises
held forth to the assured in the policies in general use were
too often a delusion and a snare, and, as the courts were
powerless to correct the evil, it ought to be corrected by statute. . . . . We are of opinion that policies issued and delivered in Missouri, after that act took effect, fall within its
protective operation; and as to such policies the act is to be
treated as if incorporated therein. . . . . The general rule is
that laws in existence are necessarily referred to in all contracts made under such laws, and that no contract can
change the law."   To the same effect may be cited *Wall* v.
Equitable Life etc. Society. 32 Fed. Rep. 273; *Queen Ins. Co.*
v. *Leslie*, 47 Ohio St. 409; *Chamberlain* **v.** *New Hampshire
Fire Ins. Co.*, 55 N. H. 249; *Reilly* **v.** *Franklin Ins. Co.*, 43 Wis.
449; 28 Am. Rep. 552; *Thompson* v. *St. Louis Ins. Co.*, 43 Wis.
459; *Bammessel* v. *Insurance Co.*, 43 Wis. 463; *Cayon* v. *Dwelling House Ins. Co.*, 68 Wis. 510; *Oshkosh Gaslight Co.* **v.**
Germania Fire Ins. Co., 71 Wis. 454; 5 Am. St. Rep. 233;
Emery **v.** *Piscataqua etc. Ins. Co.*, 52 Me. 322; *Barnard* **v.**
National Fire Ins. Co., 38 Mo. App. 106.

Section 6009 of the Revised Statutes of 1879, by its terms,
applies to policies written on "real property" and to cases
where the property is "wholly destroyed."

1. The defendants, the insurance companies, insist that
the statute has no application to cases of concurrent insurance, but governs only in cases of single policies.   This last
contention we regard as untenable.

[418] We hold that where several concurrent policies of
insurance upon real property have been written with the consent of the respective companies, and the property is wholly
destroyed by fire, the aggregate amount of such insurance
must, under section 6009 of the Revised Statutes of 1879, be
taken conclusively to be the true value of the property

insured, and the true amount of the loss and measure of damages when so destroyed.

We think there can be no valid reason why the mere fact that several companies assume each a part of the whole risk should affect the operation of the statute. If, in order to induce good faith on the part of the insured, and thus give greater security to the insurer, the companies desire to make the owner bear a portion of the risk, this protection can readily be secured by limiting the amount of concurrent insurance.

The insurance is written by the consent of all the companies, and it must be presumed that, when each consented to the additional insurance by the others, in its opinion and estimation the total insurance was not excessive or disproportioned to the value of the property. The amount written in each policy is expressly assented to by all the other insurers, and they must be held to agree that the aggregate of their several policies is the value of the property. To hold otherwise is to repeal the statute in every case where there is more than one policy on the same property, whereas it was intended to apply to all. When we consider the well-known custom of the different agencies representing often a number of companies, and distributing the insurance they write equitably among their several principals, we can readily see how easily under this contention they can render the statute nugatory in the most important risks. We think the statute is as obligatory in concurrent as in a single policy: *Barnard* v. *National Fire Ins.* [419] *Co.*, 38 Mo. App. 106; *Oshkosh Gaslight Co.* v. *Germania Fire Ins. Co.*, 71 Wis. 454; 5 Am. St. Rep. 233; *Queen Ins. Co.* v. *Jefferson Ice Co.*, 64 Tex. 578.

2. We next inquire whether the subject matter of the insurance brought it within the statute. It was and is an elementary principle of common law that land includes all houses and buildings standing thereon; that whatever is affixed to the soil is thereby made a part of it, and passes by a grant of the land without other designation. Personal property prepared and intended to be used with the land, having been affixed to it and used with it, becomes a part of it by accession. To this general principle are the equally well-settled exceptions as to trade fixtures and the relaxation in favor of the tenant as between landlord and tenant, and tenants for life and remaindermen, with which we are

not concerned in this case. While the diversity of opinions on the subject of fixtures is bewildering, it is generally held that millstones, hoppers, and bolting apparatus, as usually adjusted in a mill or machinery in a factory, constitute a part of the real estate, and will pass by deed or mortgage of the mill itself, and descend as real estate to the heirs at law: *Rogers* v. *Crow*, 40 Mo. 91; 93 Am. Dec. 299; *Thomas* v. *Davis*, 76 Mo. 72; 43 Am. Rep. 756; *Teaff* v. *Hewitt*, 1 Ohio St. 528; 59 Am. Dec. 634; *Winslow* v. *Merchants' Ins. Co.*, 4 Met. 306; 38 Am. Dec. 368.

So that we take it that a deed or mortgage of the land upon which the Waldron mill stood would *prima facie* have passed not only the building, but all of the machinery described in the policies in suit.

Affixed as it was, and constructed and adapted as it was, and placed in the mill to be used in and as a part of it, it would have passed by a grant of the real estate as a part of it. This, we think, is not seriously questioned as a general rule, but the contention is that while this is true, yet there are cases in which property so used has by consent and agreement of the owner and [420] mortgagees been treated as personal property, and that in such case the law will regard their agreements, and so consider it.

Unquestionably there are many such cases, but they depend upon the peculiar facts in each, and do not controvert any positive statute: *Smith* v. *Waggoner*, 50 Wis. 155, and cases cited. Two reasons occur to us why this exception should not apply in this case. The first, and by far the most cogent, is that such a construction is against the policy and spirit of the statute. In construing this and similar statutes the authorities already cited announce with great clearness that this statute is founded upon reasons of public policy, and, where provisions of the policy run counter to those of the statute, the statute controls. Thus, when the policies provide that " the loss shall be estimated according to the true and marketable value," it was held the stipulation could not stand because the statute fixed the amount written in the policy as the amount of recovery, and precluded an inquiry into value, nor was an agreement to submit to arbitration allowed in the face of such a statute: *Thompson* v. *Citizens' Ins. Co.*, 45 Wis. 388; *Thompson* v. *St. Louis Ins. Co.*, 43 Wis. 459–463; *Seyk* v. *Millers' Nat. Ins. Co.*, 74 Wis. 67. And in *Queen Ins. Co.* v. *Leslie*, 47 Ohio St. 409, the supreme court

of Ohio, discussing a similar statute requiring the companies
to examine the premises before issuing their policies, and
then providing that the amount named in the policy should
fix the damages in the absence of intentional fraud, in reply
to the claim that the parties might make a different agreement, says: "The statute cannot be treated as conferring
upon the assured a mere personal privilege which may be
waived or qualified by agreement. It has a broader scope.
It molds the obligation of the contract into conformity with
its provisions, and establishes the rule and measure of the
[421] insurer's liability. Terms and conditions embraced in
the policy inconsistent with the provisions of the statute are
subordinate to it, and must give way."

In *Wall* v. *Equitable etc. Soc.*, 32 Fed. Rep. 273, Judge
Brewer, in discussing the right of the parties to waive the
Missouri statute as to forfeiture after the payment of two
annual premiums, held that a provision in a policy which
required three annual payments before the insured was entitled to temporary insurance was void, and in contravention
of the statute.

Keeping in view, then, the manifest purpose of our legislature to give greater security to the insured, we hold that it is
not competent for insurance companies under this statute to
avoid their fixed liability for losses on real property by agreeing with the owner to denominate it personal property, and
thus by a mere stroke of the pen deprive its owner of the protection of this statute, when for all other purposes in law it is
real estate.

But, secondly, independent of the policy of the statute, it
is clear this statute was enacted for the benefit of the insured,
and if a waiver be allowed, it ought to clearly appear that it
was his intention to give up the protection secured by the
statute, and we do not think these policies evince such a
design. The separate valuation is the only foundation for
this claim; but it will be observed that it nowhere designates
it as personal property. While the policy specifies the property insured it leaves it to the law to define its character,
and, by the description given, the law denominates it real
property.

Reading the whole policy together, it was, after all, simply
the insurance of the Waldron mill, and not the several elements that went to constitute it. We think the fair and rea-

sonable construction of the policy is that [422] it was written
on real property and is within the protection of the statute.

3. Was the property "wholly destroyed," within the meaning of section 6009 of the Revised Statutes of 1879? ·

The facts themselves largely determine this question.   All
the property insured, the mill building and all of the machinery in it, was wholly destroyed, but it so happened that,
pending the repairs, Sage had removed a part of the machinery, and stored it in another building which was not exposed
to the fire.   The portion thus saved was found by the circuit
court to be of the value of three hundred and eighty dollars.
Does the fact that this small amount was not destroyed,
under the circumstances, take the loss out of the statute?
The property was valued at eight thousand four hundred
dollars in the policies, and the right to repair and make improvements was expressly given.   This small amount of
machinery was removed for a legitimate purpose, and in
strict accordance with the terms of the policies, and was a
mere trifle compared to the whole.   Had it been in the mill
at the time of the fire and been saved by the exertion of the
owner or his neighbors, would it have been a total loss?   It
seems to us there ought to be but one answer to this contention.

If defendant's contention be carried to its logical conclusion, if a manufacturer should be compelled to remove a piece
of his machinery and send it to a repairer, and his mill burn
before its return, it would not be within the protection of the
statute.

The terms of purchase by Sage from Havens stipulated for
a change to a roller-mill.   If, in effecting this change, some
of the old machinery was useless, and not adapted to the
roller process, and had been stored in this other building
pending the repairs, and the mill had burned with all the
remaining machinery, would it be seriously contended that it
was not a total loss?   Surely [423] not.   The useless machinery that was not exposed to the risk would reduce the valuation to that extent, but certainly would not affect the risk
otherwise.

We do not think that the question of partial loss can arise
under these circumstances.   All the property covered by the
policy at the time of the fire was wholly destroyed.   The
property insured was a mill, and the fire destroyed its identity and specific character as such.

The words "wholly destroyed" have been placed in statutes like this in many of the states of the union, and, so far
as we have been able to find, the construction appears to be
uniform that, as applied to buildings, they mean totally
destroyed as a building, although there is not an absolute
extinction of all its parts.

It matters not that some debris remains which may be
useful or valuable for some purposes.   Such was the construction given in the subjoined cases, and such is our construction: *Williams* v. *Hartford Ins. Co.*, 54 Cal. 442; 35
Am. Rep. 77; *Seyk* v. *Miller's Nat. Ins. Co.*, 74 Wis. 67; *Barnard* v. *National Fire Ins. Co.*, 38 Mo. App. 106; *Oshkosh etc.
Co.* v. *Mercantile Ins. Co.*, 31 Fed. Rep. 200; *Globe Ins. Co.* v.
Sherlock, 25 Ohio St. 59; *Wallerstein* v. *Columbian Ins. Co.*,
44 N. Y. 204; 4 Am. Rep. 664; *Insurance Co.* v. *Fogarty,* 19
Wall. 640.

We think the circuit court erred in not applying section
6009 of the Revised Statutes of 1879 to the facts, and in not
holding that the aggregate of the policies conclusively fixed
the value of the mill and machinery and the measure of
damages, less the sum of three hundred and eighty dollars,
the amount of machinery not exposed to the fire: 1 Wood on
Insurance, 100; *Lewis* v. *Rucker*, 2 Burr. 1167. As the circuit court found the insured had complied with all the conditions on their part, and the only question being whether
the statute applied, it would appear unnecessary to put the
parties to the cost of another trial; hence the judgment is
reversed, with directions to [424] the circuit court to render a
decree for the aggregate amount of said policies, less three
hundred and eighty dollars, with interest at six per cent
thereon from the time of filing the cross-bill by Sage and his
assignees, and distribute the fund as the rights of the plaintiffs and Sage, McAdams, and Harrington to the same shall
appear.

BLACK, C. J., BRACE, BURGESS, MACFARLANE, and SHER-
WOOD, JJ., concur.

BARCLAY, J., dissents.   ___

INSURANCE—CONCURRENT POLICIES—VALUE OF PROPERTY.—Where concurrent policies of insurance on property afterward destroyed were written
with the consent of the respective companies the aggregate amount of such
insurance written in the policies is the value of the property as stipulated
in each policy, and must be regarded as conclusive under the Wisconsin

statute, which must be regarded as a part of the contract: *Oshkosh Gas etc. Co.* v. *Germania etc. Ins. Co.*, 71 Wis. 454; 5 Am. St. Rep. 233, and note. See *Reilly* v. *Franklin Ins. Co.*, 43 Wis. 449; 28 Am. Rep. 552.

INSURANCE—"TOTAL DESTRUCTION" DEFINED.—In case of insurance upon a building, if the building loses its identity and specific character by fire, although a large part of the walls and some of the iron attached thereto are left standing, it is a "total destruction" within the meaning of the policy: *Williams* v. *Hartford Ins. Co.*, 54 Cal. 442; 35 Am. Rep. 77. If a building has lost its identity and specific character, and has become unfit for use by fire, it is a total loss: *Hamburg etc. Ins. Co.* v. *Garlington*, 66 Tex. 103; 59 Am. Dec. 613.

INSURANCE ON REAL AND PERSONAL PROPERTY—DIVISIBILITY.—If a policy includes real property and also personal property in the same building thereon, the risk being distributed, a misrepresentation in respect to the buildings, and which avoids the insurance thereon, also avoids it as to the personal property: *Stevens* v. *Queen Ins. Co.*, 81 Wis. 335; 29 Am. St. Rep. 905, and note; but see *German Ins. Co.* v. *York*, 48 Kan. 488; 30 Am. St. Rep. 313, and *State Ins. Co.* v. *Schreck*, 27 Neb. 527; 20 Am. St. Rep. 696.

FIXTURES—MACHINERY.—Machinery placed in a factory with the intention that it shall remain as a part thereof, though attached by screws so that it may be removed, becomes a permanent fixture: *Fifield* v. *Farmers' Nat. Bank*, 148 Ill. 163; 39 Am. St. Rep. 166, and note. See the note to *Lansing Iron etc. Works* v. *Walker*, 30 Am. St. Rep. 491.

CASES

IN THE

COURT OF APPEALS

OF

NEW YORK.

HEALTH DEPARTMENT *v.* RECTOR.

[145 NEW YORK, 32.]

AN ACT TO BE JUSTIFIED AS AN EXERCISE OF THE POLICE POWER of a state must tend in a degree that is perceptible and clear toward the preservation of the lives, the health, the morals, and the welfare of the community. It must not be exercised ostensibly in favor of the promotion of some such object while in reality it is an evasion thereof, and for a distinct and different purpose, and the courts will not be prevented from looking at the true character of the act as developed by its provisions by any statement in the act itself, or in its title showing that it was ostensibly for some object within the police power.

CONSTITUTIONAL LAW—RIGHT TO A HEARING.—In enacting what shall be done by a citizen for the purposes of promoting the public health and safety it is not usually necessary to the validity of the legislation upon that subject that he shall be heard before he is bound to comply with the direction of the legislation.

CONSTITUTIONAL LAW—POLICE POWER.—Laws and regulations of a police nature, though they may obstruct the enjoyment of individual rights, are not unconstitutional, though no provision is made for compensation for such obstruction.

CONSTITUTIONAL LAW.—THE FACT THAT A PERSON MUST INCUR EXPENSES in complying with a law, and that he is not entitled to a hearing before becoming liable to incur such expense, does not render such law unconstitutional if it is an exercise of the police power of the state.

CONSTITUTIONAL LAW—POLICE POWER—REQUIREMENT THAT TENEMENT HOUSES SHALL HAVE A WATER SUPPLY.—A statute requiring that tenement houses shall have water furnished in sufficient quantity at one or more places on each floor occupied, or intended to be occupied, by one or more families, and all tenement houses shall be furnished with a like supply of water by the owners thereof wherever they shall be directed to do so by the board of health, is a justifiable and valid exercise of the police power with respect both to the public health and the public safety.

ACTION in which the plaintiff sought to recover a penalty imposed by the legislature for violating a statute in not supplying water in several tenement houses owned by the defendant. The statute under which the right to recovery was claimed is as follows: " SEC. 663. Every such house erected after May 14, 1867, or converted, ... shall have Croton or other water furnished in sufficient quantity at one or more places on each floor, occupied, or intended to be occupied, by one or more families; and all tenement houses shall be furnished with a like supply of water by the owners thereof whenever they shall be directed so to do by the board of health. But a failure in the general supply of water by the city authorities shall not be construed to be a failure on the part of the owner, provided that proper and suitable appliances to receive and distribute such water are placed in said house; *provided*, that the board of health shall see to it that all tenement houses are so supplied before January first, eighteen hundred and eighty-nine." The houses of defendant were numbered 77 and 84 Charlton street. They were originally constructed as dwelling-houses, and had never been altered in their internal arrangement, and on this account it was claimed they were not tenement houses, though, as a matter of fact, they were occupied by tenants, there being three families in one and six families in the other. The defendant at the trial sought to introduce testimony as to the necessary cost of complying with the directions of the board of health. The evidence was excluded and a judgment rendered in favor of the plaintiff, from which the defendant appealed.

Roger Foster, for the appellant.

S. P. Nash, for the respondents.

[38] PECKHAM, J. The recovery in this case is founded upon that portion of the Consolidation Act which requires that all houses of a certain description, upon the direction of the board of health, shall be provided with Croton or other water in [39] sufficient quantity at one or more places on each floor occupied, or intended to be occupied, by one or more families. The defendant, among other things, alleges as a defense that the order of the board of health directing the defendant to furnish the water as provided by the statute was made without notice to it, and that, as it could not be com-

plied with, excepting by the expenditure of a considerable amount of money, the result would be to deprive the defendant of its property without a hearing and an opportunity to show what defense it might have, and that it in fact deprived the defendant of its property without due process of law. There was no arrangement in either of these houses in question for the supplying of the Croton or other water to the occupants of each floor at the time when the order of the board of health was made; such order could not, therefore, be complied with on the part of the defendant without the expenditure of money for that purpose. That fact must be assumed, and even upon that assumption we do not think the act is invalid on the alleged ground that it deprives the defendant, if enforced, of its property without due process of law. The act must be sustained, if at all, as an exercise of the police power of the state. It has frequently been said that it is difficult to give any exact definition which shall properly limit and describe such power. It must be exercised subject to the provisions of both the federal and state constitutions, and the law passed in the exercise of such power must tend in a degree that is perceptible and clear toward the preservation of the lives, the health, the morals, or the welfare of the community, as those words have been used and construed in many cases heretofore decided. Numerous cases have arisen in this state where the power of the legislature was questioned, and where the exercise of that power was affirmed or denied for the reasons given therein: See *People* v. *Marx,* 99 N. Y. 377; 52 Am. Rep. 34; *Matter of Jacobs,* 98 N. Y. 98; 50 Am. Rep. 636; *People* v. *Gillson,* 109 N. Y. 389; 4 Am. St. Rep. 465; *People* v. *Arensberg,* 105 N. Y. 123; 59 Am. Rep. 483, and many cases cited in these cases. See, also, *Slaughter House cases,* 16 Wall. 36, 62; *Barbier* v. *Connolly,* 113 U. S. 27; *New Orleans Gas Co.* v. *Louisiana Light Co.,* 115 [40] U. S. 650; *Boston Beer Co.* v. *Massachusetts,* 97 U. S. 25. The act must tend in some appreciable and clear way toward the accomplishment of some one of the purposes which the legislature has the right to accomplish under the exercise of the police power. It must not be exercised ostensibly in favor of the promotion of some such object while really it is an evasion thereof, and for a distinct and totally different purpose, and the courts will not be prevented from looking at the true character of the act as developed by its provisions by any statement in the act itself or in its title showing that it was ostensibly passed for some object within the police power. The court must be enabled to see some clear and real connection between the assumed purpose of the law and the 'actual provisions thereof, and it must see that the latter do tend in some plain and appreciable manner toward the accomplishment of some of the objects for which the legislature may use this power.

1. Assuming that this act is a proper exercise of the power in its general features, we do not think that it can be regarded as invalid because of the fact that it will cost money to comply with the order of the board for which the owner is to receive no compensation, or because the board is entitled to make the order under the provisions of the act without notice to and a hearing of the defendant. As to the latter objection it may be said that, in enacting what shall be done by the citizen for the purpose of promoting the public health and safety, it is not usually necessary to the validity of legislation upon that subject that he shall be heard before he is bound to comply with the direction of the legislature: *People* -v. *Board of Health*, 140 N. Y. 1, 6; 37 Am. St. Rep. 522. The legislature has power and has exercised it in countless instances to enact general laws upon the subject of the public health or safety without providing that the parties who are to be affected by those laws shall first be heard before they shall take effect in any particular case. So far as this objection of want of notice is concerned the case is not materially altered in principle from what it would have been if the legislature had enacted a general law that all owners [41] of tenement houses should, within a certain period named in the act, furnish the water as directed. Indeed, this act does contain such a provision, but the plaintiff has not proceeded under it. If in such case the enforcement of the direct command of the legislature were not to be preceded by any hearing on the part of any owner of a tenement house no provision of the state or federal constitution would be violated. The fact that the legislature has chosen to delegate a certain portion of its power to the board of health, and to enact that the owners of certain tenement houses should be compelled to furnish this water after the board of health had so directed, would not alter the principle, nor would it be necessary to provide that the board should give notice and afford a hearing to the owner before it made such order. I have never understood that it was necessary that any notice should be

given, under such circumstances, before a provision of this nature could be carried out.

As to the other objection, no one would contend that the amount of the expenditure which an act of this kind may cause, whether with or without a hearing, is within the absolute discretion of the legislature. It cannot be claimed that it would have the right, even under the exercise of the police power, to command the doing of some act by the owner of property and for the purpose of carrying out some provision of law, which act could only be performed by the expenditure of a large and unreasonable amount of money on the part of the owner. If such excessive demand were made the act would without doubt violate the constitutional rights of the individual. The exaction must not alone be reasonable, when compared with the amount of the work or the character of the improvement demanded; the improvement or work must in itself be a reasonable, proper, and fair exaction when considered with reference to the object to be attained. If the expense to the individual under such circumstances would amount to a very large and unreasonable sum that fact would be a most material one in deciding whether the method or means adopted for the attainment of the main object were or were not an unreasonable [42] demand upon the individual for the benefit of the public. Of this the courts must, within proper limits, be the judges. We may own our property absolutely and yet it is subject to the proper exercise of the police power. We have surrendered to that extent our right to its unrestricted use. It must be so used as not improperly to cause harm to our neighbor, including in that description the public generally. There are sometimes necessary expenses which inevitably grow out of the use to which we may put our property and which we must incur, either voluntarily or else under the direction of the legislature, in order that the general health, safety, or welfare may be conserved. The legislature, in the exercise of this power, may direct that certain improvements shall be made in existing houses at the owners' expense, so that the health and safety of the occupants, and of the public through them, may be guarded. These exactions must be regarded as legal so long as they bear equally upon all members of the same class, and their cost does not exceed what may be termed one of the conditions upon which individual property is held. It must not be an unreasonable exaction either with reference to its nature or its cost. Within this reasonable restriction the power of the state may, by police regulations, so direct the use and enjoyment of the property of the citizen that it shall not prove pernicious to his neighbors or to the public generally. The difference between what is and what is not reasonable frequently constitutes the dividing line between a valid and void enactment by the legislature in the exercise of its police power. In commenting on the difference of degree in any given case which would render an act valid or otherwise, Mr. Justice Holmes, in *Rideout* v. *Knox*, 148 Mass. 368, 12 Am. St. Rep. 560, speaking for the supreme court of Massachusetts, said: "It may be said that the difference is only one of degree; most differences are when nicely analyzed. At any rate, difference of degree is one of the distinctions by which the right of the legislature to exercise police power is determined. Some small limitations of previously existing rights incident to property may be imposed for the sake of preventing a manifest evil; larger [43] ones could not be except by the exercise of the right of eminent domain": *Rideout* v. *Knox*, 148 Mass. 368, 372; 12 Am. St. Rep. 560. See, also, *Miller* v. *Horton*, 152 Mass. 540, 547; 23 Am. St. Rep. 850. The case of *Stuart* v. *Palmer*, 74 N. Y. 183, 30 Am. Rep. 289, is an example of the exercise of the taxing power of the state and other considerations obtain in such cases.

Laws and regulations of a police nature, though they may disturb the enjoyment of individual rights, are not unconstitutional, though no provision is made for compensation for such disturbances. They do not appropriate private property for public use, but simply regulate its use and enjoyment by the owner. If he suffer injury it is either *damnum absque injuria*, or, in the theory of the law, he is compensated for it by sharing in the general benefits which the regulations are intended and calculated to secure: 1 Dillon on Municipal Corporations, 4th ed., sec. 141, and note 2; *Commonwealth* v. *Alger*, 7 Cush. 83, 84, 86; *Baker* v. *City of Boston*, 12 Pick. 184, 193; 22 Am. Dec. 421; *Clark* v. *Mayor of Syracuse*, 13 Barb. 32, 36. The state, or its agent in enforcing its mandate, takes no property of the citizen when it simply directs the making of these improvements. As a result thereof the individual is put to some expense in complying with the law, by paying mechanics or other laborers to do that which the law enjoins upon the owner, but, so long as the amount exacted is limited as stated, the property of the citizen has not been taken in any constitutional sense without due process of law.

Instances are numerous of the passage of laws which entail expense on the part of those who must comply with them, and where such expense must be borne by them without any hearing or compensation because of the provisions of the law: *Thorpe* v. *Rutland etc. R. R. Co.*, 27 Vt. 140–152; 62 Am. Dec. 625. One of the late instances of this kind of legislation is to be found in the law regulating manufacturing establishments: Laws of 1887, c. 462. The provisions of that act could not be carried out without the expenditure of a consid- erable sum by the owners of a then existing factory. Hand- rails to stairs, hoisting-shafts to be inclosed, automatic doors to elevators, automatic shifters for throwing off belts or pul- leys, and fire [44] escapes on the outside of certain factories, all these were required by the legislature from such owner, and without any direct compensation to him for such expen- diture. Has the legislature no right to enact laws such as this statute regarding factories unless limited to factories to be thereafter built? Because the factory was already built when the act was passed, was it beyond the legislative power to provide such safeguards to life and health as against all owners of such property unless upon the condition that these expenditures to be incurred should ultimately come out of the public purse? I think to so hold would be to run coun- ter to the general course of decisions regarding the validity of laws of this character, and to mistake the foundation upon which they are placed: *Coates* v. *Mayor etc.*, 7 Cow. 585, 604; Cooley's Constitutional Limitations, 5th ed., c. 16, p. 706.

Any one in a crowded city who desires to erect a building is subject at every turn almost to the exactions of the law in regard to provisions for health, for safety from fire, and for other purposes. He is not permitted to build of certain materials within certain districts, because, though the mate- rials may be inexpensive, they are inflammable, and he must build in a certain manner. Theaters and hotels are to be built in accordance with plans to be inspected and approved by the agents of the city; other public buildings also; and private dwellings within certain districts are sub- ject to the same supervision, and in carrying out all these various acts the owner is subjected to an expense much greater than would have been necessary to have completed

his building if not compelled to complete it in the manner
of the materials and under the circumstances prescribed
by various acts of the legislature. And yet he has never
had a hearing in any one of these cases, nor does he receive
any compensation for the increased expense of his building,
rendered necessary in order to comply with the police regulations. I do not see that the principle is substantially
altered where the case is one of an existing building, and it
is to be subjected to certain alterations for the purpose of
rendering it either less exposed to the dangers from fires or
[45] its occupants more secure from disease. In both cases
the object must be within some of the acknowledged purposes
of the police power, and such purpose must be possible of
accomplishment at some reasonable cost, regard being had
all all the surrounding circumstances. There might at first
seem to be some difference as to the principle which obtained in enacting conditions upon complying with which the
owner might be permitted to erect a structure within the
limits of a city or village, or for certain purposes, and the enactment of provisions which would necessitate the alteration
of structures already in existence. In the first case it might
be urged that the discretion of the legislature in enacting
conditions for buildings might be more extensive, because
the owner would be under no necessity of building; it would
be a matter of choice and not of compulsion, and in choosing to build it might be said that he accepted the condition,
while in the second case he would have no choice and would
be compelled to alter or improve the existing building as
directed by law. The difference, however, is, as it seems to
me, really not one of principle, but only of circumstances.
Although the owner in the one case is not compelled to build,
yet he is limited in the use to which he may put his property by the provisions of the law. He cannot build as he
wishes to, unless upon the condition of a compliance with the
law, and he may very probably be so situated, as to location
of property and in other ways, that it is really a necessity
for him to use his property in the way proposed, and which
he cannot do without expending considerable sums above
what he otherwise would be called upon to do in order to
comply with those provisions. They must, therefore, be reasonable, as already stated. When one's use of his property
is thus circumscribed and limited, what might otherwise be
called his rights are plainly interfered with, and the justifica-

tion therefor can only be found in this police power. So, when the owner of an existing structure is called upon to make such alterations, while the necessity may seem to be more plainly present, still it may exist in both cases, and the only justification in either is the same. [46] Under the police power persons and property are subjected to all kinds of restraints and burdens in order to secure the general comfort and health of the public.

The citizen cannot, under this act, be punished in any way, nor can any penalty be recovered from him for an alleged noncompliance with any of its provisions, or with any order of the board of health without a trial. The punishment or penalties provided for in section 665 cannot be enforced without a trial under due process of law, and upon such trial he has an opportunity to show whatever facts would constitute a defense to the charge; to show, in other words, that he did not violate the statute or the order of the board, or that the statute itself or the order was unreasonable and illegal. He might show that the house in question was not a tenement house within the provision of the act, or that there was a supply of water as provided for by the act, or any other fact which would show that he had not been guilty of an offense with regard to the act: *City of Salem* v. *Eastern R. R. Co.*, 98 Mass. 431, 447; 96 Am. Dec. 650.

The mere fact, however, that the law cannot be enforced without causing expense to the citizen who comes within its provisions furnishes no constitutional obstacle to such enforcement, even without previous notice to and a hearing of the citizen. What is the propriety of a hearing and what would be its purpose? His property is not taken without due process of law, within any constitutional sense when the enforced compliance with certain provisions of the statute may result in some reasonable expense to himself. Any defense which he may have is available upon any attempt to punish him or to enforce the provisions of the law.

An act of the legislature of Massachusetts which provided that every building in Boston used as a dwelling-house, situated on a street in which there was a public sewer, should have sufficient water-closets connected therewith, was held valid as to existing houses, and applied in its penalties to their owners if such houses continued without the closets after its passage: *Commonwealth* v. *Roberts*, 155 Mass. 281, and see *Train* v. *Boston Disinfecting Co.*, 144 Mass. 529; 59 Am.

Rep. 113. No notice or [47] hearing was provided for in the above statute as to water-closets before the act could be enforced, and yet to enforce it would, of course, cost the owner of the building some money. The same may be said as to the disinfecting of the rags in above case in 144 Massachusetts. If the citizen be charged with any violation of such a statute, and any penalty or punishment is sought or attempted, then is the time for a hearing and then is the time he can make defense if any he may have. But to assert that he must be heard before the authorities assume or endeavor to act under and to enforce the law as against him is to say, in substance, that each citizen is to be heard upon the general question whether it is right to enforce the law in his particular case. This is not to be permitted: *Commonwealth* v. *Alger*, 7 Cush. 53, 104; *City of Salem* v. *Eastern R. R. Co.*, 98 Mass. 431, 443; 96 Am. Dec. 650. Every thing that the individual could urge upon the hearing, if given prior to the attempted enforcement of the act by the making of the order in question, can be said by him when he is sued, or when the attempt is made to punish him for the alleged violation of the law. Upon the prior hearing, if granted, it would be no defense to him if he showed that the law could not be complied with unless at some reasonable expense to himself. That would have been matter to urge upon the legislature prior to the enactment of the statute, as a question of reasonable cost and of public policy: *Boston etc. R. R. Co.* v. *County Commrs.*, 79 Me. 386, 393; *State* v. *Wabash etc. Ry. Co.*, 83 Mo. 144–149; *Thorpe* v. *Rutland etc. R. R.*, 27 Vt. 140, 149, 156, note; 62 Am. Dec. 625.

We do not think that the cost of making the improvements called for by this act exceeds the limits which have been defined, assuming the amount thereof which the defendant offered to prove.

This is not the case of a proceeding against an individual on the ground of the maintenance of a nuisance by him, nor is it the case of an assumed right to destroy an alleged nuisance, without any other proof than the decision of the board itself (with or without a hearing) that the thing condemned was a nuisance. Nor is it the case of the destruction [48] of property which is, in fact, a nuisance, without compensation. Where property of an individual is to be condemned and abated as a nuisance it must be that, somewhere between the institution of the proceedings and the final result, the owner shall be heard in the courts upon that question, or else that he shall have an opportunity when calling upon those persons who destroyed his property to account for the same to show that the alleged nuisance was not one in fact. No decision of a board of health, even if made on a hearing, can conclude the owner upon the question of nuisance: *People* v. *Board of Health,* 140 N. Y. 1; 37 Am. St. Rep. 522; *Board of Health etc.* v. *Copcutt,* 140 N. Y. 12; *Miller* v. *Horton,* 152 Mass. 540; 23 Am. St. Rep. 850; *Hutton* v. *City of Camden,* 39 N. J. L. 122; 23 Am. Rep. 203. We are, therefore, of the opinion that the act, if otherwise valid, is not open to the objection that it violates either the federal or state constitution, in the way of depriving the defendant of its property without due process of law.

2. We think the act is valid as an exercise of the police power with respect to the public health, and also with respect to the public safety regarding fires and their extinguishment. We cannot say, as a legal proposition, that it tends only to the convenience of the tenants in regard to their use of water. We cannot say that it has no fair and plain and direct tendency toward the promotion of the public health, or toward the more speedy extinguishment of fires in crowded tenement houses. That the free use of water, especially during the summer months, tends toward the healthful condition of the body, by reason of the increased cleanliness occasioned by such use, there can be no reasonable doubt. The supply of water to the general public in a city has become not only a luxury, but an absolute necessity for the maintenance of the public health and safety. The city of New York itself has spent millions upon millions of dollars for the purpose of securing this great boon for the inhabitants thereof. The right of eminent domain in the taking of land around the sources of the water supply has been granted to and exercised by that city to a very large [49] extent, so that all sources of supply of this necessity of life should be rendered as free from contamination and danger to health and life as it possibly could be. This use of the water is not confined, so far as the necessities of the case are concerned, to the public hydrants. The water is brought into the city, so that it may be used in every house and building within its limits, and although we may, and, indeed, must, admit that no health law could practically be enforced which should provide that every individual inhabitant of the tenement houses should use the water, yet

we think it is perfectly clear that facilities for the use of the water will almost necessarily be followed by its actual use in larger quantities, and more frequently than would be the case without such facilities, and to the great benefit of the health of the occupants of such houses. Those occupan's require it more even than their more favored brethren living in airy, larger, more spacious and luxurious apartments. Their health is matter of grave public concern. The legislature cannot in practice enforce a law so as to make a man wash himself; but, when it provides facilities therefor, it has taken a long step toward the accomplishment of that object. That dirt, filth, nastiness in general, are great promoters of disease, that they breed pestilence and contagion, sickness and death, cannot be successfully denied. There is scarcely a dissent from the general belief on the part of all who have studied the disease that cholera is essentially a filth disease. The so-called ship fever or jail fever arises from filth; most diseases are aggravated by it. That opportunities, conveniences for the use of water in these tenement houses will unquestionably tend toward and be followed by more cleanly living on the part of the occupants of those houses cannot, it seems to me, admit of any rational doubt; and, if so, then the law which provides at a reasonable cost for the furnishing of such facilities is plainly and honestly a health law.

The learned counsel for the defendant asks where this kind of legislation is to stop. Would it be contended that the owners of such houses could be compelled to furnish each room with [50] a bathtub, and all the appliances that are to be found in a modern and well-appointed hotel? Is there to be a bathroom and water-closet to each room, and every closet to be a model of the very latest improvement? To which I should answer, certainly not. That would be so clearly unreasonable that no court, in my belief, could be found which would uphold such legislation, and it seems to me equally clear that no legislature could be found that would enact it. The tenement house in New York is a subject of very great thought and anxiety to the residents of that city. The numbers of people that live in such houses, their size, their ventilation, their cleanliness, their liability to fires, the exposure of their occupants to contagious diseases, and the consequent spread of the contagion through the city and the country, the tendencies to immorality and crime where there is very close packing of human beings of the lower order in intelligence and morals—all these are subjects which must arouse the attention of the legislator, and which it behooves him to see to in order that such laws are enacted as shall directly tend to the improvement of the health, safety, and morals of those men and women that are to be found in such houses. Some legislation upon this subject can only be carried out at the public expense, while some may be properly enforced at the expense of the owner. We feel that we ought to inspect with very great care any law in regard to tenement houses in New York, and to hesitate before declaring any such law invalid so long as it seems to tend plainly in the direction we have spoken of, and to be reasonable in its provisions. If we can see that the object of this law is, without doubt, the promotion or the protection of the health of the inmates of these houses, or the preservation of the houses themselves, and consequently much other property from loss or destruction by fire, and, if the act can be enforced at a reasonable cost to the owner, then, in our opinion, it ought to be sustained. We believe this statute fulfills these conditions. We think that in this case it is not a mere matter of convenience of the tenants as to where they shall obtain their supply of water. Simple convenience, we admit, would not authorize [51] the passage of this kind of legislation. But where it is obvious that, without the convenience of an appliance for the supply of water on the various floors of these tenement houses, there will be scarcely any but the most limited and scanty use of the water itself, which must be carried from the yards below, and when we must admit that the free use of water tends directly and immediately toward the sustaining of the health of the individual, and the prevention of disease arising from filth either of the person or in the surrounding habitation, then we must conclude that it is more than a mere matter of convenience in the use of water which is involved in the decision of this case. The absence of the water tends directly toward the breeding of disease, and its presence is healthful and humanizing.

Looked at in the light of a fire law and the act is also valid. The section of the Consolidation Act in question belongs to title 7, which treats of tenement and lodging houses, and various provisions are made in the preceding sections looking toward the prevention and the prompt extinguishment of fires, as well as toward the protection and promotion of the health of the occupants of such houses. And it seems to me

that the facility for the extinguishment of fires which would
result from the presence of a supply of water on each floor
of these houses is plain, and the act must be looked upon
as a means for securing such an important result. We are
inclined, therefore, to the belief that the act may be upheld
under both branches alike as a health law, and as one calculated to prevent destruction of property from fires which
might otherwise take place. The act is somewhat vague as
to what shall be regarded as a sufficient quantity of water on
each floor, but it must have, in this respect as in others, a reasonable construction, and when an appliance for its supply is
placed on a floor where it might be open and common to all
those on that floor, and easy of access, and the supply sufficient in amount for general domestic purposes, then and in
such case there would be a full compliance with the provisions of the act.

⁵² Some criticism is made in regard to the wording of the
order of the board of health. The order directed that suitable appliances to receive and distribute a supply of water
for domestic use should be provided at these various houses,
and it is claimed that there is no language in the act which
requires appliances for the distribution of water, nor that the
water shall be furnished for domestic use. The act provides
that the water shall be furnished in sufficient quantity at
one or more places on each floor occupied, or intended to be
occupied, by one or more families. This necessarily requires
some appliance for that purpose. The statute must also
mean that the water is to be provided for the use of the one
or more families that are to be occupants of the floor, and
that must include a sufficient quantity of water for domestic
purposes.

The provision in the law that the water shall be furnished
in sufficient quantities at one or more places on each floor
cannot be so construed as to leave the number of places of
supply entirely to the discretion of the board of health. As
the water is to be supplied in sufficient quantity for domestic
and not for manufacturing purposes, when that point is
reached the law is satisfied. Looking at the purpose of the
supply, it is, as I have said, reasonably apparent that one
such place on each floor, fairly accessible to all the occupants
of the floor, would be all that could usually and reasonably
be required, and any thing further would be unreasonable,
and, therefore, beyond the power of the board to order. The

facilities thus given would at the same time furnish the means necessary for obtaining water to extinguish such fires as might accidentally break out, and before they had obtained such headway as to render necessary the aid of the fire department.   This is clearly a most important safeguard.

The question alluded to in the brief of the respondent's counsel, whether the penalties might not be said to have commenced running immediately after the passage of the amended act of 1887, because of the provision requiring all tenement houses to be supplied with suitable appliances before January 1, 1889, and so have amounted to a confiscation of property, [53] is not before us, as the proceeding herein was to recover only those incurred since the order was made by the board. If such a case arises where penalties so enormous in amount are claimed, there will probably be not much difficulty in refusing enforcement under the circumstances of that case.

Upon the whole, we think the order of the general term of the court of common pleas should be reversed, and judgment directed to be entered upon the verdict ordered in the trial court, with costs.

———

BARTLETT, J., dissented, saying: "I am unable to discover the limit of legislative power if this act is to stand.

"Upon the face of the proceeding it is not an exercise of the police power to promote the safety of property by the prevention of fire.   The order of the health department served upon the defendant directs that suitable appliances 'to receive and distribute a supply of water for domestic use be provided,' on certain floors in the houses named.

"The act provides that tenement houses 'shall have Croton or other water furnished in sufficient quantities at one or more places on each floor,' etc.

"The order undertakes to construe the act, and requires the landlord to distribute a supply of water for domestic use on each floor.

"The board of health is not confined to compelling one place on each floor at which water may be obtained, but the act reads 'one or more places on each floor'; so that it is left with the board of health to determine how many water faucets upon each floor shall be provided by the landlord for the use and convenience of his tenants.   In other words, the legislature seeks to vest in one of the departments of the city government the power to decide the extent of the plumbing in tenement houses for Croton water purposes.

"It must, of course, be admitted that water is essential to the public health, and more particularly in crowded tenement districts.

"It would undoubtedly be a legitimate exercise of the police power to compel the introduction of water into tenement houses at some convenient point where all the tenants could obtain an adequate supply, and it may be that the legislature could go so far as to require a faucet upon each floor of the large tenement houses in the public hall in order to encourage the free use of water by enabling the tenants to procure it without too great exertion, but certainly it cannot be possible that the legislature may leave the number and location of faucets on each floor for the domestic use of water to be determined by the board of health. There is no limitation as to whether the faucets shall be in the public hall or in the room of the tenant. To my mind such an exercise of the police power is spoliation and confiscation under the forms of law; it deprives the landlord of the control of his property, and leaves it to a stranger to decide in what manner the house shall be plumbed.

"It is a direct interference with the right of the landlord to regulate the rental value of his property.

"It is a matter of common knowledge that in rented apartments in the city of New York the convenience and volume of the water supply is regulated by the rental value of the premises, and that in the cheap tenement districts the convenience of the tenants is not and cannot be consulted to the same extent as in first-class localities.

"The vice of the act we are considering lies in the fact, already pointed out, that it is too general in its terms, and clothes the health department with unlimited and undefined powers.

"If it be the legislative intent to compel the introduction of a more abundant supply of water into tenement houses, either to promote the public health or to provide for the timely extinguishment of fires, I think this very proper exercise of the police power should be manifested in an act containing details and limitations, so that capitalists may understand the burdens imposed upon tenement property, and decide, with a full knowledge of the facts, whether they care to embark their money in that class of buildings.

"This court has held (*Matter of Jacobs*, 98 N. Y. 108; 50 Am. Rep. 636), that the limit of police power 'cannot be accurately defined, and the courts have not been able or willing to definitely circumscribe it.'

"Each case must be decided very largely on its own facts.

A sound public policy certainly dictates that at this time, when the rights of property and the liberty of the citizen are sought to be invaded by every form of subtle and dangerous legislation, the courts should see to it that those benign principles of the common law which are the shield of personal liberty and private property suffer no impairment.

"I think the judgment should be affirmed with costs."

POLICE POWER— PROPER EXERCISE OF.—Under the exercise of their police power the states may legislate to promote domestic morals, order, and safety, to secure general comfort, health, and prosperity, to prevent crime, pauperism, disturbance of the peace, and all forms of social evils, and to protect the lives, limbs, quiet, and prosperity of all their citizens: *Burdick* v. *People*, 149 Ill. 600; 41 Am. St. Rep. 329; *New Orleans etc. Co.* v. *Hart*, 40 La. Ann. 474; 8 Am. St. Rep. 544; *State* v. *Heineman*, 80 Wis. 253; 27 Am. St. Rep. 34, and note.

CONSTITUTIONAL LAW—RIGHT TO A HEARING.—A hearing or an opportunity to be heard prior to a judgment is absolutely essential: *State* v. *Billings*, 55 Minn. 467; 43 Am. St. Rep. 525; *Larson* v. *Dickey*, 39 Neb. 463; 42 Am. St. Rep. 595, and note.

BOARDS OF HEALTH ARE NOT REQUIRED TO GIVE NOTICE OF HEARING to any person before they can exercise their jurisdiction for the public welfare, unless the statute under which they are authorized to act expressly requires such notice or hearing, but they cannot make any final determination of a nuisance resulting in the destruction of property, or the imposition of penalties, unless the party whose interests are to be affected is entitled, as a matter of right, to a hearing as a condition precedent to the making of such determination: *People v. Board of Health*, 140 N. Y. 1; 37 Am. St. Rep. 522, and note.

PEOPLE v. GIRARD.

[145 NEW YORK, 105.]

POLICE POWER—ARTIFICIAL COLORING IN VINEGAR.—A statute prohibiting every person from manufacturing or keeping for sale any vinegar containing any artificial coloring matter is constitutional and enforceable though the coloring is harmless and not injurious to health, and the vinegar so colored is in all respects equal to the best vinegar of the class which it is colored to represent, if the object of the coloring is to deceive purchasers into believing that the vinegar was of this latter class.

F. G. Fincke, for the appellant.

C. D. Adams and Fred C. Schraub, for the respondent.

106 FINCH, J. The argument in this case concedes the undoubted rule that the police power of the state may be exerted to protect the public health or prevent a fraud upon the people, but that the law professing to intend that result must indicate by its terms that such was its real and actual purpose, and exhibit a capacity to operate in the asserted direction. The defendant sold vinegar containing artificial coloring matter in violation of the law of 1889 (Laws 1889, c. 515, sec. 4), which provides that "no person shall manufacture, produce, sell, or keep for sale, or offer for sale, any vinegar which shall contain any preparation of lead, copper, sulphuric acid, **107** or other ingredients injurious to health, or any artificial coloring matter." It is evident that the last clause has relation to the prevention of fraud, not only because of the form and mode of expression, but also because if limited to an effect upon the public health, it would become a mere useless repetition. Any ingredients so injurious had already been prohibited, and the further limitation must be assumed to have a further purpose, and relate to the prevention of fraud in the production and sale of vinegar. It must be also assumed that the legislature acted with knowledge of this particular food product, of its appearance, and the modes of its manufacture. Everybody is familiar with cider vinegar, for it goes into all households. Its color and

appearance are as well understood as its taste. But another
vinegar has come upon the market made by a distillation
from grain. It is said to be entirely healthy and safe as a
food product, and that may be granted. No law forbids its
manufacture or sale. The markets of the state are open to
it freely and without restraint, and the only prohibition is
against the fraud of a false color. Its natural color, when
honestly made, is much lighter than that of cider vinegar,
and gives it rather a resemblance to water with some faint
trace of color or to a white wine. Purchasers had a natural
preference for the old familiar article, and were more or less
averse to an experiment with the new. They could tell the
difference at a glance by the marked difference in color. The
new product probably made its way slowly for that reason,
and the greed of profit, which has adulterated or disguised
almost every article of food, led to the device of coloring it
so as to change its appearance from almost white to a brown
or amber color, which is that of the ordinary cider vinegar.
Thus changed the new product might easily deceive purchasers. They would accept it supposing it to be cider vinegar, when, if its natural color had remained, they would have
refused it. Obviously, the artificial coloring matter is used
for some purpose. It adds to the cost and labor of preparation, and such expense would not be incurred unless it
improved the salable quality of the article. The coloring
[108] matter does not affect the taste or actual quality of the
vinegar when, as here, it is burnt sugar or carmel which is
used, but it does change the appearance. It masks the truth;
it effects a disguise; it naturally deceives and is intended to
deceive; for the new color is that of cider vinegar, and enables
the substituted product to be foisted upon those who prefer
and seek the old. We can see how it operated in the case
before us. The defendants are Italians. They say they knew
nothing about cider vinegar, and that such an article is not
found in Italy. They were good subjects for the manufacturer to use. They bought a barrel of vinegar and got the
distilled product having an artificial amber color. A purchaser comes and asks for cider vinegar. The sellers give
him the new, claiming that vinegar is vinegar, and very possibly not appreciating the word cider as a qualification. But
whether they were the mere tools of the manufacturer or
themselves cognizant of the situation it is apparent that the
vinegar was colored for purposes of deception, and to defraud

the buyer. The legislature had a right to forbid that device
and put a stop to the fraud, but how were they to do so?
They might forbid specially the use of a coloring matter
creating a resemblance to cider vinegar, or accomplish the
same purpose by forbidding the use of any coloring whatever. By the first process they would remit the question of
imitation to a jury; by the second they would decide it themselves conclusively and once for all. So far as the present
facts are concerned either form of prohibition effects one and
the same precise result, for there is no proof that distilled
vinegar is ever colored or even likely to be colored in any
other way than so as to resemble cider vinegar; and the form
of the law, judged by the situation it was framed to meet, is
identical in its results in either case.   But beyond that the
legislature might make the prohibition absolute for two reasons: One, the difficulty of enforcing a special provision
limited narrowly to an imitation with intent to deceive, in
which event there would always be a question of fact more
or less hampering the effective execution of the law; and the
other, that any tampering [109] with food products which adds
ingredients not natural or essential is fraught with danger
to the public health, or, at least, involves the intent and
result of a fraud upon the community.   Food should be
pure, absolutely and unquestionably pure. No tricks should
be played with it. The legislature may resolutely protect it.
No artificial color can ever be added to distilled vinegar for
any good or honest purpose that I can imagine.   Counsel
say it might be colored blue or green so that no purchaser
would take it for cider vinegar, and yet the law is broad
enough to forbid that. I grant it. The case is imaginary,
but assume it to be real. The blue or green color would, at
least, disguise the actual product, and permission to color at
all opens the door to coloring matters which might well be
dangerous to health. Must the legislature wait for the experiment and until some number of people are made sick or
die of it? In so serious a matter as the absolute purity of
food we ought not to say that a general law which simply
compels that absolute purity is beyond the power of the
legislature.

There is talk here of interference with the vested rights of
the individual. Sometimes it is pertinent and weighty, but
in this case it is neither. It becomes the assertion of a vested
right to color a food product so as to conceal or disguise its

true and natural appearance; in plain words, a vested right
to deceive the public.

This is by no means the first time that the legislature has
acted by a general law in seeking to protect the public health
and safety. It has provided a fixed standard for the purity
of milk, judging for itself, absolutely and conclusively, what
that standard should be, instead of leaving it to the varying
judgment of different juries. We sustained that law in the
case of Cipperly, adopting as our own the dissenting opinion
of Judge Learned at the general term: *People* v. *Cipperly*, 37
Hun, 319; 101 N. Y. 634. There it was claimed that the
law was too broad and inflexible; that instead of merely forbidding the sale of impure or unhealthy milk it prohibited
the sale of all below an arbitrary standard of purity, and so
that milk which was perfectly [110] pure and healthy might
fall within the prohibition because below the standard. We
sustained, nevertheless, the constitutionality of the act, and
the right of the legislature to judge for itself of the danger
and the remedy. The right of the legislature to that effect
was well illustrated in *Commonwealth* v. *Alger*, 7 Cush. 96,
where the case of a powder-mill or slaughter-house endangering the safety or health of the people was used as an
illustration. The legislature is not bound merely to enact
that such a structure shall not be put so near to a city or
village as to endanger the citizens, but may judge for itself,
and decide what is that distance, and not leave it for a
jury to say. A municipal corporation may in like manner
fix authoritatively and by a general ordinance the rate of
speed of railroad trains through its streets. These cases
are referred to only as showing the right of the legislature
to judge for itself of the character and extent of the danger which is shown to exist, and to apply the remedy by
a definite rule of prohibition. Every general law may work
harshly in a few particular instances. If that were true in
the present case it would not determine the constitutional
question. Adding a foreign and artificial ingredient to a food
product, even for purposes of color merely, is, in effect, an
adulteration, and whether it be so described or forbidden by
more specific terms is not material. The present law does
not in the least interfere with the honest manufacture and
sale of the distilled vinegar. It simply provides that it shall
not be falsely colored. I think the legislature did not in this
case, and under the circumstances existing, exceed its power.

The judgment should be affirmed.

All concur, except BARTLETT and HAIGHT, JJ., dissenting, the latter on the construction of the statute.

Judgment affirmed.

ADULTERATION—POLICE POWER.—Laws prohibiting the adulteration of articles of food, or preventing imposition or fraud in the sale of such articles, are valid exercises of the police power of the state: *State* v. *Campbell,* 64 N. H. 402; 10 Am. St. Rep. 419, and note. To the same effect see *State* v. *Fourcade,* 45 La. Ann. 717; 40 Am. St. Rep. 249, and note.

ROCA *v.* BYRNE.

[145 NEW YORK, 182.]

PRINCIPAL AND AGENT—TRUST FUNDS.—A principal is entitled in all cases when he can trace his property, whether it be in the hands of his agent, or of his representative, or of a third person, to reclaim it, and it is immaterial that it has been converted into money if it is in condition to be distinguished from other property or assets of the agent.

PRINCIPAL AND AGENT.—IF AN AGENT RECEIVED OF HIS PRINCIPAL bills to be collected and thereafter used to satisfy such obligations as the principal may incur, and which, when collected, the agent deposited in bank to his own credit, the equitable title remains to the moneys so deposited in the principal, and on the agent's insolvency the principal may recover them in preference to the other creditors of such agent.

ACTION against the executrix of Anna D. Byrne and the Corn Exchange Bank to recover a judgment directing the latter to pay to plaintiff certain moneys standing on its books in the name of the deceased. He, in his lifetime, was the agent of the plaintiffs, who were partners in business in Ecuador. They were accustomed to consign to decedent merchandise for sale, and also to have him, as their agent, ship goods to them from New York city to be paid for either from goods consigned to him or by bills of exchange sent to him. The parties were accustomed to have a settlement semiannually, and on their settlement, June 30, 1891, a balance was due the decedent of $24,953.63. Subsequently plaintiffs remitted to decedent sundry bills for collection, the amounts of which were by him collected and deposited in his name in bank. The moneys were deposited with the Corn Exchange Bank in an account in which decedent deposited his own moneys as well as those collected by him for the plaintiff. In July, 1891, Byrne received further bills for collection amounting to $4.774.26, and after the death of Byrne other persons, claim-

ing to act for his estate, received and collected further bills
of the plaintiff amounting to nearly $1,500. When the action
was commenced the aggregate due the plaintiffs from bills
collected as aforesaid, and the proceeds of which had been
deposited in the bank, was, after paying all moneys due the
decedent, $4,514.05. Judgment for the plaintiffs. The de-
fendants appeal.

Theron G. Strong, for the appellant.

Michael H. Cardozo, for the respondents.

[186] Gray, J. This is a somewhat peculiar case upon its
facts, and the question is whether the plaintiffs, having traced
the avails of the drafts which they had remitted to their
agent, shall have them, as against the claims of other creditors upon the insolvent estate of Byrne. The general and
well-recognized rule is, and has been, that a principal is entitled in all cases, when he can trace his property, whether
it be in the hands of the agent, or of his representatives, or
of third persons, to reclaim it, and it is immaterial that it
may have been converted into money; so only that it is in
condition to be distinguished from the other property or assets
of the agent: Story on Agency, sec. 231; *Thompson* v. *Perkins,*
3 Mason, 232; *Robson* v. *Wilson,* 1 Marshall on Insurance, 295;
Van Alen v. *American Nat. Bank,* 52 N. Y. 1; *Importers' etc.
Bank* v. *Peters,* 123 N. Y. 272. The difficulty here supposed
to prevent the application of the general rule arises in the
nature of the course of dealing adopted; which, as it is argued
on behalf of the appellant, shows that the relation of debtor
and creditor only existed between the plaintiffs and their
deceased agent. The moneys, it is insisted, proceeding from
the drafts remitted to Byrne, were not [187] impressed with
any trust, but were in part payment on account of a balance
due from the plaintiffs. It is undoubtedly true that the
relation of debtor and creditor existed, according as the state
of the accounts showed the balance to be one way or the
other, but that fact was not inconsistent with, and could not
affect, the fact that the relation was also of a fiduciary character. Byrne received all drafts in virtue of his agency and
they, or the proceeds, were received for purposes connected
with that agency. It was not necessary that they should
have been remitted against any specific obligations. They
may have been remitted generally, and generally credited in
the account; but their purpose was to discharge obligations

incurred, or to be incurred, or disbursements made by their
agent for them. What was the evident, the indisputable fact
here? Plainly, that there resulted an excess over what was
incumbent upon the plaintiffs to pay, of a sum of money,
which was not Byrne's, but which belonged to the plaintiffs. This excess being unused, or not required for the
purpose for which remitted, how could Byrne or his representatives claim it in equity? The legal title to the moneys
may have been in him, but the right, in equity, to follow
them, as the proceeds of their drafts, was in the plaintiffs.
If Byrne or his representatives placed the moneys in the
bank to the credit of his account that would not affect the
question as to whom they belonged beneficially; a question
which equity, in a proper case, will always inquire into. If
received, as here, in the course of transactions between the
principal and the agent, the character of the moneys would
be unchanged by the deposit, provided they could be identified. They would still be moneys held for the principal.
However peculiar the circumstances here, from the particular
course of dealing, the cardinal fact stands out that the
plaintiffs' property was sent to their agent as such, and for
purposes comprehended within the agency. The case cannot
be likened to that of bills sent on general account between a
merchant and his correspondent, nor to the case of the deposit of bills on a general running account with a banker and
without specific [188] appropriation to other bills. It is more
like the case supposed by Lord Chancellor Cottenham, in his
opinion in *Jombart* v. *Woollett*, 2 Mylne & C. 390, who, stating
the result of the law as laid down in some cases cited, said:
"Unless there be a contract to the contrary, if a person,
having an agent elsewhere, remits to him, for a particular
purpose, bills not due, and that purpose is not answered, and
then the agent carries them to account, and becomes a bankrupt, the property in the bills is not altered, but remains in
the party making the remittance." In *Veil* v. *Administrators
of Mitchel*, 4 Wash. C. C. 105, the plaintiffs sent the defendant's intestate two bills of exchange, with instructions to
remit the proceeds. The intestate sold the bills, remitting a
part of the proceeds of one, but keeping the rest and a post-
dated check which had been taken for the other. He died
before the maturing of the check, which was collected by
his administrators. On another account the plaintiffs were
indebted to the intestate in a certain balance. The intestate

died insolvent, and the question reserved for the court was whether the plaintiffs are entitled to recover the amount of the check and of the unremitted portion of the proceeds of the other note, after deducting what was due upon another account to the intestate. Mr. Justice Washington rendered judgment for the plaintiffs, upon the principle that, "where the principal can trace his property into the hands of his agent or factor . .   . he may follow it, either into the hands of the factor, or of his legal representatives, or of his assigns, if he should become insolvent or a bankrupt."

If it be objected that the proof here is that the bills were not remitted for a particular purpose, but generally on account of all obligations incurred and disbursements made by Byrne on account of plaintiffs, I think that is not a substantial distinction. The remittances were, in fact, to an agent for a purpose within the scope of the agency, and to meet the obligations or expenditures incurred for the remitters by the agent. I think, within the stipulated facts, the purpose of the remittance may be regarded as a particular one. We might paraphrase it as a general remittance for the particular purpose [189] of furnishing moneys to the agent to cover the obligations and liabilities incurred by him as such.

If the business relations between the plaintiffs and Byrne had been of the character of such which ordinarily exist between merchants and their correspondents, there would be no case; but it is because Byrne was the plaintiffs' agent that property received by him for them became impressed with a trust character, and, if not disposed of in good faith, to others, and if distinguishable from the agent's property, could be reclaimed by the principal, as against the general creditors of the agent. I am unable to see that, in truth, the nature of the dealings between the parties, of which so much has been made, necessarily did deprive their relations of their fiduciary character. The manner of his keeping the account, or of stating half yearly balances, and the general nature of a remittance to him upon account, are facts which need not have changed, and, in my opinion, did not change, the fiduciary nature of the relation held by Byrne to the plaintiffs. Under the conceded facts of the case, whatever he did, he did as their agent. The duties enumerated as devolving upon and performed by him were all consistent with his acting therein as agent.

In the account of June 30, 1891, showing a balance against the plaintiffs of $24,953.63, was included $9,721.58 of acceptances by Byrne, maturing after that date, and which were not paid by him, but which were eventually paid and taken up by the plaintiffs. The plaintiffs' indebtedness to him was therefore only $15,232.05. The drafts remitted by plaintiffs between June 20, 1891, and August 1, 1891, and realized upon and credited to Byrne's account in the bank, amounted to $18,313.69. There was, therefore, an excess over the amount necessary to discharge the indebtedness to the agent of $3,081.64. Can it be said that these moneys did not in equity belong to the plaintiffs? I cannot see it otherwise than in that light. I think it is a very plain case, where the principal has been able to trace a remittance of bills, made for the purpose of putting his agent in funds to meet expenditures [190] and liabilities incurred on his account, and in excess of what was needed to discharge their indebtedness in account, and where it has been possible to distinguish the moneys in bank as the avails of those bills with absolute certainty. That the proceeds of plaintiffs' draft did not, by being deposited to the credit of Byrne's bank account, lose their character is indisputable. In *Van Alen* v. *American Nat. Bank*, 52 N. Y. 1, the money sought to be recovered was mingled with some of the agent's own money; but this was deemed of no consequence. The controlling fact was that the plaintiffs' moneys were in the bank. In that case the authority of *Ætna Nat. Bank* v. *Fourth Nat. Bank*, 46 N. Y. 82, 7 Am. Rep. 314, was not deemed in point, inasmuch as there was no question of title in the plaintiff, but merely of the discharge by the defendant bank of an obligation to a depositor.

I think the affirmance by the general term was correct, and that the judgment should be affirmed, with costs.

All concur.

Judgment affirmed. ―――

AGENCY—RECOVERY BY PRINCIPAL OF MONEY DEPOSITED IN BANK IN AGENT'S NAME.—Money deposited in bank by an agent as an ordinary deposit, the agent stating that it was his principal's money, but desiring the officer to place it to his credit on the books of the bank, may be followed by the principal in a court of equity: *Whitley* v. *Foy*, 6 Jones Eq. 34; 78 Am. Dec. 236, and especially note.

TRACING TRUST FUNDS.—This question will be found fully discussed in the following line of cases: *Mutual Acc. Assn.* v. *Jacobs*, 141 Ill. 261; 33 Am.

St. Rep. 302, and note; *Springfield Institution* v. *Copeland*, 160 Mass. 380; 39 Am. St. Rep. 489, and note; *Homes* v. *Gilman*, 138 N. Y. 369; 34 Am. St. Rep. 463. See, further, the extended notes to *Union Nat. Bank* v. *Goetz*, 32 Am. St. Rep. 125, and *Bolling* v. *Kirby*, 24 Am. St. Rep. 800.

KEENAN *v.* NEW YORK, LAKE ERIE & WESTERN RAILROAD COMPANY.

[145 NEW YORK, 190.]

MASTER AND SERVANT—VICE-PRINCIPALS, WHO ARE NOT.—A gang boss is in no sense a vice-principal, and, if he makes a suggestion that an inferior servant go underneath a car standing on a track and procure an article required by the former in the discharge of his duties and no other person has been designated by the employee to furnish or look for such article, such boss does not, in making such suggestion, represent the principal, and, if injury results from his negligence in making the suggestion, it is the negligence of a fellow-servant for which no recovery can be had.

MASTER AND SERVANT.—A SERVANT SUSTAINING AN INJURY FROM THE NEGLIGENCE OF A SUPERIOR AGENT engaged in the same general business cannot maintain an action against the common employer, although he was subject to the control of such superior agent, and could not guard against his negligence or its consequences.

ACTION brought by John Keenan to recover for injuries received by him while in the employ of the defendant. He recovered judgment in the trial court, and, pending an appeal by the defendant, died.

George W. Cothran, for the appellants.

Adelbert Moot, for the respondent.

198 BARTLETT, J.   The plaintiff's intestate, who was a car repairer, brought this action to recover damages for personal injuries received by him while working in defendant's repair-yard in Buffalo.

·194 The jury rendered a verdict in his favor for ten thousand dollars, and the general term of the superior court of Buffalo reversed the judgment on questions of law, ordering a new trial, and the intestate's administratrix (he having died after verdict rendered) appeals to this court, giving the usual stipulation for judgment absolute in case of affirmance.

The facts in this case are simple, and will be assumed as stated by the intestate for the purposes of this appeal.

There were three tracks running east and west at the place
in the repair-yard where deceased was working on the day of
the accident; the southerly track was No. 21; the middle
track, No. 2; the north track, No. 8. It is undisputed that
the only entrance to these tracks was from the east; that No.
21 and No. 2 were used exclusively for repairing cars, and
No. 8 was known as the "cripple track," on which were
placed cars needing repairs; that the repairing tracks were
protected by flags when men were at work under the cars,
but no such precaution was adopted on track No. 8, as no
repairing was done there, and cars were shunted thereon at
all hours of the day.

The deceased testified: "I was working right next to
track No. 8 and within a short distance for three months,
and saw cars on that track every day, and the way they did
business there."

From five hundred and fifty to nine hundred men were
employed in the repair-yards, and one Robert Gunn was foreman in charge of the repairs of cars; O'Day was assistant
foreman and Getz was the man who distributed the various
articles of hardware, such as bumper-springs, braces, etc., to
the men when at work.

The men were divided up into small gangs, and one Tracy
was foreman or gang boss of the gang in which the intestate
worked.

On the day of the accident the intestate and another man
were at work repairing a car on track No. 2, and found they
needed an eight-inch bumper-spring; the intestate applied
to Getz for the spring, and was informed that he did not have
one; he then went to what was known as the scrap pile,
195 which contained second-hand material of all kinds, and
failed to find the required article there; he then reported these
facts to the gang boss, Tracy, who told him he had better go
down to No. 8 track and take one from a car there; in company with his fellow-workman intestate followed out this suggestion, and, while under a car on track No. 8, in this act of
removing a bumper-spring, some cars were backed in on that
track, moving the car under which intestate was working, and
inflicting upon him very serious and permanent injuries.

The only legal question in this case is, Did the gang boss,
Tracy, in suggesting to the intestate to go down on track No.
8 and get the spring, represent the defendant?

It is admitted by the learned counsel for the appellant that there is no direct evidence in the case showing that it was any part of Tracy's duty to furnish materials required by the workmen under him, but he insists that the defendant having failed to designate any one person whose duty it should be to borrow springs from other cars for temporary use, and still continuing the business of car repairing, it not only acquiesced in the gang foremen procuring such materials, but impliedly authorized them to procure them wherever they could.

The appellant's counsel also admits that Tracy was the fellow-servant of the intestate in every thing except in the performance of a duty which the law imposed upon the defendant, viz., procuring materials for use.

We are unable to adopt these views.

It would lead to the establishment of an exceedingly unsafe rule to hold that a gang boss over forty or fifty men could, without direct authority from the company, change the safe and proper rules in pursuance of which the work in the repair-yards was conducted, and direct workmen to prosecute their labors under cars standing on tracks other than the regular, duly protected repair tracks.

Tracy was in no legal sense the representative of the defendant when he suggested to the intestate that he should procure a spring from a car standing on track No. 8; he was a fellow-servant making a very unwise and dangerous suggestion.

[196] A servant who sustains an injury from the negligence of a superior agent, engaged in the same general business, cannot maintain an action against their common employer, although he was subject to the control of such superior agent, and could not guard against his negligence or its consequences: *Sherman* v. *Rochester etc. R. R. Co.*, 17 N. Y. 153; *Loughlin* v. *State*, 105 N. Y. 159.

The order appealed from should be affirmed, and judgment absolute directed for the defendant, with costs.

All concur.

Ordered accordingly. ____

MASTER AND SERVANT—VICE-PRINCIPAL—FOREMAN.—A foreman may be, and ordinarily is, but a mere fellow-servant. The burden is upon an injured servant to show by allegations in his complaint that such foreman whose negligence caused the injury is a vice-principal, and not a fellow-servant: *New Pittsburg Coal etc. Co.* v. *Peterson*, 136 Ind. 398; 43 Am. St. Rep. 327, and note, with the cases collected.

MASTER AND SERVANT—SUPERIOR SERVANT—LIABILITY OF MASTER.—
A master is liable to an inferior servant for injuries resulting from the negligence of a superior servant if such negligence was in regard to some duty imposed by law upon the master, and by him intrusted to the negligent superior servant: *Railroad* v. *Spence,* 93 Tenn. 173; 42 Am. St. Rep. 907, and note; *New Pittsburg Coal etc. Co.* v. *Peterson,* 136 Ind. 398; 43 Am. St. Rep. 327, and note.

ANSTETH *v.* BUFFALO RAILWAY COMPANY.

[145 NEW YORK, 210.]

STREET RAILWAYS, LIABILITY OF FOR ACT OF CONDUCTOR IN FRIGHTENING A BOY.—If, seeing a boy upon the car, the conductor calls out to him and makes a movement of a nature to justify the boy in believing that he is about to receive punishment or bodily injury, and he thereupon lets go and falls and is injured, and brings an action for such injury, he may recover if, in the opinion of the jury, the act of the conductor was done for the purpose of removing the boy from the car, and was improper, unnecessarily dangerous, and the proximate cause of the injury.

Porter Norton, for the appellant.

Adolph Rebadow, for the respondent.

[212] HAIGHT, J.   This action was brought to recover damages for injuries sustained by the plaintiff in alighting from one of defendant's street railroad cars on Plymouth avenue, in the city of Buffalo, on the twenty-first day of October, 1892.

[213] The plaintiff was a boy ten years of age, and was at the time of the accident stealing a ride upon one of the defendant's cars.   He stood, as he testified, upon the step of the front platform with one hand upon the handle of the dashboard and the other upon the handle on the corner of the car.   While standing in this position the conductor passed through the car out upon the front platform, and with one hand reached out toward him (the witness indicating) and cried " Hey!"   At this he let go of the handle upon the dashboard, fell from the step, and his body swung around against the side of the car, he still holding to the handle upon the corner, and in that position remained whilst the car proceeded ten or fifteen feet.   He then dropped, falling by the side of the car in such a manner that the wheels passed over one of his legs.

Upon the trial motions for nonsuit and for direction of verdict were made and denied.

In *Clark* v. *New York etc. R. R. Co.,* 40 Hun, 605, affirmed in 113 N. Y. 670, the plaintiff was a boy of the age of thirteen years. He caught on to the forward end of the caboose of a moving freight train. One of the company's employees saw him, and dashed a cup of water in his face, causing him to fall from the car in such a manner as to have his knee crushed by one of the wheels. It was held that he could recover.

In *McCann* v. *Sixth Ave. R. R. Co.*, 117 N. Y. 505, 15 Am. St. Rep. 539, a boy, in crossing the street, whereon were two tracks of the defendant's road, in order to get out of the way of a truck passing upon the street, jumped on to the rear platform of a car which had stopped at the crossing, and, as he was passing across the platform, the conductor kicked at him, and, to avoid the kick, he jumped from the car, landing in the other track, without looking, and was struck by a car moving upon that track. It was held that a nonsuit was improper.

In *Hogan* v. *Central Park etc. R. R. Co.*, 124 N. Y. 647, a boy twelve years of age was stealing a ride upon the rear platform of one of the defendant's cars, which [214] was managed by the driver alone. A number of boys had jumped on to the car for the purpose of stealing a ride, but at the command of the driver they all got off except the decedent, who continued to sit upon the left side of the rear platform. As the car crossed Second avenue another lad jumped on to the right side of the platform, for the purpose of obtaining a free ride, and thereupon the driver started toward the rear platform for the purpose of compelling the boys to leave the car, but before he reached them they jumped off, the plaintiff's intestate on the left side of the car, and in doing so fell under one of the defendant's cars running on the other track, and was killed. The driver did not let go of his lines, with which he managed his horses, nor approach within several feet of the boys, nor threaten them with violence. It was held that the judgment in favor of the plaintiff should be reversed.

The plaintiff was a trespasser, and the defendant owed him no duty of protection. Its servants had the right to remove him from the car, but in doing so were required to subject him to no unnecessary hazard. They had no right to seize him and throw him from the car whilst it was in motion, or to so violently assault or frighten him as to cause him to fall from the car. In order to justify a recovery the act of the defendant's servant must have been improper, unnecessarily dangerous, the proximate cause of the injury, and done for the purpose of removing the plaintiff from the car.

As we have seen, the conductor went out upon the front platform, extended his hand toward the plaintiff, and cried out "Hey!" The boy tells us that it frightened him, and that he fell off. The record does not give us much information with reference to the character of the act, whether it was violent or threatening. It does give us to understand that the witnesses indicated to the jury, by illustrating with the arm, the manner and character of the act. We consequently may assume, in aid of the judgment, that the act was of such a nature as to justify the plaintiff in believing that he was about to receive punishment or bodily injury.

²¹⁵ The case may be close and upon the border, but we incline to the view that we cannot interfere.

The judgment should be affirmed, with costs.

All concur, except ANDREWS, C. J., and GRAY, J., dissenting.

Judgment affirmed. ____

MASTER AND SERVANT—GENERAL LIABILITY OF MASTER FOR SERVANT'S ACTS.—A master is not liable 'for the act of a servant unless it was done for the purpose and as a means of doing what the servant was employed to do. An act done by the servant while engaged in his master's work, but not done as a means or for the purpose of performing the work, is not deemed to be the act of the master: *Bowler* v. *O'Connell*, 162 Mass. 319; 44 Am. St. Rep. 359, and note. See the note to *Ritchie* v. *Waller*, 38 Am. St. Rep. 370.

————

PEOPLE v. MILK EXCHANGE.

[145 NEW YORK, 267.]

CORPORATIONS — UNLAWFUL RESTRICTIONS OF TRADE — FORFEITURE OF CHARTER.—If a corporation adopts by-laws declaring that its directors shall have power to make and fix the standard or market price at which milk shall be purchased by the stockholders of the corporation, and acting under these by-laws the directors, from time to time, fix the price of milk to be paid by dealers, and the price so fixed largely controlled the market in and about the city in which the corporation had its place of business, these facts support a verdict or finding that the corporation as thus managed constitutes a combination inimical to trade and commerce, and therefore unlawful, and are sufficient to sustain a decree forfeiting the charter of the corporation.

Alfred Ely, for the appellant.

T. E. Hancock, attorney general, for the respondents.

269 HAIGHT, J.   This action was brought to have the defendant, a domestic corporation, dissolved, its charter vacated, and its corporate existence annulled.   This relief is sought upon two grounds: 1. Nonuser; 2. An unlawful and illegal combination and conspiracy made in restraint of trade to limit the supply of milk, and to fix and control the price thereof in the city of New York and elsewhere.

The defendant was organized on the twenty-first day of October, 1882, for the purpose, as stated in its certificate of incorporation, of "buying and selling of milk at wholesale and retail, the purchase of dairies of milk when deemed advisable, and the sale of the same to milk dealers."   The complaint charges that the defendant was not engaged in this business.   Upon **270** the trial at the close of the evidence it was conceded by both counsel for the plaintiff and for the defendant that the question whether the defendant had been engaged in buying or selling milk, under the evidence, was a question of law for the court, and not for the jury.   We so understand the evidence.   There is no conflict, and we have but to ascertain the meaning and intention of the witnesses. The plaintiff's chief witness was Woodhull, the secretary and treasurer of the defendant.   In his testimony he makes use of the expression that the exchange "has bought and sold milk"; but he then proceeds to state that he is familiar with the operations of the Milk Exchange in buying milk of the farmers and selling it to dealers, and then states the manner in which the business was conducted.   He says: "It is this: a farmer brings his dairy into the exchange to be sold; I go out and find him a dealer who can use the milk, and write the farmer how to mark his milk; I make the collection of the dealer and pay it to the farmer, and we guarantee him the collection."   He further testified that their commission was three per cent; that the milk was never shipped to the exchange, but was shipped directly to the dealer; that they sold the milk for the farmer at the exchange price, which they guaranteed to collect and turn over to the farmer, less their commissions.   Numerous witnesses speak of their arrangement made, or attempted to be made, with the exchange for the sale of milk, and in each case it was distinctly stated that the exchange did not buy milk; that they merely looked up a dealer who would purchase it at the exchange price, and that they guaranteed the collection for three per cent commission.

We think, therefore, that there can be no question as to
the meaning of the witness Woodhull as to the expression
made use of by him above referred to, for he immediately
proceeded to explain how the milk was purchased and sold,
and this evidence establishes the fact that the milk was not
purchased by the exchange, but that it was sold in the manner described for the commission stated.   The transactions,
therefore, constituted a commission business, and were not,
strictly speaking [271] the "buying and selling of milk at
wholesale and retail."   Whether the engaging in a commission business, such as we have described, is authorized by
the defendant's charter, we do not deem it necessary now to
determine.   It may be that the commission business is so
closely allied to that of buying and selling as to make the
former legitimate and permissible under the defendant's certificate of incorporation.

We are thus brought to a consideration of the charge of
unlawful conspiracy in restraint of trade.   We have only
called attention to the charge of nonuser for the purpose of
showing the precise nature of the business conducted by the
defendant, as bearing upon the latter question.   If the defendant was the purchaser of milk, or of dairies of milk, it
had the right to fix the price from time to time that it would
pay therefor.   If, however, it was engaged only in the selling of milk upon commission, then its duty as a commission
merchant, as ordinarily understood, was to get as high a
price for the seller as could be reasonably obtained, and it
was no part of its duty to otherwise fix the price of milk.

It appears that the Milk Exchange when organized, or
shortly thereafter, had ninety-odd stockholders, a large
majority of whom were milk dealers in the city of New York
or creamery or milk commission men doing business in
that vicinity; that at the first meeting of the exchange after
its incorporation the following, among other, by-laws was
adopted: "The board of directors shall have the power to
make and fix the standard or market price at which milk
shall be purchased by the stockholders of this company, and
to declare the stock of any and every stockholder herein who
purchases milk at any other than the price so named by the
board forfeited, subject to the conditions set forth in article
3, sections 4 and 5, of these by-laws.   All stock so forfeited
by said board of directors shall be subject to the order of the
board of directors, and shall be disposed of as they direct."

This by-law remained in force for a number of years, and until after there was an investigation as to the character and nature of the defendant's business and a report made by a [272] committee of the senate. The by-law was then amended by striking out that part thereof which authorized the forfeiture of the stock of a stockholder who purchased milk at another price than that fixed by the exchange. It was again amended in April, 1890, but that part thereof which provided that the board of directors shall have the power to determine and fix from time to time the exchange price of milk was retained. Acting upon these by-laws, the defendant's board of directors have from time to time, during its corporate existence, fixed the price of milk to be paid by dealers, and the prices so fixed have largely controlled the market in and about the city of New York and of the milk-producing territory contiguous thereto.

These facts are significant, and we are unable to escape the conviction that there was a combination on the part of the milk dealers and creamery men in and about the city of New York to fix and control the price that they should pay for milk. Was this lawful?

In *Judd* v. *Harrington*, 139 N. Y. 105, certain parties who were dealers in sheep and lambs, entered into an agreement, by its terms organizing an association for the declared purpose of guarding and protecting their business interests from loss by unreasonable competition. The agreement was to pool their commissions, except such as should be agreed to be paid to a butchers' association with which they had agreed only to sell to the butchers and the butchers to buy only of the dealers belonging to their respective associations. It was held that the real nature and purpose of the agreement was to suppress competition in an article of food, and to so control the market that they could enhance the price of the article.

In *People* v. *Sheldon*, 139 N. Y. 251, 36 Am. St. Rep. 690, certain coal dealers organized a company known as the "Lockport Coal Exchange." The object of the organization was to prevent competition in the price of coal among the retail dealers in that city, by constituting the exchange the sole authority to fix the price which should be charged by the members for coal sold by them. Sheldon and others, members of the exchange, [273] were indicted, charged with the offense of doing an act injurious to trade or commerce.

The trial judge submitted the case to the jury upon the theory that if the defendants entered into the organization for the purpose of controlling the price of coal and managing the business of the sale thereof, so as to prevent competition in the price between the members of the exchange, the agreement was illegal. The jury found the defendants guilty. It was held that the principle upon which the case was submitted to the jury was sanctioned by the authorities. Andrews, C. J., in delivering the opinion of the court, said: "The question is, Was the agreement, in view of what might have been done under it, and the fact that it was an agreement, the effect of which was to prevent competition among the coal dealers, one upon which the law fixes the brand of condemnation? It has hitherto been an accepted maxim in political economy that 'competiton is the life of trade.' The courts have acted upon and adopted this maxim in passing upon the validity of agreements, the design of which was to prevent competition in trade, and have held such agreements to be invalid.' Again he says: "Agreements to prevent competition in trade are, in contemplation of law, injurious to trade, because they are liable to be injuriously used. The present case may be used as an illustration. The price of coal now fixed by the exchange may be reasonable in view of the interests, both of dealers and consumers, but the organization may not always be guided by the principle of absolute justice. . . . . If agreements and combinations to prevent competition in prices are or may be hurtful to trade the only sure remedy is to prohibit all agreements of that character. If the validity of such an agreement was made to depend upon actual proof of public prejudice or injury it would be very difficult in any case to establish the invalidity, although the moral evidence might be very convincing."

In *Arnot* v. *Pittston etc. Coal Co.*, 68 N. Y. 558, 23 Am. Rep. 190, the Butler Colliery Company and the Pittston & Elmira Coal Company were corporations engaged in mining and selling coal. For the purpose of monopolizing the trade and maintaining [274] a high price for coal the two companies entered into a contract by which one agreed to take all of the coal which the other should desire to send north of the state line at the regular market price, and agreed not to sell coal to any other party to be shipped in that direction. It was held that the agreement was entered into for the purpose of enhancing the price of coal north of the state line, and that it was against public policy and void. Rapallo, J., in the opinion, says: "That a combination to effect such a purpose is inimical to the interests of the public, and that all contracts designed to effect such an end are contrary to public policy, and, therefore, illegal, is too well settled by adjudicated cases to be questioned at this day": See *People v. Fisher*, 14 Wend. 9; 28 Am. Dec. 501; *Hooker* v. *Vanderwater*, 4 Denio, 349; 47 Am. Dec. 258; *Stanton* v. *Allen*, 5 Denio, 434; 49 Am. Dec. 282; *Saratoga County Bank* v. *King*, 44 N. Y. 87; *Leonard v. Poole*, 114 N. Y. 371; 11 Am. St. Rep. 667.

Applying the rule thus established to the evidence under consideration, it appears to us that a case is presented in which the jury might have found that the combination alluded to was inimical to trade and commerce, and, therefore, unlawful.

It may be claimed that the purpose of the combination was to reduce the price of milk, and that it being an article of food such reduction was not against public policy. But the price was fixed for the benefit of the dealers, and not the consumers, and the logical effect upon the trade of so fixing the price by the combination was to paralyze the production and limit the supply, and thus leave the dealers in a position to control the market, and at their option to enhance the price to be paid by the consumers. This brings the case within the condemnation of the authorities, to which we have referred.

It is asserted that this litigation was instituted upon the petition of members of the "Milk Producers' Union," and that the purpose of that association was to enhance the price of milk. This may be, but the action was brought by the attorney general, and the influences that operated upon him to induce his prosecution of the defendant are now unimportant. The questions for our determination are presented by the [275] pleadings, and the parties have the right to have them determined upon the merits. If the "Milk Producers' Union" is engaged in an unlawful business, which is a restraint upon trade and commerce, it may be dealt with in another action.

The order appealed from should be affirmed, and judgment absolute ordered in favor of the plaintiff upon the stipulation, with costs.

All concur (ANDREWS, C. J., and BARTLETT, J., on the ground of nonuser), except PECKHAM, J., who dissents upon the ground that there was proof sufficient of user, and that the action of the defendant did not fairly tend to enhance the price of milk to the consumer.

Order affirmed and judgment accordingly.

COMBINATIONS—UNLAWFUL RESTRICTIONS OF TRADE.—A contract is unlawful as in restraint of trade if injurious to the public interests, as where it provides that the signers will not sell any article of prime necessity or even of frequent use in a certain city, or to be used therein to persons other than such signers except at a price therein specified. Hence a pool or combination to control the price of beer in a city is unlawful: *Nester v. Continental Brewing Co.*, 161 Pa. St. 473; 41 Am. St. Rep. 894, and note with the cases collected.

WALSH *v.* FITCHBURG RAILROAD COMPANY,
[145 NEW YORK, 301.]

LANDOWNER, DUTY OF, TO PERSONS ON HIS PREMISES BY HIS SUFFERANCE.—If premises are open and unguarded, and the public is permitted to cross and to be upon them at will, the landowner owes to every person coming thereon the duty to abstain from injuring him intentionally, or by failing to exercise reasonable care, but does not owe him the duty of active vigilance to see that he is not injured while on such premises for his own convenience.

RAILWAYS—TURNTABLES, DUTY OF, TO GUARD FROM CHILDREN.—A railway maintaining a turntable upon land which the public is in the habit of crossing and being upon at pleasure, but not by invitation, does not owe the duty to children to keep such turntable fastened or locked when not in use, so as to prevent access to it by children. If it is on the land of its owner, and is used by him for the sole purpose of conducting his business, and is fit and proper for that purpose, and is not built in any improper or negligent way with reference to the transaction of his business, he does not owe any further duty to persons, whether children or adults, who have no business on his land, and who are there unasked, and whose presence is merely tolerated.

T. F. Hamilton, for the appellant

Henry T. Nason, for the respondent.

304 PECKHAM, J. The defendant owned a plot of ground in the northern portion of the city of Troy, bounded by four different streets. Quite a large portion of its land was unfenced, and the public had, for a number of years, been accustomed to walk across this plot for the purpose of shortening the distance, instead of going around by the public

streets.   The land was approached from the north on the
same grade as the public street, and the defendant laid its
tracks through the street and onto the plot for the purpose
of using it in the ordinary transaction of its business.   It was
not used for the purpose of a depot, and the land itself was
rough, uneven, overgrown with weeds and grass, and not fit
for use by horses and wagons, and was not so used.   The
public were not invited upon the land in any sense further
than that the defendant had not taken occasion to prevent
the public from using a portion of it as a footpath for the
purpose already stated.   The footpath thus marked out by
use ran within fifteen or twenty feet of the turntable of the
defendant, which was used by it in the ordinary course of its
business.   The surface of the table was in some places about
three feet above the grade of the plot, and at others it was
eight or nine feet above grade.   The only way to approach
it on the level was by the use of the tracks of the defendant,
which led onto the table, and it was used for the purpose of
taking the defendant's engines and turning them around.
The turntable was built in the usual manner, and was in
perfect repair.   The main tracks of the defendant ran through
the eastern portion of the plot.   The turntable was west of
the main tracks. -

305 On the 31st of August, 1888, the plaintiff, who was at
that time a child of the age of five years and nine months,
had come upon the defendant's premises, and, in company
with several other and elder boys, was playing on the turntable, and, in the course of turning the table around, the
plaintiff had his leg caught between the rail on the table and
the rail on the adjoining earth, and he was severely injured.
This action has been brought for the purpose of recovering
damages for those injuries, and a recovery has been had,
which has been sustained by the general term.

Plaintiff bases his right to maintain this action upon the
allegation that the defendant, by permitting the public to go
upon its land in the manner stated, had, in effect, invited
such entrance, and was bound on that account to use greater
care to prevent an accident of this nature.

A further ground is stated that, in using the turntable,
even upon its own property, under circumstances which rendered it probable that children would come upon the land
and play upon the turntable, it was bound to the exercise of
greater care than it had observed; that it was bound to guard

the table in such a way that children could not come upon it, or to station a man there to prevent their entrance, or else the defendant should have used some kind of a device which would or might prevent the turning of the table while it was not in use by defendant. The defendant contends that the plaintiff had not been invited to come upon its grounds, either expressly or by any implication arising from its conduct in simply permitting the public to cross a portion of its grounds as a short cut between two streets, and that it was not bound to any active vigilance in the matter, and was only bound to such reasonable care and caution as any one ought to take to prevent injury to another, and that, guided by that rule, it had not, as matter of law, been guilty of any negligence.

As to the assumed invitation held out to the public, there is nothing in the facts found in this record which justifies any such assumption. The plaintiff was not on the land by invitation of the defendant, nor in its business, but for his own purposes, [306] totally disconnected with the defendant's business. He was not a trespasser in the sense of his being unlawfully upon the premises, because the defendant, by its course of conduct, had impliedly granted a license to the public to use the land for the purpose above mentioned. This license, of course, could at any time have been revoked, and then any one going upon the land would have been a trespasser. But, under the circumstances, treating the plaintiff as an adult, and simply upon the question of the invitation held out to him, he was there by sufferance only. The defendant had no right intentionally to injure him, and it would be liable if it heedlessly or carelessly injured him while performing its own business. It owed him a duty to abstain from injuring him either intentionally or by failing to exercise reasonable care, but it did not owe him the duty of active vigilance to see that he was not injured while upon its land merely by permission for his own convenience: *Nicholson* v. *Erie Ry. Co.*, 41 N. Y. 525; *Byrne* v. *New York Cent. etc. R. R. Co.*, 104 N. Y. 363; 58 Am. Rep. 512; *Splittorf* v. *State*, 108 N. Y. 205; *Cusick* v. *Adams*, 115 N. Y. 55; 12 Am. St. Rep. 772. We think there is no proof whatever that the defendant, so far as its duty to plaintiff is concerned, failed to exercise reasonable care in the conduct of its business with regard to this machine.

We are of the opinion that the defendant has not been shown guilty of a violation of its duty, nor has a question been made for the jury in that respect by proof that it used the turntable in the manner it did. It is true that some means might have been adopted which possibly might have prevented the happening of this accident. The proof is that turntables are not generally constructed with bolts for the purpose of keeping them steady. Such bolts do not come with the table from the factory. Nothing of that kind is essential to the machine or for its legitimate and proper use. The table might have been kept so fastened or locked when not in use that people could not turn it without unfastening or unlocking it, and the defendant might even have built a wall around it so high, and guarded it so closely, as to prevent any access to it [307] by children at any time. But was defendant bound to do so? Did it owe any such duty to the public or to this plaintiff? The turntable was on its own land; it was used by the defendant for the sole purpose of properly conducting its own business; it was a fit and proper machine for that purpose; it was not of the nature of a trap for the unwary; it was not built in any improper or negligent way with reference to the transaction of the business of the defendant. What further duty did it owe to those who had no business upon its land, who came there unasked, and whose presence was simply tolerated?

Upon the question of alluring plaintiff, we do not think it can be correctly said defendant either enticed or allured him to come upon its land.

The whole case in this aspect rests upon the doctrine that the turntable was, as to children of tender years, a dangerous and at the same time an enticing machine, one which, when seen, would inevitably and infallibly allure children to come upon it for the purpose of playing upon it, and that the natural and probable result of such play would be the injury of the child. Under such circumstances it is claimed that a person owning such a machine, although it be used on his own land, is bound to exercise extra vigilance for the purpose of preventing injury to children who come upon the defendant's land allured by the machine and ignorant of its dangers. We do not think the facts of this case bring it within any such principle. The leading case in this country, and one which undoubtedly sustains the plaintiff's contention that it is a case for the jury, is that of *Railroad Co.* v. *Stout,* 17 Wall. 657. That case has been followed in many states. In Missouri: *Koons* v. *St. Louis etc. R. R. Co.,* 65 Mo. 592; in Kansas: *Kansas Cent. Ry. Co.* v. *Fitzsimmons,* 22 Kan.

686; 31 Am. Rep. 203, reporter's note at 206; in California:
Barrett v. *Southern Pacific Co.*, 91 Cal. 296; 25 Am. St. Rep.
186; and in some other states. The contrary principle has
been announced and held in *Daniels* v. *New York etc. R. R.
Co.*, 154 Mass. 349; 26 Am. St. Rep. 253, and *Frost* v. *Eastern
R. R. Co.*, 64 N. H. 220; 10 Am. St. Rep. 396.

We think the better rule is laid down in the two cases last
808 cited. We do not assert that the defendant owed no
duty to the plaintiff under the circumstances existing, but
we think it did not owe the duty of such active vigilance as
would be necessary to exist in order to send the case to the
jury, and permit it to find the defendant guilty of negligence
in this case. The court, in *McAlpin* v. *Powell*, 70 N. Y. 126,
26 Am. Rep. 555, while distinguishing it from *Railroad Co.*
v. *Stout*, 17 Wall. 657, expresses doubt of the correctness of
the application of the principle in the latter case.

We have not had occasion to decide the question up to this
time, but now that it is presented we not only reiterate the
doubt which we expressed in *McAlpin* v. *Powell*, 70 N. Y. 126,
26 Am. Rep. 555, but we think that the question of the
defendant's negligence was erroneously submitted to the jury
in the Stout case, and that we ought not to follow it as a
precedent. We think it is not a question of fact to be submitted to the jury for its determination whether the defendant has or has not been guilty of negligence under such
circumstances as appear in this case. Upon such facts we
hold the defendant has violated no duty it owed the plaintiff.
It is not contended for a moment that a person on his own
land may under all circumstances do any thing that he
chooses without being held liable to answer in damages for
injuries which are direct and probable and natural results of
his action. We only say this is no such case. The case of
Bird v. *Holbrook*, 4 Bing. 628, is cited as analogous in principle to that which plaintiff urges in this case. We do not
think so. The defendant in that case for the protection of
his property, some of which had theretofore been stolen, set a
spring gun, without notice, in his walled garden at a distance
from his house. The plaintiff, who climbed over the wall in
pursuit of a stray fowl, having been injured, it was held that
the defendant was liable to him in damages. In that case
the plea was made that the defendant had the right to protect his own property, and that one who was injured without
having been invited upon the land, and who was unlawfully

there, could maintain no action. It was held that the action was [309] maintainable, for otherwise it might result in a mere trespass being made a capital offense. Chief Justice Best said that the practice (without giving notice) was inhuman, and the proof showed that the defendant had placed the spring gun on the wall for the express purpose of doing injury, and that he had refused to give notice of its existence on the ground that if he gave notice he would fail to catch any one. The chief justice said that the defendant intended that the gun should be discharged and that the contents should be lodged in the body of his victim, and that he who sets spring guns without giving notice is guilty of an inhuman act, and if injurious consequences ensue he is liable to yield redress to the sufferer. The difference in the two cases is so plain as to require no discussion.

Cases are also cited where the defendant, for the purpose and with the intention of enticing his neighbor's dogs upon his premises, set traps very near the line of the highway, and then baited them with decaying meat, so that the scent was cast not only in the highway but upon the private premises of the plaintiff, whose dogs, taking the scent, came upon the defendant's grounds, and were taken in a trap and thereby killed. One of such is the case of *Townsend* v. *Wathen*, 9 East, 277. The court held the defendant liable upon the ground that one who sets traps to catch his neighbor's dogs, although the traps were set on his own ground, was liable for his wrongful intent and act, and it was fit to be left to the jury whether it was not defendant's intention to catch the plaintiff's dogs, and it was held that a man must not set traps of a dangerous description in a situation to invite, and for the particular purpose of inviting, his neighbor's dogs, as it would compel them, by their instinct, to come into the trap. The act of the defendant in that case was not done in the prosecution of his immediate and proper business, but, as the court held, was a mere malicious attempt, successful in its result, to entice his neighbor's animals upon his property, and the enticement was effected by the means spoken of.

Quite a discussion upon the subject of the acts of an owner [310] upon his own land, directed to the preservation of game or to the destruction of dogs, etc., is to be found in the case of *Deane* v. *Clayton*, 2 Eng. Com. L. 183. In that case the court was equally divided, and so no judgment was rendered. The distinction is clear between acts of the nature spoken of in this case and those which are performed by an individual in the legitimate and honest conduct of his own business upon his own land. As is said by Mr. Justice Cowen in *Loomis* v. *Terry*, 17 Wend. 497, 31 Am. Dec. 306: "The business of life must go forward, and the fruits of industry must be protected. A man's 'gravel-pit is fallen into by trespassing cattle; his corn eaten or his sap drunk, whereby the cattle are killed; his unruly bull gores the intruder, or his trusty watchdog, properly and honestly kept for protection, worries the unseasonable trespasser. Such consequences cannot be absolutely avoided." The case of *Clark* v. *Chambers*, L. R. 3 Q. B. D. 327, is also cited as in some degree applicable. In that case the defendant erected a barrier along a way which it was admitted he had no legal right to erect. It was erected for the purpose of keeping people from traveling where they had a right to travel. The barrier which he erected was armed with spikes, and was a dangerous obstacle. Some person, without the defendant's authority, removed a part of the barrier from where the defendant had placed it, and put it into an upright position across a footpath. The plaintiff, on a dark night, was lawfully passing along the road on his way from one of the houses to which the footpath led, when he came in contact with the spikes in the barrier and injured one of his eyes. The jury found that the barrier was in the road and dangerous to the safety of a person using it. It was held that the defendant, having unlawfully placed a dangerous instrument in the road, was liable in respect of injuries occasioned by it to the plaintiff, who was lawfully using the road, notwithstanding the fact that the immediate cause of the injury was the intervening act of a third party in removing the dangerous instrument to the footpath from the carriageway where defendant had placed it. In that case you start out with the admission that the act of the defendant [311] was unlawful, and all that follows thereafter was held by the court to be the natural and probable result of his unlawful act.

In *Lynch* v. *Nurdin*, 1 Ad. & E., N. R., 29, the plaintiff was a child seven years of age, and the cartman of the defendant went into a house in London, and left his horse and cart standing at the door, without any person to take care of them, for about half an hour. The plaintiff got into the cart during the cartman's absence, and another boy led the horse on, and as plaintiff was about getting off the shaft the horse

started, and plaintiff fell, and was run over by the wheel, and
his leg broken.   The trial justice left it to the jury to say: 1.
Whether it was negligence in the defendant's servant to leave
the horse and cart for half an hour; and 2. Whether that
negligence occasioned the accident.   There was a verdict for
the plaintiff.   On the return of an order to show cause why a
new trial should not be had, Lord Denman, chief justice,
held that the case was properly submitted to the jury, and
the defendant was properly held negligent by the jury, and
although the child had no business on the cart, and if an
adult it would be said that his own negligence contributed to
the injury, yet the child merely indulged his natural instinct
in amusing himself with the empty cart and the deserted
horse, and, therefore, it could not be said that he was negligent, or that his action contributed to the injury within the
legal sense of that term, and, therefore, the defendant could
not be permitted to avail himself of that fact.   In the course
of his opinion the chief justice said there was a clear distinction to be taken between the willful act done by the defendant in the spring gun case, deliberately planting a dangerous
weapon in his ground with the design of deterring trespassers,
and the mere negligence of the defendant's servant in leaving
his cart in the open street.   In the latter case the liability of
defendant is simply for negligence.   There is a great difference
in the facts between the case of *Lynch* v. *Nurdin*, 1 Ad. & E.,
N. R. 29, and the present case.   Leaving a horse and cart
in a public street unattended and loose, subject to natural
observation and interference from [312] children passing along
the street, might be held a proper question for the jury to say
whether it was or was not negligence, while in the case of a
defendant engaged upon his own land in simply doing that
which it is necessary to do in order that he may carry on his
business properly, and who fails to exercise the highest vigilance in order to protect from possible harm children who
may stray upon his land for no other purpose than recrea-
tion, we think there is an absence of any fact upon which
a jury ought to be permitted to find negligence.   The defendant in the one case was not upon his own land, nor was he
engaged in the proper transaction of his business thereon, but,
on the contrary, he was in a public street, and improperly
left his horse and cart therein unattended, and where
others, and among them children, had the same right to be
that he had.   In the case of this defendant, on the other

hand, the turntable was on its own land it was a proper and appropriate machine for the carrying on of its business it was properly made, and it was properly used by the defendant.   To liken such a case to the allurement of dogs by the spreading of tainted meat over traps on defendant's lands, done for the very purpose of injury, is, as it seems to me, to lose sight of the different principles upon which the cases rest.

At any rate, we think that the plaintiff failed to show any actionable negligence on the part of the defendant, and a submission to the jury of the question of such negligence was error.   All that can be said on either side of the question has been set forth in *Railroad Co.* v. *Stout*, 17 Wall. 657, and the various other cases cited above, and a continuation of the discussion would be fruitless.

We think the judgment for plaintiff must be reversed and a new trial granted, costs to abide the event.

All concur.

Judgment reversed.   ⸺

REAL PROPERTY—LIABILITY OF LANDOWNER TO LICENSEES.—The owner of premises is under no legal duty to keep them free from pitfalls or obstructions, for the accommodation of persons who go upon or over them without invitation, express or implied, and merely for their own convenience or pleasure, even when this is done with the owner's permission: *Faris* v. *Hoberg*, 134 Ind. 269; 39 Am. St. Rep. 261, and note. To the same effect see *Railway Co.* v. *Ferguson*, 57 Ark. 16; 38 Am. St. Rep. 217, and note. See the extended discussion of this case in the monographic note to *Plummer* v. *Dill*, 32 Am. St. Rep. 467.

RAILROADS—TURNTABLES.—A railroad company leaving a turntable in an exposed and unprotected position will be liable for any injuries to children received by riding thereon: *Barrett* v. *Southern Pac. Co.*, 91 Cal. 296; 25 Am. St. Rep. 186, and note. The contrary doctrine, and that maintained by the principal case, is supported by *Daniels* v. *New York etc. R. R. Co.*, 154 Mass. 349; 26 Am. St. Rep. 253, and note.   The cases on this subject are collected in the extended note to *Westbrook* v. *Mobile etc. R. R. Co.*, 14 Am. St. Rep. 595.

CITY OF SCHENECTADY *v.* FURMAN.
[145 NEW YORK, 482.]

MUNICIPAL CORPORATION—NON-NAVIGABLE WATERCOURSE.—A municipality cannot compel the owner of land through which a non-navigable watercourse flows, to widen or deepen it, and a resolution purporting to establish the width of the stream and to authorize the entry upon the land of a private proprietor for the purposes of cutting down the banks and widening the natural channel is, in so far as it assumes to justify the taking and appropriating lands along the natural and permanent banks of the stream without compensation, void.

S. W. Jackson, for the appellant.

Robert J. Landon, for the respondent.

486 HAIGHT, J. This action was brought to recover the expenses incurred by the plaintiff in removing certain alleged obstructions and deposits from Mill creek where it runs through the lands of the defendants' testator. Mill creek is a non-navigable, natural watercourse, not a public highway, running through the plaintiff's boundaries. On the sixteenth day of April, 1889, the plaintiff's common council adopted a series of resolutions, in and by which they declared that obstructions and deposits existed in Mill creek running through the defendants' testator's lands, and that such obstructions and deposits caused large bodies of stagnant water to accumulate, detrimental to health, the removal of which was proper and necessary, and that such removals should be made at the expense of the owners or occupants of the lots adjoining that portion of the creek. The resolution then proceeded to describe the width and depth of the creek, and concluded by adjudging the description so given to constitute the natural and normal channel and grade of the creek, and that all earth and other matter lying in and above such grade and channel, as described, to be obstructions and deposits in the stream. The description, however, does not locate the center line of the stream or the banks thereof farther than to specify the width of the channel. The five days' notice required by the charter of the final adoption of these resolutions was then given, and on the twenty-third day of April they were ratified and confirmed. Subsequently, and on the seventh day of May, 1889, the common council adopted another resolution amending that adopted on the 16th and confirmed on the 23d by **487** reducing the width of the stream and changing the slopes of the banks. Thereafter, and in August, 1889, the plaintiff's superintendent of streets entered Mill creek where it flows through defendant's premises, cut down banks and widened the natural channel of the stream, excavating the earth therefrom, and in so doing cut several trees growing on the banks thereof, and dug out the stumps, making a new channel for the creek. Can the plaintiff recover for the expenses incurred in doing this work?

The trial court has found as a fact that after the adoption of the resolutions alluded to, and during the month of July, 1889, and before the plaintiff's superintendent entered upon the excavation of the creek, the defendant's testator cleaned out the creek where it flowed through his lands from bank to bank to the hardpan thereof, and to the natural and normal bed and banks of the stream. These findings are based upon the testimony of the witness McGowan, whose statement we do not understand to be controverted. To our minds these findings dispose of the plaintiff's case, for, assuming the resolutions of the plaintiff's common council to be regular, these findings show a compliance therewith on the part of the defendant's testator. He caused the channel of the creek to be cleaned to the natural and normal banks and bed thereof. This is all that the common council had the power to require. If by its resolutions it required more, they were unauthorized and void, for the city had no right or power to take and appropriate his lands along the natural and permanent banks of the stream without rendering him compensation therefor either under the constitution or the statutes. This question was fully discussed by Learned, P. J., when this case was first considered in the general term: *City of Schenectady* v. *Furman,* 61 Hun, 171. We fully approve of the views then expressed with reference to this branch of the case.

The judgment should be affirmed with costs.

, All concur.

Judgment affirmed.

———

EMINENT DOMAIN—WHAT IS NOT A TAKING FOR.—An improvement in a river consisting of a dam erected by legislative authority which causes an increased flow at times whereby the channel is deepened and widened, and the soil worn away, is not a taking of the lands of a riparian proprietor through which the river flows, and whose soil is thus carried away: *Brooks* v. *Cedar Brook etc. Imp. Co.*, 82 Me. 17; 17 Am. St. Rep. 459, and note. The diversion of a small and private watercourse by a city for the purpose of drainage and sewerage with the consent and approval of the landowners through whose land it runs is not an exercise of the right of eminent domain: *Murphy* v. *Mayor*, 6 Houst. 108; 22 Am. St. Rep. 345.

GRANT *v.* WALSH.

[145 NEW YORK, 5J2.]

BANKS—INSOLVENCY, FRAUD IN PERMITTING DEPOSIT AFTER.—To permit a deposit in a bank in reliance upon its supposed solvency is a gross fraud if its officers know at the time of its insolvency, and the depositor is entitled to reclaim the deposit or the proceeds.

BANKS, CHECK DEPOSITED IN INSOLVENT, DEFENSE TO.—If a check drawn by a depositor in his own favor is deposited in bank, and he is subsequently sued thereon, it is error to reject evidence by him tending to prove that when the deposit was received the officers of the bank had notice of its insolvent and failing condition.

NEGOTIABLE PAPER.—BURDEN OF MAKING OUT GOOD FAITH IS ALWAYS UPON THE PARTY ASSERTING HIS TITLE as a *bona fide* holder in a case where the proof shows that a paper has been fraudulently, feloniously, or illegally obtained from its maker or owner.

BANK, WHEN MUST PROVE THAT IT IS A BONA FIDE HOLDER.—If a check is deposited in a bank whose officers then know it is insolvent and about to fail, and is afterward transferred to another bank, the latter is not presumed to be a *bona fide* holder, and cannot recover without first showing that it received such check without notice of the fraud in the due and regular course of business and had paid value therefor.

Thomas C. Ennever, for the appellant.

Smith & White, for the respondent.

503 HAIGHT, J. This action was brought upon a check drawn by the defendant on the eighth day of August, 1893, upon the Farmers' Loan & Trust Company, payable to his own order 504 and indorsed by him "for deposit." About 2:30 o'clock in the afternoon of that day he caused the same to be deposited to his credit in the Madison Square Bank, in which bank he then had an account with a balance still standing to his credit. At 3 o'clock of that day the Madison Square Bank closed its doors and never thereafter opened for business. The officers of the Madison Square Bank then caused the check in question with others to be delivered to the St. Nicholas Bank which was then acting as the clearing house agent of the Madison Square Bank. On the next morning the St. Nicholas Bank caused the check to be presented to the Farmers' Loan & Trust Company for payment, which was refused, the defendant having in the mean time learned of the failure of the Madison Square Bank, and notified the Farmers' Loan & Trust Company not to pay it.

The answer of the defendant alleges that at the time of the deposit so made by him in the Madison Square Bank it was hopelessly insolvent, and that that fact was well known

to the officers, agents, and employees of the bank; that he
did not know of its condition, but supposed it to be solvent,
and that, in taking his check upon deposit without notifying
him of its condition, a fraud was committed upon him. The
answer also alleges that the St. Nicholas Bank did not lawfully obtain possession of the check, and is not the owner
thereof in good faith or for value; that the St. Nicholas Bank
knew, prior to the time of the making of the deposit of the
check by the defendant, that the Madison Square Bank was
hopelessly insolvent; that such insolvency was known to its
officers, and that the check had been obtained from the defendant by fraud.

Upon the trial the plaintiff produced the check, offered it
in evidence, and rested. The defendant then, after showing
the circumstances under which the check was drawn and deposited by him, called as a witness the receiving teller of the
Madison Square Bank, and asked him the following question:
"On August 7, 1893, or prior thereto, had any of the officers
of that bank told you any thing about the financial condition
505 of the bank?" This was objected to by the plaintiff as
immaterial and incompetent. The objection was sustained,
and an exception taken by the defendant. The witness then
testified that he did not hear from any person connected with
the Madison Square Bank at any time prior to August 7,
1893, that the bank was insolvent and would have to dis-
continue business. The question was then asked: "Did you
on August 7, 1893?" This was objected to as immaterial
and incompetent. The objection was sustained and an exception was taken. The discount clerk of the Madison Square
Bank was also sworn as a witness for the defendant, and
asked if he was present at a conversation on the day preceding August 8th, when the directors stated that the bank was
busted, and that they would have to stop business. This
question was also objected to upon the same grounds, excluded, and an exception taken. The cashier of the St.
Nicholas Bank was also sworn as a witness for the defendant,
and testified that he knew Mr. Judson, the bank examiner,
and was then questioned as to whether he knew that Mr.
Judson had examined the affairs of the Madison Square
Bank prior to August 8, 1893, and as to whether he had had
a conversation with him relative to the financial condition of
the bank prior to that time. Each of which questions was

objected to upon the same grounds, excluded, and exceptions taken.

At the conclusion of the defendant's evidence the court directed a verdict for the plaintiff for the amount of the check, to which direction an exception was also taken.

We think the rulings alluded to were erroneous, and that a new trial is required. It was shown that the Madison Square Bank was insolvent; that an action had been brought against it by the people and judgment entered dissolving it on the ground of insolvency, and appointing a permanent receiver. It is, therefore, apparent that no action could have been maintained upon the check by that bank if, as is claimed, the check was received after the officers of the bank knew of its condition, and of their inability to continue its business. The rule appears to be well settled that one who has been [506] induced to part with his property by the fraud of another, under guise of a contract, may, upon the discovery of the fraud, rescind the contract and reclaim the property, unless it has come into the possession of a *bona fide* holder.

In *Cragie* v. *Hadley*, 99 N. Y. 131, 52 Am. Rep. 9, an action was brought by the plaintiff against the receiver of the First National Bank of Buffalo to recover the amount of a draft deposited with the bank at a time when the managers thereof knew that it was insolvent. It was held that permitting the plaintiff to make the deposit in reliance upon the supposed solvency of the bank was a gross fraud upon the plaintiff, and that the latter was entitled to reclaim the draft or its proceeds.

The same rule was recognized in *Metropolitan Nat. Bank* v. *Loyd*, 90 N. Y. 530–537, but in that case there was no allegation of fraud in the answer, and, consequently, it was held that the evidence offered, tending to show fraud, was properly excluded. In this case, as we have seen, fraud on the part of the officers of the Madison Square Bank is alleged, and it appears to us that the defendant had the right to establish his allegations in this regard, and that they might have been sustained by the evidence excluded.

If the Madison Square Bank fraudulently procured possession of the defendant's check the plaintiff could not recover without showing that the St. Nicholas Bank was a *bona fide* purchaser and holder.

In *Canajoharie Nat. Bank* v. *Diefendorf*, 123 N. Y. 191–

206, Ruger, C. J., in delivering the opinion of the court, says:
"The burden of making out good faith is always upon the
party asserting his title as a *bona fide* holder, in a case where
the proof shows that the paper has been fraudulently, feloniously, or illegally obtained from its maker or owner. Such
a party makes out his title by presumptions, until it is impeached by evidence showing the paper had a fraudulent
inception, and when this is done the plaintiff can no longer
rest upon the presumptions, but must show affirmatively his
good faith.

In *Vosburgh* v. *Diefendorf*, 119 N. Y. 357–364, 16 Am. St.
Rep. 836, O'Brien, [507] J., says: "In this state it must be regarded now as a settled rule that, when a maker of negotiable paper shows that it has been obtained from him by
fraud or duress, a subsequent transferee must, before entitled
to recover on it, show that he is a *bona fide* purchaser."

In *First Nat. Bank* v. *Green*, 43 N. Y. 298, it was held that
a party suing upon a negotiable note purchased before maturity is presumed, in the first instance, to be a *bona fide*
holder, but, when the maker has shown that the note was
obtained from him under duress, or that he was defrauded
of it, the plaintiff would then be required to show under what
circumstances and for what value he became the holder.
The reason of this rule, as stated by Rapallo, J., is that
"where there is a fraud the presumption is that he who is
guilty will part with the note for the purpose of enabling
some third party to recover upon it, and such presumption
operates against the holder, and it devolves upon him to
show that he gave value for it": *Farmers' etc. Nat. Bank* v.
Noxon, 45 N. Y 762; *Ocean Nat. Bank* v. *Carll*, 55 N. Y. 440;
Wilson v. *Rocke*, 58 N. Y. 642; *Nickerson* v. *Ruger*, 76 N. Y.
279; 2 Greenleaf on Evidence, sec. 172; *Bailey* v. *Bidwell*, 13
Mees. & W. 73. If, therefore, the defendant had been permitted to show that a fraud had been practiced upon him by
the officers of the Madison Square Bank, the presumption
that the St. Nicholas Bank was a *bona fide* holder would no
longer obtain, and then the St. Nicholas Bank could not recover without showing that it had received the check without
knowledge of the fraud, in the regular course of business, and
had paid value therefor. This it has failed to do. Not only
has it failed to establish these facts, but the trial court excluded the evidence offered tending to show that its officers
had knowledge of the actual condition of the Madison Square

Bank and the circumstances under which that bank received the defendant's check.

The judgment should be reversed and a new trial granted, with costs to abide the event.

All concur.

Judgment reversed. ___

SLOANE *v.* MARTIN.

[145 NEW YORK, 524.]

INFANTS, JURISDICTION OVER.—THE FACT THAT PROCESS WAS NOT SERVED ON INFANT DEFENDANTS does not render void a judgment against them in the courts of the United States if a guardian *ad litem* was appointed, a solicitor appeared for them, and the proceeding did not seek a personal judgment against them, but was to obtain a judgment declaring that certain property which had been attached as belonging to a partnership, though it stood in the name of another, was held in trust for that partnership, and should be applied to the satisfaction of its obligations.

SUIT for the specific performance of a contract to purchase real property. The defendant had refused to complete his purchase under a claim that the title was not good and marketable, because it had been acquired through a judicial sale under a decree in a circuit court of the United States in a suit in which certain infant defendants were not served with process. It was admitted that, on petition of their mother, a guardian *ad litem* had been appointed and a solicitor had appeared for the infants. The judgment of the trial court was in favor of the plaintiff. The defendant appealed.

William G. Choate, for the appellant.

Charles I. McBurney, for the respondent.

[527] FINCH, J.   The very elaborate and exhaustive opinion of the learned referee, before whom this action was tried, so states the argument upon the fundamental question involved as to simplify our duty of review and enable us to narrow the discussion, which has taken a wide range, to the single ground on which our decision should rest.   The jurisdiction assailed is that of a federal court over infants not served with process, but for whom an appearance was entered and a guardian *ad litem* appointed, who defended in their behalf.   The question thus is one of federal jurisdiction and practice, taking us away [528] from our own procedure and into somewhat unfamiliar territory, and where the decisions of the United States courts should be our authority and guide.   The precise question involved came before one of those courts, and was decided in favor of the validity of the judgment.   The decision has not been reported and does not appear in the books, but what it was the record before us distinctly and accurately shows.   The action was brought in equity in the circuit court by Drake and others against Goodridge and others, among whom, named as defendants, were the infant children of Goodridge.   The plaintiffs alleged in brief that they were creditors of the copartnership of Goodridge & Co., and had obtained judgment for specified amounts; that in such actions attachments had been issued and duly levied upon the land here in controversy; that the legal title stood in the individual name of one or more of the partners, but was in truth held in trust for the firm to which it actually belonged, and asked judgment that the land be declared to be partnership property, and that a receiver be appointed to sell it and apply the proceeds to the payment of plaintiff's debt.   Judgment was rendered to that effect, and, in pursuance of its directions, the receiver sold the land at a judicial sale.   The purchasers thereafter refused to take the title tendered, alleging it to be defective and not marketable.   Thereupon the receiver presented a petition to the court setting forth the facts, and praying that the purchasers be required to accept the deed and pay the purchase price.   For the purposes of the motion it was stipulated, among other things, that the infant defendants were not in fact served with a subpœna or other process.   Judge Blatchford, before whom the judgment had been obtained,

decided that the title proffered was good, and the purchasers
were bound to accept it. Deciding thus, with the stipulation
before him, he necessarily ruled that the court obtained jurisdiction even though there had been no actual service of
process upon the infants, but instead merely the appointment
of a guardian *ad litem* upon the petition of their mother.
What we are now asked to do is to disregard that **529** decision and hold it to be erroneous, upon a presentation of the
same question, founded upon the same alleged defect in the
same judgment, and affecting the same land. I am very
sure we ought not to do that unless upon some strong and
clear conviction that the circuit court went astray and in
opposition to the decided and manifest trend of federal
authority. It is to that inquiry that the learned counsel for the appellant has addressed himself in an extremely
able argument.

His principal reliance is upon the case of *Woolridge* v.
McKenna, 8 Fed. Rep. 650, decided by Judge Hammond in
the circuit court of the western district of Tennessee. If I
regarded the language of the decision as applicable, or intended to be applicable, to a case like the present, where,
instead of a mere personal action against infants, we have
one in the nature of a suit *in rem*, prosecuted against property in which they had or claimed an interest, seeking to
impress upon it a partnership character and devote it to the
discharge of the partnership debts, I should feel bound to
admit that it held service upon the infants to be imperative,
without which the application of the mother and consequent
appointment of a guardian *ad litem* would be ineffectual to
confer jurisdiction. But I observe that the learned judge
himself drew the distinction between the two classes of cases,
and held the one at his bar to be a personal action against
the infants. I am not sure that he was entirely right in so
holding, but that for the present is an immaterial inquiry.
He did so hold, and I think intended to confine his ruling to
the class of cases in which he ranked the one before him.
Speaking of the character of the action, he said: "It is rather
in the nature of a personal suit against her to cancel as void
the deeds under which she claims than a proceeding against
the land." After some further argument, he says again: "If
this were a case originally brought in this court, standing
as to parties in the shape it now does, there is no doubt
whatever that this infant defendant, like all other defend-

ants, assuming that she is a citizen of Kentucky, would
have to be [530] sued in the district of her residence, so that
process could be personally served on her, if the case is to be
treated as a personal action to cancel the deeds of conveyance." He had already said that it should be so treated,
and, therefore, was correct in the assertion that she would
have to be sued in the district of her residence, irrespective
of the possible fact that the land itself might be in another
district, and in holding that personal service was required.
He then proceeds thus: " Or if it be a suit *in rem*, or of that
nature, against the land, there might be substituted process
under the act of March 3, 1875, which is understood to dispense with the requirement of personal service as well in the
case of infants as other defendants." Here again the distinction between the two classes of cases is recognized, and
when it is finally held that actual service is essential to the
jurisdiction the ruling must relate to merely personal actions
such as the one before the court was assumed to be. It,
therefore, decides nothing as to the necessary mode of obtaining jurisdiction in a suit against the land. If what is
said as to such an action permits an inference that where
there is no service on the infants the only other mode of obtaining jurisdiction is under the act of 1875, there are three
answers to be made: 1. The opinion does not so declare. The
reference to the act of 1875 grows out of the nonresidence of
the infant in the district of the litigation, and assumes the
necessity of making her a party against her will or without
movement or intervention on the part of her natural guardian; 2. If the opinion had so declared, the statement would
have been *obiter*, because relating to a class of cases not before the court; and 3. In that event the decision would stand
wholly and entirely unsupported by the authorities cited to sustain it. If on examining them it shall become apparent that,
so far as they are applicable at all, they do sustain the court
in holding that actual service on the infants is imperative
in a merely personal action, but do not support the decision,
indeed tend to contradict and overthrow it, if regarded as
applicable to a suit against the land, we shall be bound to
understand the learned judge as I [531] think he meant to be
understood, and not put upon him a decision which he did
not need or undertake to make.

The first case which he cites is *Bank of United States* v.
Ritchie, 8 Pet. 128. That was a bill of review and a direct

attack upon a judgment decreeing the sale of property in
which infants had an interest. It did not appear that process
had been served upon them. It did appear that a stranger
had been appointed guardian *ad litem*, on the motion of counsel for the plaintiffs, without bringing the minors into court
or issuing a commission for the purpose of making the appointment. As to that, Chief Justice Marshall said: "It is not
error, but is calculated to awaken attention." After pointing
out other defects in the procedure, he affirms the reversal of
the decree, citing many departures from correct usage, but
never once intimating that the judgment was absolutely void
for want of actual service of process on the infants. It is
inconceivable that so great a jurist should have overlooked
such a defect if he so regarded it at all. The learned counsel
for the appellant perhaps weakens the suggestion by an
explanation that something in the law of Maryland following
the cession of the District of Columbia may have saved the
jurisdiction. I do not know how that is, but obviously
the authority, if not positively adverse, does not support
the decision of Judge Hammond as the appellant would construe it.

The second case cited is *O'Hara* v. *MacConnell*, 93 U. S.
150. That was a case in which the assignees of the bankrupt
sued to set aside his conveyance as fraudulent against creditors, making his wife, who was an infant, a party defendant.
The subpœna was served only on the husband, but that was
held sufficient before 1874, while yet it was decided that the
decree should be reversed because no appearance for the wife
had been entered and no guardian *ad litem* had been appointed. The reversal was for the lack of the very steps
which were taken in the judgment assailed on this appeal.
The case, therefore, does not sustain the doctrine for which it
is claimed to have been cited.

⁵³² The third case cited is *New York Life Ins. Co.* v. *Bangs*,
103 U. S. 435. The question involved was the validity of a
judgment pleaded as a defense, and it was adjudged void as
against an infant not actually served with process, although
a guardian *ad litem* had been appointed and had answered.
But the court specially point out with constant reiteration the
character of the action as having been purely personal. It is
said that the infant had no property in Michigan; that the
suit did not concern any property, real or personal, and that
it was brought to cancel a contract of insurance made with

the infant's father. Then it was added that "In all cases
brought to enforce or cancel personal contracts, or to recover
damages for their violation, the statute requires a personal
service of process upon the defendants or their voluntary
appearance." So far it is clear that the case is authority for
the doctrine, in support of which Judge Hammond cited it,
that is, as applicable to personal actions, but not at all to the
opinion imputed to him as covering also actions in the nature
of a proceeding *in rem.* But the opinion cited goes further.
The attention of the court was called to three cases which held
that nonservice upon the infant did not render the judgment
void where a guardian *ad litem* had been appointed. It is
important to observe the attitude of the court toward these
cases. They are in no respect criticised or even doubted, but,
on the contrary, are said to be consistent with the doctrine
asserted. One by one their facts are developed, and it is
shown that the actions were in the nature of suits *in rem,* and
then the court added that there was nothing in them inconsistent with the doctrine asserted as applicable to a case which
did not touch any property in the district, but to one brought
to cancel a personal contract. I think this case fairly holds
that the need of service on the infant exists in personal
actions, but does not exist in those *quasi in rem.*

There is still another case cited by Judge Hammond, which
is *Carrington* v. *Brents,* 2 McLean, 174. Speaking of a judgment obtained by Carrington, the court said: "It does not
appear that in the above suit process was served on the infant,
[533] nor that the guardian *ad litem* was appointed by the court,
and for these omissions or errors in the proceedings the decree
might be reversed by an appellate court; but when the decree
is used as matter of evidence it cannot be disregarded or
treated as a nullity."

This examination of the cases cited by Judge Hammond
makes it very clear, I think, that the rule which he formulated
was a rule applicable only to personal actions, and that he
did not at all intend or contemplate its extension beyond
those. The difference between the two classes of cases was
clearly noted in *Mohr* v. *Manierre,* 101 U. S. 422. In discussing the mode in which the federal courts acquired jurisdiction
Mr. Justice Field said: "This necessarily depended upon the
nature of the subject upon which the judicial power was called
to act. If it was invoked against the person to enforce a liability the personal citation of the defendant or his voluntary

appearance was required. If it was called into exercise with reference to real property by proceedings *in rem*, or of that nature, a different mode of procedure was usually necessary, such as a seizure of the property with notice by publication or otherwise to parties having interests which might be affected." He proceeds to say that these rules were "part of the general law of the land," and were to be applied by the courts of the United States. The words of the learned jurist indicate to my mind what is the vital difference between the two classes of cases, and the distinctive directions in which we should approach the question of jurisdiction. In the case of merely personal actions, there is no possible ground upon which that jurisdiction can attach except the service of process upon the individual. The court must lay hold of him. In suits *in rem* it may lay hold of the land, aided as in this case by an attachment and *lis pendens*, and thereby the jurisdiction may attach, but can only be exercised upon notice to the parties interested. If they have that notice in fact, any irregularity in giving it may, indeed, be reversible error, but does not necessarily render the subsequent judgment void.

A similar, though not the same, distinction runs through [534] our cases in this state. On the one hand we held in *Ingersoll* v. *Mangam*, 84 N. Y. 622, by force of an explicit statute, that in foreclosure actions service of the summons must precede the appointment of a guardian *ad litem;* while, on the other hand, in an action of partition, which that statute did not govern, we also held that such precedent service was not essential to the jurisdiction: *Gotendorf* v. *Goldschmidt*, 83 N. Y. 110.

It seems to me, upon this review of the subject, that the decision of Mr. Justice Blatchford pronouncing the title good under the judgment authorizing the sale, is not contradicted, and not even made doubtful, by the other federal authorities, but that, on the contrary, their manifest drift is toward the result reached by that decision. I think, therefore, we ought to follow it, and that, if it is to be overruled at all, it should meet that fate, not at our hands, but from the ultimate federal tribunal, carefully considering the nature and limits of its own jurisdiction.

I have said nothing of the rules of the United States court, because I do not think that they at all settle the question or bear very seriously upon the argument, and also because they have been sufficiently discussed in the report of the referee.

Nor have I adverted to the position sustained by him and adopted by the general term that the jurisdiction is saved by the presumptions which attach to the judgment in view of the condition of the record; not because I disapprove of the conclusion which has been reached, but because I think we ought to put our decision upon the ground which I have already stated.

The judgment should be affirmed, with costs.

All concur.

Judgment affirmed.

INFANTS—JURISDICTION OVER.—A judgment against an infant without service of process on him in an action in which he appeared by attorney will be upheld as fully as if he had appeared in person: *Childs* v. *Lanterman.* 103 Cal. 387; 42 Am. St. Rep. 121, and note.

CASES

IN THE

SUPREME COURT

OF

PENNSYLVANIA.

THEISS *v.* WEISS.

[166 PENNSYLVANIA STATE, 9.]

SALE—MEASURE OF DAMAGES—ORDINARY RULE.—In an action for damages for a failure to deliver goods where no part of the price has been paid, the measure of damages is the difference between the contract price and the market price of the goods at the time and place of delivery.

SALE—MEASURE OF DAMAGES WHERE VENDEE HAS SUPPLIED HIMSELF WITH OTHER GOODS.—The true measure of damages in an action to recover damages for a failure to deliver goods which the defendant agreed to sell to the plaintiff, and where the vendee has supplied himself with other goods out of which to fill his orders, is the difference between the contract price and the real price at which he obtained such goods. He should be allowed to recover only his actual loss, and to show this the defendant will be allowed to prove what the goods actually cost the plaintiff.

ASSUMPSIT to recover damages for a failure to deliver flour under a contract in writing. The amount sold was one hundred cars of straight flour, two hundred barrels to be put on each car, and two cars to be delivered each day. The contract price was four dollars per barrel bulk. The evidence on behalf of the defendant tended to show that when he signed the contract he was considerably under the influence of liquor, but that he knew perfectly well what he was doing. The parties had been bargaining over the sale of two carloads of flour at four dollars and thirty-five cents and four dollars and forty-five cents per barrel. Finally, according to the defendant's testimony, he said to the plaintiff, "If you will not sell me flour I will sell you some. I will sell you all the flour you want at four dollars." This, the defendant testified, was said in a bantering way; but the plaintiff accepted the proposition, and defendant signed the contract.

J. J. Miller and John Wilson, for the appellant.

Willis F. McCook, for the appellee.

[15] GREEN, J.   The plaintiff testified on the trial, very positively and directly, that he sold all the flour he bought from the defendant to various firms and individuals immediately after the contract in suit was made.   He also said he was obliged to purchase the flour to fill those orders.   He was permitted to prove, and did prove, the market price of flour during the time he was making the sales.   He admitted, however, that he got most of the flour with which to fill these orders from his own firm.   The defendant asked the plaintiff what the flour he thus obtained cost [16] him, and whether he made or lost money on the flour he obtained to fill these orders.   The court rejected these offers of proof; and the assignments of error to the rejection of the offers and to what the court below said on the question of the measure of damages give rise to the question, What is the true measure of damages applicable to the facts of this case?   The court charged that it was the difference between the contract price named in the contract in suit and the market price of the same grade of flour at the time and place of delivery.

There is no doubt that this is the general rule in cases where the vendor of goods refuses to deliver and no part of the price has been paid.   But the defendant contends that the rule is different where the vendee supplies himself with other goods in order to fill orders which he has taken for the resale of the goods which he contracted to receive from the vendor.

In 2 Benjamin on Sales, section 1327, the writer says: " It is submitted that these decisions establish the following rules in cases where goods have been bought for the purpose of resale, and there is no market in which the buyer can readily obtain them: 1. If, at the time of the sale, the existence of a subcontract is made known to the seller, the buyer, on the seller's default in delivering the goods, has two courses open to him: 1. He may elect to fulfill his subcontract, and for that purpose go into the market and purchase the best substitute obtainable, charging the seller with the difference between the contract price of the goods and the price of the goods substituted; 2. He may elect to abandon his subcontract, and, in that case, he may recover as damages against the seller his loss of profits on the subsale and any penalties he may be liable to pay for breach of his subcontract. . . . . If, at the time of the sale, the existence of a subcontract is not made known to the seller, a knowledge on his part that the buyer is purchasing with the general intention to resell, or notice of the subcontract given to him subsequent to the date of the contract, will not render him liable for the buyer's loss of profits on such subcontract; the buyer may either procure the best substitute for the goods as before and fulfill his subcontract, charging the seller with the difference in price, or abandon his subcontract and bring his action for damages, when the ordinary rule, it would seem, will apply, and the jury must estimate as well as they can the difference between the contract price [17] and the market value of the goods, although there is no market price in the sense that there is no place where the buyer can readily procure the goods contracted for. In every case the buyer, to entitle him to recover the full amount of damages, must have acted throughout as a reasonable man of business, and done all in his power to mitigate the loss."

In the case of *Kountz* v. *Kirkpatrick*, 72 Pa. St. 376, 13 Am. Rep. 687, the opinion delivered by Mr. Justice Agnew contains a very able and exhaustive discussion of the subject of the measure of damages, in actions by the vendee of goods, against the vendor, where delivery has been refused. The case turned upon the question of the effect of a combination, after the sale, and before delivery, by the buyer with others to put up the price of the commodity sold, oil, the buyer having in the mean time assigned his contract to a stranger. It was held that the assignee was not bound by the acts of his assignor, but nevertheless the rule as to the measure of the seller's liability was shown not to be the current market price.

After stating the general rule that the true measure is the difference between the contract price and the market value (not price) at the time and place of delivery, the opinion proceeds: "Ordinarily, when an article of sale is in the market and has a market value, there is no difference between its value and the market price, and the law adopts the latter as the proper evidence of the value. . . . . Value and price are, therefore, not synonymous, or the necessary equivalents of each other, though commonly market value and market price are legal equivalents." Citing the rule as stated in Sedgwick on Damages, fourth edition, 260, that the true measure of damages in such cases is the difference between the contract price and the market value, and "that this is the plaintiff's real loss, and that, with this sum, he can go into the market and supply himself with the same article from another vendor," the opinion further proceeds, quoting from *Smethurst* v. *Woolston*, 5 Watts & S. 109. "The value of the article at or about the time it is to be delivered is the measure of damages, in a suit by the vendee against the vendor for a breach of the contract. . . . It is therefore proper to inquire into the true legal idea of damages in order to determine the proper definition of the term 'value.' Except in those cases where oppression, fraud, malice, [18] or negligence enter into the question, 'the declared object (says Mr. Sedgwick in his work on Damages) is to give compensation to the party injured for the actual loss sustained': Sedgwick on Damages, 4th ed., 28, 29, 36, 37. Among the many authorities he gives he quotes the language of C. J. Shippen, in *Bussy* v. *Donaldson*, 4 Dall. 206, 'as to the assessment of damages (said he), it is a rational and legal principle that the compensation should be equivalent to the injury.' 'The rule,' said C. J. Gibson, 'is to give actual compensation, by graduating the amount of the damages exactly to the extent of the loss, *Forsyth* v. *Palmer*, 14 Pa. St. 97; 53 Am. Dec. 519. Thus compensation being the true purpose of the law, it is obvious that the means employed, in other words, the evidence to ascertain compensation, must be such as truly reaches this end. It is equally obvious, when we consider its true nature, that, as evidence, the market price of an article is only a means of arriving at compensation; it is not itself the value of the article, but is the evidence of value. The law adopts it as a natural inference of fact, but not as a conclusive legal presumption. . . . . But to assert that the price asked in the market is the true and only test of value is to abandon the proper object of damages, viz., compensation, in all those cases where the market evidently does not afford the true measure of value."

In *Seely* v. *Alden*, 61 Pa. St. 302, 100 Am. Dec. 642, we said: "If there be different modes of measuring the damages, depending on the circumstances, the proper way is to hear the evidence, and to instruct the jury afterward according to the nature of the case."

In *Wehle* v. *Haviland*, 69 N. Y. 448, it was held that the "market price" within the meaning of the rule, is the price at which the goods can be replaced, and not their retail value.

In *Haskell* v. *Hunter*, 23 Mich. 305, it was held that in an action for the nondelivery of lumber the true measure of damages is the difference between the contract price and what it would have cost plaintiffs to procure it at the place of delivery and at the time or times when it was reasonably proper for them to supply themselves with lumber of the kind and quality they were to receive under the contract.

In the case of *Arnold* v. *Blabon*, 147 Pa. St. 372, which was an action by the vendor of a quantity of cork to recover the contract price of cork delivered, the defense was that the plaintiffs [19] were bound by the contract to deliver a much larger quantity than they did, and refused to deliver the residue, and the defendant claimed that he had been obliged to procure cork to supply the deficiency at a higher price than the contract called for, and asked for a certificate of damages against the plaintiff, the court below charged as follows: "Undoubtedly if you find there was this contract as claimed here by the defendant, and if you find that the plaintiffs broke it, the defendant would have the right then to his damages, which damages are fixed; but, if the defendant was able by any acts on his part to lessen his damage, he could not, of course, recover more than his actual damage. . . . . Then comes the question whether this defendant, in obtaining these goods from other people, did lessen his damages, whether he made them any less than the difference between the price agreed upon in the contract and the market price at the date of the breach. . . . . If you find for the plaintiffs you will find for this amount, one hundred and fifty-one dollars. If, on the other hand, you find for the defendant, you will give him a certificate of the amount that he actually paid out, that is the difference between the alleged contract price and the market value of that amount, three hundred and forty tons of cork, on the day of the breach of the contract, unless you find from the evidence that what he bought cost him less than that, in which case you will find for the lesser sum." This ruling was affirmed by this court in a per curiam opinion in which we said we found no error on the part of the court.

And the ruling was manifestly correct, because, while it is true that the ordinary rule of damages in such cases would have entitled the defendant to recover the entire difference between the market value of the cork and the contract price, yet, as the proof was that he had supplied himself with cork at a less cost than the market price, he could recover only for his actual loss. This is in accord with all the authorities above cited, and is perfectly sound law. The rule of actual compensation for the loss of the goods to be delivered requires that the actual loss only should be allowed to be recovered.

We are therefore of opinion that the defendant should have been allowed to prove what was the actual cost to the plaintiff of the flour which the plaintiff said he bought from other parties to fill his orders. We sustain the sixth, seventh, tenth, eleventh, and thirteenth assignments of error.

[20] We do not feel that we can sustain any of the other assignments. The case necessarily had to go to the jury on the main questions of the condition of the defendant at the time he signed .the contract in suit, and whether it was a mere bantering proposition, never intended to be carried into execution; and the learned court below fairly and correctly left these questions to the jury. The verdict was against the defendant, and, after reading carefully the whole of the testimony, we feel constrained to say that we regard the verdict as against the weight of the evidence on this latter question. The case, in its circumstances, is very much like the case of *Brown* v. *Finney*, 53 Pa. St. 373, which received the condemnation and reversal of this court after a verdict of two thousand dollars had been recovered in the court below.

The defendant in this case unfortunately and most unwisely put his name to a written proposition, and, while it is manifest that he did so while considerably under the influence of liquor, it is very plain that he knew perfectly well what he was doing, and that he was not impelled to affix his signature by any act of fraud, deceit, imposition, mistake, or undue influence. On the contrary, his partner, who was present, refused to become a party to such an act of drunken folly; but, after that refusal, the defendant did consciously and knowingly put his name to the paper, with a recklessness and a silly disregard of consequences, which, no doubt, he has bitterly regretted ever since.

Nevertheless, a calm review of the circumstances indicates clearly, as we think, that the making of the offer to sell twenty thousand barrels of flour at four dollars a barrel, at the same time when he actually bought four hundred barrels, in good business earnest, at four dollars and forty-five cents a barrel, and the signing of a memorandum in writing of such a sale, was never regarded or intended by either party as more than a mere bluff or banter, without any serious intention that it should be performed as a real *bona fide* contract. It was perfectly evident, and was abundantly proved, that the defendant, who was a small retail dealer with limited means, was utterly unable to carry out such a contract, even if the flour could have been obtained in sufficient quantity, and was also unable, without a large advance in the price, to make deliveries at the rate of four hundred barrels daily, for fifty consecutive days. There is very grave reason to doubt [21] the correctness of the plaintiff's statement that he immediately called upon the defendant to perform the contract, in view of the defendant's positive denial, and, what is more important, the continuance of their ordinary business relations, and the customary purchases by the defendant from the plaintiff of flour at the regular market rates, which were considerably above four dollars per barrel. One of the witnesses present, and entirely disinterested, testified that he heard and saw the whole transaction; that the defendant's statement to the plaintiff that he would sell him the flour was made in a bantering, joking way, and that his understanding was that the plaintiff regarded it as a joke.

But of course all of these things were matters for the consideration of the jury, and it is out of our power to change the verdict, no matter what we may think of the effect of the testimony. We do not think the court committed error in the instructions given to the jury upon these subjects, and therefore, as to all the assignments of error, except those which relate to the measure of damages, we dismiss them as not being sustained.

Judgment reversed, and new *venire* awarded.

SALE.—MEASURE OF DAMAGES for breach of a contract to sell and deliver personal property when the purchase price has not been paid is the difference between the contract price and the market price at the time and place of the promised delivery: *Austrian v. Springer*, 94 Mich. 350; 34 Am. St. Rep. 350, and note. But, if similar goods can be procured in the market, the defendant will be liable only for the difference between the amount for which he had agreed to sell and the amount which plaintiff was compelled to pay in order to supply the deficiency: *Trigg v. Clay*, 88 Va. 330; 29 Am. St. Rep. 723, and note.

THATCHER *v.* CENTRAL TRACTION COMPANY.

[166 PENNSYLVANIA STATE, 66.]

STREET RAILWAY COMPANIES—CARE REQUIRED OF—NEGLIGENCE.—It is not negligence *per se* for a citizen to be upon the tracks of a street railway. So long as a common user of the tracks exists in the public it is the duty of passenger railway companies to exercise such watchful care as will prevent accidents or injuries to persons who, without negligence on their part, may not at the moment be able to get out of the way of a passing car.

STREET RAILWAY COMPANIES HAVE NOT AN EXCLUSIVE RIGHT to the highways upon which they are permitted to run their cars, or even to the use of their own tracks; and, while the driver of a wagon must yield the track promptly on sight or notice of an approaching car, he is not a trespasser because upon the track, and only becomes one if, after notice, he negligently remains there.

STREET RAILWAY COMPANIES—CARE AND LIABILITY.—If the speed of a street railway car is a dangerous and negligent one the natural consequence is that, on a much traveled street, those in peril will obstruct each other's movements in attempts to escape; and this is one of the very contingencies which the company is bound to foresee and avoid by due care, or it will be liable for the result.

STREET RAILWAY COMPANIES—NEGLIGENCE OF, IS QUESTION FOR JURY, WHEN.—In an action against a street railway company to recover damages for personal injuries the question of defendant's negligence is for the jury, where it appears that there was a double track on a steep grade; that plaintiff was driving a light wagon up one track while a heavy wagon was coming down the other, followed by a cable-car running at a very high rate of speed; that in order to avoid standing wagons ahead of him the plaintiff turned upon the track of the down-coming car; that an effort was made to get both wagons off the track, but that the heavy one so interfered with the light one that the latter did not clear the track; and that, in consequence thereof, the light wagon was struck by the car, and the driver thereof injured. In such a case there is no question of proximate or remote cause, or the interposition of an independent responsible cause which produced the result.

STREET RAILWAY COMPANIES—NEGLIGENCE OF, IS QUESTION FOR JURY, WHEN.—In an action against a street railway company to recover damages for personal injuries the question of the company's negligence is for the jury, where it appears that the gripman ran his car at a high rate of speed, when the probable consequence would be a collision with wagons ahead of the car on the track, and there is evidence that the car could not have been stopped until it reached a point three hundred feet beyond the point where it did collide with a wagon.

TRESPASS for personal injuries. There was a verdict and judgment for the plaintiff for six thousand dollars.

Thomas Patterson and E. W. Smith, for the appellant.

T. T. Donehoo, L. K. Porter, and W. A. Boothe, for the appellee.

⁶⁸ DEAN, J. On the 12th of February, 1891, about 3 o'clock in the afternoon, the plaintiff, while driving with a companion in a light sewing-machine wagon on Wylie avenue, Pittsburg, was run into by a cable-car and very seriously injured. Wylie avenue has a very steep grade for about six hundred feet from the foot of Minersville hill to the top. Fulton is a cross street at the foot of the hill and Arthur a cross street at the summit level. Between these are three other cross streets, Vine, Tannehill, and Crawford, about one hundred and fifty feet apart. Wylie avenue is about thirty to forty feet wide, being seven or eight feet narrower above Fulton street than below; above Vine it curves toward Arthur. The defendant occupies, with double tracks, the middle of the avenue, and operates its railway by cable. Looking up the avenue from Fulton the ascending cars take the right-hand track and the descending cars the left hand one. Thatcher and his companion, John Crusan, the latter having the lines, drove on Wylie avenue and up across Fulton street in the direction of Crawford, the next cross street, keeping on the right-hand car track, when, hearing a car behind them, and seeing wagons standing on the space between the rails and curb on the street to the right, they turned off on the left-hand track for the car to pass; it passed them between Crawford and Tannehill, when they attempted **⁶⁹** to get back on the right-hand track, at a point near Tannehill, but, before they were entirely clear of the track, a car coming down struck the wagon, throwing both out, and Thatcher, falling under the car, had his left arm crushed, so that it is permanently useless. He brought suit for damages against defendant, averring negligence in running the car on a much-traveled street at a high rate of speed, and of giving no notice of its approach to vehicles driven on the rails, so that they might avoid a collision. The evidence as to the circumstances tending to show negligence or absence of it was conflicting; it was submitted to the jury to find the fact by the learned judge of the court below in a very full charge. Of the six written points presented by counsel for defendant he peremptorily affirmed four; the two negatived practically requested him to direct a verdict for defendant. There was a verdict and judgment for plaintiff in the sum of six thousand dollars.

On appeal, error is alleged in negativing defendant's fifth and sixth points. The first of these asked the court to instruct the jury that if the direct cause of the collision was owing to the fact that a wagon coming down the avenue turned to the left just as plaintiff turned to the right and thus prevented him clearing the track and avoiding the collision, it was the negligence of the driver of the wagon which was the cause of the injury, and the company is not answerable.

As the plaintiff himself testified: "We attempted to pull back, and, in getting back on the other track, there was a wagon turned in front of us from the left-hand track, and cut our way off from getting back, and the car that was coming down was coming at such a rate of speed that we couldn't get.out of the way and it ran into us," an. affirmance of this point would have been, in substance, an instruction that plaintiff could not recover. The assignment is without merit; as the driver coming down on the, to him, right-hand track, suddenly made an effort to escape from the rapidly approaching car behind and turned to his left just as plaintiff turned to his right, the driving of the wagon off the track was not the negligent interposition of an independent responsible cause which produced the result. On this question Wharton on Negligence, section 134, illustrates the application of the rule thus: "I am negligent on a particular subject matter as to which I am not contractually bound. Another person [70] moving independently comes in, and, either negligently or maliciously, so acts as to make my negligence injurious to a third person. If so, the person so.intervening acts as a non-conductor and insulates my negligence so that I cannot be sued for the mischief which the person so intervening directly produces." And the same rule is, in substance, laid down in Bigelow's Cases on Torts, 611. The case in hand in its facts is wholly outside the rule. The wagoner was moved by the same impelling motive as the plaintiff; both sought escape from the same impending danger; he neither acted maliciously nor negligently; both displayed prudence in acting with the utmost promptness. If the speed of the car was a dangerous and negligent one the natural consequence was that, on a much-traveled street, those in peril would obstruct each other's movements in attempts to escape. This was one of the very contingencies which defendant was bound to foresee and avoid by due care, for it would be the natural and probable result of high speed; under such circumstances one driver will not remain on the track and be run over that he may not impede another in his movement toward safety.

There is no question of proximate or remote cause raised by the facts, nor of the interposition of an independent act of negligence to which the injury is lawfully attributable.

As to the second assignment, it is argued there was not sufficient evidence of negligence of defendant to submit to the jury.

Taking the statements of witnesses on both sides, it seems the gripman did sound the gong at about Vine street, but did not lessen speed, although then plaintiff's wagon was in full view and the up car passing them; it must have been plain to the gripman then that the vehicle was on the left-hand track, because it must get out of the way of the car going in the same direction; but there is the significant testimony as to the speed of the car, that it could not be stopped until it reached Fulton street, three hundred feet beyond the point of the accident. It is not our duty now, nor was it that of the court below, to pass on the credibility of plaintiff's witnesses as to the rate of speed and the absence of effort to stop the car when the danger was manifest. That was for the jury. If the gripman recklessly ran on at a high rate of speed, when the probable consequence was a collision, that was negligence for which defendant is answerable. [71] As is held in *Ehrisman* v. *East Harrisburg etc. Ry. Co.*, 150 Pa. St. 180: "It is not negligence *per se* for a citizen to be anywhere upon such tracks (railways on streets). So long as the right of a common user of the tracks exists in the public, it is the duty of passenger railway companies to exercise such watchful care as will prevent accidents or injuries to persons who, without negligence on their own part, may not at the moment be able to get out of the way of a passing car." Or, as is said in *Gilmore* v. *Federal St. etc. Ry. Co.*, 153 Pa. St. 31, 34 Am. St. Rep. 682: "Street railway companies have not an exclusive right to the highways upon which they are permitted to run their cars, or even to the use of their own tracks." In both these cases the court is speaking of the relative rights of the public and the railway companies on the streets of cities and boroughs where the grant is of the right to occupy the surface in common with the public. The construction of the track and the form of the rail are with a view to a user in common. The right of the wagon, in certain particulars, is subordinate to that of the railway; the streetcar has, because of the convenience and exigencies of that greater public which patronizes it, the right of way; whether going in the same direction ahead of the car, or in an opposite one to meet it, the driver of the wagon must yield the track promptly on sight or notice of the approaching car; but he is not a trespasser because upon the track; he only becomes one if, after notice, he negligently remains there.

A careful examination of the whole evidence satisfies us there was no error committed in leaving the question of negligence to the jury. The assignments of error are over-ruled and the judgment affirmed.

STREET RAILWAY COMPANIES—RIGHTS, DUTIES, AND LIABILITIES—NEG-LIGENCE.—A street railway company has no exclusive right to the use of a public street in which its tracks are laid. It is bound to know that men, women, and children have an equal right to the use of the street, and will be upon it. The servants of the company are, therefore, bound to be on the lookout and to take reasonable means to avoid accidents: See monographic note to *Western etc. Co.* v. *Citizens' St. R. R. Co.*, 25 Am. St. Rep. 475, 481, discussing the rights, duties, and obligations of street railway corporations with respect to the streets. This note, at page 475, also shows that a traveler on a city street has the right to drive his vehicle either upon or across the track of a street railway company; and that the only limitation of this right is, that he must not unnecessarily interfere with the passage of the cars. It is the duty of a street-car driver to exercise a reasonable degree of care and diligence in watching the street ahead of him, so as to prevent collisions and avoid injury to pedestrians lawfully traveling thereon whether adults or children: See note to *Johnson* v. *Reading City Passenger Ry.*, 40 Am. St. Rep. 756; and a failure to do this is negligence: See note to *Benjamin* v. *Holyoke St. Ry. Co.*, 39 Am. St. Rep. 449. As no exclusive right to the use of its track is vested in a street railway company, a person driving upon it is not negligent, or a trespasser, but must get off to give a car precedence: *Rascher* v. *East Detroit etc. Ry. Co.*, 90 Mich. 413; 30 Am. St. Rep. 447; *Gilmore* v. *Federal St. etc. Ry. Co.*, 153 Pa. St. 31; 34 Am. St. Rep. 682. In cases where a street-car comes into collision with a team in the street the contributory negligence of the driver of the team will defeat a recovery against the street-car company: *Gilmore* v. *Federal St. etc. Ry. Co.*, 153 Pa. St. 31; 34 Am. St. Rep. 682; but the question of contributory negligence, unless the case is a clear one and presents some decisive act in regard to the effect of which ordinary minds cannot differ, must go to the jury: See note to *Thoresen* v. *La Crosse City Ry. Co.*, 41 Am. St. Rep. 68; *Benjamin* v. *Holyoke St. Ry. Co.*, 160 Mass. 3; 39 Am. St. Rep. 446: *Rascher* v. *East Detroit etc. Ry. Co.*, 90 Mich 513; 30 Am. St. Rep. 447; note to *Connelly* v. *Trenton etc. Ry. Co.*, 44 Am. St. Rep. 428. With reference to railroads, in general, the running of a train at a high rate of speed is not negligence *per se*, though it is always proper to submit to the jury whether such act is negligent or not: *McDonald* v. *International etc. Ry. Co.*, 86 Tex. 1; 40 Am. St. Rep. 803, and note; but a street railway company, in running its cars in a public street, must exercise such care and precaution, for the purpose of avoiding accidents to person or property, as a reasonable prudence would suggest: See note to *Western Paving etc. Co.* v. *Citizens' St. R. R. Co.*, 25 Am. St. Rep. 481.

O'NEIL v. AMERICAN FIRE INSURANCE COMPANY.

[166 PENNSYLVANIA STATE, 72.]

THE WORDS "LEGISLATIVE POWER" mean the power or authority, under the constitution or frame of government, to make, alter, or repeal laws.

STATUTES—REQUISITES OF VALID LAW.—A law must be complete in all its terms and provisions when it leaves the legislative branch of the government, and nothing must be submitted to the judgment of the electors or other appointee of the legislature except an option to become, or not to become, subject to its requirements and penalties.

INSURANCE—LEGISLATURE—DELEGATION OF POWER.—Whether the legislature itself may prescribe a form of contract of insurance or not, it cannot delegate the power to an insurance commissioner to prescribe a standard policy of insurance.

INSURANCE — UNAUTHORIZED DELEGATION OF POWER — CONSTITUTIONAL LAW.—A statute providing "for a uniform contract or policy of insurance to be made and issued by all insurance companies taking fire risks on property within the state," directing the insurance commissioner to prescribe a standard policy of insurance, and forbidding the use of any other, is unconstitutional, as an unauthorized delegation of legislative power.

ASSUMPSIT on policy of fire insurance. Each of the defendant companies had executed and delivered to plaintiff a policy on a certain building in McKeesport, one for sixteen hundred dollars and the other for five hundred dollars. While these policies were in force the building was entirely destroyed by fire, being a total loss. The court entered a compulsory nonsuit.

W. B. Rodgers and J. H. Beal, for the appellants.

Edwin Z. Smith and J. S. & E. G. Ferguson, for the appellees.

[76] WILLIAMS, J. The compulsory nonsuit entered in this case must stand or fall with the act of the 16th of April, 1891 (Pub. Laws, 22), entitled "An act to provide for a uniform contract or policy of insurance to be made and issued by all insurance companies taking fire risks on property within the state." The action is upon a policy in the form prepared by the insurance commissioner under the directions of that act. At the trial the plaintiff gave his policy in evidence, and then offered the testimony of witnesses for the purpose of showing a waiver by the company of the conditions in the policy relating to proofs of loss and an appraisement of the value of the property destroyed. These offers were objected to upon the ground that the conditions were prescribed by a statute, and could be waived only in the manner which the statute

provided. The learned judge of the court below assumed, with evident reluctance, the constitutionality of the act of 1891, sustained the objection to the evidence offered, and left the plaintiff to stand upon the letter of what was thus held to be a statutory form of contract. The compulsory nonsuit was the logical result. This appeal brings us face to face with the question whether the provisions of this policy are to be construed as those of a voluntary contract entered into by the parties, or as the requirements of a positive statute imposed upon the parties by the lawmaking power.

The answer to this question must depend on whether the act of 1891 is a valid exercise of legislative power. The words "legislative power" mean the power or authority, under the constitution or frame of government, to make, alter, and repeal laws: 13 Am. & Eng. Ency. of Law, 272. Under the constitution of this state this power is vested in, and must be exercised by, the legislative branch of the government: *Parker* v. *Commonwealth*, 6 Pa. St. 507; 47 Am. Dec. 480. It is a power that cannot be delegated. This principle was stated with great vigor by Chief Justice Gibson in *Borough of West Philadelphia*, 5 Watts & S. 283, in these words: "Under a well-balanced constitution the legislature can no more delegate its proper function than can the judiciary." It is suggested that *Parker* v. *Commonwealth*, 6 Pa. St. 507, 47 Am. Dec. 480, is an overruled case. While this is true, it is equally true that the cases that overrule it distinctly recognize the principle on which it was decided. They deny only the applicability of that [77] principle to the facts then before the court. The question raised in *Parker* v. *Commonwealth*, 6 Pa. St. 507, 47 Am. Dec. 480, was the constitutionality of a local option law, and it was held to be unconstitutional because the reference of the question of its going into effect in a given locality was thought to be a delegation of legislative power. In subsequent cases, and particularly in *Locke's Appeal*, 72 Pa. St. 491, 13 Am. Rep. 716, it was held that, inasmuch as the law with all its provisions and its penalties was complete when it left the legislature, and the only question submitted to the electors of the locality was whether they desired this law to become operative in the subdivision of the state in which they lived. such submission did not amount to a delegation of legislative power. No provision or requirement of the law was left to be supplied in order to make it complete in all its parts, but the vote of the electors served

to give expression to their wish in reference to the subjection
of the locality they represented to its already finished provisions. It has frequently been held that local questions may
be submitted in this manner to those who are to be directly
affected by their decision. The division of a county is such
a question, and a law submitting the question to a popular
vote, and making the division depend on the result of the
vote, was sustained in *Smith* v. *McCarthy*, 56 Pa. St. 359. So
is the location of the county seat: *Commonwealth* v. *Painter*,
10 Pa. St. 214. So, also, is the granting of licenses to sell
intoxicating drinks: *Locke's Appeal*, 72 Pa. St. 491; 13 Am.
Rep. 716. Such laws are in form and in substance laws *in
presenti*, to take effect *in futuro* upon the ascertainment of the
wish of those most directly affected thereby.

The effect of our cases is to settle firmly the rule that the
law must be complete in all its terms and provisions when it
leaves the legislative branch of the government, and that
nothing must be submitted to the judgment of the electors or
other appointee of the legislature except an option to become
or not to become subject to its requirements and penalties.
In the light of this line of well-considered cases let us examine the act of 1891 in order to get its provisions before us.
Section 1 declares "That the insurance commissioner shall
prepare and file in his office on or before the fifteenth day of
November, 1891, a printed form in blank of a contract or
policy of fire insurance, together with such provisions, agreements, or conditions as may [78] be indorsed thereon or added
thereto, and form a part of such contract or policy; and such
form when filed shall be known and designated as the standard fire insurance policy of the state of Pennsylvania." Section 2 provides, among other things, for the incorporation of
the provisions of the standard policy into the contracts of
insurance made on property within the state by foreign insurance companies. Section 3 makes the use of this standard
form of policy obligatory on all fire insurance companies
doing business in this state from and after the first day of
May, 1892. Section 4 provides the penalties to be imposed
upon any insurance company, its officers, or agents, or either
of them, for failure to comply with the requirements of the
act or with the form of policy which the insurance commissioner may devise and file in his own office.

It may be well to say in this place that we do not now
deny the power of the legislature to direct the form of a policy

of insurance against fire.   We held in *Commonwealth* v. *Vrooman*, 164 Pa. St. 306, 44 Am. St. Rep. 603, that the business of insurance against loss by fire was, by reason of its nature, its magnitude, and the temptation to improper practices which it presented, a proper subject for legislative regulation and control.   The power to prohibit technical and unjust conditions intended to open the way to vexatious litigation and to defeat the just expectations of the insured, belongs to the police control which *Commonwealth* v. *Vrooman*, 164 Pa. St. 306, 44 Am. St. Rep. 603, asserted.   The question is not therefore one of power over the subject, but of the manner in which the conceded power must be exercised.   Upon this question our judgment is with the appellant for reasons that we will state as concisely as possible and without any attempt at elaboration.

The act of 1891 is a delegation of legislative power because: 1. The act does not fix the terms and conditions of the policy the use of which it commands; 2. It delegates the power to prescribe the form of the policy and the conditions and restrictions to be added to and made part of it to a single individual; 3. The appointee clothed with his power is not named, but is designated only by his official title. He is the person who may happen to be insurance commissioner when the time comes to prepare the form for the standard policy for insurance against fire; [70] 4. The appointee is not required to report his work to the body appointing him, but simply to file in his own office the form of policy he has devised.   It does not become part of the statute in fact, is not recorded in the statute-book, and no trace of it can be found among the records of either branch of the legislature; 5. The act was approved in April, 1891. The appointee had until the following November to prepare and file the form of policy over which when filed the legislature had no control whatever.   They did not consider, they had no knowledge of, the form which they required all companies doing business in the state to adopt, and the use of which they compelled by heavy penalties.

The elementary books divide a statute into three parts: the declaratory, the directory, and the vindicatory.   In this statute the legislature furnished the first and third.   It delegated the preparation of the second.   It declared in effect the need of a standard form of policy.   It provided punishment for the failure to use such form when provided; but it turned the preparation of the form over to its appointee and gave him six months in which to do his work and file a copy of it in his own office. Whoever might be interested in knowing the directory part of the statute and understanding what it was he was required to do had to go beyond the act of assembly and inquire of the appointee of the legislature what it was he had filed in his own office, of which the people of the commonwealth were bound to take notice at their peril.

It will not do to say that the preparation of the form was an unimportant matter of detail, or an act partaking of an executive or administrative character. It was the sole purpose of the act. It was the only subject named in its title. The enforcement of the standard form of policy was the only object of its penalties. Take out the form prepared by the insurance commissioner and to be found in some pigeonhole in his office and the act is without meaning or effect: it is completely eviscerated.

We do not see how a case could be stated that would show a more complete and unconstitutional surrender of the legislative function to an appointee than that presented by the act of 1891. By its provisions the legislature says in effect to its [so] appointee: "Prepare just such a policy or contract as you please. We do not care to know what it is. The governor shall have no opportunity to veto it. File it in your own office, and we will compel its adoption, whether it is right or wrong, by the punishment of every company, officer, or agent who hesitates to use it."

We do not take time to examine the voluminous conditions loaded upon the back of a very simple and concise contract of insurance. The assignments of error do not bring them before us for this purpose. The learned judge of the court below gave them careful consideration, and he was of opinion that they were unjust and oppressive. Speaking of the form of the standard policy as a whole, he said: "I look upon it as infamous." Again he said: "The conditions put in that policy go beyond almost any policy that ever was exhibited in the courts before. Numerous provisions were put in that the courts had declared void because they were so unjust and inequitable." Speaking of its general character and effect, he said: "It seems to be framed in the interest of dishonest companies and insurance brokers, and puts an honest insurance company and honest officers of a company at a very great disadvantage."

This is a very serious arraignment of the "standard policy," to which we refer without comment of our own, for the purpose of showing the impolicy of such delegation of legislative power as might make it possible to fasten upon the people of the commonwealth a form of contract, open to such grave objections.

It is not to be supposed that a law really mischievous in its operations could pass both houses of the legislature unchallenged. If, by reason of any complication of circumstances this should happen in any given case, then the people have a remaining safeguard in the veto power possessed by the governor. The act of 1891 steered past both legislative discussion and executive veto, and vested in the insurance commissioners the power to fill in its directory provisions, and supply the form of insurance contract it was to enforce, without even the knowledge of the legislature or the governor of a single one of its many provisions that were to be bound by fines and penalties on insurers and insured all over the commonwealth.

[81] Our conclusion is that the act of 1891 is void, because clearly unconstitutional. The compulsory nonsuit is set aside and a procedendo awarded. ____

DELEGATION OF LEGISLATIVE POWER.—Legislative power cannot be delegated to the people at large, or to any portion of them: *Parker v. Commonwealth*, 6 Pa. St. 507; 47 Am. Dec. 480, and note. In general the legislature cannot submit a law to the people in such a manner as to make its final enactment depend on the popular vote, unless specially authorized by the constitution: *Ex parte Wall*, 48 Cal. 279; 17 Am. Rep. 425; *Barto v. Himrod*, 8 N. Y. 483; 59 Am. Dec. 506; note to *Harbor Commrs. v. Redwood City*, 22 Am. St. Rep. 321.

INSURANCE.—That the subject of insurance is a proper one for legislative regulation and control is undoubted: *Commonwealth v. Vrooman*, 164 Pa. St. 306; 44 Am. St. Rep. 603; *State v. Stone*, 118 Mo. 388; 40 Am. St. Rep. 388. The only question is, How shall it be exercised?

SHINN'S ESTATE.

[166 PENNSYLVANIA STATE, 12L]

EXECUTORS AND ADMINISTRATORS ACTING IN ANOTHER STATE—DEVASTA-
VIT—SURCHARGE.—The mere fact that an administrator expends money
in a reasonable effort to save the property of his intestate situated in
another state is not sufficient to convict him of a devastavit. To hold
that such fact warrants a surcharge is carrying the doctrine which
confines the administration of assets to the jurisdiction of the domicile
too far.

EXECUTORS AND ADMINISTRATORS—DUTY OF, AS TO ASSETS BEYOND JURIS-
DICTION.—To hold that the representative of the personal estate within
the domicile owes no duty whatever, either to creditors or next of kin,
with reference to personalty outside the jurisdiction is to invite neglect
and consequent waste and dissipation of assets.

EXECUTORS AND ADMINISTRATORS—SURCHARGE FOR LOSS IN DEALING WITH
ASSETS BEYOND THE JURISDICTION.—An administrator who deals with
personal assets beyond the jurisdiction must exercise prudent business management, but speculative ventures are not such management.
Therefore, where an administrator in one state takes a large amount of
money from the general fund in his hands, and expends it upon the
advice of the next of kin, without consulting creditors, and without an
order of court, in working a tract of iron ore in another state, upon
which the decedent had a lease, and upon which he had expended a
large sum of money, he should be surcharged with the loss to the estate,
in case of disastrous failure, especially if all of the facts concerning the
working of the ore showed that the undertaking was of a highly speculative and hazardous nature.

EXECUTORS AND ADMINISTRATORS—COMMISSIONS—MANAGEMENT OF ASSETS
IN FOREIGN JURISDICTION.—Though an administrator, in dealing with
personal assets beyond the jurisdiction, as in working a tract of iron
ore, meets with loss, yet if he manages the estate of the domicile with
such skill as to increase largely the value of the assets, he is entitled to
his commissions, particularly where he has spent a large amount of time
and labor upon the estate, and is under heavy bonds.

EXCEPTIONS TO ADJUDICATION.   The principal question involved grew out of expenditures made by the administrator
on account of a certain leasehold in the state of New York.
The error assigned by the administrator was the decree
surcharging him. The error assigned by the Trenton Iron
Company was the allowance of commissions to the administrator.

Willis F. McCook, for the appellant.

James Balph, R. A. Balph, A. M. Brown, John S. Lambie,
and *J. E. McKelvy,* for the creditors.

John S. Lambie, A. M. Brown, and *John Sparhawk, Jr.,* for
the Trenton Iron Company.

124 Dean, J. William P. Shinn died intestate May 5, 1892, leaving as his next of kin, Joseph A. and John K. Shinn. The assets, real and personal, in Pennsylvania amounted to $211,126.92, and debts, $202,648.27. Before his death he had taken the leasehold interest of a tract of iron ore land in Westchester county, **125** New York, granting the right for twenty years to mine and remove the iron ore therefrom at a price or royalty of fifty cents per ton, and fixing a minimum production of not less than ten thousand tons, or $5,000 per year. William P. Shinn, in his lifetime, had expended more than $100,000 in improvements and patents for the production and preparation of the ore for furnaces. Besides the royalties and certain rentals stipulated to be paid, there was upon the leasehold a chattel mortgage and other charges amounting to about $40,000. To make this operation a success the administrator took from the general fund $44,736.36 and expended it in patents, test or exploring shafts, and for other purposes in and about the ore lease, and claimed credit therefor in his account. The auditing judge surcharged him with these expenditures, and the administrator appeals.

We are not disposed to affirm this decree on the opinion of the learned judge of the court below. In that opinion the surcharge is sustained for two reasons; the first and controlling one, because the accountant had no authority to go beyond the limits of the state and attempt to manage a part of the estate in a foreign jurisdiction, and to that end appropriate a part of the assets realized in the state of the domicile. As to this, the court says: "The action of the accountant was therefore clearly a breach of official duty."

Neither the facts in this case, nor the law applicable to them, warrants such a sweeping conclusion. The question raised here is not being tried in the courts of New York, with adverse claimants of that state against the right of the administrator to remove the assets to another jurisdiction. Nor is it being tried in the courts of this state, with home creditors contesting the right of a New York administrator to remove the fund beyond the reach of our court. In either case the legal title of the administrator, and his intermeddling with the fund, might be effectually denied. But the question here is, What may an administrator do with reference to personal assets beyond the jurisdiction, without sub-

jecting himself to the peril of a surcharge? It is answered
that he should have immediately converted the asset into
money, and for that purpose should have raised an ancillary
administrator within the jurisdiction of the New York courts,
whose duty it would have been to sell and distribute the
fund, first, to the creditors there, and then pay [126] over to
him the balance for distribution among the general creditors
in Pennsylvania. But suppose an immediate sale would
have been impossible or unwise, and that the expenditure of
a limited amount would have made the asset marketable at
a fair price, and thus have saved a large sum for the estate?
If it had been reasonably probable, as appellant claims, that
the expenditure of about $7,000 in completing a shaft would
have made the property worth in the market at least $75,000,
and thus have saved the larger part of the more than
$100,000 already expended upon it, certainly a court of
equity would not have surcharged such a trustee with the
$7,000, merely because the money had come out of the gen-
eral fund, and had been paid outside the state. Even an
executor *de son tort* is entitled to reimbursement for payments properly made in relief of the estate. It is argued, an
ancillary administrator should have been appointed to do
this. If he had been first appointed he would have had
no money to expend, unless he received it from the Pennsylvania administrator, and the same fund would have
been depleted for the same purpose. When an administrator assumes the office and has delivered to him assets of the
character of these, the exigency may require that he, within
a limited extent, shall act beyond the jurisdiction. The
intestate here had pledged, in New York banks, collateral,
largely exceeding in value the amount of the obligations for
which they were pledged; the administrator paid off the obligations out of the general fund, lifted the collateral, sold it,
and thereby swelled the general fund. No one of the creditors claims that he be surcharged with the amount paid on
the notes, because the money to pay them was taken from
the general fund, and paid outside the jurisdiction. If he
had paid no attention to the matter, and permitted the collateral to be sacrificed, the creditors could properly have claimed
a surcharge because of neglect of a plain duty. This leasehold was a chattel in New York state, and is so treated there,
and a chattel mortgage under the laws of that state given
upon it. The administrator finds the instrument among the

other personal assets of his intestate. To decide that the mere fact that he expended money beyond the state to save valuable assets warrants a surcharge is carrying the doctrine which confines the administration of assets to the jurisdiction of the domicile too far, and beyond any thing ever intended to be decided by this court.

[127] As early as 1803 it was decided in *McCullough* v. *Young,* 1 Binn. 63, that it had "been uniformly understood, both before and since the revolution, that letters of administration granted in a sister state are a sufficient authority to maintain an action here; and such has been the practice without regard to the particular interstate laws of the state where they have been granted. There may be, indeed, great inconveniences from the law, but it lies within the legislature to remedy them." This case was virtually overruled in *Brodie* v. *Bickley,* 2 Rawle, 431, decided in 1830, in which it was held that an action would not lie against an administrator in this state on a judgment obtained against another administrator of the same estate in another state. The court says: "The authority of an administrator under letters granted in a sister state to meddle with the assets here is an anomaly produced by an unexampled spirit of comity in the courts of this state, which will probably be attended in this respect with perplexity and confusion." This was followed by *Mothland* v. *Wireman,* 3 Pen. & W. 185, 23 Am. Dec. 71, decided in 1831. The real question for decision in this case was whether Wireman, an administrator in Pennsylvania, was chargeable with assets received by his coadministrator, who was both a resident of Maryland and surviving partner of decedent in certain iron works in that state, and by reason of his survivorship had received money belonging to the estate. This court held the Pennsylvania administrator was not liable except for assets received within the jurisdiction, although the bond was joint. That the money received from the iron property by the surviving partner and coadministrator must be accounted for in the courts of Maryland. The decision is grounded on *Brodie* v. *Bickley,* 2 Rawle, 431, decided the year before. It is true Gibson, C. J., in delivering the opinion, says he is unable to see why, if even the assets in Maryland had come into the hands of the administrator in Pennsylvania, the latter should be charged with them; but this was wholly outside the case, for there was no pretense that the Pennsylvania administrator had actually received any part of the fund. The decision is

good law for just what is decided, that the Pennsylvania administrator was not liable for the fund received by his co-administrator, a resident of Maryland, on assets located in Maryland. The court again speaks in deprecatory terms of **128** that "injudicious spirit of comity" which prevailed in the courts of this state, evidently having in mind the decision in *McCullough* v. *Young*, 1 Binn. 63.

Then, apparently moved by these criticisms, the legislature passed the act of March 15, 1832, in which it is enacted that: "No letters testamentary, or of administration or otherwise, · purporting to authorize any persons to intermeddle with the estate of a decedent, which may be granted out of this commonwealth, shall confer on such person any of the powers and authority possessed by an executor or administrator under the letters granted within this state." This was a severe blow to the doctrine of comity on which *McCullough* v. *Young*, 1 Binn. 63, was based, and which Gibson, C. J., in the subsequent cases thought insufficient to warrant the decision.

But this act was found inconveniently rigorous, so it was amended by that of June 16, 1836, enacting that it should not apply to shares of stock in any incorporated company within this state; and then again by act of 15th of May, 1850, that it should not apply to any loan of any incorporated company within this state. So that, in a spirit of comity, a foreign administrator could come into this state and manage and collect such assets without having ancillary letters issued.

A number of cases arose requiring an interpretation of the act. *Dent's Appeal*, 22 Pa. St. 514, held that although distribution of foreign assets must be made according to the law of the domicile, it was not required that such distribution should be made in the place of the domicile; that this was a question, not of jurisdiction, but discretion. In *Moore* v. *Fields*, 42 Pa. St. 467, it was decided that where a debt against an administrator of an estate in New York had been settled by final decree of the surrogate court, an action would lie against the administrator in this state by the public administrator of New York without the issue of ancillary letters in this state. In *Shakespeare* v. *Fidelity etc. Deposit Co.*, 97 Pa. St. 173, it was held that United States bonds on special deposit could be sued for by a foreign administrator in the courts of this state. In *Musselman's Appeal*, 101 Pa. St. 165, it was decided that letters testamentary to a Pennsylvania citizen, upon the estate of a resident of another state, gave no jurisdiction to Pennsylvania courts over the accounts. *Lines* v. *Lines*, 142 Pa. St. 149, 24 Am. St. Rep. 487, held that a court of equity in this state [129] had no jurisdiction over the personal property of a decedent of another state which would authorize it to take such property out of .the hands of those in possession.

But in no case has it been decided that the mere fact of an administrator expending money in any reasonable effort to save the property of his intestate situated in another state is sufficient to convict him of a devastavit. As is said by Justice Sharswood in *Shakespeare* v. *Fidelity etc. Co.*, 97 Pa. St. 173, "the point has never been decided in this state."

A voluntary payment by a debtor of this state to a foreign administrator, when no ancillary letters had previously issued, would not be that offensive "intermeddling" with the assets in this state as would make it a mispayment under our statute; and we will not assume that, in a spirit of comity, the mere payments by this administrator beyond the jurisdiction, from that fact alone should be declared unlawful.

Nor will we assume that, if he had sold the property and had paid the claims upon it, he would not be answerable in this state for the surplus. The argument to the contrary has nothing to support it but the dictum in *Mothland* v. *Wireman,* 3 Pen. & W. 185, 23 Am. Dec. 71, and is not in accord with any of the adjudicated cases. The ruling in *Wilkins* v. *Ellett*, 9 Wall. 740, is sounder in principle: "The foreign administrator's title is recognized to receive a voluntary payment and to give a valid acquittance therefor, provided no ancillary letters have been previously granted. The payment being voluntary, the executor has not intermeddled." In *Potter* v. *Hiscox*, 30 Conn. 508, a guardian had among his ward's assets the note of a citizen of another state. He made no effort to collect, because the debtor was not within the jurisdiction. The court surcharged him with it, saying, with persuasive reason, that the domiciliary guardian was bound to use reasonable care and diligence in endeavors to save his ward's estate. To hold that the representative of the personal estate within the domicile owes no duty whatever, either to creditors or next of kin, with reference to personalty outside the jurisdiction is to invite neglect and consequent waste and dissipation of assets. That he has no

standing as a suitor in a foreign jurisdiction does not alone
fix the measure of his duty, nor has it ever been so regarded
in practice.   In thus holding we do not intimate that he
must go into a foreign jurisdiction and [130] institute suits
which could not be sustained, or offensively intermeddle
with assets, so as to defy or disregard the jurisdiction of the
courts of the situs.   There are often many things he may do,
many things he ought to do, which suggest themselves to the
prudent business man, tending toward the preservation of
the estate, and are neither obnoxious to the law nor antagonistic to the interests of foreign creditors.

But while we do not sustain the decree of the learned judge
of the court below on his first reason, we think it fairly supported by the second.   On the facts found, the action of the
administrator was wholly unwarranted.   The iron ore operation was a speculative venture which the decedent, in his
lifetime, had a perfect right to enter upon; his business was
to accumulate an estate; if his ventures turned out successful he reaped the profits; if unsuccessful, no others were
interested or had a right to complain.   But the business of
this administrator was not to make money for the estate by
hazardous ventures, but to save that which came into his
hands for creditors and kin by prudent business management.
Speculative ventures were not prudent business management.
The ore was uncertain, both as to quantity and quality, as is
apparent on a mere reading of the stipulations in the lease;
the cost of production was not known with even approxi-
mate certainty, for the methods of mining and cleaning were
purely experimental.   Besides these risks the value of the
ore when ready for the furnace was wholly uncertain, because
it was certain to be subject to the wide fluctuations of the
iron market.   Without consultation with the creditors, with
no cautionary order from the court on a statement of the facts,
he put into this plant, in hopes of profit, this large sum of
money — money realized from the estate in Pennsylvania.
The business proved a most disastrous failure.   The whole was
sold under legal proceedings in New York and did not bring
the amount of claims against it.   He advised with no one as
to the judiciousness of expending this $45,000 of the creditors'
money, except those whose interests were, in a certain sense,
antagonistic to the creditors.   His New York advisers were
interested in keeping the plant in operation whether it made
money or lost.   Joseph A. and John K. Shinn, next of kin,

examined the property, and they advised him to continue it in operation. It was their interest [131] to do so. They doubtless knew, as did the administrator, that, unless at least a portion of the large amount invested in this operation by decedent in his lifetime was saved, the estate was practically insolvent. If it proved successful there would be a surplus to go to them, the next of kin; if unsuccessful, they were no worse off, as the loss would fall upon the creditors. · Yet the administrator took the creditors' money and invested it in a wild speculation. He might, almost as safely, have invested it in stocks on the prospect of a rise. This was not ordinary business sagacity or prudent management. His conduct, on the facts found by the auditing judge, therefore, warranted the surcharge.

The decree is affirmed, and the appeal is dismissed at costs of appellant.

TRENTON IRON COMPANY'S APPEAL.

DEAN, J. The facts in this case are about the same as in the appeal of William H. Shinn, administrator, opinion filed this day. The appeal here, however, is from that part of the decree which allows the administrator commissions.

The court, although surcharging the administrator with a large sum of money expended on an iron ore operation in New York, nevertheless finds that he acted in good faith, and allows him his commissions. We are not inclined, on the facts, to disturb this decree. The appellee was compelled to give very heavy bonds, covering nearly $200,000 worth of property, for which he paid to the surety companies $500. For this the court allowed him no credit. While we saw much to condemn in his conduct with reference to the New York property, we see nothing but diligent, astute business management of the Pennsylvania property. With no cash on hand, except about $1,500, he saved from peril $103,000 of stocks pledged by the decedent for small loans both within and without the state; these he then sold for about $21,000 more than they were appraised at—more than twice as much as they would have sold for at any time since. The appellant claims that it was through the aid of reputable bankers he accomplished this; let that be so; a trustee who has the sagacity to select efficient aids in the management of delicate and responsible interests intrusted to him is all the more deserving of remuneration, especially as the [1327] bankers charged for their services less than $400. Besides these stocks he performed most vexatious labor in the sale and management of the real estate, which was heavily mortgaged, and realized on that $64,500, an amount considerably in excess of the liens. His commissions, as allowed, amount to about $7,000. The court below did not think, in view of the actual services and time devoted to his duties, and the large responsibilities involved, that this was unreasonable. We are not convinced there was any error in the allowance.

The decree is affirmed, and the appeal is dismissed at costs of appellant.

POWER AND DUTY OF ADMINISTRATOR OR EXECUTOR AS TO PROPERTY OUTSIDE OF STATE—*General Observations as to Authority and Duty.*— There are two kinds of administration, one domiciliary and the other ancillary. Whenever authority to administer the estate of one deceased, testate or intestate, is granted in two or more competent jurisdictions, the principal administration or appointment must be that where the deceased had his last domicile; and that administration or appointment granted elsewhere, because of local property or assets, is ancillary merely. This division grows out of the international doctrine that the law of the domicile of the owner of personal property governs in regard to the right of succession, whether such owner dies testate or intestate. And, while this rule as to the succession and distribution of personal property is founded on international comity, it is equally obligatory upon our courts as a legal rule of purely domestic origin: *Parsons* v. *Lyman,* 20 N. Y. 103; *Marcy* v. *Marcy,* 32 Conn. 308, 316; *Denny* v. *Faulkner,* 22 Kan. 96; *Citizens' Nat. Bank* v. *Sharp,* 53 Md. 528. The right which an individual may claim to personal property in one country, under title from a person domiciled in another, can only be asserted by the legal instrumentalities which the institutions of the country where the claim is made have provided. The foreign law furnishes the rule of decision as to the validity of the title to the thing claimed; but in respect to the legal assertion of that title it has no extra-territorial force. As a result of this doctrine it is now generally held everywhere that an executor or administrator has not, as such, any positive authority beyond the sovereignty by virtue of whose laws he is appointed: *Parsons* v. *Lyman,* 20 N. Y. 103, 112, per Denio, J.; *Glenn* v. *Smith,* 2 Gill & J. 493; 20 Am. Dec. 452; note to *Ela* v. *Edwards,* 90 Am. Dec. 176; *Fletcher* v. *Sanders,* 7 Dana, 345; 32 Am. Dec. 96; *Burbank* v. *Payne,* 17 La. Ann. 15; 87 Am. Dec. 513; *Schneller* v. *Vance,* 8 La. 506; 28 Am. Dec. 140; note to *Doolittle* v. *Lewis,* 11 Am. Dec. 394. We understand this, however, to mean active, living, legal authority; that the right of the administrator or executor to recover the property or the debts due to the decedent out of the territorial jurisdiction of the government where the grant of administration is obtained, and which property or debts cannot be reached through the medium of its courts, depends upon the comity of the state or country where the property is situated, or where the debtor of the intestate resides, or where the estate upon which such debt is a lien is found; and that in order to bring a suit in relation to the decedent's property in another state or country than that in which the decedent was domiciled, the domiciliary executor or administrator must first obtain ancillary letters testamentary or of administration in such state or country: *Vroom* v. *Van Horne,* 10 Paige, 549; 42 Am. Dec. 94; *McNamara* v. *Dwyer,* 7 Paige, 239; 32 Am. Dec. 627; *Fugate* v. *Moore,* 86 Va. 1045; 19 Am. St. Rep. 926; *Durie* v. *Blauvelt,* 49 N. J. L. 114; *Leonard* v. *Putnam,* 51 N. H. 247; 12 Am. Rep. 106; *Doolittle* v. *Lewis,* 7 Johns. Ch. 45; 11 Am. Dec. 389; *Riley* v. *Riley,* 3 Day, 74; 3 Am. Dec. 260; *Goodwin* v. *Jones,* 3 Mass. 514; 3 Am. Dec. 173. The subject of ancillary administration is treated in a monographic note to *Goodall* v. *Marshall,* 35 Am. Dec. 483–490.

It is of frequent occurrence that persons die leaving large and valuable property interests in different states, and debts due them from persons in other states, and these occurrences are constantly increasing. State lines are becoming dimmer in this class of cases, and the questions arising therein are of great practical importance. Executors, administrators, and courts of probate must act respecting them, and the law should be clearly defined. Unfortunately this seems not to have been done, at least as to many of the questions growing out of this complicated subject. While an administrator or executor cannot sue in a foreign jurisdiction without clothing himself with the authority of ancillary administration, he must not disregard the interests of the estate, and must take timely and prudent measures to protect them, or run the risk of being charged for loss.

Title—Removal of Property—Duty of Creditors and Effect of Their Laches. It is said in *Luce* v. *Manchester etc. R. R.,* 63 N. H. 588, 590, that "Letters of administration confer no extraterritorial authority as matter of right; hence the power of an executor or administrator is limited to the state or country of his appointment, and, being so limited, the general rule is that he cannot sue or defend in his representative capacity in a foreign jurisdiction—not, however, from want of title to the assets of his decedent situate in such jurisdiction, but because of his personal incapacity to enforce it. And it is upon this ground of title that it has been so often decided by courts of the highest authority that, in the absence of ancillary administration or statutory prohibition, the domiciliary administrator or executor has authority to take possession of and remove the goods or effects of the decedent in another jurisdiction, or to collect a debt due from a debtor residing therein, if voluntarily given up or paid, and give a good acquittance and discharge therefor." To the same effect is the note to *Doolittle* v. *Lewis,* 11 Am. Dec. 395. It is not material in such cases to consider the distinction between the rights of a foreign executor and a foreign administrator, as both have title. The executor derives his title from the will, while his letters testamentary are merely the due and proper authentication of his office; and the administrator derives his title and authority entirely from the letters of administration. Again, so far as the right to institute suits is concerned, or to administer assets outside of the state or country in which the probate of the will has been made and the letters granted, an executor and administrator stand on the same footing: *Shaw* v. *Berry,* 35 Me. 279; 58 Am. Dec. 702; *Murray* v. *Blatchford,* 1 Wend. 283; 19 Am. Dec. 537; and have no power to maintain suits for the collection of assets in their official capacity in any other state or country than that from which they derive their authority to act by virtue of the probate and letters of administration there granted: *Citizens' Nat. Bank* v. *Sharp,* 53 Md. 521, 528; *Marcy* v. *Marcy,* 32 Conn. 308, 316. As an administrator takes his title by force of the local law and the grant of administration, the title of an executor may be somewhat better, because he derives it, as to all movable property of his testator wherever situate, not from a grant of administration, but from the will as a recog-

uized instrument of conveyance at common law. His title accrues at the
instant of death, and without probate he may do many acts which pertain
to his office, such as the collection of debts, sale of property, and payment
of debts, etc., and his acts will be legal. This distinction as to title, however, is unimportant. Each has title, and either an executor or administrator
may go into a foreign jurisdiction, and, so long as he does not violate the
laws of such jurisdiction, or interfere with the rights of creditors therein,
may take possession and assume control of the property of deceased, receive
payment of debts, and remove the assets to the state of the domicile. Expressed in different language: "The current of decision is now to the effect
that, in the absence of an ancillary administration, a principal administrator,
and *a fortiori* an executor, can collect and remove debts or property due or
situate in another state if voluntarily paid or given up": *Marcy* v. *Marcy*,
32 Conn. 308, 322; *Denny* v. *Faulkner*, 22 Kan. 96; *Luce* v. *Manchester etc.
R. R.*, 63 N. H. 588, 590; *Parsons* v. *Lyman*, 20 N. Y. 103; *Upton* v. *Hubbard*, 28 Conn. 274; 73 Am. Dec. 670; and, in the absence of any opposing
administration, the courts of the latter state will, *ex comitate*, recognize the
title and possession of personal property therein to be in the administrator
appointed in the domicile of the decedent: See cases last cited. This doctrine was recognized by Judge Ellsworth, in *Upton* v. *Hubbard*, 28 Conn.
274, 73 Am. Dec. 670, where he said: "If indeed the principal executor or
the assignee go there (into the sister state), and, without acquiring local
authority, collects a debt or receives property belonging to the estate, it is
well enough, we suppose, if the creditors or legatees there do not interpose
and object; for, in such a case, the same end is accomplished which could
be reached through an ancillary administration, and the law does not require
any unnecessary formality and expense, but looks at the substance of the
thing." "This dictum of the learned judge," says Butler, J., in *Marcy* v.
Marcy, 32 Conn. 308, 322, "contains the gist of the whole matter. It
implies a title in a foreign executor which the debtor may recognize. It
implies the right and duty of the executor to collect without the unnecessary expense of local administration if he can, that is, if the debtor is willing
to pay and the creditor does not interpose and object. How may he interpose and object? Objection is dissent expressed by words or conduct.
Interposition and objection then are both active, and cannot consist in lying
by, relying on a supposed right, incident to the debt, which may be enforced
at any time. According to the decisions in New York such interposition
must be by taking administration, and clothing himself with a title, and a
right to appropriate the debt in payment by administering it. And this he
may do at any time before it has been fully administered at the place of
domicile by the principal administrator. So I think he may sue the principal executor or administrator and hold him to the extent of the assets so
collected or removed, at any time before they have been fully administered
at the place of domicile. But, if he lies by and neither takes administration
nor brings suit until the principal executor or administrator has fully
administered, he waives his rights, and the principal administrator should be
protected."

Collection of Debts.—While letters of administration do not confer any
extraterritorial legal authority, the one who accepts them voluntarily
assumes certain obligations and responsibilities from which he cannot escape. He must exercise that diligence and attention to the business of
others which every discreet man should and would bestow upon his own.
His duties and responsibilities in reference to a foreign debt are well ex-

pressed by George, C. J., in *Klein v. French,* 57 Miss. 662, 670, where he says: "It thus appearing that, at least as to the debts due the decedent, the securities for which are in possession of his principal and original administrator, the title and ownership are in the latter, with the right to receive payment and give acquittances therefor, it follows that he would be held responsible for their due administration, as in case of domestic debts, if there were no other obstacle to their collection than exists in relation to domestic debts. Such an obstacle does, however, exist, and to the extent that it is insurmountable by the use of ordinary and reasonable diligence by the administrator, it will furnish a legal excuse for a failure to collect a foreign debt. This obstacle is the want of power in the principal administrator to sue for and recover the debt in the foreign state. For reasons of policy, recognized in the comity of nations, each state in which a debtor of a foreign decedent may reside generally, though not universally, refuses aid through its courts to a foreign administrator to collect the debt, because it will not allow the transmission of the property within its limits to a foreign state, until the claims of its own citizens on it have been discharged. Hence, every state has usually required an ancillary administration within its own jurisdiction, before it will afford aid through its courts to the collection of the debts due to foreign decedents; so that the creditors within that state may be first satisfied, before the transmission of the assets to the place of the principal administration; but it so far recognizes the rights of the principal administrator as to give to him or to his nominee the appointment of ancillary administrator, and to direct the surplus, after paying its own citizens, to be transmitted to the place of the principal administration.

"The principal administrator's duties and responsibilities in reference to a foreign debt, the evidence of which he has in his possession, can be easily ascertained from the foregoing principles. He has the title and the possession; he has the right to receive voluntary payment; he has the right to apply for and receive the appointment of ancillary administration, or to secure it to his nominee. He cannot, therefore, hold the evidence of debt, and do nothing; for this would be most unjust to the distributees, and would result in a loss of the debt to them, unless voluntary payment was made. He should therefore take such reasonable steps as are within his power to collect the debt. He should, except where the debt is too small to authorize the expense, attempt, in good faith, either to secure the appointment of ancillary administrator for himself, or for some discreet and suitable person to be selected by him. Should he be unable to comply with the terms—as giving security—required for the appointment, that would excuse him from making application for a personal appointment. He should then take proper steps to have another appointed, and turn over to him the collection of the debt. He will be held to be excused only when he has shown that he has done all that was reasonably within his power to secure the collection of the debt. He has not done his duty when, as in this case, he has merely transmitted the claim to a lawyer in the foreign state for collection, when he has been apprised in ample time that no steps have been taken for collection by his attorney; nor has he done his duty when he accepts as a compromise whatever sum the debtor or his legal representative shall voluntarily pay."

It is settled that where there are no debts due from the estate in the jurisdiction where a foreign debtor of the estate resides, and no ancillary administration has been granted there, the principal administrator may, in such foreign state, receive a voluntary payment from the debtor, which

SHINN'S ESTATE. [Penn.

will be a good discharge of the debt, even if an ancillary administrator should
be afterward appointed: *Wilkins* v. *Ellett*, 9 Wall. 740; 108 U. S. 256; *Klein*
v. *French*, 57 Miss. 662, 669; *Marcy* v. *Marcy*, 32 Conn. 308, 321; *Citizens'
Nat. Bank* v. *Sharp*, 53 Md. 521, 529; *Luce* v. *Manchester etc. R. R.*, 63 N. H.
588, 591; *Selleck* v. *Rusco*, 46 Conn. 370, 372; *Stevens* v. *Gaylord*, 11 Mass.
256, 271; *Rand* v. *Hubbard*, 4 Met. 255, 257; *Hutchins* v. *State Bank*, 12
Met. 421; *Mackey* v. *Coxe*, 18 How. 100, 104; *Hooker* v. *Olmstead*, 6 Pick.
481; *Williams* v. *Storrs*, 6 Johns. Ch. 353; 10 Am. Dec. 340; *Doolittle* v.
Lewis, 7 Johns. Ch. 45; 11 Am. Dec. 389; *Brown* v. *Brown*, 1 Barb. Ch. 189,
214; *Vroom* v. *Van Horne*, 10 Paige, 549; 42 Am. Dec. 94; *Shakespeare* v.
Fidelity Ins. Dep. Co., 97 Pa. St. 173, 178; *Parsons* v. *Lyman*, 20 N. Y. 103;
Petersen v. *Chemical Bank*, 32 N. Y. 21; 88 Am. Dec. 298; *Deringer* v. *Deringer*, 5 Houst. 416; 1 Am. St. Rep. 150; *Mackay* v. *St. Mary's Church*, 15
R. I. 121; 2 Am. St. Rep. 881; *Schluter* v. *Bowery Savings Bank*, 117 N. Y.
125; 15 Am. St. Rep. 494; note to *Vaughn* v. *Barrett*, 26 Am. Dec. 309,
criticising earlier cases.   Such payment is a bar to the claim of the domestic administrator afterward appointed: *Citizens' Nat. Bank* v. *Sharp*, 53
Md. 521, 529; *Klein* v. *French*, 57 Miss. 662, 669; *Marcy* v. *Marcy*, 32 Conn.
308, 324; though it would not be where domestic letters of administration
are granted before the payment is made: *Vaughn* v. *Barrett*, 5 Vt. 333; 26
Am. Dec. 306.   The payment to the foreign administrator is good, although
he has neither given security nor recorded his letters of administration:
Deringer v. *Deringer*, 5 Houst. 416; 1 Am. St. Rep. 150.   Hence, payment to a foreign administrator is a legal payment of a deposit which, by
the laws of the bank, was payable to the personal representatives of the
depositor in the event of his decease: *Schluter* v. *Bowery Savings Bank*, 117
N. Y. 125; 15 Am. St. Rep. 494.   The voluntary payment of a note by the
promisor to a notary public authorized by the foreign executor to receive
payment, the notary giving up the note, would be a good payment: *Rand* v.
Hubbard, 4 Met. 252, 257.   So, such an executor may convert shares of bank
stock into money: *Hutchins* v. *State Bank*, 12 Met. 421; and one with whom
the bonds of a deceased depositor have been deposited without the state
is justified upon surrender of the receipt of deposit in giving them up to a
foreign executor: *Shakespeare* v. *Fidelity Ins. etc. Dep. Co.*, 97 Pa. St. 173.
If, however, a foreign executor or administrator gathers assets of the deceased and takes them into the state of decedent's domicile, he must there
administer them, and the weight of authority is that a foreign administrator, though having no authority as such to coerce the collection of assets in
a sister state, is equally accountable to the tribunal appointing him where
they are voluntarily paid or delivered to him as if they were collected within
the jurisdiction of the domicile: *Parsons* v. *Lyman*, 20 N. Y. 103; *In re Ortiz*, 86 Cal. 306; 21 Am. St. Rep. 44.

Inventory—Taking Charge of Property—Accounting.—It is sometimes held
that a domestic administrator can be held accountable only for the assets
found within the state of his appointment: *Governor* v. *Williams*, 3 Ired.
152; 38 Am. Dec. 712; *Mothland* v. *Wireman*, 3 Pen. & W. 185; 23 Am.
Dec. 71; and Mr. Justice Story, in his work on Conflict of Laws, eighth
edition, section 514 *b*, has pointed out the fallacy of holding a domestic
administrator or executor answerable for foreign property, which it is admitted that he can neither collect nor sue upon, nor compel its payment or
delivery to himself, by virtue of his domestic appointment, and of the existence of which he may be in total ignorance, as well as of steps taken toward foreign administration: See notes to *Petersen* v. *Chemical Bank*, 88

Am. Dec. 310; *Molyneux* v. *Seymour*, 76 Am. Dec. 669. But, on the other hand, "to let external assets knowingly escape his control," says Professor Schouler, in his treatise on Executors and Administrators, second edition, section 175, "and be lost to the estate, when with reasonable diligence they might have been procured, seems a plain dereliction of duty in the principal or domiciliary representative, whose function, as rightly understood, is to grasp the whole fortune, as the decedent did during his life, save so far as the obstructive law of foreign *situs*, or the limitations of his own appointment, may restrain him." "If, therefore," he says, "assets cannot be collected and realized for the benefit of the estate without a foreign ancillary appointment, the executor or administrator of the decedent's last domicile ought, so far as may be consistent with his information, the means of the estate at his disposal, and the exercise of a sound discretion, to see that foreign letters are taken out, and that those assets are collected and realized, and the surplus transmitted to him. If, as frequently happens, the domestic representative may collect and realize such property in the domestic jurisdiction, by selling as negotiable bonds, bills, notes, or other securities, payable abroad, or by delivering bills of lading or other documents of title (indorsing or assigning by acts of his own, which would be recognized in conferring the substantial title in such foreign jurisdiction), or otherwise, by effectually transferring property of a chattel nature situated or payable elsewhere, which is capable, nevertheless, of being transferred by acts done in the domestic jurisdiction, he should be held accountable for due diligence as to such net assets; and so, too, he may enforce the demand against the debtor, without resort to the foreign jurisdiction. If, however, foreign letters and an ancillary appointment at the situs be needful or prudent in order to make title, and to collect and realize such assets, the principal representative should perform the ancillary trust, or have another perform it, observing due diligence and fidelity, according as the laws of the foreign jurisdiction may permit of such a course; and if, in accordance with those foreign laws, a surplus be transmitted to the principal and domiciliary representative, or otherwise transferred, so as to be held by him in such capacity for payment and distribution, he will become liable for it accordingly. Whether, then, the principal or domiciliary representative be required, *pro forma*, or not, to include in his inventory assets which come to his knowledge, either situate in the state or country of principal and domiciliary jurisdiction, or out of it, his liability as to assets of the latter sort depends somewhat upon his means of procuring them and the fact of an ancillary administration in the situs of such assets. In any case, he is bound to take reasonable means, under the circumstances, for collecting and realizing the assets out of his jurisdiction; nor is his liability a fixed, absolute one, but dependent upon his conduct, and it is getting the foreign assets into his active control that makes a domestic representative chargeable as for the property or its proceeds, rather than upon the duty of pursuing and recovering such assets. If assets situated in another jurisdiction come into the possession of the executor or administrator in the domiciliary jurisdiction, by a voluntary payment or delivery to him, without administration there, it follows that he should account for them in the domiciliary jurisdiction whose letters were the recognized credentials in the case. And it is held in several American cases, consistently with this rule, that, no conflicting grant of administration appearing, the domiciliary appointee of another state may take charge of and control personal property of the deceased in the state of its situs." These views are well supported by authority, as well as principle, and have been adopted in some of the later cases. As supporting the doctrines stated, see *In re Ortiz*, 86 Cal. 306; 21 Am. St. Rep. 44; *Fox* v. *Tay*, 89 Cal. 339; 23 Am. St. Rep. 474; *Vroom* v. *Van Horne*, 10 Paige, 549; 42 Am. Dec. 94; *Brown* v. *Brown*, 1 Barb. Ch. 189; *Shultz* v. *Pulver*, 3 Paige, 182; affirmed in 11 Wend. 361; *Parsons* v. *Lyman*, 20 N. Y. 103; *Klein* v. *French*, 57 Miss. 66 *Marcy* v. *Marcy*, 32 Conn. 308.

It is the duty of a domiciliary executor to gather in and account for foreign assets of his testator, to the extent of his ability to do so, and the court of the domicile may compel him to account for his willful neglect to perform such duty: *In re Ortiz*, 86 Cal. 306; 21 Am. St. Rep. 44; *Shultz* v. *Pulver*, 3 Paige, 182; affirmed in 11 Wend. 361. So, where the assets of an estate situated within a jurisdiction come into the hands of a foreign executor while residing within that jurisdiction by voluntary payment or administration, he is bound to account for them in the domiciliary jurisdiction: *Fox* v. *Tay*, 89 Cal. 339; 23 Am. St. Rep. 474; *Parsons* v. *Lyman*, 20 N. Y. 103. The case of *Shultz* v. *Pulver*, 3 Paige, 182, affirmed in 11 Wend. 361, is a very strong one in holding the executor or administrator to a strict degree of diligence and accountability in collecting debts due from nonresidents. In that case the administrator was held to be negligent and personally liable for his failure to collect. One equitable and invulnerable principle running through the cases is that an executor or administrator is liable for all assets of the decedent received by him, whether with or without authority: *Fletcher* v. *Sanders*, 7 Dana, 345; 32 Am. Dec. 96.

There must, however, be no attempt to evade the testamentary system of a foreign jurisdiction. For example, a foreign testator's appointment of trustees here to act literally as such without letters testamentary or of administration would be a nullity as to his personal estate here: *Hunter* v. *Bryson*, 5 Gill & J. 483; 25 Am. Dec. 313.

Under a statute requiring the executor to make an inventory of all the goods, chattels, and credits of the testator, and which must include every species of personal property belonging to the testator, the executor may be required to include therein assets belonging to the deceased and which are situated in another state, where the only qualification of the statute is, that the property must have belonged to the testator at the time of his decease, and that the same should have come to the hands or knowledge of the executor: *In re Estate of Butler*, 38 N. Y. 397; note to *Doolittle* v. *Lewis*, 11 Am. Dec. 395. Being thus required by statute to inventory debts and administer them, the executor or administrator may collect them in a foreign jurisdiction by receiving payment without taking out ancillary letters: See note to *Vaughn* v. *Barrett*, 26 Am. Dec. 309, criticising earlier cases.

It has been held that neither an administrator nor his bondsmen are liable for his intermeddling with his intestate's property in another state: *Cabanne* v. *Skinker*, 56 Mo. 357; that an executor or administrator in one state cannot receive or be made to account for rents and profits of lands lying in another state: *Smith* v. *Wiley*, 22 Ala. 396; 58 Am. Dec. 262; *Morrill* v. *Morrill*, 1 Allen, 132; and that he is not obliged to make any effort to collect a judgment in a foreign jurisdiction: *State* v. *Sloan*, 64 N. C. 702. But these comparatively early cases must, in the light of the more recent decisions, be considered as against the weight of authority. A court of chancery has power to compel a foreign executor or administrator to account for trust funds, in the form of assets of his decedent, received by him abroad and brought with him into this state; and letters of administration here on the estate of the decedent are not necessary for such action: *McNamara* v.

Dwyer, 7 Paige, 239; 32 Am. Dec. 627. There is a possible distinction, as to the rights of creditors here, between the case of decedent's property brought into the state by the executor and that of property already here, and which a foreign executor comes here to secure. It has therefore been held that a foreign executor who comes here to reside, bringing with him a portion of his testator's estate, cannot be made liable here at the suit of a creditor of the testator, even to the extent of property so removed: *Hedenberg* v. *Hedenberg*, 46 Conn. 30; 33 Am. Rep. 10. The probate of the will of the decedent, or the grant of letters testamentary, or of administration, by the proper tribunal of his domicile, is sufficient, in New York, to authorize his executor or administrator to take charge of the property of the decedent and to receive debts due to him in that state, where no suit is necessary, if there is no conflicting grant of letters testamentary or of administration in that state: *Vroom* v. *Van Horne*, 10 Paige, 549; 42 Am. Dec. 94. A foreign administrator acts in Delaware by virtue of the power originally granted to him, and the laws of that state recognize him as such upon the mere production of his duly authenticated commission, and thereupon concede to him the powers of administrator appointed by the courts there: *Deringer* v. *Deringer*, 5 Houst. 416; 1 Am. St. Rep. 150. And, under the Revised Statutes of Wisconsin, a foreign administrator may have the same rights and remedies as one appointed in the state, upon filing his appointment or an authenticated copy thereof in any county court in the state, though it be one in which the decedent had no property, or not one in which suit is to be brought: *Murray* v. *Norwood*, 77 Wis. 405. Statutes, such as these, which remove almost every impediment in the way of an executor or administrator who desires to act in a foreign jurisdiction, are merely a reflex of the judicial mind on the subject, and the question of procuring ancillary letters of administration becomes a matter of small importance to the executor or administrator who can acquire full power by a very simple act.

General Principles—Suits—Assignments.—While different executors may be appointed in different countries where the testator has effects, or as to different parts of his estate in the same country (*Hunter* v. *Bryson*, 5 Gill & J. 483; 25 Am. Dec. 313), there is no privity between administrators of different states: *Braithwaite* v. *Harvey*, 14 Mont. 208; 43 Am. St. Rep. 625; note to *Ela* v. *Edwards*, 90 Am. Dec. 175. The general rule is that letters of administration confer no extraterritorial authority, and have no extraterritorial effect: *Governor* v. *Williams*, 3 Ired. 152; 38 Am. Dec. 712; *Fletcher* v. *Sanders*, 7 Dana, 345; 32 Am. Dec. 96; *Vroom* v. *Van Horne*, 10 Paige, 549; 42 Am. Dec. 94; *Fugate* v. *Moore*, 86 Va. 1045; 19 Am. St. Rep. 926; *Smith* v. *Howard*, 86 Me. 203; 41 Am. St. Rep. 537. That, when a party dies leaving property in two or more states or countries, his property in each is considered a separate succession, for the purposes of administration, the payment of debts and the decision of the claims of parties asserting title thereto: *Burbank* v. *Payne*, 17 La. Ann. 15; 87 Am. Dec. 513; *Succession of Taylor*, 23 La. Ann. 23. That the assets in each jurisdiction must be administered separately and independently, and under authority of the local law, see note to *Ela* v. *Edwards*, 90 Am. Dec. 176; *Fletcher* v. *Sanders*, 7 Dana, 345; 32 Am. Dec. 96. And that an executor can administer only upon property situate within the state from whose courts he derives his powers: *Succession of Packwood*, 9 Rob. (La.) 438; 41 Am. Dec. 341; *Glenn* v. *Smith*, 2 Gill. & J. 493; 20 Am. Dec. 452; *Lucas* v. *Byrne*, 35 Md. 494; *Burbank* v. *Payne*, 17 La. Ann. 15; 87 Am. Dec. 513; *Mason* v. *Nutt*, 19 La. Ann. 42; *Succession of Taylor*, 23 La. Ann.

23; *Succession of Packwood*, 12 Rob. (La.) 334; 43 Am. Dec. 230; *Schneller* v. *Vance*, 8 La. 506; 28 Am. Dec. 140; note to *Doolittle* v. *Lewis*, 11 Am.
Dec. 394. The authority of the domiciliary executor or administrator does
not extend to the property in a foreign jurisdiction, nor to the doings of the
executor or administrator there. Nor does the authority of the foreign
executor or administrator extend to the property here, nor to the doings of
the executor or administrator here: See note to *Ela* v. *Edwards*, 90 Am·
Dec. 176. As letters of administration granted in another state give no
authority to sue or administer assets here, one selling property under
them will not be protected from an action by the domestic administrator:
Glenn v. *Smith*, 2 Gill & J. 493; 20 Am. Dec. 452. The general rule,
sustained by the weight of authority, is that no action or suit can be
maintained either by or against an administrator outside the state of his
appointment, until he has first taken letters in the foreign jurisdiction:
Vroom v. *Van Horne*, 10 Paige, 549; 42 Am. Dec. 94; *Goodwin* v. *Jones*, 3
Mass. 514; 3 Am. Dec. 173; *Riley* v. *Riley*, 3 Day, 74; 3 Am. Dec. 260;
Doolittle v. *Lewis*, 7 Johns. Ch. 45; 11 Am. Dec. 389; *Leonard* v. *Putnam*,
51 N. H. 247; 12 Am. Rep. 106; *Fugate* v. *Moore*, 86 Va. 1045; 19 Am. St.
Rep 926; *McNamara* v. *Dwyer*, 7 Paige, 239; 32 Am. Dec. 627; *Durie* v.
Blauvelt, 49 N. J. L. 114. While a foreign executor or administrator cannot maintain a suit here by virtue of letters testamentary or of administration
granted abroad, he may sue here in his own name, if he sues in his own right,
as where he is the real owner of the chose in action sued upon: *Petersen* v.
Chemical Bank, 32 N. Y. 21; 88 Am. Dec. 298; note to *Goodall* v. *Marshall*,
35 Am. Dec. 485. So foreign executors may sue or be sued upon contracts
made with them in their capacity of executors, though the rule is otherwise
with respect to contracts made by the testator in his lifetime. Such executors may be compelled to specifically perform a contract made by them in
one state to sell and assign a judgment recovered by their testator in
another state: *Johnson* v. *Wallis*, 112 N. Y. 230; 8 Am. St. Rep. 742. And
an administrator appointed in the state in which the decedent had his domicile succeeds to all rights of action arising out of the statutes of another state.
Hence, if the statutes of another state give a right of action for injuries to
the person, whether they instantaneously result in death or not, and declare
that the right shall survive to the executor or administrator, an action may
be maintained by the administrator in this state for injuries suffered in the
other by his intestate from the negligence of a railway corporation and
resulting in death, if the decedent was domiciled in this state at the time of
his injury and death: *Higgins* v. *Central etc. R. R. Co.*, 155 Mass. 176; 31
Am. St. Rep. 544. But a foreign administrator cannot maintain an action
in another state for the negligent killing of his intestate, where he cannot
maintain such an action under the law of the state of his appointment:
Limekiller v. *Hannibal etc. R. R. Co.*, 33 Kan. 83; 52 Am. Rep. 523. So,
where a foreign executor, as trustee, has taken a note and mortgage from his
coexecutor for a fund received by the latter as belonging to the estate, he
may maintain an action to recover the fund, and to foreclose the mortgage
as mortgagee, without taking out letters testamentary in the jurisdiction
where the mortgaged property is situated: *Fox* v. *Tay*, 89 Cal. 339; 23 Am.
St. Rep. 474. But a mortgage upon real property in one state, belonging to
a person who dies in another state, and whose estate is in course of regular
and valid local administration in the former state, cannot be sold by a foreign administrator to a stranger. The title thereto is in the local administra-

tor for purposes of administration, and he alone can sue on it, or assign or discharge it of record: *Reynolds* v. *McMullen*, 55 Mich. 563; 54 Am. Rep. 386. An administrator cannot, by virtue of appointment in another state, assign a mortgage of land situated here: *Cutter* v. *Davenport*, 1 Pick. 81; 11 Am. Dec. 149. The reason of this is that such a mortgage, though in many respects a pledge for a debt, is also a conveyance in fee to the mortgagee, and an assignment of the mortgage is a conveyance of real estate to the assignee. It is also a well-settled rule of law that where it is necessary to make title to real estate, through the official act of an executor or an administrator, it must be by letters testamentary or letters of administration from some domestic probate court; because titles to real estate must be regulated, governed, and established by the *lex loci rei sitæ: Hutchins* v. *State Bank*, 12 Met. 421, 424. For example, an administrator's sale of Ohio lands by a Virginia court is void for want of power: *Salmond* v. *Price*, 13 Ohio, 368; 42 Am. Dec. 204. The disability of a foreign administrator to sue in our courts is a personal one, but he has a perfect right to assign the choses in action of his decedent, so as to confer title against every one but creditors and legatees. The assignee may, therefore, maintain a suit, in our courts, upon a chose in action so transferred to him: *Petersen* v. *Chemical Bank*, 32 N. Y. 21; 88 Am. Dec. 298; although there has been no probate or administration granted here: *Campbell* v. *Brown*, 64 Iowa, 425; 52 Am. Rep. 446. And, as a result of this principle, it has been held that an executor or administrator under the laws of one state can indorse a promissory note so as to enable the indorsee to sue in another state: *Riddick* v. *Moore*, 65 N. C. 382; *Barrett* v. *Barrett*, 8 Me. 353. Especially where there are, in the latter state, no claims against the estate of his intestate: *Mackay* v. *St. Mary's Church*, 15 R. I. 121; 2 Am. St. Rep. 881. There are cases holding a contrary doctrine: *Thompson* v. *Wilson*, 2 N. H. 291; *Stearns* v. *Burnham*, 5 Greenl. 261; 17 Am. Dec. 228. But those in support of the rule as stated seem to stand upon the better reason: Compare opinion in *Mackay* v. *St. Mary's Church*, 15 R. I. 121; 2 Am. St. Rep. 881. An administrator or executor appointed in one state may maintain an action in another state in his own name upon a judgment recovered by him as such executor in the former state: *Lewis* v. *Adams*, 70 Cal. 403; 59 Am. Rep. 423. "A debt due to the estate of a deceased person," says Mr. Freeman, in his work on Judgments, fourth edition, section 217, "if sued upon and recovered by an administrator is, in law, the debt of him who recovers it and in whose name the judgment is rendered. He holds the legal title, subject only to his trust as administrator. He may sue upon the judgment in his own name, without describing himself as administrator, and may therefore pursue the judgment defendant, by action on the judgment, in a different state from that in which the letters of administration were issued; and there can scarcely be a doubt that a judgment rendered in favor of an administrator so merges the debt that it may be treated as his personal effects so far as to authorize him to maintain suit thereon in a foreign country, without there taking out letters of administration." But as an administrator has no authority to act for, or bind the estate outside of the jurisdiction of the state of his appointment, he cannot, therefore, be bound by a judgment entered against an administrator of the same estate in another state, on the ground that he participated in the defense of the action in the other state: *Braithwaite* v. *Harvey*, 14 Mont. 208; 43 Am. St. Rep. 625.

One appointed executor in another state, but who resides in this state,

and who has collected assets in the state where he was appointed, which he
has not brought into this state, cannot be sued here for the purpose of
recovering a legacy to which the complainant claims to be entitled under the
will of the defendant's testator: *Fugate* v. *Moore*, 86 Va. 1045; 19 Am. St.
Rep. 926.

WILLOCK v. PENNSYLVANIA RAILROAD COMPANY.

[166 PENNSYLVANIA STATE, 184.]

COMMON CARRIER IS VIRTUALLY AN INSURER AGAINST ALL PERILS OF
TRANSPORTATION, except the act of God or public enemies. He is
bound to guard against perils arising from the use of defective or inadequate instruments of carriage, and from the employment of incompetent, negligent, or criminal servants.

CARRIERS.—LIMITATIONS UPON THE COMMON-LAW LIABILITY OF CARRIERS
do not decrease the degree of care which they are bound to exercise
toward the subject of transportation.

CARRIERS—STIPULATION AGAINST PUBLIC POLICY.—A stipulation in a bill
of lading that is intended to protect a common carrier in the violation
of his contract, and in disregarding a settled rule of public policy, will
not be sustained.

CARRIERS—STIPULATIONS AGAINST NEGLIGENCE.—It is contrary to public
policy to allow a common carrier to stipulate for immunity from the
consequences of his own negligence or fraud, or that of his employees.

CARRIERS—BILL OF LADING—CLAUSE VOID AS AGAINST PUBLIC POLICY.—
A clause in a bill of lading stipulating that the owner, shipper, and
consignee severally shall cause the goods to be insured, and look only
to said insurance for compensation in case of loss, the carrier in such
case being allowed the benefit of the insurance, where the loss occurs
from any cause rendering the carrier or its agents liable therefor, is
void as against public policy. The shipper will not be compelled to
insure for the carrier's benefit.

CARRIERS—INSURANCE—RECOVERY BY SHIPPER.—If goods are lost by the
negligence of a carrier, the shipper may recover the amount of the loss
notwithstanding his failure to insure the goods as provided for by a
stipulation in the bill of lading. The carrier cannot compel the shipper
to insure the goods for his benefit.

ASSUMPSIT to recover the value of sixty barrels of petroleum,
shipped by the plaintiff from Oil City to Richmond, Virginia.
Plaintiff's statement averred that the oil was lost by reason
of the defendant's negligence. The plaintiff attached to and
made a part of his statement the bill of lading, containing
the stipulation named in the opinion. The affidavit of defense set up the loss by fire, and averred that plaintiff had
failed to insure, as he agreed to do, in the bill of lading.
There was a rule for judgment, for want of a sufficient affidavit of defense, made absolute.

George B. Gordon and William Scott, for the appellant.

James S. Young and S. U. Trent, for the appellee.

[187] WILLIAMS, J.   Who shall be deemed a common carrier, and what are the nature and extent of his undertaking, are questions that were settled centuries ago upon common-law principles.   A common carrier is bound to employ safe and sufficient means of carriage, trustworthy and competent servants, and, by himself or his agent, to exercise an intelligent supervision over the system of [188] carriage which he employs.   He is therefore, to all intents and purposes, an insurer against such perils of transportation as it is his duty to provide against; and these include all the perils of the journey, except such as arise from "the act of God or the king's enemies."

Our forefathers brought this definition of the duties of a common carrier with them when they came to this continent, and its outlines remain substantially the same to this day. Some limitations upon his common-law liabilities have been sustained to protect the carrier against unjust and fraudulent claims on the part of customers; but the measure of care due from him to those whom he serves has not been abated in the slightest degree.   He is still held to be an insurer against such perils as it is his duty to provide against, and among these are such as arise from the use of defective or inadequate instruments of carriage, and from the employment of incompetent, negligent, or criminal servants: *Farnham* v. *Camden etc. R. R. Co.*, 55 Pa. St. 53.

What are commonly spoken of as limitations of the liability of the carrier, and have been upheld by the courts of this state as such, are, when carefully considered, undertakings of the shipper, implied from the nature of the contract, and enforced against him at the instance of the carrier.   Thus, a stipulation that the carrier shall not be liable to the shipper for the loss of certain packages in a greater sum than that named in the receipt or bill of lading, unless the actual value of the package was fully disclosed to the carrier when it was delivered to him, so that he might know the amount of risk involved, and charge accordingly, has been upheld, because good faith on the part of the shipper requires such full disclosure by him.   So, also, if the contents of a package are perishable, or easily broken, or explosive, so that the danger of loss is increased, and the exercise of an unusual degree of care is made necessary, good faith requires the shipper to make the facts known to the carrier; and a failure to do so ought to affect the extent, and in some cases the right, of recovery for the loss of goods so shipped.

The carrier is relieved in these cases, not from the duty to exercise care and diligence in the transportation of his customer's goods, but from the consequences of the failure of the shipper to advise him fully of facts and circumstances material [189] to the contract, the suppression of which is in effect a fraud upon him. His obligations as a common carrier are not reduced. He is bound to the exercise of great care by the nature of his undertaking. He must not be negligent. It is against public policy that he should be. It is also a violation of his contract, which is to carry safely. A stipulation that is intended to protect him in the violation of his contract as a carrier, and in disregarding a settled rule of public policy, will not be sustained. The cases in which this doctrine is recognized and applied in this state are very numerous. Among them may be named the following: *Beckman* v. *Shouse*, 5 Rawle, 179; 28 Am. Dec. 653; *Bingham* v. *Rogers*, 6 Watts & S. 495; 40 Am. Dec. 581; *Laing* v. *Colder*, 8 Pa. St. 479; 49 Am. Dec. 533; *Goldey* v. *Pennsylvania R. R. Co.*, 30 Pa. St. 242; 72 Am. Dec. 703; *Powell* v. *Pennsylvania R. R. Co.*, 32 Pa. St. 414; 75 Am. Dec. 564; *American Express Co.* v. *Sands*, 55 Pa. St. 140; *Pennsylvania R. R. Co.* v. *Miller*, 87 Pa. St. 395; *Grogan* v. *Adams Express Co.*, 114 Pa. St. 523; 60 Am. Rep. 360; *Pennsylvania R. R. Co.* v. *Raiordon*, 119 Pa. St. 577; 4 Am. St. Rep. 670; *Western Union Tel. Co.* v. *Stevenson*, 128 Pa. St. 442; 15 Am. St. Rep. 687; *Phœnix Pot. Works* v. *Pittsburgh etc. R. R. Co.*, 139 Pa. St. 284; *Buck* v. *Pennsylvania R. R. Co.*, 150 Pa. St. 171; 30 Am. St. Rep. 800.

It is a sufficient answer to an argument in favor of changing the rule in Pennsylvania, and permitting carriers to stipulate for a release from the consequences of their own negligence or fraud, that the question is not an open one. It has been settled by the cases cited and many others, and we are bound by the rule *stare decisis*. The attempt to overturn the common-law doctrine fixing the liability of carriers was made in England by act of Parliament. The result is, after several statutes upon the subject, that the carrier may make a contract limiting his liability on two conditions. The first is that the contract be actually signed by the shipper. The second is that the courts shall adjudge the limitation to be

"just and reasonable." This works no substantial change in
the law. It makes a contract for carriage of persons or property tripartite. The carrier and the shipper are the ostensible parties, but the public, as represented by the courts of
law, is the third party, and may refuse its consent to stipulations on which carrier and shipper have agreed. When
such a contract comes before the courts the question is, not
what terms have the parties incorporated into their agreement, but are the terms so incorporated "just and reasonable," so that they ought, on grounds of public policy, [190] to
be enforced? In determining this question the courts have
been constrained to apply common-law principles, and hold
that to be just or unjust which was so held at common law.
Thus in *McManus* v. *Lancashire etc. Ry. Co.*, 4 Hurl. & N.
327, the contract provided that the livestock shipped over
the defendant's railroad should be carried at the risk of the
owner, and that the company should in no case be liable for
any loss or injury sustained. The contract was signed by
the shipper, but the court held it to be both unjust and unreasonable, and refused to enforce it. In *Kirby* v. *Great Western
Ry. Co.*, 18 L. T., N. S., 658, the contract provided that the
carrier should not be liable for injury to the goods shipped
occasioned by delay, no matter what the cause of the delay
might be. The courts, representing the public, the third
party to the agreement, declined to give assent, and held the
provision relieving the carrier from the consequences of his
own negligence to be unjust and unreasonable. Still nearer
to the question in the case before us is *Peek* v. *North Stafford-
shire Ry. Co.*, 10 H. L. Cas. 473. The carrier in that case
had a contract with the shipper containing a stipulation that
he should not be liable for loss of the goods unless their value
was declared at the time of the delivery of the goods to him,
and they were then insured to their full value by the shipper.
This was held to be neither just nor reasonable, and its enforcement was refused. The courts of England have thus
held in substance that the public have a greater interest in
the transportation of persons and property than any individual shipper, and that public policy requires of a common
carrier the exercise of constant care over his vehicles or
means of transportation, and over his servants and employees
in charge of them. They further hold that it is against the
public good that he should be allowed to contract for immunity from the consequences of his own negligence or fraud, or

the negligence or fraud of his employees; and that stipulations to that effect are incapable of enforcement because unjust and unreasonable.

The supreme court of the United States holds to the same doctrine upon this subject as the courts of Pennsylvania: *Railroad Co.* v. *Lockwood*, 17 Wall. 357; *Liverpool etc. Steam. Co.* v. *Phœnix Ins. Co.*, 129 U. S. 397.

The public is interested in securing the highest measure of safety in the transportation of passengers and goods, and to [191] this end public policy requires that common carriers be held to the highest measure of care in the conduct of their business. Greenhood, in his treatise on Public Policy, 573, says: "It is obvious, therefore, that if a carrier stipulate not to be bound to the exercise of care and diligence but to be at liberty to indulge in the contrary, he seeks to put off the essential duties of his employment; and to assert that he may do so seems almost a contradiction in terms."

The carrier and the shipper do not stand on equal terms. The latter cannot afford to refuse that which the carrier demands as a condition to the transportation of his goods, and, in ninety-nine cases out of every hundred, if he does so refuse he will find himself discriminated against until his business is ruined and he has nothing·left to ship. The rule that stipulations, insisted on by carriers or other persons who stand in such a position toward their customers as enables them to compel compliance with their demands or destroy their customer's business should be judged of by their fairness, and be held void whenever they are unreasonable or oppressive, is one of very general acceptance. Public policy compels its acceptance in all civilized countries.

The learned counsel for the appellant cite *Phœnix Ins. Co.* v. *Erie etc. Transp. Co.*, 117 U. S. 312, as tending to sustain their contention. But an examination of that case shows that it was begun by libel filed by the insurance company, asking subrogation to the rights of the shipper against the carrier. The first question to be determined was, therefore, What could the shipper recover upon the facts of that case? He had contracted that any insurance he might obtain should inure to the benefit of the carrier. He obtained insurance on the goods shipped, suffered a loss, and was paid the insurance money. The question presented on these facts was whether the right of the shipper to recover against the carrier was not extinguished to the extent to which his loss had been paid by the insurer. If so, subrogation must necessarily be refused, and it was refused for this reason. This point was elaborated in *Provident Ins. Co.* v. *Morse,* 150 U. S. 99, in which it was said that in case of loss the carrier is primarily liable to the shipper, and the position of an insurer is substantially that of a surety. The insurer can recover, therefore, after payment [192] of a loss by subrogation to the rights of the shipper, and upon no other ground; so that whatever amounts to an extinguishment of the right of action of the shipper against the carrier must defeat the insurer's right to subrogation. The general proposition that the surety who pays the debt of his principal succeeds only to the rights of the creditor whom he pays is beyond all doubt; and in *Phœnix Ins. Co.* v. *Erie etc. Transp. Co.,* 117 U. S. 312, it was held to be applicable to contracts that, as we have seen, are tripartite, having the public as a third though unnamed party.

In the case at bar the carrier inserted in its bill of lading a stipulation that the owner, shipper, and consignee severally shall cause the goods to be fully and sufficiently insured, and that in case of loss the carrier shall have the benefit of such insurance if such loss "shall occur from any cause which shall be held to render this line or any of its agents liable therefor." No insurance was effected. A loss occurred as the result of a collision by two of the carrier's trains. The shipper sues to recover the amount of his loss. The only defense set up is under the condition in the bill of lading; and the question raised is, Will the courts compel the performance of a contract between shipper and carrier requiring the shipper to protect the carrier against the consequences of its own negligence? There is no doubt about the carrier's having an insurable interest in the goods, or about his right to protect himself from loss by procuring a policy of insurance for that purpose, but the question here presented is, Can he compel the shipper to insure the goods for his benefit? If so he can compel the shipper to release him entirely, and so stipulate for complete immunity from the consequences of the negligence and fraud of himself or of his servants and employees. This, in the language of the English courts, would be "unjust and unreasonable." In the language of our own cases it would be "contrary to public policy." The thought is the same.

Our own mode of expressing it is preferable, in this, that it suggests the reason on which the rule rests.

The judgment is affirmed.

———

COMMON CARRIER.—LIABILITY OF, IS THAT OF AN INSURER against all losses except those caused by the act of God, the public enemy, or the contributory negligence of the consignor: See note to *Richmond etc. R. R. Co.* v. *Benson*, 22 Am. St. Rep. 452.

COMMON CARRIER CANNOT BY CONTRACT EXEMPT HIMSELF FROM NEGLIGENCE.—A common carrier cannot, by any special contract, exempt himself from liability for loss occasioned by his negligence, and it makes no difference whether the contract provides for partial or limited exemption, or contemplates total exemption from liability: *Georgia etc. R. R. Co.* v. *Keener*, 93 Ga. 806; 44 Am. St. Rep. 197, and, note.

COMMON CARRIERS—LIMITATION OF LIABILITY.—A common carrier may, by contract, limit his common-law liability so far as is reasonable, but it is unreasonable to allow him to contract against his own negligence: *Davis* v. *Central etc. R. R. Co.*, 66 Vt. 240; 44 Am. St. Rep. 852, and note. Such a contract would violate the policy of the law: *Railway Co.* v. *Cravens*, 57 Ark. 112; 38 Am. St. Rep. 230, and note.

CARRIER IS NOT LIABLE FOR NOT EFFECTING INSURANCE: *Lancaster Mills* v. *Merchants' Cotton Press Co.*, 89 Tenn. 1; 24 Am. St. Rep. 586.

———

MILLER *v.* BAKER.

[166 PENNSYLVANIA STATE, 414.]

RESULTING TRUST IN LAND ARISES IN FAVOR OF WIFE, WHEN. If a farm is purchased for a wife with her money, upon an understanding between her and her husband that she shall receive title to it, and the deed is by mistake made to him without her knowledge, there is raised a resulting trust in favor of the wife, and the husband becomes a trustee of the legal title for her.

CESTUI QUE TRUST CAN DERIVE NO BENEFIT FROM LAPSE OF TIME, WHEN.—If the holder of a legal title, subject to a resulting trust, permits the *cestui que trust* to occupy and enjoy the land as owner, the latter can derive no benefit from the lapse of time.

RESULTING TRUSTS—HUSBAND AND WIFE—WIFE'S RIGHT NOT DEFEATED BY HER LACHES.—If a husband by mistake in a deed becomes the holder of the legal title to land in which his wife has a resulting trust by reason of her payment of the purchase money, and understanding that she should have title, his continuous recognition of his wife's title will defeat any claim by him on the ground of his wife's laches in asserting her equitable rights.

JUDGMENT CREDITOR, RIGHT OF, AS AGAINST EQUITABLE OWNER.—A judgment creditor is not entitled to the protection of a purchaser of the legal title against an equitable owner or his creditors, or to any advantage which his debtor had not.

RESULTING TRUST— HUSBAND AND WIFE— RIGHTS OF PURCHASER OF
LEGAL TITLE AT SHERIFF'S SALE AS AGAINST EQUITABLE OWNER.—
In case a husband by mistake in a deed becomes the holder of the legal
title to land in which his wife has a resulting trust arising from her
payment of the purchase money, a purchaser of the property at a
sheriff's sale under a judgment against the husband with notice of the
wife's equity takes no title as against the wife.

EJECTMENT.   It appeared from a former report of the case
(*Miller* v. *Baker*, 160 Pa. St. 172), that plaintiffs claimed title
as purchasers at a sheriff's sale under a judgment against
the defendant.   The defendant claimed that he was entitled
to possession in right of his wife; that the property had been
purchased with her money; and that the deed had been
made by the vendors to him through a mistake.   In each
case there was a verdict for the defendant in the trial court,
and the plaintiffs appealed.

*H. M. Dougan, M. L. A. McCrackens, B. L. McCrackens, and
James Q. McGiffen,* for the appellants.

*Boyd Crumrine, J. M. Garrison, J. I. Brownson, Jr., and E. E.
Crumrine,* for the appellees.

[419] McCOLLUM, J.   We reversed the former judgment in
this case because the [420] court below rejected the plaintiff's
offers to prove acts and declarations of William J. Baker inconsistent with and tending to discredit his testimony.   We
were then asked to reverse the judgment on the broader
ground that, upon the evidence in the case and the law
applicable to it, the court should have directed the jury to
find for the plaintiffs.   This, for reasons then stated, we
declined to do.   We thought the evidence was sufficient to
establish a resulting trust, and that the sixth section of the act
of April 22, 1856, was not applicable to the case of a *cestui que
trust* in possession.   We thought also that the plaintiffs being
purchasers at a sheriff's sale upon a judgment against the
trustee, and having notice of the trust, acquired such title
only as their debtor had and could enforce against the *cestui
que trust*.   This appeal invites us to reconsider these conclusions, and to hold that upon all the evidence in the case and
the law governing it the plaintiffs are entitled to recover the
land in dispute.   In accordance with their request, we have
carefully read and duly considered all the testimony with a
view to determine whether it is sufficient to authorize a finding
of the facts essential to the existence of a resulting trust.   It
occupies three hundred and eighty-eight pages of their paper-

book, and it would serve no useful purpose to insert it, or any portion of it, in this opinion. It relates principally to the ownership of the money with which the farm was purchased, to the understanding between the husband and wife in reference to the purchase, and to the alleged mistake in the deeds. We think it is clearly sufficient to warrant a finding that the farm was purchased for the wife and with her money upon an understanding between her and her husband that she should receive the title to it, and further, that the deeds were made to him without her knowledge, and by mistake. Two juries have found these facts, under careful and correct instructions in regard to the character of the evidence required to establish them. The facts, so found, raised a resulting trust in favor of the wife. By virtue of them she became the beneficial owner of the farm, and her husband became a trustee of the legal title for her.

We do not care to add any thing to what was said in our former opinion respecting the wife's possession of her farm, her husband's continued acknowledgment of her claim to it, and the relation of the act of April 22, 1856, to the case. It is clear [441] that, under the circumstances shown, the husband could not have successfully maintained that his wife's title was extinguished by her laches. Aside from the common-law rule that laches cannot be imputed to a married woman during coverture we have in this case his continuous recognition of his wife's title which alone would defeat any claim by him on this ground. In *Clark* v. *Trindle*, 52 Pa. St. 492, as in this case, there was a resulting trust arising from the payment of the purchase money, and it was sustained after the lapse of twenty-five years. In that case the heirs of the trustee brought ejectment against the widow of the *cestui que trust*, and she defended her possession on the ground that her husband paid the purchase money, and his mother, to whom the deed was made, was a mere trustee of the legal title for him. In *Douglass* v. *Lucas*, 63 Pa. St. 9, Sharswood, J., said: "There is great reason and justice in holding that when the holder of a legal title, subject to a resulting trust, permits the *cestui que trust* to occupy and enjoy the land as owner, that he shall derive no benefit from the lapse of time." But inasmuch as the plaintiffs appear to think they acquired by their purchase greater rights against the *cestui que trust* than their debtor had, a brief reference to some of our decisions on this point is deemed proper. Their position

in regard to the property in dispute is clearly and correctly
defined in the following excerpts from the opinion of Chief
Justice Gibson in *Reed's Appeal*, 13 Pa. St. 475: "If any
thing is settled by reason and authority, it is that a judgment
creditor is not entitled to the protection of a purchaser of the
legal title against an equitable owner or his creditors, or to
any advantage which his debtor had not. . . . . It has always been supposed that notice of a resulting trust or an
encumbrance is early enough at the sheriff's sale of the legal
title; but, if the judgment creditor had the immunity of a
purchaser, notice would then be too late to impair the value
of his security. A sheriff's vendee with notice buys exactly
what the judgment creditor can sell; and, if he can sell no
more than the interest of the debtor, it follows that he stands
in the place of the debtor": See, also, *Shryock* v. *Waggoner*,
28 Pa. St. 430; *Smith* v. *Tome*, 68 Pa. St. 158, and *McLaughlin* v. *Fulton*, 104 Pa. St. 161, to the same effect. We would
not have cited any of the long list of cases in which this
familiar principle has been recognized and enforced but for
the persistence of the plaintiffs in ignoring it.

422 We are not convinced of error in the rulings complained of in the third, fourth, and fifth specifications, or in
the instructions in regard to the effect of the acts and declarations of William J. Baker inconsistent with his testimony. It follows from these views that we overrule all the
specifications.

Judgment affirmed. ____

On the former hearing of this case (*Miller* v. *Baker*, 160 Pa. St. 172, 178),
McCollum, J., in rendering the opinion of the court, said: "The possession
by a husband and wife of the wife's land is referable to her title and the
marital relation. His occupancy of it results from and accords with his
relation to the owner, and it is not in any sense adverse to hers, nor, as
between them, will the mere continuance of such occupancy for any space
of time operate in equity, or by force of any statute, as an extinguishment or
bar to the assertion of her title. In such case her possession is the domi-
nating one, and as against him will protect her, although through his inatten-
tion and the mistakes of her vendors he is clothed with the bare legal title
to the property. In other words, in a situation such as we are considering,
her possession is sufficient to prevent the limitation from running in his
favor. If, after the deeds were recorded, and before the conveyance to her
of the title acquired by them, he had sold the land to a *bona fide* purchaser,
the latter would have taken a title unaffected by the trust. But the appellants are not such purchasers. They bought at a sheriff's sale upon a
judgment against the husband, and with notice of the wife's equity. They
have, therefore, his title only, and that, as we have seen, cannot prevail
against her."

HUSBAND AND WIFE—RESULTING TRUST.—A purchase of land by a husband with the money of his wife, taking the title in his own name, creates a resulting trust in favor of the wife: *Beam* v. *Bridgers*, 108 N. C. 276; 23 Am. St. Rep. 59, and note; *Fawcett* v. *Fawcett*, 85 Wis. 332; 39 Am. St. Rep. 844. As long as there is a continuing and subsisting equitable trust acknowledged or acted upon by the parties the statute of limitations does not apply. The statute of limitations does not run against claims between husband and wife. The statute of limitations does not begin to run in cases of express trusts until a repudiation of the trust. The trusts against which the statute of limitations does not run are those technical and continuing trusts not cognizable at law, and falling within the peculiar and exclusive jurisdiction of equity: *Fawcett* v. *Fawcett*, 85 Wis. 332; 39 Am. St. Rep. 844, and note. For an application of the doctrine of laches as applied to trusts see case last cited: *Seculovich* v. *Morton*, 101 Cal. 673; 40 Am. St. Rep. 106, and note; *Gutch* v. *Fosdick*, 48 N. J. Eq. 353; 27 Am. St. Rep. 473, and note; note to *Reynolds* v. *Sumner*, 9 Am. St. Rep. 530.

LEWEY *v.* FRICKE COKE COMPANY.

[166 PENNSYLVANIA STATE, 536.]

THE STATUTE OF LIMITATIONS BEGINS TO RUN, as a general rule, from the act done, but this rule has exceptions.

THE MISCHIEF WHICH THE STATUTE OF LIMITATIONS IS INTENDED TO REMEDY is delay in the assertion of a legal right which it is practicable to assert.

THE STATUTE OF LIMITATIONS DOES NOT BEGIN TO RUN AGAINST A PLAINTIFF, who has been kept in ignorance of his rights by fraudulent practices on the part of the defendant, until discovery of the fraud. The discovery of the fraud gives a new cause of action.

STATUTE OF LIMITATIONS.—COURTS OF EQUITY decline to apply the statute if plaintiff neither knew nor had reasonable means for knowing of the existence of a cause of action; but, if the cause of action was known, or might have been known by the exercise of vigilance in the use of means within reach, equity follows the law and applies the statute.

STATUTE OF LIMITATIONS—WRONGDOER.—MERE IGNORANCE will not prevent the running of the statute in equity any more than at law; but there is no reason, resting on general principles, why ignorance that is the result of the defendant's conduct, and not of the stupidity or negligence of the plaintiff, should not prevent the running of the statute in favor of the wrongdoer.

LAND IS SUSCEPTIBLE TO DIVISION INTO AS MANY ESTATES in fee simple as there are strata that make up the earth's crust, and courts will protect the owners of these separate estates from each other.

STATUTE OF LIMITATIONS—MINING COAL ON ANOTHER'S LAND.—The equitable rule that the statute should run only from discovery or a time when it might have been made should be applied by courts of law in an action of trespass to recover damages for the unlawful mining of coal in a lower stratum of another's land, especially where plaintiff's ignorance as to what was going on was due to the defendant's conduct, and was without fault of the plaintiff.

EQUITY AND LAW — COMPENSATION FOR COAL MINED AND TAKEN FROM ONE'S LAND.—In jurisdictions where equity is administered through the common-law forms of action, the plaintiff should not be turned out of a court of law in order to be admitted at the equity side of the same court. He may, therefore, in an action of trespass for the illegal mining of coal on his land, recover compensation in the same manner that he could on a bill for an account, though he might not be able to recover statutory damages.

THE STATUTE OF LIMITATIONS MAY BE AVAILABLE AS A DEFENSE, in an action of trespass for the illegal mining of coal upon one's land, as against the penal consequences of the trespass; but it is not available as a defense against payment for the coal actually taken and converted to defendant's use, and the jury should be so instructed.

THE STATUTE OF LIMITATIONS WILL RUN AGAINST A CLAIM FOR COMPENSATION FOR COAL unlawfully mined and taken from one's land from the time the existence of the claim was or might have been known to the plaintiff, the owner and occupier of the surface.

TRESPASS for illegal mining of coal. Plaintiff averred in his statement that the defendant had entered into and under the surface of his land, and mined and converted to its own use coal to the value of thirty thousand dollars. Plea, not guilty. The statute of limitations was also pleaded.

V. E. Williams, A. M. Sloan, W. A. Griffith, and Atkinson & Peoples, for the appellant.

James S. Moorhead and John B. Head, for the appellee.

[541] WILLIAMS, J. The legal question on which this appeal depends is beset with difficulty. The interests to be affected by it must increase in magnitude as the value of the minerals, in which this state abounds, increases. It is not directly ruled by any of our own cases, and we are at liberty not to treat it as a question of first impression. The facts are in dispute. The plaintiff is the owner in fee simple of a lot of land lying in the outskirts of the borough of Connellsville containing about one acre and a quarter. This lot is underlaid with coal which has not been severed from the surface by lease or sale, and which the plaintiff has made no effort to mine or remove. The defendant company owns a considerable body of coal lands in the same neighborhood [542] which adjoins and practically surrounds the plaintiff's land, and is engaged in mining and removing its coal through openings upon its own lands.

In 1884, in the progress of its mining operations, the defendant company made an opening or passageway through the plaintiff's coal under one corner of his lot, which was from seventy-five to one hundred feet in length, about six feet height, and eight to nine feet wide. The coal removed, in amounting to more than four thousand bushels, was brought to the surface through the defendant's pits or openings on its own lands and used or disposed of as its own. The plaintiff had no knowledge of the trespass upon him or the removal of his coal, and no means of knowledge within his reach. In 1891, some seven years after his coal was taken, as he alleges, he first became aware of his loss. In the following year he brought this action, and is met with the statute of limitations as a defense. The contention is that it began to run in 1884 when the coal was taken and had barred his remedy one year before he knew that a cause of action had accrued. The court below so ruled. The correctness of this ruling is the only question now to be considered. When did the statute begin to run? The general rule is, as stated by the learned trial judge, that it begins to run from the act done, but this is not of universal application. The statute makes certain exceptions. As to all persons who may be when the cause of action accrues " within the age of twenty-one years, *feme covert*, *non compos mentis*, imprisoned, or beyond sea," it is provided that the statute shall not begin to run until such disability ceases. In 1842 a supplementary statute restrained the running of the limitation still further so as to include a resident plaintiff laboring under no disability whatever, if the defendant debtor or wrongdoer should be beyond sea when the cause of action arose. As to such a plaintiff the running of the statute does not begin until the return of the debtor or trespasser to this country so that proceedings against him become possible. It is easy to see that the mischief which the statute was intended to remedy was delay in the assertion of a legal right which it was practicable to assert.

The remedy provided was a denial of process to one who had slumbered for six years, during which process was within his reach. The cases in which this denial would work a positive [543] and an apparent hardship, so far as they were foreseen by the lawmakers, were provided for by the exceptions to which we have referred and by the act of 1842. These have been extended by the courts so as to include other cases which, while not within the letter of the statute, were held to be within the spirit of the proviso. Thus it was held in *Hall* v. *Vandergrift*, 3 Binn. 374, that " It is the spirit of the statute of limitations to allow twenty-one years from the time that a person might make entry on land and support an action" before taking away his remedy. For this reason it was decided that it did not run against one who had a possibility of title but no present right of entry. Again, it was held that when the plaintiff had been kept in ignorance of his rights by fraudulent practices on the part of the defendant the statute did not begin to run against him until discovery of the fraud.

The earliest case I have found in which the courts of this state applied this doctrine in a common-law action in *Jones* v. *Reese*, found in 1 Smith's Laws, 80. The case was tried at circuit before Yates and Smith, justices. It appeared that Reese had sold a negro to Jones in 1786, alleging him to be a slave. The negro was in fact a free man, but had been kept in ignorance of it by the fraudulent practices of Reese. He discovered the fraud and his own freedom in 1801, and brought an action against Jones for the purpose of having his freedom established in a court of law, and of recovering damages for his deprivation of it. He recovered. Jones then brought an action against Reese to recover the price paid for the negro some sixteen years before, and for damages. Reese set up the statute of limitations. The court refused to sustain the plea, giving as a reason therefor that " whenever there is a fraud the act of limitations is no plea unless the fraud be discovered within the time"; that is, within the time fixed by the statute, or six years before suit brought. To make this entirely clear it was added that "while the slavery of the negro was uncontested the plaintiff had no ground to suppose he had been injured or deceived, but when he obtained his liberty in a due course of law the plaintiff's cause of action accrued against the defendants." This rule was applied in an action of ejectment in *Thompson* v. *Smith*, 7 Serg. & R. 209, 10 Am. Dec. 453, and was stated by Tilghman, C. J., at page 214, as follows: "After the [544] discovery of the fraud a man has a right to avail himself of the statute; but so long as the fraud is unknown, pending the concealment of the fraud, the statute ought not to run. The discovery of the fraud gives a new cause of action." This rule has long been applied in equity, where two good reasons are given for it. The first is that it would be inequitable to permit a defendant to profit by his own fraud. The other is that one who cannot assert his right, because the necessary knowledge is improperly kept from him, is not within the mischief the statute was intended to remedy, but is within the spirit of the proviso that restrains its operation. Courts of equity go a step farther still, and decline to apply the statute where the plaintiff neither knew, nor had reasonable means for knowing, of the existence of a cause of action. But if the cause of action be known, or might have been known by the exercise of vigilance in the use of means within reach, equity follows the law, and applies the statute: *Hamilton* v. *Hamilton*, 18 Pa. St. 20; 55 Am. Dec. 585; *Neely's Appeal*, 85 Pa. St. 387. Mere ignorance will not prevent the running of the statute in equity any more than at law; but there is no reason, resting on general principles, why ignorance that is the result of the defendant's conduct, and not of the stupidity or negligence of the plaintiff, should not prevent the running of the statute in favor of the wrongdoer. It seems to be the general doctrine in courts of law that the plaintiff is bound to know of an invasion of the surface of his close. The fact that his land is a forest and that the defendant goes into the interior to trespass by the cutting of timber does not relieve against its operation. What is plainly visible he must see at his peril, unless by actual fraud his attention is diverted and his vigilance put to sleep. But ought this rule to extend to a subterranean trespass? The surface is visible and accessible. The owner may know of its condition without trespassing on others, and for that reason he is bound to know. The interior of the earth is invisible and inaccessible to the owner of the surface unless he is engaged in mining operations upon his own land; and then he can reach no part of his own coal stratum except that which he is actually removing. If an adjoining landowner reaches the plaintiff's coal through subterranean ways that reach the surface on his own land and are under his actual control, the vigilance the [545] law requires of the plaintiff upon the surface is powerless to detect the invasion by his neighbor of the coal one hundred feet under the surface.

The case at bar affords an excellent illustration of ignorance due to the defendant's conduct and without fault on the part of the plaintiff The defendant was mining its own coal through its own shafts or drifts opened on its own lands. In the course of its operations and for its own convenience it pushed an entry or passage under the plaintiff's lands and appropriated the coal removed therefrom. It was bound to

know its own lines and keep within them. If by mistake
or for any other reason it did invade the mineral estate of
another and remove and appropriate the coal therefrom, good
conscience required that it should disclose the fact and pay
for the coal taken. Its failure to do this is in its effects a
fraud upon the injured owner, and, if he has no knowledge
of the trespass and no means of knowledge, such a fraud,
whether it be called constructive or actual, should protect
him from the running of the statute. We have felt constrained to recognize the susceptibility of land to division
into as many estates in fee simple as there are strata that
make up the earth's crust, and to protect the owners of these
separate estates from each other. Thus the possession of one
who has a title to the surface only does not extend to or
affect any subjacent estate. The occupancy of a coal stratum
for more than twenty-one years will not give title to the surface above it or the oil or gas stratum below it. The law
does not require impossibilities. It recognizes natural conditions, and the immutability of natural laws. The owner of
the surface cannot see, and, because he cannot see, the law
does not require him to take notice of what goes on in the
subterranean estates below him with which he has no communication through openings within his inclosures or under
his control. On the other hand, one who is in possession of
a lower stratum is not bound to know, nor can he be affected
by, what is going on upon the surface above him, or in a still
lower estate under his feet. The owner of each stratum
must, however, take notice of what affects his own estate, so
far as he is in possession of or has access to it. In the case
before us no severance of the coal from the surface has taken
place. The title of the plaintiff extends from the surface to
the center; but actual possession [546] is confined to the surface. Upon the surface he must be held to know all that the
most careful observation by himself and his employees could
reveal, unless his ignorance is induced by the fraudulent
conduct of the wrongdoer. But in the coal veins deep down
in the earth he cannot see. Neither in person nor by his servants or employees can he explore their recesses in search
for an intruder. If an adjoining owner goes beyond his own
boundaries in the course of his mining operations the owner
on whom he enters has no means of knowledge within his
reach. Nothing short of an accurate survey of the interior of
his neighbors' mines would enable him to ascertain the fact.

This would require the services of a competent mining engineer and his assistants inside the mines of another, which he would have no right to insist upon.   To require an owner under such circumstances to take notice of a trespass upon his underlying coal at the time it takes place is to require an impossibility; and to hold that the statute begins to run at the date of the trespass is in most cases to take away the remedy of the injured party before he can know that an injury has been done him.   A result so absurd and so unjust ought not to be possible.

In the English courts this question has arisen quite frequently.   The old rule applied in the courts of law was that the statute might be successfully pleaded as running from the date of the trespass.   In the courts of equity where an account for the coal that has been taken was asked for it was applied only from the discovery of the trespass: McSwinny on Mines, 543; see, also, *Hovenden* v. *Lord Armsley*, 2 Schoales & L. 634. If, after discovery, or the happening of any circumstance calculated to put the owner on notice, he slept on his right till the statutory period had expired, he was held bound by the statute in equity precisely as he would have been at law.   If he knew, or if by the exercise of reasonable care he might have known, of the trespass, the statute ran from the discovery, or the time when discovery could have been made: Bainbridge on Mines, 515, 516.   It was against good conscience to permit one who had taken the property of another without the owner's knowledge, and who had failed to disclose or to account for what he had taken, to avail himself of the statute while the owner remained in ignorance of his loss.   When compensation was sought by means of a bill for an account it was held that [547] the statute began to run at the time of discovery regardless of the time of taking.   The same question was also encountered in actions to recover for injuries done on the surface by subsidence due to the withdrawal of support.   When the action was trespass it was generally held that the statute ran from the date of the removal of the support which was the trespass to which the injury was due; but when the action was case the subsidence was treated as the consequence of the wrongful removal of the coal or other underlying stratum and the damages suffered as consequential.   The happening of the injury was upon this ground held to give a cause of action against which the statute would run only from its date.   The removal of the supports might not be known to, or be discoverable by, the owner of the surface until the subsidence revealed it; and unless the injury consequential to the trespass could be treated as creating a cause of action, in most cases redress for a substantial injury would be denied altogether: *Backhouse* v. *Bonomi*, 34 L. J. Q. B. 181; 9 H. L. Cas. 503; *Smith* v. *Thackerah*, L. R. 1 C. P. 566; 15 Am. Law Reg. (N. S., vol. 5) 761, and note. The reason for the distinction exists in the nature of things. The owner of land may be present by himself or his servants on the surface of his possessions no matter how extensive they may be. He is for this reason held to be constructively present wherever his title extends. He cannot be present in the interior of the earth. No amount of vigilance will enable him to detect the approach of a trespasser who may be working his way through the coal seams underlying adjoining lands. His senses cannot inform him of the encroachment by such trespasser upon the coal that is hidden in the rocks under his feet. He cannot reasonably be held to be constructively present where his presence is in the nature of things impossible. He must learn of such a trespass by other means than such as are within his own control, and until these come within his reach he is necessarily ignorant of his loss. He cannot reasonably be required to act until knowledge that action is needed is possible to him. We are disposed to hold, therefore, that the statute runs against an injury committed in or to a lower stratum from the time of actual discovery or the time when discovery was reasonably possible. But it is enough for the purposes of this case to hold that inasmuch as equity is administered in this state through [548] the common-law forms of action, the plaintiff need not be turned out of a court of law in order to be admitted at the equity side of the same court. He may not be entitled to statutory damages, but he is entitled to compensation in the same manner that he would have been on a bill for an account. For this purpose the equitable rule that the statute shall run only from discovery, or a time when discovery might have been made, should be applied by courts of law. It follows that the judgment in this case must be reversed, and a new trial had, in which the jury should be instructed that while the statute may be available as against the penal consequences of the trespass, it is not available as a defense against payment for the coal actually taken and converted to the use of the defendant. The statute will run against a claim for compensation from the time the existence of the claim was, or might have been, known to the plaintiff, the owner and occupier of the surface.

The judgment is reversed, and a *venire facias de novo* awarded.

MITCHELL, J., dissents.

THE STATUTE OF LIMITATIONS begins to run when the cause of action accrues, not from the time the knowledge of the fact comes to the plaintiff: See note to *Lattin* v. *Gillette*, 29 Am. St. Rep. 120. The only exception to the general rule that a party's want of knowledge does not prevent the running of the statute against an action that has accrued in his favor is where there has been fraud or concealment on the part of the defendant: *State* v. *Standard Oil Co.*, 49 Ohio St. 137; 34 Am. St. Rep. 541, and note. The statute begins to run from the discovery of the fraud, or from the time when it ought to have been discovered by the exercise of proper diligence and inquiry: See note to *Connecticut Mut. Life Ins. Co.* v. *Smith*, 38 Am. St. Rep. 671; *Jacobs* v. *Snyder*, 76 Iowa, 522; 14 Am. St. Rep. 235. The plaintiff must, however, show that he used due diligence to detect the fraud complained of, and should state when he discovered it, how the discovery was made, and why it was not made sooner: *Lataillade* v. *Orena*, 91 Cal. 565; 25 Am. St. Rep. 219, and note. Fraud will be deemed to have been discovered when such facts are known, either actually or constructively, as amount to knowledge or which would naturally suggest such inquiries as, if followed up, would lead to such knowledge: *Wright* v. *Davis*, 28 Neb. 479; 26 Am. St. Rep. 347. If a party has, by his fraudulent acts, attempted to obtain an unconscientious advantage by the lapse of time, he will not be allowed to avail himself of the statute in a court of equity: See note to *Thorndike* v. *Thorndike*, 142 Ill. 450; 34 Am. St. Rep. 92. The statute does not protect a defendant who has fraudulently concealed the plaintiff's cause of action: See monographic note to *Snodgrass* v. *Branch Bank*, 60 Am. Dec. 513, discussing fraud at law as preventing the operation of the statute of limitations; but the burden is upon the party who relies upon the fraudulent concealment of a cause of action to take it out of the operation of the statute: *Wood* v. *Williams*, 142 Ill. 269; 34 Am. St. Rep. 79, and note.

ACTIONS—LAW AND EQUITY.—Equitable relief may be granted in a legal action in those states in which law and equity are administered by the same tribunal: See note to *Kirkwood* v. *First Nat. Bank*, 42 Am. St. Rep. 692.

COAL MINING — OWNERSHIP IN LAND—STRATA.—"The mining of coal and other minerals is constantly developing new questions. Formerly a man who owned the surface owned it to the center of the earth. Now the surface of the land may be separated from the different strata underneath it, and there may be as many different owners as there are strata": *Chartiers Block Coal Co.* v. *Mellon*, 152 Pa. St. 286; 34 Am. St. Rep. 645, 648; *Lillibridge* v. *Lackawanna Coal Co.*, 143 Pa. St. 293; 24 Am. St. Rep. 544, and monographic note thereto showing the severability of title to the surface of land and minerals therein. A locator working subterraneously into the dip of the vein belonging to another is a trespasser, and liable to an action for taking ore: See monographic note to *McClintock* v. *Bryden*, 63 Am. Dec. 109, on the right to mine.

RINER *v.* RINER.

[166 PENNSYLVANIA STATE, 617.]

A CAUSE OF ACTION DOES NOT EXIST, unless there is a person in existence capable of suing, or of being sued.

LIMITATIONS OF ACTIONS IN CASE OF DEATH.—If no cause of action accrued prior to the death of the party entitled, the statute of limitations does not commence to run until administration is granted.

LIMITATIONS OF ACTIONS—RECEIVING MONEY OF INTESTATE AFTER HIS DEATH.—When one receives money belonging to the estate of an intestate after his death, and before administration granted, the statute of limitations does not run from the date of receiving the money, but from the grant of administration.

LIMITATION OF ACTION BROUGHT BY AN ADMINISTRATOR TO RECOVER MONEY PAID by an insurance company to a person who had no insurable interest in the life of plaintiff's intestate begins to run only from the date of the grant of letters of administration to the plaintiff, and the right of action is not defeated by gross laches in taking out administration.

INSURANCE — ACTION BY ADMINISTRATOR TO RECOVER MONEY PAID TO ONE HAVING NO INSURABLE INTEREST—JUDGMENT.—In an action by an administrator to recover money paid, before grant of administration, by an insurance company, to a nephew who was named as a beneficiary in a policy of insurance upon the life of his aunt, and who paid all the premiums and assessments due under the policy, judgment should be rendered in favor of the plaintiff for the full amount so paid by the company, less such premiums and assessments, with legal interest from the date of payment.

ASSUMPSIT to recover insurance money alleged to have been wrongfully paid to defendant. It appeared that on November 11, 1879, Rebecca Riner had her life insured for three thousand dollars, making George Riner, her nephew by marriage, beneficiary in the policy. He paid all the fees, charges, and assessments. On November 6, 1880, Rebecca Riner died, and, in the following March, George Riner received two thousand one hundred and seventy-one hundred dollars and twelve cents from the insurance company in full payment of the policy. The deceased left surviving her a husband and seven children, all over age. On August 15, 1887, the plaintiff took out letters of administration on the estate. On December 20, 1886, George Riner died, and on August 15, 1887, the defendant was appointed his administrator. This suit was brought on August 22, 1889, eight years and four months after payment of the insurance money. There was a verdict and judgment for plaintiff for three thousand five hundred and seventy-six dollars and sixteen cents, being the amount received by George Riner, less the premiums, assessments, etc., paid by him, with lawful interest thereon from April 11, 1881.   The defendant appealed.

J. W. Moyer and J. W. Ryon, for the appellant.

A. W. Schalck and Nicholas Heblich, for the appellee.

621 GREEN, J.   After a most attentive study of the very able argument of the learned counsel for the appellant we feel obliged to say that we regard both the questions discussed on this appeal as settled and controlled by our previous decisions. *Marsteller* v. *Marsteller*, 93 Pa. St. 350, decided that, if no cause of action accrued prior to the death of the party entitled, the statute of limitations did not commence to run until administration was granted.   In the opinion Mr. Justice Trunkey said: " A cause of action does not exist, unless there be a person in existence capable of suing or of being sued.   When one receives money belonging to the estate of an intestate, after his death, and before administration granted, the statute runs not from the date of the receipt, but from the grant of administration."   The decision was put upon this broad ground and not upon the special facts of that case.   In *Amole's Appeal*, 115 Pa. St. 356, we again affirmed this doctrine, and in other cases before and since, and the same rule is held by the English courts: *Murray* v. *East India Co.*, 5 Barn. & Ald. 204.   In this case it was not possible that any right of action could have accrued during the life of Rebecca Riner, nor indeed until after the money was received by George Riner.   Hence, when the cause of action did accrue, it could only be to her administrator.

It must be conceded that there was gross laches in taking out administration, but that circumstance does not seem sufficient, under the authorities, to defeat the right of action.

We make this decision with the greatest reluctance and only by the sheer force of our prior rulings.   But it is intolerable that there shall be a right of action continuing for an indefinite time simply because those who are entitled to take out administration neglect or refuse to do so, and it is to be hoped that the legislature will grant relief by extending the statute of limitations to such cases and providing that it shall commence to run from the death of the decedent.   This will give six years in which to take out letters before the claim will be barred, and that length of time is surely enough.

On the subject of the illegality of the contract our decisions in numerous cases, beginning with *Gilbert* v. *Moose*, 104 Pa.

St. 74, 49 Am. Rep. 570, and followed by *Downey* v. *Hoffer,*
110 Pa. St. 109, *Ruth* v. [622] *Katterman,* 112 Pa. St. 251, and
many other cases, leave us no alternative but the affirmation
of the judgment of the court below, except the reversal of all
of them.   This we are unwilling to do.

Judgment affirmed.

STATUTES OF LIMITATION—ADMINISTRATION.—A CAUSE OF ACTION cannot be said to have accrued until an action can be instituted thereon: *City
of Fort Wayne* v. *Hamilton,* 132 Ind. 487; 32 Am. St. Rep. 263.   Statutes
of limitation begin to run at the time when a cause of action accrues, and
there must be some person or persons capable of suing or being sued upon
the claim to be affected by the statute, in order that it may then begin to
run: See note to *Miller* v. *Surls,* 65 Am. Dec. 594.   Therefore, when a
person in favor of or against whom a cause of action may exist dies before
the cause of action accrues, the statute will not begin to run before an
administrator of his estate is appointed; for until that time there is no one to
sue on a claim in favor of the deceased, or be sued on a claim against him.
Hence the cause of action cannot accrue until that time: See monographic
note to *Miller* v. *Surls,* 65 Am. Dec. 595, on the statute of limitations against
estate of decedent before administration granted.

CASES

IN THE

SUPREME COURT

OF

TENNESSEE.

BRADLEY *v.* CARNES.

[94 TENNESSEE, 27.]

DEVISE—ESTATE IN FEE OR FOR LIFE.—If the first taker under a will is
given an estate in fee or for life, coupled with an unlimited power of
diposition, the fee or absolute estate vests in the first taker, and any
limitation over is void. If the power is dependent upon a contingency,
or definitely qualified, the estate of the first taker is limited to life,
and the remainder over takes effect.

DEVISE—WORDS CREATING ESTATE IN FEE.—Under the will of a husband
bequeathing all of his property to his widow "for her special comfort, benefit, and support," with power to sell and convey the land
devised, "if she thinks it advisable," and, "if any thing remains at
her death, it shall go to" specified remaindermen, the widow takes an
absolute estate in fee, with unlimited power of disposition, and the
limitation over to the remaindermen is void, and of no effect.

Lucky & Sanford, for the complainants.

Green & Shields, W. M. Cocke, and W. L. Ledgerwood, for
the defendants.

28 WILKES, J. The question before the court in this case
is the proper construction of the will of G. W. Carnes, especially the third clause of the same. This item is as follows:
"I give and bequeath to my wife, Sarah J. Carnes, all the
remaining property, both personal and real, for her special
comfort, benefit, and support. If she thinks it advisable she
may sell and convey the right of the land. If any thing
remains at her death it shall go into the hands of my executor, and shall and divide equally in half of the proceeds
between my wife's, Sarah J. Carnes, brothers and sisters,
and the other half shall be divided equally between my own,

G. W. Carnes, brothers and sisters, with the exception of the heirs of Martha B. Hill, and I will them one dollar, and no more."

As thus copied into the transcript the language of the third clause is quite obscure, but counsel have treated the clause as though it read as follows: " If any thing remains at her death, it shall go into the hands of my executor [who shall sell the same], and shall divide equally [one] half of the proceeds between my wife's, Sarah J. Carnes, brothers and sisters, and the other half shall be divided equally between my own, G. W. Carnes, brothers and sisters, with the exception of the heirs of [29] Martha B. Hill, and I will them one dollar, and no more."

The obscurity in the clause as copied into the transcript doubtless arises from some clerical error in copying, and the clause will therefore be considered as counsel have treated it, which is doubtless the true copy of the clause, as is shown in the final decree construing the clause in the court below. The other parts of the will are not material in this investigation.

The chancellor held that Sarah J. Carnes, the wife, took an absolute estate in all the property, both real and personal, devised in the clause of the will to her, and that the devise over was void and of no effect, and that the property, upon the death of said Sarah J., descended to her heirs, to the exclusion of the heirs of the husband, G. W. Carnes.

A. C. Carnes, one of the defendants, and a brother of the testator, G. W. Carnes, appealed, and it is now insisted that the chancellor erred in construing the clause as he did.

G. W. Carnes, the testator, died in 1874, leaving his widow, Sarah J., but no children. Immediately upon his death Sarah J. went.into possession of the land and personal property given to her by the will, used it as her own, conveyed a part of the real estate devised, purchased other lands, and died intestate in March, 1892, leaving no children.

Complainants are the brothers and sisters of Sarah J. Carnes and their descendants, while defendants are [30] the brothers and sisters of George W. Carnes and their descendants.

There is no difference between counsel as to the general principles of the law applying to this clause in the will, but, like the cases in which the class doctrine is involved, the difficulty is in deciding whether this case falls within the

rule which gives the first taker an absolute estate and renders the remainder inoperative and void.

The general principle is tersely stated as follows: If the
first taker is given an estate in fee or for life, coupled with
an unlimited power of disposition, the fee or absolute estate
vests in the first taker, and the limitation over is void. If
the power is dependent upon a contingency, or if the power
be definitely qualified, the estate of the first taker is limited
to life, and the remainder over takes effect.

Under the first head may be found a large number of cases,
of which some are: *Smith* v. *Bell,* Mart. & Y. 302; 17 Am.
Dec. 798; *David* v. *Bridgeman,* 2 Yerg. 558; *Davis* v. *Richardson,* 10 Yerg. 290; 31 Am. Dec. 581; *Bean* v. *Myers,* 1 Cold.
227; *Davis* v. *Williams,* 85 Tenn. 651; *Troup* v. *Hart,* 7 Baxt.
188; *Turner* v. *Durham,* 12 Lea, 316.

The principle underlying these cases is that, in order to
constitute a valid remainder or executory devise, the first
taker must not be given power to defeat and extinguish it by
sale or otherwise at his will and pleasure. It is held that
this unlimited power of disposition must be given by the
will, and [31] cannot arise as a mere incident to the estate
granted: *Booker* v. *Booker,* 5 Humph. 507; *Brown* v. *Hunt,*
12 Heisk. 409; *Read* v. *Watkins,* 11 Lea, 161.

Still, the power of disposition may be given not only in
express words, but also by words necessarily implying such
power: *Sevier* v. *Brown,* 2 Swan, 112, 116; *Howard* v. *Carusi,*
109 U. S. 725; *Jones* v. *Bacon,* 68 Me. 34; 28 Am. Rep. 1;
Ballentine v. *Spear,* 2 Baxt. 273. The other class of cases is
illustrated in *Deadrick* v. *Armour,* 10 Humph. 588; *Pillow* v.
Rye, 1 Swan, 185; *Downing* v. *Johnson,* 5 Coldw. 229; *Mc-
Gavock* v. *Pugsley,* 1 Tenn. Ch. 410; 12 Heisk. 689; *Pool* v.
Pool, 10 Lea, 486; *Jourolmon* v. *Massengale,* 86 Tenn. 81.

In all the cases, whether the will expressly gives a life
estate or simply uses words implying such limited estate,
the controlling question is, Does the will give an unlimited
or only a contingent and modified power of disposition to
the first taker?

In the case of *Deadrick* v. *Armour,* 10 Humph. 588–594,
the conveyance was to a trustee for a married woman, and the
power was to sell, use, and dispose of it as she may think
fit, but by and with the consent of the trustee.

In *Pillow* v. *Rye,* 1 Swan, 185, the gift was of the use of the
property, that is, its rents and profits, but, if for any cause it

became necessary for her ease and comfort to use any portion of the principal, then it should be done. The court held [32] that the power in this case was contingent upon its becoming necessary for her ease and comfort.

In *Downing* v. *Johnson*, 5 Cold. 229, it was held that the life tenant had the right to consume the corpus of the estate, except the land, if her support and maintenance, in her discretion, require it, and yet the devise over the "balance" of property on hand at her death was good.

In *McGavock* v. *Pugsley*, 1 Tenn. Ch. 411, 12 Heisk. 689, the authority to sell was for the convenience and support of the life tenant "and our two daughters," and the chancellor held that the power of disposition was limited, and hence the limitation over was good.

With these illustrations of the rule before us it only remains to determine whether the power of disposition in Mrs. Carnes was unlimited. The property was willed to her for her special comfort, benefit, and support, "and, if she think it advisable, she may sell and convey the right of the land." This is equivalent to saying she may sell and convey if she wishes or wills to do so. If she had disposed of the land in her lifetime can it be doubted that the purchaser would have taken a good title? The language of the devise over is: "If any thing remains at her death it shall go," etc. This must necessarily mean that during her life she could have consumed and disposed of it all.

In this case the gift is of a fee, and the words "for her special comfort, benefit, and support," cannot [33] be held to curtail or limit such estate. It is not a case of a life estate with power of disposition, in which, it may be, the rule will be more strictly applied, as is said in *David* v. *Bridgeman*, 2 Yerg. 576, note. Her power of disposition does not depend on the concurrence of a trustee, as in *Deadrick* v. *Armour*, 10 Humph. 588. Nor is the power contingent upon its becoming necessary for her ease and comfort, as in *Pillow* v. *Rye*, 1 Swan, 185; nor upon its being required for her support and maintenance, as in *Downing* v. *Johnson*, 5 Cold. 229; nor upon the convenience and support of the life tenant and her daughters, as in *McGavock* v. *Pugsley*, 1 Tenn. Ch. 411. But the power is unlimited, and to be exercised whenever she deems it advisable.

We are of opinion the power of disposition was unlimited in the first taker, and, this being so, the remainder over was inconsistent with it, and void, and the estate of Mrs. Carnes was absolute, and descended on her death to her heirs, and the decree of the chancellor is affirmed, with costs.

ESTATES—REMAINDER LIMITED UPON ESTATE FOR LIFE WITH POWER OF SALE.—A power of sale added to a life estate does not raise the estate to a fee. Hence, although a will creates a life estate with power to sell and convey the fee, it may at the same time limit a remainder after the termination of the life estate: *Ducker* v. *Burnham*, 146 Ill. 9; 37 Am. St. Rep. 135. But in *Bowen* v. *Bowen*, 87 Va. 438, 24 Am. St. Rep. 664, and *Combs* v. *Combs*, 67 Md. 11, 1 Am. St. Rep. 359, it was held that when a will gives the legatee therein an estate for life, with power to sell and to possess and enjoy it during life as if she enjoyed a fee-simple estate therein with remainder to certain specified remaindermen, the legatee takes an estate in fee simple absolute, and the remainder over is void for repugnancy. The cases on this subject are collected in the note to the latter case.

DEVISE TO WIFE—CONSTRUCTION OF.—If a testator gives and devises all his property to his wife, "to her use and behoof forever," but provides that if any of such property shall not be expended by her during her lifetime it shall be disposed of in a manner designated in the will, it does not vest the property absolutely, but merely confers on her a right to use it for her support and to dispose of it for that purpose, leaving whatever she has not so disposed of to vest after her death in the persons provided in the will: *Chase* v. *Ladd*, 153 Mass. 126; 25 Am. St. Rep. 614, and note; *Ken* v. *Morrison*, 153 Mass. 137; 25 Am. St. Rep. 616; to the same effect see *Taylor* v. *Bell*, 158 Pa. St. 651; 38 Am. St. Rep. 857, and note. See, also, the note to *Larsen* v. *Johnson*, 23 Am. St. Rep. 409.

SHIELDS *v.* CLIFTON HILL LAND COMPANY.

[94 TENNESSEE, 123.]

CORPORATIONS—PERSONAL LIABILITY OF PROMOTERS.—A complaint simply alleging that the charter of a corporation is void because defectively acknowledged, and that the promoters of the corporation are personally liable on its contract, is insufficient to charge them personally on any other ground, such as that of a partnership liability antecedent to the attempted incorporation.

CORPORATIONS—PERSONAL LIABILITY OF PROMOTERS.—If land is purchased in the name of a corporation whose charter is invalid because defectively acknowledged, and if the purchase money notes are signed by a person described as president of such corporation, although no formal organization or election of officers has at that time been made, such president or the other promoters of the corporation are not personally liable for such notes, especially when the corporation at its first regular meeting has approved the purchase, and the vendor has recognized the corporation as the purchaser in foreclosure proceedings.

CORPORATIONS—LIABILITY OF PROMOTERS.—Persons assuming to act under a corporate charter, invalid because some positive requirement of the law has not been complied with, are liable as individuals for all debts contracted by them in the name of the corporation.

CONSTITUTIONAL LAW—IMPAIRMENT OF CONTRACTS.—REMEDIAL STATUTES, though of a retrospective nature, are valid, provided they do not impair contracts or disturb absolute vested rights, and only go to confirm rights already existing and in furtherance of the remedy by curing defects, and adding to the means of enforcing existing obligations.

CONSTITUTIONAL LAW.—PARTIES HAVE NO VESTED RIGHT IN A RULE OF LAW which gives them an inequitable advantage over another. Such rule may therefore be repealed, and the advantage thereby taken away.

CORPORATIONS.—LEGISLATIVE RATIFICATION of the acts of an invalid corporation may not only legalize the existence of the corporation, and authorize it to act in a corporate capacity thereafter, but may also cure the illegality of corporate acts performed before the act of ratification was passed, and render such acts as valid as if authority to perform them had been previously granted by the legislature.

CORPORATIONS—STATUTES LEGALIZING EXISTENCE OF—IMPAIRMENT OF CONTRACTS.—A statute ratifying the acts and legalizing the existence of a corporation illegally organized, thereby defeating the personal liability of the incorporators as to a contract entered into with the corporation before its existence is thus legalized, does not impair any contract obligation of the parties to such contract.

CONSTITUTIONAL LAW — IMPAIRMENT OF CONTRACTS. — A statute which facilitates the intention of the parties to a contract by giving it validity never impairs its obligation nor divests nor impairs any vested rights thereunder.

CORPORATIONS—ESTOPPEL OF CREDITORS TO DENY LIABILITY OF.—Creditors of a defectively organized corporation who have sold it land and taken its purchase money notes therefor are estopped from denying its liability, and from holding the incorporators personally liable on such notes, if, for more than five years, and until after the corporate existence and contracts have been legalized by statute, such creditors have recognized the notes as corporate obligations by attempting to enforce them against the corporation.

CORPORATIONS—STOCK AS TRUST FUND.—The capital stock of a corporation is a trust fund for the payment of corporate debts, and, in case of the insolvency of the corporation, subscribers are liable to corporate creditors for unpaid subscriptions, so far as required for the satisfaction of corporate liabilities.

CORPORATIONS—STOCK AS TRUST FUND.—Under the Tennessee statute all unpaid corporate stock, whenever subscribed, is a trust fund for the payment of all corporate debts, whether created before or subsequent to such stock subscriptions.

CORPORATIONS—CONTRACTS OF—PRESUMPTION.—A contract whereby a corporation receives needed property in the payment of stock subscription is presumed, in the first instance, to be valid and binding upon all parties concerned, and must stand as made, and operate as intended, until impeached by appropriate pleading and proof.

J. T. & J. K. Shields, White & Martin, and Pickle & Turner, for the complainants.

Andrews & Barton, Watkins & Bogle, Cook, Frazier & Swaney, Barr & McAdoo, and Neil W. Caruthers, for the defendants.

[SUP]125[/SUP] CALDWELL, J.   This is a suit by vendors of real estate
to collect balance of purchase money remaining unpaid
after enforcement of vendors' lien, by resale of the land and
application of proceeds.

On February 3, 1887, Mrs. Anna N. Watkins, a widow lady,
and her daughter, Miss Alice M. Watkins, in consideration of
$1,000 to them paid, executed to Charles A. Lyerly, presi-
dent of the East End Land Company, an option on their
farm of 190 acres of land, near Chattanooga, [SUP]126[/SUP] Tennessee.
By the terms of the option the ladies bound themselves to
execute to said Lyerly, "or his indorsee" of the option, a
warranty deed to said land, if said Lyerly "or his indorsee"
should, within twenty-five days thereafter, pay to them,
$35,000 in cash, and, further, execute to them five several
promissory notes for $18,000 each, due respectively at one,
two, three, four, and five years, "with interest from date at
six per cent, payable semiannually, and secured by a vendors' lien on the land."

On February 28th (the day the option expired) the directors of the East End Land Company, in regular meeting,
decided that their company would not purchase the land,
and, upon motion regularly made and carried, directed that
the option "be transferred to another company, or purchasers," preferring the stockholders of the East End Land Company.

On the same day Charles A. Lyerly paid to J. A. Caldwell,
agent and attorney for the vendors, $8,500, as a part of the
·cash payment for the land.   A few days later, on March 7,
1887, he made a still larger payment to the same person, and
ten days thereafter he paid the balance, taking a receipt in
the words and figures following:

"$10,350.00.   Received of Chas. A. Lyerly, ten thousand
three hundred and fifty dollars ($10,350), balance cash pay-
ment on his purchase of our Oakland farm in Ninth and
Seventeenth Districts, upon the [SUP]127[/SUP] terms and conditions
mentioned in our contract, dated fifth (5) February, 1887.
Deed to be made as therein stipulated, upon the request of
said Lyerly or his assignee.   This the seventeenth of March,
1887.   [SIGNED]   MRS. A. N. WATKINS,
                    "ALICE M. WATKINS,
                    "By J. A. Caldwell, Agent."

On the day this last payment was made the persons who
had decided to organize "another company" to purchase the

land, and who had furnished Lyerly the money with which to make the cash payment of $35,000, procured the same Mr. Caldwell to draft a charter for such other company, the latter to be known as the Clifton Hill Land Company. The charter was drawn as desired and signed by six incorporators on that day. It was acknowledged on March 22, 1887, recorded March 24, 1887, filed for registration with the secretary of state March 28, 1887, and thereafter finally registered in the register's office of Hamilton county, where the corporation was to have its chief business office, on March 30, 1887.

Charles A. Lyerly, the owner of the option, assigned or transferred it to the Clifton Hill Land Company, and on the fourteenth day of April, 1887, the vendors, in pursuance of the terms of the option, executed a deed, whereby they conveyed the land to the said company as his "indorsee" or "assignee." The notes were made to run from the first day of March, 1887, though dated April 14, 1887. Except [128] as to date of maturity, the notes were the same. The one maturing first is in the following words:

"CHATTANOOGA, TENN., April 14, 1887.

"On first March, 1888, next after date, we promise to pay to Mrs. Anna N. Watkins and Miss Alice M. Watkins, or order, eighteen thousand dollars, value received, with interest at 6 per cent per annum from March 1, 1887, payable semiannually.

"This note is given for part consideration for and its payment is secured by a vendors' lien on the following real estate . . . . described in deed of this date. If necessary to resort to law to enforce the payment of this note or protect the security for its payment, we agree to pay all costs of necessary litigation, together with a reasonable attorney's fee.

"$18,000.00.   [SIGNED]   E. WATKINS,
"President Clifton Hill Land Company."

Mr. E. Watkins, whose name appears upon the notes, was one of the incorporators, and it was understood between him and his associates that he should be the president of the company though no organization was in fact effected by the election of officers until the 9th of June, 1887, at which time he was elected president.

E. Scott was elected secretary and treasurer of the Clifton Hill Land Company at the same time, and thereafter, in September and November, he, as such officer, paid to the vendors $2,700, the first semiannual interest [129] on said five purchase money notes. These payments were made to J. A. Caldwell, and receipted for by him as agent and attorney.

On April 9, 1889, the principal of two of the purchase money notes being then due and unpaid, the vendors filed their bill against the Clifton Hill Land Company and E. Watkins, to enforce their vendors' lien, E. Watkins being made a party for the reason simply that his name appeared upon the notes. He demurred to the bill because it contained no allegation whereon he could be charged with personal liability. His demurrer was sustained, and the bill was dismissed as to him.

Thereafter, on the 19th of March, 1890, the vendors and W. S. Shields, who had intermarried with Miss Alice M. Watkins, filed a supplemental bill, whereby they sought to hold the incorporators of the Clifton Hill Land Company personally liable for the balance of purchase money that might remain unpaid after exhaustion of the land, upon the alleged ground that the charter obtained by them was invalid, and that their attempted incorporation thereunder was, as a consequence, ineffectual.

Pending these bills the Clifton Hill Land Company filed a bill against the vendors and others, seeking to rescind the sale of the land to that company, on account of alleged fraud and deceit practiced in the sale of the land. This bill was answered, and all charges of fraud and deceit were denied. Of this last bill it need only be further [130] said at this place that it was dismissed upon final hearing; and, from the decree of dismissal, there has been no appeal or writ of error.

In the progress of the litigation the vendors voluntarily dismissed their supplemental bill, so far as it sought "any personal relief or recovery against the individual defendants, but no further or otherwise." And, upon the hearing of the case as it then stood, decree was rendered against the Clifton Hill Land Company for the balance of unpaid purchase money, attorney's fees, etc., and the master was directed to sell the land in satisfaction thereof, unless the amount due should be paid into court within a time named. The money was not paid, and the land was sold, and purchased by the original vendors, at the price of $47,000. The sale was confirmed, and title divested and vested.

From these decrees the Clifton Hill Land Company appealed to this court.

The case was considered, and the decree below affirmed, upon grounds appearing in the opinion of this court reported in 91 Tennessee, at pages 683 to 692, inclusive.

On March 1, 1892, while the appeal in that cause was still pending, W. S. Shields and his wife, formerly Miss Alice M. Watkins, and her mother, Mrs. Watkins, commenced the present proceeding by what the pleader termed "an original bill in the nature of a supplemental bill," to establish personal [131] liability upon E. Watkins and various other defendants, and to collect from them individually the balance alleged still to be due on the decree rendered against the Clifton Hill Land Company under the vendor's bill.

In an amended and supplemental bill, filed by the same parties on February 3, 1893, they allege that the said balance, as ascertained by decree of this court in the other case, is $77,916.50; and that an execution has been issued for the same and returned *nulla bona*. The grounds upon which individual liability is claimed on the one hand in these bills, and denied on the other hand in the answers thereto, will properly appear hereafter. At this point it is sufficient to say that each and every defendant, except the Clifton Hill Land Company, strongly denies his liability upon any ground, and that the chancellor, with the pleadings, proof, and decrees in all the cases herein mentioned before him, deemed the defenses good, and therefore dismissed these bills. Complainants have appealed and assigned errors.

The first assignment of error is as follows: "The court erred in refusing to hold the said individual defendants who composed the syndicate, or partnership, liable for the balance due complainants on the purchase price of said lands. The notes given therefor were those of the partnership, and not the notes of the corporation. They antedate the corporation."

This assignment, and the argument in support of [132] it, are based upon the contention that the incorporators of the Clifton Hill Land Company, and their associates, were, in the first instance, partners under that name, and that as such they purchased the land and gave notes for the purchase money before incorporation, and, in doing so, became individually liable for the purchase price. If this contention be true as to the facts of the case it is also true as to the legal result, nothing else appearing.

"It is well settled," says Judge Wright, "that where an

association, which has existed as a mere copartnership, becomes incorporated, and the corporation then accepts an assignment of all the property of such association, for the purpose of carrying out their object, they are primarily and jointly and severally liable for all the debts incurred before the act of incorporation. In such a case the responsibility of the corporation for contracts previously made with the association does not become substituted so as to exempt the members from individual liability, and it does not change the case that the members of the company had it in view to procure a future act of incorporation when it was formed ": *Broyles* v. *McCoy*, 5 Sneed, 603.

But these complainants can have no relief upon that view of the case, because neither alleged in the pleadings nor established by the proof.

It is true that "when the language of a bill is susceptible of a limited or enlarged construction as to its object and extent of relief sought, but the subsequent [133] proceedings show that the complainant, the court, and the defendant construed the words in the enlarged sense, that meaning will be considered as the one intended ": *Brandon* v. *Mason*, 1 Lea, 615.

That rule, however, will not save the present case on the point made in the first assignment of error. The bills proceed upon two, and only two, distinct and alternate grounds of personal liability: 1. Because the attempt to incorporate was ineffectual; and 2. Because, if effectual, subscriptions to stock have not been fully paid. The proposition of liability upon any other ground is not advanced in either of the bills. Those parts of the very lengthy original bill most directly in point are the following: "Complainants are informed, and upon such information charge, that the defendant, Clifton Hill Land Company, was intended to be chartered and organized as a corporation under the act of 1875 and amendatory acts of the Tennessee legislature. A charter was attempted to be obtained on March 30, 1887, and is in substantial compliance with said act, except that the signatures of the persons applying for the charter to the same were acknowledged before W. G. McAdoo, Jr., a notary public, instead of the county court clerk, as then required by law.

"Whether said defendant is a corporate body, under which its promoters can escape personal liability, or a partnership, these complainants submit to the wisdom and decision of the learned court, and, in view of the uncertainty attending a solution of this question, [134] ask to be allowed to file its bill in a double aspect, as more fully set forth hereafter.

"The charter members of said defendant company are defendants E. Watkins, E. Scott, I. Noa, Jas. S. Pinkard, S. W. Divine, and Jno. A. Hart, now deceased.

"Acting upon the supposition that they had a valid charter, the promoters and projectors of the Clifton Hill Land Company fixed its capital stock at $250,000, divided into 2,500 shares of the par value of $100 each, and opened books for stock subscription. The stock was all subscribed, officers elected, and all steps taken necessary to fully organize and equip a corporate body for business. The officers elected were as follows: Defendant E. Watkins, president; I. Noa, vice-president; and E. Scott, secretary and treasurer. The $250,000 of stock was subscribed for by the following persons, as shown by the minute-book kept by the secretary and treasurer, Scott:

NAME	NO. SHARES	AMOUNT
Jno. A. Hart	250	$25,000
W. P. Richardson	500	50,000
E. Watkins	250	25,000
T. C. Catchings	250	25,000
I. Noa	250	25,000
E. Scott	250	25,000
H. A. Bussick	250	25,000
Little & Brown	250	25,000
Jas. S. Pinkard	250	25,000
Making in all		$250,000

Again: "Complainants are advised and insist that [135] the defendant, Clifton Hill Land Company, at the time it became indebted to complainants, was not a valid and legal corporation, by reason of having its charter defectively acknowledged, the acknowledgment having been taken before a notary public, instead of the county court clerk, as the law at that time required; and that said Clifton Hill Land Company was a voluntary association, and that all those who were interested in the same and agreed to take stock therein are liable to complainants individually and personally, each for the entire amount of the notes heretofore sued upon, as hereinbefore stated.

"Complainants are further advised and insist that complainants' rights having been acquired and vested when said notes were executed, in the year 1887, that the subsequent act of the legislature, attempting to legalize corporations whose charters were acknowledged before notaries public, could not affect rights then vested, and, regardless of the effect of said act upon the rights acquired subsequent to its passage, said act could in no way affect or disturb complain- ants' vested rights to hold said projectors of said corporation as partners personally liable upon such notes; and complain- ants ask that said defendant stock subscribers hereinbefore named be held personally liable for the balance due upon the decree hereinbefore left unpaid after crediting the net amount received from the sale of the 190 acres of land. But if complainants are mistaken in this position, and said defendant company is a valid corporation, [136] and must be treated as such in these proceedings, then complainants insist that said defendant stockholders hereinbefore men- tioned are liable to them upon their various and sundry stock subscriptions. . . . . Said company, as its name indi-⟨ cates, was a land company, organized for the purpose of speculating in real estate, having for its object the buying of large bodies of land and subdividing the same, and selling it off into lots and blocks at an advanced price."

These allegations, briefly stated, are that the charter of the Clifton Hill Land Company was invalid because defect- ively acknowledged, and that the defendants are, therefore, personally liable for the company's debts; and, in the alter- native, that, if it should be adjudged valid, then defendants are personally liable for unpaid stock. Whether they were liable upon the one ground or the other complainants, filing their bill "in a double aspect," are pleased to "submit to the wisdom and decision of the learned court." That the com- plainants themselves so understood their original bill is fur- ther shown by the face of the amended and supplemental bill. In the latter bill, among other things, they say: "Said orig- inal bill further charged that the defendant company had attempted to procure a charter of incorporation under the laws of Tennessee, pursuant to the provisions of the act of 1875 and amendatory acts, but that the acknowledgment of the charter was had before a notary public, and [137] not the clerk of the county court, as the law required; and the ques- tion of the legality of said charter was submitted to the court, the bill being brought in two aspects: 1. To hold the pro- jectors of the said Clifton Hill Land Company personally liable in the event it was ascertained that the attempted corporation was illegal; and 2. To hold them liable as stock-holders for non-paid-up stock in the event the Clifton Hill Land Company was ascertained to be a body corporate."

The theory of partnership or syndicate liability, otherwise than as the legal result of a futile effort at incorporation, is not put forth in either of the bills. The answers did not enlarge the scope of the bills themselves. Their denials of personal liability, though in the broadest language, are to be applied only to the grounds upon which such liability was charged in the bills.

If it were conceded, however, that the bills state facts sufficient to charge defendants with personal liability as part-ners in the purchase of the land, prior to a grant of the charter, and without reference to its validity or invalidity the result would still be the same, upon this branch of the case; for the reason that the proof introduced fails to show that the land was so purchased.

Undoubtedly some of the defendants, who were stockhold-ers in the East End Land Company, contemplated the pur-chase of this land, in some form, from the time that company declined to buy it. The [138] idea among them was to find ten men who were willing to become equally interested in the matter. Nine were found, and one of them agreed to take a double part. They accordingly furnished to Charles A. Lyerly, in three installments, $35,000, with which he made the cash payment. At first there was no distinct agreement or understanding, even among those parties themselves, and much less with Mrs. Watkins and her daughter, as to the form in which the purchase should be made, or who should become the owner of the land, receive the deed, and make purchase-money notes. It was soon determined, how-ever, that a corporation, to be organized and known as the Clifton Hill Land Company, should be the purchaser; and, on the day the last installment of the $35,000 was paid to the agent and attorney of the vendors, he was apprised of that fact, and employed to prepare the charter, which he did with-out delay. The charter was signed, acknowledged, filed with the secretary of state, and then finally registered, with his cer-tificate attached. Assuming all of those steps to have been regular, as they were unquestionably intended and supposed by all parties to be, the formation of the company as a body politic was then complete; and its validity as such could not thereafter be collaterally questioned: Milliken and Ventrees' Code, 1693.

Soon thereafter the Clifton Hill Land Company, as the assignee of Lyerly, completed the purchase of the land, by taking a deed thereto, and executing notes for the unpaid purchase money. The vendors [139] never thought of the nine promoters, if they be termed such, as their vendees. They were not concerned as to who the purchaser should be. All they wanted was to have the terms of the option complied with, for their own security; and whether that should be done by Lyerly or by another as his assignee of the option was a matter of indifference to them. They, in fact, supposed, as they repeatedly say in their depositions, that the East End Land Company was their vendee. This supposition on their part was no doubt due to the fact that Lyerly, the holder of the option, was president of that company. Certain it is that they did not think they were selling to a mere partnership or syndicate, and that they did not rely upon the personal liability of these defendants as original purchasers.

Mr. Caldwell, their agent and attorney, who represented them intelligently, faithfully, and honestly, from first to last, in this whole matter, and who was conversant with all the important stages of the transaction, had no thought that these defendants were purchasing the land and assuming to pay for it, either as a copartnership or as individuals. He knew that the Clifton Hill Land Company, but recently incorporated, was in fact the real purchaser and vendee. He wrote the charter with that fact in view, and subsequently drafted the deed and purchase-money notes. The name "Clifton Hill Land Company" was used for the first time in the charter; and there was no prior copartnership or syndicate [140] by that name. The vendors, by the terms of the option, as has already been seen, bound themselves to convey the land to Lyerly "or his indorsee," whoever or whatever that might be. Prior to the final registration of the charter of the Clifton Hill Land Company all business with respect to the option and the land was transacted with Lyerly, as the owner of the option and purchaser of the land. He made the cash payment and took receipts for the different installments thereof, in his own name. In the last of these receipts the vendors referred to the sale as "his purchase" and again stated that they would make a deed to him "or his assignee."

After the grant of its charter the vendors dealt with the Clifton Hill Land Company as Lyerly's assignee. They conveyed the land to it, and received its notes for unpaid purchase money. Only Lyerly, the person to whom the option had been granted, and the Clifton Hill Land Company (his assignee) were known in any of the writings with respect to the land or the purchase price thereof. Before the time came to make the deed Lyerly was on one side of the contract and the vendors on the other. After that time the Clifton Hill Land Company, Lyerly's assignee, was on one side of the contract and the vendors on the other. In view of the terms of the option only Lyerly "or his indorsee" could properly have been thought of as vendee. Only he "or his indorsee" could lawfully [141] have demanded and received a deed to the land. There was no room for any intermediate purchaser. Lyerly assigned the option to the Clifton Hill Land Company as a corporation, not as a syndicate or copartnership, and the vendors conveyed their land to it and took its notes for unpaid purchase money in the same way. Though the assignment by Lyerly and the signature to the purchase-money notes fail to characterize the Clifton Hill Land Company as a corporation in so many words, and though the deed to the land has been lost, so that its exact language cannot be known, it is conclusively shown by other proof that the name was used in those instruments as that of a corporation, and not otherwise. There was no voluntary company or copartnership or association by that name. Besides the other proof on the subject the signature, "E. Watkins, President Clifton Hill Land Company, of itself indicates a corporate contract, and suggests corporate rather than personal liability: *Case Mfg. Co.* v. *Soxman,* 138 U. S. 437.

Mr. Cook, citing that case, says: "The corporation alone is liable where its note was given in fulfillment of a contract entered into in its name, although such contract was prior to its incorporation: Cook on Stocks and Stockholders, sec. 707, p. 1046.

At the first formal meeting of the stockholders of the Clifton Hill Land Company on June 9, 1887, after the election of officers and capitalization on the same day, the following action was taken: "On [142] motion of John A. Hart it was

resolved that this company buy from the original purchasers
of the Watkins farm all their interest therein, and pay them,
in paid-up stock of this company, the sum of $250,000, and
assume their liability of $90,000 due to Mrs. Watkins, the
original vendor."

This minute entry is said to afford "unequivocal evidence"
that the notes given to the vendors of the land were the notes
of a "syndicate." Such would seem to be true if that were all
the evidence on the point, but, in the light of the other evidence in this record, it cannot be so. The object of the
motion, judged by the other writings and proof, to which reference has already been made, must have been simply to
formally approve the purchase already made for the corporation, and to provide for the issuance of stock to those who
had furnished money with which to make the cash payment.
The language used is not the most appropriate for the accomplishment of such an end, still, that must have been
the purpose.

Treating the organization as not entirely complete when
the deed was made to the Clifton Hill Land Company, and
the notes executed by it, approval or disapproval, and compensation to those who had advanced the $35,000, were the
only questions with respect to the purchase of the land that
could have been open for the consideration of the stockholders
when that motion was made and carried. At the most the
stockholders then had power only to say [143] that they would,
or that they would not, ratify what had previously been done
for the corporation, and in its name. Whatever they may
have intended, they could not have changed the fact, otherwise abundantly established, that the land was in reality
purchased in the corporate name.

Moreover, after the 9th of June, as before, all parties treated
the notes previously executed as the obligations of the corporation. The vendors continued to hold the notes, received
interest on them from time to time from the corporation
through Scott, its secretary and treasurer, and, after maturity
and default, filed their bill against the corporation as purchaser of the land and maker of the notes; sold and repur-
chased the land, and, after application of proceeds, obtained
decree for balance against the corporation alone.

Though not expressly so called in the bill and decrees in
that cause, it is entirely manifest that the Clifton Hill Land
Company was proceeded against as a corporation and not

otherwise. Indeed, the decree for balance now sought to be collected could be valid upon no other idea; for a merely voluntary syndicate, company, or partnership by that name, had there been such, could have been bound only by naming the individual members thereof in the bill and decree.

As a concluding observation, with respect to the first assignment of error, it is well to say that complainants not only fail, both in their pleadings [144] and in their testimony, to assert that they sold their land to the defendants as partners, but they plainly negative such an idea in many ways, and distinctly state in the tenth section of their present original bill that they conveyed it to the Clifton Hill Land Company as a corporation. That statement is in these words: "The said defendant, Clifton Hill Land Company, as a corporation, is absolutely, utterly, and notoriously insolvent. It never had any assets, real or personal, except the 190 acres of land conveyed to it by complainants, Mrs. Watkins and Mrs. Shields, and that, as already shown, was never paid for by it, and, as has already hereinbefore been shown, the same has been sold at public outcry for $47,000, and bid off by complainants, Mrs. Watkins and Mrs. Shields, and, since the sale of said property, defendant company has not a cent of property of any kind left." And in section 12 they refer to the notes for the land as "the notes held by complainants, Mrs. Watkins and Mrs. Shields, against said defendant company."

The second assignment of error is as follows: "Treating the notes given for the purchase price of said land as those of the corporation, by adoption, the said individual defendants are, nevertheless, personally liable thereon, and the court erred in refusing so to hold: 1. Because the corporation did not, by any perfected act, assume this liability of its promoters, or substitute itself in this respect for its promoters; 2. But if it had done so there is no [145] proof of the acceptance by complainants of this substituted liability. At most, complainants only accepted the additional liability of the corporation; 3. And, in any event, the Clifton Hill Land Company never had power to do any lawful act, its charter being void for want of proper acknowledgment."

The controlling thought underlying the first and second subdivisions of this assignment is readily seen to be that of primary liability on the part of the individual defendants, as the result of their having been the original purchasers of the land, in the capacity of promoters and partners. The question there raised is substantially the same as that presented in the first assignment of error, which has just been so elaborately considered as to render further discussion of the question unnecessary. It is sufficient to say, briefly, that the pleadings do not assert and the proof does not sustain such a proposition. The contract of purchase was that of the corporation as such, and its liability for the purchase price was primary and exclusive, provided, only, that all preliminary steps necessary to incorporation were validly taken.

This brings us to a consideration of the third subdivision, which presents the primary ground of relief sought in the bills, viz., that the charter of the Clifton Hill Land Company was invalid, because not acknowledged before the proper officer, and that, as a legal consequence, the supposed incorporators became liable, as individuals, for the contract made in the corporate name.

[146] There can be no doubt that persons, assuming to act under a charter invalid because some positive requirement of the law has not been complied with, are liable as individuals for all debts contracted by them in the name of such corporation. Such persons so contracting in such a case stand in the room and stead of the corporation, and must answer personally for its obligations to third persons: 2 Spelling on Private Corporations, secs. 832–838; 1 Beach on Private Corporations, sec. 16.

The statute in force at the time the charter of the Clifton Hill Land Company was obtained imperatively required the acknowledgment of the proposed incorporators to be taken before the clerk of the county court of the county where the main business of the corporation was to be conducted, and permitted it to be taken by no other official: acts 1875, c. 142, sec. 3; Milliken and Ventrees' Code, sec. 1989. The acknowledgment was, in fact, made before a notary public, and, for that reason, the charter was invalid: *Teasely·* v. *State* (oral); *Brewer* v. *State*, 7 Lea, 682. As a result of that defect the incorporators at once became personally liable for the balance of the purchase price of the land conveyed to the supposed corporation. But defendants, conceding the defective acknowledgment, say that it was effectually cured, the charter made good, and all contracts and obligations of the corporation made valid, by the act of March 10, 1890. Such, beyond question, [147] was the intent and meaning of that act, whose language is as follows:

"*Be it enacted by the General Assembly of the State of Ten-*
nessee, That all charters or articles of incorporation heretofore taken out under the general corporation laws of this
state which were or have been acknowledged or proven before notaries public, are hereby ratified and confirmed, and
shall have and possess the same validity and effect as if they
had been acknowledged or proven before the county court
clerk; and the acts, contracts, and obligations of all such
corporations so organized shall have and possess the same
validity, force, and effect, as if the charters of such corporations had been acknowledged before the county court clerk."
Acts Extra Sess. 1890, c. 17, sec. 1.

Complainants deny, however, that this legislation is constitutional, and say that it cannot be held to operate so as to
affect them or their rights in this case.   The substance of
the position is that, because of the invalidity of the charter
on the day the land was conveyed to the corporation, the
defendants then became personally liable for the payment of
the purchase-money notes; that such personal liability was
a vested and fixed right of the vendors, which could not be
taken away or impaired by legislative enactment, as would
be the effect if the act in question be applied in this case.

The constitutional provision upon which this contention is
made is as follows: "That no retrospective [148] law, or law
impairing the obligation of contracts, shall be made": Const.,
art. 1, sec. 20.

This does not mean that absolutely no retrospective law
shall be made, but only that no retrospective law which
impairs the obligation of contracts, or divests or impairs
vested rights, shall be made: *Townsend* v. *Townsend*, Peck,
15, 17; 14 Am. Dec. 722; *Wynne* v. *Wynne*, 2 Swan, 405;
58 Am. Dec. 66; *Collins* v. *East Tennessee etc. R. R. Co.*, 9
Heisk. 847.

It does not inhibit retrospective laws made in furtherance
of the police power of the state; and, generally, it does not
prohibit remedial legislation, nor stand in the way of statutes
passed to cure some defect or omission in former proceedings
or enactments, or in the case of parties attempting to comply
therewith: *Ib; Marr* v. *West Tennessee Bank*, 4 Lea, 585;
Knoxville v. *Bird,* 12 Lea, 121; 47 Am. Rep. 326; *Demoville*
v. *Davidson County*, 87 Tenn. 223; *Munn* v. *Illinois*, 94 U. S.
113; *Beer Co.* v. *Massachusetts*, 97 U. S. 25; *Stone* v. *Missis-*
sippi, 101 U. S. 814; Wade on Retroactive Law, secs. 23, 257;

1 Kent's Commentaries, *456; 2 Story on the Constitution, 674; Cooley's Constitutional Limitations, 5th ed., 443, 448, 455–458; *Ewell* v. *Daggs*, 108 U. S. 150, 151; *Gross* v. *United States Mortgage Co.*, 108 U. S. 488; *Satterlee* v. *Matthewson*, 2 Pet. 412; Sutherland on Statutory Construction, secs. 206, 207.

We quote from each of three distinguished authors:

"A retrospective statute affecting and changing vested rights is very generally considered, in this [149] country, as founded on unconstitutional principles, and consequently inoperative and void. But this doctrine is not understood to apply to remedial statutes, which may be of a retrospective nature, provided they do not impair contracts, or disturb absolute vested rights, and only go to confirm rights already existing, and in furtherance of the remedy, by curing defects and adding to the means of enforcing existing obligations. Such statutes have been held valid, when clearly just and reasonable and conducive to the general welfare, even though they might operate in a degree upon existing rights—as a statute to confirm former marriages defectively celebrated or a sale of lands defectively made or acknowledged": 1 Kent's Commentaries, *455, 456.

"A party has no vested right in a rule of law which would give him an inequitable advantage over another, and such rule may therefore be repealed, and the advantage thereby taken away. To illustrate this remark, if by law a conveyance should be declared invalid if it wanted the formality of a seal; or a note, if usurious interest was promised by it; or, if in any other case, on grounds of public policy, a party should be permitted to avoid his contract entered into intelligently and without fraud, there would be no sound reason for permitting him to claim the protection of the constitution, if afterwards, on a different view of public policy, the legislature should change the rule, and give effect to his conveyance, note, or other contract, [150] exactly according to the original intention. Such infirmities in contracts and conveyances are often cured in this manner, and with entire justice; and the same may also be done with defects in legal proceedings, occasioned by mere irregularities. When a court or its officers, in a case of which the court has full jurisdiction, have failed to observe strictly the rules of procedure which are prescribed for the orderly conduct of affairs, and, in consequence thereof, a party who was in no way injured by the irregularity, is nevertheless in position to take advantage of the error to avoid the proceedings, it is often not only just but highly proper that the legislature shall interfere and cure the defect by validating the proceedings. And, if this may be done in proceedings which concern only private parties, it may be done in case of errors in the proceedings of corporations, and of public bodies. Retrospective legislation to cure their irregularities is not forbidden": 2 Story on Const., 5th ed., 674.

"If the thing wanting, or which failed to be done, and which constitutes the defect in the proceedings, is some thing the necessity for which the legislature might have dispensed with by prior statute, then it is not beyond the power of the legislature to dispense with it by subsequent statute. And, if the irregularity consists in doing some act, or in the mode or manner of doing some act, which the legislature might have made immaterial by prior law, it is equally competent to make the same immaterial [151] by a subsequent law": Cooley's Constitutional Limitations, 5th ed., 458.

Referring to the subject of legislative ratification another learned author makes this remark: "Such subsequent ratification will not only legalize the existence of a corporation formed without authority of law, and authorize the association to act in a corporate capacity thereafter, but it may also cure the illegality of corporate acts performed before the act of ratification was passed, and render such acts as valid and binding as if authority to perform them had been previously granted by the legislature": 1 Morawetz on Private Corporations, 2d ed., sec. 20.

A stipulation in the face of a note for usurious interest affords the maker a perfect defense to any action for the collection of the note; yet he has no such vested right in the defense or the contract, or the usury statute, as that the latter may not be repealed, and the obligation made collectible by a retrospective law: *Ewell* v. *Daggs*, 108 U. S. 150.

So, likewise, a loan of money made in one state by a corporation of another state, though not collectible at the time, because then contrary to the law of the former state, may be rendered collectible by a subsequent law. The latter law, though destroying a complete defense to any suit brought for the collection of the loan, does not impair the obligation of the contract. "It rather enables the parties to enforce the contract they intended to make": *Gross* v. *United States Mortgage Co.*, 108 U. S. 488.

[152] Clearly the act of 1890 does not impair the obligation of any contract with complainants, for they had no contract with the individual defendants.   Their contract was with the corporation; hence that act, which gives life to the corporation, effectuates rather than impairs the obligation of its contract.   No more does that act divest or impair any vested right of complainants.   They had no vested right in the defect in the charter of the Clifton Hill Land Company; hence, the cure or removal of that defect did not divest or impair any vested right of theirs.   The right to sue the defendants personally was not a vested right in legal contemplation.   It was but a consequential right, resulting from the disability of the corporation, and not a right flowing from any contract with the individuals as such.   The mutual intention was to bind the corporation, not the incorporators, for the price of the land; and no vested right could arise contrary to that intention.   A law which facilitates the intention of the parties to a contract never impairs its obligation or divests or impairs any vested right thereunder.

As forcibly remarked by Mr. Justice Washington in an early case: "It is not easy to perceive how a law which gives validity to a contract can be said to impair the obligation of that contract": *Satterlee* v. *Matthewson*, 2 Pet. 412.

Complainants had no vested right in the law which permitted only clerks of the county courts to take acknowledgments to charters, nor against defendants [153] on account of that law.   Our conclusion is, that the act of 1890 is valid, both as a retrospective and as a prospective law.   Besides, if it were held that the act in question can operate only as a prospective law, complainants would now be estopped to assert personal liability of the incorporators upon the ground that the charter of the company was originally invalid.   The continued prosecution of their vendors' bill against the company, as a corporation, after the passage of that act, must be assumed in law to have proceeded in recognition of that act, and upon the idea that it had validated the notes sued upon.   Complainants received those notes from the supposed corporation, as their vendee, April 14, 1887; held them continuously before and after the completed organization of the company, on June 9, 1887; collected interest on them from time to time; filed their vendors' bill against the corporation in April, 1889, and prosecuted the same to final decree in this court at the September term, 1892, when they obtained, against the corporation alone, the decree made the basis of the present action. This course of conduct, in court and out, running through a period of more than five years, and continuing more than eighteen months after the charter of the company and its contracts had been expressly validated by the legislature, conclusively estops them from now claiming and obtaining relief on any theory inconsistent with the validity of the corporation or of its notes for the land.

The case of *Broyles* v. *McCoy*, 5 Sneed, 603, is [154] not controlling in this case, because the personal liability there enforced was predicated upon a completed written contract, executed by the defendants before any steps were taken to procure a charter.

The third and last assignment of error—that which brings forward for consideration the second or alternate aspect of the bills—is as follows: "Again, treating this liability as that of the corporation alone, the court erred in not giving decree against said individual defendants upon their stock subscriptions to said Clifton Hill Land Company. There was no valid payment of said subscriptions."

Since the case of *Wood* v. *Dummer*, 3 Mason, 308, decided by Judge Story in 1824, it has been the general doctrine of American courts that the capital stock of a corporation is a trust fund for the payment of corporate debts; and that, in case of insolvency, stock subscribers are liable to creditors of the company for unpaid subscriptions, so far as required for the satisfaction of its liabilities: *Sawyer* v. *Hoag*, 17 Wall. 611; *Ohio Life Ins. Co.* v. *Merchants' Ins. Co.*, 11 Humph. 31; 53 Am. Dec. 742; *Wetherbee* v. *Baker*, 35 N. J. Eq. 501; *Sanger* v. *Upton*, 91 U. S. 60; *Thompson* v. *Reno Sav. Bank*, 19 Nev. 103, 3 Am. St. Rep. 797, and note, 808; *Kelley* v. *Fletcher*, 94 Tenn. 1; Cook on Stock and Stockholders, sec. 199; 2 Morawetz on Private Corporations, sec. 780; 1 Beach on Private Corporations, secs. 113–116; Thompson's Liability of Stockholders, sec. 10; Taylor on Private Corporations, secs. 701–704; 2 Spelling on Private Corporations, sec. 784.

[155] Conceding this doctrine, defendants say that it is available only to those persons whose debts were contracted after subscription made, and in reliance upon it, and that it cannot be successfully invoked by these complainants, because

their debt was created before the capitalization of the company, and before any subscriptions to stock were made.

Counsel for complainants admit the facts stated, but dispute the legal proposition. They contend that the true reason of the doctrine is, that unpaid subscription to capital stock is the property of the corporation, liable in the last resort to the payment of all of its just debts; that, being such, it stands upon the same ground, with respect to creditors, as any other corporate property; and, like any other property, may be subjected, in case of insolvency, to antecedent and subsequent debts alike.

It is further said that if corporate creditors can be denied resort to stock subscriptions, because made after the creation of their debts, they may, upon the same reasoning, be denied resort to any other after-acquired property; that there is no difference, in this respect, between the liabilities of corporations and of natural persons; that, inasmuch, as in case of credit extended to a natural person, the creditor has a right to look not only to the property he then has, but also to all that he may thereafter acquire, the corporate creditor should have the same right; and, finally, that all property of natural or artificial persons, whenever or however acquired, unless [156] expressly exempted by law, is liable for all valid debts of the one or the other whenever created.

Those are very forcible views, and, were the question a new one, we would adopt them as the surest means of doing justice in every case. The doctrine seems, from its inception, however, to have been rested on actual or presumed reliance by the creditor, at the time his debt was created, upon the then capital stock of the corporation for payment: *Wood* v. *Dummer*, 3 Mason, 308; *Adler* v. *Milwaukee Brick Co.*, 13 Wis. 60; *Allen* v. *Montgomery R. R. Co.*, 11 Ala. 437; *Wetherbee* v. *Baker*, 35 N. J. Eq., 501; *Sanger* v. *Upton*, 91 U. S. 56; *Sawyer* v. *Hoag*, 17 Wall. 611; *Hospes* v. *Northwestern Mfg. & Car Co.*, 48 Minn. 174, 31 Am. St. Rep. 637; 2 Morawetz on Private Corporations, sec. 781; *First Nat. Bank* v. *Gustin etc. Min. Co.*, 42 Minn. 327; 18 Am. St. Rep. 516, and other cases too numerous to mention.

In the last case the court said: "While the courts have not always had occasion to state the limitation upon the doctrine that 'the capital stock is a trust fund for the benefit of creditors,' yet we think that it will be found that, in every case where they have impressed a trust upon the subscription of the shareholders, it has been in favor of creditors becoming such afterwards; and hence fairly to be presumed as relying upon the amount of capital which the company was represented as having": *First Nat. Bank* v. *Gustin etc. Min. Co.*, 42 Minn. 334; 18 Am. St. Rep. 516.

[157] In a late case the supreme court of the United States said: "We have no doubt the learned circuit judge held correctly that it was only subsequent creditors who were entitled to enforce their claims against the stockholders, since it is only they who could, by any legal presumption, have trusted the company upon the faith of the increased stock": *Handley* v. *Stutz*, 139 U. S. 435.

But the rule of nonliability of stockholders for antecedent debts does not apply where the amount of capital stock is definitely fixed in the charter, for, in that case, the creditor is presumed to have contracted with reference to the charter capitalization: 2 Morawetz on Private Corporations, sec. 781.

The "trust fund doctrine," as thus far considered, may well be termed the American common law on the subject, originated, developed, and enforceable by the courts of equity in this country. Many of the states have statues on the subject, some of which are merely declarative of that common law, some restrictive in their nature, and others more comprehensive and imperative. The Tennessee statute is in these words: "The amount of any unpaid stock due from a subscriber to a corporation shall be a fund for the payment of any debts due from the corporation; nor shall the transfer of stock from any subscriber, release him from payment, unless his transferee has paid up all or any of the balance due on said original subscription": Acts, 1875, c. 142, sec 5, p. 237; Milliken and Ventrees' Code, sec. 1708.

[158] This provision was properly incorporated into the charter of the Clifton Hill Land Company, and is binding on all stock subscribers. What does it mean? What is made a fund for the payment of debts? "Any unpaid stock." What debts are contemplated? "Any debts due from the corporation." "Any unpaid stock" means all unpaid stock, and "any debts due from the corporation," means all debts due from the corporation—that is to say, all unpaid stock shall be a fund for the payment of all debts of the corporation. No subscriber for unpaid stock can escape liability, and no corporate debt shall go unpaid, so far as the capital stock is concerned. The liability attaches to all subscribers; the

security extends to all creditors. No subscriber whose stock remains unpaid can escape liability, and no creditor who has a valid debt can be denied his security. Nothing is said in the statute with respect to the time the subscription shall be made, nor as to the time the debts shall be created. No limitation is made in either case. The clear and plain meaning of the statute is that all unpaid stock, whenever subscribed, shall be a fund for the payment of all corporate debts, whenever created.

Under this statute it is clear that all subscribers to stock in the Clifton Hill Land Company would be individually liable, in a proper proceeding, for the debt of complainants to the extent that their respective subscriptions may be shown to remain unpaid. A similar statute was so construed [159] by the supreme court of Illinois in the case of *Root* v. *Sinnock,* 120 Ill. 350; 60 Am. Rep. 558. See, also, 2 Morawetz on Private Corporations, sec. 870.

Some of the defendants, notably Catchings and Richardson, deny that they were ever subscribers for any part of the stock in the Clifton Hill Land Company, and all of them say that all the stock has been fully paid.

The proof on the issue of payment is that certain of the defendants, collectively, furnished the aggregate sum of $35,000 in money, which was used by Lyerly in making the cash payment on the land before the Clifton Hill Land Company was actually incorporated; and that, on the 9th of June following the incorporation the stockholders took the action indicated by the following entry upon the minutes: "On motion of John A. Hart it was resolved that this company buy from the original purchasers of the Watkins farm all their interest therein, and pay them, in paid-up stock of this company, the sum of $250,000, and assume their liability of $90 000, as due Mrs. Watkins, the original vendor."

So far as the question of payment is concerned this action of the stockholders can have no other meaning, in law, than that the company was to give those particular defendants $250,000 of paid-up stock for their equity in the land, or against the corporation, by reason of the fact that they had so furnished the $35,000 already mentioned. It [160] cannot mean, in legal contemplation, nor was it in fact intended to mean, that such persons were selling the land itself to the company and taking as consideration therefor the $250,000 of paid-up stock; for, as we have seen heretofore, the land was already the property of the corporation, subject to the lien for unpaid purchase money. That the parties concerned might then reasonably have considered the land, encumbered as it was, as fairly worth $250,000 in cash, or even more, is satisfactorily established by the proof; hence there could be no doubt, in view of the settled rule that property needed by the company may be taken at a fair valuation in payment of stock subscriptions: *Kelley* v. *Fletcher*, 94 Tenn. 1. That, if the subscribers had been vendors of the land, the stock was in fact fully paid; but whether the mere equity of the contributors of the $35,000 used for the cash payment could properly have been given so large a purchasing value is quite a different question. It is clear to our minds that the company had the legal right to issue full-paid stock in extinguishment of that equity, yet the record fails to show that it was worth so much as $250,000.

But it is said that the question of overvaluation is not raised in the pleadings, and that for that reason it cannot be considered by the court. It is plain law that a contract whereby a corporation receives needed property in the payment of stock subscription is presumed, in the first instance, to be [161] valid and binding upon all parties concerned, and that it must stand as made, and operate as intended, until impeached by appropriate pleading and proof: *Phelan* v. *Hazard*, 5 Dill. 50; *Clow* v. *Brown*, 134 Ind. 287; *Coit* v. *Gold Amalgamating Co.*, 119 U. S. 345; *Kelley* v. *Fletcher*, 94 Tenn. 1.

The allegation in the original bill before us is as follows: "Complainants are informed and charge that those who subscribed for stock in the defendant company have paid very little upon their stock subscription, and perhaps some have paid nothing at all. Complainants are informed that one or more small assessments were made upon the stock subscribers, which were paid, at least in part, said stock assessment being levied for the purpose of collecting money from the subscribers to pay the annual interest due upon the notes held by complainants, Mrs. Watkins and Mrs. Shields, against said defendant company; and that, with this exception, none of said stock subscriptions have been paid in, and the same are due and owing to the corporation."

This is merely an allegation of nonpayment, and is not claimed to have been intended for more. It does not even refer to the transaction whereby the stock was paid, and can, by no construction, be taken as an impeachment of it. Hence, under the authorities last cited, the question of overvaluation cannot be considered, but the court must assume upon this record, that the equity of the subscribers [162] in the land was worth as much as the par value of the stock, that being the price at which it was taken, and that the subscriptions are full paid. The question of pleading was elaborately considered in *Kelley* v. *Fletcher*, 94 Tenn. 1.

Let the decree be affirmed.

MR JUSTICE WILKES dissented, and said: " I am of opinion that the individual defendants in this case are personally liable, as parties composing the purchasing syndicate known as the Clifton Hill Land Company, for the balance of the purchase money for the Oakland farm, after exhausting the proceeds of the land upon which the lien was retained, and that complainants, under their pleadings, are entitled to a recovery.

"With all due respect for the exceedingly able opinion of the majority, I think it proceeds upon an erroneous idea in holding that certain acts done and transactions made were the acts of the corporation, when, as a matter of fact, they were the acts of the individuals operating under the name of the Clifton Hill Land Company, as a partnership designation, before it was incorporated under the same name. In my view the corporation, as such, did no act to connect it with this transaction until the ninth day of June, 1887. Up to that time all that was done was done as individuals, and not as a corporation. The change to a corporation was made June 9, 1887, when the shrinkage in value had set in, and it was important to interpose the corporation to shield from individual liabilities. No one but these promoters had any interest in the land, or had incurred a liability to Mrs. Watkins for the purchase money up to that time.

" We have not the opportunity to carefully analyze the pleadings in the two cases with a view of showing that complainants all the time have proceeded upon the idea of the original liability of the partners individually, supplemented by that of the corporation after it came into existence.

"The substance of it all is, that complainants insisted all the time upon individual liability, and the main contention by them was that the subsequently formed corporation could not relieve from this liability. I think there is an utter absence of proof that the defendants stipulated against individual liability, nor do I understand the opinion of the majority to so hold or intimate.

" In this connection I remark that I can place but little weight upon the acts of Mr. J. A. Caldwell as working an estoppel upon complainants. If he was agent for them, he was at the same time agent and attorney for the defendants individually and as a corporation.

"The formation of the corporation did not relieve the individuals, but the corporation assumed the debt of the individuals, and, as to the creditors, became surety for the individuals": Citing *Broyles* v. *McCoy*, 5 Sneed, 603.

" In the second place I am of opinion that the individual defendants who were stockholders of the defendant corporation were severally liable upon their respective subscriptions to the capital stock of the corporation in a sum sufficient to pay the balance of the purchase money due the complainants, the said stock being for the most part unpaid.

"The act of 1875, chapter 142, section 5, page 237, contains a provision in these words: 'The amount of any unpaid stock due from a subscriber to the corporation shall be a fund for the payment of any debts due from the corporation; nor shall the transfer of stock by any subscriber relieve him from payment, unless his transferee has paid up all or any balance due on said original subscription': Code, sec. 1708.

"This provision is incorporated in the charter of this corporation, and is binding on all subscribers for stock. I think the language of the statute and charter is clear and plain, and that all stock, whenever subscribed, is liable for all debts whenever contracted. The charter virtually declares on its face, to the world, that, when the stock shall be subscribed and paid, it will constitute a fund for the payment of the debts of the corporation. Independent of the statute, the same rule results under the general principles of equity and the trust fund doctrine. All unpaid original subscriptions are assets for the payment of debts. I need not consider the question where there is an increase of stock after the original subscriptions are paid. In this case, however, the stock was subscribed at the same time and by the same instrument under which the corporation assumed the debt. I think the fact abundantly shown that the capital stock of this company had been fixed and subscribed before complainants extended credit to it, or at the time the contract was assumed by the corporation. . . . . The remaining question is whether the defendants are liable for any unpaid subscriptions. As I understand the opinion of the majority, they are not, because their stock has been paid in full in property which the stockholders agreed to receive in satisfaction of the subscriptions, and whether this was a *bona fide* actual payment cannot be questioned, inasmuch as the stockholders agreed to so regard it, unless the transaction shall be directly impeached for fraud by proper allegations in the bill. In other words, it matters not what fictitious values shall be placed upon property received in payment of stock it will be treated as payment if the stockholders so regard it, and it cannot be questioned except upon an allegation of a fraudulent combination and purpose of the stockholders.

"It is well settled that corporations may receive in payment of stock subscriptions property which it may lawfully purchase, and which is suitable and applicable to the purposes for which it was organized; but it must be taken in good faith, at its fair *bona fide* value: *Searight* v. *Payne,* 6 Lea, 285; *Albitztigui* v. *Quadalupe etc. Min. Co.,* 92 Tenn. 605.

"The transaction must be free from fraud. The property must be of such character and value that the corporation would be authorized to purchase it with money if the stockholders had first paid the amount of their subscriptions into the treasury of the company. It must be received at money's worth, and, if it have no settled and ascertained value, it cannot be received at all, unless under special circumstances: Morawetz on Private Corporations, secs. 425, 426, 428, 825; Cook on Stocks and Stockholders, 2d ed., sec. 13; *Camden* v. *Stuart,* 144 U. S. 105."

"Indeed, this case will come within the doctrine laid down in *Camden* v. *Stuart,* 144 U. S. 104, where it is held that if the property turned in is practically worthless, or is unsubstantial and shadowy in its nature, the court will hold that there has been no payment at all, and that the stockholders are liable on the stock.

"But it is said that, unless the transaction is impeached for fraud, directly and pointedly alleged in the pleadings, the question of overvaluation cannot be made effectual. In other words the subscribers say: 'We are stockholders, and have paid for our stock.' 'How have you paid for it?' 'In property.' 'Did you pay that property in at its fair cash value, as the statute prescribes?' 'I need not answer that further than to say my associates agreed to receive it as payment, and it must stand as such, unless you impeach it for fraud on my part and that of my associates.'

"This rule may apply between the stockholders, but it should not prevail as against creditors. I am ready to concede that fraud may be charged, and should be in all proper cases, and the question thus raised; but I do not think relief can be denied because of the failure to charge fraudulent overvaluation, where the proof abundantly shows fraud or an excessive overvaluation. The plea in this case is payment. The burden of proving it is on the party setting it up. It devolves upon him to affirmatively show payment. This he can do by showing that money was paid. Until that is done the plea of payment is not sustained. It may also be sustained under the statute by showing that property, instead of money, was paid; but it must be property at a fair cash valuation. . . . .

"The case of *Elyton Land Co.* v. *Birmingham Warehouse and Elevator Co.,* 92 Ala. 407, 25 Am. St. Rep. 65, is an able presentation of this doctrine, and, in my opinion, correctly lays down the law as far as this feature is involved. It is there held that any arrangement between stockholders and the corporation to issue stock as fully paid, though only partly paid in fact, either in money or property, and by which the corporation does not get the benefit of the full price of the stock in good faith, may be valid and binding between the stockholders and the corporation, but it is invalid as to creditors, and may be set aside at their instance, and full payment of the stock enforced for the satisfaction of corporate debts. . . . .

"Such being the case, the individual defendants are still liable on their stock subscriptions to the extent that the attempted payment falls short of a *bona fide* compliance with the terms of the contract, and the allegations as to excessive valuations of the property were sufficient under the rules above stated: To the same effect see *Crawford* v. *Rohrer,* 59 Md. 599; *Carr* v. *Lefevre,* 27 Pa. St. 413; *Scovill* v. *Thayer,* 105 U. S. 143; *Jackson* v. *Traer,* 64 Iowa, 469; 52 Am Rep. 449; *Osgood* v. *King,* 42 Iowa, 478; *Douglass* v. *Ireland,* 73 N. Y. 100; *Wetherbee* v. *Baker,* 35 N. J. Eq. 501; *Bailey* v. *Pittsburg etc. Coal Co.,* 69 Pa. St. 334. See, also, *Gogebic Investment Co.* v. *Iron Chief Min. Co.,* 78 Wis. 427; 23 Am. St. Rep. 417; *Thompson* v. *Reno Sav. Bank,* 3 Am. St. Rep. 817, note; *National Tube Works Co.* v. *Gilfillan,* 124 N. Y. 302.

"The cases relied upon in the opinion of the majority of the court are commented on in this case of *Elyton Land Co.* v. *Birmingham Warehouse and Elevator Co.,* 92 Ala. 407, 25 Am. St. Rep. 65–83, and, I think, with fatal effect.

"The case of *Kelley* v. *Fletcher,* 94 Tenn. 1, decided at the present term, did not meet my approval, and I reserved the right to file a written dissent, and I make this my dissent in that case, as well as in this, on the points involved."

CORPORATIONS—PERSONAL LIABILITY OF PROMOTERS.—This question is fully discussed in the extended note to *Pittsburg Min. Co.* v. *Spooner,* 17 Am. St. Rep. 162. The promoter of a corporation is liable on his promise to refund a stock subscription if building of a railroad is not completed within a certain time: *Allison* v. *Wood,* 147 Pa. St. 197; 30 Am. St. Rep. 726. The question of the liability of the corporation on contracts entered into by its promoters before its organization is discussed in the extended note to *Moore etc. Hardware Co.* v. *Tomers Hardware Co.*, 13 Am. St. Rep. 28.

STATUTES—REMEDIAL—VALIDITY OF.—A law which binds a party by contract which he had attempted to make but failed by reason of some inability on his part to make it or through neglect of some legal formality is not unconstitutional: *Town of Bellevue* v. *Peacock,* 89 Ky. 495; 25 Am. St. Rep. 552, and note. The cases discussing this question will be found collected in the notes to *Donley* v. *Pittsburgh,* 30 Am. St. Rep. 739; *Whitney* v. *Pittsburgh,* 30 Am. St. Rep. 741, and *Sutherland* v. *De Leon,* 46 Am. Dec. 107.

CONSTITUTIONAL LAW—IMPAIRING OBLIGATIONS OF CONTRACTS.—A contract obligation is protected from impairment by state legislatures by the federal constitution: *People* v. *Common Council,* 140 N. Y. 300; 37 Am. St. Rep. 563, and note, with the cases collected.

CORPORATIONS. — ESTOPPEL of persons dealing with to deny corporate existence: See the notes to *Pittsburg Min. Co.* v. *Spooner,* 17 Am. St. Rep. 161, and *Schloss* v. *Montgomery Trade Co.,* 13 Am. St. Rep. 55.

CORPORATIONS.—Capital stock of a corporation is a trust fund for the benefit of creditors: *Commercial etc. Ins Co.* v. *Board of Revenue,* 91 Alabama, 1; 42 Am. St. Rep. 17, and note.

NASHVILLE LUMBER COMPANY *v.* FOURTH NATIONAL BANK.

[94 TENNESSEE, 374.]

NEGOTIABLE INSTRUMENTS—VOID INDORSEMENT—RIGHTS AND LIABILITIES OF ACCOMMODATION INDORSER.—If the holder of negotiable paper, upon which there is a void accommodation indorsement, transfers it to a third person who has no knowledge of the infirmity, for the express purpose of enabling the latter to collect it against such indorser for the use and benefit of the transferrer, thus imposing a new liability on the indorser, the transferrer is liable to the indorser for the damages sustained by him, and he may maintain suit before the collection of the note.

NEGOTIABLE INSTRUMENTS—RIGHTS AND LIABILITIES OF INDORSER.—A holder of negotiable paper upon which he cannot legally recover against an indorser, and who transfers such paper to a third person, so as to enable the latter to collect from the indorser, not for the transferee's benefit, and in due course of trade, but for the use and benefit of the transferrer, thus holding the indorser liable when the transferrer could not regularly so hold him, is liable in damages to such indorser before the collection of the note.

Granbery & Marks, for the complainant.

P. D. Maddin, for the defendant.

374 WILKES, J. This is a suit for damages for wrongfully transferring negotiable paper to an innocent holder for the purpose of imposing upon the complainant, as indorser, a liability that would not **375** have existed if the note had not been so transferred, and thereby securing an advantage for the transferrer of the paper. There was a demurrer to the declaration, which was sustained by the court, and plaintiff appealed, and has assigned errors.

The case, as made out by the declaration, is that certain notes made by the Bond Lumber Company had placed upon them the indorsement of the Nashville Lumber Company. This indorsement was made by the secretary of the Nashville Lumber Company, not only for accommodation, but without any legal authority, and was *ultra vires* and void. The defendant bank held the notes thus indorsed, with legal notice of their infirmity when made and indorsed, and, while so holding them, the plaintiff company further notified it that the indorsement was without consideration, illegal and void, and that the company would recognize no liability on account of the same.

Prior to maturity the defendant bank indorsed the notes to the Merchant's National Bank of Louisville, and had them rediscounted by that bank. The maker of the notes was insolvent when the notes were transferred to the Louisville bank, and the declaration states that the Nashville bank fraudulently rediscounted the notes for the sole purpose of creating a liability against the plaintiff company which did not before exist, and, because of the creation of this liability, plaintiff claims the right to sue. Judgment has been rendered in favor of the Louisville bank against plaintiff company for the amount of the [376] notes, it not being able to defend against the Louisville bank, and a part of the same has been paid. Such is the case as made out in the bill. Several of the grounds of demurrer are not well laid, but we treat them together, as raising the real question at issue in the cause, which may be briefly stated as follows:

Can the holder of negotiable paper, upon which there is the void indorsement of a corporation, known to be void by the holder, transfer it to a third party with no knowledge of the infirmity, and thus create a liability against the indorser, which did not exist in the hands of the holder before transfer? The gist of the action is the knowingly transferring the paper for the express purpose of creating such liability as did not exist before the transfer, and by which the transferrer is to be benefited.

While some special objections are raised by the demurrer to the form of the declaration and the statements contained in it, these objections are more technical than real, and the effect of the demurrer is virtually to concede that the defendant bank had no right to recover upon the paper when it made the transfer, and that it was transferred to the Louisville bank, apparently in due course of trade, for the express purpose of enabling that bank to collect the note despite the infirmity in it, the proceeds held for the use and benefit of the Nashville bank, and thus imposing a liability on the indorser that did not exist while the Nashville bank held the note.

[377] On the other hand, plaintiff concedes that the Nashville bank might, if holding in good faith, have transferred the note in due course of trade, and made plaintiff liable to the transferee, without liability against it, for such transfer; but the gravamen of the charge is that the transfer was made not in due course of trade, so far as the Nashville bank was concerned, but fraudulently, to enable the Louisville bank, as an apparently innocent holder, to collect the proceeds and hold them for the use and benefit of the Nashville bank, thus enabling the Nashville bank, through the Louisville bank, to collect the note from plaintiff as indorser, which it could not do if it retained the note in its own possession.

The plaintiff insists that, while the notes affected by this infirmity, so far as the Nashville bank is concerned, were in the hands of that bank, it had two remedies to protect itself —one to enjoin the transfer of the notes till the indorsement was erased, and the other to notify the holder of the illegality of the indorsement, and of its nonliability on account of it. It is said the former course was doubtful and embarrassed, as the plaintiff company could not allege insolvency of the Nashville bank, nor that it was about to make the transfer. Hence the latter course was pursued, and the claim now is for damages for making the transfer under the circumstances. We have been cited to no case directly in point, and perhaps there is none to be found, [378] though we think the principles involved have been settled upon a somewhat different state of facts in several cases.

The case of *Metropolitan Elevated Ry. Co. v. Kneeland*, 120 N. Y. 134, 17 Am. St. Rep. 619, is relied on. That was an action for damages by the corporation against its directors, first, for illegally voting a salary to the president of the company, and, second, authorizing the issuance of negotiable notes therefor, which went into the hands of an innocent holder. The court held that no liability attached to the directors for voting the salary, for that, being illegal, created no liability, but that such of the directors as voted to issue the negotiable notes were liable, because such notes did create a liability when they came into the hands of an innocent holder. The court said: "We think the cases relating to this subject rest upon the principle that a person who fraudulently places in circulation the negotiable instrument of another, whether made by him or his apparent authority, and thereby renders him liable to pay the same to a *bona fide* purchaser, is guilty of a tort, and liable for the value of the note. The essential injury common to all cases of this character is the fraudulent imposition of liability. Hence, there should be a common remedy, whether it is called an action for conversion, or in the nature of a conversion, or a special action on the case."

The case proceeds: "In what respect do the wrongful acts of the directors who negotiated the [379] notes differ from those cases which were held to authorize an action for conversion or an action in the nature of conversion of negotiable paper? Is there not in each the same presumption of damages springing from a liability wrongfully imposed? Were not all of these actions founded on the fact that the maker, real or apparent, of a negotiable instrument had, through the wrongful acts of another, become chargeable, so that he could be compelled to pay such instrument, which would not have ripened into a valid obligation against him but for such wrongful act?"

There are numerous cases holding a party liable for the unauthorized conversion of negotiable paper. In *Decker* v. *Mathews*, 12 N. Y. 313, it is said, in substance, that the gravamen of such action is the wrongful act of the defendant in causing a note without value, except to a *bona fide* holder, to become valuable by a sale thereof to such a purchaser as could enforce it against the plaintiff, and the right of action accrues as soon as the transfer is made, and before payment enforced.

In *Thayer* v. *Manley*, 73 N. Y. 305, defendant fraudulently induced plaintiff to execute and deliver to him these notes, but, before they matured, plaintiff demanded their return to him, which was refused. It was held that, as defendant had it in his power when suit began to dispose of the notes to a *bona fide* holder, in whose hands they would have been valid, plaintiff was entitled to recover their full [380] value, which might be discharged by a return of the notes.

In *Farnham* v. *Benedict*, 107 N. Y. 159, defendant being in possession, without title, of certain town bonds that had been fraudulently issued through his procurement, and which were void in fact, but apparently valid, sold them to *bona fide* purchasers, and thus rendered them valid and binding on the town, which was compelled to pay them. It was held that he was liable to the town for the amount of the bonds, and that an action lay either in the nature of trover for the face of the bonds or for money had and received for the money realized therefrom, according to the rule laid down in *Comstock* v. *Hier*, 73 N. Y. 269, 29 Am. Rep. 142.

In *Betz* v. *Daily*, 3 N. Y. St. Rep. 309, it was held that, in an action by a partner against his copartner and others for fraudulently making notes in the name of the firm and negotiating them to innocent holders, the cause of action was complete when the wrong was done, and that payment of the notes was not essential to recovery, the court holding that the injury was done when the notes were first negotiated.

In *Ontario* v. *Hill*, 33 Hun, 250, the defendants were held liable for wrongfully issuing the negotiable notes of a town, some of which had gone into the hands of innocent holders. This case was afterward reversed, but not on this point: See *Ontario* v. *Hill*, 99 N. Y. 324. See, also, [381] *Haas* v. *Sackett*, 40 Minn. 53, and cases there cited.

In the case at bar it is proper to remember that the Nashville bank had title to this paper as against the maker, and so far as the maker is concerned, its transfer was in no sense a conversion of the paper, but it did not have the legal right to the plaintiff's indorsement, nor any right to pass it to another. Nevertheless, the transfer put the legal title of the paper and its indorsement in the Louisville bank, which had no notice of the infirmity of the paper, and hence the plaintiff could not defend against its suit. It must be borne in mind that the case at bar is not the case of an indorser who has received value for his name and credit, and who then seeks to avoid the contract, in which case he must refund the money or be denied relief, and hence many of the cases cited for the bank do not apply, and need not be commented on.

The case of *Freeman* v. *Venner*, 120 Mass. 424, is specially relied on by defendant bank, but in that case the plaintiff, upon his own showing, could not impeach the defendant's title to the note, nor his right to transfer that title to another, and it is not therefore analogous to this.

The case of *Solinger* v. *Earle*, 82 N. Y. 396–400, is also relied on, but in that case the party who sought damages for the unauthorized use of his note was denied relief because he was guilty of a [382] legal wrong in putting the note into existence, and the court repelled him because of this wrong.

In this case at bar, however, the plaintiff company did not put its indorsement into circulation, but it was made without consideration, for accommodation, and without authority by its secretary, and without knowledge of the directory.

The case, as presented to us by the declaration and demurrer, is that of a holder of paper upon which it cannot legally recover against an indorser transferring that paper to a third person so as to enable such person to collect the paper from the indorser, not for the transferee's benefit and in due course of trade, but for the use and benefit of the transferring bank, and thus indirectly holding the indorser liable when the transferring bank could not regularly so hold it. The principle would be the same if the bank at Nashville had held the note of the plaintiff on which it was maker, and which for any reason was void, and had, before maturity, transferred it to the Louisville bank in order to enable it to collect it for account of the Nashville bank. In each case it is an appropriation to its own use by forms of law of the credit and money of the indorser or maker to which the Nashville bank had no right, and we think the case falls within the reason of the cases here cited.

We are of opinion there is error in the ruling of the court below, and it is reversed and cause remanded for trial.

———

NEGOTIABLE INSTRUMENTS—ACCOMMODATION INDORSERS—LIABILITY TO BONA FIDE PURCHASERS.—An accommodation indorser is liable to a holder in good faith, although the indorsement was procured by the maker's fraud: *Marks* v. *First Nat. Bank*, 79 Ala. 550; 58 Am. Rep. 620. See also the extended note to *Credit Co.* v. *Howe Machine Co.*, 1 Am. St. Rep. 136, 138.

STRINGFIELD v. HIRSCH.

[94 TENNESSEE, 425.]

DAMAGES—ATTORNEYS' FEES AS ELEMENT OF.—In an action on an attachment or injunction bond to recover for the wrongful suing out of the attachment or injunction, attorneys fees are not a proper element of damages.

DAMAGES FOR BREACH OF ATTACHMENT OR INJUNCTION BOND—TAXES AS ELEMENT OF.—If a fund in the hands of a receiver is impounded by wrongful attachment or injunction taxes accruing on such fund and paid out thereof, pending the litigation are not a proper element of damages to be recovered in an action on the attachment or injunction bond.

DAMAGES FOR BREACH OF ATTACHMENT OR INJUNCTION BOND.—RECEIVER'S COMPENSATION AS ELEMENT OF.—If a fund in the hands of a receiver is impounded by wrongful attachment or injunction the receiver's commissions accruing from loaning out the fund during the litigation are not a proper element of damages in an action upon the bond.

DAMAGES FOR BREACH OF ATTACHMENT OR INJUNCTION BOND.—JOINT JUDGMENT WHEN ERRONEOUS.—If several creditors successively and wrongfully attach or enjoin the distribution of the same fund of their debtor, each giving a separate bond, a joint judgment against all of them in an action on such bonds, or a judgment against each for the full amount of the damages resulting from such wrongful attachment and injunction is erroneous. The damages should be apportioned according to the amount thereof caused by each creditor.

J. S. Pilcher, for Stringfield, Einstein & Co.

Champion, Head & Brown, and L. R. Campbell, for Etlinger & Co.

N. Cohn, and Steger, Washington & Jackson, for Fechheimer.

J. W. Gaines and E. A. Price, for Mendil, Bremen & Co.

J. Ruhm & Son, for Jonas, Lowenheim, and Petri.

Colyar, Williamson & Colyar, and J. S. Pilcher, for Margaret G. Neal.

Daniel & Watt, for Henry E. Neal.

[426] WILKES, J.   On July 3, 1891, attachments were separately sued out in the chancery court of Davidson county by Jonas & Co., Lowenheim and Petri, creditors of I. Mihalovitch, and levied on a stock of goods as the property of I. Mihalovitch, [427] a resident of Cincinnati, Ohio, but in possession of his son-in-law, Joseph Hirsch, in the city of Nashville. The clerk and master was appointed receiver, and took charge of the goods attached, and sold them, under the orders of the court, on July 27, 1891, for ten thousand dollars,

the sale being confirmed July 31, 1891, by the court. After the property had thus been attached as the property of Mihalovich, and placed in the hands of the receiver and sold, various creditors, some eleven in number, filed bills seeking to impound the proceeds of sale, alleging that Hirsch was the real owner of the property, and enjoining the paying over the proceeds to the creditors of Mihalovitch.

The bill of Stringfield, Einstein & Company was filed August 1, 1891, and is especially referred to as raising the issues in this case. The prayer of their bill was that enough of the proceeds of sale of the goods be impounded to satisfy complainant's debt. An order was granted, upon complainants giving bond in the sum of one thousand dollars, conditioned to pay all damages for the wrongful procuring of the restraining order, that a sufficient amount of such proceeds be impounded to satisfy complainants' debt. Bond was given payable to Hirsch & Co., and other defendants, not naming them, but no injunction was issued in that special case. In other case s creditors attached the proceeds as the property of Hirsch & Co., and enjoined Jonas, Lowenheim, and Petri from receiving the proceeds of the sale. Answers [428] were filed, and an order was obtained dissolving the injunction and removing the restraining order upon the execution of refunding bonds, but, in the mean time, other bills attaching and impounding the funds and enjoining their payment, followed in rapid succession, so that the refunding bonds were never, in fact, executed, and the funds remained in the hands of the receiver and under the custody of the court until final hearing, when the attachments were dismissed, injunctions dissolved, and impounding orders removed, so far as they interfered with Jonas, Lowenheim, and Petri, the court holding their bills to be properly filed, and that the property should be applied to the debts of Mihalovitch, instead of to the debts of Hirsch & Co. The cause was appealed to this court, and, at a former term, this court dismissed the appeal, holding that Mihalovitch was a fraudulent vendee and Hirsch & Co. were fraudulent grantors; that, as between the creditors of the fraudulent vendee, Mihalovitch, and the fraudulent vendor, Hirsch & Co., the goods should go to the creditors of Mihalovitch, inasmuch as they were first attached as his property.

The cause was remanded to the chancery court to execute all unexecuted orders, and for a reference to the clerk and

master to report the damages sustained by the wrongful
suing out of the injunction writs and impounding orders.
The clerk and master executed the order of reference, and
reported as damages the following items:

Counsel fees in securing dissolution of injunction and impounding orders...............................	$250 00
Taxes for 1892 and 1893 on fund impounded...............	120 00
Costs incurred under injunction and impounding proceedings... .	11 40
Commissions to receiver on impounded fund loaned out to attaching creditors..................................	68 70
Total..................♦..................	$440 60

429 Exceptions were filed to this report, but the account
was finally confirmed, and it was decreed by the court that
Petri, Jonas, and Lowenheim, attaching creditors of Mihalovitch, recover of the complainants who attached as creditors
of Hirsch & Co., and the sureties on their bonds, the amount
of four hundred and forty dollars and sixty cents and costs,
for which execution might issue.   The decree further provided: " But, as between said original complainants, the court
is of opinion, and so decrees, that each should contribute
to the recovery against them herein had for damages and
costs an amount which would be equal in proportion to the
amount of the respective debts of each upon which suits
were brought, and, if complainants so desire, they may, as
between themselves, have a reference to the clerk and master
to ascertain their proportion on the above basis, and a reference was ordered accordingly, the clerk and master to report
as soon as practicable.   From this decree the several complainants, creditors of Hirsch & Co., appealed, the order of
reference being unexecuted, and they have assigned errors:
These errors are, in substance: 1. That attorney's fees are not
a proper element **430** of damages for wrongfully suing out
attachment or injunction writs and obtaining impounding
orders; 2. That taxes paid by the receiver on the fund while
in his hands under impounding orders are not proper elements of damage in such cases; 3. That the item of eleven dol-
ars and forty cents costs was not a proper matter of damages;
4. That the commissions of sixty-eight dollars and seventy
cents to the receiver should not have been allowed as damages; 5. That it was error to allow damages against parties
who reached nothing by their attachments on account of the
fact that the entire fund was absorbed by prior attachments;

6. That it was error to give a joint judgment against all the creditors, and against each for the full amount of the entire fee allowed for all the cases; 7. That the court erred in adjudging against appellants the costs of the reference to the clerk and master.

The first and most important question presented is, Are counsel fees proper elements of damage in cases where attachments and injunctions are wrongfully sued out and impounding orders wrongfully obtained? Upon this question there is an abundance of authority and an irreconcilable conflict of decisions in the courts of the several states and the federal courts.

In High on Injunctions, section 1685, it is held that, according to the great weight of authority, reasonable [431] counsel fees, incurred in procuring the dissolution of an injunction, is a proper element of damages, the amount being limited to the fees paid for procuring the dissolution, and not for the general defense of the case. This holding proceeds upon the idea that the defendant has been compelled to employ counsel to rid himself of an unjust restriction which the plaintiff has placed upon him, and hence such fees will only be allowed when motion is made to dissolve pending the litigation and before the hearing on the merits: Sec. 1686. Again: Fees will not be allowed to cover the entire expense of the defense, but only for such as was incurred about the injunction: Secs. 1688–1690. See, also, 1 Sedgwick on Damages, sec. 257; 1 Sutherland on Damages, sec. 85; 2 Sutherland on Damages, secs. 524, 525; Beach on Injunctions, secs. 203–210. In these text-books the principal authorities pro and con are cited and collated. A well-considered case holding the majority view is *Cook* v. *Chapman*, 41 N. J. Eq. 152.

This rule thus stated, with minor modifications, is laid down in some twenty-six states of the union, among them the following: Alabama, California, Colorado, Florida, Georgia, Illinois, Indiana, Kansas, Kentucky, Louisiana, Michigan, Minnesota, Missouri, Montana, Nevada, New Hampshire, New Jersey, New York, Ohio, Virginia, and West Virginia. In some of these states the matter is regulated by statute, as in Iowa, Mississippi, and Washington state. But [432] the rule is held otherwise in Arkansas, Maryland, North Carolina, Oregon, Pennsylvania, South Carolina, South Dakota, Texas, Vermont, and is settled by neither statute nor decision in Connecticut, Massachusetts,

North Dakota, and Rhode Island, so far as we have been able to ascertain. In the United States supreme court and in the federal courts such fees are not allowed.

The case of *Oelrichs* v. *Spain*, 15 Wall. 211, sets forth the holding of the supreme court of the United States in a case very similar to the one at bar. In that case injunction was granted upon a bond conditioned to prosecute the writ with effect, or pay and satisfy the damages and charges which should be occasioned by such writ. The injunction was dismissed, and suit was brought upon the bond to recover damages, including counsel fees. The court below allowed two thousand five hundred dollars counsel fees, and the case was appealed. The court referred to the cases of *Arcambel* v. *Wiseman*, 3 Dall. 306; *Teese* v. *Huntington*, 23 How. 2; *Day* v. *Woodworth*, 13 How. 370, 371, and other cases, as being analogous, and continued: "The point here in question has never been decided by this court, but it is clearly within the reasoning of the case in 13 Howard, and we think it substantially determined by that adjudication. In debt, covenant, and assumpsit damages are recovered, but counsel fees are never included. So in equity cases, where there are no injunctions, only taxable costs are allowed complainants. The [433] same rule is applied to the defendant, however unjust the litigation of the other side may be, and however large the *expensa lites* to which he may have been subjected. The parties, in this respect, are on a footing of equality. There is no fixed standard by which the honorarium can be measured. Some counsel demand more than others, more counsel may be employed than are necessary; when client and counsel both know that the fees are to be paid by the other party there is danger of abuse. A reference to a master, or an issue to a jury, might be necessary to ascertain the proper amount, and the grafted litigation might be more animated and protracted than that in the original cause. It would be an office of some delicacy on the part of the court to scale down the charges, as might some times be necessary." The court continues: "We think the principle of disallowance rests on a solid foundation, and the opposite rule is forbidden by the analogies of the law and sound public policy."

In Tennessee we have the following cases bearing more or less directly on the controversy:

In *Littleton* v. *Frank Bros.*, 2 Lea, 301, Deaderick, C. J., delivered the opinion of the court: "This is an action at law by plaintiff against defendants, who were sureties on an attachment bond executed in a suit in chancery court. The attachment was issued wrongfully, although on probable cause. The damages sued for are counsel fees, one hundred and twenty-five dollars, and costs, two dollars and fifty cents, incurred in defending said attachment [434] suit. The circuit judge, deciding the case without a jury, held the plaintiff not entitled to recover, and she appealed. As to the one hundred and twenty-five dollars counsel fees, we have held in an unreported case such fee is not recoverable in cases like this. But plaintiff, for the wrongful suing out of the injunction, is entitled to recover some damages, and the judgment of the circuit court will be reversed, and judgment entered here for plaintiff for two dollars and fifty cents damages, with costs": *Littleton* v. *Frank Bros.*, 2 Lea, 301.

In *Williams* v. *Burg*, 9 Lea, 456, suit was brought to recover upon an alleged breach of warranty in a deed, where the title had failed. In such case, of course, the defendant must make defense, and the eviction must be by legal process, in order to entitle the vendee to proceed upon the covenant of warranty. It is a matter of necessity that he shall defend, and, in such defense, the services of an attorney are necessary. In regard to the right to recover attorney's fees in making such defense this court used this language:

"If the employment of counsel be necessary, upon principle, it is not easy to see why the expense is not as much a legitimate part of the damage sustained as the costs of the cause. The common-law doctrine that the services of counsel are honorary and gratuitous does not prevail in this state: *Newnan* v. *Washington*, Mart. & Yerg. 79. Yet, if such expense is put upon the same ground as the costs, the plaintiff would in every case recover his [435] necessary counsel fees in protecting a rightful claim against a defendant precisely as he recovers his costs. There would be some justice in the claim, and, in some states and in the federal courts, a tax fee is, in some instances, allowed. But such fees have never been allowed in the courts of this state. It is within the recollection of some of the members of this court that we have decided against the claim in a case precisely of this character. We have certainly so decided analogous cases, and the chancellor's decree on this point will be affirmed: *Williams* v. *Burg*, 9 Lea, 456, 457.

In the case of *Davenport* v. *Harbert*, 1 Leg. Rep. 172, it was sought to recover attorney's fees as damages upon an injunction bond. This court refused to allow such damages, and in deciding the case used this language: "To hold her responsible for fees to adversary's counsel would be to establish precedents under which all successful defendants might claim reimbursements for fees paid their attorneys": *Davenport* v. *Harbert*, 1 Leg. Rep. 173.

In *White* v. *Clack*, 2 Swan, 231, this court declined, in an action for mesne profits, to allow counsel fees incurred in the prosecution of the action of ejectment.

It is insisted that the cases of *Davenport* v. *Harbert*, 1 Leg. Rep. 173, and *Oelrichs* v. *Spain*, 15 Wall. 211, are not exactly similar to the case at bar, inasmuch as they do not show that [436] the fees claimed in those cases were properly fees incurred about the injunctions alone, and not in the general defense of the cases; and this criticism is just, so far as we can see from the meager reports of these cases; but at last the question, if not settled by these cases on analogies, is one of broad public policy, and should be settled in accordance with the general trend of our decisions in similar cases and with the wisest public policy.

It is difficult to see upon what ground counsel fees incurred by the adverse party should be charged up to the defeated party any more in attachment and injunction cases than in other litigations upon contracts or for damages for torts. The litigation may be equally unjust and oppressive in other cases as in the case of attachments and injunctions. It is true the latter cases are, in some respects, more summary, and may entail damages arising out of the seizure of defendant's property; but all this is provided for by the terms of the bond required to cover damages sustained. But counsel fees are as necessary in the one class of cases as in the other, and are neither peculiar nor more onerous in cases of attachments and injunctions than in other cases.

It is said that additional fees are required to remove the attachment and injunction, and relieve from the impounding orders, but this is more imaginary than real, as the attention necessary to protect and guard against the injunction or attachment is in a vast majority, if not all, the cases merely incidental [437] to the defense upon the merits, and it is practically impossible to distinguish between services rendered about the attachment or injunction and that about the de-

fense of the case generally. Any apportionment of the fees
between these different services is more or less arbitrary and
fanciful. But, if it were otherwise, it is at least but counsel
fees of the opposite party which his adversary is called upon
to pay.

It is said that in attachment and injunction cases a bond
is required, the conditions of which are to pay all such damages as occur by the wrongful suing out of the writs, and
that this creates virtually a contract on the part of the defendant to pay such damages. But we think that this is a
mistaken view of the office and reason of the bond. The liability for damages for wrongfully suing would be the same
so far as the principal in the bond is concerned, whether
the bond were executed or not, and the office of the bond is
not to create or regulate the liability of the principal, but to
bring in the bondsmen, as the securities of the principal, to
answer for such damages as are proper. While the liability
of the sureties arises out of the execution and condition of
the bond the liability of the principal in nowise depends
upon the bond or its conditions.

We think that the analogies of the law, as well as the
soundest public policy, demand that counsel fees, in suits
upon contracts, or for damages for torts, or upon attachments
or injunctions, should not be regarded as a proper element
of damages, even where [438] they are capable of being apportioned so as to show the amount incurred for the attachments
and injunctions as separate and distinct from the other services necessary in the case. It is not sound public policy to
place a penalty on the right to litigate; that the defeated
party must pay the fees of counsel for his successful opponent in any case, and especially since it throws wide the
doors of temptation for the opposing party and his counsel
to swell the fees to undue proportions, and, in cases of
attachment and injunction, to apportion them arbitrarily
between the fees pertaining properly to the attachment and
injunction and that relating to the merits of the case.

We think the second assignment of errors is well made.
The funds in the hands of the receiver were subject to taxation. There is no evidence or intimation that they were
doubly taxed. The parties entitled to the funds were residents of the state, and the funds were taxable, and would
have been so, we must assume, even if the complainants had
realized them, and put them into their business, or otherwise

invested them. We cannot presume that they would have so disposed of the funds as to escape taxation if they had been realized and paid over to them.

We think the item of sixty-eight dollars and seventy cents commissions to the clerk and master and receiver was not a proper element of damages. This was commission upon the interest which accrued from loaning out the impounded fund. Whether this should have been allowed [439] to the receiver is a question not now before us, but it appears that this fund was loaned to the creditors who were adjudged entitled to it on final hearing, and it was never, in fact, paid into the hands of the clerk, nor paid out by him, and was simply charged up to the attaching creditors on final settlement of their accounts. It was a mere incident to the receivership which was instituted by these creditors, and before the defendants appeared in the case. The fund could have been drawn out on refunding bond instead of being loaned.

It was error to charge each attaching party the full amount of these damages, or to give a joint judgment against them. There was no joint tort by the several attaching creditors. There was no joint liability between the principals and sureties in the several bonds executed, and no connection between them at the time the attachment and injunctions were sued out and the damage done. The fund in the case was originally impounded by the creditors Jonas, Petri, and Lowenheim. It remained tied up by them, as well as by the subsequent attachments, until the final hearing in the case. It is apparent that the liability of the first attaching creditors may be very different from that of one who subsequently attaches a fund already tied up in court. One may cause the loss of credit and damage to business, the other may not affect either. One creditor may reach no fund, while another may realize the whole of it. Each case must stand on [440] its own merits and facts. If wrongfully suing, each creditor is liable for his own tort. There is no joint liability for distinct and different torts. There is no right of contribution if one should have the whole of the recovery to pay. The attempt of the chancellor to apportion this joint judgment between the creditors in proportion to their debts proceeds upon a theory entirely untenable. It cannot be assumed, and certainly is not shown, that the damages were caused by the several creditors in the proportion of their respective debts. On the contrary, it clearly appears that it is impossible to show how much of this damage was incurred in each particular case, and hence the necessity for apportionment, but this necessity does not make the apportionment right and proper, but shows its incorrectness in theory.

The item of eleven dollars and forty cents purports to be made up of certain cost items taken from the tax journal, a book kept by the clerk and master in his office. The items are not specified and described so that we may know what they are. It is said these are items of cost, accruing alone upon account of the injunction and attachment proceeding in the several cases while being heard together. This may be so, but the nature of the items does not sufficiently appear, and, moreover, the joint judgment for them cannot be sustained in this case even if they were proper elements of damage. There are other reasons in these cases which make the decree of the chancellor [441] erroneous as to the different creditors, each having some facts peculiar to his case, but we deem it proper to pass over minor irregularities, and decide the matter involved on the broad grounds of the correctness or incorrectness of the items.

We are of opinion the chancellor was in error, and we reverse his decision and discharge the reference, and dismiss the proceedings at the cost of the complainants, Jonas & Co. Lowenheim, and Petri.

The case of *Margaret G. Neal* v. *Henry E. Neal* is entirely distinct and separate from the other cases, and has no connection with them in any way whatever, but involves the question alone of whether counsel fees paid for services rendered about the injunction only are legitimate elements of damage in a suit, or upon reference against the enjoining complainants and his sureties. The question is presented in this case clearly, and uncomplicated by any other question, and it is reported with the former cases to show the same holding and result.

The chancellor in the court below allowed the fee on reference, and we think this was error, and the decree of the chancellor is reversed, with costs against appellee.

———

ATTORNEYS' FEES AS ELEMENT OF DAMAGES GENERALLY: See the extended note to *Winkler* v. *Roeder*, 8 Am. St. Rep. 158.

ATTORNEYS' FEES AS ELEMENTS OF DAMAGES IN SUITS ON INJUNCTION, ATTACHMENT, AND OTHER BONDS: See the extended note to *Winkler* v. *Roeder*, 8 Am. St. Rep. 161.

GOODWIN *v.* GUILD.

[94 TENNESSEE, 486.]

MALICIOUS PROSECUTION—LIABILITY OF PUBLIC OFFICER—ENFORCEMENT OF VOID LAW.—A mayor of a city is not liable for malicious prosecution in attempting to enforce a void municipal ordinance before it is judicially declared invalid if he acts in good faith, without malice, oppression, or wanton disregard of the rights of any person, although at the time he may have notice that legal opinion as to the validity of the ordinance is divided.

MALICIOUS PROSECUTION.—PUBLIC OFFICERS ARE NOT LIABLE for malicious prosecution if they fall into an error in a case where the act to be done is not merely ministerial but is one requiring the exercise of judgment and discretion, even though an individual may suffer by the mistake, unless malice, oppression, or wanton prosecution, with an absence of all probable cause or excuse, is clearly proved against such officer.

Colyar, Williamson & Colyar, and *J. W. Gaines,* for the complainant.

Smith & Dickinson, Barthell & Keeble, and *J. D. Wade,* for the defendant.

486 WILKES, J. This is an action for false imprisonment and malicious prosecution. It was tried before a special judge in the court below without the intervention of a jury, and a judgment rendered **487** for fifteen hundred dollars— one thousand dollars of which were awarded as actual, and five hundred dollars as exemplary, damages—and defendant has appealed, and assigned many errors, which need not be treated in detail.

A short statement of the facts in the case is that plaintiff entered into a contract with the board of public works and affairs to construct a sewer in the city of Nashville. This contract, while dated April 14, 1892, appears to have been executed on the part of the board on April 18, 1892, and was in pursuance of a public letting to the lowest responsible bidder had before that date, and about April 2, 1892. The plaintiff secured the contract, and expected and intended to use convict labor in its execution; and there is proof tending to show that this fact was known to the board of public works and affairs at the time the contract was let to the lowest bidder. After the public letting, on the 2d of April, the mayor and city council of Nashville, on the fourteenth day of April, 1892, passed an ordinance making it unlawful for any person to use or employ convict labor on

any work to be executed under contract with the city of
Nashville, under a penalty of fifty dollars for each violation.
Defendant Guild was mayor of Nashville, and, being notified
that plaintiff was using convicts upon the work under his
contract with the city, on April 23, 1892, went before the
recorder, and procured Mr. Cleary, street overseer, to make
the necessary affidavit that plaintiff was violating the [488]
city ordinance by working convicts in the city limits under
his contract; and thereupon the recorder and judge of the
city court, at the suggestion of the said Guild, issued a warrant for plaintiff's arrest, which was given to a member of
the police force, who met the plaintiff, read the warrant to
him, and cited him to appear before the recorder on the next
morning, which he agreed to do. No actual arrest was made
by touching the plaintiff or taking him into custody, and no
bond for his appearance was required. He did appear, was
fined fifty dollars, appealed to the circuit court, and was in
that court tried and acquitted December 15, 1892, on the
ground that the city ordinance was in contravention of an act
of the general assembly, and hence was void, and gave no
authority for plaintiff's arrest. Thereupon, November 16,
1893, plaintiff brought this action for damages for false imprisonment and malicious prosecution against the defendant
personally, and against the members of the board of public
works individually, and the mayor and city council of Nashville. On demurrer, the action as to the mayor and city
council was dismissed. The cause was tried, and resulted
in the acquittal of the members of the board of public works,
and in judgment against defendant, Guild, as before stated.

It is conceded that the ordinance of the city under which
the mayor proceeded was in contravention of the law, and
was, therefore, void, but, at the time these proceedings were
taken, it had not been so [489] declared by any judicial tribunal, and defendant insists that he acted in perfect good faith
in attempting to execute the ordinance as it was passed and
stood upon the books of the city, and was actuated by no
malice. The circuit judge, in his written opinion, found that
defendant was actuated by no feelings of malice.

It is said, however, that previous to this time the board of
public works had considered this ordinance and come to the
conclusion that it was illegal, and had declined to enforce it,
and so notified the mayor, and such is the fact. It is also
said that the city attorney had given an opinion adverse to

the legality of the ordinance, and that this had been sent by
the board to the mayor along with a record of their action
declining to enforce the ordinance. The proof in regard to
this opinion is quite indefinite. It appears that such opinion was prepared by J. C. Bradford for the city attorney,
Anderson, who felt himself incompetent to pass upon the
matters, but at whose instance it was prepared, or to whom
it was given, or by whom it was called for, does not definitely
appear from the record. The defendant states emphatically
that it was not called for by him, or given to him, and that
he never saw it; but, on the contrary, that he applied to the
city attorney for an opinion, which the regular city attorney,
Anderson, declined to give, because of relationship to some
party indirectly interested. The opinion of the board of public works had no [490] judicial force, but was merely the expression of a divided board upon a legal question, which
they could pass upon for themselves, but could not settle for
any one else, and the record wholly fails to fix the defendant
with the receipt of the opinion of the city attorney, or the
special attorney, whose opinion appears to have been given
and afterwards lost in some unexplained manner. It does
appear that there was a division of opinion as to the validity
of the ordinance, and defendant states that his only object
was to test the law and execute it, if valid, and that he had
no other motive. It does not appear that he took any part
in the proceedings after they were first instituted, but merely
set on foot the proceedings to test and execute the ordinance.
It is evident that this void ordinance could not justify the
arrest of the plaintiff and his prosecution, still, it was the
duty of the mayor as the chief executive of the city, to see
its ordinances enforced, and, so long as he acted in good
faith, and with no malice or improper motive, he cannot be
held personally liable for a mere error in judgment. If he
took advantage of his official position to oppress the plaintiff, either from ill-will towards him, or because of any other
improper motive, he would be liable.

The doctrine is tersely stated in *Kendall* v. *Stokes*, 3 How.
87, 98, by Chief Justice Taney, in these words: "A public
officer is not liable to an action if he falls into an error in a
case where the act to be done is not merely a ministerial one,
[491] but is one in relation to which it is his duty to exercise
judgment and discretion, even though an individual may
suffer by his mistake."

In Bishop on Noncontract Law, section 787, it is said: "By the express or implied terms of an officer's authority he is to act honestly, carefully, and after the dictates of his own judgment, which, of necessity, being a human judgment, may err; therefore, when he has done what is thus commanded, whether the result is correct or not, he has exactly discharged his duty, and the law which compelled this of him will protect him, whatever harm may have befallen individuals."

In 14 American and English Encyclopædia of Law, page 41, it is held that "public officers, called upon to act officially, may be held liable for a malicious prosecution upon the same grounds as other persons. But malice and want of probable cause ought very clearly to appear in such case. The presumption being strongly in their favor, mere ignorance of the law or overpersuasion by others is not sufficient." While we would not be understood as going to this latter length, still it will not do to apply the same strict rules of liabilty to an executive officer, whose duty it is to see the laws executed, if he makes a mistake in judgment, that would be applied to an individual who has no public duty to perform in executing its laws. To hold this strict rule would paralyze the arm of every executive and peace officer; and while such officer, for any wanton or malicious **492** abuse of legal process which is set on foot for the oppression of a citizen, must be held liable to the same, or possibly a greater, extent than a private individual, still there must be undoubted evidence of malice, oppression, and wanton persecution, with the absence of all probable cause or excuse, to hold a public official liable for errors in the execution of his official duties.

We cannot concur in the suggestion that the control of the police and the enforcement of this ordinance against convict labor rested exclusively with the board of public works. While it was made their immediate duty to execute the ordinance, the mayor was not thereby relieved, as chief city executive, from his duty under the charter to see this, as well as all other ordinances, enforced.

The management of the penitentiary is vested in the superintendent, warden, and other officials in immediate charge, and it is their primary duty to see the laws enforced; but the governor of the state, as chief executive, is not thereby relieved from the duty of seeing that the laws in regard to the penitentiary and its convicts are enforced. He can neither delegate this duty to the prison officials, nor can they take it from him.

The action taken by the mayor was not, in the strict, technical sense, a criminal prosecution against the the plaintiff. As was said in *Sparta* v. *Lewis*, 91 Tenn. 374, "it is not a trial between the state and defendant, nor on a presentment or indictment by [493] and before a jury; but it is in the nature of a suit for debt. It is not a prosecution, but a suing in court to recover a penalty for the violation of a city ordinance." It in no sense imputed to the plaintiff any corrupt, infamous, or degrading act, or any moral turpitude, but simply a disregard of an ordinance standing upon the records of the city; and, while the warrant was in form an order for the arrest of plaintiff, still it was executed by simply reading it to him, and citing him to appear before the recorder the next morning, which he agreed to do. He was not taken into custody; was subjected to no indignity; was not required to go to jail, or even give a bond for his appearance before the recorder. He was not restrained of his liberty, or hindered in going where he pleased. He was virtually unknown to defendant, who had no personal ill-will toward him. While this is not necessary, still it is a circumstance throwing light upon the question whether the defendant had any improper motive of any kind in doing what he did.

We do not mean to be understood as holding that this ordinance was valid. It has already been held to be invalid. But, while it stood among the ordinances of the city, the mayor cannot be held liable personally if, in good faith, he attempted to execute the same in the discharge of his duty as he understood it, and in the absence of any malice, oppression, improper motive, or wanton disregard of the plaintiff's rights, and we are unable, from this [494] record, to find any evidence of such malice, oppression, or improper motive on the part of the defendant

For these reasons the judgment of the court below is reversed, and the cause dismissed at plaintiff's cost.

MALICIOUS PROSECUTION—LIABILITY OF PUBLIC OFFICER.—An action against a district attorney and another person for maliciously contriving to have the plaintiff indicted and by false representations obtaining an indictment against him for perjury, they knowing that he had not committed it, and by their false testimony obtaining a verdict of guilty against him which was afterwards set aside cannot be maintained: *Parker* v. *Huntington*, 2 Gray, 124.

NASHVILLE TRUST COMPANY *v.* SMYTHE.

[94 TENNESSEE, 513.]

NEGOTIABLE INSTRUMENTS SECURED BY LIEN — RIGHTS OF BONA FIDE HOLDERS.—An innocent holder for value and before maturity of negotiable notes secured by mortgage or vendor's lien, takes the notes as well as the security, freed from equities arising between prior holders and the mortgagor and mortgagee or the vendor and vendee.

NEGOTIABLE INSTRUMENTS.—ASSIGNMENT OF NOTES SECURED BY VENDOR'S LIEN is governed by the same rules as govern the assignment of notes secured by mortgage.

NEGOTIABLE INSTRUMENTS.—ASSIGNEES OF SEVERAL NOTES SECURED BY MORTGAGE OR VENDOR'S LIEN share *pro rata* in a proceeds thereof, irrespective of their dates of maturity or assignment, in the absence of contract or intention of the parties to vary this rule.

NEGOTIABLE INSTRUMENTS—ASSIGNMENT OF NOTES SECURED BY LIEN— PRIORITIES.—A parol or written agreement given in connection with the assignment of part of a series of negotiable notes secured by mortgage or vendor's lien, to prefer and give a priority to the assignee as to payment out of the proceeds of the security, is void as against subsequent innocent assignees for value of other notes in the same series.

NEGOTIABLE INSTRUMENTS—ASSIGNMENT OF MORTGAGE OR VENDOR'S LIEN TO SECURE NOTES.—A vendor or mortgagee may, by contract in writing or parol, assign the whole or any part of the mortgage or vendor's lien to secure any part of assignee's notes secured thereby, whether such notes be the first or last maturing or the intermediate notes of the series.

NEGOTIABLE INSTRUMENTS—ASSIGNMENT OF NOTES SECURED BY LIEN— BONA FIDE PURCHASER.—A purchaser or assignee of part of a series of notes secured by mortgage or vendor's lien, without notice but without inquiry, is not a *bona fide* purchaser as against a prior assignee of a part of the same series of notes under a contract with the lienholder giving a preference and priority in the proceeds of the security.

Granbery & Marks, for the complainant.

Smith & Dickinson and *J. S. Pilcher*, for the defendants.

⁵¹⁴ SNODGRASS, C. J. The question in this case arises under a bill filed July 30, 1892, by the Nashville Trust Co., as agent of Mrs. Martha M. Reed, against J. C. Smythe, *et al.*, to enforce lien for the purchase money evidenced by negotiable promissory notes, executed as consideration for certain real estate, sold and conveyed on the 20th of December, 1890, by defendant, Everett, to Mrs. Marlin. There were one hundred and twenty-six of these notes for twenty dollars each, except the last, which was for twenty-five dollars, payable ⁵¹⁵ by Marlin and wife to Everett. They bore interest from date, and matured, respectively, on the first day of each succeeding month after their date, until the end of one hundred

and twenty-six months. They were secured by lien, expressly
reserved on the face of the deed of Everett to Mrs. Marlin.
The complainant alleged that Mrs. Reed became the owner of
forty of said notes, maturing on and after April 1, 1898. The
bill was filed on her behalf, and that of all other holders of
said notes, and sought to sell the real estate for the amounts
due on all.   Other note-holders came in by petition, among
them Miss C. L. S. Crowninshield, as guardian of C. G.
and Caroline Underhill, and James S. Pilcher.   They alleged
that thirty of said notes, the thirteenth to the forty-second,
inclusive, were assigned by said Everett to C. L. S. Crowninshield, as said guardian, on January 22, 1891, to secure the
payment of three hundred and sixty-six dollars and sixty-
seven cents she, on that day, lent Everett; that at that time
Everett was the owner of the entire series of notes, and that
in the assignment of said thirty notes a preference was given
over the other notes as to the vendor's lien to secure the
same.   The instrument giving the preference was in writing,
and was as follows:

"NASHVILLE, TENN., January 22, 1891.

"Twelve months after date we promise to pay to the order
of Miss C. L. S. Crowninshield, as guardian of C. G. and
Caroline C. Underhill, three hundred and sixty-six dollars
and sixty-seven cents [516] ($366.67) for value received, hav-
ing pledged on deposit as collateral security for the payment
of this note thirty notes out of the series of one hundred and
twenty-six notes given by A. J. Marlin and Ella May Marlin
for lot number thirty-one in B. F. Brown's subdivision.   Said
thirty notes being numbers thirteen to forty-two, inclusive,
of said series, and preference is given to said thirty notes
over the other notes of the said series as to the vendor's lien
to secure the same."   [SIGNED]

These petitioners show that the remainder of said sixty-
five notes held by said guardian and Jas. S. Pilcher were
also held as collateral on said loan for three hundred and
sixty-six dollars and sixty-seven cents, and that all of said
sixty-five notes, after satisfying said loan of three hundred
and sixty-six dollars and sixty-seven cents, were the property of James S. Pilcher; and they asserted priority for the
thirty notes.   Proof was taken, and it appeared that, at
the time of the execution of this instrument, Everett was
the owner of all the notes of the series, all of which were
transferred by him before maturity for valuable considera-

tions, after January 22, 1891, the date of the assignment quoted, and no other preferences were attempted to be given. The assignees of the other notes had no actual notice that the preference had been given as to the thirty notes assigned to Miss Crowninshield. The property was sold, and the amount brought was insufficient for the payment of all the notes. The chancellor decreed that no preference should be ⁵¹⁷ allowed to petitioner Crowninshield, guardian, and that all the note-holders were entitled to share equally in the proceeds of the sale.

Petitioners Crowninshield and Pilcher appealed, and assign as error that the court did not decree that, as to so much as was due to C. L. S. Crowninshield on said note for three hundred and sixty-six dollars and sixty-seven cents, she was entitled to be first paid out of the proceeds of the property, basing said assignment on the following propositions of law:

" 1. A vendor of lands who holds a series of notes given for the purchase money, where a lien is expressly retained upon the face of the deed, or a mortgagee who holds a number of notes which are secured by mortgage, in assigning one or more of such notes, has the power, by parol contract, to give to the assignee of such note or notes a preference as to payment out of the proceeds of the property, and the subsequent assignees of the other notes can take no higher rights than the vendor himself had; and citing *Menken* v. *Taylor*, 4 Lea, 445; *Hicks* v. *Smith*, 4 Lea, 459; *Hill* v. *McLean*, 10 Lea, 107; *Christian* v. *Clark*, 10 Lea, 630.

" 2. The right and power of a vendor or mortgagee to give a preference as to the vendor's or mortgagee's lien by parol contract, in the assignment of a part of the secured notes made at a time when the vendor or mortgagee is the owner and holder of all the other notes, is a rule of property in Tennessee, citing ⁵¹⁸ *Nichols* v. *Levy*, 5 Wall. 438; *Gelpcke* v. *Dubuque*, 1 Wall. 176; *Lee Co.* v. *Rogers*, 7 Wall. 181; *Chicago* v. *Sheldon*, 9 Wall. 50; and averring that the assignment of the notes in question, made January 22, 1891, when Everett held all other notes, wherein the preference was given to Miss Crowninshield, guardian, etc., was a contract, which, in effect, embodied the rule established in the cases in 4 and 10 Lea, cited above, and the same was and is a rule of property as to all such contracts made since said decisions."

The question of the case, therefore, involved in this assignment is, whether the assignee of the last assigned notes, they being negotiable promissory notes taken before maturity without actual notice of prior assignment and lien contract, and for valuable considerations, took them subject to any equity between the vendor and vendee of the land or the prior assignee of the first notes assigned. The assignment of error treats it as though it were only a question whether the assignor passed his rights; and it is assumed, that being settled affirmatively, that the subsequent assignee takes no higher right than the assignor himself had.

In support of this assumption and contention appellants lay down two propositions: That the assignee of a mortgage or deed of trust does not occupy the position of an assignee of commercial paper, but takes and holds the same subject to all the equities that could be urged against it in the hands of the original owner: Citing *Olds* v *Cummings*, 31 Ill. [519] 188; *Walker* v. *Dement*, 42 Ill. 272; *Cramer* v. *Willetts*, 61 Ill. 481; *Haskell* v. *Brown*, 65 Ill. 29; *Shippen* v. *Whittier*, 117 Ill. 282; *Abele* v. *McGuigan*, 78 Mich. 415; *Harrison* v. *Burlingame*, 48 Hun. 212.

And that the privileged character of negotiable paper does not extend to a mortgage by which it is secured: Citing *Oster* v. *Mickley*, 35 Minn. 245; *Johnson* v. *Carpenter*, 7 Minn. 176; *Hostetter* v. *Alexander*, 22 Minn. 559; *Blumenthal* v. *Jassoy*, 29 Minn. 177; *Richardson* v. *Woodruff*, 20 Neb. 132; *Crane* v. *Turner*, 67 N. Y. 437; *Horstman* v. *Gerker*, 49 Pa. St. 283; 88 Am. Dec. 501; *Twitchell* v. *McMurtrie*, 77 Pa. St. 383; *Atchison* v. *Butcher*, 3 Kan. 104; *Shippen* v. *Whittier*, 117 Ill. 282; *Fernon* v. *Farmer*, 1 Harr. (Del.) 32; Edwards on Promissory Notes, 165; 2 Daniel on Negotiable Instruments, 432.

These propositions will be found advanced and maintained in many of the cases cited, to which more could be added, if necessary. They are based, to some extent, on a failure to discriminate between the case of a mortgage to secure a debt expressed merely in the face of the mortgage, or to secure accounts or other non-negotiable debts, and that of a mortgage to secure negotiable paper. Respecting those which hold that the same rule prevails where the debts secured are negotiable notes, they are based upon the theory that, although the mortgage notes [520] are negotiable, the mortgage itself is only assignable in equity, and, therefore, the assignee, having to resort to equity to enforce his rights, is compelled to do equity toward the mortgagor, and allow him all the rights of defense he had against the mortgagee. Courts so holding make no distinction between mortgages securing negotiable and non-negotiable paper.

But this view Mr. Jones, in his work on Mortgages, fifth edition, section 838, says and shows is contrary to the general doctrine; and that the assignment of negotiable paper carries with it the security of the mortgage, and is unaffected by the equities between the mortgagor and the mortgagee. This latter he declares to be the generally accepted doctrine: Sec. 840. This has been recognized and declared by the supreme court of the United States: *Carpenter* v. *Longam*, 16 Wall. 271.

In that case Judge Swayne, who delivered the opinion of the court, calls attention to the distinction between the assignment of claims secured which were negotiable and non-negotiable, and to the confusion which has resulted from ignoring the character of claims secured by lien or mortgage. He thoroughly explodes the fallacy that an assignment of such negotiable paper for a valuable consideration, before maturity, without notice, does not carry to the assignee a right superior to that of the assignor. "The transfer of the note," he says, "carries with it the security, without any formal assignment [521] or delivery, or even mention of the latter. If not assignable at law it is clearly so in equity. When the amount due on the note is ascertained in the foreclosure proceeding equity recognizes it as conclusive, and decrees accordingly. Whether the title of the assignee is legal or equitable is immaterial. The result follows irrespective of that question. The process is only a mode of enforcing a lien. All the authorities agree that the debt is the principal thing and the mortgage an accessory. Equity puts the principal and accessory upon a footing of equality, and gives to the assignee of the evidence of the debt the same rights in regard to both. There is no departure from any principle of law or equity in reaching this conclusion. There is no analogy between this case and one where a chose in action standing alone is sought to be enforced. The fallacy which lies in overlooking this distinction has misled many able minds, and is the source of all the confusion that exists. The mortgage can have no separate existence. When the note is paid the mortgage expires. It cannot survive for a moment the debt which the note represents. This dependent and incidental relation is the controlling consideration, and takes the case out of the rule applied to choses in action where such relation of dependence exists. *Accessorium non ducit, sequi-tur principale.*" This case was followed and approved by the same court in the case of *Kenicott* v.`Board of Supervisors,* 16 Wall. 452.

[522] The whole subject will be found treated and cases collected in the nineteenth chapter of Mr. Jones' work on Mortgages, before referred to. We do not deem it necessary to go into a more extended citation or discussion. It is sufficient to say that we have no hesitation whatever in holding that such assignee of such notes does stand on higher grounds than the assignor, both in respect to the note assigned and to its mortgage security. If this were a question, therefore, merely between the assignee of the note and the payor of the note who had paid it to the assignor before the assignment, there would be no question that the right of the assignee would be superior, although the assignor's right would, of course, be inferior, or rather, the assignor's right to collect the note out of the payor would not exist. It remains to inquire later on whether this concession is a settlement of the question involved in this case. Before reaching that question, however, it is proper to consider the rights of parties generally under such assignments of debts secured by vendor's lien or mortgage.

Counsel for appellants treats, properly, the assignment of notes secured by vendor's lien as governed by the same rule as the assignment of notes secured by mortgage, the two being analagous, and governed by the same principles, so far as the question under consideration is concerned; but, as has been shown, he erroneously treats the question as though there were no distinction in the character of claims assigned. [523] On the general subject the law of the case is very fully cited, and the observation is just that there is, perhaps, no question on which there is greater conflict of authority than that relating to the rights of different assignees of a series of notes which are secured by mortgage, vendor's, or other liens. There are three different views taken by the courts, and many decisions can readily be found to support each view.

The supreme court of Arkansas has clearly set forth this matter in the following language and citations: "One class holds that the notes shall be paid in the order of their assignment: *McClintic* v. *Wise,* 25 Grant, 448; 18 Am. Rep. 694; *Cullum* v. *Erwin,* 4 Ala. 452; *Grigsby* v. *Hair,* 25 Ala. 327; *Waterman* v. *Hunt,* 2 R. I. 298. Another, that the notes should take precedence in the order of their maturity: *Mitchell* v. *Ladew*, 36 Mo. 526, 530; 88 Am. Dec. 156; *Sargent* v. *Howe*, 21 Ill. 148; *Vansant* v. *Allmon*, 23 Ill. 30; *Koester* v. *Burke*, 81 Ill. 436; *State Bank* v. *Tweedy*, 8 Blackf. 447; 46 Am. Dec. 486; *Doss* v. *Ditmars*, 70 Ind. 451; *Marine Bank* v. *International Bank*, 9 Wis. 57, 64; *McVay* v. *Bloodgood*, 9 Port. 547; *Richardson* v. *McKim*, 20 Kan. 346, 350; *Hinds* v. *Mooers*, 11 Iowa, 211; *Walker* v. *Schreiber*, 47 Iowa, 529; *Wilson* v. *Hayward*, 6 Fla. 171, 190; *Kyle* v. *Thompson*, 11 Ohio St. 616; *Winters* v. *Franklin Bank*, 33 Ohio St. 250. And a third class, that the proceeds should be applied *pro rata* in part payment of the several notes, irrespective of their dates of maturity or assignment: [524] *Donley* v. *Hays*, 17 Serg. & R. 40J, 404; *Cowden's Estate*, 1 Pa. St. 278; *Mohler's Appeal*, 5 Pa. St. 418, 420; 47 Am. Dec. 413; *Perry's Appeal*, 22 Pa. St. 43, 45; 60 Am. Dec. 63; *Grattan* v. *Wiggins*, 23 Cal. 16; *Dixon* v. *Clayville*, 44 Md. 575, 578; *English* v. *Carney*, 25 Mich. 178, 181; *McCurdy* v. *Clark*, 27 Mich. 445, 448; *Parker* v. *Mercer*, 6 How. (Miss.) 320, 324; 38 Am. Dec. 438; *Cage* v. *Iler*, 5 Smedes & M. 410; 43 Am. Dec. 521; *Pugh* v. *Holt*, 27 Miss. 461; *Andrews* v. *Hobgood*, 1 Lea, 693; *Parish Exchange Bank* v. *Beard*, 49 Tex. 363; *Delespine* v. *Campbell*, 52 Tex. 4; *Wilson* v. *Eigenbrodt*, 30 Minn. 4; *Penzel* v. *Brookmire*, 51 Ark. 105; 14 Am. St. Rep. 23."

The rule adopted in Tennessee is that the assignees of the several notes share *pro rata*, if there is nothing in the contract of assignment or in the intention of the parties to vary the rule; *Graham* v. *McCampbell*, Meigs, 52; 33 Am. Dec. 126; *Roberts* v. *Francis*, 2 Heisk. 133; *Andrews* v. *Hobgood*, 1 Lea, 693; *Ellis* v. *Roscoe*, 4 Baxt. 418; *Ewing* v. *Arthur*, 1 Humph. 537; *Wicks* v. *Caruthers*, 13 Lea, 353.

This rule is in accord with the great weight of authority. Among the cases above cited, to which many others might be added in affirmance of the rule as to equality of lien of note-holders, we call special attention to *Parker* v. *Mercer*, 6 How. (Miss.) 320, as reported in 38 Am. Dec. 438.

To this case the editor of the American Decisions appends a most valuable and elaborate note, in which many cases are collected. The question and cases are thus stated:

[525] "Several notes may be secured by one mortgage or deed of trust, and, when so secured, may be assigned to different persons. The question then arising is, Which note is entitled to precedence in payment out of the proceeds of the

security?   The answers to this question are irreconcilable, and may be arranged under three classes:

"1. Those which, like the principal case, affirm that the proceeds should be applied *pro rata* to the several notes, irrespective of their dates of maturity or of assignment, on the ground that each note, according to the proportion it bears to the whole debt, is secured by the whole mortgage, and continues so secured, whether assigned or not, in the absence of any stipulation to the contrary: *Keyes* v. *Wood*, 21 Vt. 331; *Pattison* v. *Hull*, 9 Cow. 747; *Phelan* v. *Olney*, 6 Cal. 478; *Donley* v. *Hays*, 17 Serg. & R. 400; *Betz* v. *Heebner*, 1 Pen. & W. 280; *Hancock's Appeal*, 34 Pa. St. 155; *Cooper* v. *Ulmann*, Walk. Ch. 251; *English* v. *Carey*, 25 Mich. 178; *McCurdy* v. *Clark*, 27 Mich. 445; *Wilcox* v. *Allen*, 36 Mich. 160; *Dixon* v. *Clayville*, 44 Md. 573; *Cage* v. *Iler*, 5 Smedes & M. 410; 43 Am. Dec. 521; *Henderson* v. *Herrod*, 10 Smedes & M. 631; *Trustees etc.* v. *Prentiss*, 29 Miss. 46; *Bank of England* v. *Tarleton*, 23 Miss. 173; *Stevenson* v. *Black*, 1 N. J. Eq. 338; *Page* v. *Pierce*, 26 N. H. 317; *Ewing* v. *Arthur*, 1 Humph. 536; *Andrews* v. *Hobgood*, 1 Lea, 693; *Smith* v. *Cunningham*, 2 Tenn. [526] Ch. 568; *Tinsley* v. *Boykin*, 46 Tex. 592; *Paris Exchange Bank* v. *Beard*, 49 Tex. 358.

"2. Those which affirm that, in the event of the assignment of the notes, or of any of them, the assignees take precedence over the assignor with respect to the notes retained by him, and that, as between several assignees, they are entitled to precedence in the order of their several assignments: *McClintic* v. *Wise*, 25 Gratt. 448; 18 Am. Rep. 694; *Grigsby* v. *Hair*, 25 Ala. 327; *Salzman* v. *His Creditors*, 2 Rob. (La.) 241; *Barkdull* v. *Herwig*, 30 La. Ann. 618; *Waterman* v. *Hunt*, 2 R. I. 298.

"3. Those which treat several notes secured by one mortgage as having precedence in the order in which such notes mature: *Richardson* v. *McKim*, 20 Kan. 346; *Wilson* v. *Hayward*, 6 Fla. 171; *Vansant* v. *Allmon*, 23 Ill. 30; *Funk* v. *McReynolds*, 33 Ill. 481; *State Bank* v. *Tweedy*, 8 Blackf. 447; 46 Am. Dec. 486; *Murdock* v. *Ford*, 17 Ind. 52; *Isett* v. *Lucas*, 17 Iowa, 503; 85 Am. Dec. 572; *Grapengether* v. *Fejervary*, 9 Iowa, 163; 74 Am. Dec. 336; *Mitchell* v. *Ladew*, 36 Mo. 526; 88 Am. Dec. 156; *Thompson* v. *Field*, 38 Mo. 320; *Ellis* v. *Lamme*, 42 Mo. 153; *Wood* v. *Trask*, 7 Wis. 566; 76 Am. Dec. 230; *Marine Bank* v. *International Bank*, 9 Wis. 57; *Lyman* v. *Smith*, 21 Wis. 674.

"Of course, there may be special equities arising out of the assignments, or out of the intention of the parties as manifested therein; and, when this is the case, the general rule of law will be considered inapplicable, and the special equities will be recognized and enforced. It will be seen from the [527] foregoing citations that the conflict of decisions on this subject is remarkable; that the cases falling within the first and those falling within the third class are so nearly equal that no decided preponderance appears. Those belonging to the second class are less numerous."

It will be observed that all these cases recognize the right of the vendor in the one case, or mortgagee in the other, to give a priority among notes secured by liens in a vendor's deed or in a mortgage, accordingly as he may contract with any assignee. This doctrine is well recognized in Tennessee. Here it is also held that such an assignment is good as between the assignor and the assignee, and that it need not be in writing, as appears to be the general rule: *Hicks* v. *Smith*, 4 Lea, 459. In this connection it is proper to say that to the extent noted, and only to that extent, have the Tennessee cases gone. It has not been established as the law of this state, and therefore, of course, not as a rule of property, that the transfer of a negotiable promissory note secured by mortgage, made in connection with contract giving to such assignee a prior lien, will vest in such assignee an equity superior to that of a subsequent assignee of one of said notes, who is a purchaser for value, and without notice of the former assignment and lien contract. The two cases cited in 4 Lea, and urged as holding that doctrine, were not cases of assignments to purchasers for value, but were assignments to pay [528] pre-existing debts. So far, therefore, the question here presented is an open one in this state.

We return now to a discussion of that question. Without regard to conflict or difference of opinion in cases cited, it appears that several questions are definitely settled, the principal one with which we are concerned being that the vendor or mortgagee may, by contract, in writing or parol, assign the whole or any part of the mortgage or vendor's lien to secure any part of the notes assigned, whether they be the first or last maturing, or the intermediate notes of any series.

It has been seen also that without respect to the question of the effect of the assignment of a portion of one note, or of a part of a series of notes secured in a mortgage (conditions

involving other and different considerations), many cases
assert the proposition that an assignment, when made, of a
single note, though negotiable, and the entire debt secured,
does not carry the equity of the mortgage security so as to
prevent an assertion of the equities between the original parties.

We have, however, shown that the weight of authority is,
and the clear rule of reason is, that as between the original
parties, the vendor and the vendee and the mortgagor and
mortgagee, the assignment of such a negotiable note by vendor or mortgagee may vest in the assignee a right superior
to that of the assignor, the vendor, or mortgagee.

There is, however, a different condition of fact [529] which
requires the assertion of a different equity between the subsequent assignee of one of a series of negotiable notes, without
actual notice of a prior assignment with lien of contract
priority, as between the two assignees, than that which would
prevail between such an assignee and the mortgagor.

It does not follow that, because the assignee of one of a
series of mortgage notes, which had been transferred and
delivered to him by the mortgagee, and which had been paid
by the mortgagor before such transfer and delivery, takes
such note freed of all equities of the mortgagor, that he would,
therefore, take it free from all equities of a prior assignee of
another note of the same series, which had been transferred
with a preference lien contract.

In the first case, the assignee's right would undoubtedly
be superior to that of the mortgagor, because, as between
these parties, the note itself is a single and perfect obligation. If the mortgagor had paid it off he should have taken
it up, and not left it in the hands of the mortgagee with
power to transfer to one who might be a *bona fide* purchaser
before maturity upon a valuable consideration, thus enabling
the mortgagee to give to such *bona fide* purchaser a perfect
title secured by the mortgage, upon which the purchaser had
a right to rely without actual notice of any thing to the contrary, and without any condition of facts which would put
him upon inquiry and charge him with notice.

When the assignee found such note so secured [530] still in
the hands of the mortgagee apparently unpaid he had the
right to assume that it was unpaid, and no duty devolved
upon him, as between him and the payor, to make further
inquiry. But such is not the rule if condition of facts

requiring its application do not exist—as between a subsequent and a prior assigneee of one of a series of negotiable notes secured by the same mortgage.

If the mortgagee holding any part of said notes proposed to assign them to another assignee, and, at the same time, to give to such assignee a preference over the lien of all other notes to the amount of those to be assigned, the assignee has notice that the note proposed to be indorsed to him is one of a series of notes secured by the same deed; he is presumed to know the law that the mortgagee can give to another assignee priority of lien. As a matter of fact, he knows that the mortgagee either has the other notes in his own hands unassigned, or that they are out of his possession and in the hands of others claiming them with or without preference of lien. He may not know the actual fact that any such notes have been assigned, or he may not be informed of it at the time by the assignor, but the mortgage deed itself, securing a number of notes, gives him notice that all are outstanding. He is charged, therefore, with constructive notice of another prior assignment, if one has been made, for he can demand of the mortgagee the production of the other notes of the series, and, if the mortgagee cannot [531] produce them, he will know that they either have or may have been assigned, and, being presumed to know the law, will know that they may have been assigned under contract giving preference of lien. He is, therefore, charged with constructive notice of what, upon such investigation, he might have discovered. If, for instance, he calls upon the mortgagee to know where the other notes are, and the mortgagee produces them unassigned, he could, of course, then buy those of the series proposed to be sold to him without danger of subjecting himself to loss on account of prior equity. If the mortgagee failed to produce the other notes, but insisted that they were not transferred to others, and that no prior liens had been given, the assignee could, but only at his peril, take the notes proposed to be assigned to him. The mortgage itself was notice of the existence of the other notes, and his presumed knowledge of the law is that some of them may have been assigned with lien preferences. These conditions require him, so far as the equities between him and the prior assignees are concerned, to ascertain, before purchasing, whether any prior assignment had been made, and whether, in connection with it, a superior lien had been, by contract, given to any prior assignee. A failure to make such inquiry is at the peril of such assignee. If he purchases one or more of the series of such notes without such inquiry, and loses the benefit expected therefrom, by reason of prior assignment of lien, it is his own fault. He was not, as between himself [532] and a prior assignee, about whose rights the facts and the law require inquiry, a *bona fide* purchaser: *Wilson* v. *Eigenbrodt*, 30 Minn. 4; *Moore* v. *Ware*, 38 Me. 496; *Phelan* v. *Olney*, 6 Cal. 478; *Keyes* v. *Wood*, 21 Vt. 331; *Roberts* v. *Halstead*, 9 Pa. St. 32; 49 Am. Dec. 541.

Upon the theory, therefore, that the assignees of such of the one hundred and twenty-six notes as were assigned after the transfer of the thirty-two notes and prior lien to Miss Crowinshield were not *bona fide* purchasers without notice of such assignment, we hold that her equity is superior to theirs, and she is entitled to have those notes fully paid before any portion of the proceeds of the sale is applied in satisfaction of the other notes.

The argument that this holding impairs the negotiability of paper is not well founded. The conclusion itself is based upon the fact that purchasers of such notes (parts of a series secured in a mortgage) are charged with notice that the others may have been, or may be, assigned under a special contract giving priority. Such a result may be avoided by mortgage drawn in such form as to prevent preferential assignments. Where this is not done, however, it is clear that the courts, under the rules of law established, are compelled to give these assignments effect according to the contract and intention of the parties.

The decree of the chancellor is, therefore, reversed, [533] and decree will be entered here in accordance with this opinion. The costs of the court below will be apportioned between the parties according to their respective interest in the notes, and the costs of this court will be paid by the appellees.

NEGOTIABLE INSTRUMENTS SECURED BY LIEN OR MORTGAGE—RIGHTS OF ASSIGNEES.—The transfer of a debt transfers the property conveyed to secure it: *Mitchell* v. *Ladew*, 36 Mo. 526; 88 Am. Dec. 156. Collateral security given by the maker to the indorser of a note for his indemnity inures to the benefit of the holder: *Phillips* v. *Thompson*, 2 Johns. Ch. 418; 7 Am. Dec. 535; *Moses* v. *Murgatroyd*, 1 Johns. Ch. 119; 7 Am. Dec. 478, and note. If a promissory note given for the purchase money of land is secured by a lien on the land, a *bona fide* purchaser of the note before maturity is entitled to the benefit of the lien, without regard to the equities between the original parties: *Duncan* v. *Louisville,* 13 Bush, 378; 26 Am. Rep. 201. See, also, the note to *New London Bank* v. *Lee,* 27 Am. Dec. 720.

NEGOTIABLE INSTRUMENTS SECURED BY SAME MORTGAGE — PRIORITY. When a mortgage is made to secure several notes which mature at different times and are assigned to different persons, and the proceeds of the mortgaged property are not sufficient to pay all the notes, such proceeds must be distributed among the different holders *pro rata,* irrespective of the dates of the assignments or of the maturity of the notes: *Penzel* v. *Brookmire,* 51 Ark. 105; 14 Am. St. Rep. 23, and note, with the cases collected. See the notes to *Parker* v. *Mercer,* 38 Am. Dec. 440, and *Terry* v. *Woods,* 45 Am. Dec. 277.

McFARLAND *v.* BUSH.

[94 TENNESSEE, 538.]

WILLS—SUBSCRIBING WITNESS.—A signature of a witness to a will, who does not write his name, make his mark thereon, or touch the pen in the hands of the other subscribing witness, who signs his name for him in his presence and at his request, and in the presence and at the request of the testator, is not sufficient to attest a will devising real estate.

WILLS—ATTESTING WITNESS.—A subscribing witness to a will devising real estate must make some kind of a mark upon the instrument in order to make it his signature thereto.

APPEAL—DICTUM.—Two or more questions properly arising in a case under the pleadings and proof may be determined, even though either one would have disposed of the entire case upon its merits without the other, and neither holding is a dictum, so long as it is properly raised and determined.

Thomas & House and J. H. Henderson, for the complainant.

Smith & Dickinson and H. P. Fowlkes, for the defendant.

539 WILKES, J. This case presents an issue of *devisavit vel non* over the will of Mrs. S. T. McFarland. There was a verdict in favor of the will in the court below, and the contestant has appealed and assigned errors.

The only question involved is as to the attestation of the will by one of the subscribing witnesses, James R. Barnes. The will purports to convey both personalty and land. It is admitted to be good and valid as to the personalty, but it is claimed to be inoperative as to the land because one of the subscribing witnesses, James R. Barnes, did not write his name, nor did he make his mark or touch the pen in the hands of the other subscribing witness, Battle, who signed his name for him in his presence and at his request, and in the presence and at the request of the testatrix. All other

requirements as to request by the testatrix, and the other
formalities necessary to make the execution of the instrument valid and perfect as a will, were complied with, the sole
question being, whether the attesting witness must make a
mark upon the will to answer for and stand in place of his
signature, where he is unable to write or sign his name himself and requests another party to write it for him.   Barnes
was examined as a witness on the trial, and stated that, while
he could neither read writing nor write, still he could recognize his name when written, and [540] he did indentify the
paper in controversy as the paper to which he authorized his
name to be subscribed.   He made this identification both
from the appearance of the name and the general appearance of the paper.

The court was requested to charge the jury that if they
found the paper writing in question was witnessed by one
witness, Battle, subscribing his own name as a witness at the
request of the testratrix, and that this witness subscribed
the name of another party, Barnes, at his request and that
of the testatrix, the said·Barnes not touching the pen nor
guiding the hand of the party signing the same, or making
his mark, this would not be sufficient attestation to pass real
estate, but this was refused.   We think this was error.

It has been held by this court, in *Ford* v. *Ford*, 7 Humph.
96, that a person whose name is written by another, and who
makes his mark thereto, is a good attesting witness to a will.
This practice, however, is not to be encouraged or extended:
1 Jarmin on Wills, 213.

This case is apparently based on the idea that not only is
the witnesses' name written by his authority, but, in addition, he takes a part in the signing, similar to that where
another person guides his hand, and he thus makes his own
signature through another.   But we are not inclined to extend the rule any further than it has already gone, and it
has been expressly held that a writing of the name [541] by
authority is not sufficient, unless it is accompanied by some
mark or sign of the person, who thus makes it his own signature: *Simmons* v. *Leonard*, 91 Tenn. 183; 30 Am. St. Rep.
875.

It is said this decision is a dictum on this point, the argument being that there were other questions involved in it
upon which the decision could have been, and would have
been, rested.   Grant this to be so, it does not make the hold-

ing and opinion in that case a dictum. The question was fairly and directly involved, fully considered, and deliberately passed upon. The fact that the decision may have been rested on a different ground, even though one more satisfactory, does not place the decision in the category of a dictum, if the question was fairly raised and duly considered and decided, as was the case in *Simmons* v. *Leonard,* 91 Tenn. 183; 30 Am. St. Rep. 875; see *Clark* v. *Thomas,* 4 Heisk. 422; *Bates* v. *Taylor,* 87 Tenn. 324, 325; *Porter* v. *Lea,* 88 Tenn. 791.

Two or more questions properly arising in a case under the pleadings and proof may be determined, even though either one would have disposed of the entire case on its merits without the other, and neither holding will be a dictum so long as it is properly raised and considered.

It is said that making a mark, thus (X), and touching the pen is of practically no importance, and does not serve to aid the witness in identifying the paper in any way. This may be so, and it would be an argument against allowing marksmen to [542] be attesting witnesses at all, but this is not the question before us, that having been decided in *Ford* v. *Ford,* 7 Humph. 96, and recognized in *Simmons* v. *Leonard,* 91 Tenn. 183; 30 Am. St. Rep. 875. But the witness must make some kind of mark upon the instrument in order to make it his signature and in place of his signature.

The judgment must be reversed and remanded and the costs will be paid out of the estate.

———

WILLS—ATTESTATION—SUFFICIENCY OF THE SIGNING BY SUBSCRIBING WITNESS.—Writing a witness' name in his presence, and at his request, is not sufficient where he does not affix his mark: *Simmons* v. *Leonard,* 91 Tenn. 183; 30 Am. St. Rep. 875, and note, with the cases collected.

MILLS v. BENNETT.

[94 TENNESSEE, 651.]

EXEMPTIONS,—WAIVER IN ADVANCE.—A person, whether single or the head of a family, if entitled to exemptions, cannot, at the time of contracting a debt, waive the benefit of the exemption laws by a contemporaneous agreement.

B. F. Booth, for the complainant.

M. D. Fleming, for the defendant.

[651] MCALISTER, J. The only question presented for determination in this cause is whether a debtor may [652] waive his exemptions for the benefit of his creditor. The stipulation for a waiver of exemptions was incorporated in the following note, viz:

"MEMPHIS, TENN., August 23, 1894.

"Thirty days after date I promise to pay to the order of G. M. Anderson five dollars. I do hereby agree to waive my rights to exemption under the laws of the state of Tennessee until the bill is paid in full. Value received.

"H. H. BENNETT.

"Witness: J. M. Simms,
          "Wm. H. Mills."

[Indorsed]: "I do hereby transfer the within note to W. H. Mills.   G. M. ANDERSON."

The defendant, Bennett, is a daily laborer in the employment of Stewart, Gwynne & Co., a mercantile firm in the city of Memphis. The creditor is seeking, by these proceedings, to subject to the payment of his judgment wages due Bennett, which are exempt by law from execution, seizure, or attachment: Code, sec. 2931.

It appears from the record that Bennett is the head of a family, with a wife and three children. This consideration, however, is immaterial, since it is not necessary, in order to entitle the defendant to this particular exemption, that he should have been the head of a family. Of course, this fact only emphasizes the necessity for such exemption, but it is not material as a matter of law. There are other exemptions which are dependent upon this condition, [653] and the validity of contracts entered into by the head of the family is considered from this point of view. It will be observed that the defendant in this case, upon the face of the note, waives all his exemptions—those secured to him as the head of a fam-

ily, and those which he is entitled to independently of the
family. Is such a contract valid and enforceable? It was
held in the case of *Denny* v. *White*, 2 Cold. 283, 88 Am.
Dec. 596, "that the property exempt from execution in the
possession of the head of a family is held by him for the use
and benefit of the family; and, while he has the right to sell
or exchange such property, it cannot be levied on and sold
on execution by his consent, this being a privilege he cannot
waive." Said the court, viz: "The language of the act is
imperative. The property exempt shall not be liable to seizure and sale by execution, and the head of the family cannot
waive the right, as those dependent on him are under the
protection of the law, and secured in the enjoyment of the
property."

In the case of *Cox* v. *Ballentine*, 1 Baxt. 362, it was held
that "the head of the family has the right to sell, exchange,
or mortgage the exempt property, and the legislature has
no power to prohibit him": See, also, *Cronan* v. *Honor*, 10
Heisk. 534. It is suggested that these cases are somewhat
contradictory, and, perhaps, irreconcilable. The conflict, we
think, is more apparent than real.

" There is an essential difference," says the supreme ⁶⁵⁴
court of Kentucky, " between an executed contract, by which
the owner is divested of title, and an executory agreement,
by which the debtor merely promises that, in the future, he
will not take advantage of or claim the benefit of a particular
statute. . . . . The law, in its wisdom, for the protection of
the poor and needy, has said that certain property shall not
be liable for debt, not so much to relieve the debtor as to protect his family against such improvident acts on his part as
would reduce them to want. . . . . If such a contract is
upheld, the exemption laws of the state would be virtually
obsolete and the destitute deprived of all claim they have to
its beneficent provisions": *Moxley* v. *Ragan*, 10 Bush, 156;
19 Am. Rep. 61.

Says the supreme court of Illinois: "That such a waiver,
where the same is attempted to be made by an executory
contract, is ineffectual and will not be enforced, is definitely
settled. . . . . Such contracts contravene the policy of the
law, and hence are inoperative and void. The owner may,
if he choose, sell or otherwise dispose of any property he may
have, however much his family may need it, but the law will
not aid in that regard, nor permit him to contract, in advance,

that his creditors may use the process of the courts to deprive his family of its use and benefit, when an exemption has been created in their favor. Laws enacted from considerations of public concern and to subserve the general welfare cannot be abrogated by mere private [655] agreement": *Recht* v. *Kelly,* 82 Ill. 147; 25 Am. Rep. 301.

Says Judge Denio: "The maxim, '*modus et conventio vincunt legem,*' is not of universal application. It applies only to agreements in themselves legal. Where no rule of law or principle of public policy is concerned the parties may, by contract, make a law for themselves. One object of municipal law is to promote the general welfare of society. The exemption laws seek to accomplish this by taking from the head of the family the power to deprive it of certain property by contracting debts which shall enable the creditors to take such property on execution." The parties to this contract sought to set aside those laws so far as this debt was concerned. This they could not do. The learned judge says: "I am of opinion that a person contracting a debt cannot agree with the creditor that, in case of nonpayment, he shall be entitled to levy his execution upon property exempt from execution by the general laws of the state. . . . . If effect shall be given to such provisions it is likely that they will be generally inserted in obligations for small demands, and, in that way, the policy of the law will be completely overthrown. Every honest man who contracts a debt expects to pay it, and believes he will be able to do so without having his property sold on execution. No one worthy to be trusted would, therefore, be apt to object to a clause subjecting all his property to levy on execution in case [656] of nonpayment. It was against the consequences of this overconfidence and the readiness of men to make contracts which may deprive them and their families of articles indispensable to their comfort, that the legislature has undertaken to interpose. When a man's last cow is taken on an execution on a judgment rendered upon one of these notes it is not sufficient to say that it was done pursuant to his consent, freely given when he contracted the debt. The law was designed to protect him against his own improvidence in giving such consent. The statutes contain many examples of legislation based upon the same motives. The laws against usury, those which forbid imprisonment for debt, and those which allow a redemption after the sale of land on execution,

are of this class": *Kneetlle* v. *Newcomb,* 22 N. Y. 249; 78 Am.
Dec. 186.

The supreme court of Iowa, after a full consideration of the
subject, said, viz: "Without pursuing the discussion of the
subject further, we are agreed in the conclusion that a person
contracting a debt cannot, by a contemporaneous and simple
waiver of benefit of the exemption laws, entitle the creditor,
in case of failure to pay, to levy his execution, against the
defendant's objection, upon exempt property. Such an agreement is contrary to public policy, and will not be enforced:
Curtis v. *O'Brien,* 20 Iowa, 376; 89 Am. Dec. 543.

In the case of *Branch* v. *Tomlinson,* 77 N. C. 388, a similar
waiver, incorporated in a promissory [657] note was attempted
to be enforced. The court said: "The agreement is to waive
a right in contravention of state policy, which agreement this
court cannot undertake to enforce." In *Levicks* v. *Walker,* 15
La. Ann. 245, 77 Am. Dec. 187, a similar conclusion was
reached.

The supreme court of Florida, in *Carter* v. *Carter,* 20 Fla.
558, 51 Am. Rep. 618, in a most able and elaborate opinion,
held, viz: "In view of the recognized policy of the states in
enacting exemption laws, and of the practically universal
concurrence of the authorities on the identical question, our
conclusion is that the waiver of the benefit and protection of
the exemption laws contained in this note is not valid to
defeat a claim of exemption": See, also, *Crawford* v. *Lockwood,* 8 How. Pr. 547.

The result of our examination is, that the main current of
judicial enunciation is against the validity of such contracts.
Possibly the only court out of line is that of Pennsylvania.
Such contracts are also sustained in Alabama, but under the
authority of an express statute: *Brown* v. *Leitch,* 60 Ala. 313;
31 Am. Rep. 42. We think the weight of reason, as well as
authority, is opposed to such stipulations. In our view it is immaterial whether the contract is made by a single man or the
head of a family. In either case it contravenes a sound public policy, and, if enforced, abrogates the exemption statutes.

The judgment is affirmed.

WAIVER OF EXEMPTION RIGHTS—LEGALITY OF.—An executory agreement
by a debtor to waive all benefit under the exemption laws is void: Note to
Burke v. *Finley,* 34 Am. St. Rep. 133, where the cases are collected. This
question is fully discussed in the extended note to *Bowman* v. *Smiley,* 72
Am. Dec. 741.

QUINN *v.* RAILROAD.

[94 TENNESSEE, 713.]

MASTER AND SERVANT.—PHYSICIAN OR SURGEON EMPLOYED BY A RAIL-
ROAD COMPANY to attend employees injured in its service is not a
servant of the company so as to render it liable for his carelessness or
negligence in rendering professional services.

MASTER AND SERVANT—RELATION OF, WHEN EXISTS.—For the relation of
master and servant to exist, so as to make the master liable, he must
not only have the power to select and discharge the servant, but to
direct the mode of executing, and to so control him in his acts in the
course of his employment as to prevent injury to others.

RAILROAD COMPANIES—LIABILITY FOR NEGLIGENCE OF ITS PHYSICIAN OR
SURGEON.—A railroad company employing a physician or surgeon of
ordinary competency and skill to care for employees injured in its
service is not liable for his carelessness, negligence, or malpractice in
the performance of his professional duties toward an injured employee
placed in his charge by the company.

J. M. Greer and C. D. M. Greer, for the complainant.

Adams & Trimble, for the defendant.

714 BEARD, J.   One Quinn, the intestate of plaintiff in
error, was an employee of defendant, and was seriously
crushed by the driving-wheel of one of its engines while
engaged in the discharge of his duty as switchman in the
yards of the railroad at Holly Springs, Mississippi. Immediately after the injury he was taken in charge by a surgeon employed by the defendant to render surgical attention
to such of its employees as were injured at that place while in
its service.   He at once placed himself in communication by
wire with the chief surgeon of the railroad, whose duty, under
his employment, was to render personal attention in such
cases, and to exercise supervisory care over its local surgeons,
including the one in personal charge of Quinn.   This chief
surgeon lived, and, at the time was, in Memphis, in this state.
The result of this communication was that, the latter having
decided it was best for the wounded man that he should be
brought to his father's home in Memphis, where he could
more safely and intelligently receive surgical care, announced
his decision to the railroad authorities, and requested them
to prepare at once to bring him in.   In obedience to this
direction a special train was made up without unnecessary
delay, and Quinn, accompanied by the Holly Springs surgeon, was taken on board, and, after a rapid run, was delivered over, at the depot of the railroad in Memphis, into the

keeping of the chief surgeon. Within a few hours thereafter the intestate of plaintiff died.

[715] This action was brought to recover damages against the railroad for negligence in various particulars, resulting in his death. Among other grounds of negligence laid in the declaration was that defendant failed to provide the intestate with proper medical service, and that this failure greatly aggravated his condition and largely contributed to his death.

On the trial of the case the court below excluded certain evidence offered by plaintiff in error, which tended to show that these surgeons were unskillful in their treatment of the patient, and that this unskillfulness was one of the active causes contributing to his death.

When he came to instruct the jury the trial judge, among other things, said to them: "If deceased was put in charge of physicians of good reputation it was their business to stop the flow of blood, if any, and defendant is not liable for any failure to stop this flow while the patient was in charge of, or after he was put in the charge of, the physicians. If deceased was put in the hands of competent surgeons of good reputation and standing in their profession defendant is not liable for any treatment given the patient by them, or by others under their advice." The action of the court below in excluding this testimony and in giving this instruction is now assigned as error.

Before considering this assignment it is proper to say the record tends to show that both these [716] surgeons were men of fine reputation for learning, skill, and experience in their profession, and that for the service rendered to the deceased, as in all other similar cases, they were paid by the corporation, without cost or charge to him or to his estate.

The question presented by this assignment is new in this state. It is almost as new to the courts outside the state. The diligence of counsel in this cause, and the investigations of this court, have resulted in finding but few cases involving it, and these of so recent a date that neither they, nor the rule announced by them, have been carried into the latest text-books on railway law.

Plaintiff in error insists that the defendant in error is liable for the mistakes or malpractice of the surgeons in question; that their employment by the railroad created the relation of master and servant; and that the ordinary rule, which makes the master liable for the negligent acts of his

servant within the scope of his employment is to be applied
in this case. If he be correct in his contention that the relation between the railroad and these surgeons was that of
master and servant, then his conclusion would properly follow. But was that the relationship? We do not think so.
The term " servant," as it is used in connection with the rule
invoked, has a well-defined meaning. It "is applicable,"
says Mr. Thompson in his work on Negligence, volume 2, page
892, "to any relation in [717] which, with reference to the
matter out of which an alleged wrong has sprung, the person
sought to be charged had the right to control the action of
the person doing the alleged wrong; and this right to control
appears to be the conclusive test by which to determine
whether the relation exists."

" For the relation to exist, so as to make the master responsible, he must not only have the power to select the servant,
but to direct the mode of executing, and to so control him in
his acts in the course of his employment as to prevent
injury to others": *Robinson* v. *Webb*, 11 Bush, 464. To the
same effect is *Mound City etc. Co.* v. *Conlon*, 92 Mo. 221;
Wiltse v. *State etc. Co.*, 63 Mich. 639; *Andrews* v. *Boedecker*,
17 Ill. App. 213.

The term "master" is equally well defined in the law. A
" master," in the sense of the rule, is "one who has the superior choice, control, and direction; whose will is represented
not merely in the ultimate result in hand, but in all its details; one who is the responsible head of a given industry;
one who has the power to discharge; one who not only prescribes the duty, but directs, and may at any time direct,
the means and methods of doing the work ": 14 Am. & Eng.
Ency. of Law, 745.

If it be, as these authorities indicate (and it cannot be
otherwise), that the decisive test of this relationship, or even
one of its decisive tests, is that the master has the right
to select the end of the [718] servant's employment, and
that the master's uncontrolled will is the law of the servant
"in the means and methods" by which this end is to be
reached, then it cannot be maintained that these surgeons
were the "servants" of this corporation. They were not
employed to do ordinary corporate work, but to render services requiring special training, skill, and experience. To
perform these services so as to to make them effectual for the
saving of life or limb it was necessary that these surgeons

should bring to their work not only their best skill, but the right to exercise it in accordance with their soundest judgment, and without interference. Not only was this the right of these surgeons, but it was as well a duty that the law imposed. If the railroad authorities had undertaken to direct them as to the method of treatment of the injured man, and this method was regarded by them as unwise, they would have been " bound to exercise their own superior skill and better judgment, and to disobey their employers, if, in their opinion, the welfare of the patient required it ": *Union Pac. Ry. Co.* v. *Artist*, 60 Fed. Rep. 365.

In accordance with this view it has been uniformly held, so far as we have been able to discover, that, having selected surgeons skilled and competent in their profession, the corporation has discharged every duty that humanity or sound morals impose, and that it is to no extent liable for the mistakes they may subsequently commit.

[719] In *South Florida R. R. Co.* v. *Price*, 32 Fla. 46, the declaration averred that the surgeon employed by the defendant to render surgical aid to its employees injured in its service set the plaintiff's arm in an "unskilled and negligent manner," and that for this the corporation was liable. To this claim the court says: "Even though we should admit it to be within the corporate powers of such a company to obligate itself to the rendition of medical or surgical aid to its sick or injured employees, by assuming it as a duty or otherwise, or to become liable under any circumstances for any negligence of any such surgeon acting in the line of his profession, still, it seems to be well settled that it will have performed its entire duty in that respect, when it employs a person of ordinary competency and skill in that profession, and that, having done so, it cannot be made liable for the carelessness or negligence of such surgeon in the performance of his duties as such."

In *Union Pac. Ry. Co.* v. *Artist*, 60 Fed. Rep. 365, the facts were that each employee of the railroad was required to contribute out of his wages twenty-five cents a month, and the corporation, out of its general treasury, contributed from two thousand to four thousand dollars per month to establish a hospital and employ physicians and surgeons for the care of its wounded and sick employees, without any charge to them or profit to the railway. On these facts, it was held that the [720] company was not liable for an injury to one of its employees from the malpractice of a surgeon doing service in the hospital. The court says, through Judge Sanborn: "The result is, that the doctrine of *respondeat superior* has no application to this case. The only contract the law implies here is the agreement on the part of the company to use reasonable care to select and obtain skillful physicans and careful attendants; and, if the company performed that contract, it was responsible no further."

In accord with these are the cases of *Laubheim* **v.** *De Koninglyke etc. Steamship Co.*, 107 N. Y. 228; 1 Am. St. Rep. 815; *O'Brien* **v.** *Cunard S. S. Co.*, 154 Mass. 272; *Secord* **v.** *St. Paul etc. Ry. Co.*, 18 Fed. Rep. 221; *McDonald* **v.** *Massachusetts General Hospital*, 120 Mass. 432; 21 Am. Rep. 529, and *Richardson* **v.** *Carbon Hill etc. Co.*, 6 Wash. 52.

We think the sanction of authority and of reason is with the ruling of the circuit judge on this point. Other objections have been disposed of orally. The judgment is affirmed.

PHYSICIANS AND SURGEONS—SHIPOWNER'S LIABILITY FOR NEGLIGENCE OF. A physician employed by a shipowner in obedience to law is not the shipowner's servant, and the shipowner is not liable to a passenger injured by his negligence: *Allen* v. *State S. S. Co.*, 132 N. Y. 91; 28 Am. St. Rep. 556. While the shipowner would not be liable for the physician's negligence, he would be liable for negligence in the selection of a physician: *Laubheim* v. *De Koninglyke etc. S. S. Co.*, 107 N. Y. 228; 1 Am. St. Rep. 815, and particularly note.

MASTER AND SERVANT.—WHEN THE RELATION EXISTS: See the extended note to *Brown* v. *Smith*, 22 Am. St. Rep. 459.

CASES

IN THE

SUPREME COURT

OF

WASHINGTON.

ISAACS *v.* BARBER.

[10 WASHINGTON, 124.]

WATERS.—THE RIGHT TO APPROPRIATE WATERS FOR MINING AND OTHER BENEFICIAL PURPOSES was recognized by the courts and the lawmaking power as to that portion of the state of Washington east of the Cascade mountains prior to the passage of the act of Congress of July 26, 1866. Such right was established by custom so universal that the courts must take judicial notice thereof.

WATERS, APPROPRIATION OF, ON PUBLIC LANDS.—The United States, as the owner of the public lands in a locality where the use of water was required had the power to establish such rights in relation to its use and appropriation as it saw fit, and, to the extent that it recognized the right of appropriation, the common law was modified or abrogated.

WATERS—APPROPRIATION OF—PURCHASER OF PUBLIC LANDS TOOK SUBJECT TO.—Even prior to the act of Congress of July 26, 1866, the right to appropriate water had been recognized in Washington territory, and therefore a purchaser of lands from the United States acquired his title subordinate to any appropriation of waters previously made. The act referred to was rather a recognition of pre-existing rights than a statute conferring such rights for the first time.

WATERS—MILLING PURPOSES—APPROPRIATION FOR.—The appropriation of the waters of a stream for use as a propelling power to a mill is a valid appropriation, and the purchaser of public lands, after such appropriation has been made, acquires title subject thereto.

Thomas H. Brents, Wellington Clark, and M. M. Godman, for the appellant.

B. L. & J. L. Sharpstein, and Crowley, Sullivan & Grosscup, for the respondent.

126 HOYT, J. This action was brought by respondent to restrain the defendant from interfering with a dam which had been erected for the purpose of diverting water from Mill creek into a race, or flume, which led to his flouring-mill. Defendant justified his action under a claim of the right to have the waters flow past his place situated on said creek between the point where the water was diverted and respondent's mill. Respondent claimed the right to divert the water, and founded such claim upon several distinct grounds. The cause was tried before a referee, who reported the testimony with his findings of fact and law. Such findings were set aside by the superior court, and new ones made as the foundation for the decree which was entered. Defendant, not being satisfied with such decree, prosecutes this appeal, and asks for a reversal, for the reason that the findings of fact were not warranted by the proofs and also because the facts found did not warrant the conclusions of law founded thereon.

We have carefully examined all the proofs, and although, upon some points, they are not as full as they should have been, we are not satisfied that they were insufficient to warrant every finding of fact made by the lower court. It follows that such findings must stand, and that in the light thereof the rights of the parties must be here determined.

It appears from such findings that the waters of Mill creek were, in the year 1861, diverted by plaintiff into his mill-race, and conducted to his mill for use as a propelling power to substantially the same extent as they are now [127] diverted, conducted, and used. It, however, appears therefrom that there had been a slight increase in the amount of water diverted at certain seasons of the year, and upon the fact of such increase that portion of the decree in favor of the appellant is largely based. We are not satisfied that the fact of such increase was established by the proofs, but, the plaintiff not having appealed, we are not called upon to investigate as to that portion of the decree adverse to him. It further appears from the findings that at the time the water was so diverted by the plaintiff, all of the land, on both sides of the creek, from the place of its diversion to a point below the land now owned by the defendant, was a part of the public domain, and that it so remained until 1863, at which time the tract of which defendant's land is a portion was entered and purchased at private cash sale by one Artemus Dodge, who, in 1865, received a patent therefor. It further appears that said Dodge, prior to such entry, gave the plaintiff oral permission to conduct the water across the tract of land, and

that George J. Dodge, to whom he deeded it, executed to
plaintiff a written instrument in the shape of a lease formally
conferring the right to so conduct the water by means of the
race and flume as then constructed for the period of ninety-
nine years; that the operation of the mill and the source of
its power, and the means by which it was diverted from and
conducted to the mill, were open and notorious, and known
to every one in the vicinity, including said Artemus Dodge
and those holding under him, including the defendant, and
that no complaint was ever made in reference thereto until
the year 1885.

Upon these material facts, among others, found by the
court, respondent contends that, as between himself and the
defendant, he is entitled to the use of the water for the purpose of propelling his mill to the extent to which he had
used it from the time of its original diversion. He makes
this contention for the reasons: 1. That he is the owner of
the water for the purpose of running his mill by reason of
his prior appropriation thereof; 2. That the grantors of the
land, by the giving of the permission to construct the [128]
flume, and the making of the lease, as above stated, and by
standing by and seeing money expended by virtue of such
permission and lease, estopped themselves, and those holding
under them, from interfering with such flume, or the diversion of the water to effect which it was constructed; and
3. That there had been such open, continuous, and adverse
user as to give title by prescription.

The first claim is met by the appellant by two principal
propositions, one that it was not shown that any right to
prior appropriation existed as a part of the law or local customs of the locality; the other, that if the court could take
judicial notice of the existence of such customs, or so find
from the facts proven, they had no force as against the defendant, for the reason that the grantor through whom he claims
by mesne conveyance acquired title to the land by grant
from the government prior to the passage of the act of Congress of July 26, 1866. If the first proposition is determined
adversely to appellant, he substantially concedes that the
plaintiff would have been entitled to the use of the water
appropriated in 1861, if the grant of the land of which his
was a part had not been made by the government until after
the passage of said act.

Each of these propositions raises questions of the utmost

importance, and we have given them such careful consideration as our opportunities would allow, and have come to the
conclusion that this state, or at least that portion of it east
of the Cascade mountains, was included within the territory
where the right to prior appropriation of water for mining
and other beneficial purposes was recognized by the courts
and the lawmaking power, and that such right was established by a custom so universal that courts must take judicial notice thereof.

We therefore hold that the right to prior appropriation as
recognized by said act of Congress existed as a part of the
laws and customs of the locality., Such holding compels a
consideration of the second proposition above suggested. It
is argued by appellant that by absolute grant of the land
before the passage of said act of Congress the title passed
[129] with such riparian rights as were recognized by the common law of England, and that such rights, having become
vested before its passage, could not be affected thereby. If
the right to appropriate water from streams upon the public
domain is derived from the passage of the act in question,
and if, before that time, such acts of appropriation were, as
against the government of the United States, trespassers upon
the public domain, it is clear that this contention must be
sustained. But, in our opinion, such was not the fact. The
United States, as the owner of nearly all the lands in the
locality where such use of the water was required, had
the power to establish such rights in relation to its appropriation and use as it saw fit, and, to the extent that it recognized
such rights, the common law in relation thereto was modified
or abrogated. That this could be done by direct act of Congress is not disputed by appellant, and we think it could also
be done by such action on the part of the government as
clearly disclosed its intention, though not evidenced by act
of Congress, and that such modification or abrogation would
have force as against the grant of the government, though
not expressly embodied in the instrument or legislation by
which the grant was made. If the action of the government
was of such a nature as to evidence its intent to inaugurate
such a modified system as to rights to waters upon the public
domain, it was of such a nature as to convey notice to all
persons interested of that fact. If from such action such
intent could be presumed it must be because it had substantially the same effect as direct legislation by Congress; and,

since every one must take notice of such legislation, they must likewise take notice of a practice having the force thereof.

The material question, therefore, is as to whether or not, prior to the act of 1866, the practice in the locality referred to of appropriating the waters of running streams by means of their diversion for mining and other beneficial uses had been so sanctioned by the practice of the government that it had become lawful. It is not necessary for us to enter into any extended discussion as to this question, nor to enlarge [180] upon the situation of the localities in which the custom of so diverting waters prevailed, nor to speak of the absolute necessity of such customs, for the reason that'the supreme court of the United States has ably discussed and fully decided the question. And such question is a federal one, upon which such decision is controlling in the courts of the states as well as in those of the United States.

A reference to a few cases will establish the above-stated conclusions as to the position of said supreme court upon this question. In *Atchison* v. *Peterson,* 20 Wall. 507, Mr. Justice Field, speaking for the court, made use of the following language: " By the custom which has obtained among miners in the Pacific states and territories, where mining for the precious metals is had on the public lands of the United States, the first appropriator of mines, whether in placers, veins, or lodes, or of waters in the streams on such lands for mining purposes, is held to have a better right than others to work the mines or use the waters. The first appropriator who subjects the property to use, or takes the necessary steps for that purpose, is regarded, except as against the government, as the source of title in all controversies relating to the property. As respects the use of water for mining purposes, the doctrines of the common law declaratory of the rights of riparian owners were, at an early day, after the discovery of gold, found to be inapplicable, or applicable only to a very limited extent to the necessities of miners, and inadequate to their protection. . . . . This doctrine of right by prior appropriation was recognized by the legislation of Congress in 1866."

And in *Basey* v. *Gallagher,* 20 Wall. 670, the court, speaking by the same learned jurist, referring to the case of *Atchison* v. *Peterson,* 20 Wall. 507, stated that, among other things, it was held in that case " That the doctrines of the common law declaratory of the rights of riparian proprietors were inapplicable, or applicable only to a limited extent, to the necessities of miners, and were inadequate to their protection." And further on in the same case, after having reviewed several other decisions of the supreme court, and [131] speaking of the act of Congress in question, the following language was used: "It is very evident that Congress intended, although the language used is not happy, to recognize as valid the customary law with respect to the use of water which had grown up among the occupants of the public land under the peculiar necessities of their condition."

And in *Forbes* v. *Gracey*, 94 U. S. 762, and in *Jennison* v. *Kirk*, 98 U. S. 453, the doctrine that said act did not create the rights therein referred to, but was simply in affirmation thereof, is distinctly recognized. And in *Broder* v. *Water Co.*, 101 U. S. 274, the court, speaking by that distinguished judge, Mr. Justice Miller, seems to have put this question fully to rest. He made use of the following pertinent language: " It is the established doctrine of this court that rights of miners who had taken possession of mines and worked and developed them, and the rights of persons who had constructed canals and ditches to be used in mining operations and for purposes of agricultural irrigation, in the region where such artificial use of the water was an absolute necessity, are rights which the government had, by its conduct, recognized and encouraged and was bound to protect, before the passage of the act of 1866. We are of opinion that the section of the act which we have quoted was rather a voluntary recognition of a pre-existing right of possession, constituting a valid claim to its continued use, than the establishment of a new one. This subject has so recently received our attention, and the grounds upon which this construction rests are so well set forth in the following cases, that they will be relied on without further argument."

Then follows a citation of the cases to which we have referred. This language, and that of the other cases, would seem to make it unnecessary that any thing further should be said to show that, in the opinion of the said supreme court, the government had, by its acquiescence or consent, so recognized acts of this nature on the public domain as to make them lawful and a basis of right which the government and its grantees must respect.

[132] It is true, as suggested by the supreme court of California, in *Lux* v. *Haggin*, 69 Cal. 255, that the exact question

involved in the case at bar was not involved in any of the cases above cited, but the positive language used therein, and the emphasis of the proposition that the right was not created by the act of 1866 but simply recognized and continued, is sufficient to clearly show that such rights would have been protected as well before the passage of that act as after. If it was a right which it was worth while for the court to talk about it was a vested right, and if a vested right, and of such a nature that every one must take notice thereof, it would not be taken away by any grant made thereafter, for the reason that the courts would construe such grant as though the right had been in express terms excepted from its force.

It has been held by all of the courts that have considered this question that after the passage of said act all grants must be construed in connection with the rights therein provided for, and such rights protected as above stated. There is no provision in the act for the protection of the rights therein recognized, and, if they existed before as well as after its passage, they were excepted from grants made after their inception, before such passage the same as after. It is only because of their existence as rights of which every one must take notice that they are held to modify grants thereafter made. And if rights under the statute thus modify grants, rights of the same nature established by acquiescence should also be held to modify such grants made after their acquisition.

There are decisions by the courts of some of the states which directly sustain the contention of the appellant, and go to the full extent of holding that, where the grant took effect before the passage of the act in question, the rights acquired by the custom of the locality were lost unless expressly reserved by the terms of the grant. The principal case of this kind is that of *Vansickle* v. *Haines*, 7 Nev. 249, in which it was directly held, as above stated, after careful consideration, and nearly or quite all the other cases upon [133] the subject refer to this one and found their decision largely upon its authority. It follows that when this case was overruled by the court in which it was decided the authority of all of the cases upon that side of the question was greatly lessened.

In the case of *Jones* v. *Adams*, 19 Nev. 78, 3 Am. St. Rep. 788, in which the case above referred to was overruled, the court carefully reviews the whole question, and founds its holding to the effect that the rights should be given effect against grants before the date of the act of 1866 as well as after, not only upon a well-considered course of reasoning, but also upon the fact that such was their understanding of the inevitable conclusion to be drawn from the language of the supreme court of the United States in the cases hereinbefore cited. Some of these decisions were founded upon the conditions which existed in a mining country, and related to the acquisition of mining interests, and the necessary water for the prosecution of the mining business, but enough appears to show that the same rule would apply as to the diversion of water for any other necessary and beneficial use. It does not follow, as has been well observed by Mr. Pomeroy, in his treatise on Riparian Rights, that the common law of England as to riparian rights has been abrogated in the localities affected by the cases above referred to, but only that it has been so far modified as to give the rights acquired by virtue of the customs of the country force.

The United States, as owner of all of the domain, including the waters in its running streams, could, by its legislation as applied thereto, or such acquiescence and practice as should be given the force of legislation, change the rule of the common law so far as it thought necessary, but it would not follow therefrom that if no rights had been acquired by virtue of the modification of the common-law rule until after the land had passed from the government the common-law rule would be at all affected thereby. On the contrary, so soon as the government had parted with its title its right to change the rule in reference to the rights and incidents growing out of the ownership of the land would be entirely determined, [134] and its grantee would take his title burdened with all rights conferred by such action or consent on the part of the government.

The government, while the owner of the land, allowed the streams to be changed by the diversion of a portion of their waters. This had the effect of modifying the right to have the water flow in its natural channel, except as to the portion not diverted at the time the title passed from the government, and it was only upon this portion that the common-law rule could apply. The government had changed the streams, as it had the right to do by virtue of its ownership of all the land through which they flowed, and while they were so changed conveyed the land. It must follow that its grantees took title subject to the changed condition of the streams and to the rights growing out of such change.

In the case at bar the right to the use of the water had been fully acquired while the land now owned by the defendant was held by the government, and its grant of the same thereafter was subject to such right. It follows that plaintiff is entitled, as against the defendants, to have such right protected by the courts.

The conclusion to which we have come as to this question makes it unnecessary for us to discuss the other grounds upon which plaintiff seeks to found his right to divert the water.

Some criticism is made as to the form of the decree, but we think it sufficient to substantially protect the rights of both parties to the action. There is not as exact a measurement of the water to which the plaintiff is entitled as there might have been, but the substance of the decree in that regard is to establish and protect him in the use of the water necessary to run his mill as at present constructed, and for that reason we think it sufficient.

The decree of the superior court will be in all things affirmed. The respondent will recover his costs on appeal.

DUNBAR, C. J., and SCOTT, J., concur.

ANDERS, J., not sitting by reason of disqualification.

WATERS—APPROPRIATION OF ON PUBLIC LANDS.—The right to the use of a watercourse in public mineral lands and the right to divert and use the water taken therefrom may be acquired by appropriation and user: *Union Water Co.* v. *Crary,* 25 Cal. 504; 85 Am. Dec. 145, and note; *Conger* v. *Weaver,* 6 Cal. 548; 65 Am. Dec. 528, and note. The appropriator of water of a stream for irrigation acquires a right prior thereto as against the riparian owner of land along such stream who obtained patent for such land after such appropriation had been made, but before the operation of the amendment of July 9, 1870, to the act of Congress of July 26, 1866, requiring that patents to public land thereafter to be issued shall be subject to any vested or accrued water rights: *Hammond* v. *Rose,* 11 Col. 524; 7 Am. St. Rep. 258, and note. Water rights on public lands, as fixed by priority and extent of the respective appropriations, are to be regarded as perfect and absolute as if they had been acquired by prescription or by express grant from the riparian owner: *Kidd* v. *Laird,* 15 Cal. 161; 76 Am. Dec. 472. See the further discussion of this subject in the extended note to *Heath* v. *Williams,* 43 Am. Dec. 279.

REDDISH *v.* SMITH.

[10 WASHINGTON, 178.]

VENDOR AND PURCHASER—CONVEYANCES, TENDER OF, WHEN NOT RE-
QUIRED.—If a contract for the sale and purchase of lands requires the
purchase price to be paid in installments, and the vendor wishes to forfeit the rights of the vendee for nonpayment, it is not necessary that
a tender of a conveyance precede the exercise of the right to declare a
forfeiture, if the vendee would not then be entitled to such conveyance,
even if he paid the amount then due under the contract.

VENDOR AND PURCHASER.—THE WAIVER OF A FORFEITURE FOR NONPAY-
MENT OF INSTALLMENTS due on a contract to purchase land is not
implied from the fact that the vendee permitted three of such installments to become due before exercising his right to declare a forfeiture.

VENDOR AND PURCHASER—FORFEITURE OF PAYMENTS.—If a contract for the
sale and purchase of land provides that if the vendee shall fail to pay
the monthly installments after demand made on him for thirty days,
the vendor may, at his option, declare the contract forfeited, and enter
upon and repossess himself of the premises, the payments are forfeited
if the contract is not complied with, and the forfeiture is not restricted
to the land only.

RESCISSION.—THE RIGHT TO RESCIND A CONTRACT cannot be allowed to a
party in default. Therefore, when he has contracted for the purchase
of land, and fails to make his payments as stipulated in the contract, he
is not entitled to rescind it.

H. W. Lueders and John Leo, for the appellants.

Walter M. Harvey and Shank, Murray & Dresbach, for the
Respondents.

[179] DUNBAR, C. J. This is an action of ejectment based
upon a contract for the sale of land, entered into by the
respondents and the appellant, G. W. Smith, on March 18,
1891. The contract in question was as follows:

" This contract, entered into this 18th day of March, A. D.
1891, by and between Eugene A. Reddish, and Jennie E.
Reddish, his wife, of the city of Tacoma, state of Washington, the parties of the first part, and George W. Smith, of the
same place, the party of the second part, witnesseth:

" The parties of the first part agree to erect a dwelling-house
on lots number fourteen and fifteen (14, 15), in block number
two (2), in Ross' Addition to Tacoma, and to sell and convey
the said lots, with the appurtenances, to the party of the second part, subject to one mortgage in the sum of $800, and all
street assessments. The parties of the first part also agree to
advance to the party of the second part the sum of $400,
the receipt of which is hereby acknowledged by said party of
the second part. The said house so to be erected on said

lots shall be such an one as is indicated by the plans and specifications hereto attached and made a part of this contract. The said lots are to be sold and conveyed by the parties of the first part, with general warranty deed, subject to the before-mentioned encumbrances, as soon as the party of the second part shall have [180] paid the parties of the first part the full sum of $1,325 as herein specified, and after the said party of the second part has duly assigned and transferred to the parties of the first part a certain contract which he holds for the sale to him of lots five and six (5, 6), in block numbered nineteen (19), in Coulter's Addition to Tacoma, on which contract there is yet due and owing the sum of $50, which the parties of the first part agree to pay. The party of the second part agrees to pay the parties of the first part the above-mentioned $1,325, and ten per cent per annum interest from this date in monthly installments, each payment to be so made shall be the sum of $20, and the amount of interest that has accumulated at the date of each payment, on the whole of the said deferred payment. If the said Smith shall fail to make any one or more monthly payments as herein provided, then all sums of interest due by the terms of this contract shall be added to the principal, and draw like interest as the principal sum. In case the party of the second part shall fail to pay promptly the monthly installments herein provided for, after a demand made on him for the same of thirty days, then the party of the first part may, at his option, declare this contract forfeited, and he shall enter upon and repossess himself of the said premises, and thereupon this contract shall be at an end.

[SIGNATURES]

The payments were made by appellant Smith according to the terms of the contract until the last of June, 1893. After a default in the monthly payments provided for, respondents gave notice to appellants that, if they did not pay the amount due within thirty days, they would elect to forfeit the contract, and take possession of the land sold, the appellants having gone into possession of the land under the contract.

The complaint alleged ownership of the land in controversy, the execution and delivery of the contract, the performance of the conditions of the same on the part of the plaintiffs, the breach of the contract by the defendant Smith in failing to pay certain installments for the purchase price of the land, the service of notice of election to forfeit, and demand for the possession of the premises.

The answer was a general denial of the allegations of the complaint, and an affirmative allegation of noncompliance [181] with the contract on the part of the respondents; also alleging defective title in the respondents. Appellants also demanded compensation for permanent improvements made by them before the forfeiture, and asked that respondents should refund the installments of the purchase price of the land previously paid. Upon the issues thus brought a trial was had which resulted in findings and judgment in favor of the respondents. The appellants, however, interposed a demurrer to the complaint to the effect that it did not state facts sufficient to constitute a cause of action, which demurrer was overruled by the court.

The first contention of the appellants as to the deficiency of the complaint is that the complaint should have alleged the tender of the deed by the plaintiffs to the defendants prior to the commencement of the action. We do not think that the authorities cited by the appellants to sustain this contention are in point. They sustain the general rule that in a contract of this kind, where the payment of the purchase price and the giving of the deed are concurrent acts, the vendor before declaring a forfeiture must make a tender of the conveyance; but, in this instance, the purchase price was to be paid in installments, and the whole amount of the purchase price to be paid under the contract was not yet due. Consequently the time for conveying land under the contract had not yet arrived, and the vendor could not, under any principle of law, be compelled to make a deed before he had received his pay. If this theory of the law were to obtain it would either compel the tender of a deed without the payment of the full amount of the purchase price, or would compel the vendor to wait until the full amount of the purchase price had become due before he would have a right to elect to forfeit or to bring his action. Neither proposition is tenable, and neither is supported, we think, by the authorities. The covenants to make specified payments at different times are independent covenants, and the vendor can move against them as breaches of the independent covenants, or he can wait until all the purchase price is due and bring his action then.

[182] It is claimed by the appellants that inasmuch as three

months' installments had become due before the action was
brought, the respondents were guilty of laches, and that it
was thereby an indication of a waiver of their right of forfeiture. The contrary doctrine was laid down by this court
in the case of *Wooding* v. *Crain*, 10 Wash. 35, and the reasons for the rule were there discussed, and it is not necessary
to repeat them here: See, also, *Phelps* v. *Illinois Cent. R. R.
Co.*, 63 Ill. 468.

Probably it might be as well before proceeding further,
however, to construe that portion of the contract which provides for a forfeiture. By reference to the contract it will be
seen that the provision is as follows: "In case the party of
the second part shall fail to pay promptly the monthly installments herein provided for after a demand made on him
for the same of thirty days, then the party of the first part
may, at his option, declare this contract forfeited, and he shall
enter upon and repossess himself of the said premises, and
thereupon this contract shall be at an end."

It is contended by the appellants that there is no forfeiture
clause in the contract providing that the purchase money
paid under the contract and improvements made by Smith
should be forfeited and inure to the benefit of the vendor;
that the provision simply is for the forfeiture of the contract,
and not for the forfeiture of the payments made under the
provisions of the contract.

We do not think this is a legitimate construction of the
contract. While it is true that the courts will not supply
language to create a forfeiture where the forfeiture is not specially provided for by the parties themselves, yet it seems to
us that it was the clear, unequivocal intention of the parties
to this contract, as expressed by the contract, that the payments made by the appellants should be forfeited in case the
respondents elected so to do, upon the nonperformance of the
contract by the appellants. The option of forfeiture is for
the benefit of the vendor, but it would be difficult to conceive
what benefit would accrue to the vendor in a [183] case of this
kind if he were not allowed the benefit of the payments which
had been made. As was well said by the counsel for respondents in this case: "If the property, by fluctuations in the real
estate market, should increase in value, the purchaser would
insist upon a strict performance, but if, perchance, by the
opposite conditions the land should depreciate in value, the
vendee would cease his payments, allow the vendor to re-enter

upon the premises and insist that the latter should refund all payments previously made. The vendor would be completely at the mercy of the purchaser, and the very object and purpose of the agreement would be defeated."

It would certainly place the vendor in a very embarrassing position if he were to be called upon at any time during the life of the contract to refund payments which had been made to him under the contract of sale. He would never know whether his land was sold or not, and would always have to hold himself in readiness to refund the money until the life of the contract had ceased. We do not think that such is a reasonable construction of this contract, and it is not supported by authority. The rule is thus laid down by 2 Warvelle on Vendors, pages 835, 836: "A neglect or refusal of either party to perform on his part will, as a rule, place him in the power of the other party, where he is not also derelict, to avoid the contract or not at his pleasure. Hence, a failure to meet payments at the time or times reserved may be treated by the vendor as an abandonment, and he may rescind the contract and sell the land to another. And in such case the vendee will not be entitled to recover back the money he may have advanced in part performance": .Citing *Green* v. *Green*, 9 Cow. 46.

There seems to be nothing unconscionable in allowing the forfeiture in this case, as no sudden demand was made upon the vendee, but he was given thirty days' notice to make the payments that were due, and if he did not make them within that time and the further time allowed by the vendor in this case, it was presumably for the reason that he did not desire to proceed under the contract, but was willing to forfeit the payments which he had made and end the contract.

We think there is nothing in the contention that Emma [184] Smith, the wife of G. W. Smith, was not a proper party. The allegations of the complaint were that the relation of husband and wife existed between the defendants; that they were both in the possession of the premises sued for, and that they both refused to surrender said possession to the plaintiffs. Certainly, under these allegations, the wife was a proper, if not a necessary, party to the action.

The demand of the appellants in their answer that they be allowed a rescission of the contract cannot be sustained, for even though this were a proper case for the trial of such an issue, it plainly appears from all the testimony in the case, and is not denied, that the appellants were in default so far as carrying out the conditions of the contract were concerned, and a party who is in default will not be allowed to rescind a contract. The rule is thus laid down in 21 American and English Encyclopedia of Law, 77: "The right to rescind belongs only to the party who is himself without default. Thus, if one having sufficient ground therefor wishes to avoid a contract, but has done some act which hinders performance by the other, or has failed in any way to perform his own part of the stipulation, his right is thereby lost to him," citing many cases in support of this proposition.

In this case, too, the appellants are further precluded by the fact that they have never tendered any portion of the amount due the plaintiffs, and, until that is done, it can scarcely be contended that they would be entitled to a rescission of the contract: See *Drown* v. *Ingels*, 3 Wash. 424.

So far as the objection raised by the appellants to the findings of fact by the court is concerned we think it was without foundation, and that the court was justified in making all said findings. We have examined all the other errors alleged, but are unable to find any substantial error.

The judgment will therefore be affirmed.

SCOTT, ANDERS, HOYT, and STILES, JJ., concur.

———

VENDOR AND PURCHASER—TENDER OF DEED.—Where a vendor of land agrees to convey legal title on the payment of a certain number of installments of purchase money, and, before those are paid, other installments become due, he may retain his legal title as security for the full amount due when the payment is made, and may use such title to compel performance: *Thompson v. Carpenter*, 4 Pa. St. 132; 45 Am. Dec. 681.

VENDOR AND PURCHASER—FORFEITURE OF PART PAYMENTS.—One who purchases real property and makes a deposit of money under an agreement that it shall be forfeited if he fails to comply with the terms of the sale cannot recover it if the sale is not completed through his fault: *Donahue v. Parkman*, 161 Mass. 412; 42 Am. St. Rep. 415, and note, with the cases collected.

CONTRACTS.—RESCISSION of a contract cannot be sought in equity by a party whose own default caused the only obstacle to its completion and the other party is entirely without blame: *Salmon v. Hoffman*, 2 Cal. 138; 56 Am. Dec. 322. This question is fully discussed in the extended note to *Johnson v. Evans*, 50 Am. Dec. 675.

MULDOON v. SEATTLE CITY RAILWAY COMPANY.

[10 WASHINGTON, 811.]

RAILWAYS—FREE PASSES—ESTOPPEL.—One to whom a free pass is issued in contravention of law, and who avails himself of its privileges, is estopped from alleging that such pass was unlawful, for the purpose of recovering compensation for injuries suffered by him while riding upon such pass.

RAILWAYS—FREE PASS, DUTY TO READ CONDITIONS.—One who accepts a free pass from a railway, on the back of which is printed a condition exempting the corporation from liability for injuries which may be sustained by him while using such pass, cannot avoid such condition by alleging that it was printed on the back of the pass, which was inclosed in a leathern case so constructed as to conceal all parts of the pass except its face. The recipient of such a favor ought to take the trouble to look on both sides of the paper before attempting to use it.

RAILWAYS — FREE PASS — FAILURE TO READ. — The fact that one who accepts a free pass has not read the conditions printed thereon exempting the corporation from liability should he be injured, and is ignorant of them, does not relieve him from such condition.

Thompson, Edsen & Humphries, for the appellant.

812 STILES, J.   Upon the remittance of this case after the former decision (*Muldoon* v. *Seattle etc. Ry. Co.*, 7 Wash. 528; 38 Am. St. Rep. 901) the plaintiff filed a reply containing two defenses to the matter concerning the free pass set up in the answer.   In the first it is alleged that at the time of receiving the pass appellant was a duly elected, qualified, and acting member of the common council of Seattle, being a member of the house of delegates from the second ward; that the pass was issued and delivered to him by respondent, with full knowledge of all the facts, and for the reason and cause that appellant was such public officer, and not otherwise.   It is further alleged that appellant received and accepted the pass so tendered as a public officer in his official capacity, and used the same to ride upon respondent's cars because of his being such public officer, and not otherwise.   In the second it is alleged that the pass was delivered to appellant bound and inclosed in a leather case so constructed as to conceal all portions of the pass except the face, so that in using it in riding to and fro upon respondent's road it was unnecessary to remove it from the case, but it was only necessary to exhibit the exposed face of the pass to the conductors.   It is further alleged that neither at the time of receiving the pass, nor at any time thereafter prior to the injury complained of, did the appellant ever have any knowledge, notice, or information that there was printed upon the back of said pass, or upon any part thereof, the conditions and charges set forth in the answer.

To these defenses a demurrer was sustained, and this appeal calls for a decision as to their sufficiency. It is maintained, in the first place, that because the constitution of the state, article 12, section 20, forbids transportation companies [313] to grant passes to public officers, when that prohibition was violated by the respondent, both the pass and the condition were void, and the parties were placed in the position that the street railroad company was carrying the appellant as though he were an ordinary free passenger, and was subject to its ordinary liabilities in such cases.

Conceding the constitutional provision to be self-executing, we are unable to arrive at the conclusion from the premises. The appellant received the 'pass which he knew the corporation had no right to give him, and he availed himself of its privileges, and he ought to be estopped from saying that that which was the very means by which he occupied a place in the respondent's car was unlawfully given him. He was there under the license of the pass, and he cannot now be heard to say that his relation to the respondent was any other than that which he voluntarily made it.

As to the second point, it seems to us but little stronger than if the plea were that the appellant had not read what was printed, or had not looked on the back of the pass because it was not necessary for the satisfaction of the conductors. It is not alleged that the leather case was contrived so that the pass could not be easily removed from it. We think it may be fairly held that a person receiving a ticket for free transportation is bound to see and know all of the conditions printed thereon which the carrier sees fit to lawfully impose. This is an entirely different case from that where a carrier attempts to impose conditions upon a passenger for hire, which must, if unusual, be brought to his notice. In these cases of free passage the carrier has a right to impose any conditions it sees fit as to time, trains, baggage, connections, and, as we have held, damages for negligence; and the recipient of such favors ought at least to take the trouble to look on both sides of the paper before he attempts to use them.

In *Griswold* v. *New York etc. R. R. Co.*, 53 Conn. 371, 55 Am. Rep. 115, a minor was held bound by such conditions which he did not read. So in *Quimby* v. [314] *Boston etc. R. R.*

Co., 150 Mass. 365, it was said of the passenger: "Having accepted the pass he must have done so on the conditions fully expressed therein, whether he actually read them or not."

Judgment affirmed.

DUNBAR, C. J., and HOYT and SCOTT, JJ., concur.

RAILROADS—PERSONS RIDING ON PASSES—BINDING EFFECT OF CONDITIONS THEREIN.—A person accepting and riding upon a free railroad pass containing stipulations absolving the carrier from liability for negligence is bound by its terms, and cannot recover for personal injuries suffered by him through the negligence of the carrier or his servants: *Muldoon* v. *Seattle etc. Ry. Co.*, 7 Wash. 528; 38 Am. St. Rep. 901, and note; *Ulrich* v. *New York etc. R. R. Co.*, 108 N. Y. 80; 2 Am. St. Rep. 369, and especially note.

SPEARS *v.* LAWRENCE.

[10 WASHINGTON, 368.]

MECHANIC'S LIEN, CLAIM FOR.—A statement in a notice of lien incorporating a contract to furnish materials and do work necessary to the painting of the building in accordance with a contract between the landowner and the principal contractor, is a sufficient statement of the terms of the contract under which the lien is claimed.

MECHANIC'S LIEN.—THE SEPARATE PROPERTY OF A WIFE is subject to a mechanic's lien for the erection of a building thereon though she did not join in a contract therefor, if, during the progress of the work, she was about the premises with her husband and helped select the colors of the paints to be used thereon.

EVIDENCE.—IF A WRITING IS SHOWN TO BE LOST secondary evidence of its contents may be received.

MECHANIC'S LIEN.—A SURETY FOR THE PERFORMANCE OF A CONTRACT by the principal contractor, and who stipulated against the enforcement of any lien upon the building, cannot himself as a subcontractor claim and enforce such a lien, though it does not appear that the property owner will be injured should the lien be enforced.

Bruce, Brown & Cleveland, for the appellants Lawrence.

Dorr, Hadley & Hadley, for the appellant Morse.

J. J. Weisenburger and J. R. Crites, for the respondents Spears & Leonard.

[370] HOYT, J. The questions raised by this appeal relate to the sufficiency of the proceedings of the lower court in the foreclosure of certain liens against the property of F. C. Lawrence and his wife, Ada L. Lawrence. Such proceedings were had in a consolidated case involving a large number of

liens, all growing out of the contract of one R. C. Jordan to erect a certain building for the defendant F. C. Lawrence. The parts of the decree which are here for review relate to claims growing out of two of such liens. One in favor of plaintiffs Spears & Leonard was sustained, and a decree of foreclosure rendered thereon, from which the defendants F. C. Lawrence and Ada L. Lawrence have [371] appealed. The other relates to the claim of R. I. Morse, which was disallowed by the superior court, and a foreclosure denied, and from that part of the decree said Morse has prosecuted an appeal.

We will first examine that part of the decree relating to the lien of Spears & Leonard. It is attacked upon only two substantial grounds. The first relates to the sufficiency of the lien notice, and the other to the alleged facts that the improvement was upon the separate property of the wife, Ada L. Lawrence, and that no authority was shown from her to her husband to enter into the contract under which it was made.

As to the first we have only this to say: The lien notice set out a special contract by Spears & Leonard to furnish the materials and do the work necessary to the full completion of the painting of the building in accordance with the contract between the principal contractor and said Lawrence. And while it is true that the owner of the building would not be bound by the contract made between his contractor and the subcontractor, if it was shown to be fraudulent or improvident, yet, in the absence of such showing, it must be presumed that the contract is such as would be enforced by the courts. This being so, we think the statement of the contract in the lien notice was sufficient. There was no separate contract for the labor and for the materials, but one gross contract for every thing required in the prosecution of that particular work, and this being so there could not well be set out a claim under said contract for separate amounts for materials and for labor.

As to the fact that the improvement was upon property alleged to be the separate estate of the wife, we are not satisfied from the proofs that the real estate in question was her separate estate; but, if it was, her objection to its being subjected to the lien cannot be sustained, for the reason that such acts on her part, in connection with the erection of the building, were shown as should estop her from claiming that she was not bound by the contract of the husband for its erection. The decree foreclosing this lien was warranted by [372] the proofs, and to that extent it is affirmed; but in so far as it purports to render any personal judgment against said F. C. Lawrence and Ada L. Lawrence it must be modified, as the pleading and proofs would authorize a personal judgment against no one but the contractor R. C. Jordan.

As to the claim of said R. I. Morse, some objections are made to the form of the lien notice, but the principal contention grows out of the alleged fact that said Morse was a surety in the bond given by the contractor Jordan to F. C. Lawrence, which bond was so given for the purpose of securing said Lawrence from any liens being enforced against the building. This objection to the enforcement of the lien is combated by the appellant Morse for two reasons; one, that it does not appear that he ever signed such bond, and the other, that if he did he is not thereby precluded from enforcing his lien.

Before the cause went to trial a proper demand was made upon the counsel for Lawrence for said bond or a copy thereof. This demand was not complied with, nor was any reason given before the trial for noncompliance. For this reason it is contended on the part of appellant Morse that neither the bond nor the fact of its loss could be given in evidence upon the trial. This contention cannot be maintained. The bond having been lost, it, or a copy, could not be furnished in accordance with the demand, and there is no rule which requires the showing to that effect to be made before the trial. Upon the trial a sufficient excuse for noncompliance with the demand was shown, and thereby the right accrued to introduce the secondary evidence upon proof of the loss of the primary.

This leaves but one question, and that is as to the effect upon the lien claim of the claimant having been a surety for the performance of the contract by the principal contractor, Jordan. It would be inequitable to allow a person to enter into a solemn agreement to protect another from certain contingencies, and thereafter, and while such agreement was in full force, to himself seek to enforce the special liability which he had obligated himself to protect against. [373] No authority has been cited which, in our opinion, tends to sustain the contention of appellant that he could maintain his lien under these circumstances. He seeks to found this right in the particular case at bar upon the fact that it was not made to appear that the defendants Lawrence would be injured by having this lien enforced. However that may be, a sufficient answer is that what he guaranteed to the defendant was that no lien should be filed against the building, and, in the face of such guaranty, he will not be permitted to do that which would raise a direct liability on his part if done. If, as a matter of fact, there is some thing still due to the contractor Jordan from the defendants Lawrence, it can be reached without the aid of a lien against the building. He can prosecute his action against Jordan, and, under the judgment recovered against him, reach any moneys which may be due him from the owner of this building, or from any other source.

It follows that that portion of the decree finding against the defendant R. I. Morse must also be affirmed. The cause will be remanded, with instructions to affirm the decree when modified as to the personal judgment against the defendants Lawrence as hereinbefore suggested. The respondents will recover their costs on appeal.

DUNBAR, C. J., and STILES and SCOTT, JJ., concur.

MECHANIC'S LIENS—SUFFICIENCY OF NOTICE OF LIEN, GENERALLY.—The certificate of a mechanic's lien must give reasonable notice to purchasers and creditors of the existence and extent of the lien: *Bank v. Curtiss*, 18 Conn. 342; 46 Am. Dec. 325. Notice of mechanic's lien required to be filed in the recorder's office need not set out the items of the account, a general statement of the demand, showing its nature and character, being sufficient: *Brennan v. Swasey*, 16 Cal. 140; 76 Am. Dec. 507.

MECHANIC'S LIEN ON PROPERTY OF MARRIED WOMAN.—Under a statute authorizing a married woman to hold, bequeath, and convey her property, real and personal, the same as if she were a *feme sole*, she may enter into a contract for its improvement, and such contract may be the basis of a mechanic's lien for labor and materials: *Hoffman v. McFadden*, 56 Ark. 217; 35 Am. St. Rep. 101, and note. If a husband enters into a contract for the erection of a building on his wife's land with her knowledge, she participating in conversations between her husband and the contractors relative to the work during the time it is being done, and making no objection at any time, such land is liable for mechanics' liens arising out of the work done: *Jobe v. Hunter*, 165 Pa. St. 5; 44 Am. St. Rep. 639, and note.

MECHANICS' LIENS—STIPULATIONS AGAINST, UPON WHOM BINDING.—A building contract, under which the contractor agrees to keep the lot and building free from mechanics' liens and any and all manner of charges, precludes the principal contractor, subcontractor, or any other person, from filing and foreclosing any lien or charge on the building: *Fidelity etc. Life Assn. v. Jackson*, 163 Pa. St. 208; 43 Am. St. Rep. 789, and note; *Waters v. Wolf*, 162 Pa. St. 153; 42 Am. St. Rep. 815, and note. See, also, the note to *Benedict v. Hood*, 19 Am. St. Rep. 699.

EVIDENCE—SECONDARY OF LOST INSTRUMENTS.—Secondary evidence of the contents of a record may be given if such record has been lost or destroyed: *Kreitz* v. *Behrensmeyer*, 125 Ill. 141; 8 Am. St. Rep. 349; *Pruden* v. *Alden*, 23 Pick. 184; 34 Am. Dec. 51, and note; *Eakin* v. *Doe*, 10 Smedes & M. 549; 48 Am. Dec. 770, and note; *In the Matter of Will of Warfield*, 22 Cal. 51; 83 Am. Dec. 49.   The contents of a lost instrument may be proved by parol: *Jackson* v. *Cullum*, 2 Blackf. 228; 18 Am. Dec. 158.   See the notes to *Bell* v. *Byerson*, 77 Am. Dec. 144; *Wiseman* v. *North Pac. R. R. Co.*, 23 Am. St. Rep. 140, and *Georgia Pac. Ry. Co.* v. *Strickland*, 12 Am. St. Rep. 285.

NEUFELDER v. NORTH BRITISH AND MERCANTILE INSURANCE COMPANY.

[10 WASHINGTON, 393.]

GARNISHMENT—JURISDICTION.—By a suit against an insurance company in a state wherein it has a general agent, and by the garnishment of such company, courts acquire jurisdiction over the debt due a defendant who resides in another state, and to whom such company is indebted for a loss suffered by him in the state of his residence for the destruction of property there situate.

ATTACHMENT IN ANOTHER STATE—EFFECT OF INSOLVENCY LAWS UPON.—A statute of this state, providing that a general assignment by the debtor for the benefit of his creditors shall dissolve prior attachments against him cannot dissolve an attachment issued in another state by virtue of which a debt due to the assignor has been garnished.

INSOLVENCY PROCEEDINGS—WAIVER OF LIEN ACQUIRED IN ANOTHER STATE. A creditor who has in another state attached a debt due to his debtor does not, by filing in this state a claim against such debtor in proceedings in insolvency, waive or abandon his attachment lien.   The amount which he may receive under and by virtue of such lien may be deducted from the amount of his claim, and the balance is the true amount of indebtedness upon which he is entitled to dividends in this state.

Strudwick & Peters, for the appellant.

Stratton, Lewis & Gilman, for the respondent.

394 ANDERS, J.   The respondent is a corporation organized and existing under and by virtue of the laws of the kingdom of Great Britain and Ireland, and, at the times hereinafter mentioned, was lawfully conducting the business of insurance in this state, and was represented by a local agent in the city of Seattle.   It was also engaged in similar business in California and in all the other states and territories on the Pacific Coast, and had a general agent for the management thereof in all of said states and territories, including this state, whose office and place of business was at San Francisco, in the state of California.   All moneys collected by

local agents were remitted to this general agent, and the
funds of the company for the payment of losses were kept in
San Francisco and disbursed by him only, the local agents
throughout said states and territories having no authority to
settle or pay losses on account of the company, except as
requested and directed by him.

On July 2, 1890, the respondent, by its agent at Seattle,
delivered a properly executed policy of insurance to one C. H.
Knox, a citizen of this state, whereby it agreed to insure him
against loss or damage by fire, to the amount of one thousand
dollars, on a stock of merchandise owned by him in Seattle,
for the period of one year from said date. On September 19,
1890, and while the policy was in full force and effect, the
property so insured was totally destroyed by fire. Thereafter
the respondent adjusted the loss at one thousand dollars, but
before the same was paid, and on October 1, 1890, certain
creditors of Knox, residing in San Francisco, commenced
actions in the superior court of the city and county of San
Francisco to recover the [395] amount of their respective
claims, and on the following day caused the amount due
from respondent to Knox on the policy of insurance to be
attached by process of garnishment, in the manner prescribed
by the laws of California. Subsequently, and on October 25,
1890, the said Knox made a general assignment to appellant,
in this state, for the benefit of his creditors. After having
qualified according to law, as assignee, the appellant brought
this action in the superior court of King county to recover
from the respondent the sum due on the policy issued to his
assignor, Knox. The respondent admitted its liability on
the policy upon which the action was brought, and disclaimed
any desire to evade payment, but asked the trial court to
stay this proceeding until its liability in the attachment suits
in California should be determined. The cause was tried by
the court without a jury, and, upon the facts found and conclusions of law based thereon by the court, a judgment was
entered staying further proceedings in accordance with the
prayer of the defendant.

It is disclosed by the record that other insurance companies
besides the respondent, indebted to Knox on policies of insurance covering the burned stock of goods, were likewise garnished in the attachment proceedings in the California court.
The total amount of indebtedness so attached, including the
amount due from the respondent, was four thousand five hun-

dred dollars. The total amount of the claims of the California creditors, upon which suits were brought, and in which garnishments were served upon respondent, was five thousand and seventy-eight dollars and fifteen cents. Two of the creditors who caused garnishment process to be served upon the respondent in California, namely, Wheaton, Luhrs & Co., and Esberg, Bachman & Co., afterward filed their claims in this state with appellant as the assignee of Knox.

From what we have stated it will be observed that the facts in this case are almost identical with those involved in the case of *Neufelder* v. *German-American Ins. Co.*, 6 Wash. 336; 36 Am. St. Rep. 166. In that case this court held that the California court acquired jurisdiction of the debt owing by the insurance company to Knox, and, having acquired jurisdiction, could enforce its payment by [396] the garnishee. The appellant does not seek to have us reconsider our ruling in that case, but contends that this appeal presents for decision points not raised in the former case.

The first and most material point made is that the trial court in rendering its judgment overlooked one of the provisions of our insolvent law, to the injury of the appellant, or rather of the creditors in this state. The claim, more specifically stated, is that, inasmuch as, by virtue of our Insolvent Debtors' Act, then in force, prior attachments were dissolved, in this state, by a general assignment, the court should have held the law operative to the same extent upon the California attachments, and permitted the action to proceed without any regard whatever to the proceedings in that state. The appellant's contention is based upon the general proposition, that the laws of a state have no binding force beyond its territorial limits, and are only permitted to operate in other states upon the principle of comity, and when neither the state where the foreign law is sought to be applied, nor its citizens, would be injured by its application. We have no disposition to dispute this proposition, for it may be said to be the statement of an elementary principle of law: Sutherland on Statutory Construction, 12; *Dunlap* v. *Rogers*, 47 N. H. 287; 93 Am. Dec. 433.

But, while it is true that if writs of attachment had been levied upon the property of Knox at the suit of creditors in this state they would have been dissolved by his assignment by operation of law, it does not necessarily follow that the court erred in recognizing the California attachments as valid and binding there. It is said by the learned author above cited (page 12), that the observance and recognition of foreign laws rests in comity and convenience and in the aim of the law to adapt its remedies to the great ends of justice. And courts, in furtherance of justice, do recognize the validity of acts done under foreign laws, which would not be valid if done in the jurisdiction of the forum, as will be hereafter shown.

The learned counsel for the appellant cite the case of [397] *Upton* v. *Hubbard*, 28 Conn. 274, 73 Am. Dec. 670, in support of their contention. It was there decided that if a debt due from a person domiciled in Connecticut to a person domiciled in Massachusetts is attached in Connecticut by a creditor of the payee, and the payee, between the levying of the attachment and the judgment entered thereon, makes an assignment, this assignment will not pass the debt as against the attachment creditor, even though, by the laws of Massachusetts, such an assignment operates to dissolve prior attachments. And from this the conclusion is deduced by appellant that, in no event, will a court of one state give effect to the laws of another state, which are not in harmony with its own. But, suppose the assignment in Massachusetts had been made, in that case, prior to the levying of the attachment in Connecticut, what would then have been the decision of the court? It appears that this question has been answered by the same court, in accordance with the view hereinbefore indicated, in the later case of *Clark* v. *Connecticut Peat Co.*, 35 Conn. 303. In that case a debt due from a citizen of Connecticut to citizens of Massachusetts was attached by a citizen of the former state, to whom the Massachusetts creditors were indebted. Before the attachment the debt had been assigned, in good faith, by the Massachusetts creditors to a citizen of Massachusetts. It seems that the assignment would not have been valid under the law of Connecticut, for want of notice; yet the court held that, being good in Massachusetts, where made, it was good in Connecticut, and passed the debt attached to the assignee. It can hardly be said that the court disregarded or overlooked the laws of Connecticut by giving effect to the assignment in Massachusetts. It simply decided, in effect, that, after a valid transfer of the debt had been there made, it was not subject to attachment in Connecticut.

So, in this case, the trial court merely held that the debt

sued upon, having been lawfully attached and held for the satisfaction of any judgments the California creditors might recover against Knox, prior to the assignment, passed to the appellant, as assignee, subject to those attachments. Nor ³⁹⁸ was the effect of this ruling, as suggested by counsel, tantamount to enforcing a lien claim under a foreign law, which would be ineffectual under the provisions of our own statute. The court simply took into consideration the status of the debt at the time of the assignment, and thereby gave "full faith and credit" to the judicial proceedings of a sister state.

That the conclusion of the court below was not improper will also, we think, be disclosed by an examination of the decision of the supreme court of the United States in the well-considered case of *Green* v. *Van Buskirk,* 7 Wall. 148, wherein the court said: "Attachment laws, to use the words of Chancellor Kent, are legal modes of acquiring title to property by operation of law. They exist in every state for the furtherance of justice, with more or less of liberality to creditors. And, if the title acquired under the attachment laws of a state, and which is valid there, is not to be held valid in every other state, it were better that these laws were abolished, for they would prove to be but a snare and a delusion to the creditors."

If the title to property acquired by attachment in one state, and which is valid there, is to be deemed valid in every other state, it would seem logically to follow that an attachment, valid in the state where it is levied, ought to be held valid in every other state. Nor, as we understand it, does the case of *Cole* v. *Cunningham,* 133 U. S. 107, cited by appellant, overrule or modify the court's former decision in 7 Wallace, above cited.

Under the circumstances, therefore, we are unable to perceive wherein the appellant was injured by the judgment complained of. If the respondent is compelled to pay the sum of money here claimed, or any part of it, to the creditors in San Francisco, of course it ought not to be obliged to pay it again to appellant. But if it is not compelled to pay there, then the final judgment of the court in this state will be in favor of the appellant for the amount due upon the policy.

It is further claimed by the appellant that Wheaton, Luhrs & Co., and Esberg, Bachman & Co., by filing their ³⁹⁹ claims with the appellant as assignee, abandoned any rights they might otherwise have had under the attachments. But we do not think the position is strictly tenable. A creditor may prosecute two actions against his debtor for the same cause in different jurisdictions: *Stanton* v. *Embrey*, 93 U. S. 548, Bliss on Code Pleading, 410; and, therefore, the waging of one action cannot be said to be a waiver or an abandonment of another. But those creditors, by filing their claims with the assignee, became parties to the insolvency proceedings, and will be bound by them. Should the insolvent assignor be discharged from his debts, they cannot thereafter maintain an action against him for the recovery of the debt proved by them, and their claims will be paid *pro rata* with those of domestic creditors, if any payments are here made. But the amount, if any, which may be received by them by means of the attachments in California, ought to be deducted from the claims as filed with the assignee, and the balance treated as the true amount of indebtedness: *Fay* v. *Jenks*, 78 Mich. 304.

We perceive no error prejudicial to appellant, and the judgment is therefore affirmed.

DUNBAR, C. J., and SCOTT and STILES, JJ., concur.

HOYT, judge, dissented, referring to the fact that he had also dissented in the case of *Neufelder* v. *German-American Ins. Co.*, 6 Wash. 336, 36 Am. St. Rep. 166, and that in so dissenting he had failed to state his reasons therefor. He declared that the rule as announced in that decision and in the principal case was one which would lead to much inconvenience and hardship to residents of the state who held policies in insurance companies, because suits might be brought in any of the states of the union, and attachments there made of the debts due from such companies upon losses incurred in this state; and that the result would be that any one having the semblance of a claim would be tempted to bring suit in some state remote from the residence of the defendant, hoping that the difficulty of making a defense would lead to some compromise, or that, from want of pecuniary ability, or some other reason, defense would be impossible, and that the entire amount of the policy might frequently be absorbed in the payment of unjust claims, and frittered away in paying the expenses incident to making a defense against them. He declared that "A simple solution of the whole question would be to hold that a corporation has only one domicile for the purposes incident to its organization; that rights and liabilities in general must be prosecuted by or enforced against it in the state where it has such domicile, that is, in the state under the laws of which it has been incorporated; that it has a special and limited domicile in each of the states in which, under the laws thereof, it may be allowed to do business; that its domicile in those states is only for the purposes of the business transacted there. The result would be that, as to all of the business transacted in a state, and rights and obligations flowing therefrom, the courts of that state would have full jurisdiction of the corporation, but would have no jurisdiction whatever over it in relation to business not transacted in the state."

GARNISHMENT—JURISDICTION.—Garnishment proceedings must be instituted in the state where the debt is payable or the property is to be delivered, and a garnishment in one state of a debt due and payable in another is void. So, an insurance company indebted for a loss payable in one state cannot be garnished in another, where it has no money or property of the debtor within the jurisdiction of the court: *American etc. Ins. Co. v. Hettler,* 37 Neb. 849; 40 Am. St. Rep. 522, and note.

ATTACHMENT.—ASSIGNMENT FOR THE BENEFIT OF CREDITORS MADE IN ANOTHER STATE by a resident thereof, if valid where made, is also valid in this state, unless detrimental to its citizens. Hence, an assignment for the benefit of creditors executed in Iowa takes precedence over a garnishment subsequently levied in Illinois at the instance of a resident of Ohio to attach indebtedness due from a resident in Illinois to the assignor in Iowa: *Consolidated Tank Line Co.* v. *Collier,* 148 Ill. 259; 39 Am. St. Rep. 181, and note. A voluntary assignment by a debtor of all of his property for the benefit of his creditors, valid by the law of his domicile, will prevail against the lien of an attachment subsequently issued in another state in favor of a creditor there, whether citizen or nonresident, upon a debt of the original assignor embraced in the assignment, provided the recognition of the title under the assignment does not contravene the statutory law of the state, nor is it repugnant to public policy: *Barth* v. *Backus,* 140 N. Y. 230; 37 Am. St. Rep. 545, and note.

McQuillan *v.* City of Seattle.

[10 WASHINGTON, 464.]

WHAT IS CONTRIBUTORY NEGLIGENCE is generally a question for the jury to determine from all the facts and circumstances of the particular case, and only in rare cases is the court justified in withdrawing this question from the jury.

CONTRIBUTORY NEGLIGENCE.—A COURT MAY, AS A MATTER OF LAW, determine whether contributory negligence existed: 1. Where the circumstances of the case are such that the standard and measure of duty are fixed and defined by law and the same under all circumstances; and 2. Where the facts are undisputed, and but one reasonable inference can be drawn from them.

NEGLIGENCE, KNOWLEDGE OF DEFECT.—The mere fact that a person injured from a defect in a sidewalk was aware of such defect is not conclusive of negligence on his part, though it is competent evidence on the question of his contributory negligence.

NEGLIGENCE, CARE REQUIRED OF ONE HAVING KNOWLEDGE OF A DEFECT. One having knowledge of the defective condition of a street is bound to use more care in passing over it than if he had been without such knowledge, but is not bound to use extraordinary care. All required of him is to use such care and caution as a person of ordinary prudence would use under such circumstances. If the evidence does not show that he did not exercise ordinary care it should be left to the jury to say whether he did or not.

NEGLIGENCE, CONTRIBUTORY.—MOMENTARY FORGETFULNESS is not necessarily conclusive evidence of negligence.

STREETS—CONTRIBUTORY NEGLIGENCE.—Though a sidewalk in a city is in a defective and dangerous condition, and a person knowing of this condi-

tion, passing along the street on a dark night, and believing himself to
have passed the dangerous portion, stepped upon a loose plank, which,
breaking, precipitated him through the sidewalk to the ground below to
his great injury, it should be left to the jury to determine whether,
under the circumstances, he was guilty of such contributory negligence
as precluded his recovery from the municipality through whose negligence the sidewalk was left in its defective condition.

Byers, McElwain & Byers, for the appellant.

W. T. Scott, for the respondent.

⁴⁶⁴ Aɴᴅᴇʀs, J.   About 8 o'clock on the evening of March
8, 1892, the appellant left the Villard House, at the corner
of Railroad and Yesler avenue, to go to his home on South
Fifth street, between Main and Jackson streets, in the city of
Seattle.   When he reached the corner of Fourth and Jackson
streets he walked eastward, on the south side of Jackson
street, in the direction of his house, nearly one hundred feet,
and then crossed over to the sidewalk on the north side.
The sidewalk on that side of the street was in such a defective and dangerous condition for the space of about one hundred feet immediately east of Fourth street that it was unsafe
to travel upon it, and had been in the same condition for
more than a year previous to the date above mentioned, and
the appellant was cognizant of it, ⁴⁶⁵ having passed along
that portion of the street almost daily, in going to and from
his home, for a period of two years or more.   The defects in
the sidewalk consisted of openings caused by the removal of
one or more planks at several different places, which were
not replaced, but were laid loosely across the open spaces, in
some instances, if not all, near the outer edge of the walk.
There was no railing or other safeguard around this defective
portion of the walk, nothing to give warning of danger, and
the night was dark, and the street in that vicinity was but
dimly lighted.   The appellant, thinking he had passed all
the dangerous places, approached the sidewalk and stepped
upon a loose plank which was lying partially across an open
space, about two feet wide, at the eastern extremity of the
defective portion.   The board suddenly tipped downward,
and the appellant fell through the sidewalk to the ground
beneath, a distance of eighteen or twenty feet, thereby receiving serious bodily injury.   Thereafter he instituted this action
against the city to recover damages for the injuries sustained.
The cause proceeded regularly to trial, and, at the close of
plaintiff's evidence, a nonsuit was granted on motion of the

defendant, on the ground of contributory negligence on the part of the plaintiff. Judgment for costs was thereupon entered against the plaintiff.

The sole question to be determined on this appeal is whether the learned trial court erred in granting the nonsuit. Generally the question of contributory negligence is for the jury to determine from all the facts and circumstances of the particular case, and it is only in rare cases that the court is justified in withdrawing it from the jury: *Railroad Co.* v. *Stout,* 17 Wall. 657; *Grand Trunk Ry. Co.* v. *Ives,* 144 U. S. 408; *Lowell* v. *Watertown,* 58 Mich. 568; *Detroit etc. R. R. Co.* v. *Van Steinburg,* 17 Mich. 121; Jones on Negligence of Municipal Corporations, secs. 221, 222; *Maloy* v. *St. Paul,* 54 Minn. 398; *Ladouceur* v. *Northern Pac. R. R. Co.,* 4 Wash. 38; *City of Denver* v. *Soloman,* 2 Col. App. 534; 2 Thompson on Negligence, 1236.

⁴⁶⁶ There are two classes of cases in which the question of negligence may be determined by the court as a conclusion of law, but we think the case in hand does not fall within either of them. The first is where the circumstances of the case are such that the standard of duty is fixed, and the measure of duty defined, by law, and is the same under all circumstances: *City of Denver* v. *Soloman,* 2 Col. App. 534, and authorities cited. And the second is where the facts are undisputed and but one reasonable inference can be drawn from them: Cooley on Torts, 670, 671; 2 Thompson on Negligence, secs. 1236, 1237. If different results might be honestly reached by different minds then negligence is not a question of law, but one of fact for the jury: *Grand Trunk Ry. Co.* v. *Ives,* 144 U. S. 408.

The mere fact that the appellant was aware of the defective condition of the sidewalk when the accident occured is not *per se* conclusive of negligence on his part, though it was competent evidence on the question of contributory negligence: *Monongahela Bridge Co.* v. *Bevard* (Pa., Nov. 7, 1887), 11 Atl. Rep. 575; *Millcreek Tp.* v. *Perry* (Pa., Nov. 7, 1887), 12 Atl. Rep. 149; *Kelly* v. *Blackstone,* 147 Mass. 448; 9 Am. St. Rep. 730; *Frost* v. *Waltham,* 12 Allen, 85.

Having knowledge of the defect he was bound to use more care in passing than if he had been entirely ignorant of it, but he was not bound to use extraordinary care. All that the law required was the exercise of such care and caution as a person of ordinary prudence would use under similar circumstances. This, we think, is the doctrine maintained by all of the authorities. And, as the evidence does not indisputably show that the appellant did not exercise ordinary care, it should have been left to the jury to say whether he did or did not.

Several cases are cited by the respondent in support of the ruling of the court below, but, in our opinion, none of them refutes the correctness of the propositions we have here announced. *Wright* v. *St. Cloud*, 54 Minn. 94, is one of the cases relied on by the respondent (and the others are of similar character), but in that case [467] the plaintiff plainly saw the condition of the way and yet unnecessarily and deliberately attempted to pass, and the court very properly held that the plaintiff was not entitled to recover because of contributory negligence. No other legitimate conclusion could have been drawn from the facts before the court. But that that was an exceptional case is shown by a later decision in the same court, in *Maloy* v. *St. Paul*, 54 Minn. 398, wherein an order of the lower court granting a new trial on the ground that the plaintiff had knowledge of the defect in the walk causing her injury was overruled.

The testimony of the appellant discloses that at the moment he supposed he was stepping upon the sidewalk he was not thinking of the hole through which he fell, but momentary forgetfulness is not necessarily conclusive proof of negligence in cases of this character: *Kelly* v. *Blackstone*, 147 Mass. 448; 9 Am. St. Rep. 730; *Maloy* v. *St. Paul*, 54 Minn. 398. The judgment is reversed and the cause remanded, with directions to deny the motion for nonsuit, and for further proceedings.

DUNBAR, C. J., and STILES and SCOTT, JJ., concur.

HOYT, J., dissenting. I think the motion for nonsuit was properly granted. Appellant's own testimony showed him to have been familiar with the locality and with the defects in the sidewalk; that it was to avoid the defective places that he went up the other side of the street; that he knew that there was safety in continuing on that side; that he would have done so had it not been for the presence upon the sidewalk on that side of the street of a crowd of men, which made it a matter of some little inconvenience for him to continue thereon; that to avoid this crowd he crossed over, as he thought he had already passed the defects in the side-

walk. So much appearing, the only inference to be drawn
was that he was guilty of negligence in crossing the street
until he was certain he had passed the place where the sidewalk was defective.   His thinking he had passed was not
sufficient, in the light of the fact that perfect safety, with
slight inconvenience, could have been had by continuing [468]
upon the side on which he was traveling.   In my opinion
the judgment should be affirmed.

CONTRIBUTORY NEGLIGENCE—WHEN QUESTION FOR JURY.—When considerable doubt exists as to whether or not the plaintiff is guilty of contributory negligence, that question should be submitted to the jury for its
determination: *People's Bank* v. *Morgolofski*, 75 Md. 432; 32 Am. St. Rep.
403, and note.

CONTRIBUTORY NEGLIGENCE—WHEN QUESTION FOR COURT.—Proof of
contributory negligence must be clear and decisive to warrant a nonsuit or
an absolute direction to the jury on that ground: *Thoresen* v. *La Crosse etc.
Ry. Co.*, 87 Wis. 597; 41 Am. St. Rep. 64, and note, with the cases collected.

CONTRIBUTORY NEGLIGENCE—DEFECTIVE SIDEWALKS.—A person passing
over a defective sidewalk is bound to exercise ordinary care to avoid injury:
City of Sandwich v. *Dolan*, 133 Ill. 177; 23 Am. St. Rep. 598, and note; *Turner* v. *City of Newburgh*, 109 N. Y. 301; 4 Am. St. Rep. 453, and note.   A
person who, knowing the dangerous condition of a sidewalk, deliberately
goes upon it without necessity, is guilty of contributory negligence, and
cannot recover for injuries received thereby: *Town of Gosport* v. *Evans*, 112
Ind. 123; 2 Am. St. Rep. 164; but one is not necessarily negligent in walking on a sidewalk which he knows to be unsafe, as the nearest way to his
destination, instead of taking another way which is also unsafe: *City of
Altoona* v. *Lotz*, 114 Pa. St. 238; 60 Am. Rep. 346.   A person is not guilty
of contributory negligence because, assuming a sidewalk in a city to be safe,
she permitted her attention to be momentarily attracted in another direction, and fell into a hole in such sidewalk from which the covering had been
removed: *Barry* v. *Terkildsen*, 72 Cal. 254; 1 Am. St. Rep. 55, and note.

PUGET SOUND NATIONAL BANK *v.* LEVY.

[10 WASHINGTON, 499.]

JUDGMENT, WHETHER BY CONFESSION OR BY ACTION.—If a debtor, desiring to prefer certain of his creditors, caused them to assign their
claims to his attorney, and, after the filing of a complaint thereon
and the issuing of summons, immediately caused it to be served
on himself and signed a notice of appearance and a consent to the
entry of judgment, after which the papers were taken to the clerk's
office, presented to one of the judges, and a judgment entered thereon,
such judgment must be regarded as by confession and not as taken in
an action, and, therefore, unless the confession is verified and contains
a statement of the facts out of which the indebtedness arose, as required by law, the judgment is void.

JUDGMENT BY CONFESSION in which the confession does not contain a statement of the facts out of which the indebtedness arose is void, though
the statement shows that it is based upon the promissory note which is
set forth therein.

ASSIGNMENT FOR THE BENEFIT OF CREDITORS, WHAT IS NOT.—A confession of a judgment in favor of certain creditors with intent to prefer
them cannot be recognized as amounting to a general assignment for the
benefit of creditors.

Metcalfe & Jurey, for the appellants.

*Carr & Preston, W. R. Bell, Stratton, Lewis & Gilman, and
Emmons & Emmons,* for the respondents.

500 STILES, J.   This action was brought by the Puget
Sound National Bank of Seattle, as an attachment creditor
of Samuel Levy, to have certain judgments rendered upon
the confession of the said Levy in favor of Samuel Latz and
Carmi Dibble set aside and declared void.   Other subsequent
attachment creditors intervened in the action for the purpose
of obtaining a similar remedy.   The grounds upon which the
action was brought were: 1. Actual fraud, in that it is alleged
that no indebtedness existed between Levy and the persons
in favor of whom the judgments were confessed; and 2.
That the manner of taking the judgments did not comply
with the statute, in that the statement filed was not verified
by oath of the judgment debtor, and did not state concisely
the facts out of which the indebtedness arose, as required by
the Code of Procedure, section 419.

Upon the first ground the court held with the appellants,
and found the relation of debtor and creditor existed in good
faith between Levy and Latz and Dibble; and we shall not
investigate that question, deeming the findings of the court
below to be justified by the evidence.

501 But upon the second point the court held with the
respondents, and decreed the judgments to be void as against
the creditors of Levy.   The manner in which these judgments were taken made it impossible for the plaintiff in the
case to rest its suit upon the face of the paper constituting
the judgment-roll, and compelled it to take evidence showing
the manner in which the judgments came to be apparently
valid judgments of record in the county of King.

In form the judgments were not entered without action,
as provided by the Code of Procedure, sections 418 to 420,
but they were in the form provided by sections 414 and
417.   The evidence taken was for the purpose of showing

that while in form the judgments were entered in pending actions, they were in fact judgments by confession entered voluntarily by the debtor, and that the plan adopted was a scheme whereby the pendency of the actions would be concealed from other creditors and the debtor would not be required to set forth the particulars of the indebtedness confessed or verify the confession.

Samuel Levy was doing business as a merchant in the city of Seattle, engaged in the sale of toys and notions. He had a stock of goods worth some ten or fifteen thousand dollars. His debts to other creditors than Latz and Dibble amounted to about five thousand dollars. Latz, Dibble, and one other creditor whose claim was included in these judgments, were all relatives by marriage. The alleged indebtedness was upon notes given at various times from one to three years prior to the date of the judgments. All of the notes drew interest, and little or nothing had been paid, either of principal or interest, upon any of them. The whole amounted to about ten thousand dollars. On or about December 20, 1893, Levy, being then pressed by his general creditors, sought out certain attorneys at law who had theretofore been his regular counsel, and advised with them concerning the circumstances and how he could best prefer Latz, Dibble, and Matilda Guttman out of his estate. He was advised that the preferable way to accomplish this was by means of confession of judgments and the levy of [502] executions thereunder by the sheriff. His attorneys advised him, however, that if he should make voluntary confession without the knowledge of the judgment creditors, other creditors might be able to get precedence by reason of the fact that the acceptance of the judgment creditors would be necessary before the judgments would become binding. It was also suggested that, if the creditors whom he desired to prefer were to commence actions against him under the law prescribing the method of commencing actions, the whole matter could be kept out of the records of the court until such time as the papers were all prepared and the judgments ready for entry. Up to this time there had been no correspondence or communications whatever between the attorneys and the creditors. The plan last mentioned was adopted, and it was arranged that Levy's attorneys should act for the creditors. This was on December 21st. Levy thereupon caused each of the three creditors to be notified to send their notes to his attorneys, and advised them of what was proposed. As soon as the papers arrived the plan was put into effect, and on the twenty-sixth day of December his own attorneys, acting not only as the attorneys for the creditors but for himself, prepared a complaint in the ordinary form against Levy, summons directed to Levy, notice of appearance to be signed by him, the consent to entry of judgment and assent of plaintiff's attorneys, motion for judgment, and a judgment entry in blank. Levy being present, the summons was handed to an attorney occupying an office in the same building, who was called in to do the notarial work in the case, and he served it on Levy. Levy thereupon signed the notice of appearance and consent to the entry of judgment, which he acknowledged before the notary, plaintiff's attorney signed the assent, and the papers were carried at once to the clerk's office and filed, and immediately afterward were presented to one of the judges of the court, who thereupon signed the judgment entry. This was done in each case, and executions were forthwith issued and delivered to the sheriff, who levied upon Levy's stock, and [503] was proceeding to sell the same when this action was brought, and further proceedings enjoined.

Upon the face of the record the judgments were valid, and · were voidable, if at all, only by the creditors. We have stated only the salient facts pertaining to this matter; a great many others are contained in the evidence, which go to sustain the view of the judge of the lower court, that the real object of these proceedings was to enable Levy himself to take such steps as would place his property beyond the reach of any of his creditors excepting those preferred in this manner.

The appellants lay great stress upon the fact that these proceedings were taken in an action within the meaning of those words as they are used in section 414, but, in our view of the case, their position cannot be sustained. There was no action pending against Levy at any time, not even after the summons and complaint were served upon him. The attorneys for the nominal plaintiffs had no rightful control over them. They were retained by Levy, and were under his direction and control; so much so that had he so directed them they would have, and must have, entirely discarded these papers at any time before they were filed with the county clerk. Nominally, the attorneys were acting for Lata and Dibble, but in fact Latz and Dibble were merely the pliant assistants of Levy in carrying out his own plan. Latz was not even in the state, but was in the state of California, and in nowise directed the attorneys what to do. He merely sent the notes in compliance with the request of Levy. Dibble was present, but he assumed no direction over the matter, and merely complied with the request of Levy to put his notes into the hands of Levy's attorneys.

Now, it is possible for a debtor to make a confession of judgment in a pending action. It is possible, also, that such action may be brought at his suggestion, but when brought it must be in the usual sense a hostile action, and the debtor must have no control over it at any stage. In such an action the confession need only be acknowledged, [504] and the statute does not prescribe what it shall contain. There are probably many other ways in which a debtor may practically confess a judgment, as by default or by answer admitting the truth of the facts alleged in the complaint, but in such cases there is nothing secret about the proceeding, and creditors have an opportunity to become aware of what is going on and take steps accordingly. But, in this case, as we view it, the only really substantial document filed in the court, so far as the rights of other creditors are concerned, was the purported confession itself; the other papers were mere forms, and nothing more, used as covers for the actual proceedings. The judgments rested solely upon the confessions, except as between the parties.

Having come to that conclusion, but little more need be said. The confessions were not verified, and, for that reason, were absolutely void as confessions for want of compliance with section 419. And for another reason they were voidable, viz., because they did not contain a concise statement of the facts out of which the indebtedness arose. Each cause of action was stated to be upon a promissory note duly made and executed by Levy for a valuable consideration, and delivered to plaintiff, by which Levy agreed and promised to pay a certain amount with interest. It is settled law, wherever the method of confessing judgments contained in our statute prevails, that the confession must contain a statement of fact constituting the consideration for a promissory note: *Chappel* v. *Chappel*, 12 N. Y. 215; 64 Am. Dec. 496; *Freligh* v. *Brink*, 22 N. Y. 418; *Dunham* v. *Waterman*, 17 N. Y. 9; 72 Am. Dec. 406; *Richardson* v. *Fuller*, 2 Or. 179;

Bernard v. *Douglas*, 10 Iowa, 370; *Bryan* v. *Miller*, 28 Mo. 32; 75 Am. Dec. 107; *Nichols* v. *Kribs*, 10 Wis. 76; 76 Am. Dec. 294; *Wells* v. *Gieseke*, 27 Minn. 478; *Davidson* v. *Alexander*, 84 N. C. 621.

Counsel for appellants suggest that the fact that the court found the indebtedness of Levy to Latz and Dibble to be *bona fide* ought to make a difference in the judgment in this case, but it will be found that in all the cases cited there is no question of the good faith of either party to the judgment. 505 A confession in this manner is a statutory proceeding, and the interest of creditors requires it to be strictly followed. The object of stating the facts constituting the consideration is, that creditors taken at such a disadvantage may inquire into the *bona fides* of the transaction, and take such steps as they may be advised they are entitled to to avoid the effect of such judgments. The only cases which have come to our notice where a different rule has been adopted are in California.

Richards v. *McMillan*, 6 Cal. 422, 65 Am. Dec. 521, and *Cordier* v. *Schloss*, 12 Cal. 147, held that upon a direct attack upon a judgment similar to the one at bar the failure to state the facts showing the consideration for the debt confessed was *prima facie* evidence only of the invalidity of the judgment, and that the judgment creditor might show the actual sufficiency of the consideration as a defense. *Cordier* v. *Schloss*, 18 Cal. 576, was a second hearing of the case in 12 California, and the former rulings of the court on this question were adhered to under the doctrine of *stare decisis*, but a doubt is expressed as to the correctness of the rule. In *Wells* v. *Gieseke*, 27 Minn. 478, it was pointed out that the proper way to sustain such a judgment, attacked for the deficiency named, was by amending it, and it was held that no amendments could be made which could affect the rights of creditors which had been fixed by attachment. We think this to be the better rule. But, however this question might be determined, the fact remains that these confessions were not verified, and they were, therefore, void upon their face. We therefore hold that upon the main point in issue the decree should be affirmed.

It is also suggested by the appellants that the court erred in appointing a receiver of the property levied upon by the sheriff, and also in authorizing him to take it from such officer, which was done. Had we reversed this case upon the merits we should have set aside the order appointing a receiver, but, as the receiver was appointed at the instance of the attachment creditors to preserve the property and avoid certain expenses in connection with its preservation, and as [506] the appellants had no rights as judgment creditors, we shall not interfere with the order made. The attachment law authorizes the appointment of a receiver in cases arising under it.

The plaintiff and intervenors also appealed from the decision of the court which directed the receiver to hold the property for the benefit of all the creditors of Levy, as though the action of Levy in confessing the judgments to Latz and Dibble had amounted to a general assignment for the benefit of creditors. Had Levy's confession of these judgments been followed by a voluntary assignment, it might have been open to us to sustain this decision, but, in this state, the mere act of the debtor in preferring one creditor over another has not been recognized as amounting to a general assignment: *Furth v. Snell*, 6 Wash. 542.

We think the position taken by respondents on their appeal is a correct one. They brought the suit, procured an attachment, endured the burdens of the action, and are entitled to its fruits. The suit was brought by the plaintiff for itself and such other creditors of Samuel Levy as might intervene. What they ask here is that the first lien be awarded to plaintiff, the Puget Sound National Bank, the second to the intervenor, Cohen, Davis & Co., and the third to the intervenors, Bawo & Dotter. The appellant objects that at least the plaintiff and intervenors should share in the proceeds equally; but, inasmuch as they ask for a different adjustment, we do not deem it proper to interfere, even did propriety require a different arrangement. At the prayer of the plaintiff and intervenors the cause on its merits will be affirmed, but it will be remanded to the superior court for an entry of a new decree requiring the receiver to sell the property, or sufficient thereof to satisfy the judgments of the plaintiffs and intervenors, in the order specified, with their costs of this cause, and to return any unsold portion of the property to the sheriff for sale under the executions of Latz and Dibble; or, should all the property be sold by the receiver, and there be an excess over the judgments of the [507] plaintiff and intervenors, then such excess will be paid to the sheriff for a like purpose.

DUNBAR, C. J., and HOYT, J., concur.

JUDGMENT BY CONFESSION—NECESSITY FOR STATEMENT OF INDEBTEDNESS.
Under a statute requiring a statement of the facts out of which an indebtedness arose there is no authority in an action upon a note to enter a
confession of judgment, where the note is merely described, but such statement is not made.   As to third persons such a judgment is void: *Woods* v.
Bryan, 41 S. C. 74; 44 Am. St. Rep. 688, and note.   See the extended
notes to *Lee* v. *Figg,* 99 Am. Dec. 275, and *Chappel* v. *Chappel,* 64 Am. Dec.
501.

JUDGMENT BY CONFESSION—WHEN VOID—PREFERENCES.—A judgment
confessed by an insolvent debtor in favor of a creditor without his knowledge, and entered at the instance of the debtor alone, and upon which execution is levied on the latter's property to enable such creditor to obtain
priority over other creditors, is null and void as to subsequent attaching
creditors: *Wilcoxson* v. *Burton,* 27 Cal. 228; 87 Am. Dec. 66, and note.

CONOVER *v.* HULL.

[10 WASHINGTON, 678.]

CORPORATION.—THE ASSETS OF A CORPORATION ARE A TRUST FUND in the
hands of its managers for the benefit of its creditors.

CORPORATION, PREFERENCE BY. — AN INSOLVENT CORPORATION HAS NO
RIGHT to make a preference as between its creditors.

CORPORATIONS, PREFERENCE BY, WHEN COLLUSIVE.—If the business of a
corporation is known to its officers to be a losing one, and debts are
pressing which it is unable to pay, and actions are instituted by near
relatives of its managers through the procurement of one of them, and
the process served is practically kept secret until judgment is entered,
such judgment must be regarded as a collusive preference, and, as
such, denied effect.

CORPORATIONS—COLLUSIVE PREFERENCE. — If an insolvent corporation
notifies one of its creditors of its real condition and that an action is
pending against it by another creditor, as a result of which a suit is
brought and kept secret until the entry of judgment, this is sufficient
to prove an intent of the corporation to make to the creditor thus
receiving information a collusive preference.

INSOLVENCY.—THE INTENT TO GIVE A PREFERENCE MAY BE INFERRED
when such preference is the natural and probable result of the acts
done.

Arthur, Lindsay & King, and Strudwick & Peters, for the
appellants.

Struve, Allen, Hughes & McMicken and White & Munday,
for the respondent.

673 DUNBAR, C. J.   The Bennett-Hull Furniture Company
is a corporation organized under the laws of the state of **674**
Washington, and for the last five years has been engaged in
the furniture business in the city of Seattle.   Since its organ-

ization H. J. Hull has been its president, and H. F. Bennett
its secretary and treasurer, and Alonzo Hull, vice-president,
who was at the time of the commencement of this action
one of its trustees. On March 13, 1894, Stephen P. Hull
commenced an action on a note held by him, by serving summons and complaint on Bennett, as secretary and treasurer
of the company, the service being made on the evening of
March 13, 1894. The next morning Mr. Bennett notified the
Boston National Bank, one of the appellants here, of the
service of the papers in the Hull suit, and, on the same day,
March 14, 1894, the bank commenced its action by a similar
service. No appearance was made by the company in either
of these actions.

On April 3, 1894, the company was in default in the Stephen P. Hull suit, but, by agreement between his attorneys
and the attorneys of the bank, judgment was not entered
until the next day, April 4th, when the company became in
default in the bank suit, and the complaints in both cases
were placed on file, judgment entered, and execution immediately issued and placed in the hands of the sheriff, and at
once levied. By further agreement between the attorneys
for Stephen P. Hull and the bank the levy of the Hull execution was returned as a prior levy. Said levy was upon the
entire stock and fixtures of the company, which constituted
the entire available assets of the company, practically all
the book accounts and bills receivable of any value having
been previously assigned to the bank. On April 5, 1894,
application was made by one of the creditors of the company for the appointment of a receiver. On April 6, 1894,
before said application was heard, Walter & Co., a creditor
of the furniture company, demanded payment of its claim,
represented by promissory notes some of which were not yet
due, and to enable suit to be brought the furniture company
took up said notes, and gave a demand note instead, next
upon which suit was begun at once; and, on the day, the
furniture company filed its answer in said [675] suit, confessing judgment, and judgment was entered and execution
issued and levied immediately.

On April 13, 1894, the application for a receiver was heard
and granted, and the receiver at once commenced these
actions to enjoin the appellants and defendants from further
proceeding on such judgment and execution. He secured
the decree that they had no right to the prior payment out

of the property levied upon, to the end that the assets of the
insolvent company might be equitably distributed by the
receiver among all the creditors of said company. Decree
was rendered in favor of the receiver in each case, from which
this appeal is prosecuted.

Before adverting to the facts in this case we will notice
the law propositions involved. The discussion, especially the
oral argument, assumed a wide range, and counsel for appellants, with great earnestness, vigor, and ability, assault what
is frequently termed the "trust fund theory," viz., the doctrine enunciated by many of the courts that the property of
a corporation is a trust in the hands of the managers of the
corporation for the benefit of its creditors, insisting that the
theory is an illogical and unjust one, and that there should
be no distinction made in this respect between the property
of a corporation and the property of an individual. The
respondent insists that this court has allied itself with the
advocates of the trust fund theory by its decision and
announcements in the case of *Thompson* v. *Huron Lumber
Co.*, 4 Wash. 600. We will not, in this connection, discuss
the question whether the facts in that case were similar to
those in the one at bar. We however held, on the legal
proposition, that a voluntary preference by an insolvent corporation was void; and that principle is the essentially distinguishing feature between the responsibilities and rights of
a corporation and a private individual.

A further investigation of the subject and of the authorities
contents us with the rule announced in that case; and we are
satisfied that it can be amply sustained, not only by authority, but by the clearest principles of right reasoning. To
begin with, our statute law recognizes a distinction between
676 the remedies of creditors as applied to their dealings with
corporations, by providing for the appointment of receivers to
take charge of the property of corporations under certain circumstances and conditions; and, of course, after the receiver
is appointed, the property is in the custody of the court, and
the funds will be equitably distributed among the creditors,
while the liberty of a private individual is in this respect in
nowise circumscribed or controlled by law, so far as statutory enactments are concerned, and his creditors are left to
run a race of energy to obtain a vantage ground.

The law having made this wise and equitable provision,
it is the duty of courts of equity to see that the provision is

carried out to some practical effect; and the reason for this distinction is manifestly a just one.   The creditor of an individual debtor has more and better opportunities to keep himself advised concerning his debtor's business and financial standing; there are no limitations on the debtor's financial responsibilities.   It matters not how little he may embark in the enterprise, he is individually responsible for the debts which he incurs, no matter how great the amount, and the creditor can safely disregard the particular business in which he is engaged and rely on his individual estate, which he may know to be ample, and which, with the exception of a small exemption, must respond to his debts.   All this outside of the fact that an individual is liable to recuperate his fortunes in the future, after he has failed, and that there is hope of his paying his debts as long as he lives.   But not so with a corporation.   It is an artificial creature of the law.   It is favored with certain limitations, and its responsibilities are only such as are made by statute.   No matter what enormous debts it may incur the stockholders are only individually responsible to their creditors for the amount of the capital stock which they own, and when the indebtedness incurred exceeds the amount for which the stockholders are responsible, then the unfortunate condition exists of a debt for which no one is responsible.   If the venture of a corporation proves a successful one the stockholders [677] receive the benefit; if it prove unsuccessful their liabilities, as we have before said, are limited.   Hence, it behooves the law to throw some additional safeguards in the interest of creditors around a business thus conducted, for, when the corporation fails and goes out of existence, all chance for compensation to the creditor is forever gone.   When the corporation is dissolved, as it will be dissolved when it no longer is a profitable enterprise, the creditor finds himself struggling with a myth or a nonentity, and is therefore absolutely helpless.   There is no sentiment, either, in cases of dissolved corporations, which prompts the stockholders in after years to pay off the debts which they incur in the prosecution of the business of the corporation as there is in the case of individuals; and altogether it seems to us that no violence is done in making this sharp distinction between the debts of an individual and of a defaulting corporation.

But, whatever may be said concerning the reason of this distinction, it has become so permanently ingrafted in the law that it cannot now be disregarded. It was decided in *Bartlett* v. *Drew*, 57 N. Y. 587, that the assets of a corporation are a trust fund for the payment of its debts, and its creditors have a lien thereon and the right to priority of payment over its stockholders; that, where the property of a corporation had been divided among its stockholders before all its debts had been paid, the judgment creditor, after the return of an execution unsatisfied, could maintain an action in the nature of a creditor's bill against the stockholder to reach whatever was so paid; and that it was immaterial whether the stockholder got it by a fair agreement with his associates or by a wrongful act.

In *Hastings* v. *Drew*, 76 N. Y. 9, the court said: "The proposition is well settled, that the stock and property of every corporation is to be regarded as a trust fund for the payment of its debts."

The appellants cite section 864 of 2 Morawetz on Corporations, opposing this doctrine. That section seems to lay down the general proposition that a creditor of an insolvent corporation is entitled to pursue the ordinary legal and equitable 678 remedies for the enforcement of his claims, unless he is restrained from doing so at the suit of the corporation or other creditors; that he could not be prevented, except by instituting proceedings for the purpose of securing a general distribution of the assets; that an execution may undoubtedly be levied upon the property of a corporation, although it may be insolvent at the time, unless a receiver or assignee in bankruptcy of the company's property has been appointed, or a restraining order has been issued in a proceeding to wind up the company. So far the text does not seem to affect the principle which we are discussing; but the latter part of this section provides, or rather states the rule, that the appointment of a receiver or assignee in bankruptcy, after an execution has been levied upon the property of a corporation, would clearly not affect the right of an execution creditor to be paid out of the property levied upon; and that, outside of the statutes affecting the law in such cases, the general rule is that, after the lien of an attachment has vested upon property of a corporation, it will not be divested by subsequent proceedings for winding up the company, unless the contrary be expressly provided.

This proposition seems to be based upon one case, viz., *In re Glen Iron Works*, 20 Fed. Rep. 674, where it was held that the lien of judgment creditors of an insolvent corporation, who had levied writs of attachment execution under the laws of Pennsylvania, was not affected by the subsequent appointment of an assignee in bankruptcy of the corporation. We are not aware what the statute of Pennsylvania was under which this ruling was made, but the announcement here does not seem to reflect the sentiment of the author, Morawetz, on this interesting subject, for, after stating the law as announced in *Ringo* v. *Biscoe*, 13 Ark. 563, which is that, in the absence of a statutory prohibition, a corporation has the same power to make a preference amongst its creditors as an individual, the author, in section 803, in the following vigorous language, proceeds to give his views:

"This doctrine, in the opinion of the writer, is wholly ⁶⁷⁰ indefensible on principle. The capital provided for the security of the creditors of a corporation is a fund held for the benefit of all the creditors equally. That the unsecured creditors of a corporation are entitled to an equal distribution of the common security has often been recognized by the courts of equity in adjusting the rights of creditors among themselves and in relation to the company's shareholders. After a corporation has become insolvent, and has ceased to carry on business, the rights of its creditors become fixed. If a corporation, whose assets are not sufficient to satisfy all of its creditors in full, can prefer certain creditors, leaving others unpaid, this must be by virtue of a power reserved by implication to the company and its agents. But this power cannot justly be included in the general powers of management which a corporation must necessarily possess over its property in order to carry on its business and further the purposes for which the company was formed. The purposes of a corporation are not furthered in any manner by giving it or its agents the power, after the company has become insolvent and has ceased to carry on business, and after his shareholders have lost their interests in the corporate estate, to prefer a portion of the creditors, according to interest or mere whim, and to pay their claims in full, leaving the others wholly without redress."

And, indeed, this doctrine does seem to be so entirely without reason as to be properly characterized as monstrous. When we come to think that this preferred distribution is made by the managers, who represent the stockholders who are in no way responsible for the debt, or at least that por-

tion of it which is in excess of their liabilities, why should
they, thus disinterested, be allowed to confer these benefits
upon favorites to the exclusion of the rights of other honest
creditors who have helped to furnish the means which constituted the very fund which is now being distributed to the
exclusion of their interests?   Certainly, it is but a just provision of law which holds that this fund, under such a condition, must be held intact as a trust fund for the equal
benefit of all the creditors.   The author above referred to,
after asserting that the doctrine that the corporation may
prefer certain creditors at the expense of others was first
announced in *Catlin* v. *Eagle Bank*, 6 Conn. 233, proceeds to
680 say that it is a doctrine which is at variance with the
whole theory of the law concerning the rights of creditors of
insolvent corporations, and that it is contrary to the plainest
principles of justice: Citing *Robins* v. *Embry*, 1 Smedes & M.
Ch. 207; *Richards* v. *New Hampshire Ins. Co.*, 43 N. H. 263;
Hightower v. *Mustain*, 8 Ga. 506; *Marr* v. *Bank of West Tennessee*, 4 Cold. 471.

One of the earliest American cases sustaining the trust fund
doctrine was *Wood* v. *Dummer*, 3 Mason, 308.   The opinion
was written by Judge Story, and, among other things, the
learned judge says: "It appears to me very clear, upon general principles as well as the legislative intention, that the
capital stock of banks is to be deemed a pledge or trust fund
for the payment of the debts contracted by the bank. . . . .
Credit is universally given to this fund by the public, as the
only means of repayment.   During the existence of the corporation it is the sole property of the corporation, and can be
applied only according to its charter, that is, as a fund for
payment of its debts upon the security of which it may discount and circulate notes.   Why, otherwise, is any capital
stock required by our charters?   If the stock may, the next
day after it is paid in, be withdrawn by the stockholders,
without payment of the debts of the corporation, why is its
amount so studiously provided for, and its payment by the
stockholders so diligently required?   To me this point appears
so plain upon principles of law, as well as common sense, that
I cannot be brought into any doubt that the charters of our
banks make the capital stock a trust fund for the payment
of all the debts of the corporation. . . . . On a dissolution of
the corporation the billholders and the stockholders have
each equitable claims, but those of the billholders possess, as

I conceive, a prior exclusive equity": Citing *Vose* v. *Grant,* 15 Mass. 505; *Spear* v. *Grant,* 16 Mass. 9; and some English cases, viz., *Taylor* v. *Plumer,* 3 Maule & S. 562, and *Hill* v. *Simpson,* 7 Ves. 152.

In Taylor on Private Corporations, section 655, the author says: "There seems to be no longer the slightest question as to the firm establishment of this doctrine"; citing *Sanger* v. *Upton,* 91 U. S. 56, where the court says: "The capital [681] stock of an incorporated company is a fund set apart for the payment of its debts. It is a substitute for the personal liability which subsists in private copartnerships. When debts are incurred, a contract arises with the creditors that it shall not be withdrawn or applied, otherwise than upon their demands, until such demands are satisfied. The creditors have a lien upon it in equity."

It would seem to us that if this statement be true, that the creditors have a lien upon the property which comprises this fund, such lien would be absolutely worthless, if the stockholders, through their managers, were allowed to disburse the property through the medium of preferred creditors. Mr. Pomeroy, in his work on Equity Jurisprudence, volume 2, section 1046, in discussing the question of trust funds, says courts regard property of private corporations, especially after their dissolution, as a trust fund in favor of creditors, citing *Wood* v. *Dummer,* 3 Mason, 308, and many other cases.

"These statements," says the author, "may be sufficiently accurate as strong modes of expressing the doctrine that such property is a fund sacredly set apart for the payment of partnership and corporation creditors, before it can be appropriated to the use of the individual partners or corporators, and that the creditors have a lien upon it for their own security; but it is plain that no constructive trust can arise in favor of the creditors unless the partners or directors, through fraud or a breach of fiduciary duty, wrongfully appropriate the property and acquire the legal title to it in their own names, and thus place it beyond the reach of creditors through ordinary legal means."

We cite this statement of Pomeroy for the reason that it is noticed and commented upon as opposing the trust fund doctrine by the supreme court of the United States in *Hollins* v. *Brierfield Coal & Iron Co.,* 150 U. S. 371; but while the learned author, Pomeroy, in dealing exclusively with names, says that the expression of trust in such cases is mostly

metaphorical and that there is certainly nothing in the relation resembling a constructive trust, he has announced the
doctrine that the creditors have a lien upon the funds for the
payment of their debts, and so long as that [682] fact exists
the substance of the trust fund theory is maintained, no matter by what name it may be called, whether it be a trust
fund, a constructive trust, or what not.

Judge Story, in 2 Story's Equity Jurisprudence, section
1252, discussing this question, says: "Perhaps to this same
head of implied trusts upon presumed intention (although it
might equally well be deemed to fall under the head of constructive trusts by operation of law) we may refer that class
of cases where the stock and other property of private corporations is deemed a trust fund for the payment of the debts
of the corporation; so that the creditors have a lien or right
of priority of payment on it, in preference to any of the
stockholders in the corporation. Therefore, if a corporation
is dissolved, the contracts of such corporations are not thereby
deemed extinguished, but they survive the dissolution of the
corporation. . . . . This, however, is a remedy which can be
obtained in equity only, for a court of common law is incapable of administering any just relief, since it has no power of
bringing all the proper parties before the court, or of ascertaining the full amount of the debts, the mode of contribution, the number of the contributors, or the cross-equities
and liabilities which may be absolutely required for a proper
adjustment of the rights of all parties as well as of the creditors."

If the theory of the appellants were true, that the trustees
of the corporation could prefer its creditors, and, if they can
prefer them at all, they can prefer them to the extent of all
the funds of the corporation, the court of equity before whom
the case was brought for adjustment would sit helpless and
with empty hands; for it would be but a mockery of justice
to bring the affairs of an insolvent corporation to a court for
adjustment and distribution when all the substance of the
corporation had been transferred to the pocket or till of the
favored creditor. The supreme court of the United States, in
Curran v. *Arkansas*, 15 How. 304, in arguing this proposition
and discussing the rights of the bank, says: "That the charter, followed by the deposit of the capital stock, amounted to
an assurance, held out to the public by the state, that any
one who should trust the bank might rely on that capital for

payment, we cannot doubt. And [683] when a third person acted on this assurance, and parted with his property on the faith of it, the transaction had all the elements of a binding contract, and the state could not withdraw the fund, or any part of it, without impairing its obligation."

And so it is with the corporations in this state. Parties who deal with these corporations under the law rely exclusively upon the funds of the corporation, recognizing the fact that they have no redress upon the private means of the stockholders; and every principle of fair dealing demands, under such circumstances, that the fund upon which they rely and to which they extend their credit should be held as a sacred trust, and equitably and justly distributed by the court for their benefit.

The same doctrine was announced in *Sanger* v. *Upton*, 91 U. S. 56. In Perry on Trusts, section 242, the author says: "Analogous to the gift or sale of the trust property by trustees is the right of dealing with its property by a corporation. A corporation holds its property in trust: 1. To pay its creditors; and 2. To distribute to its stockholders *pro rata*."

In Wait on Insolvent Corporations, section 162, is found the following tersely expressed opinion: "The rule that the property of a corporation is a trust fund, to be applied for the equal benefit of all its creditors, is, as we have seen, constantly struggling for recognition in the cases. The funds of a corporation may be regarded as pledged exclusively for the payment of the debts of the corporation. The private property of the stockholders is not liable, nor is there at common law any individual responsibility on the part of the directors for corporate obligations. The corporate property is, then, the sole source to which the creditors must resort. The assets, as we have seen, might properly be considered as a special fund or property, set apart in law, in lieu of the private property of the corporators, to which resort may be had for the payment of the debts of the corporation. The directors and managers of an insolvent corporation are regarded as trustees of the corporate funds, and for that reason should make a *pro rata* distribution among the various creditors, and hence it has been held that the trustees will not be permitted to prefer debts for which they are themselves personally liable. The struggle, [684] both in the statutes and in the cases, has been to suppress preferences, which are justly regarded as a crying evil with which our insolvency and bankruptcy laws seem inadequate to cope. A court of equity, it may be observed, will interfere and appoint a receiver of a bank when the officers have been making preferential payments. While the existence of the right of a failing debtor to prefer one creditor to another in the distribution of his property has often been regretted, it is recognized both in courts of law and of equity. Cases may be cited upholding the right of a corporation, unrestricted by statute, to make a preferential assignment. The rule is quite firmly established. The practical working of the rule sustaining corporate preferences is monstrous. The unpreferred creditors have only a myth or a shadow left to which resort can be had for payment of their claims; a soulless, fictitious, unsubstantial entity that can be neither seen nor found. The capital and assets of the corporation, the creditors' trust fund, may, under this rule, be carved out and apportioned among a chosen few, usually the family connections or immediate friends of the officers making the preference. This rule of law is entitled to take precedence, among the many reckless absurdities to be met with in the cases affecting corporations, as being a manifest travesty upon natural justice."

This language, though seemingly turgid and vehement, is, notwithstanding, we think, justified by the injustice which is frequently effected by sustaining the rule criticised.

In *Rouse* v. *Merchants' Nat. Bank*, 46 Ohio St. 493, 15 Am. St. Rep. 644, it was held that a corporation, after it had become insolvent and ceased to prosecute the objects for which it was created, could not, by giving some of its creditors mortgages on the corporate property to secure antecedent debts, without other consideration, create valid preferences in their behalf over the other creditors, or over the general assignment thereafter made for the benefit of creditors. This case, it seems to us, is on a level with the case under consideration. It is true that the corporation in that instance was insolvent, but, as we shall hereafter see, the corporation in the case at bar, as we view it, was practically insolvent also. In the case above referred to the court said:

685 "It is obvious that the corporate property cannot, with propriety, be said to be owned by the corporation, in the sense of ownership as applied to property belonging to natural persons. The latter may without restriction acquire and dispose of property for any lawful purpose, while both the power of acquisition and disposition of the former are limited to spe-

cial objects already mentioned. The corporate property is in
reality a fund set apart to be used only in the attainment of
the objects for which the corporation was created, and it cannot lawfully be diverted to any other purpose. As soon as
acquired it becomes impressed with the character of a trust
fund for that purpose, and the shareholder or creditor may
interpose to prevent its diversion from the objects of the
incorporation, injurious to him."

To the same effect are a very large majority of the cases
that have been adjudicated on this subject. It must be admitted that there are courts which have held the contrary
doctrine, and the cases of *Hollins* v. *Brierfield etc. Co.*, 150
U. S. 371, and *Varnum* v. *Hart*, 119 N. Y. 101, are notable
instances; but, with the most profound respect for the United
States supreme court, we are unable to indorse the logic of
their decision in the case last mentioned, and think that the
result of such logic would be to destroy the efficacy of statutory law which is made distinguishing the collection of debts
from private individuals from the collection of debts from
insolvent corporations. It is insisted by the court in *Hollins*
v. *Brierfield etc. Co.*, 150 U. S. 371, that the doctrine of trust
funds is not to be disregarded, but that it only attaches
after the corporation has actually become insolvent, and
the property of the corporation has passed into the hands of
the court through its agent, the receiver. This, as we have
said before, it seems to us would practically destroy the doctrine altogether, and render the appointment of a receiver
for the purpose of justly distributing the estate of the insolvent corporation a useless task. And it is opposed to the rule
announced by this court in *Thompson* v. *Huron Lumber Co.*,
4 Wash. 600, that "when a corporation has reached a point
where its debts are equal to or greater than its property, and
it cannot pay in the ordinary course, and its business is **686**
no longer profitable, it ought to be wound up and its assets
distributed."

Discussing the case, then, upon the theory that an insolvent corporation has no right to prefer creditors, two questions
are presented: 1. Was this corporation insolvent at the times
these judgments were obtained? and 2. Was there collusion
between the corporation and the judgment creditors? On the
first proposition, we think the corporation was practically
insolvent at the times these actions were commenced. It is
true that, according to the showing made to the bank of the

company's business, the assets exceeded the liabilities; but the book accounts and bills receivable were computed at their face value, and every business man knows that such a computation falls far short of representing the actual assets of a mercantile establishment; and the result in this instance abundantly proves the unreliability of the showing made. Hence the anxiety to maintain these preferences.

We are also of the opinion that the testimony, construed by the light of all the circumstances, shows a collusion between the corporation and the judgment creditors. According to all the testimony the business had been a losing one for several months; debts were pressing, which the company was unable to pay; and it is noteworthy that the first action which was instituted was instituted by Stephen P. Hull, the father of H. J. Hull, who was the president of the corporation; and that the plaintiff in the action was the brother of Alonzo Hull, who was a trustee and vice-president of the corporation, and who was really the moving factor in the suit, he having brought the suit as agent for his brother. Most confidential relations may be presumed to have existed between the plaintiff and defendant, and, under ordinary circumstances, a father would be the last person to take the initiative in instituting legal proceedings against the interests of the son, especially when, under the circumstances, such proceedings would surely inaugurate a series of suits which could but result in financial ruin.

This case strikingly presents the pernicious doctrine contended [687] for that a corporation, under the circumstance, has a right to prefer its creditors. The vice-president and trustee of the company, who is presumed to know all about its condition, brings the action at a critical juncture for his brother, and serves the summons on the president of the company, who is the son of the claimant and nephew of the agent. No complaint was filed and the service was practically a secret one, and the claim could go to judgment and a preference lien be established before other creditors were aware that the fund was in danger; the practical result would be the same as if the corporation had confessed judgment in favor of the claimant.

While there is no law, either civil or moral, which will deprive a citizen of his legal remedies against a corporation which is owned and controlled by his relatives, yet the circumstances of this case convince us that the managers of the corporation were satisfied that they could not weather the financial storm which had overtaken them, 'and they proposed to make their relatives good at the expense of the other creditors. The next morning after the service of the Hull summons the secretary of the company' notified the appellant bank of the commencement of the Hull suit, and immediately the bank commenced suit by serving summons in the same manner in which it had been served in the Hull suit. No notification was given to any other creditors, although some of them were engaged in business in the same block in which the business of the defaulting corporation was carried on.

It is insisted upon by the appellants that, as long as a corporation does no affirmative act to assist the creditors to obtain their judgment, no inference of collusion can be drawn, and that the obligation does not attach to make a helpless or dilatory fight on a suit to which there is no defense. Certainly we think it was not the duty, or even the right, of this corporation to expend its funds in unavailing litigation; but the company did some affirmative act, in the case of the bank at least. It discriminated in favor of the bank in the knowledge it imparted of its real condition. It affirmatively [688] notified it of that condition, which resulted in the bank commencing proceedings to secure its indebtedness. And, if the theory of the appellants should be sustained, no matter what the intention was, the practical result would be that, by reason of this affirmative action of the company, the bank would recover its whole claim, to the exclusion of the rights of the other creditors.

Of course there is no absolute or definite proof here that there was an attempt to prefer. The company did not say to Hull and the bank, "We want to prefer you," and they probably did not say in so many words that they wanted to be preferred; but the bank at least was furnished by the company with data sufficient to inspire desire in it to be preferred, and its prompt and vigorous action in response to that information speaks with more emphasis than any mere form of words.

In *Giddings* v. *Dodd*, 1 Dill. 116, it was held that creditors who receive an illegal preference are liable to the assignee of the bankrupt, and that the intent of the debtor to give, and of the creditor to secure, an unauthorized preference may be

shown by circumstances. Of course this must be true, for
such intentions could never be proven.

In *Buchanan* v. *Smith*, 16 Wall. 277, it was held that a
creditor has reasonable cause to believe his debtor insolvent
when such state of facts is brought to his notice respecting
the affairs and pecuniary condition of his debtor as would
lead a prudent business man to the conclusion that he, the
debtor, is unable to meet his obligations as they mature in
the ordinary course of business. It is insisted by the appellants that the doctrine announced in this case was overturned
in *Wilson* v. *City Bank*, 17 Wall. 473. There were some announcements made in *Buchanan* v. *Smith*, 16 Wall. 277,
which seem to have been overruled in *Wilson* v. *City Bank*,
17 Wall. 473, although the court undertook to distinguish
that case from the case of *Buchanan* v. *Smith*, 16 Wall. 277.
The principal correction, however, made by the court to the
principles stated in the former case was as to the necessity
of any affirmative action on the part of the bankrupt to prevent the judgment and [689] levy, it having been announced
in *Buchanan* v. *Smith*, 16 Wall. 277, that a debtor who suffers
his property to be seized on execution, when knowing himself
to be insolvent, should apply for the benefit of the bankrupt
act; and the court in *Wilson* v. *City Bank*, 17 Wall. 473,
decides that there is no legal obligation on the debtor to file
a petition to prevent the judgment and levy, and that a failure to do so is not sufficient evidence of an intention to give
a preference to the judgment creditor and to defeat the operation of the bankrupt law. But the court in the latter case
says that: "Very slight circumstances, however, which tend
to show the existence of an affirmative desire on the part of
the bankrupt to give a preference or to defeat the operation
of the act, may, by giving color to the whole transaction,
render the lien void"; and that these special circumstances
must be left to decide each case as it arises.

In *Little* v. *Alexander*, 21 Wall. 500, it was held that when
the issue to be decided is whether a judgment against an
insolvent was obtained with a view to give a preference, the
intention of the bankrupt is the turning point of the case,
and all the circumstances which go to show such intent
should be considered. In that case the insolvent debtor
gave his son and niece notes for an old debt so as to enable
them to procure judgments before his other creditors; and it

was held that the preference growing out of the transaction was void.

In *Denny* v. *Dana*, 2 Cush. 160, 48 Am. Dec. 655, it was held that a preference will be avoided, if made by one who is insolvent with intent to give a preference to a creditor who had a reasonable belief that the debtor was insolvent or in contemplation of insolvency; and that the intent to give a preference would be inferred where such preference was the natural and probable result of the acts done.

As we have before said, the preference established by the bank in this case, if the result of the litigation is to establish a preference, which is what the bank maintains here, was the direct result of the act of the corporation in informing it of the commencement of the suit by Hull. It also [690] appears that when the company was in default in the Hull suit an agreement was made between the attorneys of Hull and the attorneys of the bank that judgment should not be entered in the Hull suit until the next day, when the company would become in default in the bank suit; and the complaints in both cases were placed on file, judgments entered, and executions immediately issued and placed in the hands of the sheriff and at once levied.

An affidavit setting up this state of facts was objected to and excluded by ruling of the court. We think that this testimony should not properly have been excluded; that it was one of the circumstances tending to show a collusion and a suppression of knowledge, so far as the public was concerned, until the judgment of the bank could be obtained.

All the circumstances surrounding this litigation convince us that the insolvent condition of this company was known to the appellants; that there was a desire on the part of the company to prefer these appellant creditors, and that the condition of the company was made known to them for the express purpose of warning them that they should not delay in the commencement of their actions; and that the result of this knowledge and action on the part of the company and of these appellants was to obtain liens upon the property of this corporation in fraud of the rights of other creditors.

The judgment will, therefore, be affirmed.

HOYT and STILES, JJ., concur.

Preferences by Insolvent Corporations.

That it is ordinarily inequitable for a corporation in failing circumstances to, in effect, turn over all or the greater portion of its assets to a few of its creditors, leaving others holding claims equally just without any means of redress, except such as may be sought by an action against its stockholders, cannot be doubted; nor is there room for denying that the power, when it is affirmed, is commonly employed to further the interests of the directors or other managers of the corporation or that of their relatives or special friends. These objections equally exist against the sustaining of preferences made by debtors who are natural persons, and have resulted in statutes, in many of the states, withdrawing the power to make such preferences. Independently of such statutes, the power has rarely, if ever, been denied in the case of natural persons, and, as a corporation is but an artificial person, endowed, with respect to the business it is authorized to transact and the property it is allowed by law to acquire and manage, with the attributes of a natural person, there is no reason why the one as well as the other may not pay one creditor, leaving another without payment and without means of compelling it, or may not make a general assignment for the benefit of creditors, and declare therein which creditor or class of creditors shall first be entitled to participate in the proceeds. The policy of denying debtors the power to make preferences has been in some instances extended by statute to certain corporations when insolvent or in contemplation of insolvency: *Robinson* v. *Bank of Attica*, 21 N. Y. 406; *Atkinson* v. *Rochester Printing Co.*, 114 N. Y. 168; *Brouwer* v. *Harbeck*, 9 N. Y. 594. Even under these statutes it has been adjudged that an insolvent corporation was not under any obligation to do any act for the purpose of preventing a creditor from obtaining a preference by his action, and that corporations, like insolvent persons, might "permit the creditor to take hostile proceedings and allow those to obtain preferences who are the most vigilant": *Varnum* v. *Hart*, 119 N. Y. 101. In the absence of statutes of this purport the courts of a few of the states have seized upon the general statement made by courts of high character to the effect that the assets of a corporation constitute a trust fund for the payment of its creditors, and have reasoned thence that it was not within the power of the directors or other managers of an insolvent corporation to make such a disposition of its assets as might leave some of its creditors without any right to participate therein: *Thompson* v. *Huron Lumber Co.*, 4 Wash. 600; *Ford* v. *Plankington Bank*, 87 Wis. 363; *Marr* v. *Bank of West Tennessee*, 4 Cold. 471; *Rouse* v. *Merchants' Nat. Bank*, 46 Ohio St. 493; 15 Am. St. Rep. 644; *Smith* v. *St. Louis etc. Ins. Co.*, 3 Tenn. Ch. 502; *Smith etc. Co.* v. *McGroarty*, 136 U. S. 237. These cases are in entire harmony with the principal case, though that cited from the supreme court of the United States does not express the views of that court upon the subject, but merely follows a decision of the supreme court of Ohio in determining the rights of the creditors of a corporation existing and doing business within that state.

The courts using the general language to which we have referred did not, so far as we are aware, ever declare that the assets of a corporation must be treated as a fund held for the *equal* benefit of all its creditors, and, even had a trust existed of the general character implied by that language, it might perhaps have been satisfied by the appropriation of the entire assets of the corporation to the payment of certain of its obligations, though others had been left entirely unsatisfied and unprovided for. It must, however, be admitted that any characterization of the assets of a corporation as a trust

fund existing for the benefit of its creditors, while it served to emphasize
the general principle that the stockholders were not entitled to withdraw
any part of such assets while obligations of the corporation remained unsatisfied, was in other respects unfortunate and misleading, because it
naturally led to decisions like that in the principal case.　Strictly speaking, a corporation does not hold its assets in trust for the benefit of its
creditors in any other sense than a natural person or a partnership holds
his or its assets in trust for the benefit of his or its creditors.　If a corporation, a partnership, or an individual undertakes to withdraw its or his
assets from the reach of creditors, the act will not be sustained, and creditors will be afforded every appropriate remedy, legal or equitable, to
thwart this dishonest purpose, but each of the creditors is at liberty, if he
can do so by superior diligence, to create a lien or receive payment to the
extent of his individual claim without making provision for his fellow-creditors, because there is not, strictly speaking, any trust existing in favor
either of him or of them.　In some of the cases already cited much reliance
was placed upon language employed in decisions of the supreme court of the
United States which it was believed fully committed that august tribunal
to what is known as "the trust fund theory," and to the extension of that
theory so far as to deny to insolvent corporations the right to make any
transfer, payment, or assignment which would in effect operate as a preference of some of its creditors and as an exclusion of others from participating in its estate.　In explaining its views upon this subject, and in
attempting to correct the misapplication of some of its previous decisions,
that court subsequently said:

"The case of *Fogg* v. *Blair*, 133 U. S. 534, 541, presented a similar question, and this court, by Mr. Justice Field, observed: 'We do not question
the general doctrine invoked by the appellant, that the property of a railroad company is a trust fund for the payment of its debts, but do not perceive any place for its application here.　That doctrine only means that
the property must first be appropriated to the payment of the debts of the
company before any portion can be distributed to the stockholders; it does
not mean that the property is so affected by the indebtedness of the company that it cannot be sold, transferred, or mortgaged to *bona fide* purchasers for a valuable consideration, except subject to the liability of being
appropriated to pay that indebtedness.　Such a doctrine has no existence.'
In the case of *Hawkins* v. *Glenn*, 131 U. S. 319, 332, which was an action
brought by the trustee of a corporation against certain of its stockholders
to recover unpaid subscriptions, and in which the defense of the statute of
limitations was pleaded, Chief Justice Fuller referred to this matter in these
words: 'Unpaid subscriptions are assets, but have frequently been treated
by courts of equity as if impressed with a trust *sub modo*, upon the view
that, the corporation being insolvent, the existence of creditors subjects
these liabilities to the rules applicable to funds to be accounted for as held
in trust, and that, therefore, statutes of limitation do not commence to run
in respect to them until the retention of the money has become adverse by
a refusal to pay upon due requisition.'　These cases negative the idea of
any direct trust or lien attaching to the property of a corporation in favor
of its creditors, and at the same time are entirely consistent with those
cases in which the assets of a corporation are spoken of as a trust fund,
using the term in the sense that we have said it was used.　The same idea
of equitable lien and trust exists to some extent in the case of partnership
property.　Whenever, a partnership becoming insolvent, a court of equity

takes possession of its property, it recognizes the fact that in equity the
partnership creditors have a right to payment out of those funds in preference to individual creditors, as well as superior to any claims of the partners themselves. And the partnership property is, therefore, sometimes
said, not inaptly, to be held in trust for the partnership creditors, or that
they have an equitable lien on such property. Yet, all that is meant by
such expressions is the existence of an equitable right which will be enforced
whenever a court of equity, at the instance of a proper party, and in a
proper proceeding, has taken possession of the assets. It is never understood that there is a specific lien or a direct trust. A party may deal with
a corporation with respect to its property in the same manner as with an
individual owner, and with no greater danger of being held to have received
into his possession property burdened with a trust or lien. The officers of
a corporation act in a fiduciary capacity in respect to its property in their
hands, and may be called to an account for fraud, or sometimes even mere
mismanagement, in respect thereto; but, as between itself and its creditors, the corporation is simply a debtor, and does not hold its property in
trust, or subject to a lien in their favor, in any other sense than does an
individual debtor. That is certainly the general rule, and, if there be any
exceptions thereto, they are not presented by any of the facts in this case.
Neither the insolvency of the corporation nor the execution of an illegal
trust deed, nor the failure to collect in full all stock subscriptions, nor, all
together, gave to these simple contract creditors any lien upon the property
of the corporation, nor charged any direct trust thereon": *Hollins v. Brierfield etc. Co.*, 150 U. S. 384.

These views are in accord with the decisions in the state courts other
than those already cited, and fully sustain the power of a corporation, however insolvent, to pay or secure one or more of its creditors to the exclusion
of others and to make any form of preference which might be sustained
were it a natural, instead of an artificial, person, with the exceptions hereinafter noted: *Worthen v. Griffith*, 59 Ark. 562; 43 Am. St. Rep. 50; *Allis v.
Jones*, 45 Fed. Rep. 148; Morawetz on Corporations, sec. 802; *Hollins v.
Brierfield etc. Co.*, 150 U. S. 371; *Smith v. Skeary*, 47 Conn. 47; *Ashhurst's
Appeal*, 60 Pa. St. 290; *Coats v. Donnell*, 94 N. Y. 168; *State v. Bank of
Maryland*, 6 Gill & J. 205; 26 Am. Dec. 561; *Sargent v. Webster*, 13 Met.
497; 46 Am. Dec. 743; *Brown v. Grand Rapids etc. Co.*, 58 Fed. Rep. 286;
Stratton v. Allen, 16 N. J. Eq. 229; *Catlin v. Eagle Bank*, 6 Conn. 233; *Ringo
v. Biscoe*, 13 Ark. 563; *Dana v. Bank of United States*, 5 Watts & S. 223;
Albany etc. Co. v. Southern Agr. Works, 76 Ga. 135; 2 Am. St. Rep. 26;
Warfield v. Marshall County Canning Co., 72 Iowa, 666; 2 Am. St. Rep. 263;
Garrett v. Burlington Plow Co., 70 Iowa, 697; 59 Am. Rep. 461; *Rollins v.
Shaver Wagon etc. Co.*, 80 Iowa, 380; 20 Am. St. Rep. 427; *Warner v.
Mower*, 11 Vt. 390; *Burr v. McDonald*, 3 Gratt. 215; *Ex parte Conway*, 4
Ark. 348; *United States v. Bank of United States*, 8 Rob. (La.) 262; *New
Haven Bank v. Bates*, 8 Conn. 505; *Gould v. Little Rock etc. R. R. Co.*, 52
Fed. Rep. 680; *Reichwald v. Commercial H. Co.*, 106 Ill. 439; *Warren v.
First Nat. Bank*, 149 Ill. 9; *Wilkinson v. Bauerle*, 41 N. J. Eq. 635; *Buell v.
Buckingham*, 16 Iowa, 284; 85 Am. Dec. 516; *Planters' Bank v. Whittle*, 78
Va. 737; *Town v. Bank of River Raisin*, 2 Doug. (Mich.) 530; *Ragland v.
McFall*, 137 Ill. 81; *Peterson v. Brabrook T. Co.*, 150 Ill. 290; *Breene v.
Merchants' Bank*, 11 Col. 97; *Foster v. Mullanphy etc. Co.*, 92 Mo. 79; *Bergen
v. Porpoise F. Co.*, 42 N. J. Eq. 397; *La Grange etc. Co. v. National Bank*,
122 Mo. 154; 43 Am. St. Rep. 558; *Schroeder v. Mason*, 25 Mo. App. 190;

Manhattan Brass Co. **v.** *Webster etc. Co.*, 37 Mo. App. 145; *Pyles* **v.** *Riverside F. Co.*, 30 W. Va. 123; *Pairpoint Mfg. Co.* **v.** *Philadelphia O. Co.*, 161 Pa. St. 17; *Sweeney* **v.** *Grape Sugar Co.*, 30 W. Va. 443; 8 Am. St. Rep. 88; *Albany etc. Co.* **v.** *Southern Agr. Works*, 76 Ga. 135; 2 Am. St. Rep. 26. In some of the states this doctrine has been modified, largely under the influence of special statutes, in cases where a corporation has already ceased to do business, or the assignment or preference in question is of such character and extent that its operation must be to compel such ceasing: *Lyons-Thomas Hardware Co.* **v.** *Perry Stove M. Co.*, 86 Tex. 143; *Larrabee* **v.** *Franklin Bank*, 114 Mo. 592; 35 Am. St. Rep. 774; *State* v. *Brockman*, 39 Mo. App. 131; *Currie* **v.** *Bowman*, 25 Or. 364; *Sabin* **v.** *Columbia Fuel Co.*, 25 Or. 15; 42 Am. St. Rep. 756. These decisions, as we understand them, do not apply to corporations rules not equally applicable to partnerships or natural persons in the same states, the policy of their laws being to deny to debtors the power to make preferences in view of insolvency.

The case last cited from the supreme court of Texas is entitled to special consideration. The opinion of the court was in response to questions certified to it by the court of civil appeals in a suit brought to set aside chattel mortgages executed by the Lyons-Thomas Hardware Company. The questions thus presented were: 1. "Whether or not a preferential deed of trust executed by a private trading corporation (chartered in July, 1884, under general law) after it has become insolvent, and consequently ceased to carry on its business, without any intention of resuming the enterprise, is void as against the unsecured creditors of such corporation; and 2. If a private corporation, under such circumstances, has the same power to prefer its creditors as an individual, whether such preferential deed is void in law because of the fact that the stockholders, directors, and other officers of the corporation, who executed it in the name of the corporation, are liable as sureties and indorsers on preferred claims." The answer of the court resulted in the denial of the right to make the preferences in question. The opinion relied, to a great extent, upon the statutes of the state, though the general argument made by the court leads us to the conviction that such denial would have resulted had there been no statute which, in the opinion of the court, bore directly upon the question and strengthened the argument against permitting preferences. It should, however, be remembered that in the case presented for decision, the claims in favor of which preferences had been attempted were claims upon which the directors and other officers of the corporation were liable as indorsers and sureties, and, while the opinion of the court apparently treated this circumstance as immaterial, and dealt with the general right to make preferences, yet, in so far as it purported to formulate rules applicable to preferences of a class not then in question, what was said was not necessary for the determination of the case, and the actual judgment of the court could be sustained under the authorities hereinafter cited with respect to the right to make preferences in favor of directors and other officers. The court, after referring to the contention of the counsel that a corporation, unless specially restricted by statute, had the same power to give preferences as a natural person, replied: "The broad proposition that a corporation created by the general laws of this state may do any act in reference to its property which a natural person may do with his is expressly negatived by the statute," and in support of this assertion the court cited article 589 of the Revised Statutes of the state providing that "no corporation created under the provisions of this title shall employ its stock, means, assets, or other property,

directly or indirectly, for any other purpose whatever than to accomplish
the object of its creation." "The purposes of its creation," said the court,
were those named in the charter of the corporation, and the essential difference between the powers of a corporation and those of a natural person is,
the latter may contract and do such acts as are not specially forbidden by
law, while the former, in the disposition of its property, is restricted by its
charter and the general statutes applicable to it.   The powers conferred by
the statute of the state were "to hold, purchase, sell, mortgage, and otherwise convey such real and personal estate as the purposes of the corporation
shall require; and also to take, hold, and convey such other property, real,
personal, or mixed, as shall be requisite for such corporation to acquire in
order to obtain and secure the payment of any indebtedness due or belonging to the corporation."   From the fact that the statute declared that the
powers thus enumerated should be exercised "as the purposes of the corporation shall require," and that those powers were such as were ordinarily
"necessary to be exercised while the business is in active operation with a
view to obtain the result contemplated when the corporation is created,"
the court reasoned that they were not entitled to be exercised when the corporation had become insolvent and consequently ceased to carry on its business.   That a corporation may, in effect, make a preference by selling or
mortgaging its property seems to have been conceded by the court, for it
said, at page 153, "The power of a trading corporation to sell or to mortgage property to raise means to pay its debts during its active life, or after
it has become insolvent and ceased business, is not controverted, but that
is not the immediate question under consideration; for the present inquiry
is, does the statute now under consideration, as claimed, expressly or by
necessary implication confer upon a corporation circumstanced as was the
hardware company power to make the conveyance in question?"   "The
conveyance in question was a preferential deed of trust executed by a corporation after it had become insolvent, and consequently ceased to carry on
its business, without any intention of resuming the enterprise."   The statute of the state further authorized every corporation "to enter into any
obligation or contract essential to the transaction of its authorized business."
The court said that the corporation whose act was in question was in such
circumstances when the preferential deed was executed that it had no business, and that "the mere act of paying or securing indebtedness can never
become a business."   The court, after referring to the laws of the state
regarding preferences in view of assignments for the benefit of creditors,
added: "Under the statutes in force in this state, if an insolvent corporation, in contemplation of an assignment under the statute, with intent to
give preference to one creditor, should convey to him property of the corporation, this would be invalid as to other creditors, and the property would
pass to an assignee under a subsequent assignment for the benefit of all creditors, unless the person so taking took under circumstances that would constitute him a *bona fide* purchaser, which could not well be if the corporation
was insolvent, and was known to have ceased business on that account; for
such knowledge, of itself, would seem sufficient to put the purchaser on
inquiry: Sayles' Civil Statutes, art. 651.   This statute further illustrates
the fact that the property of an insolvent corporation is deemed in this state
a trust fund, and emphasizes the right of all its creditors to equality in distribution of its assets, as against all other creditors who had not acquired
superior right prior to known insolvency.   In the application of principles
illustrated by this statute, ought the fact that the insolvent corporation

subsequently made no general assignment, and made, in effect, only mortgages conveying all of its property, as, from the papers certified by the court of civil appeals, appears to have been the case, to affect the rights of parties? The mortgages, if sustained, would give preferences as fully as would absolute conveyances, and all of the corporate property, if not more than sufficient to pay the preferred claims, would pass from the corporation as fully as it would by subsequent assignment. These statutes have been referred to, not because any of them, in terms, declare the law applicable to the questions propounded, but because they indicate the trend of legislation on some essential matters involved in the questions, and tend to support the proposition, through analogies, that the assets of an insolvent corporation, which has ceased to carry on business, and does not intend to resume, is a fund from which all creditors not secured by valid liens existing before the condition was fixed have the right to be paid on terms of perfect equality. If such a fund be a trust fund, then the assets of a corporation so circumstanced are trust funds, and those whose right and duty it is to administer such a fund are trustees. We have seen that such corporations as the hardware company, in England and in this state, have not the same powers in reference to property owned by them for corporate purposes as have natural persons, and that in this state there is no statute, expressly or by necessary implication, conferring on such corporations power to make preferential mortgages or like conveyances, when in the condition assumed in the questions propounded; and the question arises whether, under the general principles of law or equity applicable to such a condition, such a power exists. No English decision has been furnished in which the questions involved arose or were discussed; and it is probably true that the laws of that country in regard to insolvent corporations and persons have been such, for three centuries past, that no claim would be made in the courts of that country that such conveyances as the questions submitted refer to were valid against other creditors. We take it for granted that all English courts, under the laws of that country, would hold all such attempted preferences unauthorized and illegal, when made by an insolvent corporation circumstanced as was the hardware company, and therefore seek no further authority from that source. It would be a useless consumption of time to review the many American decisions bearing on the questions submitted, for it must be conceded that they are clearly in conflict, and that on each side of the question may be found many decisions made by courts eminent for learning and conservatism; but reference will be made to a sufficient number of each side of the question to show the grounds on which these conflicting decisions rest."

The court then cited and considered numerous decisions of the state and national courts and summarized the conclusions sustained by them as follows: "The line of decisions first referred to, in substance, holds that insolvent corporations, even though they have ceased to do business, have the same power to give preferences as have natural persons, on the theory that unless their charters forbid this, it is an implied power; but this seems indefensible under the rules applicable to the construction of charters such as may be granted to private corporations under the general laws in force in this state. The power is not expressly given, and it cannot be implied, for it is not necessary to the accomplishment of any purpose for which such corporations may be created. While such a corporation is carrying on its business it has power to buy on credit such property as to secure such services or funds as may be reasonably necessary for the transaction of its

legitimate business, and, to secure indebtedness thus incurred, may give
mortgages or other security, and thus give preferences, although in fact
insolvent. The exercise of such a power may often be, not only beneficial,
but necessary for the continuance or prosperity of the business; but no such
necessity can exist where the business has been abandoned. Self-interest,
while the business is honestly carried on, will ordinarily be sufficient to
prevent abuse of what is then a right; but where the business has ceased,
on account of insolvency, stockholders have no further beneficial interest
in the corporate assets, and they have no right or power, directly or through
the managing officers, through preferences, in effect, to pay or secure some
of the creditors at the expense of others, if the law be that the assets of an
insolvent corporation, that has ceased business, with no intent ever to
resume, are a fund held in trust for creditors, for in such a fund all creditors have equality of right, unless, prior to the condition which gives that,
one or more have acquired right to priority. The second class of cases
to which reference has been made seems conclusively to establish the proposition that the assets of a private corporation circumstanced as was
the hardware company at the time its directors attempted to give preferences are a trust fund held for the benefit of creditors—a fund which
they have the right to have converted into money, and that distributed
among them ratably." The final conclusion of the court was expressed as
follows: "In so far as the rights of creditors of insolvent corporations
are concerned there exists no good reason for making any distinction between unpaid subscriptions for stock and other corporate assets; for each
belong to the fund from which creditors are entitled to be paid. As we
have before seen, in so far as the rights of creditors are concerned, the consequences of technical dissolution occur when the corporation is in the condition set forth in the questions propounded, and in addition to the authorities cited on that point the following are now added: *Graham* v. *La Crosse
etc. Ry. Co.*, 102 U. S. 161; 26 L. ed. 111; *Wabash etc. Ry. Co.* v. *Ham*, 114
U. S. 587; *Corey* v. *Wadsworth*, 99 Ala. 68; 42 Am. St. Rep. 29. We feel
safe in declaring that when a corporation's assets are insufficient for the
payment of its debts, and it has ceased to do business, or has taken, or is
in the act of taking, a step which will practically incapacitate it for conducting the corporate enterprise with reasonable prospect of success, or its
embarrassments are such that an early suspension and failure must ensue,
then such corporation must be pronounced insolvent.' The case made by
the questions propounded bring it clearly within so much of the rule thus
stated as may be safely adopted, and it is not now necessary to inquire
whether other parts should be qualified. The condition of the corporation,
set forth in the questions propounded, under the long-recognized rules of
equity, conferred upon every unsecured creditor of the corporation the
right to a ratable share of the proceeds of all the assets of the corporation, not subject to priorities lawfully existing when this condition arose;
and we therefore answer that neither the stockholders nor the directors of
the insolvent corporation had lawful power, under the facts stated, to make
a preferential deed of trust, whereby any creditor, whether a stockholder,
director, or other officer of the corporation, or not, could acquire a preference, and that the attempted preference would be invalid as to other creditors of the corporation."

There can be no doubt that the doctrine that a corporation when insolvent
cannot prefer any of its creditors is gaining ground and finding support in the
decisions of some of the courts where, until recently, there was substantial

harmony, but it is not gaining ground as rapidly as its adherents are willing to believe. They rely on general expressions found in opinions considering preferences in favor of directors and other officers. Thus Judge Thompson, at section 6492 of his work on Corporations, cites, in support of his views, cases from Alabama, Illinois, Michigan, New York, Rhode Island, and West Virginia, which, on examination, will be found either to consider only preferences in favor of officers, or to apply special statutory provisions, and other decisions from four of those states affirm that, with respect to creditors, who are not also its officers, an insolvent corporation may prefer one creditor, or class of creditors, to the same extent as a natural person: *Warren* v. *First Nat. Bank*, 149 Ill. 291; *Glover* v. *Lee*, 140 Ill. 102; *Kendall* v. *Bishop*, 76 Mich. 634; *Town* v. *Bank of River Raisin*, 2 Doug. 530; *Coats* v. *McDonald*, 99 N. Y. 78; *Sweeney* v. *Great S. Co.*, 30 W. Va. 473; 8 Am. St. Rep. 88; *Pyles* v. *Furniture Co.*, 30 W. Va. 123.

Preferences of Stockholders.—The exceptions to the general rule arise in cases of preferences made to creditors who are officers or stockholders of the corporation, and who are themselves either in such a position as to have special knowledge of the affairs of the corporation, and are thereby afforded special opportunities to take advantage of their knowledge of its embarrassed condition, or who as stockholders are under an obligation to contribute to the payment of its debts. A stockholder does not, except in the exercise of his right to participate in the selection of its officers, have any control over a corporation not equally open to its creditors, nor is he ordinarily forbidden to do business with it on the same conditions open to persons who are not stockholders. If he becomes a creditor he has the same right to receive payment and the same means of redress in case it is not made as have other creditors. A preference by the corporation in his favor is valid to the same extent as if he were not a stockholder: *Lexington Life etc. Ins. Co.* v. *Page*, 17 B. Mon. 412; 66 Am. Dec. 165; *Reichwald* v. *Commercial H. Co.*, 106 Ill. 439; *Whitwell* v. *Warner*, 20 Vt. 425; *Lexington Life Ins. Co.* v. *Richardson*, 7 B. Mon. 412; 66 Am. Dec. 165, except under special circumstances bringing him within the principle of the cases refusing to permit such preferences in favor of directors, as where he is also a director, or is a sole stockholder, or his position has been such as to give him special information not usually possessed by stockholders and to impose upon him duties with the discharge of which his receiving a preference is inconsistent *Swepson* v. *Exchange Bank*, 9 Lea, 713; *Roan* v. *Winn*, 93 Mo. 503.

Preferences of Directors and Other Officers.—Directors of a corporation, unlike its stockholders, are its managers, and, in so far as they undertake to prefer themselves, assume to represent interests which are necessarily conflicting. There is no doubt that an agent is not authorized to act for his principal and for himself at the same time, and that this rule, applied to the law of corporations, disqualifies a director from voting in a matter in which he is personally interested, and makes any order or resolution, to the carrying of which his vote was necessary, void, for the reason that as such vote cannot be counted, the order or resolution should be regarded as lost: Note to *Beach* v. *Miller*, 17 Am. St. Rep. 300; *Smith* v. *Los Angeles I. & L. C. Co.*, 78 Cal. 289; 12 Am. St. Rep. 53; *Bennett* v. *St. Louis C. R. Co.*, 19 Mo. App. 349; *Wardell* v. *Union P. Co.*, 103 U. S. 651; *Chamberlain* v. *Pacific W. G. C. Co.*, 54 Cal. 103; *Thomas* v. *Brownsville R. Co.*, 109 U. S. 522. This rule disposes of all attempted preferences to which the vote of a preferred director was necessary. There is not, on the other hand, any absolute disqualification of a director to contract or otherwise deal with his corporation, and contracts and other transactions between him and it which his vote was not necessary to sanction are generally enforceable both by him and by it: *Little Rock etc. Co.* v. *Page*, 35 Ark. 304; *Buell* v. *Buckingham*, 16 Iowa, 284; 85 Am. Dec. 516; *Ashhurst's Appeal*, 60 Pa. St. 290; *Deane* v. *Hodge*, 35 Minn. 146; 59 Am. Rep. 321; *Beach* v. *Miller*, 130 Ill. 162; 17 Am. St. Rep. 291; *Garrett* v. *Burlington P. Co.*, 70 Iowa, 697; 59 Am. Rep. 461; *Twin L. Co.* v. *Marbury*, 91 U. S. 587. When, in the ordinary course of business, money becomes due to him, the corporation has a right to make, and he to receive, payment thereof: *Hoit* v. *Bennett*, 146 Mass. 437, and in default of such payment he may prosecute appropriate remedies to coerce it, and may thereby acquire valid liens by attachment, judgment, or execution: *Hallam* v. *Indianola Hotel Co.*, 56 Iowa, 178. When, however, the corporation becomes insolvent, or its directors, if fairly attentive to their business, must know that it is in failing circumstances, and that any payment made, or transfer or security given, to one of their number will probably result in preferring him to the prejudice of the other creditors, the right of the director to deal with the corporation becomes questionable. All the directors are, under such circumstances, in most of the states, treated as trustees of the creditors of the corporation and as such prohibited from receiving any preference which will give them any advantage over their fellow-creditors. There are, indeed, decisions which place the right of a director of an insolvent corporation to receive and retain preferences on the ground of his good faith, and, where that cannot be denied, the preference is permitted to stand: *Garratt* v. *Burlington P. Co.*, 70 Iowa, 697; 59 Am. Rep. 461; *Warfield* v. *Marshall County C. Co.*, 72 Iowa, 666; 2 Am. St. Rep. 263; *Foster* v. *Mullanphy Planing Mill Co.*, 92 Mo. 79. Where this rule prevails the doctrine that the directors are trustees of the creditors, and, as such, incompetent to act otherwise than for the equal benefit of all the creditors is denied, and preferences and other transactions are sustained, in the absence of bad faith or an intent to delay or defraud the other creditors: *Buell* v. *Buckingham*, 16 Iowa, 284; 85 Am. Dec. 516; *Bank of Montreal* v. *Potts Salt etc. Co.*, 90 Mich. 345; *Hills* v. *Furniture Co.*, 23 Fed. Rep. 434; *Smith* v. *Skeary*, 47 Conn. 54; *Central etc. Co.* v. *Claghorn*, 1 Spear Eq. 545; *Planters' Bank* v. *Whittle*, 78 Va. 737; *Brown* v. *Grand Rapids etc. Furniture Co.*, 58 Fed. Rep. 286. It is manifest that actual bad faith can rarely be proved in preferences of this class, unless, as a matter of law, a director of an insolvent corporation must be adjudged to act in bad faith whenever he receives a preference which must result in the payment of his claims to the exclusion of others equally just and valid, and that the only sound public policy upon this question is one which will not tempt him or his fellow-directors to act when the interests involved are necessarily conflicting. The rule now recognized by a decided preponderance of the authorities, with the reasons for its adoption, was thus stated in *Rosebloom* v. *Whittaker*, 132 Ill. 87: "So long as a corporation remains solvent its directors may, with the knowledge of the stockholders, deal with the corporation, loan it money, take security, and buy property of it, the same as a stranger. During the solvency of the corporation the directors are the agents or trustees of the stockholders, and owe no duties or obligations to others, but, the instant the corporation becomes insolvent, their relations and duties become materially changed. The assets of the corporation then become a trust fund for the payment of its creditors, and the directors can no longer deal with them for their own advantage, or in such way as to gain advantage for themselves over other creditors. They are then within the scope of that wise and equitable rule adopted by courts of equity for the protection of *cestuis que trust* or beneficiaries, which prohibits trustees and persons standing in similar fiduciary relations to exercise their powers or manage or appropriate the property of which they have control for their own profit or emolument, or, as it is sometimes expressed, shall not take advantage of their situation to obtain any personal benefit to themselves at the expense of the *cestui que trust.*"

If a payment is made or a security given to a director when the corporation is solvent its subsequent insolvency cannot operate retroactively so as to defeat the security or preclude him from taking the measures necessary to make it effective: *Mullanphy Bank v. Schott,* 135 Ill, 655; 25 Am. St. Rep. 401. When a corporation has become insolvent every director must, as a general rule, be chargeable with notice of such insolvency, either because he actually has such notice or because his failure to have it cannot exist without his being negligent in the discharge of the duties of his office. The very fact that he has taken special measures to secure himself is indicative of his knowledge of the necessity of security. The usual rule of allowing a race between creditors, and of rewarding the most diligent by permitting him to retain the fruits of his diligence, cannot fairly be applied between creditors, some of whom are directors or managing officers of a corporation and others of whom are not. The early start which the special knowledge of the director would permit and incite him to make will but rarely fail to enable him to distance all competitors. The only just and equitable rule, therefore, is one which will wrest from him the fruits of every form of device by which a preference may be sought, whether it be payment, security, assignment, or by judicial proceedings taken by him, whether actively aided or not by his fellow-directors: *Throop v. Hatch etc. Co.,* 125 N. Y. 530; *Corey v. Wadsworth,* 99 Ala. 68; 42 Am. St. Rep. 29; *Beach v. Miller,* 130 Ill. 162; 17 Am. St. Rep. 291; *Olney v. Conanicut Land Co.,* 16 R. I. 597; 27 Am. St. Rep. 767; *Hill v. Pioneer Lumber Co.,* 113 N. C. 173; 37 Am. St. Rep. 621; *Adams v. Kehlor Milling Co.,* 35 Fed. Rep. 433; *Atwater v. American etc. Bank,* 40 Ill. App. 501; *Lowry Banking Co. v. Empire Lumber Co.,* 91 Ga. 624; *Kankakee Woolen Mill Co. v. Kampe,* 38 Mo. App. 229; *Williams v. Jones,* 23 Mo. App. 132; *Lippincott v. Shaw Carriage Co.,* 25 Fed. Rep. 577; *Consolidated Tank Line Co. v. Kansas City Varnish Co.,* 45 Fed. Rep. 7; *Haywood v. Lincoln L. Co.,* 64 Wis. 639; *Sweeney v. Grape Sugar Co.,* 30 W. Va. 443; 8 Am. St. Rep. 88; *Howe v. Sanford etc. Co.,* 44 Fed. Rep. 231; *Smith v. Hopkins,* 10 Wash. 77; *Bradley v. Farwell,* 1 Holmes, 433; *Richards v. New Hampshire Ins. Co.,* 43 N. H. 263; *Clay v. Towle,* 78 Me. 86; *Smith v. Putnam,* 61 N. H. 632; *Hays v. Citizens' Bank,* 51 Kan. 535; *Koehler v. Black River etc. Co.,* 2 Black, 715; *Corbett v. Woodward,* 5 Saw. 403; *Hopkins' Appeal,* 90 Pa. St. 69; *Stratton v. Allen,* 16 N. J. Eq. 229; *Gibson v. Trowbridge Furniture Co.,* 96 Ala. 357; *Goodyear Rubber Co. v. Scott Co.,* 96 Ala. 439; *Lamb v. Cecil,* 25 W. Va. 288; *Lamb v. Pansell,* 28 W. Va. 663.

CASES

IN THE

SUPREME COURT

OF

WEST VIRGINIA.

STATE *v.* FLANAGAN.

[38 West Virginia, 53.]

SALE, WHERE DEEMED MADE—INTOXICATING LIQUORS.—A sale of intoxicating liquor, ordered by express, is complete, and property passes to the purchaser, when the liquor is delivered to an express agent for transportation, and not when it is received of the express agent by the purchaser.

SALE, WHERE DEEMED MADE—INTOXICATING LIQUORS—INDICTMENT FOR RETAILING WITHOUT LICENSE.—A licensed wholesale liquor dealer, doing business as such in one county, is not liable to indictment in another county for retailing liquors therein without a license, where he shipped by express, C. O. D., to a person in the latter county, a package of whiskey, as per his order by postal-card, sent through the mail, and which was received in the former county. Such facts show that the sale was made in the former county and not in the latter.

T. S. Riley, attorney general, for the state.

John Bassell, for the appellee.

53 ENGLISH, P. At the November term in the year 1890 W. H. Flannagan was indicted in the circuit court of Doddridge county for unlawfully selling spirituous liquors in said county **54** without having obtained a license therefor, as required by law. A motion was made to quash the indictment, which was overruled. The plea of not guilty was interposed. Issue was joined thereon, and the matters arising thereon were submitted to a jury, which resulted in a verdict of "not guilty," whereupon the attorney for the state moved the court to set aside the verdict of the jury and grant the state a new trial, because said verdict was contrary to the law and evidence, which motion was overruled, and the

state excepted and tendered three bills of exceptions, which
were signed, sealed, and saved to it, and made a part of the
record in the cause.

The facts upon which said indictment was predicated, and
about which there appears to be no controversy, are set out
in said first bill of exceptions as follows:

"On the 17th day of September, 1890, H. McCally, a resident of West Union, Doddridge county, W. Va., mailed to
the defendant, W. H. Flanagan, a duly licensed wholesale
and retail dealer in spirituous liquors at Parkersburg, Wood
county, W. Va., not licensed in said Doddridge county, a
written order or postal-card to send him (McCally) one-half
gallon of whiskey, collect on delivery; that said defendant
received said order and caused said spirituous liquors so
ordered to be packed and delivered to the express agent at
Parkersburg, with instructions to express same to the said
McCally at West Union, C. O. D., or collect on delivery, to
West Union; that the same was so expressed and received by
said McCally at West Union from the express agent, B. H.
Maulsby, and that said agent returned the price of said
liquor—one dollar and fifty cents—paid by the said McCally
to the said agent at West Union, Doddridge county, to the
said defendant at Parkersburg; and that he received the
same—which were all the facts shown in evidence to the jury
on said trial, and thereupon the prosecuting attorney of Doddridge county moved the court to instruct the jury that,
under the state of facts above detailed, reciting them, if they
believed them beyond all reasonable doubt, they must find
the defendant guilty as charged in the indictment; but the
court refused to give said instruction, and the state excepted,
and thereupon the [55] defendant asked the court to instruct
the jury that, if they found from the evidence the facts above
detailed, they should find for the defendant, to the giving of
which instruction the state by its attorney objected, but the
court overruled said objection, and gave said instruction,
and the state excepted; and, the jury having found a verdict
for the defendant, the attorney for the state moved to set
aside the verdict because the same was contrary to the law
and the evidence, which motion was overruled, judgment
was rendered upon the verdict, and the state applied for and
obtained this writ of error."

The action of the court with reference to said instructions
and upon said motion to set aside the verdict of the jury is

assigned and relied upon as error. In order to reach a correct conclusion in this case, it is necessary to determine where this sale was made. The defendant is charged with selling spirituous liquors in the county of Doddridge without a license; and, if the proof shows the sale to have been made in the county of Wood, he is not guilty of the offense charged, and should have been acquitted. This indictment does not charge the defendant with soliciting orders for whiskey in Doddridge county, and, if it did, the charge would not be sustained by the proof. It merely charges an unlawful selling without a license in the county of Doddridge.

The order for the whiskey was sent by postal-card through the mail. The knowledge that the whiskey was desired was communicated to the defendant, Flanagan, by the postal-card after it was taken from the postoffice in Wood county. He then received the order in Wood county, and complied with it in Wood county by packing the whiskey and delivering the same to the express agent in said county. It is true the package was sent C. O. D., but that only authorized the express agent to receive the purchase money on delivering the package. The postal-card directed the package to be sent by express, C. O. D., and the defendant, Flanagan, in pursuance of this request, delivered the same to the express agent, who acted in a dual capacity, to wit, as the agent of McCally, the consignee, in receiving and carrying the package to its destination, [56] and as the agent of Flanagan, the consignor, in collecting the purchase money.

In the case of *Garbracht* v. *Commonwealth*, 96 Pa. St. 449, 42 Am. Rep. 550, which is cited by Judge Green in the case of *State* v. *Hughes*, 22 W. Va. 755, the facts were very similar to those in the case we are considering. A party was indicted for selling liquor without a license. The defendant was the agent of a wholesale dealer in liquors, who was doing business in the city of Erie, and as such took orders for liquors from parties residing in Mercer county; and it was held in that case that "the place of sale is the point at which goods ordered are set apart and delivered to the purchaser, or to a common carrier, who, for the purpose of delivery, represents him"; and that, under the circumstances, the sale was made in the city of Erie, and not in Mercer county. Again, in the case of *Pilgreen* v. *State*, 71 Ala. 368, where whiskey was shipped from Calera to Columbiana, C. O. D., the court held the place of sale to be Calera, the beginning of the route. The court said:

"All the dealings between the buyer and the seller were at Calera. There the offer of the buyer was received, accepted, and acted upon, and there every act was done which it was intended the seller should do. The general property in this thing sold there passed to the buyers by the delivery to the carrier of his own appointment, though he could not entitle himself to possession until he paid the price to the carrier. The carrier was his agent to receive the thing sold at Calera, and was the agent to the seller to receive the price. . . . . The general property, however, passed to the buyer by the delivery to the express company at Calera. The risk of the loss then passed to him, though there may have remained in the seller a special property, and though the buyer could not, without payment of the price, entitle himself to the absolute property and to the actual possession."

The same doctrine is laid down in the case of *Krulder* v. *Ellison*, 47 N. Y. 36, 7 Am. Rep. 402, where "plaintiff, a merchant in New York, received from N. & T., of Rochester, an order in writing for certain goods, to be sent by canal. The goods were delivered to defendant's common carriers upon the [57] canal, consigned to N. & T., pursuant to the order. The goods were lost en route. It was held that upon the delivery to the carrier the title passed absolutely to the consignees, subject only to the rights of stoppage in transitu; and the plaintiff, the consignor, could not maintain an action for their loss."

In Benjamin on Sales, section 362, the author says: " In 1803, in the case of *Dutton* v. *Solomonson*, 3 Bos. & P. 582, it was treated as already settled law that, where a vendor delivered goods to a carrier by order of the purchaser, the appropriation is determined, the delivery to the carrier is a delivery to the vendee, and the property vests immediately."

This question was before this court in the case of *State* v. *Hughes*, 22 W. Va. 744, above referred to, and it was held in that case that, where orders for whiskey were solicited by the defendant, who resided in Wood county, in the county of Taylor, and the whiskey to fill these orders was delivered in jugs to an express agent in Wood county for transportation to the purchaser in Taylor county, who received the whiskey in Taylor county, and paid the express charges, and subsequently paid the purchase money to one of the firm in Taylor county, the seller could not be indicted in Taylor county for selling spirituous liquors without license, as the sales were made in Wood county, when the jugs were delivered to the express agent. Until then there was only an executory contract for the sale of the whiskey, and the sale became complete and the property in the whiskey was transferred to the purchaser, when it was delivered to the express agent for transportation, and not when it was received of the express agent by the purchaser.

Other cases might be cited to show that this sale was made in Wood county, but these are regarded as sufficient.

In Wood county the proposition was made to purchase the whiskey; it was there accepted; and the goods were packed and delivered to the expressman, the appointed agent of McCally, in Wood county; so that every element necessary to constitute a valid and complete sale was present in the county of Wood, and all of the elements were wanting in the county of Doddridge, so far as the defendant, [58] Flanagan, was concerned. To hold otherwise would prevent a wholesale merchant in Wheeling, Parkersburg, or Charleston from shipping liquors in response to a letter or telegram from a neighboring county, although he had fully complied with the law licensing him as a wholesale dealer, and would confine his wholesale business almost exclusively to the limits of his own county. Such a construction does not, in our opinion, accord with either the letter or spirit of the law, and, entertaining these views upon the statement of facts presented, our conclusion is that the circuit court committed no error in refusing to give the instruction asked for by the state, or in giving the instruction asked for on behalf of the defendant, or in refusing to set aside the verdict and grant a new trial.

For these reasons the judgment complained of must be affirmed.

————

SALES—DELIVERY TO COMMON CARRIER AS PASSING TITLE.—If goods are delivered to a common carrier for transportation to the purchaser without any condition, such delivery passes the title, although the purchase money is afterward collected by the vendor or agent at the place from which the goods were ordered: *State* v. *Wingfield*, 115 Mo. 428; 37 Am. St. Rep. 406, and note. A delivery of goods to a carrier indicated by the vendee is a delivery to the vendee: See note to *Dyer* v. *Great Northern Ry. Co.*, 38 Am. St. Rep. 508.

INTOXICATING LIQUORS—PROSECUTION FOR RETAILING WITHOUT LICENSE.—SALE, C. O. D., WHEN COMPLETE.—A licensed liquor dealer who receives an order from a purchaser residing in another county, where the dealer has

no license to send him liquor C. O. D., and accepts the order, and delivers
the liquor to a carrier under agreement to collect on delivery, cannot be
convicted of selling liquor without a license in the county where the purchaser resides, as the sale is complete on the part of the dealer when he
delivers the liquor to the carrier at his place of business: *Commonwealth* v.
Fleming, 130 Pa. St. 138; 17 Am. St. Rep. 763, and note.

DAVIS v. NOLL

[38 WEST VIRGINIA, 66.]

NEGOTIABLE INSTRUMENTS OVERDUE — TRANSFER — SETOFF — EQUITIES. —
The indorsee of an overdue bill or note takes it subject to equities
growing out of the transaction and existing at the time of the transfer, but not to a setoff arising out of collateral and wholly independent
matters; and this, though the indorsee had notice, gave no consideration for, and took the paper on purpose to defeat the offset.

SETOFF—NEGOTIABLE INSTRUMENTS OVERDUE.—The right of setoff was
unknown to the common law, but is of modern statutory creation, and
is neither an equity nor a lien recognized by the law merchant as
attaching to a negotiable instrument. Hence, the *bona fide* purchaser
of an overdue negotiable note is not required to take notice of existing
setoffs in the absence of legislative enactment.

NEGOTIABLE INSTRUMENTS OVERDUE ARE HELD SUBJECT TO WHAT EQUI-
TIES.—A *bona fide* purchaser for value of an overdue negotiable instrument holds it subject only to such equities as attach to the note itself at
the time of the transfer. He takes it in the same manner that he
would take any other personal property.

NEGOTIABLE INSTRUMENTS OVERDUE—TRANSFER OF, IN FRAUD OF CREDIT-
ORS IS VOID AS TO SETOFF, WHEN.—Negotiable paper, like any other
property, may be the subject of fraudulent transfer, as the law merchant cannot protect a transaction *mala fides* from the operation of
statutory law. Hence, the transfer of an overdue negotiable note with
the fraudulent intent to delay, hinder, or defraud the maker of such
note out of a just setoff, is void as to such setoff under the laws of this
state, unless made to a *bona fide* purchaser for value, without notice of
such intent.

NEGOTIABLE INSTRUMENTS—TRANSFER OF, WHEN VOID AS TO EXISTING
CREDITORS.—Every gift, assignment, or transfer of a negotiable instrument, on consideration not deemed valuable in law, is void as to existing creditors in the hands of such donee, assignee, or transferee, but
not in the hands of a *bona fide* holder for value.

Henry M. Russell, for the appellant.

White & Allen, for the appellee.

[66] DENT, J. This is a suit instituted by George S. Davis,
the indorser of two certain negotiable promissory notes,
against M. F. Noll, [67] the maker, in the circuit court of Ohio
county. Defendant appeared and demurred to the declara-

ration, which demurrer was overruled. Two special pleas in
writing were tendered and rejected. *Nil debet* was pleaded,
and an account of an offset filed. On the trial defendant
offered to prove his offset, but the court refused to admit his
proof and gave judgment against him for the full amount of
plaintiff's demand.

From this judgment defendant obtained a writ of error to
this court on the following assignment of errors: 1. The overruling of the demurrer to the declaration; 2. The rejection
of the two special pleas; and 3. The exclusion of the evidence and the overruling of the motion for a new trial.

The first of these assignments is not relied on in the argument and appears to have been interposed as a mere matter
of precaution. The evidence tendered was not proper under
the plea filed, but would have been admissible under the
pleas rejected. So the error in this case, if there is any,
arises from the rejection of the pleas tendered.

Plea No. 1 is, in substance, that the notes sued on were
transferred to the plaintiff by A. C. Patterson, the payee,
after maturity, and, that at the time of such transfer, defendant held a just offset against the indorser, which he was
entitled to have allowed against such notes, and therefore
raises the question of law included in point 2 of syllabus,
Smith v. *Lawson*, 18 W. Va. 213, 41 Am. Rep. 688, which is
as follows, to wit:

"(2) Query: If the equities, to which such overdue note
is subject in the hands of the transferee, are such equities as
attach to the note itself, as illegality, or want or failure of
consideration, or a release or payment only, or whether it
includes all offsets?"

This query has never been answered in this state, but is
an unsettled question. The matter of setoff appertains to the
remedy, solely, and is controlled by the law of the forum.
The plaintiff, in submitting himself to the jurisdiction, must
be satisfied with such remedies as the law affords to all suitors alike: 1 Daniel on Negotiable Instruments, sec. 890, p.
904. The legislature of this state has never passed any law
relating to offsets against negotiable notes specially, as has
been done in other states; but we are to be governed in
the determination of this question by the common law as
provided in article 6, section 21, of the constitution.

The common law, declared by modern English decisions,
is that the indorsee of an overdue bill or note takes it subject

to equities growing out of the transaction and existing at the time of the transfer, not as to a setoff arising out of collateral and wholly independent matters; and this though the indorsee had notice, gave no consideration for, and took the paper on purpose to defeat the offset. This is now held to be a fixed principle of commercial law, although several of the states repudiate the doctrine and allow offsets to be pleaded which existed at the time, but not those procured after the transfer: 1 Daniel on Negotiable Instruments, sec. 725; 2 Daniel on Negotiable Instruments, secs. 1435 *a*, 1436.

According to the uniform decisions and leanings of the courts of this state and Virginia we cannot do otherwise than accept the decisions of the English courts as declarative of the common law and hence the law of this state, except in so far as modified by statute. In the case of *Davis* v. *Miller*, 14 Gratt. 1, it is held "that the law merchant, which is part of our law, has made certain paper negotiable. The payee, or person legally entitled to it, may pass the legal title to another, and the title of that other is just as perfect as if he had been the original payee, or just as perfect as would be his title to any other kind of property legally transferred to him." After maturity and dishonor it is still negotiable, but the transferee takes it subject to such equities as attach to the note itself, in the same manner as he would take any other personal property. The right of offset being of modern statutory creation is neither an equity nor lien recognized by the law merchant as attaching to a negotiable instrument; and therefore the *bona fide* purchaser of an overdue negotiable note is not required to take notice of existing offsets, in the absence of legislative enactment. The legislature of this state has remained silent on this subject, except in so far as it has actually excepted negotiable paper from the operation of the provisions of section 4, chapter 126, of the code, in relation to non-negotiable paper, thus refusing to place commercial paper on the same footing, so far as the right to offset is concerned, with non-negotiable paper, which by this section was made more nearly to approach negotiable paper. It is not the province of judicial bodies to change, but only declare, what the law is; and, this being the sole question presented by plea No. 1, the circuit court could not do otherwise than reject it.

Plea No. 2 in substance alleges that the plaintiff and A. C. Patterson combined and confederated together to de-

fraud the defendant out of the amount of his debt, and cause
him to lose the same, and that the one made, and the other
received, the transfer of said negotiable notes without consideration for the purpose of preventing defendant from recovering said offset, and for no other purpose; thereby, while
not in express terms, yet virtually, alleging a fraudulent
transfer of these negotiable notes under the code, chapter
74, sections 1, 2.

1. "Every gift, conveyance, assignment, or transfer of, or
charge upon, any estate, real or personal; every suit commenced, or decree, judgment, or execution suffered or obtained, and every bond or other writing given, with intent
to delay, hinder, or defraud creditors or purchasers, or other
persons of or from what they are or may be lawfully entitled
to, shall, as to such creditors, purchasers, or other persons,
representatives, or assigns, be void."

2. "Every gift, conveyance, or assignment, transfer, or
charge, which is not,. on consideration, deemed valuable in
law, shall be void as to creditors whose debts shall have
been contracted at the time it was made."

The defendant's plea alleges this to be a transfer without
consideration, for the purpose of defrauding him out of an
existing and just debt. If these allegations are true, then
the transfer is void as to the defendant's offset. Negotiable
paper, like any other property, may be the subject of fraudulent transfer; and, if the fraudulent intent exists, and is
participated in by the transferee for or without value, his
title is void as to existing creditors, as the law merchant
cannot protect a transaction *mala fides* from the operation of
the wholesome and wise provisions of the statutory law. No
man can give away negotiable securities to the detriment of
existing creditors, any more than he can give away [70] his
horse or house. In such cases the law, avoiding the illegal
transfer, treats the fraudulent holder as the agent or trustee
secretly suing for the benefit of his principal, and allows all
just offsets against such principal: 2 Daniel on Negotiable
Instruments, 451; *Pates* v. *St. Clair*, 11 Gratt. 24; *Smith* v.
Lawson, 18 W. Va. 240; 41 Am. Rep. 688.

Offsets were unknown to the common law. Our statute on
the subject (Code, c. 126, sec. 4) provides: "In a suit for
any debt the defendant may, at the trial, prove, and have
allowed against such debt, any payment or setoff which is so
described in his plea, or in any account filed therewith, as

to give the plaintiff notice of its nature, but not otherwise,"
"between the original parties to a negotiable note, or parties
between whom there is a privity—that is, between the maker
and payee, drawer and acceptor, indorser and immediate
indorsee—a setoff may be pleaded to negotiable securities, as
well as any other kind": 2 Daniel on Negotiable Instruments, sec. 1435.

This, then, being a void assignment or transfer under the
law of this state, the defendant has the right to plead and
have allowed any setoff he may hold against the fraudulent
assignor or transferrer. Plea No. 2 clearly describes such an
offset.

We therefore conclude the court erred in rejecting said
plea, for which reason the judgment of the circuit court is
reversed, the order rejecting plea No. 2 is set aside, and the
plea filed, and this case is remanded to the circuit court to
be further proceeded with according to law.

———

NEGOTIABLE INSTRUMENTS OVERDUE—DEFENSES—SETOFF—FRAUD.—The
indorsee of an overdue bill or note is liable to such equities only as attach
to the bill or note itself, and not to claims arising out of collateral matters.
Thus, if a debt is due from the payee to the maker, it cannot be set off
against the note in a suit by the indorsee: See note to *Robinson* v. *Hyman*,
25 Am. Dec. 56. The negotiability of an instrument does not cease when
the paper matures. It is only subject to such equities as exist against the
paper at the date when negotiated, and the equities which affect the
indorsee are only such as attach directly to the note itself, and do not
include collateral matters. If indorsed after maturity the indorsee takes it
subject to all defenses to which it was liable in the hands of the payee:
Carpenter v. *Greenop*, 74 Mich. 664; 16 Am. St. Rep. 662, and note. In the
note to *Woodruff* v. *Garner*, 89 Am. Dec. 484, it is said that where promissory notes are assigned after maturity, the assignee takes them subject to all
existing equities between the maker and payee, and that, under such circumstances, they cannot be the subject of a counterclaim, but must be set up
as an equitable defense, on the ground that the assignee takes them subject
to an existing equity. Those who purchase negotiable paper after maturity from an innocent holder for value take it free of all equities and
defenses existing between the original parties to it; but one who purchases
a negotiable note after maturity from the payee is not an innocent holder,
and takes the paper subject to the same defenses that existed between
the original parties: *Koehler* v. *Dodje*, 31 Neb. 328; 28 Am. St. Rep. 518.
The maker of a note indorsed when overdue cannot set off an independent
demand due him from the indorser at and before the indorsement, where
the indorsee took it *bona fide*, without notice, and for value: *Annan* v.
Houck, 4 Gill, 325; 45 Am. Dec. 133. A maker of a note may set up
against the indorsee after due any defense he has against the payee: *Cochran*
v. *Wheeler*, 7 N. H. 202; 26 Am. Dec. 732. Setoff is a statutory right in
derogation of the common law, and must be strictly construed: *Bradley* v.
Smith, 98 Mich. 449; 39 Am. St. Rep. 565. One who takes negotiable paper

in bad faith can claim no recovery from the defrauded party; and the same would be true if he paid no value, or if he took after maturity, unless, in any of these cases, he acquired the instrument from one in whose hands it is not subject to the defense, obtaining thereby the title of such transferrer: See monographic note to *Bedell* v. *Herring*, 11 Am. St. Rep. 810.

Barnes Safe & Lock Company *v.* Bloch Bros. Tobacco Company.

[38 West Virginia, 158.]

Consignment for Sale—Contract of—How to be Construed.—In construing a contract of consignment for sale the court must determine from the wording of the contract itself and the circumstances surrounding it the true intention of the parties in making it. If the contract was entered into in the form of an agency contract for the purpose of evading the statute requiring all reservations of title to be recorded, then it should be held void as to creditors.

Consignment for Sale—Title—Sale with Reservation of Title.—A consignment of goods to be paid for at a fixed price out of the proceeds of the goods when sold, where the contract is one of pure agency, and there is no attempt at evasion, is a bailment for sale, and not a sale with reservation of title. The title remains in the consignor until the goods are sold to a *bona fide* purchaser for value, and they cannot be sold on execution to pay the debts of the agents. If so sold the purchaser gets no title as against the consignor.

Sale—Consignment for Sale—Distinction.—Ordinarily, if goods are "consigned" for sale, it is a bailment, and not a sale to the consignee. The goods do not become his property or liable for his debts, though consigned on a *del credere* commission. And the fact that the goods were invoiced at a stated price does not itself constitute the transaction a sale unless the terms of the consignment are such as to make the consignee, when the goods are sold, the purchaser and principal debtor for the goods.

Consignment for Sale—Lien for Commission.—Under a contract of consignment for sale, where the contract is one of pure agency, the agent's right to a lien for commission and expenditures is one personal to himself, not transferable, and he alone has the right to take advantage of it.

Factors — Dealing With — Notice of Powers. — Persons dealing with factors concerning goods intrusted to them are charged with notice of the extent and limitations upon their powers. If a transaction is brought in question by the owner of the goods the burden of proving the factor's authority is upon the party dealing with him.

The Barnes Safe & Lock Company, on April 21, 1890, entered into a written contract of agency with the Globe Contract Company, whereby the latter company obtained the privilege of selling the former company's fire and burglar proof safes, vault doors, etc. The Globe Contract Company was a corporation of the state of West Virginia, and the other company did business in Pittsburg, Pennsylvania. Safes were consigned to the Globe Contract Company as agent of the other company, and not in any sense a purchaser. The Barnes Company agreed to paint the name, "The Globe Contract Co., Genl. Agts., Wheeling, W. Va.," beneath their own name, "The Barnes Safe & Lock Co.," on all safes shipped, and this was plainly painted on every safe handled by the Globe Contract Company as such agents. The Globe Contract Company were to have the safes on hand to sell for the Barnes company whenever a purchaser could be secured on not exceeding thirty days' time. If no sales were made, then there was no purchaser, and the safes could only be returned to the consignor. If a sale was made, the title passed, not through the consignee, but direct from the consignor to the purchaser, and the price passed through the hands of the consignee to the consignor, after deducting all over a given amount to pay commissions and expenses. It was provided in the agreement that it might be terminated by either party upon thirty days' written notice, and that, at the end of thirty days after such notice, the agreement should be considered as canceled. At the instance of the Barnes company it was canceled on November 3, 1890. The accounts between the two companies remained unsettled. On July 9, 1891, the safe in controversy, being one of the safes consigned to the Globe Contract Company under said agreement, was levied on and sold by an execution creditor as the property of the Globe Contract Company, and the defendant in error, the Bloch Bros. Tobacco Company, became the purchaser, and immediately notified the Barnes company of that fact, and expressed a desire to exchange the safe for a smaller one that they could get into their vault. The Barnes company at once brought an action of detinue for the safe or the value thereof, two hundred dollars, and recovered judgment before a justice of the peace. On appeal the circuit court gave judgment for the defendant, and plaintiff then sued out a writ of error bringing the controversy before the supreme court.

White & Allen, for the appellant.

W. P. Hubbard, for the appellee.

[163] DENT, J. The counsel for the defendant in error maintains that the judgment of the circuit court should be affirmed because: 1. The safe had been sold by the plaintiff to the

Globe Contract Company; 2. If that were not so, and the
safe was in the hands of the Globe Contract Company as
plaintiff's agents, the latter had a lien for the general balance
due them, and the plaintiff, not having paid that balance,
cannot recover; 3. The plaintiff stood by and saw the safe
sold as property of the Globe Contract Company without
making any claim; 4. The Globe Contract Company, a trader,
not having complied with the provisions of chapter 100, section 13, of the code, this safe, acquired and used in its business, was liable for its debts; 5. If the contract was as claimed
by plaintiff, it was an attempt to sell goods reserving the title,
and such reservation is void under chapter 74, section 3, of
the code.

On an examination of many decisions relating to contracts
of this kind we find them apparently contradictory and hard
to reconcile, some holding that goods delivered under similar
contracts are mere bailments for the purpose of sale; others,
that they are sales with reservation of title, and therefore
void under the usual recording acts as to creditors. But
from all the general rule is deducible that the court must
determine from the wording of the contract itself and the
circumstances surrounding it the true intention of the parties
in making it; and if the contract was entered into in the form
of an agency contract for the purpose of evading the statute
requiring all reservations of title to be recorded, then it should
be held void as to creditors. Such was the determination of
the court in the case of *Chickering* v. *Bastress*, 130 Ill. 206;
17 Am. St. Rep. 309.

But where there is no attempt at evasion, but the contract
is one of pure agency, providing for a consignment of goods
to be paid for at a fixed price out of the proceeds of the goods
when sold, this is a bailment for sale, not a sale [164] with
reservation of title, and the title remains in the consignor
until the goods are sold to a *bona fide* purchaser for value:
Walker v. *Butterick,* 105 Mass. 238; *Weir Plow Co.* v. *Porter,*
82 Mo. 23; *Middleton* v. *Stone,* 111 Pa. St. 589; *Dando* v.
Foulds, 105 Pa. St. 74.

"Ordinarily, if goods are 'consigned' for sale, it is a bailment, and not a sale to the consignee. The goods do not
become his property or liable for his debts," "even though
consigned on a *del credere* commission." And the fact that
the goods consigned were invoiced at a stated price does not
itself constitute the transaction a sale, unless the terms of

the consignment be such as to make the consignee, when the goods are sold, the purchaser and principal debtor for the goods: Benjamin on Sales, 6th ed., 7; also 3 Am. & Eng. Ency. of Law, 340.

Applying these principles to this case we find that the contract entered into was one of pure agency without any attempt or thought of evading the statutory law relating to the recordation of instruments, when sales are made reserving the title, but a consignment of safes was made to the Globe Contract Company as such agent, not in any sense a purchaser, to have on hand to sell for the Barnes Safe & Lock Company, whenever a purchaser could be secured on not exceeding thirty days' time. If no sales were made, then there was no purchaser, and the safes could only be returned to the consignor. If a sale was made the title passed, not through the consignee, but direct from the consignor to the purchaser; and the price passed through the hands of the consignee to the consignor, after deducting all over a given amount to pay commissions and expenses.

It is true that the consignee could have become the purchaser of any of the safes, at any time it might wish to do so, by accounting for or paying the fixed price according to the contract to the consignor; and, when the consignor gave notice of cancellation, it gave the opportunity to the consignee to become the purchaser of any unsold safes, but this the consignee refused to do, and notified the consignor that the safes were at its disposal as soon as the accounts between them were properly adjusted.

[165] The consignor may have been guilty of some negligence in not taking steps at once after the cancellation of the contract to recover possession of the safes, but not as to divest it of its title, as it was waiting for the statement from its agent. There is no sufficient evidence to show that it stood by and saw the safe sold as the property of the Globe Contract Company without making claim. On the contrary, the proof clearly shows, that it had no knowledge of the levy or sale until the letter written it by the defendant in this case, informing it of the purchase, and asking to trade it for a safe of a different size.

It is hardly worth while to notice the fourth proposition of defendant's counsel—that the Globe Contract Company was a "trader," within the provisions of chapter 100, section 13, of the code—because the Globe Contract Company did not

do business as a trader with the addition of the words "factor,"
"agent," and "company," or "& Co.," within the meaning
and contemplation of the statute; but it was doing business
in its corporate name, and while transacting other business
it undertook to act as an agent for the Barnes Safe & Lock
Company, which fact was plainly painted on every safe
handled by it as such agents.

This being a bailment, not a sale with reservation of title,
as heretofore determined, does not come under the provisions
of chapter 74, section 3 of the code.

To sustain the position taken by the defendant its counsel quotes the law virtually as set out in the syllabus 1:
Chickering v. *Bastress*, 130 Ill. 206, 17 Am. St. Rep. 309: "1.
Contract: Whether a Sale or Mere Bailment. Where the
identical thing delivered is to be restored in the same or an
altered form the contract is one of bailment; but when there
is no obligation to restore the specific article, and the person
receiving it is at liberty to return another thing of equal
value, he becomes a debtor to make a return, and the title to
the property is changed—it is a sale."

The same law is laid down in Benjamin on Sales, sixth
edition, page 5, in these words: "On the other hand it is now
well settled that if the contract clearly contemplates, either by
express provision or by established usage of the business, that
the identical thing received will not be returned, but [166] only
its equivalent, either in the same form received, or in some
manufactured condition, or else paid for in money, at the
option of the receiver, the transaction is a sale or exchange.
The title passes immediately on delivery, and the risk is on
the receiver."

This law, while it holds good as to certain kinds of bailments, has no application whatever to that class of bailments
known as "consignments for sale," and was therefore improperly applied in the Illinois case above referred to. To so
apply it is to do away with all bailments with power to sell,
because there is no obligation in such case to restore the specific article, but only the value thereof in money, after a sale
is made by the factor or consignee, or, in case no sale is
made, then to restore the specific article; and the law quoted
above from the fifth page of Benjamin on Sales would be
directly in conflict with the law quoted from the seventh
page of the same work, but to give the construction given in
this opinion is to render both pages harmonious.

The only other point urged by the defendant's counsel is the one on which the circuit court appears from the briefs to have decided this case; and that is that the appellant was not entitled to recover possession of the safe in controversy, because the Globe Contract Company had a lien on it for unsettled commissions. It nowhere appears that such is the true state of affairs. Accounts appear to be unsettled, but which way the balance will fall is not made evident. Neither is the Globe Contract Company claiming any such lien. If it had one it was personal to itself, and was waived when it permitted the safe to be taken from its custody and it cannot be asserted by a third party. "None but the factor himself can set up this privilege against the owner. It is a personal privilege, and cannot be transferred, nor can the question upon it arise between any but the principal and the factor": 3 Am. & Eng. Ency. of Law, 339; *Holly* v. *Huggeford*, 8 Pick. 73; 19 Am. Dec. 303.

The constable in this case levied on the safe by direction of the general manager, and apparently the only secured creditor of the Globe Contract Company, then wholly insolvent. [167] This is no protection to the officer, nor to the purchaser who bought at the sale, because the doctrine *caveat emptor* applies in such cases with full force, and the inscription on the safe, "The Barnes Safe & Lock Co.," "The Globe Contract Co., Genl. Agts., Wheeling, W. Va.," was sufficient to put any reasonable man on his guard, especially as it was a new safe that had never been used; and it can hardly be doubted that such shrewd business men as compose the defendant company were fully informed as to the true state of the title to the safe, and purchased it as a matter of pure speculation. If not so informed, it was their own fault, as they knew where to find the owners of the safe. But whether they were or not does not alter the law of this case.

"Persons dealing with factors concerning goods intrusted to them are charged with notice of the extent and limitations upon their powers; and, if they deal with them as if they were acting for themselves, or if they were dealing with their own property, such persons do so at their peril that such is the fact, or that the factor has special authority from the owner, or that, by the well-established and recognized usage and customs of trade in that line, the factor is authorized to deal with and dispose of the goods in the manner proposed. If the transaction is brought in question by the owner of the goods, the burden of proving the factor's authority is upon the party dealing with him": *Kauffman* v. *Beasley*, 54 Tex. 563; Story on Agency, sec. 225.

There is no pretense or claim in this case that the Globe Contract Company, through its general manager, was authorized by the Barnes Safe & Lock Company to turn this safe over to the constable to be sold, and applied on the debts of the Globe Contract Company, and he in so doing acted wrongfully toward the true owners of the safe and the purchaser at the sale, but could not thereby deprive the true owners of their title, nor confer any title on the purchaser, because he was exceeding the authority conferred by the agency.

For the foregoing reasons the judgment of the circuit court is reversed, and judgment is rendered for the appellant, the Barnes Safe & Lock Company, for the safe [168] in question, or, in lieu thereof, the sum of one hundred and twenty-five dollars, the agreed value, with interest thereon until paid, and his costs in this and the circuit court and before the justice of the peace expended.

SALE—BAILMENT—CONSIGNMENT FOR SALE.—The agency to sell goods and return the proceeds, or the specific goods if not sold, stands precisely upon the same footing as a bailment. The title is not changed in either case, and the recognized distinction between bailment and sale "is that when the identical article is to be returned in the same form, or in some altered form, the contract is one of bailment, and the title to the property is not changed. On the other hand, when there is no obligation to return the specific article, and the receiver is at liberty to return another thing of value, he becomes a debtor to make the return, and the title to the property is changed; the transaction is a sale." In a consignment for sale the title ordinarily remains in the consignor, and the goods are not subject to the debts of the assignee or agent: See monographic note to *Ætna Powder Co.* v. *Hildebrand*, 45 Am. St. Rep. 203-210, citing the principal case, and showing when a consignment for sale vests title.

FACTOR'S LIEN.—A factor has a general lien on goods of his principal in his possession, their proceeds and securities taken for the price, for advances, expenses, and commissions, and extending to the general balance of his accounts, but not to debts outside the agency: See monographic note to *Bigelow* v. *Walker*, 58 Am. Dec. 167, on factors; *Vail* v. *Durant*, 7 Allen, 408; 83 Am. Dec. 695, and note. The lien, however, is a personal privilege, which the factor alone can set up against the owner. It cannot be transferred, and the question can only arise between the principal and the factor: Note to *Bigelow* v. *Walker*, 58 Am. Dec. 168.

FACTORS, LIMITATION UPON POWER OF.—The authority of factors and brokers, acting in the line of their employment, cannot be limited by private instructions not known to the party dealing with them: *Lobdell* v. *Baker*, 1 Met. 193; 35 Am. Dec. 358.

GIBSON *v.* CITY OF HUNTINGTON.
[33 WEST VIRGINIA, 177.]

MUNICIPAL CORPORATIONS—NEGLIGENCE AS TO REPAIRS—DAMAGES.—A municipal corporation is liable for injuries caused by its failure to comply with the statute requiring it to keep its streets, alleys, sidewalks, roads, and bridges in repair. Negligence, in such cases, is presumed from injury, and notice of the defect is not required.

MUNICIPAL CORPORATIONS—NEGLIGENCE AS TO MINISTERIAL DUTIES—DAMAGES.—A municipal corporation is liable for injuries caused by its negligence in the discharge of ministerial or specified duties assumed by its charter. In such cases negligence must be alleged and fully proved.

MUNICIPAL CORPORATIONS AS PRIVATE OWNERS OF PROPERTY ARE LIABLE to the same extent that individuals are liable. In such cases negligence must be alleged and fully proved.

MUNICIPAL CORPORATIONS—NEGLIGENCE IN GOVERNMENTAL OR DISCRETIONARY MATTERS—DAMAGES.—A municipal corporation is not liable for injuries caused by the negligence of its agents and officers in the discharge of duties purely governmental or discretionary.

NEGLIGENCE—MUST BE PROVED, WHEN.—In all cases where a remedy is not given by statute, but by the common law, negligence must be proved by the party alleging it.

NEGLIGENCE, WHEN A QUESTION FOR THE COURT AND WHEN FOR THE JURY.—If the facts of a case are indisputable, and there can be no fair difference of opinion as to whether the inference of negligence should be drawn, the question becomes one of law alone, and the court may decide it, if appealed to for this purpose. But, even where the facts are not disputed, if there may be a fair difference of opinion as to whether the inference of negligence should be drawn, or as to whether the facts sustain the charge of negligence, the jury are the sole judges, and their verdict cannot be disturbed, although the court may be of the opinion that the facts do not sustain it.

MUNICIPAL CORPORATIONS—ACTION FOR DAMAGES FOR WRONGFUL DEATH CAUSED BY FALLING EMBANKMENT—BURDEN OF PROOF.—In an action against a municipal corporation to recover damages for the death of a child in the highway, alleged to have been caused by the defendant's negligence in maintaining a dangerous embankment at the side of such highway, the burden of proving negligence is on the plaintiff; and, if the jury finds that the facts are not sufficient to sustain the charge of negligence, the court cannot disturb the verdict, although it may be of a different opinion. To do so would be a denial of the right of trial by jury guaranteed by the constitution of the state.

MUNICIPAL CORPORATIONS—ACTION FOR MAINTAINING DANGEROUS EMBANKMENT, GROUND OF—NEGLIGENCE.—An action may be maintained against a city for damages for wrongful death caused by the falling of an embankment maintained as a barrier, at the side of a highway therein, not upon the ground of a violation of its statutory duty to keep its highways in repair, but upon the ground of negligent management of its corporate property or violation of a duty assumed by its charter. The city has no more right, even for a public purpose, to maintain a dangerous barrier by the side of a road, though placed there by nature, than a citizen has; but questions of notice and negligence, in such a case, in order to fasten liability, are for the consideration of the jury.

APPEAL—REVIEW OF JURY'S FINDING—VIEW OF PREMISES.—The supreme court will not disturb the finding of a jury, unless all the material evidence touching the matter at issue that was considered by the jury is before it. Hence, where the jury have viewed the premises, and undoubtedly taken into consideration matters material in the case, but which are not before the supreme court, it will not disturb the verdict.

Gibson, Hutchinson & Gibson, for the appellant.

Campbell & Holt, for the appellee.

[178] DENT, J. Mary Lewis, an infant four years and five months old, while playing on the side of a road in the city of Huntington on the —— day of May, 1892, was killed by the falling of an embankment, which had been kept along the street or road as a barrier to keep travelers along the highway from driving into the adjacent creek. This embankment had been undermined to some extent by persons digging out sand and gravel, and was in a dangerous condition, as the death of the child bears witness. The street commissioner, after some excavating had been done (how much, the evidence does not disclose), put up a notice forbidding the taking of sand and gravel from this place; but afterward (how long does not appear, nor how long before the accident) a man by the name of Brown excavated sand and gravel and hauled it away; for what purpose is not revealed, but, so far as the evidence shows, it was without the knowledge of the municipal authorities. The jury were taken to view the place of the accident.

It is now firmly established, by a long line of well-considered decisions, that a municipal corporation is liable for injuries occasioned by its negligence in the following three classes of cases: 1. Failure to keep its streets, alleys, sidewalks, roads, and bridges in repair under the statute; 2. In the discharge of ministerial or specified duties, not discretionary or governmental, assumed in consideration of the privileges conferred by charter, even though there be the absence of special rewards or advantages; 3. As a private owner of property to the same extent as individuals are liable. It would be impracticable to cite all the authorities settling these propositions, but the following are referred to as leading cases: *Mendel* v. *City of Wheeling,* 28 W. Va. 233; 57 Am. Rep. 664; *City of Richmond* v. *Long,* 17 Gratt. 375;

94 Am. Dec. 461; *Orme* v. *City of Richmond,* 79 Va. 86; *Mackey* v. *City of Vicksburg,* 64 Miss. 777; *Barnes* v. *District of Columbia,* 91 U. S. 540.

In the first class of cases negligence is presumed, and [179] notice of defect is not required. In the second and third classes negligence must be alleged and fully proven: *Chapman* v. *Milton,* 31 W. Va. 385; *Biggs* v. *Huntington,* 32 W. Va. 55.

This suit is not proper under the first class, or statutory provision, because it was not caused by any defect or obstruction in the roadbed; but it can be maintained under the two latter classes, because it is made the ministeral duty of the municipality by law to protect the public and individuals from any thing dangerous, and the embankment that caused the injury was maintained by the city as its property in lieu of other barrier along and within the boundaries of a public highway. The city has no more right to erect or keep within or along a public highway an unnecessarily dangerous structure, even though it be for some public purpose, than a citizen has. It is true that the city did not erect this embankment, but, as the witness said, it was placed there by nature, and the city adopted and maintained it as a barrier to prevent travelers from driving into the creek. Had there been an artificial structure so rudely constructed of stone, wood, or iron as to fall of its own weight and crush this child, the liability of the city would not have been questioned; and it certainly ought to make no difference whether the city builds or adopts one already there, even though nature was the original builder. It was its ministerial duty, neither governmental nor discretionary, to see that it was not dangerous to any one lawfully using the road or any part thereof. By leaving the embankment there as such barrier the council fixed the limits of the road, and any one using it had the right to lawfully use it, up to the limit so fixed, whether it was the traveled part of the road or not.

Was the child using the road for a lawful purpose? Children are not responsible for the choice of their parents nor the place or condition of their birth. God decides these for them when he breathes into them the breath of life. Poor parents are unable to provide a place of healthful exercise and play for their children, for it requires all their earnings to clothe, feed, and shelter them. The law prohibits them, under the penalty of being trespassers, [180] from entering on

the lands of others; and now to forbid them to use the road
to its utmost boundary for the purpose of play, when not
interfering in any manner with the traveling public, would
savor too much of the dark ages of barbarism, when children
were subjected to inhuman and diabolical punishments, and
their lives were at the mercy of those having charge over
them. The roads are the only commons children now have,
and to confine them in the narrow limits of their cheerless
tenement houses would be cruel, unjust, and oppressive,
blight their young lives and render their bodies weak, sickly,
scrofulous, and vile; and, if they could manage to escape the
long list of contagious diseases so fatal to their kind, they
would grow up to adult age morbidly despising laws so
tyrannous and unworthy a civilized and liberty loving people. It is a right they have immemorially enjoyed, and
should continue to enjoy as long as the public fails to provide them other free commons, where they can have the pure
air, bright sunshine, and sportive exercise so necessary to the
healthful growth of their sensitive bodies. Horses, cattle,
hogs, dogs, and other domestic animals are all at large in
the streets, unless prohibited by special ordinance, and why
not children? The public highways can be put to no better
use. I am clearly of the opinion the child had the right to
be there, even though out of the beaten path, and only for
play. Neither was it old enough to realize the danger it was
in, or the dangerous condition of the embankment, and
could not possibly be guilty of contributory negligence.

The most troublesome question is that of negligence. In
all cases where the remedy is not given by statute, but by
the common law, negligence must be proved by the party
alleging it. Where the facts are indisputable, and there can
be no fair difference of opinion as to whether the inference of
negligence should be drawn, the question becomes one of law
alone, and the court may decide it, if appealed to for this
purpose. But, even where the facts are not disputed, if there
may be a fair difference of opinion as to whether the inference of negligence should be drawn, or as to whether the
facts sustain the charge of negligence, the [181] jury are the
sole judges, and their verdict cannot be disturbed, although
the court may be of the opinion that the facts do not sustain
it. The litigants have the constitutional right to a trial by
a jury of fair and impartial men under the rules of law.
Having demanded and had it, they have no right to com-

plain, and the court has no right to interfere. It is a tribunal of their own choosing.

It has been held in cases of this character "that notice to the corporate authorities, either express or implied, must be shown. If the defect causing the injury had existed for such length of time that proper diligence would have discovered it, then no notice need be proven; but, if the defect arise otherwise than from faulty structure or the direct act of said authorities or other agents, and be a recent defect, it is generally necessary to show that the town authorities had knowledge thereof a sufficient time before the injury to have by reasonable diligence repaired it, or that they were negligently ignorant of it": *Curry* v. *Town of Mannington*, 23 W. Va. 14.

The embankment was on the side of the road, in a remote part of the city. The authorities had the right to leave it there as a barrier, provided it was not dangerous to the lawful users of the road. There is no evidence tending to show that it was dangerous when left there, but the evidence shows it afterward became dangerous by reason of the excavations made under it. The street commissioner, when he found that persons were removing the sand and gravel, posted a notice warning them from so doing, not because he regarded it dangerous, but to prevent it from being destroyed as a barrier—the city's property. After this notice was put up (how long the evidence does not disclose, nor how long before the accident, except as a mere conjecture) a man by the name of Brown, without the knowledge or permission of the authorities, and against the express notice posted as aforesaid, did further excavating of sand and gravel, and hauled it away, which, presumably, was the excavating that rendered the bank dangerous. It is not shown that the authorities had notice of this last excavating. On the contrary, it appears from the evidence that they had no notice of it.

182 The witness Brown, for some unexplained reason, is not introduced to show when or by what authority he did the excavating. It is true the street commissioner says he passed along there frequently, but it does not appear that he passed there after Brown had done his work, nor does it appear that there was any thing to indicate to him that the embankment was in danger of falling; and none of the plaintiff's witnesses testify that they had any knowledge beforehand of the dangerous character of the embankment that produced the injury; and one of his principal witnesses says: "I consider it dangerous from falling on top. I did n't know it would cave down on them."

From this evidence the jury certainly had a right to conclude that the structure was not rendered dangerous by the direct act of the city authorities; that they had no notice of its dangerous character a sufficient time before the injury to have by reasonable diligence repaired it; and that they were not negligently ignorant of it. While we might have found a different one, we have no right to disturb their verdict. Their decision is supreme and final.

But, even if this did not conclude us, there is another question that would; and that is the jury were taken to view the spot and its surroundings. The counsel deemed it necessary. What effect this had on the minds of the jury in reaching a conclusion this court cannot say; but that it was material cannot be doubted. The remoteness of the place, the situation and character of its surroundings, and the nature and condition of the embankment would obviously all be taken into consideration in making up a verdict. None of these things are before this court, and the settled rule is that this court will not disturb the finding of a jury, unless all the material evidence touching the matter at issue that was considered by the jury is before it, as otherwise the case, as presented to the two tribunals, would be materially different.

No instructions were asked, and no points of law raised; and, there having been a fair hearing before an impartial jury, this court is legally powerless to interfere, and the judgment of the circuit court must be affirmed.

MUNICIPAL LIABILITY FOR NEGLIGENCE.—If the charter of a city requires it to keep its streets in repair it is liable in damages to one who is injured by reason of its neglect of such duty: *Farquar v. City of Roseburg*, 18 Or. 271; 17 Am. St. Rep. 732. No recovery can be had, however, against a city for its negligence in failing to perform a legislative, judicial, or discretionary duty, or in simply performing such a duty in an improper method. If a wall or other standing object is in a dangerous condition, and therefore liable to fall, and the city has notice of the danger, it may become answerable to one injured from its failure to demolish or strengthen the object: See monographic note to *Goddard v. Inhabitants of Harpswell*, 30 Am. St. Rep. 379, 386, where the whole subject of municipal liability for negligence, and misconduct of its officers and agents, is discussed.

NEGLIGENCE—PLEADING AND BURDEN OF PROOF.—To recover for injuries or loss occasioned by negligence the negligence must, as a general rule, be alleged and proved by the plaintiff. The mere happening of an accident is not sufficient evidence to be left to the jury. And the negligence is not to be presumed: See note to *Farish v. Reigle*, 62 Am. Dec. 680. But where a remedy is given by statute the plaintiff need only prove the fact that caused the injury, and the *onus* is thrown upon defendant to excuse or justify his act: *Johnson* v. *Barber*, 5 Gilm. 425; 50 Am. Dec. 416.

NEGLIGENCE—AS QUESTION OF LAW OR FACT.—Negligence is usually a mixed question of law and fact, and is never purely one of law, unless the facts are wholly undisputed and admit of no conflicting inferences: *Isham* v. *Post*, 141 N. Y. 100; 38 Am. St. Rep. 766.

OSBORNE v. FRANCIS.

[38 WEST VIRGINIA, 312.]

SALES—PROPERTY TO SATISFY PURCHASER.—An option to purchase if the buyer likes is essentially different from an option to return the property if he does not like it; but, in either case, he may peremptorily return within the time without giving any reason, if he acts honestly.

SALES—WHETHER COMPLETE OR EXECUTORY.—The question whether a sale of personal property is complete or only executory is to be determined from the intent of the parties, as gathered from the contract, the nature and situation of the thing sold, and the circumstances surrounding the sale.

SALES—"SALE ON TRIAL"—SATISFACTION OF PURCHASER.—A promise by a purchaser to do a thing only in case it pleases himself may be no promise at all, yet it is what the books call a "sale on trial," and may become, by mere lapse of time, a binding promise; and there appears to be nothing unreasonable or unfair in such every-day quasi contracts of sale.

SALES—SATISFACTION OF PURCHASER.—One who buys a harvesting-machine called a "binder" upon the condition that if it does not work to his satisfaction, he may return it, has an absolute right to reject the machine, if he so wills, without assigning any reasons.

APPEAL—WHEN ERROR WILL BE DISREGARDED.—When the court can clearly see affirmatively that error has worked no harm to the party appealing it will be disregarded.

INSTRUCTIONS.—The court cannot instruct upon the weight of evidence or the credibility of witnesses, but, when there is any competent evidence fairly tending in some appreciable degree to prove a party's case, he has the right to have the law applicable to such evidence correctly declared to the jury by the court.

INSTRUCTIONS—REVERSAL OF JUDGMENT.—An erroneous instruction on a material point is presumed on appeal to have been to the prejudice of the exceptant, and will justify a reversal of judgment, unless it clearly appears from the record that it was harmless.

D. B. Evans, for the appellant.

J. L. Parkinson, for the appellee.

312 HOLT, J.　This action was for one hundred and thirty-three dollars and fifty cents, the price and value of one right-hand binder and fifty pounds Manilla binding twine, which

plaintiffs claimed to have sold to defendant. It was originally brought before a justice, where the defendant confessed
judgment for eight dollars and fifty cents for the twine, which,
together with the costs, he paid. On the 9th of January,
1891, the justice gave judgment against Francis for one hundred and twenty-five dollars, the price of the binder. **313**
From this judgment the defendant appealed to the circuit
court of Marshall county, where the case was tried before a
jury, and a verdict found for plaintiff for one hundred and
thirty-three dollars and fifty cents. During the progress of
the trial the court, on motion of plaintiff, gave three instructions. To the giving of the one marked "No. 2" defendant
objected, but the court overruled the objection, and defendant
excepted. On motion of defendant the court then gave the
jury three instructions, to which plaintiff objected, but the
court overruled the objection and gave the same, and plaintiff excepted. After the verdict the defendant moved the
court to set the same aside and grant him a new trial, because the verdict was not in accordance with the law and
the evidence, and because the court erred in giving plaintiff's
instruction No. 2 to the jury; but the court overruled the
motion for new trial, and defendant excepted, and the court
signed, sealed, and made part of the record the defendant's
bills of exceptions, and also certified and made part of the
record the instructions given and refused, and all the evidence in the case.

There are two points assigned as error: 1. That plaintiff's
instruction No. 2 is erroneous; 2. That it is inconsistent with
defendant's instructions, especially defendant's instruction
No. 2.

Plaintiff's instruction No. 1 is as follows: "The jury are
instructed that if they believe from the evidence that the
machine was sold on a guaranty, and that after a fair trial it
did do the work as guaranteed, then the verdict should be
for the plaintiff."

Plaintiff's instruction No. 2 is as follows: "If the jury
believe from the evidence that the machine was to give satisfaction to the defendant, then it should be a fair and reasonable satisfaction, and not a whimsical or unreasonable satisfaction." This is the only one to which defendant objected.

The instruction No. 2 given for defendant reads as follows:
"The court instructs the jury that if they find from the evidence that the machine, price of which is in question, was

sold to the defendant with the understanding and [314] agreement that if it did not give satisfaction to the defendant the seller would take it back, then the defendant had a right to refuse to keep the machine if it did not in fact give him satisfaction, and the burden of proving that it did give him satisfaction is on the plaintiff.'

Now, the appellant must make it manifest from the record that the ruling complained of is wrong.

The first question is: What were the terms, the language, the words, of the contract of sale? The parties, instead of committing it to writing and thus giving us a stable and trustworthy memorial that could speak for itself, have seen fit to commit it to the uncertain, slippery memory of man as to the terms, the words used; for on some of the very words the meaning and scope of the contract in large part depend. For this we have to look to the evidence, what the parties said and did, the nature of the subject of sale, and the surrounding circumstances. There is no controversy that the cultivated land on defendant's farm was sideling, sloping, some of it steep. He had an old reaper that did not bind. Whether a binder could be used on it safely, usefully, was in his mind doubtful, and up to that time unknown.

The two agents of plaintiff who were together and made the sale were examined as witnesses on behalf of plaintiffs. The first one said defendant was to give for the binder his old reaper and one hundred and twenty dollars; one-half payable in a year and the balance in two years. "We guaranteed for the machine to do as good work as any other machine of the same nature, to be as light running as any other reaping-machine, and to do as good work in every particular. Defendant was to take the machine out, and, if it did not do the work we guaranteed it to do, defendant was to bring it back, and we were to pay him for hauling it out ten miles and back. He got the machine June 26th. It was set up and started June 30, 1890." On July 3, 1890, witness got a card from defendant, saying: "My binder does not work right. You can come and get it"; and, on the 18th of July, 1890, another card saying, "Your reaper is here at your order." He told defendant that their machine would [315] not go on a certain sloping field with the platform on the upper side without upsetting, but could not be upset with the platform on the lower side. He said that the machine was not sold on the condition that it was to give satisfaction, but defendant was to take the machine and try it, and, if it did not do its work well, the plaintiff was to pay for hauling it out and back.

The second agent, who helped to make the sale and was present, and seemed to be principal agent, in answer to the question, "What was the cause of the upsetting?" said: "Well, the weight is always on the left-hand side, and in a right-hand binder the binding attachment don't make weight. To put the platform up the hill the sideling will turn it over. It will not turn clear over, but it will upset, and stop the binder, stop the running of the shoes." On the question of giving defendant satisfaction, he said: "In guaranteeing the machine to do its work properly we always guarantee it to give the man satisfaction, because a machine doing its work properly must always give satisfaction. If a man has a farm that would n't be fit for any binder, that is some thing else. Of course, we can't satisfy every farm, but we can the man."

Defendant testified that it cut the grain off as nice as any machine, and tied the grain, but told plaintiff's agents that it worried his horses too much. On the main item here involved—the terms of the contract—he testified that he was to haul out the machine, and, if it gave him satisfaction, he was to take it; if it did not, he was to haul it back, and plaintiff was to pay for hauling it out and back; and when plaintiff's agents came out to see him about it, after receiving the cards, he told them in substance that he did not intend to take the machine. They replied, " You will have to keep the machine and pay for it." This was not denied.

Another witness, not interested, as far as appears, who was present at the sale, examined for defendant, said, by the contract defendant was not to take the machine if it did not give him satisfaction. The evidence, therefore, at least tended to show that kind of conditional sale called in the books a "sale on trial," or "a sale or return": See [316] Benjamin on Sales, Bennett's 6th ed., sec. 595, et seq., and notes, p. 568, notes, 10, 11, et seq; 21 Am. & Eng. Ency. of Law, 647, 648, 714, cases cited; Tiedeman on Sales, sec. 213, and cases; *Wood etc. Machine Co.* v. *Smith,* 50 Mich. 567; 45 Am. Rep. 57; *Seeley* v. *Welles,*120 Pa. St. 75; *Gray* v. *Bank,* 10 N. Y. Supp. 5.

If it is a "sale on trial," it is said to be a sale on condition precedent—to buy if satisfied; that is, the title does not pass until the condition prescribed is fully performed, although the possession is delivered; being rather a bailment with an

option to buy than a sale.   If it is a "sale or return" it is
said to be a sale on condition subsequent; that is, the title
passes with the possession, but to be divested if the condition
is not performed, and the property returned.   "If the condition of the sale be that the property may be returned if it do
not prove 'satisfactory' to the buyer, or if the buyer is not
satisfied with it after trial, the condition must be fully performed; that is, the buyer must in fact be satisfied; if the
buyer expresses himself to be dissatisfied it matters not how
unreasonable or groundless his dissatisfaction may be; he
cannot be required to keep the property.   The buyer is not
obliged to be satisfied, although the property delivered con-
forms to his order.   But some of the cases require that the
dissatisfaction shall be real (not feigned) in order to relieve
the buyer from liability, although they recognize that the
dissatisfaction may be unreasonable without affecting the
right of rejection": Tiedeman on Sales, sec. 214; 1 Wharton
on Contracts, sec. 590; Benjamin on Sales, Bennett's 6th ed.,
sec. 595, et seq; American notes, 569; 2 Addison on Contracts, top p. 53, Abbott's ed., notes 1883

"Sales are not always absolute.   The acceptance is sometimes made conditional, and delivery given accordingly, and
then no complete execution of the contract can take place
until the condition is fulfilled.   Instances of this are found
in sales 'on trial' and the bargain of 'sale or return.'   It
is obvious that one may take a chattel on the understanding that he is to try it before the purchase shall take full
effect; or, again, upon a complete present bargain, with the
reservation of a right on the buyer's part to return it at his
option within some period; and the main object of [337] either
provision is to give the buyer a chance to test the thing, and
find it satisfactory, before he shall be finally bound to the
bargain.   But the concession thus made by the seller is not
coextensive in the two cases, for the one puts the test as a
condition precedent to divesting the seller fully of his property, while the other seems rather to carry property to the
buyer defeasible on the condition subsequent of a test which
proves unsatisfactory, though this application of a test must
be, after all, a matter often within the buyer's own breast,
and a sort of ill-defined ingredient in determining his satisfaction or dissatisfaction.

"The point toward which these decisions gravitate is
doubtless that of mutual intention, but, using the terms

above stated in no technical sense, since common-sense men will every day make bargains of either character without designating them by any particular names, we find the distinction quite marked, as regards the immediate passing of property, between sales 'on trial,' 'on approval,' and the like, and the bargain of sale or return. There is a buyer's option to be sure, but, as it has been fitly said, an option to purchase if the buyer likes is essentially different from an option to return a purchase if he should not like it. In the one case the property will not pass until the option is determined; in the other the property passes at once, subject to the right to rescind and return": 2 Schouler on Personal Property, 2d ed., sec. 310. In the one case the buyer is a bailee rather than a buyer in fact, the title not having passed; in the other the title has passed by the delivery of possession, subject to defeasance by the exercise of the option reserved to rescind and return. But on the point here involved each may, as a general rule, return peremptorily within the time without giving any reason, if he acts honestly—a question to be determined by the intent of the parties. It is a question of intention of the parties, and of the construction of the meaning of the conditional sale according to its terms, its subject matter, and the surrounding circumstances.

"In the one class of cases the right of decision is completely reserved to the promisor, without being liable to disclose reasons or account for his course; and a right to inquire into the grounds of his action and overhaul his determination [318] is absolutely excluded from the promisee and from all tribunals. It is sufficient for the result that he willed it. The law regards the parties as competent to contract in that manner, and, if the facts are sufficient to show that they did so, their stipulation is the law of the case": *Wood etc. Machine Co.* v. *Smith,* 50 Mich. 567; 45 Am. Rep. 57; although the dissatisfaction may appear to be "whimsical or unreasonable," if expressed in good faith: *Seeley* v. *Welles,* 120 Pa. St. 69.

In such cases it is generally for the buyer to decide for himself; to decide whether a refusal to accept is or is not reasonable; because he uses for that purpose a term which indicates the state of his own feelings, which it is hard for any one to know so well as himself, and he may have prescribed the term for the purpose of protecting the gratification of some whim or fancy of his own—at all events, to

protect himself from the necessity of rendering any reason
for his conduct. Such sales on trial are almost universally
so construed in the every-day affairs of life. But there may
be cases—have been cases—where, owing to some peculiarity
of subject matter or other peculiarity, such optional contract
may be construed as binding the buyer to decide on fair and
reasonable grounds, or to the extent of ascertaining whether
the dissatisfaction be real; that is, whether it in fact exists.
But generally his own feeling of dissatisfaction is enough,
and his own announcement of it is to be taken as true. So
that if the defendant took the binder on the condition that
if it did not give him satisfaction,—which the evidence certainly tends to prove, and which is the basis of the instruction given for defendant—then instruction No. 2 given for
plaintiff is erroneous; for there is nothing to show that defendant intended the question of his satisfaction or dissatisfaction to be canvassed, or his decision reviewed. Such a
doctrine would upset the whole law of sales on trial, and
breed infinite uncertainty and confusion.

Defendant testified, in substance, that after trial he was
dissatisfied with the binder; that it did not suit his farm;
his team could not handle it; it worried his horses; told
plaintiff's agent that he did not propose to worry his horses
[319] any more with it, and the agent replied, "You will have
to keep the machine and pay for it." " His objections to the
reaper may have been ill-founded; indeed, they may have
been in some sense unreasonable in the opinion of others;
yet, if they were made in good faith, he had a right, if his
testimony is believed, to reject it. If he wanted a machine
that was satisfactory to himself, not to other people, and
contracted in this form, upon what principle shall he be
bound to accept one that he expressly disapproved? What
the learned court said to the jury on this point was equivalent to saying that, although the reaper may have been
wholly unsatisfactory to the defendant, yet if the jury thought
he ought to have been satisfied, he was bound to take it;
whereas, if he the defendant's testimony is true, he was to
judge of the merits of the machine himself, not the bystanders or the jury; and, if he exercised his own judgment in good
faith in the refusal to accept it, he was certainly not bound
for the price": Clark, J., delivering the opinion in *Seeley* v.
Welles, 120 Pa. St. 69–75; see *Baltimore etc. R. R. Co.* v. *Bry-
don*, 65 Md. 198; 57 Am. Rep. 318, opinion of Alvey, C. J., on

motion for rehearing, and cases cited; *Gibson* v. *Cranage*, 39 Mich. 49; 33 Am. Rep. 351; *McCarren* v. *McNulty*, 7 Gray, 139; *Brown* v. *Foster*, 113 Mass. 136; 18 Am. Rep. 463; *Zaleski* v. *Clark*, 44 Conn. 218; 26 Am. Rep. 446; *McCormick Harvesting Machine Co.* v. *Chesrown*, 33 Minn. 32; *Silsby Mfg. Co.* v. *Town of Chico*, 24 Fed. Rep. 893; *Pierce* v. *Cooley*, 56 Mich. 552; *Goodrich* v. *Van Nortwick*, 43 Ill. 445; *Duplex etc. Boiler Co.* v. *Garden*, 101 N. Y. 387; 54 Am. Rep. 709, and notes.

Nor is the bad instruction given for plaintiff cured by the good one given for defendant; nor can we regard the one given for plaintiff as thereby plainly withdrawn: *McKelvey* v. *Chesapeake etc. Ry. Co.*, 35 W. Va. 500, 517. The general rule is that the court may cure errors in its instructions by withdrawing, explaining, or correcting them. When a material instruction is given that is erroneous, it should be effectively withdrawn: Elliott's Appellate Procedure, sec. 705; *Kirland* v. *State*, 43 Ind. 146; 13 Am. Rep. 386, and other cases cited in note to said section 705. "The court cannot, without fatal error, give contradictory instructions to the jury, [320] since that would impose upon them the duty of determining the law as well as the facts": Elliott's Appellate Procedure, sec. 705; *City of Logansport* v. *Dykeman*, 116 Ind. 15. Nor could the court have intended instruction No. 2 given for plaintiff as a modification or qualification of No. 2 afterward given for defendant, for that would not be readily comprehended, even if so intended; and, if intelligible to the jury, would make the last instruction erroneous as well as the first (see *Carrico* v. *West Virginia etc. Ry. Co.*, 35 W. Va. 389–404), as the error would be in the correction.

It is claimed on the part of plaintiff that the jury would be justified in finding that the contract was one of guaranty, as claimed by the plaintiff; and, if so, the court could not set the verdict aside. It is true, that the inquiry is: "What was the intention of the parties? And when that intention is ascertained the law will respect it. The question whether a sale of personal property is complete or only executory is to be determined from the intent of the parties as gathered from the contract, the nature and situation of the thing sold, and the circumstances surrounding the sale": *Morgan* v. *King*, 28 W. Va. 1, 14; 57 Am. Rep. 633.

That there was a guaranty or warranty, I think, is clearly shown, and that, so far as the cutting and binding were con-

cerned, and the lightness of draught on ground well suited to
the use of such binder, the machine was all that it was guaranteed to be. But it is past contradiction that there was
competent evidence tending to prove that the buyer who cultivated sideling and steep land was expressly reserving the
right to reject and send back the machine if, on trial, it
should not be satisfactory to him positively and generally
without saying in what respect. His mind was fixed im-
movably, that no chance should be left to force the article
upon him, unless he finally chose to take it; and this condition was added to meet this purpose, and, we may infer, was
the one thing which induced the defendant to take it: See
Wood etc. Machine Co. v. *Smith*, 50 Mich. 565; 45 Am. Rep.
57, cited above. Promising to do a thing only in case it
pleases himself may be no promise at all, yet it is what the
books call a " sale on trial," and may become by mere lapse
321 of time a binding promise; and I can see nothing unreasonable or unfair in such every day quasi contracts of sale.
It is the custom and habit of the people, especially with
regard to certain kinds of property. On the contrary, it would
be harsh, if not unreasonable, to compel such a buyer without his fault to keep a binder which could not be safely or
profitably used on such land as his, to which important
item the guaranty did in nowise relate; and it shows the
importance, as well as the motive, of such qualifying reservation. The agents who sold the machine say in their testimony on this head, "Of course, we can't satisfy every farm,
but we can the man."

It is also contended that the meaning and scope of the
term "satisfaction" as it was used in this contract have been
already fixed by this court in interpreting and construing it
in a like contract in the case of *Kinsley* v. *County Court*, 31
W. Va. 464. Here the contractor, Kinsley, entered into a written contract with the county court to make a road and build
a bridge according to certain specifications set out, and "to
the satisfaction of the county court of Monongalia county."
On demurrer the court held that the declaration was not
faulty in not alleging that the work was not done to the
satisfaction of the court; that "it means in that contract
that it must be done according to the specifications, and that
would be to the satisfaction of the court; that is, that the
county court was to accept it as completed, when it was
satisfied that the work had been done and the bridge com-

pleted according to the specifications"—a very reasonable construction, so far as necessary on general demurrer to notice it in the declaration, and very likely in any construction of the contract.

But such a contract is very different from a "sale on trial," with the absolute and unqualified option to return if not satisfactory. A man might sell his horse on the latter terms, as is often done; but they seldom or never knowingly build bridges on such terms. In the bridge case, the subject matter, the finality of the written contract at its inception, its reason and object, rebutted the idea of the reservation of the arbitrary power of refusal to accept and to pay; whereas the same things in part, and [322] the want of some of them, show such reservation in an ordinary sale on trial of a horse or machine to have been intended by the parties, which is at last the decisive test.

Counsel for plaintiff also contends that the instructions given for defendant were erroneous. The plaintiff could waive such error if it saw fit, and let the verdict in its favor stand; or, if dissatisfied, it could move the court to set it aside, and grant it a new trial. It elected to let it stand, and a judgment for plaintiff ought not to be affirmed on the ground that the court, at the instance of the defendant, gave an erroneous instruction to the jury: See *Murrell* v. *Johnson*, 1 Hen & M. 450.

But the point urged with greatest force on behalf of plaintiff is that the error, if any, in giving its instruction No. 2, was a harmless error; "that the facts and circumstances certainly warranted the verdict of the jury." It is held in many cases that when the verdict is clearly right on the evidence, errors in instructions may be treated as harmless. This is made so by statute in the state of Indiana: Ind. Rev. Stats. 1881, sec. 658. See a full and able discussion of the subject in Elliott's Appellate Procedure, c. 4, sec. 643; *Standard Oil Co.* v. *Bretz*, 98 Ind. 231, and other cases cited; 3 Graham and Waterman on New Trials, 862. There has been and is a tendency no doubt to advance and widen the doctrine of harmless error. It is due in part to the desire constantly pressing upon appellate tribunals to reach the substantial merits of the case in spite of errors that are for the occasion deemed immaterial or to have done no harm. Hence the rule has long been settled that when the court can clearly see affirmatively that the error has worked no harm to the party appealing it will be disregarded: *Gilmer* v. *Higley*, 110 U. S. 47; and the judgment ought not to be reversed on the ground that the court below admitted illegal evidence, or gave an erroneous instruction to the jury, unless it appears that some injury could possibly have resulted therefrom to the party appealing: *Preston* v. *Harvey*, 2 Hen. & M. 55; for the appellant must make it manifest from the record in some way that the ruling against him is wrong. But, that being done, it is taken to be to his prejudice until the contrary is made to appear, and it [323] must appear so clearly as to be beyond all fair ground of questioning that the error did not and could not, with any reasonable degree of likelihood, have prejudiced the party's rights: See *Deery* v. *Cray*, 5 Wall. 795, 807. This qualification of the general rule or this cautious and sparing application of it rests upon the ground that the court cannot instruct upon the weight of evidence or the credibility of witnesses, and upon the settled rule that, when there is any competent evidence fairly tending in some appreciable degree to prove his case, the party has the right to have the law applicable to such evidence correctly declared to the jury by the court. "Their superintendence in explaining and deciding legal questions is essential to the proper administration of justice, and ought to be exercised when either party requires their interference": *Picket* v. *Morris* (1796), 2 Wash. (Va.) 325–346; *Hopkins* v. *Richardson*, 9 Gratt. 486. Our own cases on the general subject are numerous and indicate a tendency sometimes to extend the rule, at others to adhere strictly to the limitation of the rule. See the following cases on the subject: *Hall* v. *Lyons*, 29 W. Va. 410–420; *State* v. *Douglass*, 28 W. Va. 298; *Mason* v. *Harper's Ferry Bridge Co.*, 20 W. Va. 224–239; *Clay* v. *Robinson*, 7 W. Va. 350, 358; *Beaty* v. *Baltimore etc. R. R. Co.*, 6 W. Va. 388–395; *Preston* v. *Harvey*, 2 Hen. & M. 55; *Pitman* v. *Breckenridge*, 3 Gratt. 127; *Wiley* v. *Givens*, 6 Gratt. 277; *Colvin* v. *Menefee*, 11 Gratt. 87; *Kincheloe* v. *Tracewells*, 11 Gratt. 587; *Rea* v. *Trotter*, 26 Gratt. 585–600; *Binns* v. *Waddill*, 32 Gratt. 588, 593.

In *McKelvey* v. *Chesapeake etc. Ry. Co.*, 35 W. Va. 500–517, it is said: "This court has repeatedly held that an erroneous instruction is presumed to prejudice a party, and will cause reversal, unless it clearly appears that the instruction could not have been prejudicial" to the exceptant. The court will not reverse on account of an erroneous instruction on an immaterial point: *Pitman* v. *Breckenridge* 3 Gratt. 127.

In *Davies* v. *Miller* (1797), 1 Call, 110, upon the trial of a writ of right, both parties claimed under John Miller, who died seised in 1742; the demandant claiming under Christopher, his grandson and heir at law; the tenants, under a *324* devise from Christopher, the son. After certain evidence was given on behalf of the demandant the tenants moved the court, without going into evidence on their part, to instruct the jury that for reasons apparent the said devise was void; and the court, being of that opinion, instructed accordingly. The jury found for the tenants, and demandant on bill of exceptions appealed. The court of appeals, though of opinion that the grounds of the ruling of the court below were wrong, and to that extent the language of the instruction given, yet, as it appeared by the demandant's own showing that Christopher, the grandson, had neither seisen, possession, nor title, so that demandant could derive none from him, the opinion and verdict were substantially right, and the court affirmed the judgment. "The instruction there bore upon the question which was decisive of the cause": *Wiley* v. *Givens* (1849), 6 Gratt. 277–285, opinion of Judge Allen. The instruction involved a question of law upon a state of facts about which there was no dispute.

It is said in the syllabus of *Wiley* v. *Givens*, 6 Gratt. 277 (made by the reporter): "When an appellate court is of opinion that an instruction given to the jury by the court below is erroneous the appellate court cannot undertake to determine that the verdict, notwithstanding the erroneous instruction, is right upon the evidence, and therefore to affirm the judgment; but the judgment must be reversed, and the cause remanded for a new trial." This is correct, as applied to the facts of this particular case; but Judge Allen did not mean to announce any such general proposition. On the contrary the implication is, that it would be otherwise, if the instruction were substantially right, and therefore could work no injury; but, in a case where the jury may have been warranted in their verdict by the whole evidence, yet where they may have been misled by the erroneous instructions in regard to so much of the case as the instruction referred to, the verdict must be set aside, and the cause sent back for a new trial.

This case is much stronger, for, if the jury followed plaintiff's instruction No. 2, given by the court, they were misled in regard to what, in our view, was the vital point [325] in the case; for there is at least evidence tending to show that the agents of plaintiff, by their conduct and declarations, had dispensed with and virtually waived the necessity, if any such existed, of defendant returning the machine to them at Cameron. But the case is reversed for the reason that instruction No. 2, given on motion of plaintiff, was erroneous; and no opinion is intended to be given on the merits other than is necessarily involved, for on a new trial the evidence even as to that point may be different.

Judgment reversed, verdict set aside, and a new trial awarded.

———

SALES—"SALE ON TRIAL," OR SALE OR RETURN—"SATISFACTION" OF PUR-CHASER.—An agreement of sale or return is upon a condition that the buyer may return the goods within a fixed or reasonable time at his option. They pass to the purchaser subject to his option to return them, and, if he fails to exercise his option within the proper time, the price of the goods may be recovered as upon an absolute sale: *House* v. *Beak,* 141 Ill. 290; 33 Am. St. Rep. 307, and note. The buyer of a harvesting-machine, upon condition that if it does not work to his "satisfaction" he may return it, has an absolute right to reject it and his reasons cannot be investigated: *Wood etc. Machine Co.* v. *Smith,* 50 Mich. 565; 45 Am. Rep. 57. The buyer in such cases must, however, act honestly, and in accordance with the reasonable expectations of the seller, as implied from the contract, its subject matter and surrounding circumstances. His dissatisfaction must be actual, not feigned; real, not merely pretended: See monographic note to *Gibson* v. *Cranage,* 33 Am. Rep. 354, discussing the rule of "satisfaction" as applied to contracts to do work. A sale is not complete, but remains executory, where any thing is yet to be done by either party before delivery, as, for example, to determine the price, quantity, or identity of the thing sold: *Foley* v. *Felrath,* 98 Ala. 176; 39 Am. St. Rep. 39, and note.

APPEAL—ERROR—INSTRUCTIONS.—Error without prejudice is no ground for a reversal of judgment: *Joseph* v. *Smith,* 39 Neb. 259; 42 Am. St. Rep. 571; *Frost* v. *Wolf,* 77 Tex. 455; 19 Am. St. Rep. 761. A judgment will not be reversed on an erroneous instruction, when it appears affirmatively that the defeated party was not injured by the error: *Gray* v. *Merriam,* 148 Ill. 179; 39 Am. St. Rep. 172. So, a failure to submit a material issue to the jury, and upon which there is no conflict of evidence, is not reversible error: *Pasewalk* v. *Bollman,* 29 Neb. 519; 26 Am. St. Rep. 399. But the giving of an instruction which is misleading as to the issue, inapplicable to the evidence, and calculated to prejudice the substantial rights of the losing party, entitles him to a reversal: *Perot* v. *Cooper,* 17 Col. 80; 31 Am. St. Rep. 258. And a refusal to correctly instruct the jury is reversible error: *Young* v. *Kellar,* 94 Mo. 581; 4 Am. St. Rep. 405.

CRUMLISH *v.* CENTRAL IMPROVEMENT COMPANY.

[38 WEST VIRGINIA, 390.]

PAYMENT, VOLUNTARY, BY STRANGER — RIGHT TO MAKE. — One under no obligation to pay the debt of another, cannot, without the latter's request, officiously pay his debt and charge him with it.

PAYMENT, VOLUNTARY, BY STRANGER—EFFECT OF, AS TO DEBTOR AND CREDITOR.—The payment of a debt by a stranger, if accepted as such by the creditor, discharges the debt so far as the creditor is concerned; and, if the debtor ratifies such payment, it also discharges the debt as to him, and he becomes liable to the stranger for money paid to his use.

PAYMENT, VOLUNTARY, BY STRANGER—RIGHT TO MAINTAIN ACTION.—A stranger who voluntarily, and without request, pays the debt of another cannot sustain an action at law against the latter if the debtor has in no way ratified such payment.

PAYMENT, VOLUNTARY, BY STRANGER—SUIT IN EQUITY.—If the voluntary payment of another's debt by a stranger is not ratified by the debtor, the one who pays it may sue in equity praying that, if the debtor does not ratify such payment, the debt may be enforced in his favor as its equitable assignee, or that, if the debtor does ratify it, the plaintiff may be repaid the amount paid for the use of the debtor.

PAYMENT, VOLUNTARY, BY STRANGER—ASSIGNMENT BY CREDITOR—PURCHASE OF DEBT.—A stranger who voluntarily pays the debt of another may take an assignment of it from the creditor and enforce the debt against the debtor. And, if, at the time payment is made, the creditor agrees to assign him the debt, though no assignment in writing is made, the stranger will be regarded in equity as the equitable assignee of the debt, and the transaction as a purchase of the debt.

JUDGMENT OF SISTER STATE—"FAITH AND CREDIT."—Under the constitution of the United States the judgment of a sister state must be accorded in this state the same faith and credit which it has in the state where it was rendered.

JUDGMENT OF ONE STATE—ENFORCEMENT OF, IN ANOTHER—JURISDICTION.— The court has power, where it is sought to enforce, in this state, the judgment of a sister state, to look into the record of the court rendering the judgment to see whether it had jurisdiction. If it had, the judgment is valid and binding here; but, if it had not, the judgment is void in this state.

JUDGMENT OF SISTER STATE, WHEN VOID.—The judgment of a court of a sister state without any service of process, and without appearance, is void in this state.

CONFLICT OF LAWS—LEX LOCI.—The obligation of a contract made and to be performed in another state must be determined by the laws of that state.

CORPORATIONS—LIABILITY OF, FOR SERVICES OF OFFICERS.—Corporations are not liable on a *quantum meruit* for services performed by their officers. There must be an express contract for compensation or there can be no recovery. Hence, the president of a private corporation, and the treasurer and secretary thereof, both being stockholders of the company, cannot, in the absence of a by-law or resolution authorizing compensation, recover on a *quantum meruit* for their official services. An executive officer, however, who is not a stockholder, may get compensation, for the law raises an implied promise that he shall be paid for his services.

Barton & Boyd, U. L. Boyce, W. M. Stewart, Jr., and
George Baylor, for the appellants.

F. P. Clark, for the appellees.

[892] BRANNON, J.   In a suit in equity in the circuit court
of Jefferson [893] county by H. H. Crumlish's administrators against the Central Improvement Company there was a
fund for payment of creditors of that company and then for
division among stockholders.   A commissioner was directed
to ascertain the debts having right to be paid out of the fund.
Various demands were presented before the commissioner for
audit as debts; and among them was a judgment in favor of
B. K. Jamison & Co. against the Central Improvement Company, an account in favor of R. D. Barclay against same company, and an account in favor of John P. Green against same,
which three demands having been disallowed by the commissioner and court, Jamison & Co. and Barclay and Green
united in this appeal.

THE JAMISON JUDGMENT.

A judgment was rendered in 1877 in the court of common
pleas, No. 3, of the county of Philadelphia, Pennsylvania, in
favor of B. K. Jamison & Co. against the Central Improvement Company for twenty-five thousand one hundred and
sixty-eight dollars and eighty-five cents and costs; and afterward, in 1890, upon a writ of *scire facias* upon this judgment another judgment was rendered by the same court for
twenty-six thousand three hundred and seventy-eight dollars
and eight cents and costs.   Jamison & Co. and U. L. Boyce
and the Fidelity Insurance Trust & Safe Deposit Company
each claimed the right to said judgment before the commissioner; and the Norfolk & Western Railway Company, being
a large owner of stock in the Central Improvement Company,
pleaded payment.

Jamison & Co. and Boyce having excepted to the report
and appealed, what we have to decide is whether they have
any cause to complain of the refusal to allow them the judgment.

Jamison & Co. by process on said first judgment had
attached two hundred and fifty thousand dollars of second
mortgage bonds and one hundred and seventy-five thousand
dollars of income bonds of the Shenandoah Valley Railroad
Company, held in the hands of a third party for the benefit of
the Central Improvement Company.   The Shenandoah Valley

Railroad Company desiring to make a contract for its completion and make another mortgage to [394] raise money to complete it, and desiring to cancel and retire the bonds so attached, Boyce, the vice-president of the Shenandoah Valley Railroad Company, opened negotiations with Jamison & Co. looking to securing those bonds, and Jamison & Co. expressed their willingness to take any step which would get their money advanced to the Shenandoah Valley Railroad Company represented by said judgment. Boyce made an arrangement with E. W Clark & Co., bankers—who were financial agents of the Shenandoah Valley Railroad Company and wished to obtain said bonds for cancellation out of the way of a new series—to furnish the money.

Thereupon, on July 12, 1879, Jamison & Co. and E. W. Clark & Co. made a written agreement providing that Jamison & Co. should transfer to Clark & Co. all their right, title, and interest in and to the bonds aforesaid, as also some others; that Jamison & Co. should proceed to get judgment upon their attachments, levy on said securities, and sell the same so as to pass title to the purchaser; that, if they should not be bid up to a figure above Jamison & Co's judgment, Jamison & Co. were to buy them at the sale, and transfer them to Clark & Co., that " the said E. W. Clark & Co. are to pay B. K. Jamison & Co. the amount of their judgment against the Central Improvement Company with interest and costs, the amount of said judgment being twenty-five thousand one hundred and sixty-eight dollars and eighty-five cents, with interest from July 10, 1877, the said payment to be made as follows: Ten thousand dollars in cash, and the balance in the notes of E. W. Clark & Co., drawn in equal amounts," etc.

The said bonds were sold to Jamison & Co. under said attachments at eleven thousand dollars, which was credited on the judgment, and Jamison & Co. transferred the bonds to Clark & Co., and received from them the ten thousand dollars cash and their notes in full payment of the amount of said judgment. By reason of said agreement the commissioner reports the judgment as paid "so far as claimant is concerned "; that is, Jamison & Co. The only object of Jamison & Co. being to get their money, and the language of the writing being, "The said E. W. Clark & Co. are to [395] pay [note the word " pay "] B. K. Jamison & Co., the amount of their judgment," these facts lead me to the conclusion that the parties contemplated it as a payment, so far as Jamison & Co. were concerned.

But this payment was made by a stranger, without request or ratification by the debtor, so far as appears. Does it satisfy the judgment? As it seems to me, the answer depends upon whether you mean as to the creditor or debtor. It remains a correct legal proposition to the present, that one man, who is under no obligation to pay the debt of another, cannot, without his request, officiously pay that other's debt and charge him with it. If the debtor ratify such payment the debt is discharged, and he becomes liable to the stranger for money paid to his use. If he refuse to ratify it he disclaims the payment and the debt stands unpaid as to him. In the one case the stranger would at law sue the debtor for money paid to his use; in the other enforce the debt in the creditor's name for his use. If his payment is not ratified he may go into equity praying that, if the debtor ratify it, said debtor may be decreed to repay him, or, if the debtor do not ratify the payment, that the debt be treated as unpaid as between him and the debtor, and that it be enforced in his favor as an equitable assignee: *Neely* v. *Jones*, 16 W. Va. 625; 37 Am. Rep. 794; *Moore* v. *Ligon*, 22 W. Va. 292; *Beard* v. *Arbuckle*, 19 W. Va. 135.

But how as to the creditor? When a stranger pays him the debt of a third party without the request of such third party, as in this case, can the creditor say the debt is yet unpaid and enforce it against the debtor, as is attempted to be done by Jamison & Co? Can he accept such payment and say, because it was made by a stranger, it is no payment? Is his acceptance not an estoppel by conduct *in pais*, as to him?

There has been a difference of opinion in this matter. The old English case of *Grymes* v. *Blofield*, Cro. Eliz. 541 (decided in Elizabeth's reign), is the parent of the cases holding that even the creditor accepting payment from a stranger may repudiate and still enforce his demand as unpaid. That case is said to have decided that a plea of accord and satisfaction by a stranger is not good, while [396] Rolle's Abridgment, 471, condition F. says it was decided just the other way. Denman, C. J., questioned its authority in *Thurman* v. *Wild*, 39 Eng. Com. L. 145. Opposite holding has been made in England in *Hawkshaw* v. *Rawlings*, 1 Strange, 24. Its authority is questioned at the close of the opinion by Creswell, J., in *Jones* v. *Broadhurst*, 67 Eng. Com. L. 197, as contrary to an ancient decision in 36 Henry VI. and against reason and justice. Parke, B., seemed to think it law in *Simpson* v. *Eggington*, 10 Ex. 845. It was followed in *Edgcombe* v. *Rodd*, 5 East, 294, and *Stark* v. *Thompson*, 3 T. B. Mon. 296. Lord Coke held the satisfaction good: Coke on Littleton, 206 *b*, 207 *a*; see 5 Robert's Practice (New), 884; 7 Robert's Practice (New), 548. The cases of *Goodwin* v. *Cremer*, 83 Eng. Com. L. 757, and *Kemp* v. *Balls*, 28 Eng. L. & Eq. 498, seem to hold that payment must be made by a third person as agent for and on account of debtor with his assent or ratification. In New York old cases held this doctrine: *Clow* v. *Borst*, 6 Johns. 37; *Bleakley* v. *White*, 4 Paige, 654. But later, in *Wellington* v. *Kelly*, 84 N. Y. 543, Andrews, J., said that the old cases were doubtful, but had not been overruled, but it was not necessary in that case to say whether it should longer be regarded as law, and the syllabus makes a query on the point. It was held in *Harrison* v. *Hicks*, 1 Port. 423, 27 Am. Dec. 638, that "payment of a debt, though made by one not a party to the contract, and though the assent of the debtor to the payment does not appear, is still the extinguishment of the demand." The opinion says that, as between the person paying and him for whose benefit it was paid, a question might arise whether it was voluntary, which would depend on circumstances of previous request or subsequent express or implied. This doctrine is sustained by *Martin* v. *Quinn*, 37 Cal. 55; *Gray* v. *Herman*, 75 Wis. 453; *Cain* v. *Bryant*, 12 Heisk. 45; *Leavitt* v. *Morrow*, 6 Ohio St. 71; 67 Am. Dec. 334; *Webster* v. *Wyser*, 1 Stew. 184; *Harvey* v. *Tama Co.*, 53 Iowa, 228. Bishop on Contracts, section 211, holds that, if payment "be accepted by creditor in discharge of debt, it has that effect": See 2 Wharton on Contracts, sec. 1008.

It seems utterly unjust and repugnant to reason, that a creditor accepting payment from a stranger of the third [397] person's debt should be allowed to maintain an action against the debtor pleading and thereby ratifying such payment, on the technical theory that he is a stranger to the contract. The creditor has himself, for this purpose, allowed him to make himself a quasi party, and consents to treat him so, so far as payment is concerned. To regard the debt paid, so far as he is concerned, is but to hold him to the result of his own act. Shall he collect the debt again? In that case can the stranger recover back? What matters it to the creditor who pays? As the supreme courts of Wisconsin and Ohio in cases above cited said, this doctrine is against common sense and justice. It does not at all infringe the rule that one cannot at law make another his debtor without request to allow such payment to satisfy the debt as to the creditor; and this court, while recognizing the rule that one cannot officiously pay the debt of another and sue him at law, unless he has ratified it by allowing the stranger to go into equity and get repayment, makes the payment in the eyes of a court of equity to operate to satisfy the creditor, and render the stranger a creditor of the debtor: *Neely* v. *Jones*, 16 W. Va. 625; 37 Am. Rep. 794. I know that in that case it is held that, "if a payment by a stranger is neither ratified nor authorized by the debtor it will not be held to be a discharge of the debt"; but, though this point is general, that was a case of the stranger seeking to make the debtor repay, and the case and opinion intended to lay down the rule at law only as between the stranger paying and the debtor, not as between the creditor and debtor. So I hold that, when Jamison & Co. received the money for this judgment, it operated as a discharge as to them.

But it is said that such payment, though a payment, is inoperative, because, after it was made, a writ of *scire facias* issued to revive the judgment, and a judgment was rendered thereon, that the plaintiffs recover their debt, and thus such payment amounts to nothing. This judgment is not, as with us, according to common law, a simple award of execution, but a judgment *quod recuperet*, as in an original action. Such a judgment would be void here by some authorities: 2 Barton's Law Practice, 1031; *Lavell* v. *McCurdy*, 77 Va. 763. I have entertained doubts whether it would be void, [898] as distinguished from voidable, though I have not fully examined the subject. But in Pennsylvania a *scire facias* is a substitute for an action of debt, and the judgment is properly *quod recuperet: Duff* v. *Wynkoop*, 74 Pa. St. 300; 1 Black on Judgments, sec. 499. We must, under the United States constitution, give it the same faith and credit here which it has there: *Black* v. *Smith*, 13 W. Va. 780; *Gilchrist* v. *West Virginia Oil Land Co.*, 21 W. Va. 115; 45 Am. Rep. 555; *Stewart* v. *Stewart*, 27 W. Va. 167. If it were a valid judgment it would nullify the payment above spoken of, on familiar principles. Such would be its effect in Pennsylvania, and it is to its effect there that we look: *Custer* v. *Detterer*, 3 Watts

& S. 28; *Mc Veagh* **v.** *Little*, 7 Pa. St. 279; *Potter* **v.** *Hartnett.*
148 Pa. St. 15; *Mills* v. *Duryee*, 7 Cranch, 481.

But while a judgment of a sister state, if valid, is given
here the same effect it has there, yet, consistently with this
rule, we can look into its record and see whether it had jurisdiction of the defendant; and, looking into the record of this
judgment, we find no service whatever of the *scire facias* personal or by return of *nihil*, or any appearance, and therefore
the judgment is void, as would be a judgment here for that
cause: *Gilchrist* v. *West Virginia Oil Land Co.*, 21 W. Va. 115;
45 Am. Rep. 555; *Stewart* v. *Stewart*, 27 W. Va. 167; *D'Arcy*
v. *Ketchum*, 11 How. 165; *Thompson* v. *Whitman*, 18 Wall.
457; *Knowles* v. *Gaslight etc. Co.*, 19 Wall. 58; *Guthrie* v.
Lowry, 84 Pa. St. 533; *Steel* v. *Smith*, 7 Watts & S. 447; *Noble*
v. *Thompson Oil Co.*, 79 Pa. St. 354; 21 Am. Rep. 66; Story
on the Constitution, sec. 1297; 1 Greenleaf on Evidence, sec.
548. This is a good reason for disallowing the judgment.

Argument is made that in Pennsylvania judgment upon
two returns of *nihil habet* is good, and as effective as a return
of *scire feci*. As I find no return whatever of the *scire facias*,
I have not so closely examined this question as otherwise I
would have done. There seems some authority for the proposition that two returns of *nihil* will sustain a judgment *in
personam: Compher* v. *Anawalt*, 2 Watts, 490. The cases
cited by counsel (*Warder* v. *Tainter*, 4 Watts, 274; *Taylor* v.
Young, 71 Pa. St. 85; *Colley* v. *Latimer*, 5 Serg. & R. 211;
Edmonson v. *Nichols*, 22 Pa. St. 74; *Chambers* v. *Carson*, 2
Whart. 9; *Hartman* v. *Ogborn*, 54 Pa. St. 120; 93 Am. Dec.
679; *Allison* v. *Rankin*, 7 Serg. & R. 269) were cases of *scire
facias* [399] *sur mortgage*, as to which the rule of judgment of
foreclosure upon the two *nihils* seems established in Pennsylvania. The practice of taking judgment on two returns of
nihil is properly perhaps confined to *scire facias* upon a mortgage. The case of *Compher* v. *Anawalt*, 2 Watts, 490, says,
in the opinion, that it is liable to abuse; and, I notice, in the
case of *Custer* **v.** *Detterer*, 3 Watts & S. 28 (decided only
seven years after the former case), the opinion says that, as
a judgment on *scire facias* is a new judgment, two returns of
nihil will not do. I should doubt as to personal judgments.
But, though such a judgment would be good in Pennsylvania,
it does not follow that it would be good here, for the supreme
court of Pennsylvania. in *Steel* v. *Smith*, 7 Watts & S. 447,
in an opinion delivered by the eminent Chief Justice Gibson

held, that a judgment of Louisiana on attachment of property and summons served on one of the joint owners, which by the Louisiana law was good as to all defendants, was a nullity in the courts of Pennsylvania as to parties not served. The only Pennsylvania statute to which I have access provides that service of process on a corporation shall be on its president or other chief officer, cashier, treasurer, secretary, or chief clerk. No service of any kind appears here. For this reason the judgment was properly disallowed.

No plea of *nul tiel* record was necessary. It is a chancery suit, and concerns the audit of debts on reference before a master; and, when the judgment creditors presented the judgment, adverse interests could contest it on any legal ground without formal plea. I remark that it was not this *scire facias* judgment which was considered on the appeal reported in *Fidelity Ins. etc. Co.* v. *Shenandoah Val. R. R. Co.,* 33 W. Va. 761, but the original one.

But let us suppose that the judgments were valid, and that, treating Clark & Co's payment simply as a payment, it would be cut off by the judgment so the payment could not now be pleaded. What then? Jamison & Co. are no longer its owners, but Clark & Co. are assignees of it, and they are not asking its allowance, but Jamison & Co. are claiming for their own use. When Clark & Co. paid it the law implied that Jamison & Co. would assign it to [400] them, and without assignment actual a court of equity treats them as its equitable owners. The case of *Neely* v. *Jones*, 16 W. Va. 625, 37 Am. Rep. 794, in point 4 of the syllabus clearly supports this position. Boyce's evidence, uncontradicted, is that Jamison & Co., in the agreement which they made with him, promised to assign the judgment to him, and their attorney did transmit him a copy of the judgment. Now, if this evidence is not forbidden from consideration by the execution of the writing between Clark & Co. and Jamison & Co., then either Clark & Co. or Boyce have an express agreement to assign, tantamount to an assignment, and, though no actual assignment be made, equity regards it as an equitable assignment; and this is the letter of point 5 in *Neely* v. *Jones*, 16 W. Va. 625, 37 Am. Rep. 794, and *Beard* v. *Arbuckle*, 19 W. Va. 135.

It may be with some force said that, as between Jamison & Co. and Boyce, the assignment should' go to Boyce, and then there would be no ground for saying that the oral agree-

ment to assign would be excluded by the writing.   In fact,
Jamison & Co. admit in their petition for the appeal that
they assigned it to Boyce; so this court ought not to decree it
to them.   Thus, I think, law excludes the allowance of this
judgment to Jamison & Co., and this conclusion accords with
the real justice of the case.   Jamison & Co. only wanted
the amount they advanced to the Central Improvement Company.   They got it.   They do not deny, but admit, they received all the company owed them, but they want now to
hold it as collateral for a merely personal loan to Boyce.

And now as to U. L. Boyce's claim to said Jamison & Co's
judgment.   He has no title to it, to his own use.   Any shadow
of interest that may be vested in him was for other use than
his own: 1. He negotiated for the acquirement of it from
Jamison & Co. for Clark & Co. as financial agents of the
Shenandoah Valley Railway Company, whose vice-president
Boyce was at that very time, and in whose service and interest he acted touching this judgment.   Clark & Co. paid for
the judgment, and took the contract in their name.   Boyce
explicitly says, as a witness, and in a letter to Doran, that he
was to get assignment of it, [401] and transfer it to the parties
furnishing the money, and that Clark & Co. furnished the
money.   Never was a resulting trust more plainly established
than that any show of technical right in Boyce was for the
use of Clark & Co.   And then further consider that Clark &
Co. were agents of the Shenandoah Valley Railroad Company
and Boyce its vice-president.   And that he was acting for it
he does not deny, but admits; and a receipt to his company
for hotel bill on the trip to acquire the judgment confirms it.

Thus we conclude that neither Jamison & Co. nor Boyce
have right to this judgment.   It is urged by counsel that the
Shenandoah Valley Railroad Company, in a certain answer,
stated that a balance was due on this judgment, treating it
thus as not paid.   If it belonged to the Fidelity Company,
under its mortgage, could the Shenandoah Valley railroad
Company, by this admission, prejudice the right of that company?   It could not.   But, if the Shenandoah Valley Railroad Company owned it, it could say, with entire consistency
with the fact that Clark & Co. had paid it as regards Jamison & Co., that a balance was due on it from the Central
Improvement Company, as it had never paid it.   As assignee
it could say that the Central Improvement Company yet
owed a balance.

BARCLAY'S AND GREEN'S DEMANDS.

Barclay filed before the commissioner, and asked payment out of the fund, an account of ten thousand dollars, for services for four years and one month as president of the Central Improvement Company, and Green filed an account for six thousand two hundred and fifty dollars for two and a half years' service as treasurer and secretary. Both these gentlemen were stockholders and directors of the company. The commissioner rejected the claims.

The Central Improvement Company is a Pennsylvania corporation, having its habitat and chief office there, and there the services were performed and were to be paid for, if at all; and, if any contract were implied by law to pay compensation for services of those officers of the corporation, it would be a Pennsylvania contract. Hence the law of that state operates upon the case specially. We must therefore see whether the law of Pennsylvania would raise [402] an implied contract to pay for such services: *Klinck* v. *Price*, 4 W. Va. 4; 6 Am. Rep. 268; *Stevens* v. *Brown*, 20 W. Va. 450; *Hefflebower* v. *Detrick*, 27 W. Va. 16. There was no express contract to pay for such services, and, if there can be any recovery therefor, it must be on the theory that the law raises an implied promise to pay for the services.

I think the case of *Kilpatrick* v. *Penrose etc. Bridge Co.*, 49 Pa. St. 118, 88 Am. Dec. 497, uncontrollably decides against the allowance of these accounts. It holds that "corporations are not liable on a *quantum meruit* for services performed by their officers. There must be an express contract for compensation, or there can be no recovery." In that case Sersill claimed for service as president and Kilpatrick as treasurer, as in this case, and the court held that they could not recover. The court said:

"The salary or compensation of corporate officers is usually fixed by a by-law or by a resolution either of the directors or stockholders, but, where no salary has been fixed, none can be recovered. Corporate offices are usually filled by the chief promoters of the corporation, whose interests in the stock or in other incidental advantages is supposed to be a motive for executing the duties of the office without compensation, and this presumption prevails until overcome by an express prearrangement of salary. Hence, we held in *Loan Assn.* v. *Stonemetz*, 29 Pa. St. 534, as a general principle, that a director of a corporation, elected to serve without compensation, could not recover in an action against the company for services rendered in that capacity, though a subsequent resolution of the board, agreeing to pay him for past services, was shown. . . . . And the rule is just as applicable to presidents and treasurers and other officers as to directors. . . . . It is well the law is so. Corporate officers have ample opportunities to adjust and fix their compensation before they render service, and no great mischief is likely to result from compelling them to do so. But if, on the other hand, actions are to be maintained by corporate officers for services, which, however faithful and valuable, were not rendered on the foot of an express contract, there would be no limitation to corporate liabilities, and stockholders would be devoured by officers."

403 In the later case of *Martindale* v. *Wilson-Cass Co.*, 134 Pa. St. 348, 19 Am. St. Rep. 706, it is held: "The general rule on the subject of compensation to the directors of a private corporation is that they are not entitled to compensation for official services unless it is provided for in the corporate charter or by-laws. In the absence of such provision, a director or president of such corporation cannot recover pay for official services, when no agreement for compensation preceded them, no presumption of such agreement arising from their performance."

A by-law of the Central Improvement Company provided that the directors "shall have power to appoint all other officers or agents of the company, and fix the compensation and define the duties of all their officers or agents," but the directors never fixed any compensation. This was a mere power, given to be exercised or not, as the directors might choose, and does not itself give compensation; and the very fact that the directors, having this power, never exercised it, negatives the idea that any compensation was intended: *In re Bolt & Iron Co.*, 14 Ont. 211.

So it is clear that, under the Pennsylvania law, these officers can recover nothing.

Though not necessary to go further, my examination has led me to the conclusion that the decisions in Pennsylvania reflect the true rule applicable nearly everywhere, in denying pay without express provision or contract, not only to the president, but a treasurer or secretary, when stockholders or directors. The authorities have led my mind to the conclusion that the law raises no implied promise to pay compensation to directors, president, or vice-president of a private corporation, in the absence of provision in by-law or order of the directors.   They are trustees charged with the funds, and cannot recover on a *quantum meruit: Gridley* **&** *Lafayette etc. R. R. Co.*, 71 Ill. 200; *Cheeney* v. *Lafayette etc. R. R. Co.*, 68 Ill. 570; 18 Am. Rep. 584; *Santa Clara Min. Assn.* v. *Meredith*, 49 Md. 389; 33 Am. Rep. 264; *Citizens' Nat. Bank* v. *Elliott*, 55 Iowa, 104; 39 Am. Rep. 167; *Sawyer* v. *Pawner's Bank*, 6 Allen, 207; *New York etc. R. R. Co.* v. *Ketchum*, 27 Conn. 180; *Ogden* v. *Murray*, 39 N. Y. 202; 1 Beach on Private Corporations, sec. 208.

And if the treasurer, secretary, or other executive officer be a stockholder or director, no such promise is raised by [404] law in his favor; but, if not, then the law does raise such promise, and presume that pay was intended from the fact of appointment, and he may get compensation: *Smith* v. *Long Island R. R. Co.*, 102 N. Y. 190; *Holder* v. *Lafayette etc. R. R. Co.*, 71 Ill. 106, 109; 22 Am. Rep. 89; *Cheeney* v. *Lafayette etc. R. R. Co.*, 68 Ill. 570; 18 Am. Rep. 584; 1 Beach on Private Corporations, sec. 200; note to *Grundy* v. *Pine Hill Coal Co.*, 23 Am. & Eng. Corp. Cas. 616.   Of course, I do not here speak of the mere employees of corporations, they being entitled to compensation.

Therefore, so much of the decree of March 2, 1891, as rejects the claim of B. K. Jamison & Co. and U. L. Boyce to said judgment, and the said accounts of R. D. Barclay and John P. Green, is affirmed.

VOLUNTARY PAYMENT, EFFECT OF.—Payment of a debt by one who is not a party to the contract, although made without the assent of the debtor, extinguishes the debt: *Harrison* v. *Hicks*, 1 Port. 423; 27 Am. Dec. 638. But money voluntarily paid cannot be recovered in an action for money had and received: *Kenneth* v. *South Carolina etc. R. R. Co.*, 15 Rich. 284; 98 Am. Dec. 382.   Money voluntarily paid for the use of another does not impose a liability on such other to repay unless the payment was made at his request: *Kenan* v. *Holloway*, 16 Ala. 53; 50 Am. Dec. 162.

JUDGMENT OF SISTER STATE—ATTACKING HERE—"FAITH AND CREDIT." A judgment rendered in another state, if sued upon here, must be given the same force and effect as it is entitled to in the state wherein it is entered: *Dow* v. *Blake*, 148 Ill. 76; 39 Am. St. Rep. 156, and note, showing that a judgment of a sister state obtained in an action wherein the defendant has been served with process, or appeared, is conclusive, and that an action may be maintained thereon.   But the "full faith and credit," demanded by section 1, article 4, of the federal constitution, which provides that full faith and credit shall be given in each state to the public acts, records, and judicial proceedings of every other state, is only that faith and credit which the judicial proceedings had in the other state in and of themselves require. It does not demand that a judgment rendered in a court of one state, without the jurisdiction of the person, shall be recognized by the courts of another state as valid, or that a judgment rendered by a court which has jurisdiction of the person, but which is in no way responsive to the issues tendered by the pleadings, and is rendered in the actual absence of the defendant, must be recognized as valid in the courts of any other state: See monographic note to *Falls* v. *Wright*, 29 Am. St. Rep. 80, where the subject is further discussed. Hence, the judgment of a sister state rendered without service of process or appearance is void when called in question here: *Foshier* v. *Narver*, 24 Or. 441; 41 Am. St. Rep. 874, and note; *St. Sure* v. *Lindsfelt*, 82 Wis. 346; 33 Am. St. Rep. 50.

CONFLICT OF LAWS.—The validity of a contract should be determined by the laws of the state in which it was made and was to be performed: *Forepaugh* v. *Delaware etc. R. R. Co.*, 128 Pa. St. 217; 15 Am. St. Rep. 672; *Miller* v. *Wilson*, 146 Ill. 523; 37 Am. St. Rep. 186.

CORPORATIONS—SALARY OF OFFICERS.—The director of a corporation is not entitled to compensation for his services as a director, in the absence of any agreement in advance that he shall receive it; but for attending to matters outside the duties of his office he is entitled to claim compensation upon a *quantum meruit*, although his compensation has not been fixed by the corporation prior to the performance of the services: *Wood* v. *Lost Lake Mfg. Co.*, 23 Or. 20; 37 Am. St. Rep. 651, and note.

STATE *v.* ANDREWS.

[39 WEST VIRGINIA, 35.]

EVIDENCE.—THE DECLARATIONS MADE BY THE GRANTOR in a deed of trust at the time of its execution are always admissible in evidence as part of the *res gestæ*.

DAMAGES—MEASURE OF, FOR BREACH OF CONTRACT.—One injured by a breach of contract is entitled to recover all his damages, including gains prevented as well as losses sustained, if they are certain, and such as might naturally be expected to follow the breach.

DAMAGES—LOSS OF PROFITS AS, FOR BREACH OF CONTRACT—EVIDENCE.— If a person is engaged under contract in doing a very profitable piece of scraper work, and is using his teams and utensils in removing the dirt at a given sum per cubic yard, when his teams and utensils are wrongfully seized and sold under attachment, whereby he is prevented from performing his contract, the profit of the contract of which he has been thus deprived is a proper element of damage in an action of debt upon the attachment bond, where such profit is easily and certainly ascertainable.

Campbell & Holt, for the appellant.

Marcum & Peyton and Simms & Enslow, for the appellees.

86 ENGLISH, J. This was an action of debt upon an attachment bond brought in the circuit court of Wayne county in

the name of the state of West Virginia, which sued at the
relation and for the use of C. D. Mundy, against W. W.
Andrews, Isaac Bates, Chapman Fry, and B. J. Prichard.
The defendants demurred to the declaration, which demurrer
was overruled, and thereupon the defendants pleaded conditions performed and conditions not broken and *non damnifi-
catus,* which pleas were replied to generally.   The case was
submitted to a jury, who found a verdict for the defendants.

The facts which gave rise to said action were as follows:
On the sixteenth day of January, 1891, W. W. Andrews and
Isaac Bates, Jr., doing business under the firm name of
Andrews, Bates & Co., brought an action of assumpsit against
J. A. Mundy, Jr., and C. D. Mundy, partners, doing [37] business as J. A. Mundy, Jr., & Co., in the circuit court of Wayne
county, and sued out an order of attachment against the estate
of said defendants sufficient to pay two thousand six hundred
and twenty-three dollars and seventy-four cents and costs of
suit, on the ground that said defendants were nonresidents of
the state of West Virginia.   The defendants filed a plea in
abatement to said attachment, and a trial thereon was had
before a jury, which resulted in a verdict in favor of the defendants, and the circuit court entered a judgment thereon abating
said order of attachment.   From this judgment an appeal
was taken to this court, which resulted in an affirmance of
the same.   The bond given to authorize the taking possession of the property in said attachment proceeding being
defective, the plaintiffs were allowed to give a new bond under
the statute with Chapman Fry and B. J. Prichard as sureties, and, upon this new attachment bond, said C. D. Mundy,
claiming to be the owner of the property attached and sold,
brought the action of debt first above mentioned.

On the trial of said last-named action the plaintiffs introduced the records in said action of assumpsit with the
mandate of this court affirming the judgment abating said
attachment, together with the order directing the sale of the
attached property pending the writ of error, which property
consists of mules and wagons and harness, with proof of the
ownership of the property attached and of damages claimed
by reason of the seizure and sale of the property.   Among
other things, the plaintiff offered to prove that at the time
his property was attached and seized, he was engaged under
contract in a very profitable piece of scraper work, estimated
to contain twenty thousand cubic yards, and that but for the

seizure of his property he would have earned large profits therefrom; but the court excluded such evidence from the jury. The defendants sought to prove that the estate so attached and sold belonged to J. A. Mundy, Jr., and the said C. D. Mundy, jointly, and not to the said C. D. Mundy alone, and, for this purpose, they introduced a trust deed given after the institution of said attachment suit to certain of their creditors in Catlettsburg, Kentucky, which purported to have been executed in the name of [38] J. A. Mundy, Jr., & Co., and the plaintiff offered to show that C. D. Mundy had nothing to do with the preparation of said trust deed, and that, when the same was presented to him in that form for execution, he refused to execute it, because neither J. A. Mundy, Jr., nor the firm of Mundy & Co., had any thing to do with the property, but that it was his individually, and the trust deed should be executed in his own name, and that not until considerable parleying did he give his assent to execute it in this form; but the court refused to allow these facts to be proved, and the plaintiff excepted.

Thereupon the defendants moved the court to give to the jury the following instructions:

"The court instructs the jury that, if they believe from the evidence that the property levied on by the sheriff of the county under the attachment issued in the case of Andrews, Bates & Co. against J. A. Mundy, Jr., & Co., was the property of J. A. Mundy, Jr., & Co., then the jury cannot assess any damages in the case for the plaintiff, for the said levy and for the sale of said property under said attachment.

"The court instructs the jury that, if they believe from the evidence in this case that J. A. Mundy, Jr., and the plaintiff, C. D. Mundy, were partners operating and doing business together under the firm name of J. A. Mundy, Jr., & Co., and that said J. A. Mundy, Jr., and the said C. D. Mundy were brothers, and, as such partners, they were largely indebted, and insolvent, at the time of suing out of the attachment by Andrews, Bates & Co. against them, then the jury are required to scrutinize carefully any and all transactions between them in relation to the disposition of the partnership effects by them, and especially should the jury carefully weigh and consider all dealings between the said Mundys in relation to the partnership property, in so far as such dealings and transactions seek or tend to place such property beyond the reach of the creditors of said firm."

To the giving of said instructions, and each of them, the plaintiff objected, which objections were overruled by the court; and thereupon the court gave said instructions to [39] the jury, as above set out. The case was submitted to the jury, and a verdict was rendered for the defendants. A motion was made to set aside the verdict and grant the plaintiff a new trial, which motion was overruled, and a judgment rendered for the defendants, and from this judgment this writ of error was obtained.

The first error assigned is that the court erred in refusing to allow the plaintiff to prove his objection and protest to executing the trust deed aforesaid in the form presented, in order to rebut the inference as to the joint ownership of the property conveyed. Did the court err in excluding this testimony? The deed of trust which was executed after the levy of the attachment, as above stated, was signed: "J. A. Mundy, Jr., & Co. [L. s.]   C. D. Mundy [L. s.]   J. A. Mundy, Jr. [L. s.]   By C. D. Mundy [L. s.]" This deed of trust was executed after the alleged sale to C. D. Mundy of the property levied upon, and included said property. This deed of trust was offered in evidence by the defendant, with the view of showing that, subsequent to the time of the levy of said attachment, and previous to the institution of this suit, the property levied upon had been granted and conveyed to a trustee by J. A. Mundy, Jr., & Co. In support of the effort the defense was making to show that the property levied upon was the property of J. A. Mundy, Jr., & Co., and not the property of the plaintiff, C. D. Mundy, and, in order to rebut the presumption or inference that the jury might draw from that fact, the plaintiff sought to show that the said trust deed was prepared and presented to him for execution in that form, and that he objected to signing and executing it because the partnership did not own the property, and insisted on executing it in his own name, because the property belonged to him alone, and that he did not sign it until after considerable persuasion and argument.

The plaintiff wished to show this fact, not with a view of adding to, or in any manner detracting from, the effect of the deed, but merely for the purpose of showing what he claimed at the time the deed was executed as a part of the *res gestæ*. He sought to show his declarations accompanying the act, and this, we think, he should have been allowed to do.

⁴⁰ In the case of *Kenney* v. *Phillipy*, 91 Ind. 511, it was held that "the statements of the grantor in a deed which is in evidence, made at the time of its execution, are always admissible in evidence as part of the *res gestæ*."

So, also, in the case of *Bushnell* v. *Wood*, 85 Ill. 88, it was held that declarations made by the mortgager at the time of executing a chattel mortgage are a part of the *res gestæ*, and admissible in evidence.

The law is stated in the case of *McLeod* v. *Ginther*, 80 Ky. 403, as follows: "The general rule is that all declarations made at the same time the main fact under consideration takes place, and which are so connected with it as to illustrate its character, are admissible as original evidence, being what is termed a part of the *res gestæ*; in other words, a part of the thing done."

So, also, in our state, in the case of *Lawrence* v. *Du Bois*, 16 W. Va. 443, sixth point of syllabus, it was held that "the declarations of an agent, made while he is performing the act authorized by the principal, which qualify and characterize the act, are admissible in evidence against the principal as part of the *res gestæ*"; and, in point 4 of the syllabus in the same case, that "a deed absolute on its face, if shown to have been originally a mortgage by parol proof and the surrounding circumstances, may be declared a mortgage," etc.

This ruling of the court was manifestly prejudicial to the plaintiff in error, for the reason that, if the property levied upon under the attachment belonged to the firm, and not to C. D. Mundy, then C. D. Mundy could not sustain the action in his individual name.

The next assignment of error relied upon is that the court erred to the prejudice of the plaintiff in error by excluding from the jury the proof offered as to the profits secured by contract, and which would have been earned, had the property not been seized, by carrying on the scraper work at which he was engaged. The question raised by this assignment is as to what may be taken into consideration in estimating the damage sustained by the plaintiff. This question was passed upon in this court in the case of *Hare* v. *Parkersburg*, 24 W. Va. 554. The syllabus in that case reads as follows:

⁴¹ "In a suit for a breach of contract the damages should not be based on a conjectural estimate of the profits which might have been made out of the contract, but, if the con-

tract is for the delivery of a certain quantity of gravel, the jury may legitimately ascertain the damage sustained by a breach of contract, whereby the plaintiff was prevented from delivering the gravel by an improper cancellation of the contract by the defendant, by subtracting from the price to be paid for the gravel when delivered the cost to the defendant of delivering this quantity of gravel; and, in determining this, the jury may properly consider what had been the actual cost of delivering a like quantity of gravel by the defendant to the plaintiff."

Now, the testimony in this case discloses the fact that the plaintiff in error had sixteen mule teams engaged in the work of removing dirt at sixteen and one-fifth cents per cubic yard. It had been ascertained by actual experiment how much each team could remove per day, the costs of feed and driver had also been ascertained in like manner, and, deducting these costs, it is found that each team was earning six dollars and sixty-six cents per day, and the sixteen teams, in the aggregate, one hundred and six dollars and fifty-six cents per day. This amount the plaintiff was realizing under his contract each day, and, while the contract was not actually rescinded, yet the mules and harness and scrapers were seized and taken from him, and he was thus deprived of the entire benefit of his contract, and the result was precisely as if it had been rescinded. By subtracting the cost of removing a cubic yard of dirt from the amount he was to receive for removing the same, as was done with reference to the gravel in the case of *Hare* v. *Parkersburg*, 24 W. Va. 554, the damage can be easily and properly ascertained.

Now, in the case under consideration, the rule for ascertaining the damages to which the plaintiff was entitled is precisely the same as if the plaintiff was prevented from enjoying the benefits of his contract by reason of the fact that the party with whom he contracted refused without cause to allow him to proceed with the work in accordance with the terms of his contract; and the rule in ascertaining [42] such damages is laid down by this court in the case of *James* v. *Adams*, 8 W. Va. 569, ninth point of syllabus, as follows:

"The general rule seems to be that the party injured by a breach of contract is entitled to recover all his damages, including gains prevented as well as losses sustained, provided they are certain, and such as might naturally be expected to follow the breach. It is only uncertain and con-

tingent profits, therefore, which the law excludes, not such
as, being the immediate and necessary result of the breach
of contract may be fairly supposed to have entered into the
contemplation of the parties when they made it, and are
capable of being definitely ascertained by reference to established market rates, or like other definite criteria, according
to the case": Citing *Griffin* v. *Colver*, 16 N. Y. 489; 69 Am.
Dec. 718.

In 2 Greenleaf on Evidence, fifteenth edition, page 262,
note *b*, it is said: "The rule has not been uniform or very
clearly settled as to the right of a party to claim a loss of
profits as a part of the damages for breach of a special contract. But we think there is a distinction by which all questions of this sort can be easily tested. If the profits are such
as would have accrued and grown out of the contract itself,
as the direct and immediate results of its fulfillment, then
they would form a just and proper item of damages to be
recovered against the delinquent party upon a breach of
the agreement," etc., referring to numerous authorities, and,
among others, citing the case of *Masterton* v. *Brooklyn*, 7 Hill
(N. Y.), 61, 42 Am. Dec. 38, where it is held that, "where one
party to an executory contract puts an end to it by refusing
to fulfill, the other party is entitled to an equivalent in
damages for the gains or profits which he would have realized from performance."

In 2 Sutherland on Damages, second edition, section 512,
the author says, in speaking of damages recoverable under
attachment bonds: "In the absence of statutes authorizing
the recovery of exemplary damages the obligor and his sureties are not liable for any thing beyond such actual damages
as are the direct result of the attachment. The question of
malice is not an issue. If an attachment has been obtained
without just cause, the terms of the bond secure to the
defendant all [43] costs and damages that he has sustained in
consequence thereof. The condition is satisfied, and its terms
substantially complied with, by awarding him damages adequate to the injury to the property attached, and the loss
arising from the deprivation of its use, together with the costs
and expenses incurred. . . . . The actual damages have generally been stated to be the injury to the plaintiff by being
deprived of the use of its property, or its loss, destruction,
or deterioration, together with the costs and expenses incurred
by him in the defense of the suit. . . . . The expense which

the owner of horses incurs by hiring others to do the work of those taken from him, in order that he may perform a contract previously entered into, may be recovered, and the recovery may be for such sum as the use of the property was worth to him, though that is in excess of the market value": Citing *State* v. *McKeon*, 25 Mo. App. 667.

In the second point of the syllabus in that case it is held that "counsel fees and other expenses incurred in obtaining a dissolution of an attachment, together with the value of the use of the attached property during its detention, where such property, consisting of work animals and utensils, is restored to the defendant, may be recovered in an action on the bond."

In that case Thompson, judge, delivering the opinion of the court, said: "The next assignment of error is that the court erred in admitting evidence in behalf of the plaintiff as to the value of the services of the animals taken by the sheriff under the writ of attachment during the time they were in the possession of the officer, and also in instructing the jury as to the measure of damages in suits on attachment bonds, as set forth in the following instruction, given at the request of the plaintiff: 'The jury are instructed that the defendants are liable for all costs the relator, John W. Burton, incurred in defending the attachment suit brought by Thomas W. McKeon against him, including all costs of his own attendance and such reasonable attorneys' fees in defending said attachment, and also for all damages occasioned to him by loss of time, and all delays and expenses the direct result of said attachment.' [44] The evidence objected to was evidence to the effect that, at the time of the seizure of property under the attachment, which property consisted of nine head of mules and horses and four or five wagons, shown by the testimony to be what was called four teams and a half—that is, four double teams and one single team—the defendant in the attachment was engaged with his teams in the performance of certain contracts for the building of levees, and was obliged, in order to perform his contracts, to hire other teams to take the place of those seized by the sheriff, at an expense of three dollars and fifty cents per day for each full team. . . . . The inquiry thus is whether the expense to which the defendant in the attachment suit was put by reason of having to hire other animals to replace those which were seized under the writ is to be regarded as natural and proximate damages resulting from the suing out of the attachment. We are of opinion that it is to be so regarded."

In the case at bar the plaintiff in error had a contract, the value of which, while in possession of his teams and utensils, was easily ascertainable. With them he had the ability to remove so many cubic yards of dirt each day, and the value of the work was fixed by his contract; without them he was unable, so far as appears from the record, to proceed with his contract. The loss of the profit which he could have made by the use of his teams and harness and utensils, was the direct result of the seizure of said property under said attachment. The condition of the attachment bond provided that the plaintiffs in the attachment should well and truly pay all costs and damages which might be awarded against them, or either of them, or be sustained by any person by reason of the suing out of the said attachment, and should pay to any claimant of any property seized or sold under or by virtue of said attachment all damages which he might recover in consequence of such seizure or sale; and, in looking for the damage sustained by the plaintiff in error by reason of the seizure and sale of the said property under the attachment, the fact that the profitable undertaking in which the plaintiff in error was engaged was brought to an end, and he was deprived of all [45] the benefits secured to him by his contract at once challenges our attention, and must be considered and regarded as one of the principal elements of damage.

Our conclusion is that the court erred in excluding from the jury the evidence offered as to the profits secured by said contract. As to loss occasioned by seizure of property under attachment, see *Hoge* v. *Norton*, 22 Kan. 374, in which it appeared that a herd of cattle was wrongfully seized under attachment, and placed on an inferior range, and it was held that the gain prevented by the remnant of the cattle could be shown and considered as an element of damage.

As to the first instruction asked for and given at the instance of the defendants, over the objection of the plaintiff, in which the court instructed the jury that, "if they believed from the evidence that the property levied upon by the sheriff under the attachment issued in the case of Andrews, Bates & Co. against J. A. Mundy, Jr., & Co. was the property of J. A. Mundy, Jr., & Co., then the jury cannot assess any damages in the case for the plaintiff for the said levy, and for the sale

of said property under said attachment"—we think it was
not proper, in view of the fact that the court had excluded
the testimony offered by the plaintiff as to his declarations
and remonstrances as part of the *res gestæ* at the time said
deed of trust was executed, and the testimony of C. D. Mundy
shows that he was a subcontractor under Mason, Hoge &
Co., and he was recognized as the contractor by the engineers
on the work in Logan county; that his brother was at one
time interested in the work in Logan county, but not at the
time this attachment was levied on the work in Wayne county.
It appears that the mules were purchased by C. D. Mundy
from his brother; that the contracts, both in Logan and
Wayne, were made by C. D. Mundy; and, whether the purchase of the mules was fraudulent or not as to creditors, it
was good and valid as between the parties, and I see no good
reason why C. D. Mundy could not sustain the action; and,
for these reasons, the first instruction should have been
rejected.

As to the second instruction it also should have been
rejected [46] for the reason that the transfer of property between the Mundy brothers was not prejudicial to the rights
of the creditors of J. A. Mundy, Jr., & Co. It was as much
liable in the hands of C. D. Mundy as it was before the transfer, and, as the dealings between them had no tendency to
put the property beyond the reach of the creditors of the
firm, there was no evidence in the cause to justify the instruction, or on which it could be properly predicated, and the
instruction would have a tendency to mislead the jury.

For these reasons, my conclusion is that the judgment
complained of must be reversed, the verdict set aside, a new
trial awarded, and the case remanded, at the costs of the
defendants in error.

DECLARATIONS OF GRANTOR.—Declarations made by the grantor to the
grantee after the execution of a deed of trust but before its acceptance by
the grantee, are evidence to alter or contradict the trust: *Drum* v. *Simpson*,
6 Binn. 478; 6 Am. Dec. 490.

DAMAGES—MEASURE OF, FOR BREACH OF CONTRACT—GENERAL RULE—
LOSS OF PROFITS PREVENTED BY ATTACHMENT.—A party injured by a
breach of contract is entitled to recover all his damages, including gains
prevented as well as losses sustained; but "profits," to be recoverable, must
be definite and of an ascertainable nature; they must be such as would have
naturally resulted from the contract, and such as were within the contemplation of the parties when the contract was made. Profits which can be
made reasonably certain by evidence, and profits which would have been

made are recoverable as damages for a breach of the contract: See monographic note to *Griffin v. Colver*, 69 Am. Dec. 725; note to *Crater v. Binninger*, 97 Am. Dec. 746; *Hamilton v. McPherson*, 28 N. Y. 72; 84 Am. Dec. 330, and note; note to *Passinger v. Thorburn*, 90 Am. Dec. 760; note to *Barker v. Mann*, 96 Am. Dec. 378; monographic note to *Sitton v. Macdonald*, 60 Am. Rep. 488; *Hitchcock v. Supreme Tent*, 43 Am. St. Rep. 423; note to *Martin v. Deetz*, 41 Am. St. Rep. 163; monographic note to *McKinnon v. McEwan*, 42 Am. Rep. 461. One who violates his contract with another is liable for all the direct and proximate damages which result from such violation: *Paducah Lumber Co. v. Paducah Water etc. Co.*, 89 Ky. 340; 25 Am. St. Rep. 536, and note. Loss of profits may be recovered as damages for the nonperformance of a contract if the loss results directly from the breach of the contract itself: Note to *Brownell v. Chapman*, 35 Am. St. Rep. 330. The defendant in an attachment wrongfully sued out is entitled to recover such damages as result to him from being dispossessed of his property during the time the levy was in force: See note to *Empire Mill Co. v. Lovell*, 14 Am. St. Rep. 274. As to whether loss of profits or of business may be considered in an action for damages for a wrongful attachment, the cases are not harmonious: See *Pollock v. Gantt*, 69 Ala. 373; 44 Am. Rep. 519, note to *Sitton v. Macdonald*, 60 Am. Rep. 489.

WATTS v. NORFOLK & WESTERN RAILWAY CO.

[39 WEST VIRGINIA, 196.]

DAMAGES—GRANT OF RIGHT OF WAY—INJURY TO RESIDUE.—If one grants a right of way over his land to a railroad company, all damages to the remainder of the land arising from construction of the road, past, present, and future, are released, and neither he nor his subsequent alienee can recover therefor against the company.

DAMAGES—GRANT OF RIGHT OF WAY—INJURY TO PRIVATE FERRY.—If one grants a right of way over his land to a railroad company, damage to a private ferry thereon, as incident to or consequential upon the proper construction of the road or use of the right of way, is covered by the grant, and cannot be the subject of an action by the landowner or his subsequent alienee against the company.

DAMAGES—GRANT OF RIGHT OF WAY—INJURY TO PUBLIC ROAD OR PRIVATE WAY.—The grant of a right of way over one's land to a railroad company will not justify the destruction of a public highway in the construction of its road. Hence, such destruction is an actionable injury. But in the case of a private way it is different, and no action lies, because such injury is presumed to have been considered when the grant was made.

DAMAGES—GRANT OF RIGHT OF WAY—BLASTING OF ROCK.—After one has granted a right of way over his land to a railroad company, injury to a dwelling-house upon the residue caused by the blasting of rock, where proper precautions have been taken, is not actionable; but the leaving of rock and other material deposited on such residue by the blasting would be actionable, unless the debris is removed within a reasonable time.

DAMAGES—GRANT OF RIGHT OF WAY—NUISANCE.—If one has granted a
right of way over his land to a railroad company, a "fill," or "bar,"
made in a stream by blasting and throwing into it rock and other refuse
matter in the work of constructing the road which is not necessary for
the construction and maintenance of the railroad, and which injures a
mill situated on the residue of the land, is an injury in the nature of a
nuisance, and a ground of action against the company.

DAMAGES—FULL RECOVERY IN SINGLE ACTION—NUISANCE—DIFFERENT
ACTIONS.—If the cause of an injury is in its nature permanent, and a
recovery for such injury would confer a license on the defendant to
continue it, the entire damages may be recovered in a single action;
but where the cause of injury is in the nature of a nuisance, and not
permanent in character, but such that it may be supposed that the
defendant would remove rather than suffer at once entire damages,
which it might inflict if permanent, then the entire damages, so as to
include future damages, cannot be recovered in a single action, but
actions may be maintained, from time to time, as long as the cause of
the injury continues.

DAMAGES—NOMINAL AND COMPENSATORY.—If the plaintiff shows an actionable wrong by the defendant he is entitled, as of course, to nominal
damages; but, to recover compensatory damages, he must in some way,
and by evidence, furnish to the jury a basis from which they can ascertain and fix the amount of damages, as they cannot act arbitrarily and
by mere conjecture in making such assessment.

DAMAGES—DAM IN FLOATABLE STREAM—MILL—PUBLIC NUISANCE.—If a
dam is erected, under authority of the county court, in a floatable
stream, and for the purpose of furnishing power to operate a mill useful to the public, such dam is not a public nuisance, though it is without sluices and floodgates, and obstructs navigation. Hence, a railroad
company which inflicts injury upon the mill by any unlawful act in the
construction of its road cannot justify its wrong upon the plea that such
dam is a public nuisance.

RIPARIAN OWNER—RIGHT TO ERECT DAM AND MILL.—A riparian proprietor
may erect a dam and mill under his right of dominion over his own
property without an order of court, even though the stream is floatable.

PUBLIC NUISANCE—ABATEMENT OF, BY PRIVATE ACT.—There is a grave difference of opinion as to the abatement of a purely public nuisance by
the mere act of the party; but all the authorities agree that, where the
right of abatement by private act does exist, it must go no further than
to remove that which works the nuisance, doing injury no further than
is necessary to accomplish that end.

A NEW TRIAL WILL NOT BE ALLOWED upon the ground that the jury disregarded an instruction erroneous in law.

Campbell & Holt, for the appellant.

Marcum & Peyton, for the appellee.

198 BRANNON, P. In an action of trespass on the case by
Harrison Watts against the Norfolk & Western Railroad
Company in the circuit court of Wayne county, Watts recov-
ered judgment for one thousand and seventy-four dollars,

and the company brought the case to this court by writ of
error.

In his declaration Watts complains of several wrongs done
him by the company. The first wrong complained of is that
the railroad company built a stone wall below his milldam,
extending into and above the same, and filled in on both
sides of said wall with earth, stones, and other substances,
whereby the current of Twelve Pole creek was diverted,
impeded, and obstructed, and caused to run against the
plaintiff's gristmill and sawmill, and that caused the bank
on which the same are built to be cut away and undermined,
thereby diminishing and destroying the capacity of the water-
wheel to operate and propel the machinery of said mills, and
their capacity to grind grain and saw lumber, and injuring
his land. Let us take up, first, this ground of action.

[199] By deed dated March 20, 1890, Chapman Fry conveyed
to the West Virginia & Ironton Railroad Company a strip of
land for the construction of its railroad, which strip was
transferred to the Norfolk & Western Railroad Company, being a strip out of land owned by Fry; and afterward, on May
5, 1891, Fry conveyed to the plaintiff, Watts, the said land,
reserving and excepting the right of way conveyed to said
railroad company by said deed of March 20, 1890. Thus the
company had the older and better right to the land conveyed
to it for right of way, with all rights and privileges going
with such right under the law. It had the right, as owner
thereof, to use it as it pleased for the purpose of the construction of its road, provided it used the same in a prudent,
reasonable way, considering the nature of its use, and not in
an improper, negligent way, inflicting unnecessary injury on
others. It had the right, as against Fry, to build a wall, to
stay and support its roadway, and protect it against the
inroads of the stream. Suppose this wall, if built in a
proper manner, did entail permanent injury upon Fry by the
diversion of the stream's current against his mills, lessening
their capacity, or injuring the banks, he can recover no damage on that score.

If, instead of acquiring the right of way land by purchase,
the company had caused it to be condemned for its use, the
compensation to Fry would include, not simply pay for the
land actually taken, but damages to the residue of the tract.
I will not enter upon any elaborate argument to prove that
such injuries or damages as are complained of as resulting

from said wall would be considered and taken into the assessment of damages upon an inquisition in a condemnation proceeding under chapter 42, section 14, of the code of 1891, they being such as might be reasonably anticipated from the use to which the land was to be devoted, and naturally, directly, and proximately resulting from such use of the land. I will refer to the following authorities touching the subject of what elements are to be considered in fixing compensation, not for the land taken, but for damages to the residue: *Shenandoah etc. R. R. Co.* v.·*Shepherd*, 26 W. Va. 672; 2 Wood's Railway Law, secs. 258, 259. The sum is to cover past, present, and prospective damages to such residue [200] that are the natural, necessary, or reasonable incident to the work: 3 Sedgwick on Damages, 164. From such damages to the residue, but not from compensation for the land actually taken, may be deducted peculiar benefits to be derived in respect to such residue from the work; not benefits of a general character, shared by the owner of the residue in common with other owners.

Authorities bearing on the question of what benefits may be so deducted are the following: *James River etc. Co* v. *Turner,* 9 Leigh, 313; *Muire* v. *Falconer,* 10 Gratt. 18; *Mitchell* v. *Thornton,* 21 Gratt. 164; *Railroad Co.* v. *Tyree,* 7 W. Va. 693; *Railroad Co.* v. *Foreman,* 24 W. Va. 662. Injury, though unforeseen, is yet presumed to have been considered in the assessment: 2 Wood's Railway Law, 1034; *Aldrich* v. *Cheshire etc. R. R. Co.*, 21 N. H. 359; 53 Am. Dec. 212.

As Fry could not recover for injury from such wall, neither can Watts, as he purchased from Fry later, and in law, and by the reservation in his deed, in fact subject to the railroad company's right. The fact that the company claims not under condemnation, but under purchase or grant, does not alter the case, and entitle Watts to recovery for injury from the wall, because a grant of right of way is a waiver of all such damages as are assessable under an inquisition, as, in such case, if the grantor did not intend to waive damages he should have provided against injury: Opinion in *Hortsman* v. *Covington etc. R. R. Co.*, 18 B. Mon. 222; Mills on Eminent Domain, sec. 110; *Norris* v. *Vermont Cent. R. R. Co.*, 28 Vt. 99; *Babcock* v. *Western R. R. Co.*, 9 Met. 553; 43 Am. Dec. 411; 1 Wood's Railway Law, 698; *Hatch* v. *Vermont Cent. R. R. Co.*, 25 Vt. 49, 69; 2 Redfield on Railways, 23; Pierce on Railroads, 133; *Conwell* v. *Springfield etc. R. R. Co.*, 81

Ill. 232; *Boothby* v. *Androscoggin etc. R. R. Co.*, 51 Me. 318. Though, in such case, there be damage, it is *damnum absque injuria*—damage without violation of a right: *Rood* v. *New York etc. R. R. Co.*, 18 Barb. 80.

The case of *Chicago etc. Ry. Co.* v. *Smith*, 111 Ill. 363, is very apt in this case. It held on common-law principles that, " when any thing is granted, all the means to attain it, and all the fruits and effects, are granted· also by presumption of law, and will pass inclusive together with the thing by the grant of the thing itself, without the words ' with its [201] appurtenances,' and any like words"; that when the grant is for a certain use, neither the grantor nor one claiming under him can object to such use, and recover damages resulting therefrom; that, "where a person conveys a right of way over his land, it will be conclusively presumed that all the damages to the balance of the land, past, present, and future, were included in the consideration paid him for his conveyance, the same as an assessment of damages on a condemnation would be presumed to embrace."

It was a grant of a right of way to a railroad. What can be the difference for present purposes between a grant and condemnation? The one is a voluntary grant, the other is a legislative grant. They both equally divest the owner of his rights. The voluntary alienation should go at least as far as the compulsory one, and be favorably construed in favor of the alienee. In reason the above proposition must be true, since it would be unreasonable to say that a free and voluntary grant of right of way would not confer immunity against damage incident to its proper use, while a compulsory condemnation would do so.

If this wall had been built in a negligent and improper way, imposing injury upon the residue of the land, which, in the exercise of due and proper care, could have been avoided, it would be different; for neither a right of way conferred by grant, nor one conferred by condemnation, will give exemption from damages consequential upon the improper or negligent exercise of the right and not from the fair, proper, and reasonable exercise of it, for the reason that neither in making such grant nor in the assessment upon an inquisition are damages contemplated or included that are to be solely attributed to such misuse of the right. The grant is a defense as to all acts done within it, not outside it: *Southside R. R. Co.* v. *Daniel*, 20 Gratt. 344, 375; Lewis on Eminent Domain, sec. 482;

Mills on Eminent Domain, sec. 220; 2 Wood's Railway Law, 1004; 3 Sedgwick on Damages, sec. 1100.

Authorities that for negligent construction the party is liable outside the statute by common-law action, unprotected by the condemnation, are found everywhere; and, as Mr. Sedgwick says, *ubi supra*, the rule is universal. There is no evidence that such wall was not in itself a prudent [202] construction in building the railroad, or that it was not properly constructed, or that any injury it worked was avoidable. No damage could be recovered on account of it.

The second wrong imputed by the declaration to the defendant is that a private ferry over the milldam in Twelve Pole creek had long existed, used by the patrons of the mill in passing to and from the mill with grain, and its products when ground, and by the construction of the roadbed the approach to it on one side of the creek had been destroyed. The principles above stated apply to this private ferry. Damage to it, as incident to or consequential upon the use of the right of way, was covered by its grant. No recovery could be had for the destruction of this ferry.

These principles were not observed in the instructions given in the case, at least as to the wall. In instruction No. 8, given as one of three in lieu of certain ones asked by plaintiff which the court rejected, the court tells the jury that if the defendant in building its road " committed any of the acts set out in the declaration," whereby the channel of the creek was diverted from its natural course, and thereby caused the water to flood the water-wheels running the machinery of the mills, diminishing their power and usefulness, they must find for the plaintiff. This included the wall as a factor in the work of injury in the very wide and general statement of the hypothesis of the instruction, and, without regard to the question whether it was properly or improperly constructed under the grant of right of way, seeming to brand it as an unlawful structure imperatively calling for damages.

Instruction 10 is that, if the defendant committed "any other act" complained of in the declaration, injuring the plaintiff's property, it was liable. What other acts are referred to? Instruction 9 spoke of injuries to the ferry and to the road below spoken of, and perhaps " other act " refers to acts other than those injuring the ferry and road; but it is indefinite, and not plainly intelligible to a jury. But, give it that construction, and it is wrong, for the additional reason that it includes all other acts, including the wall, propounding unreservedly the proposition of the [203] absolute liability of the company for any act injuring the property.

A third wrong complained of is that a public road crossed said creek just below the mills, affording a crossing to the public, and enabling patrons of the mills to reach them, and that in constructing its road the company had destroyed this road and crossing. Neither a condemnation by law nor grant of right of way will justify destruction of a public highway in the construction of a railroad. The statute on the subject (Code, c. 54, sec. 50, cl. 6) provides that, when the work interferes with a highway, it shall be restored to its former condition: *State* v. *Monongahela etc. R. R. Co.*, 37 W. Va. 108.

As the law thus contemplates that the company will provide for the continued usefulness of the highway, of course, at the time of condemnation, it is not anticipated that a highway will be destroyed or left materially injured in the work, and nothing is or can be assessed for damages thereto, except the proceeding be to condemn it as a highway under chapter 54, section 50, clause 6, and therefore the condemnation gives no protection against indictment or civil action for its destruction or injury beyond that contemplated by law to a highway: *Gear* v. *C. C. & D. R. R. Co.*, 43 Iowa, 83. Neither does one who grants right of way contemplate that a highway will be destroyed. In fact, the party whose land is granted or taken does not own the highway. He may own the mere land or soil, but not the way. The public owns that. He has only a citizen's interest in it. By no reasonable argument can it be maintained that he intended to waive his right in the highway.

But in the case of a private way it is different. Injury resulting to it from the proper, reasonable, and lawful use of the land granted or condemned is covered by the assessment or grant, unless provided against in the grant. By express provision of the code of 1891, chapter 42, section 14, no damages can be assessed for private crossings in condemnation of land for railroad use; but the company must construct and forever maintain them. This is a prudent provision, since without it likely the landowner would have no right to cross, as the assessment of the compensation would, [204] legally speaking, include the injury resulting from inconvenient access or nonaccess to the divided parts: 2 Wood's

Railway Law, 1045; Lewis on Eminent Domain, sec. 496; 3 Sedgwick on Damages, sec. 165; *Mason* v. *Kennebec etc. R. R. Co.*, 31 Me. 215.

It seems that where there is no such provision, and where the condemnation vests in the appellant only an easement, leaving title in the owner, he may cross by means of crossings made by himself at proper times, and in proper places, so as not to hinder the operation of the railroad; but where the absolute title goes out of the owner and vests in the applicant he cannot cross. This distinction is plainly drawn in the two cases of *Housatonic R. R. Co.* v. *Waterbury*, 23 Conn. 109, and *Kansas Cent. Ry. Co.* v. *Allen*, 22 Kan. 285, 31 Am. Rep. 190, cited in 2 Wood's Railway Law, 903. The grantor must provide for crossings in his grant. So, where one conveys to a railroad company the absolute estate in a strip of land, why does it not confer absolute dominion, and what gives him right to exercise a privilege that may seriously detract from the use for which it was required? In this state the entire estate vests in land condemned for railroad purposes: Code 1891, c. 42, sec. 18.

The grant in this case was of the fee in the land. Therefore, if the way be private, there can be no recovery of damages for it, as the owner cannot, on his own land, have a private way, independent of his right to the land; and the way goes with the land by condemnation or grant, and injury to it is presumed to have been considered: 2 Wood's Railway Law, sec. 261, p. 1067; *Clark* v. *Boston etc. R. R. Co.*, 24 N. H. 114. There was no evidence that said road was public, other than mere long user by the public, which is insufficient to establish it as a public road: *Talbott* v. *King*, 32 W. Va. 6.

The court gave instruction No. 9, saying that, if the defendant constructed its road upon the location set out in the deed from Fry, then it was not liable for damage to the road or ferry, unless the road and ferry were public, and, if public, it would be liable. This instruction is faulty, first, because it submitted a question of fact not in issue—that is, whether the ferry was a public ferry, and, if so, directed the jury to award damages for injury to it, [205] when there was no pretense in the declaration that it was a public ferry; and faulty, secondly, because it submitted the question of fact whether the road was public, and, if so, directed the jury to award damages for its injury, when there was no evidence to establish it as a public road save mere user.

A fourth point of complaint in the declaration is that the defendant company, by blasting rock, and throwing them through and into the dwelling-house and mills, did damage thereto. Is this a ground of recovery? It is not. The distinguished Chief Justice Shaw discussed this subject, saying: "An authority to construct any public work carries with it authority to use the appropriate means. Authority to make a railway is an authority to reduce the line of the road to a level, and for that purpose to make cuts, as well through ledges of rocks as through banks of earth. In a remote and detached place, where due precaution can be taken to prevent danger to persons, blasting by gunpowder is a reasonable and appropriate mode of executing such a work, and, if due precautions are taken to prevent unnecessary damage, is a justifiable mode. It follows that the necessary damage occasioned thereby to a dwelling-house or other building, which cannot be removed out of the way of such danger, is one of the natural and unavoidable consequences of executing the work, and within the provisions of the statute. Of course, this reasoning will not apply to damage occasioned by carelessness or negligence in executing the work. Such careless or negligent act would be a tort, for which an action at law would lie against him who commits or him who commands it. But where all due precautions are taken, and damage is still necessarily done to fixed property, it is alike within the letter and spirit of the statute, and the county commissioners have a right to assess the damages": *Dodge* v. *County Commrs.,* 3 Met. 380. The damage to buildings, being simply incidental to the construction of the work contemplated in the condemnation or grant of land for right of way, is presumed to have entered into consideration, and recovery is barred thereby, whether in fact regarded or not. The same doctrine is maintained in 2 Wood's Railway Law, sec. 260, pp. 1058, 1066; *Brown* v. *Providence etc. R. R. Co.,* 5 Gray, 35; *Whitehouse* v. *Androscoggin R. R. Co.,* 52 Me. 208; *Sabin* v. *Vermont Cent. R. R. Co.,* 25 Vt. 363; *Dearborn* v. *Boston etc. R. R. Co.,* 24 N. H. 179.

This doctrine is based on the principle above stated, that, in condemning, entire damages are allowed—a sum to cover all damages, past, present, and prospective, that are the natural, necessary, or reasonable incidents of the work; but not such as may arise from negligent or otherwise improper construction or use: 3 Sedgwick on Damages, sec. 1164. To avoid misconstruction I will say that above I speak of damage to lands of an owner, part of whose lands have been condemned by legal process to the public use, not to one whose buildings are injured by blasting, and none of whose land has been condemned; for, in the latter case, there is no inquisition to protect the party doing the injury, and he is liable for such injury: *Hay* v. *Cohoes Co.*, 2 N. Y. 159; 51 Am. Dec. 279; *St. Peter* v. *Denison*, 58 N. Y. 416; 17 Am. Rep. 258; *Carman* v. *Steubenville etc. R. R. Co.*, 4 Ohio St. 399; 3 Sutherland on Damages, sec. 1051.

Another point of complaint in the declaration is that rock and other matter blasted into the creek and there remaining, and rock and other material thrown over the bank, narrowing the creek channel, did injury by diverting the water against the mill and opposite bank, lessening the power of the water-wheels, and destroying the bed of said road and the crossing of the creek, and a part of said road. Now, rock blown upon the remaining land of Fry in the creek or elsewhere could not be suffered to remain, though the original casting of them there was lawful, but they must be removed within a reasonable time: *Sabin* v. *Vermont Cent. R. R. Co.*, 25 Vt. 363; 2 Rorer on Railroads, 784; 2 Wood's Railway Law, sec. 260, p. 1066. So any debris not fairly necessary for the construction and maintenance of the road, inflicting injury, would be actionable, and would sustain this action. It would be negligent, improper exercise of the right granted. Under the record I see no other ground of recovery; but I think that ground does sustain the action to the extent of recovery for damage attributable to such rock and other debris not necessary as a part of permanent structure.

The evidence of the defendant, by its engineer, makes it **207** clear that the "fill," or "bar," as called in the evidence, made up of rock and other material, was not at all necessary for the support or benefit of the railroad, and could not be justified under its authority to build the road if it has injured the plaintiff. But, as to the injury from such debris, we think there is error as to instructions.

The defendant asked, but was refused, instructions 1, 2 and 4, which announced the position that, if there was a liability on that score, recovery could be had for only such damage as resulted from such debris prior to the commencement of the suit. The position taken by counsel for defendant before the trial court, as evinced by those instructions, was that any injury flowing from rock, earth, or other material cast into the creek, and left there, not necessary in the construction of the railroad, was not permanent in nature, but remediable with the removal of the same, and that in this one suit there could not be a recovery of damages for all time to come as for a lasting and permanent injury; and this position was, I think, correct. The doctrine is exemplified in cases of our own.

Take the case of *Hargreaves* v. *Kimberly*, 26 W. Va. 787; 53 Am. Rep. 121. The syllabus lays down the law conformably to authority generally that, "where the cause of the injury is in its nature permanent, and a recovery for such injury would confer a license on the defendant to continue the cause, the entire damage may be recovered in a single action; but where the cause of the injury is in the nature of a nuisance, and not permanent in character, but of such a character that it may be supposed that the defendant would remove it, rather than suffer at once the entire damage which it might inflict if permanent, then the entire damage cannot be recovered in a single action, but actions may be maintained from time to time as long as the cause of the injury continues": See *Smith* v. *Point Pleasant etc. R. R. Co.*, 23 W. Va. 451; *McKenzie* v. *Ohio River R. R. Co.*, 27 W. Va. 306.

To recover for permanent injury the declaration must show an intent to claim for permanent injury (cases just cited), and here the declaration, we may say, so claims as to injury wrought by such debris; but, the nature of the cause of injury being impermanent, the character of the declaration [208] could not entitle the plaintiff to recover for future injury, and thus take away from the defendant the right to remove the source of injury upon a judicial determination that his action was indefensible, and burden him at once and irrevocably for damage in future, not yet accrued. The case of *Hargreaves* v. *Kimberly*, 26 W. Va. 787, 53 Am. Rep. 121, will support this position. All the acts imputed to the defendant, defensible and indefensible, are not permanent causes of injury in nature, and most certainly the debris not part of or necessary to the stability of the railway are not.

The two following instructions were refused, and, I think, ought to have been given. While no one questions that a jury must judge of the amount of damages, yet to give any thing more than merely nominal damages—to give compensatory damages—the jury cannot act arbitrarily, but must have data according to the nature of the subject, so as to have some measure or standard to go by. There is some basis for estimation, perhaps, as to the sawmill, but as to the mill there is only evidence to show a certain per cent of diminution of capacity, and what the usual earnings were is not shown, and there is no showing of loss of earnings, and no evidence of how much more time was consumed in grinding for custom from loss of capacity, or what its cost, or how much was the loss incident to the diminution of the mill's capacity. Not even opinion evidence or estimate appears. The jury would have to conjecture in fixing a sum.

"No. 5. The jury are further instructed that the burden is upon the plaintiff to prove to them the damages, if any, which he has suffered by reason of the alleged wrongful act of defendant, and wherein and what such damages are; and, if the plaintiff has failed to prove any damages, although he proves the wrongful act by defendant whereby his water-power was diminished, the jury can give only nominal damages."

"No. 6. The jury are further instructed by the court that if the plaintiff would recover for loss of profits in operating said mill consequent upon the alleged wrongful act of defendants, it is his duty to prove wherein, when, and what profit he lost, and the amount thereof, as near as may be; [209] and it is not sufficient for him to prove simply that his water-power has been diminished, thus lessening the amount of work done in a given time, but he must go further, and show that custom and work were tendered and refused because of capacity to meet the demand, or that it took him so much longer to accommodate the custom so offered and prove with some degree of certainty or approximation the extra time so required and cost expended."

The court, on defendant's motion, gave the following instruction: "No. 7. If the jury believe from the evidence that plaintiff's milldam extends from shore to shore in Twelve Pole creek, and is of an average height of six feet; that the same is without sluices or floodgates, and is an obstruction to the passage of fish and the navigation of said creek, and that the said creek is a navigable stream—then they are instructed that said milldam is a public nuisance, and the plaintiff cannot recover for any injury thereto caused by the defendant."

This mill was erected under an inquisition taken in 1839. The dam was nearly all washed away by freshet, and rebuilt between 1870 and 1875, without leave to rebuild, and again washed out in 1884, and rebuilt under leave of county court. It is contended that, as this dam was without sluice or flood-gate, it was an obstruction to navigation and the passage of fish, and that the county court was without jurisdiction to authorize its original erection, or the reparation of the dam; and, if so, there is no authority to justify the existence of the mill, and it is a nuisance, and no injury done to it by the defendant is actionable. The county court had jurisdiction to grant leave to erect mills. It would be going far to say that if it authorized a mill in a proper proceeding which would obstruct navigation or fish, or omitted due provision against such obstruction, its action would be utterly void, and confer no authority.

But the mill act existing when this mill was allowed (Code 1819, c. 235), required the inquisition to report whether a mansion house would be overflowed, and whether, and in what degree, the passage of fish and navigation would be obstructed, and whether the health of the neighborhood would be annoyed; and, if a mansion should be [210] over-flowed, or health of the neighborhood annoyed, there was a positive prohibition against granting authority, but not so as to hindrance of navigation or passage of fish, but, as to that, the matter was left to the discretion of the court, and, if the leave was given, it only commanded that the party be put under condition for preventing obstruction of navigation or passage of fish, if the dam would be an obstruction. Would you say that leave to erect would be void for that cause after the court exercised its discretion and judgment? I think not. But, if you could possibly say so in such case, you cannot in this instance, for the reason that the inquisition found and reported that the mill would not obstruct navigation or pas-sage of fish. Surely the order of the court would not be void, if afterward it was found that the inquisition did not speak the truth.

This view is expressly held in *Crenshaw* v. *Slate River Co.*, 6 Rand. 245, laying down that, as the law required the inquisition to report whether the passage of fish or naviga-tion would be obstructed by the proposed mill, if it reported that the mill would not obstruct them, "then leave is granted to erect the mill, without any condition as to navigation";

and that "such a grant, under such precautionary proceedings, is a perfect one, and vests in the grantee all the public rights to the stream, or so much thereof as is necessary to the full enjoyment of the mill erected under such order."

Thus it seems that the public right of navigation was subordinate to the right of the millowner. Mills were of prime necessity, and, before the use of steam, water-power was indispensable; but now, since the wide use of steam-power has been adopted, and use of streams for floatage of timber has become more productive of reward, the old water gristmill has been almost relegated to the past, and is denominated a nuisance.

But the mill involved in this case had a lawful title under lawful grant in the start, and unto this day that title is preserved by not merely its original force, but by the letter of Code, chapter 44, section 24, providing that any dam or other thing in a watercourse obstructing navigation or [211] passage of fish shall be deemed a nuisance, "unless it be to work a mill, manufactory, or other machine or engine useful to the public, and is or has been allowed by law or order of court." Can it be that important mills and manufactories, built under due process of law, vesting title and property rights in their owners, can be assailed by any one in collateral proceedings, even if they could be assailed by the state itself or a citizen personally interested by a direct proceeding?

In *Crenshaw* v. *Slate River Co.*, 6 Rand. 245, it was held that even the legislature could not authorize the abatement of such a dam under the constitution. I am expressing no opinion as to the right of the state, or even of persons peculiarly interested in navigation, by proper proceedings under reservations as to navigation in the complicated statute law of the present and former years, to remove such dams; but I speak of the right of a railroad company, or of anybody not so interested, in this collateral way, to damage a millowner's right, and justify under the plea that the mill is a nuisance.

A reference to the opinion by Judge Green in *Gaston* v. *Mace*, 33 W. Va. 14, 25 Am. St. Rep. 848, will show that the millowner's right is fully recognized as coexisting along with the right of floatage, not as a nuisance, but a lawful right under the law. It is there recognized as a right resident in the riparian proprietor. This dam was rebuilt by leave of court, and the leave was not void. At any rate, it could not justify the defendant for a wrong: *Smart* v. *Commonwealth*, 27 Gratt. 950. And, suppose there were no order of court to build the dam, I think with Judge Bouldin in *Field* v. *Brown*, 24 Gratt. 93, that there may be a dam in a stream without order of court by grant or prescription. And a riparian proprietor may erect a dam and mill under his right of dominion over his own property without order of court, even though the stream be floatable. So spoke Judge Green in *Gaston* v. *Mace*, 33 W. Va. 25, 26; 25 Am. St. Rep. 848. The owner may be punishable for taking toll, and his right may be subject to the right of the state or of persons personally interested in navigation, but not as to others. Even one exercising [212] the right of floatage cannot willfully or negligently injure such a dam.

But, for argument, say that this dam is a public nuisance. What then? Suppose the state or an individual having a personal interest in the use of the stream for floatage (for the evidence shows it to be a floatable stream, under *Gaston* v. *Mace*, 33 W. Va. 14, 25 Am. St. Rep. 848,) suppose they could by judicial proceedings abate it, it does not follow that the defendant could injure the plaintiff's property, and claim immunity because the dam is a nuisance. The defendant was not using the stream for floatage, nor shown to be peculiarly interested in it as a floatable stream. Were it a nuisance, there the dam was in fact in possession of plaintiff as property. Could the defendant, without process, abate it as a nuisance?

We must take the statement often met with in the books, that a public nuisance may be abated by any person, with many grains of allowance. No one can maintain a civil action for a public nuisance, unless he sustain special damages therefrom different from that sustained by the rest of the public: 3 Blackstone's Commentaries, 2191; 4 Blackstone's Commentaries, 167; Wood on Nuisances, sec. 618; *Talbott* v. *King*, 32 W. Va. 6; Sedgwick on Damages, sec. 34, p. 946; 3 Sutherland on Damages, sec. 1057. And it is said that no one can by his own act abate a public nuisance, unless he have such interest as to give him an action: Wood on Nuisances, sec. 730. There is a grave difference of opinion as to abatement of a purely public nuisance by the mere act of the party. Some contend that no one not interested personally and peculiarly otherwise than other persons can do so, while others hold that any one may do so. Mr. Wood and Judge Cooley hold the former, and Mr. Bishop and Mr. Hilliard the latter, view.: Woods on Nuisances, sec. 729, et seq; Cooley on Torts, 45, 46; 1 Bishop's Criminal Law, 828; 1 Hilliard on Torts, 605.

It seems to me that, except in particular cases where emergency of some kind calls for it, and delay is dangerous, or at least inconvenient, the former is the more logical and reasonable view looking at the preservation of peace and the security of private property. It would be endless and useless to pursue this point further here. It cannot be said that there is any absolute general rule on the subject universally **313** applicable, but each instance stands on its own features, as will appear from the many cases enunciating diverse opinions, many of which will be found collected in 16 American and English Encyclopedia of Law, 991, note 4. As to highways, under the decisions, the right of abatement by the mere act of the party prevails. The reason here applies, given in 3 Blackstone's Commentaries, 5, as the basis of the right in any one to abate a public nuisance, that the law allows a summary remedy of abatement of nuisance to do one's self justice, because injuries of this kind, which obstruct or annoy such things as are of daily convenience and use, require an immediate remedy and cannot wait for the slow progress of the ordinary forms of action: Angell and Durfee on Highways, sec. 274.

The Virginia case of *Dimmett* v. *Eskridge*, 6 Munf. 308, sustains this right to any one to abate an obstruction in a highway by exonerating parties tearing out a dam not built at the point where it was authorized, which destroyed a ford which was part of a public road. So it seems to me that, if this dam were a nuisance, the railroad company, having no special interest in navigation, could not abate the dam directly. There would be no emergency calling for such action without legal process. If it could not do so directly, it could not do so indirectly by the acts charged against it. Nay, even if it could abate the dam itself directly, it could not go further and injure the mill-building and tear away the bank of the creek, for the right of abatement vested in it or in citizens' floating rafts would be only to remove the dam itself. But its action in making the fill, if it injured the plaintiff, operated to injure, not the offending dam, but the mill and soil. In the abatement no means could be lawfully used to work such injury. All the authorities agree that, where the right of abatement by private act does exist, it must go no further than to remove that which works the nuisance, doing injury no further than is necessary to accomplish that end: Cooley on Torts, 48; Wood on Nuisances, sec. 834; *Smart v. Commonwealth*, 27 Gratt. 950; 16 Am. & Eng. Ency. of Law, 994. So instruction 7 does not state the law correctly.

It is said that the jury disregarded it in their verdict, and for that reason the appellant asks that the verdict be [214] set aside. Being incorrect, though the jury found contrary to it is no ground for new trial: *Armstrong v. Keith*, 3 J. J. Marsh. 153; 20 Am. Dec. 131, and note: *Peck v. Land*, 2 Ga. 1; 46 Am. Dec. 368; *Wellborn v. Weaver*, 17 Ga. 267; 63 Am. Dec. 235; Hilliard on New Trials, sec. 4.

For these reasons the judgment is reversed, the verdict set aside, a new trial granted, and the case remanded.

RAILROADS—GRANT OF RIGHT OF WAY—INJURIES CAUSED IN CONSTRUCTION OF ROAD—DAMAGES.—A person owning land may grant a right of way across it to a railroad company, and the grant will imply a right to all the means of enjoying it which the grantor was possessed of at the time of the grant: *Charleston etc. R. R. Co. v. Leech*, 33 S. C. 175; 26 Am. St. Rep. 667. The company has a right to construct its road in a suitable and proper manner, whatever may be the injury to the residue of the lands of the same owner; and the latter can maintain no action against the company for any loss or injury which results from building its road in a suitable and proper manner: *Johnson v. Atlantic etc. R. R. Co.*, 35 N. H. 569; 69 Am. Dec. 560, and note. But even where the land is taken for a right of way under the right of eminent domain, the company is liable for unnecessary injury done in the construction of its road. Hence, the blasting of rocks in an imprudent or unskillful manner, or not removing the stone in due time, whereby injury occurs, is actionable: See monographic note to *Ohio etc. Ry. Co. v. Wachter*, 5 Am. St. Rep. 537, 538; *Blackwell v. Lynchburg etc. R. R. Co.*, 111 N. C. 151; 32 Am. St. Rep. 786, and note. The privilege of endangering lives of persons or property in the vicinity does not pass with the right of way as a necessary incident: *Blackwell v. Lynchburg etc. R. R. Co.*, 111 N. C. 151; 32 Am. St. Rep. 786. Injuries arising from blasting without negligence would not, however, be actionable: *Booth v. Rome etc. R. R. Co.*, 140 N. Y. 267; 37 Am. St. Rep. 552, and note. The company would be answerable for injuries produced by destroying or injuring a public highway: *Louisville etc. Ry. Co. v. Whitley County Court*, 95 Ky. 215; 44 Am. St. Rep. 220. Any one unlawfully interfering with a highway creates a nuisance, and is liable in damages to one who suffers a special injury: *Evansville etc. R. R. Co. v. Crist*, 116 Ind. 446; 9 Am. St. Rep. 865; *Evans v. Chicago etc. Ry. Co.*, 86 Wis. 597; 39 Am. St. Rep. 908, and note.

NUISANCE—ACTIONS—ABATEMENT.—All damages for a nuisance are recoverable in one action, when it is of such a character that its continuance is necessarily an injury, and it is of a permanent character which will continue without change from any cause but human labor: *Hodge* v. *Shaw*, 85 Iowa, 137; 39 Am. St. Rep. 290, and note; *Joseph Schlitz Brewing Co.* v. *Compton*, 142 Ill. 511; 34 Am. St. Rep. 92. But, where the nuisance or trespass is a continuing one, and the wrong may be apportioned from time to time, separate actions may be brought to recover the damages sustained: See notes to *Cooke* v. *England*, 92 Am. Dec. 628; *Ohio etc. Ry. Co.* v. *Wachter*, 5 Am. St. Rep. 540; *Joseph Schlitz Brewing Co.* v. *Compton*, 34 Am. St. Rep. 99. And see monographic notes to *Hargreaves* v. *Kimberly*, 53 Am. Rep. 138; *Chicago etc. R. R.* v. *Loeb*, 59 Am. Rep. 351, 369, where the cases on the subject are discussed. A nuisance, whether public or private, may be abated without notice by a party aggrieved, if done without a breach of the peace, but he must do no unnecessary damage in abating it: *Hickey* v. *Michigan Cent. R. R. Co.*, 96 Mich. 498; 35 Am. St. Rep. 621, and note. He runs the risk, however, of being deemed a trespasser, unless the existence of the nuisance is established: *Graves* v. *Shattuck*, 35 N. H. 257; 69 Am. Dec. 536.

DAMAGES—NOMINAL AND COMPENSATORY.—Nominal damages are those recoverable where a legal right is to be vindicated from an invasion that has produced no actual present loss of any kind. If there has been any actual loss, then the damages must be compensatory, and, if the plaintiff is entitled to have his case go to the jury at all, every thing which goes to ascertain the amount of actual compensation for the injury is proper evidence for the jury, and should be considered by them in estimating the compensation: *Duggan* v. *Baltimore etc. R. R.*, 159 Pa. St. 248, 253; 39 Am. St. Rep. 672, 674; *Seely* v. *Alden*, 61 Pa. St. 302; 100 Am. Dec. 642.

FLOATABLE STREAMS—RIPARIAN RIGHTS—DAMS.—A landowner has a right to build a mill, and erect a dam across a stream to accumulate water to run the mill; but the maintenance of a dam across a floatable stream, so as to prejudice the right of the public to float logs therein, and without providing suitable sluices to allow the logs to pass around the dam, is a public nuisance: *Gaston* v. *Mace*, 33 W. Va. 14; 25 Am. St. Rep. 848, and note; *Mumpower* v. *City of Bristol*, 90 Va. 151; 44 Am. St. Rep. 902, and note.

NEW TRIAL—DISREGARD OF ERRONEOUS INSTRUCTION.—If the verdict is right, though the instructions are wrong, it is no ground for a new trial that the jury disregarded erroneous instructions: See monographic note to *Strohn* v. *Detroit etc. R. R. Co.*, 99 Am. Dec. 129, on how to obtain the giving of instructions to the jury, and to obtain the review of errors in the giving or refusing to give instructions on certain points: *Chicago etc. R. R. Co.* v. *Kneirim*, 152 Ill. 458; 43 Am. St. Rep. 259.

EVANS *v.* JOHNSON.

[39 WEST VIRGINIA, 299.]

NOTICE—JURISDICTION—STATUTES—JUDICIAL PROCEEDINGS.—No man can be lawfully condemned unheard; and statutes will not be construed to authorize proceedings affecting a man's person or property without notice to him.

JUDGMENT—JURISDICTION—NOTICE OF JUDICIAL PROCEEDINGS.—The sentence of a court without hearing the party or giving him an opportunity to be heard is not a judicial determination of his rights, and is not entitled to any respect in any other tribunal.

INSANE PERSONS—JURISDICTION—NOTICE.—The appointment of a committee, by a county court, for a person as insane, without notice to him, is void, even where the statute does not expressly require notice. The power of the court to act depends upon the jurisdictional fact as to whether insanity exists; and, though the court has jurisdiction of the subject matter, insanity, it has no jurisdiction over the person without notice to him.

INSANE PERSONS—APPOINTMENT OF COMMITTEE—ORDER, HOW AFFECTED BY WANT OF NOTICE.—The appointment of a committee for an insane person is a summary proceeding, and notice must appear. Hence, where the county court, being a court of limited jurisdiction, makes such appointment, it must affirmatively appear not only that it had jurisdiction of the subject matter, but also over the person by service of process or notice.

EXECUTORS, ADMINISTRATORS, AND GUARDIANS CANNOT RESIGN unless permitted to do so by statute. The same rule applies to a committee for the insane, as they are not officers.

JUDICIAL SALES—VOID DEED RESERVING LIEN FOR UNPAID PURCHASE MONEY, AND ITS EFFECT.—If the court in a judicial sale of land directs the legal title to pass on actual payment, or by reservation of a lien, and a deed is given retaining a lien for deferred installments of purchase money, the lien is not lost, and the purchaser does not get the land for nothing, because the deed, having no scroll or seal, is no deed, and does not pass the legal title. It is not the deed which creates the lien. There is an implied lien springing from the sale and existing until the legal title is passed by deed.

LIMITATIONS OF ACTIONS—LIEN FOR UNPAID PURCHASE MONEY FOR LAND. The statute of limitations has no application to bar a lien for unpaid purchase money reserved in a conveyance of land. Though an action on a note given for the purchase money might be barred as a personal debt, yet the lien against the particular land is not barred.

LIMITATIONS OF ACTIONS—PURCHASE PRICE OF LAND—PRESUMPTION OF PAYMENT.—No time bars the right, either under the statute of limitations or presumption of payment, of a vendor to recover unpaid purchase money for land, if he has not parted with the legal title. Even a presumption of payment for twenty years would not be a positive bar, as it might be repelled by proof of the continued existence of the debt.

Berkshire & Sturgiss, for the appellant.

Keck and Okey Johnson, for the appellee.

300 BRANNON, P. Evan Morgan owned an interest in a tract of land in Monongalia county. Omer B. Johnson, as his guardian, upon petition obtained from the circuit court of that county an order to sell his ward's interest in the land, and did sell it to Elza S. Morgan, who executed to said guardian two notes for deferred installments of purchase money. Under authority of the order of sale a special commissioner made to the purchaser a deed conveying said infant's interest in the tract of land, retaining a lien for said notes. Afterward, when said infant had become of age, the clerk of the county court of Taylor county appointed Hiel J. Evans committee of said Evan Morgan as an insane person, and said committee brought this chancery suit against said Johnson, Elza L. Morgan, and others, for the purpose of charging Johnson, as guardian of said Evan Morgan, with liability to his ward for the amount of said notes made to him by the purchaser of said interest in said land, because he had been chargeable with their collection, and to settle his account as guardian, and also to enforce the lien existing for the notes under said sale and deed to the purchaser, the bill alleging that they had not been paid.

The notes were dated December 3, 1868, and this suit to collect them was brought in 1887. By deed of May 30, 1887, from Elza L. Morgan, for himself and as attorney in fact for a brother and coparcener, to Thornton Pickenpaugh and a deed of October, 20, 1887, from Minerva A. Fleming, another coparcener, to said Pickenpaugh, Pickenpaugh became owner of the entire tract, including the share of **301** said Evan Morgan, which had been sold under said court order and purchased by Elza L. Morgan. Pickenpaugh is a party to the cause.

The court entered a decree holding the said interest in said tract of land liable for the payment of said notes given by Elza L. Morgan for said interest, and subjecting it to sale in enforcement of said lien, and from this decree Pickenpaugh appeals. Pending the suit, Hiel J. Evans resigned his office of committee, and Justus F. Ross was appointed in his place by the county court of Taylor, and the suit was ordered to proceed in the name of said Ross as committee in place of Evans.

The brief of appellant's counsel in its opening presents what in its nature is the first question for us to decide, by insisting that the plaintiff has no right to recover in this suit

or any suit. The first reason given by counsel for this contention is, that the appointment of Hiel J. Evans to be committee of Evan Morgan as an insane person is void for want
of notice to said Evan Morgan. In *Lance* v. *McCoy*, 34 W.
Va. 416, the opinion is expressed that such an appointment
by a county court without notice, as required by the code,
chapter 58, section 34, is void. A re-examination of this
question in this case has confirmed me in the view then
expressed.

The question is of importance, both because of its frequent
occurrence and of its effect upon persons alleged to be insane.
So far as my observation has gone, the practice has been, in
clerks' offices of the county courts and in county courts, to
make such appointments without such notice. It lies at the
foundation of justice in all legal proceedings that the person
to be affected have notice of such proceedings. As such an
appointment takes from the person the possession and control of his property and even his freedom of person, and commits his property, his person, his liberty, to another, stamps
him with the stigma of insanity, and degrades him in public
estimation, no more important order touching a man can be
made, short of conviction of infamous crime. Will it be
said, in answer to this, that he is insane, and that notice to
an insane man will do him no good? The reply is, that his
insanity is the [302] very question to be tried, and he the only
party interested in the issue. In many cases, if notice be
given him, he will be prompt to attend and, in person, be the
unanswerable witness of his sanity. In some cases, if notice
be not given him, those interested in using his property or
robbing him of it will effectuate a corrupt plan. Almost as
well might we convict a man of crime without notice.

There is abundant authority for this position. Even
though the statute be silent regarding notice, as ours is in
the matter of appointment of committees by the county
courts, though the statute providing for the appointment by
circuit court requires notice, yet the common law steps in
and requires it: See *Chase* v. *Hathaway*, 14 Mass. 222, 224;
Hathaway v. *Clark*, 5 Pick. 490; *Hutchins* v. *Johnson*, 12
Conn. 376; 30 Am. Dec. 622; *McCurry* v. *Hooper*, 12 Ala.
823; 46 Am. Dec. 280; *Board, etc.*, v. *Budlong*, 51 Barb. 493;
Eslava v. *Lepretre*, 21 Ala. 504; 56 Am. Dec. 266; *Dutcher* v.
Hill, 29 Mo. 271; 77 Am. Dec. 572; Buswell on Insanity, sec.
55; *Stafford* v. *Stafford*, 1 Martin, N. S., 551. In *Molton* v.

Henderson, 62 Ala. 426, it was held that "inquisition of lu-
nacy without personal notice to the alleged *non compos* is void,
and so is the appointment by the probate court of a guardian
for said lunatic, and the proceedings by such guardian for
a sale of lands belonging to said lunatic." A statute authorizing an inebriate to be committed to a hospital on *ex parte*
proceeding was held void by the New York supreme court:
In re Janes, 30 How. Pr. 446.

In Georgia the statute required notice to three relatives
of the person before appointment of a guardian over him as
an insane person. Judge Bleckley delivering the opinion,
thought there ought to be also notice to the person. He
said: "It is, to say the least, doubtful whether the property
of an adult citizen can be taken out of his custody and
committed to guardianship without previous warning served
either upon him or some person duly constituted by law or
some legal tribunal to be notified in his stead: *Morton* v.
Sims, 64 Ga. 298. If it was unreasonable in the opinion of a
Roman governor to send up a prisoner and not signify withal
the crimes alleged against him, the law judges it to be equally
so to pass upon the dearest civil rights of the citizen without
first giving him notice of his [303] adversary's complaint.
The truth is that at the door of every temple of the law in
this broad land stands justice with her preliminary requirement upon all administrations: You shall condemn no man
unheard. The requirement is as old, at least, as Magna
Charta. It is the most precious of all the gifts of freedom
that no man be disseised of his property or deprived of his
liberty or in any way injured *nisi per legale judicium parium
suorum, vel per legem terræ*. It is a principle of natural
justice, which courts are never at liberty to dispense with,
unless under the mandate of positive law, that no person
shall be condemned unheard." He said that in that case
there was "action, trial, and judgment in two days, and no
previous notice." In our practice it often occurs in ten minutes.

This practice, I say, as was said by the Louisiana court in
Stafford v. *Stafford*, 1 Martin, N. S., 551, might put "the
wisest man in the community under the control of a curator,
and hold him up to the world as an adjudged insane." Both
constitution and statute confer this power on the county
courts as a jurisdiction. Before appointing the court must
determine whether or not the fact, which alone gives it power

to act, exists; that is, whether the party is, in any of the phases or conditions of mind, to be considered insane under the statute. It must inquire into the fact, and, in deciding, exercise judgment, and of this legal investigation, all important to him, he ought to have notice. He wants to deny the very basis of the proposed order—his insanity. It is an important transaction to him. Shall he have no notice of it? Am I told that the statute does not in terms require notice? I answer as shown in *Lance* v. *McCoy*, 34 W. Va. 416, as a circuit court cannot appoint without it, so, by proper construction of the code, neither can a county court. I answer, further, that a statute will not be construed to authorize proceedings affecting a man's person or property without notice. It does not dispense with notice: Bishop on Written Laws, secs. 25, 141; *Chase* v. *Hathaway*, 14 Mass. 222, 224; *Arthur* v. *State*, 22 Ala. 61; Endlich on Interpretation of Statutes, sec. 262; *Boonville* v. *Ormrod*, 26 Mo. 193; *Wickham* v. *Page*, 49 Mo. 526. Chief Justice Marshall held void a judgment of even a court-martial imposing fines on militiamen, because [304] without notice: *Meade* v. *Deputy Marshal*, 1 Brock. 324 (Fed. Cas. No. 9372). This statute is one of summary proceeding.

If the case were one of mere error or irregularity it might be said that the order was good against collateral attack, and must be reversed by a direct proceeding; but the question is one of jurisdiction—a want of authority to make the order for want of jurisdiction over the person to be affected. How can his property be affected, or title given the committee, to enable him to sue for it, if the order is void as to the person? If he is not affected by the order, how is his property? If the committee would restrain the person of the *non compos*, could he not release himself by treating the order as void? I cannot see how an order of a clerk fixing the personal status of a person without notice can rob him of his property, and vest title in another person. A tribunal may have jurisdiction of cases *ejusdem generis* with the matter involved in a proceeding before it, and it may have jurisdiction of the particular matter involved in that particular case; but if it have no jurisdiction of the person by service of process or appearance, if the proceeding is not *in rem*, it cannot go on. Though the Taylor county court has jurisdiction to appoint committees for insane persons, and though it had lawful jurisdiction to act on the matter of the appointment of a committee in the particular instance of Evan Morgan, yet it could not act without notice to him, unless we say notice was not required by law, which I have above sought to show is not the case.

A sentence of the court without hearing the party, or giving him an opportunity to be heard, is not a judicial determination of his rights, and is not entitled to any respect in any other tribunal. Jurisdiction is indispensable to the validity of all judicial proceedings. Jurisdiction of the person as well as the subject matter are prerequisites, and must exist, before a court can render a valid judgment or decree; and, if either of these is wanting, all the proceedings are void. So said the court literally in *Haymond* v. *Camden*, 22 W. Va. 180, syll., pts. 5, 9. So it has often held, as shown by Judge Green in the opinion in *McCoy* v. *McCoy*, 29 W. Va. 807. No court has more sturdily [305] held the rule of necessity of process or appearance than this court, whether as to proceedings of superior or inferior courts. Must there be process before a superior court can render merely money judgment, and yet no notice before a clerk can stamp a man with insanity, and take from him his property and freedom of person? Cases may exist of appointment of committees or guardian for *non compotes mentis* without notice appearing, in which they were held good against collateral attack; but it will be found that they were, in courts of probate, held to be courts of general jurisdiction, or where, after inquisition, the party traversed the finding, or had opportunity to do so.

The next question is: If, as in this case, it does not appear from the order of appointment, that such notice was given, can want of notice affect the order? The county court is a court of limited jurisdiction, not a court of record; and, as to such courts, the rule applies, that their jurisdiction must appear and will not be presumed; whereas, as to courts of general jurisdiction, their jurisdiction will be presumed and need not affirmatively appear, unless the want of jurisdiction does appear: *Mayer* v. *Adams*, 27 W. Va. 244; *Davis* v. *Town of Point Pleasant*, 32 W. Va. 294; *Wandling* v. *Straw*, 25 W. Va. 692; 1 Cooley's Constitutional Limitations, 406. It is a summary proceeding, and notice must appear: *Arthur* v. *State*, 22 Ala. 61. The county court being a court of limited jurisdiction, it must appear, not only that it had jurisdiction as to the subject matter, but also over the person by service of process or notice: *Mayer* v. *Adams*, 27 W. Va. 244; 2 Black on Judgments, secs. 282, 633.

When we say there must be jurisdiction we mean both that the matter and the person to be affected must be within the jurisdiction of the court by service of notice upon him: Cooley's Constitutional Limitations, 403. I maintain that such action as the appointment of a committee for one as insane without notice is so grave in its effects upon his personal status, his right to vote, liberty, and property, that it is not due process of law. It violates the definition by Mr. Webster in the Dartmouth College case, generally received as a proper one, of due process of law, that "it hears before it condemns."

306 The committee in this case resigned, and another was appointed in his room. Invested with no authority he had none to resign. But, if he had been regularly appointed, could he resign, and could the county court accept his resignation? At common law I think not. An executor or administrator, once having taken his office, cannot resign it. Schouler says, that if precedents can be trusted, they cannot resign unless under statute; "for the English rule always discountenanced such a practice as to these and similar fiduciaries": 1 Woerner on Administration, sec. 273; Schouler on Executors, sec. 157. In *Hensloes' case*, 9 Coke, 36 *a*, the law is stated thus: "For after the executors have once administered, and so have taken upon them the charge of the executorship, they cannot afterward refuse." And on page 37 *a* it states that the ordinary cannot accept their resignation. So held, also, in *Wankford* v. *Wankford*, 1 Salk. 308. So in *Parten's case*, 1 Mod. 213. So in *Sitzman* v. *Pacguette*, 13 Wis. 291; *Ford* v. *Travis*, 2 Brev. 299, cited with approval by Chief Justice Marshall in *Griffith* v. *Frazier*, 8 Cranch, 27; *Washington* v. *Blunt*, 8 Ired. Eq. 253; *Haigood* v. *Wells*, 1 Hill Eq. 59; *Sears* v. *Dillingham*, 12 Mass. 358. In *Flinn* v. *Chase*, 4 Denio, 86, held that the surrogate had no jurisdiction to accept an administrator's resignation and appoint another. At common law a guardian cannot resign: Schouler's Domestic Relations, 426. Under our code, chapter 82, section 7, a guardian may resign. I have met with only one case (*Morgan's case*, 3 Bland Ch. 332) holding that a committee may resign; but there is no opinion or authority cited, and the facts are not given. I conclude that without statute leave a committee cannot resign. An act passed in March,

1891 (Code 1891, c. 118, sec. 1), allows a committee and
fiduciary to resign on filing a petition and proceeding as
therein directed; but this resignation was in 1889. The resignation being ineffectual, it left Evans yet in office, and, the
office being full, the appointment of Ross in his place would
be void and confer no authority on Ross. Per Moncure, J., in
Andrews v. *Avory*, 14 Gratt. 236; 73 Am. Dec. 355; *Griffith* v.
Frazier, 8 Cranch, 9; *Hayes* v. *Meeks*, 20 Cal, 288. It is not
meant to say that public officers of government may not resign.
As to them the general rule is that they may resign: Mecham
on Public Offices, sec. 409; [307] *Edwards* v. *United States*,
103 U. S. 471. Evans, having no office, could resign none;
and derivatively from him, as filling his place, no power
vested in Ross.

But it may be thought that the appointment of Ross ought
to be treated, not as filling a vacancy caused by Evans' resignation, but as an original appointment. If so, it would be
subject to the same objection for want of notice as the appointment of Evans.

What is the consequence of neither Evans nor Ross being
a committee? A want of title to prosecute this suit. What
title has either to enforce the lien, or to the notes secured by
it? None. Evans could not bring the suit. It could not be
ordered to proceed in the name of his successor, Ross, and
the debt could not be decreed to Ross. Would a payment to
him be good? If the appointment be void as to the insane
person, if he could resist or disregard it, would a sale or payment under decree in this case protect against resale at the
demand of a lawfully appointed committee, or Evan Morgan
himself? Ought the court to impose these dangers on the
late guardian, the purchaser, and his alienee, Pickenpaugh?

The defense was made that there is no lien for unpaid purchase money, because the deed reserving it has no seal. The
order giving the guardian authority to sell the land of the
infant provided that, either on payment of purchase money
or earlier by retaining a lien for it, Hough, as special commissioner should convey the land to the purchaser. As there is
no scroll or seal to the deed, we must say it is not a deed and
does not pass legal title, but does the purchaser get the land
for nothing? Is there no lien? Viewing the said paper
alone, if it is effective to pass any interest in the land, it is
effective equally so to reserve a lien on that interest. If we
treat it as a contract to convey passing equitable title, of

course there is a lien, as a vendor has a lien for purchase
money as long as he retains title: *Yancey* v. *Mauck,* 15 Gratt.
300, and citations.   If another deed were made, a lien could'
be reserved in it, for without reserving right in a sale of
realty to reserve a lien in the final deed of conveyance that
right exists: *Findley* v. *Armstrong,* 23 W. Va. 113.   The vendor can never be compelled to part with [308] the legal title
without payment or security.   It seems to be thought in this
case that it is the deed which creates the lien, and, as the
paper is not a deed, it creates no lien; but there is an implied
lien springing from the sale existing until the legal title is
passed by deed, and that deed reserving it only reserves an
already existing antecedent lien and does not originate it.
That paper, so far as it might be deemed necessary to look
to it, is competent to preserve that lien.   But the sale under
the decree was attended with a lien.   The court only directed
the legal title to pass on actual payment or by reservation of
a lien.   The title has not passed to the purchaser, Elza L.
Morgan, and the lien exists.   The commissioner could not
convey free of lien.   Pickenpaugh took it, of course, subject
to the lien, because he took only what his vendor, Elza L.
Morgan, had—an equitable, inchoate title; and, also, because
he is affected with notice of encumbrance on the face of the
papers, under which Morgan derived title, and both decree
and the defective deed told of the lien.   If, as suggested in
the brief, it be viewed as a private sale by one guardian, the
same principle would apply; the lien would exist.
    Time is relied on to defeat the debt.   In no view can this
position prevail.   Viewed as a case where the legal title has
not passed to the vendee, as it is to be viewed, the statute of
limitations has no application: *Hopkins* v. *Cockerell,* 2 Gratt.
88; *Hanna* v. *Wilson,* 3 Gratt. 243; 46 Am. Dec. 190.   The statute has no application to a lien reserved in a deed passing legal
title: *Hull* v. *Hull,* 35 W. Va. 155, 165; 29 Am. St. Rep. 800;
Barton's Chancery Practice, 111, note 5.   Though the note
given for purchase money be barred as a personal debt, yet the
lien remains unaffected by the statute operations against the
land: *Coles* v. *Withers,* 33 Gratt. 194.   The statute, perhaps, is
not intended to be specifically relied upon, but laches and
staleness of demand are.   This defense cannot be maintained.
One note fell due December 8, 1869, the other December 8,
1870, and this suit began May 17, 1887.   Only a presumption of payment of twenty years would operate, and that had

not elapsed. Besides, that is not a positive bar, but only a presumption which may be repelled by proof of the continued existence of the debt. [309] The paper signed by Elza L. Morgan July 5, 1880, admits both notes to be then unpaid.

As to the release dated July 5, 1880, by the mother and brothers of Evan Morgan, it is contended for by Pickenpaugh that it precluded a recovery of said debt. It recites the sale; that Omer Johnson had as guardian never collected the two purchase-money notes of Elza L. Morgan; that recovery was barred as to the surety in them; that said guardian was not at fault for not collecting them, as his omission arose out of an agreement between the brothers and mother of Evan Morgan that Elza L. Morgan should keep Evan when required, and have enough of the notes applied to reimburse him; and that to indemnify and save harmless the late guardian, Johnson, said mother and brothers released him from all liability as guardian, and on account of such sale and delay of collection, unless he should collect said notes. Now the whole purpose of this instrument was to release the guardian, not Elza L. Morgan. Instead of releasing him it closed with a proviso looking to the probability of the collection of valid notes. As to any agreement between the mother and brothers of Evan Morgan, how could it release a debt due him? Who gave them power to stay the enforcement of the debt? The fact that they would be distributees in the event of Evan Morgan's death gave them no vested interest whatever to sell, release, or in any manner to affect the debt. The mother of Evan Morgan has kept him, not Elza L. Morgan. It is claimed he paid her some money for keeping him. She positively denies it on oath. Why did not Elza Morgan give evidence of it? A witness states a circumstance—a mere circumstance—tending slightly to show the probability that he made a payment; but it is inconclusive, very weak in effect. The amount is not shown. He must make it certain. No payment of the debt by Elza L. Morgan by paying Mrs. Morgan for keeping Evan or otherwise is shown.

The argument that the fact that there is an adequate remedy by suit on the guardian's bond, forbidding a chancery suit, is without force. Equity is the proper forum in which to enforce the liens, and it is proper to enforce that [310] lien to collect the debt before going on the guardian to make good the debt. There stands the land for the debt. The ultimate responsibility rests on Elza L. Morgan and the land; and no court of justice would lodge the liability in the first instance on the guardian, Johnson, and exonerate the land at the instance of Elza L. Morgan, the debtor, who agreed to pay Johnson and never paid him, or at Pickenpaugh's instance, claiming under Elza L. Morgan, even without the existence of said paper releasing Johnson, which paper Elza L. Morgan executed; and, more surely yet, no court would do so in view of that release. With what justice can he, or one claiming under him, ask that the liability at the first step be saddled on Johnson? To do so would be inequitable and against the contract of the parties.

It is suggested, if I am not in error as to the brief of counsel, that there is no privity between the plaintiff and Elza L. Morgan and Pickenpaugh, as the notes were made to Johnson as guardian. If it is meant to say that, because the notes were made to Johnson, a lawful committee of Evan Morgan cannot sue on them, I cannot concur in that view. When the guardianship ended upon the majority of Evan Morgan he was entitled to the debt, and, even if we could say that the legal title to the debt under the notes was in Johnson, which I doubt, but have not examined the question, because it is immaterial, I am very sure that a court of equity would entertain a suit by a lawful committee, and, having Johnson and other proper parties before it, would decree the debt into the hands of the committee.

The decree is reversed and bill dismissed without prejudice to any other suit by Evan Morgan or any lawful committee. No prejudice against the collection of the debt shall result from this decision.

———

DENT, J., dissented from the majority opinion so far as it determines that a conceded idiot must have notice before the clerk of the county court can appoint a committee for him. In making a distinction between cases of known idiocy and those of suspected insanity, and in showing the futility of serving notice in cases of known idiocy, his honor said: "Evan Morgan is conceded in this case to be a helpless idiot from his birth, never having been able to hear, speak, or take care of himself. This is undeniable. Such being his undisputed state, a committee was appointed for him by the clerk of the county court of Taylor county at the instance of those having him in charge. This appointment is held void because the order of the clerk does not show that the idiot had been served with notice. Why give him notice? His capacity was less than a child's three months old, yet the court would hardly hold that a child of such an age must have notice before a guardian could be appointed for it. A dumb brute has more intelligence, and a notice served on such would be just as effective. The court answers, 'So that, in case he is not an idiot or his sanity is in question, he may defend himself.'

"In cases of doubtful sanity or insanity the clerk has no jurisdiction, and an order appointing a committee made by him with or without notice would be a nullity just as if he should appoint a guardian for an adult. The jurisdiction in cases of suspected insanity is conferred exclusively on justices and the circuit courts by sections 9, 33-35, of chapter 58, of the code, and there is no statutory enactment conferring such jurisdiction on county courts or their clerks. The clerk acts merely in a ministerial capacity in appointing a committee for a known idiot, and therefore a notice is neither required nor would it be other than useless. An idiot needs no adjudication to establish the fact, but he is so by nature, known and recognized by all men; and, whenever notice is necessary, the clerk is without jurisdiction, and his proceedings are void, as in such a case the subject of the notice would not be an idiot.

"It is true that this court in the case of *Lance* v. *McCoy*, 34 W. Va. 416, under a misconception of the jurisdiction of the county court and finding a supposed hiatus in the law, proceeded to legislate, at least impliedly, in favor of the jurisdiction of said court in cases of suspected insanity, and enacted, by a kind of parity of reasoning, that the county court should not appoint a committee without first giving five days' notice to the suspected; and now, by this decision, the provisions of this enactment are extended to include well-known idiots as well as suspected lunatics, not, however, for the purpose in its result of protecting the idiot or his estate, but to allow the appellant to escape his liability temporarily with the sure promise of bringing him to certain justice later on. The justification of this exercise of legislative functions is section 24, article 8, of the constitution, to wit: 'They shall have jurisdiction in all matters of probate, the appointment and qualification of personal representatives, guardians, committees, and curators.' And this is construed, without legislative enactment, to include authority to examine into cases of suspected insanity. The legislature did not so consider it, and hence it conferred exclusive power in such cases in the justices, and the circuit courts. If it had deemed it wise or necessary to do so it would have conferred this power on the county courts by legislative enactment as it was formerly under the laws of Virginia, but never has been the law of this state except by judicial construction as aforesaid directly in contravention of the will of the legislature. To my mind such decisions as these are an unjustifiable and unnecessary usurpation of legislative powers on the part of this court."

Notwithstanding what the learned dissenting judge said with respect to the uselessness of serving notice on a known idiot, it is not entirely clear why notice should not be served in such a case. In fact, if we apply the fundamental principles of the law and of personal rights to the question, we see no escape from the proposition that notice should be served in such a case. It is hardly satisfactory to say that the notice would not be understood, and would, therefore, be useless, upon the ground that the law does not require idle acts to be performed. This predetermines the whole matter. Rules of law are supposed to be uniform, and to operate upon all alike where personal rights are involved. There is no law which takes away or detracts from the personal rights of a known idiot, and he, like all others, would apparently be entitled to notice of any judicial proceeding against him. Every person is presumed to be sane until the contrary appears, and courts are not interested in the consequences of enforcing the law, or as to the personal effect on the individual of serving process or notice of judicial proceedings upon him. Courts can act only in a judicial way. They cannot take judicial notice of insanity or of any other fact except in some judicial proceeding before them. As a matter of fact, a person may be a known idiot, but the court cannot judicially know it until the question is before it in a judicial way, and the only way known to our laws of acquiring power to act where jurisdiction of the person is required is by service of process or notice. If process or notice is, in fact, served upon an insane person, no harm is done, and, if the one upon whom process or notice is served is not insane, nothing more is done than what the party is legally entitled to have done. The issue in the whole controversy is insanity, and the court cannot predetermine it.

INSANE PERSONS—NOTICE OF JUDICIAL PROCEEDINGS—DUE PROCESS OF LAW.—No man should be condemned without having an opportunity to defend himself. He should be personally served with notice of judicial proceedings against him: Note to *City of Grand Rapids* v. *Powers*, 28 Am. St. Rep. 293; and have the benefit of the due course of legal proceedings. In other words, it is a constitutional guaranty that he shall not be deprived of "life, liberty, or property" without "due process of law": See monographic note to *State* v. *Billings*, 43 Am. St. Rep. 531–541, on due process of law as applied to insane persons, showing that no adjudication of a court in such cases is supported by due process of law if rendered without jurisdiction of the subject matter and notice to the party, and that the question of sanity is the very one to be adjudicated, and, therefore, jurisdictional.

RESIGNATIONS.—Officers may resign: See monographic note to *People* v. *Williams*, 36 Am. St. Rep. 523–527. But a trustee who accepts cannot renounce (*Ross* v. *Barclay*, 18 Pa. St. 179; 55 Am. Dec. 616) without the consent of the *cestui que trust* or the direction of the court: *Shepherd* v. *McEvers*, 4 Johns. Ch. 136; 8 Am. Dec. 561. An executor or administrator cannot resign except so far as permitted to do so by statute: *Haynes* v. *Meeks*, 10 Cal. 110; 70 Am. Dec. 703, and note.

VENDOR AND PURCHASER—LIEN—DEED.—A vendor's lien need not be reserved in the deed to land. In the absence of any thing showing an intention to waive it, such a lien is always implied. And a lien for purchase money exists between a vendor and purchaser, even though it is not apparent from the deed that some or all of the purchase money remains unpaid: Note to *Bell* v. *Pelt*, 14 Am. St. Rep. 61.

LIMITATIONS OF ACTIONS—LIEN FOR PURCHASE MONEY.—The statute of limitations does not run against a lien for purchase money of land reserved in a deed: *Hull* v. *Hull*, 35 W. Va. 155; 29 Am. St. Rep. 800.

PAYMENT.—PRESUMPTION, after the lapse of twenty years, that a debt has been paid is a disputable one: *Barker* v. *Jones*, 62 N. H. 497; 13 Am. St. Rep. 586; and monographic note to *Alston* v. *Hawkins*, 18 Am. St. Rep. 879–888, discussing the presumption of payment from lapse of time.

ROHRBOUGH v. BARBOUR COUNTY COURT.

[39 WEST VIRGINIA, 472.]

COUNTY—LIABILITY OF FOR ACCIDENT CAUSED BY FRIGHTENED ANIMAL AT DEFECTIVE APPROACH TO BRIDGE.—A county is answerable to a person who was driving up the approach of a public bridge, when his horse suddenly became frightened át a pile of large rock beside the roadway, and began to turn round, and, before he could arise to his feet or do any thing to control the horse, it backed over the unprotected wall of the approach, falling upon and destroying the buggy, and inflicting personal injury on the driver, if the accident would not have happened had a suitable railing been placed along the approach.

W. T. Ice and C. F. Teter, for the appellant.

V. Woods, for the appellee.

⁴⁷³ DENT, J. The plaintiff in this case obtained a judgment against the defendant in the circuit court of Barbour county for the sum of one hundred and twenty-five dollars, for injuries alleged to have been occasioned by the negligence of the defendant. The facts in the case are as follows, to wit: About 8 o'clock P. M., on a very dark night, the first Sunday in August, 1890, the plaintiff was driving up the approach of a county bridge at the town of Philippi in the county of Barbour, when his horse became suddenly frightened at a pile of large rock lying beside the roadway, and began to turn around, and, before plaintiff could arise to his feet or do any thing to control it, backed over the unprotected wall of the approach to the bridge, throwing plaintiff out, and falling upon and destroying the buggy. If a suitable railing had been placed along the approach the accident would not have happened. The horse was spirited but not vicious, and, as the evidence appears to indicate, the whole matter was almost an instantaneous occurrence, there being not sufficient time between the fright of the horse and the accident to enable the plaintiff, a man of ordinary prudence, to regain control of his horse.

The only question presented is the liability of the defendant for the damages sustained by the plaintiff. In the case of *Smith* v. *County Court,* 33 W. Va. 713, this court held that the county was not liable for injuries sustained by reason of a horse, frightened at two calves, backing a buggy over the side of a narrow road, as the accident was not occasioned by a failure to keep the road in proper repair, but the unmanageableness of the horse, which was caused by the sudden appearance of the calves, and by the unskillfulness of the driver.

The supreme court of Massachusetts, in the case of *Titus* v. *Northbridge*, 97 Mass. 266, 93 Am. Dec. 91, says: "When a horse, by reason of fright, disease, or viciousness, becomes actually uncontrollable, so that his driver cannot stop him, or direct his course, or exercise or regain control over his movements, and in this condition comes on a defect in the highway, or upon a place which is defective for want of a railing, [474] by which an injury is occasioned, the town is not liable for the injury, unless it appear that it would have occurred if the horse had not been so uncontrollable. But a horse is not to be considered uncontrollable that merely shies or starts, or is momentarily not controlled by the driver."

The same court in the case of *Palmer* v. *Andover*, 2 Cush. 608: "It is the ordinary course of events, and consistent with a reasonable degree of prudence on the part of the traveler, that accidents will occur; horses may be frightened; the harness may break; a bolt or screw may be dropped. To guard against such accidents the law requires suitable railings and barriers, a proper width to the road, and whatever may be reasonably required for the safety of the traveler." The law is also stated as follows, to wit: "Where the injury is the combined result of an accident and a defect in the highway, and would not have happened but for the defect, the town is liable": *Palmer* v. *Andover*, 2 Cush. 608; *Kelsey* v. *Glover*, 15 Vt. 708; *Davis* v. *Dudley*, 4 Allen, 557.

From these authorities the proposition is deduced that, if sufficient time elapses between the fright of the horse and the accident to permit the driver, being a man of ordinary prudence, to make a proper effort to regain control of the frightened animal, even though he should fail, the county would not be liable for its negligence, as the injury must be attributed to the viciousness of the horse rather than to the defect in the highway. But if no such time intervenes, but the fright and accident are concurrent events, then the county would be liable; for the very purpose of the law in requiring dangerous approaches to bridges to be protected by a sufficient railing is to guard against just such accidents, rendered unavoidable by reason of their suddenness.

In this case it is not made to appear whether any time intervened between the fright of the horse and the accident; but it appears to be conceded that they were both almost simultaneous occurrences. Before he was able to make any effort to control the horse the driver, buggy, and horse had gone over the wall of the approach to the bridge. Neither want of due care in the circumstances can be imputed [475] to the driver, nor viciousness to the horse. It is true that the accident would not have occurred, if the horse had not become frightened; neither would the fright of the horse have occasioned the accident if the legal guard-rail had been there to prevent it. The plaintiff was not guilty of contributory negligence in attempting to cross the bridge after night. It was open for travel, and he had the right to presume, in the absence of knowledge to the contrary, that the county had discharged its duty and made it safe for travelers, even on a dark night. The best of horses will become suddenly frightened, and no human foresight can foresee and guard entirely against such fright; but dangerous bridge approaches can and should be protected by suitable railings.

From the certificate of facts as ascertained by the judge of the circuit court, who visited and viewed the place of the accident, we are unable to say that his conclusion and judgment are wrong in the light of the foregoing decisions; and therefore the judgment is affirmed.

———

COUNTIES—LIABILITY FOR DEFECTIVE BRIDGES—PROXIMATE CAUSE— FRIGHTENED HORSES.—A county is not liable for injuries caused by a defective bridge, in the absence of a statute creating such liability, either expressly or by necessary implication: *Heigel v. Wichita County,* 84 Tex. 392; 31 Am. St. Rep. 63. A hole under the end of a bridge does not render a county liable for injury received by the driver of a buggy, when his horse, becoming frightened after stepping with his forefeet upon the bridge, backs and turns the buggy over, thus throwing the driver violently down an embankment, in the absence of any evidence, except the opinion of the party injured, that the fright of the horse was caused by the hole under the bridge: *Mason v. County of Spartanburg,* 40 S. C. 390; 42 Am. St. Rep. 887, and note. While counties are bound to so maintain their bridges that they may be safely used by persons traveling on the highways, they are not bound to so maintain them as that horses will not take fright at them: See monographic note to *Morse v. Town of Richmond,* 98 Am. Dec. 609, treating of the liability of cities and towns for injuries caused by horses becoming frightened at objects in streets and highways. Where objects ordinarily calculated to frighten road-worthy horses are placed and suffered to remain in the public highway they are regarded as defects in the road, and the public authorities, after due notice, are liable for injuries caused thereby: *North Manheim Township v. Arnold,* 119 Pa. St. 380; 4 Am. St. Rep. 650. But, to render such authorities liable, the defect must have been the sole and efficient cause of the injury: *Schaeffer v. Jackson Tp.,* 150 Pa. St. 145; 30

Am. St. Rep. 792. Where an accident is produced by two causes not concurrent, one of them must be the proximate and the other the remote cause,
and the law will regard the proximate as the efficient and responsible cause,
disregarding the remote cause: *Herr* v. *City of Lebanon*, 149 Pa. St. 222;
34 Am. St. Rep. 603.

GILL v. STATE.
[39 WEST VIRGINIA. 479.]

EXECUTION FOR A FINE SHOULD RUN AGAINST LAND, GOODS, AND CHATTELS.
A JUDGMENT FOR A FINE IS A DEBT, and enforceable by execution.
JUDGMENT.—AWARD OF EXECUTION IS NOT an integral part of a judgment.
STATUTES IN PARI MATERIA—CONSTRUCTION.—Two sections of different
  statutes, both relating to remedy by execution on state recoveries, are
  to be construed together as in *pari materia*.
MARRIED WOMEN—EXECUTION—SEPARATE ESTATE.—A state's fieri facias
  upon a judgment for a fine against a married woman may be levied
  upon her separate estate, personal or real.
MARRIED WOMEN—TORTS.—A married woman is liable for her tort, and,
  having property, it is subject to execution to satisfy a judgment establishing such liability.
JUDGMENT—EXECUTION.—When a judgment is valid against a defendant,
  an execution upon it, unless expressly forbidden by statute, must be
  equally valid.

John Bassel, for the appellant.

T. S. Reiley, *attorney general*, for the state.

479 BRANNON, P.   Eleven writs of fieri facias were issued
from the circuit court of Harrison county in favor of the
state against Mrs. Thomas Gill upon judgments against her
for fines imposed for misdemeanors; and she made a motion
to quash the same and levies of them, which being overruled,
she has brought the case here.

Her ground for quashing the writs of fieri facias is, that
upon their face they require the fines and costs to be levied
480 on the goods, chattels, and real estate, and she says that
an execution for a fine cannot be levied out of real estate.
Is this so?   At common law an execution for a debt or liability of a private person to another could not be levied of
realty, but one in favor of the king or state could be: Opinion in *Leake* v. *Ferguson*, 2 Gratt. 434; Freeman on Executions, sec. 172; *Jones* v. *Jones*, 1 Bland, 443; 18 Am. Dec. 327.
Our code, in chapter 35, section 5, expressly enacts or continues this common-law prerogative of the state by providing
that "in a writ of fieri facias upon a judgment or decree

against any person indebted or liable to the state," the command shall be to levy the money out of the " goods, chattels, and real estate" of the defendant.

It is contended that this provision applies, not to fines imposed for criminal or penal offenses, but to debts or some mere money liability; that it is found in a chapter of the code, whose very title imports such debt or money liability, not money penalty imposed for crime, the title of the chapter being "Of the Recovery of Claims Due the State," and that the chapter provides motions and actions as means of recovery of the claims here meant, "processes" not meaning the recovery of fines by indictment; and that the words in section 5, "indebted or liable to the state," must be given the same meaning as in section 3, which provides, that "the action or motion at law may be against any person indebted or liable in any way whatever to the state."

These considerations have force, but they are not conclusive and are outweighed by others. In the first place, chapter 35, section 5, is to be liberally construed, because it is purely a remedial enactment giving process of execution to enforce judgments for money in favor of the public, and, as its purpose is to realize public dues, it should not be given a narrow technical application. Its broad language is, that a writ of fieri facias "upon a judgment or decree against any person indebted or liable to the state" shall run against real as well as personal estate. Its use of the words, " person indebted or liable to the state," would include not only a simple debt, but also any money liability existing by judgment, no matter on what the judgment is based. When the prosecution for a public offense has ended in a [481] judgment imposing a fine, it is no longer an unascertained penalty or liability, but has become fixed in amount and has become a debt and that of the highest character—a debt of record payable instanter—and the lawful process of execution may go upon it at common law and under our statute: *Rex* v. *Woolf*, 1 Chit. 401; 18 Eng. Com. L., 225, 229, 230; *Kane* v. *People*, 8 Wend. 203; 1 Bishop's Criminal Procedure, sec. 1304; Code, c. 36, sec. 12.

The position taken above—that a judgment for a fine is a debt—is not only supported by cases just cited, but our case of *State* v. *Burkeholder*, 30 W. Va. 593, supports it, as it holds the state under its claim to a fine to be a creditor, and the demand such a debt as will authorize the state to appeal to

a court of equity to avoid a deed to the prejudice of the state
as to its fine. Award of execution is not an integral part of
a judgment, as it need not contain it, and such execution as
the law points out may issue upon it; and the well-considered cases, cited above, of *Rex* v. *Woolf*, 1 Chit. 401, and
Kane v. *People*, 8 Wend. 203, hold that by common law on
a judgment for a fine a writ of capias ad satisfaciendum to
take the body, or of levari facias to take the goods and the
issues of the whole land of the defendant, could be issued
just the same as on a judgment for a debt; and it seems to
me that our legislature does not intend to deprive the state
of the right given by the common law to go against the land
and so delay its steps in collection of money due the public
treasury by compelling it to resort to chancery to enforce its
recovery.

A large fine is just as much a debt and just as essential
to the treasury's needs as a debt against a defaulting sheriff.
Why withhold from the state an efficient remedial process
in the one case and grant it in the other? Such a judgment
for a fine being a fixed debt and liability, it falls under the
wide letter of section 5, and, as I have shown, it falls within
what must be considered its spirit and remedial purpose.
From the mere circumstance that section 2 of chapter 35
provides that claims due the state may be recovered by
motion or action, and that section 3 says that it may be
against "any person indebted or liable" to the state, we are
not bound to conclude that, as the words [482] "indebted or
liable" are found in both sections, we must give them exactly
the same construction for all purposes, and restrain the beneficial operation of the section to not giving execution, but
defining what property shall be liable to recoveries by action
or motion, and excluding recoveries by indictment. We must
look at all the statutory provisions, and the objects they contemplate. Chapter 35 of the code treats of the recovery of
claims due the state, while chapter 36 treats of the mode
of recovering fines, but they both relate to the recovery of
moneys due to the state. We may say that, when chapter
35 says that claims due the state may be recovered by action
or motion, it means in respect to the process of recovery of
judgment, claims other than for fines, and that when chapter 36 says that, where fines are imposed by law, they may
be recovered by indictment or presentment and warrants
before justices, it means fines, not other claims. But these

provisions relate in terms to the form of proceeding, and I
suppose only those forms can be used, because the language
is express; but, as to fines, chapter 36, section 12, authorizes
a fieri facias to issue without saying what property it shall
run against.   Does it run against land?   We turn to section
5 of chapter 35, and find that it commands that a writ of
fieri facias upon a judgment against any person indebted or
liable to the state shall run against land.   The two sections
afford a remedy for gathering the fruits of the same thing—
a recovery by judgment by the state; and, as one simply
gives a fieri facias without limiting it to goods and chattels,
and the other makes a state's execution run against goods
and lands, we do not make the sections clash by saying that
an execution for a fine shall operate upon land, since there
would be no inconsistency between them, as they are to be
construed together as *in pari materia,* both relating to remedy by execution on state recoveries.

The argument is made by counsel, that if we allow executions for fines to operate upon lands, then, as some fines
are recoverable before justices, land may be sold under executions issued by justices.   This is not so; for section 5 of
chapter 36 enacts that proceedings before justices for fines
shall conform to section 219 to 230 inclusive of chapter [483]
50; and we find that one of those sections (227) limits the
collection of such justices' executions to personal estate.
This, so far as it does go, goes to support the position taken
in this opinion, that an execution for a fine runs against
land, because it imports that the lawmakers, when limiting
a justices' execution for a fine to personal property, thought
that without such limitation it would bind land.

The law allows a state's execution to be levied on land
only in default of the defendant's having personalty.   If he
has not personalty, must he be allowed to avoid payment of
fine, though he has land?   It may be said every execution
for a petty amount might be enforced against land.   So
might a chancery suit be brought for a petty amount to sell
land, since, I suppose, no one would deny that a judgment
for a fine is a lien on land under section 5, chapter 139,
and the state has like remedy to enforce it as individuals:
State v. *Burkeholder,* 30 W. Va. 593; *Commonwealth* v. *Ford,*
29 Gratt. 683.

In the opinion in *State* v. *Burkeholder,* 30 W. Va. 593,
Judge Johnson pointedly expresses the opinion that, under

section 5, chapter 35, an execution for a fine runs against
land, and under it land can be sold. This is said to be an
obiter dictum. It was germane to the discussion of the subject before the court, if not in point, and, I think, expresses
the correct construction of the statute. So we conclude that
a state's fieri facias for a fine ought to run against goods and
chattels and land, and therefore the fact that those involved
in this case did so is no ground for quashing them.

Another ground relied upon for quashing the levies made
under these executions is, that they are upon real estate
which is the separate property of a married woman; and it is
contended that an execution cannot be levied on the separate
estate of a married woman.

A judgment at law against a married woman upon a contract made during coverture is void: *White* v. *Foote etc. Mfg.
Co.*, 29 W. Va. 385; 6 Am. St. Rep. 650. But these judgments
are for fines for public offenses, not on contract. We are not
considering the question of the married woman's liability for
the offenses, as that was a matter to be raised before the judgment, but only whether her property [484] can be taken to pay
the judgments. Simple as this question seems, it is not without difficulty of decision. No authority bearing on it is cited;
and I have found little pointed authority upon it. We can
find everywhere authority upon the question of when and how
a married woman is answerable for torts and crimes; when
the husband is alone liable for her acts; when they are jointly
liable; when she is separately liable; but not much exactly
on the question whether her separate estate can be taken for
fines against her. One would hastily say that, if a judgment
can be rendered against her, execution can be levied upon
her estate. We are not here considering how far contracts
bind her estate. For her torts I understand the common-law
rule to prevail in this state—that the husband is liable for
them. If he is present he is liable for her tort, though he
protest against it. If he is absent, and knows nothing of it,
he is liable to satisfy her torts. There is a case in Illinois
holding that the acts enabling married women to take and
hold separate estate impliedly repealed the common-law rule
making a husband liable for the torts of the wife done by her
without his consent or in his absence without his instigation,
but the court was nearly evenly divided: See *Martin* v. *Robson*, 65 Ill. 129; 16 Am. Rep. 578. In *Norris* v. *Corkill*, 32
Kan. 409, 49 Am. Rep. 489, it is also so held. Mr. Freeman,

in note to *Brazil* v. *Moran*, 83 Am. Dec. 777, seems to see it likewise.

This opinion is based on the theory that at common law by marriage the husband becomes in short entitled to all his wife's personalty and her earnings, and the rents and profits of her realty during coverture, and was clothed with power to restrain and direct her conduct even by personal chastisement, and therefore it was reasonable he should be responsible for her wrongful conduct; but as since the statutes touching her separate estate and earnings, he gets nothing of her estate by marriage, and his right of chastisement is gone in these more civilized and polite times, and he is not entitled to her earnings, the whole reason for the rule ceases, and so, too, ought the rule itself to cease under the maxim of law, "*Cessante ratione cessat et ipsa lex*" (the reason ceasing the [485] law itself ceases); and thus these statutes repeal or abrogate the common-law rule by implication. But this is nothing but judicial repeal—a dangerous road, in so important a matter, for courts to travel. If there ever was reason for the rule, much of it yet continues. The husband still, outside of the property rights, has a potential influence over the wife. His counsel may restrain her from wrong, his counsel may instigate her to it. He might encourage her to the grossest wrong against others secretly, and it would be utterly out of the power of the victim of her wrong to prove his agency in it. We may say that his moral influence over her, his capacity through her to injure others with impunity, was an element that entered into the adoption of the common-law rule somewhat or largely, and it yet exists. So the unity of person is not entirely gone. She could not contract generally. The rule did not arise solely from the consideration that by marriage he was invested with her property rights. And so it seems that not all the reasons suggesting the rule are gone,

Courts do not favor repeals of settled principles by mere implication. The New York, Pennsylvania, and Iowa courts have held that these married women's acts do not change the common-law rule of the husband's liability for the wife's torts: *Baum* v. *Mullen*, 47 N. Y. 577; *Mangam* v. *Peck*, 111 N. Y. 401; *Fitzgerald* v. *Quann*, 109 N. Y. 441; *Quick* v. *Miller*, 103 Pa. St. 67; *McElfresh* v. *Kirkendall*, 36 Iowa, 228; Wells on Separate Property, 560; 1 Bishop on Married Women, sec. 909. Thus it seems that sufficient reason exists against uniting in such judicial repeal. But, as remarked in

Withrow v. *Smithson*, 37 W. Va. 761, and by Mr. Bishop in his work on Married Women (vol. 1, sec. 909), this liability of the husband is unjust, and ought to be repealed.

As the husband is liable for the wife's torts committed before and during coverture, it might be inferred that she is not liable; but that is not so. If her tort is committed in his presence and by his coercion he alone, not she, is liable; and, where he is present, such coercion is presumed, until it appear that he objected, or she acted from her own impulse as the more active party, and then both are liable. **486** If the act be done not in his presence, both are liable, no matter whether he did or did not instigate it; and, where she is liable, both are sued jointly, and judgment goes against both: 1 Minor's Institutes, 345; *Roadcap* v. *Sipe*, 6 Gratt. 213; *Commonwealth* v. *Neal*, 10 Mass. 152; 6 Am. Dec. 105, and full note; *Wheeler etc. Mfg. Co.* v. *Heil*, 115 Pa. St. 487; 2 Am. St. Rep. 575, and full note; *Appeal of Franklin*, 115 Pa. St. 534; 2 Am. St. Rep. 583; *Brazil* v. *Moran*, 8 Minn. 236; 83 Am. Dec. 773, and full note; 2 Kent's Commentaries, 149; Schouler on Husband and Wife, sec. 134; Schouler on Domestic Relations, 103; 1 Bishop on Married Women, secs. 43, 905; 2 Tucker's Blackstone's Commentaries. If he die before suit she remains liable to suit alone. If he die before judgment pending suit she remains liable: 2 Bishop on Married Women, sec. 254. It is even said he may be acquitted and she found guilty: Opinion in *Roadcap* v. *Sipe*, 6 Gratt. 213; 1 Minor's Institutes, 346. Thus she is liable to judgment. How is it to be paid? Take a judgment against husband and wife for tort, she owning land, before the separate estate act, in which he has a life estate and she the reversion in fee. Surely the whole fee, including her reversion, would be liable. Otherwise the judgment would be vain as to her: 1 Bishop on Married Women, sec. 908; *Fox* v. *Hatch*, 14 Vt. 340; 39 Am. Dec. 226; *Moore* v. *Richardson*, 37 Me. 438. But is her separate estate liable to such civil judgment for tort? It must be so, else all the law just stated, which asserts her liability for tort, would be unmeaning. She owns a legal estate under our statute in her separate estate. She is a single woman as to it. The statute making her estate separate in words says it shall be separate to her as if she were a single woman. A judgment for a tort is a personal judgment: *Van Metre* v. *Wolf*, 27 Iowa, 341. Why does it not bind her separate estate? It would seem to be an anomaly and absurdity to implead her in court and render judgment against her, and yet say that judgment is fruitless, though she is legal owner of estate to satisfy it. The power to give judgment implies the power to enforce it. Authority, which I regard adequate to support this position, has come under my observation.

In *Merrill* v. *City of St. Louis*, 83 Mo. 244, 53 Am. Rep. 576, it was held that " a general judgment against a husband and wife for a tort of the latter not committed in the husband's presence [487] or by his coercion is binding upon both, and the separate property of the wife may be taken in execution." In the opinion it is said: "It is suggested that such a judgment could not be enforced on general execution. In the present attitude of married women in this state, and specially toward their separate estate, I perceive no such difficulty and embarrassment as the ancient common law threw around them. It does seem to me that learned judges have exhibited too much timidity, or reverence for legal antiquities, in adhering to rules after the reason for their existence has given away before our advancing civilization and broadening jurisprudence."

In *Smith* v. *Taylor*, 11 Ga. 22, the judge said, in a tort suit: "If there is a recovery the judgment passes against both. If the wife has a separate estate it may be taken in execution, and she may be, together with her husband, arrested on final process": See 1 Bishop on Married Women, sec. 908; *Musgrave* v. *Musgrave*, 54 Ill. 186; opinion in *Richmond* v. *Tibbles*, 26 Iowa, 475.

Freeman on Executions, 128, says: "Judgments against them (married women) are generally binding to all intents and purposes, and are capable of being enforced in the same manner as judgments similar in other respects. Hence, when a personal judgment for money is entered against a married woman, either alone or in conjunction with other defendants, it is commonly conceded that execution may be issued, under which the sheriff may seize and sell her separate property."

What reason can be given to show the nonliability of her separate estate for torts? Is it that it required a statute to enable her by implication to make a contract to bind her estate, and that it is bound only so far as statute allows, and there is none declaring it bound for torts? There was necessity for legislation to enable her to hold separate estate and

to contract, as her contracts are void at common law; but
when was the time that the common law did not assert her
liability to tort? It required no legislation to enable her to
become liable for her tort, and being liable, and having property, it logically follows that it must answer that liability.
There is no prohibition in any statute.

488 Is she liable for fines for her offenses against the state?
If, as I have sought to show above, she and her estate are
liable in civil actions for tort, more so is she liable for penal
offenses. I need not cite authority to show her responsibility
for crime. She is a jurisdictional person in a criminal law
court. It can take jurisdiction over her and render judgment
against her. It can hang or imprison her. It can impose a
fine upon her. The very power to impose the fine of necessity implies the power to collect it. It is a personal judgment beyond doubt, and binds her estate as such. There is
no statute limiting the liability. It requires none to declare
it. It occurred to me that the very power to give judgment
carried with it as a consequence the liability of her estate to
it. And so I find Mr. Freeman, in his work on Executions,
section 22, says:

"It would be a contradiction in terms to say that all persons may be bound by judgments, and then to declare that
some persons are exempt from having executions issued
against them. The decisions in regard to the persons who
may be parties to judgments are not perfectly harmonious;
but wherever, under the law as understood in any particular
state, a person, or class of persons, may be made parties litigant, and bound by judgments against them, it must follow,
in the absence of statutes to the contrary, that the same persons may by executions be made to satisfy such judgments.
In other words, when a judgment is valid against a defendant,
an execution upon it, unless expressly forbidden by statute,
must be equally valid. Execution may therefore issue against
a lunatic and also against a married woman."

Mr. Bishop, in 1 Criminal Procedure, section 1304, says:
"A fine is treated as a judgment debt, and binds a married
woman."

In this state we assess separate fines against husband and
wife for one act of selling liquor, or assault and battery under
a joint indictment: *Commonwealth* v. *Hamor*, 8 Gratt. 698; *Commonwealth* v. *Ray*, 1 Va. Cas. 262. Who pays the wife's fine?
I find it stated in 1 Hawkins' Pleas of the Crown, chapter 1,

section 13, and Tyler on Infancy and Coverture, 359, that the husband is liable for a forfeiture under a penal statute for the offense of the wife. And in *Hasbrouck* v. *Weaver*, 10 Johns. 247, in a *quitam* action, a husband was [489] held liable for a penalty for a liquor sale made by his wife. But I should doubt his liability, and, even though he were liable, it does not follow that her estate is not liable.

I conclude that these executions were leviable out of the separate personal or real estate of the defendants. Therefore we affirm the judgment. ____

MARRIED WOMEN—CRIMES AND TORTS OF—EXECUTION AGAINST SEPA-RATE ESTATE.—A married woman who acts independently in the commission of a crime may be convicted as if she were a *feme sole:* See monographic notes to *Bibb* v. *State*, 33 Am. Rep. 94; *Commonwealth* v. *Neal*, 6 Am. Dec. 108, treating of the liability of a married woman for crimes committed in her husband's presence.   She is also liable for torts committed by her, when not committed in the presence of, or by direction of, her husband: *Wheeler etc. Mfg. Co.* v. *Heil*, 115 Pa. St. 487; 2 Am. St. Rep. 575, and note.   For torts committed by the wife, not in the presence of her husband, and not by his coercion, they are jointly liable, and must be joined in the action.   If there is a recovery the judgment passes against both; and, if the wife has separate property, it may be taken in execution: *Merrill* v. *City of St. Louis*, 83 Mo. 244; 53 Am. Rep. 576, 580; note to *Brazil* v. *Moran*, 83 Am. Dec. 776, on torts of married women.   Land could not be sold on execution at common law for the debt of a private creditor, but this rule has been changed by statute in many of our states: *Jones* v. *Jones*, 1 Bland, 443; 18 Am. Dec. 327; *Duvall* v. *Waters*, 1 Bland, 569; 18 Am. Dec. 350.   For a debt due the state or king land could always be taken in execution.   The king's preference devolved upon the state at the revolution: *Jones* v. *Jones*, 1 Bland, 443; 18 Am. Dec. 327.   One violating a statute regulating weights and measures may be fined, and the fine may be collected either by commitment to prison or by fieri facias: See monographic note to *Ex parte Bryant*, 12 Am. St. Rep. 203, on right to imprison until fine is paid.

STATUTES IN PARI MATERIA—CONSTRUCTION.—Acts *in pari materia* should be construed together as if they were one law: *St. Louis* v. *Howard*, 119 Mo. 41; 41 Am. St. Rep 630, and note.

Boggess v. Richards.

[39 West Virginia, 567.]

Contract.—Marriage is a Valuable Consideration for an Antenuptial Contract, and where a man, in consideration of marriage, conveys all of his property to his intended wife, it is not on that account
void, and the transfer is good as against existing creditors, unless it is
shown that there was fraud, and that she had notice of or participated
in it.

Limitations of Actions—Contracts.—A statute of limitations providing
that "no gift, conveyance, assignment, transfer, or charge not on consideration deemed valuable in law shall be avoided, either in whole or in
part, for that cause only unless within five years after it is made, suit
be brought for that purpose," has no application to contracts founded
on a valuable consideration, but is expressly limited to contracts on
consideration not "deemed valuable in law." It does not apply to a
marriage contract.

Husband and Wife—Separate Estate of Wife Acquired by Skill of
Husband not Charged in Law with His Debts—A husband who is
skilled in any particular branch of labor has the right in law to bestow
all his time, labor, and skill to the increase of his wife's separate estate,
and allow his just obligations to go unpaid. The property is hers still
and cannot be levied on by execution, or attached for his debts.

Husband and Wife—Separate Estate of Wife Acquired by Skill of
Husband is Charged in Equity With His Debts.—If a man skilled
in any employment does business in his wife's name with the capital furnished by her, and large profits over and above the necessary
expenses of the business including the support of himself, wife, and
family accrue therefrom, owing to his skill and experience, and he turns
such profits over to his wife or invests them in property for her, a court
of equity will treat such arrangement as fraudulent, and will make an
equitable distribution of such profits between the wife and existing
creditors of the husband.

Husband and Wife—Action Against—Personal Decree Against Wife.
If the husband dies pending a suit against him and his wife, and the
plaintiff prevails, a personal decree may be rendered against her.

J. Bassel, for the appellant.

E. Maxwell and M. M. Thompson, for the appellee.

568 Dent, J. In the circuit court of Harrison county, at
April rules, 1890, plaintiff filed his bill in chancery against
the defendants, alleging, among other things, that on the
thirtieth day of May, 1887, he obtained a judgment against
the defendant, Wilbur F. Richards, for the sum of four
hundred and twenty dollars, with interest from date, and
twenty-two dollars and seventy cents costs, because of a libel
published on the twelfth day of July, 1884, which judgment
was in full force and wholly unpaid; that said Richards, at
the time of such libelous publication, was the owner of a

large amount of property, but that on the seventeenth day of
November, 1885, with intent to delay, hinder, and defraud
the plaintiff, he entered into a pretended marriage contract
with defendant, at that time Melissa McCleary, now Richards, by which, in consideration of marriage, he transferred
and conveyed all his known property to her, she participating
in his fraudulent intent; this contract was not admitted to
record until May 26, 1886; that after the marriage said Richards retained possession of all said property, amounting to
about seven thousand dollars, and used and managed the
same as though it were his own; that he was a practical
printer, and with part of the money realized from said property, or rather, with part of the property itself, he purchased
the fully equipped plant of the paper known as the *Clarksburg Telegram,* and printed and edited a paper, and so used
and managed the property conveyed by said marriage settlement, that from about seven thousand dollars in 1885 it
amounted to upward of fourteen thousand dollars in 1890,
all due to the skill, labor, and management of said Richards;
that with a part of the proceeds of said property he purchased in his wife's name a certain lot, and erected a valuable
house thereon—all which he alleges was in fraud of his rights
as a creditor of said Richards, and was fully participated in
by his said wife; and he prays for a sale of said property
and the payment of his debt, interest, and costs thereof.
Numerous interrogatories are propounded for the defendants
to answer.

The defendants file their separate answers under oath to
the bill and interrogatories, in which they virtually [569] admit the facts as herein repeated from said bill, but deny
all fraud or knowledge of fraud, or that any of the various
transactions fully set out in said answers were made or done
with any fraudulent intent. All of plaintiff's interrogatories
are fully and at length answered. Plaintiff replied generally. Afterward, by leave of the court, and over the objection of plaintiff, respondents filed a supplemental answer
setting up and pleading the statute of limitations.

At the September term, 1893, the court entered a final
decree dismissing plaintiff's bill, from which this appeal is
taken.

The first question presented is: Did the court err in allowing the defendants to file a supplemental answer pleading the
statute of limitations? Section 14, chapter 104, of the code,

on which defendants rely, is in these words: "No gift, conveyance, assignment, transfer, or charge not on consideration deemed valuable in law shall be avoided, either in whole or in part, for that cause only, unless within five years after it is made suit be brought for that purpose," etc. This section does not apply to contracts which are upon consideration deemed valuable in law, but is expressly limited to voluntary contracts. The contract in this case was not only on consideration deemed valuable in law, but on the highest consideration known to the law, to wit, marriage. As has been said, though the common law abhors every sort of cheating, it loves matrimony. The law regarding such contracts is laid down in these words, to wit: "However much a man may be indebted, an antenuptial settlement, made by him in consideration of marriage, is good against his creditors, unless it appears that the intended wife was cognizant of the fraud. And, even though it conveys his whole estate, it is not simply, on that account, void; and, when a settlement is made in contemplation of marriage, the law presumes it was an inducement to it, and the courts cannot assume the contrary to be the fact": *Herring* v. *Wickham,* 29 Gratt. 628; 26 Am. Rep. 405; *Coutts* v. *Greenhow,* 2 Munf. 363; 5 Am. Dec. 472.

Such being the nature of this contract, it could not be avoided under section 2, chapter 74, of the code, but only under [570] section 1 of the same chapter, because it was made with intent to delay, hinder, and defraud, and the statute of limitations is no bar to such a charge: See *Hutchinson* v. *Boltz,* 35 W. Va. 754. The statute of limitations was improperly pleaded; but was the plaintiff prejudiced thereby? Mrs. Richards, née McCleary, was a purchaser for valuable consideration, and, to make the property transferred to her liable, it must be alleged and shown that she had notice of or participated in the fraud, if any, of her intended husband. This the plaintiff has wholly failed to do, and for all the purposes of this suit the marriage contract must be held valid, binding, and unimpeached, and all the property transferred thereby as the sole and separate property, including the rents, issues, and profits thereof of the female defendant, wholly free and acquit from any liability to her husband's indebtedness.

The plaintiff objects that this contract, not being identified by date in the certificate of acknowledgment, was improperly admitted to record.   In the case of *Adams* v. *Medsker*, 25 W. Va. 127, this court has completely answered this objection.

The plaintiff further insists that, the property in controversy being the property of a married woman, notwithstanding the fact that the bill propounds interrogatories under oath, and the answer responds to the interrogatories under oath because there is a general replication, under the holdings of this court the female respondent must prove that the property was purchased with funds not derived from her husband.   Now, the bill alleges, and the respondent admits, that the funds were derived from her husband, and states the manner of the derivation directly in accord with the discovery sought.   If the answer admits the facts stated in the bill, what is left for the defendant to prove?   The defendant admits that she received the property through the very transactions which the plaintiff alleges she had with her husband; but she denies that these transactions were fraudulent, either in fact or law.   The facts being undisputed, it devolves upon the court to say whether they are such, that fraudulent intent on the part of the husband with fraudulent knowledge on [571] the part of the wife can be inferred, or, if not, whether constructive legal fraud can be imputed to her.

Taking the whole history of the transactions of the husband as set out in this case, it clearly appears that it was the intention of the defendant husband to place his property in such condition that the plaintiff could not possibly succeed in making his judgment; and nowhere is this more apparent than in the duplicate answers which he has had prepared—one, no doubt, as agent, and the other as principal—for himself and wife, and filed herein.   It is plain from these answers that the husband, either through information from his legal advisers, or through his own study of the subjects, believed that he had all the property in controversy thoroughly armor plated against the assaults of the plaintiff, and therefore he appears to take special delight in showing how skillfully he has managed to increase the value of his wife's separate estate magnificently, and yet secured it beyond the reach of the clutches of his own creditors.   The exultation at the success of his scheme, and the fraudulent intent of the husband, are nowhere more apparent than when he gives utterance to the following false profession: " Respondent regrets that his financial circumstances are so poor, but he hopes that with the blessing of good health, industry, and economy he will yet be able, not only to pay his legal debts, or to have property of his own out of which the same may be made or paid, for it is disagreeble and annoying to respondent to owe any debt to any person." This, coming from a man who in the same answer apparently prides himself on the fact that by his ingenuity, skill, and good management he has succeeded in getting over fourteen thousand dollars in his wife's name in less than five years, besides supporting his family, and who owes less than one thousand and five hundred dollars, evidences a lack of sincerity on his part that amounts to almost positive proof that he considers himself under no obligation to pay the plaintiff's claim but justified in evading it in any available manner. It is true this debt was not one of his own contracting; but the law has made him liable for it, and therefore it is just as binding on him as a law-abiding citizen as any other obligation.

672 But it is not so with the defendant wife. She is guilty of no fraud in fact, nor has she been shown to have any knowledge of his fraudulent intent; on the contrary, she appears to be wholly innocent even from the suspicion of actual fraud; and the only question is, Will the law impute to her fraud from the fact that she became the substantial beneficiary of her husband's fraudulent purpose?

Having reached the conclusion that the marriage settlement was good and valid from at least the day of its recordation, May 26, 1886, against all creditors of the husband, both existing and subsequent, it becomes unnecessary to investigate any of the transactions of the husband, except such as were subsequent to that date. The property, which became the sole and separate property of the defendant wife by virtue of said contract, was as follows, to wit: Three notes known as the "Hustead notes," amounting to three thousand two hundred and fifty dollars; three notes known as the "Thompson notes," amounting to one thousand and seven hundred dollars; a judgment against E. T. Baldwin, six hundred dollars; one note on Joseph Murray, one thousand dollars; one note on Stewart Webster, one thousand dollars; also, a rental interest in a two-story brick block on Main street, Clarksburg, West Virginia. This property the husband took possession of, as he had a right to do under the law, and continued to manage for her use and benefit, and realized therefrom the sum of six thousand five hundred and twenty dollars. The amount that was never collected does not appear; but it was certainly some thing which under the marriage agreement he would be in duty bound to make good to her, as it is to be presumed that, when he made the transfer in consideration of marriage, he represented that all said claims were as good as gold, after the usual manner of men in similar circumstances. He made several investments in real estate, and gas and electric-light stock, which were all legitimate, and from none of which she received much more in return than the principal invested. It is therefore unnecessary to consider any of these, as there is no pretense that any of them could be treated as fraudulent, with the single exception of the transaction in relation to the newspaper plant.

573 About the first day of April, 1886, the husband, having caused the newspaper plant known as the *Telegram* to be sold under a deed of trust given to secure the Hustead notes of three thousand two hundred and fifty dollars, and the same having been bought in for the wife at the price of fourteen hundred dollars, credited on said notes, began in the name and as the agent of his wife to carry on said newspaper business, and continued the same up until the first day of December, 1890, when he sold the whole plant, including the balance of the lease on the building, for the sum of three thousand five hundred dollars, which he turned into his wife's estate, and which probably fully compensated her for her loss on the Hustead notes.

In the answer of the wife, repeated in the answer of the husband, is the following statement: "Respondent had confidence in the honor and integrity of her said husband as her agent, and committed to him, as her agent, the conduct and management of said newspaper, its presses, etc., to a very great extent, depending upon his honesty and integrity and skill in the correct and proper management of said newspaper, presses, etc., in her interests and as her property and business"; and "respondent, in answer to the ninth interrogatory of plaintiff, says that the amount of profits made from the *Telegram* newspaper property, including job work connected with said newspaper office, from the 1st day of April, 1886, until December 1, 1890, was at the average rate of from one thousand two hundred dollars to one thousand five hundred dollars per annum. Respondent is satisfied that the amount of said profits per annum during the time last aforesaid was upon an average not less than one thou-

sand two hundred dollars, nor more than one thousand five
hundred dollars; so that the aggregate amount of said profits
made from the said *Telegram* newspaper, including the job
work connected with said newspaper office, was, as respondent verily believes, during said last-mentioned time, not less
than five thousand and six hundred dollars, nor more than
seven thousand dollars."

In another part of their separate answers it is stated that
part of this amount was used in support of the family, leaving a net balance, however, of not less than five thousand
⁵⁷⁴ dollars. Now, it is easy to be seen that the husband's
labor and skill, he being an efficient and practical printer,
produced this large profit. The question presents itself,
Has a husband who is skilled in any particular branch of
labor the right to bestow all his time, labor, and skill to the
increase of his wife's separate estate, and allow his just legal
obligations to go unpaid? It has been settled by numerous
and repeated decisions that it matters not how much of his
labor and skill a man may devote to his wife's property; and,
although it may be changed from a rude to a manufactured
state, it remains her property still, and cannot be levied on
by execution or attached for his debts: *Miller* v. *Peck*, 18
W. Va. 99; *Atwood* v. *Dolan*, 34 W. Va. 563.

A court of law affording no remedy, what will a court of
equity do? In Bump on Fraudulent Conveyances, page 250,
the law is stated to be " an arrangement by which the husband acts as his wife's agent without any compensation, or
for a compensation that is insufficient, is, in effect, an attempt
to make a voluntary conveyance of the products of his skill
and labor in her favor, and is void against his creditors"; and
on page 251: "A debtor may; therefore, bestow his skill and
labor upon his wife's estate, so far as may be reasonably
necessary, without rendering the products liable to his creditors. He may do even more than that. As his first obligation is to support his family, the products of the land will
not be liable for his debts, until that obligation is discharged,
and even then they will not be liable, unless the portion not
needed for the support of the family is the result of his labor;
but, if there is any such surplus that is the result of his skill,
there is no reason why it may not be reached in equity and
appropriated toward the payment of his debts": *Shackleford*
v. *Collier*, 6 Bush, 150; *Glidden* v. *Taylor*, 16 Ohio St. 509;
91 Am. Dec. 98. In the latter case it is said: "The arrange-

ment between the husband and wife, whereby he undertook
to carry on business in her name and for her exclusive benefit, was, in effect, an attempt to make a voluntary settlement
of the products of his skill and industry in favor of his wife."

575 In the case of *Penn* v. *Whitehead*, 17 Gratt. 527, 94
Am. Dec. 478, Judge Moncure says: "Now, I take it to be a
sound principle of law that by no agreement or arrangement
between husband and wife alone, founded on no valuable
consideration, can the profits of the future labor of either of
them, much less of the husband alone, be secured to the use
of them or either of them, or their family, in exclusion of the
claims of their creditors existing at the time such agreement
or arrangement is made; and any such agreement or arrangement entered into for the purpose of having that effect would
be a mere contrivance to hinder, delay, and defraud creditors, and would be null and void as to such creditors, according to the true intent and meaning, if not the literal terms, of
the statute. . . . . No one will contend that such profits can
thus be secured to the husband alone, in exclusion of the
claims of his creditors. Nor can they any more be thus
secured to the use of his wife and family, at least in exclusion of the claims of existing creditors. . . . . To be sure,
the law cannot, or does not, compel a man in advance to
labor for his creditors." They have no lien or mortgage on
his person. "And if he chooses to be so dishonest as to idle
or give away his time, rather than labor for the means of
paying his debts, the law cannot and does not attempt to prevent it. . . . . A man is not apt to give away his labor, or even
idle away his time. If he is not honest enough to wish to
pay his debts, self-interest prompts him to do some thing, and
to try to secure to himself and his family the profits of his
skill and labor. This motive of self-interest is generally
sufficient, without being assisted by legal means, to stimulate a man into action, and prevent him from throwing or
giving away his time, instead of trying to make a profitable
use of it; and the law, instead of attempting to apply such
stimulus, contents itself with subjecting any profit he may
make for himself or family to liability to the payment of his
debts aforesaid."

In the case of *Trapnell* v. *Conklyn*, 37 W. Va. 242, 38 Am.
St. Rep. 30, this court stated the law as follows: "4· The
fact that an insolvent husband voluntarily bestows his labor
and skill in the business of farming carried **576** on by his

wife upon land which is her separate property, and operated
with her separate property, will not, in the absence of fraud,
render the products the property of the husband and liable
for his debts. If such product's, after the support of the family, leave a surplus in property attributable to his skill and
labor equity would make a just apportionment between wife
and creditors."

From these and other numerous authorities examined there
can be no other conclusion reached than that if a man skilled
in any employment does business in his wife's name with the
capital furnished by her, and large profits over and above the
necessary expenses of the business, including the support of
himself, wife, and family, accrue therefrom, owing to his skill
and experience, and he turn such profits over to his wife or
invest them in property for her, a court of equity will treat
such arrangement as fraudulent, and will make an equitable
distribution of such profits between the wife and existing
creditors of the husband. Not that the wife is guilty of any
actual fraud, but her hand, be it ever so chaste, is polluted by
receiving as a gift from her husband the funds which he is
endeavoring to fraudulently conceal under the cloak of her
separate property from the searching eyes of his creditors.

According to the admission of both of the defendants in
this case the husband doing business with his wife's capital,
and in her name and for her benefit, by his skill, labor, and
management during a period of four years and nine months,
succeeded in making a net profit of not less than five thousand
dollars above all necessary expenses including the support of
himself, wife, and family, partly supplemented by the revenues of the husband from other sources. The only way
that the law furnishes for the ascertainment of how much of
this handsome profit is due to the skill and labor of the husband is to deduct therefrom the legal interest on the amount
of the capital invested. The plant, which was worth much
more, was purchased for the wife at the price of fourteen
hundred dollars; but, as she lost the balance of the Hustead notes of three thousand two hundred and fifty dollars,
and the plant was afterward sold for her at the price of
three [577] thousand five hundred dollars, it is no more than
equitable that her investment should be treated as this latter
sum. The legal interest on three thousand five hundred dollars for four years and nine months—the time the business
was carried on in her name—is nine hundred and ninety-

seven dollars and twenty cents, which, deducted from the
five thousand dollars, leaves the net balance of four thousand and two dollars and eighty cents, representing the husband's skill and labor, which he voluntarily and gratuitously
merged into her separate estate for the evident purpose of
evading the legal liabilities incurred by him, though small
in amount, for his wrongful and illegal treatment of the
plaintiff and others.   He justifies his course for the reason
that they were not debts of his own contracting but liabilities
imposed upon him in legal proceedings, in which he was not
dealt with justly, and therefore he is under no moral obligation to pay them, but has the right to fight the law with the
law, and evade them if possible.

The maxim of the moral law is tooth for tooth, eye for
eye, reputation for reputation, property for property, and life
for life, or what is called "restitution in kind."   Human
ingenuity and wisdom could not devise a practical plan for
carrying out this maxim without the infliction of the greatest
cruelties, and oftentimes the greatest injustice.   So, leaving
the equality which this law demands to the final arbitrament
of Him who can weigh the motives and intentions, and from
whom no secret is hidden, and on whom no deception can
be successfully practiced, the common law, in cases of injury
to property, person, or reputation provides a pecuniary reparation in the way of compensation to the injured party, and
also furnishes the means of ascertaining the damage inflicted;
and, when that is once fixed and determined by its judgment,
it regards the duty of payment just as sacred and binding as
any voluntary obligation assumed by the party, nor will it
lend its aid in any manner whatever to him who is endeavoring to hinder, delay, and defeat the collection of such a judgment.   Owing to its feeble administration, it may sometimes
appear impotent; but inconsistency and duplicity are no
⁵⁷⁸ part of its nature.   On the contrary, it hates fraudulent
pretenses and practices and loves honesty and fair dealing
and will furnish every means to ferret out and bring to light
the hidden resources and property of him who is endeavoring
to defeat the collection and escape the payment of a legal
obligation, be it the result of a contract self-imposed or a forfeiture for a wrong self-committed.

Since the institution of these proceedings death has sum-
moned the husband defendant before a higher tribunal, where
we can expect equal retributive justice mercifully meted out,

but the property which resulted from his skill and labor, and with which he should have satisfied his legal obligations, is still in the hands of his widow and commingled with her estate, and the plain though painful duty devolves on the court of requiring her to surrender a sufficient amount thereof to pay the plaintiff's judgment. Her coverture being removed, there is no legal barrier to a personal decree against her; but, if she prefers the proceedings to continue against the property in controversy, it will be proper and necessary for the plaintiff to amend his bill and bring James M. Lyon, who appears to be a purchaser not *pendente lite* of said property, before the court, that he may defend his interest therein.

The decree of the circuit court is therefore reversed, and this cause is remanded for further proceedings in accordance with this opinion and the rules of law and equity.

MARRIAGE SETTLEMENTS—CONSIDERATION OF CONTRACT.—Marriage is a valuable consideration and will support a marriage settlement. A person may convey the greater part or even the whole of his property to his intended wife upon consideration of marriage, and the conveyance is unimpeachable by creditors unless fraud is brought home to both of the parties: See monographic note to *Hagerman* v. *Buchanan*, 14 Am. St. Rep. 741; *National Exchange Bank* v. *Watson*, 13 R. I. 91; 43 Am. Rep. 13; *Otis* v. *Spencer*, 102 Ill. 622; 40 Am. Rep. 617, and monographic note thereto discussing the subject; *Sanders* v. *Miller*, 42 Am. Rep. 237; *Herring* v. *Wickham*, 29 Gratt. 628; 26 Am. Rep. 405; *Coutts* v. *Greenhow*, 2 Munf. 363; 5 Am. Dec. 472. *Contra*, *McGowan* v. *Hitt*, 16 S. C. 602; 42 Am. Rep. 650.

HUSBAND AND WIFE—ADDITION TO WIFE'S SEPARATE PROPERTY BY SKILL AND LABOR OF HUSBAND—APPORTIONMENT OF PROFITS.—If a husband carries on business with money of his wife, as her agent, she giving no personal attention to the conduct thereof, and by his skill and personal services makes large profits, part of which he applies to the support of the family, and the surplus of which he invests in property purchased in her name, she cannot, in a suit by his creditors to subject the property so purchased to the payment of his debts, claim the whole of the property as profits arising from her separate money: *Glidden* v. *Taylor*, 16 Ohio St. 509; 91 Am. Dec. 98. If, in such cases, substantial property, traceable to the skill and labor of the husband, is found to exist, courts of equity will make a just apportionment thereof between the wife and her husband's creditors: *Trapnell* v. *Conklyn*, 37 W. Va. 242; 38 Am. St. Rep. 30, and note. The fact that a husband has the management of his wife's separate personal property as if it belonged to him, and not to the wife, will not affect her title to it, so far as the creditors of the husband are concerned: *Second Nat. Bank* v. *Merrill*, 81 Wis. 151; 29 Am. St. Rep. 877; *Wood* v. *Armour*, 88 Wis. 488; 43 Am. St. Rep. 918.

INDEX TO THE NOTES.

INDEX.

ABATEMENT.
See NUISANCE, 2.

ACCIDENTS.
See NEGLIGENCE, 6; RAILROADS, 16.

ACCOUNTING.
See EXECUTORS AND ADMINISTRATORS, 10.

ACTIONS.

1. A CAUSE OF ACTION DOES NOT EXIST, unless there is a person in existence capable of suing, or of being sued. *Riner v. Riner*, 693.

2. NEGLIGENCE—TRANSITORY ACTION—PROOF OF LEX LOCI.—A common-law action against a railroad company by an employee to recover for injuries caused by the negligence of the company is transitory in its nature, and may be maintained in a state other than that in which the injury is received without proof of the law of the latter state. *Burdict v. Missouri Pac. Ry. Co.*, 528.

ADOPTION.

CONFLICT OF LAWS—ADOPTED CHILDREN.—Though children adopted in a foreign country may have acquired the status of children and heirs at law of a person there residing, yet, if he subsequently removes to another country, and there acquires property, it is subject to the laws of that country, and the right of the owner to dispose of it by will, though by so doing he may disinherit the children. *Long v. Hess*, 143.

ADULTERATION.

POLICE POWER—ARTIFICIAL COLORING IN VINEGAR.—A statute prohibiting every person from manufacturing or keeping for sale any vinegar containing any artificial coloring matter is constitutional and enforceable though the coloring is harmless and not injurious to health, and the vinegar so colored is in all respects equal to the best vinegar of the class which it is colored to represent, if the object of the coloring is to deceive purchasers into believing that the vinegar was of this latter class. *People v. Girard*, 595.

See MUNICIPAL CORPORATIONS, 20.

ADVERSE POSSESSION.
See CROPS.

AGENCY.

1. TRUST FUNDS.—A principal is entitled in all cases when he can trace his property, whether it be in the hands of his agent, or of his representa-

(959)

tive, or of a third person, to reclaim it, and it is immaterial that it has been converted into money if it is in condition to be distinguished from other property or assets of the agent. *Roca* v. *Byrne*, 599.

2. IF AN AGENT RECEIVED OF HIS PRINCIPAL bills to be collected and thereafter used to satisfy such obligations as the principal may incur, and which, when collected, the agent deposited in bank to his own credit, the equitable title remains to the moneys so deposited in the principal, and on the agent's insolvency the principal may recover them in preference to the other creditors of such agent. *Roca* v. *Byrne*, 599.

3. CONSIGNMENT FOR SALE—LIEN FOR COMMISSION.—Under a contract of consignment for sale, where the contract is one of pure agency, the agent's right to a lien for commission and expenditures is one personal to himself, not transferable, and he alone has the right to take advantage of it. *Barnes Safe etc. Co.* v. *Bloch Bros. Tobacco Co.*, 846.

See INSURANCE, 39, 40.

ALTERATION.
See NEGOTIABLE INSTRUMENTS, 16, 17.

AMENDMENTS.
See APPEAL, 20.

ANTENUPTIAL CONTRACTS.
See MARRIAGE AND DIVORCE.

APPEAL.

1. APPEAL DOES NOT LIE from a discharged and satisfied judgment *State* v. *Conkling*, 270.

2. JUDGMENTS—DISCHARGE OF—RIGHT TO APPEAL.—One found guilty of contempt, who pays, under protest, the fine adjudged against him, cannot reserve the right to appeal. No appeal lies from a discharged judgment. *State* v. *Conkling*, 270.

3. JUDGMENT—REVIEW.—If a complaint is fatally defective, and does not support the judgment, alleged errors occurring upon the trial cannot be examined upon appeal at the instance of the plaintiff. *Kennett* v. *Peters*, 274.

4. JUDGMENTS—REVIEW.—A judgment, if shown to be correct by the pleadings and evidence, cannot be disturbed on appeal, notwithstanding errors may have occurred upon the trial. *Kennett* v. *Peters*, 274.

5. To bring before the supreme court of Illinois for review the rulings of the trial court upon a question of law, written propositions must be submitted to it to be held as law in the decision of the cause, and the court must then write on such proposition either "refused" or "held," and the party objecting to the action of the court in this respect must except thereto. *Niagara Ins. Co.* v. *Bishop*, 105.

6. AN ADVERSE PARTY WITHIN THE MEANING OF THE STATUTE REGULATING APPEALS is a party whose interest in relation to the subject of the appeal is in conflict with the reversal or modification of the judgment or order from which the appeal is prosecuted. *Green* v. *Berge*, 25.

7. ADVERSE PARTY, WHO IS—CODEFENDANTS.—Under a statute requiring every notice of appeal to be served on the adverse party or his attorney, a plaintiff against whom a judgment has been entered in favor of

had been submitted to arbitration by the parties and a certain compensation agreed upon, though inadmissible in evidence, is not reversible error if the jury is cautioned by the court not to take the matter into account, and the issues are clearly defined and set forth in the charge. *Talmage* v. *Smith*, 414.

17. WHEN ASSIGNMENT OF ERROR MAY BE CONSIDERED AS A WHOLE.— On an appeal from a judgment of the superior court in general term, reversing a judgment of that court in special term overruling a motion for a new trial, the assignment of error in general term being that the court in special term erred in overruling appellant's motion for a new trial, which was sustained as a whole, and not by piecemeal, the supreme court may consider such assignment as a whole. *Springer* v. *Byram*, 159.

18. BILL OF EXCEPTIONS — MOTION FOR NEW TRIAL. — The supreme court is not precluded from considering a statement of offered evidence in a motion for a new trial, because of a slight difference between the phraseology of the motion and that of the bill of exceptions relating to the statement of testimony offered to be proved, if the substance is the same in each. *Springer* v. *Byram*, 159.

19. INSTRUCTIONS—REVERSAL OF JUDGMENT.—An erroneous instruction on a material point is presumed on appeal to have been to the prejudice of the exceptant, and will justify a reversal of judgment, unless it clearly appears from the record that it was harmless. *Osborne* v. *Francis*, 855.

20. PRACTICE—AMENDMENTS—PRESUMPTION.—In the absence of exceptions it is to be presumed on appeal that amendments to pleadings permitted by the court below were properly permitted and made. *Nichols* v. *Stevens*, 514.

21. IF DEPOSITIONS ARE ADMITTED IN EVIDENCE against the objections of a party, but upon all the evidence judgment is rendered in his favor, from which his adversary appeals, the appellee, if he assigns no cross-errors, must be deemed to have acquiesced in the decision of the trial court, and the depositions must be treated as having been rightfully admitted in evidence. *Long* v. *Hess*, 143.

22. CHANGE OF VENUE.—Unless some abuse of discretion is shown on the part of the trial court in denying the defendant's motion for a change of the place of trial for the convenience of witnesses its ruling thereon will not be considered on appeal, as the matter is purely discretionary. *Sims* v. *American etc. Barge Co.*, 451.

23. DAMAGES—EXCESSIVE VERDICT—REMITTITUR.—If damages awarded are excessive, but the excess is not due to passion or prejudice of the jury the appellate court may designate such excess, and allow the plaintiff to remit it and take an affirmance for the residue, or submit to a new trial. *Burdict* v. *Missouri Pac. Ry. Co.*, 528.

24. VERDICT—INCONSISTENCY OF WHEN NOT GROUND FOR EXCEPTION.—An officer who directs another officer to make an arrest, and is found guilty of false imprisonment therefor, cannot complain of the verdict on the ground of its inconsistency in finding that the officer who actually made the arrest is not guilty of the false imprisonment charged against both jointly. *Burroughs* v. *Eastman*, 419.

25. DICTUM. — Two or more questions properly arising in a case under the pleadings and proof may be determined, even though either one would have disposed of the entire case upon its merits without the ether, and neither holding is a dictum, so long as it is properly raised and determined. *McFarland* v. *Bush*, 760.

26. STARE DECISIS.—The decision of an appellate court on appeal as to a question of fact does not become the law of the case. *Mattingly* v. *Pennie*, 87.

ARBITRATION.
See INSURANCE, 11-15.

ARREST.
See APPEAL, 24; MUNICIPAL CORPORATIONS, 4; STATUTES, 6.

ASSAULT.
LIABILITY FOR UNINTENTIONAL INJURY.—One who throws a stick of wood at a trespasser on his premises with intent to inflict an unwarranted injury upon him, though he misses the party intended to be struck, is liable for an injury inflicted upon another trespasser who is struck by such stick. *Talmage* v. *Smith*, 414.

See RAILROADS, 9-13.

ASSESSMENTS.
See CLOUD ON TITLE, 3; INSURANCE, 33; WATERS, 5.

ASSIGNMENT.
See MORTGAGES, 2; NEGOTIABLE INSTRUMENTS, 6-10.

ASSIGNMENT FOR THE BENEFIT OF CREDITORS.

1. WHAT IS NOT.—A confession of a judgment in favor of certain creditors with intent to prefer them cannot be recognized as amounting to a general assignment for the benefit of creditors. *Puget Sound Nat. Bank* v. *Levy*, 803.

2. INSOLVENCY.—THE INTENT TO GIVE A PREFERENCE MAY BE INFERRED when such preference is the natural and probable result of the acts done. *Conover* v. *Hull*, 810.

3. RIGHTS OF CREDITOR HOLDING COLLATERAL.—In case of an assignment for the benefit of creditors, a creditor who holds collateral security for his debt is entitled to participate in the distribution of the insolvent estate only to the amount of his debt remaining due after deducting the value of his collaterals. *National Union Bank* v. *National Mechanics' Bank*, 350.

4. RIGHTS OF CREDITOR HOLDING COLLATERAL. — A creditor who, after the execution of an assignment for the benefit of creditors, sells collaterals held by him as security for his debt, is entitled to participate in the distribution of the insolvent estate only to the extent of the balance remaining due him. *National Union Bank* v. *National Mechanics' Bank*, 350.

See APPEAL, 11; ATTACHMENT, 2; PARTNERSHIP, 8; PAYMENT, 5.

ASSIGNMENT OF ERROR.
See APPEAL, 17.

ATTACHMENT.

1. GARNISHMENT—JURISDICTION.—By a suit against an insurance company in a state wherein it has a general agent, and by the garnishment of such company, courts acquire jurisdiction over the debt due a defendant who resides in another state, and to whom such company is indebted for a loss suffered by him in the state of his residence for the destruction of property there situate. *Neufelder v. North British etc. Ins. Co.* 793.

2. ATTACHMENT IN ANOTHER STATE—EFFECT OF INSOLVENCY LAWS UPON. A statute of this state, providing that a general assignment by the debtor for the benefit of his creditors shall dissolve prior attachments against him cannot dissolve an attachment issued in another state by virtue of which a debt due to the assignor has been garnished. *Neufelder v. North British etc. Ins. Co.*, 793.

See CREDITOR'S SUIT; DAMAGES, 1, 9–11; INSOLVENCY.

ATTESTATION.
See WILLS, 1–3.

ATTORNEY AND CLIENT.

1. ATTORNEYS, FREEDOM OF SPEECH, ABUSE OF.—A brief filed in the supreme court which, in effect, denounces one of the judges thereof, and attributes to him vile motives, and charges him with being *particeps criminis* to a scheme of villainy of which his election as such judge was a part, when there is nothing in the evidence to support such charge, is contemptuous and unbearable, and an entirely unwarranted abuse of the freedom of speech. *In re Philbrook*, 59.

2. ATTORNEY AT LAW, DISBARMENT OF FOR LANGUAGE USED IN ARGUMENT. An attorney who, in a brief, charges a member of the court with being while an attorney, *particeps criminis* in a vile scheme and conspiracy against justice, and declares that unless the other judges pronounce the transaction in question illegal and void, all persons to whom knowledge of the case may come will no longer suspect, but will know, that the courts may be corrupted, and will point to their decision as proof, is guilty of a breach of his duty as an attorney at law to maintain the respect due to courts of justice and judicial officers, to abstain from offensive language, and to advance no fact prejudicial to the honor or reputation of a party or witness unless required by the justice of the case, and may, as a punishment, be suspended from his office as an attorney at law. *In re Philbrook*, 59.

See MASTER AND SERVANT, 1.

ATTORNEY'S FEES.
See DAMAGES, 1.

AUCTIONS.

AUCTIONEER'S LIABILITY.—An auctioneer who takes property into his possession from one not the true owner, and sells it in good faith, paying over the proceeds, less his commissions, is liable in trover to the true owner, although such auctioneer has no knowledge of want of title in the party for whom he sells. *Kearney v. Clutton*, 394.

BAILMENT.

CONTRACT OF BAILMENT, ENTIRETY OF.—A contract to store hay for a specified period is an entirety, and no compensation therefor can be recovered when, because of the destruction of the warehouse, the contract to keep the hay for the time designated has not been, and cannot be, performed. *Cunningham* v. *Kenney*, 30.

See SALES, 3.

BANKS.

1. **INSOLVENCY, FRAUD IN PERMITTING DEPOSIT AFTER.**—To permit a deposit in a bank in reliance upon its supposed solvency is a gross fraud if its officers know at the time of its insolvency, and the depositor is entitled to reclaim the deposit or the proceeds. *Grant* v. *Walsh*, 626.

2. **CHECK DEPOSITED IN INSOLVENT, DEFENSE TO.**—If a check drawn by a depositor in his own favor is deposited in any bank, and he is subsequently sued thereon, it is error to reject evidence by him tending to prove that when the deposit was received the officers of the bank had notice of its insolvent and failing condition. *Grant* v. *Walsh*, 626.

3. **WHEN MUST PROVE THAT IT IS A BONA FIDE HOLDER.**—If a check is deposited in a bank whose officers then know it is insolvent and about to fail, and is afterward transferred to another bank, the latter is not presumed to be a *bona fide* holder, and cannot recover without first showing that it received such check without notice of the fraud in the due and regular course of business and had paid value therefor. *Grant* v. *Walsh*, 626.

4. **TITLE TO DRAFTS LEFT AT BANK FOR "COLLECTION AND CREDIT."**—A deposit being made by a customer in a bank, in the ordinary course of business, of money drafts or other negotiable paper, received and credited as money, the title vests in the bank, which immediately becomes the owner of the property and a debtor of the depositor for the amount. In the absence of any special agreement this course of dealing would be held to show conclusively that such was the intention. *In re State Bank*, 454.

5. **TITLE TO DRAFTS LEFT AT BANK FOR "COLLECTION AND CREDIT"—AGREEMENT.**—The question as to whether money drafts or other negotiable paper, deposited by a customer in a bank, is the property of the bank, is really one of agreement between the parties, as neither an unrestricted indorsement of the paper by the customer, nor crediting him with the amount of his account, with the privilege of drawing against it, is conclusive on the question of ownership. If it is, in fact, delivered to the bank for collection, or for "collection and credit," a credit to the customer before collection will be deemed merely provisional, which the bank may cancel if the paper is not paid. *In re State Bank*, 454.

6. **BANK HOLDS DEPOSITOR'S PAPER FOR COLLECTION AS AGENT, WHEN.**—If drafts are left at a bank for collection and credit under circumstances indicating no understanding that the title shall pass, a finding is justified that the bank holds the paper for collection, as agent of the depositor. *In re State Bank*, 454.

BENEFICIAL ASSOCIATION.

See INSURANCE, 30–38.

BROKERS.

1. WHEN ENTITLED TO COMMISSIONS.—To entitle a broker, under a contract authorizing him to sell stocks and to receive as his commission all he could obtain above a designated price, to recover such commission when no sale is actually consummated, he must prove that he found a purchaser ready, willing, and able to buy the property on the terms fixed, and either that he procured from that person a valid contract binding him to make the purchase, or that he brought the vendor and the proposed purchaser together so that the vendor might have secured such contract had he so desired. Readiness and willingness to purchase can be shown only by an offer on the part of the purchaser to the vendor to enter into the contract of purchase, or by the execution on the part of the purchaser of a valid contract of purchase. *Mattingly v. Pennie*, 87.

2. CONTRACT WITH BROKER PREVENTING PERFORMANCE.—A broker authorized to sell property, and who informs his principal that there is a party willing to purchase on the terms upon which the principal had authorized the sale to be made, but without stating who is the proposed purchaser, cannot recover his commissions, though the principal refused to make the sale, if the purchaser never entered into any valid and enforceable contract of purchase, and never made any offer to the principal to do so. The refusal of the principal does not entitle the broker to the benefit which would have accrued to him upon performance, if he on his part had not so far performed his contract as to obtain a valid contract of purchase. *Mattingly v. Pennie*, 87.

See EVIDENCE, 7.

CHECKS.
See BANKS, 2; LARCENY, 2–4; PAYMENT, 1.

CHILDREN.
See INFANTS.

CLOUD ON TITLE.

1. WHO MAY MAINTAIN BILL TO REMOVE.—A bill to remove a cloud on title cannot be maintained unless the plaintiff has both the legal title and the possession. *Helden* v. *Hellen*, 371.
2. RIGHT OF EXECUTION PURCHASER TO MAINTAIN BILL TO REMOVE.—One claiming title to land under an execution sale cannot maintain a bill against a party in possession claiming under a deed of trust to have such deed declared void and vacated as a cloud on his title. His remedy is by ejectment. *Helden* v. *Hellen*, 371.
3. VOID STREET ASSESSMENTS. — An action may be sustained to remove, as a cloud upon plaintiff's title, a street assessment valid upon its face, but void because of informalities in the proceedings preceding it. Though the plaintiff has a perfect defense in an action for the enforcement of the assessment he is not required to wait until such action is brought, but may himself invoke the equitable aid of the court to remove the cloud, and enjoin the holder of the assessment from asserting any claim based thereon. *Bolton* v. *Gilleran*, 33.

CODICIL.
See WILLS, 7.

COLLATERAL ATTACK.
See JUDGMENTS, 9–11; PROCESS, 4, 5; TAXES, 2.

COLLATERAL SECURITY.
See ASSIGNMENT FOR THE BENEFIT OF CREDITORS, 3, 4; NEGOTIABLE INSTRUMENTS, 1, 15.

COLLECTION.
See BANKS, 4–6.

COMBINATIONS.
See CORPORATIONS, 1.

COMMISSIONERS.
See INSURANCE, 2.

COMMISSIONS.
See AGENCY, 3; BROKERS; EXECUTORS AND ADMINISTRATORS, 2.

COMMITTEE.
See INSANE PERSONS.

COMMON LAW.
See EVIDENCE, 2.

CONFLICT OF LAWS.

LEX LOCI.—The obligation of a contract made and to be performed in another state must be determined by the laws of that state. *Crumlish* v. *Central Improvement Co.*, 872.

See ADOPTION; CORPORATIONS, 22–26.

CONSIGNMENT.

See SALES, 1–5.

CONSTITUTIONAL LAW.

1. THE FACT THAT A PERSON MUST INCUR EXPENSES in complying with a law, and that he is not entitled to a hearing before becoming liable to incur such expense, does not render such law unconstitutional if it is an exercise of the police power of the state. *Health Department* v. *Rector*, 579.

2. DUE PROCESS OF LAW—POLICE POWER.—A constitutional guarantee against the taking of private property without due process of law cannot be construed as abridging or interfering with the power of a state or city to pass such laws or ordinances as may be necessary to protect the health and provide for the safety and good order of society. *Deems* v. *Mayor*, 339.

See POLICE POWER; STATUTES.

CONSTITUTIONS.

See HOMESTEAD, 3; JUDGMENTS, 4; OFFICERS, 1.

CONTEMPT.

1. CONSTITUTIONAL LAW.—A statute authorizing a county attorney to punish for contempt any witnesses disobeying process or refusing to answer questions when commanded by subpoena issued by such attorney to appear before him as provided by the statute is unconstitutional and void. *In re Sims*, 261.

2. POWER OF EXECUTIVE OFFICER TO PUNISH FOR.—The power to punish for contempt is never exercised except by legislative bodies or judicial officers, and cannot be conferred upon an executive officer while acting in his executive capacity. *In re Sims*, 261.

3. CONSTITUTIONAL LAW.—The legislature has no power to confer on an executive officer, charged with the searching out violations of law, and inquiring into facts prior to instituting prosecutions, the power, at the same time and as ancillary to the performance of his duties as such prosecuting officer, to commit persons to jail as for a contempt of his authority. *In re Sims*, 261.

See APPEAL, 2; ATTORNEY AND CLIENT, 1.

CONTRACTS.

RESCISSION.—THE RIGHT TO RESCIND A CONTRACT cannot be allowed to a party in default. Therefore, when he has contracted for the purchase of land, and fails to make his payments as stipulated in the contract, he is not entitled to rescind it. *Reddish* v. *Smith*, 781.

See DAMAGES, 4, 5; EVIDENCE, 8–11; INFANTS, 2–5; LIMITATIONS OF ACTIONS, 14; STATUTES, 3, 4.

CONVERSION.
See TROVER, 4-6.

CORPORATIONS.

1. UNLAWFUL RESTRICTIONS OF TRADE—FORFEITURE OF CHARTER.—If a corporation adopts by-laws declaring that its directors shall have power to make and fix the standard or market price at which milk shall be purchased by the stockholders of the corporation, and acting under these by-laws the directors, from time to time, fix the price of milk to be paid by dealers, and the price so fixed largely controlled the market in and about the city in which the corporation had its place of business, these facts support a verdict or finding that the corporation as thus managed constitutes a combination inimical to trade and commerce, and therefore unlawful, and are sufficient to sustain a decree forfeiting the charter of the corporation. *People* v. *Milk Exchange,* 609.

2. PERSONAL LIABILITY OF PROMOTERS.—A complaint simply alleging that the charter of a corporation is void because defectively acknowledged, and that the promoters of the corporation are personally liable on its contract, is insufficient to charge them personally on any other ground, such as that of a partnership liability antecedent to the attempted incorporation. *Shields* v. *Clifton Hill Land Co.,* 700.

3. PERSONAL LIABILITY OF PROMOTERS.—If land is purchased in the name of a corporation whose charter is invalid because defectively acknowledged, and if the purchase money notes are signed by a person described as president of such corporation, although no formal organization or election of officers has at that time been made, such president or the other promoters of the corporation are not personally liable for such notes, especially when the corporation at its first regular meeting has approved the purchase, and the vendor has recognized the corporation as the purchaser in foreclosure proceedings. *Shields* v. *Clifton Hill Land Co.,* 700.

4. LIABILITY OF PROMOTERS.—Persons assuming to act under a corporate charter, invalid because some positive requirement of the law has not been complied with, are liable as individuals for all debts contracted by them in the name of the corporation. *Shields* v. *Clifton Hill Land Co.,* 700.

5. CONTRACTS OF—PRESUMPTION.—A contract whereby a corporation receives needed property in the payment of stock subscription is presumed, in the first instance, to be valid and binding upon all parties concerned, and must stand as made, and operate as intended, until impeached by appropriate pleading and proof. *Shields* v. *Clifton Hill Land Co.,* 700.

6. LEGISLATIVE RATIFICATION of the acts of an invalid corporation may not only legalize the existence of the corporation, and authorize it to act in a corporate capacity thereafter, but may also cure the illegality of corporate acts performed before the act of ratification was passed, and render such acts as valid as if authority to perform them had been previously granted by the legislature. *Shields* v. *Clifton Hill Land Co.,* 700.

7. STATUTES LEGALIZING EXISTENCE OF—IMPAIRMENT OF CONTRACTS.—A statute ratifying the acts and legalizing the existence of a corporation illegally organized, thereby defeating the personal liability

26. FOREIGN —CONFLICT OF LAWS — STOCKHOLDER'S LIABILITY.—A statute of this state providing that foreign corporations doing business shall be subject to all the liabilities, restrictions, and duties that may be imposed upon corporations of like character organized under the general laws of this state does not prohibit a citizen of this state from becoming a stockholder in a foreign corporation, nor relieve him from liabilities imposed by the laws of the country in which the corporation was created, and to which he has submitted by his voluntary action in becoming a stockholder. *Mandel* v. *Swan Land etc. Co.*, 124.

27. A STOCKHOLDER'S LIABILITY FOR CALLS UPON HIS SUBSCRIPTION to the corporate stock, though created by statute, is contractual in its nature. *Mandel* v. *Swan Land etc. Co.*, 124.

28. THE LIABILITY OF STOCKHOLDERS TO CREDITORS IS SEVERAL. Hence a creditor of a corporation may maintain a suit against a stockholder who has not paid for his stock in full, and may compel him to pay the balance due, if it does not exceed the amount of the liability of the corporation to the creditor, and the stockholder has no right to have the other stockholders made parties to the suit, nor to restrict a recovery against him to his proportion of the debt due such creditor. *Coleman* v. *Howe*, 133.

29. STOCKHOLDERS' LIABILITY CONTINUES UNTIL THEIR STOCK HAS BEEN IN GOOD FAITH FULLY PAID UP, and cannot be avoided by agreements between themselves that shares of the capital stock shall be regarded as fully paid up. *Coleman* v. *Howe*, 133.

30. JUDGMENTS AGAINST CORPORATIONS—CONCLUSIVENESS AGAINST STOCKHOLDER.—In the absence of fraud or collusion a judgment against a corporation is valid and binding against a stockholder as to his liability for unpaid stock subscriptions, until reversed by him in some direct proceeding for that purpose, and cannot be collaterally attacked. *Nichols* v. *Stevens*, 514.

31. STOCKHOLDER'S LIABILITY—RELEASE.—The officers or directors of a corporation cannot release a stockholder from liability thereto, to the prejudice of corporation creditors. *Nichols* v. *Stevens*, 514.

32. JUDGMENTS AGAINST CORPORATIONS OBTAINED BY FRAUD—ATTACK BY STOCKHOLDER.—Fraud in obtaining a judgment against a corporation, to enable a stockholder to attack it, either directly or collaterally, must be actual fraud as distinguished from a judgment obtained on false evidence or a forged instrument. *Nichols* v. *Stevens*, 514.

See ATTACHMENT, 1; EVIDENCE, 5.

COTENANCY.

JOINT TENANCY—EXECUTION AGAINST ONE TENANT.—The individual interest of one of two or more joint tenants is subject to levy and sale upon execution running against such tenant. *Midgley* v. *Walker*, 431.

COUNTIES.

LIABILITY OF FOR ACCIDENT CAUSED BY FRIGHTENED ANIMAL AT DEFECTIVE APPROACH TO BRIDGE.—A county is answerable to a person who was driving up the approach of a public bridge, when his horse suddenly became frightened at a pile of large rock beside the roadway, and began to turn round, and, before he could arise to his feet or do any thing to control the horse, it backed over the unprotected wall of the approach, falling upon and destroying the buggy, and inflicting personal injury on the driver, if the accident would not have happened had a suitable railing been placed along the approach. *Rohrbough* v. *Barbour County Court,* 925.

COURTS.

See EVIDENCE, 1; REMOVAL OF CAUSES.

CREDITOR'S SUIT.

1. SUFFICIENCY OF.—A creditor who attaches land previously conveyed by the debtor to his sons, and, after obtaining judgment, files a creditor's bill in aid of an execution issued on such judgment, need not allege the insolvency of the judgment debtor, nor have the execution returned *nulla bona* in order to maintain the bill. The only question to be determined is whether the transfer by the debtor was in fraud of creditors. If the attachment is not dissolved, the lien is good as against the debtor, regardless of how much property he may own. His vendees alone can contest the title. *Gibbons* v. *Pemberton,* 417.

2. ALLEGATION OF OWNERSHIP.—An allegation in a creditor's bill that the judgment debtor executed a deed to the land levied upon to his sons for a pretended consideration is a sufficient allegation, in the absence of demurrer, that the judgment debtor owned the land at the time that the conveyance was made. *Gibbons* v. *Pemberton,* 417.

CRIMINAL LAW.

See ASSAULT; INTOXICATING LIQUORS; LARCENY.

CROPS.

1. RIGHT OF ADVERSE POSSESSOR.—The owner of land who is not in possession thereof is not entitled to the fruits of the land, and if the disseisee rents it to another, and enters into a cropping contract with him, and he raises crops thereon, he is entitled to them, and they cannot be recovered from him, though subsequently in an action of ejectment a judgment is given in favor of the landowner for the possession of the property. The owner's remedy after the disseisin is restricted to the recovery of the value of the use and occupation of his land. *Johnston* v. *Fish,* 53.

2. GROWING CROPS OF LANDS IN ADVERSE POSSESSION.—The fact that one who rents lands from a disseisee and raises crops thereon knows that another person claims to be the owner of such land does not entitle the latter, though found to be such owner, to such crops, because the disseisee is entitled to all crops grown while he maintains his adverse possession, and his tenant or other successor in interest has the same right. *Johnston* v. *Fish,* 53.

CROSSINGS.

See RAILROADS, 18–23.

CUSTOM.

See WATERS, 6.

DAMAGES.

1. ATTORNEYS' FEES AS ELEMENT OF.—In an action on an attachment or injunction bond to recover for the wrongful suing out of the at-

tain and fix the amount of damages, as they cannot act arbitrarily and by mere conjecture in making such assessment. *Watts* v. *Norfolk etc. Ry. Co.*, 894.

9. DAMAGES FOR BREACH OF ATTACHMENT OR INJUNCTION BOND—TAXES AS ELEMENT OF.—If a fund in the hands of a receiver is impounded by wrongful attachment or injunction taxes accruing on such fund and paid out thereof, pending the litigation are not a proper element of damages to be recovered in an action on the attachment or injunction bond. *Stringfield* v. *Hirsch*, 733.

10. DAMAGES FOR BREACH OF ATTACHMENT OR INJUNCTION BOND—RECEIVER'S COMPENSATION AS ELEMENT OF.—If a fund in the hands of a receiver is impounded by wrongful attachment or injunction the receiver's commissions accruing from loaning out the fund during the litigation are not a proper element of damages in an action upon the bond. *Stringfield* v. *Hirsch*, 733.

11. DAMAGES FOR BREACH OF ATTACHMENT OR INJUNCTION BOND.—JOINT JUDGMENT WHEN ERRONEOUS.—If several creditors successively and wrongfully attach or enjoin the distribution of the same fund of their debtor, each giving a separate bond, a joint judgment against all of them in an action on such bonds, or a judgment against each for the full amount of the damages resulting from such wrongful attachment and injunction is erroneous. The damages should be apportioned according to the amount thereof caused by each creditor. *Stringfield* v. *Hirsch*, 733.

See APPEAL, 23; LIBEL, 7, 8; RAILROADS, 9–13; TRIAL, 4.

DAMS.

See MILLS; NUISANCE, 1; WATERS, 10.

DEATH.

See LIMITATIONS OF ACTIONS, 7, 8.

DEBTOR AND CREDITOR.

1. JUDGMENT CREDITOR, RIGHT OF, AS AGAINST EQUITABLE OWNER.—A judgment creditor is not entitled to the protection of a purchaser of the legal title against an equitable owner or his creditors, or to any advantage which his debtor had not. *Miller* v. *Baker*, 680.

2. NOVATION—REINSURANCE.—A mere agreement whereby one party agrees, upon a consideration moving from the other, to pay a debt due from the latter to a third person is not a novation upon the mere consent to or adoption of such agreement by such third party creditor. This applies to contracts of reinsurance, and the doctrine of novation is not applicable. *Barnes* v. *Hekla etc. Ins. Co.*, 438.

See ASSIGNMENT FOR THE BENEFIT OF CREDITORS; INSOLVENCY.

DECLARATIONS.

See EVIDENCE, 6, 7.

DEEDS.

1. CONVEYANCE—DESCRIPTION—CONFLICT IN.—If a parcel of land is described as being subdivision No. 25, as designated on a map of a block of land on file, and is also described by metes and bounds, and there is

a conflict between the two descriptions, the former prevails. *Masterson v. Munro*, 57.

2. The Rule in Shelley's Case is this: Where a freehold is limited to one for life, and by the same instrument the inheritance is limited, either mediately or immediately, to heirs, or heirs of his body, the first taker takes the whole estate, either in fee simple or fee tail; and the words "heirs" or "heirs of the body" are words of limitation, and not of purchase. This rule is the law of Indiana, but courts everywhere are inclined to circumscribe its operation within the strict limits of its own boundaries. *McIlhinny v. McIlhinny*, 186.

3. Rule in Shelley's Case—Remainders, Vested and Contingent.— A deed creating a life estate in a daughter, with remainder over to the issue of her body born alive, but in the event of her dying without such issue, then with remainder over to another, is not within the rule in Shelley's case, the word "issue" being a word of purchase and not of limitation. Under such a deed there is limited on such life estate a contingent remainder to the issue of the daughter's body born alive, and on such life estate there is also limited to such other person a remainder contingent on "issue" not being born alive of the body of the daughter. Upon "issue" of her body being born alive, the contingent remainder as to such issue becomes a vested remainder by such birth, and the contingent remainder of such other person ceases to exist, and the remainderman has, and can have, no further interest. The remainder limited to the "issue" of her body born alive, though it becomes vested in such "issue" by the birth, is subject to be opened up to let in those afterward born alive of her body, before the termination of her life estate. *McIlhinny v. McIlhinny*, 186.

4. "Issue" as a Word of Purchase or Limitation.—In Applying the Rule in Shelley's Case there is a material distinction between wills and deeds. As to wills the rule will not be allowed to override the manifest and clearly expressed intention of the testator, which will always be carried into effect if it can be ascertained. The word "issue," when used in a will, may be a word of purchase, or it may be a word of limitation, depending on the testator's intention; but when used in a deed it is always a word of purchase. *McIlhinny v. McIlhinny*, 186.

See Judicial Sales.

DE FACTO.
See Officers, 3.

DEFINITIONS.
"Bed of the water." *In re Minnetonka Lake Improvement*, 494.
"Heirs." *McIlhinny v. McIlhinny*, 186.
"High-water mark." *In re Minnetonka Lake Improvement*, 494.
"Issue." *McIlhinny v. McIlhinny*, 186.
"Legislative power." *O'Neil v. American etc. Ins. Co.*, 650.
Lottery. *Davenport v. Ottowa*, 303.
Negligence. *Harker v. Burlington etc. Ry. Co.*, 242.
Newspaper. *Lynch v. Judge of Probate*, 404.
"Proportionate measurement." *Caylor v. Luzadder*, 182.
"Sale on trial." *Osborne v. Francis*, 859.

the sureties on the bond of her son in law, who is threatened by them with criminal prosecution for a defalcation of public funds, after persistent and uninterrupted importunities by such sureties, without an opportunity on her part to advise with disinterested friends, and only to save the son in law from such prosecution, she is entitled to have the mortgage canceled in equity for fraud, and she is not *in pari delicto* with such parties so as to bar her of such relief. *Bell* v. *Campbell*, 505.

2. FRAUD—UNDUE INFLUENCE—EQUITABLE RELIEF.—A party is entitled to relief in equity whenever undue advantage is taken of him under circumstances which mislead, confuse, or disturb the just result of his judgment, if proper time is not allowed him, and he acts improvidently, or is importunately pressed, and if those in whom he places confidence make use of strong persuasions, and he is not fully aware of the consequences, but is suddenly drawn in to act without being permitted to consult counsel or disinterested friends. *Bell* v. *Campbell*, 505.

3. PARTIES IN PARI DELICTO.—Equity interferes for the relief of the less guilty of parties *in pari delicto*, whose transgression has been brought about by the imposition or undue influence of the party on whom the burden of the original wrong principally rests. *Bell* v. *Campbell*, 505.

4. JUDGMENT, RELIEF AGAINST IN EQUITY.—Though a party against whom a judgment was procured by fraud was entitled to be relieved therefrom by motion in the case in which judgment was entered, this does not preclude a court of equity from granting relief after such motion has been made and denied. *Merriman* v. *Walton*, 50.

5. EQUITY AND LAW—COMPENSATION FOR COAL MINED AND TAKEN FROM ONE'S LAND.—In jurisdictions where equity is administered through the common-law forms of action, the plaintiff should not be turned out of a court of law in order to be admitted at the equity side of the same court. He may, therefore, in an action of trespass for the illegal mining of coal on his land, recover compensation in the same manner that he could on a bill for an account, though he might not be able to recover statutory damages. *Lewey* v. *Fricke Coke Co.*, 684.

See HUSBAND AND WIFE, 4; INJUNCTIONS; INSURANCE, 30, 35; LIMITATIONS OF ACTIONS, 2.

ESTATES.

1. DEVISE—ESTATE IN FEE OR FOR LIFE.—If the first taker under a will is given an estate in fee or for life, coupled with an unlimited power of disposition, the fee or absolute estate vests in the first taker, and any limitation over is void. If the power is dependent upon a contingency, or definitely qualified, the estate of the first taker is limited to life, and the remainder over takes effect. *Bradley* v. *Carnes*, 696.

2. DEVISE—WORDS CREATING ESTATE IN FEE.—Under the will of a husband bequeathing all of his property to his widow "for her special comfort, benefit, and support," with power to sell and convey the land devised, "if she thinks it advisable," and, "if any thing remains at her death, it shall go to" specified remaindermen, the widow takes an absolute estate in fee, with unlimited power of disposition, and the limitation over to the remaindermen is void, and of no effect. *Bradley* v. *Carnes*, 696.

See DEEDS, 2–4; REAL PROPERTY, 1.

ESTOPPEL.

EVIDENCE.

be surcharged with the loss to the estate, in case of disastrous failure, especially if all of the facts concerning the working of the ore showed that the undertaking was of a highly speculative and hazardous nature. *Shinn's Estate*, 656.

4. DUTY OF, AS TO ASSETS BEYOND JURISDICTION.—To hold that the representative of the personal estate within the domicile owes no duty whatever, either to creditors or next of kin, with reference to personalty outside the jurisdiction is to invite neglect and consequent waste and dissipation of assets. *Shinn's Estate*, 656.

5. PARTNERSHIP, EFFECT OF CONTINUANCE BY EXECUTORS.—If executors in compliance with a provision of a will, continue to carry on a partnership business, in which the testator was a partner, upon the same terms that the business was conducted in his lifetime, a new partnership is thus created, composed of the executors and the surviving partner. *Insley* v. *Shire*, 308.

6. INDIVIDUAL LIABILITY.—In an action against an executor in his representative capacity it is not competent to establish and adjudge an individual liability against him. *Insley* v. *Shire*, 308.

7. LIABILITY OF COEXECUTOR.—If one executor by his negligence suffers his coexecutor to waste the estate, when, by the exercise of reasonable diligence, he could have prevented it, he is responsible for the loss. *Insley* v. *Shire*, 308.

8. JOINT LIABILITY.—Coexecutors who give a joint bond are treated in law as one and the same person, and whatever each one does is to be taken as the act of all. *Insley* v. *Shure*, 308.

9. LIABILITY—MISJOINDER OF ACTIONS.—An action by one executor against a coexecutor alleging negligence and dereliction of duty, and asking that he be removed from his trust, cannot be joined with an action for an accounting by a partnership in which the estate has an interest with other persons not connected therewith. *Insley* v. *Shire*, 308.

10. ACTIONS BY—PARTIES.—All of the executors should join as plaintiffs in an action for an accounting by a partnership in which the estate is interested, but if the action is brought by one executor, and his coexecutors are made parties defendant, and appear without objection to the misjoinder of parties before judgment, the failure to name them as parties plaintiff is not fatal. *Insley* v. *Shire*, 308.

11. ACTIONS BETWEEN.—One executor cannot sue his coexecutor for money or property in his hands belonging to the estate. *Insley* v. *Shire*, 308.

See INSANE PERSONS, 3; INSURANCE, 5; LIMITATIONS OF ACTIONS, 6, 7; PARTNERSHIP, 1.

EXEMPTIONS.

See EXECUTION, 5–7.

EXPERTS.

See WITNESSES, 4.

FACTORS.

DEALING WITH — NOTICE OF POWERS. — Persons dealing with factors concerning goods intrusted to them are charged with notice of the extent and limitations upon their powers. If a transaction is brought in question by the owner of the goods the burden of proving the factor's authority is upon the party dealing with him. *Barnes Safe etc. Co.* v. *Bloch Bros. Tobacco Co.*, 846.

FALSE IMPRISONMENT.
See Appeal, 24.

FALSE REPRESENTATIONS.
See Insurance, 29.

FELLOW-SERVANTS.
See Master and Servant, 10, 11.

FINES.
See Execution, 1, 2, 4.

FIXTURES.

1. Tests.—One of the tests of whether personal property retains its character or becomes a fixture is the use to which it is put. If it is placed on the realty, to improve it and make it more valuable, it is generally deemed a fixture. If it is placed there for a use that does not enhance the value of the realty it generally retains its character of personal property. *Winslow* v. *Bromich*, 285.
2. Machinery constructed and placed in a mill to be used in and as a part of it, and which would pass by a grant of the mill, is part of the real estate upon which the mill is situated, and not personal property. *Havens* v. *Germania etc. Ins. Co.*, 570.
3. Sugar-wagons used in a sugar-mill for the purpose of holding syrup and conveying it from place to place by being pushed by hand on the floor of the mill, if similar to wagons used in other sugar-mills, and necessary to their operation, and not run upon rails, nor actually nor constructively annexed to the realty, or to any thing appurtenant thereto, but merely furnished for necessary use in the mill, and not to enhance the value of the realty, are personal property and not fixtures. *Winslow* v. *Bromich*, 285.

FORFEITURE.
See Corporations, 24, 25; Insurance, 6, 16, 17, 18; Vendor and Purchaser, 2, 3.

FRAUD.

1. Fraud cannot be Predicated upon the decision of a tribunal constituted by the parties themselves, either as to the equity or the law of the case considered, unless such tribunal has acted in bad faith and oppressively. *Hembeau* v. *Great Camp*, 400.
2. Pleading.—The facts constituting fraud must be clearly stated, whether it is alleged in a petition as a cause of action or in an answer as a ground of defense. *Nichols* v. *Stevens*, 514.

See Banks, 1; Corporations, 18, 32; Equity, 1-4; Infants, 2-5; Mortgages, 3-7; Release.

FRAUDULENT CONVEYANCES.
See Marriage and Divorce, 1; Negotiable Instruments, 12, 13.

FREEDOM OF SPEECH.
See ATTORNEY AND CLIENT, 1.

FREEHOLDERS.
See OFFICERS, 1.

GARNISHMENT.
See ATTACHMENT, 1.

GUARDIAN AND WARD.

ESTOPPEL — HEIRS — ACCEPTING PROCEEDS OF UNAUTHORIZED SALE OF LANDS.—Heirs who, with knowledge, accept the proceeds of an unauthorized sale of their lands, are estopped from disputing the validity of the sale. They cannot retain the purchase money and also recover the land. Hence, where the guardian of a woman of unsound mind sold certain land, under order of court, having alleged, under oath, that it all belonged to his ward, when in fact she owned but a one-third interest therein with her children, the heirs of her deceased husband, and the guardian, after the death of his ward, paid to the heirs their full share of such proceeds, after they became of age, which they accepted, knowing what their interest in the land was, and that such money was the proceeds of the sale of their interests therein, and their full shares thereof; such facts show a ratification of the sale by the heirs, and estop them from attacking its validity. They cannot retain the proceeds of the sale, and recover their two-thirds interest in the land. *Wilmore* v. *Stetler*, 169.

See INSANE PERSONS, 3.

HEIRS.
See GUARDIAN AND WARD.

HOMESTEAD.

1. CONVEYANCE OF.—A deed jointly executed by husband and wife conveying their homestead, though made subsequently to a lease of the homestead, signed by the husband alone, conveys a perfect title to the purchaser. *Wea Gas etc. Co.* v. *Franklin Land Co.*, 297.
2. LEASE OF BY HUSBAND.—A lease for years of a homestead is an alienation of an interest therein, to which the joint consent of husband and wife is essential. Such a lease, if signed by the husband alone, though with the knowledge and consent of the wife, and though she

to do, is null and void. *Wea Gas etc. Co.* v. *Franklin Land Co.*, 297.
3. EXEMPTIONS FROM TORTS.—A constitutional provision exempting a homestead from "forced sale on execution or any other final process from a court, for any debt contracted after the adoption of this constitution," exempts the homestead from execution and sale upon all judgments, whether founded in tort or in contract. *Mertz* v. *Berry*, 379.

See EXECUTION, 6; HUSBAND AND WIFE, 6.

HOMICIDE.
See NEW TRIAL, 1.

HOSPITALS.

LIABILITY FOR NEGLIGENCE OF MANAGERS OF EMPLOYEES OF.—An incorporated eleemosynary hospital, organized and maintained for no private gain, but for the proper care and medical treatment of the sick, and for that purpose made the manager of a donated trust fund, is not liable for injury received by a patient therein, through the negligence of its managers or their employees, and the fact that patients who are able to pay are required to do so does not deprive the corporation of its eleemosynary character, nor permit a recovery for damages on account of the existence of contract relations. *Downes* v. *Harper Hospital,* 427.

HUSBAND AND WIFE.

1. CONFLICT OF LAWS.—If an antenuptial contract is entered into between parties living in a foreign country, which does not purport on its face to provide respecting acquisitions to be made by them after their marriage, such acquisitions, if made in this country, will be controlled by its laws, and be in no respect affected by the antenuptial contract. *Long* v. *Hess,* 143.

2. MARRIED WOMEN—TORTS.—A married woman is liable for her tort, and, having property, it is subject to execution to satisfy a judgment establishing such liability. *Gill* v. *State,* 928.

3. ACTION AGAINST—PERSONAL DECREE AGAINST WIFE.—If the husband dies pending a suit against him and his wife, and the plaintiff prevails, a personal decree may be rendered against her. *Boggess* v. *Richards,* 938.

4. SEPARATE ESTATE OF WIFE ACQUIRED BY SKILL OF HUSBAND IS CHARGED IN EQUITY WITH HIS DEBTS.—If a man skilled in any employment does business in his wife's name with the capital furnished by her, and large profits over and above the necessary expenses of the business including the support of himself, wife, and family accrue therefrom, owing to his skill and experience, and he turns such profits over t ohis wife or invests them in property for her, a court of equity will treat such arrangement as fraudulent, and will make an equitable distribution of such profits between the wife and existing creditors of the husband. *Boggess* v. *Richards,* 938.

5. SEPARATE ESTATE OF WIFE ACQUIRED BY SKILL OF HUSBAND NOT CHARGED IN LAW WITH HIS DEBTS.—A husband who is skilled in any particular branch of labor has the right in law to bestow all his time, labor, and skill to the increase of his wife's separate estate, and allow his just obligations to go unpaid. The property is hers still and cannot be levied on by execution, or attached for his debts. *Boggess* v. *Richards,* 938.

6. HOMESTEADS—ALIENATION OF ENCUMBRANCE OF BY HUSBAND UNDER POWER OF ATTORNEY.—A power of attorney given by a wife to her husband to "sign deeds and mortgages, with full power and authority to do and perform all and any acts whatsoever requisite and necessary to be done in and about the premises, as fully and to all intents and purposes as I might or could do if present, with full power of substitution and ratification, hereby ratifying and confirming all that my said attorney or his substitutes shall lawfully do, or cause to be done, by virtue hereof," but not describing any real estate, nor referring in any way to their homestead, is too general and indefinite to authorize the husband

to execute a mortgage on the homestead signed by him for himself and as attorney in fact for his wife. A mortgage so executed is void. *Wallace* v. *Travelers' Ins. Co.*, 288.

See HOMESTEAD, 1, 2; LEGACY; MARRIAGE AND DIVORCE; MECHANIC'S LIEN, 4; TRUSTS, 1–3; WITNESSES, 1.

ICE.

See LANDLORD AND TENANT, 1.

INDEPENDENT CONTRACTORS.

See MASTER AND SERVANT, 4, 5.

INDICTMENT.

See INTOXICATING LIQUORS, 2.

INDORSEMENT.

See NEGOTIABLE INSTRUMENTS, 1–3.

INFANTS.

1. JURISDICTION OVER.—THE FACT THAT PROCESS WAS NOT SERVED ON INFANT DEFENDANTS does not render void a judgment against them in the courts of the United States if a guardian *ad litem* was appointed, a solicitor appeared for them, and the proceeding did not seek a personal judgment against them, but was to obtain a judgment declaring that certain property which had been attached as belonging to a partnership, though it stood in the name of another, was held in trust for that partnership, and should be applied to the satisfaction of its obligations. *Sloane* v. *Martin*, 630.

2. CONTRACTS OF—FRAUD.—If the personal contract of an infant involves the element of actual fraud or bad faith, as where it is improvident or calculated to squander his estate, he may recover all that he has parted with or paid. *Johnson* v. *Northwestern etc. Ins. Co.*, 473.

3. RECOVERY UPON CONTRACTS OF INSURANCE — BURDEN OF PROOF. — If the personal contract of an infant, beneficial to himself, is fair and reasonable, and free from any fraud, overreaching, or undue influence by the other party, and has been wholly or partly executed on both sides, and the infant has disposed of what he has received, or the benefits recovered by him are such that they cannot be restored, as in a contract of insurance, he cannot recover back what he has paid; but the burden is on the other party to show that such was the character of the contract. *Johnson* v. *Northwestern etc. Ins. Co.*, 473.

4. INSURANCE — VALIDITY OF CONTRACT. — A contract of life insurance between an infant and a solvent insurance company, at the ordinary and usual rates, for an amount reasonably commensurate with the infant's estate, or his financial ability to carry it, is a provident, fair, and reasonable contract, which it is proper for the company to make with him, so long as it practices no fraud or other unlawful means to secure it. *Johnson* v. *Northwestern etc. Ins. Co.*, 473.

5. CONTRACTS OF—RECOVERY OF EXCESS.—If the personal contract of an infant, beneficial to himself, is free from any element of fraud or bad faith, and is reasonable and fair except that his payments exceed the

value of what he has received, his recovery should be limited to such excess. *Johnson* v. *Northwestern etc. Ins. Co.*, 473.

See NEGLIGENCE, 8; REAL PROPERTY, 6–8.

INJUNCTION.

1. INJUNCTION LIES TO RESTRAIN ENFORCEMENT OF MUNICIPAL ORDINANCES admitted to be invalid, the execution of which injuriously affects private rights. *Deems* v. *Mayor*, 339.

2. JUDGMENT, RELIEF AGAINST FOR FRAUD.—If, contrary to the agreement of counsel for both parties, judgment is entered in a justice's court, and the fact of its entry is concealed from the defendant by the joint misrepresentation of the plaintiff and of the justice of the peace until the time for appeal has expired, equity will grant relief by enjoining the assertion of such judgment. *Merriman* v. *Walton*, 50.

3. JUDGMENT, RELIEF AGAINST IN EQUITY.—Though a party could have had a judgment against him annulled by certiorari he was not compelled to resort to that remedy in preference to proceeding in equity to have the enforcement of such judgment enjoined. *Merriman* v. *Walton*, 50.

4. JUDGMENT, PARTIES TO SUIT FOR RELIEF FROM.—Though a judgment is entered against two defendants, one of them may maintain an action to enjoin its assertion against him on account of fraud practiced upon him without joining his codefendant as a party to such action. *Merriman* v. *Walton*, 50.

See DAMAGES, 1, 9–11.

IN PARI DELICTO.
See EQUITY, 1, 3.

IN PARI MATERIA.
See STATUTES, 5.

INSANE PERSONS.

1. APPOINTMENT OF COMMITTEE—ORDER, HOW AFFECTED BY WANT OF NOTICE.—The appointment of a committee for an insane person is a summary proceeding, and notice must appear. Hence, where the county court, being a court of limited jurisdiction, makes such appointment, it must affirmatively appear not only that it had jurisdiction of the subject matter, but also over the person by service of process or notice. *Evans* v. *Johnson*, 912.

2. JURISDICTION—NOTICE.—The appointment of a committee, by a county court, for a person as insane, without notice to him, is void, even where the statute does not expressly require notice. The power of the court to act depends upon the jurisdictional fact as to whether insanity exists; and, though the court has jurisdiction of the subject matter, insanity, it has no jurisdiction over the person without notice to him. *Evans* v. *Johnson*, 912.

3. EXECUTORS, ADMINISTRATORS, AND GUARDIANS CANNOT RESIGN unless permitted to do so by statute. The same rule applies to a committee for the insane, as they are not officers. *Evans* v. *Johnson*, 912.

INSOLVENCY.

INSOLVENCY PROCEEDINGS—WAIVER OF LIEN ACQUIRED IN ANOTHER STATE. A creditor who has in another state attached a debt due to his debtor does not, by filing in this state a claim against such debtor in proceedings in insolvency, waive or abandon his attachment lien. The amount which he may receive under and by virtue of such lien may be deducted from the amount of his claim, and the balance is the true amount of indebtedness upon which he is entitled to dividends in this state. *Neufelder* v. *North British etc. Ins. Co.*, 797.

See ASSIGNMENT FOR THE BENEFIT OF CREDITORS; BANKS, 1–3; CORPORATIONS, 10; INSURANCE, 10.

INSTRUCTIONS.

See APPEAL, 19; LIBEL, 6; TRIAL, 1–3; TROVER, 5, 6.

INSURANCE.

1. WHEN GOVERNED BY STATUTE.—If the facts involved in an insurance loss bring the case within regulations prescribed by statute, such statute enters into and forms part of the contract of insurance as completely as if written into it. *Havens* v. *Germania etc. Ins. Co.*, 570.

2. LEGISLATURE—DELEGATION OF POWER.—Whether the legislature itself may prescribe a form of contract of insurance or not, it cannot delegate the power to an insurance commissioner to prescribe a standard policy of insurance. *O'Neil* v. *American etc. Ins. Co.*, 650.

3. UNAUTHORIZED DELEGATION OF POWER—CONSTITUTIONAL LAW.—A statute providing "for a uniform contract or policy of insurance to be made and issued by all insurance companies taking fire risks on property within the state," directing the insurance commissioner to prescribe a standard policy of insurance, and forbidding the use of any other, is unconstitutional, as an unauthorized delegation of legislative power. *O'Neil* v. *American etc. Ins. Co.*, 650.

4. CONCURRENT POLICIES—EFFECT OF STATUTE UPON.—If several concurrent policies of fire insurance are written with the consent of the respective insurers, and the property is wholly destroyed by fire, such policies as well as single policies are governed by a statute making the amount of insurance written conclusive as to the value of the property insured and the true amount of loss and measure of damages when so destroyed. In such case the aggregate of the concurrent policies must be taken as the true value of the property destroyed, and each insurer is liable for the full amount of his policy. *Havens* v. *Germania etc. Ins. Co.*, 570.

5. ACTION BY ADMINISTRATOR TO RECOVER MONEY PAID TO ONE HAVING NO INSURABLE INTEREST—JUDGMENT.—In an action by an administrator to recover money paid, before grant of administration, by an insurance company, to a nephew who was named as a beneficiary in a policy of insurance upon the life of his aunt, and who paid all the premiums and assessments due under the policy, judgment should be rendered in favor of the plaintiff for the full amount so paid by the company, less such premiums and assessments, with legal interest from the date of payment. *Riner* v. *Riner*, 693.

6. FORFEITURE—WAIVER.—Without any forfeiture of a policy of insurance there can exist no waiver of a forfeiture. *Shaeffer* v. *Farmers' etc. Ins. Co.*, 361.

7. VOID CONTRACT AS TO REAL AND PERSONAL PROPERTY.—Under a statute making the amount of insurance written on real property conclusive as to its value insurance companies cannot avoid their fixed liability

and loss by fire caused thereby, the insurer, in the event that no additional premium note has been given, is released from liability, unless it has neglected for an unreasonable time after notice to appoint the committee and to make the examination provided for. *Schaeffer* v. *Farmers' etc. Ins. Co.*, 361.

24. ALTERATION IN PREMISES. — The placing and operating an engine fifty feet away from an insured building is not an alteration of the insured premises, nor the use of them for carrying on a trade or business increasing the risk, unless expressly so declared hy'the terms of the contract of insurance. *Schaeffer* v. *Farmers' etc. Ins. Co.*, 361.

25. "WHOLLY DESTROYED" — DEFINITION. — The words "wholly destroyed," as used in statutes regulating fire insurance and fixing the liability of the insurer, mean the total destruction of a building as such, although there is not an absolute extinction of all of its parts. *Havens* v. *Germania etc. Ins. Co.*, 570.

26. TOTAL LOSS. — Under an insurance upon a mill and the machinery therein against loss by fire the fact that a small part of the machinery has been removed pending improvements prior to the burning of the mill and machinery then in it does not prevent the mill from being "wholly destroyed," nor reduce the loss from a total to a partial one; but the value of the machinery thus removed should be deducted from the total amount of the policy. *Havens* v. *Germania etc. Ins. Co.*, 570.

27. INSURABLE INTEREST. — PAYMENT OF PREMIUMS on life insurance by the insured renders the policy valid, even though the beneficiary named in the policy has no insurable interest in the life of the insured. *Heinlein* v. *Imperial etc. Ins. Co.*, 409.

28. PAYMENT OR TENDER OF PAYMENT OF PREMIUM on a life insurance policy is not necessary if the insurer has already declared the policy forfeited, or done any act which is tantamount to a declaration of refusal to receive the premium if tendered, or if he has failed to keep his agreement to notify the insured of the amount of such premium and the day when due. *Heinlein* v. *Imperial etc. Ins. Co.*, 409.

29. SURRENDER OF POLICY—RIGHT TO REVIVE. — If, after a mother has secured a policy of insurance upon her life payable to her son, if he survives her, and, if not, to her estate, the son pays the premiums on the insurance for and as the agent of his mother, and the insurance company then induces him, through false representations that the policy is a wagering contract and void, to surrender it upon receipt by him of the premiums paid, he is entitled to maintain a bill in equity to revive the policy. *Heinlein* v. *Imperial etc. Ins. Co.*, 409.

30. BENEFICIAL ASSOCIATIONS. — A CHANGE IN BENEFICIARIES cannot be made except by a substantial compliance with the regulations of the society and yet courts of equity recognize exceptions to this general principle. Equity does not demand impossible things, and will consider as done that which should have been done, and, when a member has complied with all the requirements of the rules for the purpose of making a substitution of beneficiaries within his power, he has done all that a court of equity demands. *Jory* v. *Supreme Council*, 17.

31. BENEFICIAL ASSOCIATIONS. — A BENEFICIARY CANNOT PREVENT a change of beneficiaries by obtaining a benefit certificate of a member of a beneficial association and refusing to surrender it to him for the purpose of making that change of beneficiary which he was entitled to make. If the member does all that is within his power to do to effect a change in beneficiaries, and fails to surrender the certificate and have a new one issued only because such certificate is in the possession of the original beneficiary, who refuses to surrender it, the beneficiary thus thwarting the wishes of the member will not be allowed to profit thereby, and his rights to the proceeds of the certificate are subordinate to that of the new beneficiaries selected by the member, and to whom the issue of a proper certificate was prevented only by the act of the original beneficiary in refusing to surrender the old certificate. *Jory v. Supreme Council*, 17.

32. BENEFICIAL ASSOCIATIONS—VESTED RIGHTS.—A BENEFICIARY, designated as such by a member of a mutual benefit association, does not thereby acquire any vested rights so as to defeat a subsequent change of beneficiaries effected at the instance of such member, unless the original, beneficiary was made such on account of some contract, or has some equities recognized by the courts, and which it would be inequitable to disappoint. *Jory v. Supreme Council*, 17.

33. BENEFICIAL ASSOCIATIONS.—THE PAYMENT OF ASSESSMENTS of a member of a beneficial association by a person whom he has designated as a beneficiary in the event of his death does not give such person any vested rights in the certificate, nor deprive the member of the power to change the beneficiaries, unless such payments were made pursuant to some contract. Otherwise they are to be regarded as mere gifts. *Jory v. Supreme Council*, 17.

34. BENEFIT ASSOCIATIONS.—IF A BENEFICIARY HAS EQUITIES DERIVED from a member of a mutual benefit association, and which it would be inequitable for him to disregard, he cannot disregard or weaken them by a change of his beneficiary; at least, when the second beneficiary is a mere volunteer or acquires his interest with notice of the pre-existing equities. *Adams v. Grand Lodge*, 45.

35. BENEFICIAL ASSOCIATION, BENEFICIARY MAY HOLD IN TRUST.—If a member of a beneficial association designates a person as beneficiary for the purpose of securing a debt due to a firm of which the person so designated is a member, the firm is in equity to be treated as the real beneficiary, and hence the death of the person so designated does not deprive the firm or the surviving member of the equitable interest, nor entitle the heirs of such member of the association to the fund falling due on his death on the ground that the death of the person named as beneficiary resulted in there being no one named as beneficiary on the death of a member of the association, and therefore presented a case in which his heirs were entitled to the fund on account of his failure to designate a beneficiary. *Adams v. Grand Lodge*, 45.

36. BENEFIT ASSOCIATIONS—WAIVER.—A CHANGE OF BENEFICIARY in a mutual benefit association cannot be treated as invalid for the reason that the application therefor was not filed within the time, if the association has waived this condition, and the contest arising for decision is between rival claimants to the fund after it has been paid into court to be awarded to the person found entitled thereto. *Adams v. Grand Lodge*, 45.

37. BENEVOLENT SOCIETIES—BY-LAWS—CONCLUSIVENESS OF DECISIONS OF.—. A by-law of a mutual benefit association providing that the decision of a tribunal created by the association to pass upon death claims shall be final, and shall bar a suit in law or equity to recover such claims, is constitutional and valid. *Hembeau v. Great Camp*, 400.

JUDICIAL NOTICE.

JUDICIAL SALES.

VOID DEED RESERVING LIEN FOR UNPAID PURCHASE MONEY. AND ITS EFFECT.—If the court in a judicial sale of land directs the legal title to pass on actual payment, or by reservation of a lien, and a deed is given retaining a lien for deferred installments of purchase money, the lien is not lost, and the purchaser does not get the land for nothing, because the deed, having no scroll or seal, is no deed, and does not pass the legal title. It is not the deed which creates the lien. There is an implied lien springing from the sale and existing until the legal title is passed by deed. *Evans* v. *Johnson*, 912.

JURISDICTION.

See ATTACHMENT, 1; EXECUTORS AND ADMINISTRATORS, 1-4; INSANE PERSONS, 1, 2; JUDGMENTS, 1-5.

JURORS.

See NEW TRIAL.

LACHES.

See LIMITATIONS OF ACTIONS, 6; TRUSTS, 3, 4.

LANDLORD AND TENANT.

1. ICE FORMED ON A NON-NAVIGABLE STREAM of water belongs to the tenant and not to the landlord, if there is nothing in the lease restricting the tenant's use of the property. *Marsh* v. *McNider*, 240.
2. LANDLORD, LIABILITY OF, TO TRESPASSERS.—A private owner or occupant of land is under no obligation to strangers to place guards around excavations thereon. He is not required to keep his premises in a safe condition for the benefit of trespassers or those who come upon them without invitation, either express or implied, and merely to seek their own pleasure or gratify their own curiosity. *City of Pekin* v. *McMahon*, 114.

See MECHANIC'S LIEN, 6.

LARCENY.

1. THERE CAN BE NO CONVICTION FOR LARCENY WITHOUT PROOF OF THE VALUE of the stolen property. It must be shown to be of some value, for the purpose of fixing the grade of the offense, and the penalty to be imposed. The market value of the article stolen, and not its original cost, is the test by which to determine the grade of the larceny. *Burrows* v. *State*, 210.
2. PROOF OF VALUE — PRESUMPTION. — If the value of articles stolen is fixed by law, as in the case of gold or silver coin, or national currency, no other proof of their value is necessary; but, in the absence of any evidence upon the subject of value, the court cannot indulge in presumptions to supply the omission. *Burrows* v. *State*, 210.
3. PROOF OF VALUE — PRESUMPTION. — If the value of notes, bills of exchange, drafts, and checks is not *prima facie* fixed by statute, the question of their value, in case of larceny, is to be determined by the jury the same as that of any other article of personal property. The fact that the maker of a check has funds in the bank cannot give rise to any presumption affecting its validity or value. *Burrows* v. *State*, 210.

4. BANK CHECK—INSTRUCTION. —To instruct the jury, in a prosecution for the larceny of a bank check, that "a check drawn on a bank, when the drawer has money on deposit, as much or more than sufficient to pay the check, is presumptively of some value, in the hands of the person in whose favor it is drawn," is erroneous, as it usurps the functions of the jury by taking away from them the question of value, which it is their province alone to determine. *Burrows v. State*, 210.

LATERAL SUPPORT.

See REAL PROPERTY, 2-4.

LEASE.

See HOMESTEAD, 2.

LEGACY.

LEGACY TO WIFE OF ATTESTING WITNESS IS NOT VOID.—A statute making void a legacy to an attesting witness to a will does not apply to the husband or wife of such witness, as neither has, under existing laws, any present, direct, or certain interest in a legacy to the other. *In re Holt's Will*, 434.

LEGISLATURE.

THE WORDS "LEGISLATIVE POWER" mean the power or authority, under the constitution or frame of government, to make, alter, or repeal laws. *O'Neil v. American etc. Ins. Co.*, 650.

See CONTEMPT, 2, 3; CORPORATIONS, 6; INSURANCE, 2, 3.

LEX LOCI.

See CONFLICT OF LAWS.

LIBEL.

1. MALICE MAY BE DIVIDED INTO TWO DISTINCT CLASSES, to wit, malice in law and malice in fact. *Childers v. San Jose etc. Pub. Co.*, 40.

2. MALICE IN FACT IS MATERIAL in an action for libel only to establish the right to exemplary damages, or to defeat defendant's plea that the publication was privileged. *Childers v. San Jose etc. Pub. Co.*, 40.

3. MALICE IN LAW IS CONCLUSIVELY PRESUMED FROM the publication of a libel imputing to another the commission of a crime, where the publication is not a privileged one. *Childers v. San Jose etc. Pub. Co.*, 40.

4. MALICE IN LAW is implied from a wrongful act done intentionally, without just cause or excuse. *Childers v. San Jose etc. Pub. Co.*, 40.

5. FROM THE PUBLICATION OF A FALSE CHARGE OF A FELONY NOT PRIVILEGED, the right to sustain an action for the actual damages suffered thereby necessarily arises. *Childers v. San Jose etc. Pub. Co.*, 40.

6. AN INSTRUCTION in a libel suit that damages may be awarded as an example to others, and as a punishment for the act done, should not be given, if there is an issue respecting malice in fact in the publication of the libel. Malice in fact is never presumed. *Childers v. San Jose etc. Pub. Co.*, 40.

7. DAMAGES.—TWO CLASSES OF DAMAGES may be recovered in an action for libel, to wit, actual or compensatory damages and exemplary damages. *Childers v. San Jose etc. Pub. Co.*, 40.

8. EXEMPLARY DAMAGES may be awarded for the publication of a false charge which is libelous *per se*, and not a privileged communication. *Childers v. San Jose etc. Pub. Co.*, 40.

LIENS.

See JUDICIAL SALES; NEGOTIABLE INSTRUMENTS, 5-10.

LIMITATIONS OF ACTIONS.

1. THE STATUTE OF LIMITATIONS BEGINS TO RUN, as a general rule, from the act done, but this rule has exceptions. *Lewey v. Fricke Coke Co.*, 684.

2. COURTS OF EQUITY decline to apply the statute if plaintiff neither knew nor had reasonable means for knowing of the existence of a cause of action; but, if the cause of action was known, or might have been known by the exercise of vigilance in the use of means within reach, equity follows the law and applies the statute. *Lewey v. Fricke Coke Co.*, 684.

3. THE STATUTE OF LIMITATIONS DOES NOT BEGIN TO RUN AGAINST A PLAINTIFF, who has been kept in ignorance of his rights by fraudulent practices on the part of the defendant, until discovery of the fraud. The discovery of the fraud gives a new cause of action. *Lewey v. Fricke Coke Co.*, 684.

. THE MISCHIEF WHICH THE STATUTE OF LIMITATIONS IS INTENDED TO REMEDY is delay in the assertion of a legal right which it is practicable to assert. *Lewry v. Fricke Coke Co.*, 684.

5. WRONGDOER.—MERE IGNORANCE will not prevent the running of the statute in equity any more than at law; but there is no reason, resting on general principles, why ignorance that is the result of the defendant's conduct, and not of the stupidity or negligence of the plaintiff, should not prevent the running of the statute in favor of the wrongdoer. *Lewey v. Fricke Coke Co.*, 684.

6. LIMITATION OF ACTION BROUGHT BY AN ADMINISTRATOR TO RECOVER MONEY PAID by an insurance company to a person who had no insurable interest in the life of plaintiff's intestate begins to run only from the date of the grant of letters of administration to the plaintiff, and the right of action is not defeated by gross laches in taking out administration. *Riner v. Riner*, 693.

7. RECEIVING MONEY OF INTESTATE AFTER HIS DEATH.—When one receives money belonging to the estate of an intestate after his death, and before administration granted, the statute of limitations does not run from the date of receiving the money, but from the grant of administration. *Riner v. Riner*, 693.

8. LIMITATIONS OF ACTIONS IN CASE OF DEATH.—If no cause of action accrued prior to the death of the party entitled, the statute of limitations does not commence to run until administration is granted. *Riner v. Riner*, 693.

9. THE STATUTE OF LIMITATIONS MAY BE AVAILABLE AS A DEFENSE, in an action of trespass for the illegal mining of coal upon one's land, as against the penal consequences of the trespass; but it is not available as a defense against payment for the coal actually taken and converted to defendant's use, and the jury should be so instructed. *Lewey v. Fricke Coke Co.*, 684.

have notice that legal opinion as to the validity of the ordinance is divided. *Goodwin v. Guild*, 743.

2. PUBLIC OFFICERS ARE NOT LIABLE for malicious prosecution if they fall into an error in a case where the act to be done is not merely ministerial but is one requiring the exercise of judgment and discretion, even though an individual may suffer by the mistake, unless malice, oppression, or wanton prosecution, with an absence of all probable cause or excuse, is clearly proved against such officer. *Goodwin v. Guild*, 743.

MARRIAGE AND DIVORCE.

1. CONTRACT.—MARRIAGE IS A VALUABLE CONSIDERATION FOR AN ANTE-NUPTIAL CONTRACT, and where a man, in consideration of marriage, conveys all of his property to his intended wife, it is not on that account void, and the transfer is good as against existing creditors, unless it is shown that there was fraud, and that she had notice of or participated in it. *Boggess v. Richards*, 938.

2. DIVORCE—CRUEL AND INHUMAN TREATMENT.—Ill-treatment by the husband, long continued, and consisting of continual scolding and fault-finding, the use of unkind language, and of many other little acts, if studied and malicious, and the wife is sensitive, may be cruel and inhuman treatment if it has a serious effect on her health, or causes her great mental suffering; but, to be a ground for divorce, the effect on her must be of a serious character. It is error to refuse to admit evidence of such acts in an action for divorce, although no act of violence is proved, or any act which would, of itself, prove cruel and inhuman treatment. *Marks v. Marks*, 466.

See LIMITATIONS OF ACTIONS, 14.

MARRIED WOMEN.

See EXECUTION, 4; HUSBAND AND WIFE, 2.

MASTER AND SERVANT.

1. EMPLOYEE, WHO NOT ENTITLED TO PRIVILEGE OF.—Under a statute providing that when a person or corporation shall make an assignment for the benefit of creditors, be adjudged insolvent, or have his or its property taken possession of by a receiver, all moneys due and owing therefrom for wages or salaries to clerks, servants, or employees, contracted not more than three months prior thereto, shall be paid in full, an attorney at law engaged by such person or corporation is not an "employee," nor entitled to any priority for the payment of fees for services rendered. *Lewis v. Fisher*, 327.

2. RELATION OF, WHEN EXISTS.—For the relation of master and servant to exist, so as to make the master liable, he must not only have the power to select and discharge the servant, but to direct the mode of executing, and to so control him in his acts in the course of his employment as to prevent injury to others. *Quinn v. Railroad*, 767.

3. PHYSICIAN OR SURGEON EMPLOYED BY A RAILROAD COMPANY to attend employees injured in its service is not a servant of the company so as to render it liable for his carelessness or negligence in rendering professional services. *Quinn v. Railroad*, 767.

4. INDEPENDENT CONTRACTOR—LIABILITY FOR NEGLIGENCE OF.—Although work is being performed by an independent contractor, and an injury,

been designated by the employee to furnish or look for such article, such boss does not, in making such suggestion, represent the principal, and, if injury results from his negligence in making the suggestion, it is the negligence of a fellow-servant for which no recovery can be had. *Keenan* v. *New York etc. R. R. Co.*, 604.

12. A SERVANT SUSTAINING AN INJURY FROM THE NEGLIGENCE OF A SUPE- RIOR AGENT engaged in the same general business cannot maintain an action against the common employer, although he was subject to the control of such superior agent, and could not guard against his negli- gence or its consequences. *Keenan* v. *New York etc. R. R. Co.*, 604.

See RAILROADS, 25–29.

MECHANIC'S LIEN.

1. IMPERFECT DESCRIPTION, HOW AIDED BY EXTRINSIC EVIDENCE.—Under proper allegations in the pleadings of an action to enforce a mechanic's lien, an imperfect description of the property in the lien notice may be aided by extrinsic evidence. That is certain which can be made cer- tain. *Coburn* v. *Stephens*, 218.

2. SUFFICIENCY OF NOTICE.—A mechanic's lien notice is sufficient if it describes the premises, and states the amount due, to whom and from whom, and for what it is due. *Coburn* v. *Stephens*, 218.

3. CLAIM FOR.—A statement in a notice of lien incorporating a contract to furnish materials and do work necessary to the painting of the building in accordance with a contract between the land-owner and the principal contractor, is a sufficient statement of the terms of the con- tract under which the lien is claimed. *Spears* v. *Lawrence*, 789.

4. THE SEPARATE PROPERTY OF A WIFE is subject to a mechanic's lien for the erection of a building thereon though she did not join in a contract therefor, if, during the progress of the work, she was about the premises with her husband and helped select the colors of the paints to be used thereon. *Spears* v. *Lawrence*, 789.

5. CONTRACT WITH OWNER.—If a materialman is seeking to enforce a mechanic's lien against land of the owner, there can be no recovery unless the lien is perfected, and this cannot be done unless a contract is shown to have been made with the owner or his agent. *Coburn* v. *Stephens*, 218.

6. LANDLORD AND TENANT.—Except as to his own interest, a tenant, as such, cannot subject the real estate of his landlord to a mechanic's lien. *Coburn* v. *Stephens*, 218.

7. A SURETY FOR THE PERFORMANCE OF A CONTRACT by the principal con- tractor, and who stipulated against the enforcement of any lien upon the building, cannot himself as a subcontractor claim and enforce such a lien, though it does not appear that the property owner will be in- jured should the lien be enforced. *Spears* v. *Lawrence*, 789.

See MERGER.

MERGER.

MORTGAGE—MECHANIC'S LIEN.—If the holder of a purchase money mort- gage, having priority over a mechanic's lien, takes from his grantee a quitclaim deed to the property after the mechanic's lien has attached, in consideration of such grantee's release from personal liability on the notes secured by the mortgage, a merger does not take place, and equity will preserve the prior lien of the mortgagor. It is only where the fee simple and the lien center in the same person, and where there are no intervening equities, that a merger of the title and the lien will take place. *Coburn* v. *Stephens*, 218.

MILLS.

RIPARIAN OWNER—RIGHT TO ERECT DAM AND MILL.—A riparian proprietor may erect a dam and mill under his right of dominion over his own property without an order of court, even though the stream is floatable. *Watts* v. *Norfolk etc. Ry. Co.*, 894.

See FIXTURES, 2, 3; NUISANCE, 1; WATERS, 7.

MINES.

See LIMITATIONS OF ACTIONS, 9-11; WATERS, 6.

MISTAKE.

See SUBROGATION, 1.

MORTGAGES.

1. TWO SECURITIES FOR SAME DEBT.—One holding a real estate mortgage and a chattel mortgage, as security for the same debt, does not lose any right under the former by not enforcing the latter. *Coburn* v. *Stephens*, 218.

2. PAYMENT OF MORTGAGE OPERATES AS AN ASSIGNMENT, WHEN.—The payment of money due upon a mortgage by one who is not an intermeddler or volunteer operates as a discharge of the mortgage, or in the nature of an assignment of it, as may best serve the purposes of justice and the just intent of the parties. *Heisler* v. *Aultman*, 486.

3. CANCELLATION FOR FRAUD—RECONVEYANCE.—A mortgagor seeking to cancel a mortgage for fraud and undue influence in its execution must tender a reconveyance of land conveyed to him as part of the same transaction. *Bell* v. *Campbell*, 505.

4. CANCELLATION FOR FRAUD — RECONVEYANCE. — If a mortgagor in an action to cancel a mortgage for fraud and undue influence tenders a quitclaim deed to land conveyed to him as part of the same transaction the court may compel a reconveyance as the price of a decree in his favor. *Bell* v. *Campbell*, 505.

5. CANCELLATION FOR FRAUD—DEFENSES.—In an action to cancel a mortgage procured by the fraud and undue influence of the mortgagor's son in law and the sureties on his bond, and executed solely to indemnify such sureties against the result of a threatened criminal prosecution of the son in law for a misappropriation of public funds, such sureties cannot set up as a defense the fact that the mortgagor has failed to reconvey land deeded to him by the son in law as a part of the same transaction, and at the same time deny that they are chargeable with any thing done by the son in law in the same matter. *Bell* v. *Campbell*, 505.

6. CANCELLATION FOR FRAUD — PRESUMPTION. — Acquiescence in a mortgage under such circumstances as to render it voidable for fraud and undue influence cannot be presumed from a failure of the mortgagor to move for its cancellation while the same conditions which caused its execution continue. *Bell* v. *Campbell*, 505.

MUNICIPAL CORPORATIONS.

tion and to regulate the sale of milk, a municipal ordinance providing for the inspection of milk offered for sale in such city, forbidding the sale of milk not coming up to a standard or test of purity prescribed, and authorizing an inspector to destroy all milk found by him to be impure according to such standard, is a valid exercise of the police power of the city and state. *Deems* v. *Mayor,* 339.

21. ORDINANCE AS EVIDENCE AGAINST.—If in an action against a city the condition in which it had put and left its private property is claimed to have been a nuisance, an ordinance declaring a similar condition of the property of a private person within the municipal limits to be a nuisance is admissible in evidence as tending to prove that th condition of its premises constituted them a nuisance. *City of Pekin* v. *McMahon,* 114.

22. MUNICIPAL INDEBTEDNESS, WHAT IS.—If, by a statute, a park commission is created in cities of a certain class, the members of which are authorized to organize as a board, to elect a treasurer, to certify to the amount of taxes necessary for park purposes, to acquire property therefor, to make contracts, to sue and to be sued, to issue bonds for the sale of real estate, to hold in trust all property within the city dedicated to park purposes, bonds issued by such commission constitute municipal indebtedness of the city for which the commission acts, and are void if, before their issue, such city was already indebted to the full amount of the indebtedness which it was authorized to incur by the constitution of the state. *Orvis* v. *Park Commers.,* 252.

See EXECUTION, 3; MALICIOUS PROSECUTION.

MUTUAL BENEFIT ASSOCIATIONS.
See INSURANCE, 30-38.

MAXIMS.
Id certum est, quid certum reddi potest. *Coburn* v. *Stephens,* 218.

NAVIGATION.
See EMINENT DOMAIN.

NEGLIGENCE.

1. NEGLIGENCE IS A FAILURE to do what a reasonable and prudent person would ordinarily have done under the circumstances, or doing what such a person would not have done under such circumstances. The duties are dictated and measured by the exigencies of the occasion. *Harker* v. *Burlington etc. Ry. Co.,* 242.

2. CARE REQUIRED OF ONE HAVING KNOWLEDGE OF A DEFECT.—One having knowledge of the defective condition of a street is bound to use more care in passing over it than if he had been without such knowledge, but is not bound to use extraordinary care. All required of him is to use such care and caution as a person of ordinary prudence would use under such circumstances. If the evidence does not show that he did not exercise ordinary care it should be left to the jury to say whether he did or not. *McQuillan* v. *Seattle,* 799.

3. KNOWLEDGE OF DEFECT.—The mere fact that a person injured from a defect in a sidewalk was aware of such defect is not conclusive of negligence on his part, though it is competent evidence on the question of his contributory negligence. *McQuillan* v. *Seattle,* 799.

NEGOTIABLE INSTRUMENTS.

NEW TRIAL.

1. JUROR—INTOXICATION OF VITIATES VERDICT.—The conduct of a juror, during the trial of a cause, after the court has adjourned for the day, in drinking liquors until he becomes intoxicated, though he is in his seat

on the next morning, upon the convening of court, renders the verdict
invalid. Upon proof of such misconduct it should be set aside, and a
new trial granted, especially in a prosecution for murder, where such
verdict is "guilty," and fixes the death penalty. *Brown* v. *State*, 180.

2. A NEW TRIAL WILL NOT BE ALLOWED upon the ground that the jury disregarded an instruction erroneous in law. *Watts* v. *Norfolk etc. Ry. Co.*,
894.

See APPEAL, 1b.

NEWSPAPERS.

See NOTICE, 2, 3.

NOTICE.

1. JURISDICTION—STATUTES—JUDICIAL PROCEEDINGS.—No man can be lawfully condemned unheard; and statutes will not be construed to authorize proceedings affecting a man's person or property without notice
to him. *Evans* v. *Johnson*, 912.

2. PUBLICATION OF LEGAL NOTICES—NEWSPAPER, WHAT IS.—A journal
published weekly, of general circulation, devoted primarily to the interests of the legal profession and the dissemination of legal news, but
also containing matters of interest to the general public, such as personal items, notices of passing events, general trade advertisements,
and the like, is a newspaper within the meaning of the Michigan statute providing for the publication of legal notices. *Lynch* v. *Judge of
Probate*, 404.

3. PUBLICATION OF LEGAL NOTICE.—PROBATE COURTS ALONE HAVE JURIS-
DICTION to determine in what particular newspaper probate notices
shall be published. *Lynch* v. *Judge of Probate*, 404.

See APPEAL, 7; FACTORS; INSANE PERSONS, 12; INSURANCE, 39, 40; JUDG-
MENTS, 1, 7, 10; MECHANICS' LIEN, 2, 3.

NOVATION.

See DEBTOR AND CREDITOR.

NUISANCE.

1. DAMAGES—DAM IN FLOATABLE STREAM—MILL—PUBLIC NUISANCE.—If
a dam is erected, under authority of the county court, in a floatable
stream, and for the purpose of furnishing power to operate a mill useful to the public, such dam is not a public nuisance, though it is without sluices and floodgates, and obstructs navigation. Hence, a railroad
company which inflicts injury upon the mill by any unlawful act in the
construction of its road cannot justify its wrong upon the plea that such
dam is a public nuisance. *Watts* v. *Norfolk etc. Ry. Co.*, 894.

2. PUBLIC NUISANCE—ABATEMENT OF, BY PRIVATE ACT.—There is a grave
difference of opinion as to the abatement of a purely public nuisance by
the mere act of the party; but all the authorities agree that, where the
right of abatement by private act does exist, it must go no further than
to remove that which works the nuisance, doing injury no further than
is necessary to accomplish that end. *Watts* v. *Norfolk etc. Ry. Co.*, 894.

See DAMAGES, 7; MUNICIPAL CORPORATIONS, 21; RAILROADS, 4.

OFFICERS.

1. CONSTITUTIONAL LAW—INELIGIBILITY OF PART OF A BOARD OF FREEHOLD-ERS.—Under a constitution providing for the election of a board of freeholders to consist of fifteen members, and prescribing the qualifications necessary to render a person eligible to be a member of such board, the fact that two of the persons so elected are not eligible does not prevent the remainder from constituting a valid, constitutional board of freeholders. *People* v. *Hecht*, 96.

2. WORDS GIVING A JOINT AUTHORITY to three or more public officers may be construed as giving it to a majority, unless otherwise expressed. *People* v. *Hecht*, 96.

3. BOARD OF FREEHOLDERS—DE FACTO MEMBERS.—If persons elected as members of a board of freeholders for the purpose of proposing a charter for a municipality are ineligible, but receive their certificates of election, and qualify as freeholders, and enter upon the discharge of their duties, they thereby become *de facto* officers, whose acts are not less binding than those of officers *de jure* so far as they involve the public and third persons. *People* v. *Hecht*, 96.

See CORPORATIONS, 8; MALICIOUS PROSECUTION.

ORDINANCES.

PARENT AND CHILD.

PARKS.

PARTIES.

PARTNERSHIP.

1. EXECUTORS AND ADMINISTRATORS—DUTIES OF.—If, after the death of a testator, his partnership business is continued by his executors, they become partners with the surviving partner, and it is the duty of all of the partners to devote their time and best endeavors to carry on the business, and promote the prosperity of the partnership. In the absence of any special agreement between them as to a division of labor, each must give his time and attention to the conduct of the business without compensation, and without regard to the relative value of the services of the several partners. *Insley* v. *Shire*, 308.

2. NEGLIGENCE OF PARTNER.—If partners share alike in the control and labor of the partnership business, one of them cannot sit passively by, indifferent to the interests of the firm, and, after neglecting to use reasonable diligence himself, hold the others responsible to the firm for a like indifference or negligence. *Insley* v. *Shire*, 308.

3. PARTNERSHIP REAL ESTATE, WHETHER FIRM OR INDIVIDUAL PROPERTY. If real estate connected with a partnership business necessary for the convenient and proper conduct of the business is treated by the partners as partnership property, is put into the firm business as part of the common stock, and so entered on the firm books as to comply with the

PASSES.

PAYMENT.

stitutional, though no provision is made for compensation for such obstruction. *Health Department* v. *Rector*, 579.

3. AN ACT TO BE JUSTIFIED AS AN EXERCISE OF THE POLICE POWER of a
state must tend in a degree that is perceptible and clear toward the
preservation of the lives, the health, the morals, and the welfare of the
community. It must not be exercised ostensibly in favor of the promotion of some such object while in reality it is an evasion thereof, and
for a distinct and different purpose, and the courts will not be prevented
from looking at the true character of the act as developed by its provisions by any statement in the act itself, or in its title showing that it
was ostensibly for some object within the police power. *Health Department* v. *Rector*, 579.

4. CONSTITUTIONAL LAW—REQUIREMENT THAT TENEMENT HOUSES SHALL
HAVE A WATER SUPPLY.—A statute requiring that tenement houses
shall have water furnished in sufficient quantity at one or more places
on each floor occupied, or intended to be occupied, by one or more
families, and all tenement houses shall be furnished with a like supply of water by the owners thereof wherever they shall be directed to
do so by the board of health, is a justifiable and valid exercise of the
police power with respect both to the public health and the public
safety. *Health Department* v. *Rector*, 579.

See ADULTERATION; CONSTITUTIONAL LAW, 1; MUNICIPAL CORPORATIONS, 20.

POWER OF ATTORNEY.
See HUSBAND AND WIFE, 6.

PREFERENCES.
See ASSIGNMENT FOR THE BENEFIT OF CREDITORS, 1, 2; CORPORATIONS, 12–
15; JUDGMENTS, 7.

PRESUMPTIONS.
See APPEAL, 13, 20; EVIDENCE, 1–3; LARCENY; LIBEL, 6; RAILROADS, 16
WILLS, 8.

PRINCIPAL AND AGENT.
See AGENCY.

PRIVILEGED COMMUNICATIONS.
See LIBEL, 8; WITNESSES, 2, 3.

PROBATE COURT.
See NOTICE, 3.

PROCESS.

1. Publication of process in a newspaper four consecutive times, with an
interval of one week between each publication, is a publication for four
weeks. *Cruzen* v. *Stephens*, 549.

2. NONRESIDENT—SERVICE OF NOTICE BY PUBLICATION.—If a married
woman, interested in land, shifts about from place to place, and her
whereabouts have been unknown to her friends and acquaintances
for about thirty-five years, and notice in an action to quiet title to the
land is given to her by publication in her former name, by which she

was known in the state, it is sufficient, although her husband had died and she had since married, and taken the name of her second husband. *Jones v. Kohler*, 215.

3. NONRESIDENT—SERVICE OF NOTICE BY PUBLICATION—PRESUMPTION—ESTOPPEL.—If notice of a judicial proceeding is properly given to a nonresident by publication, the presumption is that the party notified becomes acquainted with the notice, and he is estopped from denying it. *Jones v. Kohler*, 215.

4. NOTICE BY PUBLICATION—COLLATERAL ATTACK.—Service of process by publication addressed to "Etta R. Fisher and —— Fisher, her husband," is valid on collateral attack. *Cruzen v. Stephens*, 549.

5. NOTICE BY PUBLICATION—COLLATERAL ATTACK.—Service by publication in a tax suit is sufficient, as against collateral attack, if it names the defendants with sufficient definiteness to plainly indicate their identity. *Cruzen v. Stephens*, 549.

6. NOTICE BY PUBLICATION.—Surplusage in an order for the service of process by publication does not render it void if it is otherwise valid. *Cruzen v. Stephens*, 549.

See INFANTS, 1.

PROMOTERS.
See CORPORATIONS, 2–4.

PUBLICATION.
See NOTICE, 2, 3; PROCESS.

PUBLIC LANDS.
See WATERS, 8, 9.

PUBLIC POLICY.
See CARRIERS, 2, 3, 6.

QUIETING TITLE.
See CLOUD ON TITLE; PROCESS, 2.

RAILROADS.

1. DAMAGES—GRANT OF RIGHT OF WAY—INJURY TO RESIDUE.—If one grants a right of way over his land to a railroad company, all damages to the remainder of the land arising from construction of the road, past, present, and future, are released, and neither he nor his subsequent alienee can recover therefor against the company. *Watts v. Norfolk etc. Ry. Co.*, 894.

2. DAMAGES—GRANT OF RIGHT OF WAY—INJURY TO PRIVATE FERRY.—If one grants a right of way over his land to a railroad company, damage to a private ferry thereon, as incident to or consequential upon the proper construction of the road or use of the right of way, is covered by the grant, and cannot be the subject of an action by the landowner or his subsequent alienee against the company. *Watts v. Norfolk etc. Ry. Co.*, 894.

3. DAMAGES—GRANT OF RIGHT OF WAY—BLASTING OF ROCK.—After one has granted a right of way over his land to a railroad company, injury to a dwelling-house upon the residue caused by the blasting of rock, where proper precautions have been taken, is not actionable; but the leaving of rock and other material deposited on such residue by the blasting would be actionable, unless the debris is removed within a reasonable time. *Watts* v. *Norfolk etc. Ry. Co.*, 894.

4. DAMAGES—GRANT OF RIGHT OF WAY—NUISANCE.—If one has granted a right of way over his land to a railroad company, a "fill," or "bar," made in a stream by blasting and throwing into it rock and other refuse matter in the work of constructing the road which is not necessary for the construction and maintenance of the railroad, and which injures a mill situated on the residue of the land, is an injury in the nature of a nuisance, and a ground of action against the company. *Watts* v. *Norfolk etc. Ry. Co.*, 894.

5. DAMAGES—GRANT OF RIGHT OF WAY—INJURY TO PUBLIC ROAD OR PRIVATE WAY.—The grant of a right of way over one's land to a railroad company will not justify the destruction of a public highway in the construction of its road. Hence, such destruction is an actionable injury. But in the case of a private way it is different, and no action lies, because such injury is presumed to have been considered when the grant was made. *Watts* v. *Norfolk etc. Ry. Co.*, 894.

6. FREE PASSES—ESTOPPEL.—One to whom a free pass is issued in contravention of law, and who avails himself of its privileges, is estopped from alleging that such pass was unlawful, for the purpose of recovering compensation for injuries suffered by him while riding upon such pass. *Muldoon* v. *Seattle etc. Ry. Co.*, 787.

7. FREE PASS, DUTY TO READ CONDITIONS.—One who accepts a free pass from a railway, on the back of which is printed a condition exempting the corporation from liability for injuries which may be sustained by him while using such pass, cannot avoid such condition by alleging that it was printed on the back of the pass, which was inclosed in a leathern case so constructed as to conceal all parts of the pass except its face. The recipient of such a favor ought to take the trouble to look on both sides of the paper before attempting to use it. *Muldoon* v. *Seattle etc. Ry. Co.*, 787.

8. FREE PASS—FAILURE TO READ.—The fact that one who accepts a free pass has not read the conditions printed thereon exempting the corporation from liability should he be injured, and is ignorant of them, does not relieve him from such condition. *Muldoon* v. *Seattle etc. Ry. Co.*, 787.

9. DAMAGES FOR ASSAULT—EVIDENCE.—In an action against a railroad company by a passenger to recover for an assault made on him by the conductor on a train, evidence to show that on some other occasion, and on a day different from that of the alleged assault, such passenger had used abusive and profane language to, and made threats against, the same conductor, is inadmissible. *Baltimore etc. R. R. Co.* v. *Barger*, 319.

10. ASSAULT ON PASSENGER BY CONDUCTOR.—A railroad company is liable for an assault made by its conductor upon a passenger, although the assault is provoked by profane and abusive language used by the passenger to the conductor without provocation. *Baltimore etc. R. R. Co.* v. *Barger*, 319.

11. LIABILITY FOR ASSAULT BY CONDUCTOR—PROVOCATION AS MITIGATION OF DAMAGES.—The provocation offered by a railroad passenger in using profane and abusive language to the conductor on the train, if of such character as to naturally arouse the passions of men of ordinary temperament, and not too remote in time, is admissible in mitigation of damages in an action against the railroad company to recover for such assault. *Baltimore etc. R. R. Co.* v. *Barger,* 319.

12. ASSAULT BY CONDUCTOR—EXEMPLARY DAMAGES.—If, in an action by a passenger to recover of a railroad company for an assault committed by its conductor, the evidence is conflicting as to the provocation offered by the passenger in using profane and abusive language to the conductor the court cannot instruct the jury, as matter of law, not to award punitive damages for the assault. The jury may properly be instructed to consider the character of the assault and the conduct of both parties, and award such punitive or exemplary damages as the circumstances may require. *Baltimore etc. R. R. Co.* v. *Barger,* 319.

13. ASSAULT BY CONDUCTOR—EXEMPLARY DAMAGES. — An assault by a railroad conductor upon a passenger, though provoked by profane and abusive language, is not justified thereby, and render the railroad company liable in exemplary damages. *Baltimore etc. R. R. Co.* v. *Barger,* 319.

14. TURNTABLES, DUTY OF, TO GUARD FROM CHILDREN.—A railway maintaining a turntable upon land which the public is in the habit of crossing and being upon at pleasure, but not by invitation, does not owe the duty to children to keep such turntable fastened or locked when not in use, so as to prevent access to it by children. If it is on the land of its owner, and is used by him for the sole purpose of conducting his business, and is fit and proper for that purpose, and is not built in any improper or negligent way with reference to the transaction of his business, he does not owe any further duty to persons, whether children or adults, who have no buinsess on his land, and who are there unasked, and whose presence is merely tolerated. *Walsh* v. *Fitchburg R. R. Co.*, 615.

15. LIABILITY OF, FOR INJURY CAUSED BY MAIL AGENT'S THROWING LOADED MAIL-BAG FROM TRAIN.—While a railway company has no right to interfere with a mail agent in the discharge of his official duties, its duty is to prevent him, while on its trains and premises, from continuing any negligent practice, of which it has notice, and which is liable to cause injury to passengers and others lawfully there. Throwing loaded mail-bags out of a moving train upon a platform occupied by the public is of itself a negligent and dangerous practice, and, where injury results from it, the company may be charged with negligence, without showing that a like injury occurred on some former occasion. *Galloway* v. *Chicago etc. Ry. Co.*, 468.

16. NEGLIGENCE—PRESUMPTION OF FROM ACCIDENT.—The fact that one while walking in a footpath beside the roadbed of a railroad, but not upon its right of way, is injured by cross-ties which fall from a car attached to a train passing on such railroad, and strike him, raises a presumption of negligence on the part of the railroad company. *Howser* v. *Cumberland etc. R. R. Co.*, 332.

17. NEGLIGENCE—SPEED OF TRAIN.—Cases may arise when the speed of a train may be considered by a jury, in connection with the location and other surrounding circumstances upon a question of negligence; but, in the absence of proof that the train in question was run at an excessive or dangerous rate of speed at the time of an accident, the submission of the question to the jury as to the liability of the railroad company

2. RELEASE OBTAINED BY FRAUD—NECESSITY FOR TENDER.—If a release is found to have been obtained by fraud practiced upon one incapable, because of mental weakness to enter into such a contract, the fruits of the release need not be refunded before action brought. *Girard v. St. Louis Car etc. Co.*, 556.

3. RELEASE OBTAINED BY FRAUD—NECESSITY FOR TENDER BEFORE SUIT. A tender of money, or other thing of value, received by virtue of a release, need not be made before bringing an action at law to recover for personal injury if the release was obtained by fraud. It is sufficient to offer its return and to account for it by the judgment. *Girard v. St. Louis Car etc. Co.*, 556.

4. RELEASE OBTAINED BY FRAUD—WAIVER OF TENDER.—If a reply of fraud is made to a plea of release, and no objection is at any time, by pleading or otherwise, made to the sufficiency of plaintiff's case for failure to tender or return the fruits of such release, and defendant insists upon its validity as a defense, he thereby waives the necessity for a tender, especially when the fruits of the release are restored to him by the judgment. *Girard v. St. Louis Car etc. Co.*, 556.

See CORPORATIONS, 31.

REMAINDERS.

See DEEDS, 3, 4; ESTATES.

REMOVAL OF CAUSES.

1. REMOVAL OF A CAUSE TO A FEDERAL COURT must be refused if not petitioned for in time. *Nichols v. Steven*, 514.

2. When a cause has been removed to a federal court, and remanded because the petition for removal does not set up the diverse citizenship of the parties at the commencement of the suit, a second removal on the same ground is not allowable. *Nichols v. Stevens*, 514.

RESCISSION.

See CONTRACTS.

RES GESTÆ.

See EVIDENCE, 6, 7.

RESTRAINT OF TRADE.

See CORPORATIONS, 1.

RIGHT OF WAY.

See RAILROADS, 1–5.

RIPARIAN RIGHTS.

See MILLS.

SALES.

1. CONSIGNMENT FOR SALE—CONTRACT OF—HOW TO BE CONSTRUED.—In construing a contract of consignment for sale the court must determine from the wording of the contract itself and the circumstances surrounding it the true intention of the parties in making it. If the contract was entered into in the form of an agency contract for the purpose of evad-

6. CONSTITUTIONAL LAW—ARREST WITHOUT WARRANT.—A statute authorizing an arrest without warrant for an offense not amounting to a breach of the peace, if committed in view of an officer, is constitutional and valid. *Burroughs v. Eastman,* 419.

See ADULTERATION; CONTEMPT, 1; INSURANCE, 1-4; NOTICE, 1; POLICE POWER; WITNESSES, 1.

STREET ASSESSMENTS.
See CLOUD ON TITLE, 3; MUNICIPAL CORPORATIONS, 14, 15.

STREET RAILWAYS.
See RAILROADS, 29-34.

SUBROGATION.

1. MORTGAGE SATISFACTION UNDER MISTAKE OF FACT.—If one not an intermeddler or volunteer causes a mortgage to be satisfied and discharged in ignorance of the existence of a judgment lien, under circumstances authorizing an inference of a mistake of fact, equity will presume such mistake, and give the party who made it the benefit of the equitable right of subrogation where no superior intervening equities are interfered with. *Heisler v. Aultman,* 486.

2. SUBROGATION OF SURETY WHO PAYS MORTGAGE DEBT—PRIORITY OF MORTGAGE AND JUDGMENT LIENS.—In a case where real property is sold subject to a mortgage the rules of subrogation will be applied when the surety upon a note, given for a part of the purchase price, and secured by a second mortgage upon the property, has paid the note, and taken a deed of the land in indemnification, if the second mortgage has been satisfied and discharged in ignorance of the fact that a judgment against the maker of the note and mortgage, and subordinate to the mortgage liens on the premises, has thereby been promoted and advanced from a third to a second lien, so as to render his interest in the property of no value. The satisfaction and record will be canceled and annulled, and the mortgage lien be placed prior and paramount to the lien of the judgment, or lien acquired by a sale on execution thereunder. *Heisler v. Aultman,* 486.

SURETYSHIP.
See MECHANIC'S LIEN, 7.

SURVEYS.

1. A DEFICIENCY IN A QUARTER SECTION OF LAND, as shown by the original survey and plat, should be borne by the several tracts in proportion to the quantities supposed to be contained therein by the government and its purchasers, who have assumed the lines to be correct. Hence, where, by the original survey and the plat of the surveyor general, the east line of a certain quarter section was 38 and 5-100 chains in length, and the west line was 38 and 48-100 chains, the half quarter line not being established, nor the corners thereof located, and the plat assigned 20 chains to the east line of said quarter at the south end thereof, 20 chains to the west line at the south end thereof, 18 and 5-100 chains to said east line at the north end thereof, and 18 and 48-100 chains to said west line at the north end thereof, when, in fact, the

east and west lines of said quarter section were each but 37 chains in
length, and contained 6 and 49-100 acres less than shown by said original survey and plat, the original plat marking the southern portion of
said quarter section as containing 80 acres and the northern portion as
containing 72 and 49-100 acres, and being each so respectively described by the government patent and subsequent conveyances; such
deficiency of 6 and 49-100 acres in said quarter section should be deducted proportionally from said north and south one-half quarters, upon
the basis of 80 and 72 and 49-100 acres respectively. *Caylor* v. *Luzadder*, 183.

2. "PROPORTIONATE MEASUREMENT" IS A MEASUREMENT having the same
ratio to that recorded in the original field notes, as the length of the
chain used in the new measurement has to the length of the chain
used in the original survey, assuming that the original measurement
was correctly made. *Caylor* v. *Luzadder*, 183.

TAXES.

1. JUDGMENT FOR TAXES.—SHERIFF'S DEED under a tax judgment conveying all the estate which the sheriff might sell under the judgment is
valid to transfer the interests of the defendant in the tax suit. *Orman*
v. *Stephens*, 549.

2. JUDGMENTS FOR TAXES—COLLATERAL ATTACK.—A tax judgment dealing
with the property as one tract instead of subjecting each subdivision to
its appropriate part of the taxes is not void on collateral attack. *Orman*
v. *Stephens*, 541.

See DAMAGES, 9; PROCESS, 5.

TENDER.

See RELEASE, 2-4; VENDOR AND PURCHASER, 1.

TORTS.

See HUSBAND AND WIFE.

TRESPASS.

See EQUITY, 5; LIMITATIONS OF ACTIONS, 2.

TRESPASSERS.

See ASSAULT; LANDLORD AND TENANT, 2; RAILROADS, 32.

TRIAL.

1. INSTRUCTIONS GIVEN WHICH FAIRLY PRESENT THE LAW of the case
need not be repeated, and if other instructions are asked they are
properly refused. *Burdict* v. *Missouri Pac. Ry. Co.*, 528.

2. INSTRUCTIONS.—The court cannot instruct upon the weight of evidence or
the credibility of witnesses, but, when there is any competent evidence
fairly tending in some appreciable degree to prove a party's case, he
has the right to have the law applicable to such evidence correctly
declared to the jury by the court. *Osborne* v. *Francis*, 859.

3. JURY TRIAL.—A court should not instruct a jury that evidence of the
oral admissions of a party should be received with caution, when it is
the only kind of evidence which in the nature of the case his adversary
could procure. *Mattingly* v. *Pennie*, 87.

4. A VERDICT IS NOT EXCESSIVE which awards plaintiff seven thousand seven hundred and sixty dollars in an action for personal injuries, where his expectancy of life is thirty-four years, he was earning sixty-five dollars per month when hurt, and his injuries confined him to his bed one week, rendered him unable to perform any labor for three months, and to perform any labor except chores for nine months, and there is evidence tending to show that his injuries are permanent and will prevent him from ever doing any but light work. *Harker v. Burlington etc. Ry. Co.*, 242.

TROVER.

1. SUFFICIENCY OF COMPLAINT.—A complaint in trover must allege that plaintiff was the owner, or in possession, or entitled to the immediate possession of, the property when converted. *Kennett v. Peters*, 274.

2. ALLEGATIONS OF OWNERSHIP.—A complaint in an action of trover by one not the absolute owner of the property must allege that he had a special ownership or interest therein at the time of the conversion and must state the facts in relation thereto. *Kennett v. Peters*, 274.

3. ALLEGATIONS OF POSSESSION.—A complaint in an action of trover brought by one not in possession at the time the chattels were converted must allege that he was entitled to the immediate possession of the property at that time. *Kennett v. Peters*, 274.

4. MORTGAGE OF CHATTELS—TROVER FOR CONVERSION—PLEADING.—A chattel mortgagee does not become the absolute owner of the mortgaged property upon condition broken, nor does he then become entitled to the immediate possession of the property unconditionally. Therefore, he cannot maintain trover for its conversion without alleging his special ownership and interest therein at the time of the conversion, and stating the facts in relation thereto. A general allegation of ownership is insufficient to maintain the action. *Kennett v. Peters*, 274.

5. —INSTRUCTIONS.—If, in an action of trover against a chattel mortgagee and an auctioneer who sold the goods at foreclosure sale, it is shown that a portion of the goods sued for were not covered by the mortgage, it is not error to refuse to submit the question to the jury, at the request of defendants, as to whether the auctioneer sold goods amounting to more than the mortgage debt. *Kearney v. Clutton*, 394.

6. DIVISION OF VERDICT—INSTRUCTIONS.—In an action of trover against several defendants for the conversion of goods, if the jury render a verdict for a certain sum against each defendant, without any evidence by which to determine that each defendant converted a specific part of the goods, the court commits no error in sending the jury back with an instruction that there is no ground for a division of the verdict against the defendant. *Kearney v. Clutton*, 394.

See AUCTIONS; WAREHOUSEMEN.

TRUST DEEDS.

See EVIDENCE, 6.

TRUST FUND.

See AGENCY, 1; CORPORATIONS, 10–12.

TRUSTS.

1. RESULTING TRUST IN LAND ARISES IN FAVOR OF WIFE, WHEN.—If a farm is purchased for a wife with her money, upon an understanding

VICE-PRINCIPAL.
See MASTER AND SERVANT, 11.

VIEWING PREMISES.
See APPEAL, 8.

VOLUNTEERS.
See MASTER AND SERVANT, 6, 7; PAYMENT, 2-6; SUBROGATION.

WAIVER.
See EXECUTION, 7; INSURANCE, 6; RELEASE, 4; VENDOR AND PURCHASER, 3.

WAREHOUSEMEN.
LIABILITY OF.—A storage company is not liable in trover for goods stored with it by a mortgagor, and taken from its custody by the mortgagee, and by him converted to his use, without the knowledge or consent of the storage company. *Kearney* v. *Clutton*, 394.

WATERS.
1. WHAT IS.—If waters from springs uniting run into a ravine, and on reaching low, level land widen and then pass still farther, forming a pond, and beyond the pond flow not into a channel with banks, but along a depression in the earth and over the grass and sod, and the waters thus running are at some places quite narrow, and at others several rods in width, but a current is visible along their entire course, and they again come into a single channel, through which they flow into a river, they form, in contemplation of law, a watercourse which the owner of lands through which they flow has no right to divert and to keep from flowing beyond his lands. *Hinkle* v. *Avery*, 224.

2. "HIGH-WATER MARK," as a line between a riparian owner and the public, on fresh-water rivers and lakes, is to be determined by examining the bed and banks, and ascertaining where the presence and action of the water are so common and usual as to mark upon the soil of the bed a character distinct from that of the banks in respect to vegetation as well as to the nature of the soil itself. It is co-ordinate with the limit of the bed of the water. *In re Minnetonka Lake Improvement*, 494.

3. "BED OF THE WATER."—That only is to be considered the "bed of the water" which the water occupies so long and continuously as to wrest it from vegetation and destroy its value for agricultural purposes. It does not include lowlands which, although subject to frequent overflow, are valuable as meadows or pastures. *In re Minnetonka Lake Improvement*, 494.

4. CHANGE IN LOCATION OF.—If for many years, and as a result of natural causes, a watercourse has flowed across the lands of the plaintiff, though it formerly flowed upon the lands of the defendant, and the change in its course came so gradually that it is not easily traced in its history, it must be regarded as a watercourse upon the lands of the plaintiff, which defendant has no right to divert so that it will again flow only upon his lands. *Hinkle* v. *Avery*, 224.

5. TO SUPPORT A SPECIAL ASSESSMENT FOR A LOCAL IMPROVEMENT the benefit for which the land is assessed must be secured. In other words, it must appear that benefits for which persons are asked to pay will be received. Hence, an assessment for a local benefit, under an act author-

In his presence and at his request, and in the presence and at the request of the testator, is not sufficient to attest a will devising real estate. *McFarland* v. *Bush,* 760.

5. IT IS NOT NECESSARY THAT A TESTATOR SHOULD HAVE ACKNOWLEDGED HIS SIGNATURE to the will if he produces a paper which he declares to be his will, and asks the witnesses to sign it, and states that it is not necessary for them to know what is in it. *Hobart* v. *Hobart,* 151.

6. PROOF OF THE HANDWRITING OF A DECEASED WITNESS is *prima facie* sufficient, especially when the signatures of the witnesses are attached to a clause stating that the will was written, signed, and sealed in their presence. *Hobart* v. *Hobart,* 151.

7. THE PROOF OF A CODICIL TO A WILL ESTABLISHES THE WILL without further proof if both are written on the same paper, and the codicil clearly and unmistakably refers to the will so as to prevent all doubt of its identity. In such case the codicil operates as a republication of the will, and gives to it the same force as if it had been executed at the date of the codicil, the two instruments being regarded as one and their speaking from the date of the latter. *Hobart* v. *Hobart,* 151.

8. PRESUMPTION OF SIGNING.—If a testator produces a paper which he declares to be his last will, and asks the subscribing witnesses to sign it as such, and they do so in his presence, it will be presumed that it was already signed by him, though the witnesses cannot remember whether they saw his signature or not. *Hobart* v. *Hobart,* 151.

See ESTATES; LEGACY.

WITNESSES.

1. HUSBAND AND WIFE—CONSTRUCTION OF STATUTE.—A statute providing that neither husband nor wife shall be examined as a witness without the consent of the other does not make them incompetent witnesses, nor are they to be classed as such, though their right to be examined is contingent upon the consent of the spouse for or against whom the witness may be offered. *In re Holt's Will,* 434.

2. PHYSICIAN AND PATIENT.—COMMUNICATIONS MADE BY A PATIENT to his physician for the purpose of professional aid and advice are privileged. The immunity extends to all facts, whether learned directly from the patient, or acquired by the physician through his own observation or examinations. *Springer* v. *Byram,* 159.

3. PHYSICIAN AND PATIENT—PRIVILEGE AS TO CONVERSATION HEARD BY THIRD PERSON.—Third persons who hear conversations between parties sustaining confidential relations to each other as physician and patient, whether such third persons are necessarily present as officers or as indifferent bystanders, may testify to what they heard. *Springer* v. *Byram,* 159.

4. EXPERT EVIDENCE.—An issue as to business negligence between parties must be determined from facts, and not from the opinions of witnesses. *Insley* v. *Shire,* 308.

See WILLS, 1-4, 6.

WORDS AND PHRASES.

See DEFINITIONS.